Great Pages of Michigan History from the Detroit Free Press

Detroit Free Press
Wayne State University Press
1987

GREAT PAGES of MICHIGAN HISTORY from the DETROIT FREE PRESS

Published by the
Detroit Free Press
321 W. Lafayette Blvd.
Detroit, Michigan 48231

and

Wayne State University Press
The Leonard N. Simons Building
5959 Woodward Avenue
Detroit, Michigan 48202

Distributed by
Wayne State University Press

Compiled by: Bill McGraw
Designed by: Randy Miller
Edited by: Clinton Baller, Joe Grimm
Copy edited by: Emily Everett, Jim Rogers
Photo preparation by: Bob McKeown
Camera preparation by: Larry Holman
Keyboarding by: Joe Rossiter, Allison Flowers, Terri Sosnowski, Vivian Giumette
Coordinated by: Michele Kapecky

Copyright by the
Detroit Free Press
1987

All rights reserved. No part of this book may be reproduced or transmitted in any form or by any means, electronic or mechanical, including photocopying, recording or by an information storage and retrieval system, without permission of the publisher, except where permitted by law.

Manufactured in the
United States of America

ISBN 0-8143-1881-9 (cl)
ISBN 0-8143-1882-7 (pbk)

Cataloging
in Publication Number:
86-050869

Looking through old newspapers is like walking through a graveyard. Scattered, in little apparent order, are the names of former residents, accompanied by tidbits about their lives.

As you turn the pages — or the handle on the microfilm machine — you might see an 1870 Free Press, in which Susan B. Anthony, the famous feminist, visits Detroit and tells women they should not consider themselves the property of men. There's a 1901 paper saying that Henry Ford has won a big automobile race at a Grosse Pointe track. Ford is not a famous man at the time. The big news seems to be the horses: They reportedly were acting resentful toward cars, their new, mechanized competition. On a 1942 "man in the street" page is Detroit policeman Bud Beaucand, who vows to get along with gas rationing by making "every date count." After the Belle Isle Love-In of 1967, counterculture leader John Sinclair discusses truth and life. Then there's a 1969 page, in which Berry Gordy talks about growing up on the east side and forming Motown Records, which influenced pop music around the world.

These are the real voices of real people who helped form the 150-year-old story of Michigan. They are brought back by this book, "Great Pages of Michigan History from the Detroit Free Press," for the state's Sesquicentennial in 1987.

1859:
The Free Press published at the northwest corner of Griswold and Woodbridge, a busy intersection at the time.

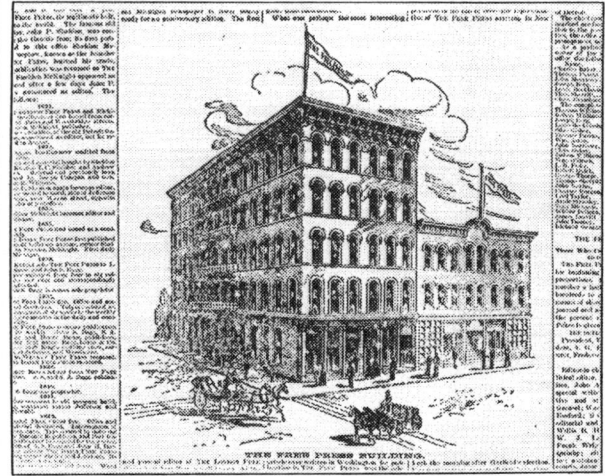

1884:
The Free Press moved to the northeast corner of Larned and Shelby.

1894:
The Free Press published at the Abstract Building on Lafayette Blvd.

The Free Press, founded in May 1831, is nearly six years older than the state, so its staff members have seen it all — the growth, the celebrations, the inventions, the buildings, the victories. They also have seen the racial, ethnic and geographic divisions, the strikes, the violence, and the natural disasters.

How long ago is 1831?

If you're 30 today, your great-great-great-great-grandfather could have been about 30 when the Free Press first hit the muddy streets of Detroit.

In 1831, there were only 24 states. There was no railroad out of Detroit and no telegraph; stagecoaches left from Ben Woodworth's Steamboat Hotel. Mail delivery was erratic. The 1830 census reported a population of only 2,222. The French were the main population group, but were dwindling. It was a tough town, even then. An early editor, Sheldon McKnight, was indicted for manslaughter (but later acquitted) after he punched a man in the head during a bar fight.

The century and a half of existence for newspaper and state might be a mere minute on the clock of world history, but the changes in Michigan have been breathtaking. The Great Lakes State has gone from a frontier outpost to a world manufacturing leader to a symbol of the decline of industrial America. By the late 1830s, nearly 200 immigrants a day were pouring into the state to stake their claims on a new life. By 1931, when the city had become the nation's leading car maker, the Free Press referred to Detroit as "Utopia on Wheels." But by 1983, West Germans were sending care packages to Detroit after hearing reports of widespread hunger.

The famous slogan of the 1890s was "Detroit — Where Life is Worth Living." The infamous nickname of the 1970s was, starkly, "Murder City."

The Free Press covered it all.

"Great Pages" is also a history of American journalism, at least as seen through the Free Press. And journalism also has changed radically in 156 years.

In the beginning, the Democratic Free Press and Michigan Intelligencer was little more than the highly partisan — and very conservative — publication of the Michigan Democratic Party.

Before the Civil War, the Free Press received its news via a circuitous route. Because the telegraph from the east stretched only as far as Hamilton, Ontario, a stagecoach took the dispatches to Windsor, where a courier in a canoe would rush them across the Detroit River. Today, reporters file their stories in seconds from around the world, using phone lines and portable computers.

Modern reporters use a spare style of writing that attempts to give busy people their news quickly by putting the important information at the beginning of the story. They try to include background information to better inform new readers about previous developments. In "Great Pages," you'll read that one hundred years ago, journalists employed a more literary style with loads of clauses and commas. They buried the news dozens of paragraphs deep in their articles. Background was an alien concept.

Papers in the 1980s use more color and graphics than a comic book in trying to appeal to eyes and brains that have been trained by television. Up until about 50 years ago, papers consisted of column after column of gray type, only rarely relieved by photos or drawings. When the Free Press began, headlines had not been invented. By the time Lincoln died, headlines ran vertically from top to bottom in a narrow column, then gradually took on their current multi-column, horizontal form. You can see this by flipping through "Great Pages."

Sensibilities also have changed. Most papers, when they publish retrospective editions, warn readers about references to ethnic groups, and especially to blacks, that seem crude by today's standards.

But scholars say the Free Press was worse than most papers. While Michigan was a leading abolitionist state and Detroit was a last stop on the Underground Railroad, the Free Press' racism and sympathy to the South gained it national notoriety during the Civil War era. Critics say the paper was bitter and often insulting toward blacks, who made up three percent of the city's 79,577 inhabitants in 1870.

Under editor Wilbur Fisk Storey, the Free Press denounced Abraham Lincoln and other abolitionists. Storey supported the Civil War as necessary to save the Union, but opposed the emancipation of the slaves, warning that freed blacks would "swarm upon us like the locusts of Egypt, devouring the whole land."

Storey was constantly controversial. According to "On Guard," Frank Angelo's history of the Free Press, a foe once referred to Storey as a "dog" who "is kept chained up ... is regularly aired, and led to his meals."

You'll read examples of the Storey-influenced Free Press in "Great Pages."

The Free Press had its progressive side during the 19th Century, and you'll see that, too. It supported the movement for statehood, became the first midwest paper to establish a foreign bureau, pioneered religion reporting and started what experts say was the first women's page in America, "The Household."

The Free Press sometimes excelled at reporting the fast-paced events of the 20th Century, winning six Pulitzer Prizes for coverage ranging from an article about a mammoth American Legion parade to a photo essay of armed inmates at the state prison at Jackson. Its editorial page developed a liberal reputation after World War II.

"Great Pages" is not textbook history. It is meant to be a scrapbook that pulls together reports of important events, such as elections and wars, and more subtle happenings, such as furniture sales and movie openings. We've tried to provide glimpses into the past that show what life was like in Michigan for our ancestors, be they assembly line workers or company presidents. To best appreciate each page, armchair anthropologists will want to read everything — especially the small print, even if it takes a magnifying glass.

By reading everything, you'll learn that:

■ On the day Lincoln was shot in 1865, the Detroit Base Ball Club completed negotiations to play its games on the grounds of the Woodward Avenue Skating Club.

■ At the turn of the century, Summerfield and Hecht's home furnishing store on Michigan Avenue sold iron beds for $4.85 and dressers for $7.98. And that the store's motto for soon-to-wed bachelors was: "You furnish the girl, we furnish the home."

■ When "Casablanca" opened during World War II, Detroiters had their choice of more than 100 neighborhood theaters.

■ Addiction to heroin and cocaine was considered a problem in Detroit as early as 1912.

■ Detroiters celebrated the new century in 1901, not in 1900, and they did it by shooting off handguns.

There are some things you won't read in "Great Pages." You won't read about the actual day Michigan became a state (Jan. 26, 1837) because a fire had shut the Free Press for six weeks. The Rev. Martin Luther King spoke in Grosse Pointe shortly before his assassination in 1968, but you won't read about that either, because the Free Press was on strike.

1913:
The Free Press moved to the Transportation Building, also on Lafayette.

1925:

The Free Press moved to its current building on 321 W. Lafayette, where the editorial and business operations remain. Below, the Free Press's riverfront printing plant opened in 1979 at a cost of $47 million.

You'll read about the first use of telegraph and telephone in Michigan and about the first State Fair, but you won't read much about the first car on Detroit streets, because it was not considered a very big deal.

"*A Horseless Carriage*" was the headline of the one-paragraph story in March 1896.

"The first horseless carriage seen in this city was out on the streets last night. It is an invention of S. B. King, a Detroiter, and its progress up and down Woodward avenue about 11 o'clock caused a great deal of comment, people crowding around it so that its progress was impeded. The aparatus seemed to work all right, and went at the rate of five or six mile an hour at an even rate of speed."

An editor made the decision to write a small story, not realizing what would develop later. That's journalism: Instant snippets of history, sometimes with little time to reflect about what might follow.

And that's "Great Pages:" Instant snapshots of Michigan over its 150 years. Today's readers have the luxury of learning what happened next. All they have to do is turn the page.

— *Bill McGraw*

A special thanks to:

The Detroit Free Press Library, especially Chris Kucharski and Ann Mieczkowski; the Detroit Public Library's General Information Department and Burton Historical Collection; the University of Michigan Graduate Library and James Wren, manager, Patent Department, Motor Vehicle Manufacturers Association.

of doubts which arise as to the validity of a deed or title bearing a date prior to that of the U. States' patent. The solicitude of all buyers of land, on account of title, will naturally suggest many difficulties in the absence of the original patent. This delay of the land patents has been owing solely to the inadequacy of the assistance which has been allowed to the Commissioner of the General Land Office, and to the unnecessary requirement of the land laws, which makes it the duty of the President of the United States to sign every patent.

About double the amount of labor has been performed by Mr. Hayward, since he was appointed Commissioner of the General Land Office, than was done, for a like period, by his predecessor; and in 1831, although *thirty thousand* patents had been filled up and signed, there still remained on hand *thirty-five thousand* to be completed. Considering the numerous and important duties which devolve upon the President of the United States, one would be led to suppose, that our legislators would find out some way to save him the time and labour of signing land patents. A simple enactment, making valid the signature of an officer appointed to sign them, or to use a stamp with the *fac simile* of the President's signature, would be of essential use in expediting the delivery of the patents after they had been filled up—but the main cause of delay is to be found in the neglect of Congress to provide adequate assistance and means to accomplish the business which for years has been accumulating in the general Land Office. The duty of providing a remedy, we should think, devolves peculiarly upon the members of Congress from the western States, and to them the land buyers of Ohio, Missouri, Illinois, Indiana, and Michigan, look for relief.

Sarcasm.—We have enquired, seriously, whether there were any grounds for the report, that A. E. Wing had changed his opinion in respect to the present administration—we have also stated our disbelief *of the fact*. Upon this subject, the delegate, speaking through the editor of the *Michigan Sentinel*, declares that our "allusions" have been "sarcastic;" and he will not, therefore, by replying, "give further currency to them, as they are no ways connected with the general politics of our Territory." We presume the people of Monroe feel about the same interest in *general* politics of any kind as the other citizens of the Territory; and if so, the delegate will find it a difficult task to convert them into *neutrals*. Our inquiries relative to the present state of the delegate's politics, are made with a view to satisfy those of our fellow-citizens who deem it important that a public man should not only have an opinion, but possess, at the same time, sufficient independence to assert it. We are free to admit that our queries, under existing circumstances, may be deemed of a nature somewhat perplexing, but it was far from our intention to offend the delegate by "sarcastic allusions."

The *delegate*, A. E. Wing, via. the Michigan Sentinel, intimates that the politics of the editor of this paper were unsettled, until "appearances indicated" the success of Gen. Jackson, and that the Detroit Gazette had "no political character." Indeed, if this be true, how wicked and false he and his political friends were in 1830 '31, when they represented the editor to the aristocrats of the Senate, as equally guilty of Jacksonism with Hill, Noah, and a score of others who have suffered for the like offence, and thus procured his rejection.

A few days ago the *delegate* would have it that we were not in favor of Gen. Jackson until *after* his election. A little chastisement urges him to a slight approximation to truth, and he admits we were never hostile to the General, and advocated his election, when "appearances indicated" his success. This shows that the delegate is not so very obstinate that he cannot be whipped in, if one will but take the trouble, whenever he strays from the path of truth.

Rev. GABRIEL RICHARD.

We are indebted to the Rev. Mr. Badin and one of our citizens for the following biographical sketch relative to the reverend deceased, whose death we noticed last week.

"Mr. Richard was born at Saintas, in France, on the 15th Oct. 1764. His father was a gentleman of distinction, and his mother a descendant of the learned Bossuet. He was educated at the college of Angers, and received ecclesiastical orders at the Catholic Theological Seminary of Paris, in 1790. On account of the Revolution he left his native land, under the direction of the rev. Mr. Emery, for America, where he had conferred upon him, previous to his departure, the appointment of Professor of Mathematics in St. Mary's College, at Baltimore, Md. Shortly after, he was called as a Missionary, and sent to Kaskaskias, Illinois, to preach the gospel to the Indians. Six years were devoted to this useful [illegible] employment with the greatest solicitude and with ceaseless industry; and his mind during that period, as he often said, seemed to have been too much enlarged and refined, to be ever spent in teaching the children of the forest the rudiments of education and of gospel freedom.

In 1798 his labors as a missionary ceased, and he came to this city and founded the present church of Ste. Anne. The difficulties which he had to encounter were great, and by many of his people are too well remembered to require detailing here.

In 1809 he visited Boston, and while on his return he purchased a printing press and types, with which he commenced the publication of a newspaper, in the French language, called the "Michigan Essay." Several numbers of this publication were issued; but there being no regular mails, and the population of the Territory being scattered, he soon found it advisable to suspend the publication. He then commenced publishing religious books for his own church. The laws of the Territory were published, and all the printing that was required was executed under his direction.

In 1812, after the surrender of Hull, he was taken prisoner and sent to Sandwich, where he remained in the discharge of his ministerial duties, and in redeeming those citizens who had been taken by the Indians. In this work of mercy his exertions were great, and many by his means were redeemed from the terrors and torments, which wait upon the death of an Indian captive. He soon returned to this place, and finding his country devastated by a foreign foe, and a remnant of his people left entirely destitute of grain and [illegible] visions, he purchased a large quantity of wheat for seed, which he refused to sell for money,—but distributed it gratuitously to the poor and destitute.

In 1817 he commenced the Stone Chapel, and could this edifice be finished according to his original draft, it would be a great ornament to our city.

In 1823 he was elected as delegate to Congress, where he faithfully discharged his duties, and his exertions for the Territory, and his success, will long be remembered by our enterprising citizens.

Notwithstanding his numerous acts of charity and duty, he has faithfully and successfully discharged his duties to the church. He has at all times been its eloquent and faithful defender, using his logical powers with the greatest precision upon all important questions. He spoke and wrote seven diferent languages; and the extent of his reading and his finished scholastic education rendered him a highly acceptable acquaintance to every man of erudition. His attachment to American Institutions and principles of liberty, has too often been manifested to need commendation at this time. During this season, and particularly while the cholera prevailed in this place, he was successful in his endeavors to assuage the disease and sooth the afflicted. He was often called from his bed to all parts of his parish to visit the sick in their last and painful struggle.

He had no fear of the disease while attending those just ready to be borne to their long homes, and such was his anxiety for his parisioners that he utterly neglected his own health, and he finally sunk under his exertions and the debilitating effects of diarhœa. The disease assumed an alarming appearance on the 9th, and the deceased, though suffering little pain, continued to grow worse until the 12th, when he was told by the Rev. Mr. Badin, that his end was near. He expressed his willingness to die, and wished that the *blessed* Sacrament might be administered; and immediately after he uttered these words—*nunc dimittis servum tuum Domine, secundum verbum tuum in pace.*" * Shortly after, he was asked if the extreme unction should be administered; he gave a silent consent, and seemed to long to be with his blessed Saviour.—His pulse continued to beat until 10 minutes past 3 o'clock, A. M. when his soul, tired and disgusted with the affairs of this fleeting world, winged its way to Him who gave it, and left the church to mourn the loss of one of her most learned Bishops.

During his sickness, his room was filled with all classes, every one wishing to aid their worthy and departing friend. His funeral was attended at 4 o'clock in the afternoon, by a numerous concourse; and by estimation more than two thousand people, of all ranks and denominations, followed the remains of this profound scholar, and firm supporter of the Catholic faith, this worthy friend and true lover of American liberty, to the cold and silent grave.

* Now thou dost dismiss thy servant, O Lord! according to thy word, in peace.—Luke 2, 29.

DIED.—At Ypsilanti, on the 7th inst. Mrs. Lydia W Champion, wife of Salmon Champion jr. Esq. aged 35 years. She was beloved by her family, particularly endeared to her intimate acquaintances, respected and esteemed by all who knew her, and by those most, who knew her best. She has left a large family to mourn her loss; but they mourn not alone: others feel the loss and with them mingle their sympathies. [Com.]

IN ATTACHMENT.

William S. Abbott, vs. Edward Tucker. } Before B. F. H. Witherell, a Justice of the peace, in and for the county of Wayne, M. T.

Wayne county, ss.

NOTICE is hereby given, that an attachment has been issued in the above entitled cause, against the goods and chattles, rights, credits, monies, and effects, of the above named defendant, an absentee debtor, and that the same will come on for trial before the above named Justice, at his office in Detroit on the 16th day of November next, at 10 o'clock, A. M.

WILLIAM S. ABBOTT.

Detroit, August 16th, 1832. 3m22.

L. BROWN & CO.

WATCH-MAKERS & JEWELER'S

AT the old stand in the Brick Building on Jefferson-Avenue, still offer for sale, a general assortment of.

Watches, Jewelry, Silver Spoons,
Plated and Britania ware,
Cutlery, Military Goods,
Indian Jewelry, &c. &c. &c.

As cheap as can be purchased this side of New-York.

Watches & timepieces of every description repaired in the best manner, and insured to perform well.——Cash paid for old Silver.

L. BOWN & CO.

Detroit Sept. 19, 1832. tf.

ATTORNEY AND COUNSELLOR AT LAW.

WILLIAM A. FLETCHER

HAS removed to the office lately occupied by Messrs. Cole & Porter, between the store of Messrs. Brown & Kellogg, and Levi Brown's house.

Detroit, Sept. 19, 1832. 6w21.

NOTICE.

IS hereby given, that I have been appointed and qualified administrator on the Estate of Joseph Cabacier, Late of Wayne County deceased, Intestate.

All persons indebted will make payment to me. Those having claims will exhibit them to me without delay.

DAVID THOMPSON.
Administrator.

Detroit, Sept. 20, 1832. 6w21.

GOOD BARGAIN AHEAD.

A LEASE of two years, of a Grocery Stand, together with its Goods, &c. for sale less than cost.—Said Stand is inferior to none in Detroit, and rent moderate.

For further information enquire at this Office.

Detroit, Aug. 30, 1832. 18tf

BRIGADE ORDERS.

Head Quarters, 3d Brigade, M. M.
Tecumseh, August 30th, 1832.

THE Officers, non-commissioned officers, and musicians of the several Regiments and battalions of the 3d brigade of the Militia will rendezvous for the purpose of Training, Disciplining, and improving in martial exercise; and the several Regiments and Battalions for Inspection and Review, and Martial Exercise, at the times and places following: to wit:—

The officers, non-commissioned officers, and musicians of the 8th regiment, on the 13th, 14th, and 15th days of September next, on the parade ground, at the Hotel of W. H. Hoeg, in the village of Tecumseh; and the said Regiment for inspection and review on the ninth day of October following, at the same place.

The officers, non-commissioned officers, and musicians of Maj. Jones' battalion, on the 20th, 21st, and 22d days of September next, at Morse's Inn, on Cold Water Prairie, in Branch County; and the said battalion for inspection and Review on the sixth day of October following, at the same place.

The officers, non-commissioned officers, and musicians of the 11th Regiment, and of Capt. John Anderson's Company of cavalry, on the 25th, 26th, and 27th days of September next, at the Hotel of A. Savary, on Pigeon Prairie; and the said regiment and company of cavalry, for inspection and review, on the fourth day of October following, at the same place.

The officers, non-commissioned officers, and musicians of the 7th Regiment, on the 25th, 26th, and 27th days of September next, at the parade ground, in the village of Niles, and said regiment for inspection and review, on the twenty-eighth day of September next, at the same place.

The officers, non-commissioned officers, and musicians of the 12th Regiment on the 27th, 28th, and 29th days of September next, on Prairie Ronde, at such place as Col. Brown shall direct; and said regiment, for inspection and review, on the second day of October following, at the same place.

Blanks will be furnished by the Inspector, and full returns will be required of the strength of each regiment and battalion; and every officer will be required to present his commission to the Inspector, that a perfect Roster can be made of the brigade.

Lieut, Col. D. Pittman has been appointed Brigade Inspector, and will respected accordingly.

By order of Brig. Gen. J. W. Brown.
D. PITTMAN,
Brig. Inspector.

[*Countersigned,*]
E. P. CHAMPLIN, *Aidecamp.*

A Brigade Court Martial will be organized, at a time and place hereafter to be specified, for the trial of all delinquents subject to said court—consisting of

Col. A. Huston, *President.*
Col. H. L. Stewart,
Col. H. M'Nair,
Lt. Col. D. Pittman, } *Members.*
Lt. Col. Daniels,
Lt. Col. N. M'Gaffee, *Supernumrary.*

By order of Brig. Gen. J. W. Brown,
D. PITTMAN, *Brigade Inspector.*

IN ATTACHMENT.

John Hale vs. Joel Seeley. } Before Robert Abbott, a Justice of the peace, in and for the county of Wayne, M. T.

Wayne County, ss.

NOTICE is hereby given that an attachment has been issued in the above entitled cause, against the goods and chattles, rights, credits, moneys and effects of the above named defendant, an absent debtor, and that the same will come on for trial before the above named Justice, at his office in Detroit, on the 27th day of November next at 10 o'clock A. M.

JOHN HALE.

Detroit, August 27, 1832. 3m20.

STEAM-BOAT FERRY.

THE STEAM-BOAT ARGO,

HAVING been fitted up and put in complete repair, will hereafter be employed as a ferry boat between the city of Detroit and the Beacon Ferry House, Sandwich. The proprietor has been at considerable pains and expense in rendering the Argo an expeditious and commodious medium of communication between the above-mentioned places; and the public may rely upon being accommodated without delay or inconvenience in the conveyance of Carriages and Wagons of all kinds, Cattle, Horses, &c. &c.

The above arrangement is intended by the proprietor to be permanent; and for the necessary and frequent communication between the Canada side and Detroit, he hopes the public will extend to him patronage sufficient to compensate him for his enterprise. The proprietor will bestow his whole attention to this business, and will spare no exertions in rendering the Steam Ferry a highly convenient and safe mode of conveyance.

The construction of the boat is such that no inconvenience will be experienced by gentlemen and ladies who may cross with teams or horses, as there is a spacious deck, gentlemen and ladies' cabin, where passengers may retire with safety and comfort.

L. DAVENPORT.

Detroit, Sept. 10, 1832. 20tf.

WHOLESALE AND RETAIL.

CHEAP FOR CASH.

JOHN TRUAX & Co. corner of Jefferson & Woodward avenue, are now receiving an extensive assortment of Groceries, Paints, Oils, Drugs, Medicines, Glas &c. To which they most respectfully invite the attention of persons disposed to purchase.

Detroit, May 22, 1832

BAROUCHE

A FIRST rate Barouche for sale, cheap for ready pay. Enquire of E. JONES.

[illegible]

IN conformity with the [illegible]

In the Township of Clinton.

Township 3	R 13	sec 25	E 1-2 N E 1-4
-	3	r 13 sec 28	e 1-2 n e 1-4
-	2	r 13 sec 21	e 1-2 n w fraction
-	3	r 13 sec 25	s fraction
-	3	r 13 sec 2	e 1-2 n w 1-4
-	2	r 13 sec 3	s e fraction
-	1	r 13 sec 2	s fraction
-	3	r 13 sec 36	e 1-2 n w 1-4
-	3	r 13	the estate of Abbott on Lake St. Clair, 1300

R. S. Rice, one village lot
Chas. Larned, one village lot
L. Cass, one village lot
P. B. Smith, two village lots
L. Kittridge, two village lots

In the Township of Harrison.

The estate of Meldrum

In the Township of Ray.

Township 4	r 13	sec 15	w 1-2 s e 1-4
-	4	r 13 sec 19	e 1-2 n w 1-4

In the Township of Shelby.

Township 2	r 12	sec 24	n e fraction
-	2	r 12 sec 15	e part n e fractional 1-4
-	2	r 12 sec 10	n e fraction
-	2	r 12 sec 6	w 1-2 s e 1-4
-	2	r 12 sec 6	e 1-2 s w 1-4
-	3	r 12 sec 32	w 1-2 n w 1-4
-	3	r 12 sec 28	s w 1-4
-	3	r 12 sec 32	w 1-2 s e 1-4
-	3	r 12 sec 20	w 1-2
-	3	r 12 sec 19	s part of n e fraction
-	3	r 12 sec 21	w 1-2 n w 1-4

In the Township of Washington.

Township 4	r 12	sec 6	e 1-2 n w 1-4 w 1-2 s e 1-4
-	4	r 12 sec 20	e 1-2 n e 1-4 e 1-2 s e 1-4
-	4	r 12 sec 1	e 1-2 s e 1-4
-	5	r 12 sec 25	w 1-2 n e 1-4
-	5	r 12 sec 27	w 1-2 s e 1-4 e 1-2 s w 1-4

HIRAM CALKINS,
Treasurer of Macomb Co.

Washington, Macomb Co. Sept. 1, 1832. *ts19

Territory of Michigan, Circuit Court for the County of Wayne, *ss:*

June term, A. D. 1832.

In the case of Adna Merritt, Perze Merritt and John Cook. vs. Jane King, late Jane M'Gee, administratrix upon the estate of William J. M'Gee, dec. and James W. King her husband. } In attachment, amount due plaintiffs from defendants as per affidavit filed, $294,-36.

NOTICE is hereby given, to all persons interested in the premises, that on the 31s day of January last, a writ of attachment was issued out of, and under the seal of the said Circuit Court, for the county of Wayne aforesaid, at the suit of the above named plaintiffs, directed to the Sheriff of said county, commanding him to attach the lands, tenements, goods, chattels, rights, credits, monies and effects of the said defendants; that the amount sworn to be due said plaintiffs from said defendants, as appears by the affidavit filed is the sum of two hundred and ninety four dollars and thirty-six cents.

JOHN WINDER, *Clerk.*

Detroit, June 22, 1832. 6w17.

GROCERIES.

Charles M. Bull & Co.

HAVE just received at their Refectory, two doors east of the Post Office, a large addition to their Stock of

CONFECTIONARIES, FRUITS,
GROCERIES, &c.

Also, a fresh supply of the choicest LIQUORS, all of which will be disposed of cheap for ready pay.

Detroit, May 24, 1832. 4tf

TOOL and HARDWARE STORE.

[*Jefferson Avenue, adjoining store of T. H. Wendell.*]

G. PAULL,

BEGS to inform the mechanics and others of this city, that he has opened the above store, with a complete assortment of *TOOLS* and many other articles in the Hardware Line, which he is now selling at New York prices.

He has also, on hand a complete assortment of fashionable *HATS*, (manufactured by himself in N. York,) which will be sold as low as at any store in the city whether a regular Hat Store or not.

Detroit, Aug. 30, 1832. tf18

ESTATE OF ORVILLE COOK.—Notice is hereby given, that a letter of administration on the estate of Orville Cook, deceased, late of the county of Wayne, has been granted to the undersigned, and that she has taken upon herself, the trust of administration, by giving bond according to law, All persons indebted to the estate are requested to make payment without delay, and those who have unsettled accounts, to present them for adjustment to John Hale, of Detroit, who has been duly constituted Attorney in fact, to the undersigned.

LYDIA COOK,
Administratrix.

Detroit, July 18, 1832. 3m15

NEW STORE.

JOHN CLARK & CO.

THE Subscribers having formed a connection under the firm of JOHN CLARK & CO. have taken the store formerly occupied by P. DAVIS, Jr. where they now offer for sale a large and well selected and general assortment of

DRY GOODS, GROCERIES,
GLASS, CHINA & CROCKERY WARE,
HARD-WARE, LEATHER,
BOOTS, SHOES, &c.

Which they will sell on as good terms as can be had in the city, at Wholesale or Retail.

JOHN CLARK,
P. DAVIS, Jr.

Detroit, April 1, 1832. 51tf

CHLORIDE OF SODA.

LABARRAQUE'S Chloride of Soda, a few bottles just received, and for sale by E. BINGHAM.

Detroit, July 25, 1832. 13tf.

WOODWORTH'S
STEAM BOAT HOTEL
[illegible]

STAGE OFFICE,

Corner of Woodbridge and Randolph Streets
DETROIT.

THE House is large and commodious, and the rooms light and airy. His table will at all times be furnished with every delicacy the season affords, and the bar well stored with the choicest liquors. Carriages will at all times be in readiness to convey passengers to and from the Boats without charge.

Seats can be taken at this establishment for any part of the country in the various lines of stages which leave the Hotel under the following

Stage Regulations.

The SANDUSKY line passing through Monroe and Maumee, leaves the Hotel every evening at 6 o'clock.

The ST. JOSEPH line, passing through Ypsilanti, Saline, Clinton, Tecumseh, Jonesville, White Pigeon, Mottville and Niles, leaves every morning at 7 o'clock During the summer season, and three times a week during the winter season. A branch of this line leaves Ypsilanti immediately after its arrival, for Ann Arbor, Jacksonburg and Calhoun.

The ANN ARBOR line, passing through Pekin, Plymouth and Panama, leaves the Hotel three times a week.

The PONTIAC line leaves daily; and a branch three times a week, passing through Rochester, Stony Creek and Romeo.

And also a line to MT. CLEMENS, three times a week.

A DAILY EXTRA will also leave the Hotel for Ypsilanti, at 12 o'clock.

As almost all of the above routes are regular mail routes, the travelling public may depend upon a safe and speedy conveyance.

EXTRA CARRIAGES

Will be furnished at all times for any part of the country.

B. WOODWORTH.

Detroit, April, 1832. 6m52

MILITARY STANDARD,
SIGN,
FANCY, AND ORNAMENTAL,
PAINTING.
GILDING, BRONZING, &C.

Jefferson Avenue, 3d door from Bates Street.

THE Subscriber will also attend to House and Sign Painting and glazing. He hopes by diligent attention, to merit a share of public patronage.

CALEB F. DAVIS.

Detroit, August 15, 1832. 16tf.

NEW STORE, NEW GOOD
AND NEW PRICES.

J. F. SHURTLEFF.

HAS opened a store in the building recently occupied by Messrs. Cole & Porter, one door east of Messrs. Levi Brown & Co. Jefferson Avenue, where he offers to the public a genteel assortment of

STAPLE AND FANCY
DRY GOODS,

of the latest style and importations, at such prices as cannot fail to please *all* who can be pleased with *Great Bargains.*

Detroit, July 11, 1832. 11tf.

NEW CLOTHING STORE.

DUNKIN & ALLYN

RESPECTFULLY inform the public that they have opened, in the Brick Building lately occupied by J. J. Garrison, & Co. one door from the corner of Griswold Street, on Jefferson Aveuue, a Large and Splendid assortment of

READY MADE
CLOTHING

made in the best style, and latest fashion. Among their goods may be found.

Fine, superfine, black, brown, blue, and green DRESS COATS.

Fine and Superfine black, brown, blue, olive, and green FROCK COATS.

Lion skin, kersey, and Petersham OVERCOATS.

Fine, black, cloth, silk Valencia, Merseilles, swansdown, bombazin and velvet VESTS.

Fine, black, brown, blue, olive, grey, and green PANTALOONS.

Camblet and plaid CLOAKS.

Shirts, drawers, gloves, hose, stocks, suspenders, mitts, silk and cotton handkerchiefs, and Cravats of every description.

They will be in receipt of Goods every two weeks during the continuance of navigation, and customers may depend upon being furnished with clothes of the latest and most fashionable style.

PAID [illegible]

The subscribers have also on hand a good assortment of

BROADCLOTHS and VESTINGS,

which they will make up to order, in the most fashionable and workmanlike manner.

DUNKIN & ALLYN.

Detroit, May 28, 1832. 5tf

REMOVAL.

H. V. DISBROW, & CO. have removed their stock of Goods to the RED STORE HOUSE on Gillet's Wharf, foot of Shelby street where they now offer a general assortment of

Dry Goods, Groceries, Hardware,
Crockery, Glass, Iron, Nails, Steel, &c. &c.

ALSO—In store on Consignment,

Pork, Whiskey, Flour, Wrapping and Writing Paper, &c.

H. V. D. & Co. inform their customers, who are indebted to them, that it is *very* necessary that their notes and accounts (particularly those of more than *four* months standing) should be *immediately* paid. By early attention to this notice *costs* may be saved.

Detroit, April 25, 1832 52tf

SEPT. 27, 1832:

The Rev. Gabriel Richard, one of Michigan's early leading citizens, dies. He was a priest, publisher and member of Congress.

"Rev. Gabriel Richard," column one.

April 29, 1835:

Local forces confront Ohio militia as the battle for the southern portion of Michigan heats up.

"The Border War," column three.

---

that translated the Old, and collected all the books of the New Testament into one, in 389. It was a Catholic that first established Trial by jury, in 846. It was the Catholic Gratian, who originated the Mariner's compass, in 1302. It was the Catholic Galileo, that first invented that compass by the first astronomical table, in that occupants the first astronomical table, in 1253. It was the Catholic of France that first invented a steam engine, in 1524. It was a Catholic monk, named Swartz, that first invented guns and gun-powder, in 1340. It was a Catholic that first traversed the Atlantic ocean, in 1492. It was the Catholic Faust that first invented Printer's types, in Mentz, in Germany, 1440. It was a Catholic that first granted free toleration of religious principles in Maryland, in 1635.

So much for Catholic ignorance. Bless me! how benighted, how idolatrous Catholics are, under their eyes and noses, that seeing they may see, and believing they may believe.

Yes, we should fix the stamp of our indignant scorn upon any man or body of men that shall undertake to blend politics and religion together. In politics, I am not a Catholic, I am an American—just as I would prove myself to be the invader of my country, should his footsteps dare pollute my native soil, though, in his country, I might happen to kneel at the same altar with him.

A NATIVE-BORN CITIZEN.

The ninth commandment is *"Thou shalt not bear false witness against thy neighbor."*

It has been asserted, written and verbally said by my neighbor *lately appointed a Justice of the Peace*—residing on the Island of Grose Isle, that the undersigned voted the Whig Ticket on Saturday the 4th day of April for delegates to the State Convention. What may have induced him to have made this erroneous statement is not for me to say—but I do say, that the assertion is wholly false and destitute of truth, and furthermore that I have not voted at any election or at any time, any other than the regular nominated *Democratic Ticket,* whenever that was made a party question.

WM. KEATH.

Detroit, April 24, 1835.

From the Michigan Sentinel.

THE TOLEDO WAR.—Our attention has been called, repeatedly, to several scurrilous, abusive and erroneous articles contained in the Toledo Gazette of the 18th inst. If an indiscriminate abuse of our public agents, a barefaced advocacy of the doctrine of resistance by force and violence to our laws and institutions, and a general and indiscriminate perversion of facts in the common history of every dry events, give a claim to celebrity and notoriety—then indeed has the Nullifying editor alluded to established for himself a most infamous and unenviable standing.

The history given in that paper of the apprehension of Goodsell and McKay is but a tissue of falsehoods, or strange perversion of trifling circumstances into glaring outrages by our officers and citizens; but taking our Toledoian neighbor upon his own statements and position, what is the state of the case?—These individuals attempted to prevent the due operation of the laws under which they had sought a temporary protection, and were apprehended in the night by civil process. We suppose if they could have reasonably called to their aid their deluded followers of the neighborhood, placed the lives of our officers and citizens in jeopardy, and had been suffered to have escaped—this organ of Nullification would have sounded it as a splendid victory, the first (except in the capture of bull frogs and cat-fish) ever achieved on the plains of Toledo !!

We have been the most amused by the *humorous picture* of a communication of Maj. B. F. Stickney, who calls it a *"horrid Border War."*—Not too fast, Major—a war must be anticipated, except a *windy war of words*, which yourself and a few of your interested neighbors may be able to create, that's all !! You have lived some time on an anticipation, lately by excitement, and you will shortly be doomed to grope quietly along upon your own resources and industry, Major. Maj. Stickney, whose fame, like that of the prophet's, shines dimmest where best known, endeavors to raise an excitement on account of a pretended insult offered to his daughter, another lady, and a certain fence. Now by the officers and citizens of Michigan. We have taken some pains to inquire into the matter; and have been assured, that although the fence-posts were capsized, by hook or crook, the ladies were offered every protection by the sheriff if they remained peaceably within doors, but were informed if they sought the street, amidst the multitude, he could not of course be accountable for the consequences.—Their desire to aid in rescuing the prisoners proved them to be in the latter course; and it was a fortunate circumstance that no other and fiercer fury, than that they were retired to follow, as I have been assured by the Nullifiers, the Major. The writer signs himself the Nullifiers, the locum of sleep, though the Major marks (absent the street) matters, is something to escape the arm of the grateful Justice. As to the idea of up-hanging, Major, or of hanging the mythical hero, I have been assured by the Major that they are both utterly without foundation.

The dragging of the Ohio flag, "at the tail of a horse," is a subject of comment by the Major—a monstrous offence, to be sure.—What a pity that our citizens should dare to resent the raising of a foreign banner upon the talest trees of their border ! what an insult to the delicate feelings of the Major and of the great western Lakes—Look out for "war, famine and pestilence," "extermination," and a most *horrid Border War*—"My kingdom for a horse!" JUPITER.

The following States have yet to elect their members of the House of Representatives, before the Congress, which meets in December next: Rhode Island 2—Connecticut 6—Virginia 21—in April. Mississippi 2—in May. Indiana 7—Missouri 2—Kentucky 13—North Carolina 13—Alabama 5—Tennessee 13—in August. Maryland 8, in October.

The political complexion of the 24th Congress, in the States that have elected Representatives, is as follows:

	Democrats	Whigs & Nullifiers
Maine	6	2
New Hampshire	5	0
Massachusetts	1	11
Vermont	0	5
New York	31	9
New Jersey	0	6
Pennsylvania	17	11
Delaware	0	1
South Carolina	2	7
Georgia	9	0
Ohio	9	10
Louisiana	3	0
Illinois	1	2
	90	58

REMOVAL.—MISS MOON respectfully informs her friends and customers that she has removed her MILLINERY STORE to the building on the corner of Jefferson Avenue and Shelby st., where she will receive, on the opening of navigation, a *large and general assortment* of Millinery and Fancy Goods.

April 26.

IMPORTANT to Western Shoe and Leather Dealers. The subscribers take this method to inform the western Shoe and Leather dealers that they are now receiving at their Shoe and Leather Store, State street, Rochester, about 100 cases gent's and ladies boots and shoes of all descriptions, and of superior quality. Having made arrangements with the manufacturers, they will be receiving from time to time, such additions to their stock as may be necessary, and which enables them to supply their customers at as low prices as they can be obtained in New York. They are also receiving a large and superior stock of Sole and Upper Leather, Kip and Calf Skins, dressed and undressed Morocco, Lining and Binding Skins, Prunella Ribbons, Colashes, Silk and Cotton Braids and Laces, Pegs and Lasts, Nails and Varnish, in short every thing that may be wanted in their line, may be had at the above stand lower than was ever before offered in this section of the country. Dealers will do well to call and examine their stock before going further, as they can more than save their expenses to New York and back, by purchasing of us.

E. PANCOST & CO.

Rochester, April 18, 1835.

To Rent.

THAT part of the building occupied as a shop for retail store in the house of the subscriber at the foot of Woodward avenue (to be let by 20) possession to be given on the 1st May. It is one of the best stands in town during the summer season, and well calculated for a Provision Retail Store.

JAMES ABBOTT.

Detroit, 24 April, 1835.

For Sale at Auction
LUMBER, TIMBER, & SPARS.

WILL be sold at public auction on Saturday the second day of May next at 10 o'clock A. M. at the lumber and timber yard of the subscriber, above the steam saw mill in this City, a large quantity of square pine timber, also about thirty thousand feet of seasoned pine timber and seasoned large spars, from 75 to 83 feet in length, all of which will be sold in lots to suit purchasers. Terms easy, and made known at the time of sale. The attention of house and ship builders is particularly called to the sale of the above mentioned property.

PETER DESNOYERS,

Agent for the late firm of Peltier and Doran.

Detroit, April 27, 1835.

TAKEN up by the subscriber at the Rising Sun Tavern, one and a half miles below Detroit, a dark BAY HORSE, about eight years old, middling size—no marks on him. The owner is requested to prove property pay charges, and take him away.

HENRY MILLER.

April 25, 1835.

FARMERS AND MECHANICS' BANK OF MICHIGAN.

NOTICE is hereby given that a meeting of the stockholders of this Bank will be held at the banking house in the city of Detroit, on the first Monday in June next, at 11 o'clock A. M. for the purpose of electing nine Directors of said Bank for the year then next ensuing. By order,

JOHN A. WELLES, Cashier.

td 1

ESTATE OF JOHN MALONEY, deceased.—Notice is hereby given that the subscriber has been duly appointed by the Hon. Benjamin F. H. Witherell, Judge of Probate of the county of Wayne, administrator on the estate of John Maloney, deceased, and has commenced the performance of his duties as such. All those indebted to the estate, are expected to make immediate payment, and all claims against the said estate will be presented for adjustment to

GEORGE C. BATES.

6w1

NOTICE.—The accounts due at this office on subscription, for Michigan Farmer and Mechanic's Bank, are in the hands of Mr. E. Clark, Ann Arbor, for collection.

R. S. RICE,

B. HOUGHTON.

Detroit, April 22, 1835.

A Lady, pleasantly situated in Sandwich, wishes to receive a few Boarders.—Apply at this office.

fw52

WANTED, by a young man a situation as clerk in a store. Enquire at this office.

April 22d, 1835.

MISS HELEN BAYNE'S DAY SCHOOL for Young Ladies in Detroit, is a building opposite the Presbyterian Session Room. April 20.

52

ESTATE OF PATRICK DONOVAN, DEC.

THE undersigned has been duly appointed by the Hon. B. F. H. Witherell, Judge of probate for the county of Wayne, M. T. executor on the estate of Patrick Donovan, late of said county. All persons indebted to the above estate are requested to make immediate payment, and those having claims to present them, duly authenticated, for settlement.

A. WHITE.

Detroit, April 25, 1835.

6w1

THE BORDER WAR.

We stop the press to announce the intelligence, that the first blow has been struck on the Border War between Michigan and Ohio. In violation of the laws of the United States, and of the sacred obligations of his State to the Union; trampling upon the laws of that Union, and upon both its rights and the rights of Michigan, the Governor of Ohio, in pursuance of an unconstitutional act of the Legislature of that State, and regardless of the admonitions he has received from the general government, perseveres in his efforts to extend the jurisdiction of Ohio over a part of the Territory of Michigan. For that purpose, early last week, he sent the Commissioners of the State, escorted by an armed force, to the west end of our Territory, adjoining Indiana, to retrace and run the boundary line through Michigan, illegally claimed by Ohio.

A penal law of Michigan, which is a law of the United States until repealed by Congress, provides for the arrest and punishment of any person accepting or exercising within our Territory any office or authority, unless derived from the government of Michigan or of the United States. This law has been pronounced valid by the Attorney General of the United States.

In virtue of this act, information having been received on Saturday last, that the Ohio Commissioners, protected by an armed escort, were engaged in running the boundary line through Hillsdale and Lenawee counties, and affidavit of the facts having been made before Charlie Hewitt, Esq. of Tecumseh, that magistrate issued his warrant for the apprehension of Patterson, Taylor, and Scely, the aforesaid Commissioners, and other persons whose names were unknown, engaged in violating the laws of the Territory. With his warrant, the sheriff of Lenawee, summoning a posse of thirty or forty persons the most respectable citizens of that county, proceeded on Saturday evening to Adrian, and on Sunday morning directed his deputies to go on with the posse about fourteen miles due south of that place, where they understood the trespassers and violators of our laws were then probably stationed.

With the knowledge that these Ohio people are armed, it became an imperative duty to arm our posse. On arriving near the house of Phillips, seven miles within the Michigan line, they found nine or ten armed men, as certained to be a portion of the Ohio party. Two of the deputy sheriffs, leaving the posse thirty yards distant, immediately proceeded towards the house, advised the party that they had a warrant for their arrest, and demanded their surrender.

The Ohio men refused to surrender, raised and levelled their arms at the Sheriffs, and threatened to shoot them. Not daunted, these officers urged forward, and came within a few feet, when it become evident that they meant to run; and orders were given to fire over their heads, and bring them to, if they did run. As was expected, they took to their heels, but were chased, and captured. They had been instructed and they had threatened not to be taken alive. Col. Hawkins, the Ohio Surveyor, and seven armed persons, nine in all, were made prisoners, and brought to Tecumseh for examination on Monday morning.

The commissioners happened to be at another house, about two hundred yards from the house of Phillips, at the time the above persons were captured. They ran into the woods, were pursued, but could not be overtaken. Gen. Taylor, one of them, made a hasty retreat to Maumee, about 30 miles, never stopping until he arrived there. The other commissioners subsequently followed him.

The Governor of Ohio, who has a force of about 500 troops collected at Maumee, has issued orders for the raising and marching of his thousand men to that point, declaring that he will never recross the Maumee Swamp until he runs the boundary line, and extends the jurisdiction of Ohio over that part of our Territory claimed by her. All this he proclaims he will effect, in despite of Michigan and any assistance which the United States may afford her. If the threat should be attempted to be executed; if the Governor of Ohio should invade Michigan with an army, in and they will commit treason against the United States, and be dealt with accordingly. One thing, at least, is certain: Michigan will never submit to be invaded, nor to have the jurisdiction of Ohio extended over any part of her territory. We presume that an invasion will be promptly repelled, not by a posse, but by all the force which can be raised. Our militia are amply provided for the emergency.

We have no doubt, however, that the President, as soon as informed of the present state of things, will promptly interpose with effect against Ohio. The authorities of that State have inflicted a blow upon the Union of these States more dangerous and destructive to it, than the Nullifiers of South Carolina aimed at it. Indeed, we are told that Gov. Lucas admits that his conduct amounts to Nullification.

RICE & HOUGHTON, PHYSICIANS AND SURGEONS, No. 62 Jefferson Avenue, one door below the Farmers & Mechanics' Bank. All persons indebted to either of the undersigned individually, are requested to settle the same without delay.

R. S. RICE,

B. HOUGHTON.

100 BUSHELS of TIMOTHY SEED of a superior quality for sale by

O. NEWBERRY.

April 28.

1tf

CITY HOTEL.

ISAAC ANDERSON would respectfully inform the public that he has taken the above ahead, well known as the GREAT VAN-SERT BOARDING HOUSE, in the most healthy and business part of the city.

The house is well fitted up to receive boarders and to accommodate travellers. The stables are large and convenient.

He is confident that his prices and fare will be such as to give general satisfaction.

A TEAM will be constantly in readiness to convey passengers and their goods to any part of the territory.

Detroit, April 25, 1835.

1tf

Valuable Furniture

AT AUCTION.

THE subscriber will sell at his residence near part of Jefferson Avenue on THURSDAY the 5th day of May next at 10 A. M. A general assortment of Household and Kitchen Furniture, amongst which, are mahogany and other materials. The sale will commence at the day previous to the sale. For particulars examined the day previous to the sale.

JOHN TRUAX.

Detroit, 29th April, 1835.

Thos. C. Sheldon
vs
Sylvester S. Hitchcock.

Before M. I. Bacon, Esq. a Justice of the Peace in and for the county of Wayne.

NOTICE is hereby given that an attachment has been issued in the above cause, returnable on the 5th day of July next, at 10 o'clock forenoon, pursuant to the statute in said case made and provided.

THOS. C. SHELDON.

Detroit, April 8th, 1835. 3m52

EAGLE TAVERN.

CHAMBERLAIN & LONG having leased the large commodious building, formerly known as Campbell's Hotel, on Woodbridge street, are now prepared to give their attention to travellers and others. The furniture of the establishment is entirely new, as is the apartments spacious, and airy, and no pains have been spared by the city, Boarders, Travellers, and Parties will always receive the best attention.—The table will be supplied with the various luxuries of the season, and the bar is of the best liquors that can be obtained. Large and convenient stables and out houses adjacent to the premises.

Detroit, April 13, 1835.

52f

TO RENT,

A convenient house, near the Capitol—Inquire of

Dr. BREACKENRIDGE.

April 21.

52f

CYRUS LOVELL,

ATTORNEY AND COUNSELLOR AT LAW,

BRONSON,

Kalamazoo County, M. T.

Elliot Gray and John Noble
vs
Sylvester S. Hitchcock

Before Marshal J. Bacon, Esq. a Justice of the Peace in and for the county of Wayne.

NOTICE is hereby given that an attachment has been issued in the above cause, against the goods and chattels, rights and credits, moneys and effects of the said Sylvester S. Hitchcock, and the trial of said cause will be held before said Justice at his office in Detroit, on the eighth day of July, 1835, at 10 o'clock in the forenoon of that day, pursuant to the statute in such case made and provided.

ELLIOT GRAY,

JOHN NOBLE.

Detroit, April 8th, 1835.

3m52

Proposals for Corn.

THE subscriber until the 15th day of May next, for delivering to the officer having charge of the Quarter Master's Department at Fort Howard, Green Bay, *sixteen hundred and forty-seven* bushels (1647) of SHELLED CORN, of a sound and merchantable quality, on or before the 30th of June next.

The proposals will be endorsed "Proposals for corn."

HENRY WHITING,

A. Q. Master, U. S. A.

Detroit, March 31st, 1835.

6w51

MICHIGAN STATE BANK.

PUBLIC notice is hereby given, that the books of subscription to the capital stock of the Michigan State Bank, will be opened at the office of the undersigned No. 2, corner of Jefferson Avenue and Bates street, on Saturday the 30th day of May next, at 10 o'clock A. M.

By the Directors,

JNO. R. WILLIAMS,

President.

Detroit, April 13, 1835. td 51

MICHIGAN STATE BANK.

PUBLIC notice is hereby given that an election for nine Directors to the Michigan State Bank, to serve the ensuing year, will be held at the office No. 2, corner of Jefferson Avenue and Bates street, on Monday the first day of June next, at 10 o'clock A. M.

By the Directors,

JNO. R. WILLIAMS,

President.

Detroit, April 13, 1835. td 51

Road Contracts:

GRAND RIVER ROAD

PROPOSALS for opening the Grand River Road from the 10th mile onwards, will be sold at public auction, at Brooks' auction room, Detroit, on the 5th of May next, at 10 o'clock A. M. The Sections will be of half miles, excluding the Bridges over the Rouge at the 13th mile, and over the Huron.

The mode of opening the road will be, in general terms, as follows, to wit: Its width will be 100 feet; it will be grubbed, cleared out and all roots removed for a space of 60 feet of the centre; 15 feet of each side will be chopped so as to receive all the rubbish &c. from the other parts of the road. Logs, 16 feet long, will be laid over marshes and miry places, so as to form a practicable cause-way, and necessary culverts will be made over the water courses which traverse the road route.

Contracts for constructing Bridges over the rivers Rouge and Huron, according to a plan, will be sold at the same time. Other bridges may be sold at a subsequent sale.

The time at which said contracts must be completed, is 31st December next. No payments will be made until they are completed. No per centage will be retained for final repairs, excepting in the cases of the Bridges. Proper security will be required in all cases. Mr. Melvin Dorr will be the immediate superintendent as heretofore.

HENRY WHITING,

Superintendent.

Detroit, April 4, 1835. 4w51

N. B.—Those jobs of the last letting which are unfinished, and which shall not be in a fair progress towards completion at the time of the sale, to be resold. H. W.

52

FOR SALE AT AUCTION, at Black River, in the county of St. Clair, on Saturday the 16th day of May next, at 10 o'clock A. M. the STORE HOUSE lately occupied by Foster & Doan; an interest in the mill materials. The terms will be made known at the day previous to the sale, for particulars inquire of

JOHN TRUAX.

Detroit, April 8, 1835.

NEW AND EXTENSIVE MILLINERY and Fancy Store.

NOTICE is hereby given that Mrs. M. O'Brien has opened a Ware House on Woodward Avenue, where they will kindly keep on hand a large assortment of every article usually kept in a Millinery establishment, and every description of Fancy Goods, which will be sold at reasonable prices.

H. C. SHELDON.

Valuable Real Property FOR SALE.

THE Mansion House in the flourishing city of Detroit will be sold, and if not sold will be rented for a term of years on the 1st day of June next.

The Mansion House is a land of stone and brick walls to a large attached frame building, one entirely new, and a still brick building. There is also a very large barn with other out houses upon the same property.

The location is the most airy and pleasant in the city, being 67 feet front on Jefferson Avenue, running back to Larned street, 200 feet. Also, Lot No. 1 and 2, where the building is located, on Larned street 36 feet front by 120 feet deep, to a 20 foot alley. This property stands upon a high elevation, and commands a beautiful view of the Canada shore, the river and the surrounding country.

A further description is unnecessary. Indisputable title will be given, and terms of sale and rent will be made known on said day of sale. The furniture along with the stock of Liquors, Horses and Cooks, will also be sold.

JOSHUA BOYER.

April 1, 1835. 2m50

The Cleveland Herald, Buffalo Republican, and Albany Argus, will please publish the above till the day of sale and forward their bills to this office.

CONTRACTS AT AUCTION.

CONTRACTS for opening and constructing the Territorial road, leading from Clinton to the rapids of Grand River, will be let to the lowest bidder, at public auction, on Tuesday the 5th of March next, at the house of P. Hooper, Clinton, and on the succeeding Thursday at Jackson burg.

As it is intended to make this road, in so far as practicable, equally good through out, its entire length. The parts most difficult of construction, commencing at its southern termination, and the bridges, will be at first reserving the residue until the last.

Copies of the contract may be seen on application to H. N. Baldwin, Clinton, or to the Postmaster at Jacksonburg, after the 27th instant. Security for the performance of the contract will be required, the name to be given to the superintendent on the day of sale.

The contracts will close on the first day of October next, and may be sooner, the amount which shall then be due, will be duct out for each month that shall elapse between the time of actual completion and the time prescribed in the contract for the same.

E. S. SIBLEY,

Ass't Eng'r. Duty.

Detroit, April 14, 1834. 3w 51

City Lots for Sale.

ONE lot on Jefferson Avenue 50 feet front by 100 feet in depth; Lot No. 2, 60 feet by 118, now the Steam Saw Mill; Lot No. 29, on section 3, lot No. 1, south side of Michigan Avenue and east side of LaFayette street; Lot No. 4, on the south side of La Fayette street; and the Mill Reservation; lot No. 6, on the south side of La Fayette street, on the Military Reservation, 2 lots on Jefferson Avenue opposite the Arsenal.

For information and particulars inquire

A. S. PORTER, under the Bank.

Detroit, March 17, 1835.

NEW CLOTHING STORE.

THE undersigned have opened, in the store recently occupied by H. Hallock & Co. a large and general assortment of READY MADE CLOTHING, which they offer for sale at as low prices as such goods can be sold in this city. Their stock embraces almost every description and quality of Clothing of the latest and most approved fashions. They have among other articles,

Olive, Brown and Mixt Cloth OVER COATS,

Brown and Drab Overcoats,

Blue and Green Blanket CLOAKS,

Kersey and Lambskin,

Green, Blue and Brown Camblet CLOAKS,

Blue and Black Goat's Hair,

Black, Brown and Olive FROCK COATS,

Black, Blue and Claret DRESS COATS,

Mix'd Cloth COATEES & HUNTING COATS,

Moleskin and Fustain ,

Striped & Fancy d & Cassimere PANTALOONS,

Fine Black and Blue Cloth do,

Blue, Mix'd and Drab Satinet do,

Moleskin, Cord and Kersey do,

Cloth, Satinet and Fustain JACKETS,

Bombazeen, Black and Fancy Silk VESTS,

Cloth, Silk Velvet and Valentia do,

Leather Merino, Cassinet & Camblet CLOAKS

All kinds of Fashionable FUR CAPS,

Fine Muslin, Gingham, Calico and Flannel Shirts,

Drawers, Handkerchiefs, Cravats, Stocks, Gloves,

Woolen Socks, etc. Also, a large lot of Hair, Seal, skin, and Leather Trunks in New York.

C. W. PENNY & CO.

No. 78 Jefferson Avenue, Detroit, Jan. 29.

L'HUILE VEGETABLE DE WARD
WARD'S VEGETABLE HAIR OIL,

RECOMMENDED and approved by the faculty, prepared only by E. A. Ward, M. D. 241 Spring street, New York. Among the many & great varieties of Oils, Cerates, Balsams, &c. to promote the growth of the hair, nothing has yet been discovered to answer the object intended so effectually as Ward's Oil. It has established a reputation never before acquired by any other preparation. It has restored the hair on heads that have been bald for many years, and in all cases where the hair is dead or beginning to grow dry and falling off, it exerts a most salutary influence in imparting life and lustre. When the hair is turning grey, the use of the Oil, and exclusive demand for the article, hitherto unknown, has and unprincipled men, to select it for imitation, thereby resorting to every kind of deception and fraud to palm the counterfeit upon the public.

The very particular to observe that except each genuine bottle is a treatise on the human hair, of about 36 pages. Sold by

BENJ. LE BRETON,

No. 107, Jefferson Avenue

Detroit, Oct. 29, 1834. 37tf

China, Glass & Earthen Ware.

WEBB, CHESTER & Co. Importers of Wholesale, No. 82 Jefferson Avenue, Shelby street, have on hand as large and complete an assortment of CHINA, GLASS, & EARTHEN WARE, as can be had east of Albany. In addition to their heavy stock, they are receiving by late arrivals at New York, further supplies direct from the Potteries, which will be sold in the original packages, or otherwise supplied to order at very low N. York prices, adding the regular rate of transportation on their goods throughout the Territory from New York. They will stock being a branch of the very well known house of Webb & Chester in N. York, and established throughout the Territory from the city, our stock will always be understood to partake of this advantage, being also determined to be undersold by any house at the West, which will always be kept manufactured in England and France, and Germany, besides the manufactured in England and France, and especially by the best manufacturers for their interest to call for sale these early fashions. Detroit, April 11, 1835. 81tf

---

Estate of the Minor Heirs of Louis Loignon, deceased.

At a Court of Probate holden in the county of Wayne, before an the office of the Judge in the city of Detroit, on Thursday of March, A. D. 1835. In the matter of the Estate of the Minor Heirs of Louis Loignon, deceased.

ROBERT ABBOTT, guardian of said minor heirs comes into court and files his proof of an order heretofore made in the premises of the second day of March last, to sell the real estate of said minors, and the said order has been shown, why said petition should not be granted, it is thereupon ordered and allowed, that the said guardian sell, at public auction, the real estate of said minor heirs, the following described parcel of land to wit; part No. Nor. See Section 11 in the range of four feet, bounded as follows: beginning at the most easterly corner, easterly corner of said lot, and running easterly along the line of said lot, forty feet, to the line between said let last mentioned and lot belonging to Robert Abbott; thence southerly along the said line, one hundred and sixty-five feet; thence westerly at right angles to the second boundary of said lot, forty feet; thence northerly on the east line of said lot to the place of beginning.

ROBERT ABBOTT, Guardian.

Detroit March 25th, 1835.

NOTICE is hereby given that the above described lot will be sold at public auction in the highest bidder, on Thursday, the 30th day of April next at the mill on said leased, in the city of Detroit, at 10 o'clock A.M. of that day. Terms made known at the sale.

ROBERT ABBOTT, Guardian.

Detroit, March 25th, 1835. 3w 41

CHINA & TEA SETTS.—PATTERSON, GARDNER, and MATHER, are opening a large assortment of fine CHINA TEA SETTS, of new patterns, which they invite their customers to call and examine, at the new Store second door below the old market.

Detroit, April 8, 1835.

50tf

ADJUTANT GENERAL'S OFFICE.

Detroit, March 31, 1835.

General Orders.

THE Rifle Battalion, commanded by Maj. J. D. Davis, and as heretofore attached to the 1st Regt., 1st Brigade, 1st Division, is now to be organized into a Volunteer Rifle Regiment, and to be attached to the 3d Brigade, 1st Division, and commanded by J. D. Davis, promoted as Colonel to the same, provided the number of companies are kept up and full, and all commissioned officers are fully equipped by the 4th of July next. Non-commissioned officers, musicians and privates to be equipped according to the uniform adopted by the Regiment within six months from this date.

The following Volunteer Companies are authorized, with the same proviso and condition as to number and uniform as stated above, viz:

In the 1st Regt. 1st Brigade, 1st Division, a Volunteer Rifle Company, at Detroit, commanded by Capt. Stevens T. Mason ; and a Volunteer Rifle Company, at Redford, commanded by Capt. Thomas Giddard.

In the 5th Regt, 3d Brigade, 1st Division, a Troop of Cavalry, at Ypsilanti, commanded by Capt. Thos. Andrews; and a Troop of Cavalry at Ann Arbor, commanded by Capt. C. Singerland.

Commandants of Regiments or separate Battalions, are hereby again directed to make their returns of election or promotion, and resignation of officers, to the commandants of the Brigade to which they belong, and that officer will make a return and requisition to the Adjutant General, according to the form prescribed in the law of 1833, page 32; as no commission will be issued, or requisition accepted, unless this rule is strictly complied with.

All companies of the line and volunteer regiments, will henceforth be designated by numbers or letters, and not by their local designation ; and these numbers or letters to be mentioned in the return of elections or promotions.

All commissioned officers of the staff, of whatsoever grade, are hereby directed to equip themselves by the 4th of July next, in uniforms fully equipped at that period, their commissions will be revoked, and their names stricken from the rolls.

The several Brigade Inspectors will report the names of all commissioned officers who are either unable or unwilling to equip themselves, in order, that their places may be filled with other such as will comply with this law.

By order of the acting Governor.

J. E. SCHWARZ,

Adjutant General.

52

Feb. 15, 1837:

Detroit celebrates Michigan's statehood with toasts, speeches and bonfires.

"The Celebration," column one.

The admission of Michigan into the Union, was celebrated in this city on Thursday last, with great manifestations of joy on the part of our citizens. The day having been previously set apart for that purpose, by the committee of arrangements, selected for the occasion, its morning was ushered in by the firing of a salute of 26 guns. In the course of the day the "Brady Guards" came out with their splendid uniformed equippage and made an elegant display of their martial discipline, in which they are already skilful tacticians. At half past 2 P.M. a large company of gentlemen repaired to Woodworth's Hotel, where they partook of a dinner prepared in "uncle Ben's" best style. After the cloth was removed, a large number of toasts were drank and several speeches made, which were received with great applause. In the evening the scene was opened with bonfires and illuminations — Jefferson Avenue presented a brilliant spectacle — bonfires flamed in the street, and lights blazed at almost every window. We regret, however, to say that the office of our Whig neighbor of the Advertiser, across the way, wore a characteristic appearance. Like the cause, of which it is the organ, it was *dark*,

"Irrecoverably dark,

"Totally eclipsed, without all hope of day."

The festivities of the occasion were closed by a "Union Ball" at Woodworth's long room, which was finely illumined and adorned with the bright eyes and manly forms of much of the beauty and chivalry of the city.

July 6, 1843:

Villagers in Royal Oak and Birmingham salute the new train as it rushes through the countryside between Detroit and Pontiac on its first run.

"Detroit and Pontiac Rail Road"

This road has in the last few days been completed, and travelers are taking advantage of it. On Tuesday last, the "glorious Fourth," the Governor, accompanied by several of his cabinet and staff, together with a number of private citizens, took a ride in the cars by invitation of the proprietors. The party left Detroit at half past eight in the morning, and after a pleasant ride arrived at Pontiac at half past ten. The road runs through a fine country, and the eye is continually delighted by flourishing and well-stocked farms. Royal Oak and Birmingham greeted the guests with salutes of artillery, and all seemed highly gratified at the success of the enterprise.

. . .

SEPT. 27, 1849:

Two of the big attractions at Michigan's first State Fair are the Fire Department and the Temple of Arts.

"The State Fair," column one.

The Fire Department, at an early hour yesterday afternoon, turned out in uniform and forming in front of the City Hall, marched to the Fair grounds, preceded by the U.S. 4th Infantry band.

They formed upon the ground around the stand built for the speakers, and with thousands of citizens listened with great interest to the address by Mr. Lothrop, which was an exceeding able production. The tremendous crowd gathered around the speaker, prevented very many, who were not fortunate enough to get near the stand, from hearing a portionn of the address.

Gov. Ransom addressed the assemblage, and paid some very handsome and deserved compliments to our Firemen. . . .

Thiss morning, great numbers were again visiting the fair grounds, although the crowd was not so great as yesterday.

One of the greatest objects of interest on the grounds this morning, seemed to be the temple of arts. It has been with great difficulty that the crowds visiting it, could be kept out, while those within had sufficiently examined the great many objects of interest which were presented there. The busts of Cass, Clay, Corwin, Taylor, McCoskry, have all excited surprise and admiration. The paintings of fruits, etc. by Dunncannson, are beautiful, and as they deserve, have elicited universal admiration. The Dagurreotypes by Martin, have also come in for their share of admiration. These Artists are all residing, for the present, in this city.

Jan. 18, 1854:

A train arrives at Windsor, linking the Atlantic Ocean and the Mississippi River with the locomotive — "the horse that never tires."

"The Great Rail Road Jubilee," column one.

Arrival of the Canada Train

At an early hour in the afternoon, immense numbers of people assembled at the foot of Woodward Avenue, and on the docks in the immediate vicinity, for the purpose of witnessing the arrival of the Great Western Cars at Windsor, and giving the guests of our city a hearty welcome. The steamer *Dart*, which was employed as a ferry on the occasion, made frequent passages to Windsor, taking over large loads. The cars should have arrived at half past 1 o'clock, but owing to various causes, were delayed till 5. Though this detention was of course vexatious, yet the throng upon our docks — which must have comprised the larger portion of our population, in addition to hundreds from the west — displayed a commendable degree of patience, and their number seemed to experience no diminution. At about 4 o'clock, the Military and Firemen, both of whom presented an exceedingly fine appearance, formed in procession and marched up Jefferson Avenue for some distance, and then countermarched down the street to Woodward Avenue, along which they proceeded to the dock. The engines were decorated in beautiful style, and their appearances reflected no small degree of credit upon the firemen. The engine of No. 2 was drawn by six horses.

About 5 o'clock, the cars came in sight, and, in a few minutes thereafter, arrived at their depot. The *Dart*, which was lying on that side of the river, immediately took on board the passengers, and, in the course of a few minutes, landed them upon our shore. The moment the train became visible, the Scott Guards commenced the firing of the salute, and it continued for some time after the guests had been landed.

July 8, 1854:

Abolitionists and like-minded politicians gather at Jackson to form what will become the Republican Party. The Free Press, a fervent Democratic paper, ridiculed the new organization.

"The Fusion Ticket," column one.

The abolitionists had it their own way at Jackson, and they drove with a tight rein. They not only constructed a platform after their own notions of architecture, containing all the anti-slavery planks, but they made such a ticket as pleased them. . . .

KINSLEY S. BINGHAM for GOVERNOR! When the democracy ran him for Congress, the whigs told so many hard truths of him that extraordinary exertions were necessary to elect him. We remember that is was especially difficult to make people believe that a man could be honest who had been guilty of an attempt to get certain naturalization papers ante-dated so that the persons who were the subjects of naturalization could vote before they had any legal right to do so . . .

Mr. GEORGE A. COE for Lieut. Governor, is an obscure individual living somewhere in Branch County. He was once a whig but we understand, makes no such profession now.

WHINEY JONES, for auditor general, is a very harmless sort of person, and is about as fit for Auditor General as a certain sooty type of person is for a preacher.

SILAS M. HOLMES, for State Treasurer, is notorious for nothing but abolitionism. When a fugitive slave was arrested in the city a few years ago, and a subscription started to raise money for his purchase, Mr. HOLMES was called upon for his mite. He indignantly refused. He didn't deal in human flesh — not he. A very *pious* philanthropy, that!

JACOB M. HOWARD, for Attorney General, was once a *whig*. He is a "republican" now . . .

Feb. 17, 1856

Of mining, snow and late mail. A report from the Upper Peninsula.

"Latest News," column three.

December 24, 1855

There is but little of interest among the miners. There is abundance of labor in the country this winter, and the mines will be worked with more economy than ever before.

The North American is opening well in the south galleries. Considerable copper has lately been met with in that part of the mine. This is especially interesting since that part of it is working in rocks farther south than anywhere else explored, or being explored, by mining in the country....

December 24th

I have just returned from a visit to the Copper Harbor mines. The snow on the highlands is four feet in depth — greater depth than I have ever known in this month....

January 1st

The mail from Keewenaw Bay came in last evening with one bag of newspapers, and the pleasing intelligence that five bags have been left, in which are our letters, on the beach of Lake Superior, midway between Marquette and the Bay, where they must await the carrier with a lighter mail, and if not destroyed, may reach us by March next....

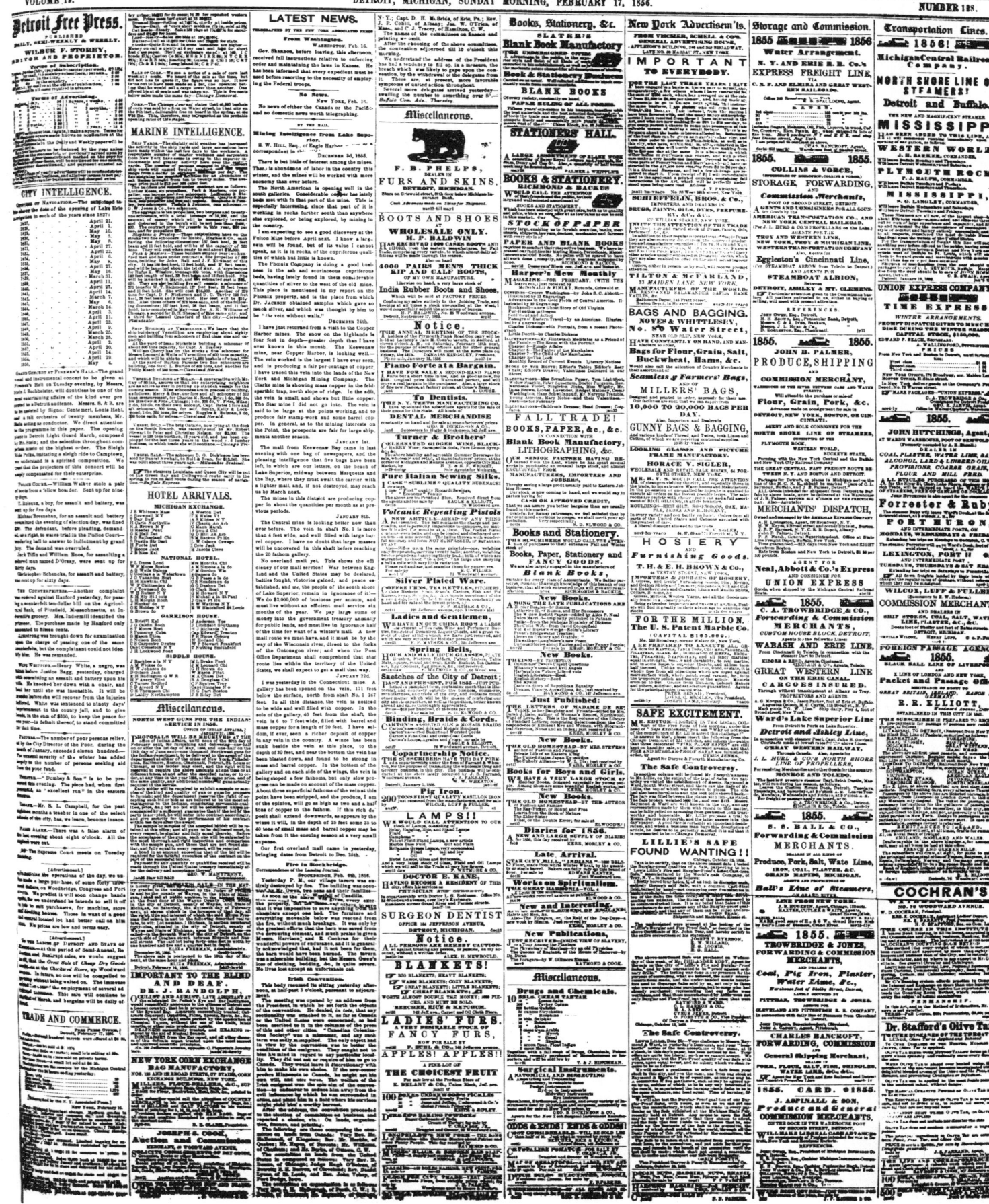

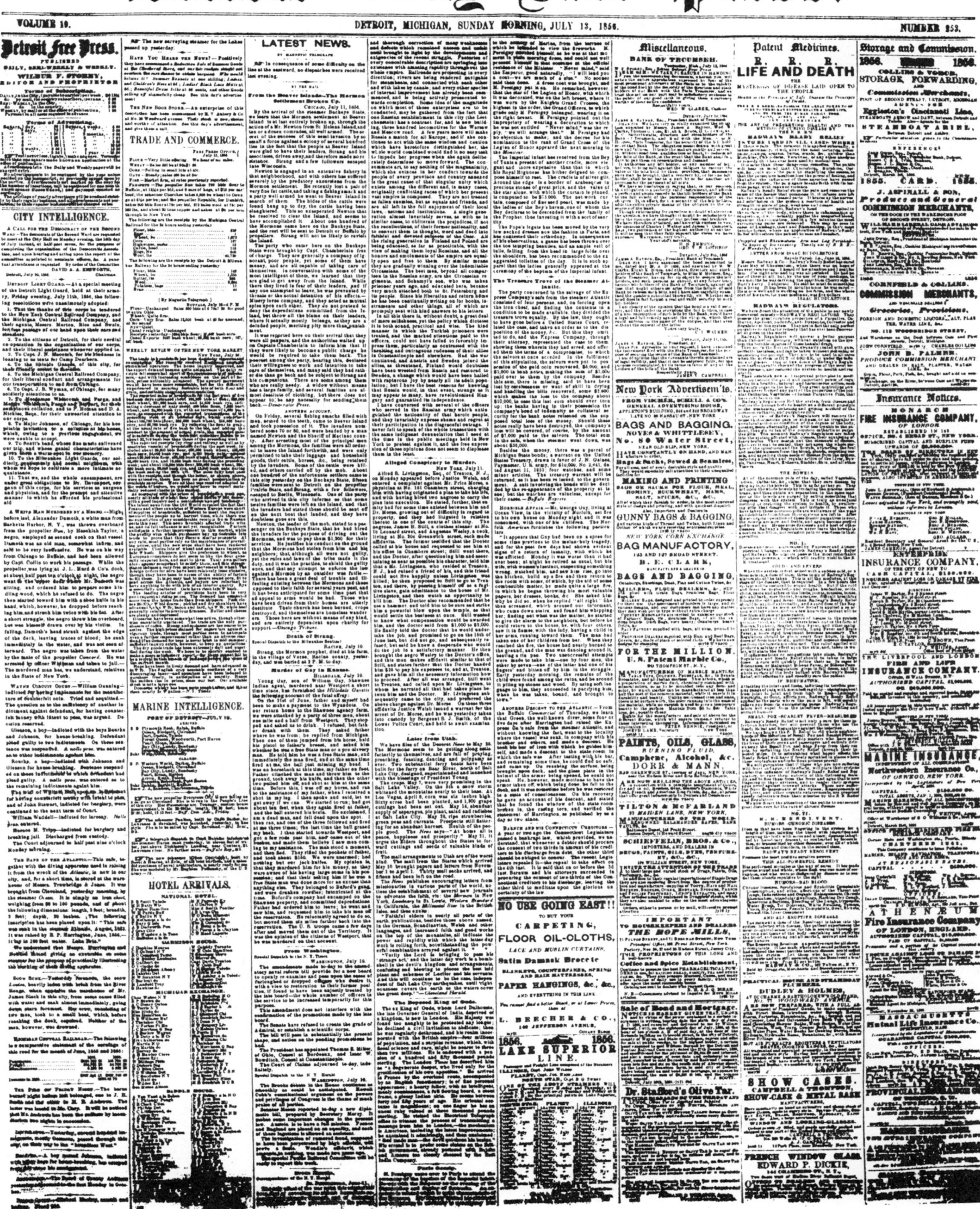

July 13, 1856:

A gang invades Beaver Island and breaks up the Mormon settlement. The leader, King Strang, is reported dead.

"Latest News," column three.

CHICAGO, July 11, 1856 — By the arrival of the steamer Buckeye State, we learn that the Mormon settlement at Beaver Island is at last entirely broken up, through the action of a Mr. Newton from St. Helena Island, and ten or a dozen comrades, all well armed. The secret of the success of this semi-invasion by so small a force against a colony of several hundred lies in the fact that the people at Beaver Island were glad to have their leaders, Strang and his associates, driven away, and therefore made no resistance. Strang and a few followers escaped into Wisconsin.

Newton is engaged in an extensive fishery in that neighborhood, and with others has suffered severely by the predatory excursions from the Mormon settlement. He recently lost a pair of very fine fat cattle, and taking a fishing smack and a party well armed he went to Beaver Island in search of them. The hides of the cattle were found hung up to dry, the cattle having been slaughtered. This so exasperated Newton that he resolved to clear the Island, and seems to have accomplished it. About one hundred of the Mormons came here on the Buckeye State, and the rest will be sent to Detroit or Buffalo by propellers. Strang will not be likely to revisit the Island.

The party who came here on the Buckeye State were brought by Capt. Chamberlain free of charge. They are generally a company of ignorant, poor people, yet some of them have money, and are all capable of taking care of themselves. In conversation with some of the most intelligent of them, we learned that they are glad to get away from the Island. While there they had lived in fear of their leaders, and if any one attempted to leave, he was prevented by threats or the actual detention of his effects. — Misery loves company, and they acted as mutual spies upon each other. They do not pretend to deny the depredations committed from the Island, but throw all the blame on their leaders, where it actually mostly belongs, as they are a deluded people, meriting pity more than punishment.

JAN. 16, 1862:

Two Michigan men tell of their captivity in a Confederate prison (Local Intelligence) while the state Senate proposes a resolution that "slavery should be swept from the land."

"Return of Two Manassas Prisoners," column two.

Sergeant Lewis Hartmeyer and Corporal Hubbard Smith, of Company A, First Michigan Regiment, who were taken prisoner at Mannasas, returned to the city on Wednesday morning, having been among those recently exchanged. They were taken after the battle of the 21st of July, having fainted and fallen through sheer exhaustion. Water was exceedingly scarce, selling as high as half a dollar by the canteen. The Confederate troops themselves nearly died of thirst, and were driven to the extremity of scooping up with their hands the puddles which were made in the road by the rain. Nothing whatever to eat was furnished them, so that they were without food from Sunday morning until they reached Richmond on Thursday, except a few hard crackers, which were only sufficient to keep life in them....

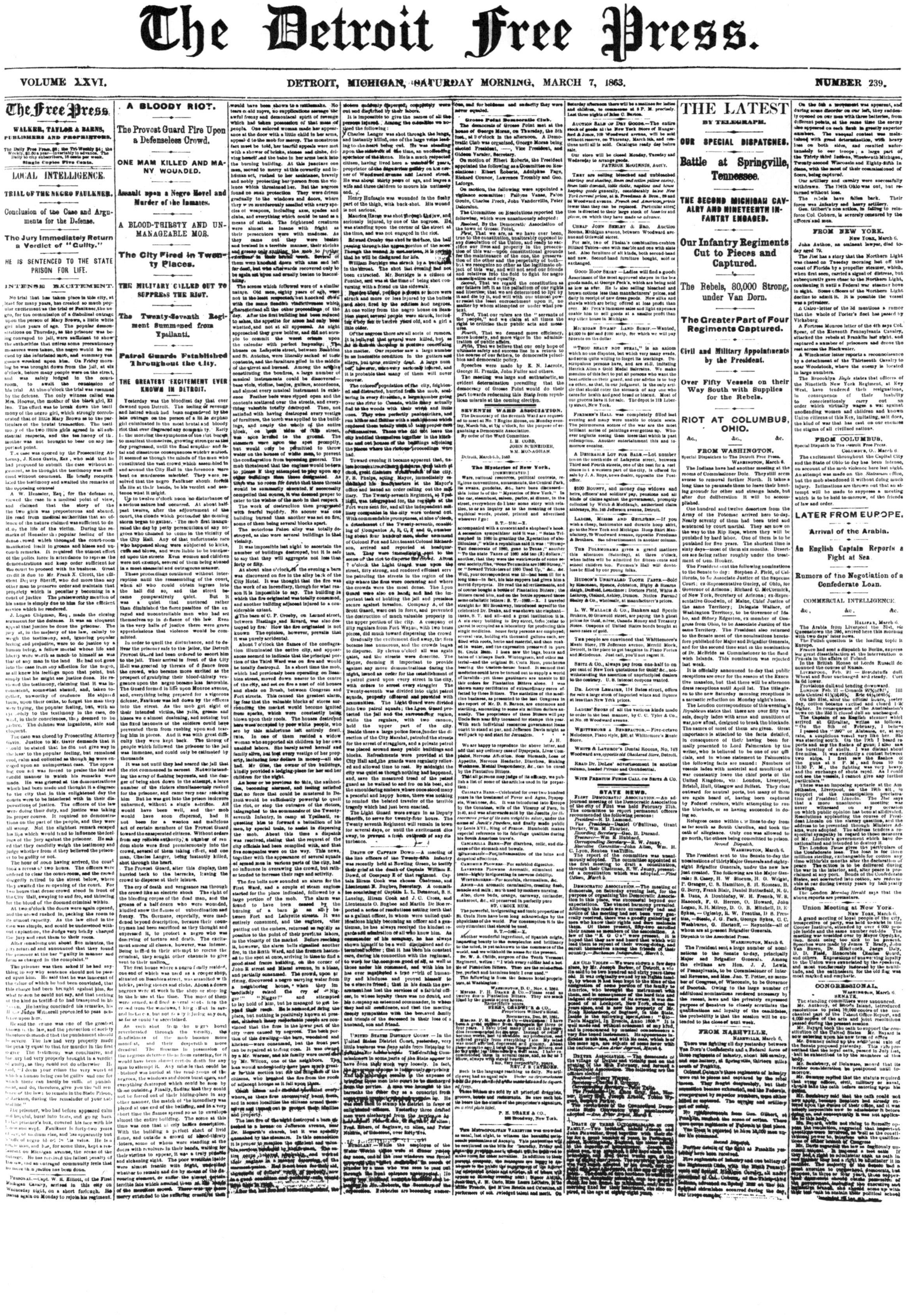

The Detroit Free Press.

VOLUME LXVI.   DETROIT, MICHIGAN, SATURDAY MORNING, MARCH 7, 1863.   NUMBER 239.

March 7, 1863:

Court proceedings involving a black man result in a riot.

"Local Intelligence," column one and *"A Bloody Riot,"* column two.

Yesterday was the bloodiest day that ever dawned upon Detroit. The feeling of revenge and hatred which had been engendered by the late outrage on the person of a little orphan girl culminated in the most brutal and bloody riot that ever disgraced any community. Early in the morning the symptoms of the riot began to manifest themselves, growing stronger as the day progressed, until the final eruption and fatal and disastrous consequences which resulted. It seemed as though the minds of the men who constituted the vast crowd which assembled in and around the City Hall in the forenoon were bent on murderous mischief. They were resolved that the negro Faulkner should forfeit his life at their hands, be his verdict and sentence what it might.

In order to quell the disturbance, and to deliver the prisoner safe to the jailer, the Detroit Provost Guard had been ordered to escort him to the jail. Their arrival in front of the City Hall was greeted by threats of defiance from the crowd, who became more excited as the prospect of gratifying their blood-thirsty vengeance upon the negro became less favorable.

It was not until they had neared the jail that the riot commenced in earnest. Notwithstanding the army of flashing bayonets, and the danger of being shot down in the attempt, a large number of rioters simultaneously rushed for the prisoner, and came very near reaching him. But he was got into the prison inclosure unharmed, without a single sacrifice. All would have been well, and the mob would have soon dispersed, had it not been for a wanton and malicious act of certain members of the Provost Guard toward the exasperated citizens. Without orders from any reliable authority, a number of random shots were fired promiscuously into the crowd, several of them taking effect, and one man, Charles Langer, being instantly killed, shot through the heart.

The cry of death and vengeance ran through the crowd like an electric shock. The sight of the bleeding corpse of the dead man, and the groans of a half dozen who were wounded, kindled anew the flames of subordination and frenzy.

June 23, 1863:

A dog leaps to the rescue when a circus hippopotamus jumps ship and flounders in the Detroit River.

"A Novel Scene," column two.

A very exciting as well as novel affair occurred about six miles down the river on Monday afternoon, being no less than a veritable chase of a hippopotamus. It seems that in the transit of the circus now performing here from Buffalo to this city, it became necessary, on account of their excessive weight, to send the elephants and the hippopotamus on a propeller and they were accordingly shipped . . .

The huge beast was shipped from Buffalo aboard the steamer *SD Caldwell* and as it was impossible to get his immense cage on board, that was sent by land while his Behemothship, accompanied by Ali, the Egyptian, his captor and keeper, proceeded by water to Detroit. During the voyage it was noticed that the animal continually looked longingly toward the water as though he would have given one of his eye teeth, (no trifle by the way) for a plunge into the depths of the lake and a ramble about its unexplored bottom. . . .

As the steamer neared the city, and when about three miles below the Fort, and as Ali and everybody else were gazing landward, a crash and then a splash were heard from the side of the bow toward the American shore. Everybody rushed to the spot. The place where the hippopotamus had been confined was empty. . . .

A large black mastiff, which had been trained to sleep in the cage with the hippopotamus, and for whom he had for a long time evinced much affection, had been keeping up a continued howling from the time his companion had escaped, was now loosened, and he instantly plunged into the river, and swam after Ali as he moved off. In about a minute the hippopotamus again stuck his huge head out of the water, and, on seeing him, the dog gave a wild bark, and swam in his direction very rapidly, Ali accompanying him in the boat. At last the dog reached the monster, and, with a series of barks, commenced swimming round the animal, and finally struck out for the shore, the hippopotamus following. . . .

The Detroit Free Press.

VOLUME XXVIII. — DETROIT, MICHIGAN. MONDAY MORNING, APRIL 10, 1865. — NUMBER 264.

SUNDAY'S MORNING EDITION

THE ENEMY PUSHED FROM THE ROAD TOWARDS DANVILLE.

They are Now Pursued Towards Lynchburg.

Grant Confident of Receiving the Surrender of Lee and What Remains of his Army.

REPORT THAT THE PRESIDENT WILL ISSUE ANOTHER AMNESTY PROCLAMATION.

&c., &c., &c.

[BY THE WESTERN UNION LINE.]

MONDAY'S MORNING EDITION

GLORY! GLORY!! GLORY!!!

THE REBELLION ENDED!

LEE'S WHOLE ARMY SURRENDERED.

THE SURRENDER EFFECTED SUNDAY AFTERNOON.

Correspondence Between Generals Grant and Lee.

ALL ARMS AND PUBLIC PROPERTY TO BE DELIVERED UP.

The Officers to Retain their Private Property and Side Arms.

EACH OFFICER AND SOLDIER TO BE ALLOWED TO GO HOME ON PAROLE.

Grant Pledges that they Shall Not Do Take Arms against the United States.

A Salute of Two Hundred Guns Ordered Fired at Every Post and Arsenal in the United States.

THE PRESIDENT'S INTERVIEW WITH REBEL OFFICIALS.

THE BOMBARDMENT OF MOBILE ACTIVELY PROGRESSING.

&c., &c., &c.

April 15, 1865:

Black borders signify the death of Abraham Lincoln.

The Detroit Free Press.

VOLUME XXVIII.   DETROIT, MICHIGAN, SATURDAY MORNING, APRIL 15, 1865.   NUMBER 269.

THE LATEST
BY TELEGRAPH

THE PRESIDENT ASSASSINATED.

He Is Shot at the Theatre

Escape of the Assassin.

HE SHOT FROM THE GALLERY, LEAPED TO THE STAGE WITH A GLEAMING KNIFE IN HIS HAND AND ESCAPED THROUGH THE BACK ENTRANCE.

HE THEN MOUNTED A HORSE AND FLED.

Before Leaving He Exclaimed "Sic Semper Tyrannus."

The President was Removed to a Private Residence and Died in a Short Time.

SECRETARY SEWARD ALSO ASSASSINATED.

HIS THROAT CUT, BUT IT IS HOPED HE WILL RECOVER.

TERRIBLE EXCITEMENT IN WASHINGTON.

THE RETREAT OF JOHNSTON.

Belief that he will Make a Stand at Augusta, Ga.

An Attempt will be Made to Form the Nucleus of Another Southern Army There.

JEFF. DAVIS PENNED A PROCLAMATION AT DANVILLE.

He Admits the Loss of Virginia, but says the War will be Carried on.

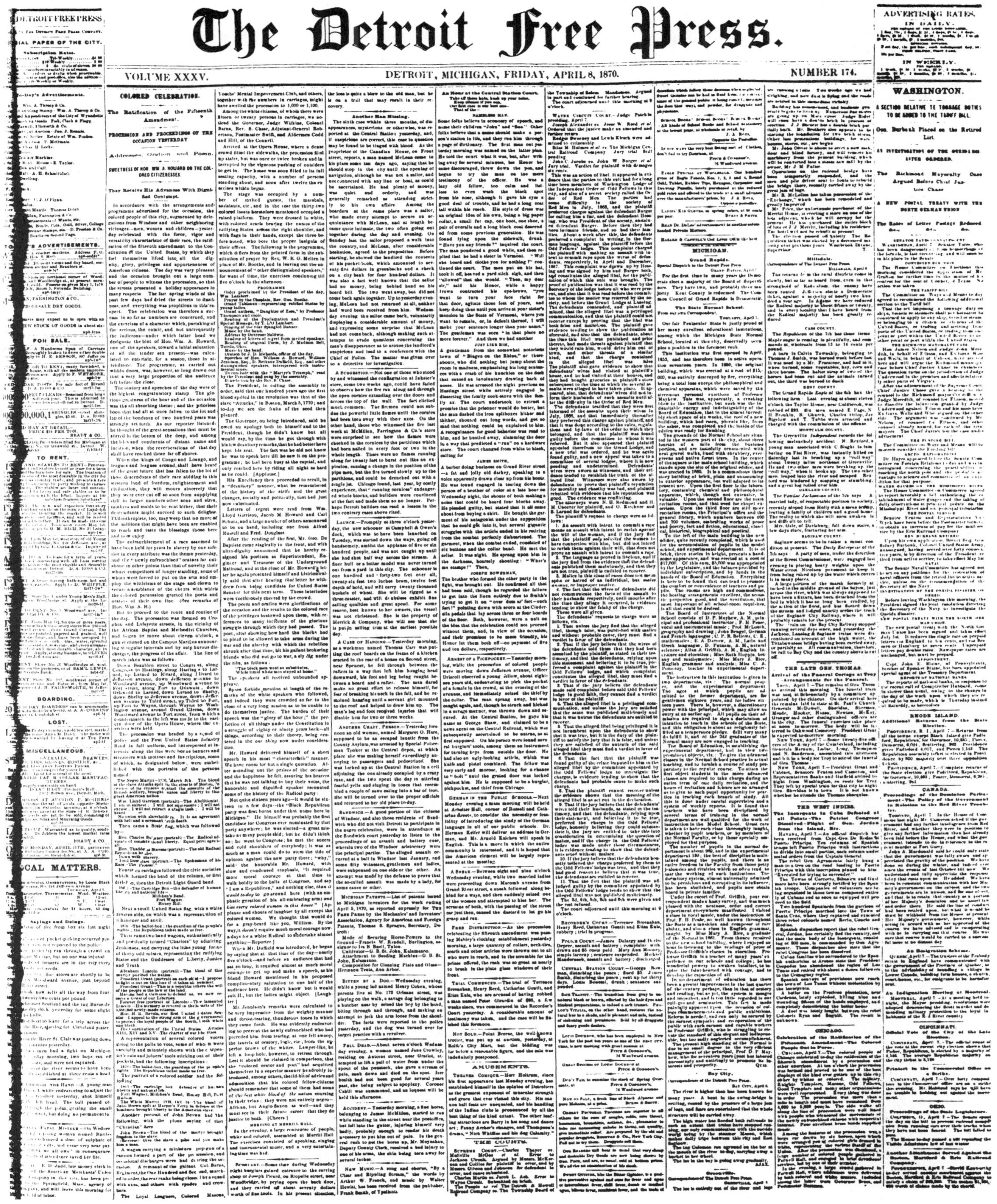

April 8, 1870:

Blacks are joined by some whites in celebrating the ratification of the Fifteenth Amendment, giving blacks the right to vote.

"Colored Celebration," column two.

In accordance with the arrangements and programme advertised for the occasion, the colored people of the city, augmented by delegations from Windsor and other neighboring vicinages — men, women and children — yesterday celebrated with the force, vigor and versatility characteristic of their race, the ratification of the fifteenth amendment to the Constitution of the United States, by which they feel themselves lifted into all the dignity, glory, privileges and appurtenances of American citizens. The day was very pleasant and the occasion brought out a large number of people to witness the procession, so that the streets presented a holiday appearance in many respects. The fair spring winds of the past few days had dried the streets to dustiness and everything was propitious in this respect. The celebration was therefore a success in so far as numbers are concerned, and the exercises of a character which, partaking of the serious, the comic, and not unfrequently the ludicrous — under which latter head we designate the hint of Hon. Wm. A. Howard, one of the speakers toward a labial salutation of all the tender sex present — was calculated to entertain, for a season, those in attendance. The programme, as carried out within doors, was, however, so long drawn out that a very large proportion of the audience left before the close.

Nov. 30, 1870:

Susan B. Anthony speaks at meeting of women demanding the right to vote.

"*Woman,*" column three.

The Northwestern Woman's Suffrage Association assembled, yesterday morning, at Young Men's Hall in this city. The attendance so far is not large. The greater part of the audience was composed, during the day session, of . . . ladies . . . celebrated throughout the land as agitators of the question, "Shall women be allowed to vote?" The meetings are presided over with great tact and ability by Mrs. M. Adele Hazlett, of Hillsdale, who is the President of the Association.

Mrs. Hazlett's manner is very gracious and her senses evidently most acute. She seizes a point with wonderful quickness and enforces her wishes in a witty and poremptory sort of way, that admits of no debate and no opposition. . . .

Upon conclusion of (the financial report), Miss Susan B. Anthony spoke, giving generally her ideas on woman suffrage, her reasons for demanding it — the abuses that women suffer for lack of it; said that the Democrats of Wyoming first granted that privilege and hoped that the Democracy all over the country would go in for it and finished by declaring that the ballot to be the key to position and independence . . .

She compared the bondage of woman to the bondage of slaves. She recited how agitation had resulted in the overthrow of slavery. There was still a slavery existing in the idea that man held property in woman. At this day and at this time men without regard to color were equal in the law. She abjured them to abolish this idea of man's property in woman. In olden times, and you, in Detroit, among them, felt that you were doing God's work when you assisted some hundreds of slaves escape to freedom. But how futile were your efforts — good as they were — when every year four hundred thousand children were born in the condition of slaves . . .

I don't like to be severe on the men, but they say I am (laughter). I know and have associated with the best and leading men of this country, and I think I know them. I do not believe that one of then, in his own home, thought that the will of his wife or daughters was quite as worthy of respect as his own. . . .

March 22, 1872:

An Oakland County farmer deals with horse theft by consulting a clairvoyant in Detroit.

"Humbugged," column three.

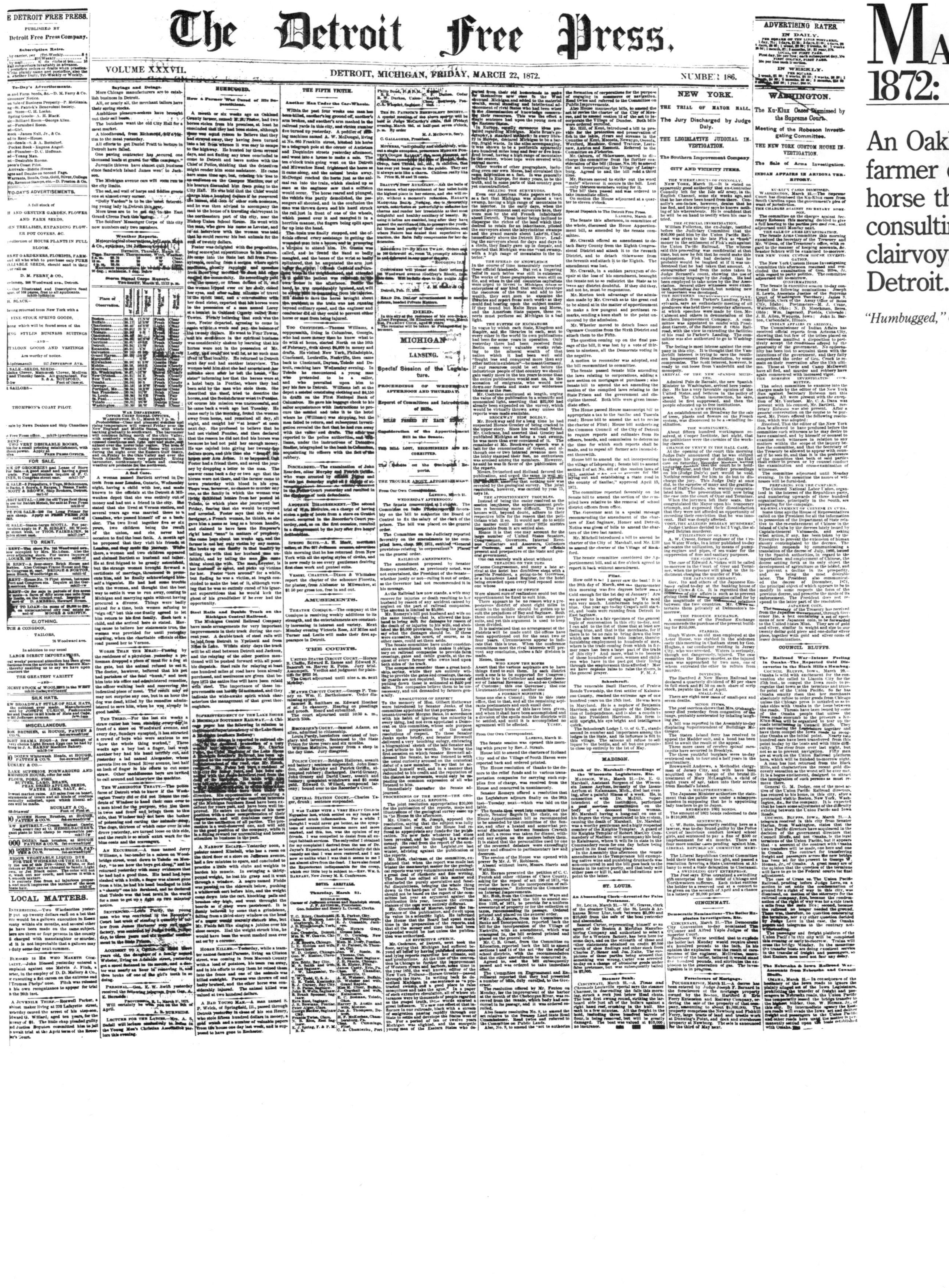

June 29, 1875:

A tornado sweeps down on Detroit's west side.

"The Tornado," column three.

One of the most startling and terrible calamities known in the history of Detroit befell the city Sunday afternoon, resulting in a serious loss of life and the wounding of nearly fifty persons, besides tremendous destruction of property.

STARTLING RUMORS

Shortly after six o'clock rumors were heard down town that a tornado had swept over a portion of the city, demolishing houses, barns, stores, etc. and killing scores of men, women, children and animals. In a very little time thereafter the city was wild with excitement. Men ran hither and thither, anxiously seeking to know precisely what had occurred or what portion of the city had suffered from the awful visitation. "Up Grand River avenue, near Fifteenth street," said one, and in that direction the crowd soon began to surge. The sidewalks were jammed, all the street cars on Grand River avenue were crowded to overflowing, and the street was literally lined.

THE DOOMED LOCALITY

Every face was blanched. Men spoke in low tones as they discussed the probable extent of the devastation, and women wept silently as the rumors of loss of life multiplied. Of course there were hundreds of stories told which had little or no foundation in fact, but the simple truth is appalling.

THE DESTROYER

Seemed to be a whirlwind which rose apparently near the southwestern limit of the city. It was first seen in that direction in the shape of a dark, smoky looking spiral mass, shaped like an inverted tunnel of enormous dimensions, and whirling with inconceivable rapidity. Its forward movement was also very rapid in a course north of east, but it did not strike the earth until it reached the vicinity of Williams avenue and Ash street. There the first evidence of

ITS AWFUL POWER

Was seen in upturned sidewalks and demolished outbuildings, but no dwellings seem to have been caught in that immediate neighborhood.

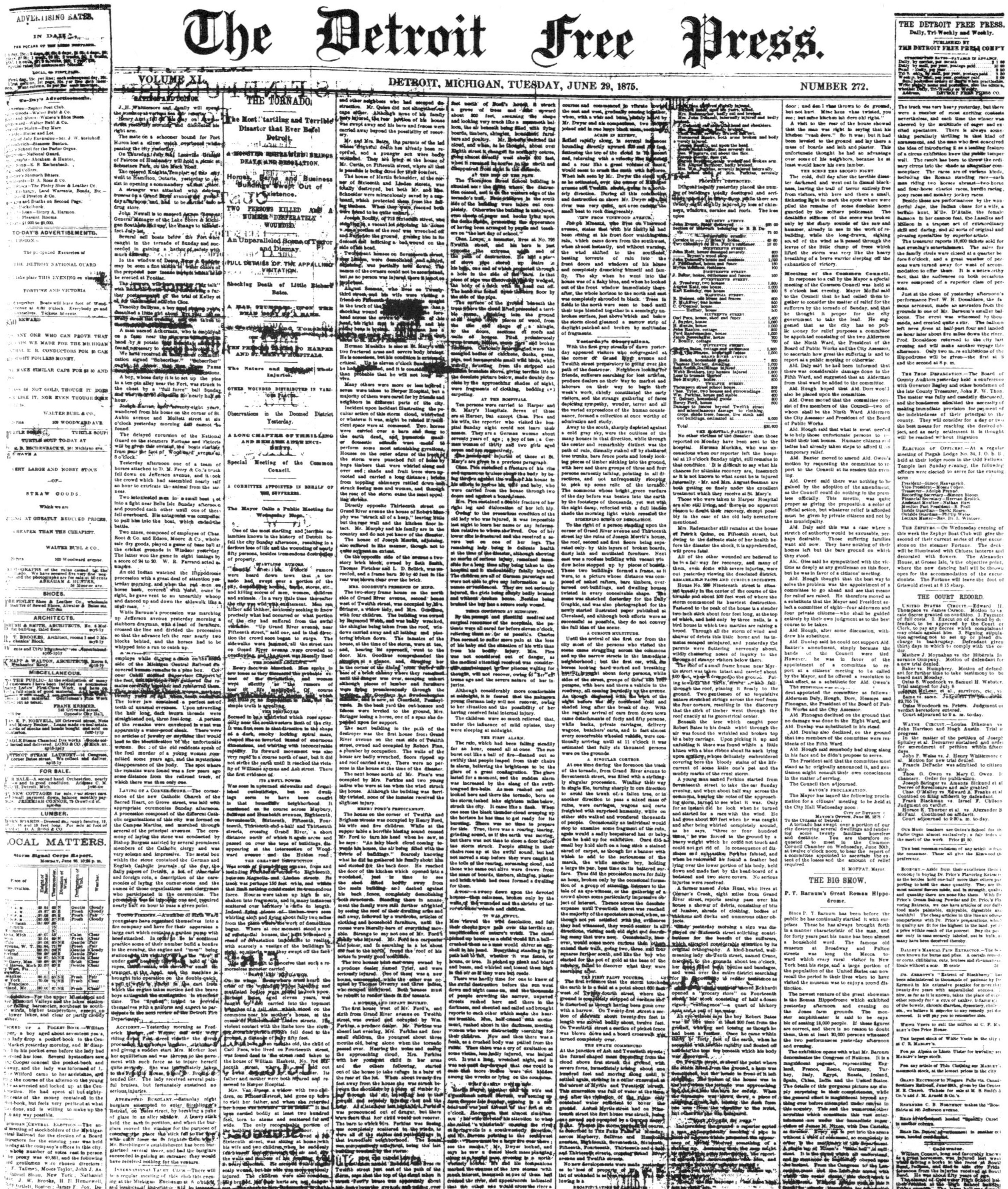

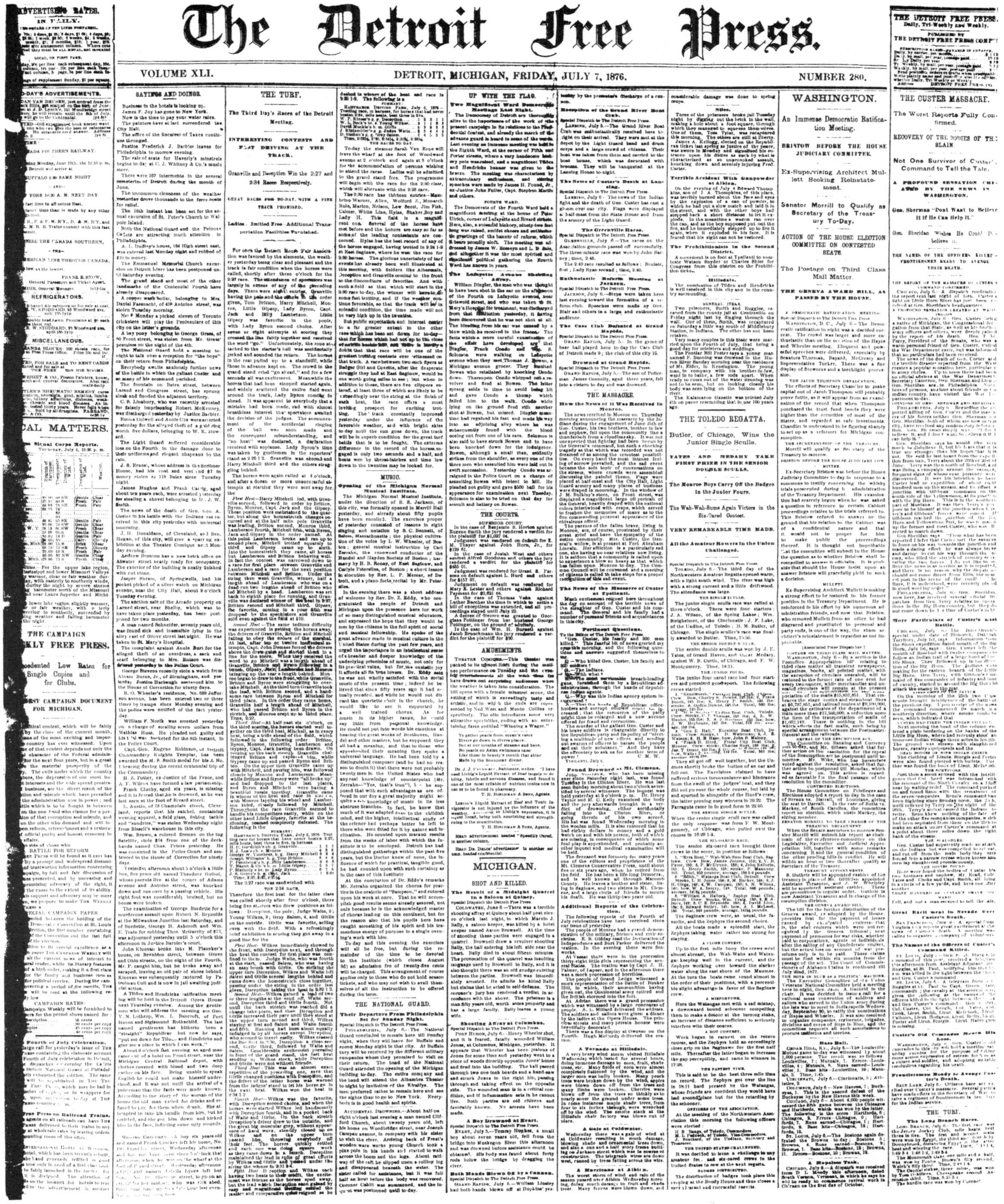

The Detroit Free Press.

VOLUME XLI. — DETROIT, MICHIGAN, FRIDAY, JULY 7, 1876. — NUMBER 280.

JULY 7, 1876:

Michigan native Gen. George Custer dies at the battle of Little Big Horn.

"The Custer Massacre," column nine.

THE REPORT OF THE MASSACRE OF CUSTER'S COMMAND CONFIRMED.

CHICAGO, July 6. — A dispatch confirming the report sent last night of Gen. Custer's fight on Little Horn River has just been received at Gen. Sheridan's headquarters.

A PROFOUND SENSATION CREATED AT WASHINGTON.

WASHINGTON, July 6 — Gen. Custer being a native of Michigan, the Congressional delegation from that State, as well as his brother army officers and others, were deeply pained by the report of his death. Hon. T.W. Ferry, President of the Senate, who was a warm personal friend of Gen. Custer, visited the War Department early, but was informed that no particulars had been received.

OPINIONS OF GENS. SHERMAN AND SHERIDAN.

PHILADELPHIA, July 6 — Regarding the reported killing of Gen. Custer and the massacre of his forces neither Gen. Sherman nor Gen. Sheridan, both of whom are now in the city, have received any confirmatory information. Gen. Sherman simply says: "I don't believe it, and I don't want to believe it if I can help it."

Gen. Sheridan says: "From what has been reported I infer that Custer met the savages in force on his way towards the junction and made a daring effort — he was always brave and daring — to cut his way through the enemy, who filled the stretch of country separating the two forces. I do not like to believe the news is as terrible as it is reported, and there is no reason why the dispatches should not come direct from Ellis, the nearest post to the scene of the conflict. The lines, it is understood, were recently placed in good working order."

March 7, 1877:

The telephone is successfully tested with a concert from Chicago.

"Musical Lightning," column six.

In response to cards of invitation, about 150 ladies and gentlemen assembled last evening at the rooms of the Detroit Club to listen to the first exhibition of the telephone, the wonderful production of Elisha Grey, electrician of the Western Telegraphic Manufacturing Company, of Chicago.

At 8 o'clock Alfred Russell announced that the Detroit Club had invited their friends to witness a simple experiment which possibly might not be a success, as eighty-four miles was the greatest distance yet traversed by means of the telephone. Now 284 miles, it was hoped, would prove no obstacle. All the Club could do was to hope for a success, but in anticipation of possible failure and by way of atonement, they had provided for their friends a little salad and coffee. In introducing M. C. Kellogg, who was to represent Mr. Grey, Mr. Russell referred to trials and ultimate success of Prof. Morse — how he labored long to secure a subsidy from Congress, until at last he was reduced to his last half dollar, and still without hope of help; how, at the very next session of Congress, he received his subsidy and constructed between Washington and Baltimore the first line of telegraph in the United States. The first message was appropriately : "What hath God wrought!" and we may well say — after witnessing the wonders of Prof. Grey's invention — with Prof. Morse: "What hath God wrought? . . ."

In order that the sounding box might increase the sound to the greatest possible extent, it was taken from the table and suspended to a chandelier in the middle of the room, and thus, with everything in readiness, Mr. Russell announced the fact and asked for silence.

Instantly chattering voices ceased their whispers, ladies and gentlemen turned their eyes and ears toward the swinging box, and in a weird, muffled sound was distinctly, though not loudly heard, the familiar air of "Comin' Thro' the Rye," which the audience listened to with wonder, almost awe. As the mysterious box gave the sounds and came near to the end of the measure the audience felt like applauding with dignity, yet when the last note of the Scotch ballad was followed with the famous theatrical "gag" of "What will you have to-night?" everybody forgot the solemn importance of the occasion, and laughing loudly, united in hearty applause.

THE DETROIT FREE PRESS, SUNDAY, NOVEMBER 10, 1878. 5

PERSONAL.

NEW ADVERTISEMENTS.

Milwaukee Beer,

M. REUTTER,

ALL THE LATEST STYLES IN WINTER MILLINERY! AT MISS MOORE'S, 1 Opera House Block.

OVERCOATS OVERCOATS

FINE WOOLENS For Gentlemen's Wear,

E. M. Burghardt & Co., TAILORS, 169 Woodward Ave.

Safety First SUCCESS AFTERWARD.

Ladies' Underclothes! A nice assortment at MISS MOORE'S, 1 Opera House Block.

NOTICE.

ANCHOR LINE. UNITED STATES MAIL STEAMERS.

Central Business Property FOR SALE

CITY OF DETROIT

LETTER HEADS AND ENVELOPES PRINTED AT THE FREE PRESS JOB ROOMS.

NEW ADVERTISEMENTS.

CAUTION TO THE PUBLIC.

ROBBINS & APPLETON.

DON'T BE HUMBUGGED

TEAS and COFFEES AT KING'S TEA STORES,

THE PERFECT LUNG AND CHEST PROTECTOR.

Made to fit the form perfectly for either ladies or gentlemen.

PRICE, $3 50. CAN BE SENT BY MAIL.

STEARNS' DURG STORE

STEARN'S DRUG STORE.

THE BEST FRIEND.

In These Times it is Hard to Find a True Friend,

Who Will Prove Helpful in Time of Need.

But Good Health is Always Possible if its Laws are Obeyed.

And Proves it to be the Best Friend in the Long Run.

The Holman Liver & Stomach Pad!

THE HOLMAN Liver & Stomach Pad

STOP DOSING

Beware of Imitations & Impostors.

BATES & HANLEY, Agents,

E. W. VOIGT, Boss Lager Beer. BREWERY, Grand River Ave., Detroit, Mich.

MUSICAL GOODS.

PIANO POLISH!

KNABE PIANOS.

ROE STEPHENS 184 and 186 Woodward Ave.

AUCTION SALES.

AUCTION SALE OF HOUSE AND LOT

CLOSING TRADE SALE OF BOOTS, SHOES & RUBBERS BY AUCTION,

Thursday, Nov. 14, 1878.

OVER 2,000 CASES

WARDELL & WALSH, Auctioneers.

AUCTION SALE OF Two-Story House and Lot

WM. W. CLARK & CO., General Auctioneers And Commission Merchants

Furniture, Pianos, &c.

Important Trade Sale

BOOTS AND SHOES BY AUCTION,

AUCTION SALE OF House No. 436 Cass Avenue,

PAWNBROKER'S AUCTION SALE.

BOOTS AND SHOES.

GENTLEMEN'S Cordovan Shoes, hand-sewed, at very low prices. Our line of Gentlemen's Shoes is very large and the best quality that the market furnishes. A large stock of Fall & Winter Goods just received, embracing all grades of Ladies', Misses', Boys', Youths' & Children's Boots, Shoes and Slippers, goods which will give satisfaction to the wearer.

McKAY & JOHNSON, Dealers in Boots and Shoes, 122 Woodward Avenue,

WM. H. DWIGHT & CO., Hardwood & Pine Lumber.

AMUSEMENTS.

Rates in Amusement Column.

WHITNEY'S OPERA HOUSE.

Monday and Tuesday Evenings,

"Eileen Oge!"

MONTGOMERY RIFLES!

Don't Fail to See It.

DETROIT OPERA HOUSE.

MAGIA, THE WATER FIEND,

FIRST GRAND CONCERT

DETROIT ZITHER CLUB, AT ARBEITER HALL, Monday Evening, Nov. 25, 1878.

THEATRE COMIQUE.

The Tigress of the West.

WHITNEY'S GRAND OPERA HOUSE. Sunday Evening, Nov. 10,

COL. ROBERT G. INGERSOLL

Some Mistakes of Moses.

COLISEUM NOVELTY THEATER.

VIM! VIM! VIM!

SPECTACLES.

PEBBLES,

At M. S. SMITH & CO.'S, Scientific Opticians.

TRAVELERS' Expense Book, FOR Business Men While on the Road.

THE DETROIT FREE PRESS CO., DETROIT, MICH.

Nov. 10, 1878:

A page of ads from 1878.

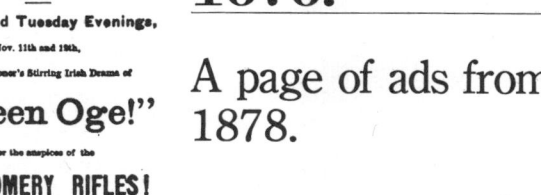

SEPT. 9, 1881:

Fire blackens thousands of square miles of Michigan land.

THE WORST IS OVER
LEXINGTON, September 8 — The fire has been more destructive than was at first supposed.

A HEAVY RAIN
fell north of Forester and resulted in quenching the fires in that vicinity, but as yet have had none here. The fires are all under subjection and people do not now apprehend any immediate danger. The losses are confined principally among the poorer class of farmers, who will suffer a long time from the effects thereof.

It is authentically reported that Moore Township was swept clear.

A BLACKENED WILDERNESS ALONE REMAINING.
Considerable property was destroyed in Flynn Township, aggregating thousands of dollars. In Elk Township, besides numerous buildings, every bridge was destroyed, and it will take over $2,000 to replace them.

Excepting the Village of Sandusky nearly the whole of Watertown was destroyed. A farmer from Austin Township related

PITIFUL STORIES
Of sights witnessed immediately after the fire. He saved his family, consisting of his wife and eight children, by taking refuge in a field of buckwheat.

MOST HORRIBLE.
A poor woman in his neighborhood endeavored to save herself and children by digging a hole and covering as best she could with her hands. They were all subsequently found dead. The little ones had their heads burned off to the shoulders.

PROBABLY 500 LIVES LOST.
Twenty dead bodies were found in Moore Township and sixty bodies brought into Sand Beach. It is estimated that 500 souls perished and that fully 5,000 are homeless and many without shelter. People here are doing all in their power to allay their distress, but they require assistance from outside.

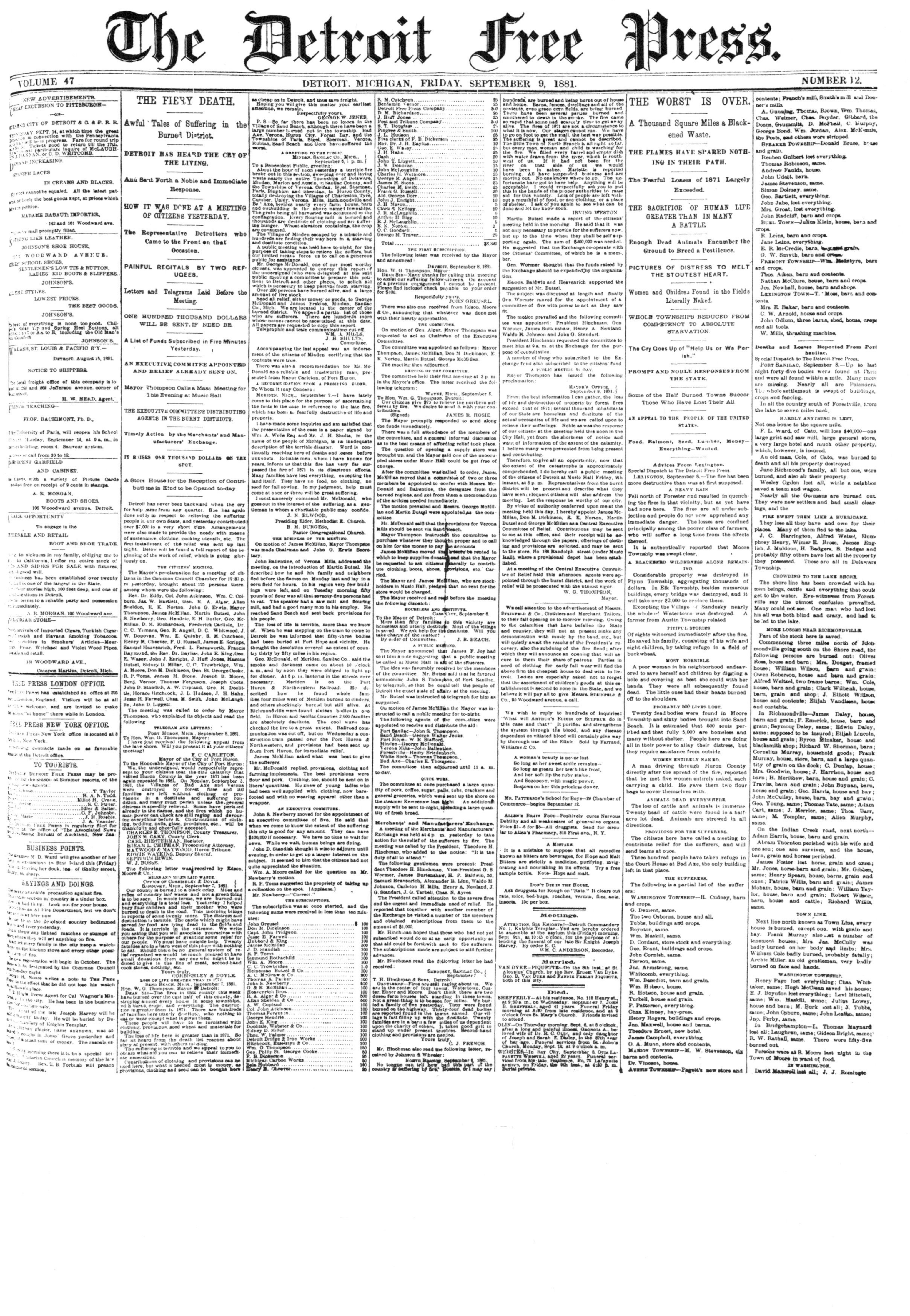

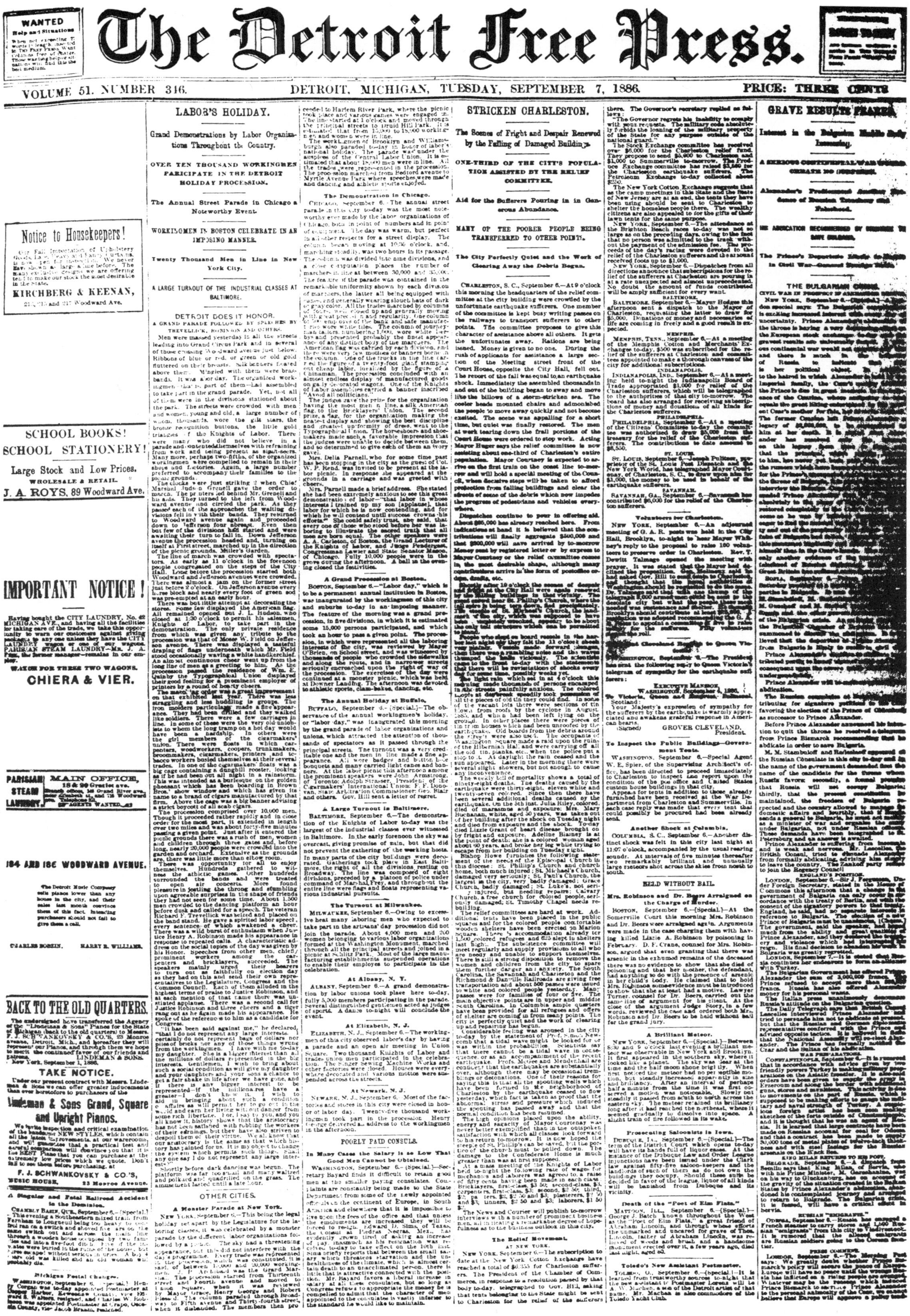

SEPT. 7, 1886:

Thousands of workers march in one of Detroit's early Labor Days.

"Labor's Holiday," column two.

Men were massed yesterday in all the streets leading into Grand Circus Park and in several of those crossing Woodward Avenue just below. Ribbons of blue or red or green or old gold fluttered on their breasts. Silk banners floated above them. Mingled with them were brass bands. It was Labor Day. The organized workingmen, that is, part of them — had assembled to take part in the grand parade. Yet, not all of them were in the divisions stationed about the park. The streets were crowded with men and women, young and old, a large number of whom, thousands, wore the gilt stars, the bronze recognition buttons, the little gold triangles of the Knights of Labor.

OCT. 7, 1887:

The charms of Michigan and Detroit are praised on the 50th anniversary of statehood.

Special section

IMPERIAL EDITION.

THE DETROIT FREE PRESS: FRIDAY, OCTOBER 7, 1887.

A GREAT COMMONWEALTH.

Michigan, the Twin Peninsulas of the Earth.

UNSURPASSED IN NATURAL AND ACQUIRED RESOURCES.

Only Fifty Years Old and Yet a Prominent Leader.

HERE'S A CYCLORAMA.

Of the City of Detroit and Her Advantages, Most Interesting.

AN OUTLINE EXPLANATION OF DETROIT'S SOCIAL, EDUCATIONAL AND OTHER ADVANTAGES.

The Reason why Detroit is the Summer Resort Par Excellence.

A BOOM AS HONEST AND PERPETUAL AS THE PRIMARY FORCES OF NATURE.

DETROIT.

DETROIT, GRAND HAVEN & MILWAUKEE RAILROAD.

THE COMMERCIAL TOURIST'S FAVORITE LINE.

Wonderful Phenomena of its Growth.

DETROIT, LANSING & NORTHERN RAILROAD.

The Shortest Route to the Famous Summer Resorts and Hunting Fields of Northern Michigan.

DULUTH, SOUTH SHORE & ATLANTIC RAILWAY.

THE SOO-MACKINAC SHORT LINE.

WHY WE PROSPER.

Because the City has the Wealth and Citizens With Pluck to Invest in.

THE PLUCK IS BORN OF APPRECIATION OF UNEXCEPTIONAL NATURAL ADVANTAGES.

An Array of Enterprises and Business Done to be Coveted by any City.

THE BANKS OF DETROIT.

MICHIGAN CENTRAL RAILROAD.

THE GREAT NIAGARA FALLS ROUTE—SHORTEST ROUTE BETWEEN THE EAST AND THE WEST.

THE WABASH ROUTE.

A COMPARATIVELY NEW LINE OUT OF DETROIT WHICH HAS GAINED WONDERFUL POPULARITY.

DETROIT, BAY CITY & ALPENA R. R.

BOOT AND SHOE BUSINESS.

THE COAL MEN.

Oct. 25, 1887:

Players parade from the train station to a Woodward Avenue hotel as Detroit celebrates its first professional baseball championship.

A GRAND FINALE, column three.

"There now! Get up, here's Detroit," was the warning that rung in the drowsy ears of the occupants of the special train which has been carrying the cream of the baseball profession around the country for the past two weeks. Curtains were lifted and sleepy eyes peered out at the vanishing scenery which was bathed in the golden light of the morning sun. Yes, it was Detroit. No one could mistake those landmarks, and when a glimpse was caught of the grandest river in the world, all doubts were set at rest.

"Well, see here, what time is it?" grumbled President Stearns as he emerged from his berth. Seven timepieces were drawn forth and a variegated assortment of time was announced. After some abstruse calculations, the opinion was arrived at that it was about 7:45 Detroit or sun time.

"This is a pretty how-de-do," said Stearns, in true ante-breakfast tones. "Here we announce that we'll arrive at 10 o'clock and get in at 8."

Without wasting much time crying over spilled milk, Stearns rushed around to repair the damage. The players were instructed to remain in the car and sentries posted to prevent desertions. Word was sent to Mayor Chamberlain that the train had arrived. The reception committee lost no time and shortly after 9 between 50 and 60 carriages had arrived at the depot, and also a large crowd of prominent citizens and enthusiasts. . . .

Despite the keenness of the air there were about 4,000 people on the grounds when Umpire Gaffney threw a new ball to Caruthers and called play. It was one of the most enthusiastic crowds that ever assembled at Recreation Park. Bubbling over with happiness owing to the magnificent achievements of the champion Detroits, the spectators laughed, shouted, applauded and danced from beginning to close. The rendering of lively airs by Hudson's Band provoked the bleaching boards and the stands to terpsichorean divertisement, and thousands bobbed up and down on one foot to the inspiring strains of Yankee Doodle or equally enlivening air. So good natured was the crowd that the least thing served to set them in a roar of laughter, and the very happy events that occurred during the game stirred up the people to a high pitch of enthusiasm.

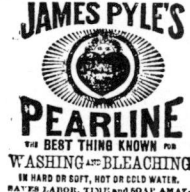

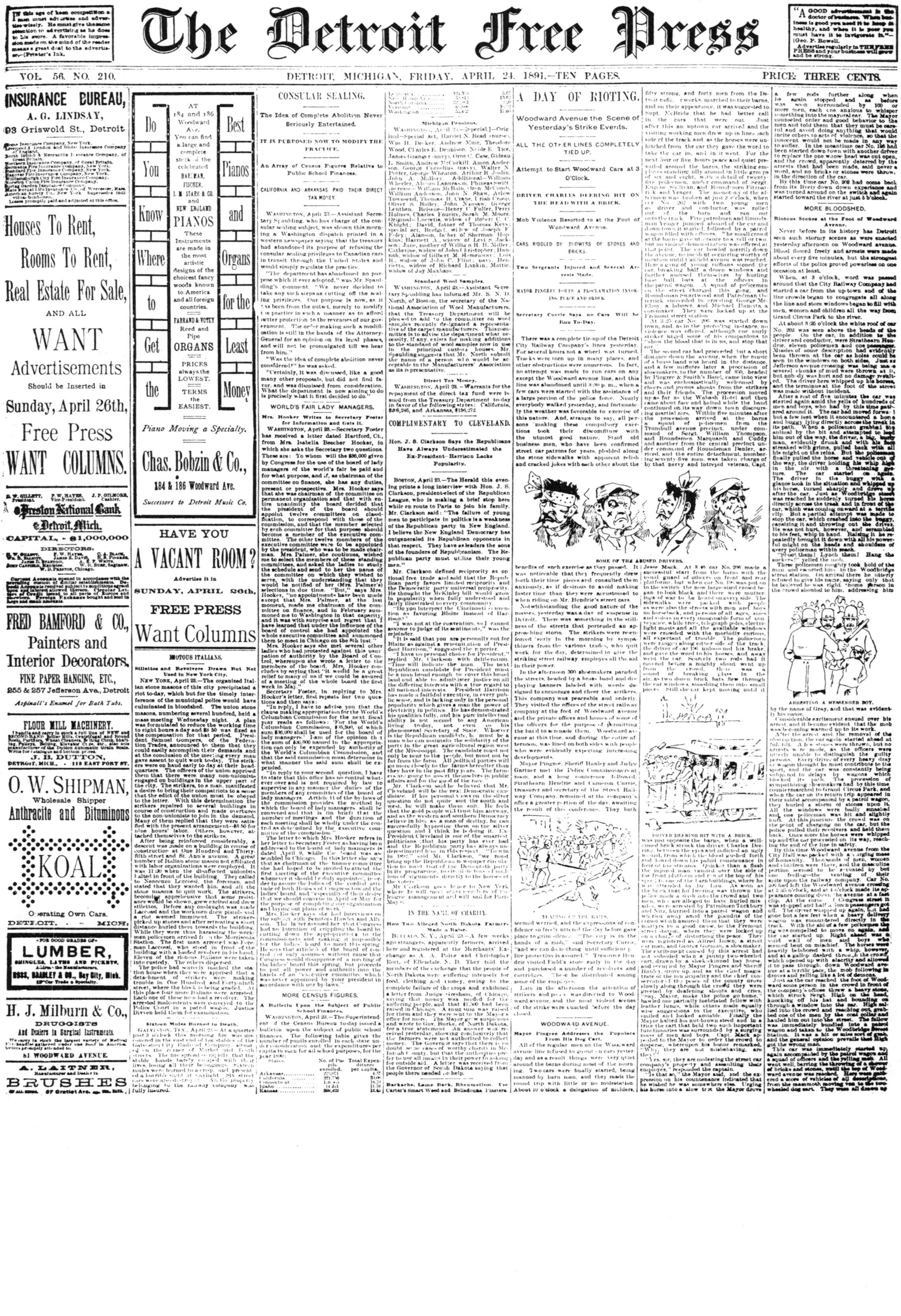

April 24, 1891:

Strike violence disrupts Detroit's mass transit.

"A Day Of Rioting," column five.

The Detroit Free Press

VOL. 56. NO. 210. DETROIT, MICHIGAN, FRIDAY, APRIL 24, 1891.—TEN PAGES. PRICE: THREE CENTS.

A DAY OF RIOTING.

Woodward Avenue the Scene of Yesterday's Strike Events.

ALL THE OTHER LINES COMPLETELY TIED UP.

Attempt to Start Woodward Cars at 3 O'Clock.

DRIVER CHARLES DEERING HIT ON THE HEAD WITH A BRICK.

Mob Violence Resorted to at the Foot of Woodward Avenue.

CARS RIDDLED BY SHOWERS OF STONES AND BRICKS.

Two Sergeants Injured and Several Arrests Made.

MAYOR PINGREE ISSUES A PROCLAMATION INVOKING PEACE AND ORDER.

Secretary Currie Says no Cars Will be Run To-Day.

There was a complete tie-up of the Detroit City Railway Company's lines yesterday. For several hours not a wheel was turned. Tracks were torn up in many places, and other obstructions were numerous. In fact, no attempt was made to run cars on any except the Woodward avenue line, and this line was abandoned until 3:30 p. m., when a few cars were started with the assistance of a large portion of the police force. Nearly everybody walked yesterday, and fortunately the weather was favorable to exercise of this nature. And, strange to say, all persons making these compulsory exertions took their discomfiture with the utmost good nature. Staid old business men, who have been confirmed

SHOT DOWN

RIOTOUS POLISH LABORERS CHARGE ON THE SHERIFF.

FORCING HIM AND HIS POSSE TO OPEN FIRE ON THEM.

A DESPERATE BATTLE ON THE GROSSE POINTE ROAD.

MANY WERE SEVERELY INJURED AND ONE KILLED OUTRIGHT.

SHERIFF COLLINS WAS RUN DOWN AND NEARLY MURDERED.

FOREMAN GEORGE CATHEY'S HEAD WAS SPLIT OPEN.

MATT STEYSKAL RAN THE GANTLET FOR HIS LIFE.

TAKING REFUGE IN THE GARRET OF A HOUSE NEARBY.

POLICEMEN FOUND SHELTER IN THE DRIVING CLUB BARNS.

THE TROUBLE AROSE OVER A PROJECTED WATER MAIN.

OWING TO A NEW METHOD OF ADJUSTING WAGES.

POLISH WORKMEN REFUSED TO LET OTHERS WORK.

TWENTY MEN ARRESTED AND LOCKED UP AT THE JAIL.

The Water Board Has Decided to Abandon the Job Temporarily.

Sheriff Collins and some of his deputies were brutally attacked by some of the striking Poles at the water works extension yesterday, and in the mêlée which followed, one man was killed, three were fatally injured and a number of others, including the sheriff himself, were seriously and made mortally wounded. It was impossible to get a correct list of all the wounded, as many of the Poles were shot and were taken away and secreted by their friends. The following is the list as far as ascertained at the time of going to press:

DEAD.

JOHN PILAT, laborer, 30 years old, St. Albertus place, married, at Geist Bros.' morgue.

INJURED.

SHERIFF C. P. COLLINS, serious scalp wounds and cuts and bruises on the shoulder, head and ankle.

ANDREW KARNOTSKI, laborer, 71 Hastings street; five shots through the stomach and bowels cannot live.

JOSEPH KABOSKI, laborer, 138 Illinois street; shot through the liver; probably fatal.

W. H. BURCH, special police officer, 854 Macomb street; left thigh broken by a blow from a pickaxe; will live.

TONY GARECHOWIAK, 61 Theodore street; bullet wound, left thigh.

LAURENCE KULWICKI, 361 Alexandrine avenue east; bullet wound, left thigh.

TONY GWASKI, 25 Leland street; bullet wound, left leg.

JOHN KAPPSCHMIDT, 21 years old, married 13 Leland street; two bullet wounds, fatal.

GEORGE CATHEY, water works foreman, 51 Champlain street; scalp wounds, serious but not fatal.

Five Poles, slightly injured; names unknown.

One of the most brutal and horrible riots which has occurred in the state for many years took place at Cathey's Creek yesterday at noon. It was a tragic consummation of the trouble existing between the water board and the laborers, in the same locality where the pipe extensions were being made east of the water works. There was a fair forewarning of the disturbance in the occurrences of the day before, but proper means of resisting the infuriated mob of unruly Poles were not provided, and a mere handful of brave men were severely and brutally dealt with. The cause of the riot makes the result more deplorable and increases the indignation against the assailants, who were simply asked to work by the piece and not by the day. It was not a case of taking the means of sustenance from the Poles and their families, by the way, have been practically maintained by public charity through the hard winter—but was a matter in which

SHERIFF COLLINS

work was offered at good wages for all. The presence of a few windy agitators precipitated a strike which was harmless enough until yesterday noon, when the mob, excited by the sophistry of some of their labor orators, fell upon the courageous men who were there to maintain the dignity of the law and like wolves would have torn them to pieces. Shovels and picks, wielded by these Polish-speaking cowards, were brought to bear against Sheriff Collins and his force, and the scoundrels like beasts attacked the men when they were prostrate at their feet, striking them again and again when life already seemed extinct. It was a spectacle of cowardly, disgraceful ferocity, showing how much of the jackal there is in human nature in its lowest order. Over fifty times more numerous than the little band, the mob, were in the interest of peace, the mob pressed upon them, held back somewhat at first by their fear of the revolvers, and gaining courage as the weapons of the assailed were slowly emptied. Of that small number not a man winced, no one shirked the responsibility of his position and standing together they retreated, fighting like bull-dogs and laying in the dust a number of the human hyenas who came toward them. Of the skirmish at the fence, the bold stand taken by the men at the electric car crossing, and the retreat across the field, it should be written that commendable valor was displayed by the police and the deputies, and atrocious revenge on the part of the mob.

THE CAUSE OF IT ALL.

Disagreement Over Piece-Work Led to the Riot.

To portray adequately the picture of the skirmish it is necessary to allude to the circumstances which led to the trouble. The Poles asserted their displeasure over the new method of working by the piece on Tuesday, when they gathered in squads about the locality and not only refused to work themselves, but would not permit others to labor. The position of these men, who had been supported more or less by charity during the hard times, disclaiming labor at a fair rate of compensation was not one to arouse sympathy in their cause, and while money is as close as it is, a strike was an affair to be regretted by honest, self-respecting workmen, who are quick to repudiate the conduct of these Poles. Engineer Williams asked that the system be tried, assuring the men that they would find it would pay them as well as could be expected. But the Poles would not listen, and when a foreman made an attempt to assign work to a laborer who was willing to accept the conditions, those who held back would interfere and forbid his employment. The foreman strove to maintain order, but the will of the mob was law for the day. At noon on Tuesday no less than 500 Poles were on the ground, apparently for the purpose of keeping their fellow-workmen out of the trenches, and the plea that they kept repeating their demands of $1.50 a day, or 25 cents an hour. Then a few of the agitators raised the cry that Engineer Williams was trying to hire the own pockets at the expense of the poor workman, and this caused them to jabber in Polish at a great rate, holding little indignation meetings in groups. Just little is needed to fan the flame of a fancied wrong, and soon

WHERE SHERIFF COLLINS FELL

for the crowd had obviously reached a lawless condition. Nevertheless adequate provision for resisting the strikers was not made yesterday.

HOW IT STARTED YESTERDAY.

Incidents That Led Up to the Cowardly Attacks.

The crowd reassembled about daybreak yesterday, and at 7 o'clock a formidable gathering of Poles, armed with their implements, were talking over their alleged wrongs and waiting to resist any attempt to put men at work at the new piece rate. The only officers called upon to keep the peace were four policemen who were especially sworn in, and the casual spectator, gazing at the sullen mob, could not but wonder what would happen if a conflict should occur over the work. In spite of the threats of the strikers, eighteen men were put to work upon a small creek beyond Connor's creek. Engineer Williams appeared, and, undeterred by the threatening attitude of the men, boldly stood his ground. The four patrolmen, acting as deputies, approached to his assistance, and the mob retreated. Meanwhile Foreman Cathey and his assistant called upon the eighteen laborers to begin work, but the mob pressed upon them, commanding the men not to use their shovels and picks. Assistant Pramstaller, followed by one man, sprang into the ditch, while the others joined the mob, not desiring to work against the wishes of the lawless crowd. But no sooner was a shovel dug into the earth than there was a rush, a wild cry and in a few moments picks and workmen

THE FOREMAN AT THE MEN'S MERCY.

wild roar of rage. Faces were contorted, shovels and picks were thrust into the air and amid the wildest shouting the mob pressed forward toward the sheriff and his assistants in the confusion Steyskal escaped, while the sheriff and his deputy, Theodore Boreman, were reinforced by the four policemen, H. Burch, Andrew Hoering, George Ely and W. E. Price. The action of the policemen was gallant in the extreme. The sheriff and his companions were being crushed by the crowd and literally overwhelmed, the sheriff and his companions began to retreat. Behind them was the fence, and through this crowd the policemen made their way until they stood shoulder to shoulder, prepared to oppose the lawlessness of the crowd. Anathemas were

MURDEROUS ATTACK.

Sheriff Collins Almost Killed by the Mob.

When about midway between the place where the men entered the field and the barn, a big fellow, armed with a long-handled, murderous-looking shovel, whose edge was almost as sharp as a sword, rushed forward with a yell, and lifting his implement, brought it down with great force upon the head of the sheriff. The sheriff's hat alone probably prevented him from being killed by the blow, but as it was, he was instantly felled and dropped into a sitting posture with head hanging down, struggling the while to get upon his feet. His companions couldn't rescue him, but what saw five men with revolvers send out without equaled a mob of several hundred? Seeing this their lives would be sacrificed, they were forced to leave their unfortunate companion to the tender mercies of the mob, who had no spark of pity for a fallen adversary. While others were rapidly making their way toward the barn, a portion of the mob closed upon Collins and struck him savage time. With a groan he sank back. But the firing of the revolvers had held him back to vent and while when first shot in the air in their efforts to avoid bloodshed now aimed to kill. During the advance from the railroad tracks over the fence and across the field, the mob fired a constant every chamber, and so dense was the crowd that several of them fell by the bullets of their assailants were of either kind or wounded, before taking to the heels. The men poured forth a volley which struck several of the mob. The spectacle of the death of a fellow workman who had been shot down with a hole in his breast aroused his companions. They yelled like beasts, an interminable throng, shouting, the officers, who pointed their looks to against the breast and kept their face turned toward the mob. Slower and slower the sheriff and the men were in the field, but the boys were skillfully led and were without effect. It is not worthy that the attack was not made upon the sheriff until his revolver was empty. As many times as the revolver had barked the weapons had lost had, and when it became necessary to withdraw down the effort and then to pour upon their

While all this was transpiring, Matt Steyskal out of breath and nearly bruised, had taken refuge in a house nearby. A portion of the crowd followed him when they instead within and the mob did not quit at him. Had not the guns of the men in the field been emptied they might have succeeded in preventing Collins, and, as it was, they were forced to burn the barn and so the weapons upon their assailants. It was a gallant sight and only to gratify men fell was the retreat accomplished with the harm of one, the men taking refuge in the barns of the new driving park. The mob tried to get in the barns but the doors were locked and they did not succeed in the attempt.

END OF THE CONFLICT.

The Bloody Fracas Lasted But a Very Few Minutes.

The conflict lasted but for a short time. Not long after it was over the vicinity was deserted, the ambulances having fled to remedy fashion to escape arrest. So remote was the place that they had no difficulty in dispersing and taking their wounded with them before the reinforcements arrived. In the very short time that the reinforcements noticed the ambulances dashing through the streets in route for somewhere, and the patrol wagons went by loaded with policemen who were gathered up here and there, but by the time that policemen and ambulances arrived in the country the country roads were deserted by wood and dead body, the injured also and his more or less injured companions were the ghastly evidences of the

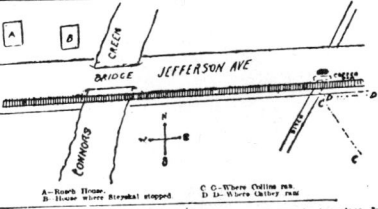

the others held their revolvers ready. Shovels were uplifted and men threatened they would have been trampled under foot. "Fire in the air!" said the sheriff. The sheriff then lifted his gun and fired. The shot was answered by half a dozen whizzed harmlessly through the body of the lights interest them. In a short time more will be here it would at the stage of the conflict when perhaps the most good. There is something peculiar in the effect of a revolver shot upon a crowd, sometimes it is resented, and at other times. It is not toll "They will continue to hide the crash of a whip lashing them to deeds of blundered and barbarity. As long as the revolvers were held in the hands of the men the mob paid little attention to them, being neither excited nor subdued by the mere act of the drawing forth of the guns. But when the first report rang out the sized of falling took its full hold, and severe conflict which had taken place. Just exactly how the riot took place the survivors seemed to but differently in explaining. No preparations had apparently been made for the sudden attack, the attack of a murderous mob when a crowd was so sudden and so spontaneous that no one knows. An angry shout, and in an instant the intention of the mob to kill was aroused, although nothing was to be gained by such action. It was the expression, of the mob manifested in the rudest forms of humanity. It was, as it were, the outer of the city, was proved in a drama which had nothing whatever to do with the difficulties between labor and capital, but was brought to an episode, of series of episodes which will be depicted either by a policeman and capitalist and employer. It was nothing more nor less than the attack of one who are criminally liable for their murder-

Nov. 9, 1895:

Thirty seven are killed in a downtown Detroit explosion. The fire still stands as one of the state's worst tragedies.

The Detroit Free Press

VOL. 61. NO. 46. — DETROIT, MICHIGAN, SATURDAY, NOVEMBER 9, 1895.—TEN PAGES. — PRICE: THREE CENTS.

LAST BODY OUT!

Three Were Taken From the Larned Street Ruins Yesterday.

MAKING THE WHOLE NUMBER OF VICTIMS THIRTY SEVEN.

Six of the Unfortunates Have Been Laid in Their Graves.

ENGINEER THOMPSON ARRESTED AND BROUGHT TO A HOSPITAL.

He Will Be Held to Await the Result of the Inquest Wednesday.

SORROW'S CALL

The Detroit Free Press

VOL. 62. NO. 177. — DETROIT, MICHIGAN, SATURDAY, MARCH 20, 1897.—TEN PAGES. — PRICE: THREE CENTS.

MARCH 20, 1897:

Hazen Pingree, one of the state's most popular politicians, cannot serve both as mayor of Detroit and Michigan governor, the state Supreme Court rules.

NO LONGER MAYOR!

GOV. HAZEN S. PINGREE NOT ENTITLED TO BE DETROIT'S CHIEF EXECUTIVE OFFICER.

SUPREME COURT DECLARES THAT IT IS UNCONSTITUTIONAL TO HOLD THE TWO OFFICES.

EXHAUSTIVE OPINION OF JUSTICE HOOKER UNANIMOUSLY CONCURRED IN BY OTHER JUSTICES.

A UNIVERSAL RULE THAT WHEN INCOMPATIBILITY EXISTS IT VACATES THE FIRST POSITION.

GOV. PINGREE'S DECLARED INTENTION TO REMAIN AS MAYOR TOUCHED UPON.

MANDAMUS GRANTED TO COMPEL THE CITY COUNCIL TO CALL AN ELECTION ON MONDAY, APRIL 5.

His Excellency May Resign as Governor and Again be a Candidate for Mayor of Detroit.

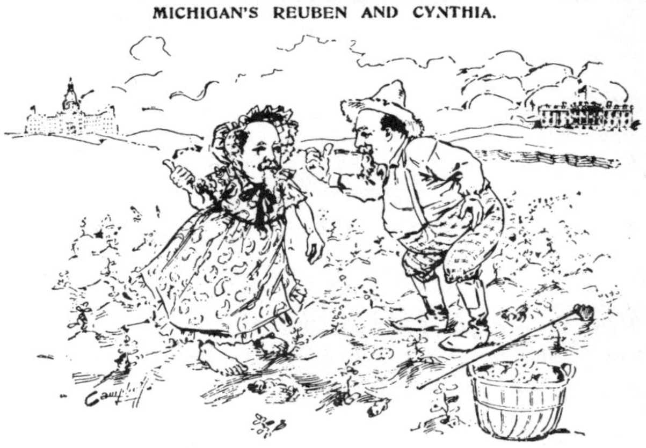

April 23, 1898:

Michigan troops assemble at Island Lake as the Spanish-American War is "now a fact."

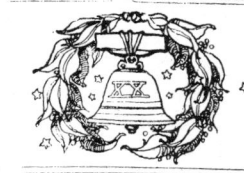

JAN. 1, 1901:

The city greets the 20th Century with gunshots, fireworks and a poem.

BRINGS GOOD RESULTS

The Detroit Sunday Free Press brings good results to mail order advertisers using its columns. —The Advisor.

The Detroit Free Press

BRINGS GOOD RESULTS

The Detroit Sunday Free Press brings good results to mail order advertisers using its columns. —The Advisor.

VOL. 66. NO. 99. DETROIT, MICHIGAN, TUESDAY, JANUARY 1, 1901.—TWELVE PAGES. PRICE: THREE CENTS.

MURDERERS AT LARGE

[illegible] More Ordered to be Released by His Excellency, Hazen S. Pingree.

WRIGHT, THE MILLIONAIRE LUMBERMAN WHO KILLED TWO OFFICERS, ONE OF THEM.

McCollum, Who Criminally Assaulted His 80-Year Old Mother, Also Made Free.

(From a Staff Correspondent.)

[illegible], Mich., December 31.—(Special.)—[illegible] Pingree extended executive clemency [illegible] less than ten murderers to-day, par[illegible] two and paroling the others, so [illegible] all but one of them will be released [illegible] as the customary formalities are [illegible]. The most sensational case was [illegible] of Charles Wright, of Benzie, the [illegible]aire lumberman, whose sentence was [illegible] from life imprisonment to seven[illegible] years and paroled with permission to [illegible] to Wisconsin, which was his former [illegible], and where he has many influential [illegible].

[illegible]presentative Ben Colvin obtained the [illegible] signature to the official docu[illegible] shortly after he arrived here this [illegible]. Uncle Ben could not restrain his [illegible] and danced about in high glee over [illegible] success. Wright was sentenced May 1, [illegible] that including the good time al[illegible] his sentence will legally expire in [illegible] a year.

[illegible] parole had evidently been prepared [illegible] some time as there was several type[illegible] pages attached to it, in which the [illegible] is reviewed at some length, and the [illegible]ernor gives his reasons for extending [illegible]mency. Attention is called to the ex[illegible] investigations that have been made [illegible] connection with the case, and the governor states that while the members of the pardon board privately urged him to extend clemency to Wright they did not have the moral courage to make an official recommendation, owing to the prejudice against Wright, and the peculiar status of the case. Reference is made to the fact that many letters were received from prominent business men in Wisconsin attesting Wright's good name as a business man. Considerable space is devoted to a review of the case by Wright's attorney, in which the claim is made that the element of self-defense enters strongly into the killing of Neal Marshall and Frank Thurber by Wright, and that he should not have been convicted of more than manslaughter.

Wright Will Have to Answer to Another Murder Charge.

The governor also points out that Wright was only convicted of the killing of Thurber. He will have to, within a year, be tried for the killing of Marshall, when he will have an opportunity of showing the part he took in the tragedy and prove that he has been injured by the courts. Wright's friends attach all blame to the attorneys who advised the officers to make the levy on Wright's logs as the latter had offered to give a bond, which was refused, whereupon he armed himself with a gun and proceeded to cut the logs. Representative Colvin had the papers properly attested and left for Jackson to-night so that Wright will obtain his freedom to-morrow.

Repke Pardoned.

Frank Repke, the last of the Molter murderers, was pardoned.

James B. Daget, who was given a life sentence from Mecoata county in 1869, was

Continued on Page Two.

BLISS TO BE SWORN IN TO-DAY

GREAT PREPARATION BEING MADE FOR HIS INAUGURATION.

GOVERNOR AND STATE OFFICERS WILL HOLD A RECEPTION.

SENATOR McMILLAN WILL GIVE A LUNCH AFTERWARDS.

TO-DAY'S SENATORIAL CAUCUS JUST A RATIFICATION.

Foregone Conclusion That Representative Carton Will Be Speaker.

(From a Staff Correspondent.)

Lansing, Mich., December 30.—Gov.-elect Bliss arrived in the city to-day and preparations are being made for his inauguration to-morrow. He will be sworn in by [illegible] Montgomery on the front [illegible] of the capitol if the weather permits, [illegible] in the executive office. To-morrow [illegible] the governor and the state [illegible] will hold a reception, when it is [illegible] Lansing society will turn out [illegible]. It is expected that all the members of the legislature will be here in the morning, [illegible] comparatively few arrived to-day.

Senator [illegible] has sent out informal [illegible] when he will tender [illegible] houses immediately [illegible] reception. The sena[illegible] will be held to-morrow after[illegible] it will be nothing more than a [illegible] meeting. [illegible] are being [illegible] get the Democratic members of the [illegible] to vote for Senator McMillan in [illegible] make his election unanimous [illegible] party, but it is certain that Sen[illegible] will not agree to any such a [illegible]

[illegible]

THE LAST DAY OF PINGREE

USED HIS PARDONING POWER UP TO THE LAST HOUR.

SEEMS TO HAVE BEEN DESERTED BY POLITICAL FRIENDS.

LEFT PRACTICALLY ALONE WITH SECRETARY AND CLERKS.

HIS USUAL SARCASM IN REFERENCE TO SENATOR McMILLAN.

Latter Gentleman's Views on the Taxation Question.

(From a Staff Correspondent.)

Lansing, Mich., December 31.—At midnight the administration of Gov. Pingree closed. There hovered over the retirement of the pardon governor the dull glow of the expiring red fire that has made Pingree's four years in office a bad dream to the people, and there was the mental falling of the sticks that were coming down after the firing of gubernatorial rockets.

The circumstances attending Pingree's withdrawal from office showed plainly the indications of an expiring political life. The crush of sycophants who crowded about Pingree when he was new and a power in state politics, and when there were offices to dole out, were missing, and when his excellency arrived at Lansing he was left alone with those that wanted a last chance to beg for a pardon and with his secretary and clerks, who had on hand the getting out of the tobacco sauce message which he is to fire at the legislature.

Singular Coincidence.

It was a singular coincidence that Gov. Pingree and Senator McMillan came to Lansing on the same train. Of the two old-time political rivals one was to be given a third term in the United States senate, while the other was to go back to private life with little chance of being galvanized back into political activity. The senator sat in the body of the parlor car on the Flint & Pere Marquette train that left Detroit at 1:10. He was flanked on either side by his son, W. C. McMillan, and by his brother, Hugh McMillan. E. W. Cottrell, the major domo of McMillan ceremonies, sat opposite to see that the senator's comforts were provided for. Some legislator going to his new duties was constantly standing near waiting to get a word or two with the leader. He sat with his gloves on and his cane in his hand.

Governor Had to Have His Little Fling.

The governor came down to the train too late to get a chair in the main part of the

Continued on Page Nine.

JEAN JAE AND OLDEN DAYS.

Memoire h'of de Past.

H'i coame fram h'ol Grosse Poin' las' night,
To de ceety beeg h'an grate;
De ceety h'of de strait she's call,
De beegest h'on de state.
De bell was ringin' loud h'an' fas',
De light was burning braight;
H'an h'evaryone was try daire bes'
To celebrate de naight.

H'as h'i look roun', h'i tink masalf,
Where's gone dem haundred year?
Where's de Frenchmans h'of de pas',
La Fleur, Saint Jean 'an Lebriere?
Where's Gabriel Chene, Prisque Cote,
De Quindre, Le Roy h'an Loranger?
Why so strange seem h'all h'aroun',
H'an no h'ol' frien' to greet;
De names h'i h'us'd to know so well,
H'are now de name h'of street.
Daire's Rivard, Riopelle h'an Chene,
Beaubien, h'an planty more;
H'all name h'of mah h'ol fader's frien',
What's gone h'on odder shore.
Where's h'ol' St. Anne, de church h'i go?
Where mah fader, too, he's went;
Why don't h'i hear de chime h'of bell?
What to me so much h'it meant.

'Where's Pere Richard, de good h'ol Pries'
Whose know me long ago?
Whose name me Touissant Eustache,
What h'all Grosse Pointe she's know.
Ah, well! H'i spose dey h'all go dead,
Fo' eets seexty year ago;
Since h'as h'a boy, h'on h'ol' Detroit
Dem Frenchman h'all h'i know.

Seemtime now, when de sleep h'i make,
H'in dream h'i saw de face,
H'of Pierre Godfroy h'an Jacques Marsac,
De grand mans h'of daire race.
No more daire face h'i see to-day,
No more h'ol' frien' h'i meet;
No mattaire where h'i walk h'along,
Aroun' Detroit's h'ol' street.

How h'i wish, when dem beil ring,
H'an dem whistle blow so loud,
Dat h'i could meet h'ol' Pierre Leboeuf
Somewhaire h'on de crowd.
Teece den dat h'i could talk h'about,
De horse race h'on de h'ice;
Where leetle pony mak' de race,
For prize so gran' h'an nice.
But nevermore h'upon deece earth,
Weel h'i fin 'Pierre h'anywhere;
He's sleep to-night, fo' h'all de time,
H'on de h'ol' French cemetaire.

Wall, h'as h'i bean here now h'all h'alone,
H'an h'of h'ol' frien' see no sign;
H'i'll greet de New Year bah mahself,
H'an drink mah glass h'of wine.
Ah! Dat's good. Wan more h'i'll take;
H'it brings to min' de pas',
H'of h'all de day h'of long h'ago,
H'of day too-good to las'.
Dat wine she's strong; h'am h'i go dream?
H'i seem to go way back;
H'an see Detroit h'as she's use to bean,
H'in de day h'of Cadillac.

H'i smell de wild-flower so sweet,
H'an de river's wave h'i see,
De summaire sun h'i see heem shine,
While h'everywhere h'is glee.
De h'ol' village Detroit h'i see,
Daire's Cadillac for sure;
H'an Tonty, his h'ol' frien' so true,
H'an de good h'ol' Pere La Tour.

Now, h'i'm walk St. Anne street down,
Where h'i see de Palisade,
H'an soljaire man dress h'up so gay,
Wid pretty trim French maid.
De garden h'all look vary bright,
Wid h'every kaind h'of flower;
H'an chil'rens voice lak music sweet,
Mak' happy h'all de hour.

De voyageur wid smilin' face,
H'an heart so fill' wid joy;
H'i see dreenk whiskey-blanc so good,
Wid Courier du Bois.
De h'ol' wind-mill, quite plain h'i hear,
H'as h'it grind de Frenchman's corn;
She's nevaire stop, but go h'all day,
From h'early h'on de morn.

De neighbor h'of de h'olden time,
He's pass him by mah h'eye;
Despre, La Porte h'an Labatier,
H'an Jean Baptiste Langlois.

H'all h'of dem be farmer mans,
Wat rent h'of Cadillac;
H'a half arpent—a ebbe more,
H'on de reever front h'or Lak'.

De h'ol' log-house h'also h'i see,
Wid eets fire-place beeg h'an great;
Where Frenchmans drink h'an smoke de pipe,
H'until de hour grow late.
Den h'up de village church shes coame,
H'an loud go soun' de bell;
For call de people h'all to hear
De prayer h'of Pere Michel.

Now Cadillac he's coame h'along,
Wid beeg sword by his side;
He's "boss" h'of h'all de settlement,
H'an' h'of h' Indian man beside.
He's mak' de law fo' h'ol' Detroit,
He's h'alway want de peace;
H'an' de h'only wan he's min' h'at all
H'am Pere Michel, de Pries'.

Den h'all de mans wid Cadillac,
H'i see lak' ghost go by;
Beauchamp, De Lisle h'an Chapaton,
Who long h'ago have die.
Den queek mah dream she mak' de change,
H'in France h'i seem to bean;
Where Cadillac h'i see go die
H'on Castel Sarrazin.

H'at las' de wine lose grand effec',
Den h'i wake h'up h'again;
When h'all h'is diffren' roun' h'about,
Bote building, scene h'an men.
Where but few tousand man she's be,
Daire's plenty tousand now;
H'an where canoe was use to sail,
Daire's stamboat wid beeg bow.

De "Griffon" wat La Salle he's sail,
To-day would 'pear lak' chip;
Shood she now pass h'upon de Lak',
Beside de great beeg ship.
H'an' where mah fader's farm she was,
De place h'i know quite well,
Daire's now beeg house, two h'acre high,
Call Cadillac's hotel.

Where wonce de farm she's use to bean,
Han' many sweet pear tree;
Daire's now beeg store h'an city hall,
Wat h'all seem strange to me.
No Commandant ees now h'around',
No Seigneur h'is h'anywhere;
De town she's run bah h'aldermans
H'an' h'a leetle bah de mayor.

No nice French sleigh h'i see h'at all,
No snug h'ol' French Caleche;
Street car she's go h'on lettle wire,
H'an' sometime go h'on smash.
H'it may be wat you call progress,
But geeve me back de day
When h'in de h'ol' log cabin dear,
De Frenchmans sing h'an' play.
Whare de story pass from lip to lip,
Bout Courier du Bois;
Where h'all was happiness h'an' joy,
No trouble, court h'or law.

Give me back de h'ol' shot-gun
Wid which h'i keill de gam',
H'an' twotree pint h'of whiskey-blanc,
H'ill happy den be h'all de tam.
Wan more glass? Well, leetle wan,
Den home h'ill go wance more;
H'an' stay—p'raps, forevaire daire,
H'on Grosse Pointe by de shore.

Befo' h'i go h'i'll look aroun',
H'an' read de h'ol' street sign;
Fo' h'it mak' me tink h'of long h'ago,
H'an' live long h'on mah min'.
Rivard street! Adieu, mon cher,
Adieu! Antoine, h'an' Chene;
Mah feeble step may never coame,
H'up h'on your way h'again.

When h'at las' mah time she's coame,
Lak' h'all dat's gone befo';
Hi' hope to fin' h'on de distant lan',.. ..
Mah h'ol' log cabin door.
H'i hope h'also h'on dat happy place,
Bon jour, Messieur, to say
To h'all de mans h'of Cadillac,
Moulin, La Fleur, Paquet.

Ring h'on', bell, ring! Blow, whistle, blow!
Let h'all be glad—no tear;
Pass roun' de wine! God bless h'us h'all,
Happy, happy New Year.

JEAN JAE (John J. Enright.)

NEW CENTURY'S GRAND WELCOME

Detroit Blazed With Fireworks and Uproar Reigned Last Night.

MUNICIPAL CELEBRATION AT CITY HALL ATTRACTED MANY THOUSANDS OF PEOPLE.

It Was a Memorable Close of the World's Most Memorable Hundred Years.

If those who a hundred years ago last night stood around the little log huts under the protecting palisades of the old log fort and saw the last hours of the old and first hours of the new century could have arisen from their graves last night to see the sunset hours of the nineteenth and the birth of the twentieth century, what astonishment would have been theirs!

Imagine the look on the faces of those French voyages and trappers, those simple-minded woodsmen and crafty Indians, could they have come back to earth last night to see the thousands and thousands of people massed on the Campus Martius, where they had herded their cattle in times of peace or fought desperately in times of strife; to see the tall buildings, the red fire, the glaring searchlights, and the myriads of electric lights; to see the electric cars and hear the clang of fire engine bells.

It is doubtful if Bedlam let loose could have produced more noise than burst forth last night when the first stroke of 12 of the city hall bell sounded forth on the frosty air. Revolvers, giant firecrackers, whistles, gongs, bombs, sky-rockets—anything, everything that would produce sound was let loose.

And it did not stop. The twentieth century had at last arrived, and it must be shown in in proper style. There was noise in plenty in those last hours of the old century, but it was the peace and quiet of the woodland compared to the tremendous outburst at midnight. One would hardly have thought that in all Michigan there were people enough, and powder and steam enough, to produce such demoniac outburst as came when gaunt old Father Time swept his scythe around him and cut down the supports of the departed century.

Woodward avenue never looked prettier than it did last night. At 10 o'clock it looked as though perhaps there had been some mistake. There were not many more people on the streets than usual and aside from a premature explosion now and then or the crack of the revolver in the hand of some messenger boy, there was nothing unusual. But when the theaters began to unload their crowds things took on a livelier tone. Then the incoming cars began to unload their crowds at the Campus and by 11 o'clock Woodward avenue was black with people from Jefferson to Grand River avenue. It was a good natured crowd however; one that slipped from side to side of the icy sidewalks and occasionally people fell, but never lost their good nature. Last night was not a night when one could walk with military precision. Square corners were very dangerous to a proper equilibrium.

By 11:30 the space in front of the city hall was a mass of people through which the electric cars passed with difficulty. The crowd extended down Cadillac square, and up Fort street, Monroe and Michigan avenues for blocks.

Earlier in the evening the "welcome" sign on the city hall had shone forth in brilliant yellow letters, "A Happy New Year to All," but later the electricians

Continued on Page Three.

UNITED STATES BONDS

BOOKS FOR EXCHANGE WERE CLOSED YESTERDAY.

REFUNDING OPERATIONS SUCCESSFUL FROM EVERY STANDPOINT.

SAVING TO THE GOVERNMENT HAS BEEN LARGE.

PUBLIC DEBT IN FAIR CONDITION FOR RETIREMENT.

Effect of the Financial Act Upon National Banks.

Washington, December 31.—Refunding operations under the financial act of March 14 last, closed to-day, the books of the department having been open to the exchange of bonds for a period of nine and one-half months. In discussing the subject to-day Assistant Secretary Vanderlip said:

"The refunding has been successful from every standpoint. Holders of the old bonds, 3s, 4s and 5s of 1908, 1907 and 1904, respectively, have voluntarily offered for exchange into 2s approximately $439,000,000 out of $839,000,000, leaving outstanding of this part of the interest bearing public debt less than one-half the amount subject to the law. Exact figures will not be known for several days, as some bonds are still in transit.

Saving to the Government.

"The net saving to the government of interest by these transactions is substantially $10,300,000. This saving has been accomplished by the payment now of the sum of $42,200,000, which is really an anticipation of $52,900,000 interest which would have had to be paid within the next eight years, in case the old bonds were permitted to run to maturity. The difference is the net saving.

"The four per cents of 1907 have been exchanged in greater amount than any other class, their total up to and including December 29 being $264,000,000. Of the 3 per cents of 1908, $95,000,000 were exchanged, and of the 5 per cents of 1904 $70,500,000.

"The secretary of the treasury still has authority under the law to resume refunding should he deem it proper to do so. Whether or not refunding will be resumed depends largely upon whether the interest of the treasury seem to require it at any time in the future.

The Public Debt.

"The public debt is now in far better condition for retirement than ever before. It may well be doubted whether the treasury

Continued on Page Nine.

TO THE PEOPLE OF 2001

MAYOR MAYBURY'S ADDRESS HAS BEEN PREPARED.

RIGHTEOUSNESS, HE SAYS, EXALTS A NATION.

HOPES CITIZENS WILL HAVE INCREASED IN THAT REGARD.

HE ASKS MANY PROFOUND QUESTIONS OF THE FUTURE.

What Wonders Will One Hundred Years Bring Forth?

Mayor Maybury's office was crowded with the city officials, members of the various municipal commissions, prominent citizens and their wives and families, last night, to witness one of the most unique and impressive ceremonies that has ever taken place in the history of Detroit. It was nothing less than the sealing of the greetings of Detroit of the present to the Detroit, its mayor and government and people, of a hundred years from now.

Mayor Maybury read to those assembled the message to the people of that far-off time which he had prepared in his position as chief executive of the city. To those gathered in the office, it was a time of great solemnity, for the mayor referred to the fact that not one of those present would be present at the opening of the box. Before he had finished the reading the city hall clock struck the first stroke of 12, and the waiting crowds outside broke into tumultuous applause and cheering as a welcome to the new century.

Then the mayor finished reading his beautiful greeting, and the listeners cheered. For a few moments the crowd went out upon the front steps of the city hall, where a flash-light picture was taken by C. M. Hayes. Then they again came within and the box, containing its many documents, was officially sealed by Benjamin Guiney to be kept unopened in the city archives until the beginning of the twenty-first century. The mayor's message to that time and generation is as follows:

Detroit, December 31, 1900.

To his honor, the mayor of Detroit in 2001 and the generation whose privilege, and, I trust, pleasure, it will be to read the contents of this box—health and greeting:

The papers herein contained, now for the first time brought to light by you, after a retirement of 100 years, were prepared at

Continued on Page Three.

MARCH 10, 1901:

The car-making efforts of Ransom Olds are dealt a setback when his factory burns. Also, a mystery surrounds a bank in Niles.

"Ten Men Jumped From Windows" and *"Cashier Johnson Missing,"* column seven.

The Detroit Free Press

VOL. 66. ON. 167. — FOUR PARTS.—DETROIT, MICHIGAN, SUNDAY, MARCH 10, 1901.—FORTY PAGES.—FOUR PARTS. — PRICE: FIVE CENTS.

TEN MEN JUMPED FROM WINDOWS

$72,700 Loss By Quick Fire at Olds Motor Factory Yesterday Afternoon.

"RUSH for your lives, the building is all on fire!" yelled one of the employes at the plant of the Olds Motor Works, 1308-1318 Jefferson avenue, about 1:35 o'clock yesterday afternoon. Then followed a scene of the wildest excitement. Men dashed for every exit. Ten of the most nervous of them threw up the windows on the second and third floors and the crowd took its breath as the frantic employes climbed out and deliberately jumped or dropped to the ground. Only one was seriously injured, but four were removed to hospitals in ambulances.

The department history recalls few such rapid fires in Detroit in a factory of the kind. The structure was in two sections and of brick. One had a frontage towards Jefferson avenue of 100 feet and this section extends back about 70 feet. The rear section was 50 feet wide and about 230 feet in depth, a court 50 feet wide being between the two sections and the plant of the Detroit Stove Works. The main section was three stories high while the remaining part of the building was but two stories.

It was near the wash room on the west side and towards the rear of the main building that the fire originated. Several theories are advanced. Some say natural gas exploded; others talk of electricity, but an investigation to satisfy most of the firemen that the explosion of gasoline was the real cause. It is at least three explosions were heard, according to the statements of men who were in the neighborhood.

OLDS MOTOR WORKS 30 MINUTES AFTER FIRE STARTED.

Flames seem to have first swept to the north and then taken a course to the river. The conductor on a south-bound Jefferson avenue line car was on the scene when the fire broke out fifteen minutes later when he returned on his trip westward, the walls had crumbled.

So great the fierceness of the tongues of fire and the excessive heat, track company had drove directly into the vacant lot.

ESTIMATED DAMAGES.

	Damage.	Insurance.
Olds Motor Works stock	$50,000	$40,000
Olds building	15,000	Cov'd
The Detroit Stove Works	1,000	Cov'd
Employes personal property	300	Cov'd
Detroit United Railway	200	—
Total	$72,700	

front of the building shortly after the alarm was turned in, and it was impossible to get closer to the structure than 100 feet. The necessary directness of the men in the building can be easily appreciated.

Building Not Strong.

Apparently, the building was weak. The walls of the first story appeared to be about thirteen inches thick, but the upper walls were considerably narrower. Of course, allowances may have had something to do with the great destruction, but a big stretch of a manufacturing building to be used by fire in such a remarkable short space of time is a surprise to men whose business it is to have burning property. The Olds Motor Works employs in the neighborhood of 300 men, but fortunately, owing to a standpoint of life and death, no more than two dozen persons were in the building at the time, owing to the fact that the place closes down at noon on Saturday.

The loss to the draughtsmen, machinists and other mechanics will probably reach as high as $1,500, with very little insurance. Groups of these sufferers gathered about the debris Saturday afternoon.

Continued on Page Two—Part 1.

BULLETIN OF THE NEWS.

PAGE ONE.
Olds Motor Works Destroyed by Fire—Stumb Controls Manchuria—Clayton-Bulwer Treaty Still in Force—Tornado in Texas—Burglar's Shrewd Scheme—Germany's Foreign Policy—Cashier Johnson Missing.

PAGE TWO.
Special Session Ended—State News.

PAGE THREE.
Maud Gonne Says Force Must be Used—Suburban Politics Warm—State News.

PAGE FOUR.
Bicentennial Appeal to Michiganders—Deaths of the Week—Local.

PAGE FIVE.
Shaftey's Business on a Solid Basis—Local.

PAGE SIX.
In the Dominion—Cut to Death by Car Wheels—Local.

PAGE SEVEN.
Marine Matters—Yachting Gossip—Local.

PAGE EIGHT.
Baseball and Bowling.

PAGE NINE.
Hunting Yarn—Harness Horses.

PAGE TEN.
Needham's Sporting Review.

PAGE ELEVEN.
Real Estate—Among the Architects—Local.

PAGE TWELVE.
Money Wanted for a Pardoned Man—Local.

Denied by Count Cassini.
Washington, March 9.—Count Cassini is very much perturbed over the tone of the press dispatches from London, and does not hesitate to add his emphatic and unqualified denial of the truth of their contents.

Commissioners Retired.
Mich. Electric Co., 151 Woodward Ave.

TREATY STILL IN FORCE

Will Not Be Abrogated by Great Britain Without a Satisfactory Equivalent.

LONDON, March 9.—The reply of the British government to the note conveying the unanimous of the United States senate to the Hay-Pauncefote treaty should be formally delivered by the British ambassadors at Washington to Secretary Hay within a few days. The foreign office here did not originally contemplate delaying the British reply until then. The plan appears to have been to transmit the answer previous to the date on which the treaty lapsed which, according to the British view of the case, would have put the onus of its lapsing on the senate. As previously set forth in these dispatches, the main object of the British government throughout has been to make an entirely new arrangement. At no stage of the proceedings has there been any inclination to accept the senate's amendments.

It is understood here that the nature of the British government's reply has already been informally communicated to Secretary Hay. Great Britain has no intention of modifying, or abrogating the Clayton-Bulwer treaty without a satisfactory quid pro quo. That treaty, according to the foreign office view of the case, remains as much in force now as the day it was signed. The speeches made in the senate do not disturb Downing street. They are dismissed with the remark that "treaties cannot be abrogated without the consent of both the contracting parties." There is, however, an apparently genuine belief here that a satisfactory arrangement will eventually be arrived at though it is scarcely thought it could be put into the requisite shape in time for discussion at the session of the senate. The government is freely expressed disinclination on this part of the British officials to commit themselves to any further treaties until they are thoroughly assured of the views of the senate holds on the matter in question.

BURGLARS' SHREWD SCHEME

GOT EMPLOYES AWAY AND THEN HAD EASY JOB.

DETROIT LIGHT & POWER OFFICE WAS ENTERED.

$1,300 SECURED BY MEN WHO KNEW SAFE COMBINATION.

CASHIER TWO MILES AWAY ON GOOSE CHASE.

Work Was Completed in Twenty-five Minutes.

ONE of the cleverest burglaries committed in Detroit in years occurred just after dark last night, when the office of the Detroit Light & Power Co., corner of Woodbridge and Randolph streets, was entered, the safe opened and $800 in cash and currency and $500 in checks carried away.

The police call it "an inside job," for the reason that the person who planned the burglary was well acquainted with the business operations of the office as well as the plan of the office building. The guilty parties were apparently in possession of the combination of the safe, opened the inner door of the safe with the key. They knew the inner door was left ajar, the outer one would not close either. The only recently locked by the burglars before they went away.

"The checks are no good to them," said Manager Phillips, "but their loss will mean an infernal lot of confusion for us. A large number of persons are represented by the checks. That place has been a sort of tempting fat to the thieves for some time. We had about been found from them. They only fear was the large number of bills and store work. Cashier Fred C. Winson was late in striking a cash balance and Charles Usery, a young employe in the office, to remain over the usual time, 6 o'clock, and assist him with his books at 6 o'clock the phone rang and Usery answered it. Mr. Visson was wanted.

"This is Detective Stinton," said the man's voice. "I have arrested two men with a wagon loaded with wire and I want you to come out at once and identify them. I am with Naveaux, 407 Jefferson avenue, near Belle Isle bridge."

"I can't come now, said Visson, "for I have quite a sum of money in the office. It is necessary," insisted the man who was impersonating Detective Stinton, "for you to come. It would be best for you to leave others than the office to clock the stuff in identify these men. Show how will it take?" Visson inquired. "Why, not long," said the supposed detective.

Visson was notified. Much thinking have he is given out at the place. A clerk, telephoned and the cousins here have been compelled to Detective Stinton and Buller. Here here in charge of most of the cases. A small product for the amount of capital invested was due largely to the fact that the receding year was a disastrous one for the best sugar company.

California has eight factories with a total capital of $16,125,000. Michigan, nine factories with a capital of $6,855,541, and the combined number of factories in other states was fourteen, with a capital of $8,385,708.

Of the thirty-one factories, twenty-nine were controlled by incorporated companies, and two by individuals. In addition to the factories operated in the present year, six were under construction of copper with a bill invested in new factories. $1,830,000, making a total of $24,535,000 for the new industry in the year 1900.

SERIOUS MOHAMMEDAN RIOT AT BOMBAY

Bombay, March 9.—The city is in a ferment and the Mohammedans are rioting. Aga Khan, chief of the Khojas, a sect of Mussulmans, arrived to-day. A collision with his arrival a portion of his followers seceded. The famatics attacked the seceders outside the mosque and as a result two persons are dead and several wounded.

ARMY PROMOTIONS.

MANY MADE THAT ARE OF INTEREST TO MICHIGAN.

Washington, March 9.—In a long list of army promotions sent by the president to the senate are the following names that are of interest to Michigan: Edwin B. Wisnon, Jr., son of the late Gov. Wisnon, now captain of the Fourth Cavalry, from first lieutenant to captain, Walter C. Short, of the Tenth Cavalry, from first lieutenant to captain, Captains to be majors: Leonard A. Lovering, of the Fourth; Wm. P. Evans and Francis B. French, of the Nineteenth. First lieutenants to be captains: Wm. M. Morrow, of the Twenty-first; John Howard, of the Nineteenth; James Romayne, of the Nineteenth; Howard B. Perry, of the Fourteenth; Wm. G. Robbins, of the Sixth; George H. Jamerson, of the Seventh; Frank H. Lawton, of the Twenty-first; F. G. Lawton, of the Nineteenth; Thomas W. Connell of the Ninth; Charles L. Best, of the Seventh; H. D. Wise, of the Ninth; Robert S. Coffey, of the Seventh; Perry L. Miles, of the Fourteenth.

Money for the St. Louis Fair.
Jefferson City, Mo., March 9.—The house to-day passed the over bill appropriating $1,000,000 for Missouri's exhibit at the Louisiana Purchase centennial exposition to be held in St. Louis in 1903. The exhibit will be under the management of a board of nine directors, to be appointed by the governor.

Gov. Dockery, to-day signed the senate bill punishing kidnapping for ransom by death. The bill has an emergency clause and is therefore a law.

CRUTCH AND CANE THROWN AWAY

The U. S. government, through the Hot Springs of Arkansas, says they cure rheumatism, gout, neuralgia, catarrh, skin and blood diseases. Write Bureau of information for illustrated book.

Sunday Dinner.
Wayne hotel, this evening, 5 to 8. Popular rate, 50c. Orchestra.
I'll bet you can't do the "U" Puzzle.

Hotel Metropole
Sunday lunch, 11 to 2:30. Sunday dinner 5:30 to 8 p. m., a la carte.
I'll bet you can't do the "U" Puzzle.

BOTHA'S SURRENDER LOOKED FOR SOME TIME NEXT WEEK

London, March 10.—Advices from two great South African financial houses confirm the press intelligence that Lord Kitchener and Gen. Botha have been in negotiation for six days. Peace, or at least a long step towards the end of the war, is looked for next week.

The war office last night declined to contribute anything to these great expectations which include, according to some, the making of a formal submission by Botha on Monday, when his force will surrender to French.

Among the versions as to what is going on there is one with some official countenance, that the government is offering Botha far more liberal terms than the parliamentary declarations have given any idea of. The only thing limiting the cheerful speculations is the fact that Delarey, Dewet and Beyers, regardless of what happens on Gen. Hill, will continue to wage guerilla warfare.

CALIFORNIA LEADS:

MICHIGAN NEXT

MANUFACTURE OF BEET SUGAR IN THE UNITED STATES.

Washington, March 9.—The report upon the manufacture of beet sugar, which was issued to-day by the census bureau, says that in 1899 the census year, there were thirty-one beet sugar factories in the United States, distributed among ten states and territories, representing an invested capital of $39,588,559, and producing 81,127 long tons of beet sugar valued at $7,375,857. This small product for the amount of capital invested was due largely to the fact that the recent year was a disastrous one for the beet sugar crop.

California has eight factories with a total capital of $16,125,000. Michigan, nine factories with a capital of $6,855,541, and the combined number of factories in other states was fourteen, with a capital of $8,385,708.

Of the thirty-one factories, twenty-nine were controlled by incorporated companies, and two by individuals. In addition to the factories operated in the present year, six were under construction of copper with a bill invested in new factories. $1,830,000, making a total of $24,535,000 for the new industry in the year 1900.

RUSSIA CONTROLS MANCHURIA

Her Flags are Also Hoisted Everywhere Throughout Mongolia.

BERLIN, March 9.—The Tageblatt's special correspondent, who has been traveling in northern Manchuria, Mongolia and on the borders of Siberia and China for a year, and whose reports, hitherto, have been correct without exception, has furnished his paper with a long letter which is published to-day, containing interesting details regarding the Russo-Chinese agreement on the subject of Manchuria, Mongolia and Turkestan. He says he is absolutely certain that the published version of this agreement is in no way the actual truth. He then proceeds to give facts covering the proposed internal administration of that part of China, demonstrating that Manchuria will become an integral part of Russia, more so than even Bokhara. In regard to Mongolia, he says there is no doubt a protectorate has been established as this is evidenced by the hoisting of Russian flags everywhere, the thorough organization of the district, the establishment of tax collecting offices and the opening of branches of Russo-Chinese banks with no one but Russian officials in charge. All this, virtually, has taken place during the past six months and began before the Boxer outbreak.

Evidence in an Army Order.
The clearest evidence, however, is contained in an army order issued by Gen. Grodekoff, to the Siberian troops, in which the general said: "You have nobly fulfilled your task of defending a line 800 hundred kilometres long, on the frontiers, of the Russian empire, from Urga (Mongolia) to Khorlmon, and have thrown back the army across this threatened line."

Bribed by Bars of Silver.

Roubles, establishing direct communications with L'Hassa (Thibet), where Dalailama scored a victory for Russia by an immense bribe of bars of silver, direct telegraph communications along cities between the Russians at Khelru and those in China. even reaching Han-Fa, where the Chinese court has been adjoining by way of Barb-al Khami, Kerschou and Lantchou. Without the knowledge of either the Europeans or Americans or that Japanese all the territory comprised between northwestern provinces of the Chinese empire, bordering on Mongolia, where the chief Chinese troops are formed from the eight millions of residents there, which troops are firmly held in China, meaning thereby paying the Boxer rebellion under Prince Tuan.

Russian Decree.
Perhaps the most important information furnished by the Tageblatt correspondent is that the Russian government has caused to be printed, distributed and placed on walls throughout trans-Baikalia, a decree informing the Chinese that the eight million of troops in trans-Baikalia, because Baikal is protected by the Russians in order to put down any disturbances which have broken out in China, meaning thereby putting the Boxer rebellion under Prince Tuan.

Severe Moros at Memphis.
Memphis, March 9.—A heavy wind and rain storm prevailed here to-night and much damage was wrought. Culverts were washed out and fences and high trees in the vicinity suffered severely. Telegraph communication with Texas and southern points are interrupted.

Several Missing.
Reports from Terrill, Tex., say that the heaviest rainfall on record occurred throughout that section this afternoon. Several persons are reported drowned or missing.

TORNADO STRUCK TEXAS TOWN

Four Persons Killed and About Twenty Injured, Many Fatally.

WILLS POINT, Tex., March 9.—A cyclone passed through the west side of this place to-day, demolishing everything in its track. Four persons are dead and many injured. Fourteen dwelling houses were entirely ruined and a number of others are badly wrecked. The public school is a total wreck. The cotton oil mill is damaged and the largest gin plant is in ruins. Wires were blown down and poles and fences uprooted. A freight car was blown off the track.

The dead:
Maggie Clouse, infant of Rev. J. H. Clouse.
Leon, 3-year-old son of J. H. Williams.
Chief of John White.
Charles Powers, painter, drowned.

Injured:
J. H. Williams and lady.
Mrs. E. H. Graham, child and brother.
Child of E. S. Gray.

Several are expected to die. The property loss is about $30,000, at a conservative estimate.

No House Left Whole.
Black clouds had been hanging in the southwest all morning. The atmosphere was heavy and at intervals there had been blistering showers of rain. It was just at noon where there was a long range of rumbling thunder, a puff of wind and then the air was thick with flying timbers. The cyclone came from the southwest and held a straight northeast course. Its path was about three hundred yards wide. It struck the northwest quarter of the town, in the residence section. No house is left whole, those that are not irremediable ruin are in the minority. Most of them are demolished, mere heaps of debris that offer no opportunity for the junkman. Household furniture and utensils are strewn further than the eye can reach and they mark the storm's path.

Struck Arkansas.
Texarkana, Ark., March 9.—A storm bearing the fury of a tornado swept over the western part of this county to-day. It is reported that many buildings were destroyed and several lives lost. Wire connections with the stricken district is interrupted.

GERMANY'S FOREIGN POLICY

CURIOSITY OVER ACTUAL CONDITION OF TRIPLE ALLIANCE.

RELATIONS WITH RUSSIA SUBJECT OF GENERAL CONCERN.

SLAVS OFFENDED BY SPEECH OF CHANCELLOR VON BULOW.

AN IRISHMAN'S ARTICLE CAUSING GREAT CRITICISM.

Said Anglo-Saxons and Russians Would Dominate Germany.

BERLIN, March 9.—Some additional interesting comment concerning Chancellor Von Buelow's enunciations of Anglo-German relations and of President McKinley's inaugural speech are about Russia. The press sees that the inference is plain that something still pending awakening for expression. The opinion is expressed by the leading newspapers that the chancellor, in his avoidance of any reference to a foreign policy. The Berlin Volks Zeitung and other papers wonder why Count Von Buelow did not answer Herr Spaffeter's (Centrist) interpellation regarding the actual condition of the triple alliance and about Russia. The press sees that the inference is plain that something still pending awakening for expression, especially as while a small party particularly has grown stronger in the last few months and an attentive ear could hear "the wires with Russia is either broken or badly in need of repairs."

Offended Russia.

One sentence used by the chancellor in his speech, about which all papers agree gave offense in that country. This was Count Von Buelow's quotation from Frederick the Great's instruction to his ambassador at St. Petersburg, saying he (Frederick) would be glad to continue Russia's friend but would never be Russia's slave. Another of the chancellor's expressions, namely, that "great monarchs no more relinquish had displeased the emperor and the Anglophiles at court and in the army, grew up with the book and lay almost without doubt to a minor extent them the expression. The German blue class newspapers recognize the fact that Count Von Buelow could not speak more plainly about foreign relations under the present delicate state of international politics. Even the Russian paper, the Cologne Volks Zeitung agrees with this comment on Von Buelow's speech.

Answered McKinley.
A number of German papers say that President McKinley in his inaugural address answer Count Von Buelow's expression's programme.

The Foreign Exchange, Monday last, printed an abusive article, in which President Von Buelow was referred to in uncomplimentary terms and to which the hope was expressed that in 1908 Mr. Bryan will be better political fences. Generally speaking, little interest is felt in the recent inaugural.

Russia's National Strength.
Advance sheets of the article written by Sir Howland Blennerhasset, commissioner of national education in Ireland, on the subject of Anglo-Saxons and Russia as the leading empires, has aroused attention and stirred great criticism. The press opinion against the view expressed in its contention impairments is that Mr. Rowland's judgments is faulty in imputing to the Slavs, particularly to Russia, so much vitality and power, it is here contended that Russia has had no serious test of her national strength for half a century and that the outbreak of the Russo-Turkish war in 1877 has not, she writes, in certain respects, than Turkey, and that without Roumania's aid at the end of the war would have been doubtful. It now remains to be seen what Russia, a sturggle with a really great power of Germany certainly does not fear, is in a position to take. The Russians were German in 1870, because the advocates has promise to future expansion and to the great expansion in either Russia or the Anglo-Saxons.

The correspondent of the Associated Press bears that Prof. DeSprech and the Russian dispatches answer Sir Rowland Blennerhasset on this interesting question.

CASHIER JOHNSON MISSING

NILES BANK FAILURE IS WORSE THAN AT FIRST SUPPOSED.

NILES, Mich., March 9—(Special).—When the First National Bank of this city closed its doors yesterday there was not as much excitement as at other times but during the day a large number of an absconding cashier was heard; nothing but words of praise for Cashier Chas. A. Johnson, who commenced with the bank as an errand boy when he was a lad, grew up with the bank and has remained with it ever since, some twenty-five years. Cashier Johnson's late Fred. Johnson leaving a wife and two small children, Johnson's habits for a bank cashier, were almost beyond reproach. He gambled, it is charged, played the races and did other cash transactions of this, as it is known that Johnson were in Peru, Ind., was a two weeks ago, at which time, it is known the on his own expense Accountant Fred Tolk, of Grand Rapids, arriving here this evening and will commence, with Bank Examiner Sadden, a right search of the night's book accounts.

During the run on the bank for two days there were first withdrew his deposit. This indicates the greatest confidence in the institution and in the bank's cashier. This city has on deposit about $200 to the counter $4,000 officer deposits have been that where a small amount, the will be reasonably and, finally or principal reasonably safe.

The statements were made public to-day with particulars of one from positions from all over announced that Cashier Chas. A. Johnson was missing. There is great excitement on the street to-night with the fact that the First National has failed and any one will get out of the wreck.

It is said that Johnson is in Chicago, it. the state of complete mental collapse but detectives fail to find him there. Johnson's father, Prof. Edward Johnson and Prof. T. T. DuSiparts and the Barth intend answering Sir Rowland Blennerhasset on this interesting question.

Cass County Must Pay the $15,000.

Cassopolis, Mich., March 9—(Special).—The United States Court of Appeals decided the application of Cassopolis for the decision of Judge Severens of the United States circuit court for the southern district of Michigan, denying the right of the United States to do with the surplus of Jordan E. Gibson, formerly contractor for the building of the new court house, the supervisors today voted to pay the bond of $15,000 to Cass county on the judgment rendered against the county. The $15,000 will be paid in cash one-half in 1902, and one-half in 1903. It is stated that several large deposits should be left in the bank on their end deposit. It is said the wire National Bank of the First National Bank the institution was in good condition according to the official reports of February 5 last, when there were as follows: Capital stock $100,000, surplus and undivided profits, $20,000; discount loans, $370,742; total liabilities, $612,566; resources, $—

The Detroit Free Press

DETROIT, MICHIGAN, THURSDAY, JULY 25, 1901.—TWELVE PAGES.

JULY 25, 1901:

The 200th anniversary of Detroit's founding by Cadillac is a spectacular pageant.

DETROIT ROYALLY WELCOMES CADILLAC ON HIS RETURN TO THE CITY HE FOUNDED TWO HUNDRED YEARS AGO.

A SECTION OF THE COURT OF HONOR ILLUMINATED.

TWO CENTURIES OF HISTORY

Detroit's Growth Traced From the Time of Cadillac.

STIRRING AND PATRIOTIC EARLY EVENTS REVIEWED IN MANY NOTED PAPERS.

CROWD AT THE DOCK WAITING FOR CADILLAC'S ARRIVAL.

OPENED WITH PAGEANT AND REJOICING

Detroit's Bicentennial Introduced With Roar of Cannon and Clanging of Bells.

THOUSANDS OF PEOPLE LINED THE RIVER AS CADILLAC'S VOYAGEURS PASSED DOWN FROM LAKE ST. CLAIR.

Steamers, Yachts and Launches Shrieked Their Noisy Welcome to the Gallant Chevalier and His Daring Crew.

CADILLAC RECEIVES KEYS OF THE CITY

Mayor Maybury Bids Him Again to Resume His Rule Over the City He Founded.

INDIANS GREETED THE FOREIGNERS AS THEY LANDED AND BADE THEM CHEERING WELCOME TO THE LAND OF THE WEST.

In the Name of the King of France the Chevalier Metaphorically Took Possession of La Ville d' Etroit.

SIOUX WARRIORS WHO HAVE COME TO HELP DETROIT CELEBRATE HER NATAL DAY.

Sept. 22, 1901:

A forerunner of the modern funny page.

PART FOUR. THE DETROIT FREE PRESS: SUNDAY, SEPTEMBER 22, 1901. 7

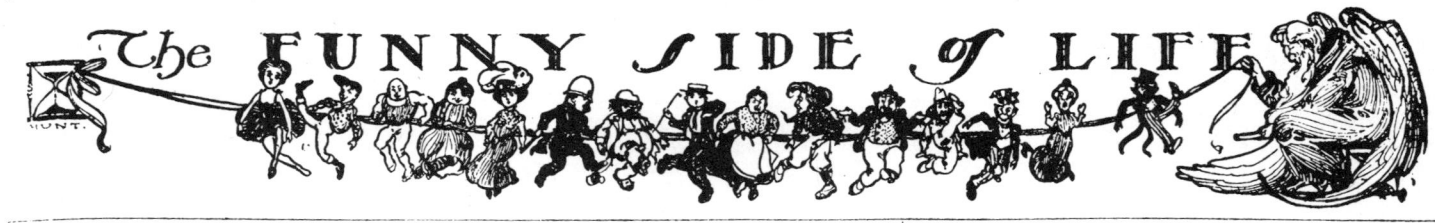

The FUNNY SIDE of LIFE

THOSE NEEDLESS QUESTIONS AND HOW TO ANSWER THEM.

Binks—"Hallo! going to play golf?"

Links—"No; going to my grandmother's funeral and this is a floral piece I am taking along. What are you doing up here; trying to avoid the cold weather in the city?"

A BAD GUESS.

A girl in a pale-pink kimona
Picked up a young fellow—a Jonah;
Said she, "Well, for lunch
I'll have reed bird and punch."
"Not much; you'll have beer and bologna."

Silas (reading telegram from his son in the city)—"Mercy, Miranda, listen to this: 'Broke. Had leg pulled. Wire me $25. Hiram.'"

Miranda (crying)—"Poor boy! I guess he must hev bin run over by one of them automobiles. Better send him $50, Silas, an' tell him to git the best doctor in town."

TAKING THEIR MEDICINE.

He—"Not everybody cares for outdoor sports."

She—"No; all those men over there seem to be quite sick."

Not the Grammatical Kind.

"What is a conjunction?" asked the teacher.

"That which joins together," was the promptly reply.

"Give me an illustration," said the teacher.

The up-to-date girl hesitated and blushed. "The marriage service," she said at last.—Chicago Post.

His View of It.

"I don't see any reason why people should interfere when fools want to go through the Niagara rapids in barrels."

"But it does seem a shameful waste of good barrels, you know."—Cleveland Plaindealer.

In This Advanced Day.

"Some men are brutes!" exclaimed the man who had been reading a newspaper.

"That is quite true," answered Mr. Meekton. "I know a man who habitually forgets to put the key under the doormat when his wife goes out to lecture. The way he keeps her ringing the bell while he wakes up out of a sound sleep, makes a light, puts on some clothes and gets down to the door is positively inhuman."—Washington Star.

What Miss Whipperly Said.

"Does Miss Whipperly ever say anything about me?" asked Gaslett, who wanted to find out where he stood.

"Well, yes," answered Goblett, "she asked me to-day where you have been keeping yourself. She said you hadn't called on her for the last two or three minutes."—Indianapolis Sun.

Not Time Enough.

Little Ethel—"Mamma, I know why you can't count th' stars."

Mother—"Why, my child?"

Little Ethel—"Coz it won t stay dark long enough."—Ohio State Journal.

"And what do you want with a match, my little man?"
"Aw! I wants ter shine me shoes with it, of course."

Little Johnnie Jones.

It scares the youngster half to death,
And yet most every chance
He gets he'll run away from home
And hang around old Nance,
And feel the goose flesh quiver while
She tells him about the "ha'nts."
Indianapolis Sun.

Incredible.

He—"This author should be ashamed of himself. A married man, too!"

His wife—"What does he say?"

He—"He says that a man's wife 'gazed at him in speechless astonishment.' Why, such a thing is unknown in matrimony!"—Tit-Bits.

Not a Wise Man.

"Why is it that so few people seem anxious to talk to Mr. Carpington? He seems very well informed."

"That's just the difficulty," answered Miss Dimpleton. "He's one of those dreadful men who know enough to correct your mistakes when you quote the classics and who don't know enough not to do it."—Washington Star.

Expensive.

Mr. Binwed—"I'd like to have hold of the fellow who invented those long coats for women."

Mr. Nebb—"Why?"

Mr. Binwed—"Why? Great Scott! they cost twice as much as one half as long."—Boston Post.

One Definition.

"What is a Bohemian?" said the young man who wants to study human nature.

"A Bohemian," answered the cold-blooded friend, "is a person who always needs two or three extra indorsements on his note when he wants to borrow money."—Washington Star.

A GOLF SET.

NOT SO EASY.

"From de cut of his trousers I should say he's from de country. I'll just shine his shoes widout askin', an' he won't have de nerve to toin me down."

"Oh! dis is too easy. I hate to take his money."

HIS CHANCE.

She—"Did you know that it is said kissing cures dyspepsia?"

He—"I am desperately ill with it."

Preacher—"When you're tempted to drink, think of your wife at home."

Henpeck—"I do—and that's what drives me to drink."

Passenger—"Are you sure there is no danger?"

Deckhand—"Yes, sir; the captain's taking a nap because it's too foggy to see anything."

"Mother, why were they named the 'Sandwich Islands?'"

"I suppose it was suggested by the fate of the missionaries who were sent there."

AN ASTONISHING LAND.

In Guatemala $1 Will Buy $6 and Railroads Have Mahogany Ties.

An American railroad man landing in Guatemala (Port Barrios) encounters various surprises, the first one of consequence being, perhaps, the answer of the ticket agent to his inquiry as to what is the railroad fare to Guatemala City, which is about 190 miles away and fifty miles beyond the terminus of the railroad. The price of the ticket to the railroad terminus ...

... $16 in Guatemala money besides. You now learn that one American dollar will buy $6 in Guatemala.

You find the passenger train a very good one. Everything is in excellent condition and the engine is a fine one. The train is equipped with air brakes. The track is very poor. The rails are heavy for a narrow-gauge road, but the track is badly out of line. The ties are mahogany, rosewood and ebony, but even ebony lasts only about two years. The train runs at about ten miles an hour and makes long stops. The road has nine locomotives, several years old; 25 passenger cars ...

... most of them receiving about $200. The operators are all natives. The chief dispatcher gets $300, which, be it remembered, is equivalent to only $50 of American money. An American cannot live here for less than $150 a month. I find that the other two roads in this country pay about the same as this one, except that on one of them enginemen get $10 a day. Any railroad man in the United States who has even the poorest kind of a position on a good road will do well to keep it rather than try Guatemala.—Guatemalan Correspondence of the Railroad Gazette.

FISHING IN LAKE KEUKA.

A Story That is Good Until the Next One is Told.

The past week has been another record-breaker in trout fishing in Lake Keuka. For several days it has been nothing unusual for fishermen to take seven or eight within an hour or so. Almost everybody who tried got full share, and some were fine specimens, weighing from five to seven pounds. It is told of a man from Corning that, while fishing near Bluff Point, he ...

... fishermen of the lake hooked a trout near the same point. As he landed the fish he was much surprised to find a second hook in the fish's mouth. He started to draw in the loose line from this second hook, and was again surprised to find that there was still another trout on the line which he had fished up. He landed this fish and was nearly overcome when, from the second fish he discovered a third line upon which was a third fish. The three fish, weighing twenty-six pounds, were safely landed, and were taken to Keuka, where it is said they were viewed by a large number of people.—Rochester Democrat.

... arise within its boundaries. In 1888 its real colonization began, when 26,000 immigrants crossed its frontiers. Now there are more than 250,000 annually. While excluding undesirable persons, the government adopts generous measures toward worthy immigrants. To every family, when desired, it advances $25 for the expenses of the journey, assigns gratuitously forty acres to each man on his arrival, and further promises to assist with a loan of $50. The only great landlord is the emperor or the state.—National Geographic Magazine.

RICHEST TOWN ON EARTH.

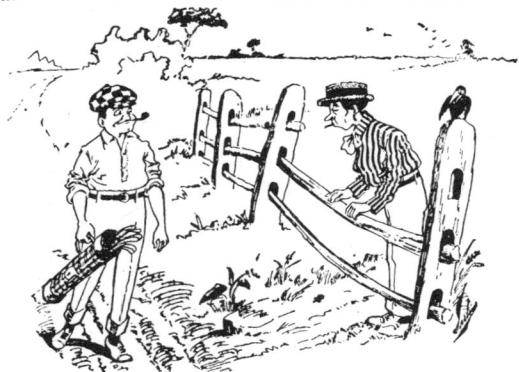

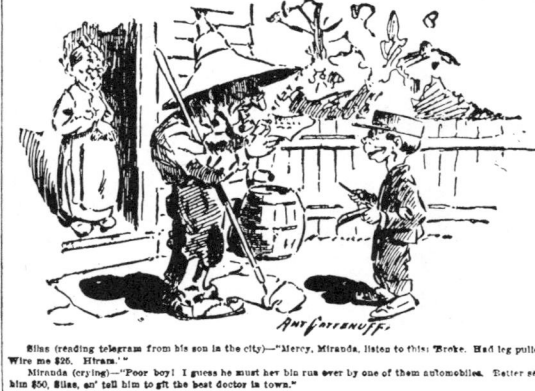

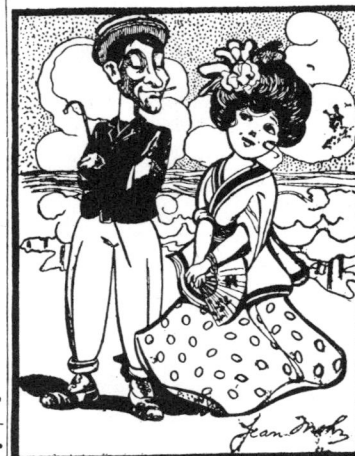

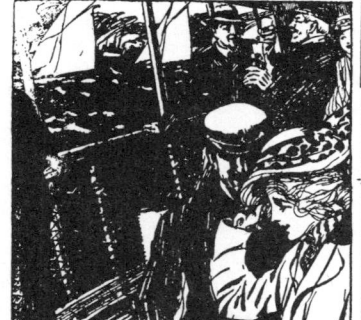

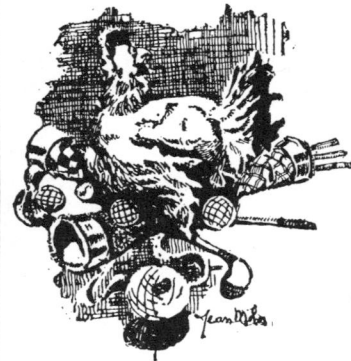

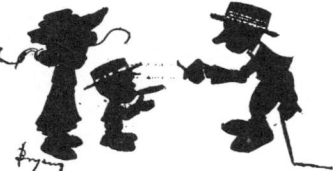

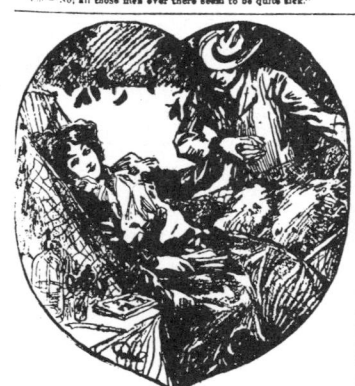

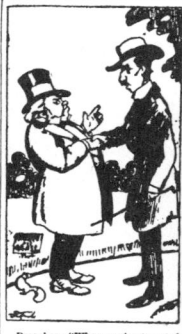

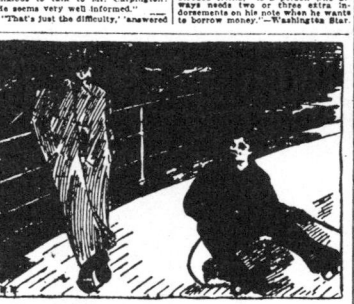

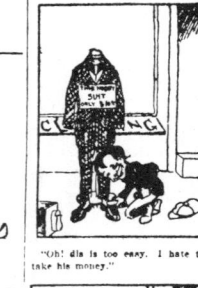

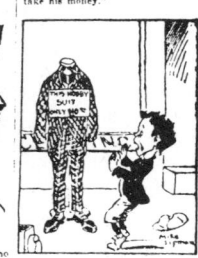

The Detroit Free Press

DETROIT, MICHIGAN, FRIDAY, OCTOBER 11, 1901—TEN PAGES.

Oct. 11, 1901:

Automobiles take over a Grosse Pointe racetrack; horses are described as dejected. A young Henry Ford wins the big race.

ALEX WINTON'S FAST MILE

A mettlesome pacer, with sleek coat, high head, extended nostrils, stood uneasily in a stall at the Grosse Pointe race track yesterday. As he pawed the floor and jerked at his halter, it was easy to see that something was wrong with his equine majesty. For the first time in his career the horse was getting no attention, though a crowd stood about, and he resented it as earnestly as a horse ever resented anything.

In the next stall was a puffing, vibrating, panting thing: a thing that emitted clouds of steam and the disagreeable odor of burning oil, and the horse objected as vigorously as repeated snorting and impatient pawing could, but it was useless. It was not his day and for the first time on Grosse Pointe's beautiful course, the horse was forgotten.

All around the horse were other things, large, small, white, black, red, yellow — making all sorts of queer noises. Outside along the fence, where usually are found tally-hos and coaches with their gay parties, were long rows of those things instead. The automobiles had at last intruded into those precincts which had hitherto been held sacred to the noble animal — and whether or not it denoted the approach of the horseless age, it certainly seemed a sacrilege — this invasion of the temple.

And when the races were over and the great crowd turned cityward, satisfied, it was of Winton's wonderful flash against time rather than of Cresceus's or some other trotter's splendid burst of speed, that the people talked.

Detroit society sanctioned automobile racing yesterday by turning out almost en masse. It was the first big race meet ever held in the west and an attendance variously estimated at from 7,300 to 10,000 was present to pass judgment.

It is doubtful whether the crowd was more pleased at the breaking of the track record for a mile, by Alexander Winton, of Cleveland, or the winning by Henry Ford, of Detroit, of the "big" race. Winton's exhibition was splendid from start to finish.

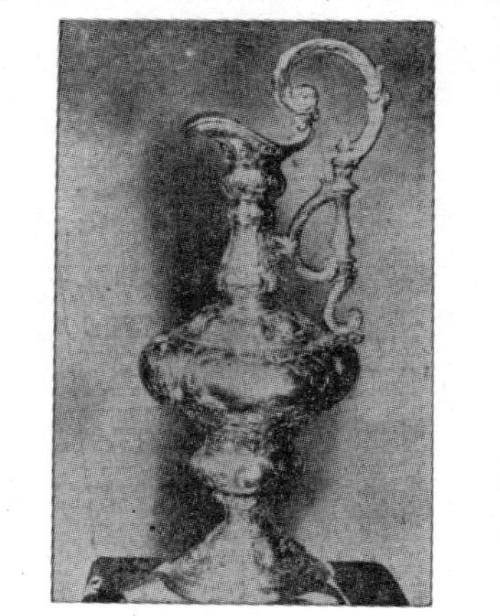

THE FREE PRESS CUP.
TROPHY WON BY EDGAR APPERSON IN A TEN-MILE RACE FOR MACHINES WEIGHING LESS THAN 2,000 POUNDS.

ALEX WINTON'S FAST MILE

Cleveland Expert Made the Distance in 1:12 2-5 at Grosse Pointe.

DETROIT FREE PRESS CUP WON BY EDGAR APPERSON, OF BUFFALO, IN A 10 MILE EVENT.

About 8,000 People Attended the First Big Auto Race Meet of the West.

EVOLUTION OF THE AUTOMOBILE

Illustrated by the Machines Turned Out at the Olds Motor Works.

Oct. 20, 1901: People take increasing notice of the automobile.

Sunday feature.

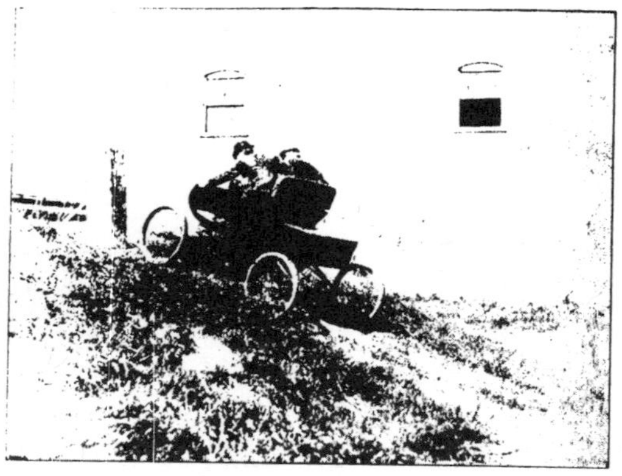

ASCENDING A 45 DEGREE INCLINE.

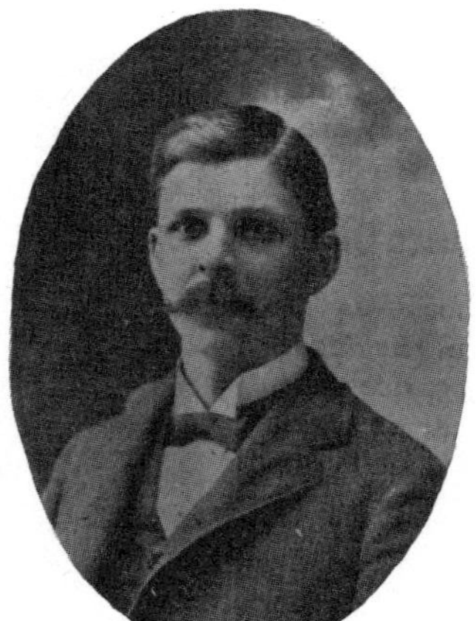

RANSOM E. OLDS.
Vice-President and General Manager of Olds Motor Works, Patentee of the Oldsmobile and Gas Engines.

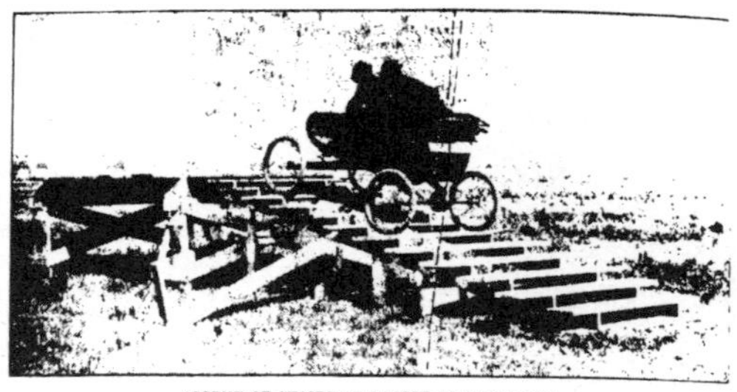

ASCENT OF STAIRS AT GROSSE POINTE RACES.

There are few people nowadays, no matter what their calling in life, that do not take an interest in the automobile. From a curio of the highway it has come to be regarded as a permanency in the matter of road locomotion, and the wonderstruck pedestrian no longer stops to gaze and comment as the horseless vehicle glides gracefully on its way, threading the devious paths of city traffic with easy motion and speed adapted to locality and circumstances. Yet while the automobile is becoming a more and more familiar object in the streets of Detroit, the interest in the industry is growing deeper and the popularity of the machine is increasing with its development. A few years back the industry was but in its experimental stage, but it has now become a most important national one.

A Well-Known Enterprise.

The purchasing public which views an automobile, buys them primarily for the same purpose for which it has always purchased any class of vehicle, viz., because a carriage or a vehicle is needed for personal transportation, convenience and comfort; and as it is among the better class of carriage users that automobiles are generally sold they demand the same diversity of design, the same elegance in finish, the same magnificence in appointment and the same easy riding qualities that they have always been accustomed to when drawn by horses. These things being true, it follows that when they decide to avail themselves of the pleasure and convenience of a machine they will place their order with a firm that has made a solid reputation in this phase of manufacturing—one whose experience and output are a guarantee of satisfaction. Such a firm is the Olds Motor Works, whose Michigan establishments have earned transcontinental fame and are well known in European manufacturing centers. The works on Jefferson avenue are always pointed out to visitors as one of the great manufacturing plants of the city, and the name is everywhere one of the familiar trademarks with which the city and state are identified.

A Modest Start.

Like many another institution whose main reliance were enthusiasm, energy and pluck, the Olds Motor Works had a modest beginning. Twenty years ago it occupied a one and one-half story frame building, 24x36 feet, with one iron planer, one engine lathe and an old drill. The plant was located at Lansing, this state, and the firm was known as Olds & Son. A few years later the senior member of the firm withdrew from taking active part in the business; this left the son, Ransom E. Olds, at the wheel, as president and general manager. The company, however, was so small at that time that Mr. Olds was obliged to be head mechanic, inventor, bookkeeper and salesman. To-day six and a half acres of floor space are required for the purposes of the firm, and the business is constantly enlarging. The new Detroit plant is located on four and one-half acres on Jefferson avenue, and this, with the Lansing gas engine plant, gives 200,000 square feet of floor space filled with the most modern machinery and equipment. There is besides another new plant in process of construction at Lansing, the grounds of which will be provided with a fine track for racing purposes. The company has also recently come into possession of 16 acres at Lansing, on which an additional plant is being erected, a cut of which is shown in three illustrations. It was in 1889 that the Olds company was first established in Lansing with the modest equipment above described. Five years later, in 1894, the company turned out its first gas engines, the demand for which increased so steadily as to necessitate the erection of a new shop, 24x110, in which the business was continued for five years. Improvements made in the Olds engine so increased its sale that at about this time a two-story building, 36x84, was added to the plant. In 1894 patents were secured on the present type of engine manufactured by the firm, which has proved to be so great a seller that each year saw the need of new buildings and increased equipment. Yet the firm was unable to meet the growing demand for this engine, notwithstanding they were working but a small number of states.

The First Olds Patent.

Mr. Olds obtained his first patent on a horseless carriage in 1894, although so far back as 1887 he built his first motor vehicle; this was a three-wheeled machine, using steam, with gasoline as fuel, the box being large enough to encase the whole of the machinery. Mr. Olds built this machine for his own use, and had no idea of putting a machine of this type on the market, as he fully realized that it would require more or less of an engineer to operate a steam machine. Later, in 1897, he built another steam machine, this being fitted with two engines, 3-inch by 4-inch cylinder, and also used gasoline for fuel. The gas engine at this time was very large and bulky, being more or less in a crude state; for instance: a three horse power engine would have a 4-foot balance wheel and weigh about 1,100 pounds. As this branch of the business progressed they were able to build a gas engine that would develop more power at less weight and in a more compact form, so that Mr. Olds' attention was turned to adapting it to the motor vehicle. They were in the engine business, and supplied them for nearly every kind of power, and there was no reason why it should not be applied to the vehicle.

The Oldsmobile of To-day.

These and similar experiments gave Mr. Olds the experience that is now so valuable to his company, which is able to avoid the experimenting being done by most builders. Devices which were found impracticable by this company many years ago are now being put on the market by other firms, while the Olds company has improved its machine until to-day it turns out one that is as near perfection as possible. To the buyer of an automobile reliability is the first requisite; a machine which is in a perfected state, and is ready to go upon a second's notice, is what the public demands. Such a machine is the "Oldsmobile," which is the name by which the gasoline runabout manufactured by this firm is known.

A description of the Oldsmobile will not be amiss to those who have determined to possess themselves of a machine. Though its weight is only 680 pounds, it has carried a load of 1,000 pounds. Its light weight enables it to run smoothly over rough roads, which would be quite impassable for a heavy machine. The weight is about one-third that of most automobiles now upon the market, thus making a much lighter load to carry, and consequently giving greater power in proportion. The expense of fuel is also here to be considered, as it decreases rapidly with the weight of the machine. The Oldsmobile has the regular wagon tread of 4 feet 8 inches; the wheels are 28 inches in diameter; the tires are four-inch cushion, which insures a regular speed. The noise usually caused by transmission gear is thereby avoided. The brake is applied to a flange which is attached to the driving sprocket. It is powerful enough to cause the driving wheels to slip along the ground when a sudden stop is necessary. Ball bearings are used in the front wheels and rollers on the rear axle. The rear driving axle is incased in a steel tube, at the center of which is an oval flange to receive the sprocket. The compensating gear is incased within the rear sprocket. This relieves the gear of all strains except that which is brought to bear for driving the carriage, making it impossible for the gear to get out of mesh. The steel tube which incases the rear axle also receives the springs. No reaches are necessary, as the springs extend from the rear to the front axle.

The Motor Power.

The two sets of batteries which are used for igniting purposes have sufficient capacity for six months to one year's use. Should one become weak or meet with an accident, the change from one set to another can be accomplished by merely throwing a switch, without stopping the machine. The expense of a new battery is about $3.

Its peculiarly curved dash is one of the patented features of the machine, which enables anyone to recognize the "Oldsmobile" wherever they may see it appear on the globe.

The motor is of the simplest possible construction, having but one cylinder, one piston, one connecting rod and crank, a balance wheel, and two valves. It is a simple proposition, one that a boy can understand. An owner of a complicated machine will find himself frequently in need of repairs. It is vastly better to have a simple machine and thereby be assured that a long trip through the country can be made without fear of a breakdown; the simpler the complication the more probable the breakage. The power is transmitted to the rear axle by a roller chain of 4,000 pounds working strength, running direct from the motor shaft. Gearing is used in hill-climbing and in backing up, but no gears are used when running at the vice. It is practically the same one that is used on their carriage motor. Its perfect working qualities avoid the usual smoke and odor which trails after many gasoline carriages now upon the market. This miser is so constructed that the most efficient gas is generated with absolute safety. There is no gasoline to shut off when through using, and there is no air to manipulate in order to arrive at a proper mixture.

The gasoline tank holds four gallons, which supply is sufficient for 150 miles of travel over good roads. There is no jar to the steering lever, as it is attached to the body and not to the running gear. The base of the steering lever is connected with the front wheels through a spring. This spring absorbs all vibration caused by irregularities in the road, yet in no way does it affect the rigidity of the steering mechanism. The motor is started, while sitting in the carriage, by means of a stationary crank at the end of the seat. The speeds are controlled by one lever, which is moved forward for the speeds ahead and backward for the reverse. The highest speed is obtained by increasing the speed of the motor; this is accomplished by an easy movement to the steering lever, and insures smooth riding on rough roads. It will speed from ten to twenty-five miles through parks, boulevards, country roads or city streets, the class of road not entering into consideration.

The body being mounted very low (only about 2 feet from the ground) does away with the possibility of upsetting when turning short corners. This also adds to the ease and convenience of getting in and out. The body is hung independent of the motor running gear, which eliminates the vibration. In the motor the same practical lines used in the Olds stationary engines, which have been built in large numbers for many years, have been followed. It is a four-horse-power motor, which, under most favorable conditions works up to six, and is ample to drive the machine under any and all fair conditions. Water is used for cooling in summer, and in winter a simple compound is added, which effectually prevents freezing.

A RUN ON BELLE ISLE.

GOING AND COMING.

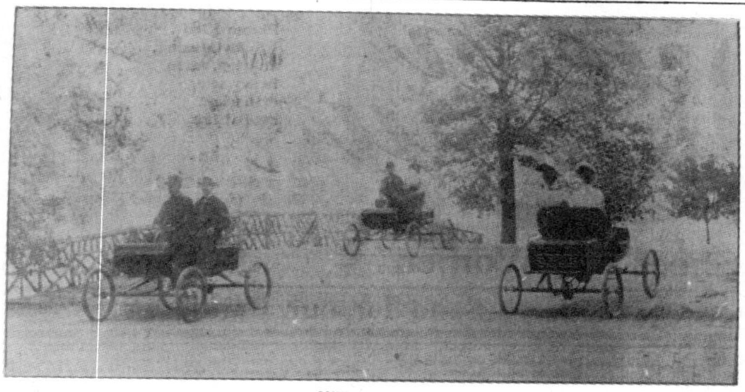

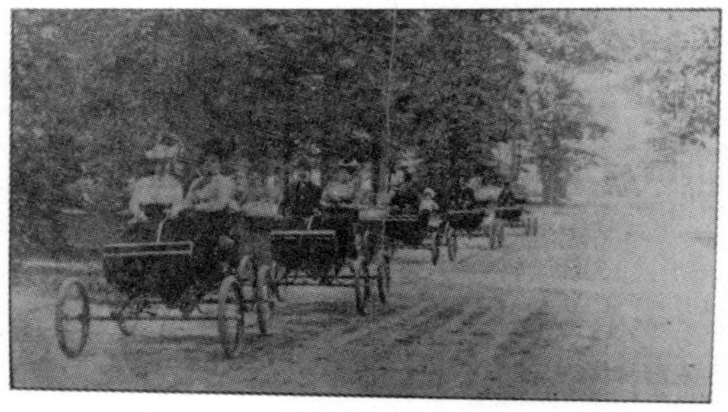

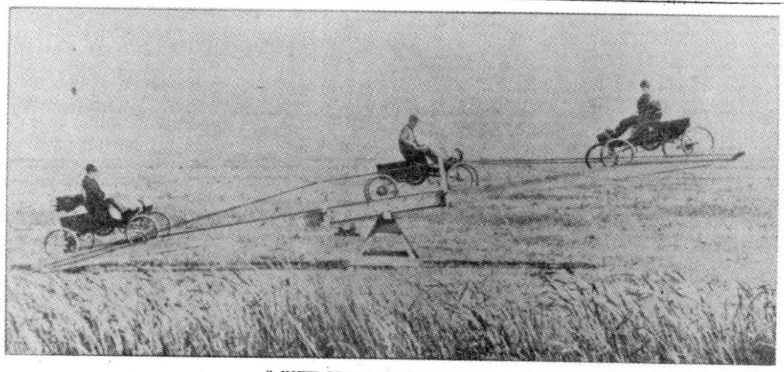

A NOVEL DEMONSTRATION OF CONTROL.

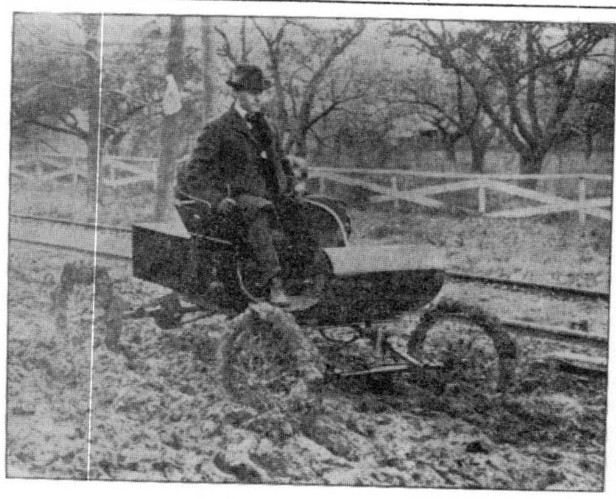

A jump spark is used, and its position is such that it can be removed without any inconvenience. It is seldom necessary to remove the igniter, however, as it is so placed that the entering gases keep it free from carbon deposits. The popularity of the Olds stationary engines is largely due to their excellent mixing means of a foot lever, which acts upon the governor, and also by varying the time at which the ignition takes place.

Adapted to Many Purposes.

The Oldsmobile is adjustable to all purposes for which a vehicle is needed. A merchant who owns an Oldsmobile may ride to his place of business in the morning. The store then adds the delivery box for the day. The box is easily removed; the merchant desires to use in exchange for other business purposes his return home, or to spend the evening riding with his family, in no time, radius being practically unlimited.

During very hot or stormy weather the top may be placed over the seat. With the top is included a set of curtains and rubber boot, permitting travel in any weather without exposure.

With the enlarged facilities for production the Olds Motor Works expect to turn out 5,000 automobiles during the coming year.

There is a separate department devoted to the manufacture of electric vehicles, in the construction of which the same accurate and careful work is employed.

An article of this nature would not be complete without mention of the patented gas and gasoline engines (both stationary and marine) manufactured by this company, which is recognized as one of the oldest and largest manufacturers of gas and gasoline engines in the world. For reliability, economy and durability, the engines have gained wide fame, and the enormous output is sufficient guarantee of their quality.

The Olds Machine at the Grosse Pointe Races.

One of the features of the big automobile racing meet at Grosse Pointe, Thursday, October 10, was the excellent showing made by the Olds machines.

Notwithstanding the fact that the Oldsmobile is not built for racing purposes, in the ten-mile racing contest it developed a speed of about two minutes to the mile, having gone over the course in 22 minutes.

Possibly the most interesting exhibition of the day was that given by several chauffeurs in Olds machines, in the field inside the track. There a high platform had been erected with a flight of steps leading to the top. Up and down these at high or low speed, as the chauffeur desired, the machines were driven, now slow, now fast, but always just where the driver wished. On a grass turfing board outside of the high platform, inclined at an angle of 45 degrees, the Oldsmobile was driven forward and then backward. The incline was so steep the dirt could scarcely hold to it, yet all these and more, with the greatest of ease.

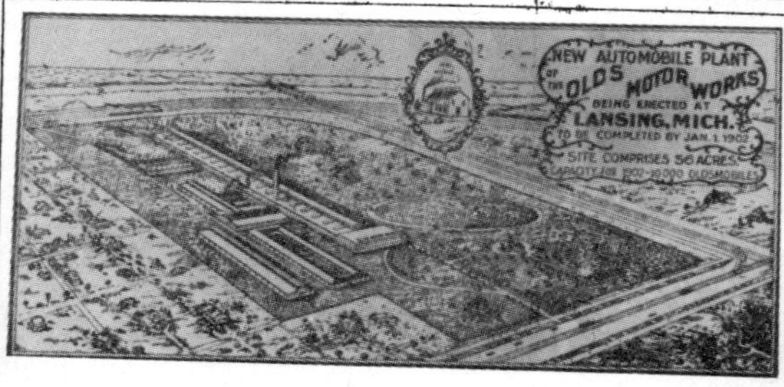

PART ONE. **The Detroit Free Press** PART ONE.

VOL. 67. NO. 54. FIVE PARTS.—DETROIT, MICHIGAN, SUNDAY NOVEMBER 17, 1901.—FORTY-EIGHT PAGES. FIVE PARTS. PRICE: FIVE CENTS.

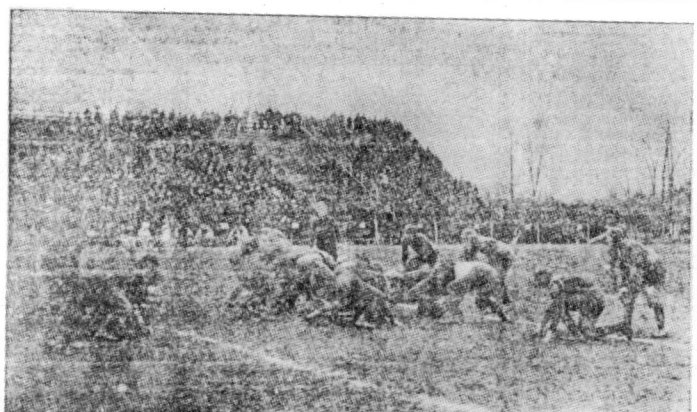

JUST BEFORE ONE OF CHICAGO'S ATTEMPTS AROUND END.

(Photographs by a Free Press Staff Photographer.)

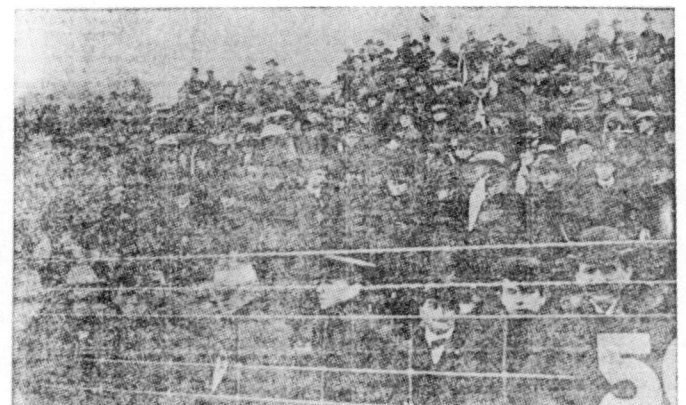

PART OF THE GREAT CROWD THAT CHEERED YOST'S MEN ON TO VICTORY.

YALE TOO MANY FOR PRINCETON

Defeated Her 12 to 0 in a Fast, Clean Game, Leading at Every Point.

HARVARD, WITH SEVERAL SUBS IN, WAS TWICE SCORED ON BY DARTMOUTH.

Carlisle All But Tied Penn., and Cornell Gave One Last Touch to Columbia's Despair.

FIGHT IN BRITISH CABINET

DISSENSION AMONG OFFICIALS SAID TO HAVE GROWN.

ROW MAY RESULT IN RESIGNATION OF HICKS-BEACH.

HIS RECENT SPEECH CONDEMNED BY HIS ASSOCIATES.

CHAMBERLAIN IS PICKED AS THE NEXT CHANCELLOR.

His Appointment Would Mean a New System of Taxation.

ASCHER JURY DISCHARGED

Two Jurors and Patrolman Placed Under Arrest.

THE FAMOUS MURDER CASE PROCEEDINGS DECLARED A MISTRIAL.

Full Statement of Judge Murphy's Finding That Caused a Sensation.

TWO MEN DROWNED IN RIVER

FRED CHASE FELL FROM STEAMER W. H. STEVENS.

CAME TO SURFACE, CRIED FOR HELP AND DISAPPEARED.

LOUIS HROMADKO JUMPED FROM BELLE ISLE BRIDGE.

IT IS BELIEVED HE DRANK CARBOLIC ACID BEFORE LEAP.

Had Lived With His Family at 201 Antoine Street.

MICHIGAN STOPS STAGG'S TRICKS

Defeated Chicago by 22-0 Score.

"WHOA BACK" DID NOT MAKE A GAIN.

Dry Field Would Mean Big Tallying.

D. A. C. Beaten in a Fierce Contest.

EACH SIDE LOST MAN ON ROUGH PLAY.

Pittsburg Scored 17 to the Detroit 5.

LEADING FOOTBALL GAMES AT A GLANCE.

At Ann Arbor—Michigan 22; Chicago 0.
At Madison—Wisconsin 18; Minnesota 0.
At Evanston, Ill.—Northwestern 11; Beloit 11.
At Lincoln—Nebraska 29; Kansas 5.
At Iowa City—Iowa 17; Grinnell 11.
At South Bend—Notre Dame 18; Indiana 5.
At Cambridge—Harvard 27; Dartmouth 12.
At New Haven—Yale 12; Princeton 0.
At New York—Cornell 24; Columbia 0.
At Philadelphia—U. of P. 16; Carlisle 14.
At Providence—Brown 24; Union 5.
At Pittsburg—Homestead 48; Lafayette 0.
At Washington—Georgetown 17; Virginia 16.
At Cambridge—Harvard '05 35; Yale '05 6.
At D. U. S. grounds—D. H. S. 17; D. U. S. 0.
At Bennett Park—D. B. U. 5; Port Huron A. C. 0.
At Kalamazoo—Kalamazoo College 15; M. A. C. 5.
At Lansing—Lansing High 63; Alpena High 0.
At Oberlin—Oberlin, 6; Ohio State, 0.

ANN ARBOR, Mich., November 16.—(Special.)—Yost is still the king. In fact his crown sits a little more squarely on his head now than ever before. ...

BY FAR the most stubbornly fought game that has been played on the D. A. C. gridiron this fall, one that kept the spectators on an edge of intense interest, which grew at times to a state bordering on wild excitement, resulted from the meeting of the representatives of the Detroit Athletic Club and a team of ex-collegiates from Pittsburg yesterday afternoon. ...

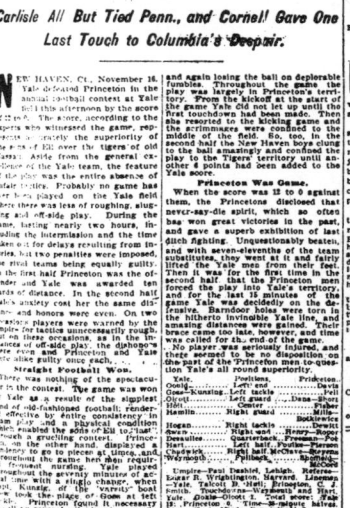

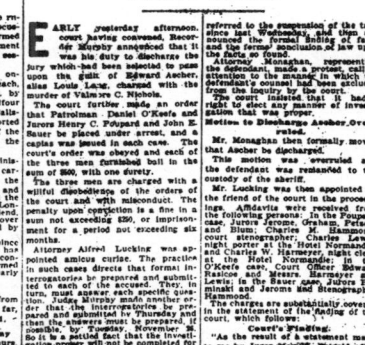

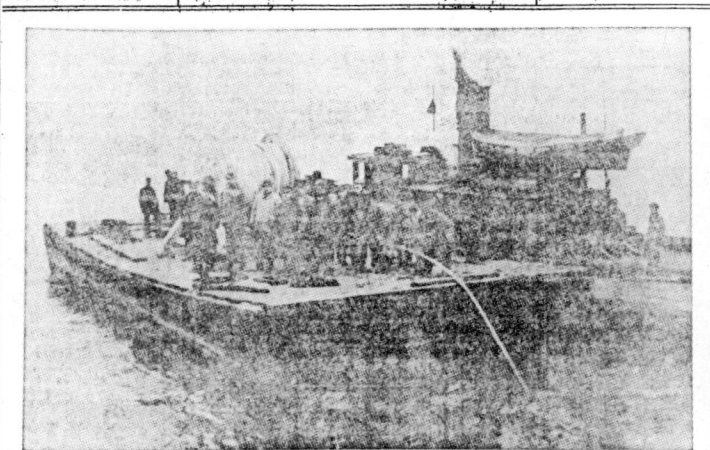

LAYING CABLE FOR THE POSTAL CO. ACROSS THE DETROIT RIVER, CONNECTING THE ATLANTIC AND THE PACIFIC

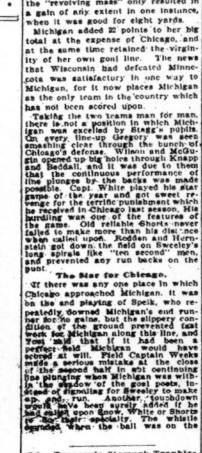

NOV. 17, 1901:

College football is big news on Sunday morning, especially when Michigan's Fielding Yost defeats Chicago's Amos Alonzo Stagg.

"Yale Too Many For Princeton," column one, and *"Michigan Stops Stagg's Tricks,"* column eight.

The Detroit Free Press

PART ONE

VOL. 67, NO. 117. — FIVE PARTS.—DETROIT, MICHIGAN, SUNDAY, JANUARY 19, 1902.—FORTY-FOUR PAGES. FIVE PARTS. — PRICE: FIVE CENTS.

JAN. 19, 1902:

The Saginaw Valley lumbering era is drawing to a close while Michigan beet sugar manufacturers meet with President Roosevelt in Washington.

"End Of Great Industry," column four, and *"Michigan Protest Delivered,"* column eight.

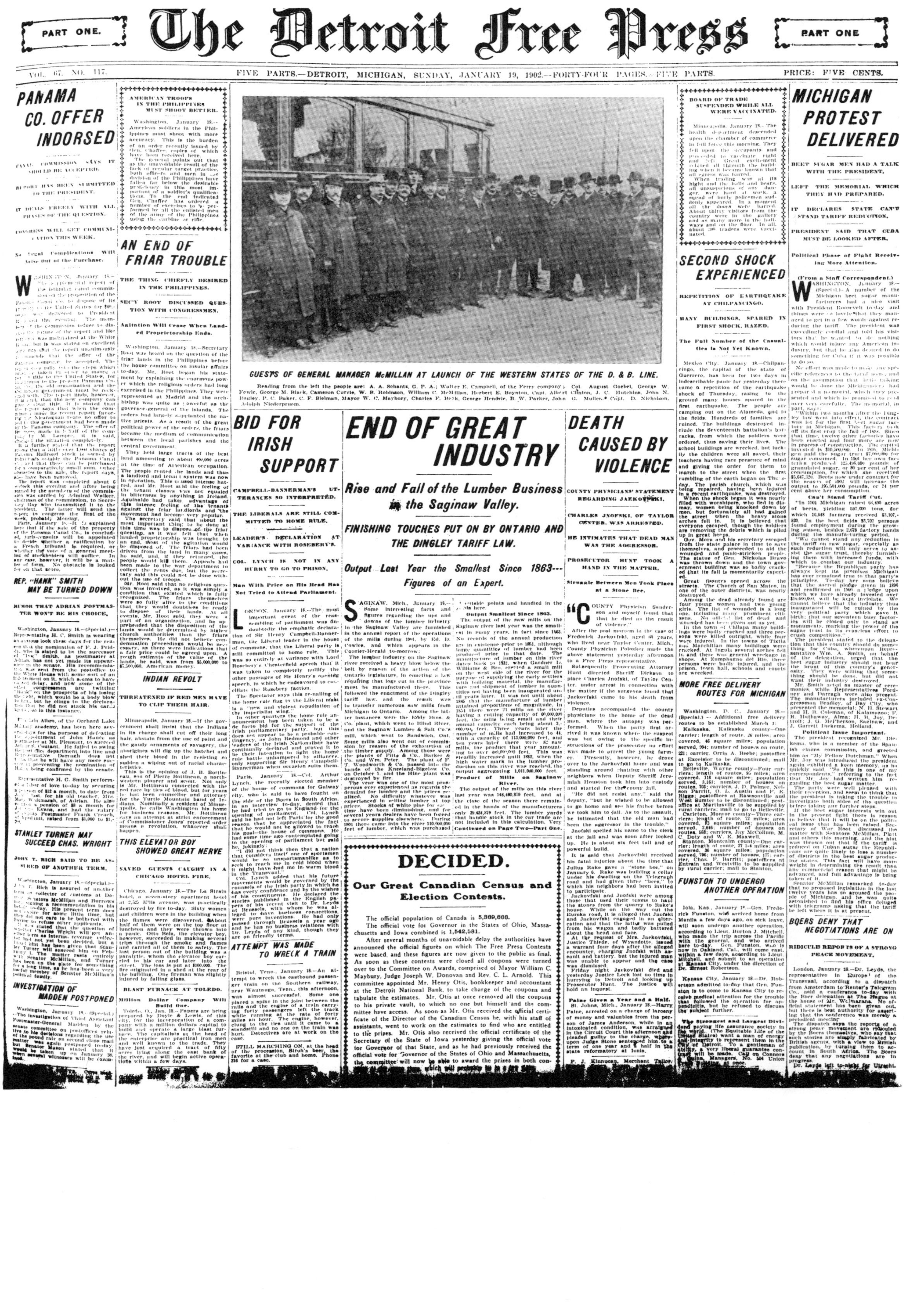

PANAMA CO. OFFER INDORSED

CANAL COMMISSION SAYS IT SHOULD BE ACCEPTED.

REPORT HAS BEEN SUBMITTED TO THE PRESIDENT.

IT DEALS FREELY WITH ALL PHASES OF THE QUESTION.

CONGRESS WILL GET COMMUNICATION THIS WEEK.

No Legal Complications Will Arise Out of the Purchase.

[article text]

REP. "HANK" SMITH MAY BE TURNED DOWN

RUMOR THAT ADRIAN POSTMASTER WON'T BE HIS CHOICE.

[article text]

STANLEY TURNER MAY SUCCEED CHAS. WRIGHT

JOHN Y. RICH SAID TO BE ASSURED OF ANOTHER TERM.

[article text]

INVESTIGATION OF MADDEN POSTPONED

[article text]

AMERICAN TROOPS IN THE PHILIPPINES MUST SHOOT BETTER.

[article text]

AN END OF FRIAR TROUBLE

THE THING CHIEFLY DESIRED IN THE PHILIPPINES.

SECY ROOT DISCUSSED QUESTION WITH CONGRESSMEN.

Agitation Will Cease When Landed Proprietorship Ends.

[article text]

INDIAN REVOLT

THREATENED IF RED MEN HAVE TO CLIP THEIR HAIR.

[article text]

THIS ELEVATOR BOY SHOWED GREAT NERVE

SAVED GUESTS CAUGHT IN A CHICAGO HOTEL FIRE.

[article text]

BLAST FURNACE AT TOLEDO.

Million Dollar Company Will Build One.

[article text]

ATTEMPT WAS MADE TO WRECK A TRAIN

[article text]

GUESTS OF GENERAL MANAGER McMILLAN AT LAUNCH OF THE WESTERN STATES OF THE D. & B. LINE.

Reading from the left the people are: A. A. Schantz, G. P. A.; Walter E. Campbell, of the Perry company; Col. August Goebel, George W. Fowle, George N. Black, Cameron Currie, W. B. Robinson, William C. McMillan, Herbert E. Boynton, Capt. Albert Clinton, J. C. Hutchins, John N. Bagley, P. C. Baker, C. F. Bielman, Mayor W. C. Maybury, Charles F. Beck, George Hendrie, B. W. Parker, John G. Muller, Capt. D. Nicholson, Adolph Niederpruem.

BID FOR IRISH SUPPORT

CAMPBELL-BANNERMAN'S UTTERANCES SO INTERPRETED.

THE LIBERALS ARE STILL COMMITTED TO HOME RULE.

LEADER'S DECLARATION AT VARIANCE WITH ROSEBERY'S.

COL. LYNCH IS NOT IN ANY HURRY TO GO TO PRISON.

Man With Price on His Head Has Not Tried to Attend Parliament.

[article text]

END OF GREAT INDUSTRY

Rise and Fall of the Lumber Business in the Saginaw Valley.

FINISHING TOUCHES PUT ON BY ONTARIO AND THE DINGLEY TARIFF LAW.

Output Last Year the Smallest Since 1863—Figures of an Expert.

SAGINAW, Mich., January 18.—Some interesting facts and figures regarding the rise and downs of the lumber industry in the Saginaw Valley are furnished in the annual report of the operations of the mills during 190l, by Ed. D. Cowles, and which appears in the Courier-Herald to-morrow.

The lumber industry in the Saginaw river received a heavy blow below the belt by reason of the action of the Ontario legislature in enacting a law requiring that logs cut in the province must be manufactured there. This followed the enactment of the Dingley tariff law, and the two combined to transfer numerous saw mills from Michigan to Ontario. Among the latter instances were the Eddy Bros. & Co. plant, which went to Blind river, the Saginaw Lumber & Salt Co.'s mill, which went to Sandwich, Ont. Some mills also went out of commission by reason of the exhaustion of the timber supply. Among these were the plants of Pitts & Co., Barker & Stewart, The plant of F. T. Woodworth & Co. passed into the hands of the Kneeland-Bigelow Co. on October 1, and the Hine plant was destroyed by fire.

The year was one of the most prosperous ever experienced as regards the demand for lumber and the prices realized. No difficulty whatever was experienced in selling lumber at the prices asked. Stocks of white pine for some time have been diminishing, and for several years dealers have been forced to secure supplies elsewhere.

Output Smallest Since 1863.

The output of the raw mills on the Saginaw river last year was the smallest in many years. In fact since 1863. No records of the annual production are in existence prior to 1863, although earlier quantities of lumber had been produced prior to that date. The manufacture of lumber on this river dates back to 1833, when Gardner D. Williams & Bro. erected a small mill on the west side of the river for the purpose of supplying the early settlers with building material, the manufacture and shipping of lumber in quantities not having been inaugurated until years later. It was not until about 1846 that the manufacture of lumber attained proportions of magnitude. In 1863 there were 21 mills on the river having a cutting capacity of 40,000,000 feet, with a total production of 21,000,000 feet. Three years ago the amount capacity each being about 1,100,000,000 feet, and two years later there were 82 saw mills, the product that year amounting to over 801,000,000 feet. This was steadily increased until 1882, when the high water mark in the lumber production on this river was reached, the output aggregating 1,011,000,000 feet.

Product of Mills on Saginaw River.

The output of the mills on this river last year was 248,400,519 feet, and at the close of the season there remained in the hands of the manufacturers only 33,424,850 feet. The lumber yards that handle stock in the car trade are included in this calculation, the yard of lumber, which was purchased

Continued on Page Two—Part One.

DECIDED.

Our Great Canadian Census and Election Contests.

The official population of Canada is 5,369,666. The official vote for Governor in the States of Ohio, Massachusetts and Iowa combined is 1,542,581.

After several months of unavoidable delay the authorities have announced the official figures on which The Free Press Contests were based, and these figures are now given to the public as final. As soon as these contests were closed all coupons were turned over to the Committee on Awards, composed of Mayor William C. Maybury, Judge Joseph W. Donovan and Rev. C. L. Arnold. This committee appointed Mr. Henry Otis, bookkeeper and accountant at the Detroit National Bank, to take charge of the coupons and tabulate the estimates. Mr. Otis at once removed all the coupons that followed the assertion for nomination for a committee have access. As soon as Mr. Otis received the official certificate of the Director of the Canadian Census, he with his staff of assistants, went to work on the estimates to find who are entitled to the prizes. Mr. Otis also received the official certificate of the Secretary of the State of Ohio yesterday giving the official vote for Governor of that State, and as he had previously received the official vote for Governor of the States of Ohio and Massachusetts, this committee will now be able to award the prizes in both contests further.

Paine Gives a Year and a Half.

St. Johns, Mich., January 18.—Harry Paine, arrested on a charge of larceny of money and valuables from the person of James Anderson, while in intoxicated condition, was arraigned in the Circuit Court this afternoon and pleaded guilty to the charge. Judge Daboll sentenced him to a sentence of one year and a half in the state reformatory at Ionia.

DEATH CAUSED BY VIOLENCE

COUNTY PHYSICIANS' STATEMENT REGARDING JACKOVFSKI.

CHARLES JNOPSKI, OF TAYLOR CENTER, WAS ARRESTED.

HE INTIMATES THAT DEAD MAN WAS THE AGGRESSOR.

PROSECUTOR HUNT TOOK A HAND IN THE MATTER.

Struggle Between Men Took Place at a Stone Bee.

[article text]

MORE FREE DELIVERY ROUTES FOR MICHIGAN

[article text]

FUNSTON TO UNDERGO ANOTHER OPERATION

[article text]

BOERS DENY THAT NEGOTIATIONS ARE ON

RIDICULE REPORTS OF A STRONG PEACE MOVEMENT.

[article text]

BOARD OF TRADE SUSPENDED WHILE ALL WERE VACCINATED.

[article text]

SECOND SHOCK EXPERIENCED

REPETITION OF EARTHQUAKE AT CHILPANCINGO.

MANY BUILDINGS, SPARED IN FIRST SHOCK, RAZED.

The Full Number of the Casualties is Not Yet Known.

[article text]

MICHIGAN PROTEST DELIVERED

BEET SUGAR MEN HAD A TALK WITH THE PRESIDENT.

LEFT THE MEMORIAL WHICH HAD PREPARED.

IT DECLARES STATE CAN'T STAND TARIFF REDUCTION.

PRESIDENT SAID THAT CUBA MUST BE LOOKED AFTER.

Political Phase of Fight Receiving More Attention.

(From a Staff Correspondent.)

WASHINGTON, January 18.—(Special.) A number of the Michigan beet sugar manufacturers had a talk with President Roosevelt to-day, and things were of a lovely kind. What they managed to get in a few words against reduction during the tariff. The president was exceedingly cordial and told his visitors that he wanted to do nothing which would injure any American industry, but that he also desired to do something for Cuba if it was possible to do so.

No effort was made to bias any opinion or reference to the tariff now, and the assumption that both talking would be done the Michiganders had proved it a moment, while they received and so many more to the tariff ways and on the floor. In all, about 30 visitors were vaccinated.

The parish church, which was being repaired, having been injured in a recent earthquake, was destroyed. When the shock began it was nearly filled with worshipers, who fled to discovery, women being knocked down by men, but fortunately all had gained the street before the heavy stone arches fell in. It is believed that everyone escaped, though the mighty gate damaged by the hurricane is said to go under 500 feet.

Gov. Mora and his secretary escaped from the state palace in time to save themselves, and proceeded to aid the wounded and panic-stricken people. The statue of Gen. Nicholas Bravo in the park was thrown down, and the town government buildings was so badly cracked that it had to be monumentally evacuated and destroyed.

Great fissures opened across the streets. The Church of San Mateo, in one of the outer districts, was nearly destroyed.

Among the dead already found are one young woman and two young girls. The list of wounded is a long one, including many prominent citizens. No one-half of the dead and wounded has been given out as yet.

In the town of Chilpa many buildings were badly cracked and three people were injured, who have since been taken to the towns of Tixtla and Matlatlan because of uncertainty. The inhabitants feared a recurrence of the shock in such large numbers, their homes, upon the uncertainty of the earthquake that they were afraid to return to their homes. The scores in the hospital have been materially increased in view of this fact.

The Jackovfski home and was standing around dancing with other neighbors when Deputy Sheriff Jeremiah Houston took him into custody and started for the town's jail.

"He did not resist any," said the deputy, "but he wished to be allowed to go home and see his father before we took him to jail. As to the assault, he intimated that the old man had been the aggressor in the trouble."

Jnofski spelled his name to the clerk at the jail and was soon after lodged to the town's jail. He is about six feet tall and of powerful build.

It is said that Jackovfski received his fatal injuries about the time that Julius Bake gave a "stone bee," on January 6. Bake was building a cellar under his house on the "Telegraph road and had given three "bees." In which the neighbors had been invited to participate.

Jackovfski and Jnofski were among those that used their teams to haul the stones from the quarry to Bake's house. While on the way out the Jnofski team, which was two days and Jackovfski rode in a great excitement about the wagon and badly battered about the head and face.

At the request of Justice Thirdel, of Wyandotte, the prosecuting attorney of Michigan county—one rich length of coast, 17 1-4 miles area covered; 50 routes; routes: 15 1-2 Palmer, Van Buren county; D. L. Austin and P. R. Biggs, postoffice at Lawsonville and M. H. Baxter will be discontinued; next offices at Martinville to be supplied by rural carriers; mail to go to Belleville.

Clinton, Newton county—Three rural carriers; 50 square miles; 12 miles area covered; 52 routes; postoffices at Churchville to be discontinued; mail to be supplied by rural carriers; mail to go to Bellevue.

Monroe, Monroe county; 50 square miles; area covered 20 miles; 82 routes; population supplied 1,120; number of houses 265; 1 Doty and W. M. Maxwell.

Stanton, Montcalm county—One carrier; length of route, 17 1-4 miles; area covered, 30 square miles; population served, 300; number of houses 125; carrier Chas. T. Harritt; postoffice at Entrican and Westville to be discontinued and mail supplied by rural carrier; mail to go to Stanton.

Can't Stand Tariff Cut.

"In 1901 Michigan raised 60,400 acres of beets, yielding 60,780 tons. For which 16,840 farmers received $1,597,416.18. It has been fields $2,727 person found employment during the growing season, besides 2,426 factory hands during the manufacturing period."

"We cannot stand any reduction in the tariff on raw sugar, especially as much reduction will only serve up as against the sugar trust, thereby formulating them with increased funds, with which to combat our industry."

"Great figures opened across the party principle. To-day he sees bodies in the last stand pledge given in 1896 as which we have already invested over $9,000,000 is to be kept inviolate. We cannot believe that the industry would be cynically destroyed, marking the power of the sugar beet in the cane-beet rise of this country so very carefully. The memorial, in part, says:"

"Within nine months after the signing we were half off, the contracts were let for the first three years after the industry. This factory the first crop of the fall of 1901. Since that time twelve other factories have been erected and four more are in progress of construction. The capital invested is $19,000,000 to No. Michigan paid the sugar trust $2,390,000 for sugar consumed. In 1901 there were $00,000,000 raised, thereby making them $2,250,000 a year for the cost of granulated sugar, at $5 per cent of consumption, for which also received $5,425,224. Beets now under contract for the season of 1902 will increase the sugar consumed to 15,500,000 pounds, or 55 per cent above last consumption."

"In 1901 Michigan raised 60,400 acres of beets, yielding 60,730 tons, for which 18,540 farmers received $1,597,216.18. It has been said $2,727 persons found employment during the growing season, besides 2,426 factory hands during the manufacturing period."

"We cannot stand any reduction in the tariff on raw sugar, especially as much reduction will only serve up as against the sugar trust, thereby formulating them with increased funds, with which to combat our industry."

"Because the Republican party has always kept its promises Michigan has ever remained true to the party principle. To-day he sees bodies in the last stand pledge given in 1896 as which we have already invested over $9,000,000 is to be kept inviolate. We cannot believe that the industry which was inaugurated by the party in 1898 will be destroyed so very carefully. The memorial, in part, says..."

Political Issue Important.

The president recognized Mr. Dickema, who is a member of the Spanish claims commission, and greeted him as "My Fellow Dutchman." When Mr. Joy was introduced, the president again exhibited a keen memory, as he quickly said: "Yo, this is the gentleman I corresponded with, referring to the facts. Mr. Joy having written his Joy regarding the beet sugar matter."

The party were well-pleased with their reception, although they think that the president is taking the trouble in calling before taking action in reference to Cuba. If the sugar increase in the price, not wait for further steps to be taken before it will be no by political change. The fact that this had been raised, however, in these interviews indicated that the future would not bring about a member in the Republican party in this state as many good predicate since. This fact will have more weight in deciding the question of the one that would really reduce the very important to the reduction of rates that might be taken up.

Senator McMillan remarked that he was proposed legislation he has twelve years has so assisted the sugar industry. In his own state, but McMillan astonished to find his office would not investigate both sides of the question as thoroughly in order to be ready he reached there as at present.

No notice of the memorial was taken by the president before the delegation left the White House. The memorial was drawn up by Senator McMillan, Platt and others this morning, and the plan was put together by Mr. Joy, while so entirely devoid of personal and emotional appeals but entirely a question of business, it is expected that it will make a deep impression on the president. The memorial was read aloud, read and considered and a copy placed in the hands of the president's secretary, Mr. Courtelyou. The Free Press to-day but any negotiations at all.

Dr. Leyde left yesterday for Utrecht.

April 28, 1907:

Five dollars down got you a lot in Hamtramck in the years of Detroit's explosive growth.

Advertisement

Cut Shows Shipman's Subdivision as it is Today. One Year Ago it was a Dairy Farm. Now we have Cement Walks, Water, Shade Trees, and Sewers are being constructed. We Know that this is

POSITIVELY THE BEST

Proposition to Get a Home or a Good Investment

SHIPMAN'S SUBDIVISION
OF THE CARPENTER FARM, HAMTRAMCK

We ask you to come out to the property and believe that you will be more than satisfied.

$250 Buys Lot 60x112 Feet | $500 Buys Lot 120x112 Feet

Including Water, Sewer, Cement Sidewalks and Shade Trees.

$5.00 Down, $5.00 Per Month Secures One of These Lots. 5% Discount for Cash

You have no interest or taxes to pay for one year. Thereafter 5 per cent on the unpaid balance. This property is free and clear. Union Trust Guaranteed Abstract given with each lot.

A BUILDING PROPOSITION UNEQUALED — ONLY $100.00 down on any lot, and we furnish you money to build your HOME. Pay it back like rent.

DON'T WAIT. To delay is a mistake. The lots are going fast. Many lots were sold last week. If your home is on this Subdivision and you are employed in the vicinity of the Milwaukee Junction district you can walk to and from your business. Just think what this means to you in the saving of car fare in one year.

Several houses have already been erected and are now occupied; others are going up rapidly, so you will have good neighbors all around you.

Agents on the ground afternoons and all day Sunday. Take Chene street car to Railroad crossing, then look for the BIG SIGN directing you to the property.

UNDERWOOD & INNIS 411 Union Trust Bldg. MAIN 85.

April 29, 1907:

Detroit blacks organize to halt the performance of "The Clansman," a controversial play dealing with the South during Reconstruction.

"'Clansman' Report May Bring Violence," column eight.

The Detroit Free Press

VOL. 72. NO. 216.   DETROIT, MICHIGAN, MONDAY, APRIL 29, 1907.—TEN PAGES   ONE CENT.

BRIDE AND GROOM TORN ASUNDER BY ASPHYXIATION

HONEYMOON OF TWO WEEKS ENDS SADLY

Man Dead on Floor and Wife Unconscious in Bed; Latter Resuscitated After Much Effort.

FOUND IN THEIR ROOM AT 170 ADAIR STREET

Constant and Lena DeKandelaere Had Come to Make America Their Permanent Home.

IGNORANCE IS THE CAUSE

Husband Committed Fatal Error of Allowing Unignited Gas to Flow.

PRESIDENT AND ROOT ARE 'OUT'

Secretary of State No Longer Roosevelt's Confidential Adviser, is Report.

CONSIDERS RECENT MOVES AS BLUNDERS

Offended by Harriman-Moyer Letter, "Conspiracy" Story and Advocacy of Taft.

SENDS BULLET THROUGH HEAD

Warner Crosby, Former Detroit Musician, Ends His Life in New York City.

DROPS OF BLOOD STAIN LATEST COMPOSITION

ROCKEFELLER PREPARES TO LEAVE THE EARTH.

Preparatory to his harp-polishing expedition to the celestial regions, John D. has started to give away all his real estate.—News Item.

HUGHES WILL BE NOMINEE OF REPUBLICANS IN 1908

Henry Watterson Picks New York's Governor as the Dark Horse Who Will Win Next Year.

REFERS TO THIRD TERM TALK AS PURE NONSENSE

SHE EXCUSES MRS. MOORE

Mrs. John Davis Says Matron of Home of Friendless Contends With Much.

INVESTIGATION INTO ABOVE CHARGES TODAY

WOMAN ROLLS UNDER TRAIN

Mrs. Minnie Wolf, of Woodmere, Loses Arm and Her Head is Badly Bashed.

WAS ALIGHTING FROM CAR AT DELRAY STATION

AMERICAN LEGATION PERHAPS ATTACKED

That in Guatemala City Reported Stoned by a Mob; Mexican Legation Also.

"CLANSMAN" REPORT MAY BRING VIOLENCE

SCIENTISTS HIDE DEATH

Attempt to Evade New York Law by a Secret Burial.

WOMAN ALLOWED TO DIE WITHOUT MEDICINES

Judge Alfred J. Murphy and Frederick F. Ingram See Play at Adrian and Inform Detroit Afro-American Ministers It Depicts the Negro as a Beast.

HUNDREDS MEET AT BETHEL A. M. E.

Make Inflammatory Speeches and Decide That if Mayor Refuses to Stop Performance Injunction Will Be Sought; Thompson Wants to See Play First.

Will Apply for Injunction.

STEALINGS AMOUNT TO ABOUT $800,000

Booty Found in Dennett's Bed $300,000 Instead of $20,000.

MME. SCHUMANN-HEINK GOES 1,200 MILES TO KISS CHILDREN

From Lincoln, Neb., to New York and Back While Her Company Makes Jump to Winnipeg, Manitoba — Wakes Them Up in Night.

HOPE TO SAVE MAN WHO HAS GLANDERS

Brooklyn Physicians Make Desperate Efforts to Cure Afflicted Veterinary.

Angry Poles Threaten Man Said to Have Felled His Young Wife With His Fist

CIGAR BANDS AND PLATES

Romances of Detroit Industries.

Thirty Miles of Motor Cars, Valued at $15,000,000, Produced Here in a Single Season.

The Auto.

WONDERFUL DEVELOPMENT OF AN INDUSTRY THAT FIVE YEARS AGO WAS PRACTICALLY UNKNOWN.

Sept. 27, 1908:

Detroit begins to realize there is something special about its booming, new industry.

Sunday feature

If the automobiles turned out in Detroit last year were placed end to end they would form a string thirty miles in length. Several thousand skilled mechanics were engaged in the production of these cars and some three and one-half million dollars of capital was invested in Detroit automobile factories alone, an investment far in excess of these figures.

The output of automobiles and accessories for the season in Detroit is conservatively placed at more than $15,000,000.

All this, and more, coming within five years makes Aladdin and his wonderful lamp of Arabian Nights fame look like a third-rate magician with a tallow candle, and should effectually silence those who insist that there is no romance in hard, practical business.

The history of the automobile industry reads like a romance, but on every hand are to be found substantial evidences of its reality.

Five years ago the suggestion that it would reach such proportions in Detroit, or elsewhere, for that matter, would have been derided, and the mental condition of the one hazarding such a prediction would have been questioned. Not without reason, either. The "horseless carriage," in spite of the fact that it had begun to demonstrate its practicability, was still a subject with which to conjure and furnished material for many a jest.

The most enthusiastic believer in this new form of locomotion never dreamed of such a result. The wildest flights of fancy stopped far short of the present mark. Yet those who pinned their faith to the motor car at a time when it was jeered at have lived to witness and participate in a development that makes things seem commonplace, and scoffers, always backbiters, must content themselves with predicting that the automobile has reached its limit, and that it is only a passing fancy-- even in the face of constant expansion in every direction.

The Small Beginning.

It seems incredible that from one small shop the manufacturer of automobiles could in the brief space of five years reach out until in point of magnitude it bids fair to outdistance any other single industry in the city, yet there are the great hives of human industry covering acres upon acres of ground, with contractors rushed to the limit building additions.

That a handful of workmen could have so much to Detroit the names of a half dozen men stand forth conspicuously, as they do in the history of the automobile industry of the country. Fame and fortune have been their portion, but the reward came only after long struggles in the face of discouragements that would have meant defeat for less determined mortals.

There are still people living on Park place, between Grand River avenue and Clifford street, who recall how some years ago they began wondering what was taking place in the little building at No. 81. The sound of hammer and file against steel greeted their ears on awakening in the morning, and it was usually the last thing they heard upon retiring at night, whatever the hour. Men--two of them--were frequently seen entering the building, across the windows of which curtains had been placed, thus adding to the mystery.

One day the noise of hammer and file was supplanted by a series of reports that brought people in the vicinity rushing to their doors terror stricken. From the building so long a source of wonderment smoke was issuing, finding its way out through crevices around the doors and windows. With the regularity and rapidity of a gatling gun came detonations that threatened to wreck the place.

But they didn't. After a time the explosions ceased, to be renewed at frequent intervals during the next few days. Excitement ran high in the neighborhood, and all sorts of wild conjectures were indulged in concerning the infernal machine it was felt confident must be secreted behind those curtains and the securely barred door that blocked the curious.

Just as the advisability of an investigation was being discussed by those who insisted that public safety demanded such a course, curiosity was aroused anew over the appearance in front of the shop of a strange looking vehicle, a sort of combination bicycle, buggy and engine, that emitted the unmistakable odor of gasoline so long in evidence in the neighborhood, threw off an oily smoke similar to that which had been noticed coming from the building, and put a battery of artillery to shame in the way of noise.

The secret was out--it was a "horseless carriage," capable of propelling itself about the streets at a fair rate of speed. The two suspected conspirators against law and order proved to be Henry Ford and C. H. Wills, two who were destined to play a leading part in the development of the automobile, whose names are famous throughout the length and breadth of the land, and who have seen the little shop on Park place grow by leaps and bounds into one of the largest plants of its kind in the world, where a few minutes is sufficient to produce a car infinitely superior in every respect to the one over which they spent months of toil and study, and whose output is found wherever civilization has left its impress.

There is no need at this time to recount what followed the appearance of Mr. Ford's first complete car, of the difficulty experienced in enlisting capital in the enterprise, how one obstacle after another was overcome with that dogged determination characteristic of Henry Ford, and how those who abruptly declined to be led into any such wildcat scheme have lived to see the men who took a chance get their original investment back time after time. How Ford fought those who sought to compel him to pay a royalty on all cars turned out, claiming priority of patents covering every conceivable means of applying a gasoline motor to a vehicle, would furnish material for a complete story of absorbing interest, but it is only one chapter in a career that has been fraught with surprises and marked by a determination to attain every desired end since the days when as a boy he took a keener interest in mastering the intricacies of the machinery employed than in performing the labor on the farm, where he was reared.

Other Pioneers.

There were other pioneers in the local field who have won a full measure of success. In the late nineties the Detroit Automobile company opened a small shop on the site and as a part of the present Cadillac plant. Curiously enough, Mr. Ford and Mr. Wills were associated with this concern at the outset, leaving because of a desire to have fuller sway than was possible here. Their departure did not wreck the company where they had been employed, for it was here that the foundation of the present Cadillac Motor Car company, with its hundreds of employes, and its volume of business annually running far into the millions, was laid.

To the unshaken faith of Henry M. Leland in the future of the automobile is due a large share of the credit for the growth of this concern, and its present prosperous condition.

There are plenty of others whose names stand forth prominently--Alanson P. Brush, for many years with the Cadillac company, and designer of more cars than possibly any other man in Detroit, if not the country; Howard E. Coffin, a few years ago a college student, now recognized as one of the foremost designers of cars; William E. Metzger, pioneer sales manager, and for years credited with being the highest salaried man in the business--their name is legion, these lights in a field that is filled with the brightest minds in the engineering world, and where to outshine others is indeed a distinction worth while.

Not all who engaged in the automobile business won fame, much less fortune. It hasn't been a bed of roses by any means. Keenness of competition and an awakening on the part of the public to what really constitutes merit have led to a survival of the fittest, and the business has settled down to a basis that should insure its continuance.

Development of the Auto.

No less remarkable than the growth of the industry is the development of the automobile from the wheezing "one lunger" of uncertain staying qualities in the earlier stages of the gasoline motor to the powerful touring car of the present time, capable of going anywhere under any conditions. The single cylinder car is still a prime favorite, but it has undergone many changes since the time it made its bow to the public.

It was back in 1901 that the first practical automobile made its appearance on the streets of Detroit. Henry B. Joy was the proud possessor of this pioneer type of a car that has since become world famous. Compared with even the runabout of the present day it presented an odd appearance. The car was provided with a horizontal single-cylinder engine, rated at 8-horsepower. It could carry two passengers, cost Mr. Joy $1,500 in New York, and was regarded as one of the most successful cars of the period.

It was some time before the local automobile colony progressed beyond the one-man stage. Those early days were full of tribulations for sales manager and purchaser, for the gasoline motor had not been developed to its present high state and was pretty much of an uncertainty. Gradually, however, other machines made their appearance, and the movement, once started, spread with astonishing rapidity until today there are thousands of automobiles in daily use in Detroit, and they no longer attract notice.

Two years after the appearance of the first automobile in Detroit the Ford Motor company was organized, with all the capital it could scrape together some $21,000. That same year, 1903, the Cadillac Automobile company entered the field, in a single season taking rank as the second largest maker of automobiles in the world.

The rest of the story is easily told, although time is required in digesting the figures involved.

Today no less than twenty concerns in Detroit are engaged in manufacturing automobiles. Eight of these pay taxes on $2,310,000 worth of property. Ten have a combined capitalization of $3,500,000, the others being capitalized at a lower figure. Last season they furnished employment to 8,000 men, including those engaged in the manufacture of accessories, disbursing millions of dollars in wages and for materials. Their output was conservatively valued at $15,000,000. If placed end to end, the cars turned out in Detroit last season would form a solid string from the city hall to Mt. Clemens and double four miles on the return trip.

Add to this showing a score of plants where bodies, tops, motors and accessories are made, not only for local concerns but whose market extends all over the country, and the magnitude of the industry that with the speed of a mushroom has sprung into a stable existence almost in a night becomes apparent.

That the automobile industry has been one of the most potent factors in aiding Detroit's growth and prosperity is certain. Its beneficial influence has not ended here, however, for the product of its factories has made Detroit famous the world over as the home of the high grade motor car, and the place where not only is life worth living but that strives to make it worth while for others less fortunately situated geographically.

SOUTH AMERICA LOCUST SWEPT.

Swarms of Insects Sixty Miles Long and Ten Miles Wide Make Desolate Vast Areas.

A CABLE DISPATCH received in France a while ago described how in the province of Catamarca, Argentina, many women took to the ground in convulsions of terror and for a time were almost bereft of reason, repeating over and over only the "The locusts, the locusts!" It was the regressive season in which they had seen the sky darkened with clouds of locusts that settled down upon their fields and plains, destroying the crops and every vestige of the vegetation on which their cattle and sheep subsist.

No other part of the world has in recent years suffered from such a plague of locusts as the agricultural states of sub-tropical and temperate South America--Argentina, Bolivia, southern Brazil, Paraguay and Uruguay share the scourge.

In some regions the swarms have been steadily increasing for a number of years. They are reported to originate in the southerly part of the Gran Chaco and in the Chaco of Bolivia, north of northern Argentina.

Then they come from the north in clouds that sometimes darken the sun, and some of the swarms have been estimated to be sixty miles long and from twelve to fifteen miles wide. The movements of flying insects are only forerunners of the greater mischief to come.

They make desolate the area in which they settle, but often jump wide areas in their flight. Before they take to the wing they lay billions of eggs in the warm earth which in a few weeks become hoppers. It is this young voracious brood, before it can fly, that utterly strips the land of everything green as though it had been burned over.

Government Fights the Evil.

All the governments are fighting the evil. Two years ago the Argentine government organized a bureau under the name of defensa general agricola para la extincion de langosta, or commission for the destruction of the locust. Last year the Argentine congress placed $4,500,000 at the disposal of this commission. Sub-committees represent the general commission in every department exposed to these invasions and they extend from the northern limit of agriculture in the republic to the Neuquen river, almost to Patagonia. Everything possible is done to minimize the damage.

A fine of 100 pesos is imposed upon any settler failing to report to the sub-committee in his district the presence of locust swarms or hopper eggs on his land. An organized service embracing thousands of men is in readiness at any moment to send a force to any place where danger is reported. The most effective war is waged against the young hoppers.

The official report is that as many as 62,000 hopper eggs have been counted in a space less than three and one-half feet square. A prodigious number of the young insects are destroyed soon after hatching by means of sprinkling carts filled with arsenic water or other poisonous liquids. Still many of them escape and the country they cover is too vast to be entirely treated with the sprinkling process. Fortunately the young hoppers have a habit that facilitates the destruction of millions more of them.

By the time they are two weeks old they have developed an enormous appetite. But they do not set out to eat up the world in thin array or scattered detachments.

Novel Methods Employed.

They collect here and there in compact masses to move forward on the food, and when an army of hoppers advances from one space to another there is nothing left to eat on the ground they have deserted. They cannot fly; they move forward only from 400 to 600 feet a day. Now is the time to trap them.

In front of them a trench is dug about six feet deep and wide and 100 or 200 feet long. From each end of the trench pieces of sheet tin about seventy-five feet long and a foot and a half high are stuck into the ground, forming two lines of fence spreading fanlike from the ends of the trench. These fences are extended till their outer ends are hundreds of feet apart, wide enough to enclose the flanks of the invading army. Then all is ready for the drive.

It is hot work, beginning at sunrise, and all the settlers and the government men sent to their aid take part in it with weapons that are effective, though they are only pieces of cloth, with which they flap the ground and urge the hoppers forward. Very often darkness falls and the rear guard of the hoppers has not yet reached the brink over which they tumble to their fate. The hoppers will not stir till sunrise, and then the flapping of the cloth is resumed till this particular army is engulfed. The crops and grass just ahead are safe for a while.

But such work as this spread over several countries is enormously expensive and is only a palliative of the terrible evil, not a remedy for it. A remedy has not yet been found. Can the plague of locusts be quenched if attacked at the head sources? Is there any parasite or natural enemy of the insect that can be introduced to quench the plague or mitigate it? Such questions as these are now being anxiously discussed in South America.

"Well, if you had a million, what should you do with it?"
"Lots of things. First, I should get married."
"You needn't tell me the other 999. That's enough."--Bouvire.

Encouragement

Christopher Ross, a rich landlord of Columbus, O., gives one month's rent free to any couple that has a baby born in one of his houses or flats.

Colors of Gold.

The yellowest gold comes from Alaska placers, the reddest from the Ural, California gold is yellow in hue, that from Australia reddish.

LOST HIS REPRIMAND.

The Judge Was Generous, However, and Gave the Boy Another.

The Children's court in New York city furnishes a variety of little life touches daily, not all of which get into the papers. An incident related by the Herald illustrates the eagerness of the youngsters to boast familiarity with big words, and the disinclination to confess himself stumped. It occurred a few days ago when a little negro boy was up before Judge Mayo for playing craps.

The whites of the little fellow's eyes rolled around in a frightened way as he took in the funeral black of the judges and listened to the big policeman, tall of his delinquencies. The boy denied having anything to do with the pernicious pastime which is popularly credited with being in such high favor with his race, but the judge couldn't quite believe him when he said he had never played craps in his life.

"That doesn't sound reasonable," said the court. "You don't know the points of the game at all? You don't know whether you win when you throw seven on the first shot?"

"No, sah," said the boy. He didn't know the rudiments of the proscribed game.

"Ever been in court before?" asked the judge.

The boy hesitated, and finally remembered that he had once before figured before the bar, when Judge Olmstead was presiding.

"What did they arrest you for," asked Judge Mayo.

"They said I was watching a craps game," said the prisoner.

"And didn't Judge Olmstead give you a reprimand?"

The boy didn't answer, but rolled his eyes more than ever. He looked helplessly around the court room. The judge repeated the question.

"Come, come," he said, "didn't Judge Olmstead give you a reprimand when you were up before him?"

"Well, yes, Judge, Your Honor," confused the boy, "he give me one, all right, but, Judge, Your Honor, I done lost it- honest I have."

So the judge gave him another, and told him not to lose that one.

Too Correct.

Richard Harding Davis, one of the deputy sheriffs of Westchester county, N. Y., went into White plains with his kennel master the other day. While awaiting his kennel master outside a dog biscuit shop, Mr. Harding Davis discussed sport.

"Sport is as good here as it is abroad," he said, "but abroad they are more punctilious. Your Englishman always is correct. He has a wardrobe of smooth, sleek, dark clothes for town; a wardrobe of knickers and thick woollens for Alpine winter sports; a wardrobe of flannels for the seashore, and so on, with other wardrobes for deerstalking, for fox hunting, for driving, even for smoking and drinking.

"I remember once, in my early youth, I was shooting over a duke's covers. A very grave and elegant young marquis was stationed near me. Suddenly the duke shouted to the marquis:

"'There goes a hare! Let him have it!'

"But the marquis shook his head.

"'I can't, duke,' he said. 'I'm in my pheasant costume.'"

Twenty Million Feathers.

Twenty million feathers are sent from Germany to England every year for millinery purposes.

Jan. 30, 1910:

This home products firm sold beds for $4.85. Its slogan: "You furnish the girl, we furnish the home."

Advertisement

The Detroit Free Press

JULY 15, 1910:

The city's first airplane flight thrills Detroit during a huge Elks convention. Another big story: The Crippen murder case.

"Elks' Parade Is Biggest Pageant Ever In City," and "Former Detroiter Is Sought As Murderer," column four.

ELKS' PARADE IS BIGGEST PAGEANT EVER IN CITY

300,000 SPECTATORS JAM LINE OF MARCH TO SEE THE LODGES

Representing Most Varied Spectacles, Serious and Comic, Beautiful and Grotesque, and All Boosting. All Happy, They Appear.

ONE STRIKING PICTURE AFTER ANOTHER PRESENTED IN LINES

ONE KILLED; TWO MAIMED

Port Huron Suburban Strikes Auto Near Roseville, Fatally Injuring Arthur Darmstaetter, Who Dies Later at St. Mary's.

BOTH VEHICLES RUNNING WITH TERRIFIC SPEED

FORMER DETROITER IS SOUGHT AS MURDERER

BELIEVED TO HAVE SAILED FOR U. S.

Practically Certain That Remains Buried in the House in London Were Those of Crippen's Wife.

AFFINITY COMING DRESSED AS BOY?

Soon After Disappearance of Belle Elmore, Typist Informed Her Folks She Had Married the Doctor.

MARY MANNERING TO WED DETROITER?

Actress Denies Engagement to F. W. Wadsworth, Recently Divorced by Wife.

SKYMEN GIVE PROOF OF THEIR MASTERY OF AIR

VICTIMS OF SUN MANY

One Hundred Persons Overcome by Heat and Exhaustion in the Crowds Watching the Big Parade Yesterday Morning.

EMERGENCY DOCTORS HAD THEIR HANDS FULL

AEROPLANE FLIGHTS, FIRST DETROIT SEES, WHOLLY SUCCESSFUL

Arch Hoxsey Soars and Swoops Over State Fair Grounds Like a Swallow; La Chappelle Circles Track Three Times.

ALTITUDE OF 2,200 FEET IS ATTAINED BY ONE AVIATOR

Only One Small Accident Mars Day; La Chappelle In Coming Down Breaks Skid of Machine But It's Quickly Repaired; Both Up Today.

DARING AVIATOR IN BEAUTIFUL FLIGHT AT STATE FAIR GROUNDS

ARCH. HOXSEY AT THE WHEEL.

APRIL 21, 1912:

Navin Field, Tiger Stadium's predecessor, is dedicated as the Tigers defeat Cleveland in extra innings.

The Detroit Free Press
SPORTING SECTION

VOL. 77. NO. 209.   DETROIT, MICHIGAN, SUNDAY, APRIL 21, 1912.   PRICE: FIVE CENTS

Immense Throng Sees Tigers Win Opening Battle

PANORAMIC VIEW OF THE FLAG RAISING THAT PRECEDED THE OPENING GAME ON NAVIN FIELD YESTERDAY

MICHIGAN TOYS WITH BUCKEYES

Wolverines Open Their Batteries Up in the First and Thereafter Never Are Headed—Score is 7 to 2.

"SMI" SMITH IS AT BEST FORM

Nourie is Declared Eligible and Holds Down the Third Sack Job—Mechling and Rogers Best at Bat.

Masons Suspended for Refusal to Take Johnson In

ATHLETES BY THE SCORE WILL RUN

Seventy Colleges Enter Teams in the Penn Relay Races Saturday.

CROWD ESTIMATED AT 26,000 PARTICIPATES IN DEDICATION OF NAVIN FIELD STADIUM; JUNGALEERS BEAT CLEVELAND IN 11 INNINGS

Mullin's Great Work in Pinches Enables Him to Stave Off Defeat. His Single Sends Winning Run Across After Bush and Stanage Have Hit Safely in Final Round.

BY E. A. BATCHELOR.

Michigan Relay Men Trying for Places on Team

Ty Cobb, Sam Crawford and Oscar Vitt Are Detroit's Stars With the Stick — Georgia Peach Makes Two Great Catches and Steals Third and Home.

'RASLIN' FEST AT 'Y' MONDAY NIGH

Put Over Amateur Tourney Will Be Decided—Big Entry List.

STATE FAIR ENTRY LIST A CORKER

Michigan Stake of $10,000 is Leader With 42 Horses and Several More Are to Come From California Stables.

PACING CLASSIC ALSO DOES WELL

STANDINGS OF THE VARIOUS LEAGUES.

JACK COOMBS INJURED BADLY; OUT MAJOR PORTION OF SEASON

NORTH RANDALL ENTRIES

JEFFERSON LASSIES WIN

May 19, 1912:

Ty Cobb is suspended, and his teammates go on strike.

Cobb Not Reinstated; Tigers Quit F

COBB'S SUSPENSION STANDS UNTIL CASE CAN BE INVESTIGATED
—BAN JOHNSON.

That is Statement Given Public by American League President—Declares Georgia Boy Pursued the Wrong Course.

ASSERTS COBB SHOULD HAVE CONSULTED UMPIRE IN CHARGE

"I Want to Hear All the Evidence, but on the Face of the Returns I Fail to See Where Cobb Can Be Justified."

Should Appeal to Umpire.

Wants the Evidence.

JIM THORPE IS INDIVIDUAL STAR

Carlisle Indian All-Around Athlete Gives Another Impressive Performance in Pentathlon.

COLUMBIA TAKES TRIANGULAR RACE

Beats Princeton and Penn, but Tigers Make Things Interesting at Finish.

R-C-H AND LOZIERS CLASH
Fast Auto Aggregations to Lock Horns at Maloney's Park

TIGERS ASK CONGRESS TO PROBE ORGANIZED BALL

PUZZLE—FIND THE RESULT.

"FOR GOODNESS SAKE, TIGE!! LISTEN TO ME!!"

ALL GEORGIA WITH COBB IN TROUBLE

So Declares Atlanta Constitution in Editorial Defending "Peach" and Fellow Players.

URGES FANS IN THE NORTH TO STAND BY THE STRIKERS

Asserts That Warm Welcome Awaits Detroit Team Should It Desire to Go South.

All Georgia With Him.

THE BURNING QUESTION.

AGGIES TROUNCE RICKEY'S TALENT

Big Fourth Permits M. A. C. to String Up Enough to Trim Michigan, 5 to 1.

DODGE DUMPS MICHIGAN WITH TRIO OF WALLOPS

Farmers Amass Ten Hits Off Baribeau and Corbin—W. Bill Donovan Umpires.

PLAYERS' MEETING MAY TERMINATE IN LEAGUE'S UPHEAVEL

George Stovall First of Rival Athletes To Arrive For Conference in Quaker City—Others Expected Before Noon.

TIGERS INTEND TO FIGHT CASE TO BITTER END

DECLARE THEY ARE GOING TO STAND PAT AND AWAIT JOHNSON'S NEXT MOVE

LEAGUE PRESIDENT AND NAVIN CONFER IN PHILADELPHIA TODAY

Athletes Request Expression of Sentiment from Other Clubs in the League Anent Their Present Action.

Conference Today.

Leave Quietly.

Protected Club.

Recruits Scared.

Hughie Is Responsible.

GEORGIA STATESMEN SEND MESSAGE COMMENDING COBB

JULY 27, 1912:

Detroit officials use a crude wiretap to trap crooked aldermen in a sensational sting operation.

The Detroit Free Press

THE WEATHER— Saturday Fair

VOL. 77. NO. 305. DETROIT, MICHIGAN, SATURDAY, JULY 27, 1912—SIXTEEN PAGES FINAL EDITION PRICE TWO CENTS.

MAYOR LAYS BARE BOLD ALDERMANIC GRAFTERS
BURNS, FAMOUS DETECTIVE, SPREADS "DRAGNET"
EIGHT UNDER ARREST; OTHERS QUAKE WITH FEAR

THIS FAMOUS SLEUTH AIDED IN DETROIT'S BIG PLUNDERBUND CASE

WILLIAM J. BURNS

CREDIT IS GIVEN TO THOMPSON

Mayor Learns From Wabash Officials Road Had Been Held Up for Six Years by Money Demands.

BUSINESS MEN PUT UP THE FINANCES

Burns Agency Operator Conducts Investigation—Evidence Procured Through Dictagraph in Room in Ford Building.

DETROIT MAYOR, WHO AS "FLY COP" CAUGHT THE "PLUNDER GANG"

WILLIAM B. THOMPSON

ARRESTS HASTENED BY GREEN'S BLUNDER

But for That Expose Would Have Been Delayed Until 25 Aldermen Had Been Paid—All Who Agreed to Take Money Will Be Arrested.

Man-Hunters Entrap Aldermen And After Money Is Accepted Arrests Follow —Glinnan Makes Full Confession

MARKED BILLS AND DICTAGRAPH EMPLOYED TO OBTAIN EVIDENCE

When Aldermen Blocked Efforts to Close Brooklyn Ave., for Wabash Railroad, Nearly Score Said to Have Been Silenced by Agreeing to Bribery.

"HE WANTED ME TO TAKE MONEY BUT I REFUSED"
—EDDIE SCHREITER

CITY OFFICIALS ARRESTED AND HELD, OR WANTED ON CHARGES OF GRAFT

Alderman	Ward	Amount
Thomas E. Glinnan	Eighteenth	$1,000
Louis E. Tossy	Ninth	$200
Alois A. Deimel	Fifth	$100
Louis Brozo	Thirteenth	$100
Martin J. Ostrowski	Ninth	$200
Andrew J. Walsh	Fourteenth	$200
Joseph L. Theisen	Eleventh	$500
Frank J. Mason	Fourteenth	$200
David Rosenthal	Fifth	$200
Secretary Council Committees E. R. Schreiter		

GRAFTERS TRAPPED BY TELEGRAPHONE

CHRONOLOGY OF GREAT SCANDAL

NAMED IN DETROIT'S STREET CLOSING DEAL

Top line, left to right—Andrew J. Walsh of the Fourteenth ward; David Rosenthal of the Fifth ward; Louis E. Tossy of the Ninth ward; Joseph L. Theisen of the Eleventh ward. Second line—Martin J. Ostrowski of the Ninth ward; William H. Mindle of the Seventh ward; Alois A. Deimel of the Fifth ward; Louis Brozo of the Thirteenth ward.

GETS JOBS FOR MEN HE SEEKS TO SAVE

Former Outcast, Now Head of a Philadelphia Mission, Does Interesting Work.

PITTSBURGH GOES TO MANUAL WORK

System of Instruction in Public Schools Will be Greatly Extended.

Dope and its Dupes

The Drug Habit Claims an Army of Victims in Detroit, and They Have Little or No Trouble Securing the Nerve Wrecking Mixtures They Crave.

WHEN THE EFFECTS OF DOPE BEGIN TO DISAPPEAR.

FAMILIAR TYPES OF "COKERS"

HERE is what an ex-dope fiend has to say: "Great quantities of 'dope' of all kinds are being sold in Detroit at the present time. A 'snorter' need have no trouble in getting all the 'coke' he wants provided he has the price, and he will get the price if he has to bargain his soul. It is an easy matter to get morphine in a number of downtown drug stores through the use of fake prescriptions. But the greatest danger lies in the rapidly increasing consumption of heroin. Once this gets you it is all off, for the habit is twice as hard to break as taking cocaine, according to my observations. Cocaine stimulates. Heroin depresses the spirits and there isn't a thing I ever encountered—and I've tried them all—which leaves such a miserable feeling. You want to get some more of it right away to relieve your sufferings, and the more you take the worse your condition. It is just as dangerous as morphine—that's what it really is—easier to take, and you can get a handful of heroin tablets for a few pennies in almost any drug store, with no questions asked. Heroin has them all beaten when it comes to putting a fellow on the bum."

Three o'clock one afternoon. Two men stood at Rivard and Macomb streets, apparently idling their time away.

From a window in a nearby tenement came the thrumming of a guitar and the coarse, if not altogether unmusical, voice of an Italian singing the songs of his native land. A little further on, from a workshop, came the strident tenor of a Sicilian baker berating his assistant for his shortcomings.

A negro, ragged, unkempt, pushing a wabbly cart, passed slowly by the street, with many a backward glance, as though fearful of being detected.

Suddenly the taller of the two men, a mere youth, whose nervous manner and twitchy eyes indicated more than a speaking acquaintance with the puce that kills, drew himself up, and a smile played about the corners of his mouth.

"There comes Wilkie Jones," he said, with a laugh.

Out of an alley in the next block shuffled the personification of shiftlessness in the form of a man of middle age, sans coat or vest, ragged overalls flapping as he shuffled along. A battered felt hat surmounted the shaggy head. His shirt was open at the neck. His feet were encased in shoes that looked as though they might have been fished from an ash barrel. Here was misery multiplied.

Down the street came the grotesque figure, looking neither to the right nor the left. His goal was a red brick building that bore its singularly appropriate sign announcing it to be a drug store. Three minutes later he re-appeared. This time his conduct was different. His first move was to look cautiously up and down the street. Then, lifting his feet high and hurrying along as though on an important mission, with frequent backward glances to see if he were being watched.

"Here comes 'King' Brady," said the look-out a few minutes later, as a sunken-faced, licensed-up in the foreground. "King's always looking for somebody or something to see that, what did I tell you?"

The man, a giant in size, halted for a moment at the alley, and glanced inquiringly in either direction. Then, he shambled along and entered the drug store.

"Let's see what he has to say," said the man who knew, leading the way up the street to a point Brady must pass in returning to his haunts.

"Hello, 'King,'" was the salutation that won a grin of recognition, and a "Howdy, boy, I ain't seen you fo' a long time."

"Whatta doing down at the 'foundry' this vernacular for a 'dope' dispensary. 'King.' Came a grin that threatened to reach clear around and lap over, while the beady eyes brightened.

"Youall 'll have to fin' out fo' yohself,'" came the reply, as Brady munched at the stub of a peanut candy with all the relish of a child. "Ah haven't bee n raw'in" fer a long time. Had to quit fo you know, 'cause Ah almos' died 'long, boy."

And Brady moved off, chuckling at the thought of how he had outwitted the would-be inquisitors.

Up and down flowed a tide of humanity, embracing many races and colors. Occasionally acquaintances stopped to chat. A woman whose gaudy attire was in ill accord with the locality swung along the street. A bit of gallery from a group of loungers on the opposite side provoked a retort that was as immodest as it was forceful, and which provoked a chorus of laughter. And from this side every now and then one would slip into the little shop, to reappear a few minutes later, invariably with a guilty glance about to see if anyone was watching.

"There comes 'Spitzy' Williams," remarked the lookout in an undertone, at the same time nodding in the direction of an unkempt fellow who was picking his way unsteadily along over the rough cobblestones with which the alley was paved. Across one shoulder was flung the coarse sack that marked him as a rag picker. It was empty save for a bit of junk in the bottom. For "Spitzy" had turned the results of his day's labor in at a nearby rag shop, and was now intent on spending the proceeds in accordance with the ideas of what constituted a good time.

Just before reaching the drug store "Spitzy" deposited his sack beside a tree at the edge of the curb. Then, unencumbered, he slipped inside. When he reappeared it was to stoop and shove something into a sock. Then he straightened up, went over to where he had left his sack, threw it across his shoulder, cleared his throat, and shuffled along.

"Spitzy got his, all right," said the lookout who recognized the symptoms.

Thus it went all the time the two men kept their vigil. Every few minutes a man or a woman whose inclinations were unmistakable would visit the store. Their reappearance was usually the signal for a hurried instance of experiences around the corner, again up a convenient alley. They were not all disreputable in appearance by any means. Some were fashionably dressed. Two women in particular, still young, with traces of youthful beauty discernible through the paint and powder employed so liberally, gave evidence of having once been accustomed to refinement.

Scarcely, every one of them," said the man who had been through the mill, and had a speaking acquaintance with nearly every one who entered the place.

The same evening, at Cass and Michigan avenues, two men, well dressed, both evidently experiencing the sensations of a "coke," when he is recovering from one of his debauches, stood arguing, while crowds of pedestrians streamed by, unmindful of the full significance of what was taking place before their very eyes.

"I tell you it's"—one of them stormed. "There's Eddie now," broke in his companion, staring unsteadily over to where a man with a straw hat and dark clothes was moving along in the shadow of a building on the opposite side of the street. "Come on, bh's got it."

On the instant their differences were forgotten. Arm in arm they reeled across Michigan avenue, calling to "Eddie," who paused in the darkness. As though by magic three other fellows appeared, and all surrounded the object of their quest.

"Shut up," was the warning, emphasized with a flood of oaths, when one of the group became too insistent in his demands. Then he led the way up Cass avenue to an alley north of Michigan, into the darkness of which the party plunged.

There were other disclosures as a result of the investigation conducted. One was that an ex-convict, whose hangout is a notorious saloon in the heart of the tenderloin, makes good money peddling "junk" as cocaine is known among its victims, to denizens of the redlight district, having an established clientele that he serves upon call, usually making the deliveries in person.

It was learned, on no less authority than the word of the victims themselves, and through the testimony of those interested in stamping out the evil, that the man who at the expiration of his sentence in the house of correction leaves that institution, has to travel but a short distance before he is afforded an opportunity to go back to the drug habit; that almost within the shadow of the institution cocaine, morphine and heroin are sold to discharged prisoners who may have the price and the inclination.

Also it was made plain that when a police officer or any other individual tells you it is the hardest work in the world to fasten guilt upon a dispenser of these drugs unless he is caught with the goods on his person he knows whereof he speaks. Which may in part account for the prevalence of the habit, and the seeming immunity its promoters enjoy.

First of all, when a man gets his system full of "junk" he imagines himself to be the craftiest mortal alive. He is a double distilled concentration of Sherlock Holmes and Old Hawkshaw. Every man he meets is a policeman intent on his capture. Every lamp post and telephone pole has a detective lurking in its shadows, waiting to seize him when he comes along. He travels cautiously, looking first to one side and then the other, glancing apprehensively down alleys, peering behind fences. Follow a "coker" for a time, and without looking around he will become aware of the fact that he is being trailed. Every few steps he will give a backward glance, and when your attention is distracted for a moment he is liable to disappear up a stairway or between buildings. When the effects of the drug have disappeared his one thought is to get a fresh supply. And quite naturally he is not exposing the source from whence it comes, or the manner in which it can be obtained.

Furthermore, the vagaries of a dope fiend are such that his testimony would count for nothing with the experienced. He will make a statement with every evidence of truthfulness, then in the next breath refute it with the most convincing sincerity. Every policeman who ever had anything to do with a beat on which a dope fiend was located has listened to lurid tales of slaughter or recitals of treachery, only to find upon investigation that they were the product of a drug-diseased brain.

A vast number of Detroiters are addicted to the drug habit in one form or another and their ranks are being augmented at an alarming rate, according to those in touch with the situation.

Two factors are the chief contributors to this condition of affairs. One is the ease with which these drugs can be obtained. The other is that because of the enormous profits they are able to make by preying upon their victims distributors of the "dope" are constantly on the alert.

Of all the despicable means of defrauding the unfortunate perhaps the worst is practiced by those who dispense cocaine, or "junk," as it is commonly referred to. It would seem that the limit of extraordinariness had been reached in selling this drug, with the demoralizing results. Not so. Cocaine is expensive, although when sold at ten to twenty-five cents a "snort" it yields several hundred per cent in profit. This is not enough, so adulteration is practiced. As cocaine is the medium that makes this possible. It is a white powder, in general appearance resembling cocaine, or "snow." It costs only a fraction as much. So the cocaine peddler, greedy for the dimes and the quarters and the dollars that come his way, adds 80 per cent of an adulterant to 70 per cent of cocaine, and sells it for the real stuff, charging full price for the mixture.

In spite of the similarity in appearance, the crafty "snorter" can detect the imposition being practiced, provided he is not so anxious to snuff the powder that he does not care to take the time. When his suspicions are aroused he withdraws to some secluded spot, takes a tiny portion of the powder in his hand, for it is too precious to waste, puts a drop of water on it and watches results. If it dissolves readily it is the coveted "snow." If only a portion becomes liquid he knows it is adulterated; and the less rapidly it dissolves the greater the degree to which he is being imposed upon by the dealer.

Heroin can be purchased by almost anybody in great numbers of Detroit drug stores with no questions asked. Heroin is in reality salts of morphine, and its effects are said by those who have formed both habits to be fully as bad as those that follow the use of morphine. Doctors agree that it presents the greatest menace of any of the harmful drugs, because of the ease with which it can be obtained.

"I am convinced from observation and my own experience that there are thousands of Detroiters addicted to the use of drugs," said one well known physician, who for professional reasons declined to permit the use of his name. "The worst part of it all is that many of the victims are little more than children in years, school boys and girls, factory workers, clerks. If there is such a thing possible as making a distinction in such classes I would say that they are of a better grade than the cocaine or morphine fiends, that is, they come from a higher strata of society. At the same time it is only a matter of time when they will sink to the same level. Either the morphine or heroin habit is harder to break away from than taking cocaine, because the depressed condition in which it leaves the tissues causes the victim to seek to repeat the performance, that his sufferings may be temporarily alleviated.

"Why do they acquire the habit and where?" I'll give it up. There seem to be almost as many causes as there are cases. I would say, however, from my investigations, that curiosity prompted most of the victims to start."

It is a well known fact that there are several downtown drug stores which do a thriving business in dispensing morphine. In their defense they assert that it can be obtained only on a prescription. The man who wants morphine will not hesitate to steal a prescription blank and forge the name of some doctor that brings him the longed-for drug. It is a provision of the law that prescriptions of this nature must be filed by the druggist and produced for the inspection of any interested party. After a brief time it is an easy matter to destroy the only evidence existing, and which is of itself a forgery, hence detection is rendered all but impossible.

Opium may be obtained in limited quantities by those who are known to the dispensers, a card of six spots, each capable of producing a dream, selling for "two bits." There are two or three "hop bells" which operate secretly, but the man who gains entry must be vouched for by someone who knows, and this form of dissipation is comparatively restricted.

Much of the cocaine sold in Detroit is said to be brought in from Toledo and points to the south by "rotterers," who find it a profitable field of endeavor. Some comes across the river, being smuggled from Canada by operatives who are secreted it on their person or have confederates working with them whose presence is unknown to the officials.

Possibly the ten best posted men in Detroit on the ways of "dope" fiends are Patrolmen Lester Potter and Royal Baker, of the police department, who are an official theater censors. Patrolman Potter for a long time covered beats on both the east and west sides of the city that were infested with dope fiends, and he was larceny instrumental in cleaning out many of the dives they frequented. Afterward the two men were assigned to the task of breaking up the operations of drug dispensers, acquitting themselves with credit. Both knew that one of the most difficult problems confronting an officer is to fasten sufficient guilt on a suspected dealer to insure conviction.

"Simply arresting a man and fining him does no good, said Patrolman Potter. "If he is doing any considerable amount of business he can make up his fine in a few days, and then to be free to go ahead again. If there was some way in which these 'junk' peddlers could be shut up it might prove effective. Although the fellow who has acquired the drug habit is going to get his 'dose' no matter what happens. He'll pawn the clothes off his back or take the very last bit from his home to raise the price of a bit of 'snow,' some heroin tablets or a 'hypo' of morphine."

THERE WAS A BAR IN POMPEII.

THEY have recently excavated in the new shop remarkable as I preserved says a writer in The Boston Herald. There is a counter of bar, with a surface of colored marble tiles. There are terracotta wine jars, a copper boiler with a hole underneath the tile cups of diaphanous glass, clay amphorae a copper tap. There is a beautiful jar of opaque glass with a beautiful neck encased in a fine print, and the lake through which the liquor passes is so small that only a drop at a time can be had, which suggests the drip absinthe or something equivalent for the jaded citizen. There is also a bargain till, a square box of bone, and in it were found gold and silver coins, while copper coins were on the counter.

Unfortunately we are not told whether there was a raft of metal or wood to support the feet of those standing in front of the bar, the rail that encourages conversation on topics of the day, stimulates good cheer, and delays the homeward-bound. We are told fondly in these old wine shops, or was there a jack-towel when there was no alarming talk about microbes? We know that ancient Romans, when they were invited to a feast, took their own napkins with them, or, if the food were particularly rich, wiped their hands on the curly head of a boy slave. Nor are we told whether any fragments of raw lunch were discovered, nor are we informed as to the character of any femals, whether the women in scant attire or wholly underaged recommended a particular vintage or some cooling drink prepared by the "Only Quintus of Pompeii."

", brant once a year some sensational act often a clergyman, lifts up his voice and denounces the town in which he lives as the wickedest one in the country. Is it not possible that trivial envy and hatred save the cities of the Plain the infamous name that still distinguishes them? Do not volcanoes cause earthquakes, floods and tidal waves, work their will on the just and the unjust. The old idea that fatal accidents implied a high degree of sinfulness on the part of the victims is not wholly extinct even among Christians in spite of the question, "Of those eighteen, upon whom the tower in Siloam fell, and slew them, think ye that they were sinners above all men that dwelt in Jerusalem?"

Looking over the letters of Pliny, Younger to see if he alluded in any way to the recklessly joyous life at Pompeii, I found, of course, his description of the eruption and that of his uncle's death, but we are caute across a story that should be pondered by any one who wishes to play the host. Pliny supped with a man "who, in his own opinion, treated us with much splendid frugality; but according to mine, in a sordid yet expensive manner." "Very elegant dishes," we quote from Melmoth's translation, were served to the host and a few of the guests; those for the rest of the company were cheap and mean. There were in small bottles three different sorts of wine. Not that the guests might take their choice, but that they might not have an option in their power." The best was for the host and a few favored. The next for those of a lower order, and so on down the table. Pliny's neighbor asked him what he thought of it, and Pliny answered: "When I make an invitation it is to entertain, not to distinguish my company; I set every man upon a level with myself whom I admit to my table, and treat even my freedmen." The pretcher added if this was not an expensive method. "I assured him not at all, and that the whole secret lay in being contented to drink no better wine myself than I gave to others."

We have known hosts in American cities who, entertaining at table, have their "distinguished" guests. Stories are told of one who has a more expensive vintage served for his sole enjoyment, while the others share in the sole enjoyment, while the others share in the cheaper wine. It was said that Nicolini, the second husband of Mme. Patti, made this distinction at their castle when giving a dinner of pomp and there was a similar distinction in the quality of tobacco smoked by the exalted tenor and his guests. We all know the man that has cheap cigars in his left upper waistcoat pocket for his friends and others in the right for himself.

The history of the free lunch has yet to be written, its origin, growth, decline, with a chapter or two on the rules of etiquette to be observed. As a boy we read in a Sunday school book that barkeepers put heating dishes within the reach of customers, victims of the Demon Rum, to increase their thirst; but we also read that early in the morning the barkeeper poured whiskey, rum, or gin on the sidewalk in front of the saloon to tempt more vigorously the passerby. Was a German the first to establish the free lunch? Where was the first free lunch of any importance in Boston, and in what year, and did it affect the death rate? These are important questions.

Just Like Some Men.

An elephant was being taken through the streets, probably as a sight. It is well known that elephants are a wonder among us, so crowds of gaping idlers followed the elephant. From some cause or other, a pug dog comes to meet him. It looks at the elephant and then begins to run at it, to bark, to squeal, to try to get at it, just as if it wanted to fight it, runs one of Krylof's fables.

"Neighbor, come to bring shame on yourself," says another dog. "Are you capable of fighting an elephant? Just see now, you are already hoarse, but it keeps straight and pays you not the slightest attention."

"Aye, aye," replies the pug dog, "that's just what gives me courage. In this way, you see, without fighting at all, I may get reckoned among the greatest bullies. Just let the dogs say:

"'Ah, look at Puggy! He must be strong, indeed, that's clear, or he would never bark at an elephant.'"

Chinese Peanut Butter.

Peanut butter in this country is an inexpensive delicacy, but there is a variety of peanut paste, made in China, for which one can pay as high as $10 an ounce. Any lovers of the peanut who refrain from eating it on account of the supposed plebeian character should be told of this royally expensive way of satisfying their taste.

WHERE THE AIR IS COLDEST.

SINCE the beginning of the twentieth century a great deal has been learned about the upper air. It is now the custom at scores of observatories throughout the world to "sound" the air at frequent intervals by means of delicate self-recording instruments attached to kites and balloons. The latter have, in extreme cases, reached a hight of twenty miles above the earth, and the records they bring back with them are interesting.

Everybody knows that the upper air is very cold. Nearly every book on physical geography contains a diagram showing how, in climbing a mountain near the equator, one passes through the same range of climates as in travelling from the equator to the pole—starting with the steaming heat of a tropical jungle and ending amid the eternal snows of the mountain summit.

Only a few years ago scientific men believed that the fall in temperature with ascent went on indefinitely. Now we know this is not the case. In the year 1902 a great number of balloons carrying self-registering thermometers were sent up in the vicinity of Paris. When the records were examined the remarkable discovery was made that in every case when the balloon reached an altitude of about 7 miles the air stopped growing colder. This discovery has since been confirmed by observations made in all parts of the world. There is always a certain level at which the fall in temperature ceases, and no matter how much higher the balloon may travel no lower temperature is recorded. The region of the atmosphere above this level has been named the "stratosphere." As observations accumulated it was found that the stratosphere begins at different hights in different latitudes. It is lowest near the poles and highest over the equator. In other words, the fall of temperature with ascent continues to a greater hight in equatorial regions than elsewhere. This explains the paradoxical fact that the lowest temperature ever recorded in the atmosphere—115 degrees below zero Fahrenheit—was found at an altitude of 12 miles over central Africa.

The lowest temperature ever recorded on the earth's surface was 90 degrees below zero, in northern Siberia. Probably the air at great hights above the polar regions is rarely as cold as this.

Glass Telephone Poles.

According to the Telephone Engineer, glass poles are now being manufactured for telegraph and telephone work. The glass is strengthened by interlacing and interwining it with strong wire threads.

Old Timbers Strongest.

Tests show that bridge timbers which had been a quarter of a century in service were stronger than selected pieces of timber a year old, which had been passed as first-class building material.

A Puzzler.

Two Minnesota youths have been sentenced to ten days in jail for calling a woman a chicken. What would have happened to them if they had called her a hen?

AUG. 11, 1912:

Drugs were seen as a problem in Detroit as early as 1912.

Sunday feature.

March 22, 1913:

A rare weather event hits the state: a hurricane.

The Detroit Free Press

THE WEATHER Snow; Colder.

FINAL EDITION

VOL. 78, NO. 177. — DETROIT, MICHIGAN, SATURDAY, MARCH 22, 1913.—SIXTEEN PAGES. — PRICE TWO CENTS

FIERCE GALE SPREADS HAVOC IN DETROIT AND GIVES BATTLE TO PEDESTRIANS

Wrecked autos, wagons, signboards and what not, piled up in Lafayette boulevard, in front of The Detroit Free Press building.

Furniture store at 890 Michigan avenue, with front blown in by gale. The wife of the owner, A. A. Haag, and her son, were on the second floor when the crash occurred, but escaped injury.

Crowds at Woodward and Michigan avenues, the Majestic corner, fighting good-naturedly against winds that make progress slow.

FISH BOATS IN BATTLE WITH 60-MILE STORM

Win Desperate Struggle, Though Nearly Swept Upon the Beach.

BLINDED BY SNOW, CREWS FOLLOW SHIP'S COMPASS TO PORT AND TO SAFETY

Two Boats Missing in Lake Erie, One on Rocks, Six Men May Be Lost.

STRAY DOGS BITE 630 PERSONS A YEAR

Cleveland May Make Some Effort to Control This Nuisance in 1913.

CONVENTION HALL WILL BE PROVIDED

Ft. Worth Will Equip to "Get Into the Game" of Catching Gatherings.

GRADE CROSSINGS WILL BE ABOLISHED

St. Louis Takes First Steps in New Policy for Safety of the Public.

POINTS TO PROFITS IN USE OF WASTE

New Yorker Shows How It Can Be Used in the Reclamation of Valuable Land.

WARNS STATE NOT TO OPPRESS RAILROADS

Stevens Declares Pere Marquette Depends on Attitude of Solons.

SQUEEZING OUT WATER WOULD HARM INNOCENT, HE TELLS INVESTIGATORS

Points Out That Many Bought Stock on Strength of Its Approval by State.

HADLEY COMING TO DETROIT TO REPLY TO COL. ROOSEVELT

Missouri Governor Will Speak Same Day as Ex-President.

BEVERIDGE CALLED TO FOLLOW UP HADLEY

Riot of Politics and Oratory Due "Greek Meets Greek," While the Public Gazes.

DETECTIVE FROM 'FRISCO COMES TO TAKE MRS. POPE

Detroit Woman Determined to Fight Extradition in Conn Case.

WILL BE ARRAIGNED IN POLICE COURT MONDAY

Sleuth Has Warrant Formally Charging Her With Being Fugitive From Justice.

STORM CAUSES HEAVY DAMAGE OUT IN STATE

Many Persons Are Injured and Buildings and Trees Suffer.

CHURCHES UNROOFED, SMOKESTACKS RAZED, WIRES HAMPERED

Losses Will Aggregate Hundreds of Thousands—Eight Hurt at Factory.

MOOSE HOTEL IS RAZED BY WIND

Detroit Residents Are Heavy Losers When Storm Hits New Baltimore.

HURRICANE SWEEPS DETROIT; DAMAGES PROPERTY $500,000

One Man Killed, Many Injured in 86-Mile Gale, Worst In City's History.

GRAND TRUNK FLAGMAN BLOWN IN FRONT OF TRAIN, CUT TO PIECES

Buildings, Trees and Wires Are Torn Down Over Wide Area; Transportation Suffers.

Wind's Velocity 86 Miles, 10 More Than Record in Detroit

By Weather Observer Norman B. Conger.

Friday's terrific windstorm cost Michigan millions of dollars. Many persons were injured, some seriously, and at the time of going to press it was impossible to reach Bay City by wire. In all parts of the state, residences, factories and churches were unroofed, miles of trees were leveled, barns and outbuildings were destroyed, cars were blown from their feet. Flint was isolated, so far as wire service was concerned, and it was necessary for the correspondent of The Free Press to bring the news to Detroit on an interurban car.

Sharp fall in the barometric pressure, causing a disturbance center that spread east from Colorado and crossed Detroit about 10 a. m. Friday, caused the hardest wind storm in 42 years' history of the Detroit weather bureau.

The disturbance was central over Colorado Thursday morning, moved southeast to Shreveport, La., during the day, and then advanced up the Mississippi valley. The barometer dropped a full half-inch during Thursday night in Detroit, and reached an unusual level of 29.42 inches, the normal for this altitude being 29.10. With the atmospheric pressure lightened, there was a swift influx of cool air to fill the partial vacuum.

The wind commenced rising about 3 a. m. Friday, and continued to increase until it reached its maximum. A high velocity was maintained all the afternoon and early evening.

Friday forenoon's storm set two wind speed records. The velocity of 86 miles an hour attained at 11:15 a. m., exceeded any previous record by ten miles an hour. The highest previous record was 76 miles November 26, 1895. On May 23, 1893, a velocity of 74 miles was registered, and April 20, 1873, a velocity of 72 miles.

The sustained velocity for one hour, from 10 to 11 a. m., was 71 miles, which was higher than ever before in the 42 years' history of the Detroit office.

The storm will be followed by a cold wave, the thermometer dropping to 15 or 16 degrees above zero by Saturday morning.

POLICE AND AMBULANCES KEPT BUSY BY FURY OF THE STORM

Death, injury and property damage, totaling at least a half million dollars in Detroit alone and several millions in the state, were borne on a hurricane that swept through Detroit from the west and southwest Friday morning, continuing with more or less intensity throughout the day and early evening.

In Detroit one man was killed, three other persons were fatally injured and at least a score others hurt.

All local wind records were broken, the gale reaching a velocity of 86 miles an hour shortly after 11 a. m.

Everything that was exposed fell prey to the blast. Roofs were torn off, steeples tilted, high electric signs demolished, street railway, telephone and telegraph wires blown down, and big wind mills smashed, while horses and motor vehicles and men, women and children in the streets were hurled like toys.

Cleveland's New Police Chief, Succeeding Kohler, Urges Square Deal Instead of Golden Rule.

HIGH WIND BLAMED FOR SUICIDE ATTEMPT

Accused in Eaton Mystery
Widow of Rear Admiral for Whose Death She Faces Trial at Plymouth, Mass., and Her Daughter

MRS. JENNIE MAY EATON AND FANNY EATON.

Stomachs As Storm Tossed As the Good Ship Promise

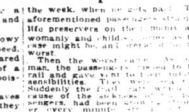
WILLIAM A. ROWE.

The Detroit Free Press

THE WEATHER: Friday—Showers.

Final Edition

VOL. 78, NO. 301. — DETROIT, MICHIGAN, FRIDAY, JULY 25, 1913.—EIGHTEEN PAGES. — PRICE: TWO CENTS.

JULY 25, 1913:

Striking Upper Peninsula miners attack their companies' properties, so Gov. Ferris orders Michigan's entire National Guard to Calumet.

DECLARES HE OPENED PURSE TO M'DERMOTT

Mulhall Swears Former Congressman "Did Not Repay Him in Cash."

DENIES HE CONSIDERED "POLITICAL FAVORS" AS PAYMENT FOR "LOANS"

Lobbyist Also Tells Probers He Paid Messengers Salary for "Stenhung."

SPEEDS TROOPS TO MINE STRIKE ZONE

ADJT.-GEN. ROY C. VANDERCOOK.
General Vandercook is one of those charged with the transportation of the Michigan National Guard to the copper country.

"HAP" WARD HAS QUIT THE STAGE
Veteran Comedian Decides to Try the Joys of Rural Life.

POLICE CRUSADE WAGING ON VICE
Atlanta is Trying to Blot Out Fake Hotels and Lodging Houses.

DETROIT PATTERN SHOP DESTROYED IN $75,000 FIRE
Huetteman & Cramer Co. Loses Models Covering 35 Years.
150 MEN OUT OF WORK; CAUSE IS NOT LEARNED
Three Other Small Blazes Cause Suspicion of Incendiarism.

MRS. YOUNG STEPS DOWN AS HEAD OF CHICAGO SCHOOLS

Famous Woman Educator Says, "I am Too Old to Fight for Myself."

UNITED STATES OPENS WAR ON 'PHONE TRUSTS'

Sues to Break Alleged Bell Monopoly on Pacific Coast.

FIRST ATTEMPT TO APPLY SHERMAN LAW TO SUCH SITUATION

Whether Single System Is Best Remains for Congress to Decide, Says McReynolds.

MAJ. E. B. BANKS IS DEAD IN ANN ARBOR AFTER VARIED LIFE
Soldier-Horseman Said to Be Stepson of First J. Gordon Bennett.
MEETS END ALONE IN HOSPITAL BED
Friends Will Take Charge of Funeral in Detroit Today.

EACH CLAIMS TO BE KEEFE'S LAWFUL WIFE

No. 1, Bitter, Declares Vows in Justice Court Only Legal Ones.

NO. 2, LOYAL, INSISTS MARRIAGE IN CATHOLIC CHURCH BY MINISTER

"Bigamist" Weeps as He Begs Second Wife's Angry Parents to Get Him Out on Bond.

THREE SLAIN, ONE INJURED IN COAL MINE STRIKE RIOT
While Watchmen Patrol Hills of West Virginia They Are Fired Upon.
TWO ASSAILANTS, DEAD, ARE NOT IDENTIFIED
Guard, Wounded, Found After Search Lying Beneath Bushes; May Not Live.

TROOPS ARE RUSHED TO COPPER COUNTRY TO PRESERVE PEACE

Michigan Troops Hitting the Trail

TYPICAL SCENE of members of the Michigan National Guard moving in easy fashion, armed and equipped to the full regalia of the soldier in action ready for a fight or a frolic as fate may decree. One of the stirring scenes of our present uncertain era.

IRON RANGE AFLAME WITH STRIKE FEVER
MARQUETTE AND surrounding districts fear that 10,000 miners will join the copper diggers; discontent is rife.

DETROIT COMPANIES START EARLY TODAY
GUARDS MOBILIZE at armory to start for Calumet via Michigan Central, fitted for long stay in the north.

CALUMET AWED BY THE ORDERS FOR SOLDIERS
HUNDREDS OF deputies armed with Colt automatic revolvers; mining paralyzed; many people leave the city.

Governor Ferris Orders Out Entire Michigan National Guard to End Rioting of Miners.

SEVERAL COMPANIES ALREADY ON SCENE

Situation Grows Acute; Calumet Fears Further Disorders and Appeals for Military Guards.

FIELD ARTILLERY IS ALSO SENT ALONG

"We Must Protect Lives and Property," Ferris Tells Officers, Urging Them Into Work.

DOREMUS NAMES NAGEL TO TAKE WARREN'S PLACE
No Opposition Expected Over Appointment to Postmastership.

MICHIGAN MAN'S TASTES GET HIM INTO TROUBLE

SCENE TO BE ENACTED IN MICHIGAN COPPER REGION

Photograph of the Wolverine guardsmen in camp, showing how the khaki tops turn out the crowd in the copper country. Under orders from Governor Ferris, commander-in-chief of the state militia, orders have been given to avoid display of hostility towards the striking miners, and to preserve peace as well among the non-striking citizens as among the disaffected miners.

Nov. 13, 1913:

Perhaps the worst storms ever on the Great Lakes take 94 lives.

94 SEAMEN KILLED IN GALE THAT SWEPT GREAT LAKES; DEATH LIST MAY INCREASE

Ninety-four lives have been lost and millions of dollars' worth of shipping damaged by the gales which swept the great lakes beginning last Friday night and not abating until early Monday morning.

From reports received at present indications are that Lake Huron's gale caused the most havoc. Near Port Huron, Mich., 18 bodies have been recovered from an overturned freighter, thought to be the steamer Regina.

Steamer on Rocks.

The steamer Howard M. Hanna went on the rocks of Point Aux Barques, and after a grueling battle with elements the crew was finally rescued, reaching Cleveland Wednesday night. They tell tragic stories of cold and starvation in their fight with the storm.

The Northern Queen with its crew of 22 men, also had a close fight for existence. The steamer was at first reported lost and 14 of its crew were reported found near Port Frank, Ont. Later the ship was reported pounding to pieces but the crew was saved.

Three bodies from the Canadian steamer Wexford were found near St. Joseph, Ont., and it is feared that the boat is a total loss. The rest of the crew has not been heard from to the present.

Six Men Perish.

Six men went to their deaths near Buffalo when Lightship No. 82 was blown off its station. A message from Captain Williams of the lost craft to his wife verifies the belief that the whole crew perished.

Lake Superior, too, claimed a merciless toll from the marine men. Turret Chief ran aground at Keweenaw Point near Copper Harbor, and after pounding on the rocks for several hours broke in two. The crew escaped in boats to land.

There they battled in the wilderness, half frozen and starved for more than a day until found by Indians who directed them to food and shelter. The Turret Chief will be a loss of $100,000.

Steamer Reported Lost With 28 Men on Board

The Detroit Free Press

THE WEATHER: Snow and Colder.

Final Edition

VOL. 79, NO. 89. — DETROIT, MICHIGAN, THURSDAY, DECEMBER 25, 1913.—SIXTEEN PAGES. — PRICE: TWO CENTS

DEC. 25, 1913:

The families of striking miners are the victims of a horrible Christmas Eve fire.

---

74 KILLED IN CALUMET AS FALSE ALARM OF FIRE THROWS HALL IN PANIC

Strikers' Families Pay Toll of Lives to Panic

SCORES OF LIVES were crushed out when an "fire alarm" cry stampeded a crowd at a Christmas tree celebration in Calumet last night. Probably some of the women shown below are the wives and mothers of miners, who paraded in the strike troubles last summer, lost children in last night's catastrophe.

Cry Stampedes Crowd of 700 at Christmas Tree Exercises For Strikers' Children

WOMEN AND CHILDREN CRUSHED AND BODIES JAMMED IN HEAP

Hysterical Mothers Rush Streets After Tragedy—Mobs Seek Unknown Man Cause of Horror

Special to The Free Press.

Calumet, December 24.—A single word—Fire!—shouted into Italian hall, where children of the striking miners were gathered around a Christmas tree early this evening, started a panic which cost at least 74 lives.

The bodies of 56 children, 13 women and five men, all the known victims of the panic, are lying in the town hall at Red Jacket, where virtually all have been identified. In many homes in the town, the authorities believe, are other bodies, snatched from the death tangle at the entrance to the hall and borne away by relatives.

Temporarily the wall between the strikers and the employers has been lowered by the tragedy and the factions are united in relief work and in efforts to find the man who gave the cry of fire—for there was not even a spark to justify the alarm.

Nearly 600 children, a few women and a number of women connected with the strike auxiliary forces—in all about 700 persons—were in the hall. The "program" of recitations and songs by the children had been finished and a tree, with its flaming candles and dangling tinsel, became the center of attraction.

A Santa Claus, red-clothed and cotton-whiskered, came from the dressing room behind the stage, bent under a heavy pack of toys. He stopped beside the tree, put down his burden and raised his head.

He was about to speak when the door in the rear of the hall opened and a man who wore a heavy beard thrust his head in.

"Fire!" he yelled.

A woman who was standing near the door, with a premonition of what was to happen, seized the man by the shoulders and called out that there was no fire. But her voice was drowned as the others in the hall took up the cry.

Cause of Panic Flees as Crowd Stampedes

The man who had given the alarm, apparently intoxicated, shook himself free and fled down the stairs as the crowd in the hall, which is on the second floor of a comparatively new building, came stampeding toward the door.

Of all the hundreds in the hall only a few kept their heads. Mrs. Annie Clemens, president of the women's strike auxiliary, who was on the platform, shouted that all was well. Others who were on the platform with her joined her, but without effect on the swirling human tide below them, beyond the footlights.

A father bent forward protectively over his little daughter. The press from behind toppled him forward and the child was crushed under his feet.

There were fire escapes at one side of the hall, but not more than 100 attempted to use them, and these for the most part were older women. Some people got more than they could carry, and, were swept with the panic crowd toward the door, the only other exit.

Human Niagara Sweeps Down Stairs of Hall

At the top of the stairs those in the forefront of the crowd, swept from their feet, spouted out from the little landing and dropped to the foot in a human Niagara. A noiseless heroine, a humane, motherly woman, lifted three small children into her arms, fought for a moment and succeeded in making a backwater in the stream. She was shot off the landing, carrying the children to death with her.

At the same time a man, a flying, rolling his wife, swept down a few steps, stamping on children, climbing over women at every pause, until at the bottom of the stairs.

Among lines of different strength held back the crowd for a few moments from the edge of the landing by sheer, desperate strength. It threw himself against the tide of the panic and appeared to be drawing his burden with him. Then the pack gave way and he was hurled down. "It's all,"

Doorway Blocked by Solid Wall of Bodies

In the meantime passing citizens had thrown up against the doors at the foot of the stairs, but the doorway...

HAMBURGER HOME, SAYS HE CANNOT REMEMBER CRIME

Asserts He Knows Nothing of Past Life Beyond 10 Years.

WILL LOOK AFTER HIS MOTHER IF PROMISED

Special to The Free Press.

Royal Oak, Mich., December 24.—"I know nothing of my past life before the last 10 years," Harry Hamberger, paroled Detroit murderer, declared tonight as he paid his little parlor of his brother-in-law's home he faced his first few hours of freedom.

"They say I killed a man. They say I was in prison years before I began to remember. I don't know anything about that. I know I have been there an endless time and I have been there long time forward to be.

"You shook my hand. I won't forgive it," I said. "You must show me the pardon papers first."

"'It's so,' she said. And it was.

"'Did they treat me well in Jackson prison?' he said to him. 'I've gained weight.

MIDNIGHT MASSES DRAW THRONGS TO CITY'S CHURCHES

Belated Shoppers, Travelers and Others at Solemn Services.

MOST VARIED CROWD ATTENDS ST. ALOYSIUS

"SAINT" DESERTED MANY WOMEN, SAYS FEDERAL AGENT

Career of "Rev." Dahlstrom, in Tacoma Jail, Being Studied.

WHITE SLAVE CHARGES MADE AGAINST PRISONER

Founded "Holiga" Religion, One Tenet Being Belief in Polygamy.

Seattle Wash., December 24.—The career of Rev. Albert Dahlstrom, who is in jail at Tacoma on a white slavery charge, is being investigated by Special Agent William H. Bryon, of the department of justice, who says the self-styled "saint" has been under scrutiny since last May. According to Bryon Dahlstrom has married and deserted probably a score of women in various parts of the United States.

Complete List of 74 Dead in Calumet Panic

Special to The Free Press.

Calumet, December 24.—Correct and complete list of dead in tonight's panic in Italian hall:

Arthur Lindstrom, 13 years.
Mrs. Laurie, 30.
Matt Mihelcich, aged 9.
Baby Joula.
Mrs. Tulpa, 40.
Mrs. Bobin.
Mrs. Abe Nicomia, 30.
Mrs. Kate Peteri.
Florence Kaliajama, 4.
Manele Tulpa, 4.
Helga Watokka, 4.
Manele Sitotti, 5.
Anton Pupch and daughter, 40.
Henry Isola, 3.
Sino Takach, 7.
Lydia Lesson, 3.
Mary Roskjana, 3.
Agnes Niemela, 20.
J. B. Woaton, secretary National Fire Insurance company, 50.
Herman Alo, 40.
Alfred Manniano, 3.
Edrun Mendacava, 3.
John Jarketta, 7.
Tonic Standaher, 10.
Mrs. Oscar Altonen, 30.
Matt Maata, 6.
Mrs. Herman Manley, 30.
Son of above, 6.
Agnes Mihelich, 4.
Nick Streekevich, 8.
Jacob Lustig, 5.
Amy Katjavia, 3.
Sylvia Altonen, 6.
Wilma Altonen, 8.
Alta Sutila, 4.
John Laari, 6.
Jennie Jarkelaka, 5.
Lempi Alo, 6.
John Kraspi, 6.
Paul Mielich, 5.
John Wyllyheathen, 5.
Henry Mentanen, 3.
Joe Ronalti, 12.
Mamie Lesson, 7.
Mrs. Peter Kaiansi, 41.
Christiana Kluefri, 5.
John Battola, 6.
Mary Karanar, 12.
Samer Runer, 5.
John Hethakner, 5.
Peter Hethkena, 4.
Sulvin Hethakena, 8.
Matt Manto, 10.
William Burt, 5.
John Lovia, 10.
Mary Tishalan, 6.
John Tishelan, 4.
Mrs. Peter Kainella.
Helka Wanitochka.
Victor Barner.
Matti Katariari, 6.
Anele Katavlara, 6.
Lena Boyle.
Leo Larrapertz, 10.
Manle Vonek, 6.
Two unidentified men.
Two unidentified women.
Four unidentified boys.
Two unidentified girls.

FOR CHRISTMAS DAY.

At Arcadia today at 2:30, Doll & Toy Party, Presents to all. Xmas Jubilee dance tonight.—Advertisement.

"PEACE ON EARTH" ON OLD CAPITOL

Big Christmas Tree in Front Another Way Uncle Sam Recognizes Festival.

(By Staff Correspondence.)

Washington, December 24.—Christmas is officially recognized by the United States. In electric letters across the main portico of the national capitol is blazoned:

"Peace on Earth, Good Will to Men."

In front of the capitol, on the spot where stood the inauguration platform, in which President Wilson took the oath of office, rises an immense Christmas tree, 75 feet high, festooned with many-colored electric lights.

Led by the marine band, children of the capital will gather about the tree this afternoon to sing time-honored Christmas carols.

NEGRO WOMAN HUGS VICTORIOUS LAWYER

Webster Grove, Mo., Wife, Freed on Charge of Slaying Husband, Causes Uproar in Court.

Special to The Free Press.

St. Louis, Mo., December 24.—Mary Carr, a 200-pound Negro woman, broke up a court in Webster Grove, a suburb, today, when acquitted of a charge of murdering her husband. She threw her arms about Samuel D. Hodgson, her lawyer and a member of the Missouri legislature and hugged and kissed him. The white man struggled to get free and finally the woman was pried loose by court attaches.

WANDERS 36 HOURS IN SEWER MAINS

Cleveland Workman, Starving and Raving, Rescued After Cries Are Heard.

Special to The Free Press.

Cleveland, December 24.—After wandering 36 hours in big sewer mains under the streets of the city unable to make his cries for help heard, Steve Holoslo, 23 years old, an employe at the Carnegie Steel plant, was rescued at noon today insane. It is believed Holoslo in some way crawled into a sewer entrance at the river bank and was unable to find his way out. Passersby finally heard faint noises under a manhole and pulled Holoslo out nearly starved and raving.

White Plague Victims Enjoy Yuletide Party

Fifty-five patients of the Detroit Tuberculosis sanatorium enjoyed Christmas festivities Wednesday through the kindness of many friends. A large Christmas tree, the gift of E. A. Bellvari, was decorated and presents were distributed by Santa Claus. Each patient received pajamas, caps, hoods, ties, fruit, nuts, etc. J. Hudson company provided the mute box, W. Brodhead and candy donated; by S. L. Hudson company, mostly starred and rains.

WAYNE GARDEN DANCING.

Christmas Matinee, 2 to 5 p. m. Christmas Night, New Year's Eve and Night, hit, Sleighride Dance—Adv.

Dancing Xmas and New Year's Night. Also New Year's Eve. The Duffy Academy.—Adv.

Diamonds, watches, jewelry, silverware, cut glass and optical goods, Hugh Connell. A. Grisworld and Statk, across from Chamber of Commerce.—Advertisement.

THE SEASON'S GREETINGS FORSYTH-MERRY COMPANY.

DAY OF CHEER AWAITS MANY DETROIT POOR

"Merry Christmas" to Be Reality for Those Forgotten Before.

LARDERS WILL BE FILLED AND STOCKINGS CRAMMED WITH TOYS AND CANDIES

Scores of Organizations and Hundreds of Individuals Plan Celebration of Yuletide.

Plenty of snow for Santa Claus' reindeers in the promise of the weather man for Christmas, the indefatigable pushing in cloudy weather and snowstorm for the day.

There was some snow throughout the lake region Wednesday and it will arrive in Detroit in time to give several thousand children an opportunity to use their new sleds and furnish a wintry setting for Christmas stories.

"Merry Christmas" will be a mockery to fewer persons in Detroit than ever this year.

The Christmas spirit of the city has grown with its population and almost everyone who is not hopelessly on the wrong side of the financial fence is playing Santa Claus for the benefit of someone who is poorer, either directly or through organizations.

Not only are most of the poor children of the city sure of getting toys, but empty larders will be scarce in the city as empty stockings. So many agencies have arranged to distribute Christmas baskets filled with food among the needy that if any go without good Christmas cheer it will be by accident.

Salaries of telephone operators and girls who work in offices are not of dimensions that go with the luxury of charity, but many poor families will benefit by the collections taken among the girls of the telephone exchange and those employed in the office of the Cadillac Motor company.

The Cadillac girls have banded together to fit out one poor family with food, clothing, coal and other supplies, sufficient to keep them warm through the winter. The girls prepared to divide baskets, each containing enough. Wood for a Christmas dinner for a large family.

More than 1,000 children received clothing, candy and toys through the committee of German women of Detroit, working under the auspices of the Daily Abend-Post. No fewer than 2,000 bills had been paid them reached $243 in the Christmas fund. The surplus was divided between the German Protestant orphan asylum, the Deutsches Home, the old folks' home, the Old People's Home, the Mute institute, St. Vincent's Orphan Asylum and the Children's Free Hospital.

HOLD 10 YOUTHS FOR GIRL'S DEATH

Chicago Police Probing Assault on Former Resident of Battle Creek.

Special to The Free Press.

Chicago, December 24.—A confession, said to have been made by a member of the Tracy Athletic club, 501 Root street, composed of young men living in the stock yards district, in connection with the death of Mrs. Ann Laughlin Dempsey caused the arrest of 10 members of the club, who are held pending investigation.

Mrs. Dempsey was found bruised and unconscious in a barn near the club. She was taken to the Bridewell hospital, where she died.

The police believe she was beaten to death. She came to Chicago from Battle Creek, Mich., recently.

FIRE DEPARTMENT IS KEPT BUSY ON CHRISTMAS EVE

Lumber Yard of J. H. A. Haberkorn Company Ablaze.

Fire broke out in the lumber yards of the J. A. Haberkorn company, 286 Fourteenth avenue, late Wednesday night. At a late hour the extent of the damage could not be determined.

Christmas eve was a busy time for the fire department, with nine alarms sent in between the hours of 6 o'clock and midnight.

A barn caught fire at the rear of Joseph Osbeski's home, 229 East Willis avenue; damage $100.

A candle on Mrs. V. Goldberg's Christmas tree started a blaze at her home, 245 Van Dyke avenue; damage slight.

Another blaze caused by a heated apparatus caused slight damage to the plant of the Crude Rubber company, Cottrell and Macky avenues.

A fire broke out in a smoke house at Parker, Webb & company's plant, causing slight damage.

Mrs. Ralph E. Burton put out a small blaze in her home at 128 Melbourne avenue to signify the Christmas spirit that was within her, and the curtains had a run when someone set off the Christmas tree curtain blaze against the same date.

Another blaze against the Christmas tree at 441 McDurry avenue, took the blaze was out by the time the engines arrived.

Christmas Dinner, Hotel Charlevoix, until 9 p. m. at $1. Hinth course, served. Christmas tree. Mid-day service and entire menu at moderate prices.—Advertisement.

THE SEASON'S GREETINGS FORSYTH-MERRY COMPANY.

GALE ACCUSED OF CONSPIRACY; ARREST SOUGHT

Missing Lawyer Charged With Fraud in Detroit Cyclecar Co.

REPORTED TO HAVE ENTANGLED OTHERS IN FINANCIAL DEAL

Officials Looking Up Noted White Slaver Believed to Be "Duke of Sutherland."

Prosecutor Shepherd Wednesday instructed the police department to arrest Philip H. Cale, attorney, who married and disappeared with his bride last Saturday, on a charge of conspiracy with intent to defraud in connection with the sale of stock in the Detroit Cyclecar company, of which Cale was vice-president.

At the same time Assistant Prosecutor Toms is investigating the record of a notorious high-grade white slaver with a criminal record, who it is believed was the "Billy F." Edegray, duke of Sutherland," who cast such a strange spell over Cale and forced the marriage between Cale and Luella Strutmann, 15 years old, and left him with the marital last Saturday night.

The white slaver in question, it is alleged, chiefly answered the description of the man who suddenly became possessed of a Pontiac estate worth millions in England.

Officers Are Questioned.

Concerning Cale's operations in connection with the Detroit Cyclecar company, it appears that Cale hired an attorney in organizing the company and was made vice-president. Prosecutor Shepherd Wednesday called in A. H. Thomas, president, S. C. Bradford and F. B. Hall of the company, and questioned them. After questioning them the Prosecutor Shepherd issued orders that Cale be arrested for violation of the new "blue sky" law. According to the report of the Prosecutor, it is believed, on the Prosecutor's statement, many individuals have not only themselves but friends, relatives, and entangled others interested in the company. Prosecutor Shepherd says that he can see no intention of allowing a shake-up in the company, and has been compelled to resign, and has been compelled to resign, and disappeared with his bride. Cale is believed to be at Detroit, and it is suspected that Cale could not have provided sufficient funds for the lavish entertainment Cale gave the "duke" and Buchers" and Luella Strutmann. Whatever Cale had was practically all gone on the day of the marriage, it is believed, as he desperately begged his friends for $5 or a $10 note, and finally sold all of his office furniture for $15. Mother believed to be the mother of Mrs. Strutmann, mother of Luella, that she will ever hear of her daughter again.

Mother is Distressed.

During the day that not a word from the little lady's will be provided tomorrow. "early Sunday morning." The officials, federal and police, had no description of the groom. Cale was known for his fine suits, was as 80 West Kirby avenue.

Continued on Page 8, Column 3.

Wellesley's Most Beautiful Girl

STUDENTS OF WELLESLEY COLLEGE recently elected Miss Maude Olive Minahan, of New York, as the most beautiful girl enrolled. To settle a question which has long been asked by visitors to the college a vote was taken which resulted in the selection of Miss Minahan.

—Photo, 1913, by Champlain & Farrar, Boston, from Underwood & Underwood, New York.

MISS MAUDE OLIVE MINAHAN.

"A rolling stone gathers no moss." Moral: Stick to the RENFRICK LUMBER COMPANY. Dietsche, 65 Woodward. Phone Main 1020.—Adv.

DEPUTIES WAGING PITCHED FIGHT IN KENTUCKY HILLS

Killing of Mountaineer's Son Among Latest Points in Conflict.

Pineville, Ky., December 24.—A pitched battle between deputy sheriffs and mountaineers, headed by John Hendrickson, opened near Hendrickson's place, four miles south of Pineville, shortly after noon today. Hendrickson shot Deputy Sheriff Haynes yesterday afternoon and later he and his friends of relatives, it is alleged, beat to death James Miller, a neighbor. This morning Deputy Sheriff John McCoy and James Smith, who attempted to arrest Hendrickson, were forced to seek shelter in an unoccupied building, which was repeatedly assaulted by the well-armed Hendrickson forces.

Deputy sheriffs C. G. Bailey and John Wilson left Pineville on a special engine at noon with a posse. One hour later word was received that in the first fusillade George Jones, one of Hendrickson's men, was killed.

Always at your feet. We ship ourselves on our delivery service. Every order delivered the same day it is given. Try us. Phone Main 886 for a case of GOEBEL'S BEER.—Advertisement.

THE SEASON'S GREETINGS FORSYTH-MERRY COMPANY.—Advertisement.

PACKARD TRUCKS FOR HIRE

Dietsche, 65 Woodward. Phone Main 1020.—Adv.

RIOT RAGES IN MONROE AVENUE CHRISTMAS MORN

Nearly 100 in Fight After Cripple Is Assaulted.

Nearly 100 men engaged in a riot in Monroe avenue between Randolph street and Woodward avenue at 12:30 o'clock Thursday morning after a cripple was hit by a man. The fight attracted every policeman. Police reports say 15 men, one of whom was a patrolman Graham, who with patrolman George Elliott and patrolman John Ossay, scattered the disturbances, but to draw his revolver to hold back the crowd of the most unruly. A dozen men were taken to Central station and later released.

XMAS MATINEE DANCE

"The Christmas Angel" and "The Boy and the Law" at the Broadway; "Christmas Carol," at the Garrick Grand Circus, 1 to 11 p. m. The great original Les Miserables, at the Forest, corner Woodward and Forrest, 2:30 and 8:15—Advertisement.

JAN. 6, 1914:

Henry Ford announces the $5 day; Gov. Woodbridge Ferris visits the bitter miners' strike in Houghton.

"New Industrial Era Is Marked By Ford's Shares To Laborers," column one, and *"Strikers And Foemen Bury Their Troubles To Welcome Ferris,"* column eight.

The Detroit Free Press

Final Edition

THE WEATHER: Fair and Warmer.

VOL. 79, NO. 101. DETROIT, MICHIGAN, TUESDAY, JANUARY 6, 1914.—FOURTEEN PAGES PRICE: TWO CENTS.

NEW INDUSTRIAL ERA IS MARKED BY FORD'S SHARES TO LABORERS

Detroit Motor Magnate's Plan to Divide $10,000,000 Profits Among 26,500 Employes is Stupendous.

MINIMUM WAGE IS DETERMINED AT $5; PRESENT ONE IS $2.34

Working Shifts Changed to Three of Eight From Two of Nine Hours, Thus Giving New Jobs to 4,000.

TANGO APPROVED BY AUDIENCE IN LONDON

Vote Taken at Matinee, 781 to 21. Dance "Morally One Woman to Tears."

TANGO AT WEDDING MAY PROVE FATAL

New Yorker Slips in Midst of Whirl, Fracturing Thigh and Injuring Brain.

TARS ARE JUDGES OF GOOD "CHEWS"

United States Sailors' Selection of Plug Tobacco for Navy Upheld by Chemical Analysis.

MITCHEL TO WAR ON MALE FLIRTS

New Mayor of Gotham Issues Order to Safeguard Women Unescorted on Streets.

PORTLAND'S HUNGRY SCORN STONE PILE

Hundreds Get Free Lodgings, but $1.50 a Day at Hard Labor is Too Little.

NEW YORK'S NEW POLICE HEAD OUTLINES POLICIES

Plans Vigorous War on All Sorts of Rogues and Will Revive Squads.

YOUNG ACTRESS KILLS SELF AFTER HER FIANCE DIES

Gotham Girl Found Dead With Throat and Wrists Cut, Day of His Funeral.

32 LOST WHEN TANK STEAMER BREAKS IN TWO

Unusual Accident Befalls Oil Carrier Oklahoma Off Sandy Hook.

ONE SECTION DRIFTS OFF IN ONE DIRECTION, THE OTHER IN ANOTHER.

After Part With Most of Survivors Aboard Soon Dives to Bottom; Seven Others Saved by Liner.

POLICE TEAMS MAY PATROL IN MURDER ZONE

Ordinance to Double Guard in Italian Quarter Planned.

NEW YORK-CHICAGO THROUGH TRAIN IS BEING ARRANGED

Michigan Central Railroad Plans 20-Hour Service.

MONROE'S COMMISSION TAKES CONTROL OF CITY

Old Council Retires; Mayor Bets Promises Business-like Administration.

ENRAGED SPANIARD KILLS THREE AND SELF

Mother, Brother and Sister Victims of Disinherited Youth's Anger.

Secretary of New Bank Committee

MILTON C. ELLIOTT

MILTON C. ELLIOTT temporarily is in charge of the secretarial work of the reserve bank organization committee. He is now in New York with Secretary of Treasury McAdoo and Secretary of Agriculture Houston.

The Committee With Which Elliott Is Working Is All Ready to Make a Flying Trip to the Principal Cities in the Race for Regional Reserve Depositories.

PORTLAND, ORE., DEVELOPS NEW MADDEN CLUE

Police Hold Man Thought to Have Driven Auto Stolen in Detroit.

BOAST CAUSES ARREST OF YOUTH SUSPECTED OF SEEING PATROLMAN SHOT

No Local Detective Ordered West but Developments Tuesday Are Awaited.

BOTH COOLEY AND ZAHM DECLINE TO AID IN PHONE WAR

Names of Two Other Experts Suggested to Council Investigators.

STRIKERS AND FOEMEN BURY THEIR TROUBLES TO WELCOME FERRIS

PERJURY IS CHARGED IN GRAFT CASE

Herman Schroeder, Talesman, Alleged to Have Sworn Falsely.

DECLARED HE HAD NO OPINION; ALLEGED TO HAVE BEEN PREJUDICED

Detectives Say He and Six Others Asserted They Would Have Voted for Acquittal.

ONE KILLED; TWO PROSTRATED BY COAL GAS FUMES

SICILIANS HELD WITHOUT BONDS IN GORDON CASE

Police Justice Refuses to Let Them Out of Jail; Witnesses Released.

Crowd Greets Governor at Houghton Depot, Miners Rubbing Shoulders With Enemies During Truce.

EXECUTIVE OFFERS ALL SQUARE DEAL DURING HIS PROBE

Denies His Investigation is Result of Federal Intervention, Saying He Seeks Facts as Head of State.

ASYLUM OR JAIL, REQUESTS FORMER COUNTY ATTORNEY

Edward Minock, Detroiter, Tells Probate Judge He Is Insane.

CROWDED INSTITUTIONS CAN'T TAKE AGED MAN

Pleads in Vain for Commitment, Declaring He is a Burden to His Family.

ROUEN HUNT

APRIL 5, 1914:

Turn-of-the-century advice: Young girls should never wear corsets.

Women's Page

THE DETROIT FREE PRESS: SUNDAY, APRIL 5, 1914.

Don't Wear Illfitting Corsets

Says Lillian Russell

The Corset Should Be Put On With Lacings Open

The Stout Woman Should Wear A Brassiere With A Low Busted Corset

Photos by Monfort

Have Your Corset Fitted to You

Beauty of Form is Prevented by Putting Corsets On a Growing Girl

The Right Sort of Waist for the Growing Girl

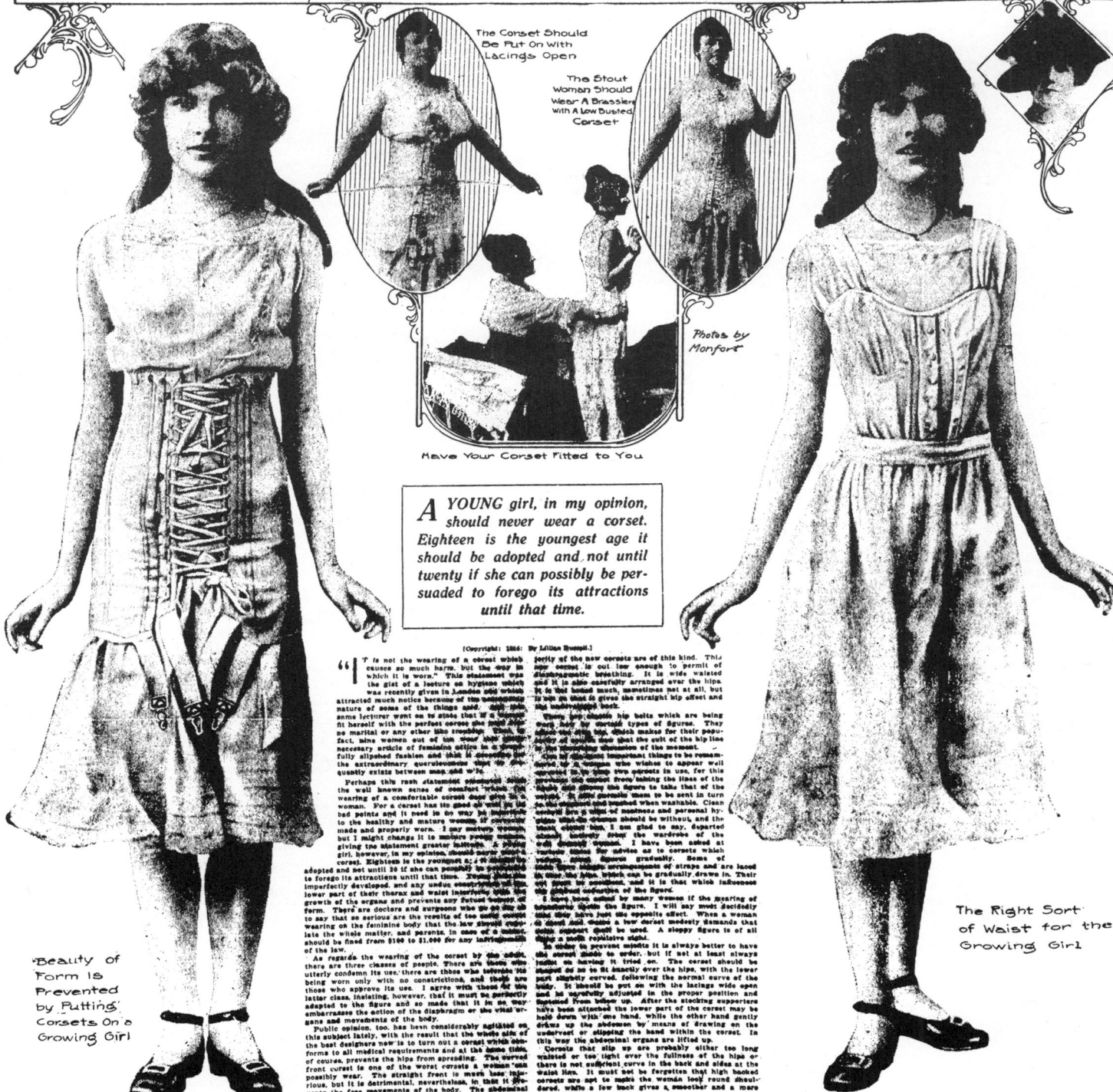

A YOUNG girl, in my opinion, should never wear a corset. Eighteen is the youngest age it should be adopted and not until twenty if she can possibly be persuaded to forego its attractions until that time.

[Copyright: 1914: By Lillian Russell.]

"IT is not the wearing of a corset which causes so much harm, but the way in which it is worn." This statement was the gist of a lecture on hygiene which was recently given in London and which attracted much notice because of the [illegible] nature of some of the things said. [illegible] same lecturer went on to state that if a woman [illegible] fit herself with the perfect corset she would [illegible] no marital or any other like troubles. [illegible] fact, nine women out of ten wear this [illegible] necessary article of feminine attire in a [illegible]fully slipshod fashion and that is [illegible] the extraordinary querulousness that so frequently exists between man and wife.

Perhaps this rash statement [illegible] the well known sense of comfort which the wearing of a comfortable corset does give to a woman. For a corset has its good as well as its bad points and it need in no way be injurious to the healthy and mature woman if correctly made and properly worn. I say mature woman, but I might change it to mature young woman, giving the statement greater latitude. A young girl, however, in my opinion, should never wear a corset. Eighteen is the youngest age it should be adopted and not until 20 if she can possibly be persuaded to forego its attractions until that time. Young girls are imperfectly developed, and any undue constriction of the lower part of their thorax and waist interferes with the growth of the organs and prevents any future beauty of form. There are doctors and surgeons who go so far as to say that so serious are the results of too early corset wearing on the feminine body that the law should regulate the whole matter, and parents, in case of a minor, should be fined from $100 to $1,000 for any infringement of the law.

As regards the wearing of the corset by the adult, there are three classes of people. There are those who utterly condemn its use, there are those who tolerate its being worn only with no constrictions, and there are those who approve its use. I agree with those of the latter class, insisting, however, that it must be perfectly adapted to the figure and so made that it in no way embarrasses the action of the diaphragm or the vital organs and movements of the body.

Public opinion, too, has been considerably agitated on this subject lately, with the result that the whole aim of the best designers now is to turn out a corset which conforms to all medical requirements and at the same time, of course, prevents the hips from spreading. The curved front corset is one of the worst corsets a woman can possibly wear. The straight front is much less injurious, but it is detrimental, nevertheless, in that it prevents the free movements of the body. The abdominal one is the only one which is perfectly safe—and the majority of the new corsets are of this kind. This new corset is cut low enough to permit of diaphragmatic breathing. It is wide waisted and it is also carefully arranged over the hips. It is not boned much, sometimes not at all, but is cut so that it gives the straight hip effect and the [illegible] back.

There are elastic hip belts which are being worn now by certain types of figures. They [illegible] hip, which makes for their popularity [illegible] that the cult of the hip line is the [illegible] discussion of the moment.

One of the most important things to be remembered by a woman who wishes to appear well groomed is to have two corsets in use, for this prevents the corset from taking the lines of the [illegible] and allows the figure to take that of the corset. It also permits them to be sent in turn to the cleaners and washed when washable. Clean corsets are a sign of neatness and personal hygiene that no woman should be without, and the [illegible] corset has, I am glad to say, departed almost entirely from the wardrobe of the well dressed woman. I have been asked at various times for advice as to corsets which reduce stout figures gradually. Some of these have [illegible] arrangements of straps and are laced [illegible] the hips, which can be gradually drawn in. Their [illegible], and it is that which influences the gradual reduction of the figure.

I have been asked by many women if the wearing of brassieres spoils the figure. I will say most decidedly that they have just the opposite effect. When a woman is stout and wears a low corset modesty demands that [illegible] support shall be used. A sloppy figure is of all [illegible] a most repulsive sight.

In order to prevent misfits it is always better to have the corset made to order, but if not at least always insist on having it tried on. The corset should be shaped so as to fit exactly over the hips, with the lower part slightly curved, following the normal curve of the body. It should be put on with the lacings wide open and be carefully adjusted in the proper position and fastened from below up. After the stocking supporters have been attached the lower part of the corset may be held down with one hand, while the other hand gently draws up the abdomen by means of drawing on the undervest or slipping the hand within the corset. In this way the abdominal organs are lifted up.

Corsets that slip up are probably either too long waisted or too tight over the fullness of the hips or there is not sufficient curve in the back and sides at the waist line. It must not be forgotten that high backed corsets are apt to make the woman look round shouldered, while a low back gives a smoother and a more desirable line.

LILLIAN RUSSELL'S ANSWERS TO INQUIRIES BY BEAUTY SEEKERS

MARGARET: The girl with red hair must be careful in the selection of the colors she wears. The dull blues, the soft shades of green, the pale lavenders, black, white, creams, and tans may be worn. The girl with red hair should never wear the baby blues. It forms too much of a contrast between the hair and skin. A girl of your type could also wear a soft shade of yellow.

* *

NELLIE: Scalp massage is the secret of keeping the hair and scalp healthy. It is easily done, and not a great tax on time or patience. The scalp is loosely attached to the underlying skull, and when the scalp becomes adherent to the bones underneath and will not move easily then the hair will fall and become dry and lifeless. By massaging the scalp you keep it flexible, promoting a flow of blood to the roots, so that it will be properly nourished. If you would faithfully massage your scalp each night when retiring, using a good hair tonic with massage, your hair would regain its luster, and in time you would find a vast difference in your hair. This will also help it to grow. I shall send you the formula for an excellent hair tonic and instructions for scalp massage if you will send me a stamped addressed envelope.

* *

PLAIN GIRL: The "peg top" skirts naturally make one look larger around the hips, but would not make you look any taller. Red should be becoming to you with your hair and complexion. You can wear all the light shades, but do not wear brown, or black, or purple. If you will send me a stamped addressed envelope I shall send you the formula for hair tonic, which will increase the growth of your hair.

* *

M. P.: You are not too old to try and improve your looks. Every woman can transform an unlovely neck, scrawny, with disfiguring hollows under the collar bones, and dry, yellow skin, into a lovely one. Cleanliness, deep breathing, massage, and feeding the skin with nourishing creams is the magic recipe. I cannot emphasize too strongly what a powerful influence deep breathing has upon the hollows about the collar bones. It is somewhat difficult to get into these places for massage, but deep breathing swells out these depressions, as you will observe by watching when you inhale deeply. Make a practice of breathing deeply at all time, but take regular exercise night and morning. Massage coconut oil or a good skin food into the hollows. I shall be glad to send you the formula for skin food if you will send me a stamped addressed envelope.

* *

RUTH: Exercise will strengthen the muscles of your back. Deep breathing will keep your shoulders straight. Be careful and watch yourself. Carry yourself erect and don't allow your shoulders to droop. A good shoulder and back exercise is as follows: Stand erect, with the heels together and toes apart. Shoulders straight, and head up. Raise the arms even with the shoulders, then without moving the feet, swing the body first to the right and then to the left. Do this five times, then rest. Increase the number of times as your back strengthens. Never exercise until the point of fatigue, for this will do more harm than good.

* *

H. M. B.: Do not fall a victim to the beauty destroying process of bleaching the hair. It is hard to bleach the hair and do it right. It ruins the hair, making it coarse and brittle, and in time it will look more like straw than anything else. It is hard to keep one color, and one must forever use the bleach, and then it is bound to turn dark and streaked at the roots, while the ends will remain light.

* *

MRS. G. J. T.: The electric needle is good for removing superfluous hair on the face. This is safe and effective and once the hair is removed it will not return. Peroxide and ammonia are good. The ammonia will gradually kill the roots of the hair and the peroxide will bleach it so that it will become less noticeable. Take two-thirds peroxide and one-third ammonia. Use the common ammonia used for laundry purposes.

* *

READER: Excessive dryness of the skin may be caused from a natural insufficiency of fat secretion or from persistent unsuitable treatment. If you have been using strong spirit lotions the present condition of cracking, peeling, and burning is easily accounted for. Stop using soap and water for a while and cleanse the face with almond meal. At night, before retiring, massage the face with a good skin food, and then allow some of it to remain on over night. This will supply the skin with the oil it lacks. I shall be glad to send you the formula for the skin food if you will send me a stamped addressed envelope.

* *

M. H.: If you wish to have pretty hair you must take care of it. Shampoo it about once a month, if it is oily shampoo it about every three weeks. Massage your scalp each night and brush your hair at least one hundred strokes. Here are a few "don'ts": Don't use a comb that is split along the teeth; don't use a steel comb, use as coarse a comb as you can get; don't sleep with the hair up stuck full of hair pins or combs in it; don't omit to rinse it thoroughly after a shampoo, and don't forget that the hair like everything else is greatly benefited by sun and air. I shall send you the formula for hair tonic upon receipt of a stamped, addressed envelope.

* *

A. C. T.: I am sorry, but I cannot give names through my columns. Pure henna may be purchased at any drug store.

APRIL 28, 1915:

The old Belle Isle Bridge is destroyed by fire. Ferry boats rescue 1,000 stranded Detroiters.

THE WEATHER Partly Cloudy.

The Detroit Free Press

MICHIGAN'S GREATEST NEWSPAPER

LAST EDITION

VOL. 80, NO. 213. DETROIT, MICHIGAN, WEDNESDAY, APRIL 28, 1915.—TWENTY PAGES. PRICE: TWO CENTS.

Belle Isle Bridge, Aflame From Draw to Island, Dies in Shroud of Black Smoke

VIEW FROM FIRE BOAT SHOWING BRIDGE NEARLY DESTROYED. AT THE RIGHT, THE ISLAND SIDE, SPAN AFTER SPAN, LICKED UP BY THE FLAMES, HAS DROPPED INTO THE RIVER, LEAVING THE STONE PIERS STANDING. THE DENSE SMOKE IS FROM BURNING OIL AND CREOSOTE.

ROOSEVELT PUTS IN MOST TRYING DAY AS WITNESS

Court Carefully Curbs His Speeches to Jury While Ivins Digs Out Political Secrets of Long Ago.

DWELLS MUCH ON AID BY "INTERESTS" IN HIS CAMPAIGNS

More Letters Read Also to Attest Colonel's One-Time Intimacy With Bosses and Their Captains.

Special to The Free Press.

Syracuse, N. Y., April 27.—Piped [illegible] their cobwebby caverns by Mr. Ivins, gnomes and hobgoblins of secret politics sprung into the [illegible] today and grimaced at Theodore Roosevelt. Ghosts that should have been decently laid low years [illegible] and squeaked and gibbered.

[illegible] that were never meant [illegible] to be spread before the [illegible] or unthinking for mere de[illegible], were snatched from old [illegible] and made to seem a [illegible] upon the good faith and [illegible] and credibility of Colonel Roosevelt. The intention of Mr. [illegible] counsel was to convince [illegible] that the colonel was as [illegible] as a witch when he turned [illegible] Barnes after 1911.

[illegible] a day sorely trying to the [illegible] self-command, because the [illegible] part of it was occupied in [illegible] of scores of letters, [illegible] intimate and private letters, [illegible] passed between him, when he was president, and Senator Platt [illegible] Barnes.

[illegible] the strategy of Ivins, for [illegible] part, to let the letters [illegible] own tale of uninterrupted [illegible] between a righteous man [illegible] bosses, and the colonel, [illegible] and glowering under this [illegible] of revealing correspondence, [illegible] small chance to explain and [illegible]

T. R. Grilled on Interests That Contributed to Fund

[illegible] Ivins possesses the faculty [illegible] snow white as smoke [illegible] of exhibiting gray as [illegible]

Continued on Page Eight, Column One.

FREE MONEY ORDERS TO WAR PRISONERS

Washington Ruling in Accordance With The Hague Convention on Such Conditions.

Washington, April 27.—Orders were [illegible] today, directing postmasters [illegible] to any applicant without [illegible] the usual fee, money orders [illegible] payable to prisoners of war in [illegible] in the European con[illegible] This is in accordance with [illegible] convention designed to [illegible] the conditions of prisoners of war.

INSURANCE RATES INDICATE LONG WAR

Lloyd's Charges $472.50 for $500 Policy, Payable if Conflict Continues After August.

Special to The Free Press.

New York, April 27.—Lloyds, of London, has increased its premium on the duration of the war, according to the word in insurance circles today.

The premium that the war will end by August 31, 1915, has now become 90 guineas per cent, or, to explain, a premium equivalent to $472.50 is being charged on every $500 policy, payable if the war continues after August 31. This would mean a profit of $27.50 to the insured if the war continued, as he only receives the face of his policy, $500. He loses the interest on his money, however, and the commission.

In betting parlance, the insurance exchange is willing to wager $27.50 against the other man's $472.50 that the war will end by August 31, the equivalent of about one to 17, the odds being given by the policy taker.

It is apparent that the great British insurance exchange looks for a long war, for a table prepared today gives the following rates for various dates up to December 31, 1916:

September 30, 1915, 80 guineas per cent, October 31, 72, November 30, 65, December 31, 55, January 31, 1916, 45, February 28, [illegible] June 30, 15, December 31, 5.

STORSTADT LIABLE FOR SINKING EMPRESS

Canadian Pacific Wins $3,000,000 Suit Following 1914 Horrors in St. Lawrence River.

Special to The Free Press.

Montreal, April 27.—The Canadian Pacific Railroad company won its $3,000,000 suit against the owners of the collier Storstadt today, when Justice Dunlop ruled that the ship was responsible for the sinking of the liner Empress of Ireland in the St. Lawrence river, May 29, 1914, an accident that cost approximately 1,000 lives. No blame whatever is attached to the captain or crew of the liner by the court.

1,000,000 EXPELLED FROM NORTH FRANCE

Germans Drive 300,000 Families From Captured Territory Because of Lack of Food.

Geneva, Switzerland, April 27.—Swiss charitable societies have been notified by Germany that 300,000 French families or about 1,000,000 people, expelled from the northern departments of France in the possession of Germany, because of the lack of food, will pass through Switzerland during the month of May. Some of the refugees have already arrived and the Swiss people are doing everything possible for their comfort and care. They are composed largely of old men, women and children, and most of them are penniless.

JASNOWSKI ASKS COURT TO DROP 8 GRAFT CASES

Gives Delay, Expense and Dearth of Evidence as Reasons.

ALDERMANIC CHARGES, THREE YEARS OLD, HIT BY GLINNAN ACQUITTAL

Judge Withholds Decision but Will Grant Request, It is Believed.

Prosecuting Attorney Jasnowski Tuesday filed a motion with Judge Phelan to nolle prosse the eight aldermanic graft cases which have been pending for nearly three years in the recorder's court.

It is probable the judge will accede to the prosecutor's request, although he made no definite announcement but took the matter under advisement. He told the prosecutor he would notify him when he was ready to pass on the motion.

Insufficient evidence upon which to obtain a conviction, the length of time that the cases have dragged and the enormous expense of trying them were among the reasons given by Mr. Jasnowski in his motion. It was practically an admission that the prosecution's base of operations was toppled into the dust by the acquittal of Alderman Thomas E. Glinnan, the first and only one of the indicted aldermen to be tried.

One Defendant Dead.

With the exception of Louis Tossy, who died some months ago, all the defendants in toto the bribery

Continued on Page Three, Column Four.

"PRINCESS" ELOPES WITH YALE STUDENT

Mrs. Hayne, of New York, Says Her Son by First Husband is an Heir to Austrian Throne.

Special to The Free Press.

New York, April 27.—Donald Shields Andrews, senior in the Sheffield Scientific school at Yale university, was married Saturday night last, after an elopement, to Mrs. George Osborne Hayne, of West Fifty-Ninth street, this city, and Pleasantville, N. Y., who asserts that she is the daughter of the late Crown Prince Rudolf, of Austria and the Baroness Vetsera.

The bride is the divorced wife of Captain George Osborne Hayne, a British army officer, who is now in France, and she says her 6-year-old child, by her first husband is an Austrian prince, and one of the heirs to the Austrian throne.

Mrs. Andrews, since her estrangement from her first husband, has maintained a house in Pleasantville and a studio in West Fifty-Ninth street. She loves to paint, she says.

MISS BREITUNG BLAMES ALL ON MAX HIMSELF

Heiress Tells for First Time of Her Romance With a Gardener.

SAYS MAID PICKED HIM OUT FOR HER HUSBAND AS CLEAN, MORAL MAN

Intended Only to Help Him, but Became Infatuated and is Glad Now It's All Over.

New York, April 27.—Juliet Breitung Kleist, in her parents' apartment in the Hotel St. Regis, told this evening the story of her "blighted love." It was with a smile that she called her romance "blighted," but she attributed her blight, not to her parents, Mr. and Mrs. Edward N. Breitung, whom her husband sued unsuccessfully for alienation of affections, but to Max F. Kleist, her youthful husband.

She related the unhappy story, beginning at the time she first was told of Kleist, running from the first meeting to the manner in which her interest in his welfare was awakened, through honest friendship to love and marriage, and then to the awakening to the fact that Kleist was not the ideal which she had built up in her heart.

With the realization of that fact—Kleist's references to her as a "lure," his placing the blame entirely upon her—her fondness for him died away. Long since she ceased to love him, and she says emphatically that it was because of his own actions.

Only a Mad Infatuation.

Miss Breitung—she is really Mrs. Kleist, but her parents and her friends never speak or think of her as married—recited the story almost as if it were a dream story.

"I did love Max at one time," she said, "but it was not a lasting love. It was a mad infatuation that really had no foundation that was real. It really was a dream. I quickly came to realize that and

Continued on Page Two, Column Two.

BANK CASHIER AND $15,000 CASH GONE

$500 Reward Offered for Indianan Who Skipped: Owns $20,000 Property.

Dugger, Ind., April 27.—Edward J. King, cashier of the Dugger State bank, has disappeared, and it was announced today by bank officials that a shortage which may reach $15,000 has been discovered in King's accounts.

King, it was said, has not been seen here since late Saturday. A reward of $500 has been offered for his arrest.

King had been in the employ of the bank for a number of years and owns about $20,000 worth of property here.

FRENCH OCCUPY ASIA TOWN ON DARDANELLES

Troops Successfully Landed on Both Sides of Turkish Straits.

ALLIES TURN TIDE OF BATTLE ON YSER CANAL AND ASSUME OFFENSIVE

Berlin Admits Repulse and German Advance is Believed Seriously Checked.

London, April 28; 2:45 a. m. (Wednesday)—The Daily Mail's Athens correspondent, telegraphing Monday, says:

"The bombardment of the interior forts of the Dardanelles, which began Sunday, continued today and resulted in heavy damage to the forts. It is reported that the forts on the coast near Smyrna also were bombarded.

BY CABLE TO THE FREE PRESS.

London, April 27.—Troops have been landed on both sides of the entrance to the Dardanelles, the general attack by land, sea and air is well under way and the first town on the Asiatic side, Kum Kaleh, has been captured.

This is the substance of reports of the Allies' new attack on the Turks as received here tonight from British and French sources.

The French land forces have been assigned to the Asiatic side of the straits and the British to the European side, which is the Gallipoli peninsula.

Enos Reported Captured.

An unconfirmed report from Athens says that the Allies have occu-

Continued on Page Three, Column Seven.

War Bulletins

BY CABLE TO THE FREE PRESS

London, April 27.—A colonial office report tonight says that a force of Germans numbering 700, with 12 guns, attacked Colonel Skinner's force at Trek-Kopjes, northern German Southwest Africa. The Germans were defeated with a loss of 250 dead and wounded.

BY CABLE TO THE FREE PRESS

Melbourne, April 27.—It is officially announced that a British warship has captured the German trading steamer Elfriede, which is believed to have been the last German ship free in the Pacific.

London, April 27.—A telegram from Stuttgart says a hostile biplane flew over Oberdorf and dropped four bombs on the arms factory. Six civilians were killed and seven severely wounded. The airmen were fired upon but escaped.

London, April 27.—A dispatch from Budapest says a Russian aeroplane has been shot down near Czobos and that three of its occupants were killed.

PLEA FOR PLAY BOARD BUDGET AGAIN IGNORED

Gordon Fights in Vain for Items Ruthlessly Cut by Estimators.

LEADER IN ATTACK AT MONDAY NIGHT SESSION, BUT REVERSES STAND

Three Motions Tabled; Request for $1,000,000 for New Jail Buildings Killed.

Spurred to action by protests from every direction against the action of the board of estimates Monday night in practically killing the recreation budget this year, Estimator Arthur E. Gordon, one of the leaders in the cutting, Tuesday afternoon reversed his attitude and made three attempts to reinstate the board in public opinion.

Gordon was unsuccessful and was opposed by Estimator Bolton, who has hitherto worked in harmony with him. They engaged in a hot dispute when Gordon moved three times that the recreation budget be passed as allowed by the common council.

All Motions Fail.

On the first motion that the budget be allowed an amendment was passed laying the matter on the table until Estimator Standish Backus was present. A motion that the budget be allowed as recommended by the committee on recreation met the same fate.

A second motion was made after the estimators adopted in committee of the whole a committee recommendation that $1,000,000 be al-

Continued on Page Three, Column Six.

MORE HELP WANTED TO QUELL TYPHUS

Head of American Commission in Serbia Sends Appeal for Aid to Washington.

Washington, April 27.—An appeal for reinforcements to aid in the campaign against typhus and cholera in Serbia was cabled to the American Red Cross headquarters here today by Dr. Richard P. Strong, head of the American commission sent to Serbia by the Red Cross in co-operation with the Rockefeller foundation.

"At least 175 more physicians, medical inspectors and fourth year students are needed to carry on the work," Dr. Strong's message said, and hospital supplies are badly wanted. "With proper means," it added, "the typhus epidemic may be controlled in a short time."

Dr. Strong announced the formation at Nish of an international board of health. He said Surgeon-General Gorgas, of the United States army, would be made the director of this board's work if he accepted the invitation of the Rockefeller foundation to become a member of its staff.

FERRY BOATS GO TO "RESCUE" OF 1,000 MAROONED

Bridge Total Loss; Fire Destroys All South-Side Spans; Debris Half Blocks Channel.

OIL-SOAKED, CREOSOTED BLOCKS BURN FIERCELY; WIND FANS BLAZE

Firemen Driven Back to Save American Side; Coals From D. P. W. Tar Wagon Are Blamed for Flames.

Eaten away by fire that swept its creosote block flooring, the Belle Isle bridge, connecting Detroit's island park with the mainland, toppled over into the river Tuesday afternoon, and is a total loss. The first alarm was sounded at 3:19 o'clock, and the last company did not leave until 7:45.

Every span between the island approach and the draw fell into the river. Half of the draw was carried away and the other portion was badly burned. Only the stone piers remained in position.

While 13 fire companies and two fire boats poured tons of water onto the floor, the wooden planking and creosoted pavement, oilsoaked by the drippings from countless motor cars that have passed over it, burned quickly, sending volumes of smoke before a stiff wind that spread the flames. The heat warped the steel beams and girders until they curled and fell with hissing splashes into the river.

1,000 Caught on Island.

On the island more than 1,000 persons and about 100 vehicles, caught in the midst of an afternoon's outing, were marooned by the fire. The Detroit & Windsor Ferry company sent the steamer Garland to the rescue and brought the visitors away. The Walkerville & Detroit Ferry company also sent the steamer Essex to help in the work, and by 7:30 o'clock all were ashore. The ferry companies carried all free of charge.

Before the embers of the bridge ceased to glow and while smoke was rising from the charred remains, the common council took the first steps toward the erection of a new structure, when Controller Engel was asked for an estimate on the cost of a special election to pass a bond issue for the work. Mayor Marx after visiting the fire, sent the council a communication asking for action in the matter.

Election Will Cost $22,500.

Controller Engel estimates $22,500 will be needed for a special election. To submit the matter an election the council will have at least 10 days, but the initiative may be resorted to in order to hasten matters. The loss of the bridge practically makes certain that the new bridge will be erected on the present site and this will be a victory for Park Commissioner Ford, who opposed the proposition for a second bridge at the head of the island. The commissioner at present has

Continued on Page Six, Column One.

HOT WAVE'S END IS PREDICTED WITHIN FOUR OR FIVE DAYS

Rain Threatened, While Mercury Ranges From 65 to 83.

MOSQUITOES ARE DOING USUAL SUMMER BUSINESS

Thunder Showers in Other Sections of State Indicate That Detroit is in Danger.

Although the summer weather spell still persisted in Detroit Tuesday, the temperatures ranging between 83 and 65, a ray of hope appeared late in the day, when dispatches from Washington announced that the hot wave would be broken, probably Saturday or Sunday.

With at least four more days of the cooking weather still in prospect, with the connecting link between Detroit and its favorite breathing spot a memory after the visit of the flames, with the skirmishers of the great annual army of mosquitoes just skirmishing into the city with all the troubles of the unexpected summer, the body politic of Detroit may be said to

Continued on Page Two, Column Four.

The Detroit Free Press

MICHIGAN'S GREATEST NEWSPAPER

VOL. 83, NO. 318. — DETROIT, MICHIGAN, SUNDAY, AUGUST 11, 1918—SEVENTY-TWO PAGES. — PRICE: EIGHT CENTS. — LAST EDITION

ENRAGED CITIZENS WRECK CARS AS FARE ADVANCE PROTEST
GERMANS BEATEN, IN FLIGHT ALONG 33-MILE BATTLE FRONT

RIOTS BREAK OUT ALL OVER CITY IN D. U. R. FIGHT

Police and Trolley Men Hurt In Battles.

ENTIRE SYSTEM IS PARALYZED

Crews Stalling Cars Are Put Under Arrest.

With the community thrown into a state almost approaching civil war by the action of Detroit United railway in jumping up traffic whenever passengers refused to pay six-cent fares, riots broke out in all sections Saturday afternoon and night, cars were overturned and wrecked, citizens, trolleymen and policemen injured in pitched battles, the city's transportation system was paralyzed and service on the Michigan and Baker lines entirely suspended by the company two hours before midnight.

Failure of Acting Mayor Guthard or Police Commissioner Marquardt to take any decisive step during the day to compel the D. U. R. to comply...

NON-PARTISAN LEAGUE TOY OF 'BOSS' TOWNLEY

Farmers Being Duped, Declares Rev. Maxwell, Who Left the Organization from Disgust With Its Methods.

MEMBERSHIP PRAISED; AUTOCRATIC MACHINE VIGOROUSLY ASSAILED

"Townley Born Gambler," He Says, "Playing Mighty Game, With Tillers of Soil and Their Dollars His Pawns."

FOE CUTS DOWN UKRAINIAN MOB

Alarmed by Revolt, Germans Massacre Peasants and Burn Villages.

"Red" Envoy in London Under Guard Due to Arrival of British Envoy at Moscow.

CARS STALLED BY CROWDS IN "PENNY BATTLE."

Refusal of passengers to pay six cents carfares resulted in street car traffic being tied up in all parts of the city. The above picture shows a crowd at Michigan and Woodward avenues, shortly after 5 o'clock Saturday afternoon.

100 DETROIT BOYS WIN ARMY CITATION

Commended by Gen. Haan for Bravery in Battle on Alsace Line.

RESIGNING FUTILE FOR JEFFRIES NOW

Court Decision Against Judge Would Keep Name Off Ballot for Mayor.

KEEP STEADY, FIGHT ON—LLOYD GEORGE

British Premier Warns That the Struggle Is Long Ways From Over.

FRENCH RUSH 8 MILES EAST IN HALF A DAY

Poilus Sweep Along on 20-Mile Line, Menace Noyon-Roye Road and Oise Salient.

YANKS BREAK TEUTONS' HOLD NEAR ALBERT, SMASH AHEAD

Enemy's Captured Wounded Exceed Haig Total; Prisoners, Guns Mounting Rapidly.

Rupprecht's divisions caught in the Allied assault from Albert to south of Montdidier apparently are concerned only in escaping to the Noyon-Nesle line and to north of the Somme. Nowhere except on the extreme northern end of their line are they offering resistance that even checks the Franco-British-American rush. Allied cavalry and tanks are operating as far as six or seven miles in advance of the infantry, so that the French and British Saturday night statements did not agree on the exact limit of the advance at the time the reports were filed. However, the British announced the line at that time almost due south from Lihons to Conchy, through Fresnoy-les-Roye. This represents an advance of about eight miles east of Montdidier. Montdidier fell to the French at midday Saturday. The French official report said a gain averaging six miles had been made on a 20-mile front. Farther north Americans, who entered the fighting Saturday, broke the German hold on Chipilly spur and are advancing eastward.

With the British Army in France, Aug. 10 (Reuter's).—The present battle has brought more Germans wounded into the Allied casualty listing stations than there are wounded among the Allied soldiers. Many German doctors and hospital attendants have been captured and they are doing good service in attending the wounded. ...

DETROITERS IGNORE PRUDDEN ATTITUDE

Manufacturers to Take Du Bois to Washington on Mission Seeking Coal.

G. O. P. STATE CHIEFS CALLED FOR SEPT. 2

Meeting at Chicago to Discuss Coming Campaign.

U-CAPTAIN WHO SENT DOWN LUSITANIA DEAD

POLICE CAN FORCE D. U. R. TO MOVE CARS, SAYS BARLOW

Assistant Corporation Counsel and Other Legal Experts Claim City Has Full Power.

SOLDIERS HURT WHEN CAR RUNS INTO TRUCK

AUG. 11, 1918:

A one-cent fare hike leads to riots across Detroit.

"Police and Trolley Men Hurt In Battles," column one.

Nov. 12, 1918:

The end of the "war to end all wars."

The Detroit Free Press

MICHIGAN'S GREATEST NEWSPAPER

WEATHER: Fair, warmer

FINAL EDITION

VOL. 84, NO. 46. DETROIT, MICHIGAN, TUESDAY, NOVEMBER 12, 1918.—SIXTEEN PAGES. PRICE: TWO CENTS

EX-KAISER REPORTED INTERNED AND CROWN PRINCE SHOT
WILSON WARNS, ALLIES FACE GERMAN BOLSHEVIKI FIGHT

ONE SCENE ALONG WOODWARD AVENUE WHEN VICTORY CELEBRATION WAS AT HEIGHT

NAVY CALLED BY "REDS" TO FIGHT ALLIES

"Defend Our Nation," Rebels Urging Sailors as Vessels of Britain Are Reported Near.

SOLF APPEALS TO PRESIDENT TO AID STRICKEN FOE PEOPLE

Berlin Officially Says Hindenburg Is at General Headquarters and Not in Holland.

London, Nov. 12.—William Hohenzollern has been interned in a Dutch chateau, the Amsterdam correspondent of the Exchange Telegraph Co. says. Prince Joachim, the kaiser's youngest son, and 50 other persons accompanied the ex-emperor on his flight into Holland, the correspondent adds. It is presumed the entire party will be interned along with the ex-monarch.

YANKEES SHELL FOE AT ARMISTICE HOUR

London, Nov. 12 (1:28 a. m.)—The former German crown prince is reported to have been shot.

HELGOLAND IS PLEDGED FOR FLEET

Iron Ring Tightened as World Waits to See Germany Win Victory Over Self.

WILSON READS DEFEAT TERMS

Enemy Must Give Up Gold Taken Out of Belgium, Russia in Compensation Plan.

What Germany Must Do.

Evacuate Alsace-Lorraine, Belgium, Luxemburg, Russia, Rumania at once.
Give up for occupation all countries on the west bank of the Rhine.
Give up for occupation Mayence, Coblenz and Cologne, principal Rhine crossings, and territory within a radius of 30 kilometres about each city.
Withdraw from all territory which belonged to Russia, Rumania or Turkey.
Disarm army and navy, hand over most of navy and quantities of war supplies.
Repatriate allied prisoners without reciprocation; return enslaved civilians.
Submit to damages for damage done.
Abandon Russian and Rumanian treaties.
Return money, securities, precious metals taken as loot.
Evacuate Black Sea ports, give up ships taken from Russia, Turks and defunct barring ones to the Cottages (entrance to the Baltic).
Release own ships to core foods, return all allied ships, and notify neutrals the sea is safe again.

BY THE ASSOCIATED PRESS.
Washington, Nov. 11.—Signing of the armistice with Germany was proclaimed today by President Wilson, who announced its terms at a joint session of congress. The terms herald the end of the war, because they take from Germany the power to renew it.
Stripped of its malicious power, the military dictatorship, its masters driven to exile, stands before the world's court of justice, having subscribed to terms of surrender which probably will be recorded in history as the most drastic and complete ever measured out to a defeated foe.
Preparations for final peace negotiations will engross American and Allied statesmen during the next few weeks, while Marshal Foch and the naval commanders see terms of armistice which ended the war.

(Continued on Page Three, Column Four)

SEVENTY FIRE ALARMS RESPONDED TO MONDAY

City firemen responded to 70 alarms Monday during the hours of the peace celebration. The majority of the blazes were of little consequence. To prevent wholesale false alarms in the business district, firemen were stationed at all hours. Although the firemen could not take part in the general rejoicing with the downtown crowds, they joined the din while answering calls, the apparatus bells and sirens blending into the great noise fest.

DETROIT HEARS TAPS SOUNDED ON WAR'S END

City Hall Bugler Tells People Great Conflict Is Concluded; Entire Municipality Rejoices in Death of Kaiserism.

Just at the exact moment that Detroit each day for months has kept heart to heart with her boys across the sea by sounding "Taps" from the sweet bugle notes were heard by the Yanks in France, when the city formally sounded "Taps" for the greatest of all wars, Monday afternoon.
The hands of the city hall clock pointed to 4 o'clock as Bugler Theodore Goebel, of the Liberty band, stepped from the van of the wagon, spontaneous "parade" which formed the keystone feature of the city's celebration, raised his bugle to his lips and blew the refrain that sends waking soldiers to their beds and is the benediction of those who are being laid away for their last, long sleep.
All down the line of the parade, which had been halted at the city hall, buglers of each band sounded the lingering refrain at the same time, and it may have been just chance, or it may have been most suspicious omen, that it was exactly 4 o'clock, "taps time," as it is known at the city hall, when Detroit's official requiem for the war drifted from the bugles.
Those who felt that Detroit had spoken the greatest force of its powers of jubilation on the preceding peace celebration of Thursday, and might meet the real

(Continued on Page Two, Column Two)

WOMEN HORSEWHIP MAN WHO HIT GIRL

Rockford Crowd Avenges Blocking of Child's Eye.

Special to The Free Press.
Grand Rapids, Mich., Nov. 11.—Accused of having struck his daughter Faith, 14, in the eye, Edwin Brooks, 41, of Rockford, was escorted to the public square in Rockford, near here, Monday, stripped of his coat and vest and horsewhipped by a dozen women while a crowd estimated at 500, including men, women and children, jeered and urged the women on.
Brooks, badly bruised, has consulted county officers. He declares he merely attempted to buy his daughter's eye when she was trying to pull a weed from his stepmother and that, when the girl threw up her hand it deflected the blow to her eye.
When the girl appeared for work at a tannery in Rockford Monday, her fellow workmen asked what had happened and when they learned she had been struck by her father, they left their work immediately and later escorted to the public square. Four horsewhips were broken across his back.
Rockford business men say the peace demonstration which was in progress excited the crowd to act.

FREE PRESS FLASHES NEWS OF PEACE TO SLEEPING CITY

It was 2:47 o'clock Monday morning when Frank J. Garrean, Associated Press telegraph operator in The Detroit Free Press editorial department, received the greatest piece of news that ever came over telegraph wires. The message contained only six words—"Flash—E. O. S.—Armistice Signed."
Chief William McGraw, of the fire department; Charles Clippert, of the fire commission; Acting Mayor Jacob Guthard and The Detroit Free Press reporter in Windsor, the Michigan Central, Wabash and Pere Marquette railroads had the news from The Free Press inside of a few minutes and by 3:10 o'clock Detroit and vicinity had started to celebrate the greatest day in history.

'FOCH' ON ALL LIPS IN VICTORY'S HOUR

Official Placards; "Maroons" Boom in London as King Announces Triumph.

Paris, Nov. 11.—Scenes of wildest enthusiasm were enacted in the chamber of deputies this afternoon when Premier Clemenceau read conditions of the German armistice. The whole chamber rose to greet the premier.
The municipal council of Paris had the following posted on walls in all parts of the city:
"Citizens! Victory is here—triumphant victory! Our vanquished enemy lays down his arms. Blood ceases to flow. Let Paris emerge from her ordered reserve. Let us give free course to our joy and enthusiasm and hold back our tears.
Homage to our great soldiers and their incomparable chiefs by fortune. We cannot let the solemn hour pass, however, without profound emotion, without remembering our glorious dead, whose sacrifice has given us the victory. To them our undying gratitude.
Let all the houses be decorated with the colors so dear to our hearts.
Long live the Republic! Long live immortal France!"

BY UNIVERSAL SERVICE
London, Nov. 11.—News of the signing of the armistice was made known to the general public in London at 11 o'clock by the firing of "maroons," guns formerly used to warn of air raids.
People broke into cheers and the streets were immediately filled by crowds of soldiers, sailors and civilians.
The king and queen, accompanied by Princess Mary and the Duke of Connaught, appeared on the balcony of Buckingham palace and were enthusiastically cheered by the vast crowd, which sang the national anthem and "Rule Britannia."
King George, addressing the throng, said:
"You are well entitled to rejoice. The people of this empire, with their allies, have won a great victory. The men and daughters of the empire have done it. It is a victory greater than any known in history. Let us thank God."
Prime Minister Lloyd George said in an address to the crowd in Downing street:
"The armistice has come to an end at 11 o'clock this morning. The food administration will be continued until the senate ratifies the treaty of peace. In the meantime, Administrator Hoover hopes against expectation that prices will drop.
The fuel administration will be continued the same length of time. There will be no slackening of the conservation program however.
The war industry and war trade boards also will be continued.
Control of wires and railways will continue for the full period of one year contracted for when they were taken over. The railways will be retained in order to insure that 'reconstruction freight' will be handled promptly through the pooling plan.
Censorship of news will be discontinued soon, as well as the Creel activities.
The government's policy of cancelling war contracts will be staked and will permit to a certain extent, regulation by the government under war risk bureau so that men will not be thrown out of work.

ALLY TERMS IMPOSED ON LAST ENEMY

Washington, Nov. 11.—Following are the armistice terms imposed on Germany, as read to congress today by President Wilson:

I. MILITARY CLAUSES ON WESTERN FRONT.
One: Cessation of operations by land and in the air six hours after signature of the armistice.
Two: Immediate evacuation of invaded countries—Belgium, France, Alsace-Lorraine, Luxembourg—so ordered as to be completed within 14 days from the signature of the armistice. German troops which have not left the above-mentioned territories within the period fixed will become prisoners of war. Occupation by Allied and United States forces jointly will keep pace with evacuation in these areas. All movements of evacuation and occupation will be regulated in accordance with a note annexed to the stated terms.
Three: Repatriation beginning at once and to be completed within 14 days of all inhabitants of the countries above mentioned, including hostages and persons under trial or convicted.
Four: Surrender in good condition by German armies of the following equipment: Five thousand guns, (2,500 heavy 2,500 field); 30,000 machine guns; 3,000 minenwerfer; 2,000 aeroplanes (fighters, bombers firstly D seventy-three and night bombing machines). The above to be delivered in situ to Allied and United States troops in accordance with details laid down in the annexed note.
Five: Evacuation by German armies of countries on the left bank of the Rhine. These countries on the left bank of the Rhine shall be administered by local authorities under control of Allied and United States armies of occupation. Occupation of these territories will be determined by Allied and United States garrisons holding principal crossing of the Rhine, Mayence, Coblenz, Cologne, together with bridgeheads at these points in 18,60 miles radius on the right bank and by

(Continued on Page 2, Column 1.)

UNCONDITIONAL SURRENDER
Celebrate our victory at Pier Carnival and souvenirs.—Adv.

AIRMAN KILLED AS AEROPLANE DROPS IN CITY

Lieut. Morrow Gives Life in Effort to Aid Peace Celebration; Many Accidents Mar Detroit's Victory Jubilation.

Killed in action—Lieutenant J. C. Morrow, of Punxsutawney, Pa.
Why should this intelligence ever be carried out of Detroit has he made his last flight. But instead of defending American honor and joy-mad celebrators sent to the victims capacity of the Yenton and Vandal, he caved into submission, he was performing aerial feats for his fellow citizens to show them how his brothers in arms would drive the marauding Hun, should the long line of "Yanks" have given...

At Night of Celebration.

If it ever any peace parade was passing the city hall at 4 o'clock Monday afternoon and the joy-mad celebrators were at the utmost of their enthusiasm, no people in the five sleeves circling the Grand Circus with the flagpole in the center were near Pyle building. Woodward avenue.
The aeroplane plunged nose down, lighted itself and plopped to the ground near...

(Continued on Page 12, Column 3)

Gives Arthur on Kaiser Front.

With the American Army on the Sedan Front, Nov. 11.—Thousands of American heavy guns fired on Sedan as a part of our drives at early 11 o'clock this morning.
On the entire American front, from the Moselle to the region of Sedan, there was artillery activity in the morning, all batteries giving forth their final...

ARMY DRAFT CALLS REVOKED BY BAKER

Edict Halts 300,000 Men Due for Camps in November.

Washington, Nov. 11.—Almost the first action of the war department today after announcement of the signing of the armistice with Germany was cancellation of all army draft calls, under which more than 300,000 men had been ordered to entrain for camps before November 30.
Urgent telegrams, prepared three days ago at the direction of Provost Marshal General Crowder, were sent to all local draft boards directing them to discontinue immediately "all work connected with the classification of men who registered September 12. General Crowder, however, directed the boards to discontinue immediately "all work connected with the classification of men who registered September 12 had attained their thirty-seventh birthdays and had attained their fortieth birthday in the year.
Since August, 1917, when the first calls were issued under the army draft law, 2,700,000 men have been inducted into the army.

U. S. TROOPS NEEDED ABROAD 2 YEARS

—TAFT

Ex-President Warns People Boys Must Do Policing.

Chicago, Nov. 11.—William Howard Taft, former President, tonight warned the people in a speech not to expect the soldiers back from France within two years, because he said, "We have two million men in Europe, and they will be kept there for some time to do police work, both in the country of our en-mies and in Russia."
"All boats in which the men were sent across will be needed to carry food and supplies to our Allies for re-building."

Britain Stops All Recruiting

London, Nov. 11.—The British government has decided to suspend recruiting.

ALWAYS THE TRUTH AND THE FACTS

Because this newspaper has always held a high regard for the truth and nothing but the truth in its news presentation, in its interpretation of the news, more than ever do its readers and advertisers appreciate the columns of The Free Press.

With "peace on earth" once more a reality and not a dream, we should even in the day to come appreciate more of the cleans being of providing for the needs of the household in a virtue that can be cultivated through a constant study of the 'advertising news' in the best newspaper Les Nouvelles, at Liege, the newspaper adds, have been deposed, and a red flag hoisted.

MAKE UP YOUR SHOPPING LIST EACH MORNING FROM THE DETROIT FREE PRESS

U. S. TAKES INITIAL PEACE PLAN STEPS

Wartime on War Contracts Eliminated; Building Ban to Go.

Special to The Free Press.
Washington, Nov. 11.—The government today took initial steps in the program for the country after the peace treaty is signed. These were phases touched on in reports of chiefs:
Secretary of War Baker has ordered all overtime and Sunday work on war contracts eliminated.
The war priorities commission will order an immediate relaxation in percentage of material available for building purposes, municipal and private. There is a possibility he will be lifted altogether.
The food administration will be continued until the senate ratifies the treaty of peace. (In the meantime, Administrator Hoover hopes against expectation that prices will drop.
The fuel administration will be continued the same length of time. There will be no slackening of the conservation program however.
The war industry and war trade boards also will be continued.
Control of wires and railways will continue for the full period of one year contracted for when they were taken over. The railways will be retained in order to insure that 'reconstruction freight' will be handled promptly through the pooling plan.
Censorship of news will be discontinued soon, as well as the Creel activities.

T. R. ILL OF SCIATICA; TAKEN TO HOSPITAL

Oyster Bay, N. Y., Nov. 11.—After suffering great pain for the last 10 days, from an attack of sciatica, Colonel Theodore Roosevelt was removed today to Roosevelt hospital, New York. He has been confined to his bed for more than a week, but has been assured that by going to the hospital and being under closer treatment there he will be able to get about in a short time.

Graceful Skating Contest, Wednesday evening, Roller Palace Rink, WOODWARD AT FOREST.—Adv.

AT THE PIER—TONIGHT
Our popular Tues., Thurs., Sat. Old Style Dancing party. Le Roy Smith's wonderful orchestra.—Adv.

CENTRAL CONCERT CO.
SECOND CONCERT TO-NIGHT
At Arcadia Bldg Circle—Macbeth (soprano), Horton (baritone), Lambois (cellist), Seats at Grinnell's.—Adv.

MILITARY DANCE AT ARCADIA
Thursday, Nov. 14, by Detachment No. 5, Air Service A. F. of Detroit.—Adv.

BETTER FOOD FOR LESS MONEY.
15 oz. Bread 18c Sugar, 5 lbs....94c
13 lb. Bread 18c Sugar, 10 lbs..1.72
14c Pancake Flr 18c Oatmeal, 5 lbs 24c
URATA LUNCH CO., 1207 Woodward

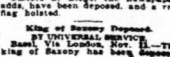

The Detroit Free Press

WEATHER Milder.
MICHIGAN'S GREATEST NEWSPAPER
FINAL EDITION

DETROIT, MICHIGAN, SATURDAY, JANUARY 3, 1920—SIXTEEN PAGES — PRICE: TWO CENTS

2,800 REDS BAGGED IN NATION-WIDE RAIDS, 500 IN DETROIT

Jan. 3, 1920:

Led by U.S. Attorney General A. Mitchell Palmer, federal officials conduct mass arrests of alleged radicals.

MICHIGAN LAW DEP AIDS QUIZ IN BROWN CASE

Witnesses Questioned in New Investigation Begun by the State.

SISTER SOLDIER HAS VICTIM'S FOUNTAIN PEN

Anonymous Letter Reveals Significant Fact; No Guilt, Says Vester Girl.

Canadian Order Halts Dumping Of U.S. Whisky

HOAX CAUSES 40 INSANITY CASES
Fear of World's End Drives Two Score Detroiters Daft, Says Health Chief.

RAILS DEFICIT OF NOVEMBER HITS $64,500,000
Government Loss for 23 Months Reaches Total of $848,000,000.

SALVAGE CHIEF SOBS IN COURT
Former Captain Nicholson is Overcome When Diary is Read to Jury.

ROUND-UP SMASHES RECORDS; AGENTS USE 4,000 WARRANTS; DEPORTATION OPENLY SOUGHT

PLOT TO ROUSE NEGROES BARED

Noted Gallery Invites Effigy Of Lady Astor

POSSE INVADES MASSES HOUSE
Police and U.S. Agents Break in on Bolshevists in Red Headquarters.

ZERO WEATHER GRIPS DETROIT
Extreme Low Temperatures to Continue Until Sunday, Conger Predicts.

RUM PLENTIFUL IN BORDER CITY
Trucks Laden With Beer and Whisky Stop at Homes of Windsorites.

ALLY-TROTZKY PEACE HINTED
Mysterious Mission of U.S. Admiral to Russia Seen As First Move.

BORDEN THANKS JOHN D. FOR GIFT OF $5,000,000

PROVIDENCE DENIES SPEECH TO BERGER
City Yields to Legion's Objection to Radical Utterance.

CARS STOLEN IN 1919 VALUED AT $3,165,000

CITY CANNOT GIVE BONUS, IS OPINION
Atkinson Holds Under Law $50 Premium is Illegal.

POWDER EXPLOSION KILLS 5 WORKMEN
Blast in Dupont Plant Rocks Wilmington, Delaware.

FOUR 12,000-TON SHIPS ARE PLANNED
American Company is to Build Them at Lorain.

MEXICO TO RESTORE RAILS TO OWNERS

A.C. GRAHAM IS NAMED PROHIBITION DIRECTOR

MOTOR STOCKHOLDERS ASK FOR A RECEIVER

ORDERS HER HUSBAND TAKE WOMAN PARTNER

NOT AN EXPENSE

PARIS HOMES ISOLATED BY SEINE RIVER FLOOD

DRYS WILL PUT 1920 CANDIDATE IN FIELD

AUTOS CRASH, TWO HURT, DRIVER HELD
Victor Garben Under Influence of Liquor, is Charge.

Fourteen Splendid New Features in Sunday's Magazine Section

TO SHIP 1,000,000 TONS SUGAR TO U.S.
Strike's End Frees New Crop Grown in Porto Rico.

SWEDEN EXTENDS TRADE TREATY WITH GERMANY

BOYDEN TO REPRESENT RED CROSS IN POLAND

G.M. BRUSH, MINNESOTA RAILWAY PIONEER

FIGHT FOR STANLEY'S SEAT WILL BE LIVELY

JUNE 14, 1923:

The Ku Klux Klan, a strong influence in Detroit politics, swears in new members at an Oakland County ceremony.

WEATHER: Fair.

The Detroit Free Press

MICHIGAN'S GREATEST NEWSPAPER

FINAL EDITION

VOL. 88, NO. 260. DETROIT, MICHIGAN, THURSDAY, JUNE 14, 1923.—TWENTY-SIX PAGES ****** PRICE: THREE CENTS

FIERY CROSS GLARES AS HOST JOINS KLAN NEAR CITY

K.K.K. BAPTISM OF 1,000 NEOPHYTES CLOSE TO DETROIT

Photo by Gene Holland, Free Press Staff Photographer.

MAN DROWNED AS DRY 'NAVY' RAMS CANOE

Girl Companion Rescued After Crash Hurls Her Into Detroit River.

YELLOWLEY RETURNS; BENT ON LIQUOR DAM

Says All U. S. Forces Will Be Used to Stem Flood; Beer Flows In.

A federal prohibition enforcement launch, patrolling the Detroit river last midnight, rammed and overturned a fragile canoe off the foot of Parkview avenue. William McNeer, 23 years old, one of the occupants of the canoe, was drowned. Helen Clark, 18 years old, 1230 McDougall avenue, pretty companion of the dead man, was saved by the first officer of the federal launch, who tossed her a life preserver and pulled her aboard.

W. J. Beamish, federal officer in command of the launch, told the harbormaster's office that the canoe was traveling across the river without lights. This later was confirmed. The men aboard the federal craft did not see the canoe until they were within a few feet of it and were unable to turn about.

Man Unable to Swim.

The canoe was capsized. McNeer, who was unable to swim, sank to the bottom. The girl managed to keep on the surface, and screamed. She paddled about for several minutes before the searchlight on the federal craft located her and the lifeline was tossed. In serious condition from exposure and the shock, she was taken to her home.

The girl said she met McNeer several weeks ago, and did not know him sufficiently well to know where he lived.

Beamish made a report to the harbormaster. A crew immediately was dispatched to seek for McNeer's body. Early today the body had not been recovered.

Beer Barges Sail On.

While E. C. Yellowley, prohibition director, in Detroit to investigate the attempt to sink one of the boats of the dry navy, together with its prize, a motorboat laden with beer, was declaring Wednesday afternoon that rum-running across the river would be stopped, a bootlegging fleet of 40 craft was making a successful dash to Detroit from the Canadian shore, according to boats openly made in rum-running circles last night.

According to assertions made by bootleggers, the 40 rum-running craft, laden with cases and kegs of beer, put off in the Detroit river from the Canadian shore, bound for Ecorse, in broad daylight. All the boats were said to have landed their cargoes safely on this side.

Monday afternoon two men attired in overalls lounged carelessly about the deck of a beer laden launch as it slowly ploughed its way up the river.

Passengers on a Windsor ferry boat, observing the launch and its freely displayed cargo of beer cases and cartons, hailed the crew as to its objective.

"Oh, just looking for a good place to run across," was the reply and

Continued on Page Three, Column Six.

HOODED GUARDS BAR ALL ROADS DURING RITUAL

Candidates Take Oath of Allegiance to Order, [illegible] and Country.

MIDNIGHT BARBECUE FESTIVITIES FOLLOW

Weird Rites Held in Oakland County; 8,000 Attend, It Is Estimated.

BY CARL MULLER.

By the lurid light of a cross rising 30 feet into the blackness of the night, 1,000 novices on bended knees swore eternal allegiance to the Ku Klux Klan, Wednesday night, while in the half light cast by an almost continuous display of fireworks thousands of hooded Knights of the Invisible Empire looked on. The Klan officials asserted 11,000 persons were present. To the reporter it appeared as if the crowd might total 8,000.

The ceremonials were conducted in a hollow on a farm of many acres in Oakland county, about 25 miles northeast of Detroit. Over them presided a lean and angular man in a voluminous cloak lined with red, whose features, when the wind brushed his mask aside, were seen to be of an ascetic and almost fanatical cast. He was introduced, together with an emissary from Imperial Wizard Hiram W. Evans, of Atlanta, Georgia, as the "Grand Goblin of the Great Lakes domain." He refused to give his name, and his followers were enjoined to utter neither it, or their own cognomens.

Comprised Three Counties.

Members of the order of mystery were present from the southeastern district of Michigan, comprising Oakland, Macomb and Wayne counties. From sundown until nearly midnight, when the gigantic cross of fire blazed against the horizon line, they arrived in long caravans of automobiles from east, north and west. Every foot of the great field was covered either with parked machines or with the fantastically-robed knights. At strategic points on the highways for miles around, and in fence corners all around the farm, outposts were picketed.

At the farthest outposts they kept alert watch for men who might be county officials. Nearer the scene of the rendezvous, which was said to be the largest ever held in Michigan, they halted all machines and allowed none to pass unless the countersign was given.

Among the vast concourse there were but two persons, both newspapermen, who were "Philistines." These two were permitted to stand at a distance from which they could not hear the mystic ritual. But even so, they were watched closely by hooded knights.

One of the "Philistines" whiled away the time which passed before the hocus pocus began, by listening to the dissertation of a Klansman, who with all the zeal of a new convert talked of the peaceful and law-abiding nature of the order.

Peaceful, But Prepared.

When the peace apostle had finished his harangue, he started toward an outlying fence to do picket duty. As he walked away, he strapped to his waist a 45-caliber army pistol.

In the throng, according to Klan spokesmen, was a delegation from Ann Arbor, among whom were said to be instructors and students at the University of Michigan.

A silence, unbroken save for the occasional hum of a motor on the

Continued on Page Three, Column Seven.

HATTIE MILLER IS JAILED AGAIN

"Underworld Queen," Recently Set Free by Jury, Once More in Law's Clutches.

Hattie Miller, "queen of the underworld," fell into the clutches of the law again early this morning, when deputy sheriffs under the leadership of John McCloud, chief deputy, raided a house-boat moored

Continued on Page Three, Column Five.

Divine Sarah's 'Family' of 100 Dolls Is Sold

Souvenir Hunters Grab Puppets Collected by Bernhardt.

Paris, June 13.—More than 100 dolls, collected by the late Sarah Bernhardt in all parts of the world, were sold at auction Wednesday, for 5,315 francs. This was the last day of the sale of Bernhardt's effects. Most of the buyers were souvenir hunters. The sales Wednesday brought 124,715 francs, making a total for the three days of 302,390 francs.

25-MILE BLAZE SWEEPS TOWNS

Forest Flames Reach, Destroy Homes; Thousands Flee. Women Rescued.

Bangor, Me., June 13.—The woods along the line of the Bangor and Aroostook railroad in Aroostook county are ablaze from Masardis to Smyrna Mills, a distance of 25 miles, and inhabitants of small set-

Continued on Page Three, Column Five.

BULGAR REVOLT FIRES BALKANS

Troops Called to Colors; Reinforcements Are Hurried to Borders by 4 Nations.

Trieste, June 13.—(By United Press.)—Jails of Bulgaria are overflowing with persons arrested during the revolution, a dispatch from Sofia reported Wednesday.

One hundred and two agrarian deputies have been arrested so far. A number fled to the woods. Countless civilians have been taken.

Athens, June 13.—(By United Press.)—Four Balkan states called troops to the colors Wednesday and rushed reinforcements to their borders.

Urgent measures were instituted to prevent the Bulgarian revolt and counter-revolt from spreading.

All Balkans Are Aflame.

Mobilization or thousands of fresh troops and extension of Civil war, reported from Sofia, caused alarm in Belgrade, Bucharest, Athens and Prague.

In Budapest, the Hungarian capital, on the other hand, it was re-

Continued on Page Three, Column One.

SHIP OWNERS DEMAND HELP TO TILT U. S. LID

French Line Officers Demand Help to Tilt Lid in United States.

British Object to American Plan to Extend Water Territorial Limits.

Washington, June 13.—French embassy officials said Wednesday they never had heard of the proposal to station a French warship in New York harbor as a storehouse for crews' wine rations. They added that they were certain no such plan had been considered.

Special to The Free Press.

New York, June 13.—The French steamship line has formally asked the French government to send warships to New York with a supply of wine for French sailors on board French merchant ships in this port, it was learned from an authoritative source Wednesday afternoon.

It was understood this action

Continued on Page Three, Column Three.

YANKS IN CHINA DEMAND U.S. AID

Foreigners Flock to Legations as President Flees, Leaving Nation in Chaos.

Pekin, June 13.—(By the Associated Press.)—President Li Yuan Hung is virtually a prisoner on the railroad at Tien Tsin, where the civil governor has surrounded his train with troops.

Pekin, June 13.—President Li Yuan Hung fled from Pekin to Tien Tsin Wednesday afternoon, fearing an uprising by dissatisfied Chinese troops. Pekin, the capital of northern China, is left without government as a result.

Many foreigners are entering the legations for safety. It is feared that troops, who have not been paid for months, will start rioting and looting. Americans in Shanghai are demanding U. S. protection, declaring their lives and property are in jeopardy.

The situation in Pekin is tense with the possibility of armed revolt by the soldiers, and foreign legations are taking special precautions to protect their nationals.

Deserted at a critical juncture by a majority of his political friends,

Continued on Page Three, Column Two.

$1,000—FREE PRESS OFFERS REWARD FOR ARREST OF BEN PURNELL—$1,000

"KING" BENJAMIN PURNELL.

One thousand dollars will be paid by The Detroit Free Press to the person who will furnish information to the managing editor or the city editor of The Detroit Free Press which will result in the capture of "King" Benjamin Purnell.

The [illegible] of the House of David and self-styled "Seventh Angel" is wanted by the state of Michigan on a criminal warrant charging him with statutory rape.

The Detroit Free Press, which exposed the conditions which have made "King" Ben's "love nest," disguised as a religious colony, a blot on the fair name of the state of Michigan, is determined to bring this alleged attacker of young girls to justice, and offers the reward to any person who will assist in this crusade by giving the tip which will land Purnell behind the bars.

There are no strings to the offer. It does not require "arrest and conviction" of the man who, shielded and aided by powerful influences which sought by every sinister means to block the inquiry started by The Detroit Free Press, is now being sought in the remote corners of the earth, to answer the revolting charges of one of his alleged child victims. The one thousand dollars will be paid, on the arrest of Purnell, to the person who gives the information resulting in such arrest to the managing editor or city editor of The Detroit Free Press. The information must be furnished to The Free Press. This is the only condition.

A telegraph tip, or information delivered over the telephone, by mail or special messenger, will be regarded the same as information delivered in person, and if your telegraphed information that Benjamin Purnell may be found at a certain place results in his arrest, you will promptly receive One Thousand Dollars. If so desired, any such information will be regarded as strictly confidential, and the source kept secret.

If more than one person shall supply the "tip" leading to "King" Ben's hiding place, the payment of the One Thousand Dollars will be left to the decision of Judge Harry J. Dingeman, presiding judge of the circuit courts of Michigan.

The Free Press is offering this reward in the same spirit in which it began the investigation of conditions in the House of David, which was forced to a successful conclusion in the face of determined and unremitting opposition. It desires to see the state purged once and for all of an institution which Judge John E. Sater, of the United States District court, has characterized from the bench as a gigantic fraud, to bring to justice the head of the institution, who in the words of the court has "systematically taught the dissemination of fraud and the commission of perjury," and to end the revolting conditions which the same court said have flourished for twenty years, "unpunished and almost unrebuked."

Following is the official description of Purnell:

Height—Five feet, eight inches.

Weight—165 pounds.

Hair—Brown and straggly, curling at the ends. Never grew more than shoulder length.

Beard—Long, dyed brown, but naturally gray.

Face—Long, straight, prominent nose.

Eyes—Brown, large, deeply sunk, usually round and piercing. Lower lips thick, with hair shaved away below the lip.

Complexion—Fair, tending to sallowness.

Teeth—Has all upper and lower teeth.

Hands—Very small for his size, and soft and of smooth texture. Purnell never did any work.

Mannerisms—Cannot sit still without fidgeting or jerking his hands. When he talks he frequently strokes his chin with his right hand.

Clothing—All of his suits were made at the House of David tailor shops, and bore no labels. He always wore a celluloid collar, and no necktie.

Shoes—Brown or white, as it was against the faith to wear black clothes or shoes.

Habits—Never smoked, but frequently chewed tobacco.

LATEST WIRE FLASHES

BALTIC RESUMES VOYAGE.

Liverpool, June 13. — The White Star line steamer Baltic, which struck submerged wreckage last Sunday on her voyage to New York and put into Liverpool for repairs, sailed for New York at midnight tonight.

RULER'S MOTHER DEAD.

San Salvador, June 13.—Dona Aurelia Quinonez, mother of President Quinonez, died tonight. All public entertainments have been suspended.

IRISH HEAR U. S. BISHOP.

Cork, June 13.—At the annual conference of the Irish Methodist church today Bishop Thomas Nicholson, of Chicago, fraternal delegate of the board of bishops of the Methodist Episcopal church of the United States, was among the speakers.

13 Workers Hurt By Falling Roof

Beaumont, Texas, June 13.—(By United Press.)—Thirteen workmen were injured, several seriously, when the roof of a 55,000-barrel steel storage tank on the Magnolia petroleum farm at Spindle Top, caved in Wednesday. All ambulances in Beaumont were called to the scene and rushed the injured to hospitals here. A checkup shows that every member of the gang, which was engaged in finishing the tank, was hurt.

Mother, 21, Saved At River's Brink

Leaving her 4-year-old baby asleep and alone, Mrs. Eva Moss, 21 years old, 487 Selden avenue, started for the Detroit river late Wednesday night, planning to end her life because, she said, her husband had left her after their first marital quarrel.

She was rescued, just as she was about to leap off the pier at the foot of Woodward avenue, by Patrolman James McGuire. After being questioned, she went home to her baby.

Safety Certificates Give Real Protection

Free Inspection Demand Increases as Drive of Police Becomes Drastic.

Drive with a Safety Certificate in your pocket!

If you are an automobile owner or driver visit the first available Free Inspection station—the Green and White signs displayed in all sections of the [illegible] reveal their location—submit your car for a Free Inspection by expert mechanics, and then secure a Safety Certificate by having all mechanical defects in your machine adjusted or repaired.

Today this advice is most valuable to all motorists of Detroit, for today the Safety Certificate has become a most important feature of the police drive to bring about an improvement in traffic conditions.

Two weeks ago the police department started a campaign that is to go on until all of the automobiles using the streets of Detroit are officially recognized as cars mechanically sound. Yesterday, at the emphatic order of Police Commissioner Frank H. Croul, the police turned this inspection campaign into a drastic drive aimed at operators of defective machines, reckless drivers, speeders, and at all violators of the Detroit traffic ordinance.

Right now is the time for all motorists to be absolutely certain as to the actual condition of their automobiles. Right now is the time to know positively that brakes will work in an emergency, and not

Continued on Page Three, Column Five.

Girl in Trousers Sought as Pal In Holdup Gang

Bob-Haired Maid Is Chauffeur for New York Brigand Band.

New York, June 13.—Police Wednesday sought a bobbed-haired girl, who, attired in male garb, acted as chauffeur for two bandits in a Brooklyn drug store robbery Tuesday night.

Sitting calmly at the wheel of a big automobile with a cigarette between her lips, the girl waited while her companions entered Harry Soladar's drug store, lined Soladar and a dozen customers up against the wall at the point of a gun and gathered in $571.

As the bandits rushed from the store, she started the car and by the time they had tumbled in, had it flying up the street at breakneck speed.

The Detroit Free Press

WEATHER Cloudy

VOL. 92, NO. 234. — DETROIT, MICHIGAN, THURSDAY, MAY 19, 1927.—TWENTY-EIGHT PAGES — PRICE: THREE CENTS.

MAY 19, 1927:

Disgruntled farmer, who had just lost his farm to a bank, plants explosives in the Bath school, killing 37 children.

CONSPIRATORS SOUGHT IN KILLING OF 37 CHILDREN

WITNESS TELLS HOW 'KING' BEN BETRAYED HER

Jersey Woman, at Colony for Year With Husband, Describes 'Purification.'

FORCED TO MAKE HOME AT SHILOH, SHE SAYS

Still on Stand Awaiting Examination by State When Court Adjourns.

BY JAMES P. POWERS,
Free Press Staff Correspondent.

Benton Harbor, Mich., May 18.—Another of the alleged feminine dupes of "King" Benjamin Purnell—married before she came into the colony—today took the stand here and timorously narrated the "blood purification" rites that the cult leader persuaded her, she said, that such was the way to immortality.

The witness was Mrs. Ruth Swanson, Orange, New Jersey. Her husband, Christian I. Swanson, also was a witness today. She said she left the colony after living there about a year in 1913 and 1914. She was 18 years old then, and after being jostled from her husband sent to live in Shiloh, the building that frequently in the past has been described as "Benjamin's harem."

Same Old Story.

The story of the "purification ceremony" is not new in stories of the mysterious doings of the now red-tail leader, whose colony base conducted in the state is successful in its attempts to remove that it was a place of immorality. But it has never been told before in such a clear-cut, dramatic fashion as Mrs. Swanson explained it in a low voice today.

Mrs. Swanson started her sensational story by describing it as the one a bond of girls were duped into the colony—from high land, where she understood they had been shunted in an attempt to help them from a pending investigation. Federal authorities were advised to make slaves and fraudulent cult usage complaints against the colony at that time.

Red First Floor Room.

She explained that while the second floor of Shiloh was occupied mostly by young girls and Benjamin, there being a few older men, there was on the first floor, near the property office in which she worked by her. Asked if she had ever visited the rooms upstairs, she said:

"I was told to go up one night, I always kept the door of my room locked so it was near the entrance to the upstairs, but when the back door was opened, I was usually at 5 o'clock, my Aunt Myrtle Taft (Benjamin's alleged brother-in-law), who was found in the room. Continued on Page Three, Column Five.

THRONGS GET RUM PERMITS

Score Waiting When Office Opens; Clerks Are Kept Busy During Day.

BY RUSSELL WHELAN.

The boys and girls blazed the trail to the great Ontario oasis yesterday.

Continental agents collected $1,950 in two dollar bills during the day for 734 import purchase permits.

Anticipate Bigger Rush.

The tide started with a rush, but drained later in the day. While the fund may have been disappointing to some, it was expected by the officials who found plenty to do. The rush anticipate a bigger rush on the day, for the sale of two-dollar high and 25-cent permits is planned on the surface as it was extended. The Woodward office sold 456 permits, which opened at 35 Broadmead road, at 3 p. m. The Butler office will be open from 10 a. m. until 5 p. m.

Main roads to seven were in line at Windsor from 8 a. m. until the public land office on the Water avenue, when the crowd surged into the buffer room offer opened at 8:30 a. m. on Windsor avenue, Windsor, and could be surprised of indignant patrons of the Moderation League of West-on Ontario.

Has Edge on Others.

Appreciatively enough, Mr. Davis is secretary. He has worked for years officially, to bring back the old boost from the other hand the attempt made in the closet to an Ontario-wide victory to make parts for these cars for five years.

E. H. Martin, assistant to the manager of the Detroit branch of the Ford Motor company, who was present, took no part in the discussion. He refused to confirm or deny the statement of Kraus.

However, Mr. Kolbe said he was informed on good authority that the Ford company would discontinue making the Model T about June 1, and would not not production of a new four-cylinder, gear-shift car about July 1.

Indications that there is to be no abandonment of the Ford business have been received from town but many weeks, but rather an increased activity instead of curtailment, was given yesterday when representatives of the Ford company called upon the hearing before the council on the rerouting of streets.

WHERE FARMER'S VENGEANCE KILLED 42

Crowds wait tearfully while rescue crews comb ruins seeking bodies of missing school children. Picture shows workers moving part of the roof of the wrecked school to facilitate their work.

CHANGE IN FORD MODELS DENIED

Company Spokesman Makes Statement After Reading Council Rumor.

A denial that any change in the Ford car was contemplated was issued by William J. Cameron, editor of the Dearborn Independent and spokesman for the Ford Motor company, yesterday, after Mr. Cameron had read a statement by Theodore J. Kolbe, secretary of the Detroit police commission, before the common council, that he had been informed that the company would put out a new model July 1.

"We got more information about the plans of the company from the outside than we do from within," said Mr. Cameron. "We have no announcement to make, and, so far as I know, there is no change to be made in the car. It seems hardly likely a change would be made with 10,000,000 of the Model T cars on the roads already and business going along as usual, if a little slow. But business has been slow in all lines."

Purchase is Approved.

Mr. Kolbe, appearing before the council in the absence of the department, urged the council to approve the purchase of all Ford cars for police scout work, to replace the present Fords. The purchase which will involve an expenditure of $26,745, was informally approved by the council.

"Police Commissioner William P. Rutledge, who appeared before the council to approve Mr. Kolbe's request, said in these new cars on hand and $10,000 worth of Ford parts, which would have to be sold at a loss, he said, if another make of car was purchased to replace the present arrival. Bert. The scout cars are used for chasing speeders and for emergency calls.

During the discussion of the gun-powder purchases, Councilman William P. Bradley asked if it were not better that the Ford company completely discontinuing the present Model T car and making a new car. Martin B. Hanna, vice-president and manager of the Detroit Motor Sales, Ford dealers, from whom the cars will be purchased, replied:

Rumor is Afoot.

"Yes, we have information that the present model is to be discontinued. We are not as king to sell these cars to the city to get rid of them, but because they will give a better service and do a better job at low cost. The Ford Motor company will continue to make parts for these cars for five years."

DEAD AT BATH

Emory H. Huyck, superintendent of schools.
Nelson McFarren, 70, a citizen.
Glen Smith, 40, postmaster of Bath.
Andrew Kehoe, 50, Bath.
Hazel Weatherbee, 20, teacher; home in Howard City.
Dorie Johns, 10, daughter of Ira Johns.
Clarence McFarren, 12, son of Wendall McFarren.
Carlyle Geisenhaver, 10, son of Walter Geisenhaver.
George Hall, 10, child of George Hall.
Willo Hall, 12, child of George Hall.
Richard Richardson, 14, son of Hall.
Don Ewing, 17, son of Simon Ewing.
Iola Harte, 13.
Vivian Harte, 12, children of Eugene Harte.
Lemoyne Woodman, 9, son of Harold Woodman.
Bobby Corcoran, 9, son of Frank Corcoran.
Earl Chapman, 12, son of Frank Chapman.
Russell Chapman, 10, son of Clarence Chapman.
Herman Bergin, 12, son of John Bergin.
Lloyd Zimmerman, 12.
George Zimmerman, 10, sons of Orla Zimmerman.
Emma Nichols, 12, daughter of Henry Nichols.
Elizabeth Witchell, 10, daughter of Roscoe Witchell.
Lucille Witchell, 10, daughter of Roy Witchell.
Catherine Foote, 11, daughter of Ben Foote.
Loren Hunter, 11, son of James Hunter.
Floyd Burnett, 12, son of Fred Burnett.
Arnold Bauerle, 8, son of Henry Bauerle.
Percy Hart, 12, son of Eugene Hart.
Robert Hart.
Marjorie Fritz.
Robert Hall.
Thelma McDonald.
Amelia Bromudt.
Robert Bromudt.
Emerson Metcoff.
Robert Dunn.
Glen Harte.
Earl Ewing.
One unidentified boy.

THE INJURED.

Bath, Mich., May 18.—(A. P.)—A partial list of the injured in the school explosion here follows:
Ardua Wilson, Nina Matson, Lillian Reed, Ruth Nichols, Lee Reiser, Helen Komm, Josephine Ercland, Donald Hoffman, Lester Stowell, Evans Duggins, Sam Eschpiuth, Earl Chapman, Gale Steebleton, Otila Nichols, Florence Hunter, Ava Sweet, Martha Richardson, F. M. Fritz, Ida Delen, Lee Mast, Steve Steavisky, Celia Zovastosky, Pauline Nichols.

Caught Smuggling Drug to Brother

Louis Hammontree, 34 years old, is charged, he attempted to smuggle morphine in a tube of toothpaste to his brother, Eddie, in the county jail.

The drug was discovered by Peter Schlaefer, assistant turnkey, and Henry Mulgrey, turnkey of the jail. Both brothers now are being held for violation of the drug act, the sheriff's office reported.

HUERTA NAMED AS SMUGGLER

Mexican Ex-President, 4 Others Charged With Plot to Run Arms.

Tucson, Ariz., May 18—(A. P.)—Adolfo De la Huerta, former provisional president of Mexico, and four other persons were charged here today with exporting arms and munitions in violation of a presidential proclamation and an act of congress. The charge was filed by United States department of justice agents.

Two of the five were arrested and are being held in the Pima county jail here. They are Louis Oxyoo, alias M. Espinosa and Francisco Partido, alias Herre. In addition to De la Huerta, Alfonso Gomez Morentin, of Los Angeles, and Enrique Brescada, of San Antonio, Tex., were named.

Denies All Knowledge.

Los Angeles, May 18.—(A. P.)—Adolfo De la Huerta, former provisional president of Mexico at his home here today, denied he had been involved in attempts to transport arms into Mexico. He said he had no knowledge of charges filed against him and four others at Tucson, Ariz.

PARLEY AVERTS PERIL OF P. M. STRIKE, RUMOR

Nine-Hour Conference Believed to Have Found Basis of Agreement.

NO DEFINITE WORD IS FORTHCOMING YET

Men Ready for Immediate Walkout, Unions Report; May Quit Today.

Flint, May 18.—Unless notification of a change of plans is received by employes of the Flint division of the Pere Marquette railroad before 6 a. m. Thursday the men will be tied up by a general strike, Clarence McNulty, secretary of the Brotherhood of Railway Clerks, said tonight. "We have received instructions from the union leaders and unless we are notified that there is some plan to arbitrate with the company officials we will go on strike at the scheduled time."

Shortly after midnight this morning, after President Frank H. Alfred of the Pere Marquette and officials of the various railroad men's unions had been in conference for nine hours, indications pointed to a likelihood that the threatened strike on the system had been averted, at least temporarily, it was learned from authoritative sources.

It was indicated that a possible basis for settlement had been reached, although the conference was still in session by an effort to prevent the tie-up voted yesterday by the eight unions involved when they failed to reach an agreement with the company after negotiations during the last three months.

However, reports which appear to be authentic, point to the fact that the railroad employes would not yet to be raised, but there was reason to believe the result is that companies retained their efforts up to the last moment.

The settlement the company was seeking against, is highly optimistic that the drive would be a success, urging the men all to continue their efforts up to the last moment.

Victory Dinner Tonight.

With today as the final day of the campaign being conducted for a $4,000,000 women's building fund, officials in charge of the drive were confident last night the end of the day would find the goal reached. Some of the workers went so far as to prophesy that the $4,000,000 mark would be exceeded.

A victory dinner tonight at the Book-Cadillac hotel, was indicated officially in an announcement. Yesterday afternoon The Free Press was informed by the general committee that it was not yet to be raised, but there was reason to believe the companies retained their willingness to proceed with the withdrawal if an agreement is not soon reached.

Last Hour Effort.

With the arrival here yesterday of Samuel E. Winslow, chairman of the federal board of mediation and arbitration, it at first appeared that the breach between the men and the company was wider than it was thought to be, but Winslow declared he was here unofficially. He said he intended to extend the benefit of his experience in similar strike cases to both sides, and probably would not act as mediator in the present discussion.

The conference between officers and the union officials began yesterday at 3 o'clock, after the announcement of the strike vote had been made public. It was indicated that the meeting, held in Alfred's office in the Pere Marquette building, at Third avenue and West Fort street, was called in a last effort to reach some equitable agreement in the protracted discussion and thus forestall the impending strike.

At six o'clock last night the conference between the men and the company officials were resumed to point to the possibility of conciliation between the men and the company. At the close of the afternoon session, however, Alfred said he had nothing to announce and refused to comment on the conference or its purposes.

Wages and Conditions.

Better working conditions and not wages alone, are said to be at the bottom of the unions' dissatisfaction. The men were recently granted an increase of seven and one-half per cent, but have demanded, also, that to be made retro-active to the date on which employes of several other railroads were granted similar raises. It is understood. The $5 fine that Intro-man Henry D. Strash attempted to serve a warrant on him, after Murphy failed to appear in court May 16 to answer to a parking violation. Murphy took the patrolman to the office of C. C. Dawn, an attorney, who at that time claimed Murphy's name was Clark.

Strash told the court that when he attempted to serve the warrant, Tuesday, Murphy denied his identity, still claiming his name was "Clark."

Murphy's home is at 83 Beverly avenue and he has offices at 713 Hammond building.

The $5 fine was imposed in lieu of the usual $5, according to the judge, because of alleged abusive language directed at the officer at the time of Murphy's arrest.

BLUES, BLACKS SCORE POINTS IN MIMIC WAR

Defenders' Flagship Sunk, Plane Carrier Langley Believed Out of Fight.

Newport, R. I., May 18.—(A. P.)—The "sinking" of the battleship Pennsylvania, flagship of the defending blue navy, a spectacular airplane "battle" over this city, headquarters of the blue defense forces, and "bombardment" of several vital coast defense fortifications in the chain along the southern New England coast, were highlights of today's fleet maneuvers between the units of 75-mile stretch of coast between Chatham, Mass., on Cape Cod, and the mouth of the Connecticut river.

Early tonight the war umpires had not announced the outcome of the torpedoing of the black aircraft carrier, Langley, a defense coup which came earlier in the day.

News of the sinking of the Pennsylvania came as a surprise to defense headquarters from the navy destroyer Lawrence. The Lawrence advised headquarters here that she fired six torpedoes at the big carrier at a range of 8,000 yards. She claimed the Langley was put out of commission with two direct hits.

SCHOOL BLAST SLAYS MADMAN AND 4 ADULTS

More Than Score of Injured in Hospitals in Critical Condition.

SLAYER WATCHES AS PUPILS HURL TO DEATH

Telephone Wires Cut Before Dynamite Is Set Off.

Lansing, May 18.—(A. P.)—An investigation by state police and the state fire marshal to determine whether Andrew Kehoe may have had accomplices in mining the Bath consolidated school, is to be launched.

State police said it would have been difficult for one man to do the wiring and plant the explosive. They pointed out that there was enough explosive to fill a small truck. It would have taken weeks of tedious work for one man to accomplish the task of placing it and wiring the connections by which it was detonated.

The state officers believed there was a possibility that other persons might have been implicated with Kehoe in a plot to destroy the schoolhouse, when it was unoccupied, and that he took advantage of his preparations to set off the charge today, when more than 200 pupils were in the building.

By Free Press Staff Correspondent.

Bath, Mich., May 18.—Seeking vengeance against society in general for the foreclosure of a mortgage on his farm, Andrew Kehoe, a childless farmer, set off a blast of dynamite, which wrecked part of the consolidated school here, just before 10 o'clock this morning, killing 37 children, five adults, including himself, and injuring more than a score of other pupils.

Under the glare of searchlights, state police and volunteer workers continued the search until it was definitely established all children reported missing were in morgues, hospitals or their homes. Forty-four seriously injured are in Lansing hospitals and between 40 and 60 children suffering minor injuries are in their homes here.

Dramatic Package Mailed.

That Kehoe's death orgy grew out of his connection with the school was indicated this evening. Continued on Page 2, Column 2.

WIND INJURES 18 IN INDIANAPOLIS

Gale Sweeps Through City at 80 Miles an Hour.

Indianapolis, May 18.—(A. P.)—Ten persons were in hospitals and eight others were injured as a result of an 80-mile-an-hour wind which swept through Indianapolis tonight. Police and ambulances were kept busy answering emergency calls.

Most of the injured were cut by flying glass, while other persons were injured when a gospel tent blew down.

FORMER DETROIT SOLON PAYS FINE

Frank E. Murphy Assessed for Parking Violation.

Frank E. Murphy, former state representative from Wayne county, was fined $10 for prohibited parking and an additional $5 for attempting to evade court, Tuesday, by Judge John M. McKay in the traffic court.

COURT AND FOG DELAY FLIGHT

Paris Dash by Bellanca Plane Enjoined; Weather Holds Back Byrd, Lindbergh.

Special to Free Press and Chicago Tribune.
New York, May 18.—Capt. Charles Lindbergh late tonight was prepared to take off for Paris from Roosevelt field in the Ryan monoplane, the Spirit of St. Louis, tomorrow morning. Charts showed good weather prevailing over the Atlantic except along the coast from Cape Cod to Newfoundland. If the fog raises so Lindbergh can get his bearings from Cape Race, N. F., he will get off at dawn.

Officers of the company say they have not yet been informed officially members of the Bellanca Columbia, of any additional members or backers of the new syndicate which was announced, at Clarence's private residence, and probably would not act as mediator in the present discussion.

The conference between officers and the union officials began yesterday at 3 o'clock, after the announcement of the strike vote had been made public. It was indicated that the meeting, held in Alfred's office in the Pere Marquette building, at Third avenue and West Fort street, was called in a last effort to reach some equitable agreement in the protracted discussion and thus forestall the impending strike.

At six o'clock last night the conference between the men and the company officials were resumed to point to the possibility of conciliation between the men and the company. At the close of the afternoon session, however, Alfred said he had nothing to announce and refused to comment on the conference or its purposes.

MR. AND MRS. DODGE HOLD CONFERENCE

Couple in Detroit Notwithstanding Contrary Reports.

Although Mr. and Mrs. Horace E. Dodge were both reported as being out of the city on Tuesday it became known yesterday that they were in conference at that time at their home, 17480 Jefferson avenue, Grosse Pointe Village, presumably in the hope of reaching an agreement over their recent domestic difficulties.

The fact of Dodge's presence in Detroit was a surprise to many of his friends. It having been supposed that he was in New York. The conference between the estranged young couple followed the filing Monday by attorneys for Mrs. Dodge of affidavits of default and regularity in her divorce suit. The papers merely certified that Dodge had failed to contest the action within the specified time after the filing of his wife's declaration and paved the way for the announcement of the decrees to Mrs. Dodge by default.

Wind Delays Start to Paris.

New York, May 18.—(A. P.)—The three monoplanes which it is hoped will fly some 3,500 miles to Paris did not yet off the ground today. Prevented from leaving for fliers, the planes were kept to the hangars by winds which made test flights inadvisable. Inclement weather prevented the final unofficial tests of the Fokker in which Byrd, Noville and Acosta are to fly. And Lindbergh's Ryan stayed in the hangar because it was unready to leave on the shortest notice and there were no further preparations to be made. Lindbergh sent to the Curtiss Bay for lunch with Theodore Roosevelt and received a letter for delivery to Ambassador Herrick in Paris.

Late today the weather bureau dispelled the last hope that the hop-off might begin early tomorrow morning.

Coliseum Cross Again Is Raised

Rome, May 18.—(A. P.)—After an absence of 45 years the cross was restored this afternoon to the Colosseum, for which thousands of martyrs hallowed with the blood during Roman times.

Queen Helena and Princess Giovanni presided at the ceremony of the unveiling of a large wooden cross above a stone black altar. Premier Mussolini had ordered to be restored to the center of the arena, from which it was taken in 1882 because of a wave of anti-clericalism.

At the moment of the unveiling a chorus of 100 voices intoned the Palestrinian hymn, while several scores of pigeons were loosed and the assemblages knelt in prayer.

WOMEN'S DRIVE NEARING GOAL

With One Day to Go Four Million Dollar Fund Is Now Well in Sight.

With today as the final day of the campaign being conducted for a $4,000,000 women's building fund, officials in charge of the drive were confident last night the end of the day would find the goal reached. Some of the workers went so far as to prophesy that the $4,000,000 mark would be exceeded.

Victory Dinner Tonight.

A victory dinner tonight at the Book-Cadillac hotel, was indicated officially in an announcement. Yesterday afternoon The Free Press was informed by the general committee that it was not yet to be raised, but there was reason to believe the companies retained their willingness to proceed with the withdrawal if an agreement is not soon reached.

Schoolboy's Prank Brings Death to 9

Berlin, May 18.—(A. P.)—Nine persons were killed, 21 seriously injured and 61 slightly injured at Cassel when a brake was released on a Ford bus down a hill. Some of those killed were women.

Finding a crowded tramcar at the foot of a hill by an incline momentarily blocking his path, the driver of the bus applied his brake and went out to converse with the tramcar conductor for a moment. In his absence a schoolboy crept into the bus and in a spirit of mischief pressed the brake release. The heavy car started rolling and, soon gathering momentum, crashed into an iron scaffolding, turned over on its side and fell upon the crowded street.

TWO FLOORS—ONE ADMISSION.
BEAUTIFUL BLUE LANTERN
Island Lake opens tomorrow evening, Straight out Grand River. JUAN GOLEKETTY IN PERSON.

Ask Me Another
SENIOR and JUNIOR
On Page 13

Green Invited To Club Dinner

Mt. Clemens, May 18.—Governor Green is expected to be the guest of honor at the Macomb County Republican club dinner at Bowen Thursday evening. Reservations for the dinner number 120. Two men who have voted the ticket for the past 52 years also will be special guests. They are Valentine Haas, of Sterling; Edward M. Pearch of Richmond; John Barber over Fred E. Porter, Dieco, C. H. Dodock, New Baltimore; Frank B. Roberts, Silas P. Spier and William L. Brake of Mt.

DANCE CLOISSELARING TONIGHT.
McKINNEY'S COTTON PICKERS.
THE PIER—DANCING NIGHTLY.

PEOPLE who have time to read in the morning are better able to entertain the proposition set forth in your Want Ad? They read the morning paper religiously—the evening paper occasionally. That's why Free Press Want Ads are especially producing more, better and quicker results—results that accomplish that which the advertiser wants accomplished.

Free Press Want Ads Produce Best Cost Less

May 22, 1927:

He was born in Detroit, and raised on W. Forest. His mother, Evangeline, taught at Cass Tech. So Detroit claimed Charles Lindbergh as its own.

"He's Our Boy!," column six.

The Detroit Free Press

DETROIT, MICHIGAN, SUNDAY, MAY 22, 1927.—136 PAGES — PRICE: TEN CENTS

WEATHER: Probably Showers

LINDBERGH, IN PARIS, ACCLAIMED WORLD HERO

AIR HERO AND HIS MOTHER

MRS. EVANGELINE L. LINDBERGH AND HER SON IN FRONT OF HIS PLANE IN NEW YORK A WEEK AGO.

AVIATOR DROPS TO SLEEP WHEN VICTORY'S WON

Lands Amid Cheering Thousands as New York-to-Paris Dash Is Completed.

MAKES EPOCHAL TRIP IN ONLY 33 1-2 HOURS

France Gives Rousing Welcome to Dauntless American, Who Wins $25,000 Prize.

JOYOUS TEARS WET HER EYES; SON TRIUMPHS

Mrs. Lindbergh Weeps for First Time on Learning Boy Landed Safe.

'WHAT CAN I SAY BUT I'M HAPPY, GRATEFUL?'

Tired by Long Vigil, Mother Receives Flood of Congratulations.

HE'S OUR BOY! DETROIT CRIES

City Celebrates Riotously; Plans Grand Homecoming.

FLIER'S LIFE LIKE FICTION

Public Had Come to Expect Much of Youth Before He Made "Hop."

ESTHER HANSEL SLATED AS CULT HEARING STAR

BULLETIN

BATH BURIES 17 VICTIMS OF MAD MURDERER

DIVORCE DELAY INTERRUPTS HER WEDDING PLANS

MISS BELLE GREEN

100-PASSENGER PLANES NEAR, FORD ASSERTS

G. O. P. MEETING MAY COME HERE

WORLD SPEED RECORD MADE BY SEAPLANE

LOOMIS FACES TRIAL MONDAY

DETROIT HAILS ITS "KID"

LINDBERGH'S LOG

FIVE AIRSHIP FLIGHTS MADE PREVIOUSLY ACROSS OCEAN

JULY 8, 1927:

Henry Ford's apology to Jews capped several years of charges that the Dearborn Independent, which Ford controlled, had printed anti-semitic articles.

"Ford Admits Jew Charges Are Not True," column eight.

JULY 31, 1928:

Dodge and Chrysler merge.

The Detroit Free Press

WEATHER — Rain, Warmer

MICHIGAN'S GREATEST NEWSPAPER

FINAL EDITION

DETROIT, MICHIGAN, TUESDAY, JULY 31, 1928—TWENTY-FOUR PAGES • PRICE: THREE CENTS

DODGE VOTE ASSURES THIRD GREATEST MOTOR COMPANY

THREE DIE IN TRAFFIC; 4 INJURED

Hit-and-Run Driver Confesses Hitting Child, Mother.

2ND MOTORIST HELD PRISONER

Woman Autoist Who Defies Court Gets Reprimand.

Traffic claimed the lives of three Detroiters yesterday, including that of a small child, and sent four others to hospitals.

One driver is held as a police prisoner at Receiving hospital while the fatal crash in which his car was involved is investigated, another has left on the downtown roads.

The dead were:
Mrs. Gladys Larr, 29 years old, 4072 Second boulevard.
Elijah Jones, 50 years old, 8716 Cameron avenue.
Pete Millcaglio, 8 years old, 2140 Chatham street.

Those injured are:
Daniel Larr, 11 years old, 4417 Second boulevard.
Albert Jarrett, 28 years old, 3800 Lowell street.
Fannie Butler, 29 years old, 3808 Lowell street.

Child, Playing Run Over.

The Milceaglio child died in Receiving hospital at 2:30 p.m. yesterday as the result of injuries received two hours earlier when he was run over by a truck in front of his home.

The boy, playing with two other children and a smaller brother, riding in a new express wagon. His brother pushed him down an inclined driveway in the path of the rear wheel of the truck, and the boy was crushed.

Cyril E. Lambert, 33 years old, of 1909 Howick avenue, driver of the truck, was released after making a statement. He said he did not see the children playing and stopped only when he heard the
Continued on Page 2, Column 1

TORAL TOOL OF PLOTTERS

Mexican Police Say Others Drove Him Into Frenzy.

Mexico City, July 30. (A.P.)—Jose de Leon Toral, slayer of General Alvaro Obregon, was held in his crime by a belief his conduct was in accord with religious problems of Mexico, a police statement today said.

That belief was fostered by a Catholic man, Concepcion Acevedo de la Lata, and a man named Manuel Trejo, who fled after the assassination. He was, says the document, assisted in Toral's presence that the difficulties of the Catholic church be solved by the deaths of President Calles, General Obregon and the patriarch of the so-called Mexican Catholic church, Trejo, by Toral's own admission, furnished the gun.

Other persons not named are also slated to have worked Toral, by suggestion, into a religious frenzy.

Statement to Press.

The youthful assassin in a confession to newspapermen today asserted no one else was responsible and particularly absolved Luis Morones and other labor leaders from the intent blame.

Calls Killing "Good Deed."

Although he denied that he had revealed his intention, to anyone he admitted that he went to mass and confession by a priest named Jimenez at a private residence in Mexico City a few hours before the slaying.

"I did not confess that I intended doing Toral said, because you only confess sin, and the killing of Obregon was a good deed and not a sin. You do not confess good deeds."

Replying to another question Toral said:
"I will not make any defense in court. I have no defense. I am tranquil. I expect to die and to go to heaven."

ROBBERS DRUG DOG TO LOOT PLACE

Special to The Free Press.
Flint, July 30. William Fraser, proprietor of a gasoline station one mile west of here, reported to officers today that burglars had drugged his German police dog, which guards the place, and escaped with auto accessories and confections valued at $150. The dog is always vicious at night, he said. The man noted a peculiar odor which permeated the place this morning. Entrance was gained by jimmying the door.

'YOU THE GUY?' ASKS LEVINE, THEN FISTS FLY

'Twas a Dull Eve at Deauville Casino' Till Charlie, Mabel and Editor Met.

Deauville, July 30. A near riot started in the fashionable Deauville casino early this morning when Charlie Levine, owner of the Come of the Ocean plane, and his aeronautical protege, Miss Mabel Boll, the "diamond queen," encountered Erskine Gwynne, Vanderbilt scion who passes his time in Paris editing the snappy monthly review called The Boulevardier.

"You the guy who edits The Boulevardier and responsible for the dirty cracks taken at me?" snarled Levine, referring to the unkindly wisecracks in the columns of the review which caused many snickers in the Paris smart set.

"Yes, I'm the guy. What about it?" came back Gwynne calmly.

"Just that!" shouted Charlie, landing his left on the debonair editor's jaw.

The sudden fisticuffs dropped a sensation into the dull evening at the casino bar. Society women, millionaires and sportsmen rushed up to separate the pair.

When the air cleared, Mabel, sparkling with diamonds as usual, took Charlie's arm gently and led him home.

SMITH OPPOSED BY M'CORMICK

Former National Chairman's Paper to Repudiate Candidate.

Harrisburg, Pa., July 30. (A.P.)—Opposition of Vance C. McCormick, former Democratic national chairman to Governor Smith as the Democratic presidential nominee is crystallized in an editorial to be carried in tomorrow's editions of the Harrisburg Patriot, which McCormick publishes.

The editorial expresses Smith for his inability even as governor of New York and his recent declaration in the Houston convention for modification of the prohibition laws, and asserts Governor Smith's belated telegram to his party's convention at Houston was a contradiction and repudiation of his party's platform.

"Mr. McCormick, as chairman of the Democratic national committee in 1916, directed President Wilson's campaign for re-election. Subsequently he was appointed chairman of the war trade board and a member of the peace commission. Four years ago he supported William Gibbs McAdoo in his fight against Smith at the New York convention.

The Patriot supported anti-Smith delegates to the Houston convention at the last primaries.

White Interprets Record.

New York, July 30. (A.P.)—William Allen White, editor of the Emporia, Kas., Gazette, tonight made public the results of the two weeks' study made by him of the New York Assembly record of Governor Smith as it affects the saloon and the allies of the saloon, made by him as assemblyman during the first dozen years of his political career.

The record shows, Mr. White says, that as a member of the assembly, Governor Smith favored the old-time "wide open, untrammeled, unregulated saloon," and voted against measures introduced for the purpose of putting restrictions upon it.

"It is inconceivable," White said, "that Smith has not changed his mind since he left the assembly. But the record is the record built in the days of his youth. It is on record before being viewed as to beliefs. That Governor Smith today is the kind of man that made that assembly record. But I am an assembly woman would consider that record and make Smith remake it if it could.

"Governor Smith has done many splendid things since then. He has grown in power and grace. But the record stands. His answer to it should not be an alibi and, lacking repudiation, the record stands as a foreshadowing portent of what may be expected from Governor Smith in the White House. I am, aware from him, now that he has the nomination of a major party, would seem to be necessary at the outset in this campaign."

Sure of South.

Hampton Bays, N.Y., July 30. (A.P.)—Governor Smith let down the bars on political discussions while he is vacationing at this long enough today to pass the word, that, as the Democratic presidential nominee, he is not worried about the south.

Although he had held a dozen reporters who accompanied him here that a vacation lid would be kept on political he commented briefly on the southern situation for the first time since his nomination, but until he had been prodded by the newspaper men. They had tried without much success to draw him out on a number of things Continued on Page 2, Column 4

Floods Inundate Siberian Villages

Moscow, July 30. (A.P.)—More than 50 villages in the Amur province of Siberia have been inundated as a result of the disastrous floods of the last few days. Blagoveschensk, capital of the province, is partly flooded. Railway lines have been washed out and much material damage has been done. The number of casualties is not reported.

AZARA HUNT IS ORDERED BY ALFONSO

All Spanish Vessels Aid Search For Detroit Ship.

FEAR FOR SAFETY OF CREW GROWS

Reported Sighting of Craft Not Yet Confirmed.

New York, July 30. (A.P.)—Fears for the safety of the Detroit-owned racing yacht Azara, which has failed to arrive in Santander, Spain, were expressed today by seamen, believers in a century old tradition that should-draft vessels, such as the Azara, are unseaworthy.

On the eve of the start of the race to Spain July 7, part of the Azara's crew deserted because of this superstition.

Boat Built in 1904.

The Azara, built in 1904, was the smallest boat entered in the class A or larger boat division. She is a three-master, manned by a professional and amateur crew, in charge of her owners, George J. and Francis E. Pabst, brothers of Detroit. They sailed the boat to New York from Detroit, through the Great Lakes up the St. Lawrence and down the Atlantic coast.

The yacht, designed by A. Cary Smith, is 113 feet over all and 85 feet water line, with extreme breadth of 23.4 feet and draft of 5.10 feet. The Kleen, winner of the race, had a draft of 15.13 feet.

Only Craft Missing.

The Azara is the only boat unaccounted for. All crafts in both classes, except the tiny Rofa, have been accounted for. The Rofa was dismasted at sea and her crew, including Mrs. William Rose, of Continued on Page 3, Column 3

OPERATE TO SAVE BRENNAN'S LIFE

Surgeons Act in Emergency as Illinoisan Sinks.

Chicago, July 30. (A.P.)—George E. Brennan, Democratic National committeeman from Illinois, was in a serious condition at a hospital here tonight with an infection which followed the extraction of two teeth. An infection of the lung has developed, lessening his vitality. Three surgeons and two physicians have been in attendance for two days.

An emergency operation was performed late tonight at the John B. Murphy hospital by Dr. Karl Meyer. After the operation Mr. Brennan's condition was reported as "fair." But still precarious.

The last sacraments of the Catholic church were given Mr. Brennan tonight.

Before the operation, physicians announced the Democratic leader was in a "very grave" condition. Mrs. Brennan, his daughter Mary, and Joseph J. Gill, a brother-in-law, remained at the hospital through the night.

Until last Thursday Mr. Brennan had been in good health and daily held conferences with political associates regarding the .... of Governor Alfred E. Smith, whom he visited a month ago.

14-MILE SWIM IS NEW RECORD OF 9-YEAR-OLD

Chester, Pa., July 30. (A.P.)—Johnny "Freckles" Levine, Jr., Philadelphia's 9-year-old swimming prodigy, swam the Delaware river from Philadelphia to Chester today, 14 miles, in 4 hour, 50 minutes.

Greeted by the mayor and cheering spectators, Johnny said he felt fine and wasn't a bit tired."

The boy has been an accomplished swimmer since he was 3 years old and holds many East Coast titles. Mrs. Lillian Meikle, 30 years old, 715 Meldrum avenue was successful at the noon at Broadway and Gratiot avenue. After treatment she was able to go home. Mrs. Ada Calbert, 27, of 5303 Mt. Hedwig street, collapsed and was taken to Receiving hospital at 6:30 p.m. She also went home after treatment.

MONROE MAYOR'S DOG 50 YEARS OLD

Special to The Free Press.
Monroe, July 30. After 50 years of life, a big collie dog, owned by Mayor Thomas Owen, died tonight at the hands of a policeman. The dog was shot because of a skin disease which his unusual age prevented curing. Mayor Owen said the dog, because of its age, prevented his entering politics some time ago, as he previously owned by another Monroe family and was extremely intelligent.

OUTLAWS TAKE TOWN.

Mexico City, July 30. (A.P.)—Dispatches from Angangueo in the State of Michoacan state that a band of about 20 rebels captured the town of Angangueo on Wednesday, occupying the place for two hours.

Eastern High Girl Named 'Miss Detroit'

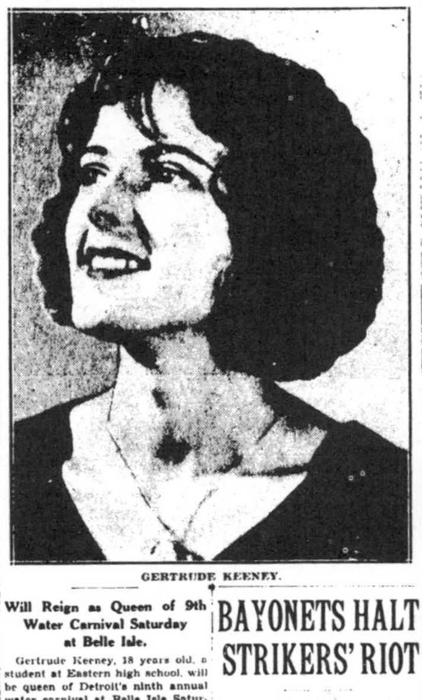

[photo: GERTRUDE KEENEY]

Will Reign as Queen of 9th Water Carnival Saturday at Belle Isle.

Gertrude Keeney, 18 years old, a student at Eastern high school, will be queen of Detroit's ninth annual water carnival at Belle Isle Saturday afternoon and evening.

The "Miss Detroit" of 1928, who resides at 3621 Field avenue, was elected by the judges from among 20 candidates who appeared in the Italian Garden ballroom of the Book Cadillac hotel yesterday afternoon. Her reward is the overwhelming majority of votes. The series of honors that will be hers because of the distinction of representing the city in the annual carnival include the gowning and costume of the queen, when a gaily bedecked automobile with banners proclaiming the new "Miss Detroit" conveyed the winner to her home. Radio fans will have opportunity to greet the city's "queen" Tuesday afternoon at 5 o'clock, when she will give a short talk from station WJR during the afternoon program.

Olive Zeller, 18 years old, 11523 Stoepel avenue, and Corinne Hawson, 20 years old, 1421 Delaware avenue, who received the next highest votes from the judges, will be the two attendants of the queen when she is crowned at the opening of the water carnival Saturday. Miss Zeller is a commercial artist and Miss Hawson a secretary in the office of R. F. Stephenson.

Judges who selected Detroit's most beautiful girl and her attendants were, in a "very grave" condition, among those who banged on the bars and the crowd continued to swell. Chief of Police McCloud decided to call for Battery E, Coast artillery, held in the armory against an emergency.

Riot Act Read.

While the guardsmen were enroute, deputy sheriffs went out to the crowd and started to read the riot act. They were greeted with jeers. The reading had not been completed when the soldiers arrived on trucks and proceeded to clear the streets.

The soldiers, with fixed bayonets, cleared the streets after the reading of the riot act by county officials had no effect. One man was injured in the fray.

Before leaving Medford for the last 40 miles of a run over the Siskiyou mountains, Mr. Hoover spent two hours cooling in the Rogue river at the Dog Creek lodge 15 miles from Medford, but photographers pursued him so closely in an effort to get a shot of him landing a steelhead trout that the fish would not bite.

Plans Hoover Meetings.

Chicago, July 30. (A.P.)—James W. Good, manager of Herbert Hoover's western campaign for the presidency, today announced he had Continued on Page 4, Column 3.

Heat Prostrates Two Women Here

Although the temperature yesterday did not go above 75 degrees, to the satisfaction of the average Detroiter, two cases of prostration because of the heat were reported.

ASK ARREST OF FORMER U.S. CLERK

Levinson Accused of Altering Federal Indictment.

OTHERS FACE PROSECUTION

Smith Is Continuing Investigation of Irregularities.

More indictments in the drive against corruption in federal court are expected as a sequel to the true bill handed down yesterday by the federal grand jury, charging Lew W. Levinson, former chief clerk in the United States district attorney's office, with forgery in connection with the disposition of one prohibition case. A capias was issued for his arrest.

This action is the first of a legal character that has followed the special commissioning of O. L. Smith, former United States district attorney, to clean up the conditions which were alleged to have permitted many bootleggers to escape trial prior to the present administration of United States District Attorney John R. Watkins.

Many Irregularities Found.

Numerous irregularities in the records of the office, such as tampering with the indictment, have been discovered by Smith during his six months' tenure as special assistant attorney general, was designated by the three judges in this federal district, Arthur J. Tuttle, Charles Simons and Edward K. Moinet, to act as district attorney pending confirmation of a regular appointment by the United States senate. The office has been vacant for a year following the resignation of Delos G. Smith.

Smith reported the discovery of irregularities in the judges' last spring and concurrently dismissed Levinson. At the same time, as an indication of his influence in a prohibition case was charged in Moinet's court, and a representative Continued on Page 3, Column 4

PILOTS ATTACK TOUR DIRECTION

Dissatisfied With Preparations, Handling of Fleet and Expenditures.

Pilots of the National Air Tour yesterday presented a petition to William B. Mayo, chairman of the tour committee, asking that next year's reliability flight be conducted under other auspices than those of the Detroit Board of Commerce. The petition, which was read at a luncheon meeting at which the prior checks were awarded, also suggested the incorporation of the tour as a proprietary organization to be managed by Captain Ray Collins, flying referee of the past four tours.

Preparations Attacked.

The fliers expressed dissatisfaction with the tour management as conducted during the handling of the fleet. They brief remarks accompanying the petition inferred that several flying operators of the schools of thought not permitting the managers to not permit the managers of the tour to leave Continued on Page 2, Column 3

MAN IS INJURED IN FALL

Pontiac, July 30. George Chase, 60 years old, of Farmington, is in St. Joseph's Mercy hospital here tonight suffering a probable fracture of the skull as the result of falling from a ladder while working at his home this afternoon.

Britain Sponsors New Key Plan To Arms Cut

Chamberlain Defines It as Separate From, But Related to Kellogg Pact.

London, July 30. (A.P.)—Sir Austen Chamberlain, British foreign secretary, announced in the house of commons today that Great Britain had reached a compromise with France over the naval disarmament question, probably later to a disarmament conference.

"Like Monroe Doctrine.**

Sir Austen indicated that the first open discussion of a compromise would probably be by the preparatory disarmament commission.

He then took up the British reservations in the recent note sent to Secretary Kellogg and said that they comprised with the Monroe doctrine of the United States. He said that no doctrine of aggression was contained in the British reservations but that, "they constituted a measure of self-defense necessitated by the geographical conditions of the empire."

Mr. Chamberlain defended himself from accusations of prolonging the delay in formulation of the British reply. He said the delay had not been unduly long and he hoped it would be no good fortune to go to Paris so as to participate in the signing of the Kellogg pact.

Fact Is Factor.

The secretary said he had hoped by having the disarmament question entirely separate from the Kellogg pact, although he admitted that this treaty undoubtedly would be a factor which would need to be taken into account.

There he announced that the government has had successful conversations with France despite differences which had arisen between the two governments over naval disarmament. He said that no matter to submit to the other principal naval powers the compromise — Adv.

HEADS MERGED MOTOR FIRMS

[photo: W.P. CHRYSLER]

FORD CHAMPION OF 'OLDER' MEN

Couldn't Do Without Those Over 50, He Says on 65th Birthday; Explains Policy.

You take all the exuberance and judgment of men over 50 and the judgment of men under 50 and you wouldn't be enough left to run it."

Thus did Henry Ford, the world's richest man, yesterday answer congratulations on his sixty-fifth birthday, and the scores of telegrams spent most of his day at work. Hundreds of congratulatory telegrams made their way from people he did not know, reached Mr. Ford's desk where he was interviewing himself in increasing production being approached.

Should Do Better Work.

"Some men of 65, persons in adjacent occupations today they were adjourning session today they were told that the required 90 per cent had not been attained in the preference shares or class A common stock, but that the necessary quota of class B was on deposit in the offices where the stock was being approved."

With a series of short adjournments, the meeting marked time in day awaiting reports from deposits, and late in the day reached for the merger plan amount of that assurance had been received from New York that at least 90 per cent was deposited to the merger plan. This assurance, the meeting proceeded to adopt resolutions approving the merger plan. The exact amount of stock deposited was not given.

Exchange of Stock.

Under the agreement, Dodge stockholders will receive Chrysler shares on the basis of allowance of each share of preference stock, one share for each five shares of class A Dodge common stock and the Chrysler corporation will receive the properties and good will of the Dodge organization and the right to use the Dodge Brothers name.

During the session it was announced that work except ornamental Continued on Page 2, Column 4

QUIZZED IN SLAYING OF GOTHAM GANGSTER

New York, July 30. (A.P.)—Parker Henderson, Jr., 26 years old, Fla., was quizzed into town today accompanied by the chief of police from the Florida city. They went to the district attorney's office in Brooklyn for questioning in connection with the slaying in this city two weeks ago of Frankie Yale, Brooklyn gangster. Police emphasized that the Florida man is not under arrest and would not be arrested.

SUFFICIENT STOCK PUT ON DEPOSIT

Barrier Once Passed, Directors Approve Quickly.

TO BE HEADED BY CHRYSLER

Dealer Organization to Be Kept Intact By New Plan.

Baltimore, July 30. (A.P.)—Merger of the Chrysler corporation and Dodge Brothers, Inc., to form one of the big motor combinations of the country, was assured today with a vote at a special meeting of the Dodge stockholders satisfying the merger plan.

Necessity of getting 90 per cent of each class of the Dodge stock deposited in exchange for Chrysler shares had loomed through several adjournments of the meeting as a condition which it might be impossible to fulfill and it was until after the July 21 time limit on the proposed agreement between the two companies gave an air of anxiety to this adjourned session, which began last Saturday.

90 Per Cent Award.

When the stockholders met in an adjourned session today they were told that the required 90 per cent had not been attained in the preference shares or class A common stock, but that the necessary quota of class B was on deposit in the offices where the stock was being approved.

With a series of short adjournments, the meeting marked time in day awaiting reports from deposits, and late in the day reached for the merger plan amount of that assurance had been received from New York that at least 90 per cent was deposited to the merger plan. This assurance, the meeting proceeded to adopt resolutions approving the merger plan. The exact amount of stock deposited was not given.

Exchange of Stock.

Under the agreement, Dodge stockholders will receive Chrysler shares on the basis of allowance of each share of preference stock, one share for each five shares of class A Dodge common stock and the Chrysler corporation will receive the properties and good will of the Dodge organization and the right to use the Dodge Brothers name.

During the session it was announced that work except ornamental Continued on Page 2, Column 4

LAY OUT ISLE BRIDGE PARK

City Councilmen O.K. Proposed Features.

Plans for the development of the property east of the Belle Isle bridge approach as a public park were approved by the council yesterday. They include the grading of the land to a slope from Jefferson avenue to the river, construction of a river-front drive from the bridge approach to Sheridan avenue, and other work necessary to make it a beautiful park. The land, formerly occupied by amusement enterprises, was condemned by the city at a cost of $4,000,000.

Plans have been secured by the city plan commission for parks and boulevards. The proposed drive will provide Jefferson as far as Sheridan, swooping eastward in a curve. North and south roads will intersect it at Field and Sheridan avenues.

Slips into the property from the river will be filled in, the council decided, and land also will be reserved for an ornamental building to be built in the future.

The council also instructed Commissioner French to place in next year's budget an item calling for construction of 2-50 bent work at Memorial Park, where the old walls are said to be falling in pieces. At present there are 190 yards and French estimated the cost of the new ones at $3,500. He said it would be built on for the wall will be about $375,000, he added.

Adolph Zukor Hurt In Auto Accident

Haverstraw, N.Y., July 30. (A.P.)—Adolph Zukor, motion picture magnate, was reported injured in an automobile accident near here today. It was understood Zukor was driving from his Now City summer home at New York City when his car was forced off the road and into a tree by a passing truck. The extent of his injuries was not known.

HORNETS FIGHT MEN COMBATING FIRE

Manistee, July 30. Several city firemen are on the hospital list as a result of a small roof fire today. In putting out the blaze the firemen disturbed a hornet's nest under the eaves. The hornets did more damage to the firemen than the fire did to the roof.

The Detroit Free Press

WEATHER — Thunder Showers
FINAL EDITION
99th Year. No. 61 — DETROIT, MICHIGAN, THURSDAY, JULY 4, 1929—EIGHTEEN PAGES — PRICE: THREE CENTS

POLICE JAIL FRIEND OF VICTIMS IN AX KILLING OF SIX IN CULT HOME

JULY 4, 1929:

Mayhem, Roaring '20s style: an anti-Prohibition riot on the east side; a racetrack fight in Windsor, and the murder of six family members on St. Aubin.

"Mob Of 500 Attacks 5 Dry Raiders," column two, *"Fans Riot Over Race In Windsor,"* column three, *"'Divine Prophet,' Wife, 4 Children Hacked to Death,"* column seven.

BERLIN HOP FLIERS AT REMI LAKE

Unable to Complete Day's Schedule Due to Delays.

CAPE CHIDLEY TODAY'S GOAL

Flight From Chicago to Europe Begins Auspiciously.

Special to The Free Press
Remi Lake, Ont., July 3.—The "Untin' Bowler, the amphibian plane that started this morning from Chicago for Berlin, landed here at 6:44 p.m., Detroit time. The plane was scheduled to reach Rupert House, on James bay, tonight, but delay at Milwaukee and at Sault Ste. Marie made it inadvisable to try for that point. The flying schedule called for a stop at Remi Lake to refuel.

The Bowler arrived at Sault Ste. Marie at 1:45 p.m. Swooping down on the St. Mary's river, Pilot Robert Gast crossed to the Canadian side to clear the customs and to take gasoline. The delay there was more than two hours and the start was made at 4:15 p.m. An earlier start would have enabled the Bowler to reach Rupert House this evening.

Cape Chidley Today.

Tomorrow's plans call for a flight to Great Whale and Cape Chidley. The flight began under the most auspicious circumstances. The weather was ideal. At Milwaukee the pilots, Gast and Parker D. Cramer, and Robert Wood, newspaperman, left the craft for an air meeting by the municipality and to lay a wreath on the statue of Leif Ericson, the Viking who came to American shores by the route which the Bowler is to take, with Greenland and Iceland as stops.

Weather indications over eastern Ontario and Labrador were not good, according to flying weather forecasts. The weather map showed that rain was prevalent over Labrador.

No attempt is being made on the trip to set speed records and the pilots plan to wait at all stops for good weather conditions. Their plan is to get into the high area following the low and to ride it down the Greenland ice cap and over the open sea to Iceland. From Reykjavik, the capital of Iceland, they are to proceed to Bergen, Norway, over the Faroe Islands.

Communications Poor.

The entire trip is in the nature of a pathfinding expedition, and the limitations in communication with the territory around Hudson Bay and in the rest of the northland were realized when the project was first taken up.

Full co-operation has been promised by the governmental radio stations at all points to be touched. The Danish government has stations in Iceland and at Angmagsalik, on the eastern coast of Greenland.

Help is to be given by the stations at Port Burwell and Mount Evans.

A crowd of several thousand at the takeoff at Chicago this morning. Only a few were permitted inside the wire fence surrounding the beach, and the ramp leading to the water.

The farewells of the trio were brief. The mothers of Gast, Cramer and Wood all were present, but after their sons had embraced them the three men climbed into the cabin and the signal to shove off was given.

There was a cheer from the crowds surrounding the beach. Pilot Gast drove the boat on the water in a northeasterly direction, until he attained flying speed, made
Continued on Page 7, Column 4

MT. RAINIER DASH KILLS 2

Six Climbers Are Swept Into Crevasse.

Tacoma, July 3.—(A. P.)—Forrest Greathouse, football coach at Lincoln high school, Seattle, and former team mate of "Red" Grange at the University of Illinois, and Edwin Wetzel, Milwaukee, were killed when six mountain climbers were swept into a deep crevasse at the 13,000-foot levels on Mount Rainier yesterday, it was learned here today.

The climbers were returning from the first attempt of the season to scale the 14,408 feet mountain when they slipped into the crevasse above Gibralter rock. Greathouse was employed by the Mount Rainier Park company as a guide during the summer. Wetzel was a visitor.

The seven injured were L. H. Brigham, Seattle, veteran summit guide and athletic director at Garfield high school, and Robert Strobel, Tacoma, assistant guide. The two
Continued on Page 2, Column 7

MAN OUT OF WORK SWALLOWS POISON

Despondent because of unemployment, Douglas Darling, 30 years old, 2149 Garland avenue, ended his life by taking poison in his home at 3:30 p.m. today.

COUNCIL FINDS LAW ENFORCED, ENJOYS LAUGH

Discovers Police Take Ordinances Seriously, When Traffic Work Is Praised.

City ordinances, several hundred of which are passed each term by the council, may yet be taken seriously. At any rate the question of enforcing traffic ordinances was brought before the council yesterday by Councilman R. W. Castator, who suggested a hearing "for the purpose of determining whether the downtown merchants want the traffic laws enforced." And then Mr. Castator's colleagues wanted to know why the police have not enforced the laws.

The matter all came about when the business interests of Washington boulevard wrote to congratulate the council upon its success in
Continued on Page 2, Column 1

MOB OF 500 ATTACKS 5 DRY RAIDERS

Police Quell East Side Riot; Take U. S. Men to Safety.

Threatened by a mob of 500 persons, some of whom were armed with clubs, knives and axes, five dry agents, who raided a garage at 2115 Philip avenue at 7:15 p.m. yesterday, were saved from violence only by the intervention of police from the Connors and McClellan avenue stations.

While police held back the mob and opened a lane through the millions of people to the street, the agents and four prisoners were hustled into a patrol wagon and driven to the Connors station, while the neighborhood bade them goodbye with hoots and catcalls. From the station they proceeded with their prisoners to prohibition headquarters.

Agents Accused of Drinking.

Neighbors who had watched the raiders insisted the agents had been drinking and acted boisterously—a conclusion in which police officers who saw them a few minutes later failed to concur.

Phillip Vandergrist and his wife, who live in the garage and operate a confectionery at 14335 Mack avenue, directly opposite the garage, were charged with violating the prohibition law. Frank Conto, 21130 Evanston avenue, and Walter Ross, 16 years old, of 3087 Manistique avenue, who were members of the mob, were also held at police headquarters at the request of the agents, although no specific charges against them were named.

Find 32 Cases of Beer.

The agents said the garage contained 32 cases of beer, and an automobile beside it held 12 cases, all of which were seized. Prohibition headquarters, in the Barium tower, refused to give out any information regarding the raid, or to answer the charges of neighbors that the agents had been drinking to excess. The name of the agents involved was withheld.

At Connors station, the agents told police they were directed to the Philip avenue address by a man whose place they raided earlier in the search of liquor, and were told they would find beer there. They found the beer, they declared, but when they attempted to arrest Vandergrist and his wife the neighborhood arose in arms and threatened to force them to release their captives.

Patrolmen Fred Gorieta and Gregory Harrington, passing by the garage, noticed the disturbance and put in a call for aid. Cruisers from the McClellan and Connors station, commanded by Patrolman Donald Allen and Sergeant Joan Conway, and the McClellan patrol wagon were sent to the scene. Within a few minutes they had pacified the mob and spirited the agents and their captives away.

When they arrived the agents had drawn their revolvers in an attempt to frighten the crowd and were backed against the wall of the garage.

Neighbors persisted in their declarations that the raiders were drunk,
Continued on Page 2, Column 7

Brain of Dead Flier Analyzed

New York, July 3.—(A. P.)—The brain of Wilmer Stultz, transatlantic airplane pilot who was killed with two other men when his plane crashed at Roosevelt field, has been subjected to a chemical analysis at Bellevue hospital.

A report of the examination was submitted today to Acting District Attorney Miller of Nassau county, who said that the analysis showed by County Judge Louis J. Smith. Mr. Miller said he could not, at this time, give a statement as to why it was made.

U. S. ENVOY RECOVERING

Washington, July 3.—(A. P.)—The American legation at Monrovia informed the state department today that William T. Francis, Negro American minister to Liberia, is slowly recovering from an attack of yellow fever.

FANS RIOT OVER RACE IN WINDSOR

Starter Is Attacked When Mistaken For Judge.

STABLE BOYS BEAT ASSAILANT

Decision in Seventh Event Is Cause of Trouble.

Rioting in which a race official was knocked to the ground with blows that cracked open his lip and discolored one eye, and his assailant was thrown to the clubhouse floor and kicked repeatedly in the stomach and face, followed the seventh race at the Devonshire race-track yesterday afternoon when Cogwheel was declared winner of the event.

George R. Kramer, veteran starter of the Western Racing association, was the official on whom the booing crowd vented its anger, apparently mistaking Palmer for one of the judges. More than a thousand race-goers took part in the mobbing of Palmer.

Row Follows Race.

Hodgefence was installed favorite in the final race of the afternoon, a claim event of a mile and one-sixteenth for 3-year-olds and upward. Cogwheel closed in the betting at 5 to 1 and Fenlight, owned by the W. L. Brodies, at 7½ to 1. The latter two horses were the ones most prominent in the sanguinary row which followed the running of the race.

Passing the clubhouse, slightly less than a furlong from the wire, Fenlight took the lead from Cogwheel and pulled away. Cogwheel closed in fast, both horses under a strong ride. They battled it out to the finish.

Men at the finish line differed in their verdict. Some said Fenlight had it. Others claimed that Cogwheel won and that Fenlight, the bid for jumps, had grazed legs tearing out. The judges announced
Continued on Page 3, Column 5

DR. W. A. GIFFEN IS HEART VICTIM

Dies in Hospital After Illness of Two Years; Was Head of National Society.

Dr. William A. Giffen, Detroit dentist and former president of the American Dental association, died yesterday in Grace hospital after an illness from a heart affection.

The remains will lie at the residence of his brother, Dr. E. L. Giffen, 86 Farrand avenue, Highland Park, until Friday, when they will be taken to the Scottish Rite cathedral where Masonic services will be conducted at 2 p.m. by Corinthian lodge. Interment will take place at Brampton, Ontario, where Dr. Giffen was born 62 years ago.

Survived by Family.

Dr. Giffen is survived by his widow, Mrs. Alberta Miller Giffen, daughter of an old Detroit family, and one son, Dr. J. Clark Giffen and Dr. Ralph P. Giffen, both of whom are practicing dentistry in Detroit. He was one of a family of eight, the remainder of whom are living. Two, Dr. E. L. Giffen and Miss Bertha Giffen reside in Detroit, another is at Bangor, Michigan, and the other four are at Brampton, Ont.

Dr. Giffen started life as a veterinary but in 1901 was graduated in
Continued on Page 2, Column 1

Kentucky Text Book Law Upheld

Frankfort, Ky., July 3.—(A. P.)—The Kentucky court of appeals today upheld the constitutionality of the state free textbook act, but enjoined the state from entering into contract for purchase of books, because funds are not available at this time.

3 Risk Lives To Get Rum 120 Years Old

110-Ton Caisson Sinks as Workers Burrow in Ground at Base for Liquor.

Special to The Free Press and Chicago Tribune.
New York, July 3.—The age of three "rum hogs" who risked their lives to dig up almost 100 bottles of rare old West Indian rum, while 110 tons of concrete sank slowly over their heads, was told today at 120 Wall street, where a 23-story office building is in the process of

SIX VICTIMS OF AX FIEND

All six of the Evangelist family, shown above, were murdered by an axman yesterday. Benjamin Evangelist, occult "prophet," and his wife, Santina, are shown in the center, with their youngest child, Mario, 18 months old, on her lap. Angelina, 7, and Margaret, 5, are shown in insets at the top right, and Jean, 4, is shown at the bottom, left.

Demand Lodge's View Of New Transit Plan

3 Councilmen Say They Will Refuse to Consider It Until Mayor Talks.

Mayor John C. Lodge must write a letter to the council stating that he favors the proposed rapid transit plan, and must further state that he will personally recommend it to the voters, before any action will be
Continued on Page 2, Column 2

ASKS FOR JURY TO TRY TUNNEY

Mrs. Fogarty Files Request in $500,000 Suit Against Ex-Fighter.

Bridgeport, Conn., July 3.—(A. P.)—Counsel for Mrs. Katherine King Fogarty, of Fort Worth, Texas, and New York City, today filed a request for a jury trial of her $500,000 breach of promise suit against James J. (Gene) Tunney, former world heavyweight boxing champion of the world.

Colonel Lewis L. Field, New Haven, attorney for Mrs. Fogarty, has not yet filed the reply to Tunney's answer, in which the retired boxer denied promising to marry the woman, and in which he charged her with an attempt to exploit an acquaintanceship with him. Tunney though he had already paid her more than $35,000 to waive any claims on him. The suit comes up in the September term of superior court.

POLISH PILOTS FINISH TESTS

Plan to Start Flight to U. S. From Le Bourget at First Opportunity.

Le Bourget, July 3.—(A. P.)—Janusz Zwirko and Kazimir Kubala, the Polish aviators who are planning a flight to New York, made their last trial flight today. They were in the air four hours.

"Both the motor and the plane behaved splendidly," said Idzikowski after the test. He said they were ready to start as soon as favorable weather was indicated.

The fliers have not decided definitely upon their route. In probability, however, will be by way of the Azores, thus following the path on which they started last year when their vessels sank in the sea near those islands.

Fliers Off for Madrid.

Algeciras, Spain, July 3.—(A. P.)—A special train tonight sped Major Ramon Franco and his three companions, rescued near the Azores from their attempted transatlantic flight last week, homeward to Madrid.

LOWMAN OUSTS DULUTH CHIEF

Customs Official Suspended on Rum, Dope and Graft Allegations.

Washington, July 3.—(A. P.)—Assistant Secretary of the Treasury Lowman today announced that Carl E. Dahly, collector of customs at Duluth, had been suspended pending hearings on charges against him. Deputy Collector Lindeberg has been placed in charge of the office.

The charges were preferred by inspectors for alleged drunkenness, conspiracy to smuggle liquor across the international boundary, conspiracy to extort money from a narcotics law violator and conspiracy to falsify government accounts.

Dahly was appointed collector of customs at Duluth on January 28, 1928, and was reappointed on March 4, 1927. He had not been in the service prior to his first appointment.

Birmingham, Ala., July 3.—(U.P.)—W. H. Gillespie, federal prohibition officer working out of Montgomery, was shot and seriously wounded today while leading state officers in a raid on a still in Coosa county, Ala. He was taken to a hospital at Sylacauga.

POPE G'EETS PILGRIMS.

Vatican City, July 3.—(A. P.)—Pope Pius today received a group of Mexican pilgrims and expressed hope that the religious situation in Mexico would ever get better. He gave them an affectionate blessing.

W E hope you don't—but if you do lose anything over the Fourth, you'll recover it more quickly by advertising your loss with a

FREE PRESS WANT AD

The finder will look in the morning paper first.

'DIVINE PROPHET,' WIFE, 4 CHILDREN HACKED TO DEATH

Father Found With Head Cut Off; Five Other Victims Believed Killed During Sleep.

WEIRD ALTAR IN CELLAR BARES MYSTIC'S RELIGION

Wholesale Tragedy Laid to Fanatic; Humble St. Aubin Avenue Home Is Scene of Murders.

(See Pictures on Page 3 and Last Page.)

Angelo Depoli, 34 years old, 2630 Pierce street, was arrested last night in connection with the slaying of Benny Evangelist, "divine prophet" of a weird cult, his wife and four children, ranging in age from 18 months to 7 years, hacked to death yesterday at 3587 St. Aubin avenue by an unknown ax wielder, believed to have been actuated by religious mania.

Depoli was arrested by Detective Lieutenant John Whitman and Detectives Charles Searle and Earl Switzer, and registered at headquarters as a disorderly person for questioning. The officers said they found a short ax in Depoli's barn, along with a keen-edged banana knife and a pair of shoes, which apparently had just been washed.

Admits He Knew Family.

The ax bore stains which will be tested to determine whether they are blood or rust. The man admitted his acquaintance with the Evangelists, but denied the murders.

Police refused to say whether these men were considered as suspects, but admitted there was a possibility they might shed some light on the case.

Police last night sought to sustain a theory Evangelist and his family were slain by the individual responsible for the deaths of Mrs. Henry Cipinski and her three children at River Rouge two weeks ago. Members of the Cipinski family were nauseated with the same savage ferocity which characterized the St. Aubin avenue slayings.

Chief Walter Hancock, River Rouge police, suggested that the killer may have consulted the "divine prophet" in connection with the downriver slayings and, fearful lest his confidence should be betrayed, returned to wipe out the Evangelist family.

The dead:

BENNY EVANGELIST, 43 years old, real estate operator and "divine prophet" of a mysterious religious cult.
SANTINA, 40 years old, Evangelist's wife.
ANGELINA, 7 years old, a daughter.
MARGARET, 5 years old, another daughter.
JEAN, 4 years old.
MARIO, 18 months old, a son.

The body of Evangelist, with the head severed and lying on the floor beside the chair in which it was slumped, was found at 10:30 a.m. by Vincent Elia, 43 years old, real estate dealer, 2334 Glendale avenue. Elia intended to pay a business call on Evangelist, also engaged in the real estate business.

Background of Religious Insanity.

The murderer worked with demoniac frenzy, apparently with the intention to sever the heads and arms of his victims. Behind the tragedy was a grotesque background of religious insanity, paralleling in its weirdness and barbarism any voodoo fetish of the West Indies.

The Evangelist home is a two-story frame structure having four rooms downstairs and five up, in addition to a basement and an attic. On the upper floor the two front rooms are bedrooms, the three back ones being unused and virtually devoid of furniture. A bathroom is located off a hallway between the two front bedrooms and one of the rear rooms. Opposite the bathroom door is the stairway leading downstairs.

Although Evangelist, slain in his office, was almost fully dressed when found, his wife and the children apparently had retired for the night when the assassin entered. Mrs. Evangelist lying on and hanging partly over her bed. Her head, horribly mutilated and nearly severed from the body, was projected over the side of the bed lying on the floor. Margaret's body was found in the bed with her, his head also badly lacerated and resting upon one of the woman's arms. The mother's other arm bore a deep laceration at the shoulder as if the murderer had sought to amputate it.

In the opposite bedroom, connected with the mother's room by a single door, lay the bodies of the remaining three children, two of them on twin beds in the room, and the third lying on the floor. Margaret's body was frightfully gashed, one of the children's bodies was found severed at the shoulders.

Nothing of Value Missing.

Insofar as is known, nothing of any value, such as money, jewelry, or papers, was disturbed, although Evangelist had the reputation of being a considerably well-to-do real estate operator among the Italian colony on the east side.

Aside from his law business activities, which cards found upon his desk indicated, included general building and repair contracting as well as real estate transactions of various kinds, Evangelist was described by neighbors as being a "confirmed religious fanatic." His religion also was something of a business, since cards found lying about the office read:

Mr. Benny Evangelist, divine prophet, author and private history writer.

He also is said to have received as much as $10 for private "readings," during which he called upon the powers of his own cult to heal various ills, either spiritual or physical, with which his "patients" were afflicted.

This cult, evidence indicated, was known as the "Union Federation of America," and apparently was founded by Evangelist himself some than 20 years ago in Philadelphia. The founder, according to a preface in his cult's "bible," which Evangelist had written, was supposed to be "with the power of God." In a flingy, but electrically lighted room of the basement, the "prophet" had set up one of the weirdest "altars" ever uncovered in Detroit.

Eight or ten wax figures, each hideous and grotesque to the extreme, and each presumably representing one of the "celestial planets," were suspended on the altar in a circle by wires from the ceiling. Above it was a huge eye, electrically lighted from the inside, which Evangelist referred to in his bible as the sun."

The walls and ceiling of this "religious sanctum" were lined with light green cloth, which bulged out in places like the walls of a padded cell. In a window of the basement, which was on a line with and visible from St. Aubin avenue, a large card bore the words: "Great Celestial Planet Exhibition."

Evangelist and his family undoubtedly were killed while the "prophet" was in his office after having "read the signs" from the celestial bodies, for in his bible states that he "saw them from 12 to 8 a.m. daily."

Planned Other Volumes.

Evangelist's "bible," which he called "The Oldest History of the World, Discovered by Occult Science in Detroit, Mich.," apparently was written, or was to be written, in four volumes, the first of which covered everything "4,000 years before Adam." Indications were this was the only one that had been published, since it was the only one found in printed form about the premises. Evangelist had written in his foreword of the second volume, which was intended to cover the "birth of Adam."

For the Evangelists, life, "My story is from my own views and signs, and that I saw from 12 to 3 a.m., I began on February 2, 1906 in Philadelphia, and completed on February 6, 1926."

SCARE GIVEN OHIO FLIERS

Endurance Plane Wing Fabric Is Torn.

Cleveland, July 3.—(A. P.)—Surviving a day of minor alarms, the monoplane City of Cleveland continued in the air tonight on its attempt to break the refueling endurance record.

Shortly after 4:30 p.m. the plane passed the endurance mark of 118 hours set by the French dirigible Italia. At 10:59 p.m., eastern time, Pilots Byron K. Newcomer and Roy L. Mitchell had topped the 19 hours toward the record of 172 hours and 31½ minutes.

Torn Fabric Causes Scare.

The sky clouded late tonight and drizzling rain fell.

An alarm was spread late in the day when a photograph of the plane revealed a rent in the fabric covering the left wing. Refueling Pilot Ernest Bashan declared, however
Continued on Page 8, Column 6

Radio Program—Page 8

Triangle Murder Warrants Issued

Batesville, Ark., July 3.—(A. P.)—Warrants were issued today for Mrs. Norma Osborne, 23 years old, and J. F. Barber, 29, former clerk, charging them with the murder of Mrs. Osborne's husband, Morris Osborne, also 21 years old, last Sunday night. Both have been in custody since her husband was found shot and beaten to death in the kitchen of his home Monday night. Barber has not been arrested.

Oct. 22, 1929:

The nation, led by President Herbert Hoover, honors Thomas Edison at Henry Ford's new Greenfield Village.

WEATHER Probably Rain

The Detroit Free Press
MICHIGAN'S GREATEST NEWSPAPER

FINAL EDITION

99th Year. No. 171 — DETROIT, MICHIGAN, TUESDAY, OCTOBER 22, 1929—THIRTY-FOUR PAGES — PRICE: THREE CENTS

WORLD'S TRIBUTE TO EDISON VOICED BY HOOVER

Thousands Hail President During His 30-Mile Ride

OVATION IS GREATEST EVER HERE

Crowds Line Streets Scores Deep Over Long Route.

FLAGS, CONFETTI MAKE GAY SCENE

Nation's Chief and Wife Bare Heads to Rain.

BY JAMES F. POWERS.

Thousands upon thousands, uncountable as they stretched away over the 30-mile route, cheered President Herbert Hoover and Mrs. Hoover Monday in the greatest demonstration that Detroit ever gave any president, and presidents have been here before.

It rained. It sleeted. It snowed, and rained again. And through all those miles President Hoover waved to the crowd until his arm must have been weary. Mrs. Hoover was with him. Her smile never failed. Her graciousness lighted the whole procession, and it was a trial for anyone who participated in it.

Bare Heads in Storm.

Scarce half a mile had been traversed out of the home of Henry Ford in Dearborn, the start of the parade, or more properly Detroit's testimonial to Herbert Hoover, when the president leaned toward Mrs. Hoover. She nodded an acquiescence. The presidential car...

First Lady Stops To Powder Nose

Although Mrs. Herbert Hoover is, first of all, a woman. She showered the city hall.

The presidential procession, planned to move swiftly from place to place, was not delayed for any stops, but Mrs. Hoover, for a few minutes anyway, stopped it. It was in the corridor of the city hall she refused to go further without stopping to take her powder puff from her handbag, and apply the universal cosmetic to her nose. She took her time to make sure the powder was on evenly, and even the protests from the secret service men failed to hurry her.

...ripped. The police escort shot far ahead on Southfield road. It turned...the front seats, got out. They were helped by police officers. The top on the president's car rolled back. Despite the rain, the snow, the sleet, President and Mrs. Hoover wanted to see Detroit, the people of Detroit and be seen by them. Every other car kept the top up.

All the way down Oakwood...hward into which the procession turned from Southfield road, the president was waving. The president waved as the first large group of school children greeted him in Melvindale. Mrs. Hoover raised the *Continued on Page 13, Column 1.*

BITE OF STRAY DOG KILLS BOY

111 Receive Anti-Rabies Treatment in Week.

Four-year-old Alfred Coppo, 15417 Hazelton avenue, succumbed to hydrophobia at Herman Kiefer hospital at noon yesterday, in a dog bite he suffered September 14. The animal that bit him was a stray public which was roaming while it turned and snapped, inflicting deep gashes in his face.

The case was reported to the board of health immediately and the boy was given the usual series of Pasteur treatments by a private physician, but who his improvement was noted, the boy early yesterday was taken to Herman Kiefer hospital. His death occurred a few hours after his admittance there.

In connection with the child's death, Dr. Frederick Meader, of the board of health, last night said 111 persons were bitten by dogs in the week ending last Saturday. Of these, 12 are receiving Pasteur treatment, four of the dogs having been found to be rabid. In the preceding week, 70 persons were bitten by dogs, none of the dogs proved positively to be rabid.

EASTERN MICHIGAN SYSTEM
Express between Detroit—Flint, Pontiac, Lansing, Grand Rapids, Ft. Huron, Toledo, Jackson, Ann Arbor, Edge 8429 information.—Adv.

CASTLE AGAIN IN BALM SUIT

Mrs. Cleavenger Refuses to Settle Case, Which is Reopened.

Attempts to settle the $750,000 breach of promise suit of Bertha B. Cleavenger against John H. Castle out of court have failed and the trial of the case will be resumed, Ralph B. Clark, defense counsel, announced yesterday.

On October 14 trial was started before a jury in the courtroom of Judge Homer Ferguson. The same day, however, counsel for Mrs. Cleavenger and the defense announced that an agreement had been reached. Though the amount of the settlement was not published, it was understood to be between $125,000 and $150,000.

Refuses to Settle.

Mrs. Cleavenger, whose bill estimates Castle's wealth at $2,000,000, asserts that when she met him he was a factory employe earning a small wage. For eight years they worked together amassing Castle's fortune, she says. During the years of their friendship, which began in 1917, they fell in love and Castle proposed marriage, the woman says.

Married in 1925.

In May, 1925, he married another woman. Mrs. Cleavenger says Castle was with her the night before the marriage and gave her no intimation that it impended. She first learned of the wedding, she asserts, when she read of it in newspapers. The breach of promise suit was filed April 5, 1927.

JOHN A. HALL'S LEAD IS 6 VOTES

Recounters Subtract From Candidate's Margin; 660 Precincts Are Counted.

The lead of about 80 votes amassed earlier by John A. Hall over Frederick Hoye in the councilmanic race was cut to a mere six as the recount of ballots cast in the October primary election progressed yesterday.

The unofficial count election night indicated Hoye had nosed Hall out for last place by five votes. The official canvass showed Hall to have been beaten by 41. The recounters have substantiated votes from Hoye standby, Councilman Arthur E. Dingeman and was less George Hingman. Other names were almost as nearly alike.

660 Precincts Counted.

With votes recounted in 660 out of the city's 852 voting precincts, the count yesterday afternoon stood: John A. Hall, plus 20; Hoye, minus 27; Kuhlman, plus 47, and Henry Kent, plus 94.

The figures indicated that Kuhlman would retain his nomination in seventeenth place, that Hall might or might not win from Hoye and that neither of the three last-named had much to fear from Kent, who he the official count ran twentieth, several hundred behind Hall.

TRIAL OF FALL NEARING JURY

U. S. Ends Arguments and Defense Starts.

Washington, Oct. 21.— (A. P.) Albert B. Fall heard himself denounced and praised today as government and defense counsel arose at the conclusion of the fourth week of his oil trial in criminal court to begin closing arguments in the case which will decide whether the former interior secretary accepted $100,000 bribe from Edward L. Doheny.

Atlee Pomerene, special government prosecutor, reviewed the government's case to the jury for nearly three hours. Frank J. Hogan, *(Continued on Page 5, Column 6.)*

WIFE OF 50 YEARS DIES AT ALTAR RE-ACTING RITE

Racine, Wis., Oct. 21.—(U. P.)—Fifty years ago today Edward and Mary Sleger were married. In observance of the anniversary, their marriage ceremony was re-enacted in St. Edward church today.

As the Rev. Bott read the last sentence, Mrs. Sleger fell dead of heart disease.

The aged couple stood in front of the altar, happy, their right hands clasped, repeating the words after the Rev. J. W. Bott.

PROOF LACKING IN FIRE PROBE

Evidence Against Marty Cohn in Study Club Investigation Weak, Says Prosecutor.

Inability to obtain evidence with which Martin Cohn, proprietor of the Study club, can be convicted on an involuntary manslaughter charge, was admitted yesterday in a letter written by Prosecuting Attorney James E. Chenot to Charles E. Wilcox, corporation counsel.

The letter read, in part: "These statements are indicative to you inasmuch as, in our opinion, of there be any possibility of prosecution it is for a violation of a city ordinance."

Chenot referred to statements given Duncan C. McRae, an assistant prosecutor, by Frederick J. Honey, of the pavement of buildings and safety engineering, and I. J. Ritchwine, of the department of recreation. The statements, with a list of ordinances under which Chenot believes Martin might be tried, were included in the letter. McRae, who conducted the investigation of the night club fire *Continued on Page 2, Column 4.*

Quintet Nabbed In Liquor Raids

Five men were arrested yesterday by federal prohibition officers. David Sonnenstahl, 5488 Lincoln avenue, was arrested at the rear of 110 Rowena street, on a charge of transporting liquor. In a saloon one door east of 15125 Kercheval avenue, two men who gave their names as Robert Hamilton and Leonard Brennan, were taken into custody. William Roethke was arrested as the proprietor of an alleged blind pig one door east of 1625 Charlevoix street. Joseph Wilhms was arrested at the side of a Mile road, where officers reported the seizure of a large assortment of liquor.

REVIEW DENIED IN KALES CASE

Income Tax on Ford Profits Allowed to Stand by Supreme Court.

Washington, Oct. 21.—(A. P.) Alice G. Kales, of Detroit, as owner of 325 shares of common stock in the Ford Motor company, was refused a review by the supreme court today on the decision of lower federal courts holding that $505,-978 in dividends received by her in 1916, representing distribution of 1916 profits, was taxable as income under the revenue act of 1916.

John F. and Horace E. Dodge began proceedings to compel the Ford Motor company to distribute 50 per cent of its $58 profits and by order of the courts a dividend of $19,275,385 was declared in July, 1919, and distributed among the stockholders. Alice G. Kales had retained her 325 shares and received $505,978 as dividend and $140,-339 as interest. The government decided the interest should not be taxed as income but imposed a tax on the 1916 revenue act on the $505,978 as income. This was opposed on the ground that the 1925 Charlevoix street, Joseph Wilhms was arrested at the side of a Mile road, where officers reported Mile road, where officers reported the seizure of a large assortment... prevailing.

HIGH COURT REFUSES TO PASS ON AIR DEATH

Washington, Oct. 21.—(A. P.) The supreme court today refused to decide whether the death of a person who crawls out on a wing of a plane in the air and jumps off is due to accident.

Five men were arrested yesterday... Alphonse R. Gits, who died in Estes Park, Colo., in August, 1923, held a $10,000 policy in a life insurance company calling for double indemnity in case of accidental death. The company claimed that Gits had while riding in an airplane crawled out on a wing and jumped. It denied double indemnity, asserting the death was not accidental.

The federal courts decided in favor of the company but the circuit court of appeals held that the trial judge should have tried the case before a jury, and remanded it.

PLANES DEFEAT FOG, RAIN; LAND

John Livingston, Winner, Leads Fifth Air Tour Pilots Into Detroit.

BY CHARLES McLEAN, Free Press Aviation Editor.

Headed by John Livingston in his Waco biplane, and flying through rain and fogs that lined the airway from Chicago to Kalamazoo and then on to Detroit, the 30 airplanes in the fifth National Air tour battled their way through the sky yesterday to land on schedule at the Ford airport for the finish of the 5,017-mile tour. Behind Livingston came his flying mate, Arthur Davis, who also flew a Waco.

About $25,000 in prize money in addition to the Ford trophy, will be awarded the 10 leaders today, and every pilot that finished will be given $200 cash.

One Mishap Mars Day.

One mishap marred the day of the last flight. W. E. Lancaster was forced down by engine trouble near Kalamazoo. He said his plane and continue here help his plane and continue here being the other pilots waiting the rule which required him to report last night or lose his contest rights.

Although the tour was shorter than any other of the five tours this year than last, interest created in $19,275,385 was declared in July, 1919, and distributed among the stockholders. Alice G. Kales had retained her 325 shares and received $505,978 as dividend and $140,- than any other of the five tours this year than last, interest created in the 16-day tour through Canada and the United States was estimated at more than 100 per cent greater. Major Clarey M. Young, head of the Air division of the department of commerce; William B. Stout, designer and builder of the two Ford all-metal planes that finished among the first five leaders; Edward F. Warner, editor *Continued on Page 2, Column 4.*

ELECTRIC 'LAMP' 'INVENTED' AGAIN IN OLD WORKSHOP

Chief Magistrate, Ford and Latter's Guests Take Part in Jubilee at Village of Greenfield.

PRESIDENT, FIRST LADY GIVE SEATS TO 'WIZARD' AND WIFE

Electrical Genius Speaks at Feast and Is Sent Home Quite 'Fatigued' by Doctor.

The complete text of President Hoover's address will be found on Page 12.

BY WILLIAM C. RICHARDS.

The world, with the president of the United States as its principal envoy of good will, turned its thoughts yesterday upon a gray old patriarch of more than 80, a story-book character of America, and joined with Herbert Hoover and Detroit in grateful acclamation of Thomas Alva Edison.

A million people watched the president ride in the downpour yesterday morning in a parade, undaunted by the rain, through packed and clamorous downtown streets.

Millions at Radio.

Millions more listened over the radio in the evening when Tom Edison, by the dim rays of an oil lamp and with the president standing silent and serious in the deep shadows behind him, recreated that first incandescent bulb which was born in old Menlo Park in 1879.

And the same millions heard Herbert Hoover, as speaking to an old friend, voice his own gratitude and that of the world in Independence Hall, in Henry Ford's new-spun village, to Mr. Edison for his gifts to the well-being and advancement of this age.

Voices were raised across the sea in a memorial that crossed many frontiers. One congratulatory cablegram was from the Prince of Wales; another from Paul von *(See Pictures on Last Page.)*

BIRD'S EYE VIEW OF THE THRONG AT CITY HALL

Jamming the streets in front of the city hall, thousands of Detroiters paid tribute to their president Herbert Hoover, when he spoke from the rostrum in front of the building. Solid masses of people, all rain drenched despite the scores of umbrellas raised in an effort to ward off the drizzle, stood for an hour waiting for the president to arrive. Some persons, unable to get within either hearing or seeing distance, clambered atop street cars, which lined the Michigan avenue side of the city hall. Only a small part of the crowd is shown here.

Hoover Gives Up Seat Of Honor to Inventor

President Hoover paid an unusual compliment to Thomas A. Edison at the banquet by relinquishing the seat of honor at his table to the famous inventor.

On few occasions in recent years has a president eat at a public dinner without the seat of honor and all citizens, no matter what the occasion, always defer to his office. Edison sought to do so, but the president would not have it thus. Mrs. Hoover paid a like compliment to Mrs. Edison.

After Fifty Years.

While the faces of the world were pressed against the window panes, figuratively, Edison in memory of the day carried out in the evening the experiment whose fruitage today, 50 years after its first accomplishment, is visible to every man who has eyes.

In a dim-lit room last night he fiddled with his materials. Behind him was the president of his country, keenly watching the movement of shadow as it puttered with things up a little old table.

Outside, a dreary rain fell. The pitch blackness was broken only by the dare, a sputter of an occasional corner lamp. Within the room, Edison and his assistant bent over their task. Thus, they hurried through the mud. Herbert Hoover at their backs, and turned a switch.

Light is Made.

As far as the eye could reach light came with the effect of an eclipse running backward. A thousand rockets sped into the sky and burst. A thousand men and women, dining in a replica of Independence hall by candle light, hurried it in strong light. An airplane raced overhead, 1879 and 1929 illumined on its wings. Bombs tore upward into the great yellow pathway in the sky built of a thousand automobile headlights.

One In Greenfield village last night, the world that Thomas Alva Edison has immeasurably befriended, paid him tribute in a manner more spectacular and far-reaching than ever was possible with human or other materials of immortalization.

The experiment done, President Hoover returned to Independence hall, and in a voice sweetened with humanness and carried by radio the distance of the land, lauded the genius of Edison to a grateful people in a formal dedication of the Edison Institute of Technology.

Gathering of Great.

As he left Edison, the patriarch, bowed his head. Boyd Edison was Ford. At the president's right was Mme. Curie, co-discoverer of radium. Nearby sat Charles G. Dawes, ambassador to Great Britain. In front of them was an assemblage gathered from all ranks and latitudes, financial, political, scientific and industrial, presidents of great railroads and universities, men of industry, men of the arts and men of the stage.

The president was enthusiastic and gay as he rose to speak. He gave himself over to homely humor. His tone was that of the whimsical fisherman of the Rapidan rather than the formal voice of the head of a great state.

In him was something of the same spirit which prompted Edison, in the morning, to gather up a bundle of papers and a basket of fruit and pass through the old-time train which carried the presidential party the last leg of its trip, insisting that everyone pay cash for his wares.

Hoover is Humorous.

With a chuckle in his voice, the president said that when Edison *Continued on Page 12, Column 1.*

BALK TARIFF BILL RETURN

Senators Defeat Proposal for Restriction.

Washington, Oct. 21.—(A. P.)— After rejecting by 64 to 10 a motion to recommit the tariff bill to the finance committee with instructions to limit proposed increases in duties on agricultural products, the senate agreed today to begin consideration of the rate schedules tomorrow.

It was the second time the senate defeated a move to restrict tariff revision to the farmers' interests. The first vote, taken last June, too, 39 to 38.

The motion today was made by Senator Thomas, Democrat, Oklahoma, who asserted the pending bill represented a general revision instead of a limited one as recommended by President Hoover. Approximately 500 committee amendments and 200 proposed changes by individual senators are pending in the rate schedules. Seven weeks were spent on the administrative provisions. Six weeks remain for consideration of rates before the special session ends.

RESULTS COUNT NOW

This is the time of year when the Want Ad user has to have the greatest number of results possible at satisfactory costs. Free Press Want Ads are read by Detroiters whose pay checks are not interrupted by industrial fluctuations. Free Press Want Ads bring results now when the advertiser most appreciates them.

Free Press Want Ads Produce Best Cost Less

RAndolph 9400

Ypsilanti Singers Win in Contest

Ypsilanti, Oct. 21.—Miss Margaret Bennett, soprano, and Chester Gooding, baritone, of Ypsilanti, today were announced winners in the state radio audition held in Detroit, October 14. Twenty-eight other contestants from Michigan entered. The two winners will go to Chicago where the state district contest will be held.

Robbery Attempt Brings Sentence

Ypsilanti, Oct. 21.—Frank Wilson, narcotic addict who lives in the vicinity of Ypsilanti, was arrested on a charge of attempted robbery and was sentenced this morning to two to six years in Ionia by Circuit Judge George Sample. Wilson has a long police record in other cities, and numerous charges of theft against him.

OLD DANCER AT ARCADIA
TONIGHT, Scotch Quadrilles, Square dances, old and new waltz.—Adv.

Radio Program—Page 20

The Detroit Free Press

WEATHER: Rain
FINAL EDITION
99th Year. No. 179 — DETROIT, MICHIGAN, WEDNESDAY, OCTOBER 30, 1929—THIRTY-FOUR PAGES — PRICE: THREE CENTS

ELEVENTH-HOUR RALLY CHECKS STOCK CRISIS; HUGE LOSSES REDUCED

Oct. 30, 1929:

A government official assures the nation that the economy is sound — on the day the stock market crashes.

DRY SEARCH AT FERRIES IS STOPPED

Drastic Change Made Along River Upon Complaints.

TAKE SHOTGUNS FROM AGENTS

Small Boats to Run Unmolested, Scare Firing Barred.

STEAM HEATED ROOMS FIXED FOR ANIMALS

Zoo's Management Gets Ready for Winter; To Close Park Nov. 18.

CHARITY FUND GAINS $318,990

Butzel Urges Greater Donations as Second Day's Results Fall Below Expectations.

INSURGENTS SEEK TRUCE WITH G.O.P.

Wish to Regain Loss in Conflict Over Tariff Bill.

WATSON TO DROP LEADER'S REINS

McNary Groomed to Assume Post; Jones in Contest.

BY F. S. LEGGETT,
Free Press Staff Correspondent.

MAY BRING END TO G.O.P. FEUD

SENATOR C. L. McNARY

'WEED'S CURSE' TOLD FARMERS

Michigan Grange Asked to Condemn Smoking, Especially of Cigarets.

BY FRANK G. MORRIS,
Free Press Staff Correspondent.

SHORNEY GETS 35-50 YEARS

Jackson Wife Slayer Will Begin Term Today.

SHIP SINKS; NEW LAKES GALES RAGE

Wisconsin Is Down; 13 Lost, Including Captain.

MICHIGAN SEAS ENGULF VESSEL

59 Rescued by Coast Guardsmen and Fishing Tug.

MAY GO FREE, EVEN IF HE DID STEAL

21-Year-Old Man Says He Took Food for Relatives.

Last Guggenheim Gift Announced

U.S. TOURISTS, CRASH-RUINED, WILD IN PARIS

Frantically Discount Jewels to Purchase Passage Back Home.

ENVOY REGAINS STOLEN RELIC

Cleveland Museum Transfers to Jugoslavia Valuable Carving Bought in Good Faith.

3RD MAN JAILED FOR BLACKMAIL

Ex-Aide of Lew Tuller's Wealthy Chef Nabbed as 'Finger Man' in $5,000 Plot.

Capone Refused Liberty Hearing

Jury Disagrees On Catts' Guilt

Rescued Officer Tells Of Tragedy on Lake

Describes Heroism of Captain and Engineer; Wept When Landed From Wisconsin.

BY EDWARD HALVERSON,
First Mate and Survivor of Steamship Wisconsin.

BUSINESS IN U.S. ON SOUND BASIS, KLEIN DECLARES

Assistant Commerce Secretary Issues Reassurance.

FACTORY, FARM OUTLOOK GOOD

Buying Power Same as Before, Radio Talk Asserts.

Powerful Aid Thrown in Market; Bankers Exert Pressure.

16,410,030 IS NEW SALES RECORD

Investment Concerns Acquire Shares at Bargain Prices.

Reach New Low Levels.

MISSING AIR LINER SAFE

Landing Made in N. M. to Dodge Snowstorm.

WIRE TAPPING CATCHES FIVE

Dry Agents Unearth Plot to Smuggle Rum.

DALADIER UNABLE TO FORM CABINET

Socialists Refuse Aid; Briand May Be Named Again.

U. S. Officials Investigate Canadian Ship, Shawnee

Wilbur Opposes Rio Grande Plan

INVESTOR DIES DURING CRASH

Collapses at Stock Ticker in Broker's Office.

Confession Strong Point.

Of Course—

I Rented my Room thru your Want Ads. Many people who have had similar experience agree with Mrs. (name on request.) This little ad did the trick!

You can get like results whenever you have a need for a Want Ad if you use

Free Press Want Ads Produce Best — Cost Less

To place a Want Ad call

RAndolph 9400

Nov. 12, 1929:

Americans and Canadians meet at mid-river during dedication of the Ambassador Bridge.

WEATHER — Rain and Colder

The Detroit Free Press
MICHIGAN'S GREATEST NEWSPAPER

FINAL EDITION

90th Year. No. 192 — DETROIT, MICHIGAN, TUESDAY, NOVEMBER 12, 1929—THIRTY-SIX PAGES — PRICE: THREE CENTS

100,000 CHEER BRIDGE DEDICATION, HAIL AMITY

UNLIMITED ARMS CUT, HOOVER BID

Says U. S. Will Go as Far as Any Nation in Reduction.

ASKS IMMUNITY FOR FOOD SHIPS

President's Armistice Day Address Is Peace Plea.

The complete text of President Hoover's Armistice Day address will be found on page 15.

Washington, Nov. 11.—(A. P.)—President Hoover appraised the world tonight that reduction in naval armaments could not be too soon to suit the United States.

"We will reduce our naval strength in proportion to any other," he asserted in an Armistice day address. "Having said that it only remains for the others to say how low they will go. It can not be too low for us."

As another contribution to the ultimate peace of the world he proposed that food ships should be made free of any interference in times of war.

Opposes Starvation Strategy.

"The time has come when we should remove starvation of women and children from the weapons of warfare," he said, adding that he will put forward the proposition of treating food ships as hospital craft as a practical step in the solution of a large part of the age old controversy of freedom of the seas.

"It would act as a preventive as well as a limitation of war," he said. "I offer it only for the consideration of the world. I have not made it a governmental proposition to any nation and do not do so now.

"This is but a proposition for the forthcoming naval conference, and if that session is for a definite purpose this proposal will not be included in it."

While advocating peace and reduction of armaments, President Hoover declared for "adequate preparedness as a guaranty that no foreign soldier shall ever step upon the soil of our country."

Speaking at an open air auditorium under the auspices of the American Legion and to an audience made up largely of men who fought in the World war, the president unfolded his ideals of a new vision of diplomacy in the world. Those present, as well as thousands of war veterans and others listening in by radio throughout the nation, also heard the legion's national commander, O. L. Bodenhamer, and a message from General John J. Pershing, who cabled greetings from Paris. The legion leader voiced a plea for the enactment of a universal draft law.

Declaring that to maintain peace is as dynamic in its requirements as in the conduct of war, Hoover said progress toward peace could be attained only through realistic, practical, daily conduct amongst nations.

"Good Will Necessary."

"Men of good will throughout the world are working earnestly and honestly to perfect the equipment of preparedness for peace," he added. "But there is something *Continued on Page 15, Column 5.*

GIRL ENDS LIFE IN PLANE LEAP

Hurls Self From Airship 2,000 Feet in Air.

Special to Free Press and Chicago Tribune
Curtiss Field, L. I., Nov. 11.—Choosing an exit from life as spectacular as it was certain, a 20-year-old girl of good family engaged an airplane this afternoon, paid a pilot to carry her high above Valley Stream, L. I., and then deliberately leaped to her death out of the poised 2,000 feet.

The girl, who achieved a grim distinction, "America's first aerial suicide," is Ruth Rockwell, of Crestwood, N. J. The man who unwittingly became the instrument of her self-destruction was Edward F. Booth, a transport pilot employed to fly passengers to Curtiss airport.

Prays, Then Jumps.

In a note found by her body, Miss Rockwell blamed a futile and fruitless search for happiness for her decision to end it all. She promised that if she could project herself in spirit from the beyond, she would communicate with members of her family tonight. She denied she was insane, expressed curiosity as to what spare the newspapers would devote to her death, and concluded her unsigned message with:

"I have no guilty conscience, whatsoever. I feel—" This was *Continued on Page 5, Column 3.*

MICHIGAN MAN IS HELD AS RECKLESS DRIVER

Special to The Free Press.
Toronto, Nov. 11.—H. D. Callahan, giving his address as 3016 Wakefield road, Berkley, Mich., was arrested tonight on a charge of reckless driving by Highway Constable Miner after he had run down and injured John Leggatt, of Islington. Leggatt received a gash in his leg and bruises.

ICE SKATING—OLYMPIA
Tonight. 8 to 11. Skates rented. Admission, 50c.—Adv.

PART OF CROWD THAT STORMED INTERNATIONAL GATEWAY

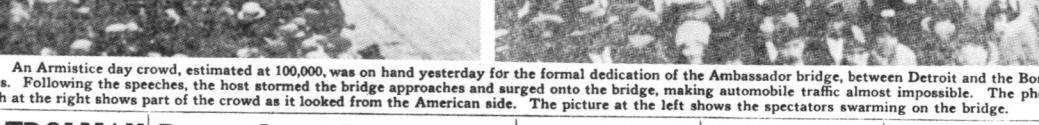

An Armistice day crowd, estimated at 100,000, was on hand yesterday for the formal dedication of the Ambassador bridge, between Detroit and the Border Cities. Following the speeches, the host stormed the bridge approaches and surged onto the bridge, making automobile traffic almost impossible. The photograph at the right shows part of the crowd as it looked from the American side. The picture at the left shows the spectators swarming on the bridge.

PATROLMAN IS HELD AS BANDIT AIDE

Three Thugs Accuse Edgar Cannane as Accomplice.

Patrolman Edgar Cannane, regarded by his immediate superiors as one of the most promising of the police department's younger men, was arrested on a charge of robbery armed at noon yesterday, stripped of his uniform and placed in a cell at the Canfield avenue station.

According to Inspector William T. Doyle, of the Central station, in which Cannane was attached as a motorcycle officer, three confessed bandits have signed statements naming Cannane as an accomplice in a holdup committed October 29.

Pistol Is Produced

When arrested, one of the three prisoners were called in the uniformed officer who accused the officer carried a revolver which he declared belonged to Cannane. This revolver, which produced Saturday evening. Before Cannane could be questioned, however, a bandit who wounded him intended victim was captured Sunday morning and the revolver which he carried was traced to Cannane through the manufacturer's number.

Anxious to develop their case as far as possible before calling in Cannane, detectives continued to question the prisoners until noon yesterday, when Inspector Doyle called the patrolman from his beat and placed him under arrest. Cannane then was taken to the Canfield station, where the thugs are held.

Three Sign Statement.

Those who signed statements naming both themselves and Cannane as bandits are Dwight Lewis, 24 years old; James Deidrich, 22, and Kay Reyes, 24. All live in a Prentis avenue apartment house.

Accompanying Doyle and Cannane to the precinct station was Philip J. Neudeck, an assistant prosecutor, who took the statements incriminating the patrolman. Before returning to headquarters, Neudeck announced that this morning he will recommend a warrant charging Cannane with robbery armed.

Describes Her Visits To Castle's Mother

Miss Cleavenger Didn't Mention Marriage Then; on Stand in Suit for $750,000.

Although she twice paid visits to the home of John H. Castle's mother in Indiana the subject of her engagement to him did not come up for discussion, Miss Bertha Cleavenger testified yesterday in the court of Judge S. Homer Ferguson, where she is suing Castle for $750,000 for alleged breach of promise to marry. The witness said she had also met the three brothers of John Castle and Mrs. Sidney Castle, the wife of one of them. When Ralph H. Clark, attorney for Castle, asked her on due cross examination whether the matter had been talked about with any of these persons she replied:

Her Private Affairs.

"I'm not referring to the public, but to the family at the time, you claim you were engaged to marry," Clark told her.

The witness said that both of the Indiana trips were made by auto and in company with Castle. Miss Cleavenger admitted she knew Mr. *Continued on Page 5, Column 1.*

BEGIN RECOUNT ON WEDNESDAY

Reading's Assistants Will Spend 2 Weeks Proving Ballots in Mayoralty Race.

A recount of all ballots cast for mayor in the election of November 5 will commence in the council chamber Wednesday morning, the city election commission decided yesterday at the regular session, where the official canvass was completed. This canvass showed that Charles Bowles was elected mayor over John W. Smith by 8,401 votes.

The petition asking for a recount was filed by Charles P. O'Neill, corporation counsel when Smith was mayor, and bore the signature of former Mayor Smith. It was the regulation petition required for a recount.

Won't Need Extra Help

Richard W. Reading, city clerk and chairman of the election commission, stated that extra help would not be employed in the recount, but that it would be made by members of his own staff.

Each of the two candidates will be allowed two men at each table to watch the count, one to check the men calling the ballots and another to keep a check on the man tabulating the result.

Will Require 2 Weeks

Reading outlined the method to be used in tabulating the count. Going to Lester F. Dunn, chief deputy sheriff, and Joseph Blythe, prospective candidates for police commissioner under Bowles, and J. DeWitt Ambrose, clerk.

It is expected the recount will require about two weeks, as the tabulators will not be required to work overtime.

Evidence Taken In Tunney Suit

Fort Worth, Tex., Nov. 11.—(A. P.)—Taking of depositions in the $500,000 alienation of affections suit of John S. Fogarty, of Fort Worth, against Gene Tunney, former heavyweight boxing champion, was begun here today. About 50 witnesses were called. The hearing may last all week. Transcripts of testimony will be sent to Bridgeport, Conn., where Fogarty's suit against Tunney at alleged attentions to Mrs. Fogarty were the cause of Mrs. Fogarty's divorce in 1925. The former Mrs. Fogarty has sued Tunney for a breach of promise. She asks $50,000.

MAMMOTH STYLE SHOW
Vanity Ballroom tonite and tomorrow nite. Gorgeous prizes. Wonderful Music. Inspiring Adm. 50c.—Adv.

RUM'S FLOW TO DETROIT HELD LESS

Only 43,400 Cases in Last Month, U. S. Figures Show.

Washington, Nov. 11.—(A. P.)—Assistant Secretary Lowman said today official Canadian reports for October showed a decrease of 119,378 cases of liquor cleared for export to the United States in the Detroit area as compared with October of a year ago.

"I don't discuss my private affairs with the public."

Lowman said only 43,400 cases of liquor cleared for United States ports in the Detroit area last month, while the clearances for the same area for the same month in 1928 were 162,778. The clearances for last October were the smallest had been established between Lakes Erie and Huron. These figures were regarded as significant because there has been an intensive campaign against rum running, he said, some months ago, in the Detroit area.

Three Before Grand Jury.

A railroad president, a hotel manager and a writer appeared before the grand jury today to testify regarding the famous "Wall street" fund, and all refused to comment afterwards on their testimony. However, the railroad president, E. E. Loomis, of the Lehigh Valley, gave an indication of what he considered the "properties" relating to private dinners.

"You don't expect me to discuss as far as he knew, the grand jury would not request the appearance of additional witnesses to testify concerning the dinner and liquor conditions for the present.

Brookhart Starts Quiz.

Senator Brookhart, of Iowa, was indirectly responsible for the appearance of Loomis and Frank Hight, manager of the Willard hotel. In a speech on the senate floor he described the dinner given at the Willard for members of congress by Walter Fahy, New York broker, and asserted he saw Loomis pour some "alcoholic stuff" from a flask and drink it. Brookhart also said that flasks were passed freely by Fahy.

District Attorney Rover said after the appearance of the trio that as far as he knew, the grand jury would not request the appearance of additional witnesses to testify concerning the dinner and liquor conditions for the present.

FEARED 'GANG,' VET A SUICIDE

Fights Off Police Siege For Fifteen Hours.

Pittsburgh, Nov. 11.—(U. P.)—Anticipating defeat, bar a miracle, the twelfth annual campaign of the Detroit Community Fund will close at noon today with a shortage anywhere from $250,000 to $300,000.

That, at least, was the outlook as fund officials saw the situation last night. This canvass showed that the need of the agencies was so acute that it was quite likely if the campaign took the now optional course of renewed after Christmas, *Continued on Page 5, Column 1.*

Carded For Bout Here, Boxer Dies

Columbus, Ohio, Nov. 11.—(A. P.)—Johnny O'Keefe, 25 years old, Columbus lightweight boxer, died in a hospital here tonight. He became ill after finishing today's training for a match Friday in Detroit with Tommy Cello, of Los Angeles. The cause of his death was not announced.

POLICE RADIO NABS 2 IN ONE-HALF MINUTE

Washington, Nov. 11.—(A. P.)—At a brief ceremony today Maj. Johnny O'Keefe, 25 years old, Columbus lightweight boxer, died in a hospital here tonight. He became ill after finishing today's training for a match Friday in Detroit with Tommy Cello, of Los Angeles. The cause of his death was not announced.

THUGS ROB MOTORIST

While putting his automobile in the garage at the rear of his home, Fred Chandler, 12134 Prairie avenue, was robbed of a wallet containing $15 and his driver's license by two thugs at 11:15 o'clock last night.

EASTERN MICHIGAN SYSTEM
Passenger-Freight-Express Service to Flint, Pontiac, Lansing, Grand Rapids, Pt. Huron, Toledo, Jackson, Ann Arbor. Edge 2120 Information.—Adv.

SENATORS MAY SHOOT IT OUT IN WASHINGTON

Washington, Nov. 11.—(A. P.)—The spirit of Armistice Day heightened, rather than diminished, a desire today on the part of friends of Senator David A. Reed of Pennsylvania, to have him settle a difference with Senator Smith W. Brookhart of Iowa, by shooting, if he troubles.

Both the senators are war veterans. Brookhart has boasted of his powers as a marksman. Reed also thinks himself a good marksman, and resents the Iowan's claim in their field. He has challenged Brookhart to shoot it out. Friends of Reed are trying to get the Iowan to accept.

The "shooting it out" will be a target, and not each other.

CROWDS GREET PARADING VETS

Thousands Join in Observing Return of Armistice Day in City.

(See Pictures on Last Page.)

Eleven years after a war-weary world embraced the dearly-won peace of November 11, 1918, the streets of Detroit yesterday again responded to the tread of marching thousands, marching this time to the music of peace.

Under the flag for which they fought, through a lane of cheering thousands, the surviving actors in the scenes played on Europe's stricken fields of war celebrated the peace that hushed the angry cannon, and paid silent tribute to the comrades who did not return.

Veterans in Line.

Rank upon rank marched the veterans of Soissons, St. Mihiel and Chateau Thierry, to whom the memories of those shambles is all too poignant.

But there were many who could not march—the disabled veterans. And in the faces of these torn men, the crowds could read the whole pitiful story of war—the story of high explosives, poison gas, shrapnel, ripping machine gun fire, bombs from the sky and the whole gray array of death-dealing devices which wrecked these courageous bodies.

Three ghosts from an unforgotten world—many misty eyes and silent a solemnity kind of Armistice Day in the city.

Side by side with the men who fought their nation's battle across the sea marched the youth of today, the cadets of the R. O. T. C. Boy *Continued on Page 3, Column 4.*

GERMANY DEMANDS PAY FROM ENGLAND

London, Nov. 11.—The British treasury has received a stiff note from the German government demanding immediate settlement of a claim for $100,000,000 due liquidated German property.

Just before the Ruhr crisis Germany paid into the London treasury money for liquidation of German claims. Then came the Dawes plan inflation, which made German settlement impossible and the matter was forgotten.

The treasury is embarrassed because the money is not available and parliament will have to be asked for a special appropriation to cover money already paid in for one purpose and spent for another.

DANCE—GRAYSTONE TONITE
McKINNEY'S COTTON PICKERS—ORCH.—Adv.

FLINT BANK SHORTAGE $3,592,000

C. S. Mott Increases Protection Fund $1,500,000.

BY OWEN C. DEATRICK
Free Press Staff Correspondent

Flint, Nov. 11.—Former officials of the Union Industrial Bank of Flint, one of the largest financial institutions in this section of the state, manipulated $3,592,000 of the bank funds in stock market speculations during the last two years before they confessed to the bank directors, according to the official statement of the new bank president, Charles Stewart Mott, vice-president of the General Motors corporation, who has assumed direction of the bank.

The entire amount has been made up by Mott, who today added $1,500,000 in actual cash to more than the $2,038,000 that was provided when the defalcation was first discovered.

Bank's Position Sound.

State banking officials and executives of the recent $75,000,000 bank merger in Detroit, of which the Union Industrial bank was a part, declared that the bank's financial status has not been impaired, due to the prompt action of Mott and the other bank directors.

"C. S. Mott has added more than $1,500,000 to the actual cash he has deposited in the Union Industrial bank further to guarantee the institution against any possible loss from the defalcations of former employes. Mr. Mott has now resumed the active presidency of the bank came forth with these additional funds when the investigation, now nearly complete, showed an increase in the net shortage to possibly $2,000,000. The gross amount there will be considerable deductions through insurance settlements and other recoveries. These developments were disclosed at a special meeting of the board of directors meeting this noon, following. *Continued on Page 2, Column 5.*

JUMPS INTO CANAL; KEEPS ON YODELING

Tall Man Found in Belle Isle Water Is Under Observation.

Although lacking the ostentation which attracted considerable attention to the Ambassador bridge yesterday, Joseph Lubinski, 42 years old, 5488 Grundy avenue, last night, in a quaint Lubinski manner, attracted considerable attention to one of Belle Isle's numerous bridges.

Lubinski's process was simple. He climbed to the summit of the bridge, and after yodeling the Canadian national anthem, plunged into the water of one of the canals. It was shallow and Lubinski's tall. The result was that three feet of Lubinski protruded above the water. The rest of Mr. Lubinski was imbedded in mud at the canal bottom.

Patrolmen Leland Rumming and Anthony Schetrach, attracted by the yodeling, discovered his discomforting position. He was hauled from the mud and transferred to Receiving hospital, and at present, is

U.S.-CANADA SPAN OPENS IN SPLENDOR

Governor Green and Judge Callender Laud Builders.

LINKS CITIES ON THE STRAIT

Huge Structure Is Built at Cost of $22,500,000.

(See Picture on Last Page.)

Severance of two white ribbons, at 4 p. m. yesterday, signalized the dedication of the Ambassador bridge, a $22,500,000 miracle in concrete and steel, which binds the United States more closely with Canada and places Detroit and the Border Cities more definitely on the map of North America.

Fittingly, it happened on Armistice day when both nations were celebrating peace, a prototype of the Pax Americana which has existed between these countries for nearly 115 years. It was the cutting of a geographical boundary which has no place spiritually.

Enthusiasm Is Tremendous.

Enthusiasm on both sides of the river was tremendous. A crowd that can only be roughly estimated at 100,000 gathered on the American shore after the Armistice Day parade and merely surmounted the bridge after the Stars and Stripes had been raised at the portals. They met another crowd, from the Canadian side, which surged not less lustily in the center. Diplomatic rapprochement could ever have equalled this commingling of two peoples.

The police, the marines, the civic and legion guards of the bridge, continued of both countries were powerless against the spontaneous burstings of either side. Only the sidewalked gates that mark the international boundary kept the two masses apart.

Planes Drone Overhead.

Between a leaden sky and the green waters of the river, amid the droning of airplanes and the hooting of sirens, Mrs. Joseph A. Bower, wife of the bridge's sponsor, and Mrs. J. W. Austin, wife of the A. Canadian lieutenant, cut the ribbon on the Canadian entrance to the bridge. At the same time, Mrs. J. J. Fozard, wife of the bridge engineer, and Mrs. C. P. McTague, wife of the Canadian attorney of the bridge company, were cutting the ribbon on the American side, and thus symbolic acts another link was forged in the wholesome relations between the United States and Canada.

The crowd sensed the spirit of this gesture of friendliness. Canadian bands were at the American *Continued on Page 2, Columns 1 and 2.*

MICHIGAN MAN HERO IN WRECK

Injured, He Flags Train; 5 Detroiters Hurt.

Chattanooga, Tenn., Nov. 11.—(A. P.)—A Michigan man who hobbled about on a broken ankle and flagged two trains that might have crashed into overturned coaches and scores of helpless injured tonight was the hero of the Southern railway Ponce de Leon wreck near Oakdale, Tenn., today.

P. A. Sherman, of Ortonville, Mich., clambered from his overturned coach, flagged a northbound train and then, walking on a broken *Continued on Page 3, Column 6.*

"It wasn't a bargain counter crowd—merely an army of young women responding to our own Free Press Want Ad"

...said Mr. Dean of the D. J. Healy Shop as he endorsed this newspaper as an ideal classified medium for filling employment needs.

This hint as to the source of so much interest and response!

SALESWOMEN have been filing into the Healy store, 1426 Woodward ave., to answer

Your employment problem can be solved to your satisfaction if you are the quarter of a million homes that receive The Free Press every day.

Free Press Want Ads Produce Well Cost Less

RAndolph 9400

DEC. 29, 1929:

A slice of funny-page life from the Roaring '20s.

Sunday feature

July 23, 1930:

Detroit recalls its mayor, and the city's No. 1 radio commentator is gunned down in a Woodward Avenue hotel.

"Bowles is beaten by 30,956" and *"Jerry Buckley Assassinated,"* a late bulletin, column six.

WEATHER Fair

The Detroit Free Press
MICHIGAN'S GREATEST NEWSPAPER
METROPOLITAN HOME EDITION

100th Year. No. 80 — DETROIT, MICHIGAN, WEDNESDAY, JULY 23, 1930 — TWENTY-EIGHT PAGES — PRICE: THREE CENTS

BOWLES IS BEATEN BY 30,956

JERRY BUCKLEY ASSASSINATED

120,863 VOTE 'YES' AND 89,907 'NO' IN RECALL CONTEST

Balloting Is Heaviest in Any Special Election Ever Held Here; Ouster Is First in Large U. S. City.

NEXT ELECTION ABOUT AUG. 27; MAYOR MUST BE CANDIDATE

Far East Side Turns on Executive After Giving Him Big November Majority; Other Reversals.

BY CLIFFORD A. PREVOST.

Charles Bowles was called from the office of mayor of Detroit by 30,956 ballots in the election Tuesday, the first of its kind ever held in a large city in the United States.

His administration was repudiated in the heaviest ballot ever cast in a special election in Detroit—more than 200,000 people having gone to the polls, of whom 120,863 voted for the recall, with 89,907 voting "No."

SCORES DIE AS BRIDGE COLLAPSES

Von Hindenburg Fete Ends in Tragedy to Celebrants.

BODIES OF FORTY ARE RECOVERED

Walk Over Pontoons to 'Security Harbor' Crashes Span.

ELECTION BODY CHECKS RECALL RETURNS

BULLETIN

Gerald E. "Jerry" Buckley, announcer for the radio station WMBC, was shot and killed in the lobby of the LaSalle hotel, Woodward avenue and Adelaide street, by an unknown assailant at 1:45 a. m. Wednesday. Buckley was walking toward the Adelaide street exit of the lobby when the gunman, who was concealed near the lobby desk, fired four bullets into the radio announcer's body. Buckley died one minute after he was admitted to Receiving hospital. The dead man had just left the studio of the radio station, which is located in the hotel.

HOOVER TELLS OF PEACE GAIN

Signs London Naval Covenant, Declaring U. S. Obtains Full Defense.

Hamer Leads Derby To Cincinnati Port

Twelve Ships Make Second Leg, Four Meet Mishaps and Two Are Missing.

BY CHARLES McLEAN, Free Press Aviation Editor.

HEAT CHASED BY SHOWERS

Maximum Temperature Here Tuesday 83; Two Die Despite Drop.

BOARD AVOIDS RUM QUESTION

School Inspectors Vote Against Official Discussion by Membership.

RED TRADERS DENY INTRIGUE

Amtorg Chiefs Disavow Secret Police in U. S.

Argentine Greets U. S. Ambassador

MOSES LOSES POST IN WEST

G. O. P. Switches Senator to Suit 'Young Turks.'

123 MILLIONS CENSUS GUESS

Estimated Population Gain of U. S. 14.9 Pct.

STRIKE IN PROTEST.

rented the first day...

113 Candidates Seek 17 Legislative Posts

Wayne County Experiences Last Minute Rush to File Petitions.

Unlike Daisies Women Tell of Carol, Lothario-Like Rumanian King

Green and Welsh Put In Race for Governor

Campaign Complicated by Unauthorized Petitions; McLeod Ruled Out.

BY JAMES P. POWERS.

WEATHER
Fair and Cool

The Detroit Free Press

MICHIGAN'S GREATEST NEWSPAPER

THIRD ELECTION EXTRA.....

100th Year. No. 129 DETROIT, MICHIGAN, WEDNESDAY, SEPTEMBER 10, 1930—THIRTY-TWO PAGES PRICE THREE CENTS

MURPHY ELECTED; PLURALITY IS NEAR 10,000

★ ★ ★

BRUCKER PILES UP BIG OUTSTATE MARGIN

WAYNE RETURNS REDUCE HIS LEAD FOR GOVERNOR

Third of Vote, Exclusive of Detroit, Indicates That Attorney General Has 100,000 Advantage.

COUZENS OUTRUNS OSBORN IN RACE FOR SENATE SEAT

Dickinson Running Far in Van for Lieutenant-Governorship; Others Are Close.

FOR SENATOR
1,793 precincts out of 3,317 in the state give:

Couzens	195,945
Osborn	139,482

FOR GOVERNOR.
1,738 precincts out of 3,317 in the state give:

Brucker	201,604
Groesbeck	139,670
Jeffries	24,402

FOR LIEUTENANT GOVERNOR.
1,452 precincts out of 3,317 in the state give:

Dickinson	115,830
Read	52,180
Breen	30,813
Thompson	26,838

BY JAMES P. POWERS.

Returns from a third of the state, exclusive of Wayne county, where the heavy vote kept tabulators working until morning hours, indicated that Attorney General Wilber M. Brucker would come to Detroit with a lead of approximately 100,000 over former Governor Alex J. Groesbeck. A handful of early Detroit returns promised to cut down the Brucker score.

Judge Edward Jeffries was badly beaten.

Brucker Carries Industrial Cities.

The Brucker advantage over his chief rival was spread over most of the counties of the state, and he was favored particularly in the rural districts. Governor Green's home county of Ionia went for him six to one, the Thumb counties almost as decisively, and the industrial counties of Saginaw, Ingham, Kalamazoo, Kent and Genesee all appeared safely in his column. The Groesbeck counties appeared to be mostly in the less populous northern territory, although Muskegon, Bay and Macomb gave him a big vote.

While trailing Senator James Couzens, former Governor Chase S. Osborn, who has campaigned for weeks from one end of the state to ...

WINS MAYORALTY --- LEADS FOR GOVERNOR

FRANK MURPHY.

WILBER M. BRUCKER.

BOWLES SECOND AND ENGEL THIRD; SMITH SWAMPED

Collapse of Former Chief Executive As Contender Feature of Hard Fought Election Contest.

CITIZENS' COMMITTEE CHOICE SUCCUMBS TO BALLOT SPLIT

Loses in Spite of Strong Showing; Winner Piles Up Greatest Lead On East Side of City.

741 precincts out of the 852 precincts in the city:

Murphy	90,420
Bowles	81,002
Engel	73,958
Smith	18,667
Raymond	2,703

BY CLIFFORD A. PREVOST.

Frank Murphy, the youthful jurist from the recorder's court, was elected mayor of Detroit, Tuesday, when approximately 26 per cent of the voters of the city expressed preference for him as against his four opponents. Murphy, who is 37 years old, is the youngest man ever elected chief executive. With the returns all but complete, it was indicated he would have a majority of at least 10,000 and possibly 12,000 ballots.

Charles Bowles, who will be remembered as the first executive of a large city to be recalled, went down to defeat in second place, approximately 7,000 ballots ahead of George Engel. The latter made the election of Murphy possible, as he cut into Bowles' support on the west side of the city and carried many precincts of the north end, in which sections Bowles piled up his tremendous leads of last fall.

Smith Vote Surprise.

Possibly the greatest surprise of the election was the collapse of the vote of former Mayor John W. Smith. Just 10 months ago Smith polled 123,000 ballots in Detroit, and his failure to rally more than 25,000 to his support in Tuesday's election amazed his supporters.

TOY, WILSON PULL AHEAD

Chenot Appears Likely to Win Place on Circuit Court Bench.

Early returns from the Republican primary contests for Wayne county offices showed Harry Toy leading P. J. M. Hally for prosecuting attorney, early Wednesday, Sheriff Ira W. Wilson maintaining a slight advantage over Henry Behrendt in the race for that office, and George T. Murphy leading a very broken field by a narrow margin in the 27-man free-for-all for the four posts of circuit court commissioner.

James E. Chenot, retiring prosecuting attorney, was running second in the contest for the four circuit court judgeships open, with Judge Lester S. Moll leading the field. Judges Homer Ferguson, Maurice H. McMahon and Allan ...

18 Planes Ready to Hop In Ford Trophy Race

First Ship Will Leave Airport at 10 O'clock Thursday on Long Flight.

BY CHARLES McLEAN,
Free Press Aviation Editor.

Walter Beech, only dual winner of the National Air tour, which carries with it the Edsel B. Ford reliability trophy, decided late Tuesday night that he would pilot his dual controlled Curtiss Kingbird in the sixth annual National Air tour.

"I think I was silly in withdrawing today," the old time flier said. "I was all excited about the Stinson withdrawal and I thought the rules would penalize me equally as much as the tri-motored Stinson entry."

... tests had started. They will be completed early Wednesday.

Fifteen ships which will accompany the tour, some carrying officials and others mechanics and aircraft representatives, had arrived by night. Several others are expected Wednesday, so that it appeared the fleet would outnumber any previous start.

Leg speed, the time required to fly between the 30 control stations, will largely determine the winner this year. Weight carried, the horsepower of engines and the time of starting and landing also figure, but not as prominently as in past years.

Edward Macauley, Luke Christopher, secretary of the National Aeronautic association contest committee; Professor Peter Altman, Walter Lees and Fred Verville were members of the contest committee who certified qualifying flights on ...

3 OF CONGRESS SEATS IN DOUBT

All Michigan Representatives Except in 4th, 6th, 7th Districts Sure of Posts.

All but three of Michigan's 13 representatives in congress appeared certain of renomination at an early hour Wednesday morning.

The only contests in doubt were in the Fourth, Sixth and Seventh districts.

Person Is Trailing.

Interest centered in the Sixth district race where the veteran representative, Grant M. Hudson, a former employe of the Michigan Anti-Saloon league, was opposed by State Senator Seymour H. Person, of Lansing. Person announced himself in favor of modification of the prohibition law. Returns from 164 precincts gave Hudson 21,288 votes and Person 16,628. However, ...

2 DEAD, 6 HURT IN AUTO CRASH

Cars Collide at High Speed at Maple and John R. Roads; All Are Detroiters.

GROW FIGHTS FOR PERU JOB

Asks U. S. Diplomats Let Him Defend Self.

First Life Episodes Will Be Published In Friday's Free Press

Read The Free Press and Listen in Over WXYZ

5 Killed, 11 Hurt In Engine Blast

WARSHIP SENT WITH RELIEF

Ordered to Santo Domingo With $20,000 Cargo.

SENATOR.

JURY TO CALL MAYOR BOWLES

Emmons' Charges to Be Aired After Buckley Case; Ex-Police Head to Testify.

RIOTERS SHOT IN ARGENTINA

Firing Squad Executes Two Alleged Leaders of Counter Revolt.

UNFIT ALIENS BAN TIGHTENS

U.S. Orders Curb on Visas to Assist Jobless.

HONOR MICHIGAN WOMEN.

SEPT. 10, 1930:

Frank Murphy would go on to become Michigan governor, governor-general of the Philippines, U.S. attorney general and associate justice of the U.S. Supreme Court.

MAY 10, 1931:

Writers see Detroit as the city of tomorrow on the 100th anniversary of the Free Press.

Special supplement

 **Detroit To-day Section** ANNIVERSARY SUPPLEMENT OF **The Detroit Free Press** 1831 ~ A CENTURY OF SERVICE ~ 1931  **Story of a City The World Watches**

101st Year. No. 6   DETROIT, MICHIGAN, SUNDAY, MAY 10, 1931

DYNAMIC CENTER OF MACHINE AGE

Detroit Leads World In Mass Production And New Democracy

BY HARVEY KLEMMER

What is Detroit?

"My country," wrote a great Frenchman, "is a state of mind." The same description well might be applied to Detroit, Wonder City of the Twentieth Century.

Superficially, it would seem a simple thing to define Detroit or any other city. Just look up the number of people, consult a map, ascertain the principal industries, delve into history a bit—and there you are. Thus Detroit is a city of 2,000,000 people, located on a river of the same name, is the automotive capital of the world, and was founded by Antoine de la Mothe Cadillac on July 23, 1701.

The task is not nearly so simple, however. We have described Detroit, to be sure, but defining the city is a different matter. None of the facts listed explains why Detroit is great among the cities of all time why the eyes of the world have turned this way for an answer to the inscrutable riddle of progress.

Is Detroit great because of natural endowments denied to other communities? Emphatically no. Few cities have been handicapped by location as has Detroit. We have come to our present commanding position over a long trail of obstacles.

Geographically, this amazing modern phenomenon which is Detroit is accurately described by the name itself—De Troit, or City of the Strait. Located between two of the Great Lakes, the city stretches for miles along the banks of the river and northward into the hinterland for additional miles.

DETROIT ISOLATED.

This does not explain why Detroit is great. Geography can claim no share of Detroit's success. Nor can weather, topography or proximity of natural resources. Chicago—at the crossroads of the nation—couldn't help becoming great. Detroit—off the main lines—became great in spite of its handicaps. Chicago, Cleveland and Toledo shut us off from the rest of the United States. We actually are north of Canada and have to cross a foreign nation to reach the seaboard markets.

New York, Boston, Philadelphia and other coast cities can thank an ocean for their position. Detroit has neither an ocean nor a lake. We have only a river through which ships pass on their way to rival ports. And we have to tunnel and bridge the river if we wish to cross into the foreign nation lying between us and the rest of our own country.

Is it because of vast natural resources that Detroit has grown to full stature in the family of cities? Hardly. Detroit has not gold or precious stones; what is more to the point, Detroit has neither the iron nor the coal so essential to the Machine Age. This city is located on the bottom of ancient Lake Maumee, which many thousands of years ago covered this area. All that we have from the past is a heritage of mud and a flat topography excellent for building roads, but hard on the landscape painters.

Surely there is no answer to Detroit's secret here.

CITY SHOWS RAPID GROWTH.

Nor is the answer to be found in the census figures, either now or at any time since that July day when the bateaux of Cadillac arrived to protect her French dandies their supply of beaver hats. Detroit has doubled its population almost every decade for the past century, until now we stand fourth in the roll call of American cities.

Still we have not discovered why Detroit should be hailed as the most significant phenomenon of our time. Other cities have risen as rapidly, some more so. We must look beyond mere size for the answer to our query.

Does agriculture explain the greatness of our city? No. Michigan ranks well among the American commonwealths in the value and diversity of its agricultural products. We consume the major share of what we produce, however, so that Detroit has little in common with Montreal, Galveston, Odessa or Buenos Aires.

Which brings us to the subject of shipping. Here we again are thwarted in our search for explanation of Detroit's importance. Although the Detroit river carries the greatest waterborne commerce of any stream in the world, few of the great ships which ply the lakes stop here. With the coming of steel to the Detroit area, more and more of the 27,000 freighters annually passing the city's door will take on or discharge cargo. At present Detroit is not predominantly important as a distribution center. We are forging ahead in the value of our exported products, but they go by way of other ports.

Does antiquity explain Detroit? Or Art? Science? Learning? Culture? Do these give Detroit its excuse for occupying the pedestal of greatness in preference to cities founded before the new world was discovered? Detroit is cultured, to be sure, yet hardly more so than its contemporaries. Nor are our scientific achievements inordinately great.

WHAT IS "DETROITISM"?

What, then, DOES explain this thing Detroit, and this more elusive but none the less real thing known as "Detroitism"? Ah, you say, the explanation is industry, converting raw materials from the ends of the earth into utilitarian products enjoyed by all the people of all the civilized world. This, then, must be the explanation which we seek.

But hold; let us proceed more slowly. Careful examination will reveal that even this explanation is inadequate to explain the whole significance of the Capital of Speed. Detroit, of course, turns out a tremendous volume of manufactured articles; the whirling wheels of industry dump into the world markets an endless profusion of products. But there are other manufacturing centers equally prolific. There is one thing more, an institution which more than any single factor has

Continued on Page 2.

Detroit is the fourth city, with a population of 1,568,662. The population of Greater Detroit (the metropolitan trading area) is 2,049,906. The population of Wayne county is 1,892,372.

The area of Detroit is 139.0239 square miles. The city is 581 feet above sea level. The mean annual temperature is 48.5 degrees; average annual rainfall, 32.05 inches. The city has 11 miles of water frontage. Detroit river is 31 miles long.

The assessed valuation of Detroit real and personal, is $3,774,851,100 (1930). The city's bonded debt is $275,991,395 net. There are about 235,000 homes in the city, exclusive of apartment houses. Building construction for 1930 was $48,369,000.

There are 26 national and state banks and trust companies in Detroit, Highland Park and Hamtramck. Bank clearings for 1930 were $8,433,000,000. Savings deposits were $559,629,000. The total capital is $39,000,000, with resources of $1,271,643,000.

There are 450,000 wage earners in Detroit, employed in 2,043 establishments. They earn $675,000,000 annually and produce goods valued at $3,500,000,000 in normal times.

Detroit has 2,650 miles of streets, of which 1,684 miles are paved. Capacity of the municipal water works is 565,000,000 gallons a day, with 2,754 miles of mains in the city proper and assessed valuation of $98,786,482. The city uses 254,121,848 gallons of water daily.

Detroit plants produce 60 per cent of the automobiles manufactured in the United States, while 77 per cent of the total number is produced within an 85-mile radius of Detroit. During 1929, the banner year, 5,358,361 cars were produced in the United States. Of this number, 4,152,729 were made in Detroit and nearby centers.

Detroit's municipally-owned transportation system carries 1,350,000 passengers a day. There are 380,000 telephones in Detroit, 2,424 miles of gas mains and 440 miles of street railway track.

The Detroit public schools include 197 elementary, 18 intermediate and 15 high schools; a college of pharmacy, a teachers' college, the College of the City of Detroit, the College of Medicine and Surgery and Detroit College of Law. Personnel is 7,693, with total enrollment of 249,877. Detroit spends 31.24 per cent of its

Here stands our City—

in one year has used raw materials to the value of $1,246,711,000. One million tons of coal are used annually by one Detroit coke plant, while the city requires 9,000,000 tons of coal for heating and manufacturing.

There are 27,600 retail stores in Detroit and 884 wholesale houses. Of the retail establishments, 3,750 are grocery stores, 628 drug, 648 hardware and 18 department stores. Detroit postoffice receipts for 1930 were $10,831,000. Retail

taxes for education. In the Catholic school system of Detroit there are 111 schools, 45 of which have high schools in addition. There are 1,602 teachers and 77,680 pupils. The board of education budget for 1930 was $39,300,057. The birth rate in Detroit for 1930 was 21.3 per thousand. The death rate was 9.2 per thousand. In 1930, 13,127 marriage licenses were issued in the city. There are 69 hospitals with 7,605 beds in metropolitan Detroit, and 2,500 registered physicians and surgeons.

Detroit is held to be the most popular tourist and convention city in America. More than 400 conventions are held here every year, bringing 450,000 delegates. A total of 3,543,000 persons visited Detroit in one year, while 6,663,000 people came in 1,881,000 cars to visit the state. A half million people annually visit one Detroit automobile plant.

There are 740 churches of all denominations in Detroit; 23 libraries and branches, containing 847,782 volumes; 200 theaters, with seating capacity of 200,000 and investment of $50,000,000; 34 city parks, containing 2,810 acres of land valued at $100,000,000; 450 hotels, with 25,000 rooms.

Michigan in one year exported goods valued at $342,645,582, exceeded only by New York, Galveston and New Orleans. Only three counties in the United States exceed Wayne county as a plant consumer. Wayne county

service serves 5,000,000 people within a radius of 30 miles; the jobbing territory, extending out 150 miles, includes 10,000,000 people.

Aircraft products of Detroit exceed $20,000,000 a year. Detroit has a municipal airport, a Wayne county airport, and 10 private landing fields in addition to the government airports at Selfridge field and Grosse Ile and Henry Ford's field at Dearborn.

The Detroit police department has 3,778 uniformed members, with 15 precinct stations and 402 pieces of motor equipment exclusive of motorcycles. The fire department employs 2,033 men, with equipment including 93 automobiles, 58 pumping engines, 7 chemical hose cars, 5 rescue cars, 31 ladder trucks and two fire boats.

Nine railroad systems serve Detroit, operating from three terminals. They are the Michigan Central, the New York Central, the Pennsylvania, the Grand Trunk, Pere Marquette, Canadian Pacific, Wabash, Detroit & Toledo Shore line and the Detroit, Toledo & Ironton.

In addition to automobiles, Detroit also leads the world in the manufacture of a score of other products. Among non-automotive products for which Detroit is noted are adding machines, pharmaceuticals, soda ash, salt, marine engines, electric fans, paints and varnish, stoves and vacuum cleaners.

Detroit Envisioned City of the Future By World Scholars

The eyes of the world are on Detroit, plowshare of progress. From every corner of the globe there converges on this city an unending stream of pilgrims come to worship at the altar of speed. Many are magnates of manufacturing in their own right, courting at Detroit the awesome secret of industrial success. They linger a few days, absorb ideas, return to their homes fired with enthusiasm. Another monument in steel soon will be reared to the mother city of mass production.

Technicians come to Detroit by thousands. They spend days and weeks studying the technique of manufacturing as developed here. They return to their homes in many lands fortified by expert counsel on every phase of production and distribution. Hundreds of plants annually are raised in the Detroit image.

Along with those who undertake the Detroit pilgrimage in order to make obeisance before the shrine of industry are others actuated by an even more significant purpose. They have no interest in multiple operations and the subdivision of labor, per se; their interest is in mankind and they come to Detroit to study the human consequences of the factory system which in this city has found its fullest expression. It is the consequences, rather than mere quantitative production, which have made Detroit great.

Thus sociologists dissecting the Machine Age almost invariably turn to Detroit as the epitome of manufacturing development. Economists find here the finest example of an industrial community, solving today the urban problems which eventually all cities must face. Their studies reveal Detroit as a many-faceted phenomenon without parallel in the whole world.

Literally tons of reading matter have been published about this Wonder City of the Twentieth Century. Every newspaperman who comes here, every novelist, essayist and scholar, is stimulated into lively expression by the throbbing pulse of Detroit's life. They disagree violently on the merits of mass production—even when accompanied by mass consumption; they rarely fail to agree that Detroit is the most significant fact of modern times.

Lexicographers have been working overtime coining words with which adequately to express the meaning of this city. Such phrases as "Modern Utopia," "Wonder City," "Industrial Democracy" and "City of Tomorrow" are sprinkled throughout contemporary literature. Interpretive writers give us a new picture of this community wherein we dwell. Let us glance through some of the more important utterances, culling out paragraphs which, placed together, yield a mosaic of Detroit as others see us.

"UTOPIA ON WHEELS."

R. L. Duffus, writing in a recent issue of Harper's Magazine, happily described Detroit as a "Utopia on Wheels." The growth principle dominates, he points out, coincidentally with the almost universal adoption of the automobile and the frantic use thereof. Duffus writes:

"Detroit is a city on wheels. I would go as far as to say of Detroit that even its buildings somehow give the impression of being parked rather than rooted in the ground. One gets a sensation of permanence only from a few ambitious edifices like the Book Tower, the Penobscot building (which would be as tall as that of the Woolworth building if it had a tower as tall as that of the Woolworth building), the Fisher building and the gargantuan General Motors office building. The gray old city hall, with its sculptured figures by Julius Melchers, father of Gari Melchers, also looks pretty stable. But in general one feels that almost anything in Detroit could be cranked up and put in motion at a moment's notice. In finding one's way about one looks not so much for street numbers as for license plates.

"There are all varieties of cars in the Detroit procession. Ingenious youngsters buy venerable relics for a few dollars and somehow contrive to make them go. Millionaires trundle around in Rolls Royces or in Fords as the mood takes them. One may see a dented Ford standing in front of a $50,000 house. Nobody wonders at that. Nobody worries.

"In short, in this city of motor cars there is a genial carelessness toward them. One is reminded a little of those bright, early days in the Far West when entire populations were bowlegged with riding and nobody cared what happened to the animal so long as the saddle was safe."

"INDUSTRIAL DEMOCRACY."

Sisley Huddleston, the English commentator, closes his recent book, "What's Right With America," with a chapter devoted to Detroit. Huddleston sees the development of an industrial democracy as Detroit's most important contribution to the advancement of man. Thus:

"In this concluding chapter, I must once more dwell upon the industrial revolution. Detroit did not begin it, but Detroit best typifies it. Perhaps Detroit is more conscious of it than any other city. Perhaps Detroit, although it is almost in Canada, is the most American part of America.

"So far as I can see, the new ideas of men like Ford do not differ greatly from the former ideas of such socialists as William Morris. In the first place, the workman is to be paid on a scale sufficiently high to enable him to purchase the goods he makes. Those goods are not reserved for a luxurious class. They are for him. That is one of the conditions of mass production.

"An industrial democracy—that is the goal to which America is pressing. It is quite irrelevant to point to bad conditions here and poverty there. I know the denigratory statistics, and they are—

Continued on Page 4.

The Detroit Free Press
1831 ~ A CENTURY OF SERVICE ~ 1931

WEATHER: Partly cloudy and warmer Tuesday; possibly showers Wednesday unsettled.

METROPOLITAN FINAL EDITION

101st Year. No. 127 — TUESDAY, SEPTEMBER 8, 1931 — 28 Pages — THREE CENTS

SEPT. 8, 1931:

Kaye Don and Gar Wood are two of the best-known powerboat racers on the Detroit River.

DON'S BOAT SINKS; U. S. KEEPS TROPHY

100 Rescued as Dock Collapses

BOY, 3, LOST AMID PANIC OF VICTIMS

Women and Children Trampled in Wild Fight to Live

OFFICER HEADS RELIEF EFFORTS

(See Pictures on Last Page)

At the echo of the cannon's boom signaling the beginning of the Harmsworth Trophy Race, a narrow dock at the foot of Water Works Park creaked and collapsed. Five hundred persons slid into the Detroit River. They were mothers and fathers who had gone there to enjoy a holiday watching the speed contest.

For a moment the water turned to froth. Then heads bobbed up. Women with children in their arms were seeking to hold a wife or sweetheart safe above the threshing arms. There were others who fought madly for a foothold or to get a grasp on a rope. Somewhere in the milling hundred, three-year-old Nelson Pattison was jostled out of his father's arms and, it is believed, swept to his death in the river.

Pulmotors Save Many

More than a dozen persons were saved by Fire Department Rescue men. Most of those who were unconscious, it was said, were aged persons who suffered from shock. They came so rapidly that firemen hurried from one victim to another without bothering to ascertain names.

As soon as revived, the victims were hurried away by drenched relatives who also had plunged into the river. Engine Company 11, Ladder Company 14, and Rescue Squads 3 and 12, all under direction of Capt. R. J. Ferry, performed resuscitation work. The Fire Tug James Battle also aided.

Fireman George Craig, of Engine Company 52 who had come to the scene, was one of the first to go to the aid of those in the water. He took in persons to shore.

The suddenness of the collapse stunned the thousands who had gathered at Water Works Park to view the race. Then rescue work started in such a rush that in the confusion. Scores of swimmers plunged into the water. Motor boats maneuvered to within swimming distance. Yacht owners dotted the waters with life preservers and safety cushions.

If there was an outstanding hero among the rescuers it was Sergt. William Burkuhl, of the McClellan Station, assigned to duty at the dock. He plunged into the water and organized a "bucket brigade" of the swimmers. He hauled out children who were being shoved under the water by stronger persons and handed them to fellow-rescuers who relayed them to shore. He shoved women within grasp of life preservers. He hoisted men within grasp of arms stretched down from the portion of the dock still standing. He was bruised and cut by persons who sought to claim him-self him.

Many Swim Wrong Direction

The unexpectedness of the fall seemed to daze most of those in the water. Instead of heading toward shore and shallower water, many headed out into the River. A raft anchored 30 feet from the dock is believed to have prevented more fatalities. Although it was crowded with persons, many in the water headed for it and gained a handhold.

When the dock collapsed, F. N. Pattison, 170 Merriweather Ave.
Continued on Page 3, Column 4

WHERE ANOTHER BRITON NEARLY MET SEGRAVE'S FATE
Kaye Don's Miss England II as she was sinking end up. Arrow shows one of crew swimming.

KAYE, CREW SAFE; BOATS RULED OUT FOR BEATING GUN

British Challenger Follows Gar Over Line Ahead of Starter's Signal; Both Disqualified

Miss America VIII With George Wood Wins Harmsworth Heat; Don Escapes Segrave's Fate

By W. W. EDGAR

Seated in the boat in which the late Sir Henry Segrave rode to his death a little more than a year ago, Kaye Don, English challenger for the Harmsworth Trophy, nearly met with the same fate Monday afternoon on the Detroit River during the second heat of the Harmsworth Trophy Race.

Miss England II capsized on the first turn after having been disqualified. Gar Wood and Miss America IX were also disqualified. Both boats had beaten the starting gun.

Rounding the lower turn, riding in the wash of the Miss America IX, the big white-hulled British challenger raised its nose in the air for an instant and rolled over.

The vast crowd that lined both banks of the course stood amazed as the ship went down and the tension was relieved only when the members of the crew came to the surface and floated about on their life belts.

Don and Dick Garner, one of Don's two mechanics, were thrown clear of the boat. The other mechanic, Roy Platford, stayed with the craft. The boat floated until a rescue party reached it and put a tow-rope on the upturned craft. A few moments later the tow-rope gave way and the British boat sank near its quarters at the Thomson boat house. None of the crew was injured seriously, although Platford was taken to a hospital for examination.

It was the same sort of an accident that had snuffed out the life of the late Sir Henry Segrave during a trial run of Miss England II on Lake Windermere. Don and his crew escaped their late only because they were thrown instead of being carried under when the boat rolled over.

They little realized that the boat was disqualified and not considered in the race when the accident occurred.

Only several seconds before the accident both boats had shot across the starting line, Miss England in an attempt to take the Trophy back to England, and Miss America IX to win and force a running of a third heat.

They were entering the turn just off the Boat Club dock with their throttles wide open when the officials announced: "Miss America IX and Miss England II, have been disqualified for beating the gun and are ruled out of the race. Miss America beat the gun by 8.52 seconds and Miss England crossed the line 7.26 seconds before the gun was fired.

Don Expected to Win

It was Kaye Don's race before it started so far as expert opinion was concerned. So much so, that the Harmsworth Trophy officially was ordered to the Detroit Yacht Club dock for presentation to the Englishmen as soon as the second heat was completed.

None foresaw the series of dramatic events that turned what seemed certain victory into glorious defeat for the challenger. The Trophy was brought to the dock just before the race. It was expected Gar Wood himself would make the presentation. Five minutes later both Wood and Don were disqualified, Miss England II had capsized and the bronze Trophy was on its way back to the club, there to repose for at least another year.

Dramatic Finish to Race

It was a dramatic finish of what was expected to be the greatest race ever run for the trophy. Added to the tragedy of the day was the charge that Wood had tricked Don out of his chance to win the trophy.

Whether intentionally or not Gar lured Don into chasing him over the starting line long before the gun was fired. He had himself and the challenger disqualified and George Wood, in Miss America which started well back, went on to complete the course and become the winner of the second heat.

Balls Warn of Time

Miss America VIII took no chances. It just maintained a steady speed, seldom went above 60 miles an hour and coasted to victory with an average of 66.635 miles an hour for the distance.

Richard W. Gray, meteorologist, said the storm carried no threat of wind damage.

Officials Rule Harmsworth Is 'No Match'

(By the Associated Press)

The following statement was issued by racing officials:

"The 17th running of the British International Trophy resulted in no match. The challenger was eliminated from the match through disqualification at the start of the second race through crossing the line 7.26 seconds ahead of the starting flag, half and gun, and her finishing could in nowise affect the second race the International Commission, under the authority opened to it by the B. I. T. deed of gift, rules that no match resulted.

"The rules of the Union Internationale du Yachting Automobile are very clear on disqualification for crossing the line more than five seconds ahead of the starting signal, being Rule No. 24, and this was fully understood by all contestants, being explained to them personally on Aug. 26, 1931.

"Miss England won the first race and Miss America VIII won the second race, but the special rules of the B. I. T. state, 'The country which first wins two races shall be adjudged the winner,' and only countries and not boats may be taken into consideration.

"The International Commission recognizes that all records established in the first race on Sept. 5, 1931, stand, despite its ruling that no match resulted from the series."

Florida Storm Passes Inland

MIAMI, Fla., Sept. 7.—(A.P.)—A tropical disturbance apparently passed inland from the Gulf of Mexico over the Southwest Florida coast tonight, its strength dissipated.

Mary Pickford Tells a Mean Fish Story

HOLLYWOOD, Calif., Sept. 7.—(A. P.)—Mary Pickford needn't listen in awe any longer to the fish stories of her energetic husband, Douglas Fairbanks. Cruising with a party of friends off Santa Monica yesterday, Miss Pickford caught a 150-pound Marlin swordfish and a 75-pound hammerhead shark. She refused assistance in both catches, playing the swordfish half an hour

TOKIO-U. S. HOP STARTS

Moyle, Allen Begin Nonstop Pacific Flight

SAMUSHIRO, Japan, Sept. 8—(Tuesday).—(A. P.)—Beginning one of the most hazardous flights known to aviators, Don Moyle and C. A. Allen, California pilots, left the Beach runway here at 5:30 a. m. Monday) on a nonstop journey of 4,465 miles over the stormy North Pacific to Seattle.

At 6:40 a. m. (4:40 Detroit time Monday) the Ochishi Radio Station reported the plane was heard from Hokkaido Island. The fliers had flown approximately 110 miles in 70 minutes.

Have Gas for 47 Hours

Their monoplane carried gasoline for 47 hours of flying, but no radio to inform the world of progress in the little traveled area over which they were flying.

The course skirted the volcanic Kurile Islands, often hidden by fog, and swung out over the North Pacific in a great circle that touched the Bering Sea and curved across the Aleutian Islands and southward over the Gulf of Alaska and off the British Columbia coast to Seattle.

The weather was reported more favorable than usual on the route. It was clear here and a storm had moderated over the Aleutians. Moyle calculated the flight would require 39 to 44 hours, depending on the weather. He said he and Allen expected to arrive in Seattle possibly before daylight of Wednesday morning.

Fliers Alter Craft

A small crowd gathered in the semi-darkness to witness the take-off. Moyle got the plane into the air much easier than experts here had expected. The wind and a smooth sandy runway were favorable. It had been predicted that the plane which called to carry Harold Bromley and Harold Gatty on a nonstop flight to America last year, and also failed Thomas Ash this year, would not rise from the beach with a heavier load than was carried on the previous attempts.

Moyle and Allen had cut one inch off the propeller at each end, giving it swifter revolutions, and had altered the tail assembly. It is...
Continued on Page 3, Column 2

NELSON — F. N. PATTISON — MARY — SALLY

THEIR HOLIDAY IS TURNED TO TRAGEDY

The boy, who is believed to have drowned, his father and two sisters were among the Harmsworth Race spectators who were plunged into the Detroit River when the dock at the foot of Motorboat Lane gave way late Monday afternoon.

FASHIONS RULE FAIR

Paris Models Appear in Revue; Holiday Draws 75,000

TUESDAY PROGRAM

8 a. m.—Gates and buildings open; Ford and General Motors Automobile Show; the Style Show and Airplane exhibit and other entertainment.
9 a. m.—Cattle judging begins.
1 p. m.—Horse racing begins, interspersed with vaudeville acts, special concerts by children's bands of Detroit and Wayne County and exhibition drill by prize winning woodsmen.
5 p. m.—Detroit Symphony Orchestra in the Grove.
6:30 p. m.—Boy's milking contest in the Coliseum.
7:30 p. m.—Parade of beef cattle, a special horse show program and concert by Detroit Symphony Orchestra in Coliseum.
7:30 p. m.—An elaborate fireworks display and outdoor show and other entertainment before the grand stand.

Two new events, of particular interest to women visitors, were provided Monday for the 75,000 persons who comprised the Labor Day crowd that attended the Michigan State Fair and Exposition.

For the followers of the turf there were harness races, which started at 1 p. m. Vaudeville and trained animal acts were interspersed in this feature.

Style Show Attracts Women

A style show, with Parisian models here especially for the Fair, was the highlight of the day for women attendants, at 2:30 o'clock they started their parade down the fashion runway.

The show was held in the Machinery Building under the sponsorship of Detroit merchants and brought to the Motor City the latest in feminine apparel. Fall wear, riding garb and numerous sport models were exhibited by the mannequins.

Judging of poultry also commenced Monday, when experts surveyed the 1,667 entries, while the contest for honors in the livestock show also got under way.

Winners in the second event will qualify for the International show in Chicago next December. More than 1,000 entries were registered in this class.

Cattle Exhibits Open

As on Sunday, the opening day, the gates swung open at 8 a. m. to admit only a handful of persons. Within a few hours, however, the grounds were teeming with visitors anxious to recapture for a few moments at least something of the small town atmosphere immortalized in the annual State Fair.

Besides the numerous features which delighted them Sunday, Labor Day gave the Fair-goers a chance to compete again. His smile was placed for him.

With a faint smile and a chair was placed for him.

The Thermoworth Race is abated in a manner designed to prevent getting away ahead of time. Five minutes before the race, a warning gun is fired and five colored balls are placed atop the judges' stand. The boats are taken to the head of Wayne Island to warm up the motors and each minute a ball drops in full view of the pilots to bridge them how many minutes remain before the starting gun.

In this way they can time their run to the line almost to the second because they know that when the fifth ball drops they will be on their way. The start of the first heat Sunday afternoon was almost perfect.

But Monday while the boats were being warmed up, Gar in Miss America IX made a sudden start for the line. In the tabulated course and came down the river at full speed.

Sensing Wood's move, Don followed him. Down they came, eager to gain the advantage to be had by getting away first, while Miss America VIII laid back, apparently biding its time.

Like a streak Miss America IX shot past the judges' stand. Ten seconds later the famous white hull of the throttle wide open, in an effort to take the lead and the advantage
Continued on Page 3, Column 1

'Just Luck of Game,' Declares Kaye Don

British Challenger Disappointed But He Smiles; Gar Expresses Regret

Kaye Don, sportsman in victory and disaster, called it "just the luck of the game."

No hint of bitterness escaped the debonaire Britisher. With the prize of a lifetime in his grasp, he failed. Curio hunters walked the streets last night with fragments of his boat, torn scraps of perhaps the finest craft that has ever graced the water. Snatched by Fate from a tragic death, Kaye Don would be happy to compete again. His smile was gay and it was sincere.

Immaculate in white flannels and blue jacket, Don sat in his room at the New Whittier and greeted friends who would not be denied a handclasp. Don was tired. His right knee was painfully wrenched when the boat turned over. But the stream of visitors seemed endless.

Three floors below Don's suite newspapermen were waiting. Shortly by 8 o'clock, accompanied by his American manager, William P. Sturm, Don stepped quietly in. Was limping slightly and a chair was placed for him.

Continued on Page 3, Column 4

Redcoats Victorious in Bloodless Battle

GROTON, Conn., Sept. 7.—(A. P.) Fort Griswold, scene of Connecticut's worst battle in the Revolutionary War, fell again today to an attacking force of Redcoats, but this time in a bloodless battle.

The occasion was the re-enactment of the Battle of Groton Heights on the 150th anniversary of that skirmish.

The First and Second Companies of the British Attackers and the Putnam Phalanx of Hartford, enacted the part of the Colonials.
Continued on Page 3, Column 1

AUTO DEATHS LACKING HERE

Two Die in Suburban Area at Week-End

Despite the record traffic that poured through Detroit streets Saturday, Sunday and Labor Day, not a fatal accident inside the city limits had been reported Monday night. John T. Fike, of Chicago, 28 years old, 2847 Banner Ave., died of injuries received in Dearborn. Detroit suffered 115 accidents over the week-end.

Last year's records show 149 accidents and six deaths in Labor Day week-end traffic.

In the car that struck Mr. Binkerd were Mrs. Irene Doney, 38, of 608 New York Ave., her daughter, Eleanor, 10, and her husband, Fred Doney, 30. Mrs. Doney and Eleanor were treated for minor injuries at Ford Emergency Hospital. Dearborn, after the light truck was struck, by a car driven by Harry A. Walker, 35, of Liverpool, O.

Driver Flees Scene

Mr. Fike was standing by his automobile at Merriam Road and Michigan Ave., near Eloise, when that stopped, but whose driver fled the scene. Mr. Fike was killed instantly, State Police said.

START THE MORNING RIGHT
with THE FREE PRESS

	Page
Edgar A. Guest, Poem	6
George Matthew Adams	6
"Good Morning"	6
Quillen's Paragraphs	6
Stage and Screen	12
Around the Town	18
"920 a Week," Serial	27
Pictorial review	20
Culbertson on Bridge	23
Grantland Rice	19
Comics	27
Dr. Evans on Health	6
Personal Problems	15
Finance	22
Society	12
Radio Programs	25
Every Day Psychology	6
"I Rise to Remark"	6

Lesson in Pitching Pennies Costs $720

CHICAGO, Sept. 7.—(U. P.)—The antics of two men in front of the Wrigley Tower fascinated Albert Glattfelder from Cairo, Egypt. He watched them toss pennies at a crack in the "walk.

"You can do, too," said one of the pitchers. Glattfelder joined in. He agreed to wager his $720 in checks against $100 in money. One of the penny pitchers held stakes. But it wouldn't be fair for you to pitch against an experienced man." said the man holding the envelope.

Glattfelder, impressed by the "Niagaraans' 'sense of fair play,' walked away. Later he opened the envelope. His checks were gone.

Flint Police Drops Dead After Crash

Special to The Free Press
OWOSSO, Sept. 7.—George Passmore, 60 years old, of 1101 Durand St., Flint, dropped dead nine miles southwest of here today, a few minutes after an automobile accident. His car had gone into the ditch but with the help of a milk truck crew he was again on his way. A heart attack caused his death. He was en route to Lansing with his family.

$638,805 PAID FOR PENSIONS

Cost of City Fund Shows Constant Increase for Several Years

Residents of Detroit pay $638,805 of their taxes this year for pensions to City employes, exclusive of the retirement fund for school teachers. The cost of the City pension fund has constantly increased during the past several years. The taxpayers this year will provide funds as follows:

Firemen's Pensions	$322,120
Policemen's Pensions	246,185
City Employees' Pensions	70,500

The police pension fund has to raise more money than any other because their occupation is the most hazardous. Policemen contribute a part of their salary each month to the pension fund. School teachers contribute a considerable portion of their salary, but not City employes. Five men draw retirement fund. Firemen contribute nothing, and neither do the general City employes.

He Picks His Turtles and They Both Place

Special to The Free Press
JONESVILLE, Mich., Sept. 7.—Wayne Shufelt, 16 years old, of North Adams, is a good judge of fast turtles. When he came over here this morning he wanted to enter the turtle derby which was a feature of the carnival, so he bought two turtles here in Jonesville boy. One of them won the race. The turtle entered by Geraldine Turrell, 10 years old, of Litchfield, placed second.

SEPT. 17, 1931:

Detroit's first large-scale gangland slaying in more than four years became known as the "Collingwood Avenue Massacre."

The Detroit Free Press
1831 ~ A CENTURY OF SERVICE ~ 1931

WEATHER: Partly cloudy, preceded by showers, Thursday; little change in temperature.

METROPOLITAN FINAL EDITION

101st Year. No. 136 — THURSDAY, SEPTEMBER 17, 1931 — 28 Pages — THREE CENTS

3 KILLED BY GANG: 5 JAILED

LEGION MEN TO PASS ON JOB CRISIS

O'Neil to Arrive Here from Conference Thursday

VARIOUS PLANS ARE SUGGESTED

Marshaling the constructive force of the American Legion's 1,000,000 members into the national drive for the relief of unemployment and distress is one of the big tasks confronting the National Convention, which will bring more than 100,000 Legionnaires to Detroit next week. National Commander Ralph T. O'Neil, of Topeka, Kan., will arrive here Thursday at 12:30 o'clock direct from the conference of the Legion's unemployment committee with national leaders in Washington. He was preceded Wednesday by Fred C. Condict, secretary of the committee, who brought word that Legion officials pledged the utmost resources of their national organization to co-operative effort with the Hoover Relief Committee headed by Walter S. Gifford.

Officials to Greet Chief

"There can be no question that unemployment problems are among the most important pressing for solution in the Convention," Mr. Condict pointed out. "Commander O'Neil has frequently asserted the job question transcends all others." Legion officials in Detroit for the Convention look upon a constructive program of unemployment relief as the one thing which will make another serious demand for repeal of adjusted compensation schedules and banish a growing tide of unrest.

Commander O'Neil will be accorded a warm welcome when he arrives at the Fort St. Station. Col. Fred A. Alger, president of the Convention Corp.; Col. Alan D. Loomis, of Marquette, department vice chairman of the executive committee, and other prominent Legionnaires, will head the reception committee. They will be escorted by a mounted police patrol and band. Commander O'Neil will be accompanied to the Statler Hotel where he will make his headquarters.

Suggestions to Be Considered

His arrival will make complete the transfer of National Headquarters to Detroit. It is expected the tempo of the preparations for the big gathering will be quickened perceptibly thereafter.

Discussions at the Washington unemployment conference will
Continued on Page 2, Column 4

The Modern Problem; Should Wives Work?

JACK WELTMAN — NAN HARDY

Nan and Ted had come to the parting of the ways. Ted's job took him to another city—hers seemed too important to give up. Their marriage fell crashing about their heads.

Read Anne Gardner's thrilling story of modern life.

WORKING WIVES
It begins Today—See page 27

Labor Insurance Urged by Swope

General Electric Head, Asking Reforms, Warns Manufacturers to Forestall Laws Menacing Business

NEW YORK, Sept. 16—(A.P.)—A co-operative management-employee plan aimed to eliminate unemployment, stabilize business, and remove the worker's fear of idleness and old age, was offered industry tonight by Gerard Swope, president of General Electric Co.

Addressing the National Electrical Manufacturers' Association, Mr. Swope warned industry it must act to forestall legislation which he said threatens the fundamental structure of American business and society.

"Industry exists basically for serving the needs of the people," he said, "and therefore production and consumption must be co-ordinated. * * * Shall we wait for society to act through its legislatures or shall industry recognize its obligation to its employees and to the public and undertake the task? Co-ordination of production is impossible under our present laws."

His plan calls for compulsory pensions, unemployment, disability and life insurance, and workmen's compensation protection, the cost to be borne equally by employer and employees.

Under the plan the employee would lose none of the accrued benefits of such protection by switching from one company to another, and if he went into business for himself, returned or changed his trade he would receive back all he had paid in, plus interest.

Plans Joint Control

"The stabilization of industry would be brought about through the compulsory formation, by law, of trade associations in virtually every business and industry in the country.

"These groups would have broad powers under Mr. Swope's proposal. They would seek to co-ordinate production and consumption by controlling each industry's output 'on a broader, more intelligent basis, thus tending to regularize employment.'

"Every effort should be made to stabilize industry and therefore stabilize employment, and when this is impracticable, unemployment insurance must be provided, and organized industry should take the lead," he said.

Program in Detail

The details of the Swope plan are: Within three years all companies with 50 or more employees shall be required to form a trade association under supervision of some Federal body.

All companies must adopt standard accounting and cost systems and earnings statements.

All companies with 25 or more stockholders shall send out quarterly statements of the condition of the business; and its earnings.

A National Workmen's Compensation
Continued on Page 2, Column 4

M'COLL DUE TO GO NEXT

Removal from Jury Board Position Is Sought

Reorganization of the Recorder's Court Jury Commission Thursday is the aim of a meeting which William M. Walker, newly appointed commissioner, said he will try to arrange with Commissioner Richard L. Shannon, and Commissioner Joseph A. Walsh, whose removal is sought in ouster proceedings now under way.

Commissioner Walker was appointed Wednesday morning by Gov. Wilber M. Brucker to succeed Thomas J. Barrell, who followed the example of James F. McGregor in resigning from the commission when investigations started Aug. 27, 1930. Judge Lester B. Moll at 9 o'clock Wednesday and ask release.

Prosecutor Harry S. Toy revealed the Grand Jury has cost $68,960.85. Immediate replacement of Lorne McColl, secretary of the commission, honors Walker admitted, because new members have control of the commission, and the Governor wants complete change of the methods. Possibility of a woman being elected secretary was discussed.

"I will seek a meeting Thursday with the other commissioners. Mr. McColl's statement is a proper subject for discussion at an early date," the Prosecutor said.

10,000 VIEW WOODWARD FIRE FIGHT

Blast at Grand River Sends Sheet of Flame in Street

BLOCK PERILED; THEATER BLAZES

(See Picture on Page 3)

A hail of shattered glass showered Woodward and Grand River Aves., when an explosion in an artificial limb factory at 1418 Woodward Ave. precipitated a fire which threatened the entire block. Damage was estimated at $100,000.

Within a few moments, 10,000 persons thronged the street to watch firemen in their spectacular fight. Traffic in Woodward Ave. was at a standstill while firemen mounted the big water tower in front of the building and directed a high pressure stream at the flames. High pressure companies Nos. 1 and 2 used their turret guns and all engine companies were worked to capacity.

Search Made for Victims

Working from the alley at the rear, other firemen scaled the structure and searched the upper floors for possible victims. At 8:50 o'clock, 45 minutes after the fire broke out, they had confined it to the roof of the Embassy Theater at 1418 Woodward Ave., and at 10 o'clock the blaze was under full control.

One fireman, William Dewitt, was slightly hurt.

The explosion occurred in the artificial limb factory of the E.H. Rowley Co., on the third floor of the four-story building. It was believed. Spontaneous combustion in the varnishes and lacquers was thought to have been the cause as the block, which contained artificial limbs, all over the street.

The Felix Predl Clothing Co., occupies the second floor and the fourth floor is vacant. The J. Black Co., opticians and jewelers, is on the first floor.

Herman Roth, one of the clothing store owners, said that his firm suffered no fire damage. Water caused what damage there was, he said.

Rope Lines Used

Five minutes after Chief Stephen J. De May and Asst. Chief Michael J. Callahan arrived at the scene two extra alarms were sounded and all apparatus near the downtown area was summoned. Ladder Companies 1 and 2 flung extension lines to aid the water tower crew.

It was the first time in more than 20 years that a fire of such proportions has occurred on Woodward Ave. during the evening rush. The crowd was so large that police were forced to use rope lines to keep them out of the danger zone.

BRITISH TARS WIN PLEDGE

Pay Cut Hardships to Be Remedied

LONDON, Sept. 16—(A.P.)—Blue jackets of the British Navy's Atlantic Fleet, through a series of demonstrations against cuts in pay, obtained from the Admiralty today a promise of re-examination of the new rates with a view to alleviation of such hardships as might be revealed.

Announcement was made in the House of Commons by Sir Austen Chamberlain, First Lord of the Admiralty, that ships of the Atlantic Fleet had been ordered to proceed to their home ports immediately. He gave no details of the origin of the trouble among the men of the fleet, which was reported to have staged a sort of non-violent mutiny in protest against prospective pay cuts but he made it clear the government had capitulated at least to the extent of investigating the complaints with a view to remedying whatever hardships might be found.

A dispatch to the London Daily Herald describes how "the proudest vessels of the navy lay idle and helpless while 12,000 sailors refused to obey orders." The officers stood helplessly by, but the strikes was carried on in orderly fashion. The men were in control of the ships and, although they refused to obey orders, they undertook to keep the ships in good order. The officers tried to raise the pickets did not try to stop them, but merely warned, that as soon as they raised one anchor the men would drop the other. Stokers, meanwhile, checked the fires in the boilers.

SUES AIMEE'S LATEST MAN

—Acme Telephoto

MYRTLE ST. PIERRE

Miss St. Pierre, a nurse, who has sued David L. Hutton for $200,000, alleging breach of promise to marry, is shown looking at a picture of Hutton and Aimee Semple McPherson taken after the couple's recent marriage. Hutton was threatened with a severe breach of promise suit Wednesday by Mrs. Roland Neece, of Long Beach, Calif., who said he proposed to her three months ago.

GANG CURB IS SOUGHT

Trust Law Revision Also Advocated at Bar Meeting

ATLANTIC CITY, Sept. 16—(A.P.)—Leaders of America's bar today urged alteration of the anti-trust laws to permit industry to control production and advocated changes in the criminal laws to curb the gangsters of gangdom.

Rush C. Butler, chairman of the Commerce Committee of the American Bar Association, addressing the mineral law section, said chaos is king in the oil industry largely because Federal laws will not permit the oil companies properly to co-operate.

Meanwhile a joint committee representing the American Law Institute, the Association of American Law Schools and the Association of American Bar Associations, recommended exhaustive and co-ordinated researches with a view finally to radical readjustments in the criminal codes.

Addressing the mineral law section earlier today, Francis B. Brownell, chairman of the board of the American Smelting & Refining Co., urged that the nations of the world restore silver as a coinage metal, at no fixed ratio to gold.

The Bar Association was told that the Wickersham report, condemning police third degree methods, had increased crime throughout the nation.

Joseph C. Smith, prosecutor for Essex County, N.J., attacked proposals made by the committee on unlawful enforcement of the criminal section of the association.

DOG CATCHING COST IS $67,310

Major Part of Annual Expense to Detroit Is Outlay in Salaries

It will cost the taxpayers of Detroit $67,310 this year to catch the stray dogs of the city, according to the budget of the City Controller's office.

Of that $51,950 of this sum goes into salaries paid the dog catchers and the men who supervise the work at the dog pound. The salary list follows:

One police lieutenant	$2,960
Senior clerks (2 at $2,400)	4,800
Dog catchers (24 at $2,400)	57,600
Food and supplies	1,950

A new dog pound was erected at the foot of Twenty-Fourth St. The Police Department receives some revenue back from the sale of dogs at the pound and also from license fees.

HIGHER PRICE LEVEL URGED

Scale of 1926 Sought at Farm Parley

CHICAGO, Sept. 16—(A.P.)—A "100-cent dollar" was the goal today of a conference of farm leaders, economists and editors of agricultural publications.

Today's session was the first of a series to formulate a legislative program designed to place the price level at the general level of 1926. This program will be presented at the December annual meeting of the American Farm Bureau Federation, sponsor of the conference.

The conferees, headed by Ralph Snyder, head of the Kansas Farm Bureau, were urged that the farm the 1926 price levels would be a stabilizing monetary influence in the current economic depression.

C.R. White, president of the New York Farm Bureau, said: "The big banking and financial interests do not want the dollar stabilized any more than do the speculators in the grain trades. This is our strongest opposition."

All the conferees agreed that no panaceas would be written overnight, although the general opinion of the conference was that the lack of money in circulation was the main ill.

C.W. Ramseyer, Iowa Representative in Congress and leader of the Farm Block, said there was no overproduction, except in wheat and cotton, and that this could not be blamed for the ills of the monetary system.

An intensive program to find jobs for the unemployed, the congressman said, would temporarily boost the prices of commodities by putting the farmers a wider market.

RECORD BROKEN IN REGISTRATION

554,480 on Final Lists; Only 513,289 in 1930

Total registration figures this year are higher than at any time in the city's history. The City Election Commission reported Wednesday, as lists closed, that 554,480 Detroiters are registered as compared with 513,289 for 1930.

The 9,040 transfers of registration Wednesday brought the total of transfers to 25,974 since last spring's elections. There were 7,368 new registrations Wednesday. To the total of new registrations since the last election is 17,008, according to Oakley E. Distin, secretary of the Election Commission.

START THE MORNING RIGHT
with THE FREE PRESS

	Page		Page
Edgar A. Guest, Poem	6	Westbrook Pegler	6
George Matthew Adams	6	Comics	27
Good Morning	6	Dr. Evans on Health	6
Quillen's Paragraphs	6	Personal Problems	6
Around the Town	10	The Marketer	13
"Working Wives," Serial	27	The Screen	17
Pictorial Review	28	Cross Word Puzzle	24
The Theater	17	Finance	21
Culbertson on Bridge	24	Society	8
Grantland Rice	17	Radio Programs	6
		Every Day Psychology	6

VICTIMS HERDED INTO APARTMENT, BODIES RIDDLED

Known to Police Here as Handbook Operators and Engaged in Rum Racket on Big Scale

Shot in Backs—Four Men Speed from Scene in Collingwood Manor at Rate of 70 Miles an Hour

Detroit had its version of Chicago's St. Valentine's Day massacre Wednesday afternoon when three liquor racketeers, who had defied a rival gang's warning, were kidnaped in the thick of W. Grand Blvd. traffic, herded into an apartment hired for the killing, and slaughtered in cold blood.

Five alleged associates of the dead men were questioned by prosecutor's officers early Thursday morning in an effort to sift out of their devious underworld dealings a clue to the reason for the murders and to the identities of the killers. The men held for investigation are: Sol Levine, 30 years old, Fort Wayne Hotel; Otis Broder, 46, of 637 Owen Ave.; David Cohen, 32, of 470 Stimson Ave.; Louis Goldberg, 30, of 9325 Broadstreet Ave, and Roy St. Clair, of 674 Brainard St.

The triple murder occurred in Apartment 211 of Collingwood Manor, 1740 Collingwood Ave. The victims were identified by fingerprints in the Police Identification Bureau as Joseph (Nigger Joe) Lebowitz, alias Leibold, 31 years old, 680 Brainard St.; Joe (Izzy) Sutker, alias Sutton, 28, of 949 Reed Place, and Hymie Paul, 31, of 881 Merrick Ave. All had police records.

Five Men Fled from Scene

The four killers fled through a rear stairway of the quiet family apartment house and made their escape in a dark five-passenger coupé, at the wheel of which a fifth man was waiting.

Three .38-caliber pistols were found back in the apartment where the slayings occurred. Police ballistics experts examined the guns and bullets taken from the bodies and reported that they were the pistols used by the killers.

Detectives said the killers apparently had carried the paint to the apartment for use as a receptacle for their guns. The pistols were being carefully cleaned in an effort to retain finger prints. Numbers of the weapons had been mutilated, but experts believe they could still be deciphered.

The three dead men were the survivors of a once powerful Detroit River rum-running gang, who had transferred their activities to the race track handbook racket and life wholesale liquor business, police said.

First Massacre Since 1927

Wednesday's murders represented the first large scale gang massacres in Detroit since March 28, 1927, when three men were cut to pieces by machine gun fire in the Miraflores apartments, 106 E. Alexandrine Ave. Isaac Riesfeld, alias Joseph Bloom; William Harris, alias George Cohen, and Frank Wright were killed. Those killings were believed to have been retaliatory gesture following the kidnaping of Meyer (Fish) Bloom, gambler. The killers were never caught.

"Gun Poked in Back"

Lebowitz, Paul and Sutker left their handbook joint at 708 Selden Ave. shortly before 3 o'clock in the afternoon, according to Levine, a hanger-on who drove the victims car to the rendezvous.

"Joe (Lebowitz) called Harry Klein's blind pig at Twelfth St. and Blaine Ave.," said Levine. "He told Harry to keep Raymond Bernstein there until he, Paul and Sutker could get there. They owed Bernstein some money for whisky and they wanted to get him to hold off until after the Legion Convention.

"We got in the car and started for Klein's place," Levine told the prosecutors. "We got to the intersection of W. Grand Blvd., and somebody shoved a gun against my back. He said 'we don't want you. Scram and don't look back.' I got out and walked away and I didn't look back. I went back to the store."

Cannot Be Found

Klein had been questioned a week ago in connection with a fire in his house, according to Asst. Prosecutor George M. Stutz, and Bernstein had been seen within the past two days by detectives. Bernstein is known to police as a member of the Purple Gang and a big silky district.

CROOKS FLEE CITY IN FEAR

Detectives' Roundup Nets No Arrests

Forty detectives of the homicide and blackhand squads assigned to arrest all members of the Purple Gang and every known Detroit hoodlum for questioning in the Collingwood Manor triple murder, returned to Police Headquarters at 3 a.m. Thursday without having made a single arrest.

"Detroit's underworld has taken it on the lam," they said.

Inspector John I. Navarre, of the homicide squad, and Prosecutor Harry S. Toy took charge of the investigation an hour after the killings and ordered all available detectives to begin a city-wide roundup.

The searchers reported the usual underworld hangouts deserted.

Militant Pastor Rues Vice Crusade

PARMA, Mich., Sept. 16—"Let them have their hellhole from now on if they want them. I'm through with trying to clean them up," the Rev. James F. Bowerman, militant pastor of the Parma United Church, said Wednesday.

The Rev. Mr. Bowerman's decision that crusading doesn't pay came after his return from Grand Rapids, where he was assigned to the Methodist Conference at Grand Rapids, where he was assigned to a pastorate paying little more than half the salary he received at Parma. The Rev. Bowerman blamed lack of support at Parma for his banishment.

The Parma pastor's pulpit crusade was credited with aiding in bringing a Jackson County Grand Jury investigation which resulted in dismissal and arrest of Police Chief Charles E. Phelps, of Jackson.

Britain Boosts Tax of 'Wedding Smithy'

GRETNA GREEN, England, Sept. 16—(A.P.)—The economy program of the new government of Great Britain has struck the famous "wedding blacksmith shop of Gretna Green." It was discovered today through court proceedings at Dumfries.

The romantic smithy and its attached museum heretofore have been assessed at about $185. That assessment this year was about $4,500 and the prospect was that the prices for its easy and quick marriages or go out of business. An appeal was argued in court today. A valuation of $2,500 was finally agreed upon.

NAUTILUS RESUMES VOYAGE

BERGEN, Norway, Sept. 16—(A.P.)—The Polar submarine Nautilus was en route southward today after storms forced it to halt on the Norwegian coast between Tromsoe and Bergen.

LEGION MEN TO PASS

M'COLL DUE TO GO NEXT
(cont.)

Forgot His Wives, So Married More

PONTIAC, Sept. 16—Fred Sturtevant, 60 years old, Milford, told the court today that he could not remember how many wives he has. Officers had records of three, so Sturtevant will spend from two to five years in Jackson Prison, Judge Frank L. Doty decided. Sturtevant kicked his most recent matrimonial acquisition from an automobile, where he learned she was coming to Pontiac to check up on his record.

Hitch-Hiking Mouse Wrecks Car; 3 Hurt

GALESBURG, Ill., Sept. 16—(A.P.)—A hitch-hiking mouse that climbed up on Mrs. A.M. Kennelly's shoulder caused a motor accident today in which Mrs. Kennelly, of Yates City, and her two children were injured. The stowaway frightened Mrs. Kennelly and she lost control of the car. The auto turned upside down in a ditch.

Flies to Give Blood; Too Late to Save Son

EVANSVILLE, Ind., Sept. 16—(A.P.)—James Short arrived by plane from Raleigh, N.C., in time to offer his blood for two transfusions, but too late to save the life of his three-year-old son, Richard, today. Richard's death climaxed a series of misfortunes which Laura LaFaber, children of the family. James, Jr., 6, is suffering from a broken collar bone received in a fall. William, 6, fell from a second story window recently and broke his leg.

First Fall Football Casualty Is Treated

The distinction of being the first person to be treated at Receiving Hospital this season for a football injury belongs to Joseph Rentropp, 16 years old, 7473 Emily Ave. Tackled in a neighborhood game at Brentwood and Veach Aves. Wednesday, Joseph suffered a broken right arm.

Private Teachers

Enroll Pupils Through Free Press Want Ads

That's exactly the method that Miss Watercrane, 320 East Grand Boulevard, used so successfully to attract music pupils. She says, "I was able to increase my enrollment considerably by inserting this want ad in the Free Press."

Phone [illegible]

Perhaps you offer a different type of service. The Free Press readers admit it with a want ad. Let the Adtaker explain how you can reach most prospects at low cost.

Phone RAndolph 2400

A Four-Page Special Pictorial Section of the Big Parade in This Issue

The Detroit Free Press
1831 ~ A CENTURY OF SERVICE ~ 1931

WEATHER — Increasing cloudiness Wednesday; cloudy and cooler on Thursday.

METROPOLITAN EDITION

101st Year. No. 142 — WEDNESDAY, SEPTEMBER 23, 1931 — THREE CENTS

SEPT. 23, 1931:

One million watch, up to 100,000 march, and the parade of World War I veterans of the American Legion lasts nine hours. Its coverage earned the Free Press a Pulitzer Prize.

BONUS AND DRY FIGHTS RAGE

CASH ISSUE CLASH DUE ON FLOOR

Delegates Also Likely to Have Voice on Beer Question

RE-REFERENDUM MAY BE ASKED

By HUB M. GEORGE

Despite the call of the President of the United States for American Legion enlistments "in the fight for the stability of our Government," the cash bonus issue will be fought out on the floor of the National Convention here, probably Thursday. It is not entirely dead and leaders were engaged in a desperate effort to rally their forces.

The prohibition issue also will crowd itself before the delegates, probably in a compromise form asking for a re-referendum to the States of a modification of the Volstead Act which will permit milder beverages, and even then probably not with the wholehearted recommendation of the Resolutions Committee whose subcommittee session Tuesday night broke up in a wrangle.

Lines Sharply Drawn

Commander Ralph T. O'Neil, who aligned himself with President Hoover against any bonus raiding which would embarrass the Government and "impose burdens upon fellow citizens," gave assurances Monday evening that "there will be no attempt either directly or indirectly to influence the decision of a single delegate or determination upon its merits after fair discussion."

Lines already have been sharply drawn for the bonus parliamentary battle, the floor leaders are selected, but both sides seemed willing to accept delay until Thursday to permit more time to corral votes.

Wide Splits Looming

Caucuses were being held by more than a score of delegations Tuesday evening, with the prospect of wide open splits in many camps. Instructions were being cast aside by some on the ground the President's presentation of facts superseded all other comments, while uninstructed delegates were taking sides individually. Estimates of voting strength, even upon cautious actions, was little better than guesswork. Unit rules generally are not upheld in Legion deliberations. Optimism prevailed among the sober-minded leaders of the convention that the situation was well in hand.

Theodore Roosevelt, governor of Puerto Rico, Samuel Reynolds, of Nebraska, and Monroe Johnson, of South Carolina, will lead the anti-bonus fight, while the cash bonus group is being rallied behind Rep. Wright Patman, of Texas; Raymond Field, Guthrie, Okla., newspaper publisher, and John Stelle, of Illinois. The two first named of the pro-bonus group were leaders of the Legion's Congressional battle, which led to the 50 per cent loan legislation last winter.

Three sub, all members of the ---- Committee when were picked

Continued on Page 9, Column 6

HENRY FORD FIDDLER UNDERGOES OPERATION

LEWISTON, Me., Sept. 22—(U.P.)—Mellie Dunham, 78 years old, the old-time fiddler made famous by Henry Ford, today underwent a major operation.

Late Tuesday night Mellie reported as resting quietly. Dr. G. A. Schneider also announced his patient probably would have to undergo a second operation shortly.

Mr. Dunham's ailment involves the complication of old age," Dr. Schneider said. "I do not consider his condition immediately critical, but is naturally serious."

LEGIONNAIRES YOU'LL WANT THIS COMPLETE RECORD of CONVENTION DAYS

Folks back home will enjoy, too, reading these 5 issues of The Free Press including last Sunday's big edition with its host of Legion features and

Next Sunday's Free Press

with gravure pictures of the Big Parade and other events. Wrapped — Mailed Anywhere for 35c

------

The Detroit Free Press
Legion Service Desk

I enclose 35c for 5 issues of The Free Press, comprising a complete record of the convention. Mail papers to:

Name...........
Street..........
City.......... State..........

AS THE EVENING SHADOWS FELL

On, on they marched, "from morn to dewy eve," Legionnaires, applauded by a crowd estimated and then on into the night, a steady line of ... at nearly a million persons.

PAY SLASHED BY STEEL, G. M.

Motors Action Affects Salaries Only

NEW YORK, Sept. 22—(A.P.)—Two of America's greatest corporations today reduced wages 10 per cent, and a third cut salaries from 10 to 20 per cent.

United States Steel and Bethlehem Steel Corps., between them responsible for more than half of America's great steel production, cut wages, effective Oct. 1. United States Steel pays wages to more than 200,000 workers.

General Motors Corp., makers of more than 30 per cent of the nation's automobiles, reduced salaries effective the same date. Hourly wages were not affected.

Salaries of $50,000 were cut 20 per cent; from $20,000 to $50,000 they were cut 17% per cent; from $10,000 to $20,000, 15 per cent; from $3,000 to $10,000, 12½ per cent, and up to $3,000, 10 per cent.

Meanwhile Youngstown Sheet & Tube Co., announced a 10 per cent wage cut. The finance committee of United States Steel in a statement said:

"For the purpose of better meeting prevailing unsatisfactory conditions in the industry, rates of wages of the subsidiary companies of the United States Steel Corp., will be reduced approximately 10 per cent, effective Oct. 1, varying somewhat with the character of the work performed."

Eugene G. Grace, Bethlehem president, in following United States Steel's lead, termed the action, "a constructive move."

Alfred P. Sloan, president of General Motors, said:

"The purpose of this action is to establish a new base of salaries in line with the standards of values now existing and in harmony with the present reduced cost of living—up to the present time the corporation has made no general change in salary rates.

"In the early stages of the depression the highest officials of these three organizations were required to meet outspoken foes of wage and salary cuts.

Some observers recalled that the final reduction in wages by United States Steel in the 1921 depression virtually coincided with the bottom both in business and the stock market.

Estimates were that the corporation will save about $50,000,000 annually on the basis of this year's operations. General Motors would be affected about 20 cents each annually, similar unofficial estimates said.

Princess Gone; King Fears She's Kidnaped

ALLENTOWN, Pa., Sept. 22—(A.P.)—An Indian Gypsy king whose people specialize in fortune telling is a worried and puzzled man over the disappearance of his 15-year-old daughter, a full-blooded Gypsy princess, and has asked local police to aid in locating her.

Samuel Evans, of Muskogee, Okla., the king, told police he fears the princess may have been kidnaped. He dropped out of sight on June 29 near here. The tribe spent the summer peeping into the future for the credulous.

Avoid Hot Dog Diet, Freshmen Are Told

KALAMAZOO, Sept. 22—"Curb your desires for varsity sweaters, refrain from a diet of 'hot dogs,' spend 48 hours a week in study or class, and 'be collegiate,'" Dr. T. S. Henry, of the faculty of Western State Teachers College, began the department of Psychology, told freshmen who are to enroll Wednesday when he addressed them today on "What Is Collegiate."

SEARCH ASKED FOR CRAMER

Sea Flier from Detroit May Be Alive

LONDON, Sept. 22—(A.P.)—The British Broadcasting Co., in its general radio service tonight, included a message to all shipping in northern waters asking that a "careful lookout be maintained in the possibility that Parker D. Cramer, American aviator whose plane was wrecked in the North Sea in August, still may be alive.

The message also was directed to the inhabitants of the islands off the northeast coast of Scotland, where it was believed the aviator and his companion, Oliver Paquette, might have taken refuge.

The wreckage of Cramer's plane, which fell in the sea during the last leg of a flight from Detroit to Copenhagen by way of Greenland, was discovered recently.

The broadcast was requested by the American Embassy, which disclosed that the action was asked by William R. Cramer, an older brother of the missing flier.

MINISTER IS INDICTED IN DEATH OF HIS SON

AUGUSTA, Ga., Sept 22—(A.P.)—An indictment charging that he murdered his 19-year-old son, Raeford Grady Williams, a sailor, was returned by the Richmond County Grand Jury today against the Rev. J. M. Williams, former pastor of a Methodist Church at Rochelle.

He was arrested Sept. 6, a month after the youth, home on a furlough, was found dead on a highway.

Officers at first believed he was killed by robbers, but an investigation disclosed the minister had collected $2,500 insurance on his son's life.

START THE MORNING RIGHT
with The Free Press

Page	Page
Legion News 9,9,10,15,28	Comics 27
Legion Pictorial ...Supplement	Dr. Evans on Health 8
Edgar A. Guest, Poem 6	The Marketeer 14
George Matthew Adams.....6	The Screen 15
Good Morning 6	Cross Word Puzzle 66
Quillan's Paragraphs 6	Finance 22
Around the Town.......11	Society 12
Personal Problems 8	Radio Programs 21
"Working Wives," Serial..27	Every Day Psychology 6
Culbertson on Bridge 21	"I Rise to Remark" 6
Grantland Rice 17	

World Gold Parley Sought by England

British Consider Need of International Concord on Government Finance; Stock Exchange Opens Today

LONDON, Sept. 22—(A.P.)—The London Stock Exchange will open tomorrow for business as usual, and Great Britain tonight was preparing to renew efforts for an international conference to deal with problems of the world gold supply.

While the country calmly continued readjustments after its temporary suspension of the Gold Standard, Lord Reading, foreign secretary, let it be known today that Great Britain again would seek to call such a conference.

Lord Reading said he thinks recent British developments may remove the objections of some nations to the conference. No time or place has been considered for such a meeting, but the Foreign Secretary said he thought the conference should include representatives of the central banks and governments.

Baldwin in Charge

Stock brokers looked hopefully to the Exchange's reopening.

The House of Commons again tackled the supplementary budget introduced by Chancellor of the Exchequer Snowden today, and the Government obtained a majority of 67 on a vote arranging the legislative program for the coming week.

Stanley Baldwin, Conservative leader and Lord President of the council, is temporary helicopter of the National Government because Prime Minister Ramsay MacDonald today went to the country for a rest, necessitated by the overstrain of recent weeks.

The Prime Minister attended a Cabinet meeting at 10 Downing St. this morning, and no alarm was felt about his physical condition.

Other moves by the Government today included a ban on the purchase of foreign exchange except for normal business transactions and for reasonable traveling or personal expenses.

Tourists Rush Home

Thousands of British tourists on the Continent are hurrying home, and numerous British winter colonies along the Mediterranean shores will be affected by the drop in the value of sterling.

The Government is taking early precautions against an undue rise in food prices and announced that drastic regulations under the Emergency Powers Act, called into force during the general strike of 1926, again will be employed if necessary to prevent speculation.

As for the effect abroad of Great Britain's six month suspension of the Gold Standard, the anxiety and uncertainty of yesterday had largely replaced today by messages of reassurance for the future from many parts of the world.

Plan Silver Association

A crowded meeting of public and business men, held under the auspices of the China Association in London decided today to form a silver association. The meeting also urged a conference of governments to consider raising the price of silver and restoring it to a place in the world's monetary system as the quickest way to stop falling prices. Sir Robert Horne, former Conservative chancellor of the exchequer, presided, expressed the belief America would participate if such a conference were called.

Better Times Seen Ahead for Great Britain by U.S.

WASHINGTON, Sept. 22—(A.P.)—Struggling England is more surely headed for better days as the result of temporarily suspending the gold standard, in the opinion of governmental authorities here.

For months the rumor grew persistent. Uncertainty causes worry. It was known such drastic action as has now been taken was contemplated. Tenseness over this is gone. Relief evidenced itself in high quarters today.

MILLION WATCH LEGION VETERANS MARCH FOR HOURS

Crowds Thrill to Martial Airs and Brilliant Uniforms; Ranks Gay with Song and Laughter

Surging Mass of Spectators Keeps Police Busy Clearing Route; Many Notables Present in Reviewing Stand

Story by William C. Richards, Douglas D. Martin, James S. Pooler, Frank D. Webb and John N. W. Sloss
Sketches by Russell Legge

The Legion marched.

The Yanks came—thousands upon thousands of them who have been sung about always as coming. Pulses quickened. Tempo moved up. The pendulum flew faster. And those who thought they had laid away the World War in a cobwebby file felt again a familiar throbbing.

The crowd that watched was estimated at a million. The number of marchers was put at 85,000 by National Commander Ralph T. O'Neil. Other estimates, among them that of Maj. Gen. Guy Wilson, field marshal, were as high as 100,000.

Still, this was nothing new. Men have marched so down the ages. They marched in Athens and Nineveh and Marathon fighting their various Armageddons, and, when these were over, they marched behind their Hannibals and Alexanders and Caesars before those they fought for.

Hour After Hour They March On and On

They, like these, fared off as were inspired by ideals and buoyed by lofty purposes and hopes. Many of war the length of time define many quests and instruments.

Up Woodward Ave. they swept, the men of our civilization, in hush impressiveness. They came, bless after hour, a part of the forces which barged out in '17 when folly took the world by the head and led it out on a sanguinary holiday to fill the meadows of France with dead.

All kinds of men, and the women they left behind them, filled the prideful, clicking columns. There were men who saw none of it and men who saw it all and played the string out. There were men too late at the final push, and men who made, in America, household names and tourist spots of tiny French villages previously unknown, unvisited, unhonored, unawakened.

There were men who have never reached an outbound gang-plank and men who knew full well the green fumes rising off the long stretches of mustard, the bitterness of Archangel and the streaked sky of Pelleau, clipped by lead and stumps standing like gallows-trees against the sky-line.

No Packs on Shoulders

Gay were these interminable columns. One realized that this, because of that gayness, was a canceled photograph. This day they needed no khaki to blend inconspicuously into the landscape. They were not going up at night into the line and toward an unknown. This could be a lark in all a lark's gaudy accouterment.

No awkward packs on the shoulders. Nothing of fear and solitude. Nothing of corruption and men crouched in mud, moaning ones matted with dust and calling to stretcher-bearers, men living and dying in dirty trenches—and away off beyond a broad sea a quaint commingling of preachment about mercy, in one breath, and the glorification of barbarity, in the next.

Thousands Upon Thousands

So the thousands upon thousands marched, swinging down E. Jefferson Ave. and turning North at Woodward into the roaring canyon. It was only occasionally one could forget the magnificence of helmets, the tranquility of flares, the hilarity of bugles, and tailor for the paraders the garb in which they journeyed shipward more than a decade ago and, finally, on some star-lit night when closer seemed the air, heard for the first time the whine of shell and saw, perhaps, no house where one had been but only a second before.

But it was no effort at times, for all we know that guns no longer grumble from the Alps to the Channel, to throw around the host its war-day aura and see its unite vividly—the sappers and bombers.

Continued on Page 8, Column 1

CASUALTY RECORD SET

1,800 to 2,000 Treated at Parade; Many Prostrated

The press of the million people who jammed the line of march for the American Legion Parade Tuesday resulted in a record-breaking number of casualties. Between 1,800 and 2,000 persons were treated at first aid stations.

Many of the cases were heat prostrations due to density of the crowd and to the exhaustion of standing for several hours. At the site of the more serious cases were taken to Receiving Hospital where, during the 24 hours up to midnight Tuesday, a new record of 341 cases was set.

Burned, Bruised by Ropes

The first aid station at Bates St. and E. Jefferson Ave. handled 106 cases of minor injuries, while the station at Cadillac Square handled more than a hundred. Many persons were burned and bruised against the ropes used to restrain the crowds, according to Dr. Burt R. Shurly, in charge. Twelve ambulances were in constant use during the parade.

Temperatures during the day remained moderate, the highest temperature 85 degrees coming between 4 and 5 p. m. Nurses and physicians at Receiving Hospital agreed that temperatures similar to the previous three days would have trebled the number of prostration cases.

A number of traffic mishaps also were caused by the crowd or were traceable to the sporadic efforts to break through the police lines. There were no fatalities during the parade, however.

Cycle Crashes Into Crowd

When Motorcycle Officer Gilbert Neff, 30 years old, of 4344 Chalmers Ave., swerved to avoid hitting a child and crashed into a crowd on Jefferson Ave., six persons were injured, one seriously. He was escorting Gov. Wilber M. Brucker to the reviewing stand.

George McIntyre, 73 years old, of 3329 Kirby St., one of those struck, is in a critical condition in Receiving Hospital and Eugene Pratt, 25, of 7043 Longyear Ave., is recovering

MRS. COLLINGS CLEARS SELF

Skeptical Prosecutor Accepts Story

NEW YORK, Sept. 22—(A.P.)—District Atty. Alexander Blue, who at first expressed skepticism at the story told by Mrs. Benjamin P. Collings about what happened the night her husband was slain in Long Island Sound, tonight said he believed her "relieved of all culpability."

She will be the first witness, he added, when the inquest into what happened aboard the Collings yacht Penguin is resumed on Friday.

Mr. Blue's apparent dismissal of suspicion with respect to Mrs. Collings followed a study of the results of a two-day questioning of the young widow by Felix Dimartini, private detective retained by authorities investigating the case.

The prosecutor admitted Dimartini's interview had developed an angle "which looks very promising." He said his investigators were searching for a maniac who was a "total stranger to the Collings."

MRS. E. D. WALKER WEDS IN NEW YORK

Becomes Bride of R. E. Clapp; Will Live Here

NEW YORK, Sept. 22—The marriage of Mrs. Elizabeth D. Walker, of Grosse Pointe Farms, to Raymond E. Clapp, of Detroit, took place in the Municipal Chapel here this afternoon. The ceremony was performed by Deputy City Clerk J. P. McCormick.

It was the bride's third marriage. Her first husband, Charles R. Walker, died Jan. 10, 1926. Her second marriage, to William A. Moran, was dissolved by divorce in Detroit, Dec. 24, 1924. She was born in that city 42 years ago, the daughter of William J. and Elizabeth Hanley Dawson. Mr. Clapp, a traffic manager, is 60 years of age. It was his second marriage. He and his first wife, Mrs. Ursula Corbett Clapp, were divorced in Detroit yesterday. He is the son of John T. and Mary Elizabeth Garrett Clapp.

Will Reside in Detroit

At the residence of the former Mrs. Walker, her housekeeper said Tuesday evening that she had just received a wire informing her of the wedding, one side of which was a surprise, though it had been expected "in the near future." Mr. and Mrs. Clapp will return to Detroit Thursday to make their home at 98 Merriweather Ave., Grosse Pointe.

Legionnaires

Should You Lose Anything

The best way to recover lost articles is with a want ad in the

LOST and FOUND COLUMN of THE FREE PRESS

Phone the Adtaker
RAndolph 9400

Three women were treated at Receiving Hospital and released. They are Mrs. Hazel Dennis, 41; Miss Norma Klosick, 23, and Mrs. Winifred Klosick, 27, all of 4737 Gladys

Continued on Page 10, Column 1

MARCH 8, 1932:

The Ford Hunger March costs four men their lives.

WEATHER
Cloudy and continued cold Tuesday and Wednesday, with occasional snow flurries.

The Detroit Free Press

1831 ~ OVER A CENTURY OF SERVICE ~ 1932

METROPOLITAN
FINAL EDITION

101st Year. No. 309 — TUESDAY, MARCH 8, 1932 — •••••• — 26 Pages THREE CENTS

4 DIE IN RIOT AT FORD PLANT

Baby's Kidnapers Send Two Notes to Lindbergh

CHILD IS SAFE, NEW LETTERS TELL PARENTS

Governor Says Mail Now Goes Directly to Family

SENATE DELAYS ACTION ON LAW

HOPEWELL, N. J., March 7—(A.P.)—Information that the kidnapers of Charles Augustus Lindbergh, Jr., have been in communication with his parents came tonight from an apparently authoritative source.

Two notes were received Sunday by the Lindberghs. One was typewritten, but handwriting experts agreed the other was in the same writing as a ransom demand left behind last Tuesday night by the kidnapers before they fled with the child

All three were on the same kind of paper, it was reported. The last two bore the same post-mark. The baby was described as safe and well.

State Police Confusing

The source of this information supplied these details despite a confusing series of public pronouncements by officials.

From a morning State Police press conference came denials both of the existence of an original ransom note being left by the kidnapers last Tuesday and of any contact with them since that time.

Later, police said "none through the police" when asked if any communication had been established with the abductors.

At the last press conference of the day, officials refused to answer any questions covering these two phases of the case.

Tonight Gov. A. Harry Moore announced that henceforth police will open none of the mail taken to the Lindbergh home, where it is known every effort is being made to deal with the kidnapers on the basis of the three appeals made by the parents.

Family to Get Mail

Police will see, the Governor said, only those letters to the family and its representatives which the Lindberghs and their agents desire to turn over to them.

Amplifying the statement a short time later, the Governor said:

"If the kidnapers wish to get into touch with Col. and Mrs. Lindbergh, they can do so by mail with perfect security. Only such mail as contains leads or tips are turned over to the police. The integrity of Col. Lindbergh is so beyond question that the kidnapers can entirely depend upon his word."

At the same time it was learned that only a skeletonized police force was being kept at the Lindbergh home, at the request of the famous flier himself.

Meantime a letter to Col. Lindbergh demanding $500,000 for the return of the child and setting a meeting place was taken from the mail at Elmira, N. Y.

Fail to Appear

It was written in red ink, and demanded that a representative of the Lindberghs be sent with $500,000 in $20 bills wrapped in a news[illegible] the Cross Trail Restaurant near Mansfield, Pa., tonight.

A message from Mansfield stated that no one had appeared at the Cross Trail Restaurant to represent the Lindbergh kidnapers. The message said that scores of persons were waiting in the street in the bitter cold for the appearance of someone who might be the kidnapers' messengers.

After the money had been delivered, it said, the child would be left at the same place.

At Newark, N. J., Henry (Red) Johnson, sailor suitor of the Lindbergh baby's nursemaid, still was being held after three days and three nights of questioning.

Supports Johnson's Story

In Bridgeport, Conn., a man told police he had ridden from New York to Bridgeport with Johnson early last Wednesday. This tended to bear out the sailor's own story of his movements.

A search of a baby farm in Saco, Me., operated by a relative of Johnson disclosed no trace of the missing child. Capt. Lamb was asked if police had a tip Johnson was on his way to the farm when arrested and replied that investigators assigned to that angle of the case "have not reported as yet."

As the confusion over conflicting reports developed here, Capt. Lamb was asked when it would be possible to obtain an interview with Col. Lindbergh to clear up the numerous discrepancies.

"There are no discrepancies given out from here," he replied.

Officials previously had said no footprints were found in the nursery.

Officials' Stories Conflict

At the noon press conference a State Police official said that footprints had been found on the nursery window sill and on the floor, and that they had been compared with the footprints of a number of persons "without identification."

"Do the State Police and Col. Lindbergh believe the baby is dead

Continued on Page 4, Column 1

TEAR GAS BOMBS HURLED AS RIOT RAGES IN DEARBORN

SHIELDS LOSES PRIMARY FIGHT

Markland Leads Race in Highland Park

John C. Shields, mayor of Highland Park, was nosed out of a place on the final ballot April 4, by 26 votes, it was announced when the last of the primary return had been tabulated late Monday night. The two candidates for the office are N. Roy Markland, member of the Council, who polled 1,354 votes, and James I. Ellman, attorney, 1,254 votes.

Mr. Shields received 1,228 votes, while Charles W. Seymour, former chief of police, trailed with 314.

Joseph M. Hackett topped the field of candidates for the four positions on the ballot for City Commissioner with 1,980 votes. R. Stanley Wilson was second with 1,601. C. Chester Mack, with 979 votes, and Colin J. McRae, with 921, were insured of having their names on the final ballot. William E. Everist and Richard Nahabedian were eliminated. The former polled 810, and the latter 744.

Robert M. Smith, running unopposed for treasurer, received 3,312 votes. Three candidates for constable all will have places in the final election. Charles J. Robinson polled 2,684 votes; Gavin D. Smith 2,398, and Arthur J. Conlin 1,215.

Two proposed amendments to the City Charter were defeated by close votes. A proposal to permit the City to borrow funds in anticipation of the collection of taxes was beaten by a margin of 492 votes. A difference of only 49 votes defeated a motion to make the office of City Controller appointive instead of elective. The result was 1,876 to 1,827.

Holmes to Spurn Party on Birthday

WASHINGTON, March 7—(A. P.)—The eve of Oliver Wendell Holmes' ninety-first birthday finds him partly even with time for forcing him from the Supreme Court bench.

Resigning recently because the work was too much for his strength, he promptly regained some of the physical vitality which kept him delivering opinions after practically all his early contemporaries were living only in memory.

The aged New Englander—he was wounded three times during the Civil War—will not attend the banquet tomorrow night in his honor. Justice Holmes hasn't gone out of his red brick house on I St. at night in years and birthdays to him aren't important enough to break any precedents.

Head of Princeton Waits for Spitale

PRINCETON, N. J., March 7—(A. P.)—In the reception room of their home here tonight, Dr. John Grier Hibben and his wife expressed a willingness to meet Salvy Spitale and Irving Bitz, underworld characters, named by their friend, Col. Charles A. Lindbergh, as his "go-betweens" in the search for the kidnaped Lindbergh baby.

The silver-haired couple explained they had heard reports the pair was coming from New York to confer with them.

The seventy-year-old Princeton University president said he was not an official agent of the Lindberghs, but he was willing to act. The whole situation seemed to puzzle the distinguished Princeton president, and the couple was frankly nervous.

GAS RATE BATTLE DUE ON TUESDAY

Attorneys to Meet on Legal Procedure

Corporation Counsel Clarence E. Wilcox will confer Tuesday morning, with Alexis R. Angell, attorney for the Detroit City Gas Co., when legal procedure in the City's fight for lower gas rates will be discussed. The meeting will mark the opening of the City's fight for lower rates.

The meeting with Mr. Wilcox was called after Mayor Frank Murphy rejected Monday a proposal submitted by the Gas company for cuts in certain rates. The offer was considered unsatisfactory, Mayor Murphy said.

The Mayor conferred with Charles W. Bennett, executive vice president of the Detroit City Gas Co., and W. G. Woolfolk, Chicago, representing the American Light & Traction Co., holding concern for the Detroit firm. They insisted it was impossible at this time to reduce the rate upon household gas, which could only follow six months after introduction of natural gas to Detroit.

The company's representatives volunteered to lower rates charged

Continued on Page 5, Column 5.

Pistol Mishap Kills Officer at Son's Crib

MILWAUKEE, March 7—(A. P.)—Policeman Harold Stroud came home today and stooped over the crib of his eighteen-month-old son to embrace the baby. Stroud's revolver fell from its holster to the floor and was discharged. The bullet struck the policeman in the head, killing him.

SCORE KILLED IN COLD WAVE

Thermometer Due to Rise Tuesday

Premature notes of spring were drowned out Monday by the roar of the March Lion. The entire nation was in the grip of a frigid wave which arrived Saturday night and indications Monday were that temperatures will flirt with zero before the passage of the storm king.

Relief from the cold within 24 to 36 hours, but not until temperatures have fallen to five or 10 degrees above zero, was forecast Monday by the Government weather bureau here.

The lowest mark of the cold wave was predicted for early Tuesday, with temperatures rising slowly during the day.

Fears that the sudden cold, which embraces the whole State, might damage crops were set at rest by Dr. Victor R. Gardner, Michigan State College horticulturist. Dr. Gardner said Michigan crops had not grown sufficiently to be damaged by cold.

Zero reading continuing throughout Tuesday and snow flurries preceding the expected drop in temperature were expected at Lansing.

According to Associated Press dispatches the frigid wave, which extended from the Florida Coast to Canada, and from the Rocky Mountains to the Atlantic seaboard, took a score of lives, including those of five coast guardsmen, who were drowned while trying to save the crew of a fishing schooner.

Highway and telephone and telegraph communications were disrupted in Eastern States.

Start the Day Right With the Free Press

	Pages
Editorials	6
Edgar A. Guest, Poem	6
Good Morning	6
Around the Town	8
The Theater	6
Finance	19
The Screen	10
Society	12
Radio Programs	14
"Dancing Feet," Serial	25
Culbertson on Bridge	14
Crossword Puzzle	23
Grantland Rice	17
Westbrook Pegler	17
Pictorial Review	26
Dr. Evans on Health	6
"I Rise to Remark"	6
Dorothy Lee	13
Personal Problems	13
Music	5
Comics	25
George Matthew Adams	6

Beer Levy Urged in Tax Measure

WASHINGTON, March 7—(A. P.)—The House today received the new $1,096,000,000 revenue bill and prepared for its fiercest battle of the session over proposals to tax beer and manufacturers' sales.

A group of members reserved the right to submit an amendment to legalize 2.75 per cent beer. They would levy $5 on each barrel. Proponents estimated the revenue from this source would exceed $350,000,000.

The proposed amendment is carefully worded and provides that the manufacture of non-intoxicating beer "shall be conducted under permits to be issued in accordance with the national prohibition act."

Meanwhile, opponents to the 2.25 per cent sale tax began to hold meetings on ways of opposing it.

WORLD MOURNS DEATH OF BRIAND

Statesmen Pay Honor to 'Peace Apostle'

PARIS, March 7—(A. P.)—Aristide Briand, France's most prominent statesman in the international field and symbol of her post-war striving for peace, died suddenly just before 1 o'clock this morning in his modest bachelor flat not far from the Arc de Triomphe.

The man who 12 times was chief of his country's government and was a leading spirit in the activities of the League of Nations passed away as a simple member of the Chamber of Deputies.

M. Briand, who would have been 70 years old May 28, succumbed to a cardiac attack.

His valiant heart, which carried him through a turbulent militant socialist and parliamentary career for 40 years, failed him just at the moment when three specialists were hoping to restore him sufficiently to partake in the coming electoral campaign for the renewal of the Chamber, in which he was expected to defend his pacific policies with his old-time oratorical vigor.

The Nation he served as premier during the dark days of Verdun as well as throughout the efforts to stabilize peace in Europe during the last 11 years, will accord him a state funeral. The services will be held at 2 o'clock Saturday after-

Continued on Page 2, Column 5

HIGH COURT REFUSES POWERS CASE REVIEW

CHARLESTON, W. Va., March 7—(A. P.)—Harry F. Powers, under sentence to be hanged March 18 for the slaying of Mrs. Dorothy Pressler Lemke, of Northboro, Mass.; was denied a review of his case by the State Supreme Court today.

BILL TO FEED NEEDY SIGNED

40,000,000 Bushels of Wheat Released

WASHINTON, March 7—(A. P.)—A huge store of Farm Board wheat—40,000,000 bushels in all—was placed late today to the credit of the Nation's unemployed and needy.

President Hoover signed the measure without comment after holding a series of conferences with Attorney General Mitchell and John Barton Payne, chairman of the American Red Cross, which will distribute the Government's donation.

Payne raised a strenuous objection to a clause of the measure permitting the Red Cross to bake the grain into bread after milling. He asserted categorically his organization would not undertake this and suggested the President might well want a legal ruling upon it. A few minutes later Mitchell was summoned, but neither he nor the President would comment.

The section to which Payne objected was:

"In cities of over 25,000 poulation the American National Red Cross or any other organization designated by it may have the flour baked into bread provided that no part of the expense incident to such baking or processing shall be paid out of said wheat or flour and no part of the expense shall be borne by the United States or the Federal Farm Board."

As Payne interpreted the section, it would require the Red Cross to pay for the baking unless this could be obtained gratis from bakeries.

The measure provides for a least 5,000,000 bushels to be used as feed for livestock.

Three Faiths Join to End Prejudice

WASHINGTON, March 7—(A. P.)—A war on religious prejudice was opened here today by Catholic, Jewish and Protestant spokesmen.

Speaking before the national conference of Jews and Christians, three church leaders—Bishop James E. Freeman, of the Washington Cathedral; Rev. Francis J. Haas, director of the National Catholic School of Social Service, and Rabbi Abram Simon, of the Washington Hebrew Congregation—broadcast nationwide appeals.

U. S. CONSUL DIES IN VENICE

WASHINGTON, March 7—(U. P.)—Bernard F. Hale, American consul at Venice, died today, the State Department was advised.

MURDER CHARGES ASKED AFTER RED MOB FIGHTS POLICE

Communists Inflamed by Foster Hurl Stones and Clubs in Pre-arranged Outbreak

Harry Bennett and Others in Hospital Following Battle Started When Agitator Fires Six Shots

Six shots fired by a Communist hiding behind a parked car were cited by police Monday night as the match which touched off a riot at the Ford Motor Co. plant, Miller Road, early in the afternoon in which four men were killed and 29 seriously injured.

Scores of others among some 2,500 rioters were beaten and bruised before they were dispersed by Dearborn and Detroit police, State troopers and deputy sheriffs with pistols, shotguns and tear gas.

Harry Bennett, head of the Ford Service Department, was wounded and is in Henry Ford Hospital, not in danger. Stories conflict as to how he was injured.

Three May Face Murder Charges

Three reported ringleaders of the mob, who may be charged with murder, are among 29 prisoners, five of whom are women, held at the County Jail and Dearborn Police Headquarters. They gave addresses in Detroit, Lincoln Park, Melvindale and Dearborn.

The riot, brewing for more than a week, is said by police to have gathered a large part of its inspiration from two meetings in Detroit Sunday addressed by William Z. Foster, radical leader, who urged the 7,000 men and women who heard him not to miss Monday's "hunger march to Ford's."

Immediate arrest of William Reynolds, Communist agitator who was identified as another inciter of the Ford plant riot, was ordered Monday night as a search continued for Foster.

Reynolds, one time candidate for Mayor of Lincoln Park, is a chronic agitator, a leader of the Unemployed Council, and only recently figured as a victim of the lashings administered to Communistic sympathizers by hooded men at Dearborn.

He was convicted of disorderly conduct following an unemployment demonstration last October and sentenced to serve 90 days in the House of Correction. The October demonstration resulted in a riot in which a Lincoln Park policeman was injured when reserves were called to quell the disturbance.

Sheriff Henry Behrendt told reporters if he could get enough information he would ask warrants for murder against John Fauth, 540 State St., Lincoln Park, former secretary of the Trade Union Unity League, whose papers have been seized; Shelley Rogers, 33 years old, 1522 Lafayette Ave., and Paul James, 27 years old, 1469 Hartford Ave.

Foster Faces Riot Action

Chief Carl Brooks, of the Dearborn police, said Monday night that he would confer with the Prosecutor Tuesday with a view to obtaining warrants charging Foster, Reynolds and others with inciting the fatal disturbance.

Meanwhile, a police guard was established at the home of Chief Brooks, who is ill in bed. Information has reached them, police say, that Chief Brooks and Bennett are the particular targets for attack chosen by the riot leaders.

Threats of the dispersing mob to return later in the night and "wreck the whole damned works" resulted in the concentration at the plant Monday night of police, troopers and deputy sheriffs, and 200 men of the First Battalion, 125th Infantry, Michigan National Guard were on call in the Brush St. Armory under command of Maj. Frank H. Rine.

At midnight, after the shifts at the Rouge Plant had changed, the bulk of the police guard maintained there was withdrawn for rest. A detail of a dozen State Troopers remained and it planned to bring the rest of the officers back at 7 o'clock Tuesday morning to be held in readiness in the event of further disturbances. The National Guardsmen in reserve downtown also were sent to their homes.

The Ford Motor Co., in a statement, expressed itself mystified over the attack, "since this company pays higher wages and employs more men than any industrial organization in Detroit."

The mob began to gather at Oakwood Blvd. and S. Fort St. about 1 o'clock in the afternoon.

Its members came afoot, by street cars and automobile. Conductors said they had fist fights in some instances trying to collect fares. Another report, unverified, was that belligerent groups commandeered 10 D. S. R. busses in the downtown district and compelled the drivers to run them as far as Oakwood.

Crowd Cheers New Arrivals

In the main, the crowd was orderly, and a squad of 70 Detroit police, detailed to the intersection to see that there was no trouble, found no reason to interfere.

There was a profusion of banners:

"Come on Workers, Don't Be Afraid!"

"Down with the Men Who Destroy Milk!"

"We Want Jobs!"

"Now Is the Time to Act!"

The crowd rushed out to meet each arriving street car, booing the police good-naturedly and cheering additions to their own ranks.

The marchers were heterogeneous. All were not Communists, although faces of familiar agitators were in the ranks. In line were known radicals, habitual demonstrators, former Ford workers, professional paraders, and jobless men hoping somehow, to obtain work by parading. The line-up, however, was a good three-quarter Red.

About 1,200 were on hand—hundreds of them women—when the marchers began to move at 2 o'clock.

They marched singing. They left Fort St. on Dearborn Ave. and swung across Baby Creek Bridge to Miller Road. It was near this point that 30 Dearborn police, armed with tear bombs, barred the way.

The first tear gas attack drove the marchers back 300 feet,

Continued on Page 3, Column 1

WEATHER
Generally fair Thursday, not much change in temperature; probably cloudy Friday.

The Detroit Free Press
1831 ~ OVER A CENTURY OF SERVICE ~ 1932

METROPOLITAN FINAL EDITION

102nd Year. No. 92 — THURSDAY, AUGUST 4, 1932 — 18 Pages — THREE CENTS

AUG. 4, 1932:

Two Detroiters make good: Eddie Tolan wins his second Olympic gold medal and Roy Chapin goes to Washington.

"Tolan Flashes To New Record," column two, and *"Vacancy Caused By Resignation,"* column eight.

Walker Lies, Says Seabury to Roosevelt

'He Is Proven Guilty,' Investigator Tells N. Y. Governor

'Mayor Is Unworthy of Belief,' He Holds

NEW YORK, Aug. 3—(A. P.)— Caustic charges of contradiction, evasion and falsification were directed tonight at Mayor Walker's defense of his Administration, by Samuel Seabury, who told Gov. Roosevelt that the New York Mayor had proved himself "unworthy of belief" about his official actions.

The Hofstadter Legislative Committee counsel, who spent a year and a half investigating the New York City Government, reviewed the whole Walker case in a 20,000-word document.

It was his rebuttal to the Mayor's defense of charges on which his removal has been asked.

'Proves Mayor Guilty'

"The record now before you clearly proves the Mayor is guilty of the acts set out in the specifications," Seabury wrote, referring to his previous analysis of the evidence produced in committee hearings.

"I submit the matter to you for such action as may be just to him (Walker) and to the great public interests that are involved."

The dispatch of the document to Albany, where Gov. Roosevelt ordered it made public, made more imminent a decision in the Walker case which has attracted even international interest.

Although the Governor has firmly stated that no political considerations would influence his decision, his Presidential campaigning has been delayed by widespread speculation about the effect the outcome might have on the State and National political situation.

Seabury dwelt at length on Walker's contention that the charges against him were not grounds for removal because they concerned his previous term.

'A Sorry Sight'

Seabury wrote:
"It is a sorry sight indeed to see a person occupying high public office, whose honor is impugned, taking the position that the people must suffer him to continue in his public office because he can fortunate enough not to be caught in time.

"There is no provision in the Constitution or elsewhere limiting the Governor's power of removal of mayors.

"To use it seems shocking that a Mayor should even be heard to urge that the sufferance of his malfeasance in office, indeed from corruption in office, he may escape removal because he succeeded in concealing his misfeasance long enough for another election to intervene."

In discussing the Mayor's contention that Russell Sherwood, missing accountant, handled nearly $1,000,000 in financial transactions for him, Seabury wrote:

"It will be readily observed that whenever expenditures were shown to have been made by Sherwood for the Mayor's benefit, the Mayor's explanation was always the same even from the safe.

"This explanation differs from those made by lesser members of the political hierarchy only, so far as Mayor Walker's great pains to emphasize that it involves.

"On a vault, not a tin box not a safe in no time."

Cites Farley Ouster

"The Governor has rejected this explanation somewhat differently expressed will it now be accepted?"

Seabury referred to the removal of Thomas Farley, Tammany leader, from the office of sheriff, after he had given a tin box in his home as the explanation of where large sums of money came from.

"What man leaves his home, his job and his friends, goes into hiding and subjects himself to an adjudication of contempt and a fine of $50,000, as Sherwood has, unless he has something to conceal? And has any suggestion from anyone that Sherwood has anything to conceal except his relations with the Mayor?"

Seabury charged that Walker could have reached Sherwood in Mexico had he wished to.

Walker's explanation that the $246,000 he obtained from a joint brokerage account with Paul Block, newspaper publisher, did not constitute a gratuity, in which he (Walker) had a joint liability, drew the comment from Seabury that it was a palpable afterthought.

Obscure Ragpicker Dies Worth Million

CHICAGO, Aug. 3—(A. P.)— William H. Kearns, in life an obscure rag collector, died a millionaire. This was revealed today when a brother and sister filed a $2,000,000 bond pending disposition of the estate.

Start the Day Right With the Free Press

Pages
Editorial 6
Edgar A. Guest, Poem.. 6
Good Morning 6
Cubberson on Bridge ... 4
The Screen 4
Radio Programs 15
Society 7
Silhouettes 8
Dorothy Lee 10
Personal Problems 9
Minute Mysteries 10
Window News 15
Financial 14
Crossword Puzzle 14
"Leap Year Bride," Serial.. 17
Comics 17
Pictorial Review 18
Around the Town 8
George Matthew Adams.. 6
Quillen's Observations .. 6
Dr. Evans on Health .. 6

TOLAN FLASHES TO NEW RECORD

Wins 200-Meter for Double Olympic Crown; American Stars Sweep Day's Events

By GRANTLAND RICE

LOS ANGELES, Aug. 3—The new crown that belongs to the "world's fastest human" now rests just 5 feet 4 inches above the ground. It is squarely planted upon the black brow of little Eddie Tolan, the midnight express, who came on like a sable flag to outrun the greatest field that ever met upon a track.

Two days ago the same Tolan won the 100-meter race. Now he adds the longer sprinting route to his list of speed achievements, doubling up just as Percy Williams did four years ago at Amsterdam.

As Tolan, Simpson and Metcalfe crossed the wire in front of the struggling Jonath, of Germany, they gave the United States its fourth victory in four finals as the Stars and Stripes spent most of the afternoon outlined against a blue sky that swung out of the Sierra Madre range.

Dynamite in Tolan's Start

Tolan's twinkling feet were too fast, much too fast, for the world to meet. They were too fast for the mighty drive of big Metcalfe. They were too fast for the flashing strides of Simpson, of Ohio; Jonath, of Germany; Luti, of Argentina, and Walters, of South Africa.

There was too much dynamite in Tolan's start. He was off and away with the striving speed of a rattlesnake's head. There was too much powder in Tolan's continued whirl from the start to the wire. He wore a broad a world's record at 200 meters around a curving track to win in :21.2, but he carried his pace to the finish as Metcalfe failed and Simpson's game challenge fell behind by a yard.

Standing only 5 feet 4 inches in height, Tolan moved his feet with incredible speed. As the starter's gun barked on the message Tolan and Jonath were the first that streaks that took the lead. They were catapults in white and black. They ran on even terms for the first 100-meters as Simpson coming on with Metcalfe struggling to catch up.

Seventy meters from the tape Tolan, still traveling like the midnight wind across an open plain, left Jonath behind. The fast German could hold on no longer. His bolt was shot. Metcalfe now made a mighty effort to overtake his darker, smaller rival but the old lunge and surge was no longer there.

Spectators Up with a Shout

It was Simpson, the veteran from Ohio, who still hung on- who still carried the dazzling pursuit to the last stride. But even Simpson, running at his best after a gallant comeback, lacked the steam needed to run down this spinning mite who was running the fastest 200-meter race around a turn the world had ever seen.

Seventy-five thousand spectators were up with a roar as Tolan took the lead and raced on in his second victory in three days.—The first time in 12 years the United States has won more than one 2nd place upon an Olympic track.

Big Metcalfe lacked the drive he had shown before when the final charge was needed. It faded and fell before the continued speed which Michigan's Midnight Express had carry of the crowd. It was the pole vault battle between Bill Miller, of Stanford, and Bitie Nishida, of Japan.

Bill Graber, who set a new world's record at 14 feet 4¾ inches, fell out at this rate at 13 feet 10 inches. Then, to the huge delight of the 75,000 souls in the stands, Little Nishida, from the Land of the Rising Sun, cleared the bar at 14 feet. The margin was

Continued on Page 3, Column 4

Vets Pack Up to Go Home

Mayor Orders Them from Johnstown

JOHNSTOWN, Pa., Aug. 3— This welcome worn out, in less than a week, the bonus army tonight voted to break camp and go home.

Many of the veterans who took cars packed up and left tonight after they were told to leave by Mayor Eddie McCloskey, who invited them here last week. But the main evacuation will start tomorrow, when most of the 5,000 veterans and their families will roll westward on special Baltimore and Ohio passenger trains.

Arrangements with the railroad to carry the veterans West were made by the Bethlehem Steel Co., whose mills are the major industry here.

Threatened by Mayor

"You mugs are leaving here in a lot better style than you came," Mayor McCloskey yelled as a disgruntled faction served notice that it intended to stay.

"And if you don't get out by tomorrow I'll chase you out myself without calling in any troops."

"The dissenters under Capt. Doak Carter, veteran commander, later announced they would form a new camp at Huntington, W. Va.

Other units of veterans were dreaming westward through Pennsylvania today. Forty-three men and women who had started to walk eastward to Washington, with Capt. W. T. Hurley, today packed their belongings and left. The camp had been condemned by Gov. Ritchie. Arrangements to carry veterans free by trucks through Ohio and West Virginia were announced by Governors White and Conley.

Hurley Denies Bonus Seekers Were Injured by U. S. Army

WASHINGTON, Aug. 3—(A. P.)—Replying to what he termed the "apparently deliberate propaganda and misrepresentations that are being circulated," Secretary Hurley today reviewed the incidents leading to the expulsion of the bonus army from Washington by Federal troops and said the action was performed with "unparalleled humanity and kindliness."

The War Department head said the bonus forces remained in the Capital ache. Congress adjourned only "to carry out orders of propagandists and radicals.

"No one was injured after the coming of the troops," he added. "No property was destroyed after the coming of the troops, except what which was destroyed by the marchers themselves."

Hermit Signs Confession in Killing of Girl

Body Found in Cellar of Abandoned Dwelling

Victim is Strangled to Death by Recluse

TRAVERSE CITY, Aug. 3—(A. P.)—Francis (Rusty) Nash, thirty-one-year-old bachelor recluse of Freesoil, confessed in the jail here tonight, officials said, that he killed Evelyn Sanford last Saturday night at the edge of Freesoil and buried her in the cellar of an old dwelling. The detailed statement which officials said he signed checked in essential details with the reconstruction investigators had made of how the pretty seventeen-year-old farm girl whose body was found today in Freesoil lost her life.

Saw Girl Go to Town

The confession, as given out by officials, said that he saw the girl walk into Freesoil from her home, half a mile out, about 8 p. m. He wandered about town during the early night, he said, went home and started to retire, then dressed again and walked out along the road Evelyn would follow going home.

Angered, he said that he struck her a heavy blow with his fist and that she fell unconscious in the roadway. He became frightened, pushed her body down an embankment, went to his home, less than half a mile away and along the same road, and returned with some rope and a gunnysack.

The confession said he felt her pulse, could detect no heart action and believed her dead. To make certain, however, he tied a piece of rope tightly around her neck.

Wheeled Body in Cart

Then he went to a neighbor's home and stole a two-wheeled cart. After trussing up the girl's body in the gunnysack and with the rest of the rope, he said, he lifted it into the cart and wheeled it to the vacant dwelling at the rear of the house he occupied and buried it in the basement.

He said he did not attack the girl.

Nash was brought here from Manistee when threats of a mob forming in Freesoil to storm the jail were heard.

Nash's confession quoted him as saying he had difficulty going to sleep after burying the body of the girl he had killed, but that he finally dozed off.

Sunday morning, he said, he had breakfast with his mother; then spent the day at various tasks about his place. His arrest did not come until Tuesday night.

Discovery shortly after noon of the girl's body buried in the cellar of the vacant house at the rear of the dwelling in which Nash lived brought to a tragic conclusion a four-day search.

An autopsy this afternoon disclosed that she had been knocked unconscious by a heavy blow across the face, then strangled by a rope tied about her throat. Examining physicians said that an attack had been attempted.

Murderous Load to Arrest

Nash, who lives by hunting and fishing, was arrested last night because of scratches on his face which a physician said apparently were caused by fingernails and because he had been apathetic about the search for Evelyn's body.

State Police are holding at Ludington as a material witness Calvin Edwards, 19, of Freesoil, who also had scratches on his face and his face while felling a tree. Later, Edwards admitted that his corroboration had been influenced by threats from Nash.

The crime aroused intense feeling. A crowd of men formed in Freesoil this afternoon after the discovery of the body and it was then that officials announced that Nash had been moved to Manistee, about 10 miles distant.

The post mortem examination was conducted in the undertaking establishment of Coroner Rupert Stephens at Scottville by Drs. J. L. Spencer, Scottville, and E. George Gray, Ludington.

Evelyn was graduated from Freesoil High School last spring. Jammed head-down into a narrow

Continued on Page 8, Column 2

Charges Husband Cost Her $60,000

SAN ANTONIO, Tex., Aug. 3—(U. P.)—Mrs. Cora S. Glassford, of San Antonio, wife of Police Superintendent Glassford, of Washington, was granted a divorce here yesterday on charges of desertion, it became known today.

ROY D. CHAPIN CHOSEN TO SUCCEED LAMONT AS COMMERCE SECRETARY

Industrial Gains Create Optimism

Bolstered by Federal Aid, Trade Shows Improvement

Stocks Up $2 to $7 on New York Mart

WASHINGTON, Aug. 3—(A. P.)—Administration of the gigantic plan enacted by Congress to speed economic recovery proceeds apace these days, and today brought optimistic soundings.

The Reconstruction Finance Corp. today devoted primary attention to the railroad situation, and how wider employment could be provided.

The Treasury felt the first effect of the billion dollar tax bill bulwark, learning it had taken in $2,631,000 in miscellaneous internal revenue the first of this month; or more than twice as much as on the same day a year ago.

New Currency Issued

The first increase in the currency under the Glass-Borah provision, which allows National banks to issue currency against Government securities until the amount of currency so issued is now $3,895,000. Although the legislation allows for expansion up to almost a billion dollars, this initial currency was very fractional, amounting to but $1,656,000 out of a total of $733,877,000 in National bank notes which were outstanding on Aug. 3.

The shoe industry was added by the Commerce Department to the list, including automobile, textile, cement and tobacco, in which it reports activity has increased.

Mr. Hoover worked on his analysis of the situation, as it will be expressed by him next week in accepting renomination.

Home Loans Discussed

Organization of the Federal Home Loan Bank System, to which Congress allotted $125,000,000 with a view toward facilitating home building, was up in a talk between the President and Dr. N. Roop, president of the Home Building and Loan Association of the United States.

The board met again with a committee of rail executives and experts from the Interstate Commerce Commission, to move out of a three-point plan for increasing employment, which would be submitted to railroad executives as a unit for approval.

Steel and Rail Issues Lead in Spurt Taken by Market

NEW YORK, Aug. 3—(A. P.)— A fresh wave of buying swept over financial markets today, sending many leading shares on the New York Stock Exchange $2 to $7 net higher, and bringing another strong advance in wheat and some grain prices.

A number of bullish rumors circulated throughout the financial district in the afternoon, and brokers who had sold yesterday on rumors of change in the nation's money policy which he was in with prominence.

As a boy his hobby was photography and it was his work as an amateur cameraman just that brought him to the attention of R. E. Olds and then up so rapidly that by the end of 1906 he organized with Mr. Howard Coffin persuaded Hugh Chalmers to put money into their venture. In 1908 the Chalmers-Detroit Co. was organized with Mr. Chapin as general manager and treasurer. He was getting closer to his goal, and there still was a vast space to traverse.

A year later he decided to try his own hand on the plan of his dreams, and then up so rapidly that by 24 he was to be at the head of department and sales manager for that pioneer maker of automobiles.

Late Trading Active

Bonds, after some irregularity in the morning, reversed themselves in the afternoon.

Trading in stocks was extremely active during the last hour, when pivotal issues pushed well above their high prices of last week. Final quotations were virtually the best. Total sales approximated 2,500,000 shares.

Stalwarts like United States Rubber common and preferred, American Telephone, Union Pacific, Allied Chemical, Santa Fe and American Can shot up spectacularly as shorts hurried to execute their repurchase orders. The final transaction did not appear on the tape until several minutes after closing time, 3 o'clock.

Many Issues Gain

American Telephone was buoyant, closing $7 higher at $96.25, while Steel common finished with a gain of $3.75, the final price being $31.87, and the preferred jumped $5 to $77. Allied Chemical at $63.50, Sears Roebuck $17.50, up $3; Corn Products Refining $23.62, up $3; American Can $42.37, up $4.62; American Tobacco "B" $73.75, up $6.50; New York Central $17.25, up $2; General Motors, $12, up $1.50.

NEW MEMBER OF HOOVER CABINET

ROY D. CHAPIN

New Commerce Secretary Grew Up with Car Industry

Chapin Started with R. E. Olds and Became President of Hudson at Age of 30

Roy D. Chapin, newly appointed secretary of commerce, is as much a product of Detroit as is the automobile industry.

In fact, the two grew together. He rise started with the automobile industry before there really was any such thing.

But long before there was a boy with a hobby. A hobby like any youngster might have, but it led him straight into the work in which he was to win prominence.

Prove to N. Y. in a Week

Mr. Chapin was born in Lansing on Feb. 23, 1880. It was while he was in Lansing High School that he became interested in taking pictures. The habit grew as he attended the University of Michigan. It was then that he met Olds and his career was twisted into the course it was to run.

The youthful Chapin decided that he wanted to become a demonstrator of those new-fangled machines, automobiles. He figured that if he was going to go into the industry the best way to learn it was to get into the cars and drive them, familiarize himself with the product. So he drove the first Olds from Detroit to the New York Show in seven and one-half days, much to the Country's amazement some 30 years ago.

He was a practical optimist, this young man who had joined a fledgling industry which was to develop into one of the leading units of the Country's industrial fabric.

The motor man, emulating the fashion of the day, decided catalogs were fine things. That gave the new recruit of the industry's opportunity.

Took Pictures for Catalog

"You know," he ventured to Olds, "I'm a bit of a photographer myself and I probably can supply the pictures to go into that catalog."

All the pictures used in the first inspirational thing and the nebulous ambitions of youth were beginning to take shape. He began to see a goal ahead and threw his whole heartedly in with the new industry.

At La Paz the Bolivian Government made public a note informing the League the Bolivia "did not decline pacific means or action of the controversy."

Following upon Paraguay's general mobilization order, Bolivia called all classes between the ages of 22 and 36 to the colors.

So great was the fever here in Asuncion that 500 volunteers not swamped a transport starting up the Paraguayan River to the Chaco boundary region since June 18.

Hundreds of Paraguayan women society girls and baby peasants involved Government officers with pleas that they be allowed to fight alongside their men.

Vacancy Caused by Resignation

Detroit Man Called to Aid in Recovery of Business

Sees Brighter Day Near for Industry

By EUGENE S. LEGGETT

WASHINGTON, Aug. 3—Roy Dikeman Chapin, chairman of the Board of the Hudson Motor Car Co., today was appointed Secretary of Commerce by President Hoover. He will succeed Robert Patterson Lamont, of Chicago. Both are natives of Michigan.

Mr. Lamont leaves the Cabinet to resume his duties with the American Steel Founders Co. His resignation has been in prospect for many months and he has urged it his post only at the insistent request of President Hoover.

Mr. Chapin, active in the development of highways and the automobile industry, has supported the work of the Department of Commerce in the last decade in developing American exports. Much of his work in the cabinet will be centered in this direction.

Sees Better Business Prospects

Mr. Chapin today was optimistic over the Nation's economic outlook. He told the President that "business prospects now seem better than at any time since the depression began." In a conversation with a newspaperman he declared that "the change in public psychology for which everybody has been praying has taken place."

Mr. Lamont was born in Detroit 61 years ago and is a graduate of the engineering school of the University of Michigan. He married in Lansing and in the practical pioneers of the automobile business. He is now 52 years old.

The change in the cabinet was decided upon the last 72 hours. Mr. Chapin agreed to take over the post when President Hoover talked to Mr. Chapin by telephone and asked if he could arrange his private affairs so as to enter the cabinet.

Mr. Chapin appeared at the White House after a lengthy conference with President Hoover at which he was seen to be serious. A few minutes after the White House announcement the appointment was made. Mr. Chapin boarded a train for Detroit.

President's Announcement

Explaining the change, President Hoover today said:

"Secretary of Commerce Robert P. Lamont has found it necessary to resign in order to re-enter private business.

"Mr. Lamont has remained in his position at great sacrifices for personal months at my request. I regret extremely his loss from the administration. His abilities and service have commanded the respect and confidence of the entire Country.

"I am pleased to announce the appointment of Mr. Roy D. Chapin, of Detroit, and Mr. Lamont's successor.

"Mr. Chapin is a manufacturer in Detroit. In 1910 he became president of the Hudson Motor Car Co., holding that office until 1923 since which time he has been chairman of the board. He has been vice president of the Lincoln Highway Association, chairman of the Highway Transport Committee of the International Chamber of Commerce and director of the Motor State Good Roads Associations.

"He was president of the National Automobile Chamber of Commerce in 1927 and 1928."

The shift is to become effective as soon as Mr. Chapin can conclude his business affairs in Detroit a few days hence.

Secretary Lamont had sought to be relieved of his office during three times before during the past year but had yielded each time to President Hoover's request that he carry on until a successor might be found.

Mr. Lamont's major business

Continued on Page 2, Column 4

Pan-Americans Demand Peace

Outlaw Spoils of War in Chaco Dispute

By The Associated Press

A policy to outlaw war and deprive offenders of the fruits of conquest was employed for the first time in the Western Hemisphere yesterday when 19 neutral American nations told disputing Bolivia and Paraguay that they would not recognize any territorial gains obtained by force of arms.

The American nations further declare that they will not recognize any territorial arrangement of this controversy which has not been obtained by peaceful means, nor the validity of territorial acquisitions which may be obtained through occupation or conquest by force of arms."

At Geneva the League of Nations secretariat announced that Paraguay had agreed to arbitrate.

At La Paz the Bolivian Government made public a note informing the League that Bolivia "did not decline pacific means or action of the controversy."

Following upon Paraguay's general mobilization order, Bolivia called all classes between the ages of 22 and 36 to the colors.

So great was the fever here in Asuncion that 500 volunteers not swamped a transport starting up the Paraguayan River to the Chaco boundary region since June 18.

Hundreds of Paraguayan women society girls and baby peasants involved Government officers with pleas that they be allowed to fight alongside their men.

NEW ANNUITIES PARLEY URGED ON FREE STATE

DUBLIN, Aug. 3—(A. P.)— The Irish Free State Senate passed a motion tonight calling for the reopening of negotiations with Great Britain regarding the Irish land annuities, of which President Eamon de Valera's government has refused to pay.

Reynolds Case Quiz Reopened

Heir's Slaying Taken Up by Grand Jury

WINSTON-SALEM, N. C., Aug. 3 — (A. P.) — Sheriff J. Transou Scott, who has been investigating circumstances surrounding the fatal shooting of Z. Smith Reynolds, young millionaire, here July 6, was closeted with the Forsyth County Grand Jury more than two hours today.

The Grand Jury will reconvene tomorrow.

Prior to going before the jury, Sheriff Scott conferred with Stewart Warnken, vice president of Reynolds, Inc., executor of the Reynolds estate. An employee of Reynolds carried to Sheriff Scott a sealed paper, which appeared to be a drawing.

Continued on Page 8, Column 2

War Exalted by Mussolini; He Calls Peace Impossible

Democracy Termed 'a Tyrannical Failure' in Duce's Exposition of Fascism

ROME, Aug. 3—(A. P.) War is exalted by Premier Mussolini as giving "the seal of nobility to peoples" in his concluding exposition of Fascism for the Encyclopaedia Italiana, which was published today in his old newspaper, Il Popolo d'Italia. Perpetual peace, the Premier says, is impossible.

His disdain on democracy is blunt:

"Fascism, as it generally regards the future and the development of mankind and apart from considerations of present policies, does not believe in the possibility of perpetual peace," the Premier writes.

"It therefore rejects pacifism, which amplifies renunciation of struggle and cravenness in the face of sacrifice. Only war carries all human energies to the height of tension and gives the seal of nobility to peoples that have the courage to confront it."

"The belief in the necessity of combat, Mussolini says, is natural by Fascism into the life of the individual. Consequently, Fascism rejects universal embrace and, although living among other peoples, it watches them and will not be deceived by changing and fallacious appearances."

"He explains the Fascist cry of empire as the will to power. "Empire is not only a territorial, military or commercial expression, it is a spiritual or moral expression," he says.

Girl Prankster Gets $1,235 for a Spanking

LOS ANGELES, Aug. 3—(A. P.)— For the pain, embarrassment and humiliation of being spanked over a comparative stranger's knee, Agnes Trahar was awarded damages of $1,235 in Superior Court.

Jack Halloween's the fifteen-year-old high school girl said that the windows of Dr. Bernard G. Traue's home.

She said he turned her over his knees and "beat" her, injuring her spine.

Wife of Glassford Is Granted Divorce

SAN ANTONIO, Tex., Aug. 3—(U. P.)—Mrs. Cora S. Glassford, of San Antonio, wife of Police Superintendent Glassford, of Washington, was granted a divorce here yesterday on charges of desertion, it became known today.

BETTY GOW SAILS HOME

NEW YORK, Aug. 3—(A. P.)— Betty Gow, nursemaid in the home of Col. Charles A. Lindbergh at the time his baby son was kidnaped, was listed as a passenger on the Mauretania when it sailed for England today.

CAR GOES

This particular car was a big one—one of the biggest of the vaunted brood of cars.

It had been owned by the West Detroit Auto Sales, of 5965 W. Fort St., and taken in trade on a new car. Knowing the value and the worth of the owner behind the wheel it was decided to sell it "as-is" through the Free Press Want Ads.

And the very first day the want ad appeared it was sold—drove away with a satisfied new owner.

So great was the fever for "Free Press Want Ads always. Dial Randolph 8600, the Free Press Want Ad taker will help write your ad."

Free Press Want Ads, 321 W. Lafayette, Downtown office, Shinola's Drug Store, Woodward Ave.

FEB. 15, 1933:

The eight-day Bank Holiday shocks Michigan residents and signals one of the worst moments in the Depression.

The Detroit Free Press

THE WEATHER — Generally fair, Wednesday and Thursday; somewhat colder.

1831 ~ OVER A CENTURY OF SERVICE ~ 1933

METROPOLITAN FINAL EDITION

102nd Year. No. 287 — Wednesday, February 15, 1933 — 22 Pages — Three Cents

Detroit Banks Ready to Pay Depositors $25,000,000 Under 5 Per Cent Plan of Withdrawal on Thursday

Ford-Couzens Conflict Revealed as a Factor in Financial Stalemate

Senator Opposed R. F. C. Loan to Trust Firm, Saying Collateral Was Not Sufficient

Insisted That Motor King Keep $7,100,000 on Deposit as 'Frozen Asset'; Magnate Refused to Sign Joint Note

(Copyright, 1933, by The Detroit Free Press)

Behind the clouds of rumors, cross-currents of semi-official statements and denials and the confusingly contradictory statements of Gov. Comstock, there loom two figures in the inside story of the difficulties of the Union Guardian Trust Co. and the subsequent bank holiday.

One is Henry Ford; the other is his old partner, James Couzens.

These always dramatic figures are so much a part of the history of Detroit as to need no introduction to them and their conflicting personalities is needed. They fought their way up in the early days of the motor car industry, when adventurous giants walked the earth and made of Detroit a dynamic Eldorado. They parted company, each going his way—and since then, their views on all political and economic matters have been as far apart as their ways.

Inside Story Is Pieced Together

What follows here is culled from the wires and a tempestuous day on Griswold St. The principals will not talk. In some of the minor details, the story may err; but in the large general outline it is all vividly true. Here it is in its essentials.

It might never have been told if Gov. Comstock had not made charges the import of which he now admits he did not understand. Out of a sleepless night of wild confusion, he talked without knowing the drama that was being enacted behind the scenes. Now he admits he did not know what he was talking about.

It began this way:

A few years ago the Union Trust Co., an old institution of the city, with heavy investments in real estate, merged with the Guardian Detroit Bank, and out of this merger came a unit of the Guardian-Detroit-Union Group Inc., which was known as the Union Guardian Trust Co. Through this latter firm a trust business was carried on.

The Official Viewpoints

Assets in Real Estate

With 72 per cent of its assets tied up in real estate, and with Detroit property rapidly depreciating in value, these assets dwindled. Depositors, feeling the stress of the depression, began at the same time to withdraw funds to meet their everyday needs. Several months ago the directors of the company reached the point where liquidation of assets to meet depositors' demands was becoming more and more difficult.

It was about this time that Henry Ford came into the picture. He had several millions on deposit, and this money was sorely needed by the trust company. He made no effort to withdraw the money, but current rumor had it that he had become much interested in the concern. Clifford B. Longley, who had appeared in court as Mr. Ford's lawyer, became president of the company. Edsel Ford is a director in the Guardian-Detroit-Union Group, Inc. and Ernest Kanzler, his brother-in-law, is chairman.

Liquidation to meet depositors' demands became extremely difficult in December, and at that time Mr. Ford is understood to have deposited several millions more. But even with this assistance, the going became even more difficult.

Provisions of Measure

The bill follows:

"The Commissioner of the State Banking Department is hereby authorized to restrict and prescribe the conditions under which deposits, both savings and commercial, may be withdrawn from any bank or trust company doing a banking business in this state.

"Any bank or trust company or any depositor in such bank or trust company affected by such decision, may appeal therefrom within 10 days after the rendering of such decision by filing an application in writing with an Appeal Board to consist of the Governor, the Attorney General, the State Treasurer and the Auditor General of the State, who shall be members of this board during their respective terms of office. Such board shall be authorized to conduct a hearing in accordance with the rules prescribed by the board, and to affirm, revise, alter or amend any decision of the Commissioner.

"The Corporation is therefore taking unusual steps to enable the employees to secure cash for their services, so that they may be promptly paid.

"Chrysler Corp. has arranged to open tomorrow, Feb. 15, a cash disbursing office in the building at

Please Turn to Page 4—Column 1

R. F. C. Asked to Aid

"The solution of the financial problems rested with the ability of the directors to organize a new company and take over the assets of the Union Guardian Trust. These plans were pushed in January, and the Reconstruction Finance Corp. was asked to take a hand.

"It was at this juncture that the former partners in the motor industry, Couzens and Ford, came into conflict. Ford had stuck to motors, Couzens had launched himself into a public career.

"Mr. Couzens, now United States Senator, is chairman of the committee named by the Upper House to inquire into the loans of the R. F. C. He questioned at Mr. Ford's wish.

Start the Day Right with the Free Press

Pages
Editorial 6
Edgar A. Guest, poem ... 6
Good Morning 6
The Theater 8
Music 8
Society 9
Silhouettes 9
Ruth Adams 10
Dorothy Lee 10
State News 11
Culbertson on Bridge .. 12
Screen 13
Grantland Rice ... 15
Cullyre's Comment .. 15
Financial 16
Radio Programs ... 19
"Folly Island," Serial .. 21
Comics 22
Picture Review ... 22
Around the Town .. 22
Minute Mysteries ... 22
Dr. Joseph Fort Newton ... 6
Quillen's Observations .. 6
Dr. Evans on Health .. 6

Dramatis Personae

JAMES COUZENS — HENRY FORD

Limits Sought on Withdrawal

Legislature to Act on Bank Relief

LANSING, Feb. 14 — A bill limiting withdrawals from both savings and commercial accounts was prepared Tuesday night at a conference in the office of Attorney General Patrick H. O'Brien. It will be introduced in the Legislature Wednesday by Rep. George J. Corn.

Gov. William A. Comstock has taken no position on the proposal, declaring that the problem is one the banks themselves must solve. Several members of the House and the Senate who attended the conference and the proposed law is one that may be useful after the bank holiday ends, but that its terms should not be mandatory.

The measure would permit varying withdrawal limitations, fixed at the discretion of the Banking Commissioner, in accordance with the requirements of each institution that elects to come under the law.

Business Carries On Despite Bank Holiday

Plans Are Made to Insure Public Against Suffering from Lack of Essentials

Detroit moved Tuesday to reduce the inconvenience of the bank holiday to a minimum and to devise ways of getting something to use for money. The state-wide moratorium, an unprecedented action to relieve a critical banking situation, precipitated countless problems of feeding and heating the entire metropolitan population and providing it with some acceptable tender.

Retail stores decided early in the morning to accept checks only in payment of accounts, and members of the Retail Merchants Association, at a meeting at the Detroit Board of Commerce in the afternoon, decided not to commit themselves to any definite merchandising program until some further word was forthcoming from Gov. William A. Comstock and the banking group. The Wholesale Merchants Bureau, following an hour's discussion, announced its members would continue "business as usual."

Chain groceries and milk and fuel companies promised liberal concessions, and three of the City's largest industrial firms announced plans to make their employees' checks negotiable.

Fears that counterfeiters would flood the city with spurious bills, once the restraint of banks was removed, were allayed Tuesday when 350 special Government Secret Service investigators were sent to Detroit from Washington. Their men will augment the force working under Bert C. Brown, chief agent, here, sufficiently to control the activities of counterfeiters and propagandists until the bank holiday period is ended, Government spokesmen in connection with the Michigan bank holiday.

Spurious Money Warning Issued

City Guards Against Counterfeiters

"The Chrysler Corp., importing funds from outside the State to meet its midmonth payroll, announced the opening Wednesday on W. Grand Blvd. of its own temporary bank to do business exclusively with the company's employees. It was understood that the corporation will be in a position to turn over to its workers in this way about $1,100,000 in cash Wednesday.

R. F. C. Is Ready to Help Banks

Confidence Voiced in State Institutions

By Eugene S. Leggett

WASHINGTON, Feb. 14 — Adequate support for the Michigan banking structure was pledged tonight by officials of the Reconstruction Finance Corp. They expressed confidence in the State's banks and the belief that business soon would be resumed under normal conditions.

$40,000,000 in Reserve Cash Reaches City and More Is Being Rushed

Officials of Nation and State Take Hand in Relieving Finance Emergency in Michigan

Other Institutions' Stability Not Involved in Trust Company's Difficulty, Executives Say; Legislature to Aid

The Detroit Clearing House Association Tuesday announced the following regulations, designed to lessen the inconvenience to the public of the bank holiday:

1 — Acting upon the supplemental proclamation by the Governor, the Detroit banks have arranged to release on Thursday morning in excess of $25,000,000.00. All depositors, both checking and savings, may withdraw for emergency purposes not in excess of 5% of the net amount on deposit in their accounts at the close of business Saturday, Feb. 11, 1933. Such withdrawals are to be made only by counter receipts which will be paid in currency.

2 — All banks and all branches will maintain facilities for making change.

3 — Safe deposit departments will be open and will operate on the regular hours.

4 — Arrangements are being made with many of the large life insurance companies whereby checks for premiums will be accepted as conditional payment in order that the policies may not lapse.

By Clifford A. Prevost

More than $25,000,000 will be available for depositors in Detroit banks Thursday morning. Any depositor may withdraw 5 per cent of his commercial or savings account. Withdrawals may be made by counter receipts and all payments will be in currency.

This relief was provided late Tuesday, when the Detroit Clearing House Association moved to relieve the financial strain which the Governor's proclamation closing all banks in Michigan imposed upon communities of the State. Plans for further releasing of the financial pressure will be formulated in several meetings Wednesday.

Branches Also Will Be Open

To facilitate the transaction of business, the branch banks also will be open, thus providing change-making facilities. Safety deposit vaults will be open as usual and will operate during the regular banking hours. Life insurance company plans to accept checks, thus preventing the lapsing of policies, were formulated.

These measures were formulated Tuesday to meet conditions brought about by the eight-day banking holiday proclaimed early Tuesday morning by Gov. Comstock. The Detroit Stock Exchange will remain closed until the holiday is ended, and all brokerage houses have been prohibited from trading in the stock of any banks.

The Federal Reserve Bank of Detroit will remain open, accepting the millions that are being poured into the City from branches of the Federal Reserve System in Chicago and New York. By Tuesday night, $40,000,000 already had arrived.

While local bankers hopefully began work upon unraveling the situation created by the financial difficulties of the Union Guardian Trust Co., the eyes of the nation centered upon Michigan. President Hoover was in telephonic communication with financiers and manufacturers in Detroit, and the Federal Reserve agents co-operated with the local bankers. Ogden L. Mills, Secretary of the Treasury, watched the Michigan situation closely and discussed it at a White House conference.

Officials Confer on Situation

George L. Harrison, governor of the New York Federal Reserve Bank, also conferred with the President as Eugene Meyer, chairman of the Federal Reserve System, discussed the situation with Mr. Mills. The latter was in constant communication with Wall Street and official Washington and A. A. Ballantine, in Detroit, while Wall Street and official Washington kept eyes upon Cleveland and Chicago.

Reports reached the White House that the Michigan situation was causing little uneasiness in the neighboring states of Ohio and Illinois. In the House, the Michigan situation was discussed and responsibility placed with the Senate for its failure to enact legislation to guarantee bank deposits.

At Lansing two bills were introduced in the House, designed to legalize the proclamation of the Governor. His action had no legal force, although all banks respected his wishes, excepting those of the Upper Peninsula, which operate under a different Federal Reserve Branch than those below the Straits.

The bill introduced are designed largely to overcome legal difficulties that may arise later. They cannot be enacted within 12 days, but will carry a retroactive clause. They were brought in by Rep. William H. Donnelly, of Detroit.

Criticizes Postal Savings

Rep. Clarence Cannon, Missouri Democrat, said the failure of 1,000 banks at the door of Congress. He was particularly critical of the Postal Savings system and the marketing of Government bonds, which he said "drain money from the small communities into the large financial centers."

Representatives Carl R. Chindblom, of Illinois, and John C. Schafer, of Wisconsin, both Republicans, joined in the criticism of publicity given to Reconstruction loans.

Rep. Edgar Howard, Nebraska Democrat and author of the publicity amendment to the Reconstruction act, defended his amendment, declaring he favored publicity for all Government business.

After 14-Story Fall, Worries About Hat

CLEVELAND, Feb. 14 — (A. P.) — Samuel Malbin fell from a window on the fourteenth floor of the Allerton Hotel here today and plunged through a skylight to the ground four of the laundry room.

"Where's my hat?" he demanded as horror-stricken employees picked him up. Still conscious, he had suffered no more than a fractured arm, hospital attendants reported.

Beware of Racketeers

BE on your guard against schemes by which racketeers will try to turn the banking holiday and the temporary shortage of currency to their profit and your loss.

Don't sell at a discount the checks you receive. Nearly all business houses are making arrangements to cash their employees' salary checks. In any case, the checks will be worth face value when the bank holiday is over and the banks reopen.

Loan sharks may try to take advantage of the present temporary condition. Don't let nervousness or anxiety lead you into their traps.

Above all, watch for disseminators of vicious rumor and false propaganda and report instances of that kind to the United States Secret Service, which has detailed 350 men to Michigan to combat such propaganda.

Please Turn to Page 4—Column 5

ICE SKATING TONIGHT—OLYMPIA 5 to 11:30. Band music—35c.—Adv.

BOXING'S BIGGEST BARGAIN

The Detroit Free Press

GOLDEN GLOVES SEMI-FINALS

Friday Night, Feb. 17 at Arena Gardens

Woodward at Hendrie

7:30 P. M.

— 32 BOUTS —

Prices: 40c, 55c, 83c, $1.10, including tax. All except 40c seats now on sale at Arena Gardens and the Free Press.

GET YOUR TICKETS NOW!

MARCH 26, 1933:

Diego Rivera's murals at the Detroit Institute of Arts spark furious arguments among citizens.

Dispute Over Worth of Rivera's Murals Divides Detroit Into Two Factions

Sneers Mixed with Cheering

Cleric Starts Firing, and City Joins In

Seldom has an artist's work evoked such a torrent of discussion, even quarrel, as the argument over the frescoes by Diego Rivera in the Detroit Institute of Arts.

Beginning a little over a week ago when the Rev. H. Ralph Higgins, curate of St. Paul's Episcopal Cathedral, wrote to Detroit newspapers a letter objecting to what he termed a "caricature" of the Holy Family appearing in a panel demonstrating the process of vaccination, the discussion quickly spread.

Meetings to air protests against the murals on religious, economic or artistic grounds have been held. Organizations and individuals have sprung forward, on the one hand, to the defense of the murals. Those attacking the murals have called the paintings sacrilegious, others have seen in them sheer Communist propaganda, others object to them as presenting a one-sided picture of Detroit life and spirit and still others call the painting simply "bad art."

The defenders of the paintings, on the other hand, consider that Rivera has presented a realistic picture of Detroit as he sees it, has not deliberately affronted any religious sect, and has painted a masterpiece that will redound to the artistic reputation of the city in that it has permitted a fine expression of the modern in art and given it suitable emphasis.

Of hundreds of letters received for and against the murals, The Free Press herewith presents some of those which seem to typify the sentiments of the opposing groups.

'True Humanity' Traced in Colors

'Era of Impressionism' Hailed by Reader

To the Editor: The controversy regarding the diabolical insinuations of Diego Rivera's murals is fast assuming asinine proportions. For the benefit of the clergy and the clubwomen engaged in this ridiculous criticism of a famous artist, allow me to say that they are laymen; the public turns to the ridicule of the world. It is about time that a halt was called on the unwonted activities of our self-appointed guardians of public education in matters of art.

Not being satisfied with laying at the doorstep of Communism every conceivable catastrophe from the stock market crash to the earthquake in California, we now have the spectacle of some learned gentlemen and a few ardent club women growing hysterical over the so-called "filth menace" symbolically (?) portrayed in Rivera's murals.

I agree that the first impression of Rivera's murals is not altogether pleasing. But if we pause for a moment and consider, first that persons are not always correct nor are they always pleasing. One is startled by the apparent realism; by a week-old child that cannot fathom the extraordinary break of history caused by the war, by its antecedents and the consequences, can expect that art, this mirror of the nation, will continue in its normal way as it did during the preceding generations. Now more than ever reflecting the spiritual experiences during a turning point in a nation's history is natural to the masses. The day of the "naturalistic" school is past. The era of "impressionism" is here.

"... there is also an art that is life itself, that rises out of the depths like a cry and in this cry carries the deepest expression of true humanity." That is the art of Diego Rivera; that is the vitalism expressed by the artist who has endeavored to paint life as he sees it in this dynamic city.

MILTON M. ROSE

Imagination Gift Termed Rivera's

Artist ... Has Created Living World Out of Mind

To the Editor: All esthetic laws begin with pereeption and final definitions. There are created by genius and distinctive imagination.

Diego Rivera is an artist who has the rare gift of this distinctive imagination.

They gave him the commission to do the murals for the "Detroit Institute of Arts"—and he completes them in due time.

Now the air seems to be disturbed by strange noises, shaping themselves into protests as to how Rivera should have done his own work. Some say: "It is beautiful!" others, "It is ugly!"

As it is, there is neither beauty nor ugliness in nature or art. Trees do not grow for the artist to please his taste. The last rays of a dying sun do not stop between two branches of an oak tree, so that you may say: "It is beautiful!" but you yourself must render these objects alive and beautiful.

Out of material stored in his mind, Rivera has created a living world; "Detroit as it is today." Facts alone do not count: they may give the wrong impression, but the imagination of an artist confronts facts with living access and presents the hidden truth.

FRANZ C. M. MEIER

Curate Is Taken to Task for Criticism of Painting

To the Editor: I wish to voice a protest to the letter of the Rev. Ralph Higgins, senior curate of St. Paul's, who attacked the murals of the Mexican artist, Diego Rivera.

In my opinion, restrictions put upon the artist, sculptor or writer, work on injustice of great moment upon the progress of the nation.

ROY SAUCH
Dearborn, Mich.

This 'Vaccination Panel' Set Off the Explosion

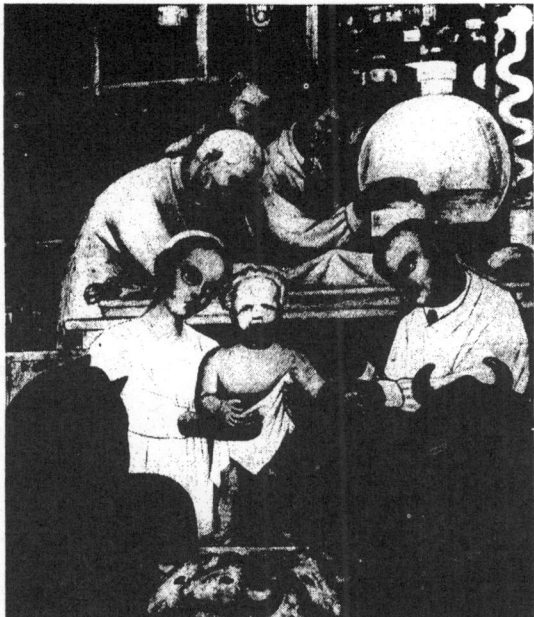

This fresco panel by Diego Rivera, first reproduced in The Detroit Free Press on March 17, is responsible mainly for the furious argument which has been waged over whether the artist has maligned the Church and the Holy Family. Officials of the Detroit Institute of Arts contend that the "Vaccination Panel" portrays merely the constructive side of medicine and is entirely scientific in subject. The controversy has grown by leaps and bounds and concerted action is threatened to have not only this panel but the entire work of Senor Rivera removed.

No Threats Found in Clenched Fist

Called Kulak Symbol, Not Communist

To the Editor: While I was gazing, admiring and trying to grasp the meaning of the murals, two ladies came up to me and remarked that the murals reminded them of jazz. Ever a moment I did not know just what to answer. How, when I came to, I said in part: "The difference is this, jazz became popular from the start, while these frescoes can no more become popular than the works by Bach and any other great master. It takes often centuries before great art becomes recognized."

I know almost nothing about the high technique you see from the first principles of painting, but intuitively I can appreciate the manner in which human energy, ingenuity and industrial life in action can be expressed by a great artist painter. They express Industrial Detroit of today, not of yesterday nor of tomorrow. Nor will these murals express Boston nor Los Angeles.

It is rather significant to read why some people denounce these masterpieces in such strong terms. One can only draw from their opinions derogatory meanings. It seems that it is out of all reason to think, that these murals have any damaging effect religiously, politically or ethnically. The worst one can claim, bringing the objector have his say, is that some of it offends his individual artistic taste.

But are not these other ultra-modern works in our Art Institute, and various other subjects, which have a peculiar effect on some the individuals? Are we to dispense with all of these, too?

Some people seem to think that the flats neutralizing in the frescoes are symbols of communism. This is quite erroneous. In the Russian language the word "Kulak" means fist. The "Kulaks" in Russia are against communism, which apparently the artist did not wish to express. The Kulaks could not possibly intend to symbolize communism.

BORIS GANAPOL

Is Panel Bad Enough to Be Called Canvas?

To the Editor: The modern interior mechanic with a toothpick—in your Tuesday issue, O. Austin Johnson, who has "devoted some 30 years to art", writes of Rivera's "Vaccination Family:" "If there is one redeeming feature of this canvas—"

Mr. Johnson doesn't recognize the difference between a canvas and a fresco mural. Or he himself as bad it must even be treated with euphemism? O.K. MAJORCA

Maybe Rivera Will Return to Give His Pictures Words

To the Editor: As a subject of Mr. Rivera's wonderful portrayal, I feel privileged to criticize my painter, more especially since my labors were exchanged for his. After inspection of his work, I am overwhelmed by a grave error; we should have exchanged places. We were misread. A vacant panel on the walls of my kitchen has long tempted me to express the inner urge of art thereon, but a sense of modesty and my wife's disapproval have heretofore forbid.

However, Mr. Rivera's exposition of art is a grand addition of civilization, and I now feel completely, nay, masterfully, superior to be undertaking.

One cannot but stand in reverence of the noble spirit in which Mr. Rivera approaches to interpret upon a few square feet of wall no less a concept than the interior of the entire Ford plant. In fact

History Cited by Valentiner

'Nature Art' Theories Are Questioned

To the Editor: When Mr. Bingay speaks about politics I do not venture to dispute with him, for I do not know anything about the subject. But when he discourses on art and art history, I should like to have my little say, too.

Mr. Bingay describes how beautifully Velazquez expresses the soul of Spain, Titian that of Venice, Rembrandt that of Holland; how they were great because they held to their own environment, and he concludes from this that no outsider artist like Mr. Bingay paint in the Louvre, I am afraid he is not well informed on the subject, for on those very walls are a great cycle of paintings which Marie de Medici, queen-mother of France, commissioned the Flemish Rubens to paint for her, and which depict scenes from French, not Flemish history. And was not Leonardo asked by Francis I to come to France, where he developed the school of Fontainebleau, at a time when there was still some discussion regarding the greatness of his art?

One could easily enlarge this list of artists who, leaving their native country, gave a better representation of the characteristics of the places to which they went than some of the native artists. Did not Greco, a Greek who studied in Venice, give a more living representation of the Spain of the Counter-Reformation than any Spaniard? And when it comes to American art history, the best portrait sculptures of Washington and Benjamin Franklin were done by the French artist Houdon. Vice versa, the American Benjamin West spent most of his life in England, where he achieved many honors, among them that of being chosen president of the Royal Academy. And is not an English painter but the American Sargent who gives us the best impression of English society of the last generation. The fact is that outsiders can sometimes see national characteristics better than those who stay in one place all their lives.

But I question whether Mr. Rivera is really so much of an outsider as Mr. Bingay thinks, even though he was born some hundreds of miles away from Detroit. In Europe he is regarded as an American artist, and seeing things once in a while from the other side of the ocean has at least the advantage—of which Mr. Bingay seems to disapprove—of viewing them at a distance and in this way arriving at the common traits which are characteristic of a continent as a whole, without regard to its geographical boundary lines. In fact I am not able to understand how American art history can be comprehended without having an idea of the polite appreciation of the titanic effort that a great artist has poured into a work of art that he calls his masterpiece.

And on top of it all, along comes the "Michigan Civic League which through its secretary voices a denunciation of the work and expresses horror at Dr. Valentiner's artistic taste. They then cap it off with the opinion that the work would have been done by the American Artists Union.

Can one Detroit ever make amends to Senor Rivera for this total type of good manners?

How can Detroit escape the ridicule that is bound to follow from every part of the world? Ridicule brought on our heads by a few hasty critics who in a paroxysm of bad taste bid their lack of numbers by the smoke they raised?

Well, I guess the only thing to do is to try to live it down.

GORDON T. HILL.

Marring of Court Charged to Artist

To the Editor: A mural decoration is a monumental building should first of all express itself with dignity, beauty and serenity.

It should make its appeal to the intellectual and emotional nature through its composition, its color and charm, without violence or exaggeration in drawing or color.

The writer submits that no decoration is justified in marring the effect of ... of a building from it ... on my distinction in composition and conclusion of motives, as has been done in the Garden Court of the Art Institute.

The Court was in that a thing of beauty, and it is to be regretted that the public spirited and generous gift of Mr. Edsel Ford should, through no fault of his, have so sadly miscarried.

ISABELLA HOLT FINNIE.
(Mrs. Haldeman Finnie.)

Wondering What Architect Thinks

To the Editor: One phase of the Rivera controversy which apparently has been lost sight of is the reaction of the architect of the Institute of Arts to these murals. Doubtless he would, for several reasons, refrain from expressing himself, but it would be interesting to take his blood-pressure before and after viewing.

One of the first and most fundamental principles of mural decoration is that the work of the artist shall be subordinate to the architecture—it shall at least be harmonious. The most learned partisans of Rivera cannot contend that a gross violation of this principle has not been perpetrated in the Garden Court of the Institute. The architect and the purpose of the room have been subordinated to a personal conception—one man's idea of what a mural, depicting the soul of Detroit, should be. Yet in the Detroit Institute of Arts thousands of people here sought spiritual uplift—they have wanted to get away from the very thing which Rivera shows them.

H. G. WENZELL.

Edsel Ford Comment Held the Best Answer to Critics

'It Is Rivera's Interpretation,' Said Man Who Paid for Work of Mexican Artist

To the Editor: For Edsel B. Ford, when asked if he thought Diego Rivera's frescoes accurately interpreted industrial Detroit, replied, "It is Rivera's interpretation."

Coming from the most artistic money paid for these frescoes, this reply seems to me to answer generously the critics of the immeasurable work of this great artist.

How many of these critics have sought to harmonize this artistic product with the destiny of art? How many have attempted to determine whether it is art by testing it according to the accepted definitions of art?

How does the great Diego Rivera meet these tests in his frescoes?

His religious feeling is manifested in his revelation of the emotional value of the common human personality and all of its related activities, aspirations, traditions, and rationalism. His precious cynicism breathes religion and a high conception of morals. For morality is solely the normal activity of a healthy nature.

What would the critics of these frescoes say of the immortal Walt Whitman, who, in "Song of Myself," declared:

"And nothing, not God, is greater to one than one's self is—"

And what would they say of this same author who thus approaches the humid flesh of his fellow beings:

"There is something in staying close to men and women and looking on them, and in the contact and odor of them, that pleases the soul well.

All things please the soul well, but these please the soul well."

"Is loveliness of body more than the external indication of its utilitarian and vital use?"

Is criticism sufficient which says that those frescoes represent a Communistic dart at the stronghold of Capitalism?—that they are the work of a foreigner? Do "Buy American" advocates, and those who are unable to understand Communism direct their criticism to Detroit, and the Arts Commission knew it. Where were these critics then? Why didn't they register their complaint at that time, instead of now, when the artist has finished his work?

My main point, however, is to protest against those who talk of destroying the frescoes. Such an attitude is as narrow, provincial, reactionary, cowardly and barbaric that I hope all literal-minded and cultured people in Detroit will rise in protest. Do we still live in the Dark Ages, when mobs were incited to destroy and burn libraries and works of art? It is another attempt to bring back the notorious Spanish Inquisition? Do we want the whole world to laugh at us as typified in the case of the State of Tennessee? Do we want our City to be known as Detroit, Destroyer of Art?

No! A thousand times, no!

Let us argue all we want pro and con, but leave it to history to decide whether Diego Rivera who is a great artist or a mere bungler. Should the verdict of history prove him to have been a great artist, Detroit would never be able to expiate its crime. On the other hand, if his work is of no value what Detroit will decide that, too, then we do not want to make him famous through martyrdom.

There is one more possibility; we may allow him to take his frescoes away from here, even though it were necessary to replace the walls of the inner court.

Civilized people do not destroy! We must not allow fanatics to gain the upper hand!

A genuine democracy obeys the mandate of the majority, and protects the rights of the minor ties. Let us be democratic, not just talk about it!

EUGENE MONDOR.

Walls Condemned as Lacking Beauty

'Acid Test' Is Applied to Work of Rivera

To the Editor: Art expressed through pictures is—as viewed by the great mass of people—an expression of the beautiful, the sublime. The acid test of a picture to most people would be, Is it of sufficient beauty and interest to be placed in my home, can I view it with pleasure and does it arouse in me the sentiments of satisfaction, restfulness, or inspiration? Surely these murals cannot squeeze into any such classification. True, some people may work themselves into a state of ecstasy over them, but the majority would not agree; and, after all, should the decorations in a public building be made for the few who think that they need this procession in art appreciation or should they be of such character that the mass of people can enjoy them?

These murals are entirely out of harmony with the beauty of the fountain court and should be removed. The walls of this court are no fit place for the display of caricatures. Why deface a noble horse by making him look so grotesque? Rivera saps the scenes glorify the workman. Heaven forbid that any workman should feel glorified by such a representation as he now depicted there where he is made to look like an emaciated gallery slave with no spark of intellect and where the faces and forms are contorted as in agony.

Out with the frescoes!

H. S. W.

U. S. to Lease Station Site on East Grand Boulevard

WASHINGTON, March 25—(A.P.)—The Postoffice Department has announced that it has accepted the proposal of Israel Seidenberg to lease its present quarters at 2405 E. Grand Blvd., near the Milwaukee Junction Station, for a ten-year term from May 15.

Outsider Derides Detroit's Culture

City Called Backward by Ann Arborite

To the Editor: It is no wonder that Detroit fails to appreciate the murals of Diego Rivera. This city is a cultural backwater and has failed to produce any art, architecture, or even a City Plan of its own which is of any consequence, or in keeping with modern ideas.

The thought of the world has changed regarding the Church, Architecture and Government and it is this new spirit of Detroit that the artist has depicted in your Art Institute. The fact that the people whose walls they adorn is too small does not overshadow the fact that Diego Rivera has painted the noon of Detroit, instead of mere "pretty pictures." This is no new field to step in art, but is being done by modern cities all over the world.

The world has gone through this new idea in Music, i. e. sonders, cycnicism; in Poetry we have the genius of Carl Sandburg; in Drama the plays of O'Neill, and as we analyze this new movement we find that it is taking place in all the life of modern man. Why, then, one of our most artistic places, the automobile, be satisfied with the thoughts of our ancestors or the art and architecture of the dark ages? C. E. R.

Ann Arbor, Mich.

Suggests Taking Word of Experts

To the Editor: The murals of the Mexican artist, Rivera, have created an orgy of unnecessary discussion. What more pitiful in a "this "quarrel" is a thing that the people who know less about an are speaking loudly about it.

An art is something which must be understood by a racial, political or religious prejudice, but through an inner conviction.

Let us leave the criticism of art to those who spend their life in studying its mysterious beauty. Let us only stop, to read the statements of Dr. Valentiner and Mr. Richardson.

Diego Rivera is an artist. The cause here as an artist of heroic proportions, and not as a propagandist of any political faith; therefore the dispute of his political affiliations is of absolute nonsense.

GENEVIEVE TROJANOWSKI.

Museum Leaders Given the Blame

'Frescoed Biliousness' Brings Attack on 'False Gods'

To the Editor: Although believing that the frescoed biliousness now defacing the once beautiful walls of our Art Museum should be removed at once the incident of controversy is not without certain benefit. It has revealed the strange conception of art held by the directors of the museum, a highly presumptuous insistence by themselves upon the virtues of their ideals, and the accusing insubordinateness of the native and recognized cultural leaders of our City. All praise is due those who have already denounced this travesty upon the City's life and good name. But it may appear that had our people been dutifully alive and awake no foreign propagandist could have been brought here to institute our public buildings and insult both our intelligence and our artistic sensibility. It cannot change to historic and eternal truth.

In view of all the facts, therefore, the only genuine issue is: shall Detroit belong to Detroiters—the legitimate heirs and respecters of our City's indisputably sounded and mental ideals, or shall we surrender to the false and repulsive gods of the money maniacs and his blind strangers within our gates.

HENRY B. SULLIVAN.

INSURE YOURSELF AND FAMILY NOW

A $10,000 Free Press Accident Policy Costs But $1.00 a Year

Covers Automobile, Street Car, Train, Bus and Pedestrian Accidents in Traffic, as Specified

Pays Up to $10,000 for Loss of Life—$7.00 to $25.00 per Week for Injuries—Indemnity for One Day or More

More Than $831,000 Paid in Claims

Send This Application to the Free Press With $1.00

Where The Free Press is delivered to the home daily and Sunday. Or by mail ... your subscription. Each must send in application and registration fee of $1.00. Age limit 18 to 69.

THIS APPLICATION MUST BE COMPLETELY FILLED OUT OR IT WILL NOT BE ACCEPTED

APPLICATION

To E. R. Hatton, Registrar:

☐ Do Not Write in This Space

I hereby apply for the $10,000 Accident Policy issued by the Continental Life Insurance Company exclusively to regular readers of The Detroit Free Press. I enclose registration fee of $1.00 and understand that said policy will not be effective until this application has been received at the main office of The Detroit Free Press and the policy actually issued; also that the policy will be kept in force only while I continue as a regular Free Press reader.

YOU ARE AUTHORIZED TO START DELIVERY OF THE DETROIT FREE PRESS, AS CHECKED BELOW, AND I WILL PAY THE CARRIER AT THE ESTABLISHED RATES.

☐ Daily and Weekly ☐ Daily Only ☐ Sunday Only
25c per week 10c per Week

I now receive The Detroit Free Press regularly as checked below:
☐ Daily and Sunday ☐ Daily Only ☐ Sunday Only

Delivered by Carrier at ....
Give Address

Procured From ....
(If not delivered by carrier, state fully the source and location from which it is received.)

Name .... Age ....

TO INSURE ACCURACY PRINT WITH PENCIL—USE BLOCK LETTERS

Street Address .... Date of Birth ....

City or Town .... State ....

Mail this application with $1.00 money order or currency to THE DETROIT FREE PRESS INSURANCE DEPT., DETROIT, MICH.

MARCH 29, 1933:

The Rev. Charles Coughlin, the "radio priest," broadcast from the Shrine of the Little Flower church in Royal Oak and became one of the most controversial public figures in the nation. Wall Street was one of his favorite targets.

The Detroit Free Press
1831 — OVER A CENTURY OF SERVICE — 1933

102nd Year. No. 329 — Wednesday, March 29, 1933 — 20 Pages — Three Cents

Fr. Coughlin's Gambling in Stocks with Charity Donations Is Revealed

'A Crap Game Played with Other People's Money'
(Excerpt from Father Coughlin's Radio Address of Sunday)

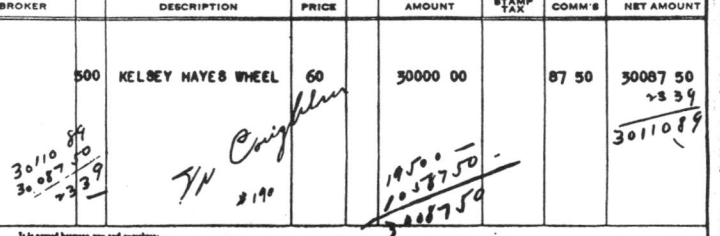

Priest Who Denounces Market Plungers Lost Thousands in Wall St.

Funds Sent in Reply to Radio Pleas Used in $30,000 Transaction; Bank Accounts Shifted

There is gold in the radio racket.

That is proven by the bank balances maintained by the Rev. Charles E. Coughlin.

Each Sunday afternoon he broadcasts over a national hookup.

The contributions which have flooded into his bank account as a result of these talks run into thousands of dollars weekly.

Leo J. Fitzpatrick, general manager of the local Station WJR, admitted Tuesday that the cost of radio stations and telephone companies, paid from these donations to charity, each Sunday reaches $8,000.

These contributions also have permitted Father Coughlin to plunge in the stock market, paying at one time as much as $30,110.89 for stocks purchased. This sort of gambling has been bitterly denounced by Father Coughlin in his radio addresses.

He lost $13,955.89 on one venture into Wall Street.

These are the records revealed in a check of the radio priest's account with the Guardian National Bank of Commerce. He controlled three accounts in one branch of that institution.

Carried Three Accounts in Bank

One of these was a personal account, under the name of C. E. Coughlin, another was known as the account of the League of the Little Flower, and still a third as the account of St. Theresa's Parish of the Child Jesus.

On Feb. 27, 1929, the account of the priest shows, the bank bought for him 500 shares of stock in the Kelsey-Hayes Wheel Corp., which was then selling for $60 a share. The stock was quoted this week at 20 cents a share.

On that day Father Coughlin transferred from the League of the Little Flower account $9,216.28; drew $4,233.72 from his personal account; cashed a check on another local bank for $6,000, and borrowed $10,587.50 on a note from the Guardian National, which was then known as the National Bank of Commerce.

Supplementing this money with a sum from his pocket the priest was able to pay the $30,110.89 for his 500 shares of Kelsey-Hayes stock. This figure includes the broker's commission.

This purchase was made by the bank through Paine, Webber & Co. The stock was delivered on March 6, 1929.

There is also on record a sale order for 200 shares of Kelsey-Hayes stock for $6,212, including commission, on June 10, 1930. The bank files, as far as could be learned Tuesday, do not list the purchase of this stock.

They reveal another sale order for 38 shares at $1,147.03 on June 9, 1930, with no record of the purchase. Still another transaction in behalf of Father Coughlin shows that he purchased 25 shares on February 27, 1929, at 60½ per share and his account was debited $1,520.01, including commission.

The 500 shares, together with 200 shares and 38 shares, were all sold on June 8, 6 and 9 of 1930, for $23,485.78. The radio priest's personal account was credited on June 10 with $23,485.78.

This sale was negotiated through the Nicol-Ford Co., brokers, by the bank. The loss on the 500 shares was $13,955.88. As the records are not available to show what was paid for the 200 shares and the 38 shares, the loss, if any, cannot be determined.

Father Coughlin had at least $80,048.04 in the Guardian National on March 19, 1931. On that day he withdrew this amount and purchased Government bonds. The bonds were purchased for him by the bank.

Large Withdrawals Appear in Records

On June 5, 1931, Father Coughlin withdrew $30,000 from the League of the Little Flower Fund.

On Oct. 16, 1931, he withdrew $27,000 more from the League of the Little Flower Fund.

On Dec. 16, 1931, Father Coughlin transferred $50,000 from the three funds to meet an indebtedness to the bank. This indebtedness was incurred in the name of St. Theresa's Parish.

Conservator B. C. Schram, in charge of the Guardian National, and Judge Frank E. Wood, his legal advisor, refused Tuesday to discuss the nature of this indebtedness, or to answer a question as to whether Father Coughlin still owes the bank money.

Father Coughlin arrived frequently at the bank, carrying his money, and accompanied by his father, C. J. Coughlin, who acts as his business manager, and who has charge of the store at the Shrine of the Little Flower.

When the heavy withdrawal of $80,048.04 was made, *Please Turn to Page 3—Column 3*

Detroit Trust Placed Under a Conservator

Harry J. Fox Is Put in Charge by State Commissioner

Financial Statements of Old Banks Issued

Bank statements showing the condition of the First National Bank and the Guardian National Bank of Commerce on Dec. 31, 1932, on Feb. 11, 1933, the last business day before the State Banking Holiday, and on March 13, the day the banks were taken over by the Federal Administration, were issued Tuesday by C. O. Thomas and B. C. Schram, Government conservators. (See tables on Page 2.)

Other developments in the Detroit banking situation during the day were:

1 Harry J. Fox, who has conducted the liquidation of the Fidelity Bank & Trust Co., now nearing completion, was named conservator of the Detroit Trust Co. by State Banking Commissioner Rudolph E. Reichert.

2 Armed with definite concessions to the First National and the Guardian National Banks, Police Commissioner James K. Watkins and a committee of Detroiters left Washington for Detroit after conferences with Treasury Department officials. They are to arrive here at 8:30 a. m. Wednesday.

3 Disclosure was made of imminent legal action by an outstate banker to recover funds impounded in the Detroit banks. The action will be filed in Detroit courts and will be based on the new National and State emergency banking legislation.

4 The National Bank of Detroit established a record for new business with 808 accounts opened during the day for a total of more than $5,500,000 of new deposits. Deposits in the bank since its opening now amount to $23,224,008.55. Commercial accounts number 2,420.

5 Prosecutor Harry S. Toy questioned four unnamed persons in connection with his investigation of the Detroit banking situation. He indicated that he would take to the outstate bankers by M. C. Eveland, president of the Michigan State Bank, who was in the city to arrange suit against the two old banks and their conservators designed to compel the return of "impounded funds."

Mr. Eveland indicated that he would fight for the release of these funds under the provisions of new National and State banking legislation. He decried the present theory of impounding state bank funds because, he said, it "pyramids backwards," making impossible the release of proportionate funds by the state banks to their depositors.

The Mayville banker asserted that his bank has only small resources on deposit in the Detroit banks and that his bank now is open. "The National Bank of Detroit," he said, "is only one of the banks since its opening."
Please Turn to Page 2—Column 5

---

15 Die as Plane Falls in Flames

BRUSSELS, March 28 — (A. P.) — The City of Liverpool, a tri-motored airplane of the British Imperial Airways, burst into flames and crashed today near Essen, killing 15 persons, every one aboard her. The cause of the accident was not established. The ship, bound from Cologne, Germany, to Croydon, England, by way of Brussels, had stopped at Haeren Airdrome here shortly before the crash.

One explanation advanced was that one of the three motors was stopped, setting fire to the plane. Witnesses said that the great ship dropped like a spent rocket, then landed in a field.

Apparently four of those aboard jumped for their lives during the wreckage some distance from the wreckage. It appeared that the others had been burned to death. Twelve of the victims were passengers and three were members of the crew. There were no Americans aboard.

California Quake Victims Given Funds by Japanese

WASHINGTON, March 28 — (A. P.) — Ambassador Debuchi of Japan today informed John Barton Payne, chairman of the American Red Cross, of a 10,000 yen Japanese gift to the California earthquake fund. The donations came from the Japanese Red Cross and the cities of Tokio and Yokohama.

Belgian Savants Welcome Prof. Einstein at Antwerp

ANTWERP, Belgium March 28 — (A. P.) — Prof. Albert Einstein, returning from the United States, was greeted today by a delegation of Belgian savants. It was said that he intends to arrive in this country and that he may be offered a chair at the University of Brussels.

Start the Day Right with the Free Press

Pages
Editorial 6
Guest, Poem 6
Good Morning 6
Walter Lippmann ... 6
State News 8
Windsor Briefs 9
The Screen 9
Society 10
Silhouettes 10
Ruth Alden 11
Dorothy Lee 12
Broadway on Bridge 12
Crossword Puzzle .. 13
Collyer's Comment 13
Financial 14
Radio Programs 17
"The Changing Bride" Serial 17
Comics 20
Editorial Review ... 20
Around the Town ... 6
"The Raven on Health" 6
Joan's Port Newton . 6
Quillen's Observations 6

NOTIFICATION

March 28, 1933.

Mr. Leo Fitzpatrick,
Manager,
Radio Station WJR,
Detroit, Michigan.

Dear Mr. Fitzpatrick:

Pending action for libel and criminal slander against Father Charles E. Coughlin, your station, and your allied group of stations, for the utterly false and vicious attacks upon Mr. E. D. Stair, The Detroit Free Press, and Mr. Stair's associates, you are hereby having called to your attention your joint responsibility and co-partnership in this campaign of vilification.

This is being officially sent to you as a matter of record for use in case of continued violation of the laws of libel. Due to the illness of Mr. Stair we are unable to proceed immediately. We wish to assure you that you personally, and your station, will be held to strict accountability in this and in future action.

Very truly yours,
Malcolm W. Bingay,
Editorial Director,
The Detroit Free Press.

(Notice similar to the above has been sent to the 26 allied stations which broadcast Father Coughlin's address Sunday.)

* * *

March 28, 1933.

Mr. Eugene O. Sykes,
Chairman,
Federal Radio Commission,
Washington, D. C.

Dear Mr. Sykes:

For your information so that you may understand future action, I am enclosing in this letter copy of a notice sent to Mr. Leo Fitzpatrick, manager of Station WJR, Detroit.

Very truly yours,
Malcolm W. Bingay.

Watkins Note Backed by U.S.

Government Contract Secures Loan

Special to Free Press and Chicago Tribune
WASHINGTON, March 28 — The note which Police Commissioner James K. Watkins has in the First National Bank is secured by the United States Government.

Disclosure of this fact Tuesday night revealed another falsehood in the address of the Rev. Father Charles E. Coughlin over the radio last Sunday, in which he bitterly attacked the head of the Detroit Police Department.

Not a Loan to Watkins

The note was not actually issued for a loan to Mr. Watkins, but for a loan to the Bagley Land Co., of which he is a trustee.

It was made in order that the Burnham-Stoepel Building, L. Larned and Bates Sts., might be renovated for the United States Government's temporary postoffice. It was originally for $178,000.

Each monthly payment made by the United States Government to date has been applied to the note, which has been reduced to approximately $165,000.

Commissioner Watkins is a trustee of the Bagley estate. His signature appears on the note as trustee of that estate.

The Postoffice Department selected the building among a large number offered. Postoffice officials suggested that the loan be made in order that the building might be placed in condition for operations of that department, pending completion of the new postoffice building.

The contract of the United States Government for the use of the building is the collateral behind the note.

Roosevelt Will Open Drive Against Speculators Today

Congressional Message to Ask Regulations for New Securities as First Step

WASHINGTON, March 28 — President Roosevelt tomorrow will take the first step in his promised campaign against stock market speculators.

The President will submit a message to Congress proposing Federal regulations to safeguard the investor against fraudulent or misrepresented stock-selling schemes. The bill to carry out his proposals will not be drafted in advance of the submission of his message to let it become known how far he thinks the Government should go in regulating new securities. It was reported that the bill would require the organizers, promoters and sellers of the issues to submit for public information complete financial statements concerning the stocks and bonds offered for sale.

The bill is expected to require that full information shall be given in every prospectus offering securities for public sale, and that similar information be made freely available at other sources.

Although Mr. Roosevelt has declared that buyers of securities were entitled to *Please Turn to Page 2—Column 1* in advance of the submission of his message to let it become known how far he thinks the Government should go in regulating new securities.

A Letter from Mr. Stair

The following letter written by Mr. E. D. Stair, president of The Detroit Free Press Co., to its editorial director, explains itself.

Mr. Stair is recovering from several weeks' illness and left Detroit yesterday afternoon for a brief rest in Florida to recuperate his strength.

Today Mr. Stair celebrates his seventy-fourth birthday. He will be greeted on his way south—at Cincinnati—by a message signed by all the members of his staff expressing their admiration and affection.

March 28, 1933.

Dear Bing:

Please correct the impression given in Monday's statement that I was prominent in the marvelous economies worked out in the management of the First National bank last May. The honor must go to the Chairman of the bank, Wilson W. Mills, and his assistant, Joseph M. Dodge, ably backed by a committee consisting of James T. McMillan, William T. Barbour and James S. Holden.

These men were working together reduced the operating expenses of the two units approximately $100,000 a month without the slightest injury to efficiency.

I hope to be back on my job with you all within a week or 10 days, but under absolute orders of Dr. Jennings I am leaving for a little sunshine after 12 days in bed with a stubborn attack of tonsillitis and its attendant difficulties.

Keep the fires burning in the interests of Detroit, and in giving your full support to the new bank please do not forget the services rendered by the Detroit Savings Bank, the Commonwealth-Commercial, the United Savings and the Highland Park State by their opening in full at the earliest possible moment.

Yours,
E. D.

Court Will Air Petition Fraud

May Prevent Vote on 21-Man Council

By John N. W. Sloan

Circuit Judge Adolph F. Marschner will hear at 9:30 a. m. Thursday evidence gathered by Prosecuting Attorney Harry S. Toy's office from which it was determined Tuesday to demand, on the ground of fraud in the initiatory petitions, that the City Election Commission be enjoined from printing the twenty-one-man Council proposal on the April 3 ballots.

A three weeks' examination of a portion of the petitions, conducted by Assistant Prosecutor I. A. Capizzi and a corps of investigators, gleaned the information on which Prosecutor Toy filed his bill of complaint Tuesday.

"There is no doubt," declared Mr. Toy, "but that the petitions are honeycombed with fraud."

A few hours after Mr. Toy had filed his complaint Assistant Prosecutor Capizzi discovered 55 more affidavits carrying 25 names each which he believed to be fraudulently notarized. Handwriting experts and detectives attached to the Prosecutor's staff will continue their work, and additional questioning of petition circulators is expected in the next 24 hours.

A formidable collection of affidavits, Mr. Capizzi said, will be presented with the sworn testimony of handwriting experts. The affidavits
Please Turn to Page 3—Column 1

Woodin Overrules Edict of Webster

BALTIMORE March 28 — (A. P.) — Not even the English language is escaping the arbitrary aspects of the new deal.

The dictionaries say it's "con-serv-a-tor" and so do other authorities. But Secretary of the Treasury William H. Woodin has decided that it should be "con-serv-a-tor" in it. In answer to a query by Harry Edward Warner, a newspaper editor and lexicographer, F. G. Await, acting comptroller of the currency, wrote: "Regardless of the pronunciation given by the dictionaries, the Secretary of the Treasury has adopted the pronunciation which places the accent on the second syllable."

Lone Gunman Rides Away on a Bicycle

A lone gunman escaped on a bicycle after he had held up and robbed Charles Noble of $14 in his grocery store at 1932 Joseph Campau Ave, Tuesday afternoon.

You're Invited to See Rabbit-Hunting Sheep

EASTON, Md., March 28 — Leavenworth Holden, Talbot County sportsman, is inviting people down to see his rabbit-hunting sheep at work.

This sheep, Mr. Holden avers, was left an orphan and was adopted by an old rabbit dog and raised with her puppies.

"One day while hunting," said Mr. Holden, "I was astounded to see the sheep running along with the hounds, hot on the trail of a rabbit. He performed his work perfectly, but he is practically useless for hunting because he cannot bark. His faint bleatings while on the trail can be heard only at a short distance."

Home Brewers Put in Moonshiner Class

CHICAGO, March 28 — (U. P.) — The home brewer will be no better than a moonshiner after April 7, according to an informal opinion given today by United States District Attorney Dwight H. Green.

Green pointed out that makers of home brew would be evading the Federal tax and would be operating without Federal license.

He also believes that there are few places where revenue laws which would ban home brewing.

Friday Deadline for 1932 Licenses

Friday will be the last day on which motorists can operate automobiles with 1932 license plates, L. Wesson Dickinson, manager of the Detroit branch of the Secretary of State's office, pointed out Tuesday that midnight Friday is the time limit for half payments.

At present, he estimated, 120,000 Detroit motorists have failed to procure their 1933 plates or the stickers issued for half payments. At the time the last time extension was granted, from March 15 to April 1, Secretary of State Frank D. Fitzgerald declared that police action would be taken against all motorists who attempted to operate their cars with old licenses. The warning was repeated Tuesday by Dickinson.

Beer Stamps Mailed to Brewing Centers

WASHINGTON, March 28 — (A. P.) — The first beer stamps were in the mails today.

The Bureau of Engraving and Printing sent the stamps to internal revenue collectors in St. Louis, Philadelphia and Hartford.

Other shipments will be on their way in time for brewers to paste the stamps on containers by April 7.

[CF SKATING TONIGHT—OLYMPIA 7 to 11:30—35c. Band Music.—Adv.]

THE WEATHER
Cloudy and warmer Tuesday; showers Wednesday.

The Detroit Free Press
1831 ~ OVER A CENTURY OF SERVICE ~ 1933

EXTRA

102nd Year. No. 335   Tuesday, April 4, 1933   20 Pages   Three Cents

AKRON WRECKED AT SEA; ONLY FOUR OF 77 RESCUED

Michigan Votes for Repeal of Prohibition

APRIL 4, 1933:

The big national story was the crash of the dirigible Akron, but locally, Michigan became the first state to vote for the repeal of Prohibition.

"Wets Win at Least 85 of the 100 Delegates; Democrats Far Ahead," column one.

Wets Win at Least 85 of the 100 Delegates; Democrats Far Ahead

Dillman Makes Strongest Showing of Republican Candidates But Apparently Is Beaten

Michigan wets early Tuesday continued to pile up a huge majority in the popular vote on repeal. With 1,982 precincts reporting in more than four-fifths of the 100 districts, electing delegates to the convention, the totals showed:

For repeal 513,398
Against repeal 154,020

By Hub M. George

Michigan voters Monday rolled up an overwhelming majority for repeal of the Eighteenth Amendment, in the statewide referendum which was the overshadowing issue of the spring election. More than 1,000,000 voters went to the polls.

The first State in the Union to act on the repeal of Federal prohibition, returns early Tuesday indicated that at least 85 of the 100 delegates named from representative districts were pledged to ratification at next Monday morning's "convention in Lansing, which will formally pass upon the Twenty-first Amendment." The majority may mount still higher.

The Democratic sweep which upset tradition in November continued in full force and shattered the hopes of all Republicans seeking re-election on the State ticket. Democratic majorities ranged from 40,000 to 60,000.

Grover C. Dillman, Republican highway commissioner, was making a valiant fight to hold on in outstate returns, but Wayne's heavy Democratic swing presented what seemed an insurmountable obstacle.

Upper Peninsula returns, which were meager, gave Dillman hope of some help there, but hardly enough to overcome the unfavorable metropolitan vote. Other Republican candidates fared even worse in Wayne. Adverse returns outstate had left them trailing even before Wayne was heard from.

Large Council Plan Is Losing

City Office Occupants Holding Own

By John N. W. Sloan

Detroiters, 275,000 of them, Monday stamped their seal of approval by a 10 to one ratio on repeal of the Eighteenth Amendment and registered in unmistakable language their opposition to the proposed Charter amendment setting up a twenty-one-man Council.

Incumbents on the municipal ballot, where two judgeships in the Common Pleas Court and two posts on the School Board were at stake, held their own, marking the re-election of School Inspectors Burt T. Shurly and A. Douglas Jamieson and of Judges Charles Rubiner and Joseph A. Gillis.

Three other proposed alterations in the City Charter which appeared on the same ballot with the twenty-one-man Council proposition seemed destined for adoption.

Democrats Appear Victors

Victory was obviously again attending the Democratic cohorts. County Auditor William H. Clements, the Republican nominee to succeed himself, trailed School Inspector Edward H. Williams, the Democratic choice. The nine Democrats who were contesting for State offices had tallied approximately twice as many Detroit and Wayne County votes as the Republican incumbents and candidates.

Greatest interest, however, was manifestly centering in the vote on the City ordinance for the ratification of the Twenty-first Amendment.

Start the Day Right with the Free Press
Editorial ... Page 6
Edgar A. Guest, Poem ... 6
Good Morning ... 6
Winchell News ... 7
Society News ... 8
Crossword Puzzle ... 9
Filmograms ... 10
Ruth Alden ... 12
Dorothy Dix ... 12
Westbrook Pegler ... 14
Colyer's Comment ... 14
The Screen ... 15
Radio Programs ... 15
Colorisms on Midge ... 15
Financial ... 18
Pictorial Review ... 19
"The Changeling Bride," Serial 19
Comics ... 19
Around the Town ... 20
Minute Mysteries ... 20
Dr. Joseph Ford Newton ... 6
Quaker Observations ... 6
Dr. Evans on Health ... 6

Of the larger districts voting emphatically for repeal-pledged delegates, Kent named 5, Genesee and Saginaw, with 3 delegates each, went heavily wet; Oakland, Jackson, Bay, Calhoun, Berrien, Houghton, Kalamazoo, Muskegon and St. Clair, with 2 delegates each, were decidedly wet. Wayne's 21 were counted as safely in the repeal column.

Repeal margins were close in the early returns from the Antrim District, from Hillsdale, Gratiot and Isabella Counties from the Mecosta and Osceola Districts and from Ottawa County. Because these districts voted dry in November it was uncertain whether the prohibition margin would stand if Oceana voted dry.

Large Districts Wet

One of the larger districts voting emphatically for repeal-pledged delegates, Kent named 5, Genesee and Saginaw, with 3 delegates each, went heavily wet; Oakland, Jackson, Bay, Calhoun, Berrien, Houghton, Kalamazoo, Muskegon and St. Clair, with 2 delegates each, were decidedly wet. Wayne's 21 were counted as safely in the repeal column.

Please Turn to Page 3—Column 3

Giant of the Sky as It Appeared on First Official Voyage

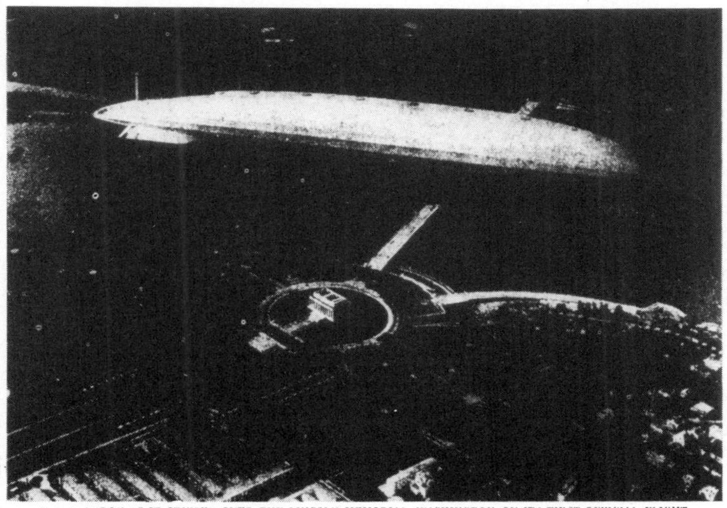

U.S.S. AKRON AS IT CRUISED OVER THE LINCOLN MEMORIAL, WASHINGTON, ON ITS FIRST OFFICIAL FLIGHT

Legionnaires Parade Here

Demonstrate Against Red Activities

One of the first and greatest obligations of the American Legion is the proper care of the disabled Shenandoah, destroyed in a thunderstorm over Ohio, the ZR-2, which exploded over Hull, England, in 1921, and the R-101, the largest ever built prior to the Akron, which crashed on a French hillside in 1930.

This last tragedy, which among its 46 victims took many high in British military circles, led to the abandonment of airship construction by the English. Pending contracts were cancelled and partially completed rigid lighter-than-air vessels ordered destroyed.

No similar reaction followed the destruction of the Shenandoah. United States ship, when it went to pieces in a thunder squall over Ava, O., Sept. 3, 1925, carrying 14 men to death.

A Navy Court of Inquiry decided that the disaster was unavoidable, that it was due to no neglect and that the operation of the ships was a proper and powerful function of the Navy.

"On the day following the Inauguration," he said, "I pledged the million men of the American Legion to give their utmost loyalty and help in the complex and difficult problems facing the Administration. I said that the American Legion wants to be of service to the Country as its members were in 1917 and 18.

'Time for Service Here'

"The time to render that service has arrived. Congress has given to the President authority to effect the economies which he believes necessary to restore the Nation's financial stability. This new legislation is fraught with grave consequences to the disabled veterans. Under the authority given him, the President has powers of life and death over thousands of men who once gladly offered their lives in a period of National emergency.

"The Legion has faith in his discretion, fairness and the justice with which he will deal with this problem. The President needs the support of every loyal American and I expect our million members to uphold the pledge I have made, as national commander."

He added that, though he may not agree with the new law, but that personal opinions should be set aside in a crisis.

"It is a time to take orders," he continued. "Our President is confronted with problems as great as any ever faced by a Chief Executive of the United States. He has not faltered in action where he deemed action necessary. He is giving us his leadership and courage, he cannot win the war on depression alone, all citizens accord him their utmost help. That requires a re-awakened spirit of unity and confidence, a willingness to follow our Chief Executive, a kind of patriotism... *Please Turn to Page 2—Column 4*

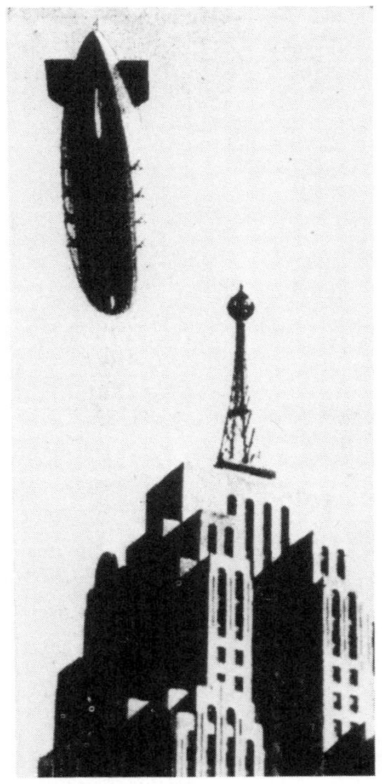

AKRON FLYING PAST PENOBSCOT TOWER, OCT. 10, 1931

Airship Crash Toll Is Heavy

U.S. Navy Men in Two Major Disasters

Airship disasters heretofore have taken heavy toll of human life. The most memorable were those of the Shenandoah, destroyed in a thunderstorm over Ohio, the ZR-2, which exploded over Hull, England, in 1921, and the R-101, the largest ever built prior to the Akron, which crashed on a French hillside in 1930.

This last tragedy, which among its 46 victims took many high in British military circles, led to the abandonment of airship construction by the English. Pending contracts were cancelled and partially completed rigid lighter-than-air vessels ordered destroyed.

No similar reaction followed the destruction of the Shenandoah. United States ship, when it went to pieces in a thunder squall over Ava, O., Sept. 3, 1925, carrying 14 men to death.

A Navy Court of Inquiry decided that the disaster was unavoidable, that it was due to no neglect and that the operation of the ships was a proper and powerful function of the Navy.

Bound from Lakehurst, N. J., to St. Paul, the ZR-2 681-foot ship ran into a storm. After battling the elements for several hours, it suddenly shot upward from 3,000 feet to an altitude of 7,500 feet where it broke into three pieces from the great pressure of cross currents.

The fore-section, measuring about 150 feet and housing seven survivors, free ballooned for more than an hour and finally was landed 12 miles away.

The ill-fated ZR-2, with a crew which included United States Navy officers and enlisted men, was cruising...
Please Turn to Page 2—Column 1

Akron Sister Ship About to Take Air

The Macon, christened in her Akron hangar in March and about to make her first flights in a few minor respects. The same engineering plans were used for both, the commissioning of the Macon, the United States Navy has constructed an appropriate base for her at Sunnyvale, Calif. It was the intention to maintain a dirigible on each coast, the Akron's base being at Lakehurst, N. J.

The Akron's former commander Capt. Alger H. Dressel, was transferred from her to take command of the Macon. The Macon was christened by Mrs. William Moffet, wife of Admiral Moffet, chief of the Naval Aircraft Bureau, who was aboard the Akron when the ship went down.

ICE SKATING TONIGHT—OLYMPIA Last skating Wed. evening. Adv.

High Death Toll Feared in Crash of Dirigible Off New Jersey Coast

Tanker Fails to Find Additional Survivors; Admiral Aboard; Navy Speeds to Scene

WASHINGTON, April 4—(A. P.)—The tanker Phoebus in a radio message at 4 a. m. to the Navy Department said the airship Akron had crashed at 12:30 a. m., "in a widespread thunderstorm" and that many men were in the water when the Phoebus had last seen the dirigible.

Copyrighted by the Associated Press

NEW YORK, April 4—(A. P.)—Definite indication that the giant airship Akron was wrecked early today off Barnegat light, with the loss of life of some if not most of her crew came today in a message to the Associated Press from Capt. Dalldorf of the German tanker Phoebus.

The message said that as the Phoebus approached the scene of the Akron's crash, he found mattresses and wreckage floating in the water. After picking up three men, he saw others sink before his men could reach them.

S. S. PHOEBUS AT SEA (By Wireless) April 4—(A. P.)—Capt. Dalldorf, master of the tanker, said at 3:58 a. m. (Eastern Standard Time) today that he had thus far succeeded in rescuing only four of the 77 men aboard the stricken airship Akron.

LAKEHURST, N. J., April 4—(A. P.)—Naval officials here early today privately expressed the opinion the dirigible Akron, down at sea 20 miles off Barnegat Light, had been struck by lightning.

NEW YORK, April 4—(Tuesday)—The Naval Dirigible Akron, greatest of the ships of the skies, crashed into the sea shortly after 1:30 a. m. today as a driving thunderstorm whipped the Jersey Coast off Barnegat light.

Among the 77 persons aboard was Rear Admiral William A. Moffett, chief of the Bureau of Aeronautics. At an early hour today only four of those on board had been saved.

A wireless message sputtering through the static which made reception difficult told of the crash. It was from the German tanker Phoebus outbound from New York to Tampico.

It said:

"Airship Akron with 77 men aboard went down near Barnegat Lightship. Keep sharp lookout. We are 20 miles from Barnegat Light now. Chief officer and three men saved."

Later messages that the tanker was cruising about the wreck in the area attempting to find more survivors.

The chief officer of the airship, Lieut. Commander Herbert V. Wiley, radioed from aboard the Phoebus.

A complete list of those aboard the Akron is on Page 2.

"The Akron crashed 20 miles east of Barnegat. Searching for survivors. Lieut. Commander Wiley, three men on board suffering from immersion and shock. Further details later. (Signed) Wiley."

Second Message Received

A second message intercepted by the MacKay Radio Station and relayed to the department from the Phoebus at 3:40 a. m. said:

"On board Phoebus (are) Wiley; Erwin, Metalsmith, second class; Deal, boatswain mate, second class, all in good condition; Copeland, chief radio man, condition serious."

Vessels raced for the scene. A swift Coast Guard craft and lifeboats from stations along the New Jersey coast. The sea was rolling with great fury after the storm. All of the mighty resources of the Navy were ordered into the rescue task by Admiral William V. Pratt, chief of Naval operations.

Static made communication difficult.

Officers at the Lakehurst Naval Station told the Navy Department in a telephone conversation that in their opinion the chances of the *Please Turn to Page 2—Column 5*

Aboard Dirigible

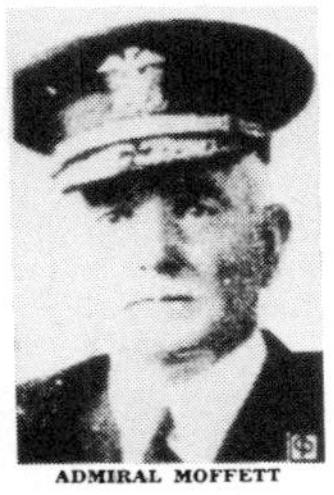

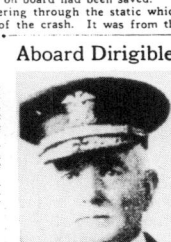

ADMIRAL MOFFETT

Akron an 'Infant,' Christened in 1931

Huge Craft as Tall as 15-Story Building

The Akron was christened by Mrs. Herbert Hoover in sight of 100,000 people at the Akron Municipal Airport on Aug. 8, 1931. The huge craft was constructed by The Goodyear-Zeppelin Co.

The frame of the Akron is a latticed web of duralumin, the principal ingredient of which is aluminum.

There are 10,000,000 individual numbered parts and 6,500,000 rivets. Her dead weight empty is about 221,000 pounds.

An idea of the dimensions of the dirigible is given in the fact that it is as long as several city blocks *Please Turn to Page 3—Column 4*

JULY 18, 1933:

Gov. Comstock is in trouble because of a friend and adviser, while three Purple Gang killers ask for a new trial.

"Purples Make Pleas For New Murder Trial," column five.

The Detroit Free Press

THE WEATHER — Slightly cloudy and cooler Tuesday; showers Wednesday

Tuesday, July 18, 1933, 103rd Year. No. 75 — On Guard for Over a Century — 20 Pages — Three Cents

METROPOLITAN FINAL EDITION

Drop Leebove, Gov. Comstock Is Told by House in United Vote of Criticism

---

Mother and Girl, 4, Are Slain in Home; Suitor Kills Himself

Assailant Is Shot During Struggle

Fires Bullet in Head When Police Arrive to Seize Him

Husband of Pontiac Victim Is Overcome

PONTIAC, July 17—Engaging in a gun duel with an unwelcome suitor bent on murder, a young Pontiac mother tonight wounded her attacker three times before being killed by bullets from his pistol. The man committed suicide a short time later when police surrounded his home.

The woman's four-year-old daughter, Helen, was fatally injured when the killer struck her in the head with a shotgun which he carried in addition to his pistol. She died in Pontiac General Hospital.

Mrs. Rose Gaylock, 29 years old, was the woman killed. The man who committed suicide was Charles King, 32.

The duel took place in Mrs. Gaylock's home at 60 N. Roselawn Drive shortly after 10:30 o'clock. King apparently followed her from a store which she kept a few doors from her home and which she had left only a few moments before by neighbors heard the shots.

Husband Furnishes Clue

George Gaylock, the woman's husband, was at work when the shooting occurred and collapsed when informed of the tragedy. He was able, however, to provide the clue which sent a squad of police to King's home at 111 N. Tasmania av.

Posting his men about the house Sergt. Frank Calvert and Patrolman Joseph Showers of Patrol No. 2. The bell was answered by King's parents. Before Showers' question as to the suspect's whereabouts could be answered, a shot rang out upstairs.

King was found stretched on his bed with a bullet from an automatic pistol through his head. In the room also were a rifle and a shotgun. He apparently fired the shot that took his life, when he heard Showers' voice.

Mrs. Gaylock was shot twice in the back of the head and in the breast.

Wounded by Revolver

Examination of King's body revealed that bullets from Mrs. Gaylock's revolver had struck him in the knee, hand and stomach. He apparently had been endeavoring to dress his wounds when police came to the house and he turned the pistol on himself.

Powder burns found on Mrs. Gaylock's hands were interpreted by police as indicating that the duel was fought at close range and that she was "up from the bed," Mrs. Gaylock's parents said that on coming home he had gone directly to his room and had not noticed he acted strangely.

The money box from Mrs. Gaylock's store was found on the dresser in the room and contained 35 in silver. Officers expressed the opinion that the killer had taken whatever bills there may have been. Early investigations, however, failed to trace any stolen money to King.

Neighbor Reports Screams

No one could be found who saw Mrs. Gaylock enter the home, but a few minutes after she left the store she was heard to scream. Mrs. Kate Elwell, 64 N. Roselawn Drive, reported that Mrs. Gaylock cried, "Oh, please don't" and then her cries were followed by the firing of four shots.

Other neighbors reported hearing both a man and woman from their beds. Their fears that something was wrong were allayed, they said, when they saw lights being turned on and off upstairs and downstairs in the home.

About 30 minutes after the screaming a man emerged from the front door and walked leisurely between the Gaylock home and the house next door.

Neighbors then called police and they entered the home, to find Mrs. Gaylock dead on the dining room floor. The child was rushed to the hospital.

Helen Morgan Weds Maurice Maschke, Jr.

NEW CASTLE, Pa., July 17—(A. P.)—Helen Morgan, blues singer of New York, and Maurice Maschke, Jr., son of Cleveland's Republican leader, were married through affidavit records revealed.

Obtaining a marriage license by proxy approximately 5,000 out of 7,000 workers were married Monday by Roy D. Chaplin, president of the Hudson Motor Co. and former Secretary of Commerce.

Peace Justice Harrison D. Reynolds in his Union Township office just...

Plan to Reopen First National Studied by U.S.

Checking of Suburban Assets for New Bank Begun

Davison Not to Give Testimony at Probe

By Clifford A. Prevost

Detroit's banking problems had the attention of high officials of the Treasury Department Monday, as an intensive study of plans for the reorganization of the First National Bank was begun.

It was believed that definite plans for the reorganization would be announced within a few days, and that the announcement would be made simultaneously by the Treasury Department and the Reconstruction Finance Corp. The latter Federal agency has agreed to loan $50,000,000 for an additional payoff, so far the reorganization of capital of the First National.

The Treasury Department's experts as to the condition of the closed institution were studied by E. H. Gough, Deputy Comptroller of the Currency, and W. R. Milford, chief of the division handling the reorganization of the National banks. The First National was represented in these conferences by R. A. MacDonald and Maxwell E. Fead.

Figures Are Examined

All National banks are under the control of J. F. N. T. O'Connor, Comptroller of the Currency, and Mr. Gough, a deputy in that department, spent Monday in going over the figures with MacDonald and Fead. Milford was to make his recommendation relative to the application of the First National Bank directly to Jesse H. Jones, chairman of the board of the R. F. C.

Comptroller O'Connor is understood to have taken the position that banks must be assured before the First National will be allowed to reopen. Assurances have been given of loans against Emory W. Clark and Col. Fred M. Alger contemplate the raising of $18,500,000 by a voluntary assessment of stockholders.

Indications Monday night were that definite action in regard to the First National Bank would be taken not later than Wednesday.

As far as the Guardian National Bank of Commerce is concerned, the Treasury officials are of the opinion that its problems will be ironed out with the opening of the new Manufacturers National Bank. This institution, with the backing of Edsel B. Ford and other industrialists, has applied for a Charter, the issuance of which awaits a check of assets which will be taken into the new institution.

Assets Being Checked

These assets were being checked by examiners of the National Banking Department Monday. They represent the holdings of the Highland Park State Bank, the Peoples Wayne County Bank, of Highland Park; the Guardian State Bank, of Dearborn, and the Dearborn State Bank.

Chairman Jones announced last week the decision of his board to make available $25,000,000 to $30,000,000 in debentures in the Guardian National. This payoff is to be made through the new Manufacturers National Bank. It represents an additional 30 per cent of the deposits, who already have received 40 per cent of the sum on deposit when the banks were closed last February.

This statement last week Mr.
Please Turn to Page 2—Column 3

Post Arrives at Novosibirsk, Ten Hours Ahead of Record

Gains Time by Refusal to Sleep at Moscow; Says Robot Steered Ship Off Course

NOVOSIBIRSK, Siberia, July 18—(A. P.)—Wiley Post hopped off towards Irkutsk, Siberia, at 9:02 a.m. today, Moscow time (1:02 a.m. Monday E. S. T.), just two hours and 35 minutes after completing the 1,818-mile hop from Moscow.

NOVOSIBIRSK, Siberia, July 18—(A. P.)—Wiley Post, American round-the-world flier, landed here at 6:27 a.m. today, Eastern Standard Time, from Moscow.

Post was seeking to better the time for a lone journey he set with Harold Gatty in 1931. He flew 1,318 miles in 13 hours and 15 minutes, at an average speed of about 138 miles an hour, as compared to the estimated hour rate of 130 miles he flew on the first lap of his journey from New York to Berlin.

He was two to 10 hours ahead of the Post-Gatty record when he arrived from Koenigsberg, where he landed Sunday. Post was four hours and 26 minutes ahead of schedule.

The American airman showed distinct signs of fatigue when he took off for Novosibirsk. He had remained in Moscow only two hours and 52 minutes after landing there from Koenigsberg.

Although swaying with weariness when he stepped out of his ship at Moscow, Post refused to take any sleep, preferring to supervise overhauling of his plane, which had developed a leak in the gasoline tank.

His robot pilot, Post asserted, had been a big disappointment, making such difficulties that he was required to steer the ship manually all the way from New York.

Post blamed his mechanical robot for a deviation of 100 miles off his course between Koenigsberg and Moscow.

Two Lithuanian Fliers Killed as Plane Crashes in Germany

SOLDIN, Pomerania, Germany, July 17—(A. P.)—After flying approximately 4,000 miles from New York, Stephen Darius and Stanley Girenas died early today in the crash of their plane on the last leg of their journey to Kaunas, Lithuania.

A Detroit Mother Sees Boy Drown

Dashes into Lake Fully Clothed in Attempt to Save Him

Dashing fully clothed into Lake Ontario, Mrs. Rowena Southwell made a desperate attempt Monday to rescue her eight-year-old son Jackson from a strong undertow off the beach at Fort Hope, Ont., only to see him drawn down before her eyes.

She rushed into the lake as she was carried back to shore by bathers, among whom were her other sons, George 13, and Lawrence, 10, who also had tried vainly to save Jackson.

Jackson's death left children of but one of the four families in the apartment building at 432 Dickerson Ave., where the Southwells live, untouched by tragedy. One of Jackson's playmates, Jimmie Boggs, 3, was run down by a milk truck recently, suffering three fractures of the left leg, and another, Frank Budd, 8, is critically ill with pneumonia and appendicitis.

Mrs. Southwell had taken her sons to Port Hope to spend Monday with her father, John McMillan, postmaster there. The three boys donned bathing suits and sought the beach immediately.

Jackson was splashing in shallow water when he was swept from his feet by the undertow.

Jackson was a second grade pupil at Keating School.

Drive to Boost Pay Will Open

U. S. Chiefs Mapping Campaign Plans

WASHINGTON, July 17—(A. P.)—Hugh S. Johnson, the industrial administrator, said today that he might be ready tomorrow to start a National movement, for immediate application of wage raising and hour limiting agreements to all business.

Johnson made the statement after a meeting with the Cabinet Advisory Committee at which the question was taken up by him following a thorough canvass of his staff this morning in checking preparations for the movement.

He indicated that a wave of publicity would be taken up at the White House tomorrow in the meeting of the Executive Council.

Proposals to the Recovery Administration have ranged from 35 to 40 working hours a week, with minimum wage levels from $12 to $14. Wholesale abolition of child labor also has been contemplated as a means not only of protecting childhood but also of making more jobs for the still unemployed millions of adults.

The plan which Johnson and his aides hope finally to announce tomorrow has contemplated simple arrangements, headed by prominent citizens, with the governors to take an honorary lead. Under these local meetings would be arranged with "minute men" speakers to stir up enthusiasm will tell business men and consumers of the National recovery objective.

Along with this, there was the prospect that a wave of advertising would prepare the campaign. It would employ all available methods of reaching public opinion, from posters to magazine and newspaper articles, and civic and patriotic organizations.

Designs for the posters, for lapel buttons for advertising slogans and emblems intended to be used by merchants and manufacturers joining the movement, were perfected.

Please Turn to Page 2—Column 4

12 Below Zero in Brazil

RIO DE JANEIRO, July 17—(A. P.)—Temperatures 10 and 12 degrees below zero were registered in Sao Paulo state today, unusually cold weather continuing.

Purples Make Pleas for New Murder Trial

Three Convicted for Massacre Present Fresh Alibis

30 Affidavits Bolster Petition by Attorney

New alibis for the three Purple Gang hoodlums serving life sentences for the Collingwood Ave. massacre were made the basis Monday of a motion for a new trial filed in Recorder's Court by Edward H. Kennedy, Jr., their attorney.

Raymond Bernstein and Harry Keywell, two of the convicted killers, were placing a $1,200 over bet with a bookmaker by long distance telephone when they were supposed to have murdered three members of the Little Jewish Navy bootleg mob Sept. 16, 1931, Kennedy declared.

Irving Milberg, the third convicted killer, did not get out of bed in his home until five minutes after the massacre occurred, it is claimed.

The motion for a new trial is the first definite move to free the notorious trio since several weeks ago, when the name of Isaiah Leebove, former New York attorney and advisor of Gov. Comstock, was linked with alleged attempts to "spring" them from the Michigan Branch Prison at Marquette.

Private Interview Sought

It was declared at that time by State Senator Ray Derham, of Iron Mountain, that Leebove had sought a private interview for another attorney with the imprisoned Purples whom prison authorities regarded as the most desperate men in their keeping. Edward N. Fremdorf, recently deposed manager of prison industries, admitted he aided the warden of Marquette in the private interview.

Abe Bernstein, brother of Raymond, Leebove, in behalf of the long-distance phone call he says his brother was making at the time of the slaying.

The petition is bolstered by affidavits. Three were made by the prisoners themselves, one by Reading (Pa.) police officers and the rest by relatives and friends of the Purples.

Try to Clear Fleisher

Their purpose is not only to demonstrate the innocence of Raymond Bernstein, Keywell and Milberg, but also to clear Harry Fleisher, who named in the original indictment of the gallery.

Arrested several months after the others, Fleisher, who was sought by police for questioning in connection with the kidnaping of Col. Charles A. Lindbergh's infant son, was released when it was found Solly Levine, the principal witness against him, had disappeared.

One of the affidavits obtained by Kennedy states that Fleisher was held for investigation by Reading Pa., police, under the name of Harry Fishman, on the day of the crime.

An affidavit by Abe Bernstein maintains that his brother and Keywell were at the home of the Bernstein sister, Mrs. Jean Winston, 1528 Delaware ave., between 4 and 5 p.m., the day of the killing. The three Little Jewish Navy gangsters were shot to death at 3:25 p.m.

Three overtures from the Michigan Bell Telephone Co., indicate that three phone calls were made from the Winston home that day to New York, Chicago and Cincinnati.

Tapes were made: Abe Bernstein is ready to testify, to make a $1,200 bet on a horse called Hindenburg at Brattleboro, Vt. Raymond Bernstein and Keywell placed the call jointly.

Says Receipts Were Mislaid

The receipts, the affidavit says, were received by Lou Burt, an employee of the telephone company, and but for Burt's death would have been produced months following Burt's death. Bernstein declares they were misplaced and have come to light only recently.

There are additional affidavits from Bernstein, Keywell and Milberg to the same effect.

Please Turn to Page 4—Column 1

Murphy Out to Enfranchise Women of the Philippines

MANILA, July 17—(A. P.)—The full right of suffrage was proposed today for women of the Philippines by Governor General Frank Murphy in his address at the opening of the Insular Legislature.

Do You Know Detroit's Traffic Rules?

What restrictions are there to govern the riding positions of motor vehicle occupants?

(For Answer See Page 19.)

Try Again

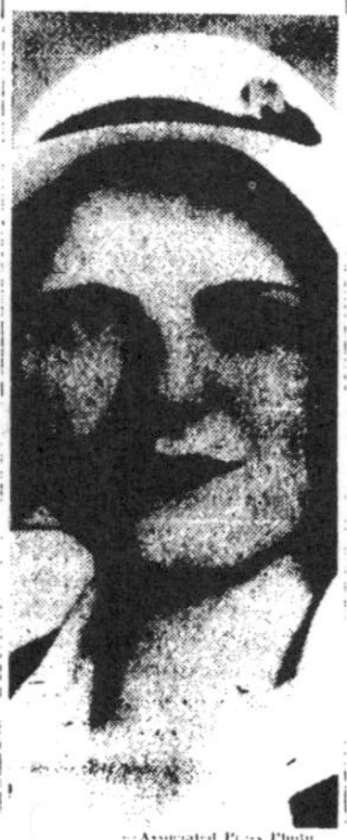

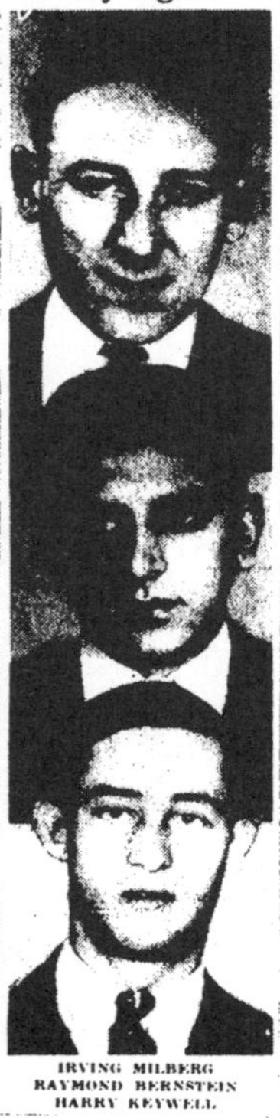

IRVING MILBERG
RAYMOND BERNSTEIN
HARRY KEYWELL

Leebove 'Interest' in Racing Denied

Action Is Held Up on First Meetings

LANSING, July 17—(A. P.)—Gov. Comstock said today that he would take no action permitting running races on pari-mutuel machines until he is sure that the betting will be bona fide, and the horse flesh of high quality.

"The Governor denied that Isaiah Leebove had any connection with the subject of horse racing. He said that Leebove has as much right to suggest things as dozens of other citizens who have written, called upon and wired me." Comstock said.

"I would have to spend my time almost exclusively denying false rumors if I were to get excited about them."

"The good horses are all tied up at other tracks for this season, the Governor pointed out, leaving for Michigan only 'horse skins' if racing is permitted at once. His demand on the State Racing Commission that 30 minutes go to the right foot even to the point of delaying the meets. "It is better to have no racing at all," he said, "than to run into the thing and spoil racing in Michigan for all time by having rackets in pony meets."

"The big syndicates now holding for the Fair Ground track are being carefully investigated, the Governor said.

Samuel T. Metzger, commissioner of agriculture, admitted he had received bids today but refused to make them public. Gov. Comstock said it was doubtful that he could make public certain members had been appointed. Gov. Comstock said he would decide on the matter of publicity on the bids when it was time to consider them.

English Players Lead Culbertson

LONDON, July 17—(A. P.)—The British team by 1,170 points to-night at the end of the second session of an Anglo-American contract bridge tournament with a team captained by Ely Culbertson, of New York.

With 50 boards played, the score was: England, 20,250; and America, 19,050.

The match is at 300 boards, 50 to be played each day, for a trophy posted by Charles M. Schwab. The members of the American team are Culbertson, Theodore A. Lightner and Michael T. Gottlieb. The British team is captained by Col. H. M. Beasy and Sir Guy Domville.

DANCE PARTNERS FURNISHED Hollywood — Woodward at Forest

Scandal Cast on State by Gangster Lawyer's Sway, Report Declares

Lobby Probers Hear Watson and Berka Tell of Bribe Attempts in Small Loan Drive

By Hub M. George

LANSING, July 17—The Democratic Legislature told Gov. William A. Comstock, Democrat, Monday, that "Leeboveism has cast scandal and suspicion on our State Government and is objected to by Michigan citizens." It told him that his friend, Isaiah Leebove, New York gangster lawyer, should be discarded as an adviser and replaced by men whose "residence and loyalty are beyond question."

The House of Representatives unanimously adopted the report of its Lobby Investigating Committee, which condemned in no uncertain terms Leebove's survey of Michigan prisons, flayed Leebove for attempting to influence private interviews with three Purple gangsters incarcerated in Marquette Prison for life for the Collingwood Apartment massacre, on behalf of Frederick Kaplan, a New York lawyer friend, and branded as falsehood the representations of Leebove and Kaplan made to former Warden James F. Corgan.

Rep. Frank J. Berka, Democrat, of Saginaw, identified B. E. Henderson, of Chicago, who told him he was vice president of the Household Finance Corp., as the Small Loan lobbyist who strolled through the capitol grounds with him at midnight, and casually offered him a $5,000 bribe if he would fix the interest rate at two and one-half per cent a month.

The First $1,000, Berka told the committee, Henderson offered to pay him on the spot, in twenty $50 bills, the rest to be paid in monthly installments until the whole amounted to $5,000.

Rep. George C. Watson, Republican, of Capac, told the committee that 30 minutes before the Small Loan Bill conference report was adopted by the House, he had received a similar $5,000 bribe offer from an unidentified person, just as he left the Capitol elevator to enter the House chamber.

"We had virtually agreed upon our report, but because it was a brief Monday night session had not been reported, the men who had attempted to bribe them sat in the gallery. They had not collaborated on the bribe offers, and while Watson was sure it was not Henderson who approached him, he having had a speaking acquaintance with Henderson, Berka felt equally sure that Henderson had an associate with him in the gallery taking notes, and the possibility that the two men had together presented their bribes as a planned program.

The offers was the second made by Berka, he was washed up in the lobby probes a few days previously, as he walked up the Kim Hotel after a golf game. The lobby probers were told by Berka, he had been approached by a man whose name he said was Steveman and who told him that a small personal obligation to a loan company in Saginaw would be taken care of by Berka's succeeding in stopping the Small Loan Bill. The amount involved was $200, an indirect obligation in the form of an unpaid family debt.

The gallery was crowded by members of the House Defense League, an organization of independent grocers who have been demanding for several years that the State repurchase competition in chain stores. They interrupted the session with cheers and applause that hurt Lieut. Gov. Allen E. Stebbins and Speaker Martin B. Bradley threatened to clear the galleries.

In his message explaining the veto, Gov. Comstock said the law will increase grocery costs, the law would bring about continuous litigation that might endanger validity of the new sales tax, inasmuch as the Constitution prohibits double taxation.

The measure provides that owners of more than one store must obtain licenses from the Secretary of State within 30 days. The fee *Please Turn to Page 3—Column 5*

Chain Stores Tax Is Voted

But Veto Is Upheld on Loan Bill

By Frank G. Morris

LANSING, July 17—The Legislature Monday night enacted the chain store tax into law. Gov. Comstock's veto after accepting his refusal to sign the measure reducing the interest on small loans from 42 per cent a year to 21 per cent.

Only two votes were overridden, although the Senate had voted to pass six measures besides the chain store bill, the lawmakers enacted a bill reducing the cost of advertising tax sales.

The key on chain ownership passed the House by a vote of 91 to 6 and the Senate concurred unanimously.

Gov. Comstock had warned that the law will increase grocery costs, inasmuch as chain organizations fix prices. He had pointed out that the tax will increase the living costs of every resident of Michigan.

Dryness of Dixie Is Tested Today

Alabama, Arkansas to Vote on Repeal

WASHINGTON, July 17—(A. P.)—Repeal forces, with 18 states already taken into camp, predicted that if the two Southern states went wet, ratification of the amendment by Christmas was a certainty.

Two other states yet to complete this week, Tennessee on Thursday and Oregon on Friday. The wets anticipate victory in both of these states, and also are running on the repeal bandwagon.

Shades of Carry Nation

MONTGOMERY, Mo., July 17—(A. P.)—Harry C. Turner, manager of a local crusader, tonight claimed vote for prohibition repeal tomorrow at least two to one and that Missouri would go wet in the coming election by three to one.

Start the Day Right with the Free Press

	Page
Editorial	6
Edgar A. Guest, Poem	6
Good Morning	6
National Whirligig	6
Obituaries	6
Crossword Puzzle	6
State News	7
Woman's World	8
Walter Lippmann	9
Society	8
Silhouettes	10
Dr. Evans on Health	10
Ruth Alden	10
Culbertson on Bridge	10
Do-ro-thy Dix	10
Westbrook Pegler	11
Children's Corner	11
The Screen	12
Manhattan	13
Financial	13
Grantland Rice	15
Radio Programs	16
Comics	17
Iffy the Dopester	17
Pictorial Review	18
Around the Town	20
Dr. Joseph Fort Newton	20
Quillen's Observations	6

City Starts War on Food Gougers

Investigating Crew Is Sent into Action

A crew of investigators started on inquiry into food prices Monday afternoon on Mayor Frank Couzens' heels his avowed warning to profiteers and mustered the City's legal forces to curb the threats of dealers who attempt to charge excessive prices for necessities of life.

In direct charge of the City's forces are Corporation Counsel Raymond J. Kelly, Purchasing Commissioner John F. Gorman and Health Commissioner H. H. Goldrick, assistant corporation counsel, who is assigned to the Police Department.

Investigators' reports will be turned to Tuesday morning, and studied with a view of canceling licenses and starting prosecution of all who have taken advantage of rising markets to charge unjustified prices.

"Maintain clean work over the possibility of profiteering in foodstuffs," Mayor Couzens directed Mr. Kelly. "I believe that any complaints should first be investigated by the commissioner of purchases and supplies, who, possibly, is the best informed person in the City Government on prices throughout the city. He should then immediately turn over any complaints which he believes should be investigated.

"Mr. Goldstick stated that the City has a 'big stick' which may be used to curb attempts at profiteering. He explained, "The City's instrument for the correction of dishonest merchants or willful profiteers is Ordinance 132-C, which permits the Mayor to suspend or revoke the license of any merchant for sufficient cause. Thus the Mayor...
Please Turn to Page 2—Column 8

Hudson Motor Co. Gives Men Raise

Wage increases for shop employees of 5 to 10 per cent were announced Monday by Roy D. Chaplin, president of the Hudson Motor Co. and former Secretary of Commerce.

"These increases are effective at once," Mr. Chaplin said, "and are in line with the constructive spirit of American industry to rebuild the buying power of the country."

The new scale will affect approximately 5,000 out of 7,000 workers whose base pay averages $35 a week, officials of the company said. The new figures represent a 7 per cent boost and will mean an annual payroll boost of $750,000.

The Detroit Free Press

WORLD SERIES SECTION

104th Year. No. 159 — Wednesday, October 10, 1934 — Free Press Want Ads Bring Best Results

OCT. 10, 1934:

The last game of the 1934 World Series is one of the wildest ever. There was a brawl on the field and a seat-cushion fight in the stands. The Tigers lost to St. Louis, 11-0.

Bleacher Fans Stage Most Tumultuous Riot Ever Seen in a World Series Game

Spikes and Bottles Fly as Cards Win Series in 11-0 Rampage

Cards to Get $5,941 Each for Winners' Share and Tigers $4,313 Per Man

Stirring Scenes of Play That Caused Storm to Break in Sixth Inning

MEDWICK STARTING HIS SLIDE INTO THIRD

CARD OUTFIELDER GOING OVER BAG JUST BEFORE OWEN FELL

PLAYERS SURROUND UMPIRES IN DEBATE AFTER SPIKES FLASHED

The Saga of the Deans
Diz the Great and Terrible Paul Carve Niche for Themselves in Baseball Hall of Fame

By Grantland Rice

When 'Omer smote his bloomin' lyre,
When Caesar sang his song of Gaul,
They blew the epic of the age—
The lyric rise of Diz and Paul.
They wrote of blokes now in a coma,
Four thousand miles from Oklahoma.

When Byron sang of Grecian Isles,
Where "burning Sappho loved and sung"
He overlooked the mighty Deans
As helpless Tiger batsmen swung.
He called the Grecian Phalanx good,
But overlooked the cottonwood.

I am no Homer at my best—
I was no Byron in my prime—
And yet I hold a better theme
That lends itself to stirring rhyme.

Let Hector fall for Trojan queens—
I sing the Saga of the Deans.
Let Alexander sleep and dream
Of Persian glory through the age—
I pick a greener laurel now
To flare along the sporting page—
Two country kids from dust and trail
Who rise to grip the Holy Grail.

IN THE WAKE of Western dust, blown up by the two cyclonic Deans, the St. Louis Cardinals take their place today on the top plateau of baseball as the new champions of the world.

Riding along on the rubbery, loose-jointed arm of the dazzling Dizzy, they cut their way to the front through six Tiger pitchers and a wild and savage barrage of beer bottles, oranges and other implements of fruit, wood, iron and glass thrown from the left field bleachers that for 20 minutes turned the seventh game into a woolly riot that looked like the two Battles of the Marne, with Verdun and Tannenberg thrown in.

Slingshot Dizzy slaughtered six Tiger pitchers, 11 to 0, in this final foray of flying spikes as he held the enemy to six scattered hits for the closing triumph of the Dukedom of the Deans. But it remained for Ducky Wucky Medwick, the Cardinal Cossack, to steal a big part of the show and start one of the wildest young riots that any World Series has ever known.

The Vesuvian explosion that came near blowing up the ball game took place in the sixth inning.

Spikes Gleam and Riot Is On

Ducky Wucky had just tripled and driven Pepper Martin over with the eighth Cardinal run. Medwick slid into Marvin Owen at third with the speed of a runaway horse. The impetus carried Owen from his feet and as they collided and fell together Medwick threw a pair of shining spikes at Owen's legs, and the riot was on.

When Medwick started for his place in left field at the close of the inning, he was greeted with a salvo from the howling left stands, 17,000 in number, that quickly littered up the field and sent the Cossack from New Jersey into a hurried retreat. For 20 minutes the enraged bleachers laid down a barrage that might have stopped the charge of First Division of the Prussian Guard.

The sunny autumn air was a whirring mass of missiles, fired from a 200-yard front, and the blue autumn skyline was almost

Please Turn to Page 18—Column 6

$299,785 Put in Player Pool
Each Club to Receive $152,738 Split

The world champion St. Louis Cardinals will receive $5,941.19 each as their share of the World Series receipts, while each of the vanquished Detroit Tigers will get $4,313.90. The shares include receipts from the radio rights, sold to the Ford Motor Co. for $100,000. The Cardinals split their receipts 25 ways; the Tigers divided theirs into 23 shares. The Cardinals also voted $3,000 in donations to club attendants, cutting their actual share to $5,821.19 each.

For the four games in which the players shared, the total player pool was $299,785.50 from the gate receipts alone. The pool was increased $51,500 by radio receipts. The commissioner received $15,000 from the radio, swelling his share to $169,811.15. Each league and each club received $144,235.57 from the gate and $8,500 each from the radio, grand total of $152,735.57 each.

Other shares, including radio receipts to major league teams finishing from second to fourth, inclusive, in their respective leagues follow:

New York Giants and Yankees, $25,808.92 each.
Chicago Cubs and Cleveland Indians, $17,205.90 each.
Boston Braves and Boston Red Sox, $8,283 each.

Showgirl Is Suing Rothrock for Ring

BOSTON, Oct. 9.—(A.P.)—While a diamond battle for Jack Rothrock, St. Louis outfielder today, a diamond halo of another type came to his fore.

Miss Jackie Coogan, Boston showgirl, filed suit in Suffolk Civil Court for the return of a diamond ring valued by her at $500 which she alleged she entrusted to Rothrock in New York two years ago during a party in her honor.

According to Miss Coogan, went and sat on Rothrock a month ago, while the Cardinals were playing in Boston and he promised to return the ring within 36 hours. Instead, she charged, Rothrock brought a counter action.

17,000 Pelt Medwick Until He Is Benched
And Landis Upholds Their Verdict After Ducky Kicks Owen

By Paul Gallico

The dizziest, maddest, wildest and most exciting World Series game played in recent years began with a seven-run batting rally in the third inning that gave the Cardinals the championship of the world for 1934, broke up in one of the wildest riots ever seen in any ball park in the sixth inning, and wound up, of all things, with the spectators engaging in an old-fashioned pillow fight in which for a half hour the populace stood around and hurled seat cushions at one another.

For the first time that I know of, the crowd forced Commissioner Landis to remove a ball player from the field. Twenty thousand people manned a stand in the left field bleachers turned into a deadly and vicious mob. Only the barrier of a steel screen and locked gates prevented them from pouring into the field and mobbing Outfielder Joe Medwick of the Cardinals, who bears the incongruous nickname of "Ducky-Wucky."

Medwick's Triple Starts It

In the sixth inning, with Pepper Martin on second and two out, Medwick hit a triple against the centerfield fence and slid into third base. Marvin Owen stepped on him, but whether by intent or accident no one could tell. But there was no mistaking Medwick's ideas as he lay on the ground on his back and suddenly began lashing out at Owen's legs with his spiked feet.

One-two-three, his feet flashed, and then he kicked with both together like Joe Savoldi. Then they were at one another with Bill Klem in the middle. The coaches stepped in, the other players ran over, and what is known as "cooler heads" prevailed.

Cards Leave Dugout

The Cardinals swarmed from the dugout, a red mob, but returned immediately. Klem must have seen provocation for Medwick, for neither man was punished. Medwick held out his hand to Owen. The Tiger third baseman refused it petulantly and returned to his station. Medwick remained on third, and scored on Collins' single, Delancey struck out, ending the inning. The teams changed places on the field, and without the slightest warning, the dangerous storm broke.

Medwick, the No. 7 showing up plainly on his back began to jog to his position in left field. In an instant, the entire bleacher section, a tall, sloping stand holding 20,000 was on its feet and literally blasted him to a standstill with a salvo of booting that broke over his head like a comber curling over a lone swimmer. He came closer, and 40,000 arms were lifted against him, waving him back.

Then a single apple, a red one flew from the crowd and rolled at his feet, and Medwick fielded it lazily and gracefully, in the way an infielder scoops up an easy grounder, and threw it back to the fans. The next moment the air was full of flying fruit, apples, oranges, bananas and beer and pop bottles, the fruit squashing and breaking into little bits, the ugly brown and white bottles striking the turf and rolling over and over. I watched the crowd and Medwick and the pelting missiles through my field glasses, and it was a terrifying sight. Every face in the crowd, women aged men was distorted with rage. Mouths were torn wide open, eyes glistened and shone in the sun. All field were clenched.

Medwick stood grinning, with his hands on his hips. Just out of range of the bottles. A green apple rolled to his feet and he fielded that too. Umpire and attendants rushed out to left field for safety. Landis didn't order Medwick from the game until Joe had made several efforts to take his position in left field, only to be chased back by the missiles lobbed by the bleacher fans. Then Landis called both Medwick and Owen, as well as the two managers and the umpires, to his box. After questioning them Landis ruled Medwick out of the game.

"When I called them to my box," Landis said, "I simply asked Medwick if Owen had done anything to him or if there was any reason for his kicking at the Detroit player. To both questions Medwick answered 'no.' Thereupon I

Please Turn to Page 18—Column 6

All Right, It's Printed

The following telegram was received from St. Louis last night:

AA544 90, ST. LOUIS, MO 9 231P.
DETROIT FREE PRESS, DETROIT, MICH.
EVEN IN OUR PRIMITIVE DAYS WE WERE ONLY PIKERS AT THROWING POP BOTTLES AND WE DARE YOU TO PUBLISH THIS.
M. FENAJA.

Joe to Blame, Landis Insists
Medwick Ban Wasn't to Appease Crowd

By M. F. Drukenbrod

Medwick, St. Louis left fielder, decided to take a kick at an opposing player he probably will look around to make certain that Kenesaw Mountain Landis, high commissioner of baseball, is not within sighting distance.

Commissioner Landis from his box near the Cardinal dugout, saw Medwick's slide into third base in the sixth inning of Tuesday's game.

After the game, Judge Landis explained after the game, was why he took Medwick out of the game. He said that it was not done to appease the wrath of the fans in the left field bleachers, who held up the game about 15 minutes while showering Medwick with fruit of every description and pop bottles when he attempted to return to his position after the kicking incident.

"I saw Medwick kick at Owen," Landis said, "and his act warranted punishment. That is why I ordered him out of the game."

At the same time Landis explained it was always anxious to have both teams at full strength in a World Series game, and that for that reason before each Series he instructs the umpires to have two kicks at Owen's stomach and started the melee.

Apparently, though, the Commissioner regarded this as one time it couldn't be done "decently" and accordingly took the action he did.

"I knew that the umpires were thinking of my instructions when Medwick kicked at Owen," Landis said, "and for that reason did not order Medwick out themselves."

Landis didn't order Medwick from the game until Joe had made several efforts to take his position in left field, only to be chased back by the missiles tossed by the bleacher fans. Then Landis called both Medwick and Owen, as well as the two managers and the umpires, to his box. After questioning them Landis ruled Medwick out of the game.

Please Turn to Page 18—Column 6

Jerome Dean Supreme in Wildest Game of All
Dizzy Toys with Bengals While St. Louis Pounds Five of Six Detroit Hurlers Used

By Charles P. Ward

THE St. Louis Cardinals won the baseball championship of the world Tuesday in one of the wildest World Series games ever played. Manager Frank Frisch, of the Cardinals, sent Dizzy Dean, his ace hurler, against the Tigers, and Dean blanked the Tigers, 11 to 0, and had a lot of fun doing the blanking.

Manager Mickey Cochrane used everybody on the Tigers' mound staff except Carl Fischer, Luke Hamlin and Victor Sorrell. If the game had lasted a little longer he might have sent them in.

Elden Auker, Schoolboy Rowe, Elon Hogsett, Tommy Bridges, Fred Marberry and Alvin Crowder pitched for the Tigers and then with a barrage of 17 basehits which included triples by Joe Medwick and Leo Durocher, and doubles by Frisch, Jack Rothrock, DeLancey and the incomparable Dean himself.

The game almost broke up in a free-for-all fight when Medwick kicked Marvin Owen after sliding into third base in the sixth inning. While sitting on the ground, Jersey Joe took two kicks at Owen's stomach and started the melee. Tigers and Cardinals came running from the dugouts shouting angrily. Medwick and Owen had a slight scuffle but the umpires soon restored order before anybody was hurt severely.

Game Takes a Recess

But the crowd which had been watching the Cardinals' rough and tumble baseball tactics throughout the series, would not permit the pageant to die out so easily. When Medwick attempted to take his position in left field at the start of the Tigers' half of the sixth, the indignant proletarians sitting in the bleachers greeted him with a bombardment of oranges, lemons, bananas and a pop bottle or two.

The demonstration continued for 17 minutes. Then Judge Kenesaw M. Landis, high commissioner of baseball, restored order by dismissing Medwick from the game. Chick Fullis took his place in left field and the crowd settled back to see the battle through to the bitter end.

The collapse of the Tiger pitching staff might be blamed for the Tigers' defeat, but it hardly deserved the blame. The cause of the setback was a four letter word meaning trouble for batsmen. The word is Dean.

Beaten by the Tigers last Sunday, Dizzy came back today and gave a greater pitching performance. The Tigers didn't have a chance. To have gained even a tie the Tiger hurlers would have had to pitch shutout ball. And none of them was up to that yesterday.

Dizzy Has Lots of Fun

The Cardinals presented Dean with a comfortable lead when they scored seven times in the third inning and from then until the finish, Dizzy just threw the ball up there and had fun. He let the Tigers get six hits in the last six innings, but when they threatened to score he just r'ared up and threw the ball past them. And when he caused them to strike out or pop up he laughed.

In the fifth inning it looked as if the Tigers might get a run when Hank Greenberg singled and Pete Fox doubled. But Dizzy threw three strikes past Tommy Bridges and caused White to ground out to end the inning. Then he turned to the hair of the despondent Tigers and grinned good humoredly. The Bengals threatened mildly again in the eighth when

Please Turn to Page 18—Column 2

Mickey Takes It ... Visions a Good Cry with Kipke

By Tod Rockwell

GORDON STANLEY COCHRANE, Tiger leader, walked smartly into the dressing room after the final World Series game Tuesday, and sat down in the wire cage surrounding his locker. For a moment he remained there looking into space, then he walked over to the Cardinal quarters.

Manager Mike, striding with dignity, walked over to Frankie Frisch, the Cards' boss.

"Congratulations, Frankie," Mike said.

"Thanks, Mike," was the reply.

The Tiger boss was brief, but sincere. After shaking hands, he left and came back to his locker. He sipped from a bottle of his favorite pop. He grinned a little.

"Well," he began, "it's been a tough Series. Dizzy was good today. He had a lot of stuff and we just couldn't stop him. But while we were taking a beating we took a good one.

"Yes, my leg felt a little better but it was just the wrong day for the Tigers. All the boys have worked hard this season but none any harder than little Tommy Bridges when he was in there today. He was pitching his head off. He's a thoroughbred ball player."

Mike turned around on his seat and fondled an excellent set of golf clubs held in a very large felt-lined leather bag.

"Walter Hagen sent them to me," Mike said. "I am going to take the Tigers to win more for Mike's sake than any other single thing. Few managers in the leagues today that course, across from the Michigan stadium. And while I'm there I'll stop in and have a little cry with Kipke.

"Within a few days Mike will leave for Honolulu with Mrs. Cochrane. Others who will make up the party are Al Simmons, Chicago White Sox outfielder, and Mrs. Simmons, and Cy Perkins, Mike's assistant, and coach.

Cy and his boss talked things over for a while. They discussed the game and then began making plans for the trip. Mickey seemed anxious to discuss it. Cy is like many other of the Tigers.

Like Deppy Carroll, Cy wasted no time in the third base coaching box at the time, was indignant. "Medwick was sliding into the

Please Turn to Page 17—Column 3

are more popular with their squads than is Mike Cochrane.

The rest of the Tigers took their beating with better grace than any of the other three during the Series as expressed by Goose Goslin.

"We gave 'em all we had to give the Cards credit."

There were many Tigers who thought Marvin Owen showed great judgment in not striking Medwick when the latter kicked at him when sliding into third base. Other Tigers thought Marv had a right to let him have it right in the teeth.

Del Baker, assistant coach who was in the third base coaching box at the time, was indignant. "Medwick was sliding into the

Please Turn to Page 18—Column 2

Sept. 29, 1935:

Michigan's most listened-to radio station converts to 50,000 watts.

Advertisement

The Detroit Free Press

Tuesday, October 8, 1935, 105th Year, No. 157 — On Guard for Over a Century — 28 Pages — Three Cents

FINAL EDITION

THE WEATHER: Cloudy and warmer on Tuesday; showers and cooler Wednesday

OCT. 8, 1935:

"Wait till next year," they said in '34: Tigers win Detroit's first World Series.

Detroit Hails Its Champion Tigers as a Symbol of the City Dynamic

League's Council Votes Sanctions Against Italy

Paris Formally Offers Britain Aid; All Quiet on the Tigre Front as Duce's Armies Dig In

The Council of the League of Nations voted unanimously Monday to apply economic and financial sanctions to Italy, as France gave its pledge of military cooperation with Britain in the Mediterranean in case of an attack on the English fleet. France's pledge was based on a condition of reciprocity.

Declaring that Il Duce was the aggressor against Ethiopia, the Council of the League unanimously adopted a report which said Italy had resorted to war in disregard of its covenants.

The decision of the Council will be placed before the full Assembly of the League Wednesday.

In Ethiopia, the Italian invaders were consolidating their advances on all fronts. A counter-attack on Aduwa was feared and in some quarters there were reports that the Ethiopians had retaken Aduwa.

Emperor Haile Selassie prepared to lead an army of 120,000 northward to meet the invaders.

Monday's dispatches from the Ethiopian war fronts, from Addis Ababa and Rome, revealed an ominous lull after the first burst of hostilities.

The Italian invaders on the Tigre front were fortifying their advances against the masses of the warrior thousands gathering in the mountains ahead.

It seemed probable that the Italians would spend several days in consolidating their lines before beginning the real push into the interior, and in the meantime Emperor Haile Selassie's troops were massing for a savage resistance behind their natural fortifications which no invader ever has penetrated.

The Italian Eritrean armies were feverishly entrenching and fortifying the northern front, from Aksum to Aduwa and Adigrat.

Crude roads swarmed with reserves, moving up to the front, established [illegible] when the blackshirt hordes poured proudly through the gates of Aduwa to blot out the shame of that thirty-nine-year-old landmark of Italian defeat.

Counter-Attack Repaired

Wary lest the crafty generals of Selassie order a sudden counter-attack on Aduwa, the Italians established strong outposts.

Planes kept a constant watch for the enemy from the sky.

There even was a report at Addis Ababa that Aduwa had been re-captured by the Ethiopians in a vicious counter-attack and that five Italian officers had been taken prisoner, but this was no stronger than rumor.

Persistent reports that Italy had proposed peace terms were scouted by all Italian sources, but an Ethiopian authority said the rumor was "almost true."

Meanwhile, Selassie himself prepared to ride forth on mule back to lead an army of 120,000 northward against his Fascist foes. The immediate Ethiopian strength was estimated at...

Please Turn to Page 5—Column 1

Cruiser of President Engages in a 'Battle'

ABOARD U. S. S. PORTLAND, Oct. 7—(A.P.)—The cruisers Houston and Portland—bearing members of President Roosevelt's party—went to war today in the Pacific under the interested gaze of President Roosevelt. But it was all for practice.

The Houston, with the President aboard, slipped over the western horizon this morning off the coast of Lower Mexico, and the crews of the two Navy fighters engaged in "battle" by long distance range finders.

Business Partnership Survives a Divorce

NEW YORK, Oct. 7—(A.P.)—A Nevada divorce decree today severed the family ties of Mrs. Hortense McQuerrie Odlum, New York department store executive, and Floyd B. Odlum, millionaire investment magnate—but their business association was uninterrupted. Mrs. Odlum a year ago became the Country's first woman president of a large retail store. She obtained her position when her husband's firm, the $100,000,000 Atlas Corp., took control of a store on Upper Fifth Ave.

Start the Day Right with the Free Press

	Pages
Editorial	6
Edgar A. Guest Poem	6
National Whirligig	6
The Day in Washington	7
Nat'l daughter Jane went through	7
Europe	7
Culbertson on Bridge	8
Around the Town	8
Manhattan	8
Radio Programs	8
The Screen	9
Society	10
Ruth Adam	11
The Chatterbox	11
Silhouettes	12
Iffy the Dopester	13
Grantland Rice	13
Paul Gallico	15
Collyers Comment	18
Financial	19
Obituaries	22
Comics	24
"Border Patrol" Serial	25
Pictorial Review	26
Music	27
Dr. Joseph Fort Newton	6
Quillen's Observations	6

Detroit Had the Dynamite; Mickey Had the Spark

Plant Is Blown to Bits; 7 Dead

Scores Hurt as Blast Rocks Chicago

CHICAGO, Oct. 7—(A.P.)—A terrific explosion, which witnesses said hoisted a six-story paint factory as a giant firecracker raises a tin can, today killed between seven and 13 men, injured at least 80 others and sent a shower of debris over a block square area.

Twenty-six men were still missing. Twenty-six of the victims were in hospitals, some in serious condition.

Laboring [illegible]—erie flood...

Please Turn to Page 5—Column 4

That Ninth Inning!

CHICAGO—Hack up. Ball one, inside. Hack smashed a long hit to deep center. The ball sailed over Walker's head, and Hack reached third standing up. Jurges up. Strike one, called. Strike two, swinging. Strike three, swinging. French up. Strike one, swinging. Strike two, s w i n g i n g. French grounded out, Bridges to Owen. Hack held third. Galan up. Ball one, low. Strike one, called. Strike two, swinging. Galan flied to Goslin in short left. No run, one hit, no error.

TIGERS—Clifton up. Strike one, called. Ball one, inside. Foul, strike two. Ball two, high and outside. Foul into upper stands. Ball three, wide. Clifton fanned, swinging. Cochrane up. Cochrane got his third hit on a hard grounder that Herman stopped, but on which he could not make a play. Gehringer up. Ball one, wide. Ball two, outside. Gehringer grounded s h a r p l y to Cavarretta, who stepped on first base for the putout. Cavarretta threw to second in an attempt to get Cochrane but the ball glanced off Mickey's shoulder and he was safe. Goslin up. Foul, strike one, against the right field boxes. Goslin singled to right and Cochrane came home with the winning run. One run, two hits, no error.

Dad Crowder Hears Son Did 'Pretty Good'

WINSTON-SALEM, N. C., Oct. 7—(A.P.)—There is a radio on Dad Crowder's farm near here, but the father of "General" Alvin Crowder didn't listen in on the World Series...

He was too busy, he said, "but Alvin must of done pretty good from what I hear."

Crowder is proud of his son but has never seen him pitch. "I've seen Alvin throwin' balls around the lot here, though," he said.

Exuberant Fans Force Tigers to Flee Homes

Only Two, Bridges the Brave and Walker, Succeed in Sticking to Firesides

Gerald Walker and Tommy Bridges were the exceptions among the Tigers Monday night. They both stayed home.

The rest of the Tigers, with the tension gone, decided to join the celebration. They disappeared.

Mr. and Mrs. Bridges kept close to their apartment at 3450 W. Chicago Blvd. with Gerald and Mrs. Walker remained at their apartments in the Seward Hotel.

The reason Gerald stayed home was that a skin infection prevented him from shaving for several days and he looked like an ad in the Garfield presidential campaign.

"We took care of our end of the celebration, though," Gerald apologized. "We sent Hubby out to do it. We told him just where to go, just what to say and just what I would like to have done if I didn't have this here beard."

Hard on the Nerves

"No, I don't blame everybody for going out and celebrating," Gerald said to his friends in the Seward lobby. "Nobody realizes what a nervous strain a ball player is under in a series. Do you know until tonight I haven't breathed naturally since the Cubs came to town last Monday."

Mrs. Walker allowed Gerald to stroll in the lobby of the hotel to receive the congratulations of his friends there. Everybody knows Gerald there and like him, beard or no beard.

Jo-Jo and Mrs. White at one time in the evening decided to join the celebration, also, but finally gave it up. They left the Seward Hotel at 11 p. m. to help the rest of Detroit celebrate its first World Series victory.

Schoolboy Rowe was another who had decided to stay home but his telephone operator said he was getting so many telephone calls, to congratulate him or to show to get some sleep.

Tommy, whose proper place in the evening was on the shoulders of the downtown celebrants, was home dosing himself with quinine and...

Please Turn to Page 2—Column 4

Seven Held in Plot to Kill Mae West

LOS ANGELES, Oct. 7—(A.P.)—Police of an asserted plot to extort $1,000 from Mae West, film actress, under threats of killing her, district attorney's investigators today announced seven men [illegible] threats were made to disfigure her with acid, police announced.

Half Million Jam Streets in Mad Victory Carnival

Celebration Bigger than 1918 Serves Notice to All the World that the Old Town's a Winner

Detroit the Dynamic exploded last night.

It exploded with a roar that rumbled and re-echoed far into the morning.

Ostensibly, it celebrated the Tigers' winning the world championship—the first world championship in baseball brought to Detroit in 48 years. Actually, it celebrated more than that. The City poured forth its emotions in a spectacle unprecedented in all of Detroit's long history.

Half a million of its citizens, police estimated, laughed, cheered, struggled, elbowed, whistled and sang their way through pack-jammed streets. They threw streamers, blew horns, yelled greetings at friends and strangers, danced and back-fired automobile exhausts.

It was an outburst of carnival spirit that gave the lie to the gloom-sayers of a few years ago who said that Detroit the Dynamic had become Detroit the Doomed.

Police said the crowd was bigger than the Armistice Day crowd of 1918. Even in that glorious moment no such crowds had choked Detroit streets; no such paralysis of transportation had ensued; no such heights of pandemonium had been reached.

Detroit Tells the World It's a Winner

Detroit, through the baseball team that is the symbol and the incarnation of its fighting spirit, had won the baseball championship of the world, and the world was to know it.

It was Detroit's salute to America.

Detroit had the dynamite; Mickey Cochrane and his Tigers provided the spark.

Detroit celebrated because it had won the world championship.

It celebrated because it was the city that had led the Nation back to recovery.

It celebrated because it was the city that wouldn't stay licked; the city that couldn't be licked.

It was Detroit the unconquerable, ready to tell the world when the moment arrived.

The moment had arrived, and the world was told.

"There's no moment," Police Inspector William Maloney said, "that it's the biggest crowd in downtown Detroit in my memory." And, he added, he has a very long memory.

Wading through the drifts of confetti and streamers which snowed from office windows when the word was flashed that the Tigers had won, the thousands sluggishly flowed up and down the streets. They carried banners, bunting, Tiger trophies and pennants and yelled. They yelled with a gusto that shook windows. They just wanted to be together to see if everybody else felt as good about everything as they did.

Downtown Traffic Lights Blink in Futility

Detroiters craved action—but the motorists didn't get it. Converging on downtown Detroit they tangled in the tightest traffic jam in the oldest traffic cop's memory. Traffic lights turned red and green, but that didn't mean a thing.

When Woodward Ave., from Eliot St. to Jefferson Ave., is a solid line of cars, how can the solid line of cars in Grand River Ave. cross? Police couldn't answer that question either. To allow the barely moving traffic more, pedestrians flowed around, through and over the cars.

But the drivers of the cars didn't seem to worry. They were in the same carnival spirit. They just kept a heavy hand on the horn to augment the din. Besides, a trail may not go very far but he sees a lot in his travels. And they came downtown to see the sights, and to let out their exuberance.

But it wasn't the motorists only who had the spirit of Detroit. It was the crowds that overflowed the sidewalks, too. They weren't happy—they were in ecstasy.

It was carnival and Mardi Gras. It was charivari and riot. Halloween, New Year's Eve and All Shout Day. It was everything an evening can be when thousands let high spirits run loose.

Drum and bugle corps filtered into the downtown section but the beat of their drums was only an undertone in the din. Impromptu musicians made cymbals out of garbage can covers. The Halloween stocks of noise makers were sold out. There even were some very sour renditions of "Take Me Out to the Ball Game." One amplifier-equipped truck moved through the streets blaring incessantly "Hold That Tiger!"

They Know a Few Carnival Tricks

Detroiters showed that they hadn't forgotten the tricks they learned from the Legion convention. They dropped paper sacks full of water out of windows onto the masses below, and laughed. They gathered up armsful of confetti and streamers from the street and entwined the next passerby in it.

Trouble? Well, the police had it. The traffic cops were trying to undo the traffic jams. The firemen were dashing out on false alarms and bonfires. The mounted police had to restrain the enthusiasm of the crowds pressing against the entrance of the Book-Cadillac Hotel for a glimpse of ball players, celebrities—anybody.

And all the enthusiasm wasn't confined to the downtown

Please Turn to Page 2—Column 3

Impulse Grips Frank J. Navin

So—He Just Goes to See His Boys

By Tod Rockwell

For the first time in the memory of even old-time Tiger adherents, Frank J. Navin, wise and kindly president of The Detroit Baseball Co., visited the clubhouse of the new World Champion Tigers.

"Just thought I'd drop in and congratulate the boys," said the Bengal president to the guard at the door. Perhaps the guard didn't know who his distinguished visitor was. But it was all right. Everybody knew.

It had been a struggle—that journey from the Navin box to the dressing room door. And the head official of the Champions had a button torn from his coat and his hat was pushed into 40 shapes but he was grinning.

The president first met Jerry Walker.

"Congratulations," he said. Then he walked to Hugh Shelly's locker. In Flea Clifton's; to old General Crowder's. The Navin handclasp was warm and friendly.

Some of the Tigers were in the...

Please Turn to Page 16—Column 4

Mickey Cochrane Is People's Choice

A movement to draft Mickey Cochrane as a sticker candidate for the Council was well under way Monday night.

Right in the midst of a downtown hotel celebration a guest got the idea and announced his plan of voting Tuesday to the crowd.

No candidacy in the history of politics ever was received with greater acclaim.

Dozens in the crowd pledged themselves to write in the full name of "Gordon S. Cochrane" on the ballot among others who would be behind the movement by the time the polls close to anybody having at least one new face in the Council.

TRILERION [illegible]

—Adv.

The World Series Money

Total Series receipts of $1,173,794, including $100,000 for the radio rights, were split as follows:

Each Detroit player's share	$6,131.86
Each Chicago player's share	4,385.72
Each club's share	153,324.15
Each league's share	153,324.15
Commissioner's share	176,072.50

Last year the total receipts in the seven-game series were $1,131,341. Each Cardinal received $5,941.19 in the winner's share, each Tiger $4,313.90.

Magician Thurston Seized by Paralysis

CHARLESTON, W. Va., Oct. 7—(A.P.)—Howard Thurston, magician, was reported improved tonight after an attack of paralysis. His daughter Jane went through scheduled performances. Mrs. Thurston said physicians believed her husband may be able to resume his stage performances "in 10 days or so."

The magician was stricken last night in a restaurant after he had appeared in four shows.

DEC. 22, 1935:

Dynamic Detroit: Good news as the state climbs slowly out of the Depression.

THE WEATHER
Cloudy Sunday and Monday; somewhat higher temperature

The Detroit Free Press

EDITION

Sunday, December 22, 1935. 105th Year. No. 232 — On Guard for Over a Century — Ten Cents

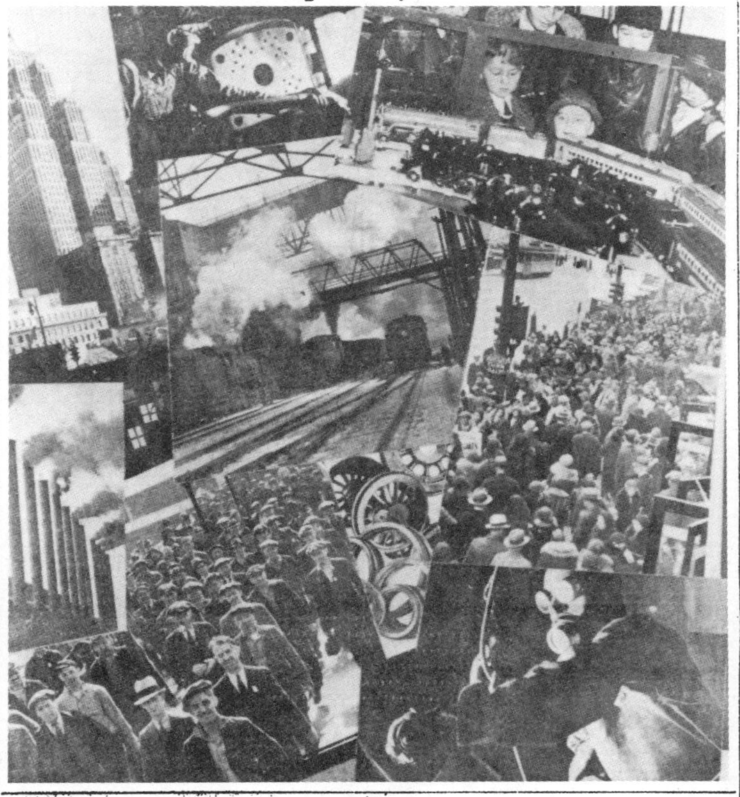

Mussolini Replies to Peace Plan by Speeding Up War

Gives a Free Hand to High Command

Snubs Powers with Casual Mention of Settlement Offer

Britain Rallies Allies to Intensify Sanctions

(By the Associated Press)

Benito Mussolini, contemptuous of sanctionist nations, drove Italy at full speed down the war path Saturday.

The advocate of the motto, "Live Dangerously," spurned any thought of peace in Ethiopia except at his own terms. He pressed the fight against the economic wall his foreign nations and former allies have built about him.

Italy went ahead despite the fact Great Britain was rallying Mediterranean League members to her side in case she is drawn into a war with Italy.

A reliable source said that Britain was considering further precautionary measures and was firmly determined to continue, even reinforce, sanctions against Italy.

Prime Minister Stanley Baldwin was expected to name a foreign secretary Sunday to succeed Sir Samuel Hoare.

Rome's reaction was eagerly studied in London and officials hoped Il Duce had been sufficiently impressed by the line-up of Mediterranean powers behind Britain in case of "a desperate Italian act."

Britain went ahead with precautionary measures, after securing agreements from Turkey, Greece, Yugoslavia and France to help her if need be. Spain debated her course but a reliable authority said that she would fully support her obligations under the League covenant.

Britain's Stand Explained

Britain's stand was explained by Neville Chamberlain, chancellor of the exchequer, in a speech at Birmingham.

"The peace proposals are dead and they have already been buried at Geneva. They will not be renewed presently, and I suppose all thinking people must regard them as having come to an end. We must go back to the policy...(of the League of Nations). They were prepared to make themselves resist any attack which may be made on any of their number."

Diplomatic sources in Paris asserted that Great Britain may propose the creation of a League of Nations Police Force to back up sanctions if necessary.

These quarters said the calling of a special session of the League Council around Jan. 10 for this purpose is being considered.

Fascist sources said, that to accomplish Italy's conquest of Ethiopia, Marshal Pietro Badoglio, chief of Mussolini's armies in East Africa, had been given a free hand in the campaign and told to get results.

Spur to Home Market

In the matter of economic siege, Fascists assured the sanctions applied by the League of Nations against Italy would revive Italian industry by increasing the home market.

Il Duce did not bother even to reply formally to the Franco-British peace formula. The Fascist Grand Council likened the British to "repudiation of the Paris proposals, spoke of 'French initiative.'"

The Grand Council issued a communique saying forth three main points:

—1. That the Italian people, in contrast to the conduct of opposition League states, remain unified and firm in their course, as exemplified by the popular contributions of gold to aid the whole-armed campaigns of war abroad and resistance at home.

—2. That the Fascist leaders are confident of victory in Ethiopia.

—3. That the Nation will prove the previously for achievement of that goal.

Accompanying his words with swift action, Il Duce dispatched 4,000 additional Blackshirts militiamen and 800 workmen aboard the steamer Lombardia to East Africa, to reinforce his armies in the field.
(Copyright, 1935)

Ethiopians Claim Capture of Two Northern Villages

ADDIS ABABA, Dec. 21 — (A.P.) — Recapture of two Northern Ethiopian towns previously held by the Italians, and the seizure of 16 Fascist tanks, were claimed today by the Government.

An official communique said troops leading the forces of Dedjamatch Ayele took Ende Nisesi, 30 miles west of Aksum, and Daga Nub Dec. 13, and that "Italian losses were considerable."

—Ende Nisesi and Daga Nub are about 35 miles northwest of the Takkaze River, scene of a three day battle at the beginning of the week. The Italians asserted more than 500 Ethiopians died in that encounter, and placed the Italian dead at 272. The victories of the Dedjamatch Ayele's men reported today apparently occurred simultaneously with the Battle of the Takkaze River fighting.

"The Government's announcement of the retaking of the two towns reported that "our forces also captured 32 machine guns, two trucks, two automobiles and seven while Italian prisoners."

Two Guilty of Taking Baubles from a Tree

Burgess Jordan, 26, of Northville, was sent to the Detroit House of Correction Saturday for 10 days. He was convicted of stealing ornaments from City Christmas trees in Northville's business district. Rupert West, 32, of Detroit, was given a suspended sentence for the same offense. They were convicted by Arthur J. Nichols, justice of the peace.

Mild Weather Predicted for Detroit Today

Snow Flurries Likely to Usher Winter in Officially

16 Deaths in Country Are Blamed on Cold

The Weather Man Freezes Fingers

Clarence J. Root Is Unable to Be at His Office

Unseeing persons who hold the weather man directly responsible for the unpleasantness of the elements will receive a morbid satisfaction out of knowing that Clarence J. Root, head of the Weather Bureau here, is at home taking care of his frozen fingers.

The accuracy of his Friday forecast, predicting the coldest weather of the season, was brought home to Mr. Root Friday evening as he was walking the two long blocks from his street car stop to his home at 181 Moss Ave., Highland Park. When he arrived, he found that his fingers had been nipped, although he had been wearing gloves. He was unable to go to his office Saturday.

a. m.	8	Noon	15
2 a. m.	6	1 p. m.	15
3 a. m.	6	2 p. m.	15
4 a. m.	6	3 p. m.	16
5 a. m.	6	4 p. m.	16
6 a. m.	7	5 p. m.	15
7 a. m.	7	6 p. m.	15
8 a. m.	7	7 p. m.	15
9 a. m.	7	8 p. m.	15
10 a. m.	7	9 p. m.	14
11 a. m.	13	10 p. m.	15

Rising temperatures will bring Detroit relief Sunday from the cold wave which swept across the Country by Saturday, directly or indirectly, causing 16 deaths, the Weather Bureau officials predicted.

The temperature Sunday, which will be the shortest day of the year and the official beginning of winter, may go as high as 30 degrees, according to the forecast. The skies will be partly cloudy and there is a possibility of snow flurries.

At 1 a. m. Saturday the mercury hit 6 degrees, the lowest of the season. By noon, with the aid of brief appearances of the sun, it had climbed to 16 degrees.

Zero weather was general from the Dakotas east to New York, and it extended as far south as Maryland, West Virginia and Kentucky. Snow flurries were reported in Texas.

Roads Coated with Ice

In South Dakota, Iowa, Wisconsin and Minnesota the mercury fell below zero. Highways were coated with ice from Illinois almost to the Eastern Coast. Fourteen of the deaths were in automobile accidents caused by the weather.

Two others died when a steam pipe exploded in an orphanage near Centralia, Ill. An apartment house fire in Chicago forced 40 persons to flee in night clothes. Thermometers at Sheboygan, Wis., braved sub-zero weather to rescue two men from a brewery fire.

The cold wave also gripped Ontario. Lower recordings there were 40 degrees below zero at White River, 32 below at Sioux Lookout, and 20 below at Port Arthur. Toronto experienced its coldest weather of the year—8 below.

Boat service between Lake Erie islands and Sandusky was being Saturday night by heavy ice on Sandusky Bay. The ice ferry between Sandusky and the islands attempted to reach the lake but was forced back. All service was ordered stopped temporarily.

Florida Vegetables Freeze

Below freezing temperatures in Florida did extensive damage to the vegetable crops but spared the citrus crop, and the weather Bureau warned of still colder weather, Saturday night and early Sunday.

Holiday traffic, which has reached a post-depression peak in the east, was impeded by snowdrifts in New York.

One railroad company, which is running 240 extra trains during the holiday season, reported that huge drifts near Utica were disrupting their schedule.

In spite of the inclement weather, major transportation companies put additional equipment into service to care for the holiday rush. Even trans-Atlantic liners reported capacity bookings. It was believed that holiday travel would be nearly 25 per cent greater than last year.

Moderating temperatures have been predicted for the large area that was in the path of the cold wave. In the Northern states, cloudy skies and snow flurries are expected.

Man Is Held in Shooting of a Friend of His Wife

Harold Lee, 26 years old, of 1930 Marentette Ave., was shot over the heart Saturday night by a small calibered rifle in the hands of Kenneth Weisner, 24, of 1120 W. Hancock Ave., after an altercation in a beer garden over Lee's attentions to Weisner's estranged wife, police reported. Lee's condition was not considered dangerous by Receiving Hospital attendants.

The shooting occurred in the beer garden at 1339 Michigan Ave. Weisner and his wife were held for investigation.

Dionne Guardians Help Quadruplets

Dig Down in Own Pockets to Save Their Home

CALLANDER, Ont., Dec. 21 — (A.P.) — The Dionne quintuplets slept outdoors in 20 below zero weather today.

Wrapped in blankets and for warmth, the youngsters slept on their verandah when the mercury fell to its lowest mark this winter and already this month have been out without an explanation.

TORONTO, Dec. 21—(A.P.)— Guardians of the Dionne quintuplets today went funds to Saint John, N.B., to prevent housing of the Mahoney quadruplets home before Christmas. They were faced with eviction unless $24 back rent was paid.

The money was donated by David Croll, Ontario Minister of Welfare; Dr. Allan Dafoe and Judge J. A. Valin, of North Bay, the guardians, after they had found that some of the Guardianship Act prevented their using the wealthy quintupletsʼ funds for the purpose.

The action was taken here before word was received from Saint John authorities that they intended to provide for Mr. and Mrs. William Mahaney and the quadruplets—three girls and a boy—Christmas Day.

Detroit's Christmas Rush Climaxes Year of Amazing Gain in Trade and Industry; City Leads Nation and Breaks Records

The Spirit of Detroit

Labor Act Held Void by U.S. District Court

Decision Given by Judge Otis of Kansas City, Who Ruled Out NRA Price Fixing

KANSAS CITY, Dec. 21 — (A.P.) — The Wagner Labor Disputes Act was held unconstitutional tonight by Federal Judge Merrill E. Otis.

The opinion was the first Federal Court ruling on the legality of the law enacted by the last Congress.

Judge Otis granted the Majestic Flour Mills, of Aurora, Mo., a temporary injunction against a National Labor Relations board complaint which cited it for alleged refusal to bargain on a wage agreement with a union of its employees.

Declaring that Congress had exceeded its Constitutional right "to regulate commerce with foreign nations, and among the several states * * *," the Judge said: "The conclusion is that the whole Act is unconstitutional."

In opposing what Judge Otis declared, treats the individual as a "recently emancipated slave." He added that "there is no way in which any of the specialized unfair labor practices in any business * * * conceivably can directly affect * * * commerce."

Judge Otis said that the bill "is engaged exclusively in manufacturing which * * * is a local business. Yet the clear intent of the National Labor Relations Act is to subject

See Pictre on Page 4

the relations between employers and employees in even such small intrastate institutions to the control of the executive branch of the National Government."

"It is inaccurate to say that under the Commerce Clause, Congress can regulate that which, of itself a part of commerce. Nothing more firmly is established in Constitutional law than that Congress, therefore, under the commerce power cannot regulate manufacturing," the decision held.

In Washington, Edwin S. Smith, member of the National Labor Relations Board, said that Judge Otis apparently disregarded the far-reaching principle on which the act is based—"that any interruption of manufacturing due to an improper labor practices would involve interstate commerce. The Board will determine next week whether an appeal is to be taken from Judge Otis' ruling.

Fruehauf Case Pending

Two NLRB decisions already are in the United States Circuit Court. They are the Fruehauf Trailer Case, of Detroit; and the Pennsylvania Greyhound Lines case.

Judge Otis, a Republican, in December, 1934, ruled against the price-fixing clauses of the NRA. Last Oct. 3 he held that AAA processing taxes became constitutional only after the August amendments. Last August after a mob assaulted a United States marshal at a farm foreclosure sale, he ordered interim treatment to Judge Otis if he kept a speaking date in Hopkins, Mo., he kept the date, made his speech, and there was no disturbance.

Kiesgen's Boy Badly Burned While Tinkering with Bicycle

Swindler, Out of Jail, Returns Home to Find More Trouble; His Fiancee Vanishes

Matthias Kiesgen Saturday found himself in a house built upon his burns.

As he was cleaning his bicycle in the garage Friday, he applied gasoline to some rust. Then he struck a match to find a tool in his small bicycle toolbox.

The gasoline exploded, igniting his clothing. His legs and feet were burned severely, white flames enveloped his body to the waist. The nine-year-old child was quarantined for scarlet fever Nov. 7, when he normally would have been released, the Board of Health inspectors ordered the warning card to remain on the house.

Kiesgen, to cut under a $5,000 bond. With Roy Gaddy, foreign grocery store manager; Mrs. Gaddy and Harry Nedelman and Louis Seigel, proprietors of a market at 4721 W. Warren Ave., he is charged with conspiracy to defraud the Wayne County Welfare Commission.

His fifteen-year-old son John, was held in John Doe and five Mary Does. Further arrests, are expected.

His nine-year-old son John was under a doctor's care with an ear infection which followed an attack of scarlet fever.

And his fiancee, Miss Eleanor Radke, had left his home without an explanation.

"But I couldn't marry her now anyway," Kiesgen said Friday. "She gave up taking this money while I was in jail. And now she's gone."

"Neighbors are telling me I have to take care of my four sons. Their mother died last March. But what will become of them?"

Meanwhile, Dean was in an upstairs bedroom swathed in bandages from the waist down and with

---

Deposits in Banks Reflect Advances

Figures Also Indicate a 26 Pct. Increase in Money Spent

Employment Feature of Surging Recovery

Detroit has great cause to rejoice this Christmas.

This City's economic revival, well under way at Christmas time last year, continued throughout 1935 and produced—in some instances—amazing results.

Highlights of the comparison of 1935 with 1934 show:

The exchange of money in Detroit, indicated by bank clearings, increased by nearly one billion dollars—25 per cent.

The automotive industry's output increased by more than 1,200,000 cars and trucks—30 per cent.

Retail sales in Michigan rose to an estimated volume of $1,000,000,000—up 18 per cent.

The value of Detroit Stock Exchange shares increased 69 per cent.

All fall, between 75,000 and 80,000 more men have been employed in industry than were employed in the fall of 1934.

All Business Benefits

The volume of mail passing through the Postoffice set a record; the consumption of electricity eclipsed the 1929 peak; Detroit wholesalers did 16 per cent greater business; hotels did 25 per cent better; movies 15 per cent better; retail stores 8 to 10 per cent better. Automobile purchases in Wayne County increased 60 per cent—built again as many cars were bought in 1935 as in 1934.

Detroit's banks made perhaps the most extraordinary record. Clearings which totaled $3,576,000,-

Detroit's Industry Adds 75,000 to Payroll; Page 7

000 in 1934 increased to $4,486,-000,000 this year. According to F. James Bear, manager of the Detroit Clearing House Association, this is 70 points better than the record of other large cities.

Bank deposits rose $113,000,000. Savings deposits of $134,000,000 in January had risen to $160,000,000 by mid-December. Demand deposits rose from $352,000,000 to $436,000,000, and total deposits from $488,000,000 to $600,000,000.

Ahead of the Nation

Bear said that Detroit bank deposits increased 61 per cent in the 13 months ended July 1, compared with the country. Up to Dec. 1, the Detroit banks showed a gain of 68.7 per cent in deposits in 17 months.

The number of accounts, too, showed Detroit ahead of the Nation. In the County at large, the number of accounts equalled 141 per cent of the population, while in Detroit, as of Dec. 1, the number of accounts in the six largest banks was $18,000, or 80.0 per cent of the city's population.

The increasing number of depositors parallels the increasing deposits," President Walter R. McLucas of The National Bank of Detroit commented.

"Bank deposits from the dark days in Detroit show successively steady, apprehension, changing to a bracing resolution to meet misfortune, and, during the past year, the old buoyancy has returned. It is tempered with reality that has characterized recovery assurance for informed responsible living.

"There are many things remaining to be done. Progress has reached the majority as the wheels of industry revolved, but its benefits must be carried further."

Briton Awakes After Four-Year Dreamless Sleep

FOLKESTONE, England, Dec. 21 — (A.P.) — Waking from a four-year sleep, Victor Cleave said today that he and his family would celebrate on Christmas what his friends call his "coming back" from the unconscious.

Cleave, a railway employee, began to doze over his meals in 1931. Then he fell asleep. Doctors, unable to rouse him, had to inject nourishment into his body. The beating of his heart was one of the few evidences that he continued to live.

Waking recently, Cleave did not recognize his own children.

"I feel so strange," he explained. "The four years have been so much like a blank in my life."

He has returned to the cottage home, after long confinement in a hospital.

Cleave now is 40 years old, but his friends say he seems younger than before his sleep.

Pretty Patricia Maguire, of Oak Park, Ill., has been asleep nearly four years. She is 24 years old and 25 pounds heavier than when her strange malady developed. She has survived an attack of pneumonia and a minor operation during her long sleep.

Her mother is hoping that she will awake Christmas morn. The first Christmas of her illness (1932) Patricia slept constantly." Now she has her eyes open from eight to 10 hours a day, can follow simple commands written on a slate, but is still far from real consciousness.

TRENTON, N.J.—Albert E. Heeplin, of Trenton, 83 years old, and hearty, has never had a single dream; he has never been torn from slumber by an alarm clock; he has never known the agony of getting out of a warm bed in a cold winter morning. He has, he insists, never been asleep.

The explanation, authorities say, is that Heeplin actually does sleep briefly while sitting in his chair but on this one subject he suffers from a hallucination; he cannot remember sleeping.

Escaping Gas Overcomes 10

Woman Dies; Several Families Periled

Illuminating gas that seeped from a street main along sewer pipes into a group of houses in Riverview, killed one woman, overcame nine others and turned seven into the street, severely ill.

The dead woman was MRS ANAN HULET, 74 years old, of 17835 Riverview Ave.

Those overcome, none of whom were in serious condition were: MRS. ANNA BOGARIAN, 25, her three children, SAMUEL, 4, KATHERINE, 8, GERALDINE, 7, and her sister-in-law, ELEANORA BOGARIAN, 12, all of 18723 Riverview Ave.

F. A. FLEGAL, 48, of 18765 Riverview Ave., his wife, MARILLA, 31, and her two children, IRVIN FOWKES, 10, and RAPHAEL FOWKES, 8.

The neighborhood alarm was sounded when Russell Bogarian returned to his home and discovered all the members of his family unconscious. In trying to summon the aid of neighbors, Bogarian himself nearly was overcome.

The Gas company and local Bogarian's assistance.

When the Gas company rescue squads arrived at the home in the neighborhood were cleared of their occupants.

At the home of Mrs. Hulet, they found Flavius Hurd, of 18767 Riverview Ave., trying to gain entrance. He had remembered that Mrs. Hulet lived alone. Forcing the door, the rescue squads discovered the aged woman reclining on a davenport in her darkened living room with the radio playing. Attempts to resuscitate her with a pulmotor were unsuccessful.

The Wyandotte Fire Department assisted in the rescue work, and after all of the residents were taken into the fresh air outdoors and treated, a guard of policemen was stationed in the neighborhood as a precaution against a possible explosion.

At Least the G.O.P. Has a Real Santa

LOGAN, O., Dec. 21 — (A.P.) — Conrad Reichley, 72 years old, who vowed in 1932 that he would let his whiskers grow until a Republican again in the White House.

Now he has a long, flowing beard beneath a pair of ruddy cheeks and a sparkling, merry eye. The Logan Chamber of Commerce said, "Reichley is just the man to be our Santa Claus."

Tired of Life at 110, Tries to Die but Can't

SOFIA, Bulgaria, Dec. 21 — (A.P.) — Police of the Village of Tchepelare reported today that Ussouf Karaibrah, 110 years old, had become tired of life.

Karaibrah, they said, tried to kill himself with a rabbit gun. His aim was bad. He — is alive.

Scotland Hit by Cold

EDINBURGH, Dec. 21 — (A.P.) — Scotland was gripped tonight by the severest winter weather in 10 years.

Start the Day Right with the Free Press

	Pages
Edgar A. Guest	6
Good Morning	6
Voice of People	6
The Day in Washington	7
Polling America	7
Around the Town	8
Stage News	9
Building News	10-11
Theater and Screen	10-11
Crossword Puzzle	11
Radio	11
Travel and Resort	12
Puzzles	13
Auto News	14

SPORT SECTION

Iffy, the Dopester	1
The Second Guess	1
Wide Life	7-8-9-10
Financial News	7-8-9-10
Oil Page	9
Business-Industrial News	10

SOCIETY-ART SECTION

Chatterbox	
Social Calendar	3-13
Tower Kitchen	
Ruth Alden	
Shopping News	13-14
Music and Books	15

LINER SECTION

Culbertson on Bridge	5
Obituary	8

Gravure and Comic Supplements and Magazine Sections. Complete novel. Christmas Tree and Screen and Radio Weekly.

The Detroit Free Press

SPORTS | FINANCE
105th Year. No. 326 | Wednesday, March 25, 1936 | Free Press Want Ads Bring Best Results

MARCH 25, 1936:

The longest game in National Hockey League history ends after 2 hours, 56 minutes in a victory for the Red Wings.

Red Wings Win Record Game, 1 to 0

Tigers' Two-Run Rally in Ninth Beats Boston Bees, 4-3

Teams Play 176 Minutes Before Bruneteau Scores

Norm Smith Is Hero in Detroit Nets, Staving Off Wearisome Threats of Sharpshooting Foes

By Doc Holst

MONTREAL, March 25 (Wednesday)—The Detroit Red Wings defeated the Montreal Maroons, 1 to 0, here this morning in the opening game of the N. H. L. first playoff series that shattered all records for longevity in hockey battles.

Mud Bruneteau, recently brought up to the Wings from the Detroit Olympics, scored the goal that decided the struggle in the 177th minute of play. The time was 16:30 for the sixth overtime period.

The longest previous hockey game was played April 3, 1933, when the Toronto Maple Leafs defeated the Boston Bruins on a shot by Ken Doraty after more than 104 minutes of overtime play. The Wings and Maroons bettered this mark by nearly 12 minutes.

While Bruneteau was the hero of the battle because of his game-winning shot, Normie Smith, the Wings' net minder, also played a heavy game. Considered the weakest link in the Wings' battle front Smith saved his mates from defeat many times during the long battle by many miraculous saves.

This play that decided the battle came when the crowd had settled back, hoping against hope for a break that would allow them to go home. It finally came when Bruneteau took a pass from Hec Kilrea and blazed it past Lorne Chabot precisely at 2:25 a. m.

Manager Jack Adams shot on his first line of Barry, Aurie and Lewis and the Maroons responded with their star attack of Northcott, Smith and Ward when the game started at 8:30 p. m. Tuesday night. The Maroons kept the Detroit line from getting a shot but the Maroons got in for two dangerous shots and two long ones. Hooley Smith, the Maroons' star center, got the first shot on goal of the game, a long one from the blue line. Ward followed with a wicked driver that Smith saved. Pettinger moved the crowd with a shot from inside the blue line that Chabot fumbled and juggled for a few seconds before he got it out of the net.

Lamb and Sorrell started to fight but Lamb yawned and Sorrell stretched. Normie Smith made the two star plays of the night when he batted down a shot from Hooley Smith and then rushed out of the net to keep Northcott from slamming in the rebound.

Hooley Smith Penalized

Hockey Smith was penalized for cross checking in the seventh period opened. The Wings rushed in five forwards. Dwise Chabot dashed out of the net to save, and again on Lewis. It was the first penalty in the four periods of overtime.

Ward dashed in with a shot and the Maroons argued he was high-sticked by Young. The game was delayed while the sweepers removed the peanuts and papers. Aurie almost scored on a quick shot from right wing.

As the game went into its eighth period it was evident that a break probably would decide it. The players were standing passes that normally would be easy. Aurie almost scored when he caught a loose puck 10 feet out and every photographer in the Forum let loose their flashlights, but Chabot saved. A minute later the camera battery did the same thing as Northcott skated in on Goalie Smith.

Barry, Lewis and Aurie got the puck in on Chabot and Young took a terrific drive at the Maroon goalie. Blinco got in on Smith and N. Kilrea was penalized for tripping. The Wings sent on Young and Goodfellow with Aurie and Lewis to break up the Maroons' idle play. They did not get a shot on Smith while Kilrea was off the ice.

Kilrea returned but only a remarkable save by Smith kept the Maroons from scoring. He stuck his knee out and the puck bounced off.

Ward and Barry were penalized for roughing after both teams had staged a wild scramble around Chabot's net. McDonald sent Hooley Smith spinning as the latter skated in on goal and Bucko was penalized.

Hec Kilrea In Hurt

Hec Kilrea was rammed into the boards and left the ice with his face bleeding. Gracie rushed in and popped a shot on Smith and the puck disappeared. The crowd went daffy, but Goalie Smith calmly pulled the puck out of his pads.

The Wings staged a mad attack on Chabot and Goodfellow clicked the goal post with a dynamiting shot. W. Kilrea crashed into the boards as his brother Hec came back on the ice with a plaster over his left eye. Wally was helped to the dressing room.

Mud Bruneteau scored the only goal of the game after a pass from Hec Kilrea at 16:30. It came three minutes before the ninth period was to have ended.

Hockey

NATIONAL LEAGUE PLAYOFFS
TUESDAY RESULTS
SERIES A
Detroit 1, Maroons 0 (16:30 overtime)
SERIES B
Boston 3, Toronto 0.
SERIES C
Americans 1, Chicago 0.
THURSDAY'S GAMES
Detroit at Maroons.
Americans at Chicago.
Toronto at Boston.

INTERNATIONAL LEAGUE
FINAL STANDINGS
WESTERN DIVISION

EASTERN DIVISION

FINAL KEEPSER GAMES
Detroit 3, Pittsburgh 1.
London 5, Windsor 3.
THURSDAY'S PLAYOFF GAMES
Buffalo at Cleveland.

The Second Guess
By W. W. Edgar

THAT fickle lady sometimes referred to as Dame Fortune has a peculiar way of reaching down in any major sports event and picking out some fellow who has been just an ordinary athlete to play the role of the hero.

One never knows just which lad she will pick. For that reason spectators always lie in wait before a big prize regarding her selections. Some times she looks down in the arena and decides to walk along with the accepted stars. At other times her friendly grasp goes out an unsung fellow—the underdog of whom little is expected.

It is just as if she says to herself, "Down there is my boy and I'm going to string along with to the finish."

That's why you'll find the underdog coming through in the pinch—reaching heights never before gained by him. Yes, this fickle lady makes stars out of run of the mine players and bums out of stars. We got to discussing her selections last night while debating which of the Red Wings would play the leading role in the Stanley Cup series that now is under way.

Her Selections Don't Follow Form

IF ONE were to string along with form the hero of the Red Wing cast could be selected from a few, for instance, on form alone, Herbie Lewis, Larry Aurie, Marty Barry, Doug Young and Ebbie Goodfellow would be the leading candidates. For Dame Fortune's selections don't always follow form.

She is apt to pick out Hec Kilrea, his brother Wally. She may even choose Gordon Pettinger, Syd Howe, Bucko McDonald or Normie Smith of each any of them in the pass raising hero that will lead the team to victory.

This is one of the things that always lend interest to a short series where a championship is at stake. Since eons ones remarked, "The race is not always to the swift." However, that's still the place to look unless Dame Fortune makes a sudden decision to pick out an unsung fellow and place him on the pedestal.

She has done this many times in the past and will continue to do so in the future. For you never can tell about the odd girl and her whims and fancies.

She Made a Hero of Pepper Martin

FOR instance, there was the time, a few years back, when she reached down and picked her arm around "Pepper" Martin of the Cardinals in the world series against the Athletics.

Until that series Martin was considered little more than an ordinary ball player. He was consistent, possessed a lot of speed, but the Cardinals' winning permit to be the pennant was not the result of any outstanding feats that "Pepper" turned in.

But were the series got under way Martin was a far different ball player. He could do nothing wrong. He slammed the ball to 31 points of the lot, ran the bases like a man possessed and in general harassed the Mackmen to no end until they were beaten.

And mind you Martin did his wild base running against one Gordon Stanley Cochrane, premier catcher of the Tigers, at the time he considered the best catcher in the league.

Mickey looked like anything but a great catcher after Martin got to the business. "Pepper" stole everything in sight and gave Mickey the most embarrassing moments he ever had on the ball field.

Little Flea Clifton Struck Her Fancy

DURING the last world series she laid another example of the working of this fickle lady. Before the series, "Flea" Clifton was one of the Tigers who was not expected to see service against the Cubs. In fact, he wasn't expected to get into the games at all.

You can recall what happened: Marvin Owen was injured and forced out of the battles. Marvin Owen was switched to first base and Clifton, that little fiend of whom little was expected, suddenly found himself in the third base.

It was a tough spot for him. But he came through. At the finish, the world wars were not Bridgeman's, Cochrane, and Goslin, but standing with the battles of the struggle was little Clifton. He performed a gigantic task down at the first corner. Had he failed then would have been no hero role for Clifton.

So you never can tell just where Dame Fortune will point her finger in the Stanley Cup series. That's why it is interesting to follow the playing of the Red Wings would play the leading role in the Stanley Cup series.

Pinehurst Course Stumps Pro Field

PINEHURST, N. C. March 24.—(A. P.)—Professional Golf's touring star found the remodeled Pinehurst No. 2 course a severe jolt of their opening round today. Edward Herman Barron of Long Island at 71 was the lowest score. He was the only one to break par for the $6,000 North and South Open Championship.

It was the first time on the "venerable layout" that no one had broken par.

Phillips Wins Own Game in Late Scoring

Benge's Wild Pitch Sends in Hayworth with Victory

By Charles P. Ward

LAKELAND, Fla., March 24.—Having trounced the plutocratic Boston Red Sox here Sunday before the anguished eyes of their free-spending owner, Thomas A. Tom Yawkey, the World Champion Tigers today demonstrated their utter impartiality in baseball matters by doing the same thing to the plebeian Boston Bees, who are the current Little Orphan Annies of the National gauge. The score was 4 to 3 and it was arrived at after the Tigers staged a thrilling ninth-inning rally to pull the game out of the Boston bag.

Although a wild pitch by Ray Benge, Boston right-hander, sent Ray Hayworth home with the deciding run, the lion's share of the glory for the triumph must go to Clarence Lemuel Phillips, the big right-handed hurler from Beaumont. Phillips not only turned in a fine hurling performance but also led the Tiger attack with a triple that got him nowhere and a single which drove home the tying run.

Big Red had to fight hard to achieve his triumph, for in the ninth inning Lady Luck implacably attempted to toss the game to the Bees when she presented them with a one-run lead by a series of lucky circumstances.

When the inning began, the teams were tied at two runs each and Red was tolling confidently, expecting his mates to score in the last of the ninth and give him a victory. But in the Bees' half, Rupert Thompson grounded to Rudy York after one was out. Phillips, covering first, took York's throw in time to retire the slugger but missed the bag with his foot when he made a blind stab at it.

Hops Over York's Head

Baxter Jordan then hit a high bounder down the first base line. York set himself to field the ball but just before it reached him, the green-eyed goddess hit it a kick and it hopped over his head like a crazy kangaroo. Thompson took third on the hit and scored a moment later when Gerald Walker hauled down Ray Mueller's fly just inside the left field wall.

Ted took command then and struck Benge out. But the Bees were ahead and it looked as if they might win and score a clean sweep in their series with the Bengals.

But Walker, who doesn't seem to know when he's licked, brought a cheer from the home fans when he opened the Tiger ninth with a slashing single to left. He was forced by York but the "meat truck" helped the Tiger cause by beating the throw to first when the Bees attempted to execute a double play.

Marvin Owen had a chance to advance York but wasn't up to it, fouling out to Jordan at first. Hayworth was better news, however. He hit a Hayworth special—a single to left center, putting York on third. That brought up Little Lem, Mickey Cochrane having decided to let Phillips hit for himself rather than use a pinch-hitter.

Phillips justified this display of confidence by singling to center, scoring York with the tying run. That must have upset Benge, for he walked Bill Rogell. Then, while pitching carefully to Pete Fox, he cut loose a wild pitch which permitted Hayworth to trot home with the run that ended the game.

Phillips Sure to Go North

Phillips has been waiting to learn his fate before telling Mrs. Phillips and their two-month-old daughter to move from their home in Oklahoma City to Detroit for the summer. But Red can send that important telegram now, for he is certain to stick at least long enough to make the trip north while.

Thus far Phillips has shown more stuff than any of the Tiger hurlers. And his work today was up to previous performances. Working the last five innings, he limited the Bees to two hits, one of which was Jordan's tainted output in the ninth. He had great control walking not a man, and at all times he was calm as a stone image.

The Bees sent another two hurlers against the Tigers, Jim (Blow Him Down) McCloskey, a left-hander, and a young friend of Bill McKechnie's named Spiesman sharing the mound duties with Benge.

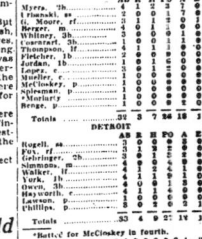

Battled for McCloskey in fourth.

Runs batted in—Benge, Owen, Mueller, Gallagher, Two-base hits—Phillips, Mueller, Three-base hit—Mueller, Sacrifices—Tamulis, York. Double plays—Phillips to Rogell to York; Lavagetto, Rogell to York; Lavagetto, Rogell to York. Left on bases—Detroit 9; Boston 7. Bases on balls—Off McCloskey 2; off Phillips 2, off Spiesman 2. Struck out—By Phillips 5, by Tamulis 1, by Spiesman 1, by Benge 1. Hits—Off McCloskey 3 in 3 innings; off Tamulis 0 in 1; off Spiesman 4 in 4; off Benge 1 in 1-3. Winning pitcher, Phillips. Losing pitcher, Benge. Umpires—Magerkurth and Basil. Time—1:50.

Here's Goal that Ended Stars' Hopes of Beating Olympics

JOHNNY GALLAGHER, NO. 4, TIES UP GAME WITH THIS SHOT IN SECOND PERIOD

Clark Assumes Charge of Lions

Richards Turns Over Reins to Coach

G. A. Richards, president of the Detroit Lions, announced last night that he had turned over the executive reins of the world professional football champions to Coach George (Potsy) Clark.

Richards said that Clark had been named general manager of the Lions in addition to would continue to coach. The president indicated that he would step completely out of the executive picture, retaining only control of the club's finances.

Richards' former title was president and general manager. His new title raises him as president in charge of finance.

The announcement followed many rumors that a new executive setup was being formulated for the Lions. It had been reported that a committee of board members, under the chairmanship of H. T. Keller, would assume command.

Made Clear to Club

And the president's statement justified this rumor. It was an amicable conclusion the alleged feud which had existed between Clark and Richards as to Clark's status.

Richards made it evident that the Lion coach now is the czar of Detroit's professional football, in complete charge of all Lion players, salaries, schedules and other matters pertaining to the club. With the exception of George Halas, who owns and coaches the Chicago Bears, Clark has become the most powerful manager in professional football ranks.

The Lion mentor is particularly well qualified to handle his new duties. He had a distinguished athletic career at the University of Illinois and later coached successfully at Butler University. He was instrumental in starting the construction of the Butler Field House, one of the largest indoor sports arenas in the Country.

Developed Many Stars

He joined professional football at Portsmouth. It was while there that he constructed the foundation for his 1935 World Champion Lions. He brought from Portsmouth some of the greatest stars of the professional gridiron. He had developed far beyond their college careers when he came to Detroit for the sum mer. He included Earl (Dutch) Clark, the outstanding quarterback in pro ranks today; Halfbacks Glenn Prannell, Ernie Cadell; Linemen George Christensen, Jack Johnson, Harry Ebding, John Schneller, Ox Emerson and Tom Hupke.

In his second year as coach of the Detroit Lions, he bought a world title to Detroit. And because he has prepared extensive plans for bolstering his 1936 eleven the Detroiters are favorites to repeat. He announced that Elmer (Red) White, 170-pound Brooklyn Dodger halfback, had been signed. Clark said that the triple-threat Dodger had been added to the roster to alternate with fleet Ernie Caddel.

Brown 'U' Picks Myers

PROVIDENCE, R. I. March 24.—Danny E. Myers, former Yale and West Virginia varsity star coach and a graduate of the University of Iowa, was named Brown varsity line coach tonight. He succeeds Paul Hodge who resigned.

O's Down Syracuse in Last Period Drive

Hughes' Men Take 4 to 2 Victory in Opening Playoff After Stars Falter

By Tod Rockwell

With Willie Starr having one of the biggest nights of his hockey career, the Detroit Olympics set back the Stars from Syracuse, 4 to 2, in the first playoff contest of the International League at Olympia last night.

It was a splendid contest, and fought throughout, witnessed by less than 3,000 spectators. Starr's contribution to the O's loud strife was a sudden burst of speed and three assists. Last night he was a backchecker, cool as a cucumber a few minutes later and Convey and Markle teamed it to even the count against the short handed O's.

Boulston and Gallagher failed to note history. But Burke standing in front of Broda after sitting minutes of play in the second stanza. He took a tough pass from Jack Markle and sent it into corner before Broda could set himself for a save.

Gallagher Knots Count

Gallagher was irked after that goal. So he blazed down the center of the ice with Starr. Both men were in high gear and wheeled past Howard with a double pass. Starr laid his next pass on Gallagher's stick right in front of the goal mouth. Gallagher easily picked a corner.

When the Stars turned on all their steam. It made a fine spectacle. Walter Broda seldom has had a busier night. He was in hot water for the Stars would have forced the game to overtime. Starr broke up the last dangerous Syracuse rally when he flashed down the left wing with Giroux following. Giroux left his mate at the blue line and skated to the goal mouth. He got there just in time to rifle home Starr's pass from the wing.

The O's will practice Wednesday in preparation for the second game with the Stars Thursday night at Olympia. The remaining games of the three out of five game series will be played in Syracuse next week.

Many Chances Missed

Several golden opportunities to score were missed by the Hawks. In the third period, Romnes found himself on top of the Amerk goal but with Worters drawn out of position the American's goal defenders closed his shot to go awry. Jerwa had taken Worters place for the moment, stretching his body across the goal mouth to block any low shot that might be aimed at the net.

Seibert missed another opportunity when with a clear shot, four feet from the goal, Oliver tied up his stick from behind.

The Hawks, try as they would, saw their every effort frustrated by the hard-playing Amerks.

Hawks Beaten by Americans

New York Piles Up a 3-Goal Margin

NEW YORK, March 24.—(A.P.)— Dave (Sweeney) Schriner, the Deadeye Dick of the National Hockey League, whipped in two goals tonight to pace the New York Americans to a 3-0 victory over the Chicago Blackhawks in the first of a two-game series in the Stanley Cup playoffs.

The speedy forward, a popular choice for all-star honors this season, scored twice in the first period and the Americans completely dominated proceedings from there on. Lorne Carr getting the third and last marker in third period.

The Americans' star line of Schriner, Art Chapman and Carr took the ice for the opening faceoff with orders to turn on the heat and keep it on until the light was lit. It did. Less than two minutes had gone by when Carr picked up the rubber near the boards, passed to Chapman and the latter fed it to Schriner who drew Mike Karakas from the Chicago net and then slipped it in behind him.

The time was 16:40 when Chapman again passed to Schriner who took Smith made a great save. Hooley Smith came around the net and the puck angered around the goal line but Normie pushed it off.

Barry, Lewis and Aurie got the puck in on Chabot and Young took a terrific drive at the Maroon goalie. Blinco got in on Smith and N. Kilrea was penalized for tripping. The Wings sent on Young and Goodfellow with Aurie and Lewis to break up the Maroons' idle play. They did not get a shot on Smith while Kilrea was off the ice.

Kilrea returned but only a remarkable save by Smith kept the Maroons from scoring. He stuck his knee out and the puck bounced off.

Ward and Barry were penalized for roughing after both teams had staged a wild scramble around Chabot's net. McDonald sent Hooley Smith spinning as the latter skated in on goal and Bucko was penalized.

Break Mark in 9th Period

Once again the two teams sent in their first lines as the ninth period opened. The two clubs were playing like a team of flagpole sitters. They were trying hard but they found it difficult to skate and shoot.

The first five minutes of the ninth period passed and the game became the longest contest in the history of hockey, organized or unorganized, passing the old Toronto-Boston mark of 164 minutes 46 seconds.

Pettinger nearly scored Chabot was jammed back into the nets by Jimmy Ward for a break and almost scored when the puck struck the skate of Herbie Lewis. Lewis a moment later grabbed the puck and Chabot made a beautiful save.

Mud Bruneteau scored the only goal of the game after a pass from Hec Kilrea at 16:30. It came three minutes before the ninth period was to have ended.

Hockey History

RED WINGS						MAROONS

(Lineups and statistics)

Hank Shows Signs of Weakening

NEW YORK, March 24.—(A. P.)—Hank Greenberg's holdout is the real McCoy, although Detroit's slugging first baseman gave signs today of weakening just a bit.

"I know where I should be and where I'd like to be," said skyscraping Hank, "but this is legitimate business. I'm no fooling and by the looks of things, neither is the club."

Hank has been apartment hunting in New York, ostensibly for a friend, and he reported this morning that he has been most of his time there except for a daily workout in a nearby park. He moves to his home several days ago.

"What worries me it the club." he confided. "I won't compromise I proposed. I won't."

"That doesn't concern me at all," broke in Hank.

So do not take a vow to finish between Greenberg and the club by the first of April there's no telling what I might do," he said.

pounds—five pounds over his playing weight.

"I should have been down in Florida with the club three weeks ago," Hank sighed. "I really don't every day I'm away from there I'm losing something, but there's a principle involved in my case. I believe I'm entitled to more money than the club has offered me.

"If this wasn't so on the level I'd tell the world in minutes how much I'm asking. What the club offered and why, but everything can consume that the club and me have both agreed to keep their counsel, so I'm keeping mine."

Hank was paid approximately $10,000 last year and was reported to have asked $20,000 for his services this year. Dizzy Dean, after asking $40,000, settled for be reported $52,500, and it is believed that Greenberg will compromise for that much or less.

Unless he suddenly weakens completely, it is unlikely that Hank will budge before his first step for his turn to the field. He's greatly interested in the promised big Tiger toys making in the South, but says he's not worried a bit by reports that Rookie Rudy York is filling the first base assignment with distinction. York recently was tagged by President Will Harridge as one of the American League's prospects.

Haynes, Godfrey Signed for Match

PHILADELPHIA, March

(Partial text illegible)

conqueror of Primo Carnera, and George Godfrey, the International Boxing Federation's world heavyweight champion, were signed to tangle here in a 15-round bout in the Arena on April 13.

JUNE 30, 1936:

Dayton Dean is a key prosecution witness in the breaking up of the Black Legion, a violence-prone cult flourishing in Michigan and the Detroit Police Department during the Depression. Legion literature says it is dedicated to "white, native-born Protestant, 100-percent Americanism."

The Detroit Free Press

THE WEATHER — Showers Tuesday; fair, with rising temperature, Wednesday

FINAL EDITION

Tuesday, June 30, 1936. 106th Year. No. 57 — On Guard for Over a Century — 26 Pages — Three Cents

McCarl Denounces New Deal's Waste as His Term Ends

Would Eliminate Tax-Eating Units

Hits Squandering

Extravagant Bureaus' Foe Hopes to Aid Reconstruction

May Assist in Work of Byrd's Committee

WASHINGTON, June 29—(U.P.)—An attack on spending activities of New Deal emergency agencies was Controller General John R. McCarl's official goodby to the office he has held for 15 years.

As he prepared to leave office at midnight tomorrow, McCarl characterized emergency agencies organized to combat depression as "loosely and extravagantly set up" and as "tax consuming in the extreme."

Much of McCarl's work during the last three years has concerned "rality of New Deal spending. He lashed repeatedly what he considered extravagant agencies with heads of alphabetical agencies who sought to spend public money in a manner which McCarl believed did not comply with congressional mandate.

May Help Reorganization

McCarl said he hopes "many if not all of the existing special or emergency agencies * * * may be promptly eliminated." He said that his plans for the immediate future are not definite, but that he contemplates remaining in Washington to assist, if possible, in a reorganization of Government agencies.

He recommended realignment of Federal bureaus so that their proper functions as may be proper assigned to the more economically organized regular establishments. Under the law, McCarl is not eligible for reappointment as the "watchdog" of the Treasury. His successor has not yet been designated, although former Senator Harry F. Byrd, Virginia Democrat, has been mentioned, and if the work is to be seriously taken up I would wish to be available to give the Senator such assistance as I can."

Senator Byrd said that he would urge the committee to use McCarl's services "to the greatest possible extent."

"System and Sense" Needed

"A systematic and sensible reorganization of the regular Governmental agencies and activities should result not only in a vast monetary saving but would eliminate duplications and overlapping operations, bring together related functions, simplify procedures, and in every respect make for better administration," McCarl asserted.

"This is a legislative problem and I am in hopes that the next Congress may be so constituted that there may be assured not only a systematic and thorough examination of the regular agencies with proper consolidations and eliminations, but that many if not all of the existing special or emergency agencies, which are the creatures who loosely and extravagantly set up and are tax consuming in the extreme, may be promptly eliminated with such of their functions as may be proper temporarily carrying on, assigned to the more economically organized regular establishments."

Mrs. Leonard to Return to Divorced Phobic Poet

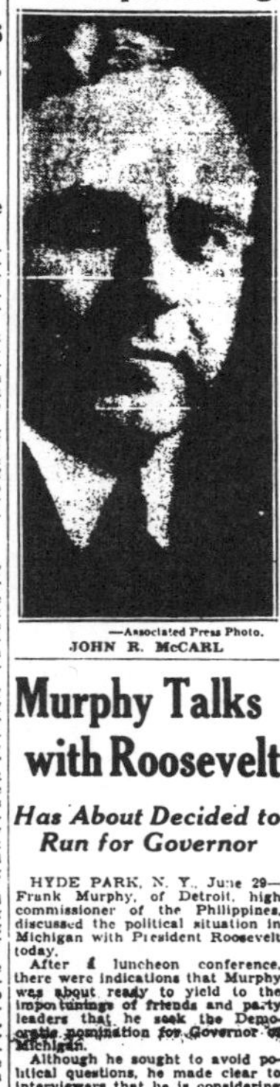

MADISON, Wis., June 29—(A.P.)—Mrs. Golden Leonard, who a month ago swore in a divorce action that she could no longer endure the strange phobias of her poet husband, Prof. William Ellery Leonard, is on the verge of trying it again.

Mrs. Leonard, 23 years younger than the sixty-year-old whiskered University of Wisconsin scholar, has been in the East only obtaining a divorce a month after 11 months of marriage.

Friends disclosed today that she is returning to Madison to "give it another try for a reconciliation. Jenna, a lonely figure Scientifically-imposed fears of which he envisions a huge family, is ready to swallow him need to comment.

Iffy...the Dopester

ARCHEOLOGISTS HAVE discovered traces of a vast city under the soil of Nebraska which they estimate flourished thousands of years before Columbus discovered America.

It must be considered that these searches have been going on for over a year and went to market find no answer to Jim Farley's remark about "typical prairie states." West isn't trying to prove that city under than New York.

Spinsters have organized in England to give other of the older citizens' pensions at the age of 10. But they don't make quite so...

—Associated Press Photo.
JOHN R. McCARL

Murphy Talks with Roosevelt

Has About Decided to Run for Governor

HYDE PARK, N. Y., June 29—Frank Murphy, of Detroit, high commissioner of the Philippines, discussed the political situation in Michigan with President Roosevelt today.

After a luncheon conference, there were indications that Murphy was about ready to yield to the importunings of friends and party leaders that he seek the Democratic nomination for Governor of Michigan.

Although he sought to avoid political questions, he made clear to interviewers that he is considering entering the gubernatorial race. When asked if he was returning to the Philippines, Murphy replied: "If I should run for Governor, I won't. That's a possibility, you know."

To Decide in Few Days

He expects to make a decision in the next four or five days on seeking the nomination.

Besides receiving Murphy's report on political conditions in Michigan, President Roosevelt got some first-hand information on the situation in Illinois from Gov. Henry Horner.

In both of these states intraparty discord has caused concern regarding the chances for a Democratic victory in November. The conferences today were interpreted as an effort by Mr. Roosevelt to iron out the dissension.

Both Murphy and Gov. Horner assured the President of their confidence that all factions of the party would be united and that he would carry their states in the election.

Going to Washington

Murphy said that he was going to Washington tomorrow for conferences with War and Navy Department officials and Philippine matters and then would spend the week-end in Michigan.

He added that he talked about Philippine and Eastern affairs with the President in addition to politics.

Murphy was one of four men indorsed for the gubernatorial nomination at the "co-operation" in state political convention in Illinois. The others were George Welsh, Perpetual lieutenant governor; George Schroeder, speaker of the House, and Theodore I. Fry, State treasurer.

President Roosevelt ended his two-day stay at his home here late tonight and left by a special train for Washington.

He Buys 1,260 Shoes; They're a Little Big

LOS ANGELES, June 29—(A.P.)—A Baiboni loves a bargain.

When he had a chance to bid in 30 pairs of shoes at an Army goods auction for $15, he seized it. Then he discovered that he had been bid on 630 pairs—all in one lot.

Baiboni took them home. The first crate was all size 14, so was the second—and the third.

Baiboni wears size 8½.

"What can anybody," he asked, "with 630 pairs of size 14 shoes?"

Live at Hotel Webster Hall—Cars...—Adv.

40,000 Cases Are Held Up in State's Courts

Judicial Council Asks Drastic Shake-Up in Circuit Districts

Wayne Suits Waiting 15 Months for Trial

With 40,000 cases pending at the beginning of 1936, and with Michigan circuit and other courts falling behind, reorganization of judicial circuits to distribute the load more equitably is recommended by the Michigan Judicial Council in its annual report.

In all courts of record in Michigan last year, 70,163 cases were started and only 62,723 disposed of, adding nearly 8,000 cases to the backlog.

With more than 20,000 cases pending, the Wayne Circuit Court was 15 months and 13 days behind schedule on law cases, and 21 months and 20 days behind in chancery matters.

The Wayne pile-up was increased by curtailment both of the number of days' service of visiting judges and of the aid furnished by Recorder's judges under authorization of a 1933 statute.

Recommends Transfers

The Judicial Council recommends that, until relief can be had through reorganization of circuits under constitutional authorization, effective results can be obtained through transferring judges.

Decreased efficiency of the courts in dealing with their civil calendars also is indicated, with only 32,886 cases disposed of last year as contrasted to 39,424 handled in 1932.

In 1932 the backlog was cut down 1,886 cases. In 1935 it increased 5,600.

On the other hand the courts have kept even with criminal cases, but the amount of criminal business has diminished. In Detroit Recorder's Court, new criminal actions fell from 38,173 in 1934 to 24,758 in 1935, and in the rest of the state the number of new criminal cases dropped from 8,126 in 1934 to 4,813 in 1935.

Thirty-two circuits lost ground last year, and only eight circuits gained ground in dealing with civil matters.

Disproportionate loads falling on different judicial circuits is indicated by the fact that in 1935, in no less than six circuits, a single judge was called upon to try more cases than confronted all three judges of the Wayne Circuit. In one circuit a single judge ended the year with as much work as the three judges of the Kent Circuit combined. Some one-judge circuits have as much as nine times as much trial business as others.

In Wayne Circuit Court, outside Visiting Circuit Judges spent 2,028 days on the bench in 1935, as contrasted to 635 days last year. With service of the resident judges, this meant a grand total of 6,098 court days in 1932 to only 4,851 days in 1935.

1935 Recorder's Aid

Although the Recorder's Court visiting calendar shows 2,400 new cases in the year, the records show that the judges of this bench gave less than half as much time in 1935 to Circuit Court assignments as in 1932, when the concurrent jurisdiction over certain types of civil cases was instituted.

In 1935 Recorder's Judges spent 684 days on Circuit Court affairs, equal to almost 10 per cent of the total court days.

Last year this help was reduced to 193 days, or less than 4 per cent of the Circuit Court total.

The Judicial Council details approvingly the pre-trial system in use in the Wayne Circuit and suggests expansion of its application.

16-Inch Rainfall

EAGLE PASS, Tex., June 29—(A.P.)—This city's streets were flooded today from rain measuring 16.27 inches which fell from 10:30 p.m. Saturday to 7 a.m. today.

Wisconsin Ready for Job Insurance

First Law of Kind in U.S. Effective Wednesday

MADISON, Wis., June 29—(A.P.)—Wisconsin's new unemployment-insurance law—the nation's first—will be eligible to receive benefits under its provisions if they lose their jobs after it begins to operate on July 1.

A $13,000,000 fund will be on hand if payments are needed on the first day.

This nest egg has been built up by Wisconsin employers since the beginning of 1934. The pioneer statute took fund laws to cover employers of 10 or more persons, long before enactment of the Federal unemployment-insurance clause in the National Social-Security act.

In 1934 the employers began contributing up to two per cent of their monthly payrolls toward reserve accounts which have now reached $12,000,000 and will increase as time goes on. Approximately 600,000 employees are affected. Eligible for assistance if they lose their jobs are those earning an average of $1,500 a year or less.

The minimum benefit is $5 a week, the maximum $10 for those whose full-time pay is $25 a week, to $12.50 for average pay of $25 to $30 a week, and to $15, the top rate, for workers who normally receive $30 a week.

The duration of the benefits depends on how long a person has worked for his employer.

Heavy Rainfall Ends Drought

Homes Inundated by Detroit Downpour

The heavy rain which broke Central Michigan's drought Monday also flooded many basements in Detroit and Hamtramck. With a continued downpour predicted for Tuesday, Detroit Public Works Department officials warned householders that they should clean their eaves troughs to prevent further clogging of storm sewers.

About 100 complaints were received up to midnight concerning damage caused by the inch of rain that had fallen up to that time. The downpour proved hazardous to traffic and was accompanied by a seven-mile northeast wind.

It was forecast that fair weather would return by Wednesday.

Nearly a month without rain ended for Michigan farmers Monday, relieving damaged pastures and spring grain crops. The heavy rain was general and caused a tremendous breeze in the slightly parched ranks. The State Meteorologist appeared that few are following the same method in the Kenyon...

Illinois and Indiana fields, which had been dry for three months, were given relief. In Michigan's worn side fields but heavy prosperity damages was reported in the Middle West. Thousands of dollars' damage was done to trees and small buildings in Clinton, Ia., and a novelty-manufacturing plant at Fulton, Ill., was destroyed by fire. In Chicago a newsboy sought shelter under a tree and was killed by lightning.

Nebraska, Kansas and Missouri farmers also were helped by the rain, although much of the South remained in the grip of the season.

Papa Swan's Spree Ends in Black Maria

SAN FRANCISCO, June 29—(A.P.)—Officer David Flamm picked up a staggering white swan on a downtown street today, took one whiff of its breath—and put him in the patrol wagon.

"Pickled," was Flamm's verdict. Flamm suspects a prankster but proved a day's celebration at "Tommy's" inland lagoon home in Golden Gate Park. The swan and his mate, Susie, are proud parents of four baby swans.

Zioncheck Is Started West After Day of Hide and Seek

Charges He Was Shanghaied to Hospital from Which He Made Escape

WASHINGTON, June 29—Thoroughly chastened and weary, Rep. Marion A. Zioncheck started by train for his home in Seattle late tonight after a day of playing hide and seek with throngs of curious persons in the House Office Building and straightening out some of his tangled affairs.

He arrived at Union Station accompanied by a squad of Capitol police. Because the Congressman's mother was reported to be seriously ill in the West he planned to take a plane from Chicago tomorrow.

The playboy Congressman was found in his office earlier today, bruised and hair starred, just 24 hours after he had walled a seven and one-half-foot wire fence at the Shepherd and Enoch Pratt Hospital for mental cases in Towson, Md., 10 miles north of Baltimore, and disappeared. Pennies, Zioncheck had hitch-hiked back to Washington.

He had appeared in the House Office Building at 9 a.m. with no key, but found a charwoman who unlocked his office. After Lenneth Romney, sergeant at arms of the House, had posted $25 bond with Washington police on an assault warrant sworn out for the Congressman by his former landlady, Mrs. Benjamin Scott Young, Capitol police escorted Zioncheck from his suite to the...

...office until train time. He was...body was found nearly a mile from the Thomas farmhouse Saturday morning, half submerged in a branch of the Au Gres River. The head was nearly cut off by what others must have been a knife-slash across the throat. The ears and tongue had been sliced off and have not been found.

Monday, Chester Corrigan, who lives near the road where the abandoned trail branches toward the river, said that at 10 p.m. last Monday he saw a car turn down the old trail.

He took notice of it, he said, because so few cars ever traverse the trail. Later, he said, he saw the car drive out again.

"That fits in with the police theory that the boy had been killed and then carried to the stream. If he were slain nearer the cliff and thrown into three miles to a police station for help.

The statement added: "Had I not escaped I am certain that I would have qualified for an insane asylum in the very near future. I have to say that they have never persecuted; nevertheless I have been called upon to endure nerve-shattering experience and the torture-destroying processes. The thirty-six-year-old Representative signed the statement which included somewhere in Virginia for the past week.

Rep. Knutson Arrested

LONDON, Ont., June 29—(A.P.)—Rep. Harold Knutson, Minnesota Republican, was fined $10 and costs today at the London police station for illegal consumption of liquor. The congressman was arrested in his parked automobile. A police constable said that Knutson was drinking in the car although he returned to his...

Officers Seek a Degenerate in Boy's Death

Tawas Doctor Thinks Lad Was Attacked Before Slaying

Countryside Combed for Telltale Signs

TAWAS CITY, Mich., June 29—Police seeking the mad murderer of ten-year-old Bobby Kenyon have narrowed the search to a degenerate in the belief that the boy was criminally assaulted and killed by a degenerate before being killed and mutilated with a knife.

Until tonight, officers had indicated that the murder seemed to be the work of a homicidal maniac.

One of the things being sought by State Police and authorities of the University of Michigan is definite evidence that the boy apparently was seized and held by a degenerate before being killed and mutilated with a knife.

O. W. Mitton, Tawas City physician, said that it was his belief that the boy had been killed before the corpse was handed over to Dr. John C. Bugher, pathologist at Ann Arbor, as definite proof regarding the attack on the boy.

It was believed that the boy "wanted to know whether anything from the river had gotten into the body."

It is known that State Police, investigating Michigan's baffling crime of the week, had begun to find it difficult at any step the unsolved Brinkler murder at Yale and have turned the slightest clues in an effort to discover if the same method in the Kenyon case was following.

Believed Slain While Nude

Deputy Sheriff Harry Rollin revealed that according to the theory now held by the police, the boy was slain while nude, and that the killer, after cutting the boy's throat, slicing off his ears and cutting out the boy's tongue, then dressed the corpse before carrying it to a branch of the Au Gres River and throwing it into the water. Authorities, it was understood, are waiting for a final report from Dr. John C. Bugher, pathologist at Ann Arbor, as definite proof regarding the attack on the boy.

Until tonight, the fact that the boy was fully clothed, except for his hat, was taken as indication that he had not been the victim of sexual degenerate but might have been killed by a man seized with a sudden deranged impulse to kill.

Indication that State Police and local authorities have discovered some new but secret clues was disclosed by Sheriff John Moran who announced that he was sending a bottle of water from the river to Ann Arbor for analysis. Later he sent the boy's clothing for a similar analysis.

Authorities refused to give any details of their new suspicions in the case except to say that they "wanted to know whether anything from the river had gotten into the body."

It is known that State Police, investigating Michigan's baffling crime of the week, had begun to find it difficult at any step the unsolved Brinkler murder at Yale and have turned the slightest clues in an effort to discover if the same method in the Kenyon case was following.

100 Police Cult Members, Dayton Dean Says After Pleading Guilty to Killing

State Witness Takes His Medicine

Dayton Dean, Black Legion trigger man (center), on his way to Circuit Judge Joseph A. Moynihan's court, where he pleaded guilty to kidnaping and murdering Charles A. Poole. Guarding him are Detectives Charles Meehan (left) and Jack Harvill.

Nine Held to Trial on His Testimony

Trigger Man Refuses to Dodge Charge He Says Is True

Death and Riot Plots Confirmed by Slayer

Dayton Dean, the trigger man whose readiness to turn State's evidence has enabled the Prosecutor to build cases against nearly two-score Black Legionnaires, pleaded guilty Monday to the murder of Charles A. Poole.

Dean provided another sensation Monday when he expressed the opinion at a Civil Service Commission hearing that approximately 100 Detroit policemen are in the ranks of the Black Legion.

"I'd say, from conversations I've had with Black Legion officers, that there are about that many," he remarked. "There are a lot of other City employees in the Black Legion who haven't lost their jobs yet."

Dean entered his plea before Circuit Judge Joseph A. Moynihan in the court of Recorder's Judge John P. Scallen as a witness in the court of Recorder's Judge John P. Scallen as a witness for the prosecution Monday.

Dean's plea makes it mandatory upon Judge Moynihan to send him to prison for life. Sentence will be passed as soon as a probation report on Dean has been completed, which will probably be next Monday.

His Attitude Changes

In Judge Scallen's court Dean seemed indifferent to the predicament in which he found himself. He waited to be called before the bar, he grinned at the testimony of a young girl in a morale case, then leaned back. But when he was summoned to the bench his attitude changed suddenly.

As Prosecutor Duncan C. McCrea read the charge, the pervious killer stood with flushed face and eyes averted, clasping his hands behind him. Almost for the first time he seemed to appreciate the gravity of his case. When the Court told him to plead, Dean seemed to hesitate and then for a few seconds. Finally he said:

"My sir, I want to do it right now."

Two Held in Koerm Plot

Dean's testimony before Judge Scallen earlier questioned him, Dean answered unhesitatingly, through in a somewhat lower voice, and invariably appended a respectful "sir" to his answers. When the Judge asked him how police, sheriff's officers and the Prosecutor's staff had treated him, he said:

"Just, sir."

From time to time he licked his lips and as the questioning continued his face became more flushed. His gray eyes shifted nervously. Only when the Judge offered him time to think it over did he hesitate and then just for a few seconds. Finally he said:

"No sir, I want to do it right now."

Bearing this plea in the Poole case continued, "are hopeful that he can return as Postmaster General after the November election. It is known that his desire to remain in the Cabinet, believing that thus his prospects of success as the party's manager for the New York in 1936 would be enhanced.

If Farley were granted a formal leave of absence by the President, it would have been necessary, in keeping with the authority of his Cabinet position, minus his $15,000-a-year salary. It was recalled that the President asked William H. Woodin, the first secretary of the treasury, in the Roosevelt administration, was granted a leave of absence without pay because of illness, while an acting secretary carried on his work. Farley told interviewers in Atlantic City:

"I have not resigned as postmaster general and beyond that, I have no comment to make."

"Do you plan to resign later?" he was asked.

"I have no further comment to make," he reiterated.

Farley, hoping to avoid recognition, walked across several hours on the boardwalk today, but was "picked up by a least 50 people," he said.

"Fortunately," he recalled, "none was looking for a job."

Suffering Prisoners Bite Hand That Freed Them

CHATTANOOGA, Tenn., June 29—(A.P.)—City Judge Martin Flanagan pondered today the ingratitude of some people.

Yesterday the thermometer registered 101.4, the highest ever reached inside the City Jail last night and Judge Fleming visited the City Jail last night and ordered the occupants of the cells released. He was greeted with a chorus of boos from the Brasos River from the "Devil's Backbone" Saturday night. He heard a young woman cry, "Don't do that," and noted as being taken home, he said. Later Hewitt said in a signed statement, there was silence followed by the sound of something heavy going over the cliff. Soon after, he said he heard an automobile being driven away.

England Continues Ban on Radio Ads

LONDON, June 29—(U.P.)—Sponsored programs as well as direct advertising will continue to be banned by the British Broadcasting Corp. under a Government decision published today. The Government recommended efforts to prevent foreign advertising programs from being received in England.

The charter of the B. B. C., which is the official and sole broadcasting agency in England, was extended for 10 years.

Roosevelt Nominators Given Tax Exemption

WASHINGTON, June 29—(A.P.)—The Treasury Department has ruled that Democrats will not have to pay a Federal tax on their tickets for the Roosevelt-Garner notification ceremony. In an informal ruling, Department officials have determined that in no way expended was in the form of "contributions" rather than for tickets, taxable.

Start the Day Right with the Free Press

Editorial
Edgar A. Guest, Poem
National Whirligig
Iffy the Dopester
Foreign News
The Day in Washington
Walter Lippmann
Radio News
Around the Town
Society
Silhouettes
The Chatterbox
Ruth Alden
Culbertson on Bridge
The Second Guess
Colyer's Comment
Financial
Radio Programs
Manhattan
Crossword Puzzle
Comics
Sher ian Road, Serial
Obituaries
Dr. Joseph Fort Newton
Quillen's Observations
The Theater

Please Turn to Page 2—Column 1

THE WEATHER
Mostly cloudy Tuesday and Wednesday; colder Wednesday

The Detroit Free Press

FINAL EDITION

Tuesday, January 12, 1937. 106th Year. No. 253 — On Guard for Over a Century — 26 Pages — Three Cents

NATIONAL GUARD MOBILIZED AFTER STRIKE RIOT IN FLINT

Scores Join Hunt for Kidnaped Boy's Killer

JAN. 12, 1937: A key year for the labor movement begins with violence in Flint.

Appeals Court Ruling Is Blow to Wagner Act

Mackay Radio Firm Upheld in Rejection of NLRB Order

SAN FRANCISCO, Jan. 11—(A.P.)—The United States Ninth Circuit Court of Appeals by a vote of two of three judges, refused today to grant the National Labor Relations Board an enforcement order directing the Mackay Radio & Telegraph Co. to reinstate five discharged employees.

Presiding Judge Curtis D. Wilbur, former Republican secretary of the Navy, declared in the majority opinion that the Labor Board's order "clearly violates the fundamental rights of respondent, the Mackay Co." guaranteed to it by the Fifth Amendment to the Constitution."

The Wilbur opinion dealt almost wholly with constitutional issues and held portions of the National Labor Relations Act unconstitutional. It expressed doubt of the right of the Federal Government to regulate employment even in interstate commerce.

Distinction on Bargaining

"It is one thing to declare and protect collective bargaining, and quite another to require collective bargaining," Wilbur ruled.

He answered in the affirmative a query whether it would be accurate to say that the opinion "stopped just short of declaring the Wagner Act unconstitutional."

The Labor Board had ordered the telegraph company to reinstate the five men who charged that their union labor leadership had caused the company to refuse to rehire them with other workers after a strike.

It had ordered the company to cease threatening discharge of other employees who might join the American Radio Telegraphists Association, to post notices for employees stating that no such discharge would be made, and to pay wages to the five men. The court ruled out every provision of the board's order.

'Contract Rights Violated'

Judge Wilbur upheld the company's contention that it would be violating its right of contract to require it to break contracts with the five men now working in the places of the discharged ones.

Judge Clifton Mathews, in a separate concurring opinion, said he agreed with Judge Wilbur that the National Labor Relations Act was "not wholly void." He ruled against the Labor Board purely on the basis of the particular case.

Judge Francis Garrecht dissented, declaring that the decision "deprives Congress of the power to establish a department of government with authority to compose the increasing strife between employers and employees."

The Best Policy

WASHINGTON, Ga., Jan. 11—(A.P.)—Luke D. Faver, 70 years old, who campaigned on the slogan "I Need the Job," was re-elected mayor of Washington for his fourth term today.

Start the Day Right with the Free Press
Pages
Allen, Ruth 11
Chatterbox 17
Collyer, Bert E. ... 17
Comics 20
Crossword Puzzle .. 22
Editorial 14
Financial 19
Foreign News 4
Good Morning 6
Guest, Edgar A. ... 6
Hillis, Marjorie .. 15
Itty, the Dopester . 9
Lippmann, Walter .. 11
Manhattan 6
Music 16
National Whirligig . 14
Newton, Dr. Joseph Fort 5
Obituaries 18
Psychology 22
Quillen, Robert ... 8
Radio Programs 8
Screen 16
Second Guess 9
Serial, "They Paid the Price" .. 28
Society 10
State News 18
Theater 16
Ward to the Wise .. 8
Washington News ... 6
What's Doing Today 8

Dancer's Case May Be Given to Jury Today

By Katherine Lynch

ANN ARBOR, Jan. 11—A jury that has heard the secret love affairs of Betty Baker, the slim married dancer on trial for the murder of her lover, may begin to consider her fate in Circuit Court here Tuesday.

The jurors must decide whether she "only intended to frighten" her victim or whether, as the State contends, she was jealous of him and murdered him because he was seeing other girls.

The jury of 14 middle-aged men heard the final summing up of both prosecution and defense Monday. Mrs. Baker, nicknamed "Bum-bum," sat expressionless at her counsel table, and Albert K. Baker, her handsome young policeman husband, from the other side of the packed court, pulled his lip nervously.

It was with Baker's service revolver that Mrs. Baker shot his best friend, Clarence Schneider, who, she has testified, was for six years her lover.

The defense contends that the shooting, which occurred on a lonely road near here on June 29, was accidental.

Each member of the jury Monday was handed the gun by Judge W. Conlin, defense attorney, and tested the pull of the trigger, to judge whether it might have been discharged accidentally.

Prosecutor Albert Rapp in his summing up attacked the dancer's character.

"It has been testified that she said that her husband was all right to support her, but that when it came to love she wasn't going to lose this man," he said. "She has called Schneider by a pet name—'Cub.' If she couldn't have him, no one was going to have him. She could not have known he was dead when she left him lying in the garage. Would any reasonable person have done that in case of an accidental shooting?

"Less than nine months after her marriage she was having an affair with Cub. Here is her husband, who has stood by her, yet she trampled down and makes a fool of him. She is a woman who must have what she wants at any cost. Jealousy was the motive for this shooting."

Head crushed and teeth broken, the nude and frozen body was discovered about half a mile from the heavily traveled Pacific Highway south of Everett.

Had Premonition of Death

The boy's father said that he had "feared something like this would happen" and, through a representative, declared that he had "made every effort humanly possible" to pay the ransom to gain the return of my son."

Please Turn to Page 2—Column 1

Woman Is Found Slain in Bathtub

NEW YORK, Jan. 11—(A.P.)—A young husband, returning to his Jackson Heights home, tonight discovered the body of his wife immersed in an overflowing bathtub.

Her skull had been crushed, and there were bloody evidences of a violent struggle in the apartment kitchen.

Her husband, Frank, was the last person known to have seen her alive. Detective Inspector John J. Ryan of the Queens County police, said.

Inspector Ryan said that Case, also 25, had left home at 8 o'clock this morning for his place of employment. At 6:55 p.m. he arrived home.

In the basement, in the unlit incinerator furnace, police discovered the pocketbook of Mrs. Case, intact with $15 in it.

They expressed the opinion that the slayer had thrown the pocketbook away to make robbery seem the motive for the killing.

He Will Be a Farmer, Says Jimmy Walker

NEW YORK, Jan. 11—(A.P.)—James J. Walker, New York's former playboy mayor, disclosed tonight that he aspires to be a gentleman farmer.

Recovered from his penthouse apartment on the fashionable East Side that he had purchased a farm at Northport, Long Island and hopes eventually to have "two of everything" on it.

Hoover Offers All Resources of U. S. Agents

Lad's Battered Body Found in Brush 50 Miles from Home

TACOMA, Jan. 11—The Federal Government tonight pledged the full strength of its manhunting resources in tracking down the kidnaper-murderer of ten-year-old Charles Mattson, whose body was found today.

J. Edgar Hoover, director of the Federal Bureau of Investigation, said in Chicago that the G-men would "use all the resources at our command to apprehend and bring to justice the kidnaper and slayer."

The nude and battered body of the son of wealthy Dr. W. W. Mattson was discovered in the snow-crusted brushlands near Everett, 50 miles from the home from which he was abducted two weeks ago.

A nineteen-year-old hunter stumbled upon the broken body of the boy who was snatched away from his Christmas tree and beaten to death by an assailant who spurned every effort of the father to pay a $28,000 ransom. The victim had been dead—perhaps four days.

Relentless Hunt Starts

The full forces of Federal, State and local authorities were united tonight in a relentless effort to track down the killer. Prior to the gruesome discovery, officers had been held in restraint in the hope of saving the child's life.

The force of 40 G-men here is in charge of Harold Nathan, assistant to Hoover, who had not decided tonight whether to come to Tacoma.

The Washington State Patrol indicated that its policemen would be given full authority to resume the search they had abandoned last week at the request of the boy's father to permit ransom negotiations.

Department of Justice agents and Seattle police, armed with shotguns, made what observers believed to be a kidnap raid within two hours after the body was found, but did not disclose their destination or exact purpose.

Officers Remove Kidnaped Boy's Body from Woods

Sheriff's deputies are shown Monday bearing the pitiful little body of Charles Mattson from the spot in the woods 50 miles from Tacoma where his kidnaper tossed it after brutally beating and killing the boy. The body was found by a nineteen-year-old hunter in snow-laden brush, frozen.

(A. P. Wirephoto)

Hitler Pledges to Keep Hands off Spanish Land

[By the Associated Press]

With Adolf Hitler taking the initiative in a move for European peace, Germany and France exchanged pledges Monday to respect the integrity of Spain and Spanish possessions.

This development served to ease international tension, but France and Great Britain did not cease to count their military and naval forces in the Mediterranean.

Hitler's pledge, coming on the heels of reports received by the British and French Governments of German activity in Spanish Morocco, was made to André Francois-Poncet, French ambassador at Berlin.

Asks for Reconciliation

Hitler told the diplomatic corps that Germany wanted "a real rapprochement and reconciliation among peoples."

Avoiding all mention of the Soviet Union or of Europe's armament competitions, the Fuehrer said his country hoped to contribute to "appeasement of the apprehension and uneasiness" besetting Europe.

Meanwhile, an announcement that Gen. Hermann Wilhelm Goering will fly to Italy Tuesday for "a brief recuperative leave" aroused speculation in diplomatic circles over prospects of Italian-German consultation on the Spanish crisis.

These two nations were among the five which Great Britain has sent notes seeking an immediate ban on the flow of volunteers to Spain.

Germany was not expected to reply for at least four days.

Maintain Precautions

Meanwhile, Britain and France, while cheered by the new note of peace from Berlin, were not relaxing precautions in the Mediterranean.

France earlier in the day gave Gen. Francisco Franco, Spanish Fascist chief, "a few days" to clear Germans out of Spanish Morocco.

France informed Gen. Franco that she was willing to wait a "reasonable time" for action to expel German volunteers. At the same time, officials at Berlin said ...

Woman Demands Injunction to Quell Persistent Admirer

Margaret Scheymanski, 22 years old, took her troubles to Circuit Court Monday, charging that the persistent attempts of a young man to visit her home "in a series of annoyances and assaults" in an effort to regain her friendship.

"He constantly annoyed me by following me wherever I went, and created scenes on the street," the bill set forth.

One Company Ordered Kept Ready in Armory; 14 Injured in Outbreak

FLINT, Jan. 12—(Tuesday)—National Guards were being mobilized in Flint early Tuesday after a strike riot at the Fisher Body plant had sent 14 men to the hospitals for treatment.

The order went out shortly after Gov. Murphy had hurried to Flint from Lansing. He went into immediate secret conference with Oscar G. Olander, State police commissioner; Col. John S. Bersey, adjutant general of the Michigan National Guard, City and County officials.

Gov. Murphy arrived at the Durant Hotel shortly after 1:30 a.m. following the riot at the Fisher Body Plant No. 2 in which the 14 persons were injured, one of them seriously.

Others in the conference were Harold E. Bradshaw, mayor of Flint; City Manager John M. Barringer, Police Chief James V. Wills and several City commissioners.

Simultaneously, Capt. Frank Millard mobilized 55 National Guardsmen at the Armory at 1101 Lewis St., on the other side of town from the plant.

A detachment of State police was called to reinforce City police although there had been no new skirmishes since before midnight.

Shortly after the secret conference began, three Federal labor conciliators, James F. Dewey, John E. O'Connor and Edward C. McDonald, and Frank X. Martel, president of the Detroit and Wayne County Federation of Labor; Capt. Lawrence Lyon, of the State Police; Sheriff Thomas W. Wolcott; Richard Bradford, vice mayor of Pontiac; Prosecutor Joseph R. Joseph, and City Attorney Hyman Hoffman entered the consultation.

Watch from Roofs

The scene of the riot apparently was peaceful early Tuesday morning. Police held their position on a bridge about 100 yards from the plant where strikers, wearing overcoats inside the cold plant, watched from the second story windows and an adjoining roof.

Others stood about in front of the plant at the front door which they had captured earlier.

Those hurt in the encounter were taken to Hurley Hospital with injuries ranging from riot-gun wounds in the legs to bruises from bricks and bottles from the gas grenades hurled by the police.

Those hospitalized were Earl DeLong, Gerhard Maw, Fred Stevens, Hans Larsen, Charles Havens, Fred Moore, John Shepherd, Claud Sheer, George Sheer, Nelson Wodley, Bob Mamero, Lawrence Hoskins, William Lightcap, and George Huber. Only DeLong, reported shot in the abdomen, was reported to be in serious condition.

Fight Starts Over a Ladder

The fight began soon after company police seized a ladder which strikers were using to get in and out of the building and on which food was carried into the strikers at the same time the heat was turned off in the plant. In the meantime strikers captured a plant gate which company police had abandoned to seize the ladder.

The first engagement lasted about 20 minutes. The police threw gas bombs at strikers crowded in front of the plant and into the second-floor windows from which the strikers were hurling bricks and milk bottles. Both sides employed fire hose to spray the opposition.

Please Turn to Page 4—Column 4

Efforts to Pay Ransom Bared

Slayer Was Yellow, Mediator Says

TACOMA, Wash., Jan. 11—(A.P.)—A vivid picture of how Dr. W. W. Mattson made "every effort humanly possible" to pay the $28,000 demanded for the return of his kidnaped and slain son was given tonight by Paul Sceva, close friend of the Mattsons.

As he emerged from the Mattson home Sceva said:

"The doctor has broken down for the first time since Charles was kidnaped, and the entire family is badly shaken. Mrs. Mattson is under a nurse's care.

"The ransom definitely was not paid, although the doctor made many attempts to pay it. The kidnaper was too yellow to come out of his hiding to obtain the money.

"Charles has been dead a long time—probably between three days and a week. When I identified his body today, the blood on his face was black and frozen.

"The kidnaper communicated three times with Dr. Mattson by mail and telephone, but no effort was made to trace the letters or calls for fear of endangering the safety of Charles.

"The kidnaper has said that he feared extreme pain in his big legs and shortness of breath early today. Reliable sources stated that his discomfort continued until 3 a.m., when doctors' treatment calmed him. He was reported later to be sleeping while a doctor rested within call in an antechamber."

(Copyright, 1937.)

Strike Report Goes to Lewis

Martin Visits Chief of C.I.O. Today

By Clifford A. Prevost

WASHINGTON, Jan. 11—The meeting between leaders in the automobile strike and John L. Lewis, chairman of the Committee for Industrial Organization, concerning the next step in the walkout in General Motors Corp. plants will be held here at 11 a.m. tomorrow.

Originally scheduled for tonight, the conference was canceled when Lewis, his immediate advisers, and Edward F. McGrady, assistant secretary of labor, had gathered at the offices of Labor's Nonpartisan League in the Willard Hotel.

Lewis declined comment tonight on the nature of the conference with Martin and Brophy, but it generally was believed that the automobile workers officials are hopeful of advising President Roosevelt of the strike situation from the White House that the President is ready to step into the controversy.

Lewis Declines Comment

Airliner Is Missing with Nine Aboard

MEXICO CITY, Jan. 11—(A.P.)—The Mexican Aviation Co. announced tonight that a transport plane carrying six passengers and a crew of three was missing between Mexico City and Minatitlan, in Vera Cruz state.

The plane, an eight-passenger Lockheed-Electra, was last reported by radio at 10:17 a.m. Prominent among the passengers was Hugh Edward Buckingham, lubrication engineer of the Aguila Oil Co. and son-in-law of Guillermo Renwow, head of the company's sales department. The others were Miles Lingstrom, Swedish general manager of a match company, and a woman.

Pope's Breathing Again Hampered

VATICAN CITY, Jan. 12—(Tuesday)—(A.P.)—Pope Pius suffered a recurrence of extreme pain in his legs and shortness of breath early today. Reliable sources stated that his discomfort continued until 3 a.m., when doctors' treatment calmed him. He was reported later to be sleeping while a doctor rested within call in an antechamber.

An official note issued Monday by the Vatican said that the Pope, favored by an improvement in his condition, has been increasing his activities.

Spider in Safe 20 Years

ROCHESTER, N. Y., Jan. 11—(A.P.)—A spider, J. H. Egerle reported, walked out of his safe today when it was opened for the first time in 20 years. Egerle said the safe was airtight.

Feb. 12, 1937:

UAW strikers march from three General Motors plants after a 44-day strike.

THE WEATHER — Cloudy Friday and Saturday; rising temperature on Friday

The Detroit Free Press

FINAL EDITION

Friday, February 12, 1937. 106th Year. No. 284 — On Guard for Over a Century — 30 Pages — Three Cents

Three Flint Plants Are Evacuated by Cheering Workers

G. M. ORDERS BIG PRODUCTION AND BOOSTS PAY $25,000,000

Milling Throngs Celebrate as Peace Comes to Flint

CROWDS CHEERING SIT-DOWNERS AS THEY LEFT CHEVROLET PLANT NO. 4 LAST NIGHT

Union Parades from Plants in the Celebration

5,000 Join Strikers in a Gay March Around City

By Allen Tenny

FLINT, Feb. 11—Jubilant strikers marched from three General Motors plants late Thursday with all the fanfare of Armistice Day 1918.

Peace had come at last to strike-vexed Flint.

The strikers came out in the most dramatic incident of the forty-four-day-old strife between the General Motors Corp. and the United Automobile Workers of America, more dramatic even than the tension that accompanied their determination to stay in, more dramatic than the court room scenes when they were ordered out.

They came out one plant at a time—first from Fisher No. 1, then Chevrolet No. 4, then Fisher No. 2. It was all over in an hour and a half.

5,000 Join March

Five thousand persons, in automobiles and on foot, accompanied the strikers from Fisher No. 1 on a march through the city's main street and to the Chevrolet plant. A sound car filled with union officials led the way. Flags, horns, toy balloons and confetti were passed out at the factory gates.

The flags and balloons contrasted vividly in the clubs, brickbats and blackjacks that had waved in the hands of mobs at some previous demonstrations in this strike. But this was a festival, not a disturbance.

The climax came on Chevrolet Ave., between Chevrolet Plant No. 4 and Fisher No. 2 stand on opposite sides of the street, with the Flint River flowing between.

Militia Stands Back

As Chevrolet Ave. began to fill, a handful of National Guardsmen drew back quietly and allowed the crowd to pass. Military passes were no longer needed to enter the area. The guardsmen gathered in a small group at the south end of the bridge over the river, just below the plant. A few minutes later they were gone.

As the crowd grew, a sound car arrived at the head of a long procession of honking, flag-carrying automobiles. It stopped in front of Chevrolet No. 4.

There the sit-downers, who had emerged from the plant, were packed tightly on the steps leading to the front high water. Speakers in the sound car applauded them.

By this time, 10,000 persons and scores of cars had jammed into the street. Night had fallen, but the brilliant flares of the newsreel cameramen made an artificial day above the river.

Please Turn to Page 2—Column 4

End of Strike to Bring Renewed Operations in 17 Plants by Tuesday

By Clarence McConnell

Wheels of many industries here and elsewhere in the nation will accelerate Friday, the goods of commerce will move more swiftly in hundreds of channels and the stress of individual uncertainty will disappear as one of the major payroll and production units of industry throws off its strike-born lethargy.

Actual operation of the 17 General Motors Corp. plants closed by the strike will not begin until Monday or Tuesday, but the positive prospect of their activity is enough to restore trade and the security of thousands to an even keel.

The scale on which the closed or impeded channels of commerce will begin to flow is revealed in the corporation's statement that its March production schedule calls for 225,000 automobiles. With this will come $25,000,000 in wage increases and a $25,000,000 expenditure for materials—$50,000,000 that will spread outward to reach out to bulwark the prosperity of uncounted thousands.

The amount was disclosed Thursday by Alfred P. Sloan, president of the corporation.

Arrangements were completed to start collective-bargaining conferences Tuesday on union demands for wage increases and changes in working conditions.

Homer Martin, United Automobile Workers' president, and other union officials flew to Flint to lead sit-in strikers out of three plants and participate in a peace parade.

Murphy Is Given Wide Praise

Meanwhile, management and union united in praising Gov. Murphy for his success as industrial peacemaker. President Roosevelt sent the Governor a telegram of congratulation. Scores of leaders in business, government and union circles did likewise.

Gov. Murphy and Dewey signed as mediators and then took the agreement to the Hotel Statler, where the bed-ridden Lewis affixed his signature.

The agreement covered the extent of recognition which General Motors would extend to the U. A. W. This was amplified in a good faith letter from Knudsen to the Governor which said:

"We will not bargain with or enter into agreements with any other union or representative of employees of plants on strike in respect to such matters of general corporate policy as referred to in letter of January fourth, without first submitting to you the facts of the situation and gaining from you the sanction of any such contemplated procedure as being justified by law, equity or justice towards the group of employees so represented."

Knudsen epitomized the situation in this way:

"There is no crowing on either side. What we think is most important is to get people back to work and get the plants running again, because you know that when a big machine is stopped you have to monkey with the flywheel a bit before you get it going again. That flywheel has got to be tolerant. There must be a desire for peace and no animosity on either side."

Conference of U. A. W. Is Called

At the same time, Martin announced that he had called representatives of every General Motors local of the U. A. W. to Detroit for a conference at 10 a. m. Friday.

Representatives will present their demands to the U. A. W. Board of Strategy, which in turn will present them to General Motors in the bargaining conferences.

Their negotiators will include Wyndham Mortimer, U. A. W. vice president, and Lee Pressman, counsel for the John L. Lewis Committee for Industrial Organization, who signed the settlement agreement.

That instrument was signed in behalf of the corporation by Knudsen, John Thomas Smith, general counsel, and Donaldson Brown, finance chief.

Letter of Knudsen Pledges Good Faith

Please Turn to Page 2—Column 8

Canadiens Hand Wings Second Defeat of Week

By Doc Holst

MONTREAL, Feb. 11 — When Jack Adams reaches Detroit late Friday afternoon he will rush right up to a statue of Abraham Lincoln and demand from the nearest policeman that he hang both Lincoln and Jeff Davis to the nearest sour apple tree.

Mr. Adams' Red Wings took the eve of Abraham Lincoln's birthday to equal their only losing streak of the season, a very tiny one. It's true, but if you know Mr. Adams he cannot stand a losing streak no matter how tiny and woe it may be.

The Canadiens beat the Wings, 5 to 2, for the Flying Frenchmen's fourth straight triumph over the Stanley Cup champions. It was only the second time this season that the Wings have been defeated twice in a row and no other club in the League has such an astounding record, including the club that vanquished them tonight.

Back in December those cold and cruel statistics disclosed that the Americans and the Chicago Blackhawks beat the Red Wings

Please Turn to First Sport Page

Start the Day Right with the Free Press

	Page
Alden, Ruth	16
Chatterbox	13
Collyer, Bert E.	21
Crossword Puzzle	26
Culbertson on Bridge	26
Foreign News	9
Financial	22
Good Morning	6
Guest, Edgar A.	6
Hillis, Marjorie	15
Iffy the Dopester	17
Manhattan	26
Obituaries	26
Radio Programs	16
Screen	14
Second Guess	13
Society	12
State News	10
Theater	6
Ward to the Wise	20
Washington News	8
What's Doing Today	8

Fascists Cross Valencia Road

Madrid Lifeline Cut 12 Miles to South

(By the Associated Press)

Fascist insurgent cavalry Thursday night swept across the Jarama River and the Madrid-Valencia Road toward an important junction of supply roads southeast of the Spanish capital, the Associated Press correspondent with the Fascists reported.

Airplane bombers, artillery and hard-riding Moorish horsemen took part in the devastating attack in which the Fascists said that the Socialist militiamen were driven from their trenches with heavy loss of life.

The advance carried the Fascists to near Arganda, 12 miles southeast of Madrid, where byways east of the capital join the Valencia Road.

Moors Lead Advance

As the militiamen retreated under the bombardment of Fascist planes and guns, Moorish cavalrymen, shooting from their saddles, splashed through the rain-swollen Jarama River.

Plunging up the heights on the enemy side, the horsemen cut a path for the infantrymen and poured into trenches newly abandoned by the militiamen.

Official statements in Madrid have not admitted that the Fascists control the Madrid-Valencia highway.

Meanwhile, Madrid's Socialist defenders, pushing through a hail of shells and bullets, shook their foothold on the city's western edge Thursday, the Military Defense Council announced.

Sloan's Decree Increasing Pay in G. M. Plants

Alfred P. Sloan, Jr., president of the General Motors Corp., issued the following statement Thursday in his announcement of the General Motors wage increase:

"In view of the corporation's expressed policy of maintaining at all times the highest justifiable wage scale, and in harmony with other increases that have just been made in the automobile industry, it will again increase wages five cents per hour in all plants in the United States now in operation, as of Feb. 15, 1937, and in all plants not now in operation, at such time as same may be reopened. Detailed announcement will be made on an individual plant basis.

It will be recalled that on Nov. 9 an increase also was granted. The total increase in wages to be disbursed on a normal yearly basis as the result of the proposed new increases now being put into effect, will be $25,000,000. November and February increases together, on the same basis, will amount to approximately $55,000,000. The corporation's average wage rate, giving weight to the above increase, will be approximately 25 per cent in excess of the highest prevailing in the predepression period.

Roosevelt Fails to Gain Norris' Help on Court

WASHINGTON, Feb. 11—President Roosevelt failed today in an effort to gain the support of Senator George W. Norris, seventy-five-year-old Nebraska independent and usually an Administration supporter, in his battle to force adoption of the plan to force retirement of Supreme Court justices who are 70 years old or above.

Senator Norris was one of several senators whom the President summoned to the White House today to discuss the Roosevelt bill, which would authorize him to increase the Court's membership by 15 by adding one justice for each one 70 or over who declines to retire, thus bringing about a majority of justices in accord with New Deal policies.

"I think the President's plan is bad," the veteran Nebraska senator said after an hour's conference with Mr. Roosevelt, pointing to several "dangers" in the proposal. He said he would not support it unless it proved to be "the only remedy left" to make possible economic and social legislation such as the New Deal favors.

Suggests Some Alterations

"And there are lots of legislative remedies we can pursue, as well as constitutional amendments," he explained. Among them, he suggested:

1—A constitutional amendment limiting the tenure of Supreme Court and other Federal judges, instead of appointing them for life. The term of office would be determined by years, instead of age.

2—An act of Congress providing that a mere majority of the Court could not declare a law unconstitutional.

Norris, listed as a Republican until the last campaign but now one of the most ardent backers of New Deal legislation. So highly has Mr. Roosevelt valued his services that he supported him for re-election, as an Independent, in last year's election as the Democratic candidate.

Although Senator Norris was five years beyond the seventy-year age limit that Mr. Roosevelt advocates for judges—and will be 81 years old when his present six-year-term expires—the President urged Nebraska's voters to keep Norris in the Senate as long as he lives, "whether he wants to or not."

Holds Precedent Is Bad

"It seems to me that giving the President power to increase the Supreme Court is a dangerous precedent," Norris commented today. "Another Congress might come along and increase the court again, until it's as big as the House of Representatives."

Please Turn to Page 8—Column 4

Steel Men Given $5-Per-Day Pact

PITTSBURGH, Feb. 11—(A. P.)—Management representatives of the Carnegie-Illinois Steel Corp., joined late today with employee representatives of 18 district mills in approving a general increase of 8¢ cents a day and establishment of a $5-a-day wage minimum.

The two groups, making up the Pittsburgh District Council and representing 50,000 of Carnegie-Illinois' 100,000 workers, also approved a forty-hour work week.

Under the company-sponsored representation plan, the raise will become binding after adoption at individual plants by employee representatives and management.

Please Turn to Page 9—Column 1

Amelia to Blaze Equatorial Route

NEW YORK, Feb. 11—(A. P.)—Amelia Earhart Putnam, conqueror of both the Atlantic and Pacific Oceans, announced tonight a new air venture — an East-to-West globe-girdling flight "as close to the equator as I can make it."

She said that the 27,000-mile flight would be started, after more than a year of planning, from Oakland, Calif., in March. Capt. Harry Manning, hero of many ocean rescues, will accompany the woman pilot on a part of the flight as navigator.

Close Call for Hurja

SAN FRANCISCO, Feb. 11—(A. P.)—Emil J. Hurja, of Michigan, political adviser and aide to Postmaster General James A. Farley, disclosed here today that he had bought a ticket for use on the United Air liner which crashed into the bay here Tuesday night killing 11 persons, but that friends prevailed upon him to remain in Los Angeles.

TONIGHT--FREE PRESS GOLDEN GLOVES SEMI-FINALS at NAVAL ARMORY
2 RINGS --- 32 FAST BOUTS --- SEATS 25c, 55c, 85c --- BE SURE TO COME!

MARCH 25, 1937:

Because of the number of strikes underway in Detroit, some believed that a revolution was starting.

"Detroit Is All Right" and other stories.

THE WEATHER
Snow and colder Thursday; cold, snow flurries on Friday.

The Detroit Free Press

FINAL EDITION

Thursday, March 25, 1937. 106th Year. No. 325 — On Guard for Over a Century — 30 Pages — Three Cents

Lewis Calls Strikers Out of Chrysler Plants; Talks Will Continue Today After Evacuation

18 Are Killed in Blazing Bus After Blowout

Roller-Skating Group Caught in Inferno in Illinois

Newlyweds Injured; Three Others Hurt

SALEM, Ill., March 24—(A.P.)—A tire blowout hurled a private bus against a concrete bridge abutment and turned it into a blazing wreck in which 18 persons, including a four-year-old girl, were killed today.

Only five persons survived one of the worst bus disasters in history and two of them were so seriously injured that they may die.

The bus, loaded with a professional roller-skating troupe, en route from St. Louis to Cincinnati, was going down a slight grade when its right front tire blew out about 50 feet from the bridge, two miles west of here.

The heavy machine careened crazily, dug into the soft shoulder of the highway and rammed the abutment. Hurled on its side, the bus burst into flames when its gasoline tank was smashed.

Bus Appears to Explode

"The survivors said that the bus appeared to explode and then there was fire all over and all were caught in it," reported Dr. H. L. Logan, of the Salem Community Hospital, where the injured were taken.

"I can still hear my pals' screams of terror," Don Flanery, of Kansas City, a professional roller skater, said. "They were trapped in a mass of fire. The boys as well as the girls were hysterical."

Flanery managed to crawl out of a window, but he suffered first-degree burns when he attempted to rescue Miss Ruth Hill, of Kansas City, his fiancee.

At the hospital, attendants quoted him:

"She called to me twice. I finally found her. I tried to pull her out, but she was pinned and I couldn't move her."

The attendants reported that he wept as he asked, "I did the best I could for her, didn't I?"

Four Others Escape

Dick Thomas, of Chicago, the driver; his bride, Mrs. Emily Thomas; John L. (Schoolboy) Creekmore, of Miami, Fla., and Ted Mullen, of Portland, Ore., also escaped.

Dr. Logan said that Mrs. Thomas and Mullen had slight chance to live.

The flames, which mounted 40 feet, turned the bus into a funeral pyre for those trapped. The bus smoldered for more than an hour.

Please Turn to Page 11—Column 8

Clipper Reaches Pago-Pago Port

PAGO-PAGO, American Samoa, March 25—(A. P.)—(Thursday)—(Via Pan-American Airways Radio)—The Pan-American clipper, pioneering a commercial airline from California to New Zealand, landed here today at 5:30 p. m. (11:30 p. m. Detroit time), only one flight removed from its destination.

The 1,546 miles from the Ting Kingman Reef was negotiated in seven hours and 51 minutes. The big flying boat passed through a variety of weather, cruising most of the time at 7,000 feet, where alternate headwinds, tailwinds, squalls and clear skies were encountered.

Start the Day Right with the Free Press

Big Snowstorm Crossing State Toward Detroit

A blinding winter snowstorm which crippled traffic in Western Michigan Wednesday afternoon and threatened to close schools was expected to moderate before striking Detroit early Thursday.

Heavy snows were expected before dawn, following a freezing rain which began in the afternoon and fell to a depth of two-tenths of an inch before midnight, accompanied by a fall in temperature from around 33 degrees at 6 p. m. to an unofficial mark of 20 degrees at midnight.

Sleet was blamed for intermittent failure of hydro power in Windsor after 9:45 p. m., when the whole city was thrown into darkness and street cars were tied up at intervals, while crews of linemen sought to repair the breaks.

Storms Sweep Over U. S.

At least two deaths were reported as storms—dust, hail, rain, snow and wind—swept 11 states in the South and Midwest. In Kentucky, a tornado lashed the outskirts of Winchester, injuring at least 30 persons. The two deaths were from a tornado which struck in Alabama.

In Detroit, 17 traffic accidents in five hours were blamed by police on icy windshields.

All air traffic was grounded at the Detroit City Airport after 4 p. m. Shortly before that time two westbound planes reached the airport. Their schedules farther west were canceled.

Radio Program Halted

The Windsor power break cut off a speech by Senator Hugo L. Black, supporting President Roosevelt's Supreme Court proposal, over Station CKLW at 10:20 p. m. Later the station used auxiliary battery power to put on the East-West Golden Gloves Tournament from Chicago, at 11 p. m.

Homes in Windsor were in darkness and street lights were out, but traffic through the Detroit & Canada and Michigan Central tunnels was not affected, as both have recourse to Detroit Edison service. Telephone service was not affected.

O. M. Perry, manager of the electric power division of the Windsor Utilities Commission, said that the power failure was due to breaks in the 26,000-volt power lines between the Essex County Substation and Windsor. Service was restored before midnight.

Please Turn to Page 11—Column 3

Kid McCoy Given Complete Pardon

Ex-Prizefighter Will Consider Stage

Kid McCoy, famous old-time prizefighter, said Wednesday night that he had received full pardon from San Quentin Prison, to which he was sentenced for 24 years in 1925 for the murder of his sweetheart. The fighter, who was paroled in 1934 to Harry Bennett, of the Ford Motor Co., consistently had denied his guilt.

McCoy, whose real name is Norman Selby, served seven years for the slaying of Mrs. Teresa Mors and the wounding of two other persons in Los Angeles 11 years ago.

"You can't realize what a yoke this takes from my neck," McCoy said. "It means a new life for me."

Immediately after receiving the information, McCoy wired Philadelphia Jack O'Brien, entertainment promoter, that he would accept a twenty-week contract at $1,500 a week for a vaudeville act. He had discussed the engagement with O'Brien two weeks ago, he said.

Girls' Easter Dreams Wrecked by the Law

NEW YORK, March 24—(A. P.)—Four little girls sobbed tonight in juvenile-detention headquarters—their dreams of finery for the Easter parade wrecked on the hard rock of police charges that they had stolen more than 100 purses from baby carriages in recent days.

Lieut. Detective Patrick O'Neil said that the girls, all 12 years old, had confessed that they watched for baby carriages in which shopping mothers had left purses. More than 100 purses were found in the girls' homes, O'Neil said, together with much small change.

When arrested the girls already had embarked on their Easter shopping.

Misstep Is Fatal

DUSTON, England, March 24—[illegible] Harrison, 8[illegible] years old, died as the result of putting both feet in the same trouser leg, an inquest disclosed today. Harrison fell and broke his thigh. Pneumonia set in,

Tests Disclose Sale of Diluted Drugs to City

Half-Dozen Lots of Hospital Supplies Found Faulty

State and U.S. Asked to Launch Inquiries

Adulterated drugs in "considerable quantities" have been sold to the City and used by Receiving Hospital, it was revealed Wednesday by Commissioner William M. Walker, Jr., of the Department of Purchases.

Walker made known the results of a series of tests conducted by the Department of Health and by the Detroit Testing Laboratories and said that he had appealed to both State and Federal authorities for further investigation.

Sixty or more drugs have been tested, Walker said, and sealed samples have been retained of a half-dozen purchases which fail to conform to the United States pharmacopeia or the City's specifications.

Nearly 50 Per Cent Off Standard

Chloroform liniment, sold to the City by the Frank W. Kerr Co., was found by the Detroit Testing Laboratories to have a chloroform content of 23.8 grams per 100 c. c., whereas there should have been 40 to 45 grams. The Laboratory memo to Walker said:

"This does not conform to U. S. P. XI requirements."

Another preparation known as cresolis liquor, described as a disinfectant, sold to the City by Century Chemical Products, revealed a 20 per cent cresol content when 50 per cent was specified.

A tincture of belladonna leaves tested well over the minimum for alkaloidal content but was found to be deficient in alcohol. The sample contained 36.9 per cent by volume although 65 to 70 per cent was specified.

A preparation described as "Medicine Formula No. 21", sold to the City by the Hammond Chemical Co., was analyzed by Fred E. DeVoist, senior chemist of the Department of Health.

One Ingredient Lacking

DeVoist reported to Walker that "his sample does not conform in that no ethyl morphine hydrochloride was found." One-quarter of a gram of this ingredient should have been present, it was said.

Redistilled mercury revealed traces of dirt, attributed to the mercury having been placed in an unclean container, and wide variation was reported by the chemists in temagami balsam tablets.

Requesting the aid of E. J. Parr, State director of drugs and medicines, Walker urged a thorough sifting by local, State and Federal agencies.

"It is evident," Walker said, "that the most generous view of this situation requires me to state that there is a carelessness in manufacture or control that is culpable.

Please Turn to Page 5—Column 1

After Eight Hours, a Truce

JOHN L. LEWIS — GOV. MURPHY — WALTER P. CHRYSLER

Fists of Envoys Fly as London Parley Totters

LONDON, March 24—(A. P.)—An angry clash in which the Italian and Russian members almost came to blows gave the European Neutrality Committee's long-sought ban on foreign intervention in Spain an inauspicious send-off tonight.

In a tumultous meeting, delegates of the 27 nations comprising the committee settled the last details of a land and sea cordon around Spain which Europe hopes will isolate the civil war.

Appointment of 16 key administrators to supervise the international patrols left only the last step, the date for the scheme to become fully operative, to be decided by Admiral M. H. van Dulm, Dutch general administrator of the arms-and-men embargo, and his aides.

The swift action of the "hands-off-Spain" committee, however, failed to allay fear that speeches yesterday by Premier Benito Mussolini and Count Dino Grandi, Italian ambassador to London presaged new Italian efforts to help the Spanish insurgents. The committee's spurt of action was believed inspired by open Italian assertions that Italians now fighting

Please Turn to Page 2—Column 1

Detroit Is All Right

DETROIT is a City on a hill. Ever since it became the cradle of the motor car industry it has been the cynosure of the world

Historians, sociologists, economists, engineers, magazine and newspaper writers, from all the nations of the earth, have been pouring in here to study Detroit, the dynamic, for the past 25 years.

This City has been hailed as the precursor of a new age, the pioneer in a mechanized civilization.

But there is a penalty to leadership.

Let us be magnanimous enough not to suggest that it is jealousy on the part of other municipalities, but in recent years every minor incident that can be distorted into a black eye for Detroit has gotten front page treatment in the other newspapers of the Country.

Newspapers and magazines from all over the United States poured men into Detroit Tuesday to report "the Revolution." Headlines blazed on the front pages of the metropolitan and country press alike across the land.

In an effort to offset this propaganda of disaster, Malcolm W. Bingay, editorial director of The Free Press, sent to the editors of the Nation, through the Associated Press, a statement Tuesday night following the peaceful gathering on Cadillac Square. It was given wide publicity in many papers. The wire follows:

> Stories and rumors floating over the Nation that there is a "revolution" starting in Detroit are as unfounded as any to the effect that Harry Lauder bought a round of drinks.
>
> The demonstration on Cadillac Square was far more orderly than the celebration of the Detroit Tigers winning the World Series—and only about one-tenth in size.

This is a young man's town, and spring is in the air.

Revolutions don't start in a City that pays the highest standard of wages of any town in the Nation.

Walter Chrysler and John Lewis—who both speak and understand the same language—will have an eyebrow lifting contest out at Lansing with Gov. Murphy, who also is quite an "eyebrow," and the controversy will be over, just as the General Motors affair was settled.

As Iffy the Dopester says in Wednesday's Free Press.

"Old Iffy ain't worrying much about any revolution in this Country when the lads who want to raise hell have difficulty finding parking space for their cars before they start their demonstrations."

There was not one violent word or action in all the two hours of the crowd's gathering. More than half the 50,000—more or less—people who gathered in Cadillac (not Red) Square, were sightseeing, out to enjoy whatever fun there might be.

If every City in the Republic was as safe and sound in its Americanism as is Detroit this would be a fine Country.

Quit hiding under the beds and don't believe the wild yarns about us. Detroit led you out of the depression and we will continue to head the parade back to prosperity.

Don't mistake vibrant, and sometimes all too ardent, youth for Communism,

1,000 Checker Cab Drivers Quit Their Wheels in Strike

Union Sends Roving Crews to Halt Taxis; Three Auto-Parts Sit-Downs Settled

A strike of approximately 1,000 drivers of Checker taxicabs was called at 11:15 p. m. Wednesday by John Lewis, chairman of the Strike Committee of the Metropolitan Chauffeurs Association.

Immediately after the strike was called roving committees were dispatched throughout the city to notify drivers and order them to attend a meeting in the Hoffman Building.

Cabs passing the building on Woodward Ave. were halted by the drivers, and the police riot squad was sent to the scene to maintain order.

Other Strikes Settled

Earlier Wednesday, two Detroit strikes, one of them affecting six plants, were settled and another was called and settled in a General Motors plant. One management imposed a lockout to forestall a threatened strike, and a strike was called by 75 employees of the Polish Daily News, 1550 E. Canfield Ave.

The cab drivers' strike committee headed by Lewis included Milton Simonds, Don Guthrie, Leo Madigan, Fred Richards and Joe Charbonneau.

The exact number of drivers who had joined the strike could not be determined at an early hour Thursday. Many of the drivers were in outlying sections and had not learned of the strike.

William Lamson, business agent for the union; the Rev. Benjamin Jay Bush, D. D., of the Governor's mediation committee, and Nicholas J. Rothe, attorney for the union, visited Udo F. Andres, president of the Checker Cab Co., in his office shortly after 5 p. m. They gave him a copy of the union demands, then left.

Lamson said that he had been given no answer by the management, and was going to report to the union meeting.

Andres said that he did not believe that the union represented the majority of the 1,000 drivers employed by his company, nor had any considerable strength.

Confers with Board

Earlier Andres had conferred for an hour with the Rev. Father Frederick J. Siedenburg, Dr. Bush and Rabbi Leon Fram, of the mediation committee; Police Commissioner Heinrich A. Pickert and Sergt. John G. Callahan, of the police Motor Vehicle Squad.

Lamson and Rothe had gone to the Hotel Book-Cadillac, but Andres refused to confer with them. After an hour's conference behind closed doors, Father Siedenburg told the union men that Andres had refused to meet with them.

"He says that you do not represent his employees and that he will not deal with you," the priest reported.

"However, he says that you have never approached him directly at his office and that you can find him there if you like."

Meeting Efforts Fail

The visit to Andres' office then was made. Previous efforts to arrange a negotiations meeting had been through the State labor board and the company attorney, Edward N. Barnard, Lamson said.

At the 5 p. m. union board meeting it was asserted that a driver had been fired for union activity after the Book-Cadillac conference. The company maintains that the drivers dismissed were fired for inefficiency or for driving fares with the meter off.

Members of the committee explained that they were empowered to call a strike without another vote of the general membership.

In a telegram sent Andres Tuesday, the union asked immediate

Please Turn to Page 11—Column 6

Ontario Repeals Tax for Schools

Act to Aid Catholics Called Unworkable

TORONTO, March 24—(Canadian Press)—The Ontario Legislature, in what was believed the stormiest session in its history, voted unanimously tonight to repeal separate school-tax legislation passed in 1936.

The 1936 legislation granted a greater share of corporation taxes to Ontario's Roman Catholic schools—called separate schools in contrast with the public school system.

Premier Mitchell Hepburn, in announcing acceptance of a Conservative bill to repeal the legislation, declared:

"So far as the act itself is concerned I say it has been a failure * * *.

"It is my responsibility at whatever the cost to forestall the possibility of a religious war in this province."

Immediately after outlining his position, the Premier moved for closure to end the debate.

Leopold, Macauley, Conservative, protested so loudly and lengthily in defiance of Speaker Norman Hipel that he was ejected by the sergeant-at-arms.

Please Turn to Page 11—Column 4

Second Detroiter Dead in Collision

LANSING, March 24—Eugene Buhrer, 31 years old, of 2704 Sixth St., Detroit, died in a Lansing hospital Wednesday of injuries suffered in a head-on collision of two trucks and trailers in Lansing Tuesday morning.

Another Detroit man, Perry K. Pooler, 33, died about two hours after the crash. Hospital attendants said that Jack Neuschaefer, 34, also of Detroit, probably would recover from injuries received in the accident. Buhrer was riding in a truck driven by Neuschaefer and Pooler was driving the other truck.

An inquest will be held when Neuschaefer recovers sufficiently to testify,

Union Chiefs to Present Truce Terms to 6,000 Who Occupy Factories

Heads of C. I. O. and Corporation Clear Way for Parley After Conference with Murphy

By Clarence McConnell

LANSING, March 24—Six thousand sit-down strikers are to evacuate eight Chrysler Corp. plants in Detroit immediately under terms of a three-part agreement which was arranged Wednesday evening by Gov. Murphy.

John L. Lewis, militant union leader; Walter P. Chrysler, chairman of the automobile corporation which bears his name, and the Governor were parties to the pact which was made after eight hours of negotiating in the State Capitol.

It was provided that strike-settlement negotiations would be resumed at 10 a. m. Thursday and would continue until an accord had been reached on collective bargaining.

There is a provision in the agreement that, while negotiations are in progress, no manufacturing operations will be attempted and no effort will be made to move tools, dies and equipment away from the struck plants.

In addition, there is a bit of good news for those of the 60,000 idle strikers who are in need of immediate cash. It was provided that payroll clerks would be permitted immediate entry to the striker-occupied administration building so that arrangements could be made to disburse $2,000,000 in payrolls delayed because the management has been unable to get to the records.

All executives, plant officials and their staffs, office help, plant police, maintenance men and engineering-department employees likewise are to be given immediate entry to the plants.

President Roosevelt called Murphy from Warm Springs, Ga., to congratulate him on the news that the strikers would evacuate the plants.

Martin Leaves Lansing

Homer Martin, U. A. W. president, and a corps of his associates left Lansing immediately to go to Detroit and present their report to the strikers.

They expected to reach their headquarters in the Hofman Building about midnight and go to the Dodge main plant, the principal center of strike activity, about 1 a. m. Thursday.

When Lewis was asked whether he expected the strikers to comply immediately with the agreement, he said that he did not care to reply.

Because of the lateness of the hour when the union officials would report to the strikers, it was considered likely that the evacuation would take until 10 a. m. Thursday to complete.

Gov. Murphy smiled broadly when he invited nearly 100 newspaper men into his executive offices for the formal announcement.

Stands Between Them

Lewis stood at his right and Chrysler at his left, with a score of corporation officials and union officers in the background, while the terms of agreement were read.

When pressed for further details, B. E. Hutchinson, corporation spokesman, said:

"The agreement speaks for itself."

Richard T. Frankensteen, former Chrysler employee who is now organization director of the U. A. W., nodded and smiled while the formalities were performed.

He and Martin then rented a bus to take the large union delegation back to Detroit.

Lewis' agreement to the immediate evacuation of the plants, after they had been held 15 days by U. A. W. militants, was interpreted as another feather in the cap of Gov. Murphy.

Insists on Obedience

Chrysler had insisted on union compliance with the terms of court orders which called for the vacation of plants by the 6,000.

In fact, he declined to enter into negotiations looking toward a compromise agreement. Enforcement of the law, he had pointed out, was a subject for discussion between the Governor and union officials.

Please Turn to Page 11—Column 1

Murphy Letter to the Chrysler Sit-In Strikers

LANSING, March 24—Gov. Murphy Wednesday night addressed the following letter to the United Automobile Workers:

As you are aware, the conference arranged by me between Mr. Walter P. Chrysler and Mr. John L. Lewis to ascertain whether the controversy between the Chrysler Corp. and the United Automobile Workers Union might be amicably adjusted is now in progress. In the event the plants are vacated the conference will be continued tomorrow morning and until a conclusion has been reached on collective bargaining.

In the meantime, I have requested that the Chrysler plants be immediately evacuated, and Mr. Lewis and his associates have agreed to this suggestion. I have been advised by Mr. Chrysler that while these negotiations are in progress, manufacturing operations will not be resumed in the Chrysler plants, and no tools, dies or machinery will be moved from any of the Chrysler plants.

In view of these circumstances, there would seem to be no reason why the men now in the plants should not be withdrawn at once, and all executives and their staffs, all plant officials and staffs, all office help, all plant protection (plant police), all maintenance men, engineering-executive heads and heads of departments and their staffs, receiving clerks, payroll clerks, timekeepers, janitors, cooks and waiters, have free and uninterrupted access to the Chrysler plants and offices. It is suggested, therefore, that appropriate steps to accomplish these objects be taken at once by the proper officials of the United Automobile Workers Union.

Rights of Pedestrian Affirmed in a Verdict

INDIANAPOLIS, March 24—(A.P.)—An Indianapolis pedestrian's right to the right of way over an automobile has been affirmed by the Appellate Court.

The court upheld a Circuit Court decision allowing $2,500 damages to Miss Catherine Lucid for injuries received when a motorist failed to stop to permit her to complete the crossing of a street intersection after the sudden change of a traffic signal.

The damages were awarded against Virgil Stinebaugh, assistant superintendent of Indianapolis schools.

General Lee Demoted on New Postal Stamp

WASHINGTON, March 24—(A. P.)—Postal officials discovered with some chagrin and more amusement tonight that they had demoted Robert E. Lee from general to lieutenant colonel.

Soon after the Postoffice Department issued a new stamp honoring the Confederate general, a newspaper stamp editor pointed out that the likeness of Lee had only two stars on the coat collar. A Confederate general should have three stars and a wreath, the editor contended.

Norman Davis Departs for World Sugar Parley

NEW YORK, March 24—(A.P.)—Ambassador-at-Large Norman Davis, sailing today on the United States liner Manhattan for the International Sugar Conference April 5 in London, said that he would seek adoption of measures regulating world sugar production and export along lines followed by the United States.

Ambassador Davis, accompanied by the Philippine delegate, Senator Felipe Buencamino, and a corps of technical advisers, said that stabilization of the sugar industry would not be possible [illegible] agreement were reached within two or three weeks for limitation of imports and exports."

MAY 27, 1937:

Walter Reuther, later to head the UAW, is among four organizers beaten in what becomes known as the Battle of the Overpass.

The Detroit Free Press

THE WEATHER — Mostly cloudy, cooler Thursday; warm Friday; probable showers

Thursday, May 27, 1937. 107th Year. No. 23 — On Guard for Over a Century — 30 Pages — Three Cents

PUBLIC LIBRARY FINAL 1937 EDITION

Doctors Optimistic Over Cochrane as Concussion Eases

Danger Still Lurks in Sinus Infection

Wife at His Bedside; Bump Hadley Tries Vainly to See Him

Mike to Play Again, One Physician Says

NEW YORK, May 26—Mickey Cochrane, who suffered a fractured skull when he was hit by a pitched ball in the Tiger-Yankee game yesterday, was reported slightly improved by doctors following a consultation tonight at St. Elizabeth's Hospital.

Although he still is in a serious condition for five more days, the three doctors attending the Detroit Tigers' catcher and manager were a little more optimistic than heretofore.

"Signs of cerebral concussion have diminished," the bulletin said. "The possibility of infection and secondary meningitis is still present."

Three Sign Bulletin

The bulletin was signed by Dr. Robert E. Walsh, club physician of the New York Yankees; Dr. Byron Stookey, of the Neurological Institute, and Dr. Alexander Nicoll, house physician at St. Elizabeth's.

Cochrane was felled by a ball thrown by Yankee Pitcher Bump Hadley in the fifth inning of yesterday's game. He was moved to the hospital, last night.

Dr. Stookey, asked if Cochrane would be able to play ball, said, "Sure, he's going to play."

He would not say whether "Iron Mike" would be able to return to the Tigers as a player this year, however.

Dr. Walsh was less optimistic. "Whether he will play ball in the future," the Yankee doctor declared, "I am concerned with saving his life."

Depends on Response

He added that different types respond to such injuries in different ways.

Mrs. Cochrane, who flew here to be with her husband, said that the catcher seemed much clearer tonight, and that he still had his team in mind.

"We lost today," he told her. She nodded and he asked, "Very badly?"

"No," she replied, "not so badly." (The Tigers were beaten, 7 to 0.)

Mickey asked his wife to spend the night in the room across the hall from his. She had stayed there last night after her flight from Detroit.

Consultation Held

Dr. Walsh held a consultation in the morning with Drs. Nicoll and Stookey. Later a bulletin was issued saying that Mickey had a fracture of the skull and mild cerebral concussions. The fracture, the bulletin admitted unfortunately into the sinus area causing the physicians to consider the possibility of an infection and operation. Thus far, it added, there has been no sign of infection.

The physicians reported to the Detroit Club that Cochrane had sustained a quadruple fracture of the skull, the most dangerous being the one that extended into the sinus area.

Coach Cy Perkins, who remained with Mickey most of yesterday and last night, said that Cochrane was conscious much of the time and seemed inclined to joke about his condition.

Hadley visited the hospital last night in the hope that he might be able to see the patient. But all visitors except Perkins and Arthur T. Sheahan, representatives of the club, were denied entrance to the room.

Tries Again in Vain

Hadley went back to the hospital today, but again was unable to see Mickey because the physicians had ordered absolute quiet for him.

"Gee, I wouldn't think of harming anybody, and last of all Mickey," said Bump disconsolately.

Please Turn to Page 2—Column 7

Al Smith Visits Pope at Palace; Two Trade Gifts

CASTEL GANDOLFO, Italy, May 26—(A.P.)—Pope Pius welcomed Alfred E. Smith to his summer palace today as a "stalwart American citizen and a true Catholic."

The Holy Father, speaking in Italian, talked to Smith privately for half an hour with Bishop Ralph L. Hayes, rector of the American College in Rome, as translator.

The former Governor of New York later presented Mrs. Smith and gave the Pope a ten-inch gold copy of the Empire State Building, made by a New York jeweler. The Pope gave a Good Shepherd Medal for both of them and a pearl rosary to Mrs. Smith.

The Holy Father also autographed a photograph bearing the words, written in Latin, "Blessing with all my heart."

Six in School Bitten by Dog

Spaniel Wanders In and Attacks Pupils

Six school children were bitten Wednesday by a spaniel that invaded the corridors of the Barbour Intermediate School, 4209 Seneca Ave. At the City pound it was said that the animal showed indications of rabies.

Entering from an open front door, the dog slashed at the six children and then scampered into a room where a class was in progress. Unaware that it was vicious, the teacher started to pet it, William B. Templeton, assistant principal, had seen one of the children bitten and ordered the room cleared.

The spaniel then was locked in the room until police arrived.

Those bitten were Louis Mielke, 15 years old, of 4439 Seminole Ave.; Pat Heiman, 15, of 5115 Burns Ave.; Carl Ward, 15, of 3832 Canton Ave.; Nancy Coffey, 15, of 4148 Seneca Ave., and George Husted, 14, of 1752 Canton Ave.

All were treated at Receiving Hospital and will be given the Pasteur treatment if the dog proves to be rabid.

Up to last Saturday, 2,570 persons had reported dogbites to the Department of Health since Jan. 1. Of the dogs involved, 76 proved rabid and as a result some 200 persons were subjected to Pasteur treatment. Besides these, about 400 others were bitten by stray dogs.

Pasteur treatment is given at Herman Kiefer Hospital and those taking it must appear there for 21 consecutive days.

Plow Wife Dead; Husband Is Held

WOODBURY, Tenn., May 26.—(A.P.)—Sheriff W. D. Davis, sixty-year-old farmer, was held on a first-degree murder charge today after his Cannon County neighbors had told Sheriff J. P. Smith that Davis had hitched his wife to a heavy plow and literally "drove her to death."

The woman, an undernourished hill wife of 44, died late Monday. A coroner's jury found that her death was the result of blood poisoning, probably resulting from an illegal operation.

The sheriff said Davis admitted that his wife had pulled a plow Friday and that she had been overcome by the heat while working in the fields.

Sooty Homing Pigeon Pops Out of Chimney

Sergt. George Miller, of Palmer Park Station, opened a flue in his home at 13460 Montcalm Ave. Wednesday afternoon and out popped a sooty pigeon.

On the leg of the bird was a band bearing the inscription "CRC 37-572." Miller washed the bird, fed it and put it in a nest in his garage.

Duke's Treatment by Church Is Hit

LONDON, May 27—(Thursday)—(A. P.)—A sharp protest that the Duke of Windsor was being treated too harshly by the Church of England over his marriage to Mrs. Wallis Warfield Simpson was voiced today in the Daily Express.

The article blamed church leaders for the present situation, emphasizing the lack of sympathy shown for Edward's friends who hold Government positions in the list of wedding guests.

Frightened by Roller; an Auto Runs Amok

Frightened when she saw a steam roller coming out of an alley, a woman driver lost control of her car Wednesday afternoon, the auto careening over the curb and crashing into the roller, police said.

Officers who placed a charge of driving without an operator's license against Mr. Elenore Oliver, 24 years old, of 9412 Richter Ave., said that she was going west on Warren Ave. near Twelfth St. when the mishap occurred.

Mrs. Oliver and Miss Bernice Smith, of 10923 Harvard Ave., operating the roller, were hurt slightly. Fred Cadette, of 10923 Harvard Ave., was operating the roller.

Trailer Called U. S. Cure for Housing Costs

Stout Offers to Drive Proof on Wheels to City Hall

Camping Regulations Will Get More Study

Extended discussion, featured by the statements of William B. Stout, research engineer, that trailers will help reduce the housing shortage, brought to a close Wednesday the Common Council public consideration of a proposed ordinance to regulate trailer camps.

The Council took the proposed ordinance under advisement, indicating that another hearing might be held next month.

Stout reported that a recent Purdue University survey showed a housing shortage in the United States of 500,000 homes.

Called 'Greatest Problem'

"The greatest single problem we're facing today is housing," he asserted. "There is a great shortage of housing, particularly for the people who aren't earning enough to buy homes at the prices for which they're now sold. The problem of the trailer manufacturer is to make permanent homes of trailers."

Stout said later that he would invite members of the Council to have lunch with him in his three-room collapsible trailer to demonstrate his point. And if the Council couldn't go to his Dearborn laboratories, he added, he would drive his trailer to the City Hall for their convenience.

Statement Corrected

Recent statements he had made to the effect that 40 per cent of trailer purchases were for permanent homes has been corrected by magazine writers who estimate the figure at 80 per cent, he said.

The average person who buys a trailer does so not because he wants to live in it because of economic conditions which prohibit him from buying a fixed dwelling, he asserted.

Principal objection to the ordinance was the provision limiting the time for which trailer owners might remain camping to 90 days.

Asks for Leniency

Arthur Sherman, president of the Covered Wagon Co. of Mt. Clemens, said he would oppose any restrictive legislation with the plea to "give us a chance to work out our destiny."

Mrs. Harold Rohrbach, 14030 Maddelein Ave., the most outspoken critic of unregulated trailer camps urged the removal of a camp near Gratiot Ave. and Seven Mile Road because of alleged unsanitary conditions.

Benjamin Robinson, attorney for a group interested in construction of a camp at the foot of S. Lakewood Ave., said that plans proposed provided even greater sanitary protection than contemplated in the City ordinance.

Councilman George Engel, a resident of S. Lakewood Ave., observed, however, that 500 cars a day would create a dust nuisance because of unpaved streets.

Broker, Hurt in Manila, Flown to San Francisco

SAN FRANCISCO, May 26.—(A.P.)—Hurried across the Pacific by Clipper plane, George Sumers, New York broker, was taken to a hospital here today for treatment of fractured vertebrae suffered in an automobile accident in Manila.

Sumers was accompanied by a nurse and by Richard Berlin, of New York, executive director of the Hearst magazines. Berlin suffered a rib fracture.

Airmen Fly a Fur-Lined Hut to Soviet North Pole Colony

Three Planes, Bearing Eight Tons of Supplies, Land Safely After 560-Mile Hop

MOSCOW, May 27—(Thursday)—The four airplanes of the Soviet Union's North Pole expedition were safely down early today, victorious and carrying eight tons of supplies to the advance party which had started on the pack ice from Rudolph Island, 560 miles from the pole, late Tuesday to carry eight tons of supplies to the advance party were reported safe after one had been missing nearly 24 hours.

The missing plane, piloted by the veteran flier I. P. Mazuruk, made a satisfactory landing about 35 miles from the pole, the expedition's leader, Prof. Otto J. Schmidt, told Soviet leaders in Moscow in brief radio messages.

First of the supply planes, with Vasily Molokoff at the controls, located the advance party easily and came down alongside the following the marks placed the day before by Pilot Mikhail Vodopyanoff and 11 others over the pole and landed them near it the pole.

The second plane, that of A. D. Alexieff, overshot the goal and came down about 12 miles from the pole.

The expedition now is confronted with the task of assembling the aircraft and landing and storing the supplies for the base which will remain as close to the pole as possible for a year.

Four men are to remain in that base for a year's scientific research under the leadership of the country's pioneer flier Ivan D. Papanin. The supply planes were carrying a special portable fur-lined hut, a year's food supply and scientific supplies.

House Votes to Bring Back the Old Saloon

Bill Also Would Spell Doom of Michigan's Beer Gardens

Increase in Age Limit to 21 Is Sought, Too

LANSING, May 26—In its first general revision of State liquor-control laws since repeal, the House tonight voted 70 to 20 to return to the old-time saloon and eliminate the present-day beer garden.

The measure, involving sweeping amendments to a Senate bill, still must win concurrence of the upper house before it is ready for the Governor's signature.

Major changes are as follows:

Elimination of beer gardens after 1938, and limitation of license to taverns selling beer and wine to Class C licensees selling spirits as well.

Authorization for standup bars, through elimination of the requirement that drinkers be seated.

Lift Age Limit to 21

Raising the age limit to 21 years, with penalties for any person who misrepresents his age.

Limiting club licenses to establishments two years old.

Establishing a forty-cent-a-gallon tax barrier against wine from other states, with a thirty-eight-cent Michigan exemption if the winery pays $50 a ton for Michigan grapes.

Retaliation excluding the beer of any state which discriminates against Michigan beer.

Elimination of the $1,200 annual-profit limit for specially designated distributors.

An increase in State stores from 97 to 200.

Vote Hamtramck Relief

Provision for relicensing Hamtramck's 28 over-the-quota establishments by lowering the population ratio to one license for each 650 persons.

Statewide 2 a. m. closing, with Sunday closing hours fixed at 2 a. m. to Sunday midnight.

Representatives who voted against the revision were Rapes, Charles P. Adams, Barto, Carter, Courier, Decker, Eaton, Faulkner, Hallwood, Herrick, Knox, Lee, Leonard, Post, Steele, Swain, and Tureman.

Sen. Murray Van Wagoner, of Grand Rapids, led a futile fight for statewide sales by the glass, with a local-option provision permitting communities, by referendum, to suspend all licenses. It lost, 55 to 40.

The House rescinded votes to substitute the auditor general for the governor as an ex-officio member of the liquor commission.

Fear that additional Michigan taxation might expose the State government to public disfavor led to a Federal income tax till the House to rescind its action Wednesday night after once having incorporated a three per cent codes on manufacturing distillers. The House reconsidered and eliminated the levy at night.

For months, representatives of the Federal Internal Revenue Department have been collecting data on the profits of the Liquor Commission as taxable under the Federal income tax, although no definite move has been made to collect.

Michigan liquor profits would have been subjected to the highest rate of Federal taxation because they aggregate about $10,000,000 annually.

The House amended the bill to eliminate the provision for "appeal" to the commission from a local governing body's failure to recommend a license.

Paris-Tokio Fliers Hurt in Nippon Coast Landing

TOKIO, May 26—(A. P.)—The Japanese (Domei) News Agency reported today that the French aviators Marcel Doret and Francois Micheletti made a forced landing along the Tobasu coast in Kochi prefecture at 7:30 p. m. tonight (6:30 Detroit time). Both were injured slightly. They were attempting a Paris-Tokio flight.

A. of L. Charters Union to Compete in Auto Plants

WASHINGTON, May 26.—The American Federation of Labor Wednesday eased craft lines in its automobile unions in order to come to grips directly with the C. I. O.

Please Turn to Page 2—Column 6

Husband Who Forgot Is Introduced to Wife

NEW YORK, May 26—(A. P.)—Adolph Renke, 28 years old, asked to be introduced to his wife when they appeared in Federal Court today to plead guilty to a charge of conspiracy to defraud the Government by a spurious marriage.

"Is that lady my wife?" he asked an attendant. He explained that he had not seen her since the wedding three years ago, and didn't remember what she looked like. Renke, an alien, obtained a preferential visa as the husband of an American citizen soon after marrying.

Severe Drought Grips Seven States in West

WASHINGTON, May 26—(A. P.)—The Weather Bureau reported serious drought today in parts of seven Western states.

The western third of the Dakotas and Nebraska, much of eastern Montana, the eastern half of Wyoming, parts of eastern Colorado and western Kansas were affected.

Elsewhere in the country weather generally was favorable to farm work and crop growth, the bureau said.

U.A.W. Organizers Are Beaten and Thrown Off Ford Property; 80,000 Called Out in Steel Strike

C. I. O. Union Hits the Independents

Picketing Under Way at Big Plants in Five States

Republic Corp. Says It Will 'Stay Closed'

YOUNGSTOWN, O., May 26—(A.P.)—A strike went into effect late tonight at plants of three major independent steel producers in five states. Approximately 80,-000 men were affected. Picketing was under way.

Leaders of the Steel Workers organizing Committee, a C. I. O. affiliate, ordered the strike to back up their demand for signed bargaining contracts with Republic Steel Corp., Inland Steel Corp. and the Youngstown Sheet & Tube Co.

The walkout applied to 34 plants located in Ohio, Illinois, Pennsylvania, Indiana and New York. Their aggregate steel production, about 10,000,000 tons, represents approximately 16 per cent of the industry's total output.

Philip Murray, of the organization which won an agreement from United States Steel Corp. said he had difficulty in its effort to obtain signed contracts from the independents, said:

"It is the purpose of our organization to conduct the strike peacefully and in a law-abiding way." Murray disclosed that two leaders of the walkout had informed unless had advised today's meeting that on what action these unions might take to assist the steel workers.

Firm Sends Letters

Advised of the action, Republic Steel Corp., in letters to its employees, insisted, that signing of a contract would "be merely the first step toward a later demand for the closed shop and the check-off."

Republic's chairman of the board, Tom Girdler, has expressed himself outspokenly on the question of unionism. He said that Republic would "shut down its plants and keep them shut" if picketing kept workers away.

Youngstown Sheet & Tube, previously indicated that it would take action similar to Republic's. Republic employs about 55,000 men and Sheet & Tube about 18,-000 men. Part of the Republic employees are in the Birmingham (Ala.) area, which was not included in today's W. O. C. action. Murray said that S. W. D. L. leaders would meet tomorrow at Birmingham to consider action in that district.

No Trouble in State

No labor difficulties were reported at the Republic's Michigan plants. In Detroit, the corporation owns the Truscon Steel Co. at Caniff Ave. and the Grand Trunk Railroad. In Ferndale it owns the Steel and Tubes, Inc.

At Monroe, 450 men went to work on the midnight shift at Newton Steel Co.

Police Take Educator Back

THOMAS E. ELDER — A.P. Wirephoto

Dr. Elder, former prep school dean, is shown at Alton, N. H., being taken to Massachusetts on a charge of assault with intent to murder a former cashier of the school near the campus.

Arrest of Ex-Dean Reopens 'Prep School Murder Case'

Held in Shotgun Attack Near Campus Where Headmaster Died in 'Perfect Crime'

GREENFIELD, Mass., May 26—(A.P.)—Charges of attempting to kill a former colleague were lodged against a gray-haired former prep school dean tonight, and New England authorities reopened the famous "Public School Murder" of 1934.

The parallel between that attack on Norton and the death of Dr. Speer was twofold. Both cases were on or near the Mt. Hermon campus, established by the late evangelist, Dwight Moody. In each the weapon was a shotgun, loaded with No. 8 shot, the dignified retired dean of Mt. Hermon School for Boys at Northfield. He is charged with a shotgun assault with intent to kill the Rev. Elliott Speer, years ago teammate of Speer, and to the murder of Headmaster Speer.

Elder's arrest followed Norton's accusation that last night a man whom he identified as Elder stepped from the shadows, pulled a shotgun from beneath his coat and said:

"Norton, I want to see you." Norton said that he fled into the house and called the police. The search for Elder began at once, and ended today on Elder's farm near Alton, N. H.

Both Mysteries Baffling

And both are cloaked in a mystery as baffling as the one told in the book, "The Public School Murder," which threads its imaginative crime through the fabric of the murder of Headmaster Speer.

Speer, on the night of his death had been reading "The Public School Murder," and the book had traveled the rounds of the Mt. Hermon faculty.

His death was grimly reminiscent of the story which accounted the murder of a headmaster.

Speer was sitting in his study in the evening as his killer crept up along the macadam path outside, fired one charge through the open window, and fled leaving no clew. His arm and breast were blasted by a charge of double-O buckshot.

"Bring a tourniquet," murmured Speer as his wife reached him. He lived for 30 minutes later without saying whether he had recognized the assailant.

Mysterious, Too

The attack on Norton was equally mysterious. For one thing, Dr. Elder insisted that he had been in another state last night, naming a hotel at Keene, N. H.

Daniel E. O'Neil, proprietor of the hotel, said that Elder and his wife had been registered in the evening and left a call for 7 a. m. this morning. Elder said that he had not left the hotel room that night.

Dr. Elder, who worked his way through Mt. Hermon, spent the greater part of his life at the school. He was made dean in 1928 by Dr. Speer's predecessor, Headmaster Henry F. Cutler.

At the Northfield Inquest into Dr. Speer's death, Dr. Elder was a witness, but from all the testimony, amounting to 500,000 words, the only verdict was "death at the hands of a person unknown."

Most officials and residents of the school put the murder down as a perfect crime although Capt. John F. Stokes, chief of Massachusetts detectives who announced Norton's arrest, always insisted that some day the case would be solved.

Authorities admitted that they had a suspect under surveillance. They said, too, that the suspect had been a witness at the inquest. Of that total, 262 left the school at the Detroit end of the tunnel, 1,652 continued to the end of the line at Woodward Ave. and Fort St.

Wage Rate Is Set by Building Union

Figures Quoted for Detroit Projects

(From the Free Press Bureau)

WASHINGTON, May 26 — The Detroit Building Trades Union informed the Public Works Administration today of the rates which its members would demand on the Brewster and Parkside low-cost housing projects in Detroit, in the event that contracts are let early in June.

The rates quoted will apply to all building operations in Detroit after July 1. Ed Thal, secretary of the union, informed R. E. Kirkpatrick, chief mediator for PWA, that the rates varied from 70 cents an hour for teamster and chauffeur, to $1.50 an hour for electric-sign workers and plasterers.

Rates quoted cover 32 building trades. Thal also informed the PWA that the union would not discriminate against contractors from outside Detroit. Bids on the projects will be opened June 3 and June 8.

Detroit Tunnel Terminal Being Studied by Council

Whether the Detroit and Canada Tunnel Co. will have to establish its own bus terminal for unloading and discharging passengers may depend upon a report submitted to the Council Wednesday by Inspector Fred W. Juergens, director of traffic.

A recent survey, ordered by the Council, showed that 180 busses and street cars used the tunnel during a twelve-hour period carried 2,809 passengers.

Auto Union Seeks Labor Board Quiz

Agents of LaFollette Look On at Fight at Rouge Plant

Battle Follows Effort to Pass Out Leaflets

By Clarence McConnell

See Pictures on Back Page

In a fist-fighting melee four United Automobile Workers organizers were beaten severely and thrown off Ford Motor Co. property Wednesday after they had attempted to distribute union pamphlets among workers there.

Immediately union officials filed a formal complaint with the National Labor Relations Board, charging the company with intimidation, coercion and interference with the workers' constitutional rights.

"This is not going to discourage us in the least," said Richard T. Frankensteen, U. A. W. organization director, who with Walter P. Reuther, West Side Local president, bore the brunt of the attack.

First Aid, Then Complaint

After their numerous cuts and bruises had been treated by Dr. J. J. Rieg in his office, at 5696 W. Vernor Highway, the organizers went to union quarters to prepare the complaint.

Others injured were J. J. Kennedy and Robert Kanter, organizers.

The biggest argument that developed out of the affray was over the identity of the men who beat the U. A. W. Union organizers-men asserted that 25 of their own men were overwhelmed by 200 Ford service men.

This was denied by Harry Bennett, Ford personnel director. "They grabbed some of our workers when they were trying to enter the plant," said Bennett. "Meanwhile a group of women wearing union insignia taunted the men who were going to work, calling them slackers, cowards and other names.

Spoke of 'Slaves,' He Says

"When a Negro appeared they told him that 'Lincoln freed the slaves.'

"Most of the organizers' attention seemed to be directed toward the incoming shift rather than the outgoing force. When the workers declined to accept the union pamphlets the organizers thrust them into the air. Then the fight started among the workers and organizers.

"When the organizers moved onto company property or attempted to go through the gates they were thrown out. Orders had been issued that no service man was to leave the gates and I do not know of any who did."

On the other hand, union officials cited the arrest by Melvindale police of three men, two newspaper men charged that the arrested trio had chased them away from the riot.

Frankensteen and Reuther, following the battle, issued a joint statement describing their part in it. It reads:

"In order to clarify all rumors and conjectures, we wish to describe exactly our actions up to the time we were assaulted by Ford service men.

"When we arrived at the plant we were not carrying handbills. We got out of our cars and started walking toward the bridge. We presumed that the bridge was public property since it spans a public highway.

"As we walked up the stairs to the bridge none of the company men attempted to stop us, nor did they say anything to us. The only union members with us were J. J. Kennedy and Robert Kanter.

Please Turn to Page 2—Column 3

Crook Pays Tribute to Crookston's Ears

ALLIANCE, Neb., May 26—(U. P.)—The Nebraska town in Gus Malmberg's self-described career as a crook was Crookston, Neb. Malmberg said that he and fellow burglars, unable to open a heavy Crookston safe, rolled it out the door and let it coast down the sidewalk for three blocks. Gus rode on top of the safe yelling "whoopee," he said.

At the bottom of the hill the safe smashed into railroad tracks and rolled over. The burglars then took it apart.

"We didn't wake anybody up," Malmberg told the court. "Not even a dog barked."

Woman, 103, Losing Third Set of Teeth

GREENCASTLE, Ind., May 26 — The only regret that Aunt Mandy Stewart had today as she headed toward her 104th birthday was that about all of her third set of teeth had been pulled.

The Detroit Free Press

THE WEATHER — Thundershowers and cooler Thursday; partly cloudy Friday

Thursday, June 23, 1938. 108th Year. No. 50 — On Guard for Over a Century — 24 Pages — DETROIT FINAL EDITION — Three Cents

JUNE 23, 1938:

Joe Louis quickly disposes of Max Schmeling in a fight that takes on global significance with Hitler's Germany preparing for war.

Woolworth Heiress Believed Guarding Son from Husband

London Gossiping of a Marital Rift

Countess and Spouse Reported in Row over Child

Scotland Yard Detail Watches Over Baby

LONDON, June 22 — (U.P.) — Scotland Yard officials indicated tonight that a "domestic affair" involving Countess Barbara Haugwitz-Reventlow, five-and-ten-cent store heiress, and her mysteriously missing Danish husband, had been responsible for a kidnaping scare centering on their baby son Lance.

The handsome forty-three-year-old Count Haugwitz-Reventlow has been absent from London for some time, supposedly on the continent, but is expected to return soon.

The Daily Mail quoted the Count as having said, in a telephone interview from Paris, that sharp differences had arisen between him and the Countess regarding the education and upbringing of their son.

Denies Kidnaping Threat

The Count said, according to the newspaper, that British police were anxious to question him should he attempt to land on British soil, but he denied any threat or attempt to kidnap his son.

If he returns, he will find the sprawling Haugwitz-Reventlow London town house, second in splendor only to Buckingham Palace itself, heavily guarded and his two-year-old son surrounded by Scotland Yard and private guards.

They called me up and told me I could not get back to keep out of the country, but they will not, and can not."

The Daily Mail said:

"This is all being done to keep me out of the country, but they will not, and can not."

The Daily Mail told the Count it reports concerning differences between himself and the Countess regarding the future education of their son.

Determined to Return

"I have done nothing a gentleman would not do," he was reported as having said and reiterated his determination to arrive in England Thursday.

The reporter who interviewed him about the telephone repeatedly the conversation to the Countess, who then replied:

"Well, all I can say is that it is lucky Lance can't read newspapers."

The Daily Mail it is understood that a visit by the Countess to the Bow Street Court had been made in connection with an application on her behalf for a summons to obtain temporary custody of the child pending litigation. The summons was granted, it was added.

The newspaper said that it understood also that there had been certain disagreements between the Count and Countess on questions of finance.

Refuse to Discuss Order

Officials of Bow Street Court, where the Countess reportedly conferred in private with the Chief Magistrate late today, refused to discuss whether the Countess had obtained a legal order safeguarding her son. The child allegedly will be heir to the $40,000,000 Woolworth fortune.

Please Turn to Page 3—Column 4

Texas Jury Dooms Murderer of Boy

ALPINE, Tex., June 22 — (A.P.) — A jury was found guilty today of pushing thirteen-year-old Marvin Dale Noblitt to his death from a 400-foot cliff in a $5,000 insurance plot.

A shirt-sleeved jury deliberated less than 30 minutes before voting to send Black, a former University of Kansas student, to the electric chair. He had confessed the plot against the boy, asserting in Black's care for the lad's widowed mother, Mrs. Bobbie Smith.

In San Antonio, Black's confession said, a bicycle was bought for the Noblitt boy in the hope that he would be killed by an automobile. That failing, a vacation in the rugged Big Bend country was decided upon. The trip to the precipice followed.

Ann Arbor Press Loses Contract with U. of M.

ANN ARBOR, June 22 — The University of Michigan has canceled a contract of nearly $35,000 annually with the Ann Arbor Press, it was announced Wednesday by President Alexander G. Ruthven.

Beset by a strike of the International Typographical Union since May 19, the printing establishment in March received an ultimatum from the University Board of Regents to settle its labor difficulties or face loss of the contract.

A National Labor Relations Board hearing in Washington for the Ann Arbor Press was found guilty of unfair labor practices on four counts.

Pontiac Fed Up on 10 Per Cent Bank Auctions

Recalls Sacrifice of Values as Result of U.S. Sale

Experience Painful to Birmingham, Too

By Hub M. George

PONTIAC, June 22 — Pontiac and Birmingham have had enough of 10 per cent auctions of bank assets. The Free Press disclosure that such a sale has been considered for Detroit, with rich pickings in prospect for the auctioneers from the $75,000,000 of real estate and mortgage assets of the old First National Bank, stirred unpleasant memories here.

Detroit's fear of sacrificed values unfairly penalizing depositors and deflated community values, is just as imaginary, say those of experience in Pontiac.

Still of Same Opinion

And depositors in both Birmingham and the county seat, who come voluntarily by high-pressure salesmanship to desist in their open opposition to the sale, are pretty generally "of the same opinion still."

One permanent performance of the sale conducted by Auctioneer Ben Temple, Oct. 20 and 21, of from $250,000 to $300,000 of realty in a shift in the requirement of from 15 to 25 per cent in down payment, at a time when the FHA is pushing 90 per cent loans on new homes. Sales activity, which probably would be none too good in any event due to economic reverses, is almost negligible now, because so few prospective buyers can shift up the down payment. The shift in down payment requirement, it is noted, represents the exact measure of the auctioneer's commission.

Brain Children

Pressure liquidation and auction sales are the brain children of the so-called "10 per cent group" in the Comptroller's office. Those active in the Pontiac sale were Temple and Walker Adams, directors of his office. Temple's sale was distinct from receivership operations. He made all arrangements, handled all expenses, and collected commissions. In practice, it is difficult to understand that the expenses could equal 5 per cent, as claimed.

How eagerly the attractive commissions are sought for is well illustrated in Circuit Court records, where in at least one instance, Temple's commission was disputed and made subject to litigation.

In Hub of Business District

The home site of the old First National Bank, a three-story brick structure, on a corner opposite the courthouse, in the very hub of Pontiac business activity.

Temple's auction of this property produced one bid of $110,500, far below the value at which it was carried on the books, from J. H. Varon, identified with Pontiac affairs of the Metropolitan Life Insurance Co.

"All of our departments are operating."

"All assets are our own and doing business."

"Ninety per cent of the regular managers are on the job. The experienced and competent managers are filling the places of those not working."

Probe of Bombings

"The identity of the persons responsible for last night's bombing has not yet been ascertained. These acts of destruction are being thoroughly investigated to the end that the persons responsible may be apprehended and dealt with according to law."

"Our store managers are grateful to their many customers for their many expressions of helpfulness and for their loyal and continued patronage."

The strike was called by the Bakers Local 126 (A.F.L.), the Teamsters and Truckdrivers Union, A.F.L.) and the United Food Handlers Local 136 (C.I.O.). The company has 350 stores in Detroit.

Please Turn to Page 3—Column 1

Shirley Stops to Play, but Isn't Recognized

LAGRANGE, Ind., June 22 — (A.P.) — Two boys and a pup had a romp with Shirley Temple as the child movie star made a brief stop today while motoring East with her parents.

The two were Tommy Keenan, whose mother operates a filling station where Shirley's party stopped for gasoline, and David Fisher, son of Lieut. Ray Fisher of the State Police.

The boys were unaware of the identity of their playmate until told by her father, George Temple.

Showers to End Heat

The temperature Wednesday afternoon crept up to 87 degrees to tie the high mark set Tuesday, but the Weather Bureau promised cooler weather in the form of showers Wednesday night and Thursday.

Phone Call Saves 300 in Cloudburst

PILOT KNOB, Ore., June 22 — (A.P.) — Torrential rains and a cloudburst poured five feet of water through this town of 360 today, flooding all stores and practically every house.

No lives were lost.

Mane Nielson, a rancher, telephoned. "Run for your lives, there's a flood on the way!"

Within 30 minutes the town was empty.

Reports reaching here said another flood, outpouring down West Birch Creek toward the heart of the town.

12 Prisoners Swelter in a Stalled Elevator

Of all the people in Detroit those suffering most from the heat Wednesday left from the courthouse elevator being taken from the County Jail Building to the County Jail, when their elevator stalled between floors for more than an hour at noon.

Henry Sawyer, operator of the County Building, referred to the brake failed to catch at the proper level, but did catch and hold the car midway between the first floor and the basement. Electricians finally released Sawyer, the prisoners and Deputy Sheriff Roy Grant.

Bank Robbers Slip Past Trap Laid by Police

Two Victims Slugged in $4,285 Holdup at Flushing

Sixth Crime of Kind in Michigan in 1938

FLUSHING, Mich., June 22 — Michigan State police and Genesee County officers searched Michigan highways for three gunmen who clubbed a bank employee and a customer into unconsciousness and then escaped with $4,285 from the First State and Savings Bank of Flushing. It was Michigan's sixth bank holdup this year.

A highway blockade, maintained by police for several hours, was lifted Wednesday night when it became apparent that the bandit gang had slipped through the cordon of officers after fleeing from this village, eight miles northwest of Flint.

Escape in Sedan

The bandits made their getaway in a late model sedan which they had parked in front of the bank on Flushing's main street. Police were hindered by scanty descriptions of the men.

Bank officials said that the thugs had missed nearly $5,000 which lay in unlocked drawers. The loot included approximately $200 in silver with the remainder in paper money. Checks were not disturbed.

Michael B. Pajtas, twenty-seven-year-old assistant cashier, was alone in the bank when the three men entered. He told State Police that one gunman walked to the rear of the bank and asked him to change a $2 bill.

Then Pulls a Gun

When Pajtas proffered the change the bandit poked a pistol through the grill and declared: "This is a stickup." Pajtas was compelled to lie face down behind the counter while the thug opened an empty drawer.

While his two companions remained near the front entrance, the first bandit forced Pajtas to open the grilled door leading to the bank vault. He then walked into the vault and scooped up the money while Pajtas stood with hands upraised.

Again ordered to lie down on his face, Pajtas was complying when Fred Russell, 34, operator of a bus line between Flint and Flushing, entered the bank.

Two Step Behind Him

The two gunmen neared Russell, stepped behind him and shoved guns into his back, ordering him to lie on the floor. The third bandit, apparently believing that Russell was an officer since he wore a visored cap, struck the prone Pajtas on the back of the head with a gun butt.

Russell was slugged a moment later, the blow being somewhat deflected by his cap. Pajtas suffered a deep scalp wound and both men were knocked unconscious by the blows, although Russell said that he heard the scuffle of feet as the men left the bank. Pajtas was the first to recover and called sheriff's officers.

Two Thugs Described

Pajtas said that one man was about 30 years old, five feet 11 inches tall, and wore a light sport jacket and grey trousers. Another wore a grey suit, was 30 to 35 years old, six feet tall and weighed about 180 pounds. No description of the third bandit was obtained.

The previous bank robberies this year included one in which bandits took $3,100 after abducting an employee of the Metamora State Savings Bank on Jan. 8.

Other robbed banks and the amounts taken include the Yale State Savings Bank, on March 21, $1,839; Farmington State Bank, on March 24, $5,700; Bloomingdale Peoples State Bank, April 19, $1,838; and a branch of the Detroit Savings Bank, $7,685.

The bandits were captured and now are serving prison terms for more than half of the 1938 holdups.

Boy Braves Belle Isle Wilds to Conquer Nature in the Raw

He Takes Hammer and Tacks to Build Cabin, Ride Home with Police Irks Woodsman

A latter-day Tom Sawyer went home yesterday on a police scout car Wednesday. He was pretty indignant.

"A fellow can't even go off to live like an Indian without the police interfering," complained twelve-year-old Bill Ashmun.

His mother, Mrs. Vera Ashmun, of 2213 Ashland Ave., was the one who found Bill camping at the head of Belle Isle. The lad searched all night for him.

"We thought you had fallen in the river," Mrs. Ashmun said, inspecting one of her best lace curtains, taken along on Bill's expedition to serve as mosquito netting.

"Why, Mother?" Bill asked. "I know the woods like a book."

His mother continued her search of his equipment. She found a small hammer, some tacks and a hatchet.

"I was going to build a cabin with," Bill explained patiently. "Out of wood found on the spot."

Bill's father's expensive fishing tackle turned up next. Bill had intended to live on fish and herbs, he explained. There was a slab of beeswax to make waxed string, which always comes in handy in the wilds.

"Well," Bill expostulated when his mother looked at the knife disapprovingly. "You've got to be prepared. What if I had to kill a bear?"

Heat Fells Minister

OTTAWA, June 22 — (U.P.) — Charles Dunning, Canadian finance minister, collapsed late today because of overwork and the intense heat. His personal physician said that there was no cause for alarm.

Louis K.O's Schmeling in First, Flooring Maxie Three Times; Fight Lasts Only 2:04 Minutes

Roosevelt Icy to Kennedy for Aiming at Presidency

Special to Free Press and Chicago Tribune

WASHINGTON, June 22 — The chilling shadow of 1940 has fallen across the blooming friendship of President Roosevelt and his two-fisted trouble shooter, Joseph Patrick Kennedy, United States ambassador to Great Britain.

This was learned here from unimpeachable sources this afternoon on the heels of the long conversation between Mr. Roosevelt and the Ambassador in Hyde Park yesterday afternoon.

The conversation, it was learned, was carried on in a frigid atmosphere because Mr. Roosevelt has received positive evidence that Kennedy hopes to use the Court of St. James's as a stepping stone to the White House in 1940.

President Learns Secret

Copies of a secret circular, which Kennedy has been forwarding to selected Washington correspondents, have been relayed to the President. The circular, according to reports, contains information on the progress of British debt and trade negotiations which have not been reported to the State Department.

It was learned also that Kennedy has brought a prominent Washington correspondent to direct his presidential boom from London. It is not known whether the offer is being considered seriously, but its tender is considered as evidence of Kennedy's ambition.

These revelations were seen here today as explaining the change in the attitude of Administration leaders toward the red-haired ambassador in the last two months. White House intimates, who once hailed Kennedy as the only representative of big business to see eye to eye with the Administration, lately have taken to characterizing him as the soul of selfishness in foreign crisp with smiles.

A New Dealer Speaks

"Joe Kennedy never did anything without thinking of Joe Kennedy," a high Administration official said. "And that's the worst thing I can say about a father of nine kids. He's put them in an orphanage one by one to give Joe Kennedy more room in the White House."

Similar vehemence has been expressed in Administration quarters against everyone who has been mentioned as a possible successor to the President. Presidential friendship has withered wherever the White House appeared on the horizon.

The most notable example is Postmaster General James A. Farley, to whom, more than to any other man, Mr. Roosevelt owes his office. When genial Jim was mentioned as his successor for the President lost faith with his party leader and took to directing party affairs through his son James, Harry Hopkins, Thomas Corcoran and other intimates.

Says Majority Backs Him

The board said that 9,557 of the 12,860 eligible workers had signed cards designating Bridges' union as their exclusive representative in bargaining over wages, hours and other conditions of employment.

The decision represented a major victory for Bridges, Australian-born C.I.O. leader against whom deportation proceedings have been instituted on grounds that he is a member of the Communist Party.

The NLRB ruling covered one of the major points at dispute in the widespread West Coast maritime strike of 1934 when the long-shoremen, then members of the International Longshoremen's Association (A.F.L.) struck for a coastwide agreement.

The A.F.L. and the reorganized I.L.A. formed from dissenting members within the old I.L.A. brought home to the longshoremen that action which is not coastwide could only be a harmful setback to their self-organization.

"The history of bargaining among the longshoremen's organizations is a vivid portrayal of the experiences of the longshoremen, they learned that, since their employers were acting together on a coast basis, they, too, would have to build a coast organization with which to parallel the organization of the employers."

The board pointed out that the Wagner Act expressly provided it could fix an "employer unit" and that the "term included one or more associations of employers."

Youth Sought in Attack on Five-Year-Old Girl

Police Wednesday were looking for a youth who attacked a five-year-old girl in her yard near Dexter Blvd. and Grand Ave. at 3:30 p.m. He was described as 17 years old, five feet eight inches tall and weighing 140 pounds. The victim's mother went to the girl's scream. The girl was taken to Florence Crittenton Hospital.

Trainer Tosses In Towel to Halt Last Count at 8

Detroiter Avenges 1936 Knockout with Speediest Finish in Title History Before 80,000 Fans

By Alan Gould

(Pictures on Pages 13, 14 and 16)

NEW YORK, June 22 — (A.P.) — The Brown Bomber came back tonight, all the way back with an explosion that electrified the fight world and smashed Germany's Max Schmeling into a helpless, sprawling figure of defeat in less than one round.

Dusky Joe Louis waited two years to avenge the one and only defeat of his professional career, but then took little more than two minutes to achieve it under the Yankee Stadium's floodlights with a devastating blast that produced the quickest ending in pugilistic history to a world heavyweight championship match.

The 24-year-old former Detroit Free Press Golden Glover, knocked out in the same ring in 12 rounds by Schmeling in 1936, turned loose an attack of such suddenness and ferocity that the German never had a chance.

Beaten to the first punch by the Bomber's snake-like left, Schmeling was knocked down three times and so badly battered that his handlers threw in the towel in token of defeat as the timekeeper tolled the count of eight on the last knockdown.

The finish came after 2 minutes 4 seconds of the first round as a howling crowd of 80,000 on-lookers, thrilled by the Negro's spectacular rush to triumph, witnessed the most sensational heavyweight title finish since Jack Dempsey flattened Luis Angel Firpo at the Polo Grounds in September, 1923.

Even Faster Than Dempsey

Dempsey's memorable conquest came after 57 seconds of the second round, a total of only 3:57 of fighting time.

Schmeling, a picture of confidence beforehand and favored by many to regain the championship he lost three years ago, never had a chance. Louis, justifying his own prediction of a short finish, achieved it one round sooner than he expected, with a two-fisted onslaught that left the huge crowd as excited as Schmeling was dizzy after it was all over.

The champion took command on the first exchange, belted Schmeling unmercifully about the head, and quickly had the German in distress. Max was on the verge of going down with the first minute, but covered and hung grimly to the ropes, near his own corner, as he tried desperately to save himself.

Max Goes Down for Three

Finally forced into the open, Schmeling went down on his side with a rolling motion after being clipped with a hard right to the head. He was already so groggy that he took no heed of either the count or warning yells from his corner. He struggled to his feet, after only three seconds, only to meet another withering blast.

On the second knockdown, Schmeling sprawled on all fours, after Louis had fired both hands to his jaw. The German's eyes were glassy, his mouth open, but his courage somehow pulled him back to his feet, after a count of only one.

Please Turn to Page 6—Column 1

In a Nutshell

Louis took the offensive at the start and missed two short lefts as Schmeling crouched cautiously. Louis nailed Schmeling with a right to the ropes and smashed Max with rights and vicious lefts. Max shot over a short right that landed on the champ's jaw. A hard right staggered Schmeling and Louis piled in as Max leaned against the ropes. Louis followed in and measured him and Schmeling went down for a count of three. The stunned Teuton arose, stretched against the ropes, only to go down almost instantly with another hard left and right. But he was up after a count of one, only to be sprawled again with a terrific right to the jaw. As he lay almost in the center of the ring, dazed and half unconscious, with the count reaching eight, his handler, Max Machon, threw the towel into the ring and ended the fight. The knockout came at 2:04 of the first round.

Start the Day Right with the Free Press

Pages
Alden, Ruth 9
Around the Town 3
Chatterbox 8
Collyer, Bert E. 6
Comics 22
Crossword Puzzle 16
Editorial 6
Financial 19
Food News 15
Good Morning 6
Guest, Edgar A. 6
Iffy the Dopester 13
National Whirligig 6
Newton, Dr. Joseph Fort 9
Obituaries 21
Quillen, Robert 6
Radio Programs 16
Screen 17
Serial, "Forgotten Bride" 11
Society 8
State News 5
Vital Statistics 21
Ward to the Wise 6
Washington News 7

Paradise Valley Dances for Joy as Its Joe Wins

Wild-eyed with enthusiasm over the crushing victory of their own Joe Louis, and echoing expression for their joy in dancing, the residents of Paradise Valley Wednesday night staged an open-air celebration around St. Antoine and Beacon Sts.

St. Antoine was roped off for the celebration from Gratiot Ave. to Adams Ave., and Beacon St. was cleared from Hastings St. to Beaubien St. Traffic was rerouted from Madison Ave. between Beacon and Beaubien Sts.

Cheering, shouting, singing and above all dancing, a crowd estimated at 10,000 gaily cavorted in the streets after the fight, in the first organized demonstration since Louis has become world champion.

Everybody's Truckin'

Couples danced, old folks danced alone and with each other, men joined hands, girls joined, and even on top of a telephone pole two men joined in keeping perfect time with their bodies in the rhythm. Feet kept time, whole bodies kept time.

The music was played by a swing rhythm band under Cecil Lee which was mounted on a truck in front of the B. and C. Club. The tune they played steadily for 20 minutes, was entitled "Flatfoot Floogie with a Floy Floy." Where Lee dug up this piece he admitted — and a tune he said it spoke more than anything else, as an incentive to the dance.

Celebration Organized

The organized celebration was sponsored by Albert Pakeman, the first mayor of Paradise Valley, who thought it would be a good idea to get everyone together, rope off the streets and let them have their fun there. After some previous Joe Louis victories the celebrations have been a trifle out of hand.

Reuben Patton, present mayor, was in New York at the ringside. Pakeman said that there was not much betting because the boys had trouble finding anyone who wanted to bet on Schmeling.

As the radio loudspeaker started the broadcast of the fight, the noise subdued and all was tense. When Louis knocked down his opponent the first time there was a lot of noise, and when the knockout was announced, there was nothing but noise and everyone just cut loose.

It went on in the small hours of Thursday morning.

Roosevelt Icy to Kennedy for Aiming at Presidency

(see article above)

JOSEPH P. KENNEDY — Taking a vacation from his duties in London, Ambassador Kennedy went to Harvard as an alumnus Wednesday to join in commencement exercises. He's shown as he smiled at antics of old grads at a reunion frolic.

All West Coast in Single Union

NLRB Makes C.I.O. Sole Dock Unit

WASHINGTON, June 22 — (U.P.) — The National Labor Relations Board tonight overruled protests of the American Federation of Labor and certified Harry Bridges' International Longshoremen's and Warehousemen's Union as exclusive bargaining agent for 12,860 longshoremen in 21 Pacific Coast ports.

The board's action was unprecedented in that it established the first major geographical bargaining unit in certifying the I.L.W.U. as sole bargaining agent for all longshoremen who work for companies which belong to the following five employers' associations: Waterfront Employers of Seattle, of Portland, of San Francisco, and of Southern California and the Shipowners Association of the Pacific Coast.

G-Man's Spy Tale Held Up by Court

U.S. Protesting Use of 'Inside' Articles

NEW YORK, June 22 — (U.P.) — Federal authorities started action today to prevent publication of articles by Leon G. Turrou, former G-man, advertised as the "authentic inside story" of the indictment of 18 members of an alleged German spy ring.

Federal Judge Murray Hulbert signed an order late today directing the New York Post to show cause tomorrow why it should not be restrained from printing the articles, scheduled to begin tomorrow.

The order was obtained by Lamar Hardy, United States attorney here. Department of Justice officials in Washington said that they wanted to prevent publication of such confidential information. For many years a star agent of the Bureau of Investigation, Turrou spent four months investigating the espionage case. As soon as indictments were returned, he announced his resignation to write a series of articles.

Announcement that Turrou's story would begin tomorrow had been made today by Johanna Hofmann, twenty-six-year-old hairdresser on the German liner Europa, and three men pleaded innocent in Federal Court to espionage indictments against them and 14 others. Trial was set for Aug. 1.

Pending the outcome of tomorrow's hearing, the Post announced that it was withholding the articles. J. David Stern, publisher, accused the Government of a violating freedom of the press."

Better Business Note

Traffic-violation tickets issued so far this year number 170,646, an increase of 46,157 over the corresponding period of last year, the Police Department disclosed Wednesday.

Kroger Stores Being Guarded

Unionists Released in Bombing Probe

Police guards were placed at Kroger Grocery & Baking Co. stores in the city Wednesday by Deputy Superintendent Louis L. Berg to prevent recurrence of bombings which damaged six stores, three of them Kroger branches, within 15 minutes shortly after midnight.

Six unionists arrested after the bombings were released Wednesday by their attorneys, to appear in the office of Inspector George Hertel Thursday morning.

Five of them were members of a committee that last Tuesday warned Mayor Reading and police officials that there might be violence unless police guards were withdrawn from Kroger trucks.

Seen as Warnings

Police interpreted the bombings as warnings to five West side branches of the company to join a strike called June 14 over an alleged wage-cut plan.

The Kroger company issued the following statement:

The Detroit Free Press

JULY 8, 1938:

Michigan's long-standing ban on capital punishment does not affect executions of those convicted of federal crimes.

THE WEATHER: Showers Friday and possibly Saturday; not so warm Friday

Friday, July 8, 1938. 108th Year. No. 65. On Guard for Over a Century. 24 Pages. Three Cents

FINAL EDITION

Roosevelt Heading West to Begin His Party Purge Drive

Four Addresses Set for First Day

President Taking Bid to Use Influence in Hot Georgia Fight

Barkley to Get Boost in Covington Speech

WASHINGTON, July 7—(A.P.)—President Roosevelt left Washington tonight for one of the greatest campaign drives of his career—a transcontinental tour on behalf of his unfinished New Deal program and of New Deal candidates for office in the 1938 Democratic primaries.

Laboring all day at top speed, the President had his desk fairly clear of official business before his departure by special train at 10:35 p. m. (Detroit time).

The train carried next to the largest crowd whichever made a presidential cross-country tour. There were 80 persons aboard, including 27 newspapermen—three times as many as usually follow the President.

One major addition was made in his itinerary—an addition which will give him an opportunity, if he chooses to use it, to lay a finger of disapproval on the renomination campaign of Senator Walter F. George, Georgia Democrat.

Accepts Georgia Bid

He accepted an invitation of a delegation of Georgians, including Lawrence Camp, of Atlanta, who is in the race against George, to speak at Barnesville Aug. 11 "on any subject you may deem of interest to Georgians."

George has opposed the Administration on numerous occasions.

The Georgia speech will be made after Mr. Roosevelt has completed his swing across the Nation and has taken a leisurely cruise down the Pacific Coast, through the Panama Canal and back to Pensacola, Fla.

The occasion for the first address of the tour will be a celebration at Marietta, O., tomorrow of the 150th anniversary of the settling of the Northwest Territory. The President arrives at Marietta about 9 a. m. and leaves about 10:30 a. m. (Detroit time.) The time of the speech has not been announced definitely, but it will be broadcast nationally.

Will Boost Barkley

Later in the day, the President will drop down to Kentucky, where he is expected to leave voters in no uncertainty about his desire for renomination of Senator Alben W. Barkley, Democratic leader. He will make a major talk at Covington between 3:20 p. m. and 4:20 p. m. This address also will be broadcast nationally.

Please Turn to Page 4—Column 1

Four Girl Hikers Killed by a Train

NEW CASTLE, Pa., July 7—(U.P.)—Four girls were killed late today when struck by a passenger train as they walked along Pennsylvania Railroad tracks en route to a bathing beach.

Police reported that the girls, two of them sisters, stepped from one track to another to avoid a freight train and were struck from behind.

The dead, all of New Castle, were: Nellie Jaworski, 18 years; Helen Orabinic, 17; Lena D... 14 and Anna Deanko, 14.

Pet Parrot of Houdini an Escape Artist, Too

HOLLYWOOD, July 7—(U.P.)—Physical bonds never proved a barrier to the late Harry Houdini, nor do they mean a thing to Pat, Houdini's twenty-five-year-old parrot.

Pat, who has escaped from everything but a whale's tummy, picked the lock on his cage and tonight was flitting through the Hollywood hills screaming six choruses of "The Big Bad Wolf." Constant companion of Houdini during the entertainer's last days on the stage, Pat was taught to carry on long conversations with his master.

Dr. Millikin Is Treated in Mayo Clinic Hospital

ROCHESTER, Minn., July 7—(U.P.)—Dr. Robert A. Millikin, Nobel prize winner, physicist of the California Institute of Technology, was a patient in a Mayo Clinic hospital tonight receiving treatment for an abdominal ailment.

The scientist was transferred to Rochester from Bismarck, N. D. where previous to his illness he had been conducting cosmic ray research with use of balloons.

Heroic Cat Honored

ALBANY, July 7—(A.P.)—Whiskey, a Buffalo cat that dashed into a burning barn to rescue its kitten, has been awarded a certificate of merit by the American Humane Association.

Relief on Way After Mercury Hits High of 91

Cooler and Probable Local Showers Is Friday's Forecast

Throngs Seek Cool of Near-By Beaches

HOURLY TEMPERATURES
6 a. m. ... 72	5 p. m. ... 90
7 a. m. ... 76	6 p. m. ... 87
8 a. m. ... 79	7 p. m. ... 85
9 a. m. ... 82	8 p. m. ... 85
10 a. m. ... 82	9 p. m. ... 82
11 a. m. ... 81	10 p. m. ... 81
12 noon ... 88	11 p. m. ... 81
1 p. m. ... 89	12 midnight 80
2 p. m. ... 90	1 a. m. ... 79
3 p. m. ... 91	*2 a. m. ... 79
4 p. m. ... 91	
*Unofficial.

Detroit may expect relief from the current heat wave Friday, the United States Weather Bureau promised Thursday. Temperatures soared to 91 degrees Thursday afternoon, but the forecast was for cloudy skies Thursday night and Friday morning and lower temperature Friday afternoon.

Showers and local thunderstorms are probable, the bureau predicted.

Thursday's highest temperature, registered at 3 and 4 p. m., was only one degree below the season's record of 92 on June 24. From 1 to 6 p. m., the mercury fell four degrees to 87.

Thursday's heat sent the season's largest weekday crowds scurrying to the City's parks and bathing beaches.

John Ireland, Belle Isle zoo director, reported an unusually large crowd of bathers at Belle Isle and similar conditions existed at other recreation centers.

Family picnics were numerous in all parks as children and adults together deserted stuffy homes in the hopes of encountering an occasional breeze under protecting shade trees.

While swimming was by far the favorite diversion, bridle paths, tennis courts and boating docks also drew more than their usual week-day quota of recreation seekers.

Neighborhood sprinkling parties cooled off hundreds of perspiring children, and soda fountains in all sections of the city reported business of near-record proportions.

Seized in Indiana, Six Confess Theft

They Admit Robbing Salesman in City

Six men captured Thursday night by Indiana State Police in a stolen car driving to Chicago confessed, police say, that they bound and gagged Charles Schnoor, of New Baltimore, stole $27 from him and threw him out of his car in Detroit.

The autopsy allegedly death to natural causes, death following a lesion of the spinal cord which resulted in oedema of the brain. The son, who left for Chicago as soon as he heard this result, is reported to have been at odds with the Toronto magnate, at whose home Mrs. Sidley had been a guest for an indefinite term of years, over the question of his mother's residence there.

Mrs. Sidley's mother and her two brothers live under curious conditions in the same house at Racine, Wis., the mother and her one son on good terms, the other son estranged from them and confining himself to another part of the house.

Mrs. Sidley's body, released after the autopsy, is now on its way to Racine for burial. Meanwhile her death has revived rumors of high finance and black hand gang tactics.

Suit by Ex-Husband

In 1931, Mrs. Sidley's husband, who had been treasurer of the Horlick Malted Milk Co., gained settlement in the Chicago courts of a $250,000 damage suit against Perkins Bull.

Divorced from Mrs. Sidley, Dr. John Streeter Sidley charged that Perkins Bull was shadowing and molesting him and that his health was ruined by his divorced wife's attorney's action.

Before the settlement was reached, Perkins Bull, tall, bearded, imposing in appearance and in his dry cleaner on his home, had waited nine days, perplexed and upset when the postman did not show up, and finally had died. The dog refused food all the while and slept by the mail box in silence of visible... ... his kennel.

Dies in Toronto

MRS. MAYBELLE H. SIDLEY

Autopsy Made Upon Heiress

Mystery Involves the Horlick Family

Special to Free Press and Chicago Tribune
TORONTO, July 7—Toronto police have been ordered to investigate the death yesterday of Mrs. Maybelle Horlick Sidley, part heiress to the Horlick malted milk millions, who died after two days of illness at the country home of W. Perkins Bull, K.C., sixty-nine-year-old internationally known lawyer and financier.

An autopsy already has been performed on the insistence of the physicians who had attended Mrs. Sidley the two days preceding her death, and on permission given by her son, Dr. W. L. Robinson, of the Banting Institute, conducted the autopsy, with two other pathologists assisting.

Asked if the brain showed evidence of mental illness, Dr. Robinson said that it was impossible to learn of any through the autopsy, but that Dr. Eric Linell, another pathologist, would make a new examination of the brain within a week of 10 days.

Son Leaves for Chicago

Borah Put to Bed After Breakdown

WASHINGTON, July 7—(A.P.)—Senator William E. Borah, seventy-three-year-old dean of the Senate, was in bed today under a physician's orders to rest for a few days after a breakdown of his work.

Stricken Sunday, the Idaho Republican was ordered to bed and today was given no permission to care for him until the return of Mrs. Borah, who had been visiting in the West. She arrived this morning.

Aides said that the Senator's condition was not serious, but that he was tired from overwork.

Clock Strikes 526

OLNEY, Ill., July 7—(A.P.)—Richland County's temperamental courthouse clock went on another tolling spree today and broke its own record with 526 gongs before it returned to normal. Its previous record was 496 strokes, boomed out April 21.

$10 Bill Will Enable Little Louise to Live Out Summer Months

There is a dark and dreary basement in Detroit that is the only home that a ten-year-old Louise knows. Summer has come and 150 children are out at the Free Press Fresh Air Camp, playing in the sunshine, swimming in the sparkling waters, eating three healthful meals a day.

Weeks ago the Free Press Camp rolls were filled and, despite the plea of a case worker for the Children's Air Society, the Camp Director was forced to reject an application from Louise.

But now a physician has added his plea for the child. Unless she can have better air, better food and better surroundings, he says, she may not live through the summer.

It costs $10 today a child in camp through a full camp period. One $10 check or bill will send Louise there today. It is such a small amount when weighed against the life of a little girl that the Free Press is cheered by the feeling that somewhere in Detroit there is a reader who will help.

Deb Gowns Shock George VI's Court

Lord Chamberlain Expected to Take Measures

LONDON, July 7—(U.P.)—Mayfair buzzed with excited tales tonight of the "shocking" dresses some of the debutantes wore when presented to King George VI at last night's royal court. An edict was expected from the Lord Chamberlain suggesting that less skin and more modesty be shown.

Members of the court were "dumbfounded" when the debs made her curtsy in a dress resembling a beach costume with brassiere and skirt.

They were "horrified" when another girl paraded before His Majesty with a dress almost backless. Then they were "speechless" when yet a third debutante appeared in a gown with a Sixteenth Century square neckline cut lower than any seen in Buckingham Palace since Victorian days when women wore off-the-shoulder gowns.

There was evidence at tonight's presentation that the debutantes invited to court had received royal hint about décolleté gowns, as many had made last-minute additions to their low-cut costumes. At least seven of the debs, unable to arrange for new gowns, fell back on scarves, while others draped about their shoulders when they curtsied to the King.

Rear-Engined Ford Patented

Disalignment Trouble Believed Overcome

WASHINGTON, July 7—(A.P.)—A patent on a new type, rear-engined automobile has been granted to Henry Ford, the United States Patent Office revealed today.

Drawings submitted with the patent application show a compact arrangement of a V-type eight-cylinder motor, with transmission, differential and other mechanical parts assembled over the rear axle. This arrangement, it is claimed, will provide a more direct drive from engine to the wheels.

The argument for rear-engined vehicles has been that the driver will have an unobstructed view of the road and thus operate in the interest of additional safety. Ford said in his application that the past considerable difficulty had been experienced with all styling uses of this feature because of the various troubles in maintaining exact alignment between the various units of the assembly.

The Ford assembly, he said, will permit an appreciable amount of out-of-line displacement and still give good operation.

No indication was given whether Ford proposes to make the new type of car. Officials said that he had obtained many patents in recent years for radical changes in his car but has not always used them.

The Patent Office added that the new patent was similar to another rear-motor idea patented by Ford a year ago.

House for $1,050 Rises in a Hurry

Mayor Sees It Built in Three Days on Screen

Motion pictures of the construction of five-room houses that can be built in three days at a cost of $1,050 were shown in Mayor Reading's office Thursday afternoon by Capt. R. B. Lord, director of construction for the Farm Security Administration.

Capt. Lord appeared at the invitation of Henry E. Beyster, D.P.W. commissioner, who is interested in low-cost housing.

As the movies were shown, Capt. Lord explained that the Government has constructed many of the prefabricated dwellings and that experience in the construction had reduced the cost of the buildings from $1,600 to the present figure. The labor cost is $471.

Also Linn Trevoit, technical director of the Detroit Housing Commission and, Carl L. Bradt, secretary, also attended the showing.

Retired Minister, at 84, To Take Seventh Wife

COLUMBUS, O., July 7—(U.P.)—The Rev. Abner B. Welch, 84 years old, retired Manzeree minister, who is convinced that "every man who isn't married by the time he is 40 should serve five years in the penitentiary," was ready tonight for his seventh wedding.

Mr. Welch will marry Miss Kate Austin, seventy-one-year-old spinster, "next week."

He is the oldest and most-married man ever to apply for a license here.

Four of Mr. Welch's wives died. The other two marriages ended in divorce.

Nazis Cut Remarque Off Citizenship Rolls

BERLIN, July 7—(A.P.)—A decree published today disclosed that Erich Paul Remark, better known as Erich Maria Remarque, noted pacifist and author of the novels, "All Quiet on the Western Front" and "The Road Back," had been deprived of his German citizenship. Remark has been living in Switzerland since 1929.

Arabs Massing on Border for Palestine War

British Rush Warships and Soldiers After Four-Hour Battle

Strife to Be General, Jewish Leaders Fear

JERUSALEM, July 7—(A.P.)—Arab tribes from Transjordan were reported massed on the Palestine frontier tonight as Britain speeded warships and troops to smash the bloodiest Jewish-Arab race outbreak in the Holy Land's recent history.

Simultaneously Jewish leaders warned their people against being "drawn into civil war."

In a pitched battle lasting four hours, British troops fought a band of 600 Arabs said to have just crossed the border from Transjordan, east of Palestine and a part of Britain's League mandate but governed by a local Arab administration.

15 Arabs Are Casualties

Five Arabs were reported killed and eight wounded. There were no British casualties.

Total casualties for the week of rioting and battling were 33 killed and 111 wounded.

A number of Arabs were said to have succeeded in entering Palestine, however, and to have joined their comrade fighting in the hills for "Arab independence."

The tribesmen were said to be massing south of Tegart's Wall, the $500,000 electrified fence recently completed along the Syrian border, north of Palestine, to keep troublemakers out of the country.

Troops Called from Egypt

The news of Arab reinforcements was received as Britain ordered two battalions, each normally consisting of more than 800 men, from Egypt at "the earliest possible date."

Already at Haifa were the British cruisers Emerald and Enterprise, each of more than 7,500 tons. Both arrived as the result of an emergency call.

On the way was the mighty 33,000-ton cruiser Repulse, detached from its Mediterranean cruise and due at Malta to relieve the Emerald, whose homeward journey from the East Indies was interrupted by the summons for reinforcements.

Violence in Palestine continued despite a constant patrol by troops and police.

There were incidents in Jerusalem and Arab workers who lived in the latter city.

Force of 11,900 on Hand

The Jewish community, after an apprehensive survey of the situation, said through Moshe Shertok, general of the Jewish Agency, that the Jews would not "allow themselves to be drawn into the streets."

Officials of Town Quit in a Dudgeon

BUCKNER, Mo., July 7—(U.P.)—Buckner's Mayor, City Marshal, Police Judge and three of the city's four aldermen—fed up with what they considered unjustified criticism—quit today and conferred with an attorney about the legal method of resigning.

The last straw for the criticized officials was a Fourth of July incident. The Marshal said that some boys had been driving around town tossing firecrackers at pedestrians. They refused to heed his shouts, so he fired a shot into the pavement. The bullet ricocheted, struck one of the boys in the leg, and in the excitement another boy fell from the car and bruised himself.

Half the town of 520 rose in indignation, charging the Marshal with exceeding his authority, and demanded that the officials resign. Today the officials decided to do so.

Clemency Refused for Cash Kidnaper

Plea to Commute the Death Penalty Fails

TALLAHASSEE, Fla., July 7—(A.P.)—The Florida Pardon Board refused today to commute the sentence of "Franklin Pierce McCall for the ransom kidnaping of five-year-old James Bailey Cash Jr., at Princeton, Fla. May 29."

Its decision followed pleas by McCall's attorney for commutation and by his prosecutor that the death sentence be carried out. Earlier, the Cash child's mother had signed to join McCall, the kidnaper's widowed mother in a plea for mercy for her son.

More than 300 persons were injured by fireworks in Philadelphia over the Fourth of July weekend.

Chebatoris to Be Hanged at Dawn Today in Milan; Murphy's Plea Refused

Clubbers Sought in Slaying and Beating on Two Farms

State police joined with officers of Huron and Sanilac counties Thursday in a search for attackers who left one man dead and another injured seriously in two separate crimes committed on Thursday morning.

The body of Byron Henry, 53 years old, a hired man on the farm of Mrs. Arzle Parker, 23 miles northwest of Sandusky near the Tuscola-Sanilac line was found Thursday morning. He was dead from a fractured neck which have been inflicted by a blow.

The second victim was Arthur Fuhrwerk, 60, a Sigel Township farmer in Huron County, who was taken to a Bad Axe hospital with a concussion and fractured ribs.

Sheriff A. T. Campbell, of Sanilac County, said that Henry failed to return to the house shortly before midnight Wednesday after going out to investigate a car which he heard drive into a field away from Fuhrwerk's car. His employer and neighbor, Mrs. Nina Chase, searched for him, but were not able to find his body until Thursday morning. It lay 400 feet from the house in an uncultivated field. Deputies said that there were tire tracks near the body. An autopsy was held Thursday afternoon and the body was taken to Ann Arbor for further examination.

A neighbor, William Smith, found Fuhrwerk in a serious condition, tied to the twine in his barn Thursday morning. Fuhrwerk told Sheriff John A. Graham and Coroner George Milligan, of the State Police, that a stranger had clubbed him Wednesday night, and, after tying him in the barn, had driven away in Fuhrwerk's car.

Sheriff Graham reported that the stolen car was found abandoned in Centerline, Mich., but that papers, including $1,500 in Liberty Bonds belonging to Fuhrwerk, were still in the car where Fuhrwerk left them.

Lack of clues in both the handicapped officers in the investigation of the crimes, which occurred in the adjoining counties within a few hours.

Sentencing Judge Calls Penalty Just

Asserts He Wouldn't Change Site Even if He Could

Slayer Awaits Hour of Death on Gallows

The execution of Anthony Chebatoris will take place at dawn Friday, despite last-minute appeals of Gov. Murphy to the President.

Federal Judge Arthur J. Tuttle, who had passed sentence, announced this case to a qualified jury of five men and seven women, all good citizens of the State of Michigan," Judge Tuttle said in a formal statement. "On Oct. 26, 1937, that jury had the courage and wisdom to return the just verdict which directed that Chebatoris be punished by death.

"That just verdict having been returned, the law was mandatory in three respects, namely, that the penalty should be death, that it should be hanging, and that it should be within the State of Michigan. Those last two requirements resulted from the fact that Michigan has one statute providing the death penalty by hanging."

Explains Terms of Sentence

"That is the kind of lawful sentence I imposed on Nov. 30, 1937. If the sentence had been different in any one of those three respects, it would have been unlawful. When my discretion, I fixed the time of execution for July 8, 1938, in order that every right of the defendant might be fully protected.

"The term of court within which that sentence was imposed has expired. I have neither the power nor the inclination to change the sentence. If I did have the power to do so, I think it would be unwise to suggest that the people of a neighboring state are less humane than are the people of our own State of Michigan.

Sees Change as Affront

"It is not a matter for my discretion, but if it were, it would not be in good taste to select the territory of a neighbor for an unpleasant duty. The Federal Court in enforcing the Federal law is enforcing the law for an offense against the United States, committed in Michigan.

Please Turn to Page 4—Column 2

Malefactor Is Hunted; He Dodged Dog Tax

In a long-distance telephone call Thursday, Sheriff John Kennedy of Livingston County asked Chief of Detectives Henry W. Piel to run down a malefactor suspected of being in Detroit—one Ken Komlaski, 40, of Green Oak Township, who has paid no dog tax for two years. Kennedy has the warrant and will come and get Komlaski when found. Piel promised to throw out a police dragnet.

---

18 Hurt in Buying Rush

BERWICK, Pa., July 7—(A.P.)—Eighteen persons were injured, two seriously, in a bargain sale rush at a department store here today. The crush of bargain hunters in the eighteen-foot entrance broke ten windows.

Philadelphia Places Ban on Cargo of Fireworks

PHILADELPHIA, July 7—(A.P.)—Mayor S. Davis Wilson ordered municipal authorities today to prevent a Japanese steamer from unloading a cargo of $500,000 cargo of fireworks consigned for transshipment to Southern cities, from unloading in the port of Philadelphia.

Wife Dies at Doorbell

BOSTON, July 7—(U.P.)—Disturbed by persistent ringing of his doorbell today, Vito Steranzer opened the front door and his wife fell into his arms—dead. She died of a heart attack while pressing the bell, a doctor said.

BULLETIN

EL PASO, Tex., July 7—(A.P.)—The six-member Nevill expedition, overdue at Lees Ferry, Ariz., on its trip down the treacherous Colorado River, was reported sighted today by two Coast Guard pilots from El Paso.

Campaign Aim Is Safe Brakes

Police to Start Tests Monday Morning

A campaign for safe brakes on every car on Detroit's streets will be launched by the Police Department in co-operation with safety councils Monday, when brake tests will be given under police supervision on specially marked streets in three parts of the city.

The tests, which will continue through July 17, will be given on Clark Ave., between W. Vernor Highway and W. Lafayette Ave.; Fairview Ave. between Charlevoix St. and Goethe Ave., and on LaSalle Blvd. between Collingwood and Webb Ave.

The tests are not compulsory, according to Police Commissioner Heinrich A. Pickert, but it is hoped that motorists will take them.

"We are inviting every driver in Detroit and the suburbs to test his brakes," he said.

"No records will be kept of results and no demands will be made regarding repairs or adjustments. We are confident that no right-thinking citizen will have to be told to get his brakes adjusted if a test shows need for it.

"It is especially important at this time of year, when many children are playing in the streets."

Neither Michigan nor Detroit has laws prescribing safe stopping distances, Pickert said. Police have found, however, that for safe driving a car going 20 miles an hour must be able to stop within 18 feet; one going 30 miles an hour should be able to stop in 40 feet, and one traveling 40 miles should stop within 71 feet of the point where brakes are applied.

Summer Illness Ascribed to Food

Department of Health Gives Seasonable Advice

The Department of Health told Detroiters Thursday how to avoid summer illnesses caused by improperly refrigerated food and by unripe and overripe fruits.

Meat should be cooked immediately after purchase if possible, and when not consumed at one meal should be kept in a refrigerator, the department warned. If refrigeration is not adequate, the meat should be cooked for the next meal.

Milk, custards and cream desserts also should be kept cold before they are served, the department also warned and Fruit should be kept in small quantities and used immediately.

The department also warned that minor disturbances often are caused by fatigue and exposure to the sun. It recommended rest periods before meals and after exercise.

The danger of heat exhaustion may be minimized by drinking small quantities of water at a time, three or four times a day, the department said.

Please Turn to Page 4—Column 4

Start the Day Right with the Free Press

Pages

Alden, Ruth	21
Around the Town	17
Chatterbox	17
Collyer, Bert E.	17
Comics	23
Crossword Puzzle	23
Editorial	6
Financial	18
Foreign News	6
Good Morning	6
Guest, Edgar A.	6
Harrison in Hollywood	15
National Whirligig	6
Obituaries	20
Quillen, Robert	6
Radio Programs	15
Screen	15
Second Coors	20
Serial, "Forgotten Bride"	21
Society	19
State News	20
Theater	15
Vital Statistics	20
Ward to the Wise	15
Washington News	15

The Detroit Free Press EXTRA

SECOND METROPOLITAN EXTRA · SECOND METROPOLITAN

Friday, September 1, 1939. 109th Year. No. 120 — On Guard for Over a Century — 28 Pages — Three Cents

SEPT. 1, 1939:

Hitler invades Poland, and the world is once again at war.

WAR

German Warplanes Bomb Poland's Capital; Nazis Annex Danzig; Heavy Border Fighting

Hitler Formally Takes Free City into Reich

BERLIN, Sept. 1 (Friday)—(A. P.)—Adolf Hitler today accepted the Free City of Danzig into the Reich.

The Fuehrer acted after Albert Forster, Nazi chief of state of the Free City and Nazi district leader there, had proclaimed the reunion of the Baltic city with Hitler's Germany, and begged the Fuehrer to accept it.

In a telegram to Forster, Hitler acknowledged the reception of Forster's proclamation and thanked him for "the loyalty of Danzig to Germans."

Hitler declared a newly proclaimed law for the reunion of Danzig to Germany "immediately effective" and named Forster, already chosen by the Danzig Senate as chief of state, to head the city government.

"I acknowledge your proclamation of the return of the Free City of Danzig to the Reich," the Fuehrer's telegram said.

Turn to DANZIG—Page 11

Hitler Gives War Orders; Nazi Navy Blockades Poles

BERLIN, Sept. 1 (Friday) - (A.P.)—The German Army was ordered to "meet force with force" and Poland was declared dangerous territory for foreigners by Adolf Hitler at 5:30 a. m. today (11:30 p. m. Thursday, Detroit time.)

At the same time a naval blockade of the Polish harbor of Gdynia was announced. The Fuehrer proclaimed that his action was because of alleged Polish violations of the German frontier.

His order of the day to the Army asserted:

"The Polish State has rejected my efforts to establish neighborly relations, and instead has appealed to weapons.

"Germans in Poland are victims of bloody terror, driven from house and home.

"A series of border violations unbearable for a great power show that the Poles no longer are willing to respect the German border.

"To put an end to these insane incitations, nothing remains but for me to meet force with force from now on.

"The German Army will conduct a fight for honor and the right to the life of the resurrected German people with firm determination. I expect that every soldier, mindful of the great traditions of the eternal German military, will do his duty to the last.

"Remember always that you are representatives of the National Socialist great Germany. Long live our people and our Reich!"

Neutral Ships Warned

The German radio announced the blockade of Gdynia before 6 a. m. and prohibited all except military-plane flights over Germany.

Another order issued shortly before 6 a. m. in Hitler's order-of-the-day issued as Hitler issued his order. Neutral ships in the Baltic were warned that they enter the Baltic Sea at their own peril. Gdynia and Danzig are but a few miles apart in the same harbor.

The Government announcement said that German military operations necessitated these measures.

The announcement said that German warships would meet foreign vessels steaming into the danger zone and instruct them where to go.

Army Massed on Border

The command to use force against Poles was issued as the order of the day to the army massed on Polish frontiers from the Baltic to the high Tatra Mountains and in East Prussia.

The radio announced immediately an indefinite closing of all schools in Germany.

Rapid-fire orders followed commanding masters of German vessels to get out of the Baltic Sea and not to enter the Danzig or Polish harbors.

The radio warned all foreigners

Fuehrer Tells Reichstag Why He Went into War

BERLIN, Sept. 1 (Friday)—(U.P.)—Adolf Hitler addressing the Reichstag, said today that he appointed Field Marshal Hermann Goering his successor "if anything should happen to me in this war," with Rudolph Hess, his deputy Nazi Party leader, as second heir.

BERLIN, Sept. 1 (Friday) (A. P.)—Adolf Hitler addressed the Reichstag at 10 a. m. today (4 a. m. Detroit time) after ordering the German Army to "meet force with force" in the conflict with Poland.

For the first time in Nazi Germany, soldiers stood guard with party formations at Kroll Opera House for the address to the Reichstag.

A crowd stood silently watching cars dash in and out of Wilhelmstrasse.

At the Propaganda Ministry a tired-looking group of about 100 foreign correspondents, most of whom had worked through the night, answered the Ministry's summons for a special conference. On entry into the conference hall, they were told that Reichstag cards would be given out by a roll call of accredited correspondents.

NEW YORK, Sept. 1 (Friday)—(A. P.)—A summary of the translation of Adolf Hitler's speech to the Reichstag, as received in this country by radio, follows:

"We have all been suffering under the torture which the Treaty of Versailles has brought us.

"Danzig was and is a German city.

"Minorities in the Polish corridor have been shamefully mistreated.

"You know the proposals that I have made to bring about the return of German territories.

"Therefore, it is understandable that action must be taken by us.

"I have tried by peaceful means to bring about a solution of the Danzig and Corridor problems.

"As always I have tried to solve the problem by peaceful means.

"For 15 years there have been opportunities to bring about these revisions but nothing has been done.

"All the proposals to remedy these unbearable conditions did not receive any consideration.

Turn to REICHSTAG—Page 10

Paris Caught by Surprise; Envoy Charges Nazi Guilt

PARIS, Sept. 1—(A. P.)—Havas (French news agency) said today that the Polish Embassy here had announced that "Germany violated the Polish frontier at four points."

"German reports of pretended violation of German territory by Poland are pure invention, as is the fable of 'attack' by Polish insurgents on Gleiwitz," the Embassy announcement said.

Earlier, Havas had disclosed that official French dispatches from Germany indicated that "the Reich began hostilities on Poland this morning."

The report caught Paris by surprise on a sunny morning when newspapers were proclaiming that "French and British Firmness Can Still Save Peace."

An hour after the first report was received there still was no official reaction.

Although officials said the Cabinet, meeting last night, had not discussed general mobilization and that no full contingents had been called to the colors since Saturday, men continued to leave for posts of duty on individual orders.

News of the mobilization of Army reserves was received with satisfaction as evidence of the joint firmness of Britain and France, who have pledged aid to Poland if she resists any attack on her independence.

Head of Army Called by Premier

The removal of civilians from the French capital continued as Premier Daladier in succession called Generalissimo Maurice Gustave Gamelin and Foreign Minister Georges Bonnet into urgent early morning consultation.

Turn to PARIS—Page 10

Bulletins

LONDON, Sept. 1— (A. P.)— Reuters (British news agency) said today in a Warsaw dispatch that the official Warsaw radio announced that German troops had launched a full scale attack against towns in the Polish Corridor.

WASHINGTON, Sept. 1 (Friday)—(A. P.)—President Roosevelt directed early today that all naval ships and Army commands be notified at once by radio of German-Polish hostilities. The White House issued the following announcement:

"The President received word at 2:50 a. m. Eastern Standard Time by telephone from Ambassador Biddle at Warsaw and through Ambassador Bullitt in Paris that Germany has invaded Poland and that four Polish cities are being bombed.

"There probably will be a further announcement by the State Department in a few hours."

The announcement was issued by William Hassett, acting White House press secretary, after the President had telephoned him at his home.

White House offices had been dark during the night, but Mr. Roosevelt himself was keeping in constant touch with European developments.

LONDON, Sept. 1 (Friday)—(A. P.)—A Reuters dispatch from Parish early today said:

"The following is given with all reserve: Accordingly to unconfirmed reports received here, the Germans have begun an offensive with extreme violence on the whole Polish front."

GLEIWITZ, Germany, Sept. 1 (Friday)—(A. P.)— An army ambulance carrying wounded soldiers arrived at the emergency hospital here today at 9:10 a. m. (3:10 a. m., Detroit time).

The men, carried in a wagon, were on stretchers. One wore a first-aid field bandage. It could not be ascertained where the ambulance came from.

BERNE, Switzerland, Sept. 1—(A.P.)—The Neue Zurcher Zeitung's correspondent in Berlin wrote today:

"It is declared here categorically that the Fuehrer's proclamation amounts to opening a state of war. Military operations were begun at 6 a. m. along the entire German-Polish frontier."

London Evacuates Children; Parliament Is Summoned

LONDON, Sept. 1 (Friday)—(U.P.)—Almost one half million school children were evacuated from the "target" areas of greater London today and transported to safe places in the country.

They assembled in the dawn in 2,000 schools and were herded by 22,000 teachers, parents, and volunteer workers to trains and busses which took them to "unknown destinations."

It was an unprecedented, dramatic spectacle—the effort of the British Government to save the new generation of Englishmen and Englishwomen from horrible deaths by bomb fragment or under the debris of tenements destroyed by aerial bombardment.

LONDON, Sept. 1—(U. P.)—The Cabinet was summoned to meet this morning and it was announced that Parliament would meet at 6 p. m. (noon Detroit time.)

Foreign Office officials were in a conference which began at midnight.

Great Britain had already mobilized her fleet, called up the entire army reserve, brought the Royal Air Force to full strength and started to evacuate 3,000,000 women, children and others from danger zones.

Adolf Hitler's final diplomatic move before the attack on Poland, a sixteen-point "peace" proposal, was declared authoritatively to be "not a reply to any British proposals."

The Berlin "peace plan" was not known in Warsaw until Thursday night, it was said here.

One British observer said that Hitler had apparently desired to was making a "magnanimous" gesture before taking military action.

The proposals were read to Sir Nevile Henderson, British ambassador in Berlin, late on the night of Aug. 30 (Wednesday). They

Turn to LONDON—Page 11

Other Towns of Poland Raked by Berlin Planes

WARSAW, Sept. 1—(A. P.)—The Foreign Office said today that German planes had bombed Krakow and Katowice, in southwestern Poland.

WARSAW, Sept. 1 (Friday)—(U.P.)—German airplanes bombed the Polish capital at 9 a. m., (3 a. m. Detroit time) today, it was announced officially, within an hour after German bombardments had been reported in five other cities in Poland.

The Foreign Office immediately charged Germany with aggression, announcing:

"Shortly after 7 a. m., Germans started military action at different points on the frontier. This undoubtedly is German aggression against Poland. Military action now is developing."

The Foreign Office did not name the places of action.

It was reported that the German bombing squadrons had not been large. The Government announced that they had bombed, among other places, the railway station at Czew, the town of Rypnic and the town of Putzk, near Czew.

Private sources here said heavy fighting was under way at Chojnice, on the northwestern border.

Military circles said that "apparently general fighting has begun at most parts of the frontier."

The bombardment at Warsaw began with heavy detonations outside the city. Apparently most of them were antiaircraft barrages but some possibly were bombs.

The explosions were almost continuous. Then the drone of big planes was heard.

In another moment there was a terrific explosion near the Central Station. Antiaircraft guns were blasting the sky, and clouds were visibly breaking up.

The antiaircraft gunners obviously could not see the planes when they began the constant fire.

The Polish army was almost fully mobilized and spread out along the full length of the German and Slovak borders; cities were streaked with newly dug air raid trench shelters; Gdynia harbor at the mouth of the Gulf of Danzig was mined, and, to the limit of its ability, the country was ready to withstand the onslaught of the German war machine.

Turn to FIGHTING—Page 10

Start the Day Right with the Free Press

	Pages
Alden, Ruth	18
Amusements	17
Around the Town	2
Chatterbox	12
Collyer's Selections	20
Comics	27
Crossword Puzzle	26
Editorial	6
Financial	22
Good Morning	6
Guest, Edgar A.	6
Iffy the Dopester	7
National Whirligig	6
Newton, Dr. Joseph Fort	6
Obituaries	24
Radio Programs	24
Serial: "The Yearling"	27
Sullivan, Ed	6
Theater	17
Ward to the Wise	19
Washington News	18
Weather Report	4

April 12, 1941:

Ford Motor Co. was the last holdout against the UAW.

The Detroit Free Press

On Guard for Over a Century

Saturday, April 12, 1941. No. 343 — BURTON 110th Year — 18 Pages — Three Cents

METROPOLITAN FINAL EDITION

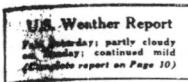
U.S. Weather Report: partly cloudy; continued mild

Panzer Forces Drive Through Flank of Allies

Push 25 Miles into Western Line as Big Fight Rages

Nazis Also Attacking Near Mount Olympus

By the Associated Press

ATHENS, April 12 (Saturday) — The Greek Command acknowledged early today that German forces, coming through a gap in the Allied front at Bitoli, had reached the Greek lines in the Phlorina area of Greece, near the Albanian frontier.

Panzer units thus plunged some 25 miles into the left flank of the Allied line, where both British and Greek units have been fighting since Thursday back of the remainder of the Yugoslav armies of Southern Serbia.

Contact Admitted

An official communique said that the German "motorized elements coming from the direction of Monastir (Bitoli) came in contact with our forces."

This was not the only point of the line at which British Imperial and Greek troops were locked in a great battle of motion. Other German divisions were attacking in force on the Allied right, within 48 miles of Mount Olympus. Tonight's communique did not mention this attack.

On the Allied left, the German forces first moved down through Yugoslavia from Prilep, and, attacking furiously at the Bitoli, or Monastir Pass, broke through and poured on to the Phlorina area. Some observers believed that the Allies might have had only a small delaying force at the pass.

Allies Making Stand

The major struggle has been in progress since Thursday, on the front where the Allies had elected to make a fateful stand to hold the Grecian peninsula and the vital ports to the south.

A British announcement said that the commander-in-chief of the British force was Lieut. Gen. Sir Henry Maitland Wilson, who commanded the Army of the Nile in its winter offensive into Libya.

The brief communiques of the British Expeditionary Force — Englishmen, Australians, New Zealanders — merely suggested the fury of the fighting, but made it clear that the Nazis were striking hardest at both flanks of the Allied line.

Athens Reports Success

The Athens radio declared that Yugoslav troops fighting northwest of Skoplje have prevented the Germans (from joining) Italian soldiers on the Albanian-Yugoslavia frontier.

The Rome radio earlier reported, however, that Italian troops occupied Ohrid, Yugoslavia.

Turn to Page 2, Column 7

Second Battle Starts in Libya

By the United Press

LONDON, April 12 (Saturday) — British troops and German-Italian mechanized columns have made contact in the "Second Battle of Libya" in the rugged desert country west of Tobruk, the war office announced early today.

The terse announcement was regarded here as indicating that the imperial forces had mustered sufficient strength after their miraculous withdrawal from Bengasi and Derna to make a stand against the rapidly advancing Axis forces.

Prior to the renewed battle, British planes, in several days of intense activity, destroyed 34 Axis aircraft, a British announcement said Friday.

(An Associated Press dispatch from Cairo, giving details of the previously announced capture by British generals and three brigadier generals, revealed that a German motorcycle patrol, wielding "Tommy" guns in "Chicago gang" fashion, had taken Lieut. Gens. Sir Richard Nugent O'Connor and P. Neame when the patrol waylaid staff cars transporting the generals and their staff on a moonlit road near Derna.)

PAYOFF ON THE WAY

Michigan Bell Taking Steps to Make Refund of $1,500,000

The Michigan Bell Telephone Co. prepared Friday for the prompt distribution of approximately $1,500,000 to 700,000 customers in accordance with a Supreme Court order upholding reduced long-distance intrastate toll rates which have been in dispute since 1938.

George M. Welch, president of the company, announced that there will be no appeal of the Michigan order to the United States Supreme Court.

Steps will be taken at once to put the new rates in effect and to establish a refund machinery. Customers using Michigan long-distance service will save $700,000 a year, Welch estimates.

The company will petition Circuit Judge Leland W. Carr, of Lansing, for a supplemental procedure of refund procedure. It was Carr's decision which the Supreme Court.

Because 65,030,000 separate toll tickets are involved, the company...

WARNING

Avoid a New Dunkerque, British Urge

Chicago Tribune Foreign Service

LONDON, April 12 (Saturday) — The Daily Mail in a long editorial in this morning's issue comes out with the warning that Britain cannot afford another Dunkerque.

"We have met with a reverse in the Balkans," says the Mail, "owing to the vast German superiority in men and metal. But if we should lose a substantial part of our Army in Greece, or all of our equipment, as we did at Dunkerque, the reverse would be turned into a military disaster. In no circumstances should this be allowed to happen."

In North Africa, the Mail points out, Britain "may lose Cyrenaica."

"It must be realized," the editorial adds, "that we are losing valuable airfields to Germany and her predominance in this element will make prolonged resistance very difficult."

Objecting to the British Army being thrown on the Continent, where Germany possesses overwhelming odds in its favor, the Mail observes: "Churchill says that wars are not won on the safety-first principle, and we agree. But neither are they won by taking foolish risks."

Turks Decree State of Siege

Civilian Evacuation of Straits Reported

By the Associated Press

LONDON, April 11 — An Exchange Telegraph Agency dispatch tonight quoted the Turkish press as reporting that a state of siege has been declared in Turkey and that civilian evacuation of the Dardanelles and a large part of European Turkey to Anatolia had been ordered.

The Army was said to be providing facilities for the removal of inhabitants from Adrianople, near the Greek and Bulgarian frontiers, and Rodosto, a town east of the Dardanelles on the Sea of Marmora, to Asiatic Turkey.

Evacuation of Istanbul was ordered yesterday.

The newspaper Cumhuriyet was quoted as saying that the evacuation step was quite normal, and that Turkey had not yet ordered any general mobilization.

"Turkey has decided not to fight unless she is attacked," the paper added.

(The Berlin correspondent of the Geneva newspaper Tribune de Geneve reported that it was believed that Germany would demand from Ankara, "henceforth isolated," the right of passage across Turkey to gain the Mosul oil fields and move toward Syria and the Suez Canal. The newspaper said that the campaign would be rapid because the Germans might need to cross Anatolia "before the rainy seasons begins next month.")

Countercoup Reported Foiled

BAGDAD, April 11 (A.P.) — An Iraq Government communique said tonight that a countercoup, engineered by former Regent Emir Abdul Ilah and three of his followers, had been frustrated by the commander of the Basra garrison.

(The Emir and members of his Government were overthrown last week by Rashid Ali Al Gailani, premier, reportedly pro-Axis, who has been termed anti-British. However, the new premier has promised to respect Iraq's engagements with Britain. Iraq is a major British ally.)

Red Decree Curbs Anniversary Parties

MOSCOW, April 11 (A.P.) — Soviet officials decided today that too many celebrations not anniversaries constitute "a very unhealthy practice" and ordered that they be sharply restricted.

F.D.R. Opens Route to Rush Balkans Arms

Lifts Ban on Red Sea and Gulf of Aden for U.S. Shipping

Craft to Run the Risk of Axis Raider Attack

BY RICHARD L. TURNER
Associated Press Correspondent

WASHINGTON, April 11 — In a new attempt to checkmate the Nazis, President Roosevelt threw open today the Red Sea and the Gulf of Aden to American vessels so that they may carry war supplies almost all the way to the embattled Balkans.

Whether Adolf Hitler would offer his surface raiders to sink the vessels as they passed through the Indian Ocean was unknown, although it was recalled that he has said that "every ship, whether with or without a convoy, that comes before our torpedo tubes will be torpedoed."

Revises Combat Zones

The President opened the way for the ships by a slight readjustment of the "combat zones" defined under the Neutrality Act. He eliminated the Gulf of Aden and the Red Sea from the area which American vessels had been forbidden to enter. They may now go clear into the Suez Canal from the east and make deliveries in Egypt.

However, it was indicated that at least some of the American vessels may not go as far as the canal. The American Export Line, announcing in New York that it was applying to the Maritime Commission for permission to operate ships to Egyptian ports via the Red Sea, said that the supplies carried in its vessels would be landed at Port Sudan for transshipment, Port Sudan is on the Red Sea Coast some 900 miles from the canal.

Have Attacked in Canal

Axis planes have attacked ships at the canal on several occasions. Foreign observers in London recalled that Axis surface raiders have been operating in the Indian Ocean in reach of the routes between the United States and the canal. British official reports from Singapore this week said that the Nazi pocket battleship Admiral Scheer had been raiding in the Indian Ocean.

Egypt Stays Neutral

The Neutrality Act prohibits American ships from delivering supplies to a belligerent. But Egypt is technically neutral. And the President, his tongue in his cheek, made it more than plain that "the Administration will not be oversensitive on the point of international relations with the belligerents and not to Britain, in particular."

One day after including Greenland within the American Hemisphere defense system, Mr. Roosevelt signed a resolution affirming a policy of nonrecognition of any transfer of Western Hemisphere land from one non-American power to another.

A Havana Conference Pact

The resolution, in accordance with an agreement reached by the 21 American republics at the Conference of Havana, provides for consultation among them in the event of a prospective change of sovereignty over non-American territory in this hemisphere.

The President was asked at his press conference whether there was any question of transferring more American destroyers to Britain at this time, and his reply was a flat no.

Mr. Roosevelt also announced that he had declared a state of war to exist between the Italian-German alliance and Yugoslavia. This was done under the Neutrality Act, preparatory to making that law apply to the new extension of the battle area.

Harriman, in London, Gets Minister Rank

WASHINGTON, April 11 (A.P.) — W. Averell Harriman, who was sent to London to "expedite" American aid to Britain, has been given the rank of minister.

The United States now has two ministers in London as well as an ambassador, John G. Winant. The ministerial rank had previously been given Herschel Johnson, embassy counselor.

BRITISH DOWN 5 PLANES

VALLETTA, Malta, April 11 (A.P.) — Two German Messerschmitts were shot down and one Junkers 88 and two Italian CR-42s of high flying over this island fortress today, a British communique said.

Ford Plant Opens to Prepare for Work After Picket Lines Dissolve and Troopers Depart

All Genial and Happy After the Dispute's Over

R. J. THOMAS — GOV. VAN WAGONER — HARRY H. BENNETT
UAW head, Governor and Ford personnel chief pose for movies after settlement.

Plunge Is Fatal to Detroit Flier

2 Hurt as Army Ship Crashes in South

Second Lieut. Wilmer Exler, 26 years old, of Detroit, attached to the 107th Observation Squadron at Camp Beauregard, La., was killed Friday and two Detroiters with him were seriously injured when the Army observation plane Exler was flying crashed at the camp airport.

The injured were First Lieut. Paul R. Smith, 42, severe head injuries and a fractured leg, and Pvt. Charles Yesalones, 26, severe head injuries.

Exler was to have been married soon to Shirley Briggs, daughter of Mr. and Mrs. Miri L. Briggs. She was visiting in Louisiana at the time of the crash.

"Taking off on a routine flight, the plane reached an altitude of about 150 feet when the motor cut out," sending the ship into a nose dive, it was said.

Ford to Pay Off 21,000 More Today

Approximately 21,000 Ford Motor Co. employees will be paid off Saturday at the temporary office at 144 W. Fort. They are the holders of the following badge numbers:

Series B – 4,001 to 10,000.
Series H – 1 to 5,000.
Series T – 5,001 to 10,000.
Series Z – 5,001 to 10,000.

On Monday, payment will be made for the period ending April 4 to the following badge holders:

Series C – 1,000 to 5,000.
Series P – 1 to 5,000.
Series R – 1 to 5,000.
Series Y – 1 to 5,000.

Head of G-Men Mum on Defense

WASHINGTON, April 11 — John Edgar Hoover declined today to testify at a House investigation of defense production, saying that a discussion of FBI information otherwise than through the courts would be "fatal to the future usefulness of the Federal Bureau of Investigation."

The FBI chief said that Attorney General Jackson concurred in his decision.

Hoover's views were made public in a letter to Chairman May, of the House Military Affairs Committee.

Iroquois Are Seeking to Get Out of the Draft

SYRACUSE, N. Y., April 11 (A.P.) — The Six Nations of the Iroquois Confederacy, comprising 4,200 of New York's estimated 6,500 Indians, named today a committee to protest to the Government a White Man's law subjecting them to compulsory military service.

GM Receives Strike Threat

Union Sets April 20 Contract Deadline

Reported to be deadlocked "on certain issues" in negotiations with the United Automobile Workers (CIO), the General Motors Corp. Friday notified the Labor Department in Washington that the union had given notice from the union that strike action would be negotiated before April 20.

James F. Dewey, Federal conciliator, was to be assigned to the case immediately, the Labor Department reported. To avert a work stoppage in the plants of the corporation, which has large defense orders.

Wouldn't Include Defense Workers

However, Walter Reuther, GM director for the union, declared that if a strike was called "it would not include workers on national defense projects."

Threatened by the strike are 13 General Motors plants, employing 165,000 workers. Negotiations on the new contract have been under way since March 11. Both sides reported that there was no breakdown in the negotiations.

"The corporation added in its advice to Washington that tentative agreement had been reached on some of the points involved."

Hope for Early Conclusion

"We hope these negotiations can be pushed through to a conclusion at the earliest date possible, and we are attempting to do our part to that end," the corporation stated.

Word that a strike was threatened also was received by Office of Production Management officials.

Corporation officials said that General motors held defense contracts aggregating more than $700,000,000. The sum does not include contracts held by subsidiaries and affiliated corporations which would swell the defense orders to more than $1,000,000,000.

Union Shop Reported Rejected

In his wire to OPM, Reuther declared that the corporation "has repeatedly attempted to force a deadlock in the negotiations on the question of union recognition." It was understood that the company had rejected a proposal for a union shop.

Other points which are in dispute, according to Reuther, are improved grievance machinery, wages and the extension of authority of the impartial umpire. The union, had sought to have the latter's powers broadened.

Fleeing Nazis Feared to Have Oil Plans

TAMPICO, Mexico, April 11 (A.P.) — The United States neutrality patrol has been requested to search for six German liner Orinoco, who escaped Tuesday night in a home-made thirty-foot yawl, it was reported unofficially today. The Germans were said to have carried detailed plans of the oil fields surrounding Tampico.

DIVORCES COWBOY

RENO, April 11 (U.P.) — Joan Biddle Polk, of Philadelphia Main Line society's younger set, her marriage to a movie cowboy, aged 10 weeks ago, divorced him tonight.

Ford Plant Opens to Prepare for Work After Picket Lines Dissolve and Troopers Depart

5,000 to Return Monday as Result of Strike's End

Pickets and State troopers faded away from the Ford Motor Co.'s Rouge plant Friday after 10 days of siege, opening the gates to a force of production workers rushing to swing the world's largest factory back into operation.

The picket lines broke up in midafternoon when the settlement became official.

The largest assemblage of State troopers in Michigan history was disbanded somewhat later, and by 5:30 p.m. was entirely gone from the plant area. Its departure meant a return to normal for the State Police posts all over Michigan, every one of which had been stripped to the limit for the strike emergency. Some of the posts were down to two men in the crisis, with the ranks of the absent troopers filled by State Department of Conservation officers and deputy sheriffs.

The process of re-establishing the plant on a production basis will take about 10 days, company officials said, except in divisions where damage to equipment may delay operations longer. The first 5,000 or 6,000 workers out of 85,000 employed in the plant will be back on the job Monday.

Plant Chiefs Confer

Efforts to get the workers turning again were begun immediately after Gov. Van Wagoner announced settlement of the Ford strike at 2:30 p. m. Friday. As the first act, Ray H. Rausch, Rouge plant superintendent, called a meeting of divisional superintendents.

Ford officials were working late Friday on advertisements that would notify workmen when they were to report. First to be called, it was indicated, will be workers in the foundry, rolling mills, coke ovens and blast furnaces.

Union Hails a Victory

The union called the settlement "the greatest of all labor victories in our generation."

A company attorney called it "a truce," adding:

"We feel that our vital part in national defense is more important than any other consideration."

Said Gov. Van Wagoner: "All parties by their unselfish and patriotic attitude have placed the public good first."

However, Sidney Hillman reported that this week has been abandoned its fight for the aircraft industry, with 38 plants now on a six-day week and two large plants working seven days a week. Three-fourths of the industry is working three shifts, a day, he said.

Hillman reported that 7,000 additional skilled workers are needed for the aircraft industry this week from production. Labor and industry are cooperating throughout the country to obtain additional training for workers in this and other industries.

By September, he predicted, an additional 200,000 workers will be required for the aircraft industry, with 250,000 needed for shipbuilding plants by November, 1942. To date 607,000 workers have passed through defense training schools and are at work.

He sent a letter today to all manufacturers with defense contracts urging them to discriminate against none on the ground that he be known against the Negro worker.

Hillman also said that William S. Knudsen, director-general of OPM, had been concerned over the week-end closing of plants, but so far no machines with which to work are made available for wider opportunity to Negro men and machines.

JUSTICE MURPHY ILL

Recorder's Judge George Murphy said Friday that he and a telephone conversation with his brother, United States Supreme Court Justice Frank Murphy, advising him that he plans to enter Johns Hopkins Hospital for surgical treatment. Judge Murphy said he plans to fly to Baltimore to be with his brother.

MASTER OF DIPLOMACY

Van Wagoner's Endless Toil Brought Ford Settlement

BY FRANK B. WOODFORD
Free Press Staff Writer

One of the highlights which long will stand out in the history of the political life of Gov. Van Wagoner is overcoming the Ford strike obstacles which many observers believed could not be accomplished without a long and bitter struggle.

Gov. Van Wagoner alone brought together the Ford people and the union so that negotiations could be carried on. For 11 days the Governor foresook all his other duties to sit at this one problem. Day and night, almost, working the clock around, he and his staff were available to both parties. Harassed and worn almost to the point of exhaustion, he carried it through with the aid of his confidential secretary, C. W. Lucas; Byron Ballard, his legal advisor and Commissioner Oscar C. Olander of the State Police.

When it was evident, on April 3, that the disorders in the Ford plant were getting out of hand, and that the whole situation was critical, Gov. Van Wagoner rushed to Detroit.

One of his first steps was to get...

Turn to Page 5, Column 4

Defense Skies Grow Clearer

Only 7,000 Now Idle in Arms Plants

BY CLIFFORD A. PREVOST
Free Press Washington Bureau

WASHINGTON, April 11 — With the settlement of the Ford strike there are now fewer than 7,000 workers connected with defense production who are unemployed, Sidney Hillman, co-director of the Office of Production Management, said at his press conference today.

He added that hours of employment are being rapidly increased in many industries dealing with defense and predicted a shortage of labor as production...

Enjoy These Exclusive Features Over the Week-End

IN THE EDITORIAL MAGAZINE

WHAT'S BEHIND HITLER'S VIOLENT SEA CAMPAIGN? — What is the deadline for the breaking of England's blockade? Why is it so vital to Germany for the collapse of the British navy? Read the Editorial Magazine Sunday.

WHO IS ROOSEVELT'S RIGHT HAND MAN TODAY? — Who is this Harry Hopkins and what has he done in "come so important in the administration?"

WANT A RINGSIDE SEAT AT THE INVASION OF BRITAIN? — Here's a mind's-eye description of what will happen, written by a veteran foreign correspondent.

DOES YOUR SON WANT TO ENTER THIS MICHIGAN MODEL AIRCRAFT MEET? — You will find an entry blank in the Model Aviation section of the Editorial Magazine.

WHAT DOES DETROIT THINK OF THE PROPOSED STREAMLINING OF COUNTY GOVERNMENT? — How much would this save the state, or would it save anything at all? The Free Press Sunday Forum gives an EXCLUSIVE picture of what Detroiters are thinking today.

IN THE SUNDAY GRAPHIC

IFFY THE DOPESTER EXPLAINS: "Tradition counts. If you don't think so, look at England." Here's Detroit's baseball tradition, in two pages of pictures, predictions and comment by Iffy the Dopester, a great collection of Tiger "Greats" PLUS a full-page drawing of Iffy Tiger, in colors, by Loyd S. Nixon.

A CARTOONIST VISITS LANSING — Arthur Poinier, staff cartoonist, drops in on the state capital.

ON THE WOMEN'S PAGES

SPRING IN THE COUNTRY — What to wear this spring for spectator sports, smart new fashions presented by Jean Pearson. In addition: Isabella Taves' New York fashion letter ... Ruth Alden's Easter message.

COMPLETE BOOK-OF-THE-WEEK

"STAND-IN FOR DANGER" — An exciting story that could easily be true — and it has happened — in England and France when this war started. A fast-moving hit by Kathleen Hewitt.

TOMORROW'S SUNDAY FREE PRESS

Balmy Breezes Due for the Easter Parade

You can put on that Easter bonnet for a nice jaunty Sunday by the looks of the weather now. The weather Bureau, while noting an increase in cloudiness for Saturday night, predicted "quite mild" weather over the Easter week-end.

As a clue to what kind of weather to expect, there was Friday, when the temperature got to the highest for 1941, 69 degrees.

Start the Day Right with the Free Press

	Page
Amusements	9
Around the Town	10
Business and Industry	14
Church News	6-5
Clapper, Raymond	6
Classified Ads	14-15-16
Crossword Puzzle	
Editorial	6
Lippman, Walter	6
My Day	14
Radio Programs	9
Society	9
State News	13
Vital Statistics	15
Vessel Almanac	10
Weather Report	10

The Detroit Free Press

Weather Report
Fair Tuesday and Wednesday; little change in temperature.
(Complete report on Page 11)

Tuesday, April 29, 1941. No. 360

On Guard for Over a Century

METROPOLITAN FINAL EDITION
BURTON
110th Year   24 Pages   Three Cents

APRIL 29, 1941:

Wayne County's ex-prosecutor and ex-sheriff are among those convicted on graft charges.

McCrea, Wilcox, Garska and Staebler Guilty with 20 Others on Vice-Graft Plot Charges

Way Clear for Ending Coal Tie-Up

Southern Operators Accept F.D.R.'s Plan; Agreement of Lewis Is Believed Assured

By the United Press

WASHINGTON, April 28— The way was cleared late tonight for ending the twenty-eight-day tie-up of soft-coal mines, which threatened the nation's rearmament drive, when recalcitrant Southern operators suddenly capitulated to President Roosevelt's proposal that all mines be reopened pending final settlement of the wage dispute.

Mr. Roosevelt's proposal was made just a week ago tonight. The Southern group, which previously had rejected the President's week-old proposal, advised Mr. Roosevelt shortly after 11 p.m. that they now accepted it "without equivocation" and that "we are ready to resume work immediately."

Agreement Previously Made

Northern operators and the United Mine Workers of America (CIO) already had agreed to the President's proposal which called for the reopening of all soft-coal mines—Northern and Southern—continuance of negotiations, and if the suggestion that any wage gains be made retroactive.

William H. Davis, vice chairman of the Defense Mediation Board and chairman of the panel which had been attempting to bring about a settlement, informed the President that it was his understanding that the offer of the Southern operators was "acceptable and agreeable to Mr. Lewis" (John L. Lewis, President of the miners' union).

Action Pleases President

A spokesman for the Southern group said "We can start digging coal Wednesday morning."

L. Ebersole Gaines, chairman of the Southern group of 13 districts, advised Mr. Roosevelt that his group was ready to put their miners back to work at once "with a wage increase of $1 a day for

Turn to Page 3, Column 1

Ten Are Shot in Indian Riots

BOMBAY, April 28—(A.P.)—At least 10 persons were killed and 135 injured when Hindu and Moslem rioters in the streets of Bombay today, wounding 10.

At least six stabbing victims were taken to hospitals. The district magistrate banned gatherings of more than five persons and clamped down a 7 p.m. curfew.

The outbreak was a spread of riots which have beset India. The situation in Bombay was said to have improved. The casualty list since the first outbreak a week ago is 10 dead and 135 injured.

Capt. Roosevelt Flies to Chungking

HONGKONG, April 29 (Tuesday)—(A.P.)—Capt. James Roosevelt and Maj. Gerald Thomas, special observers from the Washington headquarters of the United States Marine Corps, left by airplane today for Chungking, Chinese Central Government capital. They were to see Generalissimo Chiang Kai-Shek.

KILLED IN BLAST ON SHIP

NEW ORLEANS, April 28—(A.P.)—An explosion on the French freighter Angoulene killed Crewman Julian Tefel, 33 years old, and injured two others today. Coast Guard authorities are investigating.

TODAY'S INDEX

Announcements	17
Around the Town	10
Clapper, Raymond	6
Classified Ads	20-21-22
Crossword Puzzle	20
Editorial	6
Financial	18-19
Lippmann, Walter	6
Merry-Go-Round	6
My Day	9
Obituaries	
Radio Program	15
Sport News	13-14-15
State News	5
Vessel Passages	9
Vital Statistics	20
Weather	11
Women's News	6-9-10

No Breathing Spell in the Mediterranean

Blitz Already On, Germans Say; British Fear for 'Rock' Defenses

By the United Press

BERLIN, April 28—Germany is determined to destroy Britain's power in the Mediterranean without pausing for a breathing space after the twenty-one-day Balkan blitzkrieg that drove the British off the European Continent, Nazi military quarters said tonight.

German Laval units already are striking deep into the Eastern Mediterranean and bomber squadrons of the Luftwaffe are blasting British warships and troopships between the Greek mainland and the island of Crete with unbroken ferocity, it was asserted.

(Berlin newspapers indicated the Associated Press reported, that the Greek island of Crete, next seat of the Government which fled from Athens, apparently will be the next objective of the German Army after the

Turn to Page 4, Column 5

Credit Tie-Up as New Blow at Axis Hinted

U.S. May Supplement Sea Patrol Operations

By the United Press

WASHINGTON, April 28—The United States may supplement extension of neutrality-patrol operations to safeguard shipments of war materials to Great Britain in the new economic pressure against the Triple Alliance, Secretary of the Treasury Henry Morgenthau, Jr., intimated today.

He called at the White House soon after President Roosevelt had frozen Greek credits in this country estimated at $40,000,000 to $50,000,000. It was the fourteenth freezing order against funds of nations which have lost their independence and served to keep from their conquerors about $4,500,000,000.

Big Axis Credits in U.S.

Morgenthau and his aides persistently have advocated the freezing of more than $175,000,000 of German and Italian credits in this country, but the State Department has objected.

Morgenthau later told reporters that he had received encouragement for the Treasury's attitude on the foreign situation, but would not say whether reported new economic moves would include freezing of German and Italian credits.

Experts said that such an order would bring reprisals from Germany and Italy, in which this country holds a substantial part of $500,000,000 of Freezing of $175,000,000 in Japanese credits in this country reportedly is not in the immediate picture.

Could Strike at Germany

It was suggested that this Government might strike at Germany and Italy through their Axis partner by tightening export control over American shipments to Japan which British officials complain are reaching Germany via Russia.

The President will have an opportunity to outline new plans in this direction in an address to the nation Wednesday night coincident with the first sale of war saving certificates and stamps.

CHURCHILL LIKELY TO BALK

Move for New War Cabinet Is Nearing a Test in Britain

By the Associated Press

LONDON, April 28—Political observers tonight foresaw the possibility of the opening wedge being driven this week in a move to streamline Great Britain's War Cabinet.

For several weeks there have been widely whispered hints that the present eight-man War Cabinet, with five of its principal members holding departmental positions, has proved too unwieldy, and the matter is scheduled to be aired in the House of Commons this week.

Informed sources believe that if the rumored four-man cabinet is formed, its membership probably will be Prime Minister Winston Churchill, Jan Christiaan Smuts, prime minister of the Union of South Africa, W. L. Mackenzie King, prime minister of Canada, and Robert G. Menzies, prime minister of Australia.

These same sources, however, consider it more than likely that

and that Britain's personnel and that Britain will carry on with the present board who is in reality in a one-man cabinet—Churchill.

"Now, a hint by Winston Churchill is instantly put into action," this observer said. "A tight, four-man body comes three weeks would be a slowing up of the process—and Britain is counting on speed to win."

(Conservative Leader R. B. Hannon suggested in Commons at Ottawa Monday that King should go to London, leading the way for a conference of Commons premiers for the betterment of the morale of British people and the Dominions whose troops are in action.)

War Entry Threatened by Vichy

'Free French' Drive on African Colonies Irks Petain Cabinet; Army May Be Called

By the United Press

VICHY, April 28—The Petain Government tonight considered throwing France's overseas army back into the war in Africa where British and Free French forces are attacking French Somaliland in a drive against the important port and railroad terminus of Jibuti.

French defense forces, ordered to resist the Somaliland attack, were said in an official announcement to be remaining at their posts and to be refusing to enter into any agreement with the attacking Free French dissidents of Gen. Charles de Gaulle.

Warships Block Port

British warships were said to have appeared off Jibuti Sunday, completely blockading the port, in support of the land attack.

The "Free French" and British units were said to be spread all along Somaliland's southern frontier, trying to provoke the 2,800 French defense troops to desert.

Thus far, it was said, there has been no serious fighting in the drive on France's East African colony 250 miles northeast of Addis Ababa where British armored units and Free French forces have suppressed two points.

"Persuasion" Suggested

(The Associated Press report from Vichy viewed the De Gaulle move more as an attempt to "persuade" the colony to enlist with Axis African forces rather than an attack. It was said that a De Gaulle plane dropped pamphlets urging French outposts to join the British side.

(Free French headquarters in London announced that it had no knowledge of an attack by its forces on French Somaliland, and said the report of an attack issued at Vichy "should be accepted with very great reserve."

(In London, the possibility was raised that the French in Somaliland might co-operate to the extent of disarming and interning any Fascists who might slip through the British net from Ethiopia.

(A Free French column was said in an official announcement to be striking upon Daouamkoh, 70 miles south of Jibuti along the railway.)

Turn to Page 2, Column 3

British Army Makes Stand Near Salum

Attempts to Halt Axis Drive Toward Suez

By the Associated Press

CAIRO, April 28—Advance units of a British armored division were reported in combat with Axis forces near Salum, Egypt, tonight as the North African front resumed the center of the stage in the Mediterranean war theater.

German-Italian units, British headquarters said, made little or no progress with the spearhead they have established six miles inside the Egyptian frontier, and in East African Axis forces suffered another setback with the fall of Dessie, Italian-Ethiopian stronghold.

British troops entered Dessie Sunday after a few hours of tough fighting at Kombolcha Pass, 14 miles south of the plateau city, informed military circles said.

(This supported London reports that the town was taken by forces operating from the British-held capital, Addis Ababa, although Dessie had been attacked from all sides.

(There was speculation in London over the possibility that the Duke of Aosta, Fascist viceroy of Ethiopia, and his staff might soon fall into British hands. Previously it was assumed that they would attempt to escape by plane, but military sources in London said that they knew of no air fields from which a take-off is possible in the mountainous, snow-covered country along the route of the Italian retreat.)

With Dessie captured, there remain only one or two major centers of Italian resistance, Gondar, 600 miles northwest of Addis Ababa and 180 miles northwest of Dessie, and Jimma, 160 miles southwest of Addis Ababa.

SOLDIER FARE OK'D

WASHINGTON, April 28—(A.P.)—The Interstate Commerce Commission authorized railroads today to carry members of the nation's armed forces at a rate of 1 ½ cents a mile instead of the regular two-cent rate beginning May 1.

Village Flees Forest Blaze

By the Associated Press

GROTON, Mass., April 28—Fifty families evacuated their Forge Village homes as a precautionary measure tonight as a thousand soldiers battled side by side with weary firemen to stem a forest blaze that already had blackened an area estimated at about 100 square miles.

At least one home in the vicinity was destroyed and the fate of a dozen others was in doubt as the flames ate over the largest area burned in Massachusetts this year in a single woodland blaze.

As the fire swept within a half mile of the village, the Abbott Worsted Mills—only industry in the hamlet—released 500 employees on the night shift.

Panicky families were piling clothing and other valuables outside their homes in the village, which is surrounded by woodland, in the town of Westford, bordering May 1.

2 Sons of Pierlot Die in Train Fire

Free Press-Chicago Tribune Wire

LONDON, April 28—Two sons of Belgium's premier, Hubert Pierlot, were killed and another injured when a train containing 66 boys from Ampleforth College, York, caught fire between Hungerford and Claypole, Lincolnshire, today.

Six boys altogether were killed and seven injured. The cause of the fire was unknown.

KREISLER UNCONSCIOUS

NEW YORK, April 28—(A.P.)—The condition of Fritz Kreisler, the violinist, remained unconscious tonight at Roosevelt Hospital almost 60 hours after his injury by a truck Monday night. Dr. Alexander Brown said the sixty-six-year-old musician was "still unconscious..."

Facing Prison After Conviction in Graft Conspiracy

ALFRED J. GARSKA
Ex-President, Grosse Pointe Park

THOMAS C. WILCOX
Former sheriff

DUNCAN C. McCREA
Former prosecutor

Morgenthau Opposes Plan to Tax Food

Business Men Urge Lower Exemptions

By the Associated Press

WASHINGTON, April 28—Secretary of the Treasury Henry Morgenthau, who has recommended stiffly increased income taxes and other means of raising $3,500,000,000, opposed today a rival revenue proposal to tax food by declaring it would "tax the poor man's table."

He referred to a plan drawn up by experts of the joint Congressional Committee on Internal Revenue Taxation. Among other things, these experts suggested levies on coffee, tea and sugar, and Morgenthau said such taxes were contrary to "everything that Administration has stood for."

Easier on Low Incomes

Both plans are designed to help finance armaments. The Treasury had proposed surtaxes starting at 11 per cent on the lowest income tax brackets, certain increased excise taxes and other new levies. The Congressional plan would be considerably easier on most lower-income brackets.

Proposals to make many additional persons subject to income taxes by lowering exemptions were made today by representatives of two New York business men's organizations.

The lower-exemptions idea was advocated by M. L. Seidman, chairman of the tax committee of the New York Board of Trade, and William J. Schieffelin, Jr., chairman of the Chamber of Commerce of the State of New York, in testimony before the House Ways and Means Committee.

Sales Tax Also Favored

Schieffelin also suggested either a Federal retail sales tax or a defense tax collected at the source on all gross incomes. The Treasury has said that it rejected both these tax possibilities.

Seidman proposed a specific new schedule of exemptions: $500 for single persons, in place of the present $800; $1,000 for married couples in place of the present $2,000, and $250 for each dependent, instead of the current $400.

He suggested that those made subject to the income tax as a result of the taxation reduction be charged a rate one-half that levied against the next highest tax bracket.

Puts Yield at 2 Billion

Seidman estimated that about $2,000,000,000 additional would be derived from the lower exemptions.

Besides his other suggestions, Schieffelin proposed that the present normal income tax rate be increased from 4 to 6 per cent.

SCIENCE IS MAKING STRIDES

And to keep abreast of these strides, read the Sunday Free Press.

Are you taking note of the Science Column in each Sunday's Free Press? If not, you are missing one of the most informative departments available to the newspaper reader.

In Don Campbell's science department you are assured of at least one "scoop" each Sunday.

SUNDAY'S FREE PRESS

Names of 24 Convicted of Graft Plots

Those convicted in the gambling-vice-graft case before Circuit Judge Earl C. Pugsley were:
DUNCAN C. McCREA, former prosecutor.
THOMAS C. WILCOX, former sheriff.
ALFRED J. GARSKA, erstwhile president of Grosse Pointe Park and handbook operator in the suburb.
CARL J. STAEBLER, chief of the rival divisions under Wilcox.
JOSEPH BIRACH, Hamtramck handbook operator.
FRANK CHISM, Grosse Pointe Park handbook operator.
JAMES DeFALCO, payoff man for a brothel operated by Angelo Scaduto on Six Mile.
LOUIS ELLIOTT, Grosse Pointe Park handbook operator.
MICHAEL FIGURSKI, alias Ferguson, Hamtramck political figure, graft collector, former and policy operator.
CHARLES (RED) GORMAN, partner of the Rouge Combe, a Downriver gambling syndicate.
SAM (THE JAP) GROSS, Hamtramck brothel keeper.
LYLE HARTRICK, Hamtramck handbook operator.
BERTHA (JOHNSON) MALONE, Hamtramck brothel keeper.
HARRY (TENNESSEE SLIM) KIVLIN, Downriver gambler.
BENJAMIN D. LANDSBURG, former Inkster police chief, policy banker and slot-machine operator.
VICTOR OTTO, partner of Chism in a Grosse Pointe Park handbook.
WILLIAM (SLICKER) PAIGE, member of the Rouge Combe, a Downriver gambling syndicate.
GEORGE (LEFTY) QUINIFF, Downriver gambler.
ANGELO SCADUTO, outcounty brothel keeper.
JOSEPH SEMETKO, Grosse Pointe Woods slot-machine operator.
SAM (SMOKEY) SOLOMAN, Hamtramck handbook operator.
CLYDE STANBAUGH, partner of Elliott in a Grosse Pointe Park handbook.
EDDIE WAY, Downriver graft collector and gambler.
THOMAS WOODHAMS, River Rouge handbook operator.

Strike Halts Delivery of Meat in London

LONDON, April 28—(A.P.)—Distribution of meat for Greater London was tied up today by a strike of 2,500 employees at wholesale depots who protested dismissal of 60 of their number when one depot was closed by raid damage.

ANOTHER BOTTLENECK

OPM Sees City Draft Boards Bleeding Defense Industries

BY FRANK B. WOODFORD
Free Press Staff Writer

Charges that national-defense industry is being hampered by the drafting of qualified craftsmen in Michigan, particularly in the Detroit industrial area, have been brought by Army and OPM officials in Washington, it was revealed in the Detroit Monday.

These charges, in the form of complaints to National Selective Service Headquarters, have been passed on to state headquarters and through that agency to the local draft boards of Wayne and adjoining counties.

So incensed is Washington by the admittedly "tough" attitude of Wayne County draft boards on occupational deferments that Michigan officials were asked by the OPM whether they regarded Michigan as "still being in the

That the situation is serious is revealed by figures included in a recent report to local board members showing occupational deferments granted in Michigan. It was prepared by Lieut. Col. J. D. Brent of the state selective-service staff, and is as follows:

It was pointed out that in the Detroit area, where the demand for skilled men in defense industry probably is not exceeded by any other locality in the country, occupational deferments have averaged only 1½ per cent of the men classified.

In other areas in Michigan, notably agricultural districts, the occupational deferments have been as high as 18 per cent.

In the St. Louis industrial area deferments for industry have averaged 7½ per cent, and in Hartford, Conn., where there are many plane industries, they have been from 10 to 15 per cent.

Colonel Brent, a representative of manufacturers, Kreuger, the Michigan Unemployment Compensation Commission, and other agencies, indicate

Turn to Page 4, Column 1

Jury Frees Only One Defendant

Terms of 5 Years and $2,000 Fines Can Be Given; Sentencing Scheduled on May 14

BY KENNETH E. McCORMICK
Free Press Staff Writer

Former Prosecutor Duncan C. McCrea, former Sheriff Thomas C. Wilcox and 23 other defendants in the County vice and gambling conspiracy case will be sentenced May 14, Circuit Judge Earl C. Pugsley announced following their conviction at 3 p.m. Monday.

Of 25 defendants who placed their fate in the hands of a jury, only Charles Mocori, one-time owner of the Ackmur Club, in which gambling was alleged to have taken place during the time of the conspiracy, escaped conviction. Angelo Scaduto, operator of a house of prostitution, only defendant who elected to waive trial by jury, was convicted by the Court and sentenced with the others.

The jury returned the verdict consisting of seven women, and five men who have been locked up under the strict vigil of the Sheriff's Office since Jan. 27 when it was sworn.

Garska One of Guilty

Alfred J. Garska, former president of Grosse Pointe Park and Carl J. Staebler, chief of the civil division under Wilcox, were other former public officials convicted of accepting graft from vice and gambling interests.

Harry Colburn, chief investigator before Judge Pugsley several weeks ago and then took the stand as the principal witness against his erstwhile boss and close friend, will be sentenced with the others.

The defendants—convicted of conspiracy to obstruct justice by paying and accepting graft for protection of illegal enterprises—face a maximum sentence of five years' imprisonment and a fine of $2,000.

Jurors Appear Tired

The court room was comparatively empty when the solemn jury filed in and took seats in the jury box. Each member of the venire showed the strain of long jury deliberations, apparently, and looked bleary eyed.

The clerk called the roll of the venire and asked the foreman, Ralph M. Holmes, a salesman, to rise.

"Have you arrived at a verdict?" the clerk asked.

Pulling a prepared list of the defendants from his pocket, Holmes announced the verdict.

Two of the jurors, Miss Tillie M. Yanuska, a clerk, and Mrs. Ann Snooks broke down and began to weep. Other women on the jury could scarcely refrain from crying.

Poll of Jury Taken

The jury was polled and each member answered a monotonous "yes" to the inquiry of the clerk's regarding whether verdict was his.

Judge Pugsley continued the bonds of the defendants and asked only one "last desperate plea remaining to persuade Judge Pugsley to remain in the court room to arrange interviews with Fred H. Wright, chief probation officer of the Circuit Court.

The Court immediately went into an adjoining court room where sentencing arguments to Thomas A. Kenny, assistant attorney general attached to the grand jury staff, were made in the Scaduto case.

"The White House has no comment on the Lindbergh letter today. War Department officials said it would be up to Secretary of War Henry L. Stimson to accept or reject the resignation customarily rejected during emergency periods."

Scaduto, unperturbed, received Judge Pugsley and that the evidence against Scaduto was all overwhelming against him, that the others, but was still sufficient. He was sentenced with the others.

Warns Against Demonstration

Before the verdict was returned by the jury, Judge Pugsley cautioned the audience against any demonstration, intimating that others in the venire of the venire might be reached.

His orders were obeyed. The spectators sat grimly in their seats. Mrs. Mocori, wife of the only freed defendant, wept. But her emotions were probably more the result of the acquittal of her husband and grief over the fate of her brother, Michael Figurski, one of those convicted.

Bertha Johnson Malone, Hamtramck brothel keeper, who was convicted, wept long after the verdict was read. She had bought her self a fine house. Last but not one of the convicted.

Chester F. O'Hara, chief special grand-jury prosecutor, who carried the bulk of the burden of the prosecution, showed no emotion. He sat beside his assistant, Guy W. Jensen, and gazed at the floor.

"I want to thank you, ladies and gentlemen of the jury," said Judge Pugsley, in dismissing the venire, "for the splendid co-operation and consideration you have shown in this case. You are now free to go your homes."

After that, he announced that

Turn to Page 16, Column 2

Air Corps Job Is Resigned by Lindbergh

Flier Cites Remarks of F.D.R. on Loyalty

By the Associated Press

NEW YORK, April 28—Charles A. Lindbergh resigned today as colonel in the United States Army Air Corps Reserve because, he said, his commander in chief—President Roosevelt—had implied certain things about "my loyalty to my country, my motives and my character."

Thus, the thin young man who, at the age of 25, historically flew the Atlantic, became a world hero and rose at once from captain to colonel in recognition of the feat beseeched the Government at 39 to return him to private life because he had "no honorable alternative."

A reply to a speech of Col. Lindbergh by a Briton on Page 2.

defeat Great Britain. The President compared them to appeasers of Revolutionary and Civil War days who insisted that defeat was immanent and that peace should be sued for promptly.

The President thus "clearly implied," Lindbergh wrote, "that I am no longer of use to this Country as a reserve officer."

He told his Commander that he was "greatly disturbed" and that he had hoped he might "exercise my rights as an American citizen to place my viewpoint before the people of my Country in time of peace, without giving up the privilege of serving my Country as an Air Corps officer in the event of war."

Lindbergh in recent months has been a leading isolationist speaker. Wednesday night he said at a New York rally that Britain had only one "last desperate plan remaining"—to persuade American entry into the war and to have this Country share the "fiasco" with England both militarily and financially.

"The White House has no comment on the Lindbergh letter today. War Department officials said it would be up to Secretary of War Henry L. Stimson to accept or reject the resignation, customarily rejected during emergency periods."

DEC. 8 1941:

Troops move in to help secure Detroit after the attack on Pearl Harbor.

"War Guard Moves into City Plants," column one.

Weather Report
Showers changing, it snow Monday; Tuesday cloudy, continued cold.
(Complete report on Page 8)

The Detroit Free Press
On Guard for Over a Century

METROPOLITAN EXTRA

Monday, December 8, 1941. No. 218 — BURTON — 111th Year — 26 Pages — Three Cents

Army Guards Detroit Tunnel and Bridge

U.S. NAVY IS HARD HIT AS JAPAN OPENS WAR

Roosevelt Taking Message to Congress Today

War Guard Moves into City Plants

FBI Takes Action to Fight Sabotage; Workers to Have Strict Regulations

BY CLIFFORD A. PREVOST
Free Press Washington Bureau

War came to Detroit early Monday in the form of strict regulations imposed on all plants participating in the defense program.

The Federal Bureau of Investigation has a complete plan to prevent sabotage. Its agents will work in close cooperation with plant and local police and no plant will be left unguarded. It is believed that within a few days all workmen will be required to carry identification cards, similar to those now necessary to gain admittance to Army and War Department buildings here.

Borders Closed to Japs

Secretary Henry Morgenthau, Jr. tonight closed the nation's borders to Japanese nationals and imposed a strict ban on any financial transactions by Japanese aliens. Japanese assets in this country have been unofficially estimated at $1,000,000,000. The nation's major auction houses issued orders for their phases not to transport any Japanese.

Morgenthau also invoked tonight a portion of the Trading with the Enemy Act, which bars...

24-Hour Work on Arms Asked

WASHINGTON, Dec. 7 — Undersecretary of War Patterson called tonight for production of all war munitions on a twenty-four-hour basis.

Patterson issued instructions to chiefs of the War Department procurement agency that "all steps must be taken to increase the speed with which contracts are let, and to speed up maximum production."

In a memorandum follows:

"It is essential that our procurement be put into highest gear at once. All steps must be taken to increase the speed with which contracts are let, and to speed up maximum production of munitions.

"All officers and civilian employees of War Department services will be required to work as many additional hours each day as are necessary to get the day's work done."

...transportation or communication with Japan or by her allies, no matter how indirectly.

The Civil Aeronautics Authority issued orders tonight grounding all Japanese airplanes in the United States and its possessions, except commercial airliners.

The Federal Communications Commission tonight prohibited all amateur radio operation in the United States and its possessions, authorized by Federal, state and municipal authorities in connection with emergency matters.

Anticipating sabotage attempts, Secretary of War Henry L. Stimson today urged the nation's armed forces to take extra precautions immediately. With the declaration of war Monday, every worker will be closely checked in accordance with the FBI regulations.

"All with proper credentials will be charged with the utmost...

Turn to Page 11, Column 2

Joint Session Is Due to Vote a Declaration; Whole Nation Rallied

U.S. Swiftly Put on War Basis; All Military Personnel Mobilized

NEW YORK, Dec. 8 — (UP) — The National Broadcasting Co. reported from Manila tonight that reports there said that the United States transport Gen. Hugh L. Scott, formerly the President Pierce, has been sunk about 1,000 miles from Manila and that the liner President Harrison, which was used to evacuate Americans, either had been seized or sunk off Shanghai.

By the Associated Press
WASHINGTON, Dec. 8 — (Monday) — (UP) — Japanese warplanes made a deadly assault on Honolulu and Pearl Harbor Sunday in the foremost of a series of attacks without warning against American possessions throughout the Pacific.

Three hours later — while its envoys were still conferring with Secretary of State Cordell Hull — the Japanese Government declared war on the United States and Great Britain.

After President Roosevelt had conferred all last evening with his war and naval chieftains, his Cabinet and congressional...

Blackout in Washington

WASHINGTON, Dec. 8 — (Monday) — The Nation's capital was partially blacked out early today.

...leaders, it was announced just before midnight that the President would go before Congress at 12:30 p.m. today with a special message.

This was expected to be a request for a United States declaration of war on Japan, and there was no question in any quarter but what it would be promptly voted.

(Clifford A. Prevost, Free Press Washington correspondent, predicted that "Sunset today will probably see this country openly at war not only with Japan but with Germany and Italy as well.")

There were unconfirmed reports that the Japanese assault on Pearl Harbor, Hawaii, had sunk two American battleships — possibly the Oklahoma and West Virginia — and several destroyers, and that the force of 300 American warplanes there had been badly damaged.

The White House announced during President Roosevelt's conference with legislative leaders and members of the Cabinet that he had received word from Gen. Douglas MacArthur that "enemy planes were over Central Luzon in the Philippines about 8 p.m., Eastern Standard Time; that a bombing attack has been made on Davao at the southern end of the southern island of Mindanao, and that another attack has been made on Camp John Hayes at Baguio in the northern mountains of Luzon. So far no essential damage had been reported."

Otherwise, the Japanese aggression which the United States officially and unequivocally described as treacherous and utterly unprovoked bore three first fruits for the Empire, as summed up from official and unofficial sources.

Up to 350 United States soldiers killed and more than 300 wounded at Hickam Field, Hawaiian Islands.

The United States battleship Oklahoma and some of four other United States ships at Pearl Harbor attacked.

Heavy damage to residential districts, where there were unnumbered casualties.

Torpedoing of a lumber-laden United States Army transport between Hawaii and San Francisco.

Capture of the United States Pacific islet of Wake and bombing of Guam.

Seizure of the International Settlement at Shanghai.

Capture of the United States gunboat Wake at Shanghai and destruction of the British gunboat Peters near by.

The Japanese also bombed Singapore, and the British announced that the Japanese had landed in North Malaya and were being engaged. The Tokio radio said the...

Turn to Page 11, Column 6

Momentous News for the Whole Nation

Free Press Photo

Japan's bombing of Honolulu created an even greater demand for the Free Press Sunday night extras than did Hitler's invasion of Poland, which launched World War II, and set a record for copies sold. Here three news-hungry young men concentrate on one copy to read dispatches of especial significance to them. Naval trainees stationed in Detroit, they are (from left to right) Thomas Jainer, of Birmingham, Ala.; Howard Black, of Williamston, S.C., and Harry Bigelow, of Montgomery, Ala. All were intensely interested in the dispatches about the opening battles.

West Coast Girds to Repel Any Invasion

Air-Raid Listening Devices in Operation

By the Associated Press
LOS ANGELES, Dec. 7 — Air-raid listening devices went into action at scores of Southern California defense factories today, alert for any sign of a raid on this area, which contains the largest aggregation of plane building in the nation.

First to take precautionary steps were the huge aircraft factories, busily engaged in maximum capacity production of large bombers and fast fighting aircraft.

Regular air patrols in this area may be established immediately, it was understood.

All vessels capable of moving under their own power were ordered from the inner harbor at San Pedro to positions just outside the harbor. This move, it was explained was for the purpose of getting the vessels as far as possible from the harbor warehouses, oil tanks and docks.

Nearly 1,000 members of the Sixth Regiment, California State Guard, were mobilized in a Compton armory under orders by Brig. Gen. J. O. Donovan.

John S. Hugus, director of the Detroit office of the FBI, refused to comment Sunday night on the specific plans of his office for the prevention of sabotage and the treatment of local Japanese...

Turn to Page 10, Column 5

U.S. Troops Arrive to Protect City

The Army and the FBI Sunday night took over Detroit to insure protection of her vital defense industry.

Four truckloads of Selfridge Field troops arrived in the city at a late hour to set up guard at the Ambassador Bridge and the Detroit-Windsor Tunnel. Similar precautions were planned for the Michigan Central Railroad tunnel under the river and the vital car ferries.

The Detroit police, meanwhile, broadcast a notice requesting all scout cars, cruisers and patrolmen to closely watch all radio stations and radio transmitter areas.

Nearly 1,000 members of the Sixth Regiment, California State Guard, were mobilized in a Compton armory under orders by Brig. Gen. J. O. Donovan.

Simultaneously, immediate mobilization of 10,000 men in the major...

Turn to Page 11, Column 5

Army Likely to Call Reserves to Colors

WASHINGTON, Dec. 7 — Immediate and vast expansion of the nation's armed forces, now that hostilities have been thrust upon the United States, was regarded in military circles tonight as certain.

It was believed that one of the first steps would be to call all enlisted reserves to active duty. This would mean a return to Army posts for those selective service trainees who recently were discharged from active duty because of being past the age of 28 or for other reasons.

Army officials at Fort Lewis, Wash., already have issued calls to such men.

With a declaration of war by the United States, men in the age bracket between 28 and 35 and registered under the Draft Act would be liable for immediate call to training.

These men were given a de...

Turn to Page 11, Column 1

Tokio's Action Includes Both U.S. and Britain

By the Associated Press
TOKIO, Dec. 8 (Monday) — Japan went to war against the United States and Great Britain today with air and sea attacks against Hawaii followed by a formal declaration of hostilities.

Japanese Imperial headquarters announced at 6 a.m. (4 p.m. Sunday, EST) that a state of war existed among the Japanese people in a broadcast from Tokio Sunday night. "I hereby promise you that Japan will win final victory." He said that Japan was declaring war on the United States for "self-protection and self-existence."

(The broadcast was declared to have raided Honolulu at 7:35 a.m. Hawaii time (1:05 p.m. Sunday, EST).

(A broadcast from Tokio re...

...ceived in Los Angeles said that 63 American soldiers had been disarmed at the International Settlement in Tientsin China.

(Premier Hideki Tojo told the Japanese people in a broadcast from Tokio Sunday night. "I hereby promise you that Japan will win final victory." He said that Japan was declaring war on the United States for "self-protection and self-existence."

(The broadcast upon Singapore came as a mighty British force of men, guns, ships and planes stood ready for Prime Minister Winston Churchill's anticipated declaration of war against Japan today.

LOS ANGELES, Dec. 7 — (AP) — Japanese troops have invaded Thailand, the Tokio radio said today in a broadcast heard on the NBC listening post...

Turn to Page 11, Column 4

2 U.S. Battleships Reported Sunk

Pearl Harbor Base and Honolulu Bombed Heavily; Big Toll Feared

BY FRANCIS McCARTHY
United Press Correspondent

HONOLULU, Dec. 7 — War broke with lightning suddenness in the Pacific today when waves of Japanese bombers attacked Hawaii and the United States Fleet struck back with a thunder of big naval rifles.

Japanese bombers, including four-motored dive-bombers and torpedo-carrying planes blasted at Pearl Harbor, the great United States naval base, the city of Honolulu and several outlying American military bases on the island of Oahu. There were many casualties, but the number was unstated.

(An NBC observer reported tonight from Honolulu that 350 men had been killed in a direct bomb hit at Hickam Field, Army bomber base there. He said that three ships, including the USS Oklahoma, a battleship, had been attacked and set afire in Pearl Harbor. The base was said to have been heavily damaged.

(Japan's Domei news agency said in Shanghai that the Oklahoma had been sunk. Later the Berlin radio broadcast a Tokio announcement that the United States battleship West Virginia had also been sent to the bottom in an engagement between the Japanese and the United States and British navies. The Berlin broadcast said that the battle was still going on and that altogether three United States ships were hit. The third was not named.)

(Several attacking planes, believed to have advanced on Pearl Harbor from the north, were shot down, the NBC observer said. In Washington, reliable quarters said that antiaircraft fire and naval action had bagged six Japanese planes and four submarines in the Hawaiian action.)

Parachutists appeared off Harbor front, five miles from the center of Honolulu. It was assumed that they were suicide squadrons of saboteurs.)

Fleet Steams Out

Then the United States Fleet steamed out of Pearl Harbor. The sound of gunfire was heard off Oahu and gunflashes were seen from the shore. It was believed that most of the Japanese bombers operated from aircraft carriers, which might have been intercepted.

(A Japanese aircraft carrier was sunk off Honolulu today, according to a broadcast by the Panama radio heard in New York by NBC. At the same time, a Reuters dispatch from Shanghai quoted an unconfirmed report circulated there saying that Wake Island had been occupied by the Japanese. The British News agency said that the Shanghai rumors had it that the occupation of Wake was accomplished peaceably.

(The Tokio radio reported tonight, in a broadcast picked up by the NBC listening post in Los Angeles, that Japanese naval ships have surrounded the island of Guam and that a naval oil reservoir and hotel have been set afire.

(An Associated Press dispatch from Manila said that the United States bombers and pursuit planes took the air early Monday and headed northward.

"Let's Get the Japanese"

The cry, "now let's get the Japanese," was raised as the United States fleet steamed out. (Japanese sources at Shanghai reported that a Japanese-American naval battle was under way "in the Western Pacific.")

The air attacks began at 7:55 a.m., rousing most Honolulans from their beds. Some were still...

Turn to Page 11, Column 3

British and Japanese Clash in Malaya; Singapore Raided

By the Associated Press
SINGAPORE, Dec. 8 (Monday) — The Japanese bombed this British Far Eastern naval bastion today and landed troops on the Malay Peninsula to the north where they engaged British forces.

Two bombs fell in the center of Singapore and a number of others were heard in various parts of the island.

Gunfire was reported heard off Mersing, 90 miles northwest of Singapore on the east coast of Malaya.

A brief official announcement said that the Japanese had landed in North Malaya and that "the invaders are being engaged."

(Japanese planes have sunk two British cruisers in Singapore Harbor with direct hits, according to a CBS bulletin heard in New York.)

The attack upon Singapore came as a mighty British force of men, guns, ships and planes stood ready for Prime Minister Winston Churchill's anticipated declaration of war against Japan today.

(LOS ANGELES, Dec. 7 — (AP) — Japanese troops have invaded Thailand, the Tokio radio said today in a broadcast heard on the NBC listening post.

Tokio appealed to all friendly sources in Japan believes that Germany will declare war on the United States within 24 hours.

(The BBC broadcast an unconfirmed report tonight that Bangkok, capital of Thailand, had been bombed. The broadcast was heard in New York by CBS.

FASHIONS OF THE DAY

THE DETROIT FREE PRESS — SATURDAY, NOVEMBER 28, 1942

Matched Accessories and Smart New Shoes for the Holidays

Big Handbag Has Smart, Drape Line

Black Gabardine Pump Features Clever Trim

BY JEAN PEARSON

WHILE WASHINGTON bubbles and seethes, while various reports are printed in the papers and rumors run rampant about the availability of shoes, people go right on buying them with the greatest of ease from stores who have—and expect to continue to have—a good stock of them on hand.

"No more red shoes!" one report said. And that will certainly be true after the present supply is gone. But there are still a lot of shoe manufacturers with a stock of red shoe leather on hand to use. So you can be sure you won't suddenly wake up some gray dawn to discover there isn't a pair in the world.

HOWEVER, IF you have a new outfit that just cries for red accessories, you might better buy them now while there is still a selection.

And if you're anxious to have your accessories match perfectly be certain to consider the set at the far left in "Flambe" red. The shoe, handbag and glove are an identical color because the suede of which they are made was all dyed together in the same vat.

The pump "A" is a high-heeled platform pump. Open the ankle, it has a round buckle trim at the gathered, draped toe. A trim, yet dressy style, it is priced at $23.90.

THE LARGE, under-arm bag of matching suede has a clever cut and a lovely gathered softness. Beautifully finished on the inside and expertly made, it is priced at $25. The matching classic gloves are tagged at $5.95.

An early mid-winter model to appear in the shoe fashion scene is sketched in "B". It is a classic black gabardine pump with a sheer black cord and braid buckle. Open-toed, it has a scuff-less heel that may be had in either the high or medium height.

Also done in brown gabardine and brown or black calf, it is priced at $13.95 in gabardine and $15.95 in calf.

THE SHOE sketched in "C" is called the "Porthole." Why, you can plainly see. For the perforations are about as big as a porthole—well, almost!

A platform model with a high, slim-heel, it is done in bright suede, brown and black, and is priced for $19.95.

A beautiful, gleaming genuine alligator open toe and heel, the trim flat buckle is also of alligator. Designed in brown only, it is priced at $22.50.

'Mrs. Page'

Ruth Franklin Crane "Mrs. Page" of WJR, has recently been named committee chairman of Michigan and Ohio for the recently organized National Association of Women's Activities Directors of the National Association of Broadcasters. Mrs. Crane, who lives at the West end in a Red Cross canteen station, in maintaining a Victory antiseptic occupation of the skin areas of the patient, the needle and the hands of the operator before, during and after application of the process may really lead to infection of varying degrees of severity. One should never tolerate an operator in whom the least lack of sanitation is detected.

AND IN answer to your question about multiple electrolysis I again quote. There is much discussion as to whether single needle or multiple needle electrolysis (that is in which four, six, eight or more needles are connected to the negative pole) is the better. The fact is that each has its advantages and disadvantages between which the individual must choose. Multiple needles are said to be faster, but this is probably not overly true since each one must still be placed separately. Some time may be saved through being able to place one needle while another is working but this is likely offset by the fact that the single needle operator will be more careful that the other, not having several needles to confuse and distract his attention. Also there will be a smaller percentage of failure with the single needle to compensate for the apparently greater speed of the other."

COLDS
Relieve misery, as most mothers do. Rub Vicks on throat, chest and back with time-tested **VICKS VAPORUB**

Relief At Last For Your Cough

Creomulsion relieves promptly because it goes right to the seat of the trouble to help loosen and expel germ laden phlegm, and aid nature to soothe and heal raw, tender, inflamed bronchial mucous membranes. Tell your druggist to sell you a bottle of Creomulsion with the understanding you must like the way it quickly allays the cough or you are to have your money back.

CREOMULSION
for Coughs, Chest Colds, Bronchitis

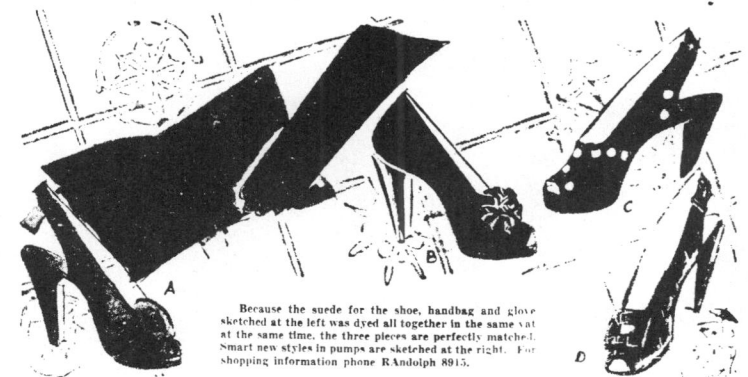

Because the suede for the shoe, handbag and glove sketched at the left was dyed all together in the same vat at the same time, the three pieces are perfectly matched. Smart new styles in pumps are sketched at the right. For shopping information phone RAndolph 8915.

Secretary Asks Advice About Looks

BY GRACE BARBER

DEAR MISS BARBER: I am eighteen and have been out of school since 1941 and am employed as a secretary. I am the only girl in an office where there are many men. Could you suggest what type of clothes I should wear? My boss definitely insists on sweaters and skirts. I have very long hair and have been contemplating having it cut into a featherbob or something similar to that. What do you suggest? Any ideas you have to offer would be more than appreciated.

The letter quoted above (accompanied by a tiny but clear photograph) poses too very sensible questions by an apparently pretty level-headed young woman. Since she is typical of a group of young women that face her problems are of general interest in a large teen-age group who are working these days.

FIRST THE hair. The young lady, who shall be known as G. P., wears her hair so long that it hangs well below her shoulders, giving too much childish an effect. Personally I believe she would do well either to do it up in some way with a braid or a roll to get it up out of the way or else go ahead and have the feather cut. In that case it is quite evident that a good permanent must be had because the photograph shows that G. P.'s hair is fine and lacks body enough to look well if cut short.

As to dress I'm not surprised about the sweater and skirt selection by the "boss." The "sweater" girl problem has upset things in more than one office and the "boss" probably has had it happen in his office. There are in my smart tailored suits which with a variety of blouses make many changes. And there are all sorts of warm tailored dresses which are not only neat and trim but very good looking.

MORE TROUBLE from another working gal Mrs. E. F. writes, "I would like to inquire about the safe removal of superfluous hair from the face. My hair is black I have tried bleaching it to no avail. I am employed at a good salary and the question itself would multiply electrolysis for removal of hair be safe with no danger of scars, infection or the like?"

The best way I can answer, E. F. is to quote from A. F. Niemoeller's book, "Superfluous Hair and Its Removal." In the chapter on electrolysis he says "Electrolysis is to date the best and safest method of permanent hair removal. This does not mean however that it is wholly foolproof or that it does not possess many very real disadvantages. In the hands of an inexperienced or bungling operator it can produce highly disfiguring pitting and scarring of the areas worked over. Since the skin is penetrated during its use carelessness in maintaining absolutely

Food for Victory
BY GERTRUDE VOELLMIG

🇺🇸

IF YOU are in a quandary about what to give to a woman whose love is her kitchen and the dishes she prepares in it, why not consider a cook book . . . perhaps two . . . one silly, one practical. Cook books make excellent gifts. Assortment—unbelievable; stocks—excellent; quality—good.

There's a new one on the list you might consider . . . "Lunching and Dining At Home" by Jeanne Owen (Alfred A. Knopf). It is a book of wonderful, mouthwatering menus with accompanying recipes for four, six and eight people . . . combined from foods which should not be difficult to locate even now. It is divided according to the seasons with Sunday breakfasts and suppers tossed in for good measure. Jeanne Owen has made a hobby of food and its preparation . . . writes for magazines . . . knows wines . . . Her "A Wine Lover's Cook Book" is the delight of many.

* * *

SWEDISH SPRITZ—It will soon be time to get started on Christmas cookies. So, while you are in the holiday mood I am giving you the recipe for Swedish Spritz requested by Mrs. Sim Harris, 617 Bennett E. Ferndale. Recipes vary . . . this is one variety.

Spritz
2½ c cake flour
¼ t salt
1 c shortening
¼ c powdered sugar
1 t almond extract
2 egg yolks, beaten
1 egg white
1 t water

Coarse sugar crystals

Mix flour and salt. Cream shortening until soft; beat in powdered sugar, add almond extract and egg yolks. Gradually stir in flour mixture; chill. Pack dough in cookie press, using various forms of discs or nozzles to make shapes such as letter S, wreaths, bows, knots, crescents, ribbons, etc. Place shapes on ungreased baking sheet; brush with egg white and water, beaten together until frothy, and sprinkle with coarse sugar crystals, colored or plain. Bake in hot 400 degree oven about eight minutes or until delicately browned. Makes five dozen.

If you have a little pumpkin left over you may wish to whip up this pumpkin chiffon pie for the week-end.

Pumpkin Chiffon Pie
1 recipe plain pastry
1 T gelatin
¼ c cold water
1½ c cooked pumpkin
1 c brown sugar
3 eggs, separated
2 t cinnamon
1 t ginger
¼ t all spice
¼ t salt
3 T granulated sugar
1 T grated orange rind
½ c heavy cream

Make nine inch pie shell. Soften gelatin in cold water. Combine pumpkin, brown sugar, egg yolks, spices and salt in top of a double boiler; cook over hot, not boiling water until thickened, stirring constantly. Add softened gelatin to hot pumpkin mixture and stir until dissolved. Remove from hot water. Chill until mixture begins to thicken. Beat egg whites stiff but not dry. Beat in granulated sugar. Fold in to cooled pumpkin mixture. Whip cream and fold in. Pour into baked shell. Top with additional cream if desired.

New Magazine for Homemakers

DRESSED UP in a gay red, white and blue cover patriotic as you please, "What's New in Foods and Nutrition" . . . a new monthly magazine for homemakers . . . appeared on stands all over the country Nov. 20. It's small, compact . . . well worth the 25-cent investment.

For some time Eleanor Howe and M. S. Harvey Jr. co-editors and publishers, have been doing an excellent job on "What's New in Home Economics (a periodical for home economists) . . . this new adventure promises to be equally successful.

Big feature: complete set of wartime menus and recipes for every day in the month. Also included: household hints plus short articles on wartime problems in which women are interested. Mary I. Barber, Food Consultant to the Secretary of War, contributes to the first edition with a bit on "Your Soldier Son's Christmas Dinner."

Food Pages from Scotland

I HAVE just fallen heiress to the food pages of The Montrose Review, from Montrose, Scotland. Scotty your friend of Fish and Game has promised to drop in on the pages and send them to the Tower Kitchen the minute they arrive.

Today's Gift Suggestion

Free Press Photo

Here's a marvelous stocking gift for dad! A little Chinese brass tray for his pipe which, if he likes, he can use for ashes too. It's shaped like an old oil lamp—miniature size, however. And due to the fact that Oriental imports are rapidly becoming a thing of the past in American shops, this delightful piece is a real find at 49 cents. For shopping information call RAndolph 8915.

Christmas for Hirohito

Having roast turkey, goose or chicken for Christmas dinner?

Save some for the Japs! Give them the drippings! Strain all waste kitchen fats into a wide-mouthed can.

When you have a pound sell it to the meat dealer.

FATS MAKE EXPLOSIVES!

Saturday's War-Time Dinner

Each day the Tower kitchen plans a beautiful dinner to help Detroit homemakers fill their families' food requirements. The Government shares the meal programs, rationed and scarce foods are taken into consideration, to make the meal practical for the home front.

Stuffed Sausage Roll
Baked Sweet Potatoes — Biscuits
Carrot Sticks
Orange and Grape Cup

MARKET LIST

Tonight's market list can be purchased for approximately $2.59 and serves six. All of these foods were included on the week-end marketing list printed yesterday.

1½ lbs sausage
4 lbs apples
2 lbs onions
2 lbs sweet potatoes
2 lbs broccoli
3 stalk celery
1 doz. oranges
1 lb grapes

CHECK THESE SUPPLIES
Bread crumbs, bran, milk, butter, bread and beverages

STUFFED SAUSAGE ROLL
2 c chopped raw apples
½ c chopped onions
1 c bread crumbs
1 c bran
1½ lbs sausage meat

Combine apples, onions, crumbs, bran to form a dressing. Pack sausage into a rectangle about a half inch thick. Spread stuffing over surface of the meat; roll up like a jelly roll beginning at the long side of the rectangle so the roll will not be too thick. Bake in a shallow pan on a moderate 350-degree oven for 45 minutes or until done. Serves six.

Marketing Tips
Bureau of Markets, Weights and Measures

Plentiful Supply: Apples, beans, cabbage, table grapes potatoes, sweet potatoes.

Moderate Supply: Avocados, beets, cauliflower, cranberries, greens, lettuce, mushrooms, onions, peppers, shallots, tomatoes.

Light Supply: Bananas, pineapples, broccoli, brussels sprouts, carrots, cucumbers, eggplant, celery, celery cabbage, parsnips, radishes, rutabagas, turnips.

Meats: In spite of the general use of poultry over the Thanksgiving holiday, the demand for other meats appears to have been just about as heavy as usual, according to wholesale dealers. There possibly may be a little better choice of cuts available for this weekend, but this will only be temporary and meats for consumer use will continue scarce.

Butter, eggs and cheese too are in very light supply for civilian use. Stocks of butter in storage have been "frozen" by the Government and all that is available for consumers is that which is in the hands of dealers plus what is being currently produced. It might be suggested here that consumers start to spread their butter thin and conserve it in every other way possible.

Poultry: With the exception of roasting chickens, the supply of poultry was ample for Thanksgiving and anyone who still wants it for the week-end should be able to purchase it freely.

Fish: Wholesale fish dealers report that plentiful supplies of fish continue to be available. King blue hake are selling at very reasonable prices. Offerings of Lake Erie whitefish are increasing in volume with the result that wholesale prices have moderated somewhat.

RUTH ALDEN
Dress Quotas Lag in Upper Age Groups

DEAR GUESTS: Since my last remarks on a new group of dresses and sizes especially needed for so many of you inquiring about these two phases of the campaign, which covers new Christmas dresses as well, I earnestly ask that you use the time up to and including December 1 to see how rapidly, rather than slowly, until the deadline of Dec. 1 for this gift is reached. I am very anxious for each of you to get a new Christmas dress as possible and to those of you among the Guests who have not yet selected their Christmas dress.

If you are planning to chase a dress in the near future I am earnestly urging that you tell your husband that it will sap your gift coffers very quickly. Perhaps he will agree to make this the big item on the gift list for you to get this week. Tell me a dollar more than he gave me gladly, when I explained about being made over into one of these cute little frocks for a little girl who has always worn faded, shabby, hand-me-downs, who has never known what it means to have a brand-new frock of her very own.

Please send me a dress or a Dress Score

3,180 Dresses Received

drab, dear guests, so devoid of the simple joys that most of us take for granted. To these little ones, who are the innocent victims of misfortune, your gift of a brand-new dress means happiness beyond belief.

A pretty, crisply-starched frock brings a thrill of pleasure to any child—think, then, of the joy it spells for a little girl who has always worn faded, shabby hand-me-downs, who has never known what it means to have a brand-new frock of her very own.

Mail Frocks Today

MAY I, this morning, at the counter of this column, ask that you send in or bring your dress, to its final destination in your office, if that is more convenient to you, or leave it at the Free Press, if that is the handier way for you. Every minute and hour of this week must be a period in which you are purchasing a frock, for a checkup of dresses received shows we are still running short of sizes 10, 11 and 12. We have not yet reached our quota in any of the smaller sizes either, but are especially lagging in the older age groups.

So if you are choosing a dress today, select it for a girl of 10, 11 or 12 years. This of course does not mean that I don't want the frocks in other sizes that you have already bought or are making. I am not counting heavily on them in any estimates.

Our eighth annual dress drive comes to a close in three days, and in all the years we have yet failed the needy children of our great city, and I am hoping, oh so fervently, that when our accounts are totaled next Tuesday we shall have gone over the top again. You can understand my anxiety, I know, for we are still so far from our goal of 11,666 frocks for little girls from 4 through 12.

Help Child Pick Friends
BY GLADYS BEVANS

MANY PARENTS of teenage daughters will, I am sure, say "Me, too," when reading the following letter, because it mentions two difficulties that are fairly usual, and which, for a reason, go hand in hand.

"Dear Mrs. Bevans:

"Will you kindly send me advice on understanding the adolescent, any information you can give me on handling a fifteen-year-old girl as to the proper picking of her girl friends and the way of too much make-up? It is a constant argument in our home because our daughter uses lipstick thick, as she says all her friends do."

TO THIS I sent the following reply.

"It is a little difficult to advise you about how to help your daughter to choose the most desirable sort of girls as friends, because young people in their teens resent this sort of thing at a time too often and in a direct, interfering sort of way.

"It seems to me, however, that there is a number of things that will influence any girl. One of these is the good taste which she finds exercised in her own home. Another is the kind of friends her parents have.

"Still another factor is the chance that she should be given to measure up her friends, by inviting them freely into her home.

"However, grown-ups have to bear in mind that sometimes what makes a friend seem undesirable to them is a quality not even noticed by the son or daughter of the family, and one which may be a very superficial thing.

"AS TO makeup, I think it should be very easy to influence your daughter not to use heavy make-up or lipstick. One way is that if they will observe the leading film stars in their most charming characterizations, they will notice that heavy make-up has been completely discarded.

RUSSEKS
1448 WOODWARD AVENUE

Evening Separates from the Fifth Floor

Star Bright Sweater
Gold-color stars twinkle on a wool and rayon chenille sweater. It's warm, gala-looking. Black, green or Christmas white. Sizes 32 to 40 in the group.
7.95

Rayon Jersey Skirt
Sleek and swirling skirt that's adroitly tucked for a smooth hipline. Black, red or white. 12 to 20.
6.50

9135

PATTERN #9135 MAY BE ORDERED ONLY in misses' and women's sizes 14, 16, 18, 20, 32, 34, 36, 38 and 40. Size 16 requires 3⅜ yards 54 inch. MARIAN MARTIN NEW FALL AND WINTER PATTERN BOOK is 15 cents, or book and pattern together, 26 cents. Send your order for a number of pattern with your name and address and 16 cents. Address your order for pattern to the Marian Martin, Detroit Free Press, Detroit, Mich. Pattern will arrive in a week or 10 days.

RUSSEKS
1448 WOODWARD AVENUE

3.95

"Sweetie Pie"
by ROPEEZ

Velvety soft black or brown busko leisure slippers with springy rope soles. They're appealingly young, wonderfully comfortable . . . an ideal gift for your "Sweetie Pie."

First Floor

Rayon Crepe Jacket
Red apple buttons sparkle on a long-sleeved blouse you'll wear for evening or with street-length skirts. Fuchsia, gold, Kelly green or black rayon crepe.

Rayon Velvet Skirt
Suave black rayon velvet in a graceful skirt that's slim and glamorous for evening. Sizes 12 to 20.
7.95

Fifth Floor

Nov. 28, 1942:

"Victory Food" recipes help wartime cooks plan menus around scarce ingredients.

Saturday lifestyle page

Dec. 11, 1942:

The war forced Detroiters to make changes in their lifestyles.

THE INQUIRING REPORTER: How Are You Getting Along on Gas Rations?

LEONARD LYONS

So King George Got Guns, Not Turkey, for a Thanksgiving Gift from U.S.

NEW YORK, Dec. 10 — CRIME: At the Walton Roof in Philadelphia, a ringsider invited the chorus-line and Henny Youngman, the Broadway comic, to his table. There he distributed money to all the girls, and to soldiers within his reach... Youngman saw Jerry Foley, a detective, enter the room, and told him: "This guy must've made a killing at the racetrack. He's giving away dough." Foley followed the man, investigated, and arrested him. Result: The New York story of Clifford M. Shoemaker, the Manhattan bank-guard, who had absconded with $11,500 and spent most of it in this spree.

CONVERSATION: Aline Bernstein, who will design Helen Hayes' costume in her new play, went to a dinner party, where the hostess warned her that she might find it difficult to hit upon a suitable topic of conversation with her dinner partner — "Why? Who is he?" asked Aline.... "He's the editor of the Encyclopedia Brittanica," explained the hostess. But Aline found a topic of conversation. "I'm the only woman you've ever met who knows the titles of the Encyclopedia set," she began. "Here they are: 'A to Anno,' Annu to Baltic; Baltim to Brail; Brain to Castin; Castir to Cole; Coleb to Damasc; Damascu to Educ; Edwa to Extract, etc."

MAPS: In Michael Straight's forthcoming book, "Making This the Last War," the author will tell the story of the late Justice Oliver Wendell Holmes. The story came from Tommy Corcoran, who once was Holmes' secretary.... Justice Holmes collected old maps of the United States. They were uncharted, beyond the known frontiers, except for the inscription: "Terra incognita, the aunt leones."... "But the brave adventurers will find there far more asses than lions," Holmes wrote on one map. "There are few lions in this world."

ENTERPRISE: Francis Albertanti is back in the sports field again publicizing the important sporting events. Albertanti retired a few years ago for the security and respectability of a movie job. He became a press agent for Warner Bros.... A short time after he began, he was summoned to the head office. "Bob Pastor just went 13 rounds with Joe Louis," he was told. "We want a story put out that our star, Wayne Morris, is being matched to fight Pastor."... Albertanti got his hat and coat, and said "Goodby," and returned to the sports field.

CHATTER: Ganna Walska has written her memoirs, and they soon will be published.... Zimbalist's accompanist, Teddy Steinberg, and Feuermann's accompanist, John Kerner, will become a piano team and will work at Cafe Society Uptown.... Ernest Hemingway's "The Fifth Column" will be produced in England next month.

SHIPMENT: Last month Amon Carter, the Texas publisher who now is in London, cabled his friends, asking them to send 38 smoked turkeys to him, at the Savoy in London. Carter wanted them sent air-express, no matter the cost, for one of the turkeys was to be sent to Buckingham Palace, for Thanksgiving Day. Carter was told that since was a priority, the turkeys couldn't be sent via plane. He cabled Sam Rayburn, the Texas Congressman. A priority was given. But then more urgent material replaced the turkeys. "One of these turkeys is for King George," the transport official was warned. "King George," he answered, "needs fresh guns more."

TRAVEL: Maurice Maeterlinck, the author of "The Blue Bird," left New York last week for Palm Beach. He went by train, to Richmond, and then made the rest of the trip by car. He was given a C card by the gas-rationing board, because he couldn't get train passage beyond Richmond, and the doctors certified that the eighty-one-year-old poet had to go to Florida for his health.... He arrived in Richmond alone. His train had been late, and neither his agent nor his wife was at the station. Maeterlinck found a large crowd, a band, and a welcoming committee. He speaks no English, and throughout the reception he muttered in French, to the committee which did not understand: "But I HATE receptions."

TRIUMPH: Joe E. Lewis, the comic now at the Copacabana, is a veteran of the Chicago gang wars. He worked in the Chicago cafes when the Capones reigned there. ... Last week an ex-member of the mob came to New York and saw Lewis. "Remember those days, Joe?" he began. "We all used to sit in the same joint. It was like a school-room class."... "Yes," Lewis agreed, "and your forehead was voted the most likely to recede."

IFFY THE DOPESTER

Or, as Shakespeare might have written it: "Lay on, McNutt, and damned be he who first cries 'Hold, this ain't enough'!"

Well, here's hoping that by Dec. 7, 1943, we'll have even more to celebrate.

Maybe by that time we will be rationing the Japs and the Nazis instead of our gasoline and food. That's what this old world needs: a shortage of Japs and Nazis.

Maybe that street the Nazis named for Mussolini has a blind alley. We said alley, not silly.

Now that the horse is coming back, the speed boys will no doubt be talking about "stepping on the oats," as they kick the old nag in the tummy.

Funny they never mention rationing turnips and parsnips and other things I don't like.

New York dispatch says that the Borough Council of Ho-Ho-Kus has installed four hitching posts. This is interesting — just to recall that there is a town of Ho-Ho-Kus.

What worries the Washington bureaucrats is that the people are beginning to ...

BUD BEAUCAND, policeman: "As far as my personal life is concerned, I won't be running around as much, and I'm going to make every date count. I walk Woodward downtown and it seems to me that everyone is getting down some way or other. There isn't much traffic but people are coming from somewhere just the same."

MRS. J. H. TEUBERT, 3310 Hogarth, housewife: "At the moment my husband and I haven't used one of our gas rationing cards. We have done this by cutting down on our driving around home. Our frequent trips to Canada are out and we are limiting our social calls. We both use public transportation a lot even though we have a car."

JOHN FIXOTT, 2646 Park, late applicant: "I'd have been down earlier to get my A card, but I've been sick in bed for several days. Now the next thing is to get a B card; I've got to have one if I'm going to be able to carry on my real estate business. I know it's late to be making application, but it's better late than never."

E. M. JOHNSTONE, 70 w. Warren, Coast Guardsman: "Gas rationing has really affected me. I used to use my car in my work in the Coast Guard publicity department throughout the state, but I travel by train now. Trips to our farm in Ohio are out, too, for the duration. My wife and I sure will miss those good chicken dinners."

WANDA KOWAL, 15826 Coran, Streetcar rider: "If I can help win the war by shivering on a street corner waiting for a car, that's OK by me. These are strenuous mornings for me. I have to walk half a mile from my home to the Wilshire bus line, then transfer to a Gratiot car for a forty-five minute trip to work each day."

SAMUEL KHOURI, 122 Westminster, filling-station operator: "There's about 300 gallons in my pumps. When that is gone, I'm closing up for the duration. My partner leaves next week and after that I'll handle the parking lot myself. I hope there'll be enough business to make it pay, but right now I have my doubts about it."

J. H. WILSON, 1440 Michigan, taxi driver: "Business is wonderful, but I'm afraid it isn't going to do me much good. They allow only 13 gallons a day for a cab and I've usually used 18 or 19 gallons. I share the cab with another driver but there's hardly enough gas for one. We are splitting the work into half days."

MRS. SADIE HURVITZ, 2953 Carter, housewife: "My husband, a defense worker, has a B book and also drives four other men to work. It's a little early for him to determine how much driving he can do, but we'll get along. We take the baby to the doctor now and then, but the office is close by so we'll probably be able to make it all right."

FRANK X. NORRIS, 376 Lenox, district attorney: "All we use the car for is family trips, so it looks like we are going to do more walking. The only thing I regret is the possibility of having to cancel the weekly trips to Belle Isle to show my three-year-old son the elephants. He'll be inconvenienced, but he can take it."

MRS. DOROTHY MASSNICK, 4378 Courville, rationing-board clerk: "Gas rationing isn't any fun for us either, but I guess we'll get by all right if they don't ration aspirin. My chief headache right now is people who call up and won't tell us where they live until we've pried it out of them in a dozen or so questions."

ALFRED FARIS, 201 Highland, parking-lot operator: "Business has been off about 75 per cent ever since gas rationing went into effect, but I'm all set. I'm going to work in a war plant next week. Cold weather may have something to do with the falling off of business, but there doesn't seem to be much hope for improvement now."

G. LESLIE FIELD, 1580 Lochmoor, swap rider: "I've been a member of a swap-ride group for about three weeks and it's worked out very well so far. There may be complications later, though, because a couple of the members have only A cards and another couple have B cards. I have a C card, because I belong to the Civil Air Patrol."

GENEVE PICKWICK, 9645 Shoemaker, secretary: "It's a little too early to notice it yet, but I think we all are going to spend much more time around home now. I don't have a car but gas ...I have been accustomed to going for rides with friends. That is going to be ...

KENNETH YORK, 4877 Hillsboro, bus driver: "I'm wondering what is going to happen to bus transportation in a few days when those full tanks run dry. There's been a 25 per cent increase ... but we've been able to handle them pretty well so far. We'll know considerably more about it next week."

DR. JOSEPH STARMAN, 18290 Woodingham, dentist: "None of my patients have complained so far about inability to keep appointments, but I'm going to be ready to accept excuses for late arrivals ... but trips to lodge meetings and the like will have to be made by other transportation arrangements."

RICHARD C. LARSON, 7836 Walnut, hotel doorman: "You're telling me that gas rationing is affecting me! I don't have as many auto doors to open, but are we having trouble trying to get cabs for people! What a time! Lots of the people leaving the hotel are on the way to catch trains and we have our hands full getting them off."

TOWN CRIER

Hodgepodge of Dope on Folks Around Detroit; How USO Will Be Finished

BY ANTHONY WEITZEL

STUFF: The local moguls are arranging a mammoth affair to honor Irving Berlin, who drops into our village next week with his show, "This Is The Army."... And the Army show sold $80,000 worth of ducats to the folks who stood in line that first long day at Masonic Temple.... Packaging of spare parts has been one of the bugs in the war operation.... That is, packaging the parts so the package will resist salt water corrosion, etc.... Les Swallow, out at Chrysler, has worked out a new paper-base package impregnated with a waxlike compound, which Sam Lebold, the paper expert, claims is tops.... The impregnating compound is similar to the stuff they use to keep salt spray from corroding the Golden Gate Bridge. Incidentally, Ted Forton, who is now with Swallow's boxing division, is the chap who used to do sky-writing for Chevrolet.... Ted says his career has taken him from "crates" (meaning those early Jennies) to crates.

SEYMOUR SIMONS, the musician, and his bride are veddy, veddy domestic these days, preferring the comfort of their own hearth to the comfort (?) of the night spots.... Seymour is also an amateur chef of parts.... So Mrs. Ben Bernie wrote to Mrs. Simons: "Write me all about what you are doing in the new house.... WHATS COOKING"... and WHO'S COOKING!"

LAST FRIDAY a rather dignified dowager had herself driven by her colored chauffeur to Sears' Highland Park shoppe.... She went with the chauffeur to the piano department and studied the assembled instruments for some time.... Finally she said, "Try that one." The colored lad sat down on the piano bench and began to play very softly one of Grieg's concertos.... "Hotter, please!" commanded the dowager.... The colored lad broke into a terrific boogie-woogie number that set feet to tapping up and down the aisles.... The dowager frowned.... "That's fine," she said to her chauffeur, "but would you mind trying that piano over there.... I can't quite make up my mind!"

A SMALL ARMY of AFL painters, carpenters and other workmen are hard at work today, putting the finishing touches on the interior setup of the new five-story USO Downtown Club at Cass and Lafayette ... and there's a story behind that. The USO HQ was opened in such a hurry that the main idea was to get it going. Along came the AFL Building Trades Council with a donation ... not in cash, but something more precious. The workers finishing the building are paid by the Council and they contribute to the USO nothing. During the gas ration, in donating his services to USO not only for the Downtown Club job, but for the duration. Add that up and it gives the Detroit USO the finest clubhouse to service men in the nation. The Downtown Club entertained 109,333 service men in November ... and expects to entertain 1,206,000 of them during the next 12 months.

NOTES: Paul Draper and Larry Adler, who performed for Detroiters yesterday, dropped in on Al Wolf at the chophouse the other night ... to chat about old times — back in 1936 when Paul and Larry were playing the Michigan.... Les Gruber, by the way, now has a frozen ear ... a decoration he won while going through training maneuvers in the snowy stretches around Wayne Airport.... It's a brother act out there now.... Sam Gruber is in charge of the officers' mess.... Les in charge of their entertainment.... By the way, what ever happened to Carroll and Gorman, the song team?

PEOPLE: Josephine Fehrenbach maintains she's as patriotic as anybody, but she figures standing in line for hours to buy tickets to "This Is the Army" is going pretty far. Why, she wants to know, couldn't there have been several boxoffices? I wouldn't know, but there's nothing can be done about it now.... Incidentally, the tickets for the New Year's Eve show start at $11 a copy, for orchestra seats, and that jump back to $3.30 and so on down.... As the finale of the waiter's ball promoted by Lou Koenig, secretary-treasurer of Local 705, handed Lieut. Col. W. H. Kite, Jr., of Army Relief, Ensign R. E. Belt, of Navy Relief, and Henry Meyers, of USO, a check for $3,457 ... to be divided three ways.... Grace Chaffee reports the Detroit MOMS (Mothers of Men in Service) will hold their ninth organization meeting Dec. 14 at the Federation of Women's Clubs Building.

SHOWS: Priorities are now worrying the Banfields ... a little man and wife who do a juggling turn out at the Palm Beach ... they use 30 balls in the act, all made of para gum, rubber ... they donated 25 worn out balls to the rubber scrap drive months ago, but are now down to their last balls, so to speak, and Banfield is worried about the situation he takes the balls home with him every night and keeps them under the bed. Ho hum.

TURNING BACK

100 Years Ago Today several states planned to vote against the annexation of Texas because slavery existed there.

50 Years Ago Today a banquet was given for President-elect Grover Cleveland in New York where he outlined his party's platform for the coming term.

25 Years Ago Today representatives of the country's largest steel mills assured war workers they would have all the steel they needed.... The promised coal from the Federal Government failed to arrive, thus leaving the city's fuel situation in a critical condition.

10 Years Ago Today a general investigation into "fraud, wrongdoing, and violations of the law" in the conduct of the Wayne County election was ordered by Probate Judge Henry S. Hulbert, chairman of the County Canvassing Board.

One Year Ago Today Japanese troops and parachutists landed off the Luzon Coast.... The Army announced that unidentified planes were "over and south of Los Angeles."

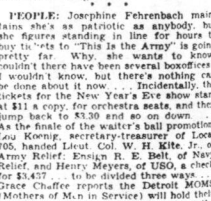

16 — Theater — THE DETROIT FREE PRESS—SATURDAY, APRIL 10, 1943 — Amusements

ROMANCE AND SENTIMENT

Tale of Tiny Refugees Pleasing Fox Feature

'The Amazing Mrs. Holliday' Has Deanna Durbin in Leading Role

BY LEN G. SHAW
Free Press Motion Picture Editor

Deanna Durbin devotees, and anyone else for that matter, should find a generous amount of enjoyment in "The Amazing Mrs. Holliday," which holds top place on the Fox screen. For Universal has wrought well in providing this personable songbird with one of the most appealing mediums of her screen career, putting her back in circulation after a considerable absence from pictures. It is a well blended mixture of sentiment and smiles, a bit saccharine in spots (but who cares for that?). It tells about a group of war orphans Deanna pilots from the little school she maintained in China to safety in the United States, after stowing them away aboard a ship whose crusty old captain turns her request for passage down cold, but who proves to be a big-hearted chap when he finds the brood installed in his palatial home in San Francisco.

Shaw

The real surprise stemming from "The Amazing Mrs. Holliday" is the discovery of Deanna in a mature role, and the development she discloses both histrionically and vocally.

POSES AS WIDOW

It is the task of Deanna to pose as the widow of old Commodore Holliday, who was supposed to have gone down when his ship, carrying the motley young stowaways, was torpedoed in mid-Pacific. The "wedding" is the invention of Barry Fitzgerald, an old retainer of the Commodore, for the purpose of insuring shelter for the refugees and their guardian angel, while the family of the supposed deceased squabble over division of his estate.

It might have gone along all right if Edmond O'Brien, grandson of the Commodore, and himself just back from the sea, had not fallen in love with Deanna, and discovered the hoax. Just about that time Commodore Holliday turned up miraculously, to learn of the plot, and decide to see it through, by announcing his intention of marrying Deanna. But true love must have its way, so the Commodore contented himself with bestowing his blessing on the young folks and adopting the refugees. Which settled everything very nicely.

DEANNA SINGS

Deanna was never more charming to look at than in her current role, in which she deftly accentuates the human interest with which the story abounds. She acts with poise and naturalness. Her lovely voice is lifted in "The Old Refrain," "Mighty Lak a Rose," a "Chinese Lullaby," "Rock-a-Bye Baby," sung in Chinese, and "Visa d' Arte," the aria from "Tosca," all of which are neatly woven into the action.

Edmond O'Brien plays the other half of the romance very agreeably. Barry Fitzgerald is amusing as the old salt. Harry Davenport is briefly but restfully on hand as the Commodore. Frieda Inescourt, Elizabeth Risdon, Grant Mitchell and Arthur Treacher are discoverable in supporting parts. You'll warm to the little refugees, including tiny Chinese Michael Chan.

The accompanying item is "Prairie Chicken," a bit of frothy nonsense that has Noah Beery, Jr., and Jimmy Rogers among its conspirators.

The Film Clock

SATURDAY

ADAMS—"Margin for Error," 11 a. m., 1:40, 4:20, 7, 9:40 p. m., 12:20 a. m. "Manila Calling," 12:19, 2:59, 5:39, 8:19, 10:59 p. m.

BROADWAY CAPITOL—"Andy Hardy's Double Life," 12:02, 2:57, 5:52, 8:47, 11:21 p. m. "Omaha Trail," 11 a. m., 1:55, 4:50, 7:45, 10:29 p. m.

CINDERELLA—"Arabian Nights," 3, 6:50, 10:25 p. m. "Gentleman Jim," 12:55, 4:40, 8:15, 11:45 p. m.

CINEMA—"Slaves of Bondage," 1:05, 3:15, 5:25, 7:35, 9:45, 11:55 p. m. "Shark Woman," 12:05, 2:15, 4:25, 6:35, 8:45, 10:55 p. m.

WORSHIP IN THEATER

With the big pipes from the Orchestra Hall organ occupying most of Calvary Presbyterian Church, the congregation will worship across the street at 10:30 a. m. Sunday in Victory Theater.

Glamorous

Alexis Smith is the high-hatting heiress who tries unsuccessfully to put Errol Flynn in his place in "Gentleman Jim," the James J. Corbett screen autobiography playing neighborhood theaters.

McClintic Asks Part in Picture Profits

CHICAGO, April 9 — (AP)—Mrs. Margaret Ayer Barnes, Chicago writer, was sued for $67,608.97 in Federal Court by Guthrie McClintic, New York producer.

The suit alleged McClintic was agent for Mrs. Barnes and Edward Sheldon of New York, who collaborated on a play called "Dishonored Lady," 'and as such was entitled to 50 percent of all movie rights.

McClintic seeks half of the $135,217.95 awarded Mrs. Barnes and Sheldon in a plagiarism suit against Metro-Goldwyn-Mayer. The authors alleged that MGM's picture, "Letty Lynton," was taken from "Dishonored Lady."

AFRICAN ADVENTURE

'Casablanca' Thrills on Michigan Screen

Humphrey Bogart, Ingrid Bergman Chief Figures in Romantic Tale

The human triangle without which dramatists would be hard put comes to the fore in "Casablanca" to provide taut drama. It also affords Humphrey Bogart opportunity to do some of his best acting, with lovely Ingrid Bergman as the object of his genuine love that comes to naught but a display of heroics quite foreign to his usual attitude. It is all available at the Michigan, and, on the whole, provides engrossing diversion, with a Nazi touch that is not overemphasized.

Bogart is the hard-bitten American proprietor of a drinking establishment in Casablanca who earlier had met and fallen in love with a girl in Paris. Their romance was rudely interrupted when the woman, without giving a plausible reason for not marrying him, dropped from view.

When she reappears, in Casablanca, where Bogart is trying to forget, it is to explain that the husband she supposed had been a victim of the Nazis because of his anti-Facist activities, was alive. She is seeking to get him to safety in America. There are watchful German officers on hand to insure his ultimate capture, and there is equivocation on the part of the French police that makes the situation particularly precarious.

It is for the help of Bogart that Ingril pleads. He alone can effect an escape, and there are memories of those happy days in Paris to prevent his taking the necessary steps. It is a situation rich in dramatic possibilities that are finally woven into an anticipated pattern, when Bogart sees to it that Paul Henreid, the Czech patriot, and his wife Ingrid, are whisked away in a plane a jump ahead of the Nazi pursuers, with Claude Rains, as the vacillating police officer, cowed into lending assistance.

While "Casablanca" is fast-moving, and the intrigue between the Germans and the French holds attention, with plenty of dramatic high spots, it is the individual performances that give the picture its real distinction.

Bogart is at his best as the proprietor of the cafe who plays no favorites—at least, until Ingrid appears on the scene. He keeps the cold, calculating American within bounds that make him believable. Miss Bergman brings charm and effectiveness to her characterization.

Excellent also are Conrad Veidt, Peter Lorre, Sydney Greenstreet, Madeleine LeBeau and Dooley Wilson, to mention only a few who populate the cafe where intrigue is rampant and the gaiety obviously forced.

"My Heart Belongs to Daddy," the accompanying feature, is a wild whip-up about a metaphysicist, a bubble dancer and a jack-of-all-trades who in the person of Cecil Kelloway furnishes many of the brighter moments, with a performance of astonishing versatility. Kellaway is a taxi driver whose cab gets stalled as he is taking Martha O'Driscoll, the dancer to a hospital to have a baby. He carries her into the home of Professor Rick (Carlson), delivers the child, and what follows defies chronicling. Hardly necessary to tell you that at the finish the metaphysicist and the bubble dancer find happiness in each others' arms. L. G. S.

Blind Marine Sells Story to Hollywood

PHILADELPHIA, April 9—(AP)—The story of Marine Sergt. Albert Schmid, of Philadelphia, who killed 200 Japs on Guadalcanal, and his romance with Ruth Hartley, who refused to break their engagement after he was almost completely blinded by a Jap hand grenade, has been purchased by a movie studio for $30,000, of which Schmid will receive $20,000. Miss Hartley became Mrs. Schmid last Saturday.

Several studios bid for Schmid's story, with Warner Brothers entering the successful offer.

Today's Program at Your Favorite Theater

WAR STAMPS AND BONDS ON SALE AT ALL THEATERS IN THESE COLUMNS
THEATERS MARKED WITH A ★ ARE CO-OPERATIVE THEATERS. **UNITED DETROIT THEATERS

April 10, 1943:

"Casablanca" opens, and 119 theaters are listed inside Detroit. In 1986, five theaters are listed within the city limits.

Theater and Amusements Page

April 11, 1943:

Some authorities consider Detroit's young women to be a home front problem during the war.

Sunday magazine feature

BEGINNING IN THIS ISSUE: YOUR WARTIME DIVORCE, AND HOW TO PREVENT IT — PAGE FIVE

PART FOUR — SUNDAY MAGAZINE — THE DETROIT FREE PRESS
SUNDAY, APRIL 11, 1943

WAR TOWN'S BAD GIRLS

BY RALPH NELSON
Free Press Staff Writer

THEIR PIQUANT, JUVENILE FACES masked by heavy make-up, the two girls stand under the brilliant marquee lights of the downtown theater. It is late in the evening, and the night life of War Town swirls around them.

Pay night. War workers crowding downtown, free for one night, the strain of sixty-hours-a-week showing in their eyes. Swing-shift girls in slacks parading by, along with police officers, and stray men whose cold eyes expertly appraise the girls' figures.

The two girls ignore them, their eyes busy inspecting the crowds. The line of service men stroll by, look, pause and come back. The girls smile and the group is an intimate little huddle in a matter of seconds.

One girl giggles, betrayed by her nervousness, but quickly stiffens her lips into a smile.

A minute more and the girls are whisked off down the street "under convoy."

Although glamour rags conceal the lumpy, immature figures, you'd swear the girls aren't yet 17. All their sophistication comes from a milliner and a pot of pancake makeup.

THIS TABLEAU is repeated a thousandfold every night, anywhere in Detroit's downtown area. Spectator reaction depends strictly on viewpoint.

The police officer watches with ill-concealed disgust. The man or woman with kids at home may feel a vague alarm. But the full weight of the truth hasn't yet hit home. The harsh, exhilarating tempo of the new Detroit, America's War Town, is throbbing in the background.

It's not enough to sit at home and tap your feet when the tempo starts to quicken. The kids will tell you that. War is driving men into the Army, women into the plants and the kids into the streets.

The record tells an alarming story. It shows a 500 per cent increase in drunkenness on the part of youngsters under 21. It shows a sharp increase in burglary, robbery armed and vandalism by young boys. It shows the development of hotel "love nests" and "booze parties" in parked cars on the outskirts of the city.

The love nest problem is strictly new. A guest at a fashionable Detroit hotel wrote the Free Press that he was unable to sleep because of the all-night parties that turned his floor into a *five parlor*.

The statement is supported by the records of Miss Jeanne Bestard, director of the Girls' Wayward Minor Division of Juvenile Court.

"The trend towards all-night hotel parties is probably a result of too much money and gasoline rationing," Miss Bestard said. "And it isn't only the furtive, side street hotels that are being patronized. We've had cases from the best hotels in the City."

Policewomen are investigating the backgrounds of two juvenile girls who were taken out of a man's hotel room last week. The girls carried cards identifying the bearer as a member of the Wolfress Patrol. One of them, at the time of arrest, had already called her parents to tell them she was spending the night with a girl friend.

Miss Bestard recently questioned a sixteen-year-old girl who insisted on staying out until 4 a.m. "Why not?" the girl said through crimson lips. "The fun doesn't start until midnight."

Last fall, the girl-problem near the Naval Armory on E. Jefferson had reached such proportions that a fence was erected along the Armory grounds to keep the young girls out of it. A brief Richard Park...

"The way those young girls went for the sailors was terrible," McClellan Station Lieutenant said. "Our cleanup squads hardly had time to patrol the precinct, they were so busy chasing juveniles in debutante clothes out of the park.

"Since the fence went up, had our worries are gone. The cleanup squads and the policewomen must concentrate on chasing the girls out of the confectioneries and drug stores now."

Back in the dawn of Repeal, when beer gardens with dance orchestras sprang up like mushrooms, the Liquor Control Commission ruled that there should be no cross-table dancing. The ruling was founded on the belief that groups of young girls would patronize taverns and dance with any likely looking young man who asked them. Sometimes the man's good looks were not the correct mirror of his soul, and the girl was introduced to the first phase of a shameful life.

In a survey covering 12 dine and dance joints in Detroit last week, the Free Press learned that not only as cross-table dancing permitted, but it is the vogue.

In fact, so adept has the A.W.O.L. (A Wolf on the Loose) become that it is almost impossible for the novice to secure a partner for a dance.

For some reason, the Commission's ruling is flatly violated, with little apparent attempt toward enforcement.

One alibi is that you must be 21 to be served drinks in a bar, and that a woman of that age should know how to take care of herself. But that isn't borne out by records, either. Central Station police have had their hands full weeding drinking youngsters out of downtown bars.

THEY HAVE NEW TRICKS . . . .

IT'S ONLY IN THE LAST few months that juveniles have begun to swarm into the Loop after nightfall. They are a headache to tavern operators, all night theater staffs and all other amusement centers.

According to John Bodenstadt, business executive of the Royal Ark Association, the juveniles have developed a bag full of tricks to use in coming drinks out of the suspicious bartender.

For one thing, they produce faked credentials proving they're 21. Another trick is for the juvenile girl to enter with an older man. She demurely orders ginger ale. The man orders whisky and a beer chaser. When the waitress' back is turned, the whisky casually flows into the girl's ginger ale and there she is with a highball.

These tricks are time-honored, and may work repeatedly until a police officer comes in and the sight of his badge scares the truth out of the kids.

"When the Royal Ark introduced legislation raising the age limit from 18 to 21, we thought we had the juvenile problem licked," Bodenstadt said. "But we've got it rig* now worse than we ever dreamed it could be."

All night theatres come in for their share of grief. Ben and Lou Cohen, owners of the Roxy, reported that during the month of March alone they turned away 3,737 kids, both boys and girls, who tried to gain admittance after midnight.

"And when we turn them away, where do they go?" Ben Cohen wanted to know. "They're back on the streets right in the middle of a tenderloin district. I don't know why these kids insist on prowling around downtown. All I know is I wish they'd stay home. We don't want them downtown."

He cited the case of an eighteen-year-old girl, a swing-shift worker, who was turned back at the door. "And when am I supposed to see a show?" she demanded. "I leave for work at 2 and don't get out until 11 p.m."

There are still some kids who don't come downtown. Tour around the outskirts of the City around midnight, investigating dead-end streets. You'll hear laughter from dark cars, and the splash of liquid. Come back in the daytime and you'll find empty bottles. It's the new creed. "You gotta be smart to be young."

Inspector William M. Johnson, of the Police Juvenile Division, recently interviewed a youth charged with attempted rape. "I belong to the younger generation," the youth stated flatly. "We believe in taking every girl we can."

One juvenile authority quoted an increase of 500 per cent in drunkenness. "It's easy for them to get liquor. They can have an older boy buy it for them in a drug store. But the easiest source is the one parents don't seem to suspect: Dad's stock in the bar in the basement.

"You've got as many wild parties going on right in kids' homes as you have in bars and hotel rooms," he said. "The parents are making money and they like to party around. They don't want to be bothered with their kids, so they leave them at home. So the kids get their own party going."

The hotel love nests and house parties characterized by abandonment are just the beginning for these young kids. Maybe it's part of the emotional fever of war. But tomorrow is coming, when the war will be over and family ties must be taken up again.

And then society, according to juvenile authorities, is going to have a bad hangover. The Victory Babies, who cater to soldiers, will be grown up then, embittered by their experiences. The Wolfress Club, a product of sex-consciousness and an adolescent yearning for scarce male companionship, will disband when former boy friends come marching home.

But the scars will be indelibly etched. She will find that favors can be sold as well as given. This opens for her the last mile in the long road—a life of a party girl. Then as she grows older and the price of her favor dwindles, she is type-cast as a common prostitute.

And even this early that trend is starting. Patrolman Philip Van Antwerp recently arrested a sixteen-year-old department store employee in a Woodward Ave. bar. She approached the officer, who was in plain clothes, offered her favor and named a price.

"These kids are coming downtown strictly on the make," a police sergeant said. "It's obvious to anybody who wants to look, and they don't seem to care. When normal times come again, a lot of these girls are going to be spoiled for men who would want to marry them. Five years from now we'll find some of them when we raid disorderly houses. Sure, the police worry about it. But why the devil don't their parents worry about it too?"

CAUSE LIES IN THE HOME

JUVENILE AUTHORITIES are prone to put the blame for increasing delinquency right, where it belongs, in the home.

Miss Hazel Tuck, head of the Girls' Juvenile Division, said that sometimes greed, masked under guise of patriotism, puts both mothers and fathers in defense plants, leaving the kids to run the streets.

She cited an interview she had with a father in endeavoring to learn what the child's home life was like. "Is it necessary for your wife to work in a factory, inasmuch as you are earning a good salary?" she asked.

"Certainly not," he replied. "But there's a lot of money around and we want to get our share."

"But what if your children go wrong because there's nobody home to care for them?"

"My kids are old enough to know better," the man retorted. He has four children. The oldest is 14. He works nights and his wife works days.

The problem of working parents leads to more than delinquency. Authorities say that it often leads to downright neglect.

In the lobby of the Roxy Theater at 4 a.m. one morning edged two kids, a six-year-old accompanied by his ten-year-old brother. The oldest boy was dressed warmly enough. The youngest was only half dressed: Coat unfastened; his pants held up only by the clutch of his grimy hand. Each was eating a slice of bread and jelly.

The manager asked what they were doing in the theater. "We want to get warm," the eldest said.

"Why don't you go home?"

"It's cold there, too."

Patient questioning revealed the fact that the boys' parents worked in defense plants and left for work at 3:30 a.m.

"But it's night yet. You don't belong on the streets."

"No, it's morning when mamma and daddy go to work. We can go out."

These two youngsters were on their own from 4 a.m. until 8 p.m. They dressed themselves and roamed the streets until time for school. (Not their own lunch at home and went back to school together.

On another occasion a boy, pale and shaking, came into the theater lobby out of a pouring rain during school hours. He was told he couldn't be admitted. "But I just want to get out of the rain," he explained. "Teacher sent me home because I'm sick. Mom and Dad are working and I can't get in the house." The Roxy manager took the soaked boy home in a taxi; found his story was true, and rented out a neighbor to care for the boy until his parents came home.

As evidence of the growing lack of parental control, Inspector Johnson points to the fact that cases involving juvenile boys have increased at the rate of 250 to 250 cases a month just since December.

"Last year we came in contact with 13,000 boys, but this year juvenile crime is skyrocketing," he said that burglary, larceny and vandalism were increasing. Also there is developing a new fad for carrying concealed weapons.

Just why a boy in his early teens should feel that a gun, blackjack or heavy hunting knife is necessary equipment for his daily life is unexplainable.

When questioned, the boys have a standard cryptic answer, delivered out of the corner of their mouths. "For protection."

Another bottleneck in juvenile investigation is the problem of getting past the defiant "I don't talk to coppers." When the speaker is a tousle-headed boy of 12, the remark is funny and paradoxically contains a wealth of tragedy.

"In many cases, we find that parents are too tired to take care of their children. They send them off to see a show just to get them out of the house," Johnson said. "But instead of giving them 15 cents, they hand them a dollar. Now the kids have found they can spend money and have many cases of youngsters robbing their own parents and setting out on wild spending sprees that include their whole circle of friends."

THE ASPECT OF NEGLECT in growing more alarming to police-women every day.

Kathryn Gisher, supervisor of the Missing Girls Department, pointed out that complaints of children left alone are a daily feature now. Investigating, officers find children whose ages range from 9 months to 7 years, crying, unfed, and alone in the home. Mother is working, or downtown shopping.

"And when the babies get in trouble running the streets, we call the parents and the tell us they're too busy to come down to police headquarters," she said.

Another problem in Detroit is the influx of unattached Southern girls. Strangers in a big city, they settle together in whatever districts are available. The districts may not be the best. One settlement, Miss Gilcher said, is springing up around Abbott and Porter, and a second on the Easter Side, where a bus line comes in direct from Kentucky.

Among these young women are many runaways, and policewomen weed them out and send them home.

"The peak in Detroit for juvenile delinquency was reached just before the crash in '29," one authority pointed out. "During the depression, the parents were home watching their children. The kids themselves had little money. There was a general restraining influence.

"Then it was a major part of the programs of civic clubs to look after underprivileged children. Send them out to summer camps. Arrange picnics and ball clubs.

"Now, with the war boom, people have forgotten the kids. The civic groups are immersed in war-supporting programs. There's less community activity. Parents are too busy making money to look after their children. The aids themselves are working at breakneck speeds and ages. They have nothing to do with their money but follow their own desires in amusement.

"Parents of children who are not working, in many cases, have never had much money to give to their children. Now they are going to the other extreme and are getting them with funds.

"The only solution is through an aroused public interest in children. Wartime is no time to forget the youngsters. They are finding out daily that there is no place for them in adult society and they're left to shift for themselves. And so they are turning to the bright lights."

(The story of juvenile delinquency in Detroit will be continued by Ralph Nelson in the Monday Free Press.)

"A minute more and the girls are whisked off down the street 'under convoy.'"

— Drawings by Floyd S. Nixon
'You'd swear the girls aren't yet 17.'

VOICE OF THE CITY — THE TOWN CRIER — BY ANTHONY WEITZEL

WAYNE CORNERS GAZETTE: The Metropolitan Opera folks from down New York way played an engagement this week in our sister city of Cleveland. They still having culture shown there, and a number of our villagers traveled to Cleveland for the event. Ye editor is no wearier than those of our other comedians we could name but won't.

ROOB ALLIE, railroad expert and connoisseur of soft coal smoke, dropped in this week, he saying it is not likely the Government will ration railroad transportation, the whole business being too complicated even for OPA to figure out. He did say, however, that it might come to the point where you might buy a lower berth from here to Podunk and then be bumped out of it by a major or even a lieutenant equipped with priorities.

THE PONY wire from the city carried a note to the effect that Fred Allen, gifted comic, etc., from down East, might take a long vacation to reel up his tired gags or whatever. We hope he does not do this, because we like Fred and besides his gags are no wearier than those of many other comedians we could name but won't.

SEVERAL STRANGERS visited our village during the week and up to press time, one and all wished to know if our Willow Run airplane shop could be in production yet. In other parts of our nation, they told a Gazette reporter, folks keep staring at each other and asking, "Is Willow Run really producing, or is it just a lot of propaganda." Our reporter hastened to assure these people that Willow Run is doing a fine job and that even the govt. folks have admitted same, and they ought to spread the word.

YE EDITOR heard tell just at press time of a dry cleaner out Wyoming way who offers to store a soldier's civilian clothing free of charge until he comes back from North Africa or wherever. This is a fine thing, say we.

MRS. HOLLIS SHELTON, our popular subscriber from out Milan way, writes ye editor that she got quite a kick out of Jack Scagnetti's letter about his brother. She can sympathize with Jack because some time back she was a reporter and wrote hundreds of obituaries without turning a hair until one day she had to write an obituary notice . . . on the passing of her father.

THE SPORTS editor of the Gazette came in the day before the paper was to go to press and he said the women were looking over everything and he was going to quit and get a job in a haberdashery or someplace where women would only come at Christmas time, and then only for loud neckties to wake up their husbands.

ROSCOE AILS, who used to be very funny in the movies, etc., is visiting in our town and we had quite a time talking about the days when he was in burlesque with Joe E. Brown and Jim Barton and a number of others who are now making big money on little gigs. Roscoe told us he is a genuine hillbilly, he being from Kentucky and remaining obscure until he was 8 years old, when somebody took him to see a performance of "Uncle Tom's Cabin," where was staged on a river showboat. Young Roscoe was so entranced by the villainy of Lawyer Marks that when he grew up and moved to the wicked city of Portsmouth, O., he got a job in burlesque, filling in with gags, etc., while the stripease got pinned up, that being before the days of zippers.

JACK DALEY, popular designer and in door architect, is in our village drawing up plans, etc., for the apartment of one of our prominent citizens. This will be the finest apartment in town, Jack says, there being every modern convenience, even a special cupboard for keeping old ration books.

A DELEGATION of citizens of here is planning to wait upon Eddie Guest, our popular and gifted poet, and ask him please not to read any more poems about apple blossoms on the radio until May 1, when the danger of blizzards is passed. Eddie read an apple blossom piece on the air April 8, the anniversary of the last of 1889, and that very same day it started to snow like anything and a number of our villagers had to run home and put their long underwear back on.

YE EDITOR ran into Mayor Ed Jeffries the other day at luncheon and His Honor looked mighty fit and even a trifle suntanned from his stay in the Southland. The Gazette photographer is instructed not to take any pictures of his honor, however, until he gets a couple of shadows blender, he now looking like the mayor of Miami or even Palm Beach.

SUBSCRIBERS WHO do not have anything better to do tomorrow at 6:15 p.m. are urged to tune in on Station WJR and hear ye editor tell a number of fascinating tales, including one about how they are giving cold cures to vegetables now and getting more of same. If you love your Victory Garden, tune in.

TRAFFIC POLICE of here were baffled this week when Cock found an auto parked at a "No Parking" spot with a note on it, windshield, "Have been here to see my going home to get duplicate." The traffic people are still waiting for the chaps to find his duplicates, and when he does they are going to give him duplicate traffic tickets.

April 18, 1943:

Ads for war bonds were far from subtle.

This Message Sponsored by These Public Spirited Firms

Advance Glove Mfg. Co.
901 West Lafayette

Berry Brothers
211 Leib

Continental Motors Corp.
12801 E. Jefferson

Craine Schrage Steel Co.
8701 Epworth Blvd.

J. P. Denison Company
7310 Woodward Avenue

Detroit Ball Bearing Co.
110 W. Alexandrine Ave.

Detrola Corp.
1501 Beard

Federal Screw Works
3401 Martin

Gear Grinding Machine Co.
3501 Christopher

James W. George Machinery Co.
3146 E. Jefferson Ave.

Giern & Anholtt Tool Co.
1308 Mt. Elliott

Giffels & Vallet Inc.
1000 Marquette Bldg.

Gray Marine Motor Co.
710 Canton St.

Hupp Motor Car Corp.
3641 E. Milwaukee Ave.

F. L. Jacobs Co.
1043 Spruce

C. E. Jamieson & Company
1962 Tromblay

Janolt Sales Co.
Machinery Dealers
6060 Woodward Ave.

Kasper Mfg. Co.
3226 Drexel Ave.

Larrowe Milling Co.
8047 Hamilton Ave.

LaSalle Tool, Inc.
1840 E. Outer Drive

LeMaire Tool & Mfg. Co.
2657 S. Telegraph, Dearborn

MURDER in Detroit...
it *CAN* happen here!

Think Detroiters! And think before it's too late. Is this to be your loved ones lying broken in the ruins of your home? Is this your child ... motherless or maimed?

If you're one of those who said we'd whip the Japs in two weeks, better think again. You ... and your loved ones here in Detroit ... and all that you hold dear .., are definitely "military objectives" on Hitler's and Hirohito's dive-bombing schedule. And why not? For Detroit is turning out more of the things Hitler fears than any other city on earth.

Think too that 3,500 Americans died at Pearl Harbor, and they were 2,500 miles from Japan. But Detroit is only 800 miles from the Atlantic coast line. Your wife, your daughter, your son, your mother, your friends ... live only 800 miles from the ocean.

There is one big protection for them ... one big guarantee that they will not know pain and suffering ... the *War Bonds that you buy during the* 2nd WAR LOAN DRIVE *will buy the bombs and shells and tanks and guns* that will carry the war *over there, away* from Detroit where it belongs. Buy Bonds to the limit of your financial endurance!

THE 2ND WAR LOAN DRIVE
★ ★ ★
THEY **GIVE** THEIR LIVES ...
YOU **LOAN** YOUR MONEY!

This Message Sponsored by These Public Spirited Firms

Long Mfg Co., Div. Borg-Warner Corp.
12501 Dequindre

McLouth Steel Corp.
300 S. Livernois Ave.

Michigan Steel Casting Co.
1999 Guoin

Modern Collet & Mach. Co.
401 Salliotte, Ecorse

Mead Screw Products, Inc.
363 Midland Ave.

Midwest Tool & Mfg. Co.
2360 W. Jefferson Ave.

Modern Die & Tool Co.
227 Iron St.

Motion Picture Eng. Co.
13540 Linwood Ave.

Motor Specialties Corp.
120 Mt. Elliott Ave.

National Machine Prod. Co.
4850 Bellevue Ave.

Sal-Way Steel Treating Co.
14034 Woodrow Wilson

Snyder Tool & Eng. Co.
3400 E. Lafayette Ave.

The Schmidt Brewing Co.
1935 Wilkins St.

Simons-Michelson Co.
Advertising Agency
12th Floor, Washington Blvd. Bldg.

Super Tool Co.
21650 Hoover Rd.

The Taylor Winfield Corp.
15120 Woodward Avenue

Temprite Products Corp.
47 Piquette Ave.

Troy Tool & Gage Co.
5736 12th Street

The Udylite Corp.
1651 E. Grand Blvd.

Welding Machines Mfg. Company
17325 Lamont Avenue

Weldit Acetylene Co.
638 Bagley Ave.

Whitehead & Kales Co.
58 Haltiner, River Rouge

APRIL 20, 1943:

As former Michigan football star Tom Harmon survives the crash of his bomber, another Michigander fights for his life after being convicted of treason.

"Tom Harmon Fought Wilds for 4 Days," column one, and *"Tuttle Bares Max's Letter,"* column seven.

The Detroit Free Press

On Guard for Over a Century

METROPOLITAN FINAL EDITION

Weather Report
Light rain or snow

Tuesday, April 20, 1943. No. 351 — 112th Year — 26 Pages — Four Cents

TUTTLE BARES MAX'S LETTER

Jeffers Repudiates OWI Rubber Report

Note Links Nagel to Krug's Escape

Says Ex-Postmaster Paid 83 for Fugitive Nazi Flier's Bus Fare

A charge by Max Stephan, convicted traitor, that former Detroit Postmaster William J. Nagel not only actively aided him in arranging the flight of Oberlieutenant Hans Peter Krug, but contributed $3 for Krug's bus fare, was made a part of Federal Court records by Judge Arthur J. Tuttle late Monday.

This charge, made by Stephan in a personal letter to Supreme Court Justice Frank Murphy, was received before the high court granted a stay of execution after Judge Tuttle had ordered Stephan hanged April 27.

Judge Tuttle filed in the Federal Court clerk's office a letter Justice Murphy sent to Stephan April 15, and the four-page letter Stephan sent to Judge Tuttle Saturday, inclosing Justice Murphy's letter to him.

WILLIAM J. NAGEL
Named by Stephan

The letters were filed after Judge Tuttle had conferred for more than two hours with District Attorney John C. Lehr and his assistant, John W. Babcock.

Judge Tuttle, in his order that the two letters be made part of the Stephan record, said he wanted "to assure the respondent every right open to him under the law."

Nagel has denied repeatedly any association with Stephan in the Krug case. The FBI found no substantiation of Stephan's allegations of Nagel's complicity when he first made the charges months ago.

BUGAS TO REOPEN CASE

John S. Bugas, head of the Detroit FBI office, said Monday night that his office had known all the details of Stephan's letter before it was sent to Judge Tuttle.

He said there would be a re-examination of "that aspect of the case."

The Free Press tried unsuccessfully Monday to locate Nagel for a statement. He was not at his home, 611 Seyburn.

Bugas said the inference that Nagel had advised Stephan went into the records during the examination of Stephan before a United States commissioner during his trial.

"As I recall the statement Stephan originally made at the time of his arrest," Bugas explained, "he said he had talked to Nagel late on the same night that Krug came to Detroit. As I recall, Stephan had talked to Nagel rather hypothetically."

Bugas said that all of the information obtained by the FBI had been turned over to the court. Asked why it had not come out in greater detail during the trial, Bugas replied, "Possibly it didn't prove of sufficient value to the prosecutor or the defense."

Justice Murphy's letter to Stephan, a reply to one the latter had written him April 10, suggested that he "bring this matter acquaintance with Judge Tuttle, if you are acquainted with him, and Judge Tuttle, in Detroit, with all possible speed."

TEXT OF STEPHAN LETTER

Stephan's letter to Judge Tuttle follows:

"Hon. Judge Tuttle:

"In 1928, business was getting bad in Germany so that I decided to sell my saloon there and come to America to start over. Oct 1928 I moved to Windsor Canada. In November 1928 I started to work for General Motors, Windsor, as a repairman, till about July 1929. I did my work to their satisfaction until not on account of illness. In the meantime I made my application for U. S. citizens papers with the consul in Windsor. In 1930 I got my papers to move to Detroit.

"But in 1930 the depression was on and for me impossible to start a business or to get any work. Thus I was forced to stay in Windsor till 1933. I kept on going back and forth to Detroit, to friends at Wabash Ave. So I had the feeling I was just as much home there as in Michigan.

"In 1933 I moved my furniture over in 1935 I got my final papers. Later I bought a restaurant at 7209 E. Jefferson. In 1936 I vested $2,000 in same to build a hall in addition. The hall was rented for banquets, meetings, weddings, birthday parties, etc. Among the ones who had meetings in this hall were the Following: Canadian-legion, immigration and custom inspectors, Arion Finging Society, Schwaben Society, German War Veterans and at for 5 times the Bund. I never was a member of the last one.

"I told the Bund no uniforms, no swastika and no hell in my place, otherwise, no hall. I belonged to the American political club, both non partisan. In the joint political committee I was treasurer and to the Schwabensociety, I was sacred vice-presidently. Both clubs did not take any money from the candidates. All

Turn to Page 4, Column 1

Labor Body Plans to Ask Court Probe

Nonpartisan League Studies Bar Report; Committee Now Revising Findings

Labor's Nonpartisan League announced Monday that it was making a study of a report criticizing the handling of criminal cases by the Judges of Recorder's Court with the view of petitioning either the Judges of the Court or the Michigan Supreme Court for a grand-jury investigation.

Ernest Bennett, secretary of the league, expressing the view that the only logical method to clarify the many charges which have been directed at the judges, said:

"I feel that the recent grand jury should never have concluded its work until such an investigation had been made. There has been a lot of smoke; there must be some fire.

SAYS JUDGES COULD ACT

"I don't understand why the Judges themselves don't get together and demand a grand-jury investigation. Those who have nothing to fear would be vindicated, and of course, the others, if any, would be properly dealt with."

Meanwhile, the Recorder's judges were informed that the report signed by eight of the 12 members of the Detroit Bar Association's committee on Criminal Law and Procedure was undergoing revision at the request of Glenn Coulter, president of the Association.

Thomas M. Chawke, one of the four who did not sign the report, informed the judges that a revised report would be submitted for their comment at an early date.

William Griffin, chairman of the committee which prepared the report, as well as the other seven members who signed the original report, would not comment Monday, having been notified that all statements were to be issued personally by Coulter.

The judges, meeting Monday to discuss the report which was published in the Free Press Saturday,

Turn to Page 10, Column 6

Police Discuss Curfew Plans

Whether curfew shall or shall not ring in Detroit was discussed Monday afternoon with Police Commissioner John H. Witherspoon by Sgt. Louis L. Berg, Councilman William Rogell and Eleanore Hutzel, of the Women's Division.

"We discussed the difficulties which would be encountered in trying to notify the juveniles of the curfew time," Witherspoon said. "In smaller towns they can be warned by the ringing of a bell, blowing of whistles or some other signal, but that would not be practical here.

"I am not in favor of passing a curfew law until we are certain that we have the facilities to enforce it."

Timely Reading for Next Week-End

HOW TO GO TO SLEEP: War workers and others will be greatly benefited by this authoritative article in the National Graphic. Millions of Americans need to learn how to slumber soundly.

MEET JOE GENTILE, favorite of radio's smartest program. A page of pictures in Sunday Graphic.

MACKENZIE HIGH SCHOOL: The Camera Caravan visits Mackenzie High and brings smashing feature for Sunday Graphic.

IN NEXT SUNDAY'S FREE PRESS

Tom Harmon Fought Wilds for 4 Days

6 in Crew Bail Out in Storm over Dutch Guiana; Natives Rescue Ex-Gridder

PARIMARIBO, Dutch Guiana, April 19 — Second Lieut. Tom Harmon, who parachuted to safety when his Army bomber crashed, found the wreckage of his plane and the bodies of two crew members while wandering in the Guiana jungle for four days, it was reported tonight.

Harmon, former University of Michigan All-America football player, was guided by friendly natives to the Army base here, where he was tired, but in good condition, the Aneta Netherlands Indies news agency said.

NOT BADLY INJURED

Hospitalization was not necessary and Harmon asked permission to accompany an Army searching force to seek other missing crew members in the jungle. Harmon had been missing since April 8, when he parachuted into the jungle from his bomber, "Old 98," named for his football player.

In Washington, according to the Associated Press, the Army said that five of the crew members of the plane piloted by Harmon, still are listed as missing. They are: Second Lieut. Edwin J. Wolf, navigator, of Philadelphia; Second Lieut. Frederick O. Wieting, of Charlotte and Lansing, Mich.; Sergt. Leonard D. Gunnells, of Deatleville, Ala.; Staff Sergt. Bernard R. Coss, of Mendota, Ill. and Staff Sergt. James F. Goodwin, of Texarkana, Tex.

RUNS INTO STORMS

(An officer said the plane took off April 8 on a South American flight, but ran into storms and the crew of six was forced to bail out, the Associated Press reported.

(Reports reaching San Juan, Puerto Rico (which is the headquarters of the Antilles Air Force) indicated that at least two of Harmon's companions parachuted to earth, according to the Associated Press.

(Fliers searching the area near the plane wreckage spotted three parachutes hanging from tree branches, the Associated Press said.)

Harmon Phones 'Mom' that He Is All Right

ANN ARBOR, April 19 — Lieut. Tom Harmon is "all right—except for a few scratches," he assured his jubilant parents today in a three-minute telephone conversation.

Listening in with Mrs. Harmon were her husband, two daughters, Mrs. James Considine and Mrs. Bertram Jensen, both of Gary, Ind., and Herbert O. (Fritz) Crisler, University of Michigan football coach.

"Hello, Mom," Harmon said. "Tom, my boy! How are you?" "I'm safe and well, mother." "That's great," she said. "Everybody here was praying for you. Is your crew all right?" "I haven't heard."

"Fritz Crisler is here. Do you want to talk to him?"

"Hello, you old ghost," he said. "Are you all right?"

"Sure," replied Harmon.

"You're not hurt, are you, Crisler asked.

"I was shaken up a little, and I got a few scratches. Otherwise I'm all right.

"Good luck, boy."

Harmon also chatted briefly with his seventy-year-old father.

Nazi Manhunter Killed, Say Poles

LONDON, April 19 — (UP) — Polish circles here reported today that Kurt Hoffmann, notorious organizer of slave labor manhunts in Warsaw, had been assassinated in accordance with a death sentence decreed by the Polish Underground. Hoffmann headed the German Labor Exchange at Warsaw for three years.

On Inside Pages

Amusements 25	Horoscope 26
Bingay 6	Iffy 26
Chatterbox 10	Lyons 26
Clapper 6	Mary Meade 14
Classified 19-24	Merry-Go-R'd 6
De Crane 11	Newton 6
Dr. Crane 11	Quillen 6
Edgar Guest 6	Radio 25
Editorial 6	Sports 16-17
Fashions 11	Town Crier 26
Financial 18-19	Washington 8
Glenn Babb 8	Women's 10-12

Crew That Plunged into Trouble with 'Old 98'

Shown beside their Army bomber, "Old 98," are Tom Harmon and six crew members who ran into trouble over Dutch Guiana. The plane crashed in the jungle, but Harmon parachuted safely to earth and was rescued by natives. The fate of the others has not been definitely determined. Left to right are Second Lieut. Edwin J. Wolf, Staff Sergt. James F. Goodwin, Harmon, Sergt. Leonard D. Gunnells, Second Lieut. Frederick O. Wieting and Staff Sergt. Bernard R. Coss.

10 Sea Scouts Drowned in Training Trip Wreck

ISLIP, N.Y., April 19 — Ten Sea Scouts drowned and their skipper was rescued today after their cabin cruiser capsized and sank in Great South Bay. All of the victims, between 16 and 18 years old, were from South Shore Long Island communities.

Scout Ship 14, had set out yesterday for a seamanship training cruise on the Legionnaire, a ship presented to the new Blue Point Belmonte L. I., were picked up by a passing vessel, which found them near an overturned dinghy. The other bodies were found later in the same manner by a Coast Guard searchers.

Police established that the boys, under Mayer, third mate of Sea

Scout Ship 14, had set out yesterday for a seamanship training cruise on the Legionnaire, a ship presented to the new Blue Point by the Rockville Centre American Legion. The craft encountered rough weather today.

The ship, police said, met rough weather today. Capt. Maynard said he thought a huge wave must have struck the 35-foot cabin cruiser, overturning it.

On five bodies recovered life preservers were found. The ship was located several hours later, sunk in 12 feet of water.

Mayer related this account of the tragedy:

A huge wave smashed the hatch door of the Legionnaire, sweeping one of the boys overboard. Two others, without stopping for their life preservers, launched the dinghy and set out after their shipmate. A wave capsized the dinghy, and Mayer saw no more of any of the three.

Meanwhile, water poured into the hatch door. The vessel's bow pointed downward and she began to sink. The boys donned life preservers, but before they could jump they were hurtled overboard as the craft's bow sank deeper.

With Mayer shouting encouragement to them, the boys clung to the side of their ship. One by one they dropped off, exhausted by the lashing waves and the bitter cold or the water, until only Mayer was left clinging to the ship. He was there almost four hours after the boat capsized before the rescue vessel arrived. By that time he was virtually unconscious.

"My legs were paralyzed," he said, "and I was just about ready to give up myself."

Allied Planes Blast 5 U-Boats in Big Battle

LONDON, April 20 (Tuesday) — Allied planes joined the defense of two important convoys in mid-March and probably destroyed five submarines and seriously damaged many others in a four-day running battle with a great pack of U-boats, the Air Ministry News Service said today.

An unspecified number of Allied ships were lost, but attacks were reduced sharply when the battle came within range of the Flying Fortresses, Liberators and Sunderlands attached to the Coastal Command. In four days, the bombers delivered 19 attacks, dropping hundreds of depth charges over thousands of square miles of the Atlantic.

The ministry claimed no actual kills.

One of the wide-ranging patrol planes sighted six submarines and attacked them within an hour. The report said it was a commonplace for planes to sight two or three submarines on each patrol.

The battle was so hot that either to charge their batteries or obtain greater speed in attempts to overtake the important ships. Often they dueled the planes with antiaircraft guns, but not one plane was damaged.

The ministry called the battle "one of the most ferocious of the war between aircraft and U-boats.

After the fight, the commander-in-chief of the Coastal Command messaged participating British, Canadian, South African, Rhodesian, Australian, New Zealand and Belgian fliers that "there is not the least doubt that you saved a number of ships."

DON'T WANT TO BE SHOWN

JEFFERSON CITY, Mo., April 19 — (AP) — A bill was introduced in the Missouri House of Representatives today to bar all motion pictures in which any actor who has been divorced appears. It also would bar any film portraying or implying a divorce.

Jeffers Repudiates OWI Rubber Report

Story Called a Blow to Public Faith

Davis Charges Critic Tried to Stop Release of Survey After Giving Approval

WASHINGTON, April 19 — Rubber Director William M. Jeffers, describing the second week of the Office of War Information report on the rubber situation as "a jumble of figures and gossip," said tonight that it had destroyed public confidence in the rubber program.

Elmer Davis, head of the OWI, countered immediately with a statement that Jeffers had "tried to stop me from telling the American people facts about rubber which had been certified as correct by his own office." He said that President Roosevelt had established OWI "in recognition of the right of the American people to be truthfully informed," and added:

"So long as I am here, I propose to tell the people the truth as accurately as I can ascertain it, whether Mr. Jeffers likes it or not."

Jeffers replied to Davis immediately, saying:

"My one concern is that the American people get the exact facts in respect to rubber in anything else. If Mr. Elmer Davis had convinced the people they are getting the facts I am delighted — but I doubt it."

In his original statement, Jeffers said that the OWI report, issued Saturday night, was not up to date.

"I do not need the OWI to advise me on the rubber situation and I can do my own talking," Jeffers declared. "That report was just a jumble of a lot of figures from my report seven weeks ago plus some gossip. Added together it doesn't make a true story because the rubber situation changes from day to day. It has destroyed a lot of the confidence I have been trying to build up in the public for the rubber program."

The OWI report said that the rubber picture would "darken before it becomes lighter," and that synthetic tires would not become available in quantity until the end of 1944. Sixteen Axis fighters were

SAFETY FIRST

NEW YORK, April 19 — (AP) — Radio France said in a Frenchlanguage broadcast from Algiers, recorded here by the Federal Communications Commission today, that the Italian Government is distributing pamphlets telling Italian citizens to be subtle to the enemy in the event of an Allied invasion.

shot down as they tried ineffectually to protect their unwieldy charges yesterday and another was destroyed today.

Of the other 81 enemy planes destroyed, five were shot down in a night raid by German bombers on Algiers.

(Military spokesmen in Cairo, headquarters for the Western Desert Air Force (where Allies will get worse before it starts improving," he said. "And in time, I do not agree with OWI that it is necessary for private motorists to further reduce their mileage. There are some other observations there that I don't agree with.

"I do not believe the situation will get worse before it starts improving," he said. "And in time, I do not agree with OWI that it is necessary for private motorists to further reduce their mileage. There are some other observations there that I don't agree with.

He characterized OWI's 14,-600-word report as "just one of those stories that confuse the public. It certainly doesn't indicate my views in respect to rubber."

The OWI story was cleared with Jeffers' rubber division as a matter of routine, but the rubber chief said that he had been "too busy" to read it all. He said the report took so long to prepare that the situation had changed.

"They'd been pecking away at that story for so long, it seemed it was out of date," he said.

Turn to Page 2, Column 2

Allies Bag 96 Planes Off Tunisia

58 Big Transports, 16 Fighters Downed in Great Clash with Sicily-Bound Convoy

ALLIED HEADQUARTERS IN NORTH AFRICA, April 19 — Allied airmen having destroyed 96 Axis planes, including 58 big transports, four freight and troop transports, in less than a day and a half of savage attacks against the enemy's aerial supply line to Marshal Erwin Rommel's troops in Tunisia, the Allied Command disclosed today.

Fifty-eight enemy transports were seen fleeing to earth and into the sea in the destructive engagement yesterday when a great Axis outbound convoy was ambushed at the northeastern tip of Tunisia, and 10 more of the three-engined aerial freighters were destroyed within a few hours today. Sixteen Axis fighters were

F.D.R. Goes on Air Tonight

WASHINGTON, April 19 — (UP) — The White House announced tonight that President Roosevelt will broadcast to the nation tomorrow night at 11 o'clock (Detroit time). All networks will carry the broadcast.

The nature of the speech was not disclosed but it was noted that it will be made on the fifty-fourth birthday of Adolf Hitler, who reportedly will make a pronouncement on a "European Charter" tomorrow.

The President's last major address was Feb. 12, when he reported to the nation on his historic journey to Casablanca.

Empire Contingent Lands in England

AN EASTERN CANADIAN PORT, April 19 — (UP) — Large numbers of Empire troops have arrived safely in Britain after an Atlantic crossing from Canada, it was revealed here tonight.

The majority of the contingent consisted of Royal Canadian Air Force personnel but included airmen from many parts of the world.

Angry Swedes Accuse Nazis

STOCKHOLM, April 19 — Sweden charged in an angry protest to Germany today that a German merchantman had fired on the Swedish submarine Draken inside territorial waters, and after demanding investigation and preventive measures, reserved the right to take such measures of its own as might prove necessary.

Sweden protested that the Draken was fired on Friday.

News of the protest caused a sensation in Stockholm in view of the fact that about the same time of the Draken's sister submarine Ulven, which sank in 200 feet of water off the Isle of Marstrand in the Skagerrak, the entrance to the North Sea. Sweden asked if German vessels could shed any light on the Ulven mishap.

Suggestions to Improve Mail Service Urged

WASHINGTON, April 19 — (AP) — More than 200,000 Postoffice employees have been asked to think up some ideas to improve the postal service and working conditions. Congress will be asked to appropriate funds to pay rewards for suggestions. Postmaster General Frank C. Walker said.

Bond Sellers to Center on Small Buyers

Half of Drive Quota Still to Be Raised

By LYFORD MOORE
Free Press Staff Writer

Detroit and Wayne County Monday ended the second week of their drive to attain their quota of $140,825,000 in War Bond sales campaign with nearly one-half the quota yet to be raised while the bigger investors in the area had already subscribed.

For that reason emphasis of the drive was newly discovered Monday to a thorough canvassing of the many thousands of smaller bonds considered a vital necessity of the quota is to be met.

Walter S. McLucas, chairman of the Treasury War Finance Committee for Lower Michigan, and Frank N. Isbey, head of the State War Savings staff, in a joint statement scored "the silly practice of trying to buy our way to victory out of money we don't have."

BIG BUYING ENDED

They agreed that the unexpectedly heavy returns of last week "could not be expected this week," and pointed out that a factor in that large figure was the purchases of bonds by banks — which will not do it again."

Pointing out that only 100,000 of the potential of 1,000,000 subscribers in Detroit and Wayne County have yet subscribed, the statement emphasized the need for bank sales of additional small bonds.

THEY **GIVE** Their **LIVES**— You **LEND** Your **MONEY**

Easing of Food-Parley Gag Predicted

WASHINGTON, April 19 — (AP) — Relaxation of restrictions on press coverage of the international food conference was predicted today by Senator Arthur H. Vandenberg, Michigan Republican, protested against the imposition of what the Michigan Senator was said to have termed a "gag rule."

Under present arrangements for the meeting, which is to begin at Hot Springs, Va., May 18, reporters would be barred from all except perfunctory opening and closing sessions and would be barred from contacts with delegates.

The Assistant Secretary reported to have asked delegates from other nations might feel slighted if American legislators were asked to be present and their own parliamentary bodies were not represented.

Democratic Leader Alben W. Barkley, of Kentucky, told a press conference that the meeting would be exploratory, with no commitments. He said the agenda would be announced soon by the State Department.

In a turbulent session behind closed doors, members of a group led by Senator Arthur H. Vandenberg, Michigan Republican, protested against the imposition of what the Michigan Senator was said to have termed a "gag rule."

Under present arrangements for the meeting, which is to begin at Hot Springs, Va., May 18, reporters would be barred from all except perfunctory opening and closing sessions and would be barred from contacts with delegates.

A demand by the Agriculture Committee for some assurance that the conference an observer brought Acheson before the group.

VANDENBERG LEADS PROTEST

were would be barred from all except perfunctory opening and closing sessions and would be barred from contacts with delegates.

The Assistant Secretary reported to have said that the State Department expected the press to be represented at the conference, pointing out that reporters certainly would be present if President Roosevelt addressed the group.

Vandenberg and some others predicted afterward that the press restrictions would be modified. This might be done, it was indicated, by permitting reporters to interview daily the heads of delegations and the chairmen of subcommittees.

A demand by the Agriculture Committee for some assurance that the conference as observer brought Acheson before the group.

KRYPO MARGARINE — rich with 9000 units Vitamin A per pound. ADV.

Weather Report — Cooler with scattered showers

The Detroit Free Press
On Guard for Over a Century

CITY EDITION EXTRA

Tuesday, June 22, 1943. No. 49 — 113th Year — 30 Pages — Four Cents

JUNE 22, 1943:
Whites attack blacks during Detroit's wartime civil disturbance.

MARTIAL LAW AT 10 P.M.
U.S. TROOPS MOVE IN

Gov. Kelly at 6 p. m. signed a proclamation declaring a state of martial law in Detroit. Military rule of the City will begin at 10 p. m. The streets were ordered cleared at that hour.

The Governor's proclamation read:

I, Harry F. Kelly, governor of the State of Michigan and Commander in Chief of the military forces of the said State of Michigan, hereby declare a state of emergency and the necessity for the armed forces of the State of Michigan to aid and assist, but in subordination thereto, all duly constituted civil authorities in the execution of the law of the state.

The necessity for such aid and assistance is declared to extend to the following counties of the State of Michigan, namely: Wayne, Oakland and Macomb.

In witness whereof, I have here unto set my hand and caused to be affixed the great seal of the State of Michigan this Twenty-first Day of June, 1943.

HARRY F. KELLY, Governor

In addition Gov. Kelly prohibited the sale of all liquor until further notice. All places of amusement were ordered closed at 9 p. m. Monday.

POLICE COME TO THE RESCUE OF TERRIFIED NEGROES CHASED AND BEATEN BY ROVING BANDS OF WHITES — Free Press Photos

3 Years of Strife Behind Disorders

Persistent Predictions of Race Rioting Become Tragic Reality

BY JAMES S. POOLER
Free Press Staff Writer

What happened in Detroit Monday was neither unexpected nor unpredicted.

For three years the rumblings of the racial eruption have been close to the surface. It was no more than passingly significant that the talk, never discreet, always set the race riot for summer and the place as Belle Isle. That is where it started on the eve of summer before it spread unwholesomely across a bridge and throughout a city of 2,000,000 purported civilized beings.

It did not take a prophet to know the riot was coming. Loose talk, blowing on hot prejudices, may have fanned it, but even the unemotional analyst could see the cumulative evidence—the housing troubles, the protest against racial discrimination in industry, the sporadic violence in high schools, and only a few days ago the Packard strike, rooted in racial antagonism. Detroit has been building steadily for three years toward a race riot and it cannot disregard the harsh fact that Monday's killings broke loose in remote sections.

15-YEAR PERIOD OF COMPARATIVE PEACE

There were nearly 15 years in which the city's white and black man lived in order. This was the period that followed the last serious rioting in 1925 when Dr. Ossian H. Sweet moved to 2905 Garland and earned the resentment of white neighbors. In an ensuing neighborhood clash Leon E. Breiner, a white man, was killed. In the celebrated trial which followed, Clarence Darrow came to Detroit to defend the 11 Negroes charged with murder and to plead eloquently for tolerance.

It was in the following years, when there was much talk of social reforms, when a depression came along to drop living conditions to new lows and aggravate the poverty of the city's Negroes, when a Negro boy named Joe Louis emerged from that poverty to become the heavyweight champion, when George Washington Carver, Negro scientist, was coming to Detroit with his honors, that the racial problem seemed to have fallen away. This did not mean that tolerance had come and resentments passed but there was no significant rioting.

It was in the last three years, when the city's industrial boom brought new settlers to Detroit and brought the Negroes' problems, both economic and in housing, into focus, that the increasing rumors

Turn to Page 7, Column 5

Riot Foes Fraternize at Hospital

Wounded Negroes and Whites Sit Side by Side as Staff Works Tirelessly

Receiving Hospital was probably the one place in Detroit Monday where Negroes and white men met on amicable terms.

Bleeding Negroes and whites sat side by side, sometimes even talking together, as the staff of 200 nurses and 60 doctors and internes battled tirelessly to staunch the flow of blood and patchup broken bodies.

A few minutes earlier the injured had been hunted or hunters in the rioting a few blocks away, but now the fight was over.

AWAIT TREATMENT

Dazed and mostly silent, they sat there mopping faces with blood-tinged handkerchiefs or strips of torn shirt until the doctors could get to them.

Attendants whose grey mops had turned red could not keep the floors of the emergency admitting and operating rooms free of it. Nurses and doctors who had worked ceaselessly since Sunday night had no time to change blood-clotted operating gowns and uniforms for fresh ones.

Grimmer still was the spectacle in the driveway at the rear of the hospital where ambulances and police cars bringing in new victims competed with the morgue wagons coming for the bodies of the dead.

WORST CALAMITY

Dr. Austin Z. Howard, senior surgeon, said that the riot, from the standpoint of dead and injured,

Turn to Page 2, Column 5

Home-Front Slump Seen by Senators

War Mobilization Committee Calls for a 'High Command'

By the Associated Press

WASHINGTON, June 21—Declaring that the home front is sagging "dangerously," the Senate War Mobilization Committee called today for a domestic "high command" to make sure that the Nation's energies shall "no longer be dissipated by loose management."

Citing what it called a "lack of centralized direction of the war effort" and "failure to mobilize fully the will and energies of all groups," the committee said:

"Establishing a high command on the home front becomes even more timely as our troops gird for great offensive actions."

6 STEPS RECOMMENDED

The report, signed by Chairman Harley M. Kilgore, West Virginia Democrat, and Democratic Senators Elbert D. Thomas, Utah; Edwin C. Johnson, Colorado; Mon C. Wallgren, Washington, and James E. Murray, Montana, recommended:

1—Across-the-board price control "at all levels of production and distribution."

2—Clear-cut direction of the distribution and allocation of basic food and clothing supplies to support rationing.

3—The formation and execution of a single policy on subsidies.

4—Establishment of a requirements committee to inquire into military, lend-lease and civilian needs.

5—Participation by management, labor and agriculture in a War Mobilization Board working under direction of the Office of War Mobilization.

6—Incentive wage plans to spur war production.

Alluding to a report made May 13, the committee said that since

Turn to Page 4, Column 5

House Passes Army Funds

By the Associated Press

WASHINGTON, June 21—Without a dissenting vote, the House passed and sent to the Senate today a $71,510,438,873 War Department appropriation bill to meet the Army's request for funds to "bring the war home to Japan, Germany and Italy."

The record vote was 345 to 0.

Biggest supply bill in history, the measure, Department officials told the House Appropriations Committee, will permit the recruiting and equipment of 7,500,000 men by the end of this year and furnish approximately 100,000 airplanes for incessant bombing of the Axis.

ENTERTAIN HEROES

Fifteen wounded veterans of the South Pacific and African theaters of war Monday were guests of employees in the aircraft building of the Ford Motor Co., touring the plant to see assembly of Pratt & Whitney aircraft engines.

D&C Lake Lines offers you a trip by water to Buffalo—all-expense—$19.95. No interference with war effort. Plenty of room, sail any day. Call CA 9800—Adv.

Mobs Rove the City to Stir Trouble

Eyewitnesses Describe Endless Series of Attacks on Negroes in Downtown Area

Free Press reporters downtown and in the Woodward-Mack sector observed a virtually endless series of attacks by white rioters upon Negroes who had wandered unknowingly into the danger zone.

Their eyewitness reports, however, are confined to the areas under white domination. In Negro neighborhoods, particularly along Hastings, stores owned by white persons were looted by Negroes and many white persons were attacked, according to police reports. Police refused to allow whites to enter this area.

A crowd of white men, mostly youths, with a sprinkling of soldiers and sailors, ranged up and down the six-block stretch on Woodward north of Peterboro, attacking every Negro man they could catch.

A northbound Woodward street car was stopped at Mack when the rioters pulled the trolley from the wire. Mobs poured in the front and side doors after two Negroes. Screaming women in the rear of the car jumped or were carried out the open back window while the mob dragged its two victims out the doors.

The two men were beaten down to the iron-grilled floor of the car stop and pounded with fists and feet into semi-consciousness before police arrived and took them to Receiving Hospital.

CARS ARE BURNED

At least a half-dozen cars driven by Negroes were turned over and burned on Woodward and adjoining streets and alleys.

One of the first—a large black Lincoln Zephyr—was turned over just east of Woodward on Stimson

Turn to Page 8, Column 1

On Inside Pages

Amusements	37
Bingo	6
Clapper	15
Classified	24-28
Crossword	24
Edgar Guest	6
Financial	18-19
Grafton	15
Horoscope	30
Jiffy	30
Lyons	
My Day	15
Merry-Go-R'd	6
Newton	
Quillen	6
Radio	29
Reporter	
Sports	22-23
Town Crier	30
Washington	15
Women's	14-16

11 Dead, 500 Hurt; Rioting Goes On

Looting and Violence Spread over City; Bars, Stores Closing

A military police battalion from Fort Custer, together with State Troops from all parts of Michigan, moved in on Detroit Monday afternoon as race riots which began Sunday night continued to spread through the North and East Sides of the city.

Brig. Gen. William E. Gunther, in charge of military police for the Army's Sixth Service Command, arrived in Detroit early in the afternoon to take charge for the military.

Looting and continued violence rocked the city.

Eleven men were dead, three white and eight Negro, at 5:30 p. m., and at least 500 had been treated for injuries ranging from bruises

Additional Riot Pictures on Pages 13, 20 and 30

to fractured skulls, at Receiving Hospital alone. No estimate was available on the number treated at other hospitals or by private physicians.

Police had arrested 614 persons in the first 20 hours of the rioting. They were charged with inciting to riot, felonious assault and reckless driving. Only one woman had been arrested. She was held at McGraw Station for disturbing the peace.

Production in some war plants was slowed as afternoon workers stayed away from work from fear of rioters, and Federal officials appealed to Detroiters to check rioting in the interest of the war effort.

The dead:

JOHN FRAILACH, 43, of 14230 Wayne, white, found at 2 p. m. on Brush near Warren, shot through the chest. He was identified through a gasoline ration book issued to a trucking company.

BILLY HARDGES, 27, of 987 Division, Negro, shot by Sergt. George Pallister, who said Hardges was looting.

ROBERT DAVIS, 29, of 620 E. Euclid, Negro, shot by police.

CARL SINGLETON, 19, of 968 E. Warren, Negro, shot by police.

ANDERSON FORD, 43, of 968 E. Warren, Negro, shot by police.

Turn to Page 8, Column 6

JAN. 12, 1945:

State Sen. Warren Hooper, a key witness in a political corruption trial, is shot before testifying.

WARMER
Warmer with Light Snow;
Gentle to Moderate Winds

The Detroit Free Press

FRIDAY, JANUARY 12, 1945 — On Guard for Over a Century — Vol. 14—No. 253 — Five Cents

FINAL EDITION
Vandenberg Speech Strengthens Hand of the President, Says Stokes—See Page 18

GRAFT WITNESS SLAIN

Senator Hooper Shot, Left in Burning Car; He Was Ready to Testify in McKay Trial

Special to the Free Press
SPRINGPORT — State Senator Warren G. Hooper, 40, Albion Republican and star witness in the Carr-Sigler Graft Grand Jury, was murdered in his car four miles north of here Thursday night.

There were three bullet holes in his head. His car was set fire after the shooting, State Police said. They found footprints leading from the left door through the snow to the pavement on the other side of the car.

THE SHOOTING occurred at about 6 p. m. (EWT) on M-99 four miles north of Springport. Springport is in the extreme northwest part of Jackson County.

Kim Sigler, special prosecutor for the State Graft Grand Jury, said at Lansing:

"Hooper was the principal witness against Frank McKay, Floyd Fitzsimmons and William Green. He had given a complete confession to the grand jury and had been granted immunity in this case."

McKay, Grand Rapids political boss; Fitzsimmons, a Benton Harbor sports promoter, and Green, former Republican State representative from Hillman, are awaiting preliminary examination on graft conspiracy charges involving horse racing legislation.

* * *

STATE POLICE reported that Hooper's wife had received three mysterious phone calls from a man with a "foreign accent" since Tuesday asking details as to her husband's movements to and from the Capitol.

The first call, she told troopers, was at 9 p. m. Tuesday.

"He wanted to know Mr. Hooper's Lansing address," she said. "He also wanted to know just what time I expected he would leave for home."

* * *

"I WAS A LITTLE suspicious and asked him who was calling. He hesitated and then said his name was 'Alex Nipenock.'"

She said it appeared quite obvious that he "made the name up."

"The same man called again Wednesday and at noon today," she said.

"I was just preparing my son's lunch. He asked again what time Mr. Hooper was leaving Lansing. I told him I didn't know and he hung up.

"The calls worried me so that I called Mr. Hooper at his Lansing office. He just laughed and said 'don't worry about it.'"

Detective Murray Young, of the State Police, said that Hooper's movement had been traced to 3:40 p. m. At that time he had visited the McLaughlin Osteopathic Hospital in Lansing.

* * *

MISS ALETA HOOD, a Senate committee clerk, said that she had taken dictation from Hooper Thursday morning, and that he seemed in an excellent frame of mind.

The last legislator who saw Senator Hooper, as far as could be ascertained Thursday evening, before he left the Capitol, was Rep. Arnell Engstrom, of Traverse City, who said he saw Hooper about noon and that, he was in "excellent spirits."

* * *

SLAYING OF HOOPER brought to light for the first time his connection with this phase of the Grand Jury. He previously had been a State witness at an examination in which William Burns, executive secretary of the State Medical Society, was charged with attempting to bribe Hooper.

Burns, alleged to have offered Hooper a trip to California if the latter would drop opposition to a Medical Society bill in the Legislature, is free on bond.

* * *

SIGLER DECLINED comment on how Hooper's death would affect the McKay-Fitzsimmons-Green case. He said that Hooper's testimony in the Burns case could be used in court, "but whether it will be is another matter."

Sigler said that Hooper had been offered police protection since his appearance before the Grand Jury figures, Sigler replied: "You can bet your bottom dollar it will." The special prosecutor added that "everyone I think should have it" will be furnished a guard.

City Speeds Postwar Plan to End Slums

Tax Exemptions to Bid for Capital

BY LEO M. DONOVAN
Free Press Staff Writer

Detroit's postwar plans for replacing vast slum areas with landscaped housing projects, privately financed, will take definite shape next week at a meeting Wednesday of the Mayor's Executive Blight Committee with representatives of several City departments.

Three proposed laws, approved by Common Council and designed to enable the City to accomplish its objectives, are in the legislative hopper in Lansing.

* * *

THE MEETING at 2:30 p. m. Wednesday, in the board room of the Board of Water Commissioners, will consider two additional bills by which the City hopes to attract private capital into the low-cost housing field. The City would acquire the property through condemnation.

Mayor Jeffries announced that attorneys in the Corporation Counsel's office, and the experts of the Detroit Housing Commission and the City Plan Commission, have been working for months on a comprehensive slum elimination program.

* * *

AMENDMENTS in three bills awaiting the Legislature were analyzed by Walter E. Vashak, assistant corporation counsel who has been working with the Housing commission. They are:

The Home Rule Act would be changed to eliminate the current necessity for a three-fifth vote of the people to dispose of City owned property or vacating streets leading to the waterfront. It also would wipe out prohibitions against the sale of park land without the vote of the people
Turn to Page 3, Column 2

AEF Ousts BBC Reporter

SUPREME HEADQUARTERS, Allied Expeditionary Force, Paris — (AP) — Supreme Headquarters announced Thursday that the accreditation of Cyril Ray, British Broadcasting Co. correspondent with the Allied expeditionary forces, had been canceled.

The cancellation was the result of an uncensored broadcast violating the security release on the Army's counter attack against the Ardennes salient.

Unionize City Supervisors

Supervisors in City departments are being organized in a local of the State, County and Municipal Workers of America (CIO).

Norman Safart, president of the newly chartered local, said its organizing drive will seek to enroll supervisors of five or more City employees up to the rank of members of departmental administrative staffs.

Berle Approved

WASHINGTON — (AP) — The Senate Foreign Relations Committee voted Thursday to recommend confirmation of Adolf A. Berle, Jr., former assistant secretary of state, to be Ambassador to Brazil.

Distillers Create N.Y. Liquor Oasis

Survey by Michigan Officials Finds Monopoly States Skipped

In an effort to discover how Michigan's system of handling and distributing liquor compares with that of other states, two representatives of the Liquor Control Commission and State Revenue Department are now making a first-hand survey in the East. James M. Haswell, staff writer of the Free Press, is accompanying Charles Parrish and Clarence Locke on their mission. This is Haswell's first article, written in New York. Others will follow daily and Sunday, as the survey proceeds.

BY JAMES M. HASWELL
Free Press Staff Writer

NEW YORK—The big bars in this town are a sight to behold. Every remembered brand of rare and quality liquor lines their shelves. Prices are low, and business is simply colossal.

There isn't any whisky shortage for these bars. Scotch, bonded ryes and bourbons, brandies and famous blended whiskies pour out in endless streams.

It has to be seen to be believed. Imagine a bartender serving 2½ ounces of Haig and Haig Scotch, with ice and soda, for 50 cents!

PROHIBITION was the law of the land during the last big boom here. The bars kept under cover in those days. They paid protection to racketeers and gunmen, and the prices for their unlawful liquor were consistently high.

That boom is out in the open today. It is brightly lighted, cheerful. Competition is brisk but not deadly. So Joe the Bartender is glad to be legitimate again, and to have the liquor supply holds out.

(The first major junction south of that town, on the Lingayen-Manila highway which flanks the Agno River, is Mangatiarem, 11 miles below Umanday and 18 miles inland.)

THIS OASIS in the American whisky desert didn't come about by chance. It was deliberately created, and is deliberately maintained by distillers and importers for a long-range merchandising purpose.

There are two other drinking oases, in Chicago and Los Angeles. These three downtown markets, highly competitive, carry great prestige. The customers of these New York, Chicago and Los Angeles bars have been hammering at bar lines from the east. The neck out of the box was left no more than two miles wide.
Turn to Page 5, Column 1

Patton Hits by Surprise

Threatens to Cave In Front in Luxembourg

BY AUSTIN BEALMEAR

PARIS — (AP) — The United States Third Army threatened to cave in the Luxembourg front with a surprise stroke Thursday that sent thousands of Germans fleeing into the woods. In Belgium, the enemy began a twenty-three-mile withdrawal maintained by distillers and importers turned loose British patrols on a ten-mile eastward sweep.

The northwestern enemy anchor of Larouche fell along with 15 other towns.

Lt. Gen. George S. Patton's troops cut in half powerful box positions southeast of Bastogne from which three enemy divisions had been hammering at bar lines from the east. The neck out of the box was left no more than two miles wide.

Resistance in the American this area was reported collapsing rapidly as the Germans floundered off into the snow drifts and woods toward the uncertain haven of Wiltz, 10 miles east of Bastogne, where other Third Army forces lay on high ground.

THE GERMAN High Command admitted that it was quitting all
Turn to Page 2, Column 1

Army Looters Get 40 Years

PARIS—(AP)—Five United States Army enlisted men accused of looting supply trains and selling cigarets and other goods were tried in cases involving 182 enlisted men and two officers. None of those sentenced Thursday were Michigan men.

The five, all of Company C of the 716th Railway Operating Battalion, were the second group to be tried in cases involving 182 enlisted men and two officers. None of those sentenced Thursday were Michigan men.

ERNIE JOINS THE NAVY

Pyle Off to War Again; This Time in the Pacific

Ernie Pyle has finished his vacation and is off to the Pacific front to resume writing his famous daily column.

Recognized as the war's greatest reporter of the human side of the conflict, Pyle again will mingle with our boys in the Pacific as he did with those on the other side of the world, sharing their hardships, winning their devoted friendship, learning what they feel and think. Into his day-by-day diary he will write the poignant little incidents that show what war means to the individual.

HIS COVERAGE of the campaigns in North Africa, Sicily, Italy and France won him enough honors for half a dozen men—the Pulitzer Prize, the Raymond Clapper Memorial Award, and the National Headliners' Club Award.

for two successive years. His columns were incorporated into two books that have been bestsellers—"This Is Your War" and "Brave Men."

Now he's going back for another taste of war. This time he will be with the Navy. Where the Navy will take him or when he will return, he doesn't know. But it's likely that, before he's through, he'll be set ashore somewhere to hobnob again with the GIs as well as with the men of our Pacific fighting fleets.

Yanks Reach Agno River on Luzon

Gain in All Sectors; Take 5 More Towns

BY WILLIAM B. DICKINSON

MacARTHUR'S HEADQUARTERS, Luzon — (UP) — American patrols have driven to the Agno River at points 18 to 20 miles inland and 87 miles from Manila, it was disclosed Friday.

The Sixth Army has expanded its main beachhead from five to nine miles, capturing five more towns and many villages.

Gen. Douglas MacArthur announced the capture of Labrador, Umanday, Calasino, Bulog and Masaoog in an advance, headed for Manila via main highways, along a solid 21-mile front.

* * *

AMERICAN FORCES, however, have advanced beyond nearly all the points mentioned.

United States reconnaissance planes are operating from the captured Lingayen airstrip. It is not known, however, when fighters can use the strip.

Ralph Teatsorth, United Press correspondent, reported from Sixth Army headquarters that troops on the right flank had seized an important road junction beyond Umanday.

* * *

THE CAPTURE of Labrador secured the mouth of the Agno. Shallow draft barges and other landing craft will be able to navigate well inland along the Agno, which is the first natural Jap defense line barring the path to Manila.

Indicative of the minor resistance met thus far, a high ranking officer said that Wednesday one prisoner was taken and United States casualties were "five or six men."

Considerable Jap concentrations are on the left flank, smaller elements on the right.

On the right flank, anchored
Turn to Page 5, Column 4

French Ready Larger Army

PARIS (AP) — War Minister Andre Diethelm declared Thursday that by summer France would have an army of 1,200,000 men equipped and armed with the latest American materiel.

Fair and Warm

WITH FIRST ARMY IN BELGIUM—(AP)—Foxhole Flash: Pin-up girl pictures new are known along this frozen front as "foxhole heaters."

SENATOR WARREN G. HOOPER
Death seals his lips

Murdered Senator Linked to Racing Bill Indictment

Frank D. McKay, Michigan political boss, and two others were named in an indictment Dec. 2, charging them with conspiracy to bribe legislators to defeat a bill to amend the Michigan horse racing law.

Rep. William Green, Hillman Republican, and Floyd Fitzsimmons, Benton Harbor dog racing lobbyist and boxing promoter were named with McKay.

* * *

HITHERTO UNKNOWN to have any connection with the McKay-Green-Fitzsimmons indictment, Senator Warren G. Hooper, whose death shocked the State, was really, a key witness.

Said Kim Sigler, special prosecutor:

"Hooper was the principal witness in the case against McKay and Fitzsimmons. That I can say now."

* * *

THE BILL TO amend the racing act was introduced Jan. 7, 1943, by Rep. George N. Higgins, Ferndale Republican, and Rep. Edward J. Walsh, Detroit Democrat. Walsh was convicted of other graft charges and sentenced.

The bill was killed in the House State Affairs Committee. It provided an increase from 7.5 to 10 per cent of the Racing Association
Turn to Page 5, Column 2

WASHINGTON—(AP)—Restricted mail service will be resumed to Leyte, Samar and Mindoro Islands in the Philippines beginning Friday, Postmaster General Frank C. Walker has announced.

Pacific Mail

WARMER FRIDAY

January's Cold at Record Low

January is running nip and tuck—mostly nip—with the coldest January on record. Clarence J. Root, Weather Bureau senior meteorologist, announced the average temperature of Detroit this month to date is 13.2 degrees.

The coldest January on record was 1918, an average of 13.2 degrees.

Weather fans are pulling mightily for 1918, hoping higher temperatures the rest of this month will raise this January's average. The lowest temperature Thursday was 4 above at 10 a. m., below normal. The lowest Thursday night probably would be 14, with Friday warmer.

The Week's Weather

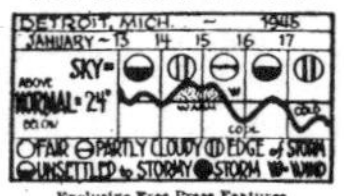

DETROIT, MICH. JAN. 12 - 19 1945

Skaters Happy

All city parks and neighborhood rinks offer good skating conditions. There is tobogganing at River Rouge.

French to Visit

PARIS (AP) Six French newspapermen and two newspaperwomen will leave soon to make a six- to eight-weeks inspection of the American war effort under OWI auspices.

HOOPER'S CAR was traveling south, indicating that he was en route from Lansing following week-end adjournment of the Legislature to his home at Albion. He was serving his first term in the Senate. Previously he had been a member of the House for three terms.

Marks on the highway indicated that the car had skidded to the left after the shooting started. The ignition was turned off. Gears were in neutral.

Floyd F. Mojeska, Springport, and M. B. Howard, of 1309 Pershing, Lansing, were first at the scene. They pulled Hooper's body from the car and dumped snow into the machine to extinguish the fire blazing in the front seat.

* * *

HOWARD SAID THAT Hooper's body was in the right front seat, slumped forward and to the left. There were two bullet holes in his hat and one through the rear right window. The latter shot appeared to have been fired from inside the car.

The body was taken to the Hoffman Funeral Home at Springport. Preliminary examination there disclosed that Hooper had been shot three times. One bullet pierced the left cheek, another entered under the left ear and a third entered the top of the head at the left. There were extensive burns on Hooper's thighs, right hand and right arm.

* * *

STATE POLICE REPORTED that there was no smell of gasoline in the murder car, although from the condition of Hooper's body and the car upholstery it was evident that some inflammable fluid had been used.

The hands of the dead man had been burned to formless stumps and his legs were charred before the crime was discovered and the body pulled from the blazing auto.

Mrs. Hooper hurried to Springport but was so hysterical that she was returned to her home.

* * *

CORONER JAMES WAY discounted any possibility of suicide with the statement that Hooper "obviously was shot by someone else."

Detective Bion Hoeg, of the Jackson State Police post, which is investigating the slaying, said that Hooper's body was still warm when officers arrived nearly an hour after the shooting. Hoeg asked that experts of the State Crime Detection Laboratory at Lansing be rushed to Springport to aid in the investigation.

Because the position of Hooper's body indicated that someone else may have been driving his car, State Police were
Turn to Page 5, Column 2

On Inside Pages

Amusements	4	Merry-Go-R'd	6	
Bingay		My Day	12	
Childs	6	Radio	17	
Classified	15-16	Rations	11	
Crossword	17	Sabo	12	
Editorials	6	Stafford	12	
Financial	14	Stokes	18	
Guest	6	Town Crier	18	
Lyons	18	Women's	8-9	

The Detroit Free Press

WEDNESDAY, AUGUST 15, 1945 — On Guard for Over a Century — Vol. 115—No. 103 — Five Cents — METRO FINAL

COOLER — Cloudy and Cooler, Showers Wednesday

AUG. 15, 1945:

Japan's surrender drives Detroiters wild.

PEACE! PEACE! PEACE!

Cruiser Goes Down in Flames; 883 Lost

HIROHITO BLAMES BOMBS

315 Rescued After Days in High Sea

Indianapolis Victim of Torpedo Attack

BY MORRIE LANDSBERG

PELELIU, PALAU ISLANDS—(AP)—The 10,000-ton cruiser Indianapolis was sunk in less than 15 minutes, presumably by a Japanese submarine, 12 minutes past midnight July 30—and 883 crew members lost their lives in one of the Navy's worst disasters.

She went down in the Philippines Sea, within 450 miles of Leyte while on an unescorted high speed run from San Francisco.

THE FATAL torpedo attack came without a second's warning. Two explosions flashed out of her bow. She quivered while flames streaked like a white, searing torch down passageways all through her main hull.

In less than 15 minutes the Indianapolis was gone; 10,000 tons of "proud and happy" ship plunged headfirst into the sea.

Nobody outside the oil-covered circle of men and debris in the water knew her fate until after a Peleliu search plane led the way to the rescue of the 315 men who survived five days in the sea.

NEARLY 700 MEN went down with the ship. Hundreds more jumped off the cruiser's rearing side in time.

But many were without life preservers or rafts, without clothing, without hope of remaining afloat for long.

Survivors believe two underwater torpedoes smashed into the starboard side near the bow of the fourteen-year-old cruiser, setting off one of the eight-inch gun magazines.

What happened in the last 15 minutes aboard the Indianapolis was a living nightmare of flames, explosions, of men screaming, of others making near-miraculous escapes, of watching the one-time Fifth Fleet flagship of Adm. Raymond A. Spruance founder helplessly, and disappear.

For the nearly 500 men who reached the water—out of the 1,196-man crew—there began an ordeal seldom equaled in modern history of lost ships.

THE MAJORITY floated in rough seas from 96 to 116 hours, supported only by kapok jackets and a few rubber life rings. Death picked off the wounded; men killed each other in frantic moments of mass hallucinations, and drowned themselves in nightmarish dreams.

Of 305 enlisted men and 10 officers who came through that battle with the sea, someone said "the weak died, the strong lived."

But there were cases like that of Radioman 3rd Class Harold J. Schesteris, 24, Shattuckville, Mass., whose appendix had been removed nine days before, and a seaman with the base of his spine shattered. Both lived.

Many died while trying to help the dying.

CRYING OUT for water, nearly everyone drank from the sea, only to torture themselves into raging ... They thought they saw ships and planes coming for them—blinking at them—flying off without them.

They ripped off their waterlogged kapoks and dived below. "To get a glass of milk in the galley."

At the peak of their hallucinations, "large numbers swam feebly off toward a mystery from ten."

Turn to Page 2, Column 8

Lest We Forget

WASHINGTON — (AP)—For the United States, the cost of victory in World War II was more than a million casualties. The world counted its dollars and lives needed at perhaps 25,000,000, plus millions more slaughtered in air raids or dead of starvation.

Says Nips Quit to Save the World

Sought No Conquest, Mikado Declares

SAN FRANCISCO—(AP)—Emperor Hirohito proclaimed to his defeated nation in an unprecedented broadcast from Tokyo Tuesday night that if Japan should continue to fight it would have resulted in the extinction of human civilization. Therefore, he announced, the empire had accepted the Allied "joint declaration."

"To strive for the common prosperity and happiness of all nations as well as the security and well-being of our subjects is the solemn obligation which has been handed down by our imperial ancestors, and which we lay close to," the Emperor said.

. . .

"INDEED, we declared war on America and Britain out of our sincere desire to ensure Japan's self-preservation and the stabilization of East Asia, it being far from our thought either to infringe upon the sovereignty of other nations or to embark upon territorial aggrandizement.

"It is according to the dictates of time and fate that we have resolved to pave the way for a grand peace for all the generations to come by enduring of the undesirable and suffering what is sufferable."

Revealing to his subjects for the first time that Japan was committed to lay down its arms against the United States, Britain, China and the Soviet Union, the Emperor said Nippon's enemies had begun to employ a "new and most cruel bomb."

He described the atomic bomb, which virtually obliterated two of his largest cities, as being so powerful that it can inflict "damage which is indeed incalculable, taking the toll of many innocent lives."

. . .

"SHOULD WE continue to fight, it would not only result in an ultimate collapse and obliteration of the Japanese nation, but also it would lead to the total extinction

Turn to Page 2, Column 2

Petain Guilty! Faces Death Unless Pitied

PARIS — (UP) — Marshal Henri Philippe Petain, eighty-nine-year-old hero of Verdun, was found guilty of treason and intelligence with the enemy and sentenced to death. But the jury recommended that the sentence not be carried out because of his great age.

The twenty-four-man jury deliberated nearly seven hours. It found Petain innocent of plotting to gain power and of plotting against the security of the state.

. . .

PETAIN HAD protested in a dramatic last statement to the judges and jurors: "My life is in your hands, but my honor you cannot take away from me."

After almost an entire night of deliberation in which the judge and jurors twice had meals brought to them, Petain, sleepy-eyed and with his white hair ruffled awry, was led back into the court at 4 a.m. Wednesday to hear his fate.

The courtroom was crowded despite the long wait.

JAPAN FACES SLOW DEATH

Loss of Stolen Lands Destroys Empire

(Relman Morin, Associated Press bureau chief at Tokyo from 1937 to 1941, and reporting from Indo-China when the Japanese struck there Dec. 7, 1941, writes of Japan's possible future.)

BY RELMAN MORIN

PARIS—Japanese surrender on terms stripping her of her overseas empire will be a warrant for the lingering but inexorably certain death of that nation as we have known her.

It is difficult to see how Japan can live as a major nation without her empire.

But that empire has been built within the last 50 years entirely from territory torn from other countries, in short by bare, unvarnished aggression.

WITHIN THE FOUR main islands that constitute Japan proper there is not even rice to feed the people. There is very little good iron or petroleum. There is virtually none of the raw materials and minerals or natural resources necessary for maintaining life in the modern manner.

All that has been coming to Japan from the areas she won by conquest.

She ripped huge chunks of territory from China. She took south Manchuria and half of Sakhalin Island from the Russians, and north Manchuria and three gigantic provinces in north China from the present Chungking Government.

THE WHOLE CHINA coast from Tientsin to Canton has been bitten off piece by piece in the 14 years since the present Sino-Japanese War began. The rich Yangtze River valley is "Japanese."

Off the coast, the great islands of Formosa and Hainan were brought under the Rising Sun.

The Japanese conquests since Pearl Harbor throw a gigantic shadow over even this whole area. French Indo-China is nearly as large as California, Oregon and Washington together. Further south lies Malaya with Singapore at its tip.

JUST BELOW THE HORIZON is Sumatra, then Java, the whole Celebes group, Borneo and the Halmaheras—all taken by the Japanese in their 1942 sweep.

The physical size of this empire is nothing by comparison with the unbelievable wealth it contains. If Japan had been able to retain possession of it she would have become the world's richest and most powerful nation within 20 years after the last gun was fired.

Without it she cannot live at all except as an impotent little oriental country. This was entirely clear 50 years ago to an astute and far-sighted group of men who became "elder statesmen" and plotted the course for modern Japan.

It was equally as clear to the man who charted the famous blue-print for conquest known as "The Tanaka Memorials." Tanaka, retiring prime minister, submitted his plan to his emperor. What he recommended Japan tried to do.

IT WAS A SPECTACULAR gamble, and it almost succeeded. Forty months ago there wasn't an effective fighting force anywhere within 3,000 miles of Japan. The Americans, British and Dutch had been swept from the Orient like leaves in a typhoon. The French were helpless in Indo-China.

And now, three and a half years later, something like the annihilation at a single stroke of an empire. The empires of Egypt, Rome and Spain crumbled piecemeal and over a period of many years.

Japan's empire will disappear, "vaporized" as though by an atomic bomb. And the process of creeping death for modern Japan will then immediately begin.

2 Holidays Proclaimed by Truman

Overtime Pay Set for Today, Thursday

WASHINGTON — (AP) — Wednesday and Thursday are days off for Government workers, and holidays for pay purposes for workers in general.

President Truman announced both rulings Tuesday night.

He directed Government agency heads to use bare skeleton staff Aug. 15 and 16 and not to charge the two days against the employees' annual leave. He said it was in "inadequate" recognition of the four-year efforts of "one of the hardest working groups of war workers."

. . .

FOR OTHER workers under wage control, Wednesday and Thursday count like Christmas and the few other accepted holidays for purposes of overtime pay in figuring the number of days worked in a week.

Postal service for the next two days will be "approximate holiday service," the Postoffice Department said. Local postmasters will have wide discretion in carrying out the President's wishes.

It was presumed, but not officially stated, that Government workers generally will be off on V-J Day, too.

The White House said the next two days are to be regarded as legal holidays.

Nudes Is News

It could only happen at war's end. Seems that crowds in Grand Circus Park were entertained by a couple of inebriates who mounted the lighted fountain, stripped to the skin, and danced around in the nude. Before the cops came they retrieved their clothes and disappeared.

Number 1

SAN FRANCISCO — (UP) — The Japanese War Minister, Korechika Anami, has committed suicide, Domei news agency reported in a Tokyo broadcast recorded by FCC.

City Greets End With Wildest Day

Hilarious Detroiters Parade in Streets in Great Celebration

BY JAMES S. POOLER
Free Press Staff Writer

Detroit greeted peace twice Tuesday.

The first was an impromptu frolic that sprang up before dawn as Japan admitted defeat.

The second—the full-blown celebration—came Tuesday night after President Truman confirmed the long-awaited end of a terrible war.

V-J Day will not be officially proclaimed until the formal signing of surrender terms by Japan. This was announced in Washington.

Although the President has designated Wednesday and Thursday as legal holidays, neither is V-J Day.

. . .

SHOWERS had dampened the first frolic, quieting the downtown streets, sending the young spearheads of uproar home and matting the confetti in the gutters.

Then in the evening, the sun broke out. At 7 o'clock, the White House ended the last of the suspense. The people sprang up in the streets like mushrooms after the rain.

Far off, the bass notes of a river boat gave the first shout. The shriller whistles of the far

Turn to Page 3, Column 2

Celebrant Killed

One fatality marred celebrations of the surrender of Japan. Donald Tomasek, 27, of 659 Lincoln, Wyandotte, died when he fell off the fender of an auto at Bennett and Biddle, in Wyandotte, police reported.

11 Pct. Drop Seen in Canned Foods

WASHINGTON — (AP) — Civilian supplies of all commercially canned fruit and vegetable products during the 1945-46 marketing season will be about 11 per cent less than last year.

This was the Commerce Department's estimate. Increases in export and war requirements were given as the principal reason.

Peace Bears Date of Atlantic Charter

WASHINGTON — (AP) — Japanese surrender came on the fourth anniversary of the Atlantic Charter.

That declaration, with its pledges of freedom from aggression and oppression, was framed by President Roosevelt and Prime Minister Churchill in conference aboard ship in the Atlantic.

Cooler Weather, That Man Says

After sweltering Tuesday, Detroiters were promised cooler weather for Wednesday and Thursday. The occasional showers will continue, the Weather Bureau predicted. About a half inch of rain is anticipated Tuesday night and Wednesday.

A warmer trend will set in again toward the week-end, it was said.

Jap Emperor Bows; Boss Is MacArthur

BY ARTHUR KROCK
New York Times Service

WASHINGTON—Japan Tuesday unconditionally surrendered the hemispheric empire taken by force and held for more than two years against the rising power of the United States and its Allies in the Pacific war.

The bloody dream of the Japanese military caste vanished in the text of a note to the four powers accepting the terms of the Potsdam ultimatum of July 26, 1945.

The Japanese surrender document was forwarded through the Swiss Foreign Office at Bern and the Swiss legation in Washington.

The note of total capitulation was delivered to the State Department by the legation charge d'affaires at 6:10 p.m. (Detroit time) after the third and most anxious day of waiting on Tokyo.

The anxiety had been intensified by several premature or false reports of the finale of World War II.

The State Department responded with a note to Tokyo through the same channel.

The American note ordered the immediate end of hostilities by the Japanese.

. . .

IT REQUIRED that the supreme Allied commander, whom the President said will be Gen. Douglas MacArthur, be notified of the date and hour of the order.

It instructed that emissaries of Japan be sent to him at once—at the time and place selected by him—"with full information of the disposition of the Japanese forces and commanders."

President Truman summoned a special press conference in the executive offices at 7 p.m. He handed to the reporters three texts.

The first—the only one he read aloud—was a statement that he had received the Japanese note and deemed it full acceptance of the Potsdam Declaration, containing no qualification whatsoever.

The statement added that arrangements for the formal sign-

Turn to Page 2, Column 1

UAW Drops Its Wartime Strike Ban

International Must Sanction Walkouts

With the end of hostilities, R. J. Thomas and other UAW (CIO) international officers announced an end to the no-strike pledge.

At the same time they warned that support would not be forthcoming to strikes called without sanction of the international body.

Thomas, president of the union, in a proclamation to the members declared that with "termination of hostilities the UAW (CIO) America's largest union, ends its wartime no-strike pledge. It returns to the union's constitutional position."

Text of President Truman's announcement of Jap surrender Thursday as legal holidays, on Page 4.

THE PROCLAMATION, sent out to 1,000 local unions in the United States and Canada, was issued following a meeting of the union's top international officers.

dure whereby strikes may be authorized by the international president and international executive board."

CITY STORES, BARS, PLANTS CLOSE

Activities Grind to a Stop

Through either official edict or voluntary consent the following places of employment announced these closing dates:

1—All major downtown retail department stores will close Wednesday.

2—Most factories will remain closed Wednesday and Thursday.

3—All Federal agencies including the postoffice will remain closed Wednesday and Thursday by edict of President Truman.

4—City, State and County Governments will close for Wednesday and Thursday except those departments which necessitate skeleton forces to keep necessary responsibilities functioning.

5—Bars will be closed and all sales of alcoholic beverages suspended until 7 p.m. Wednesday.

MARCH 14, 1946:

GM workers win an hourly wage of $1.30½ after 113-day strike.

The Detroit Free Press

THURSDAY, MARCH 14, 1946 — On Guard for Over a Century — Vol. 115—No. 314 — Five Cents — **METRO FINAL**

SHOWERS
There will be mildness too. Wednesday's showers were dew.

U. S.-SOVIET CRISIS
Walter Lippmann Sees Peril in Lack of Diplomatic Contact with Moscow
See Page 6

Stalin Warns Churchill Not to Start War

Says Reds Can Beat Any Foe; Invites Repudiation of Briton

LONDON—(UP)—Generalissimo Josef Stalin Wednesday night personally answered Winston Churchill, accusing him of fomenting "new armed intervention" against Eastern Europe.

Stalin asserted bluntly that if Churchill and his friends in Great Britain succeeded in doing so they would be beaten.

Calling Churchill's speech at Fulton, Mo., a sort of ultimatum to the non-English speaking world, Stalin said:

"There is no doubt that the setup of Mr. Churchill is a setup for war, a call to war with the Soviet Union."

STALIN TERMED Churchill's speech a dangerous act which jeopardized co-operation among nations. He said the former prime minister's attitude was incompatible with the twenty-year Russian-British alliance.

Thus, by implication, Stalin invited the British Labor Government to repudiate Churchill and even hinted he was ready to tear up the alliance treaty if necessary.

Stalin made his bitter personal and political denunciation in his wartime Big Three colleague, in an interview published in the newspaper Pravda, organ of the Russian Communist Party.

The interview was broadcast by the Moscow Radio.

• • •

(CHURCHILL, in New York, declined to comment on Stalin's tirade.

(The Mutual Broadcasting System announced that Churchill will make a national broadcast at 10:30 p. m. Friday, Detroit time.

(He will speak at a dinner in his honor in New York.)

STALIN CHARGED that Churchill organized intervention against Bolshevist Russia after the first world war.

He said he did not know whether Churchill and his friends would succeed now in organizing a new "military expedition" in Eastern Europe.

"But if they succeed in this, which is not very probable since millions of common people stand on guard over peace, then one may confidently say that they will be beaten just as they were beaten in the past, 26 years ago," Stalin said.

THE GENERALISSIMO compared Churchill in detail with Hitler.

Calling his speech a sort of ultimatum to the vast majority of peoples who do not speak English, he emphasized that Churchill was supported in his views by friends not only in
Turn to Page 2, Column 6

Mr. Truman Backs Down on Pauley

But Praises Him in Withdrawing Name

WASHINGTON—(AP)—President Truman withdrew Edwin W. Pauley's nomination for Undersecretary of the Navy Wednesday with a final vigorous defense of Pauley's "integrity and ability."

His "Dear Ed" Pauley thus went the way of President Roosevelt's "Dear Ed" Flynn and an explosive election-year squabble was ended after six weeks without so much as a cheep from the Democratic camp, at least.

EDWARD J. FLYNN had written to the late Mr. Roosevelt in 1943 that he was "unwilling to permit" his candidacy for Minister to Australia "to be made the excuse for a partisan political debate in the Senate" which "would imply most unfortunate disunity."

Similar considerations had prompted Democratic Senators to urge Pauley to retire.

But there was no mention of politics in an exchange of letters, both dated March 13, which the White House made public.

PAULEY WROTE that he believes all charges against him have been "shown to be false."

But in view of "hysteria that has been engendered by there misrepresentations," he explained, he feels he could not render "the high order of service" required.

So he asked that his nomination be withdrawn.

Mr. Truman, in a letter addressed "Dear Ed," consented to the action—only, he said, on the basis of Pauley's "feeling that there is no immediate antidote to the tactics which have been employed."

• • •

THE PRESIDENT wrote Pauley that "you stand before your countrymen after vicious and unwarranted attacks with integrity unscathed, with ability unquestioned, with honor unsullied."

Obviously as a part of the arrangement, Chairman David I. Walsh, Massachusetts Democrat, of the Senate Naval Committee issued a statement in his behalf.

It said that "the majority of the committee . . . have no doubt regarding his personal integrity and administrative competence."

Ex-Nazi Chief Blomberg Dies

NUERNBERG — (AP) — Field Marshal Werner von Blomberg, first of Hitler's cabinet, died of heart failure at the 116th General Hospital.

He was to have testified as one of an aristocratic family, started one of the major sensations of Nazi Germany when he defied social conventions of the military and took as his second wife a stenographer, Erika Gruhn.

As a result of the storm which developed he resigned his post.

Marshall Silent; Stops at Hawaii

HONOLULU — (UP) — Gen. George C. Marshall the President's envoy to China, stopped briefly here en route to Washington to confer with Mr. Truman.

He told newsmen he was saving his report on the China-Manchurian situation for the White House.

B-29 Stands Alone

WASHINGTON — (UP) — Maj. Gen. Leslie Groves said that the B-29 Superfortress is the only known plane that can carry an atom bomb.

IN EXTRA INNINGS, TOO

Oak Safe on Feeble Bunt as Pitcher Tosses a Drop

The Weather Man beat out a feeble bunt Wednesday.

The mighty W. W. Oak managed to score after the game had gone into extra innings. It gave him his second consecutive victory.

His prediction for Wednesday was: Cloudy, showers afternoon or evening.

THERE WAS no general precipitation. Free Press reporters said that a few drops of rain skirted their hair as they walked along Lafayette Blvd.

And the integrity of Free Press reporters is not to be doubted.

Besides, Oak claimed credit for showers at 6:08 a. m.

WHILE the game was in suspense, the temperature sneaked up to a record 66 degrees under overcast skies—to break the previous high of 62 set March 13, 1913.

The score:
Won Lost Percentage
Oak 2 0 1.000
Thursday Prediction
Continued mild, scattered showers, mostly cloudy.

PAY YOUR TAXES IN BY
Installment Dept.
National Bank of Detroit—30 Offices —Adv.

Army Repeats Denial of Rumors

WASHINGTON—(AP)—It's still untrue that the Army has alerted or is calling its reserves to active duty.

A fresh crop of inquiries prompted War Department officials to point to a week-old statement which said categorically that "all such rumors are completely unfounded."

World tension grows as nations keep eye on Russian moves in Middle East. See Page 3.
Top Government officials warn Congress not to cut U. S. armed forces too far. See Page 5.

Strike Settled for 18½ Cents

GM WORKERS AWAIT CALL BACK TO JOBS

SETTLEMENT SETS PICKETS TO DANCING JIGS

GM Employees Go Wild at News

It was typical of the explosion of emotions that rocked membership in the 96 locals of the 84 GM plants

REACTION AT GM'S TERNSTEDT PLANT AT THE ANNOUNCEMENT OF THE END OF THE 113-DAY STRIKE

Truman Asks U.S. to Double Vet Housing

Approval of 100,000 More Homes Sought

WASHINGTON — (AP) — President Truman asked Congress to appropriate $253,727,000 to build an additional 100,000 temporary homes for veterans.

Congress already has provided funds for 100,000 such dwellings. The President said 100,000 more are needed.

Union, Plant Officials Rush to Settle Local Differences

Meetings Are Called for Today in Preparation for Vote on Pact

After 113 days of waiting, UAW(CIO) locals exploded like a chain of firecrackers with news of the GM settlement.

Exultant shouts roared from the throats of thousands throughout the state as the long-awaited news was flashed.

It was like a home run in the ninth inning of a crucial World Series game.

Groups of card players in Detroit locals, scattered the decks like confetti when the report came in.

Pickets whacked each other on the back and danced impromptu jigs along the picket lines.

THE NEWS STOPPED the show when announced in a Flint movie theater. Wild cheering, recalling the end of the Jap war, greeted the report.

By radio, loudspeaker and word-of-mouth, the announcement swept through the locals like an electric current, galvanizing the strike-sluggish officials into action.

They bristled with plans to hurry settlement of strictly local
Turn to Page 11, Column 3

War Gas Used as Disease Cure in Human Tests

ATLANTIC CITY — (AP) — A new war gas, nitrogen mustard, that acts much like X-rays, is being tried on more than 100 human cases of cancer, Hodgkins disease and leukemia.

The medical angles were reported to the Federation of American Societies for Experimental Biology by Dr. Alfred Gilman, of the pharmacology section of the Chemical Warfare Service, Edgewood Arsenal, Md.

Gilman said the effects on nitrogen mustard have been favorable on Hodgkins disease, less favorable on leukemia, and nearly negative on cancer.

Exit Superman

NEW YORK — (AP) — The London radio reported that Dr. Karl Haushofer, 76, exponent of the Nazi superman myth and a teacher of geopolitics, had committed suicide with his wife.

KEYKO MARGARINE—a spread, seasoning, shortening—it's good.—Adv.

The children will like
Bunny With the Heart-Shaped Tail
A delightful story that will appear Saturday in
WEEK END
The Detroit Free Press

Highlights of Accord

Highlights of the settlement of the 113-day-old General Motors strike:

1—An 18½ cent an hour wage increase
2—Adjustment of wage inequities in local plants. Plant managers are to present new wage schedules to shop committees within 90 days of resumption of production.
3—Improved vacation pay.
4—Equal pay for women.
5—Higher overtime rates.
6—A new dues collection system providing for dues checkoff.
7—Reinstatement of the 1945 contract plus all gains won under War Labor Board.
8—Preference on transfers to workers with greatest seniority, "when other factors are equal."
9—Seniority preference in connection with promotions within departments.
10—Contract to run for two years from rank-and-file union ratification.
11—Reinstatement of local union agreements supplementary to national contract.
12—No wage demands for one year.
13—A retroactive clause, giving all strikers an additional 13½ cents an hour from Nov. 7 to Nov. 21.

'46 Car Output to Be Half of Original Goal

3 Million Units May Be Turned Out

BY LEO DONOVAN
Free Press Motor Writer

The automobile industry is ready to move forward again.

Assembly lines, geared to greater and greater production, may turn out not the 6,000,000 cars estimated for 1946, but 3,000,000 in the remaining nine months.

Still to be solved are the serious problems of prices and materials and parts shortages.

As the General Motors strike was settled, here was the production record of the five major GM divisions:

CHEVROLET — Produced only 12,776 passenger cars before the strike; it had been scheduled to turn out 1,800 a day by March.

BUICK—Produced 2,481 cars. In schedule was for 120,000 in the first postwar year of full production.

CADILLAC — 1,205 cars produced; 100,000 scheduled for first year.

OLDSMOBILE — Turned out an estimated 3,956; scheduled for 1,300 a day by March.

PONTIAC — Produced an esti-
Turn to Page 11, Column 3

Rail Strike Ends

LOUISVILLE — (UP) — The Transport Workers Union (CIO) announced the end of the six-day strike against the Louisville Railway Co., pending ratification of an agreement.

On Inside Pages

Amusements 15	Keeping Well 10
Bethurum 19	Lippmann 6
Classified 19-22	Merry-Go-R'd 6
Crossword 23	Miss Riley 8
Dawson 18	Radio 23
Editorials 6	Smith 16
Fashions 8	Sports 16-17
Financial 18-19	Stokes 6
Guest 6	Teenagers 9
Horoscope 23	Women's 8-10

FIRE PIPER CLEANER—fast and sure. No fuming—wipes dirt away.—Adv.

Union to Speed Approval of Pact

Locals to Vote Sunday on 2-Year Contract; Work May Start in Week

BY ARTHUR O'SHEA
Free Press Labor Writer

A contract which settled the General Motors strike in its 113th day is expected to be approved Sunday by the rank and file membership of the UAW (CIO).

On that day referendum elections will be held in 90 local union halls throughout the country.

Settlement of the dispute — longest big strike in American history — was announced at 2:45 p. m. Wednesday by Special Labor Mediator James F. Dewey after a gruelling seventeen-hour, all night bargaining session.

Agreement was reached on the basis of an 18½-cents-an-hour wage boost, adjustment of local wage inequities, a dues checkoff

Wage Rate Comparisons

	General Motors	Ford	Chrysler
Wage raise, hourly	18½ cents	18 cents	18½ cents
Workers affected	175,000	95,000	65,000
New average hourly wage	$1.30½ plus*	$1.39 plus	$1.32 plus
Old average hourly wage	1.12 plus*	1.21 plus	1.14 plus

*Includes non-automotive as well as automotive workers.

system, improved vacation and overtime pay and other contract improvements.

THE WAGE INCREASE — offered by GM on Feb. 12 — represents a 16 per cent boost. It will add an estimated $64,750,000 annually to the corporation's payroll.

Top union officials declared that they would "heartily recommend" acceptance of the terms to the UAW National GM Conference, which meets Friday in Detroit.

In view of this, ratification by the rank and file was regarded as certain.

Action of the conference, which consists of 200 elected delegates from the locals, is not binding upon the membership, but it undoubtedly will have a profound effect on the referendum vote.

WALTER P. REUTHER, UAW vice president, expressed the opinion that workers could start back to their jobs within a week after ratification.

General Motors previously had said it probably would place all of the 175,000 affected men to work within a week or 10 days after ratification.

The union said it had achieved its demands for a 19½-cent an hour raise through a face-saving formula under which GM has agreed to remove inequities.

The corporation had no official comment on this point.

Of the wage settlement the union had this to say in an official statement:

"The 18½-cent wage increase plus the agreement to remove inequities in wage rates meets the 19½-cent increase recommended by President Truman.

"In addition to those two provisions there are other economic clauses — improved vacation pay, which alone amounts to $5,000,-
000 a year; improved overtime rates and equal pay for women, which bring the total average hourly increase to well above 19½ cents."

OTHER HIGHLIGHTS of the agreement include:

The new contract will run two years — the first time the UAW has agreed to a contract of more than one year.

The wage question cannot be reopened for one year.

A retroactive pay clause will give all the 175,000 strikers an additional 13½ cents an hour from Nov. 7 to Nov. 21 — the day the strike started.

Maintenance of membership will be replaced by a system pro-
Turn to Page 4, Column 4

A history of the strike, plus pictures and sketches of the principals involved are on the back page.

General Electric workers and management reach wage agreement to end long strike. Story on Page 4.

$132,000,000 Pay Lost

More than $125,000,000 in wages was lost by 175,000 hourly-rated workers as a result of the General Motors strike, UAW (CIO) spokesmen said.

Another $7,000,000 was lost by other workers affected by the strike. An estimated total of $849,750 in union dues also was lost.

Company losses were estimated at $565,000,000; lost in dealers' commissions, $113,000,000; loss of of automobile production, 556,260 units.

Full Story of Ford's Life on Page 4; Pictures Page 5

APRIL 8, 1947:

The Detroit Free Press

TUESDAY, APRIL 8, 1947 — On Guard for Over a Century — Vol. 116—No. 339 — Five Cents

WARMER — A fair day more like spring

SECOND METRO FINAL **EXTRA**

HENRY FORD DIES

Henry Ford's death is Page One news around the world.

Succumbs Quietly at 83 with Wife at His Bedside

Henry Ford, founder and builder of the vast Ford industrial empire, died at 11:40 p.m. Monday at his residence in Dearborn. He was 83 years old.

The venerable pioneer of the automobile industry, who pumped life's blood into the economic system of Detroit and the Nation, would have celebrated his 84th birthday July 30.

His death came very suddenly and the cause was not announced immediately. Ford had been very active over the week-end, members of his family said.

Ford, in a simply phrased letter of resignation had stepped down for the second time as active monarch of his empire on Sept. 21, 1945.

EARLIER, he had relinquished the management to his only child, Edsel, but when Edsel died on May 26, 1943, he took over the reins again for two years and three months.

Then he surrendered the presidency of the Ford Motor Co. to his grandson, Henry Ford II. At that time, the elder Ford was in excellent health, but he wanted to devote more time to personal interests.

In recent months, however, his health began to fail and his public appearances became less frequent, although he enjoyed his periods of outside activity.

HE HAD BEEN able to spend some week each week at the Ford engineering laboratory where he maintained a private office and workshop, but was rarely seen about the administration building where affairs of the big company were directed.

His last formal public appearance was a week before Christmas, when he presented watches to veteran employees of his company. At the end of a bleak and cold February, Ford journeyed to his home in Richmond Hills, Ga., where he rested and sought to recapture his vitality.

He returned to Dearborn just eight days ago.

Mr. Ford's wife was the only one with him when he died. His death was announced 90 minutes later by the Ford News Bureau, which arranged a telephone hook-up with all of Detroit's newspapers and the various wire services.

* * *

ALL OF THE immediate family are in Detroit, with the exception of one grandchild, Benson Ford. Benson was rushing back from New York, where he had been on a business trip.

The other grandchildren, in addition to Henry Ford II, are William Ford and Mrs. Walter Buhl Ford II.

Ford's death started immediate speculation as to the probable disposition of the vast personal fortune, which like that of his late son, Edsel, has been estimated variously at upward of $200,000,000.

It was generally assumed, in the absence of any statement from the family, that all of the elder Ford's holdings probably would go directly to his widow, Mrs. Clara Bryant Ford.

With Mrs. Ford, the founder of the great Ford empire owned approximately 58 per cent of the voting stock of the giant enterprise.

The remaining 42 per cent was understood to be held by Edsel Ford's heirs, Mrs. Eleanor Clay Ford, his widow, her three sons, Henry II, Benson and William and her daughter, Josephine.

* * *

A LARGE PART of the Ford stock, however, was in nonvoting shares, and was held by the Ford Foundation, founded by the elder Ford more than a decade ago to promote educational interests. As such it was tax exempt.

When Edsel Ford died in 1943 it was said the inheritance tax would eat up a large part of his estate. There even was speculation that to satisfy the tax, some of the Ford stock would have to be sold outside the Ford family.

The difficulty arose immediately of determining the exact value of a share of Ford Motor Co. stock, however. So far as has been disclosed, probate of his estate has not yet been completed.

Presumably the same problem will arise in attempting to determine the exact monetary value of the elder Ford's holdings in the company.

As far as the great Ford industrial empire is concerned, however, it will go on as usual, with the second Henry Ford and nearly a dozen vice presidents directing its destinies.

1863 — 1947

HENRY FORD
His memory will live forever in Detroit

U.S. Plan on Greece Blasted by Gromyko

BY JAMES E. ROPER

LAKE SUCCESS, N. Y.—(UP)—Russia attacked American plans to send direct aid to Greece and Turkey.

The Russian spokesman demanded that the United Nations administer any American help sent to Greece.

Soviet Delegate Andrei Gromyko asked the UN Security Council to set up a special commission to make sure that any help offered Greece used only for the benefit of the Greek people.

He charged that President Truman's program, as originally proposed, was "political."

It deals "a serious blow" to the UN and "produces distrust" among UN members, Gromyko said.

President Truman has proposed to spend $250,000,000 to help Greece and $150,000,000 to help Turkey.

The program would include both military and economic aid which would be carried out independently of UN.

Gromyko charged the plan was inconsistent with UN's "purposes and principles"—the maintenance of peace. He said it would intensify the Greek civil war.

GROMYKO'S proposal for UN supervision of Greek aid apparently was intended to prevent the United States from offering military aid directly to Greece.

Turn to Page 2, Column 1

TOWN'S DILEMMA
Lights Voted; Pay Refused

Center Line voters Monday expressed a desire to have darkened city streets relighted, but disapproved raising taxes to pay for it.

The proposal to end the blackout was approved by a vote of 336 to 106, but the accompanying proposal to raise the tax limit two mills was beaten, 209 to 199.

The lights on Center Line's side streets were turned off during the early 1930s as an economy measure. A proposal to light them again was voted down several years ago.

Paraguay Chief Rejects Mediation

ASUNCION, Paraguay — (UP) — President Higinio Morinigo said that he had rejected all offers by the Catholic Church and foreign governments to act as mediators in bringing the Republic's months-old civil war to an end.

Local Issues Fail to Lure Suburb Vote
Floods Blamed for Vacant Polls

Despite contests for municipal offices and balloting on local issues, voting was generally light in suburban communities in the Detroit area Monday.

Highland Park, some downriver towns and communities in Southern Oakland and Macomb Counties were choosing city officials.

In some of the areas where moderately heavy balloting was expected flood conditions were blamed for keeping voters away from the polls.

Ferndale

Ferndale voters ousted two members of the City Commission in the lightest vote in a spring election since 1931.

The two new commissioners are Sidney G. Hill, president of the Ferndale Labor Club, and Murray A. Scott, a personnel official of the Packard Motor Car Co. They defeated Commissioners George J. Kline and Hugh R. Liddicoat.

The vote was: Hill, 1,473; Scott, 1,119; Kline, 834; Liddicoat, 753.

The two present constables were re-elected. The vote: Robert Robbins, 1,210; Willis D. Pierce, 953; Bruce P. Wheeler, 931; Zeno Crittenden, 610.

Five amendments to the City Pension plan were approved by majorities of about three to one.

East Detroit

Councilman Harry W. McMillan was elected mayor of East Detroit to succeed Mayor Richard Max-well, who was not a candidate for re-election.

McMillan defeated William H. Ryas, another councilman, 1,099 to 651.

In the race for two Council posts, the vote was: Allen D. Aschenbach, 1,078; Betty Hays, 720; Clement A. Rock, 640; A. H. Neville, 602. None is a present council member.

Charles W. Yost defeated Frederick W. Renard for constable, 725 to 642.

Hazel Park

The two incumbent councilmen seeking re-election in Hazel Park were easy victors.

John M. Gray received 804 votes, Benjamin L. Walton 800, Paul Edward Worley 461 and Warren Sturz 331.

Constable Thomas Baggs led Homer R. Pugh, 477 to 292, with one of the city's five precincts unreported.

Pleasant Ridge

Pleasant Ridge returned two incumbent city commissioners to office in a three-man race. The vote was: Edward H. Stanton 269, Harry K. Munroe 253, Ned W. Landau 147.

Dearborn

Dearborn voters registered definite disapproval of proposals to raise the pay of several City officials $1,500 a year.

A proposed increase for Council members was from 3,057 to 155; a boost in pay for the mayor, City clerk and treasurer was rejected 3,070 to 715, and raises for the municipal judges were defeated, 3,000 to 900.

The sentiment against boosting the City officials' pay carried two strictly routine charter amendments to defeat. One providing immediate effect for ordinances

Turn to Page 2, Column 1

'Pasture' Is Urged for Iowa House

DES MOINES, Ia.—(UP)—Rep. John A. Walker (R.) suggested that the Iowa House be "retired to pasture" Nov. 1, when the House membership reaches an average age of 55.

If the resolution were adopted, the representatives would be retired at half pay, $500 per biennium.

TIME TO MAKE HOME IMPROVEMENTS. No down payment required and 3 years to pay on Industrial National's F.H.A. Local Plan.—Adv.

Wallace Denies Political Ambition

NEW YORK—(AP)—Henry A. Wallace said before leaving for Europe by plane that he had "no political ambitions whatever."

Wallace said he planned a "visit to London, Stockholm and Paris and speak with European leaders "most interested in peace and in backing up the United Nations in every way possible."

Incumbent Judges Win; State Goes Republican

Late Tabulations

City Returns

RECORDER AND JUDGE OF THE RECORDER'S COURT (800 out of 1,211 Precincts)

John J. Maher	67,898
Samuel W. Barr	14,996

JUDGES OF THE RECORDER'S COURT (8 to be elected)

George Murphy	47,069
John P. Scallen	45,804
W. McKay Skillman	46,116
Joseph A. Gillis	45,283
Paul E. Krause	45,242
Christopher E. Stein	44,238
O. Z. Ide	44,215
Arthur E. Gordon	42,870
Gerald W. Groat	3,864

The two present constables were re-elected. The vote: Robert Robbins, 1,210; Willis D. Pierce, 953; Bruce P. Wheeler, 931; Zeno Crittenden, 610.

JUDGES OF THE RECORDER'S COURT—TRAFFIC AND ORDINANCE DIVISION (2 to be elected)

John D. Watts	51,783
George T. Murphy	49,560

Mary V. Beck	24,165
James R. Walsh	22,043

JUDGES OF THE COMMON PLEAS COURT (Full Term) (800 Out of 1,211 Precincts) (4 to be elected)

Thomas A. Kenney	39,692
L. Eugene Sharp	38,513
Harry J. Dingeman, Jr.	31,545
Andrew C. Baird	29,325

Charles W. Yost defeated Frederick W. Renard for constable, 725 to 642.	
George T. Cartwright	29,045
Arthur W. Sempliner	28,514
E. N. Karay	26,057
Eduard Werner	26,995

JUDGES OF THE COMMON PLEAS COURT (To Fill Vacancies) (2 to be elected)

Harry J. Dingeman, Jr.	33,072
George T. Cartwright	31,962

Andrew C. Baird	30,145
E. N. Karay	29,699

MEMBERS OF THE BOARD OF EDUCATION (2 to be elected)

Laura F. Osborn	50,373
Robert G. Foster	49,654

Michael J. O'Brien	44,674
Clark D. Brooks	43,191

CHARTER AMENDMENTS (Salaries of Councilmen)

NO	67,785
YES	21,219

(General Retirement System)

NO	50,188
YES	38,181

State Returns

JUSTICE OF SUPREME COURT (1,246 out of 3,968 Precincts)

Leland W. Carr	90,284
Henry M. Butzel	76,789

Edward T. Kane	40,508
Patrick S. Nertney	27,561

JUSTICE OF SUPREME COURT (Term Ending Dec. 31, 1953)

John B. Dethmers	78,9...
Maurice E. Tripp	65,072

PROPOSAL NO. ONE

YES	10,766
NO	65,022

PROPOSAL NO. TWO

YES	22,164
NO	55,690

REGENTS OF THE UNIVERSITY

J. Joseph Herbert (R)	84,251
Kenneth M. Stevens (R)	85,715

George D. Schermerhorn (D)	58,230
John L. Brunun (D)	55,750

SUPERINTENDENT OF PUBLIC INSTRUCTION

Eugene B. Elliott (R)	80,415
George F. Montgomery (D)	60,563

MEMBER OF THE STATE BOARD OF EDUCATION

Victor Targonski (D)	54,650
Louisa I. Durham (R)	58,705

MEMBERS OF THE STATE BOARD OF AGRICULTURE

Clark L. Brody (R)	86,446
Ellsworth B. Moore (R)	84,463

George D. Stevens (D)	60,301
William S. Lamoreaux (D)	56,482

County Returns

CIRCUIT COURT JUDGE (800 out of 1,486 Precincts) (15 to be elected)

Thomas F. Maher	52,278
Ila M. Neuenfelt	46,406
John V. Brennan	46,015
James E. Chenot	44,789
Chester P. O'Hara	44,629
Joseph A. Moynihan	43,658
Vincent M. Brennan	42,442
Murphy D. Murphy	42,392
Robert M. Toms	41,736
Arthur Webster	39,705
Thomas J. Murphy	39,620
Adolph F. Marshner	39,306
Guy A. Miller	39,215
Clyde I. Webster	39,158
Theodore R. Richter	38,574
Frank Fitzgerald	34,448
Frank B. Ferguson	32,362

William E. Dowling	30,129
Ned M. Smith	28,660
George D. O'Brien	28,279
Henry S. Sweeny	27,796
Gerald F. Fitzgerald	22,402
William Friedman	21,856
George of Mary V. Beck and	
B. E. Keldan	17,072
George Bashara	19,092
V. E. Sacre	16...
Francis X. Norris	15,976
Harry N. Nicol	15,015
James Montante	14,057
Wade M. Leib	13,861
Charles E. Merrill	13,014
Harrison T. Watson	11,920
William Brashear	10,878
George P. Coash	10,836
Francis M. Tresler	10,107

COUNTY AUDITOR

Jacob P. Sumeracki (D)	53,331
John A. Kronk (R)	41,156

City Charter Amendments Are Beaten

Sumeracki Defeats Kronk for Auditor

BY HUB M. GEORGE
Free Press Staff Writer

Michigan electors swept back into office three justices of the State Supreme Court, named Republicans for all State offices and rejected three of the four special ballot proposals.

Disturbed communications as a result of the telephone strike caused returns to trickle in.

Voting was the lightest in a decade, reflecting complications of floods and washouts as well as public apathy.

ALL INCUMBENT Circuit Judges appeared to have been re-elected with Frank FitzGerald, court commissioner, chosen for the place left vacant when Judge Sherman D. Callender decided not to seek re-election.

Traffic Judges George T. Murphy and John D. Watts, withstood the challenge of Mary V. Beck and James R. Walsh.

THE DAY'S biggest upsets were the probable defeat of Common Pleas Judge George T. Cartwright and Emanuel N. Karey, both appointees of former Gov. Kelly. Judges Thomas A. Kenney, also L. Eugene Sharpe were re-elected.

The two additional places on the bench appeared won by Harry J. Dingeman, Jr., son of the former Circuit Judge, and Andrew C. Baird, former sheriff.

The voters likewise retired Dr. Clark D. Brooks, former president of the Detroit Board of Education, but gave Mrs. Laura Osborn, a board veteran, a vote of confidence. Her associate will be Robert G. Foster, at present a teacher.

CITY CHARTER amendments to boost councilmen's pay from $5,000 to $7,500 a year and to liberalize the Retirement System were defeated.

So was the state constitutional amendment to permit corporations to hold income property for 30 instead of 10 years. The amendment to aid judicial primaries where there are no contests was approved.

Returns expressed public confidence in the conduct of recent grand juries.

JUSTICE Leland W. Carr, who was associated with Gov. Sigler as his aspirants for the Supreme Court with a substantial margin.

Judge George B. Murphy, labor-rackets grand juror, was well up among the Circuit Court candidates.

Republican and Democratic candidates for State office ran neck and neck in Wayne County, but County Auditor Jacob P. Sumeracki, Democrat, outdistanced his rival, John A. Kronk, Republican, in the only County partisan contest.

U.S. May Ask Full Fine on Miners

WASHINGTON — Government attorneys, it was learned, will ask Federal Judge T. Alan Goldsborough Thursday to restore the contempt fine against the United Mine Workers (AFL) to the full amount of $3,500,000 set by him last December.

They will ask this action as a result of the current mine "safety" work stoppage.

THE GOVERNMENT will charge that UMW Chief John L. Lewis and the union have displayed bad faith and trickery in tying up the mines in this manner after the Supreme Court upheld the lower court's injunction barring a strike against the Government.

The high court ruled that if Lewis obeyed the strike edict $2,800,000 of the fine would be returned to the union.

Lewis withdrew his strike notice after the miners had been out three weeks, but the current unofficial stoppage has curtailed operations again.

6 Drown in Gale

PARIS — (UP) — Six persons drowned when a hurricane swamped a fishing boat and France's western coast.

Strike Foiled

LISBON—(AP)—The Portuguese Government, moving to halt spreading strikes in Lisbon's waterfront and industrial areas, ordered troops to replace dock workers.

JAN. 2, 1948:

A typical New Year's Day: The roads are icy, and the Wolverines are in the Rose Bowl.

TERRIBLE Things are bad all over. Look ↘

The Detroit Free Press

FRIDAY, JANUARY 2, 1948 — On Guard for Over a Century — Vol. 117—No. 243 — 24 Pages — Five Cents

FINAL EDITION • LARGEST IN MICHIGAN Free Press Weekday Circulation Tops All Michigan Newspapers.

U-M Wallops Trojans in Rose Bowl, 49-0

★ ★ ★ ★ ★ ★ ★ ★

93,000 Watch Wolverines Roll

Weisenburger Scores 3 Times; Chappuis' Passes Play Big Role

BY TOMMY DEVINE
Free Press Sports Writer

PASADENA, Calif.—One of modern football's greatest teams, the University of Michigan, rewrote the Rose Bowl record book by trouncing Southern California 49 to 0 in the 34th renewal of this postseason classic.

An overflow crowd of 93,000 fans sat stunned as the Wolverines of Fritz Crisler rolled up the record-equaling point total at the expense of the hapless Trojans.

The precision-built Michigan team tied the Rose Bowl achievement of another immortal gridiron combination, the Wolverines of 1902.

* * *

BACK IN THE fledgling days of football, the late Fielding H. Yost brought a bemustachioed Michigan football team to Pasadena for the first Rose Bowl game. The Wolverines hammered Stanford, 49 to 1.

From that day to this, 64 other top-ranked teams have competed in this game.

One after another the football giants of the East, the West, the North and the South have shot at the point total of the Wolverines of long ago. None could equal it.

Then came the youngsters of the current outfit. With an attack of blinding speed and brilliant execution, they battered into submission the Pacific Coast Conference champions.

* * *

THE DAY was clear, with the temperature 74 degrees. There was only breeze enough to ruffle the flags atop the stands.

B-b Chappuis, Michigan's All-American fullback who was on the "doubtful list" for a time after suffering a leg injury in practice Monday, was in the Wolverines' starting line-up.

Capt. Bruce Hilkene, of Michigan, won the toss and elected to receive. Southern California chose

FIRST PERIOD

After taking the opening kickoff and returning it to the 33, Jack Weisenburger picked up three yards at center.

Bump Elliott raced 22 yards to the Trojans 42. Then Howard Yerges was smeared for a 10-yard loss.

Two plays netted 14 yards before Weisenburger punted out of bounds on the nine.

After two running plays netted only four yards, Verl Lillywhite quick-kicked to the Michigan 37.

The Wolverines then marched 63 yards in 11 plays for a touchdown, Weisenburger plunged over from the one. Jim Brieske converted.

Michigan 7, USC 0.

Three passes by Chappuis were the key plays in the drive. He hit Bob Mann for a 14-yard gain, tossed to Yerges for six and to Dick Rifenburg for 25.

In an exchange of punts, Lillywhite kicked out of bounds on the Michigan 48. Weisenburger then punted out on the Trojan one-foot line. After one play Lillywhite punted out on the Trojans 41.

* * *

WEISENBURGER hit tackle for 11. Chappuis picked up five. The quarter ended with the ball on Southern California's 28.

Michigan 7, USC 0.

SECOND PERIOD

Chappuis passed to Mann for 16 yards and a first down on the 11. Weisenburger made four at center. Chappuis passed to Yerges for six to the one. Weisenburger plunged over for the touchdown. Brieske converted.

Michigan 14, USC 0.

Southern California couldn't gain and Lillywhite punted to

Gene Derricotte on the 22. He raced back to the Michigan 40. The Wolverines were penalized to their 17 for clipping.

Elliott and Weisenburger made 10. Elliott took a lateral from Chappuis and ran 28 yards. Chappuis tossed to Rifenburg for a first down on the Trojan 35. Weisenburger made eight.

Chappuis raced 18 yards and a first down on the 13. A Chappuis pass to Bump Elliott was good for a touchdown. Brieske converted.

Michigan 21, USC 0.

After the kickoff the Trojans moved from their 19 to the Wolverine 13 where Dick Kempthorn, Michigan fullback, intercepted a pass.

The half ended without further scoring.

THIRD PERIOD

After taking the kickoff to start the second half, Southern California stalled and Lillywhite punted out on the Michigan 40.

In four plays the Wolverines advanced to the Trojan 38. A holding penalty set them back to their own 48.

Chappuis connected on passes to Rifenburg and Mann for 34 yards. Chappuis made three and then tossed to Mann for a first down on the 12.

Two plays netted five. Yerges fumbled and McCormick recovered for Southern California on the nine.

* * *

Chappuis intercepted a Rossi pass on the Michigan 20.

Dan Dworsky recovered a fumble by Dean Dill on the 15. On the second play, Chappuis tossed to Yerges for a touchdown. Brieske converted.

Michigan 28, USC 0.

Brieske's fourth conversion enabled him to tie a Rose Bowl record for the most points after touchdown in a game.

After the kickoff, Dill punted to Derricotte, who returned it to the 40.

On an end-around Ford made 16. Dill intercepted Chappuis' pass and ran to the 39 as the quarter ended.

Michigan 28, USC 0.

The Trojans punted to the Michigan 36. Chappuis sprinted around end for 38 yards. He added 11.

Weisenburger picked up 14 on two tries, then plowed through center for his third touchdown. Brieske converted for the fifth straight time, a Rose Bowl record.

Michigan 35, USC 0.

Southern California picked up two first downs before Powers fumbled and Joe Sobeleski recovered for Michigan on the Trojan 45.

Halfback Henry Fonde then passed 23 yards to Derricotte who ran for a touchdown. Brieske converted.

Michigan 42, USC 0.

After Southern California took the kickoff and couldn't gain, Dill punted to the Michigan 44. Five plays later the Wolverines scored their seventh touchdown on a pass from Yerges to Dick Rifenburg.

Michigan 49, USC 0.

There was no further scoring.

MICHIGAN		USC
Hilkene	LE	Yolonsky
Soboleski	LT	Ferraro
Pritula	LG	Manley
Wilkins	C	Burnett
Tomasi	RG	Cleary
Dworsky	RT	Nunes
Rifenburg	RE	Bell
Chappuis	QB	McCardle
Elliott	LH	Doll
Yerges	RH	Jamison
Weisenburger	FB	Lillywhite

Landing Plane Has Close Call

ATLANTA—(U.P)—An Eastern Airlines DC-3 plane narrowly averted disaster when its landing gear buckled as it touched the runway on arrival from Jacksonville.

The plane was damaged as it skidded to a halt but none of the three crew members and 13 passengers was hurt.

Tug Strike Off

NEW YORK—(A)—A threatened strike of 3,500 tugboat workers in New York harbor was averted when operators and AFL union representatives reached an agreement on a contract calling for 10-cent hourly wage increases.

On Inside Pages

Amusements	10	Lippmann	6
Bingo	8	Lyons	6
Chatter box	12	Merry-Go-R'd	6
Classified	20-22	Pringle	6
Clubs	13	Radio	23
Crossword	24	Riley	23
Editorials	6	Smith	18
Fashions	8	Sports	18-19
Food	14	Theaters	10
Guest	6	Town Crier	24
Horoscope	8	Women's	11-15

Baby Abandoned by Fleeing Parents Dies in Swamp

BAINBRIDGE, Ga.—(AP)—Abandoned by her fleeing parents, a seven-month-old girl was found dead. Her brother, 3, found with her in a desolate swamp, was near death from exposure.

Sheriff R. A. Stephens said that E. C. Cook and his brother, Eugene, had been charged with robbing and shooting a Negro taxi driver. The two men, Mrs. E. C. Cook and her children fled in a boat.

After the boat capsized, the adults abandoned the children, the sheriff said.

Trap Set for Killer on Train

Colorado Fugitive Slays Motorist

DENVER—(U.P)—Police set a trap aboard a speeding westbound train for the last of 12 prisoners who escaped from Colorado State Penitentiary.

The holdout fugitive being hunted had boarded the train shortly after killing a motorist who had given him a lift.

The desperate convict, identified by police as James B. Sherbondy, 29, "lone-wolf" killer, slipped through police at Denver's union station.

* * *

OFFICERS SAID he boarded a Denver & Rio Grande train.

Before the train passed through, police said Sherbondy had shot Robert Hutchins, a motorist who had given him a lift, and tossed the body out of the Hutchins car near Castle Rock.

Mrs. Shirley Hutchins, wife of the slain man, was shot and wounded critically. Along with her four-year-old son, she was found in the car which the killer wrecked in East Denver.

Fall Off Auto Fatal

ANN ARBOR—(A)—Five-year-old Wilburn Barwick, Jr., died of injuries suffered Dec. 29 when he fell from a moving auto.

'I WILL FOLLOW HIM'

Princess Tells of Love for Ex-King Michael

COPENHAGEN — (AP) — Princess Anne of Bourbon-Parma said, in an interview, that she was completely in love with Michael, the abdicated King of Romania.

"Wherever he goes I w'l follow him. But I will not leave Copenhagen until I have heard from him."

* * *

IF MICHAEL weds the Princess he will not marry into a wealthy family. She is heiress, however, to a small fortune left her mother by the will of a Danish millionaire who died last summer.

Michael's financial resources also are not believed large. His private income from the timber estate in Rumania recently was estimated at about 5,000,000 lei ($33,400) for this year.

This income is in addition to any allowances the Rumanian Government would settle on him.

One Flyer Rams Rear of Another

Toll in Missouri Accident May Rise

OTTERVILLE, Mo. —(AP)— At least 13 holiday travelers were killed early Thursday in a rear-end crash of two Missouri Pacific passenger trains in a blinding snowstorm near here.

One of the victims was identified by police as Mrs. Herbert W. Waddell, wife of a retired naval officer.

* * *

A STATE HIGHWAY patrolman, Lt. K. K. Johnson, said a bracelet with Mrs. Waddell's name and carrying the inscription "State Department, Washington, D. C.," was found on one of the twelve bodies removed from the wreckage.

Her husband was believed to have been aboard the train, but he could not be located.

Removal of the bodies in the subfreezing weather was tedious and nightfall added to the difficulties. State highway patrolmen said two or three more bodies may be found in a telescoped Pullman car.

ONE OF THE injured died in a hospital at near-by Sedalia, making the known toll 15 and leaving the possibility that it may reach 18.

Johnson also reported a traveling bag bearing the word "ambassador" was found near the woman's body.

The accident came about 8 a. m. and 40 of the passengers were still in bed or just arose.

Both sections of the "Missouri" were reported to have been moving slowly at the time.

Col. Hugh H. Waggoner of the State highway patrol said the tragedy apparently had been caused by failure of block signals, disrupted by the storm which had raged since Wednesday.

Kelly Scruton, reporter for the Sedalia Democrat, said "the engine of the second section of the train tore into the rear of the first train."

"Bodies were crushed into a space not more than 10 feet."

* * *

"THE TRAIN seemed to jump into the air," said J. H. Golden, a porter on the first section. "Five people were in my car, the second from the rear. All were shaken.

"After the impact I ran to the rear. It was a horrible sight. I just don't know what happened next."

Clean Gift

LONDON—The Board of Trade announced a New Year gift for plumbers working on building sites. They will get an extra ration of three ounces of soap monthly.

Assassination Attempt Fails

TEGUCIGALPA, Honduras — (AP)— Police said Thursday had frustrated an attempt by Antonio Castejon to assassinate President Tiburcio Carias after Castejon killed one man and wounded a policeman.

Authorities said that Castejon admitted that he came from his home in Tatumbla expressly to kill the President. They said that he stabbed Juan Ramon Midence to death in front of the Presidential Residence and then ran through the house before he was subdued.

MICHIGAN IS FACING PARALYSIS BY STORM

★ ★ ★ ★ ★ ★ ★ ★

Trains Crash in Snow; 13 Die

Ice Follies of 1948

MISS JANIE HAMER
Attacks windshield ice with hot water and scraper

ANOTHER VICTIM OF ICY STREETS
This car skidded into railroad viaduct at Twelfth and Lafayette

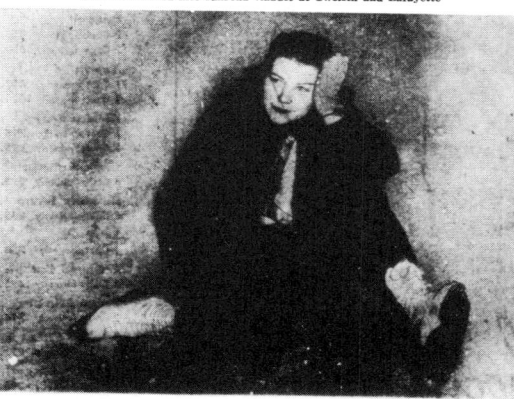

CHARLYS PIERITZ
Free Press Photos by Vince Wislak
Saginaw girl finds Detroit streets too slick for skates

Roads Icy; Stop Travel, Police Warn

Blizzard Sweeping In; Skid Causes Death

A "stop-travel" alarm was sounded by State Police Thursday after a grim warning by the Weather Bureau that a howling snowstorm was heading toward ice-sheathed Michigan.

Snow squalls with winds ranging between 40 and 50 miles an hour were expected hourly to hit roads already made perilous by Thursday's sleet-rain-hail downpour.

The Automobile Club of Michigan feared motor travel might have to be brought to a complete standstill for a 24-hour period.

THE WEATHER played havoc with holiday travel schedules. Interstate buses were running up to three hours behind schedule. Some trips were called off altogether.

Hundreds of Michigan residents who traveled to homes of relatives and friends for New Year's Day reunions were stranded.

All airline flights in and out of Willow Run airport were canceled Thursday for at least 24 hours.

In Detroit, DSR vehicles were running 10 to 15 minutes behind schedule. Sleet froze on trolley wires in some neighborhoods, temporarily knotting traffic on streetcar lines.

A SPOKESMAN for the Automobile Club said driving conditions "probably have never been so hazardous as they are now."

Extra crews were put on duty to handle calls for help coming from motorists at the rate of 150 an hour, he said.

The battering sleet, which started at 4 a. m. Thursday and changed around noon to hail briefly, and then freezing rain, dragged utility poles down, interrupting telephone communications and knocking out electric power in some parts of the state.

STATE POLICE at the Flat Rock Post received reports that flood conditions had become critical at Horse Island, off Gibraltar.

They were advised to evacuate several families from their homes as the rapidly rising Detroit River threatened to sweep over the island.

It was feared that the only bridge between Gibraltar and the island might collapse, marooning the residents.

Around 5 p. m. flashes of lightning flared in Detroit and Monroe, Mich. This report prompted weather experts to comment, "It's getting more freakish by the hour."

* * *

MOST SERIOUS communications damage occurred in Ontario.

Long-distance telephone calls between Detroit and the communities of Leamington, Kingsville, Hamilton and St. Thomas were cut off.

At least half of the circuits from Detroit to London, Toronto and Montreal were out.

Michigan Bell Telephone Co. reported that service to three Michigan communities — Milan, Flat Rock and Carleton—was disrupted.

HALF OF the circuits were out between Detroit, Howell and Tecumseh.

Between Kalamazoo and Dowagiac 90 telephone poles were pulled down by the weight of ice. Highways between Adrian and Monroe were blocked by fallen poles.

Fourteen out of the 16 circuits between Detroit and Adrian went dead. Calls from Detroit to Dundee and South Haven were being rerouted along alternate routes.

In Detroit, the telephone company was repairing 150 lines from houses to poles that had been snapped by the ice.

THE DETROIT Edison Co. reported "no major" disruption of

Turn to Page 4, Column 1

Tigers Win Opener, 5-2 — *See Story and Full Page of Pictures. Pages 21, 30*

The Detroit Free Press

COOLER Heat wave gone with the wind

METRO FINAL EXTRA

WEDNESDAY, APRIL 21, 1948 — On Guard for Over a Century — 30 Pages — Vol. 117—No. 353 — Five Cents

APRIL 21, 1948:

Walter Reuther escapes death.

REUTHER SHOT!

Lewis Orders Miners to Work

Seeks to Escape Jail Term; UMW and Boss Fined $1,420,000

WASHINGTON—(U.P.)—John L. Lewis and his United Mine workers were fined $1,420,000 for criminal contempt of Federal Court Tuesday.

A few hours later Lewis moved to halt a protest strike of miners that was sweeping the soft coal fields.

The penalties were imposed on Lewis and the UMW by Federal Judge T. Alan Goldsborough. The judge hinted strongly that further punishment would be dealt out if the miners were still on strike Friday.

More than 150,000 miners quit the pits in protest within a few hours after the fines were announced. Another 100,000 never had gone back to work from the walkout which led to the contempt conviction.

Lewis ordered them all back to work late Tuesday in a telegram to their union officials. It said:

"I do hope you will convey to each member my wish that they immediately return to work."

THE MINE union chief apparently was taking no chances on Goldsborough's imposing new fines—or even a jail sentence—if the walkout continued.

District presidents of the UMW said they were notifying the miners of Lewis' action "as fast as possible," but refused to predict what the response would be.

John P. Busarello, president of Pennsylvania's big district five, said:

"You'd have to be a magician to tell what the boys are going to do."

Goldsborough withheld sentence until Friday morning on the civil contempt charge on which he also found the defendants guilty. Lewis can be jailed and fined on that charge and the United Mine Workers Union can be fined.

THE JUDGE gave the plain implication that he might invoke the rarely used civil penalties if the protest strikes now under way are still in progress Friday.

UMW Attorney Welly K. Hopkins said he would appeal the sentences, which probably would bring the case to the Supreme Court next fall or winter.

Meantime, Lewis and the union
Turn to Page 4, Column 1

UAW Board OK's Strike at Chrysler

Negotiations May Be Resumed Thursday

The UAW (CIO) executive board approved a strike by 75,000 employees of Chrysler Corp. if and when such a step is deemed necessary to support 1948 wage demands.

The union earlier had complied with strike requirements of Federal and State laws.

Meantime, Leo Kotin, of the United States Conciliation and Mediation Service, said bargaining between the union and Chrysler probably would be resumed Thursday.

NEGOTIATIONS, which had been under way for more than six weeks, were interrupted but not broken off Friday. The interruption followed a company offer of a six-cent hourly raise.

Federal conciliators sponsored a brief meeting Monday in an effort to bring about renewal of the talks.

In a statement issued by the executive board, the six-cent offer was termed "ridiculously inadequate." It had been officially rejected Saturday at a meeting of delegates from 14 Chrysler plants.

HERMAN WECKLER, Chrysler vice president and general manager, said Tuesday that the company
Turn to Page 2, Column 5

21 Sentenced in Bulgar Plot

SOFIA, Bulgaria — (AP) — A Sofia court sentenced 21 men to prison on charges of forming an organization aimed at overthrowing the present (Communist-dominated) Government with the aid of "international sources."

Some of the men belonged to the former party of Nikola Petkov, Agrarian leader executed for alleged plotting against the State. The Government said others belonged to a Fascist group.

The stiffest sentence, life imprisonment, went to Koycho Koev. The other sentences ranged from three to 15 years.

Heads Mint Again

WASHINGTON—(AP)—The reappointment of Nellie Tayloe Ross, of Wyoming, as director of the mint was confirmed by voice vote in the Senate.

Forgotten Man?

BERLIN—(U.P.)—Tuesday was Adolf Hitler's birthday. None of the 12 daily newspapers here mentioned it.

On Inside Pages

Amusements	19	Horoscope	13
Bingay	6	Merry-Go-R'd	6
Chatterbox	6	Pringle	15
Classified	24-28	Racing	23
Clubs	16	Radio	29
Crossword	30	Riley	14
Donovan	23	Smith	20
Editorial	6	Sports	20-23
Fashions	15	Theaters	16
Financial	23-24	Town Crier	30
Guest	6	Women's	14-16

Rocky Path Led Reuther to Success

Champion of Labor Since Early Youth

Redheaded Walter P. Reuther, 40, son of German immigrant parents, started his fight for the rights of labor while in his early teens.

At the age of 15, he went to work for Wheeling Steel in West Virginia and immediately began to show the basic characteristics which have carried him to the leadership of the United Auto Workers (CIO), the world's largest union.

WHEN HE attempted to negotiate an overtime pay agreement for men in his department, he was fired.

This incident resulted in Reuther's moving to Detroit in 1927 and started his role in a turbulent two decades in the city's labor history.

As a tool and die maker he spent the years from 1927 to 1932 working for Briggs Manufacturing Co., General Motors, Coleman Tool & Die and Ford Motor Co.

He was discharged by the Ford company for labor agitation.

After attending night school for three years at Wayne University, Reuther made a world tour to visit factories and study economic systems in England, Russia, other European countries, Japan and Central Asia.

WHILE ABROAD, he heard that labor was on the march in the auto industry. He returned to Detroit immediately to join the campaign.

He organized and became president of West Side Amalgamated Local 174, raising its membership from 78 to 30,000 in one year.

The Reuther star had started its ascendancy.

He began his bid for big-time union fame by winning a seat on the UAW Executive Board at the 1936 convention in South Bend. The UAW was formally launched at that time after unhappy months in the AFL fold.

FOR THE NEXT five years, he and his brother, Victor, were in the forefront of the rough and sometimes bloody organization strikes.

In one year, 1936-37, there were 325 authorized sitdowns in Detroit alone.

By the time 1940 had rolled around, Reuther had proved himself a skilled tactician at the negotiating table as well as a labor general willing to lead his legions into battle.

HE WON HIS "wound stripes" at the gates of the Ford Rouge plant in the 1937 "Battle of the Overpass."

But his most important coup, from the labor viewpoint, was his handling of the 1939 strategy strike against General Motors which paved the way for the first corporationwide contract in the auto industry.

GM's previous contract with the union, signed in 1937, covered only 17 of the more than 90 plants. This strike also wiped out the rebellious Homer Martin faction of the UAW which had set up a competing union under the AFL banner.

REUTHER KEPT his seat on the Executive Board for six years. He was elected to one of the vice presidencies in 1942 and re-elected in 1944.

In 1946 the UAW established an office at Washington, D.C., and named Reuther one of the two national co-directors.

A convincing orator, and possessing a genius for obtaining publicity, Reuther was already a big union name when he started his final climb toward the UAW presidency in 1946.

HIS BIG MANEUVER was his declaration of a blockade against
Turn to Page 4, Column 4

GM Workers' Loss from Strike Bared

CLEVELAND — (AP) — Employees laid off at General Motors Corp. will lose between 12 and 15 million dollars in wages "even if all the coal miners return to work tomorrow," GM President Charles E. Wilson said here Tuesday.

An indefinite layoff for more than 200,000 GM workers will begin Friday.

Transit Fares in N.Y. Go Up

NEW YORK—(AP)—Mayor William O'Dwyer approved a 10-cent subway fare and a seven-cent surface-vehicle charge, signaling the end of New York's historic nickel fare.

O'Dwyer said the new rates would go into effect July 1.

His action broke all political precedents. The fare has long been a debated issue.

'Miss Ireland' Leaves for U.S.

SHANNON AIRPORT, Eire—(AP)—Violet Nolan, of Listowel, County Kerry, who was chosen "Miss Ireland" recently, left by air for a tour of the United States and a screen test in Hollywood. She was accompanied by her mother.

Boy, 13, Given 22 Years as Slayer

CHICAGO — (AP) — Howard Lang, 13, youngest murder defendant in Chicago history, was sentenced to 22 years imprisonment for killing his seven-year-old playmate.

Lang confessed he killed Loonie Fellick last Oct. 18 in a forest preserve.

141 Bitten by Dogs in City in Week

Dr. Bruce H. Douglas, City health commissioner, said that 141 persons were bitten by dogs in Detroit last week, although none of the dogs was rabid.

His statement was coupled with a warning to dog owners to have their pets revaccinated.

Blast Scene and Principals

POLICEMAN INSPECTS SHATTERED WINDOW
Assassin fired into kitchen

CLOSE-UP OF BULLET HOLE
Gun-wielder fired at close range

WALTER P. REUTHER
Arm torn by slugs

LOUIS JOHNSTONE
Saw gunman flee

Shotgun Assassin Shatters Arm

UAW President Felled in Home; Assailant Flees in Red Auto

Walter P. Reuther, dynamic young president of the UAW (CIO), was shot and seriously wounded by an assassin at 9:45 p.m. Tuesday.

His right arm was shattered above the elbow by a shotgun blast fired through a kitchen window of his home at 20101 Appoline.

Slugs also penetrated his chest and side.

DOCTORS AT New Grace Hospital described his condition as "very, very serious."

Blood transfusions were being administered and a bone specialist was called in a determined effort to save Reuther's arm.

Other Pictures Pages 4 and 10

An operation to remove the slugs from his chest and side was scheduled.

A statewide alarm was sounded for a two-door red Ford sedan, either a 1947 or 1948 model.

Witnesses said that the man who fired the shot jumped into the car and that the car immediately sped away. It was believed that another man was driving.

Reuther had just returned home from a meeting of the UAW Executive Board which adjourned at 8:30 p.m.

He had had nothing to eat, so he and his wife, Mae, went into the kitchen to prepare a meal.

MRS. REUTHER told police that she and her husband were standing at a breakfast bar and that the blast came just as she stepped away toward the stove.

She was not hurt.

Reuther said that a remark by his wife undoubtedly saved his life.

He told police that he was standing at the breakfast bar, facing the window, and that the shot was fired just as he turned to answer his wife.

Otherwise, he said, the blast would have caught him full in the chest.

Reuther said that he had had no threats. Asked who could have been responsible for the shooting, he replied "Any one of three sources—Communists, management or a screwball."

Mrs. Reuther said that her husband was bleeding profusely and that she hurriedly summoned the Reuthers' personal physician, Dr. Raymond Sokolov.

She told police that her husband had had no callers in the evening.

He made no mention of anything being wrong, she said.

Jack Livingston, Executive Board member of the UAW, was equally at a loss to explain the shooting.

He said that everything ran smoothly at the meeting.

He quoted Reuther as saying, "Those Dirty——. They had to shoot a fellow in the back; they couldn't come out in front."

Louis Johnstone, 14, of 19991 Appoline, was playing 100 feet from the Reuther home at the time of the shooting.

After hearing the shot, he ran to the rear yard of the Reuther home and saw a man dash out the back gate and leap into the car.

THE BOY RAN home to tell his father, Thomas A. Johnstone, assistant director of the UAW's General Motors department.

Johnstone said that when he reached the scene Reuther was conscious, crawling on the floor of an inclosed rear porch just off the kitchen.

He apparently had tried to learn the identity of his assailant, Johnstone said.

"Art, help me," Reuther cried. "Get me to a hospital. They've shot off my arm."

Mrs. Helen O'Keefe, 47, of 20120 Steel, was in the rear yard of her residence and heard the shotgun blast. She described the assassin as a "very small" man.

WHEN SHE GOT to the Reuther home, she said, Mrs. Reuther was trying to administer first aid to her husband.

Two Reuther children, Linda Mae, 5, and Elizabeth Ann, 9 months, were asleep at the time.

Mrs. Reuther went to the hospital to stand by her husband.

The family's minister and Reuther's personal friend, the Rev. E. T. Bernthal, of the Lutheran Church of the Epiphany, visited him in the operating room.

When he came out, he would say only, "Mine was a spiritual visit."

A police guard was established in the operating room and in
Turn to Page 10, Column 4

MAY 4, 1948:

An important Supreme Court decision on racial covenants is based partly on a Detroit case, and has widespread impact on the city.

"Court Voids Racial Housing Curbs," column one.

MILDER
About the same as on Monday

The Detroit Free Press

TUESDAY, MAY 4, 1948 — On Guard for Over a Century — Vol. 117—No. 366 — 24 Pages — Five Cents

METRO FINAL

LOSE SOMETHING?
Phone WO 2-9400
for a Want Ad
That Will Help
Get It Back.

SEEK 50-CT. BOOST AT FORD

Court Voids Racial Housing Curbs

UAW Eyes Hourly Hike of 30 Cents

Chrysler Strike Plans Held Illegal by Black

Additional economic demands totaling approximately 50 cents an hour for 107,000 workers will be served on the Ford Motor Co.

The demands, which include a straight 30-cent-an-hour wage increase, were approved Monday by the National Ford Council meeting in the Hotel Tuller.

They were revealed by Ken Bannon, national UAW Ford director.

MEANTIME, the UAW went ahead with plans for a strike against the Chrysler Corp., tentatively set for May 12.

This despite an opinion by Attorney General Eugene F. Black that a walkout will be in violation of the Bonine-Tripp Act unless a strike vote is taken under the supervision of the State Labor Mediation Board.

In addition to the straight wage boost, the UAW wants for Chrysler a Ford medical benefit plan, a company-financed pension plan, a guaranteed weekly wage, three-week vacation with pay and return of the paid 20-minute lunch period recently taken away.

ALSO APPROVED by the Council were demands for a 10-cent bonus for night workers and a discount for Ford workers buying Ford automobiles.

The union will offer a plan to finance pensions by a bonus system based on production of vehicles. The bonus would be added to a welfare fund.

The Ford-UAW contract is reopenable on economic issues after July 15.

FORD OFFICIALS are withholding comment on the demands, which are far more ambitious than those currently being made at Chrysler and General Motors.

The demands being made on Chrysler amount to a 30-cent increase and those at GM to 25 cents.

If all were granted, the hourly wage rate at Ford would be $2.06, at Chrysler $1.75 and at GM $1.80.

BLACK'S OPINION on the proposed Chrysler strike was sought by Philip Weiss, chairman of the Mediation Board.

The UAW contends that a State-conducted strike vote is not necessary because the strike would affect plants in three other states.

The union has complied with pre-strike provisions of the Taft-Hartley Law and has called a strike for May 12.

Weiss pointed out that a State-conducted vote would require 10 days to two weeks to complete, thus making a May 12 walkout impossible.

Meanwhile, contract negotiations are still in progress.

A STRIKE would affect 75,000 workers in 14 Chrysler plants, 10 of which are in Michigan.

Weiss said Black's opinion also was applicable to the Briggs Manufacturing Co., where negotiations are in progress.

Rules Segregation Cannot Be Inforced

Tribunal Finds No Violations Under Voluntary Agreements

WASHINGTON—(AP)—Courts cannot enforce real-estate agreements which bar colored persons from all-white neighborhoods, the Supreme Court ruled.

In a 6-0 decision, the Court said Government action to back up such covenants violates the "equal protection" clause in the 14th Amendment, and, in Washington, D. C., it breaks a Federal law covering similar ground.

The Court specified, however, that the clause "erects no shield against merely private conduct, however discriminatory or wrongful."

It said there is no violation so long as the agreements are carried out voluntarily.

THREE SEPARATE actions were involved—one each from Detroit, St. Louis and Washington, D. C.

The Detroit and St. Louis cases, involving state courts and laws, were consolidated.

The Washington case, purely Federal, was handled separately.

In all, however, the results were the same. Lower-court decisions upholding enforcement of covenants were overturned.

Chief Justice Fred M. Vinson wrote the two opinions handed down on the issue. In neither did he go beyond the question of excluding would-be residents on the ground of "race and color."

Solicitor Philip B. Perlman, in oral argument of the cases, also had discussed the question of exclusion of Jews.

AFTER HEARING Monday's rulings read, Perlman declined to speculate whether covenants excluding persons on religious grounds also are barred.

Justices Robert H. Jackson, Stanley F. Reed and Wiley B. Rutledge took no part in the cases.

The National Association for the Advancement of Colored People said in a statement in New York that the decision is a "blow" against segregation.

Mr. and Mrs. Orsel McGhee had appealed the Detroit case. The property they bought was under a covenant limiting occupancy to Caucasians until 1950 with no specific penalty provided.

The St. Louis case was that of Mr. and Mrs. J. D. Shelley, Negroes.

They bought property in an area covered by a covenant restricting it to Caucasian occupancy until 1961. The agreement provided forfeiture of the property as the penalty for violation.

THE WASHINGTON case involved property covered by an agreement that it should never be "rented, leased, sold, transferred or conveyed to any Negro or colored person." The covenant provided a penalty of $2,000, which

Turn to Page 3, Column 2

Texas Town Is Wrecked by Tornado

School and Hospital Flattened by Wind

By the Associated Press

Death-dealing tornadoes added Texas to their list Monday with at least three killed.

A 48-hour toll of 23 dead and more than 156 injured was listed in six states hit by the spring storms.

The Texas windstorm hit McKinney, a city of 10,000 and near-by Princeton, both about 30 miles north of Dallas.

The storm cut a 600-yard path of fury, two miles long, through McKinney.

It tore the second floor off a $2,000,000 textile mill, blew off the top floor of the city hospital, ripped off the metal roof of a grade school, damaged the High School gymnasium and smashed an estimated 150 houses.

DESPITE THE loss of its roof, the hospital continued to treat patients in the undamaged part of the building.

Barry Stroup, Associated Press newsphoto editor, took a look at the storm area. He said he added 10 or 12 square blocks in McKinney appeared to have been destroyed.

The McKinney storm was the sixth to strike the nation with devastating blows in 48 hours. Beginning Saturday night, tornadoes hit Kansas, Oklahoma, Missouri, Kentucky and West Virginia with a death toll of 20 in those five states. More than 100 persons were injured.

In Wake of Storm----A Shambles

AERIAL PHOTO OF McKINNEY AFTER TORNADO STRUCK NORTH TEXAS CITY
Two schools and hospital were damaged and many homes demolished
Associated Press Wirephoto

SAYS GOP ASSESSED THEM FOR $250,000

Black Rips Auto Dealers for Politics

Special to the Free Press

PORT HURON—Michigan automobile dealers have been assessed more than $250,000 for the Republican campaign fund, Attorney General Eugene F. Black told the Fort Huron Exchange Club.

Black said the contributions were demanded at the request of Arthur Summerfield, Republican national committeeman of Michigan.

"NOT MORE THAN two weeks ago, at a supposedly secret meeting, the automobile dealers met in Detroit on the demand of Summerfield," Black declared.

"They were informed then that their political contribution would be $1 a car sold since the factories reopened at the end of World War II.

"This political assessment alone means more than a quarter of a million dollars. What do you think the boys are buying with this fund—good government or special interest profit from invisible government?"

PRAISING Recorder's Judge W. McKay Skillman for his grand jury work, Black said that he was continuing the investigation in Flint where Circuit Judge Philip Elliott will be grand juror.

He was critical of Former Gov. Harry F. Kelly and Wilber M. Brucker, now DADA legal counsel for taking what he called "political law business."

He called the DADA Michigan's most powerful political organization and said that State officials have been giving the organization secret information about car sales.

Black said that he was amazed to find that "dues paid" membership in either the DADA or the Michigan Automobile Dealers Association means a

Turn to Page 2, Column 6

Migration of Minorities within Detroit Doubted

Interracial Committee Leader Sees No Danger to Property in Ruling

No wholesale shifting of Negroes into white neighborhoods was expected as the result of the Supreme Court's decision on restrictive covenants.

Such was the view of George Schermer, director of the Interracial Committee.

Approximately 3,000 Detroit-area subdivisions are covered by real estate agreements banning Negro occupancy. They comprise an estimated 40 per cent of the city.

JOHN POLESKI, head of the Wayne County Tract Index Department, said there were few such covenants prior to 1915.

Some developed in the last 30 years have expired.

Schermer pointed out that many of the 4,000 subdivisions not restricted do not have a Negro settlement.

"The decision is in every respect wholesome and sound," Schermer said.

"FROM THE standpoint of the Interracial Committee, it is the only kind of positive decision which the court could have made.

"Aside from the great impetus which restrictive covenants worked, it has been one of the most serious barriers to inter-racial and interreligious understanding."

Schermer deplored the fact that certain minority groups are ready

Turn to Page 2, Column 4

Auto Champ Pleads Guilty to Larceny

John L. Carroll, 38, of 12333 Byron, who admittedly purchased some 350 new automobiles in a 16-month period, pleaded guilty in Recorder's Court to larceny by conversion. He will be sentenced May 17.

Nick Nicholas, of 7612 Bingham, Dearborn, said as payee Carroll $2,056 as partial payment on a new car several months ago but has received neither the car nor a refund.

POLICE SAID 18 similar complaints against Carroll, Detroit's champion automobile purchaser, involve approximately $35,000.

Disclosure of Carroll's purchases was one of the incidents resulting from the grand jury investigation by Recorder's Judge W. McKay Skillman.

Missouri Students Heckle Wallace to Delay Speech

COLUMBIA, Mo. — (U.P.) — A crowd of heckling University of Missouri students delayed for 15 minutes Henry A. Wallace's speech on the courthouse lawn here before an estimated 3,000 persons.

The former vice president and third party presidential candidate appealed to the "good name of the State of Missouri" to stop the heckling after he bluntly exchanged remarks with the hecklers.

Wallace continued his address without further interruption although a spectator flourished a hammer and a sickle amidst laughter from the crowd.

Watered Down

NEW YORK — (U.P.) — A water main break at Madison and E. 54th flooded the basements of more than a dozen hotels, stores and other business establishments. Damage was estimated at $300,000.

Colombia Cuts Diplomatic Tie with Russia

Action Taken Month After Revolution

BOGOTA, Colombia — (AP) — Colombia broke off diplomatic relations with Russia Monday.

The action came almost a month after the unsuccessful revolution which took 1,500 lives in Colombia.

A DIPLOMATIC rupture had been expected ever since President Mariano Ospina Perez blamed international Communism for the revolutionary rioting which broke out after the assassination of Liberal Leader Jorge Eliecer Gaitan April 9.

(It was reported at the time of the revolution that relations had been broken, but the Government later denied it.)

Brazil and Chile previously had cut their diplomatic ties with Russia.

Report Mass Arrests in Paraguay Capital

BUENOS AIRES—(AP)—Newspapers at Formosa, Argentina, published reports that hundreds of persons have been arrested in the Paraguayan Capital, Asuncion, by police patrolling the streets with automatic weapons.

The reports said "grave happenings are taking place in Asuncion.

(At Washington State Department and Paraguayan embassy officials said they have no information of disorders in Asuncion.)

Mountbatten's Successor Named

NEW DELHI, India—(AP)—Chakravarti Rajagopalachari, 69, shrewd political strategist, lawyer and administrator, has been appointed governor general of India to succeed Earl Mountbatten.

The appointment had been approved by King George VI on recommendation of the Indian Government. It is effective June 21. Rajagopalachari is now governor of West Bengal Province.

Loyal to Truman

JEFFERSON CITY, Mo.—(AP)—President Truman's home-state delegation to the Democratic National Convention was unanimously instructed to vote as a unit for his nomination.

MINNESOTAN CONFIDENT IN CRUCIAL VOTE

Taft, Stassen Wind Up Ohio Drive with Radio Pleas

BY EDWIN A. LAHEY
Of Our Washington Bureau

CLEVELAND—Senator Taft (R., O.) and Harold E. Stassen made their final radio pleas to the voters Monday on the eve of Ohio's crucial primary battle.

Stassen is contesting with Taft for 23 of the state's 53 delegates to the Republican National Convention.

IF HE GETS half that number in Tuesday's election, he implied rebuff to "Mister Sen." Taft would well nigh destroy the Ohioan's chance for the nomination for President.

In a statewide radio broadcast from Cincinnati, his home town, Taft renewed his request for a vote of confidence from his fellow citizens.

He has campaigned the state as the authentic spokesman of Republican policy.

In a similar statewide broadcast from Cleveland, giving his listeners a roundup of his views and asking for support for his "fundamental liberal philosophy."

UPON HIS arrival in Cleveland, Stassen claimed that he had the first-ballot support of 240 delegates to the Republican National Convention in Philadelphia in June. That is 269 delegates short of the majority needed to win the nomination.

Stassen includes 12 delegates he left Ohio a week ago for quick forays into Oregon, New Jersey, and Rhode Island, in his estimate. He predicted that a "majority" of the 23 he has entered in Ohio will be elected Tuesday.

His campaign manager, Earl Hart, predicts that 15 Stassen delegates will be elected. Newspaper polls in Ohio tend to support the Stassen claims of a victory in a majority of the contests.

STASSEN SAID that since he left Ohio a week ago for quick forays into Oregon, New Jersey, and Rhode Island, he has received encouraging news from Colorado, Missouri and New Mexico.

Eight of the 15 delegates chosen at the Colorado Republican convention favor him, Stassen said.

He also claimed the support of 18 of the 33 delegates who have been picked in Missouri, and four of the eight delegates from New Mexico.

The Minnesotan calmly dismissed as incorrect the last-minute allegation of Rep. George Bender, the Cleveland area manager for Taft, that the Stassen people have spent $5 in Ohio for every $1 spent for Taft.

"WE HAVE HAD only a fraction of the amounts available to other candidates," Stassen said. "This will be clearly shown when the accounts are filed.

"As a matter of fact, we had poor going, financially, until after the Wisconsin primary. It has been picking up since then."

BOMB SENT IN BOOK

Mail Blast Kills Briton

WOLVERHAMPTON, England—(U.P.)—Rex Farran, 26, was killed when a parcel containing a bomb hidden in a volume of Shakespeare exploded.

The package was delivered to his brother, Capt. Roy Farran, who was acquitted recently of murdering a Jew in Palestine.

Gov. Dewey outlines views on Communism in Oregon speech.
Page 2.

THE PACKAGE was delivered by the mailman to the Farran family home in near-by Codsall and Rex opened it.

Former British Army officer Capt. Farran, much-decorated and an almost legendary figure in Palestine fighting, said he had received two threatening notes and several mysterious telephone calls since his acquittal.

Window Washers in City on Strike

An estimated 200 window washers started a strike Monday as Cleanup Week began.

The strikers are members of the Detroit Window Cleaners Union, Local 139, AFL.

They want a 40-cent increase. Present rates are $1.65 an hour unless the washer is required to work on a scaffold. It is then $1.75.

About 31 window - cleaning firms are involved.

Top Officers' Pay Brings Protest

WASHINGTON — (AP) — Rep. Miller (R., Neb.) complained that Congress was "entirely too liberal" in its grant of pay and privileges to five-star generals and admirals.

He told the House that newspaper stories say retired five-star Gen. Dwight D. Eisenhower will get full pay plus a lifetime allowance for a small group of assistants.

Top Jet Pilot Dies in Crash

WASHINGTON — (AP) — Howard C. Lilly, 30-year-old test pilot, was killed at Muroc Air Base, Calif., while taking off in the Douglas Skystreak, a single-engine jet which holds the world's speed record.

NACA's top jet test pilot.

Word of Lilly's death was received by John Victory, secretary of the National Advisory Committee for Aeronautics, the top Government agency for aviation research. Lilly was rated the NACA's top jet test pilot.

The plane was reported to have rolled over and crashed as it was taking off.

Envoy Resigns

WASHINGTON — (AP) — The White House announced the resignation of R. Henry Norweb as ambassador to Cuba to assume "another important post."

U.S. Freighter Afire at Sea

NORFOLK, Va. — (AP) — The American freighter Shell Bar reported she was afire about 15 miles off Cape Hatteras.

A message received at Coast Guard headquarters said the fire raged out of control on the 3,805-ton vessel with a crew of 35.

A cutter was sent from Norfolk to aid the Shell Bar.

Heiress Lost

NICE, France—Ski troops and St. Bernard dogs scoured the Maritime Alps for Francoise de Pelleport, 24, heiress and daughter of Marquise de Pelleport, who disappeared while skiing.

Voting Scheduled for Council Seat

Common Council approved dates for a special election to name the successor to Leo J. Nowicki, who resigned his Council post last month to become DSR general manager.

The primary will be Sept. 14 and the election Nov. 2, coinciding with State and County elections.

Violent Volcano

AUCKLAND, N. Z.—(AP)—Witnesses said that Mt. Ngauruhoe, North Island volcano, threw out "hot boulders as big as houses."

Lana and Bob in the Clouds

NEW YORK — (AP) — Lana Turner and her new husband, Henry (Bob) Topping, were having a transcontinental aerial honeymoon Monday.

Trans World Airline official revealed that Topping had bought eight seats in a compartment—at a cost of $1,453.60—so that he and his bride could enjoy privacy on their flight from Hollywood to New York.

A wine company gave them a case of champagne for the flight.

Film Star Hurt

HOLLYWOOD — (AP) — Film star Ann Sothern was slightly injured when her new car was demolished in a collision.

Other Stories of Major Interest on Inside Pages

Phone Union Acts to Prevent Strike, P. 8

New Palestine Plan Asked by Britain, P. 4

House Group OK's Two-Year Draft, P. 9

Amusements	16	Horoscope	12
Beauty	11	Lyons	24
Bingay	6	Merry-Go-R'd	6
Chatterbox	10	Pringle	11
Classified	18-22	Radio	16
Clubs	11	Riley	10
Crossword	24	Smith	11
Donovan	17	Sports	14-15
Editorials	6	Town Crier	6
Fashions	11	Women's	10-11
Financial	23		
Guest	6		

Last Port of Call

VALLEJO, Calif. — (AP) — The heavy cruiser Salt Lake City, radio-active from her target role in the Bikini atomic bomb tests, will be sunk at sea by surface units the last week in May.

The Detroit Free Press

WEDNESDAY, JUNE 16, 1948

COOL — But it will be fair with a wandering wind

METRO FINAL

CANDIDATE TAFT — Pearson Analyzes Senator Taft's Presidential Bid. See Page 6

JUNE 16, 1948:
Night baseball arrives in Detroit.

Vandenberg Doubts GOP Will Name Him

Calls Fight on ERP Bar to Race
Backers Insist He's Still Best Bet

BY WILLIAM S. WHITE
New York Times Service

WASHINGTON—Before opening his frontal assault on House Republicans for cutting the foreign recovery appropriations, Senator Vandenberg told friends that it meant his final renunciation as a Republican presidential possibility.

He has left them, moreover, with the firm impression that, in the field of his greatest interest — foreign affairs, he would not object to Gov. Thomas E. Dewey of New York as a Republican president, with John Foster Dulles as secretary of state.

WITH SUCH an administration Vandenberg would simply continue as chairman of the Senate Foreign Relations Committee.

His view plainly is that such a triumvirate could carry forward an international policy so powerful that the Republican isolationist wing would thrust against it in vain.

All this was learned as Vandenberg watched the Senate uphold

Poll Shows Editors Pick Vandenberg

WASHINGTON (AP)—The U.S. News and World Report published a poll of 815 daily newspaper editors on who they think will be the Republican presidential nominee.

The majority's guess: Senator Vandenberg of Michigan.

Vandenberg's nomination was predicted by 417 editors. Other results: Dewey 195, Taft 45, Stassen 33, Warren 7, Martin 7.

The editors also were asked whom they would prefer to see nominated. That question produced this result: Vandenberg 271, Stassen 143, Taft 141, Dewey 121, Warren 26, and Martin 10.

About four-fifths of the papers polled were Republican or Independent.

him in his fight to restore to the recovery program the money taken from it by a Republican-controlled House.

VANDENBERG'S backers rejected his reasoning that his hard and open break with a strong wing of the Republican Party would take him "utterly" out of the reckoning at the Philadelphia convention next week.

They told him, and are now telling him, that the reverse was true and that as the presidential prospect who had most directly challenged the "economy" leaders of the House, the presentation of his name at Philadelphia had become a "must."

Vandenberg feels, however, that he has alienated a large segment of the Republican Party.

Most of Cut in ERP Fund Is Restored

Free Press Wire Services

WASHINGTON—The Senate Tuesday night restored most of the $1,175,000,000 House cut in foreign aid spending by wiping out a requirement that the funds be spread over a 15-month period instead of a year.

The 64-15 roll-call vote came at the request of Senate President Vandenberg (R., Mich.). He asked that it be made "unmistakably plain" that the Senate overwhelmingly opposed the House "meat axe" technique.

CHAIRMAN Bridges (R., N.H.) of the Appropriations Committee opened debate on the measure with a plea for passage as a token of America's belief that "the free people of the world must stand or fall together."

In its present form, the bill would appropriate $6,125,710,228 for foreign relief and recovery.

It represents an increase of more than one billion dollars in the amount voted by he House for the program. It is about $408,010,-225 less than the Truman Administration asked.

Vandenberg asked for the roll call to strengthen the hand of Senate members at a joint House-Senate conference which will start work Wednesday on compromising differences in the two bills.

He said he was "profoundly grateful" for the "good faith and spirit" of Bridges' committee in recommending restoration of the House cuts.

Provision for a one-year program instead of one for 15 months eliminated what Secretary of State George C. Marshall has described as "the most unjustified cut of all."

Hal Hurls 2-Hitter Under Arcs

TIGERS ENLIGHTEN A's, 4-1

U.S. Again Enters Coal Deadlock
Calls Talks After Walkout on Lewis

BY LOUIS STARK
New York Times Service

WASHINGTON—Northern and Western soft-coal operators walked out of contract negotiations Tuesday.

Talks with the United Mine Workers were recessed as "futile" because "there has been no progress toward getting a discussion of a new agreement," the operators said.

Several hours later, Cyrus S. Ching, director of the Federal Mediation and Conciliation Service, moved to prevent a coal tie-up July 6 by requesting both sides to confer with him Thursday.

THE SOUTHERN Coal Producers Association, representing a third of the Nation's tonnage, did not agree to the recess and kept itself free to negotiate with the union.

John L. Lewis, UMW president, at a news conference, charged that the operators have "apparently elected to fight in 1948 and not to settle."

He announced that telegrams were being sent to the UMW's 200-member Policy Committee for a meeting here June 24 for "instructions."

SHOULD ANOTHER strike illegally result from Tuesday's action, it would begin July 6, when the miners are scheduled to return from their annual 10-day vacation. Their contract expires June 30.

If Ching is unable to settle the dispute or arrange for continuation of parleys with keeping the miners in the pits, recourse likely will be taken under the Taft-Hartley Law.

That means the naming of a presidential board of inquiry, a report to the President and the President's direction to the Attorney General to seek an 80-day injunction to prevent a stoppage starting in Detroit Wednesday.

IN REFERENCE to such an injunction, Lewis asserted that "men beaten back into the mines as slaves are not good producers of coal."

He said that the operators' attitude on activating the 1947 Welfare Fund meant abandoning 127,480 persons dependent on that fund for aid.

Repeatedly he said that an agreement could be written quickly if Benjamin Fairless, president of the United States Steel Corp., and George M. Humphrey, of the Pittsburgh Consolidation Coal Co., who initiated the 1947 agreement, repeated their interest in the current negotiations.

CHARLES O'NEILL, in a statement for the operators, declared that the split Tuesday came on matters relating to the Welfare Fund and the union refusal to discuss an agreement for 1948.

The talks between operators had been in progress since June 7. Called off once before, they were ordered resumed by Federal District Judge T. Alan Goldsborough.

State Probes Gouging of Car Buyers
15 Warrants Ready; Scores Investigated

Alleged gouging of automobile buyers on finance fees and insurance premiums will be subjected to a legislative inquiry starting in Detroit Wednesday.

"We want to learn how the system works and who gets the kick-back," said Senator Clarence A. Reid, of Detroit, who probably will head the probe.

THE INQUIRY gained impetus from a Supreme Court decision upholding the conviction of a Detroit dealer charged with violating the Motor Vehicle Title Act.

A deluge of new prosecutions is expected as a result of the case of Dale H. Hughes, Inc., of 17555 Livernois.

The firm was fined $100 by Recorder's Judge Paul H. Krause last Oct. 30 for failing to give a used car buyer an itemized statement of costs.

Police investigators have been working on scores of additional cases growing out of 200 complaints to the Better Business Bureau, Lt. George Ludwig, of the Auto Investigation Squad, revealed.

Service of 15 warrants has been
Turn to Page 2, Column 4

Petticoat Protest on Kilts Ignored

Chicago Tribune Foreign Service

LONDON—Arthur Woodburn, secretary of state for Scotland, informed the House of Commons that there was no ban on wearing of kilts by civil servants in Government offices.

Woodburn ignored an appeal by Mrs. Jean Mann, Laborite, that "under no consideration should effeminated, knock-kneed men be allowed to wear the kilt."

Hollywood Story: Separation Off

HOLLYWOOD (AP)—Last week Actress Sheila Ryan announced she had parted from her husband, Eddie Norris, film player.

Tuesday she said she had changed her mind, and "everything is okay again."

Under the Lights

SHORTSTOP JOHNNY LIPON IS FIRST TIGER BATTER TO TRY OUT STADIUM LIGHTS
But the effort wasn't too encouraging to Johnny. He popped up to the infield
Free Press Photo

Russia OK's Parley to Reopen Danube
Moscow Accepts U.S. Proposal; Seen as 'Peace Offensive' Move

WASHINGTON—(AP)—Russia cleared the way for possible settlement of one long-standing East-West issue—reopening the Danube River to free international commerce.

Showing an apparent new willingness to compromise, Moscow accepted an American proposal to call a 10-nation conference for July 30 to lift existing barriers to shipping.

The river is normally the main artery of trade between Eastern and Western Europe and its reopening is tied up with hopes of reviving that trade to help European recovery.

RUSSIA abandoned in part its objection to letting Austria take part in the conference. It agreed that the Austrians might send a nonvoting delegation.

The manner in which Moscow agreed to go along was viewed by some diplomatic officials as "another gesture in the Soviet 'peace offensive.'"

They noted, however, that Russia as well as the Western Powers has a stake in reopening the Danube.

Russians continue pressure on Allies in Berlin. See story on Page 9.

They further pointed out that in the conference the Soviet bloc would have a 7 to 3 voting margin.

The Big Four powers—Russia, United States, Britain and France—already have accepted that Russia's Eastern European satellites will be invited, including Bulgaria, Czechoslovakia, Hungary, Romania, the Ukraine and Yugoslavia.

THE SOFTENED Russian attitude was expressed in a note dated June 12 which was announced by the State Department.

Officials assumed that Britain and France would go along with the idea of meeting July 30 in a Balkan capital, but foresaw practical difficulties.

The United States has insisted that in all post-war conferences with Russia adequate communications and other facilities be provided for full reporting of the proceedings.

Other Stories of Major Interest on Inside Pages

Truman Proves He's Fighter, Page 4

Draft Bill Debated in Last Rush, Page 5

Amusements 22	Horoscope 9
Beauty 13	Lippmann 6
Bingay 6	Merry-Go-R'd 8
Chatterbox 6	Pringle 13
Childs 6	Racing 29
Classified 24-28	Radio 29
Crosby 30	Riley 12
Crossword 30	Sports 19-21
Editorials 6	Theaters 15
Fashions 14	Town Crier 8
Food 13	Women's 12-13
Guest 6	

OK Trade Pact

WARSAW—(AP)—Poland and Iceland signed an 18-month trade treaty.

54,480 See City's First Night Game
Homers by Mullin and Wakefield Assure Newhouser 7th Straight

BY LYALL SMITH
Free Press Sports Editor

The lights went on at Briggs Stadium at 9:30 Tuesday night. When they went off again at 11:20, the Tigers had extended their longest winning streak of 1948 to five games with a brilliant 4-1 victory over the second-place Philadelphia Athletics.

A throng of 54,480 customers jammed into the park on a chilly night to watch Detroit become the last American League club to join the ranks of teams playing after-dark games.

THEY SAW Pitcher Harold Newhouser, the lanky home-grown southpaw, run his own personal winning streak to seven games with a nifty two-hit performance while the Bengals assaulted Joe Coleman for seven safeties, including eighth-inning home runs by Dick Wakefield and Patrick Mullin.

The victory was a big one for Detroit. It not only opened the new night-time schedule for 14 games in auspicious fashion but ended the spell of Coleman, a husky right-hander, over the Tigers.

He had faced them on three previous occasions and defeated them each time.

THE ONLY sour note of the contest was a back injury suffered by popular Barney McCosky of the A's.

Barney bumped into the fence on Wakefield's third home run of the year and had to be carried from the field. His injuries were not believed to be serious.

Newhouser, who now has given up only 12 runs in his last seven games, has never been more scintillating this year. He was prevented from a shutout only by his own wildness. In the first inning, he walked two and then pitched a double to Hank Majeski.

Harold walked six batters and struck out five.

HE WAS afforded sensational support by his teammates, with Third Baseman George Kell turning in three terrific plays to thwart the A's when they could have been dangerous.

Kell received an assist from George Vico on the third inning when the A's had runners on second and third (both by walks) with one out (a sacrifice by McCosky).

THE CONTRACT was extended to Aug. 1, 1950.

Vacation pay for Hudson employees was boosted from $57 to $62.30 after one year's service and from $114 to $124.40 after five years.

There was no announcement from Hudson about raises for salaried employees.

The opening Ford-UAW wage conference lasted 2½ hours and was confined to a broad preliminary discussion.

The union is demanding a 30-cent hourly boost for 108,000 production workers.

THE TALKS will be resumed Wednesday at Rackham Memorial. The parties have scheduled three meetings for next week. No conclusive action is expected for at least two weeks.

Meantime, the strike of 5,000 workers against 75 tool-and-die shops entered its third day without development.

A spokesman for the Automotive Tool and Die Council, representing the struck shops, said the struck shops not to make separate settlements.

Ray Dooe, stormy labor figure, announced that he had received a federal charter from the AFL authorizing him to organize a new garage workers' union.

Dooe was removed from UAW (CIO) Local 415 last year after he led an ineffective strike against more than 50 Detroit garages.

Fans Roar Approval of New Lights
Thousands Gather Outside Stadium

BY RILEY MURRAY
Free Press Staff Writer

It takes a lot to awe Detroiters but the new Briggs Stadium lights did just that Tuesday night.

So thrilled were the fans that they were momentarily speechless when the eight giant lighting standards, generating 182,000,000 candlepower, were turned on at 9:29 p.m.

STRETCHING 150 feet up into the skies, 1,386 mammoth bulbs played their radiance on the gleaming green playing field.

Then a thunderous cry of acceptance that must have been heard even in the depths of the salt mines out S. Fort resounded across Mr. Briggs' brilliantly illuminated property, the lights for which cost a cool $400,000.

It was evident that Detroit had accepted and was going to like its night baseball.

Even the cool night air didn't dampen fans' enthusiasm. It took the first run of the game — scored by Philadelphia — to do that.

THOUSANDS of fans, who couldn't be persuaded to buy "standing-room" tickets, filled Michigan, National and Trumbull for an hour after the game got under way to get an exterior view of the spectacle.

The bleachers were packed to capacity by 7:30 p.m. By the same hour, fans were standing three and four deep in some unreserved sections.

Don McMillan 81, of 351 W. Mapleburst, Ferndale, a druggist, who saw his first ball game when Pittsburgh beat Detroit in the 1907 World Series in the old Bennett Park, echoed the sentiments of
Turn to Page 2, Column 4

18,000 Win 13c Raise at Hudson
Ford and UAW Open Wage Negotiations

A few hours before the UAW (CIO) entered into its first wage session with Ford Motor Co. Tuesday, a wage agreement was reached with Hudson Motor Car Co.

The Hudson wage accord came at 5:30 a.m. after an all-night session.

It provides a 13-cent hourly boost for the company's 18,000 hourly rated employees, subject to ratification by the membership of UAW (CIO) Local 154. The raise is retroactive to June 7.

2 Arrested in Holdups in Lover's Lane
Implicated Youth in County Jail

Two youths who allegedly took part in two Taylor Township lover's lane holdups June 7 were taken to Wayne County Jail.

They are Earl Warner, 21, of Inkster, who gave himself up to a Detroit parole officer, and Richard Moore, 21, of Wyandotte, who was arrested near White Pigeon by State Police.

Police said the pair had been implicated by Larry Adams, 32, of Inkster, and Warner's brother, Melvin, 32. Adams and Melvin Warner were arrested at the scene. The two stickups netted the quartet $6, police said.

13c Increase Set at Kelsey-Hayes

Kelsey-Hayes Wheel Co. and Local 78, UAW (CIO), have agreed on a 13-cent hourly raise for about 3,000 employees in two Detroit plants, the union announced.

The raise will be retroactive to June 14, if ratified by the union by June 21.

Spike Sets Date

HOLLYWOOD—(AP)—Spike Jones and his feminine singer on his touring stage show, Helen Grayco, set the date of their wedding. It's June 28.

Lansing Milk Up

LANSING—(AP)—The price of milk will be jumped 2 cents a quart to 19 cents in the Lansing area Wednesday.

PHILADELPHIA	AB	R	H	O	A	E
Joost, ss	2	1	1	3	3	0
R. Coleman, rf	3	0	0	2	0	0
McCosky, lf	3	0	0	1	0	0
White, lf	1	0	0	0	0	0
Valo, 1b	3	0	0	6	0	0
Majeski, 3b	4	0	1	2	2	0
Chapman, cf	4	0	0	4	0	0
Rosar, c	3	0	0	4	0	0
Suder, 2b	2	0	0	2	3	0
J. Coleman, p	2	0	0	0	0	0
Totals	**27**	**1**	**2**	**24**	**8**	**0**

DETROIT	AB	R	H	O	A	E
Lipon, ss	4	0	0	2	3	0
Lake, 2b	4	0	0	5	1	0
Kell, 3b	3	1	1	1	1	0
Wakefield, lf	3	1	1	0	0	0
Evers, cf	4	0	2	6	0	0
Mullin, rf	4	1	1	4	0	0
Vico, 1b	4	0	2	9	1	0
Swift, c	2	0	0	0	3	0
Newhouser, p	2	1	0	0	0	0
Totals	**30**	**4**	**7**	**27**	**9**	**0**

Philadelphia 100 000 000—1
DETROIT   002 000 02*—4

HR—Majeski, Evers 2, Wakefield, Mullin. 2BH—Majeski, Joost.
J. Coleman 5, Newhouser 5. WP—J. Coleman. Attendance 54,480.

July 29, 1951:

Detroit loves a good party when it comes to the city's birthday.

"Detroit Relives Colorful Past in Blaze of Glory," column one.

The Big Birthday Parade

BIRTHDAY CAKE is carried in triumph to symbolize anniversary.

HER IMPERIAL HIGHNESS the Empress of Detroit rode in regal splendor.

SEE NEXT PAGE

The Detroit Free Press

WARMER — An 85 high with cloudy sky

SUNDAY, JULY 29, 1951 — On Guard for Over a Century — 100 Pages — Vol. 121—No. 85 — Fifteen Cents

METRO FINAL

GEHRINGER IN Famous Ex-Tiger Named General Manager. See Sport Section

Detroit Relives Colorful Past in Blaze of Glory

Spectacular Parade Thrills 800,000 on Line of March

BY NORMAN KENYON
Free Press Staff Writer

Detroit's past came to life in a blaze of glory Saturday.

An estimated 800,000 persons stood spellbound by the brilliance and majesty of the spectacle.

It had been billed as the historical section of the birthday parade.

But what the huge throng saw was a 250-year drama packed with thrills, tears and triumph.

In 45 minutes of mobile tableaux, a two-and-a-half-century rise to greatness came into sharp focus.

DETROITERS RELIVED the tense moment when Cadillac, the French adventurer, stepped ashore to plant the flag of France.

They watched while Maj. Robert Rogers, of Ranger fame, hoisted the Union Jack over the log palisades.

Chills prickled up and down their spines as the Indian chief,

Parade Second Longest

Saturday's parade was the second-longest in Detroit's history, lasting five hours and 40 minutes.

It was eclipsed only by the gigantic American Legion parade on Sept. 22, 1931.

That one lasted exactly eight hours. An estimated 85,000 marched. A million watched.

Twenty thousand took part Saturday. And the crowd was set by police at 800,000.

Pontiac, decided to call off his campaign of blood and violence.

They cheered at the sight of the first American soldiers bringing the principles of freedom to Detroit.

Tragedy, in the form of the great fire of 1805, gripped their hearts.

At the same time, there emerged the courageous figure of Fr. Richard declaring: "We hope for better days—it shall rise from the ashes."

Spectators watched soldiers march off from Fort Wayne to preserve a union.

THE SCENE SHIFTED to Belle Isle in the 1880s, when Detroit was beautiful and living was gracious.

All of a sudden a violent chugging thundered up the street. And here came a procession of "funny-looking" cars—dawn of a new age.

Marking the turn of the century, the parade re-created the flower queen's float, a highlight of the 1901 birthday festival. Once again it proved a hit. Made of thousands of carnations, the float glowed with beauty.

Riding in the seat of honor was Mrs. Francis Lowrie, daughter of the queen who took the bows 50 years ago.

Onward the pageant moved, mounting in color.

There was the midway at the 1909 agricultural fair—and the first tractor exhibited in Michigan.

War clouds thunder. Detroit's mighty gears roll. The Motor City becomes the Arsenal of Democracy.

Then a mad dream of conquest strikes again.

Detroit amazes the world with its mighty outpouring of weapons for freedom.

THE MOTOR CITY marches into the present. It salutes great labor unions and a great dairy industry.

Into view rolls a twin vision of loveliness—the 250th birthday cake being served by the large industries and a radiant Miss America.

Now for the final piece de resistance.

On a float 50 feet long rides Pauline Gugelyk, the festival empress, and her beauteous court.

The empress' blue eyes sparkle amidst a dazzling array of jewels and royal robes.

Up and down the canyons of the metropolis rolls the thunder of a pleased people.

There is a chattering of voices lauding the mighty show— the brilliance of its 1,500 costumes, the detail of its settings, the clarity of its reproductions.

There is discussion of the sidelights—the elephants kneeling—

Turn to Page 8, Column 2

Truman Hails Detroit's Role in Struggle for Global Peace

PRESIDENT TRUMAN — MAYOR COBO — GOV. WILLIAMS
Reactions appear mixed as officials leave Willow Run Airport for President's talk
Free Press Photo by Tony Spina

CRITICIZES 'BUSINESS AS USUAL'

Wilson Gives Detroit a Pat and a Slap

Praise and censure were handed out by Defense Mobilizer Charles E. Wilson in his Birthday Festival speech at the Hotel Book-Cadillac.

The praise was for the immense contribution made by Detroit to the arming of the free world against the previous assaults of dictators.

The censure was for what he described as a "business as usual" attitude at present by Detroit industry.

Farming out of defense contracts outside Detroit could be blamed for some of the present unemployment here, Wilson declared.

"I REALIZE that Detroit is a producing center which habitually calls on other areas for a large volume of parts and subcontract items," he explained.

"But it seems that too much of the military business placed in Detroit is being so distributed by the large industries as to leave Detroit for business as usual, or, at least, for almost business as usual. This, in turn, accounts for some of the present unemployment here."

The unemployment he attributed to the shift from civilian to defense production and said "no doubt this condition will be sporadic in coming months."

He added that while it is impossible "to avoid some dislocations of this character, we are very anxious to hold them to a minimum. You can be sure that we are leaving nothing undone to avoid the waste of manpower and manufacturing facilities in this area."

The needs of the defense program are such that it is desirable for Detroit to retain a larger portion of the work it is now farming out," he said.

PARLEYS DEADLOCKED

UN Orders to Ridgway Rule Out Truce at 38th

By the Associated Press

Gen. Matthew B. Ridgway's truce instructions will permit him to make minor adjustments but no concessions in the United Nations demand that an armistice buffer zone in Korea follow the present battle line.

Informed officials in Washington said that the United States intends to stand absolutely firm on this issue, which has produced a head-on-clash with the Communist negotiators at Kaesong.

THE UNITED States also will not yield on the question of adequate system for inspection of all troops in Korea after an armistice is established, the officials added.

The present battle line is well north of the 38th Parallel, except in the west.

Ridgway's instructions were decided to be identical with the truce offer, repeated it, "It's strength that works, let's work for strength."

Wilson offered a slogan—he liked it so much he repeated it, "It's strength that works, let's work for strength."

22 Hurt in Crash

SOMERSET, Pa. — (UP) — Twenty-two persons were injured when a highway bus crashed into a steel-laden tractor-trailer.

You'll Find:

Amusements	Sec. D, Page 13
Editorials	Sec. B, Page 4
Financial	Sec. B, Page 10
Movies	Sec. D, Page 8
Radio and Television	Sec. B, Page 8
Living	Sec. A, Pages 9-13
Travel	Sec. B, Page 9

TO CALL THE FREE PRESS: WOODWARD 1-8900

Elect Leonard John Burke, City Clerk —Pol. Adv.

Nation Must Keep Guard Up, He Says

President Vows Aid on Layoffs; Warns of New Aggression

President Truman warned the throngs celebrating Detroit's 250th birthday that Russia is making rapid preparations for new acts of aggression.

But the Arsenal of Democracy again is taking the lead in meeting the threat of world conquest, he declared.

Police estimated that 30,000 persons crowded Campus Martius for his address.

Approximately 60,000 gathered to hear Mr. Truman in his last appearance in Detroit—Labor Day, 1948, when he opened his campaign.

Mr. Truman flew back to Washington shortly after his address. He arrived at 4:05 p.m. Detroit time.

Relatively quiet during the speech, the crowd let loose a volley of cheers when the President waved at them at the finish.

IN A FIGHTING mood, Mr. Truman hit out at critics of the defense program.

POINTING TO the major role Detroit will play in the dangerous time ahead, Mr. Truman asserted:

"The success or failure of the cause of freedom again depends on what is done in your factories."

While employment in Detroit is higher now than at the peak of World War II, many workers face layoffs during the conversion period, he said.

"I have told the defense agencies to do everything possible to make

"We cannot let down our guard, no matter what happens in Korea," the President declared.

Mr. Truman said his desk was flooded daily with reports of new Soviet military preparations.

Bulgaria, Romania and Hungary now have armed forces "far greater" than those allowed under the 1947 peace treaties, he said.

"That's one of our main troubles in dealing with the Soviets," the President declared.

"They have no respect for signed treaties or their given word."

"However, there are few producers in Detroit who do not have more than one production line. One production line running at 100 per cent should free a second production line for use on defense production."

"I should like to make this further point: You know and I know that you cannot operate at production line efficiency at partial capacity.

"And in this connection may I remind you that, during the last war, Detroit actually grew in size during the period when it manufactured comparatively few automobiles?

"WE HAVE always held the door open to a real and permanent settlement of the world's problems," Wilson said. "Perhaps a demonstration of America's might, such as we are building now, will cause Russia to enter that door willingly and with real meaning.

"If we can speak with a strength equivalent to the Kremlin's, perhaps at last we can make ourselves understood by the 14 rulers (the 'Politburo') behind the stone walls."

Text of Address Section B, Page 11

More Stories and Pictures of Festival

More stories and pictures of Detroit's gala birthday celebration appear on Pages 2, 3, 4, 5, 6, 7, 8, 14 of this section, and Page 12, of Section B, the Magazine. You'll enjoy all of them.

Sunday's Events in Detroit's Birthday Festival

10 A. M.–2 P. M.—The 250th Birthday Bicycle Derby in Chandler Park, a competition sponsored by the Amateur Bicycle League of America.

4 P. M.–5 P. M.—"Builders of the Spirit," depicting the growth of Protestantism and Orthodoxy in Detroit, at the Theme Center Stage in Grand Circus Park.

8 P. M.–10:30 P. M.—The fourth concert of the Festival Symphony, directed by Valter Poole and featuring the work of American composers, in Remick Band Shell on Belle Isle.

8:45 P. M.–9:45 P. M.—Canada pays tribute to Detroit's 250th Birthday at the Theme Center Stage, Grand Circus Park.

Pennsylvania Hit by Storm

California Also Has Cloudburst

BETHLEHEM, Pa. — (UP) — Torrential thunderstorms hit several areas of Eastern Pennsylvania, causing two deaths and widespread damage.

Four inches of rain fell at Allentown.

PALM SPRINGS, Calif. — (UP) — Mountain cloudbursts sent torrents of water down canyons, flooding desert communities.

Streets in Palm Springs, Palm Desert, and other desert towns looked like canals.

Turn to Page 8, Column 1

The Detroit Free Press

TUESDAY, FEBRUARY 26, 1952 — METRO FINAL — Vol. 121—No. 297 — Five Cents

The Full Story So Far: Other Stories and Pictures of Unfolding Drama of Red Hearing on Pages 2, 3, 4, 5 and Back Page

FEB. 26, 1952: The McCarthy era in Detroit: Searching for Communists is serious business.

RED PROBERS HUNTING FOR MISSING TEACHER

The Squeeze Is On

THE BIG SQUEEZE was on Monday as the corridor before Federal Judge Arthur A. Koscinski's courtroom became jammed with citizens hours before the Communist hearings were scheduled to begin. Only 15 of the waiting throng got in, one by one.

Senate Approves McDonald as RFC Chief After Battle

Detroiter Meets Stiff Opposition

2-to-1 Vote Follows Long, Stormy Debate

BY JAMES M. HASWELL
Of Our Washington Bureau

WASHINGTON—Over strong opposition, the Senate confirmed President Truman's nomination of Detroiter Harry A. McDonald as administrator of the Reconstruction Finance Corp.

McDonald, now chairman of the Securities and Exchange Commission, is a Republican. The vote was 46 to 23.

The large number of nay votes came after protests by Senator Douglas (D., Ill.) and Senator Ives (R., N. Y.).

DOUGLAS CHARGED that McDonald, though "honest and likeable," is not strong enough for the job of resisting "great pressure" for RFC loans.

Ives' viewpoint was that President Truman had pressured Congress into accepting McDonald "or else" and had "kicked around and coerced" the Senate Banking Committee.

Voting for McDonald's confirmation were 30 Democrats and 16 Republicans, including Michigan's Senator Ferguson. Against were...

Turn to Page 2, Column 5

HARRY A. McDONALD
Truman appointee confirmed

Killing, Suicide Orphans Seven

ELWOOD, Ind. — (U.P) — John Stroud, 60, father of seven, shot his wife, 36, to death as she stepped off a bus and then took his own life, police said.

One of Stroud's shots wounded a young woman passenger.

Folsom Freed

BIRMINGHAM — (AP) — Former Alabama Gov. James E. Folsom was acquitted of driving while drunk.

Stuck

LOUISVILLE — (AP) — A thief stole 288,000 safety pins from a factory here.

Find New Pentagon Waste

Probers Report Huge Leakage

BY EDWIN A. LAHEY
Of Our Washington Bureau

WASHINGTON — The general accounting office has found new and flagrant evidence of waste in military spending at home and abroad.

Details of extensive leakage from the $61,000,000,000 Pentagon kitty and the $7,300,000,000 Mutual Security Program have been put into a report by Lindsay C. Warren, the comptroller general of the United States. He has the reputation as the tightest man with a Government dollar in Washington.

THE PRELIMINARY draft of this explosive report is now in the custody of Speaker of the House Sam Rayburn and Vice President Alben W. Barkley.

It will remain a secret until Congress orders the report to be printed.

It was further learned that tax money has been thrown around Europe with such reckless abandon that Warren has decided to set up a shop on the Continent. His investigators there could keep closer watch on the foreign aid program.

A special team will leave for Europe next week to lay the groundwork for the new branch.

Even before the Pentagon became a $61,000,000,000 establishment, investigators for the comptroller general were turning up widespread instances of military waste and fraud.

A year ago the investigators gave a cursory examination to the records of 5,000 officers of the Army and Navy. They found that 20 per cent of them were cheating the Government out of dependency allowances.

The guilty officers turned up in this spot check claimed dependent parents and relatives who either didn't exist or were not dependent.

THE AVERAGE "overpayment" through these fraudulent claims was $1,500, or a total of $1,500,000. The officers found to be cheating the Government were not court-martialed, as they might have been some years ago under similar circumstances.

The records & the fraudulent claims were turned over to the inspector generals of the different branches of the military service.

The offices of these inspectors are now trying to recover the dependency allowances from the officers who perpetrated the frauds.

Demands Press-Agent Cost Data

Legislator Seeks Defense Dept. Check

WASHINGTON — (AP) — Rep. Hebert (D., La.) called on the Department of Defense to turn over to the House Armed Services Committee a list of all personnel assigned to public relations duty.

"I want to know the name and salary paid each civilian press agent, ghost writer and public relations expert and for whom and under whose direction the individual works," he said.

HEBERT HEADS an armed services subcommittee which has been investigating reports of waste and extravagance in military buying programs.

"It is about time the American public be informed as to the identity of the individuals and what it costs the taxpayers to maintain and support this gigantic and colossal propaganda machine on the banks of the Potomac," Hebert said.

Bank Bandit Gets $20,000

HOLLYWOOD — (AP) — A cool, methodical bandit robbed a Bank of America branch of $20,000 as moviegoing customers waited in line, unaware of the crime.

Manager Gilbert R. Fox said the robber came into his office, waited politely until he finished a telephone conversation, then took out a revolver and said: "Okay, start filling this briefcase."

Fox was forced to enter each of six tellers' cages and fill the briefcase.

You'll Find:

Amusements	13
Editorials	6
Financial	10-11
Radio and Television	28
Sports	16-18
Women's Page	8

TO CALL THE FREE PRESS
WOODWARD 2-8900
For Want Ads:
WOODWARD 2-9400

★ ★ ★ ★ ★ ★

Woman Named by FBI Spy Has Been Off Job Five Days

Federal agents sought Monday night to subpena a Detroit Public Schools art teacher to testify at the House Un-American Activities Committee hearings in Detroit this week.

One of the committee's surprise witnesses, Richard F. O'Hair, identified her as Eleanor Laffrey Cook Maki. O'Hair was an FBI spy in Detroit Communist circles for four years. O'Hair said Mrs. Maki was acting as membership director of the Midtown Communist Party Club, of which he was a member until 1947.

He Named Names

RICHARD O'HAIR
He was the secret witness

THE HEARING GOT under way 3½ hours late Monday. It was set to start at 10 a. m. But a wrangle on whether to allow TV coverage delayed it until 1:30 p. m. Communist pickets, carrying placards, arrived outside the Federal Building around noon and departed a little after 1 p. m.

Rep. Potter (R., Mich.), committee member, said he didn't know just when Mrs. Maki would be subpoened to testify. He said if she is located she will testify sometime, even if there isn't time to hear her during this week's hearings.

The Board of Education said a Mrs. Maki has been employed in the public schools as an art teacher since 1929. It said she has been at Dwyer School since 1944.

O'Hair said he didn't know whether Mrs. Maki still was a party member. He said, however, she was one of the persons to whom he paid his dues in 1947.

Harry H. Gragg, principal of Dwyer School, described Mrs. Maki as a "very good teacher." He said she is "quite popular with the children." Mrs. Maki lives at 2700 Rochester.

A reporter who went to the Maki home was met by a polite but stern rebuff from an unidentified man who came to the door.

The man, who seemed to know the reporter's purpose, said that Mrs. Maki was not at home. He refused to make any comment.

Gragg said Mrs. Maki called him last Thursday saying she wouldn't be in school that day, and hasn't been there since.

"I was busy at the time and don't remember if Mrs. Maki said she was sick," Gragg said.

The Board of Education members who were reached for comment expressed their surprise at the committee's naming of Mrs. Maki.

But both, Mrs. Jane H. Lovejoy and Patrick V. McNamara, said action should be taken to remove the teacher if the charges against her are bonafide.

The House committee will resume its hearings at 10 a. m. Tuesday. O'Hair, who was Monday's only witness, had previously testified at deportation hearings against Mrs. Anna Ganley, wife of Nat Ganley, former editor of the Michigan Daily Worker.

O'Hair, now 38, came to Detroit from Marion, Ind., in 1942. He said he worked for Federal Mogul Corp. in plant protection work and later as a fireman for the Pere Marquette Railroad.

WHILE AT Federal Mogul, he said, he was approached by an FBI agent and asked to join the Communist Party as an undercover agent.

O'Hair gave a detailed picture of the operations of the Midtown Club, of which he said was his cell of the Communist Party. He listed more than 20 names of persons he called party officers and members.

The Midtown Club he said was one of 17 or 18 cells which made up the party's East Side Council. The club's membership of 147 was "about average" for each cell, he said.

O'HAIR SAID HE joined the party at an Earl Browder rally at the Graystone Ballroom in 1943 at the instigation of the FBI. He said he was recruited by Harry Glasagold, an artist.

Headquarters of the club was at 10 W. Warren, he said.

"I understand a dentist by the name of Vern Piazza obtained the office and paid the rent," O'Hair said.

"At the time I knew Sis she was working in the district office. I believe it was at 2419 Grand River. Sis was married to a newspaper reporter, who I believe worked for the Detroit Times, by the name of Gordon Friesen."

Committee Counsel Frank Tavenner broke into the testimony to say that Friesen left the Times in 1944 to work for the Office of War Information.

"After that we don't know exactly where they went but they both were reported to have gone to New York," Tavenner said.

O'HAIR CONTINUED his testimony:

"Gus Anderson was financial director. He was a painter and a member of the AFL. Anne Bieswenger, as I recall, worked

Turn to Page 5, Column 1

McGRATH MAY GET ULTIMATUM

Morris to Ask Details of U.S. Aides' Incomes

WASHINGTON—(UP)—Newbold Morris announced plans to demand an income accounting from all key Government workers as the first major step in his drive against corruption.

The cleanup director said questionnaires will be handed to officials and top employes next week with orders to answer up or face immediate dismissal.

THE SENATE committee's action came on President Truman's request that Morris be allowed to grant witnesses immunity from prosecution.

Morris is anxious to have subpena powers. The President has directed all Government employes to co-operate with him fully. But subpenas would be needed for "outsiders."

PRESUMABLY, the demand for full statements of income will apply to everyone in the top echelon of the Executive branch of the Government except President Truman.

This would include Attorney General J. Howard McGrath, Morris' "boss," whose income already is a source of interest to a House Judiciary subcommittee.

The subcommittee meets Tuesday to consider Harold Stassen's charges that McGrath has become a millionaire while in public office.

The Morris plan for getting income information was coupled with these other developments:

1—The Senate Judiciary Committee voted to refuse him immunity powers and postponed action on his request for authority to subpena witnesses.

A House Judiciary subcommittee also delayed action on the subpena request.

2—Senator Ferguson (R., Mich.) disclosed he will introduce legislation tightening restrictions on ex-employes of the Internal Revenue Bureau who seek to handle tax cases before the Government.

Calm and Safe

MULLENS, W. Va.—(AP)—About 50 afternoon moviegoers walked calmly out of a burning theater here, minutes before the theater roof collapsed.

618 Volunteer

HEIDELBERG, Germany—(AP)—United States Army headquarters said that 618 American infantrymen in the European Command volunteered for duty in Korea in the last six weeks.

Free Press to Start Lenten Series Tonight

Religion — how it is interpreted and put into practice in the daily lives of 30 Detroiters — will come to life in a series of personal statements of these sermons beginning Ash Wednesday. The series, which will run through Lent, will first appear in edition of the Free Press on sale Tuesday night.

Feb. 29, 1952:

Coleman Young, 34, is defiant before the House Committee on Un-American Activities.

Page eight

Committee Loosens Reins, Defiant Witness Runs Wild

Fight over Terminology Bitterest of Hearing

BY FRED TEW
From Free Press Staff Writer

The House Un-American Activities Committee relaxed its checkrein on defiant witnesses as the first person called took the stand Thursday.

And the witness, Coleman A. Young, took the bit in his mouth and ran wild for more than an hour in the bitterest battle yet fought in hearings on Communist activities in Detroit.

He admonished both Rep. Wood (D., Ga.), chairman of the committee, and Committee Counsel Frank S. Tavenner, a native of Virginia, that they had "slurred" the word "Negro."

Each time, he was told that if a slip had been made it was unintentional.

* * *

AT ONE POINT, Young goaded Wood into saying: "This is not a vaudeville show."

Young and Wood engaged in heated arguments over the right of Negroes to vote in the South and some of the actions of former Rep. Rankin (D., Miss.), one-time member of the House Un-American Activities Committee.

At one point, Young said, in answer to a question about the difference between the National Negro Congress and the National Negro Labor Council, that he "assumed" committee members were "intelligent" enough to "see the difference yourself."

It was the first time since the hearings began Monday that the committee had allowed a witness such leeway during formal sessions.

At the conclusion of the testimony, Young was pounded on the back by other witnesses who already had testified or were waiting to.

Spectators who asked committee members why Young had been permitted such latitude were told, "It just happened."

* * *

YOUNG TESTIFIED that he was born May 24, 1918, in Alabama. He said he had lived in Detroit 30 years.

He said he had worked for the Postoffice and was discharged for attempting to organize a union. After service in the Army as an Air Force captain, he said he returned to the Postoffice for two months.

Young, who was represented by George W. Crockett, Jr., a lawyer who has been cited for contempt in defending New York Communists convicted of plotting to overthrow the United States Government, said he then became an International Representative of the United Public Workers.

In 1947-48, he was director of organization for the Wayne County CIO Council. Presently, he is national executive secretary of the National Negro Labor Council, he said.

Tavenner asked: "Our investigation has not presented any evidence that you are a member of the Communist Party. We wish to inquire, however, into your activities in some organizations which have been listed as subversive and with which you have been connected."

Young: "I have been subpenaed here. I hope that when I am asked a question, I can react fully and answer it fully. I may have answers you may not like, but I want the right to answer fully."

Q — "Are you now a member of the Communist Party?"

* * *

"I REFUSE to answer that question," Young answered, "relying on my rights under the Fifth Amendment and also under the First Amendment which gives a person the right of free speech and the privilege of privacy of thought and actions I am not here as a stoolpigeon."

Tavenner then asked: "Are you a member of the National Negro Congress?"

A — "That word is 'Negro', not 'Negra'."

"I don't think I said 'Negra,' but if I did it was unintentional and I am sorry," Tavenner said.

"Thank you," Young replied. "I resent the slurring of the name of my race. In some sections of the country it is 'Negra.' And I resent it."

Tavenner then asked: "Are you a member of the National Negro Congress?"

A — "I refuse to answer. The National Negro Congress has been labelled by this committee as subversive and I don't intend to discuss any organizations that have been labelled, properly or improperly, as subversive."

Q — "Were you a field organizer for the National Negro Congress?"

A — "I just told you that I wouldn't answer such questions. By the way, the National Association for the Advancement of Colored people has been labeled as subversive by this committee."

Q — "I think you are mistaken."

A — "All you have to do is look at your own records."

Q — "No action has ever been taken to cite the NAACP as subversive."

A — "Well, Congressman Rankin was a member of the committee and he said it was subversive."

* * *

REP. POTTER (R., Mich.) broke in to say: "Rankin no longer is a member of this committee."

Potter took up the questioning, saying: "We're not here to discuss Rankin."

A — "I consider the segregation and discrimination of Negroes un-American."

Q — "Do you consider the Communist Party un-American?"

A — "I consider the activities of this committee to be un-American."

Rep. Wood directed Young: "Answer the question."

Young refused to say whether he thought the Communist Party was un-American.

"You've got me mixed up with a stool pigeon," he told Wood, who took over the questioning.

Q — "That's enough of that. Just answer the questions."

A — "That's what you want me to do. Under the First Amendment I've got the right to free speech and I intend to exercise that right. I will answer as I see fit and if I want to say more than 'yes' or 'no' then I will say more."

TAVENNER THEN asked Young: "Would it not be correct to say that the Veterans' Council became the Detroit chapter of the National Negro Congress?"

A — "I will not answer any question regarding the Congress."

Wood: "The only truthful way to answer the question is did the Council do it or did it not become the Detroit chapter of the Congress?"

A — "I am not going to let you put words in my mouth."

"This isn't a vaudeville show," Wood reminded the witness. "You're before a committee of the House of Representatives."

Rep. Jackson (R., Calif.) broke in and said that he didn't think Young could be proud of his actions.

"Do you have anything more to say to me?" Young asked Jackson.

A — "That's a great deal to say, but in due course."

Young: "That's fine because I've got a great deal to say to you, too."

Tavenner then asked Young when the National Negro Labor Council was formed.

A — "In Cincinnati in 1951."

Q — "Who is the president of the Council?"

A — "William R. Hood is the president. You have him under subpena."

THEN BEGAN a long sparring session between Tavenner

FRANK TAVENNER COLEMAN YOUNG
Counsel and witness locked horns

and Young over the difference between the National Negro Congress and the National Negro Labor Council.

Young read the preamble of the Council which said it was formed to fight against segregation and discrimination. He added: "I take it that the Committee has in its possession the preamble of the Congress. Now you know the purpose of the Council. I assume you are intelligent enough to see the difference yourself."

"The question is, what is the difference between the National Negro Congress and the National Negro Labor Council," Chairman Wood reminded Young.

A — "You said 'Negra'."

Wood — "Well, it was a mistake. I can't help the way I talk. I do the best I can. I come from the South, you know."

A — "Yes, from Georgia where the Negroes can't vote and there are lynchings."

WOOD AND Young then engaged in a fierce verbal battle with Wood claiming that all 152 of the Negroes in his village voted for him and Young claiming that Negroes were not allowed to vote freely.

Potter then told Young: "Today there are many casualties in Korea. That proves that Communism is a cold-blooded conspiracy and you are a part of it."

Jackson asked Young: "Do you approve of United States action in Korea?"

Young said: "I refuse to answer because my opinions are private."

Young said to other questions that he had been an unsuccessful candidate of the State Senate in 1948 on the Progressive Party ticket.

He refused to say whether he attended a banquet to welcome Pat Toohey as the new secretary of the Communist Party in Michigan on May 27, 1941.

He also refused to say whether he attended a Lenin Memorial Meeting and Rally for Victory Jan. 18, 1942, in the Mirror Ballroom.

Young also refused to say whether he introduced Benjamin Davis (one of 11 convicted Communists leaders in New York) at a meeting July 27, 1948, at which Davis said: "I am proud to be an American, a Negro and a Communist."

He refused to answer many more questions regarding meetings.

AT THE CONCLUSION, Jackson asked: "Do you believe it possible for Russia and the United States to exist side-by-side in the world?"

Young — "I fervently hope that that is possible."

Jackson: "Well Stalin says they can't. I feel that anyone who takes up the cudgels of the Communist Party in the past few years is wielding a bayonet as effectively as Communist soldiers in Korea. Can you agree with any portion of what I have just said?"

A — "I have taken up the cudgels for the Negro people to obtain freedom and equality for them right now, not five years from now."

Porter Cleared of Red Tinge

A hotel porter named as a Communist appeared voluntarily before the House Un-American Activities Committee and was cleared of the Red tinge.

"I paid one month's dues back in 1943," said William A. Record. "That was all. I quit the party because they wanted 10 per cent of my earnings."

RECORD WAS named in testimony Monday by Richard F. O'Hair, an FBI informant who was planted in the party.

Committee members were told that Record had been fired from his job at the Murry Hall Hotel, 5230 Third. They said they hoped he would be rehired.

In contrast to Record was another witness, Mrs. Lorraine Faxon Meisner, a Wayne University student.

She simpered and giggled throughout the questioning.

MRS. MEISNER departed from the "standard" reason for refusal — guarantees by the Fifth Amendment of the Constitution.

She took refuge behind the legal tenet which permits a wife to refuse to testify against her husband. She was married to Morris Meisner, also under subpena, on Feb. 5.

She refused to say whether she is a Communist Party member, whether a Communist cell exists at Wayne, and whether she attended a Communist youth festival in East Berlin last summer.

Train Burns

OMAHA — (AP) — Eleven cars of a Union Pacific fast mail and express train were destroyed by fire after the train hit a gasoline truck near Morgan, Utah.

Victor Reuther to Speak in Ohio

Victor Reuther, former UAW (CIO) education director and now CIO representative in Europe, will return to the United States to address the UAW International Education Conference being held in Cleveland April 3-4.

Stabs Wife Fatally as Children Watch

SANTA ROSA, Calif. — (AP) — Joseph Dougherty, 52, a divorced real estate broker forced his way into the home of his former wife and fatally stabbed her, officers said.

Four of their five children watched the slaying in horror.

More Comfort Wearing FALSE TEETH

Watch for the new
CYCLA-MATIC
FRIGIDAIRE
on display soon at...
NED'S 10 Stores
Detroit • Dearborn • Mt Clemens • Royal Oak

Take Dad's Word for it!
...the best-tasting, mildest whisky you can choose!

FAMOUS SINCE 1894

Philadelphia
BLENDED WHISKY

$3.60 4/5 QT. $2.25 PINT

Through the Years - In the Best of Taste!

Blended Whisky - 86.8 Proof - 67½% Grain Neutral Spirits - Continental Distilling Corporation - Philadelphia, Pa.

When you get

MOTOROLA AT MEYER

You get **FULL YEAR** Warranty On **ALL** Parts Including Picture Tube

at NO EXTRA COST!

17 IN.

TREASURE CHEST PLAYHOUSE
WJBK TV (channel 2)
MOVIETIME
TUE. & THURS.
11:15 P.M.

$249.95

$37.50 DOWN
$3.00 WEEK

DOUBLE-VALUE TRADE-IN
on your old TV set or radio

You get Area Selector
Better picture wherever you live

You get Easy Tuning
Perfect picture and tone with one click. No dialing

You get Glare Guard
Eliminates 95% of reflected light

Motorola

BRAND NEW 1952 full console in newly designed rich mahogany cabinet. Meyer branches open Thursday, Friday and Saturday 'til 9.

MEYER JEWELRY COMPANY
Treasure Chest Stores

DOWNTOWN
WOODWARD AT GRAND CIRCUS PARK

WEST SIDE
9304 Grand River at Joy

EAST SIDE
13703 E. Jefferson at Chalmers

NORTHWEST
13301 Grand River at Greenfield

NORTHEAST
14403 Gratiot at 7 mile

The Detroit Free Press

TUESDAY, APRIL 22, 1952 — On Guard for Over a Century — 32 Pages — Vol. 121—No. 353 — Five Cents

METRO FINAL

QUELL NEW PRISON RIOT

APRIL 22, 1952:

Jackson Prison inmates take hostages.

STATE POLICE FLUSH INMATES FROM MESS HALL BUILDING SCORCHED BY FIRE
Two prisoners (white shirts) wade through water and debris left from fire

Uneasy Truce Reigns in Deadly Jackson Mutiny

11 Guards Still Held as Hostages by Diehards

BY KENNETH McCORMICK AND JEROME HANSEN
Free Press Staff Writers

JACKSON — A new flare-up of rioting Monday night served notice on Jackson Prison officials and State Police that they were still sitting on a powder keg.

Another convict was wounded, the eighth so far.

The disturbance was put down quickly, and comparative calm settled over the seething inmates.

Although a feeling of uneasiness and tension was apparent, Warden Julian N. Frisbie said he was satisfied that the situation was under control for the moment.

His immediate objective was to negotiate for the release of eleven prison guards still held as hostages by the unruly mob in the punishment cellblock.

Prison floodlights blazed across the shambles left by wildly stampeding convicts as the warden and State Police moved cautiously lest some new incident incite the mutineers.

"We can hold out all night and just as long as you can," yelled Earl Ward, spokesman for the rebels in Cellblock 15.

Meanwhile, the ugly toll counted one convict dead; eight

Other Stories and Pictures on Pages 2, 3, 8, 9, 21 and Back Page

wounded; two guards beaten; three State Policemen injured.

The rioters, except for the hard-bitten ringleaders in the punishment cells, had been driven back into cells with tear gas bombs and shotgun blasts.

A force of 200 State Police, drawn from every post in Southern Michigan, restored a semblance of order after 20 hours of the worst violence in the history of Jackson Prison.

PILLAGING AND rampaging, the mutinous inmates—as many as 1,000—set fires which made hollow shells of six buildings. Dr. Vern Fox, deputy warden, said the damage might run to "several million dollars."

The hard core of resistance—104 of the most desperate prisoners—held eleven guards, threatening to kill them at any moment. Another guard, released at 4:15 p. m., brought out the first news from the center of the revolt.

"The guards are getting along OK," said Guard Henry W. Curry. "The prisoners said they'd see me out of the building. I don't know why they did it. Some of the other prisoners brought in food and water and they have plenty. It will be tomorrow at least before they start getting hungry."

State Police Commissioner Donald S. Leonard reported to Gov. Williams early Monday night that his men were in control of the situation, except in Cellblock 15.

HE REAFFIRMED that he would not attempt to invade the principal danger spot before morning, still fearful for the lives of the guard-hostages.

Leonard said that the troopers who had served long hours at the riot scene were being relieved by fresh police being sent from Southern Michigan posts. The troopers who have been on the scene since Sunday night were being quartered Monday night at the Jackson armory.

With the new troopers moving into Jackson, most of the posts south of the Straits have been virtually stripped of personnel.

Leonard was the latest State Police casualty. He was struck on the head by an object thrown by a troublemaking convict from an upper tier of Cellblock 11, where Leonard was leading a detail of men to quell a disturbance. His injury was trivial.

Williams said he has been in contact with National Guard heads but no attempt will be made to mobilize the guard unless such action is requested by authorities at Jackson.

Monday night's disorders occurred in one of the corridors outside troublous Cellblock 15 as inmates started shouting and milling about.

POLICE QUIETED them quickly with a few more shotgun blasts. One struck Arthur Smith in the arm and leg. The wounded convict was serving a burglary term from Detroit.

One group of prisoners set another fire—this one in Cellblock 6—but it was quickly subdued.

Another development Monday night was the announcement of State Senator Robert S. Haggerty, Detroit Democrat, that he would demand a legislative investigation of the Jackson riot when the Legislature reconvenes May 14.

He said he will seek an explanation why Warden Frisbie, known as a stern disciplinarian, was transferred from Marquette Prison to Jackson, which had a good record for years.

He charged that one of the reasons for the riot was a lack of facilities for treatment and a lack of competent help in the mental wards.

He said he had found, during an inspection trip, that mental patients were "herded together" in one cellblock.

THE SOLITARY cells were described by Haggerty as a "dungeon-like hole."

"I was amazed at the treatment prisoners were receiving," Haggerty said.

The dead convict was Darwin W. Millage, serving 15 to 25 years from Wayne, Mich.

Millage was shot through the chest in one of three skirmishes as State Police and guards, on the one hand, battled sneering, defiant prisoners who roamed the yards.

Led personally by Leonard in the first battle, 20

Turn to Page 2, Column 1

STATE TROOPERS STAND GUARD AS CONVICTS MILL AROUND
Damage from riots may run to millions of dollars

Free Press Photos by Tom Venalock and Jerry Heiman

Senate Bars U.S. Funds in Steel Grab

44-to-31 Vote Is Censure of Truman

WASHINGTON — (UP) — The Senate ignored a last-minute warning from President Truman Monday and voted to bar the Government from using any funds in a pending appropriations bill to operate the seized steel industry.

By a vote of 44 to 31, it approved a Republican-sponsored amendment, introduced by Senator Ferguson, of Michigan, which proponents hailed as a "vote of censure" against the Chief Executive.

Opponents of the proviso said it was meaningless, except as a gesture, because none of the funds actually were earmarked for the Government-held plants.

STILL BEFORE the Senate was a more far-reaching Republican proposal, sponsored by Senator Knowland, of California. It would forbid operation of the steel industry with any funds ap-

Turn to Page 2, Column 4

Envoy Sworn In

WASHINGTON — (AP) — Ambassador Robert D. Murphy was sworn in Monday at the State Department as the first postwar United States envoy to Japan.

You'll Find:
Amusements	10
Editorials	6
Financial	16-18
Radio and Television	19
Sports	22-24
Women's Pages	14-15

For Want Ads:
WOODWARD 2-9400

8 Ex-Convicts Urge Jackson Investigation

Claim 80 Pct. of Grievances of Prison Rioters Are Correct

The common bond of former imprisonment—and "an obligation to society"—brought eight Jackson Prison ex-convicts together in Detroit Monday night.

Behind the riot-torn walls men with whom they had served time were embroiled with prison guards and State Police.

"We don't even belong together," the spokesman said. "Six of us are on parole—only two of us are 'off paper'—and we're not supposed to congregate.

"If we're caught together, we have to go back for more time, but we feel we have an obligation to society and should speak out on this."

THE MEN, each of whom served 10 years or more in "Jacktown," asked that a full-scale investigation be made of the conditions that led to the rioting.

"Six of us would be willing to appear before an investigating body set up independent of the prison," the spokesman said.

The men declared that about 80 per cent of the rioting prisoners' charges of abuse and other grievances are correct.

"A lot of the convicts are not angels," the spokesman said. "We're not tryin' to tell you they are. But there are some mighty fine men among the prisoners and 75 per cent of the cons just want to do their time and get out."

The men insisted that they meant no reflection against Warden Julian N. Frisbie and his staff.

"But sometimes things get over their heads," the spokesman said.

said. "But the other guys are a little shaky."

The group suggested that State Police Commissioner Donald S. Leonard or Detroit's Police Commissioner George F. Boos be named by the Governor to head such a probe.

"YOU MAY think it's funny, us asking for a policeman to investigate this thing," the spokesman said. "But those guys are square men and we've got faith in them."

What People Are Saying

MILLARD CALDWELL, Federal defense administrator: "We're faced with two enemies — the threat of Communism from without and the threat of inaction and thoughtlessness from within."

MOHAMMED ALI, Pakistan's ambassador to the United States: "America has proved itself to be the great champion of freedom and democracy in the modern world."

Today's Chuckle

Too many of us spend money we haven't earned to buy things we don't need, just to impress a lot of people we don't like.

SPRINKLE
Drip and breeze and less degrees
Official U. S. Weather Map on Page 21

FOR WOMEN'S WAYS
Looking for Menu Ideas? or New Hints for Beauty—Just Turn to Women's Pages.

JUNE 10, 1953:

Michigan's biggest weather disaster.

Twister Slams into Massachusetts, Killing 69

The Detroit Free Press

WEDNESDAY, JUNE 10, 1953 — On Guard for Over a Century — 40 Pages — Vol. 123—No. 36 — Seven Cents

METRO FINAL

Truce Talks Recessed Again
See Story Page 6

CLOUDY
Partly cloudy. Low 54 to 58. High 72 to 76. Rain by night.

209 DIE IN TORNADOES; FLINT TOLL MAY SOAR

Worcester Area Lists 738 Injured

Fear Death Toll May Reach 80

Free Press Wire Services

WORCESTER, Mass.—The worst New England tornado lashed through 11 central Massachusetts communities and into New Hampshire before sundown Tuesday night, claiming 69 known dead and smashing hundreds of homes and industrial buildings.

The known injured totaled 738.

Authorities said many others probably were trapped in the rubble of dwellings and factories.

State police estimated 2,500 were homeless in the area crushed by the devastating twister, which struck shortly after 4 p.m. (EST)

A Harvard University weather expert said the tornado was spawned by the same squall line that produced tornadoes in Michigan and Ohio Monday night.

A spokesman for the Worcester City Hospital said it appeared the total deaths would reach 80.

* * *

A STRIP ABOUT 25 miles long extending from Rutland through the north end of this city and southward to Southbridge near the Rhode Island state line was the hardest hit.

An off-shoot descended on

Picture on Page 6

Franklin about 25 miles due east, struck neighboring Wrentham, wrecking scores of buildings and sending 35 to an Attleboro hospital.

Meanwhile, a twin-funnel twister made a two-minute slash at Exeter, N. H. demolishing a country club, wrecking a dozen buildings and injuring about 10 persons.

* * *

DISASTER CREWS, led by Gov. Christian A. Herter, poured into the Worcester area.

Disaster relief experts were dispatched from the American Red Cross Eastern Area headquarters at Alexandria, Va. An allotment of $100,000 was allocated to care for the ill and homeless.

At least 200 homes were demolished in the Central Massachusetts area. Several huge industrial plants had roofs blown off.

* * *

PESTERED BY residents worried by equally sultry skies Tuesday afternoon a Worcester weather observer said he could see no tornado threat.

Less than an hour later, the storm struck.

Some debris from Worcester was carried 45 miles to Boston.

Five minutes before the brunt of the blast struck Norton Co.'s new $1,000,000 plant, more than 100 workers had left for the day. Winds whipped off the roof and hurled it onto some 40 automobiles that were crushed.

TWO NUNS and a priest were reported killed at Assumption College.

A convent and dormitory were demolished. Nuns with flashlights, their habits heavy with mud, probed through the debris.

Brother Maurice Allaire, A.A., of Ferndale, Mich., saw a trailer snatched up by the wind and hurled on a woman pedestrian struggling along the street outside.

Brunt of the blow was borne in Worcester County by Petersham, Athol, Barre, Rutland, Holden, West Boylston, North Worcester, Boylston, Shrewsbury, Westboro, Southboro, and Southbridge.

A Ruined Home, an Injured Child, a Picture Story of the Tragedy When Nature Went A-Riot at Flint

Survivors' Eyes Reflect the Horror

BY JACK SCHERMERHORN
Free Press Staff Writer

FLINT—One roaring, smashing moment turned the quiet evening hour of relaxation into a shocking hell of slaughter, anguish and destruction in Flint.

The air was mild and still and folks were sitting down resting after supper or taking a leisurely ride to get a bit of air.

Moments later they were dead or battered and cut or standing vacant-eyed and numb from pain and horror. For some, that moment passed and they pitched in to help the injured and pull the dead from the wreckage.

For others that moment stretched into hours and the morning light that showed the horror in all its immensity was reflected from their glazed, still-staring eyes.

IN THE CRAMMED rooms and corridors of Hurley Hospital the injured survivors had harrowing stories to tell.

There was Miss Olga Snitko, 29, of 813 Black, being treated for back injuries. She told how she had been driving alone at Clio and Coldwater in the heart of the Beecher district.

"I noticed a dark cloud," she said. "It seemed to twist. It was coming at me. I slowed down. The thing picked the car right up, twisted it and I think that I must have turned over in the air at least six times. My car was thrown across the road into a cow pasture. It landed on its top.

"Two gentlemen stopped their car and pulled me out. They brought me here to Hurley Hospital."

FRANK STODDARD, 63, started to close the back door in his home at 1189 W. Kurtz. Both sides of the house blew in, injuring Stoddard and his 63-year-old wife. But he stayed and helped pull his injured and dead neighbors out of the wreckage of their homes until friends practically forced him to join Mrs. Stoddard in the hospital.

A weird, desperate ride through the city was a heart-chilling buildup to the final, frantic moment for Mrs. Florence Morrison, 31, of G-5963 Detroit St.

"My brother, Carl Brink, and his wife, Mona, came to my house to take me to the funeral parlor to see my nephew, Donald Brink, Jr., who died Saturday. The funeral was to be Wednesday," she said.

"I saw that black thing coming. Carl said, 'Let's get in

Turn to Page 2, Column 2

A-Bomb Didn't Cause It

Experts Absolve Tests. See Page 39.

Two Pages of Pictures, Pages 10 and 40.

Other Stories and Pictures, Pages 3, 5, 6, 7, 12, 74 and 40.

Two More Marquette Felons Caught

IRON MOUNTAIN—(AP)—Two more of the desperadoes who fled Marquette Prison May 22 were captured Tuesday midnight in the railroad yard at Quinnesec, five miles southeast of here.

Taken without resistance were John McMacklin, 35, and John McDowell, 40.

Only Lloyd Russell, 31, believed to be the ringleader in the break to freedom, remained at large.

State Police took McDowell and McMacklin after receiving a tip they were hiding in the yards. The two felons are believed to be the two men with Charles Morrison when his car plunged off a bridge at Nathan Saturday.

Korea Today

TRUCE negotiators recess full parleys indefinitely until aides work out technicalities. Page 6.

ROKs again retake Luke the Gook's Castle on Eastern Front. Page 2.

Identified Victims Of Storms Listed

The identified dead among Monday's tornado victims in Michigan include, in alphabetical order:

—A—
Patrolman Arnold W. Anschuetz, 37, of 237 Florence, Highland Park, died at Indian Lake.
Mrs. Dorothy Anschuetz, 35, his wife.
Dorn Anschuetz, 6, their son.
Dana Anschuetz, 2, their son.

—B—
Mrs. Virginia Baird, 55, of 3400 Detroit, Flint area.
Muriel Baught, Flint area.
Mrs. Rose Agnes Bean, 44, Coldwater Street, Flint area.
James Ballentine, 30, of 1081 E. Kurtz, Flint area.
Verna Bonneville, 33, of 1075 W. Coldwater, Flint area.
Terry Lee Bolin, 4, of 1509 W. Coldwater, Flint area.
Daniel Boone, 6 months, of 1400 E. Kurtz, Flint area.
Jessie Lee Boone, 3, of 1400 E. Kurtz, Flint area.
Carl Brink, 28, of 1378 E. Kurtz, Flint area.
Carl T. Brook, 1166 W. Kurtz, Flint area.

—C—
Charles E. Clapp, 56, of 4136 E. Coldwater, Flint area.
David Clifford and a 5-year-old son, of 2200 W. Coldwater, Flint area.
Jeanne Bernice Coena, of 1313 E. Grand Blvd., Detroit, died in the Flint area.
Edwin Cooper, of 1175 W. Coldwater, Flint area.

—D—
Dale A. Crawford, 8 months, of 1076 E. Coldwater, Flint area.
Mrs. Rose Agnes Dean, Coldwater and Clio, Flint area.
William B. DeFossat, 70, of 5601 Lewis, Flint area.
Marjorie Deneen, 31, of 1154 E. Kurtz, Flint area.
James Dipsinski, of Spart St., Gaylord, Mich.

You'll Find:

Amusements	29
Astrology	19
Bridge	19
Editorials	8
Financial	22-24
Movies	27
Radio and Television	25-28
Sports	15-18
Weather Map	38
Women's Pages	17-20

NEW! IMPROVED KEYES—the mayonnaise that spreads smoothly when "ice box" cold.—Adv.

WOODWARD 2-8900

Stricken City Digs 112 Bodies From Ruins

Many Still Missing; Damage Is 15 Million

BY JEROME HANSEN, JACK SCHERMERHORN, RALPH NELSON AND KEN McCORMICK
Free Press Staff Writers

FLINT—Fears mounted Tuesday night that the toll in Monday night's tornado in the Flint area would rise to 200 dead, with property damage of 15 million dollars.

State Police Commissioner Joseph A. Childs gave the estimates as weary rescue workers moved steadily ahead digging through the debris and smashed homes in search of more victims.

At nightfall the toll here was 112 dead, 12 of them unidentified. Tornadoes took 10 lives elsewhere in Michigan and killed 18 in Ohio and 69 in Massachusetts.

Long lines of residents of the Beecher District, where the twister struck north of Flint, sought State Police passes to return to the devastated area in search of loved ones and personal property.

Five hundred injured jammed hospitals in Flint, Saginaw and Bay City. Scores of others were treated and sent home with painful injuries to make room for those in serious and critical condition.

Childs could not give a positive estimate of the number still missing in the wreckage. But the long lines of silent men and weeping women gave mute evidence that more were unaccounted for than the 23 first reported.

Turn to Page 14, Column 3

Death Toll Hits 209 in 3 States

A tornado smashed into Worcester, Mass., Tuesday night, leaving at least 69 dead and more than 700 injured. It followed close upon the devastation left by Monday's tornadoes in Southeastern Michigan and Northwestern Ohio. The storms in three states left 190 dead in eight hard-hit communities.

The latest toll showed:

MICHIGAN
Flint: 112 dead; 500 injured.
Erie: four dead.
Tawas City: four dead.
Pleasant Lake, (Washtenaw County): one dead.
Brown City: one dead.

OHIO
Cleveland and Elyria: 10 dead.
Cygnet: eight dead.

MASSACHUSETTS
Worcester: 69 dead; 738 injured.

The storms also caused millions of dollars worth of damage.

Officials classed the death and destruction as the greatest disaster in Michigan history.

The Detroit Free Press

TUESDAY, MARCH 16, 1954 — On Guard for Over a Century — 30 Pages — Vol. 123—No. 315 — Seven Cents

BRISK — Mostly fair, Low, 17-20; high, 34-38. Moderate winds.

METRO FINAL — BLUE STREAK

MARCH 16, 1954:

Northland Center, called the world's biggest shopping mall, prepares to open.

"Northland Center Opens Its Doors Next Monday," column five.

NUMBERS SCANDAL SUSPENDS 13 COPS

French Wilt Under Reds' Mass Attack

Rebels Near Center Of Vital Indo Fort

HANOI, Indochina—(AP)—French headquarters announced Monday night that thousands of screaming Communist-led Vietminh troops smashed through the northern defenses of Dien Bien Phu fortress at one point and were advancing toward the heart of the base.

The French said they killed 1,500 attackers before they gave up the northern defense hill position of the dustbowl fortress. The biggest and most decisive battle of the Indochina war is

now being fought. Thousands of Vietminh are pressing steadily closer to the heart of the bastion intended to stop the southward march of rebel armies.

THE FRENCH threw fresh tanks and planes into the battle. They bolstered their stronghold, 175 miles west of Hanoi, with a battalion of paratroopers.

They also sent planes almost 200 miles from the carrier Arromanches to bomb and strafe Vietminh artillery positions.

This marks the first time in the war that the Vietminh have dropped guerilla and infiltration tactics for an all-out frontal assault. The attack, with blowing bugles and shouting soldiers, was a copy of those launched on the United Nations allies in Korea.

Hint Crofutt Got $250,000 in Deals

Youngblood Links Profits To Juggled Auctions, Fakery

The late Mrs. Freda Crofutt, whose chancery court accounts showed a $58,000 shortage may have made upward of $250,000 on other questionable transactions, it was disclosed Monday.

Councilman Charles N. Youngblood, chairman of a Board of Supervisors committee investigating the shortages, said Mrs. Crofutt may have profited by juggling auction sales, selling fake chattel mortgages and forging guarantors' names on personal notes.

Youngblood said he learned from three reliable sources that Mrs. Crofutt, who died last Sept. 30, was retained during the depression by prospective bidders interested in acquiring major buildings to be auctioned under mortgage foreclosures.

BY POSTPONING the sales frequently, Youngblood confused other prospective bidders on the sales dates and left his clients free to buy the properties, Youngblood said he was told.

Mrs. Crofutt's profits from these deals were estimated at $100,000 to $150,000. Youngblood said.

Youngblood added that Mrs. Crofutt may have netted more

Turn to Page 2, Column 1

$600 GAME

Police Slowed Down By Fast Couple

When George Morris, 47, saw a man and a woman holding up Paul Matte, 44, in his grocery downstairs at 4497 Grand River Monday night, he rushed upstairs to call the law.

They were there in a jiffy, in time to catch slacks-clad Mrs. Marilyn Doogan, 22, of 3741 Third, where her husband was nor had been seen him in hours.

They waited. Parsons finally showed up.

"Where is the money and the gun?" the policemen asked. Parsons was only too willing to tell.

Mrs. Parsons had left and the gun and money with her. She had seen her husband, and she had slipped out the back door.

Parsons was held.

555 VOLUNTEER

Sports Day Donors Break Blood Record

Income-tax headquarters was not the only place that was jammed Monday.

Sports Day at the Blood Bank broke its own record as 555 sports fans and sports personalities volunteered. Of these, 513 were accepted.

Last year the Free Press originated the program in which the sports world donates vitally needed blood to war veterans still in hospitals.

At that time 455 registered, donating 382 pints of blood which was a one-day record for the Red Cross Blood Bank.

(Details on Page 23.)

IN THE CLEAR

Last-Minute Taxpayers Jam Offices

Hundreds of last-minute taxpayers jammed six Detroit offices of the Internal Revenue Service until the stroke of the midnight deadline Monday.

At the Federal Building, a stream of cars circled, double-parked, or inched in to the curb bringing new customers.

INTERNAL REVENUE experts—who started their day at 8 a.m.—said they would take care of anyone who got in line by midnight. They admitted they would not be through work until nearly dawn.

At the Federal Building officials expected 4,500 returns—a near-record single day total. Last year, only 3,282 persons filed at the downtown office on the final day.

State Faces Deficit of $6,500,000

Pay Hike for 23,000 Employees Blamed

BY HUB M. GEORGE
Free Press Political Writer

LANSING — Legislative fiscal planners Monday night faced up to the prospect that Michigan will operate about 6½ million dollars in the red in the next fiscal year.

The return of red ink, as soon after adoption of the 35-million-dollar business receipts tax and heroic efforts to wipe out a previous deficit, has disturbed Lansing.

It was brought about by the vote Saturday increasing pay for more than 23,000 Civil Service employes. The total hike will be more than 6 million dollars a year.

GOV. WILLIAMS in his mid-January budget message anticipated that after appropriations of $365,541,099 were voted, there still would be a million dollar nest egg in the Treasury.

Lawmakers have tried to trim Williams' total about 10 million, but such bills as have appeared record little progress in that direction.

The Civil Service action caught the appropriating committees by surprise.

The only remaining possibilities for budget trimming are in the capital outlay items.

SENATE BILLS Monday night set up a $11,695,350 General Fund outlay for capital improvements and $8,529,029 to be spent from the residue of the 54-million-dollar bond issue.

Wayne's hope that provision would be made for a children's mental hospital and adjunct clinic in connection with Northville State Hospital, was omitted.

While final decision still must be made the Senate Finance Committee set up $100,080 for preliminary planning for the proposed new prison.

It indicated a preference for a 1,200-inmate unit as suggested by the Corrections Commission. The wardens voiced a preference for the first of two 600-inmate institutions at a recent House hearing.

The House is ready to act Tuesday on a $118,857,252 school aid appropriation as mandated by the Constitution and also on a grant of $44,457,825 for welfare agencies.

Dig This Case

BLACKWELL, Okla.—(AP)—Sheriff's officers dug up $200 worth of beer, one can at a time, after two suspects admitted stealing the beer and burying each can individually along a river bank.

Ike Blasts Democrat Tax Plans

Calls Bid for Cuts Political, Unfair

WASHINGTON—(AP)—President Eisenhower blasted the Democrats' cut-the-income-tax proposals Monday night as unsound, politically motivated and unfair to the great majority of taxpayers.

Declaring such cuts would be "a serious blow to your Government," the President told a nationwide radio and television audience:

"In your interest I must and will oppose such an unsound tax proposal."

Speaking informally, Mr. Eisenhower appealed for support of his own tax program, which includes what he called a "modest" reduction in the tax on income from corporation stock.

HE CENTERED his fire on Democratic moves, beginning with a bill that comes up in the House Wednesday, to raise income tax exemptions.

House Democrats want an increase from $600 to $700. There is a movement among Senate Democrats to make even more of a taxpayer's income tax-free. The Democrats' reply to Mr. Eisenhower will be made Tuesday night by Rep. Rayburn, of Texas, Democratic House leader.

Rayburn said the Democratic National Committee has arranged for 15 minutes of free television time at 9 p.m. (EST) Tuesday and had asked him to present the minority party's views.

IN NEW YORK, ABC and NBC said they would carry Rayburn's speech by recording of their radio networks at 10:15 p.m. (EST) Tuesday. The two networks said no plans for TV coverage has been made yet.

The President reproached the "professionally faint-hearted" for spreading depression talk.

Mr. Eisenhower declared, "the nation as a whole continues to be prosperous" despite unemployment in some places, and conditions "at this time do not call for an emergency program that would suggest larger Federal deficits and further inflation through large additional tax reductions."

Surprising even some of his own staff members, the President made no criticism of last week's action by the House in cutting excise taxes by some 900 million dollars. He had opposed this cut and Administration leaders have voiced hope the Senate would try to reduce it.

Mr. Eisenhower said he's as strong for cutting taxes "as the

Turn to Page 2, Column 5

Birds See Light —And Can't Sleep

FORT WORTH, Tex.—(AP)—Her pigeons have insomnia, a housewife complained to police. She explained it this way:

"A floodlight burns all night in a neighbor's backyard. It keeps the pigeons awake. They just can't close their eyes because for them there is no night.

"The birds get so sleepy they often tumble off roosts. Several pigeons have been seriously injured.

You'll Find:

Interesting, informative stories and comments by some of America's top columnists—Drew Pearson and Foreign Report—Page 11.

Amusements 10
Astrology 14
Bridge 14
Editorials 10
Financial 17-19
Movies 10
Radio and Television ... 16
Sports 21-24
Weather Map 8
Women's Pages 13-15

TO HAVE THE FREE PRESS DELIVERED TO YOUR HOME PHONE WO 2-8900

DOOR TO Hudson's in Northland shopping center is unlocked by James B. Webber III, 5, using key of original J. L. Hudson store opened in 1881. Dad, James B. Webber, Jr., Hudson's vice president and general manager, watches.

Northland Center Opens Its Doors Next Monday

BY GEOFFREY HOWES
Free Press Staff Writer

The huge Northland shopping center, occupying 160 acres in the triangle of Eight Mile, Northwestern and Greenfield, will be opened to the public next Monday.

The opening will climax nearly four years of planning and building by the J. L. Hudson Co.

Every door is a "front" door. All freight is delivered underground, with trucks unloading at docks under each store.

There will be package pickup service for shoppers at Hudson's Northland and Kroger's market in the center. They can make a purchase, leave it with the clerk, and find it waiting at a station on the way drive out.

Covered walkways will enable shoppers to stay out of the weather once they have left their cars and reached the buildings.

TOGETHER THEY will provide merchandise and services ranging from clothing to food, furnishings, appliances, drugs, dry cleaning, banking, barbering and many others.

By the end of the year, Northland officials expect 20 more stores will locate in the center. Shoppers will have no trouble getting into Northland. The parking lots are arranged in a ring around the buildings, and there are nine access roads from Eight Mile, Greenfield and Northwestern.

THREE DSR lines terminate at Northland's sheltered bus stops, the Conant, Hamilton and Greenfield lines, and there will be two Greyhound suburban shuttle services to the center. Convenience and beauty are keynotes at Northland. Raised sidewalks link the parking lots and the stores. The buildings are grouped around courts and malls with terraced gardens, sculpture and other art work.

It is only a few steps from one store or building to another.

THE CENTER, said to be within a 15-to-20-minute drive for a half-million people, is so large that the Detroit Edison Co. has built a substation there to provide electric service.

It is capable of supplying the equivalent electrical needs of 25,000 homes.

Northland was inspected by press, radio and television representatives Monday after a brief ceremony in which five-year-old James B. Webber III, son of James B. Webber, Jr., vice president and general manager of Hudson's unlocked the door.

The key and lock were from the original J. L. Hudson store opened in Detroit in 1881.

Gambling Raids Bring Fast Action

13th Precinct Mess Bared by Leonard

Thirteen policemen were suspended Monday night by Police Commissioner Donald S. Leonard in what Leonard called "irregularities" involving a mutuel bet ring operation in the 13th Precinct (Woodward Station).

The suspension followed quickly a raid at 945 St. Josafats Ct. This address was raided with a search warrant. At the same time there were raids at 1803 E. Kirby and 5420 Riopelle.

LEONARD SAID the raids and suspension of the policemen were linked together.

"Certain irregularities" concerning operation of the policemen involved in the numbers operation in the precinct came to light during an investigation of gambling in the area, Leonard said.

Those suspended, all patrolmen, were: Matthew Barnes, Chester Ochenski and Paul Schlang of the vice bureau; and Edward Couse, Francis V Fraser, William Fuller, Gordon Henderson, William Hogg, William Jones, Walter Ludwig, Elmer Maglia, Joseph Walker and James Lemmon, of Woodward Station.

EQUIPMENT AND badges were taken from the policemen at the questioning in the police academy.

Lawrence said "further developments" could be expected, but hinted there would be no further suspensions.

Leonard declined to elaborate on the case, other than to emphasize that the policemen were linked to gambling operations being the cause of a careful investigation of the spots hit on the raid, particularly 945 St. Josafats Ct.

ARRESTED AT the St. Josafats Ct. address was Edwin Stephen, who was grilled by police before the 13 policemen, including three members of the vice bureau, were brought to headquarters.

Police had the 13 policemen under surveillance and quickly called them to headquarters. The policemen were questioned by Supt. Edwin Morgan, Deputy Supt. Kennedy Lawrence and Inspector Walter Wyrod.

Leonard said the policemen were suspended on the spot and are off the force until they face a police trial board.

The connection of the policemen with the gambling ring appeared to be shaping up into one of the major scandals of the police department in recent years.

WOMAN HOLDS CAR, SAVES BOY

A Mighty Mite at 86 Pounds

Police credited an 86-pound Grosse Pointe housewife Monday with saving a boy's life by wrestling a runaway car to a stop.

Bobby Emerson, 11, of 765 Washington, Grosse Pointe, was bruised and scared, but apparently not seriously hurt. He was held for observation at Cottage Hospital.

Mrs. Gloria Fair, 35, of 768 Washington, the heroine, said she wasn't sure she deserved all the praise.

"I don't believe I'm big enough to stop that car," she said.

The 5-foot 2-inch mother of two boys, Jeffrey, 11, and William, 6, is the wife of a naval commander on duty in the Atlantic. She teaches a Sunday School class of 20 at Christ Church, Grosse Pointe.

THE AUTO belonged to Mrs. Fair's mother, Mrs. W. J. Watkins, of 1182 Buckingham, Grosse Pointe Park. Mrs. Watkins parked it in the Fair driveway when she arrived for a visit.

At 5 p.m., Mrs. Fair said a neighbor boy came to her door and told her the car was rolling slowly down the driveway toward the street. She ran out to stop it.

The Emerson youngster, another neighbor, tried to help but slipped under the right rear wheel.

"I got the door on the driver's side open," said Mrs. Fair, "and I pushed as hard as I could. The car stopped, and then I was afraid to let go for fear it would roll over Bobby some more."

MRS. WATKINS ran out when Mrs. Fair screamed, got in and moved the car away from the youngster.

The woman said Bobby was not breathing.

"He was curled up in a grotesque position, all blue," said Mrs. Fair.

An unidentified man rushed up and gave the youngster artificial respiration until he gasped for air. By the time Grosse Pointe Patrolmen Jim Derseott and Robert Van Then reached the scene, he was breathing normally.

"The man was surely Heaven-sent." Mrs. Fair said. "He seemed to materialize from nowhere when I screamed. After bringing Bobby around, he walked away unnoticed."

"He was a real hero," she added. "He never said a word while working, but he was a wonderful man."

At the hospital, cursory examination showed no broken bones, only bruises.

APRIL 4, 1954:

Details of Pvt. Slovik's execution remained quiet for nine years.

"How U.S. Executed City GI as Coward," column one.

'Mamie's Life with Ike' *Read This Detroit Free Press Exclusive Starting Today on Page One, Section C*

The Detroit Free Press
SUNDAY, APRIL 4, 1954 — On Guard for Over a Century — Established in 1831 — 130 Pages — Vol. 123—No. 331 — Twenty Cents

14 ABOVE — Partly cloudy and cold. Low, 14-18; high, 31-38. West winds.

METRO FINAL — Knight Sizes Up Indochina Peril — See Page 1, Sect. B

How U.S. Executed City GI as Coward

Eddie Slovik Died a Hard Death

The Story Of Slovik, First Man To Be Shot As Deserter Since 1864

BY LOUIS COOK
Free Press Staff Writer

A Detroit GI of World War II is the only American soldier to be shot as a coward since 1864.

The firing squad was not very good. No American soldier had been ordered to shoot another in 80 years. Perhaps none ever will be again.

There were 12 infantrymen on the execution detail that killed Eddie Slovik for deserting to avoid combat duty.

One carried the traditional blank cartridge in the chamber of his M-1 rifle.

Shaking, they tried to hit Eddie's heart at 20 paces. None could. Eddie died hard, as he had lived.

• • •

MOST OF EDDIE'S 24 years were spent scrounging the streets of Detroit and Hamtramck for a living.

His grade-school education was rounded out with two terms at Ionia Reformatory, and with lots of Army KP and latrine detail.

The only official record of four United States wars executed quite a while ago — on the bitter-cold morning of Jan. 31, 1945, at St. Marie aux Mines, Belgium.

Very few people ever knew what happened to Eddie. The Army didn't make any great secret of his death. Dozens of witnesses saw him fight the straps after 11 clumsy bullets ripped him.

It was just that nobody asked. The number of people who cared whether Eddie came back from World War II was very small.

For years only one Detroiter knew what happened.

That was Eddie's wife, Antoinette, who lives at 5038 Kendall, Dearborn.

And she tried to forget. She nearly succeeded, except for the nightmares that came at night after the house quieted, and still come.

• • •

BUT THERE WAS A curious one. He is William Bradford Huie, an author who likes to sift the ashes of history.

Huie has written a book about Eddie. It will be published April 22 and on April 20 Look Magazine will run a condensation of the book which contains much exclusive material. This is the factual story as it shapes up from sources in the Pentagon and in and around Detroit.

The person who knows most about Eddie's early life is his older brother, Ray.

Ray now is married to Antoinette, his brother's widow, and is a considerably more gentle person than he used to be. Like Eddie, Ray was constantly in trouble but is trying hard to live it down.

Eddie was born Feb. 18, 1920, on Edwin street in Hamtramck. His father is dead. His mother, Anna, lives at 20101 Stoepel. Besides Ray there are three sisters.

"Eddie was the quiet one," Ray remembers. "I was the noisy one in the family. Eddie couldn't get into trouble by himself but he had plenty of guys to show him how.

"He could scrap, although he didn't much care for it. We used to put on the gloves a lot. Once he blacked my eye.

"We had a hell of a rough time as kids. We both peddled papers and ran the streets.

"Eddie was born with bad legs. When he was 8, the doctors cut them up and broke them so they would be straight. They always ached him.

"Loud noises hurt his head and he used to hold his head over some of his ears all the time."

• • •

Eddie's police record started when he was 12. There was a series of petty thefts and minor break-ins, always with other lads.

• • •

EDDIE WAS ALWAYS the one who was collared by the cop when the gang was surprised in mischief.

He was caught swiping a pack of cigarets in a drugstore in 1937. By the time the police got through with him he had drawn six months in Ionia for grand larceny and was sent to Ionia Reformatory.

Eddie was in Ionia for nearly a year. During that time he never received a visit from anybody in The Free World, as reformatory inmates call it.

Eddie lasted four months after he was paroled. The gang took a car and wrecked it.

Eddie escaped from the scene of the wreck, but trustingly turned himself in to the police that night.

He got 1 to 5 years for auto theft and 2½ to 7½ years as a habitual criminal. He served more than three years before being paroled again.

The world had been at war nearly three years when Eddie returned to Detroit and went to work in a Dearborn plumbing shop.

Eddie was so wrapped up in his own problems he scarcely knew there was a war.

Turn to Page 14, Column 1

Jobs Up 5,000 In City
But Jobless Rise Outstate

BY ED WINGE
Free Press Staff Writer

Unemployment in Detroit dropped 5,000 in the month ended March 15, after eight months of increasing joblessness.

But unemployment outstate continued to rise, the Michigan Employment Security Commission reported Saturday. Despite Detroit's gain, 7,000 were added to the jobless toll outstate.

MAX M. HORTON, MESC director, pegged unemployment in Detroit as of March 15 at 135,000, or 9 per cent of the total labor force.

Statewide, there were 216,000 out of work, or 7.8 per cent of the labor force, he added.

Horton predicted a net increase of 55,000 jobs in Michigan by July 1, and said half of them would be filled by May 15. But only 2,000 of the jobs will be in manufacturing according to employer estimates, he said.

During the last six months about 45,000 former workers have returned to their home states, Horton estimated.

In a short-range forecast Horton predicted:

"A careful weighing of all factors involved points to a moderate improvement in the labor market situation during the second quarter of 1954."

• • •

"ALTHOUGH the employment downturn has lost most of its momentum, no significant progress has been made toward the re-establishment of 182,000 jobs which have evaporated since the all-time peak was reached in June, 1953," Horton added.

Recent job losses have pushed Michigan's nonfarm employment back to the August, 1950 levels despite a growth of 130,000 in the nonfarm work forces since then, Horton said.

On the hopeful side, the MESC director noted a 4,200 drop in the average weekly volume of new claims filed for jobless benefits.

He called this "an important measure of new unemployment."

The MESC's March 15 figures showed that Port Huron, with 11.6 per cent of its labor force out of work, had the highest level of unemployment in Michigan.

"Unemployment in Muskegon and in the Upper Peninsula amounted to 11.2 per cent, followed by Battle Creek, 10.9; Bay City, 9.6, and Benton Harbor, 9 per cent.

• • •

IN THE MESC Labor Market News Letter, Horton stated that in the last eight months "Michigan's manufacturing industries have received one of the most serious employment setbacks since the end of World War II."

Successive cutbacks have trimmed factory employment by 188,000 or 12 per cent, since June, 1953, the Letter said.

"By mid-February of 1954 virtually all gains registered since the start of the Korean conflict were erased," Horton said.

Tax Law Brings Wedding Rush

LONDON — (AP) — Britain's annual rush to wed reached top gear Saturday.

Churches and registry offices across the country reported business was about three times normal. Couples queued up to take vows from 8 a.m. onward.

Spring you might think? Not a bit of it. The British tax year ends Monday, and Saturday's bridegrooms got up to £112 refund from the tax man.

Good Reading on the Inside:

Ike and Nixon Praise Ferguson	Page Three
11 Suburbs Hold Elections	Page 10
Travel and Resorts	Pages 12-13
Drew Pearson, Inez Robb, Fred Neal	Page 15
SECTION B—MAGAZINE, TV PREVUE	
Real Estate and Building	Pages 7-11
Gardening	Page 12
The Story of Senator McCarthy	Page 12
SECTION C—FOR AND ABOUT WOMEN	
Beginning the Story of Mamie Eisenhower	Page One
New Fad, the Squaw Dress	Page 14
SECTION D—SPORTS	
Stage, Screen, Music	Pages 5-6
Autos, Business, Stock Prices	Pages 7-9
Want Ads	Pages 10-16

ALSO PARADE MAGAZINE, ROTO, MOST AND BEST COMICS

Missing Socialite Is Safe
Detroit Girl Phones From Milan, Italy

Donna Di Marco

A Bloomfield Hills socialite was reported safe Saturday night after a four-day search in rugged mountain areas in Italy and Germany.

The search ended when Donna Di Marco, 27, telephoned her parents that she was safe in Milan, Italy, with her companion, Monique Le Berge, 20, of Sudbury, Ont.

Donna is the daughter of Mr. and Mrs. Rocco Di Marco, of Dunston Road, Bloomfield Hills. Miss Le Berge is the daughter of Mr. and Mrs. Joseph Alfred La Berge.

• • •

PARENTS OF both young women are in Florence, Italy, where they went some weeks ago. Donna and Monique were studying interior decoration there.

The young women phoned their parents Saturday night that they were safe in Milan and had not gone to Heidelberg, Germany, the destination they had set out for Tuesday in Miss Di Marco's new Italian-made Fiat station wagon.

No word had been heard from the missing young women from their departure until the phone call.

• • •

ITALIAN police had expressed concern for the safety of the two young women because their proposed route from Milan to Heidelberg passes through rugged country with which Miss Di Marco was unfamiliar.

The families of the girls are scheduled to sail for home Tuesday from Genoa.

2 Guilty Of Evading Taxes
Auto Dealers Hid $276,000

A Federal Court jury Saturday found the president and vice president of R. and R. Chevrolet, Inc., guilty on nine counts of income-tax evasion totalling $276,000.

The verdict against Louis T. Bohn, president, and Robert T. Bolo, vice president of the firm, was returned after more than 11 hours of deliberation by a jury of four men and eight women.

JUDGE Theodore Levin continued the defendants' $50,000 bond and referred the case to probation officers. No sentencing date was set.

Maximum penalty on each count is five years in prison and a $10,000 fine.

Three separate indictments containing nine nine counts were returned by a Federal Grand Jury in December, 1952.

It charged Bohn, 58, and Bolo, with evading $276,000 in corporate and personal income taxes during the years 1946-47-48.

CHIEF ASSISTANT United States District Attorney Joseph Moynihan, Jr., said the two men evaded taxes by manipulating car-sale records.

A number of used-car dealers testified that they were able to buy automobiles from the firm only by making under-the-table cash payments in addition to paying by check the sum listed on invoices.

Bohn lives at 731 Berkshire, Grosse Pointe, and Bolo at 81 Kercheval, Grosse Pointe Shores.

Governor Goofed---and That's That

Gov. Williams' big, black Cadillac got in trouble with the Detroit Police Department Saturday.

The car was found in a no-parking zone on Putnam, outside the Maccabees Building, where the Governor was appearing on a television show.

A motorcycle patrolman wrote out a ticket and attached it to the windshield wiper, disregarding a sign on the car visor reading: "Official Business—State Police."

THE TICKET won't require the Governor or his driver to fork over a parking fine.

It said simply:

"You are improperly parked regardless of your State Police status."

U.S. Tax Boss Forgets Own

RICHMOND, Va. — (AP) — A. Coleman Andrews, a Richmond native and all a legal resident of the city, files his state income tax return on the basis of a fiscal year ending Sept. 30.

This gives him until Jan. 15 to file, under Virginia law. In the greater rush of handling Federal tax collections, Andrews said he left his personal filing chores in Virginia to a bookkeeper, who forgot the Jan. 15 deadline.

Secret Talk Due On H-Bomb Curb

Reds Receptive To UN Parley
Disarmament Body May Meet This Week on Western Bid

UNITED NATIONS, N.Y. — (UP) — The United States, Britain and France asked the United Nations Saturday to set up secret negotiations to bring a halt to the hydrogen bomb race between the United States and Russia.

The three nations asked the United Nations Disarmament Commission to get the secret talks under way quickly.

Dr. Tingfu F. Tsiang, of Nationalist China, chairman of the commission, said the group probably would assemble by the middle of the week.

Such a meeting will get UN disarmament talks going again for the first time in two years.

THE MOVE BY the big Western powers came as the world grew increasingly apprehensive over the almost unbelievable power of the Hydrogen bomb as disclosed by United States tests in the Pacific.

The proposal was made a bare 48 hours before Britain's Prime Minister Winston Churchill must go before Parliament to face a full-dress inquiry on the H-bomb.

It followed the Labor Party demands for a Big Three meeting with Russia on disarmament. British UN delegate Sir Pierson Dixon told Soviet Delegate Andrei Y. Vishinsky of the atomic proposal Saturday morning, and it was understood he welcomed the move.

THE ACTION was taken in line with a General Assembly resolution passed last November calling for secret talks by the big atomic powers (probably the United States, Russia, Britain, France and Canada).

The unheralded request for a meeting was sent to Tsiang in three identical notes signed by American Ambassador Henry Cabot Lodge, Jr., French Delegate Henri Hoppenot and Dixon. The Assembly resolution had suggested that the Disarmament Commission set up a subcommittee of the major atomic powers.

Turn to Page 2, Column 5

Indo Reds Beaten Off By French
Defenders' Hopes Of Victory Rise

HANOI, Indochina — (UP) — Red-bereted French paratroopers jumped into the flaming battle of Dien Bien Phu Saturday.

Hopes of victory for the stand-or-die defenders rose. The tough airborne troopers went parachuting into the battle in answer to a call for help from beleaguered Col. Christian de Castries, whose grimy forces have not given an inch to human-sea Red assaults.

A terse communique from French high command headquarters said that parachute reinforcements were dropped to the besieged fortress.

THE COMMUNIQUE said De Castries' men also fought their way out of the defense perimeter and picked up some of the supplies dropped by transports near Red positions.

A French military spokesman refused to indicate how many men were dropped into the dust bowl of Dien Bien Phu.

Chances for a French victory rose after the defenders held the isolated fortress despite a ceaseless 24-hour attack.

However, a grave new threat to the French position in Indochina was posed by a rebel army knifing south into the unprotected kingdom of Cambodia, one of the three Indochinese states.

For 24 hours the Red ground forces have hurled waves of attacks against Dien Bien Phu while artillery pounded French positions.

French cooks, switchboard operators, orderlies and staff officers grabbed rifles and grenades and went into the trenches to hold off the Reds.

The weary defenders passed

Turn to Page 2, Column 1

German Band Flees to West

BERLIN — (AP) — An 18-man East German jazz orchestra, ordered disbanded by Communist authorities for playing American music, fled into West Berlin Saturday with its instruments and girl vocalist.

The band made its way to freedom from Chemnitz, 110 miles southwest of here.

Karl Walter, the leader, said he had been banned from music for life. The other musicians were told they could play in other bands but not as a unit.

To avoid suspicion, the group split up for the escape to the west. They left most of their possessions behind.

Seeing Red

FORT WORTH, Tex. — (UP) — Detective Grady Haire is working on an important—to him—theft case. His own pay check disappeared from police headquarters.

---

14 A RECORD LOW

Cold Snap to End Monday, Says Bureau

Sunday will be cold, according to the Weather Bureau, but warmer weather is in sight for Monday.

Saturday's low of 14 set a record for April 3, the previous low being 16 on that date in 1879.

The Weather Bureau predicted a Sunday morning low of 14 to 18 and a high of 34 to 38. The low Sunday night is expected to be around 20 degrees.

SUNDAY WILL be partly cloudy with south to southeast winds 10 to 17 miles an hour.

The giant air mass described as the last polar outcrop of the season produced frigid temperatures throughout the state. Cadillac was the coldest spot with an eight-below reading. It was three above at Kinross, in the Upper Peninsula.

Who'll Teach?

LAUSANNE, Switzerland — (AP) —Tenzing Norkay, the Sherpa guide, who climbed Mt. Everest, the world's highest mountain last summer, is coming to Switzerland soon to take a three-week course in mountain climbing.

Taps

NEWARK, N.J. — (AP) — Early Character was accused Saturday of clouting a neighbor over the head with a baseball bat at 3:45 a.m. to climax an argument.

Plane Cash Fatal to 26

ISTANBUL, Turkey — (AP) — A Turkish State Airways plane exploded in the air near Adana Saturday, killing 26 persons aboard.

The accident occurred shortly after the plane had taken off from Adana for Istanbul.

Reports here said that among the passengers—all Turkish— were Prof. Remzi Oguzarik, leader of the Peasants' Party, and Istanbul Deputy Salamon Adatto. The crew numbered five — including two stewardesses.

Next!

ROCHESTER, Vt. — (AP) — Grandma Huntington, 85, a farmer, is clicking her scissors again on a part-time basis after being laid up for three months by a broken arm.

The Detroit Free Press

MONDAY, MARCH 21, 1955 — METRO FINAL — BLUE STREAK

MARCH 21, 1955:

WINGS WIN ALL, 6-0

Once upon a time, the Red Wings were the greatest team in hockey.

It's 7th Title in Row; Lindsay Gets 3

Wind Drops Tent On 400 Watching Circus in Texas

UVALDE, Tex.—A sudden windstorm Sunday brought a rain-soaked circus tent down on the heads of about 400 spectators, most of them children.

No one was seriously hurt but many suffered scratches and bruises.

The gusty wind, spawned by one of many thunderstorms in the Southwest, struck shortly after the spectators settled into their seats.

If it had hit moments earlier when the Hagen Bros. Circus animals paraded around the ring, or moments later when the lion and tiger act was scheduled, dangerous animals might have been freed among the fleeing spectators.

Police Officer George O'Neall said there was little panic as the big tent began flapping loose, jerking its inside supporting poles up and down among the spectators and performers.

"When the people got outside and started wondering where their children were," said O'Neall, "that's when the panic hit."

Some mothers screamed, and children separated from their parents ran about crying.

"I MIGHT HAVE been scared if I had had time," said J. W. Stewart, Uvalde grocer who brought his two sons, Ronnie, 4, and Jimmie, 12, to the circus along with two girls, Deborah, 5, and Gail, 4, daughters of a friend, Robert Hicks.

"I told Jimmy to get Ronnie," Stewart related. "Then I picked up Deborah and Gail, one under each arm. Just after we got down from the bleachers, they ... flapped. Something

Turn to Page 2, Column 6

Two Gunmen Rob Druggist of $600

Two middle-aged gunmen tied two employes with clothesline and escaped with more than $600 from a drugstore at 19184 Grand River Sunday.

Michael Gleason, 47, druggist, said the men forced him to open a safe and two cash registers. Gleason and Miss Dolores Berger, 17, a clerk, were then ordered into a back room and bound.

BULLETIN
Airliner Crashes; 38 Aboard

Detroiter Aboard Newark-Tulsa Plane

SPRINGFIELD, Mo.—(U.P.)—An airplane identified as an American Airlines Convair crashed in an open farm field about eight miles west of Springfield late Sunday night and at least six persons were killed.

Kay J. Grankowski, of 13130 Syracuse, boarded the plane at Detroit bound for Springfield.

He was the only passenger to board the plane at Detroit.

Bib Tubert, a radio newsman who rushed to the scene, said he counted six bodies "and at least 10 others were injured."

Tubert said the plane burned after it crashed, "but she fire is all out and none of the bodies I saw were burned badly."

Ambulances rushed to the scene were moving the injured to Springfield hospitals, Tubert said.

A steady day-long rain hampered rescue efforts and ambulances were bogged down a half-mile from the crash scene, Tubert said.

THE PLANE was reported to be American Airlines Flight 711, which originated at Newark, N. J., and was en route to Tulsa, Okla.

Scheduled intermediate stops included Syracuse and Rochester, N. Y., Detroit, Chicago, St. Louis, Springfield and Joplin, Mo. The flight left Willow Run Airport at 6 p.m. Sunday.

Bonanza Asks—

Have you entered my big Cinerama Holiday Trip contest yet? Remember, every day I'll give you a question, the answer to which must be included on your entry in my crossword puzzle contest each Sunday.

My question for Monday is: According to the Dripples the season's over for topcoats but it isn't over for _____

Turn to the comics on page 42 and see what Dotty Dripple says in seven letters.

MONDAY'S ANSWER

Keep this as a reminder so you can write your answer in the space provided on your Sunday crossword puzzle, and you may win not only $700, but a fabulous $2,000 all-expense paid Cinerama Holiday vacation in Switzerland for two, plus $130 spending money!

LINDSAY SCORES! Red Wing Capt. Ted Lindsay (center) blasts the puck past Montreal Goalie Jacques Plante to get his three-goal scoring spree under way. No. 14 is Red Wing Dutch Reibel.

WHAT OUR RELIGION MEANS TO US AS A FAMILY
Life Centers on the Bible

"Our religion to us as a family means that our Christian-centered family life must be a Bible-centered life," Mr. and Mrs. Cornell A. Harrison, 13129 Borgman, Huntington Woods, agree.

Mr. Harrison is vice president of the Perring & McGowan Coal Co., 6821 Second Blvd.

Mr. and Mrs. Harrison and the four children make First Baptist Church, No. 27 Woodward at of a Pingree, Detroit, Series their church home. Mr. Harrison has been superintendent of the Sunday School for the last five years, and is a member of the board of managers of the Baptist Children's Home.

He describes Mrs. Harrison as a "home preacher extraordinary." The children are Carol Ann, 12; Janet, 9; Nancy, 3, and Barbara, 2.

Mr. Harrison elaborated on the Christian-centered family life as a Bible-centered life.

HE SAID: "As Baptists we are teaching our daughters that it is their duty to understand what the Bible says and what it means.

"We don't feel that we have the right of private interpretation even though it differs from that of other Christians (II Peter 1:20). A question we ask as we read and study the Bible as a family unit is 'Just what is God trying to tell us in this verse or chapter?'

"Too often, even among professing Christians, people are too ashamed or hesitant to sit down to an intelligent discussion of spiritual matters simply because of a lack of Bible study.

"To help remedy this we individually may employ various methods such as group study sessions, topical study, regular attendance at a church Sunday School and in other ways.

"The power of the Bible is derived from the knowledge that God inspired its writers who were speaking for God as they were moved by the Holy Spirit (II Peter, 1:21).

"The spiritual food so essential for Christian living can only be found in the Word of God. It is when we fail to take these daily spiritual calories that our spiritual virility is subdued.

"WE ARE TOLD in 1st Peter, 2:2 to 'desire the sincere milk of the Word, that ye may grow thereby.' When we pause to reflect that the more than 40 writers of the Bible were God-chosen and God-directed men from all walks of life, such as musicians, statesmen, fishermen, soldiers, poets and others, the full impact of its purpose and universality seems very simple.

"And that is 'that ye might believe that Jesus is the Christ, the Son of God; and that, believing, ye might have life through His name.'

"What John says (John 20:15 about His purpose can be said of the entire Bible, the reason why God gave us the Book."

Mr. Harrison went on to say that, "the life of any family can be enriched beyond the fondest expectation of its members when the family unit accepts the Bible as its authoritative revelation from God (II Tim. 3:16).

"We accept the Bible as the final voice on all matters of a moral nature. Its wisdom for life as an infallible as a guide of life or standard of truth, and its adoption for cultivation of faith is complete."

—Adrian Fuller
Free Press Religion Writer

THE children's hour in the home of the Cornell A. Harrison family, 13129 Borgman, Huntington Woods, is featured in Bible reading. Shown above left to right is Mrs. Harrison holding Barbara, Mr. Harrison, Carol Ann (sitting) and Nancy with Carol Ann (standing). Family belongs to First Baptist Church, Detroit.

66 on Airliner Escape Injury In Nose-Over

CHICAGO—(AP)—A four-engine American Airlines plane with 66 aboard crash-landed at Chicago Midway Airport Sunday and came to rest with its tail almost straight up.

The 60 passengers, including singer Connie Boswell, were shaken up but not injured seriously. Besides the regular crew of five and the 60 passengers, another company employe was aboard.

THE DC-7 airliner was en route from Los Angeles to New York. One of the engines failed east of Chicago and the pilot, Capt. R. A. Patterson, of Los Angeles, turned back for an emergency landing.

Miss Boswell, crippled from polio, sang: "We Came In on a Wing and a Prayer," from a song popular during World War II.

An airline spokesman said the nose wheel buckled as the plane was landing. Patterson had feathered the No. 4 engine because of minor mechanical trouble.

Oust Hoover Unit, Ruralites Demand

WASHINGTON (AP)—An organization of rural power consumers called on Congress Sunday to abolish the Hoover Commission on grounds that former President Herbert Hoover is using it to serve "the vested interests."

The National Rural Electric Co-operative Association angrily accused the 12-man Commission on Reorganization of the Executive Branch of joining with "the power lobby" and "Wall Street bankers" to try to destroy the Government program to bring electric power to farms.

Pakistan Seizes Ring of Assassins

KARACHI—(AP)—Sind Provincial Minister Ali Mohammed Rashidi said Sunday his Government has uncovered a plot to assassinate him and his colleagues.

He said six leading members of the Provincial Assembly were arrested and warrants issued for eight more.

Vezina Goes To Sawchuk

Penalties Hurt Montreal In Disastrous 2nd Period

BY MARSHALL DANN
Free Press Sports Writer

Ted Lindsay refused to miss the "kill." The fiery little Red Wing captain came out of the hospital to become chief executioner Sunday in the happiest hockey slaughter it ever has been Detroit's privilege to enjoy.

Lindsay fired three goals and Terry Sawchuk posted a valuable shutout as the fired-up Detroiters clinched their seventh National Hockey League championship in a row with a 6-0 shutout over the angry, frustrated Montreal Canadiens.

This must be called the greatest of the seven title teams. The club which the experts once counted out staged the wildest finish in the history of the NHL to win with a torrid blast of nine straight victories.

After leading most of the season, Montreal could have ended Detroit's long reign with a victory or even a tie Sunday. Yet, it was all over early in the second period.

After Lindsay caged the lone goal of the slam-bang first period—one of the most brutal 20 minutes of hockey ever seen at Olympia—the Wings exploded for four goals in the first seven minutes of the middle stanza.

The shutout by Sawchuk was an exciting $1,000 touch that will be Terry's bonus for winning the Vezina Trophy by one goal, 134 to 135, over Toronto's Harry Lumley (who won over Sawchuk last year by a single goal, 131 to 132).

Lumley lost a two-goal lead Sunday when New York nicked him, 3-2. This was known early by Sawchuk and all the spectators since the Ranger game finished while this one was in the second period.

It was a good thing there was such a sidelight, since it provided the only suspense after the Wings took a commanding lead.

Considerable pre-game suspense was supplied by some 70 policemen, who were ordered to

Other Pictures On Pages 29, 31 And Back Page

CHAMPS, ALL
No Riot, Just Hockey

Fans Ignore Extra Police

While the Detroit Red Wings polished off the Montreal Canadiens on the ice at Olympia Sunday night, Detroit fans gave the visitors a post-graduate course in sportsmanship—with the assistance of 70 policemen.

Commissioner Edward S. Piggins and top police brass led a heavy complement of officers into Olympia to prevent any recurrence of the rioting that marred Thursday night's game between the two teams in Montreal.

But the precaution was unnecessary.

Detroiters showed themselves to be hockey fans rather than rowdies. They shouted and cheered and stomped their feet enthusiastically to urge on the Red Wings.

NOT ONCE did the expert eyes of police detect anything that might be construed as an unsportsmanlike act or word.

Police blocked entrances and exits and scout cars prowled the area.

The fans ignored them. They had come to enjoy hockey.

They were content to let the fighting be restricted to the ice where tempers grew short between traditional rivals.

Only casualty among the fans was Newton Black, 30, of Sarnia, Ont., who was cut above the right eye when he fell while descending stairs.

Three Added

A combination of home cooking and Free Press Want Ads is bound to build up the patronage of a boarding establishment, as the ad below brought in three new boarders when it appeared in the Free Press.

ROYAL OAK Woodward 10 Mile—Home cooking. TV, Lincoln 7-0641.

Whatever your offer is, there are readers of the Free Press Ads eagerly watching to take you up on it.

WO 2-9400

and an experienced ad-taker will be glad to help you word your ad.

IN ADDITION to Lindsay, whose "hat trick" gave him 19 goals for the season, Dutch Reibel got his 25th goal, Tony Leswick his 10th and Alex Delvecchio his 17th.

Reibel also picked up two assists and claimed the Art Ross club scoring crown with 65 points to 62 for Gordie Howe, who held it the last five years. Held pointless by aggressive Canadiens checking, Howe still was one of Detroit's top performers.

There could be no singling out of players for this was one night all the Wings sparkled.

Turn to Page 29, Column 2

You'll Find:
Amusements	24
Astrology	42
Bridge	42
Day in Michigan	42
Drew Pearson	26
Editorials	6
Industrial	25
Mexico	8
Radio and Television	9
Sports	29-32
Want Ads	33-42
Weather Map	2
Women's Pages	22-23

Mamie in Church

WASHINGTON — (AP) — President Eisenhower took his wife to church Sunday, for her first Washington outing since her recent attack of influenza.

APRIL 1, 1955:

Detroit's most notorious kidnapping of the post-war era ends in tragedy.

The Detroit Free Press

FRIDAY, APRIL 1, 1955 — On Guard for Over a Century — 44 Pages — Vol. 124—No. 331 — Seven Cents

SHOWERS — Partly cloudy and mild. Low 60-64, high 68-84.

METRO FINAL EXTRA

BARBARA SLAIN; HUNT FOR FIEND

Detective Lt. Ed Jocque of Detroit finds Barbara's snowsuit near where her body lay (circle right)

Frank Gaca After Viewing His Daughter's Body

Barbara Gaca, victim of murder

The Fear Becomes Reality for the Gacas

BY TOM NICHOLSON and PATRICIA YAROCH
Free Press Staff Writers

Word finally came—word of Barbara Gaca.

The word her parents, Frank, 31, and Rita, 29, had expected, but prayed they wouldn't have to hear.

The father heard it from a reporter. The body of an unidentified little girl had been found.

Maybe it wasn't Barbara ... maybe.

He tried to convince himself, taking a breath of cold air, he took up a map and plotted out the area where the body was found.

Gaca heard it again on a newscast. He still kept it from his wife.

THE REV. FATHER Joseph E. Ryder, assistant pastor of Assumption Grotto Church, was summoned from a confessional. He arrived at 4 p.m. and walked directly to the rear of the white frame house at 14102 Faircrest.

Mrs. Gaca began to weep when she saw the priest go

ing at the house at 3:30 p.m. If Mrs. Gaca sensed anything wrong, she didn't show it.

She went about her housecleaning, trying to occupy her time, and remarked:

"I wonder where all this dirt comes from?"

Gaca said: "Don't say anything to Rita. I won't believe it until we know for sure ... we've had such hope."

He told Sgt. Joseph Cox: "Better get the priest up here. We'll need him for Rita."

• • •

THE STREET hummed with excitement. Housewives gathered in whispering groups, begging information from passers-by.

Gary Tucker, of 14088 Faircrest, who apparently was the last to see Barbara before she disappeared, stood gazing at the rear of the white frame home at 14102 Faircrest.

"I knew Barbara and I liked her," he mumbled.

in. She followed him. Then he told her.

Father Ryder comforted her for 10 minutes. The parents returned to the living room and sat together on the couch.

"Remember, this is what we wanted, what we were praying for ... some definite word," Gaca told his wife. She bore up.

Neighborhood children, home from school and unaware of the tragedy, played hopscotch.

Inside, Gaca hugged his youngest child, Charles, 22 months. Charles cried for a while.

Mrs. Gaca's sister, Mrs. Sophia Dunbar, and Gaca's father, Frank Sr., were at the house. They were a big measure of strength.

'GACA WAITED to hear from police. When would he be able to see the body ... to make sure?

Mrs. Gaca stayed in the kitchen surrounded by relatives.

The Rev. Father John Rozak, a teacher at St. Mary's Seminary, Orchard Lake, and the
Turn to Page 12, Column 5

Flint Rides High on GM Overtime

83,612 Employed In Its Auto Plants

BY LEO DONOVAN
Free Press Automotive Writer

FLINT — Automotive production soars ever higher into the stratosphere of overtime above this General Motors City.

All the old statistical records of prosperity have been broken, and production schedules for the next few months indicate that current peaks will be surpassed.

• • •

WHAT HAS happened to Flint would astound the automotive pioneers.

Now the second largest city in population in Michigan, Flint is experiencing a phenomenal growth, due almost entirely, of course, to General Motors Corp.

Of a population of 180,000 in Flint and 230,000 in Genesee County, GM employs 83,612. When it is considered that total nonfarm employment is 137,500, including 89,000 in the industrial work force, you get a good idea of GM's importance as an employer.

• • •

ON THE PAYROLLS of Buick alone there are 37,400 hourly and salaried workers. A call for an additional 1,500 unskilled workers earlier this week brought forth another 700 applicants. Even the workers in the personnel department hiring additional workers are getting overtime pay.

The average work week at Buick is 48.7 hours.

Last fall, when the 1955 model Buick cars were previewed, Ivan L. Wiles, vice-president of General Motors and general manager of Buick, forecast a market for 750,000 Buicks a year by 1960.

For the first two months of this year, Buick has been producing and selling the 1955 models at a rate of 750,000 cars a year, that's five months after the forecast and five years ahead of the estimate.

• • •

WHILE BUICK is the biggest of the GM family in Flint, none of the others is small, unless you consider General Motors institutions—
Turn to Page 18, Column 1

16 Die as Quakes Rock Philippines

MANILA—(AP)—The Philippine National Red Cross reported 16 persons killed near Lake Lanao on Mindanao Island Friday in a seven-hour-long series of earthquakes.

The Red Cross said a partial survey showed 56 houses were destroyed. There also were "numberless injured" and the victims were urgently in need of food, the Red Cross said.

You'll Find:

Amusements	33
Astrology	34
Billy Graham	8
Bridge	34
Day in Michigan	43
Do It Yourself	16
Dorsey Patterson	8
Editorials	6
Financial	21-23
Movies	35
Radio and Television	41
Sports	24-32
Town Crier	8
Want Ads	36-43
Weather Map	2
Women's Pages	12-37

TO HAVE THE FREE PRESS DELIVERED TO YOUR HOME PHONE WO 1-2323

Girl Strangled; Body Found In Dump

Rail Hand Spots Victim In Rural Oakland County

BY KEN McCORMICK AND TED SHURTLEFF
Free Press Staff Writers

Barbara Gaca was found Thursday, murdered. A grim manhunt for a fiend began through the wooded lakes country southwest of Pontiac. The mutilated body was found in a dump near Halstead and Pontiac Trail.

For savage brutality, the murder of the seven-year-old Detroit girl has not been equaled in many years.

An autopsy conducted Thursday night at St. Joseph's Hospital in Pontiac indicated Barbara was strangled the same day she was abducted, a week ago Thursday.

Dr. Richard E. Olsen, examining pathologist, said the girl had been raped.

In a sadistic frenzy, the murderer had stabbed the body 15 times with a small knife.

She also had been struck a heavy blow on the back of her head.

The body lay in a tangle of rusting beer cans and rotting garbage in a secluded wooded section.

Barbara's grandfather, Frank Gaca, Sr., and Father Joseph Ryder, of Assumption Grotto Church, identified Barbara about 8 p.m.

THE FATHER, Frank, Jr., insisted on seeing his daughter. Detective Lt. Thomas Cochill told Gaca, "Grab a-hold of yourself. This is a rough one."

He led Gaca into the morgue. Gaca stayed 90 seconds and came out, face contorted in agony, hands shoved deep into the pockets of his slacks.

He joined his father and the priest and the three hurried to a car.

Other stories on Pages 3, 4, 12, 19 and 22

Gaca hesitated at a question, started to shake his head, and said:

"All I can say is I hope she didn't suffer and I hope they catch the one who did it."

• • •

BARBARA DISAPPEARED from the home of her parents, Mr. and Mrs. Frank Gaca, a week ago Thursday.

The Gacas live at 14102 Faircrest, in the Gratiot-Seven Mile area on Detroit's East Side.

Barbara vanished while on her way to Assumption Grotto School, six blocks away at 13780 Gratiot.

One of the biggest and most painstaking searches in Detroit history ended when a Grand Trunk Western section crew spotted the body in the dump at 2:30 p.m. Thursday.

A Pontiac section hand, Rufus Zamora, saw a bundle on the dump 50 yards from the track.

Zamora walked over for a better look.

It was the body of a child wrapped in a grimy army blanket.

The face lay exposed to the afternoon sunlight. The eyes were closed. The light breeze ruffled her hair. It was Barbara. The hunt was over.

Zamora raced back to his crew, shouting. The railroad man ran to the nearby home of Mrs. Mary Smelser, 48, of 4975 Halstead. She phoned State Police.

STATE POLICE notified the Oakland County Sheriff's office. A sheriff's patrol car was first to the scene.

The area was immediately roped off.

Fresh tire tracks led to within 10 feet of the body. Detroit police took plaster casts of the tire marks in the muddy lane leading to the dump.

Barbara was wearing the same dress in which she disappeared. She had on an undershirt, shoes and socks.

Scattered around the dump in wild disorder was other clothing ... pants, gloves, a bloody blue-and-red babushka, a snowsuit ripped with a knife.

There were other things, too.

Her rosary. A school pad. A plastic pencil case containing—
Turn to Page 12, Column 1

A Dirt Road, A Dump, Death

The Search Ends, The Hunt Begins

BY WILLIAM SUDOMIER and RAYMOND COURAGE
Free Press Staff Writers

Two clumps of scrub oak trees, their dead leaves rippling silently, stand as sentinels over the small garbage and rubbish littered dump where the body of little Barbara Gaca was found.

The trees served to hide the tragic and gruesome scene from all directions except the railroad tracks to the north.

Less than 25 feet in diameter, the dump is about 200 yards west of Halstead Road, which runs north from W Maple in West Bloomfield Township.

• • •

IN DAYLIGHT it is used by householders who secretly violate a township ordinance against dumping. During hunting season would-be marksmen test their shooting skill, as hundreds of spent shotgun shells in the area reveal.

By night it is a lover's lane. A narrow, one-lane dirt road leads in from Halstead—the same road the killer of Barbara drove recently. Oak and elms hide the road, but police know of it and check it frequently at night.

The dirt road forks south and then north toward the railroad tracks. The first of
Turn to Page 12, Column 1

Call Police At These Numbers

Do you have information about the murder of Barbara Gaca?

Anyone having information that might help lead police to the child's slayer is asked to call:

Detroit Police—WO 2-5700. Ask for the Special Investigation Bureau.

Oakland County Sheriff—FEderal 5-8194.

Pontiac Post, State Police—FEderal 4-0519.

FIRST PICTURES OF EDSEL

Page One
Back Page

COOLER
Partly cloudy and cool.
Low 54-58, high 66-70.

Map and Details on Page 2
HOURLY TEMPERATURES

The Detroit Free Press

METRO FINAL ★

BLUE STREAK

TUESDAY, AUGUST 27, 1957 — On Guard for 126 Years — Vol. 127—No. 115 — 36 Pages — Seven Cents

REDS CLAIM THEIR MISSILE CAN REACH WHOLE WORLD

AUG. 27, 1957:

A sneak preview of the doomed Edsel, and the Soviet Union's "super weapon."

Why Detroit Has a 'DP' Problem

City Fails to Help Southern Whites

Detroit's new southern white citizens are still far from being adjusted to the city. This, the second of a series, tells why some experts think their assimilation will be slow.

BY EVELYN S. STEWART
Free Press Staff Writer

If you drive south, toward Kentucky or Tennessee, over a long holiday weekend, you will find yourself in a fast-moving line of Detroiters headed home. Driving back, the line will move more slowly, as if reluctant to return.

These are Detroit's newest citizens, still homesick for their hills and valleys and river bottoms. There are some 200,000 of them.

Of every 10 persons in Detroit, one is a southern white immigrant.

They came from the mountain counties of Kentucky, from Tennessee's hills and river beds, from West Virginia, Arkansas and southern Missouri. And more than half came from rural areas.

They came because they no longer could make a living from their worn-out farms, or from sharecropping, or from the cutover forests or worked-out mines in their native regions.

They began to come in 1941, in great waves, recruited for war industry in World War ɪɪ. They continued coming in large numbers until 1950.

THEY'RE COMING still, although in smaller numbers, due to industrial outbacks. They will continue to come, sociologists predict. Even if industrial employment declines, they will come looking for jobs in the city's labor force.

They were recruited by posters and ads in the war years. Now they get the word from friends and relatives settled here.

They live in clusters, moving first uptown and ada in the war fatally shot a Japanese woman shell salvager on a United States firing range last Jan. 30'

THE DEFENSE insists he was; the prosecution insists he was not.

The five-hour opening session before three black-robed Japanese judges here Monday set the stage for an off-and-on Monday that may last into November.

At the conclusion, the trial was recessed 12 days. The next session is set for Sept. 6.

THE CITY Government knows little about this great group of immigrants. Cincinnati has its Mayor's
Turn to Page 9, Column 1

SMILES
Girl Loses Her Dress To Train

Free Press Wire Services

A passing train snagged the dress of a shapely French girl at the Milan (Italy) railroad station Monday and left her standing there naked.

Blushing, she promptly open her baggage and climbed into a pair of pajamas. Policemen dispersed an appreciative crowd and escorted her to a private room where she changed into another dress.

No Hats This Time

Twenty Russian girl athletes went shopping in London's swank west end Monday. A similar expedition last year brought on the affair of "Nina and the Five Hats." This time the Russian girls stayed well away from the hat counters.

Discus thrower Nina Ponomareva was arrested last year on a charge of stealing five hats from a London store. The Russians canceled a scheduled meet against Britain in protest and the affair developed into a namecalling diplomatic incident.

The Russians came again this time to carry out the meet canceled because of Nina's arrest. Nina wasn't among the shoppers.

Ordered to Bed

DENVER — (/P) — Former Colorado Gov. Ed C. Johnson, 73, was admitted to St. Joseph's Hospital Monday with an acute bacterial infection.

THIS IS EDSEL, with its shield-shaped styling feature. Other pictures back page.

Japs' Right To Try GI Challenged

MAEBASHI, Japan — (/P) — The William S. Girard manslaughter trial has quickly boiled down again to a jurisdictional question.

The lingering question, raised long before the United States Supreme Court ordered the 22-year-old GI turned over to Japanese justice:

Was Girard carrying out his Army guard duties when he fatally shot a Japanese woman shell salvager on a United States firing range last Jan. 30?

THE DEFENSE insists he was; the prosecution insists he was not.

The five-hour opening session before three black-robed Japanese judges here Monday set the stage for an off-and-on Monday that may last into November.

At the conclusion, the trial was recessed 12 days. The next session is set for Sept. 6.

A ruling on the jurisdictional question, which might mean transfer of Girard's case to a United States Army court-martial, was deferred.

Girard told the Japanese court it has no right to try him for shooting the woman, Mrs. Naka Sakai, 46.

"The facts of the indictment are not correct," he said
Turn to Page 2, Column 1

Old Sub Sinks On Way to Scrap

NORFOLK, Va. — (/P) —The decommissioned submarine Tarpon went to the bottom of the ocean Monday while under tow 35 miles from Cape Hatteras, N. C.

No one was aboard the 22-year-old submarine, the Coast Guard was advised by the tug Julia C. Moran, which was towing it to Baltimore. The Navy had sold the submarine for salvage.

New Edsel Packs 300-Plus Horses

Goes on Display Sept. 4, Priced from $2,500 to $4,200

BY FRED OLMSTED
Free Press Automotive Editor

A handsome and hard-punching newcomer will officially join the Ford family of automobiles Tuesday.

The Edsel, packing 300-plus horsepower in either of two engines, is expected to deliver some telling blows in Ford's fight to capture an even larger share of the market in 1958.

It will be in the showrooms across the nation Wednesday, Sept. 4. Prices will be announced about that time. They are expected to range from about $2,500 to $4,200, plus state and local taxes and optional equipment.

Details of the Edsel, named in memory of Henry Ford's son who died in 1943, were revealed by the Ford Motor Co. Monday.

The Edsel, which stemmed from an idea to bolster Ford in the medium-price field and grew into a quarter-billion-dollar effort, became No. 20 in the current list of American-made cars.

The car's debut will take place Tuesday in Dearborn before a critical audience of 250 news, magazine, radio and
Turn to Page 2, Column 1

BESIDES, IT LACKS COLOR

Cobo's Dehoco Report Proves to Be Hazy

Mayor Cobo was distressed to learn Monday that he's no Cecil B. DeMille.

The preview of his movie production, unofficially titled "A Day at Dehoco," turned out to be a flop.

Cobo had taken along a Department of Public Works cameraman for his day-long tour of the Detroit House of Correction last Thursday.

He wanted filmed proof that Dehoco wasn't as bad as it was painted by a committee of penal experts. The committee had been asked to study Dehoco conditions after trouble erupted there.

A single take was made of the Mayor as he stooped to gather a handful of strawberries from the vegetable garden behind a woman's cottage.

The Mayor instructed the cameraman: "Get a good closeup of these so the color will come out strong."

The astounded lensman replied: "But, Mr. Mayor, I don't have any color film."

The black - and - white film showed almost nothing. Outside shots were hazy. Inside shots were mostly a blur.

Disappointed, Cobo ordered a new film to be made, this time in color and by another cameraman.

If it comes out well, he will show it next week at the administration's first report to Common Council since Dehoco was criticized by the committee.

Foe Calls Hoffa Bad For Union

LOS ANGELES — (/P) — A vice president of the Teamsters Union said Monday the election of James R. Hoffa, of Detroit, as union president would be bad for the union.

"It would show that Teamsters don't give a hoot," said Thomas L. Hickey, of New York, "and we can't afford that kind of a reputation."

Hickey, an old foe of Midwest Teamsters Boss Hoffa and his only avowed rival for the $50,000-a-year president's job held by Dave Beck, assailed Hoffa at a gathering here of top Teamsters brass.

In reply, Hoffa said:

"Hickey failed to bring wrongdoings and abuses in New York to our attention, as was his responsibility."

The Senate Labor - Management Rackets Committee has been investigating an alleged tie-up between Teamsters officials, including Hoffa, and New York labor racketeers.

The sniping between the two leaders came in separate discussions with reporters before the union executive board went into secret session to decide how it will answer AFL-CIO charges that the union is under corrupt influences.

BOARD MEMBERS refused to give any inkling of the action.

Turn to Page 10, Column 6

Extra Home Values!

House hunting? See what Detroit's leading "Bildors" have to offer in home values in today's Free Press. More home news in today's paper is a big plus for Free Press readers because you will still find the big Sunday Real Estate Section each week. These mid-week ads give you an extra chance to find just the right home for your taste and your budget.

Soviet Tests Super Weapon

Vast Distance and Height Achieved, Russia Boasts

Free Press Wire Services

MOSCOW — The official Tass news agency said Monday night that Russia has the ultimate weapon — an intercontinental ballistics missile capable of carrying a nuclear warhead "into any part of the world."

It said such a missile was successfully tested recently. It "flew at a very high, unprecedented altitude covering a huge distance," Tass said. "In a brief time, the rocket landed in the target area."

The announcement, broadcast to the world, said the intercontinental missile can reach any "distant area without the use of strategic aviation, which is at present vulnerable to anti-aircraft defense."

• • •

SUCH A MISSILE as Russia claims is referred to in the United States as "the ultimate weapon."

(In Washington, the United States Defense Department had no immediate comment. The United States has never successfully launched an intercontinental rocket — that is, one with a scheduled range of about 5,000 miles.

(However, the United States Army has covered between 2,000 and 3,000 miles with devices based on its Jupiter intermediate-range missile.

(And the United States Air Force has under production the Snark, a jet-powered pilotless bomber considered capable of spanning the distance between the American continent and Russia's heartland. Under Pentagon policy, no official word would be released about the performance of American missiles.

(The United States has been working on the Air Force Atlas intercontinental missile, now being tested at Patrick Air Force Base, Fla.)

• • •

THE TASS announcement said the test results "showed it is possible to direct rockets to any part of the world."

It added that the Soviets recently held additional high-altitude hydrogen and atomic weapons tests — a fact already known to the West.

It coupled its statements on the ICBM and the weapons tests with a fresh charge that the West is stalling on an agreement at the five-power disarmament talks in London.

Tass charged that Russia, in effect, was forced by the West into developing the city-shattering ICBM because the West refuses to agree to a disarmament pact.

Tass described the test missile as a "super, long-distance intercontinental multi - stage ballistic rocket."

• • •

THE WORD ballistic means that the missile is fired like a giant bullet and is not controlled in flight by a pilot or from the ground. The word multi-stage suggests that the weapon carries several rockets into flight, which are fired at predetermined intervals to propel the missile further along its path.

The announcement was the first official Soviet statement on the ICBM, although Russian leaders in the past have plainly hinted that the Soviets were working on the missile.

PROPAGANDA VALUE SEEN

Lawmakers Skeptical About Red Missile

WASHINGTON—(/P)—Members of Congress were mainly skeptical Monday night in their immediate reaction to the Russian claim of having developed a successful intercontinental ballistic missile.

Senator Symington (D., Mo.), former secretary of the Air Force, said that Moscow's announcement "is the ultimate step in the propaganda use of this weapon — and therefore half the battle is won by their saying they have it."

SYMINGTON SAID "it is obviously impossible for us to check this statement. In the past, however, we have all noticed that when they say they have something in the way of this type of weapon, it turned out later to be fact."

He said "Life or death of the nation may very well depend upon our activity in this field."

Senator Saltonstall, of Massachusetts, top Republican on the Senate Armed Services Committee, said the Russian statement can't be accepted at face value "until we know more about it than just their unconfirmed claims."

Hat Workers Won't Wear 'Em

LUTON, England — (/P) — Hat manufacturers are distressed because their women workers won't wear hats.

So 200 manufacturers will stage a hat parade next month in a campaign to remedy the situation. There will be prizes for the best hats.

You'll Find:

Amusements	23
Ask Andy	22
Astrology	24
Auto-Business	12-15
Bridge	24
Comics	24-25
Drew Pearson	22
Editorials	6
Movie Guide	25
Names and Faces	4
Radio and Television	23
Sports	25-29
Stock Markets	15
Want Ads	29-33
Women's Pages	20-21

TO HAVE THE FREE PRESS DELIVERED TO YOUR HOME PHONE WO 2-9000

DEC. 30, 1957:

The Lions win their third title in six years.

Pictures of Lions' Thrilling Victory on 5 Pages in This Free Press

The Detroit Free Press

COLD — Cloudy with light snow. Low 20-27, high 28-36.

MONDAY, DECEMBER 30, 1957 — On Guard for 126 Years — Vol. 127—No. 240 — 36 Pages Seven Cents

METRO FINAL ★★ EXTRA

55,263 See Browns Humbled

LIONS WIN, 59-14!

Crash Kills Fleeing Slayer
Rams Another Car In 110-MPH Chase

ATLANTA — (UP) — Henry Clay Overton, one of two fugitives wanted for a double slaying in Washington, died Sunday night in a fiery auto collision while being chased at 110 miles an hour by a Georgia Highway Patrol car, the state patrol announced.

The FBI verified the identity of one victim of the collision on US-1 near Wrens, Ga., as Overton.

OVERTON, 44, a diabetic barber with a criminal career, and his friend, Wayne Carpenter, 22, were accused of a shooting in which a Washington nightclub owner and a hillbilly musician were killed.

The Georgia Patrol said several other persons may have died in the blazing wreckage.

Carpenter was not believed to have been in the car, the patrol said.

A patrolman from the Tomson (Ga.) patrol station was chasing the car Overton was riding in at a speed of about 110 miles an hour when the car collided head-on with another, it was reported.

BOTH THE fleeing car, bearing Virginia license plates and reported stolen in Virginia, and the car with which it collided were burned beyond recognition, the patrol said.

Police said that but for the quick action of passers-by in pulling the passenger from the other car, Hugh Hagan Erwin from his burning doorway.

The owner, George P. Tolden, 32, and a hillbilly vocalist who worked in the bar, Kenneth Marion Fisher, 36, were killed. "A blind pianist, Bernard J. Mainer, 25, was wounded.

Witnesses said it appeared the men fired a pistol and a sawed-off shotgun.

LATE FRIDAY night the gunmen kidnaped a young couple in their car at Manhattan.

The fugitives released Miss Doris Mattingly, 19, unharmed at Richmond, at Alberta, Va. They abandoned the car with Pfc. Larry Monteith, 21, of South Fargo, N.D., locked in the trunk.

Monteith knocked a hole in the trunk and got out.

Mrs. Areosia G. Allman, of Richmond, told officers that two men halted her between South Hill and Petersburg, Va., and released her in Cheraw, S.C. The men continued southward in her car, she said.

Overton left Washington without his insulin supply or his hypodermic needle. The FBI had alerted all druggists in the area to be on the watch for either of the men.

You'll Find:
Amusements 23-29
Astrology 30
Ask Andy 30
Bridge 30
Comics 32-33
Dear Francee 9
Earl Wilson 9
Editorials 6
Industrial 8
It Happened in Michigan .. 11
Movie Guide 12
My Answer 15
Names and Faces 8
Radio and Television 33
Sports 33-36
The Town Crier 5
Want Ads 29-31
Women's Pages 17-19

STILL CLUTCHING football, Lion Captain Joe Schmidt is carried on shoulders of enthusiastic football fans after his team dealt out humiliating defeat to Cleveland Browns for professional football championship. Hundreds of fans stormed onto field at Briggs Stadium at conclusion of Sunday's game. Most Lion players managed to elude shouting fans, but Schmidt and championship football were held captive 20 minutes.

U.S. Budget To Be Near 74 Billion

WASHINGTON — President Eisenhower is expected to send Congress next month a budget approaching 74 billion dollars, highest in peacetime and comparable to the peak spending of the Korean War.

An official said Sunday the Administration still hopes to balance this budget—the biggest of the current decline in Federal revenue caused by a business recession.

Some budget decisions remain to be made, this high source said, including whether to ask for a special military contingency fund of perhaps 500 million dollars to be used at Mr. Eisenhower's discretion.

In nondefense categories, little if any cost reduction is foreseen in spite of Mr. Eisenhower's New Year's call for outright elimination of some "desirable" but "less essential" programs.

THIS MEANS that the Government may, starting next July 1 may stay 2½ billion or so ahead of unconfessed military spending. This sum is expected to reach 40 billion dollars, compared with the original setting of 38 billion dollars for this year and actual outlays now estimated at around 38 billions.

Officials expect no great outcry from Congress at the budget, except possibly at the failure to reduce civilian spending as had been hoped.

VISITS FORMER WORK SPOT
Invalid Gets Her Wish After 12 Years at Home

BY ROBERT SHOGAN
Free Press Staff Writer

They opened the doors at Hudson's Farmer St. entrance Sunday and led in a lady.

Mrs. Leslie Doss is paralyzed from the neck down.

But she moved her head from side to side as she lay on the stretcher and looked at the jewelry department where she had worked more than 25 years ago.

She glanced up at her husband and smiled.

"This is what I wanted to see most," she said.

Mrs. Doss, 51, hadn't seen much but the bedroom of her Livonia home for 12 years.

She was stricken with multiple sclerosis in 1945.

Doctors told her husband, Norman, 51, she would be paralyzed for life.

THE COUPLE, married in 1927, had moved into a neat frame bungalow at 19584 Farmington a few months after the wedding.

With the onset of the crippling disease, the house became Mrs. Doss' whole world.

Her husband, a worker at Ford's Rouge plant who takes home about $75 a week, did what he could to make life comfortable and pleasant.

The congregation of the nearby Livonia Methodist Church helped.

The Men's Club installed a sound system in Mrs. Doss' bedroom so she could hear the services from the church.

The Women's Society of Christian Service arranged and paid for Sunday's ambulance trip.

IT WOULD be the city's third transportation strike in less than a month and the worst transit crisis in New York history.

An overflow crowd representing 21,000 workers crammed Manhattan Center in the heart of the garment district.

They backed their leader, fiery union President Michael Quill, in his demand for a 65-cent hourly wage - welfare package. The Transit Authority's last offer was 18 cents an hour in wage increases over a two-year period.

Asks Fund Cut
HONG KONG — (UP) — Red China's vice chairman, Chu Teh, has appealed for a cut in military spending to provide more money for the industrialization of China.

"I'm so excited I think I'm going to burst," she said as she was carried into the ambulance at her home at 4 p.m.

"Mrs. Doss' eyes saw things she remembered . . .

Her childhood home on 31st near Warren . . . the Christmas decorations . . . the river.

And things they never saw before.

The Civic Center . . . Northland . . . the Expressway.

MRS. DOSS had requested the visit to the J. L. Hudson Co.

She had worked as an inspector and cashier in the jewelry department for two years, starting when she was 16.

Hudson's had a pink camellia corsage waiting for Mrs. Doss.

She smelled the flowers, looked around, wept a little. "Now I have so many more things to remember," she said.

Then the ambulance took her home.

N.Y. Faces 1958 Without Its Subway

NEW YORK — Cheering New York transit workers voted unanimously Sunday to welcome 1958 with a strike at midnight on New Year's Eve, which would paralyze all subway bus and boat service.

The strike, which by a show of hands, was taken in last-ditch negotiations between the Transit Workers' Union and the New York Transit Authority.

A Fabulous Victory Calls For —And Gets—Fabulous Coverage

A fabulous job of picture taking and presentation was done to bring Free Press readers the complete story of the fabulous Lions' victory over the Cleveland Browns.

Five picture-filled pages present all the thrills of the game. They were taken by Free Press Photographers Tony Spina, Bud Johnson, Tom Venaleck and Leo Fossch, ably supported by the Associated Press staff.

Combined with the word pictures of Sports Writers Lyall Smith, Bob Latshaw, Marshall Dann and George Puscas, all these efforts make a complete reporting job on a great and thrilling sports event.

It's Third Title In Six Years

Rote Passes for 4 TDs To Avenge '54 Fiasco

What TV blackout? Gimme a beer—Page 3.

BY BOB LATSHAW
Free Press Staff Writer

The expected struggle for the world championship of professional football was just no contest.

A razor-sharp crew of Detroit Lions ran the Cleveland Browns right out of Briggs Stadium Sunday afternoon to climax one of the greatest clutch performances in pro football history.

Detroit picked up its third world title in six years by handing the Browns their worst defeat in history, 59 to 14, before 55,263 fans.

As has been the custom, this was a tremendous team effort. The Lions rolled up their greatest point total in history on offense.

The defense took the ball away from the Browns seven times and held them to a mere two touchdowns—both of which came while Detroit was holding a comfortable edge.

The Lions were sparked by a brilliant performance by Robin Rote. He riddled the Browns' defense with his accurate passes, completing 12 of 19 for 280 yards and four touchdowns.

Detroit opened with a 17-point splurge in the first quarter and then added 14 points in each of the next three periods.

* * *

IT WAS THE PERFECT REVENGE for the Lions' humiliating defeat in the 1954 championship game, when the Browns rolled up a 56-10 verdict. Sunday's contest could be best classified as a carbon copy of that lopsided loss—in reverse.

The Browns could do nothing right. The Lions could do nothing wrong. Detroit got all of the breaks—if you could call them that—but most of them the Lions manufactured themselves. Consistent pressure by the defensive team forced the Browns into mistakes and that eventually cost them the game.

Rote's brilliant passing was the top individual performance. Disregarding the pressure of the title at stake, the lanky Texan pitched scoring passes of 78, 32, 26 and 24 yards.

Seven Lions shared in the club's eight tallies. Steve Junker picked up two on passes from Rote. Jim Doran and Dave Middleton took Rote pitches for two more.

Rote, who set up the first touchdown with an 18-yard run, scored it on a sneak and Gene Gedman picked up another on a short plunge. Howard (Hopalong) Cassady scored the other six-pointer on a 16-yard pass from Gerry Reichow.

* * *

THE DEFENSE took turns clobbering the Browns. Joe Schmidt, Jim David, Gerry Perry, Terry Barr and Bob Long each intercepted passes.

Barr and Gil Mains both recovered fumbles jarred loose by the hard tackling of the Lion forwards.

It's hard to name the key play that turned this expected battle into a rout. Actually three of them broke the back of the Browns.

Long's interception of Tommy O'Connell's pass early in the first quarter that gave the Lions the ball on the Browns' 19 and set up a touchdown and a 10-0 lead could have been the big one.

Barr's recovery of Milt Campbell's fumble on the ensuing kickoff was just as big. That gave the Lions the ball again on the Browns' 15 and they quickly hiked the lead to 17-0.

Rote's 78-yard scoring pass to Doran after the Browns

Turn Page to Column One

Scoring Timetable

FIRST QUARTER
7:36—Lions, Martin (31-yd. field goal) 3— 0
11:54—Lions, Rote (1-yd. run) 9— 0
11:04—Lions, Martin (conversion) 10— 0
13:53—Lions, Gedman (1-foot run) 16— 0
13:52—Lions, Martin (conversion) 17— 0

SECOND QUARTER
0:10—Browns, Brown (29-yd. run) 17— 6
0:10—Browns, Groza (conversion) 17— 7
7:42—Lions, Rote-to-Junker (26-yd. pass play) 23— 7
7:42—Lions, Martin (conversion) 24— 7
11:36—Lions, Barr (19-yd. interception) 30— 7
11:36—Lions, Martin (conversion) 31— 7

THIRD QUARTER
7:58—Browns, L. Carpenter (3-yd. run) 31-13
7:59—Browns, Groza (conversion) 31-14
8:45—Lions, Rote-to-Doran (78-yd. pass play) 37-14
8:45—Lions, Martin (conversion) 38-14
13:21—Lions, Rote-to-Junker (24-yd. pass play) 44-14
13:21—Lions, Martin (conversion) 45-14

FOURTH QUARTER
0:07—Lions, Rote-to-Middleton (32-yd. pass play) 52-14
0:07—Lions, Martin (conversion) 53-14
11:40—Lions, Reichow-to-Cassady (16-yd. pass play) 59-14
12:40—Lions, Martin (conversion) 60-14

Winter Returning

Winter weather was scheduled to ease back into Detroit Sunday night and Monday morning.

The Weather Bureau said the low temperature would be 16, with a high of 24 Monday.

Sunday's temperatures ranged up to 36 degrees, but a return of lower temperatures might bring light snow.

STATISTICS

	CLEVELAND	DETROIT
First downs	17	22
Rushing yardage	218	187
Passing yardage	95	296
Passes	9-22	13-21
Passes intercepted	0	4
Punts	4-35	4-36
Fumbles lost	2	1
Yards penalized	60	52

Cleveland .... 0 7 7— 0—14
DETROIT .... 17 14 14 14—59

Cleveland: Touchdowns—Brown (29, run); L. Carpenter (3, run). Conversions—Groza 2.
DETROIT: Touchdowns—Rote (1, plunge); Gedman (1-foot plunge); Junker 2 (26, pass-run from Rote; 24 pass-run from Rote); Barr (19, pass interception); Doran (78, pass-run from Rote); Middleton (32, pass from Rote); Cassady (16, pass-run from Reichow). Field goal—Martin 31. Conversions—Martin 8.

May 25, 1958:

Urban sprawl finally catches up with Grosse Pointe's last farm.

Sunday feature

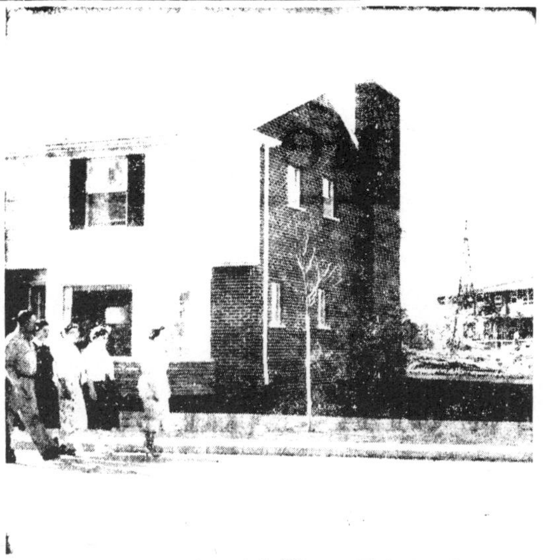

The Staelenses Inspect Building on Their 'Farm'

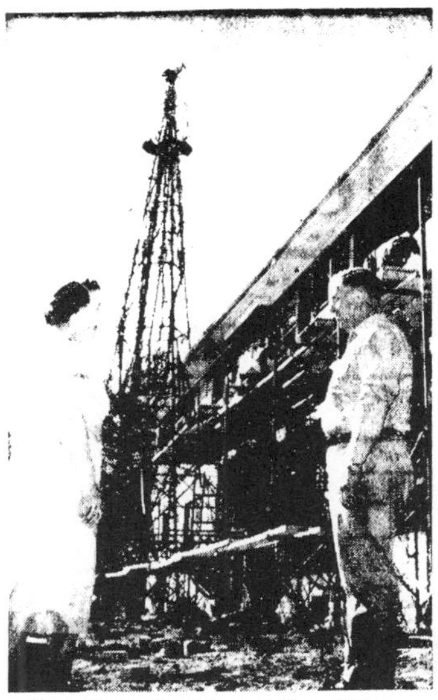

Mrs. Joseph Staelens and Son, Albert — Albert's Wife Serves Coffee in the New Home

THEY'LL BUILD $40,000 HOMES

Grosse Pointe's Last Farmer Sells His Biggest Crop—The Land Itself

BY HARRY GOLDEN
Free Press Staff Writer

A DARK-HAIRED woman of 60 watched the workmen building new apartments next to the wisteria-covered windmill of Grosse Pointe's last farm. The last Staelens "crop"—the little farm itself—was being harvested and a profit of 9,100 per cent was in sight.

Mrs. Joseph Staelens has watched stolidly as 14 marshy acres, where the first Staelens from Belgium settled 66 years ago to grow corn and tomatoes and beans, were being cleared.

She gulped just a bit when the old five-room house and rough gray barn came down to make way for 37 homes in the $40,000 price range and a $500,000 brick terrace-apartment project.

"I've worked here 40 good years," she said. "But I have no regrets. It is time for new things."

* * *

HENRY STAELENS bought the farm—on the south side of Mack, between Neff and University—for $3,300.

His descendants say the land alone is now worth $300,000—about 91 times the original investment.

But there were many long days of toil and a lot of history between Henry's arrival and today's development.

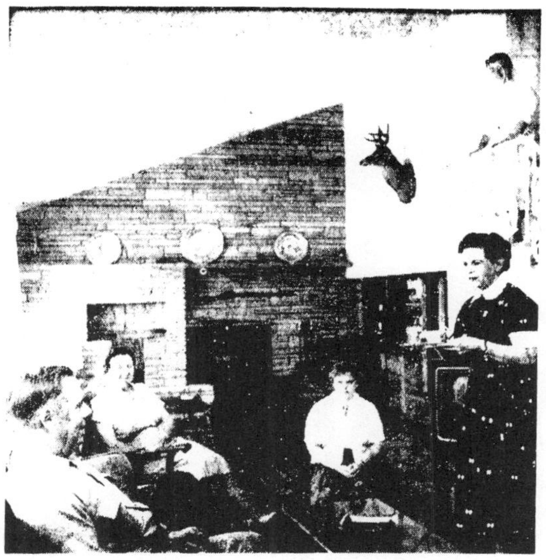

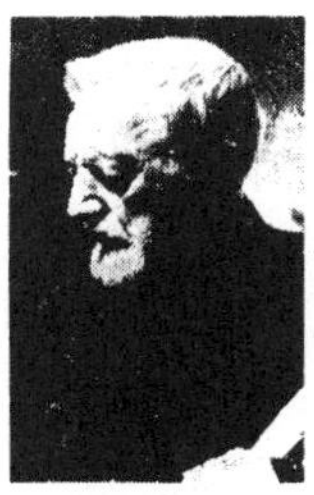

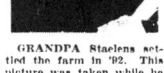

GRANDPA Staelens settled the farm in '92. This picture was taken while he picked corn in 1933 on his 91st birthday, shortly before he died.

MRS. STAELENS, widow of Henry's son, moved two months ago into the new subdivision's finest home—a modern colonial tri-level at 867 Lakeland.

SLICK PLAN

Profs Get Raise —With Interest

RENSSELAER, Ind.—Little St. Joseph's College, amid grainfields 73 miles southeast of Chicago, has found a way to eat its Ford Foundation cake and have it, too.

When in 1955 the college received word of a Ford Foundation grant of $270,000—the money to be invested and the interest on it used for at least 10 years to increase faculty salaries—the college treasurer, Father John Lefko, got an idea.

He'd use the cash twice: lend the money, at 4½ per cent interest, to members of the faculty so they could build homes, and then use the interest professors paid on their homes to hike their income.

* * *

FATHER LEFKO told a newsman that, so far as he knew, St. Joseph's is the only college thus far to put the dollars on double duty.

Perhaps, a reporter suggested, he came from a banking family.

"Yes," he replied with a smile, "my father was a janitor at the Chase National Bank."

A new salary plan to go into effect this fall is called "one of the best in the country." For nine months of work, full professors will get $9,000 to $15,000, associate professors $7,000 to $9,500, assistant professors $6,000 to $8,500, instructors $5,000 to $7,500.

A SURVEY BY THE North Central Association of 53 liberal arts colleges in the interior of the nation early this year showed top teaching salaries scaled from $9,500 down to $3,900.

Since the announcement of the new salary plan this spring, 40 unsolicited inquiries about jobs came from teachers in the Midwest and East.

Her son, Albert, 39, and his family also live in the new $60,000 house built scant feet south of where the original five-room farm dwelling stood until this spring.

Only 6 Farm Families

ACTUALLY as far back as 1892, there were only six farm families in what is now the City of Grosse Pointe. That's when Henry came with his wife and six children.

At first, he rented the farm from a Frenchman who hadn't been able to make it pay.

Henry didn't even have a horse, but he swapped his labor to get the plowing done. He weathered the loss of crops under spring floods from the since-enclosed Black Marsh Ditch at his south boundary.

He and his older children pulled a wagon across the dirt path that was Mack Road to get firewood in a forest of oak and maple. He worked at night in a chicory processing factory.

Four years after he arrived, he had a team of horses, several cows and pigs and enough money for a down payment on the property.

HIS WIFE, Louise, drove the produce-laden wagon down St. Clair to Jefferson, and Henry walked ahead with a lantern to guide her away from holes in the dirt road. That was the best route to the Eastern Market in those days.

By 1906, Henry decided he needed a barn. He bought one that stood where Grosse Pointe High School's tennis courts now are.

He and his son, Joseph, a husky young man of 20, dismantled the hand-hewn beams and put the barn up just east of their house.

Then they put the windmill to pump water from a well into a storage tank in the barn. Then came the greenhouses.

And Things Went Well

WHILE, industrial pioneers were putting the world on wheels, and new residents were stampeding into the suburbs, things went well for the Staelenses. Henry bought a motor-powered truck to haul his produce to market down Mack, which had become a narrow macadam road.

But Henry came home from the market one day in the season of 1917 with very little of his produce sold.

As it turned out, the "tough break" helped the family's fortunes. For Henry hit upon the idea of putting the produce out on benches in front of the house.

The roadside-stand idea caught on. Henry's son, Joseph, married Madeline that fall, and she helped tend the stand while the men worked in the field and the greenhouse.

BY 1923, the operation had become so big that the Staelenses no longer went to market at all. Three years later, Joseph and Madeline bought another 30-acre farm near Utica. Now the produce came from two sources. And the stand became a store.

Henry was 91 when he died in the fall of 1934.

An early riser all his life, he tended the perennial flower plants in his last season. He had slowed down only to the extent of resting under the shade of the maple

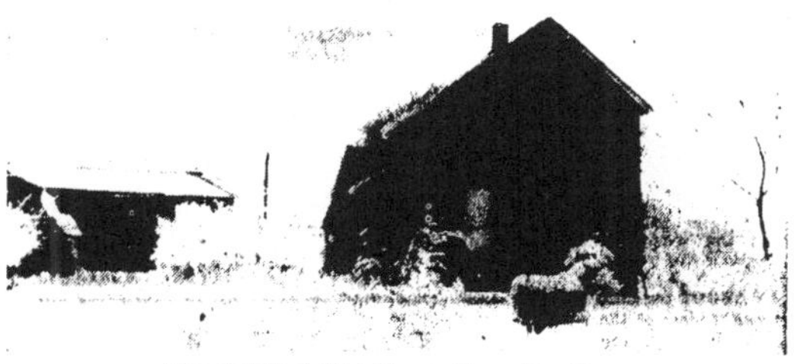

The Original Five-Room Farm Dwelling

Why Didn't It Sell?

WHY HADN'T he been able to sell his produce in 1917?

"That's the way farming

They Profit Aiding Aged

BY BEN FUNK

MIAMI—(AP)—"Would you lend the Mackle brothers a million dollars?" a Miami banker was asked.

He replied: "I've got 10 million dollars the Mackle boys can pick up today if they want it."

The Mackle boys—Elliott, Robert and Frank—run Florida's biggest real estate operation, Mackle Co., Inc., whose specialty is building low-cost homes for retired folks—particularly those with just $160 a month to spend.

A 75-year-old man can get a 25-year mortgage on a Mackle house with $210 down and $46 a month.

The Mackles, hard-working heirs of a construction business started by their British-born father in 1908, have been Florida's biggest home builders in the postwar period during which new residents have arrived at the rate of 225,000 a year.

In the six-month period ended April 30, they sold 40 million dollars worth of homes and homesites in eight pre-planned cities and subdivisions.

With a virtual monopoly on the low-price field in some parts of Florida, they expect to build 5,000 houses this year and believe the figure will reach 25,000 annually by 1965.

Speculation plays no part in their setup. They never lay a foundation until the house is sold.

What would a depression do to their grand plans?

"It would help us, I imagine," says Elliott Mackle, who at 49 is the oldest of the brothers and president of the firm.

* * *

"THE GREAT bulk of our buyers are retired people getting their first chance to enjoy life in the Florida sun. A depression actually would benefit them, because their incomes are assured and it would make their money go farther."

The Mackle operation points up the vast difference between the ridiculous Florida boom of the '20s and the phenomenal but solid growth of America's only subtropic state today.

In the '20s Florida building lots were gambled like poker

chips in a boom that exploded with a spectacular crash. Today Florida believes it is

trees out front in early afternoon.

is." Mrs. Joseph Staelens explained. "You're on the go all the time, and then there are little streaks of luck—good and bad.

"And I can remember one time when our tomato plants all burned off from the heat.

"But there was a late fall, and the plants all sprouted

from the roots. When our tomatoes came in, no one else had them, and we sold the green ones for $2 a bushel and the ripe ones for $4."

The maple trees came down when Mack was widened to a divided highway in 1948.

* * *

BEFORE the bulldozers and graders came through, Joseph and his son, Albert, found a nest of four fox squirrels in one maple.

"We tried to keep them in a box in the kitchen," Albert related. "They were only about three inches long. We even went to a veterinarian and got a formula, but they only lived about six weeks."

Joseph was busy transferring plants from the greenhouse into outside frames on the day that he died in 1949.

Sell? Not Seriously

THE surviving Staelenses (two of Henry's daughters and a daughter of Joseph also live in the Detroit area) didn't seriously consider selling or subdividing the farm until about that time.

Now Albert's daughters—Judy, 17, and Diane, 14—represent the fourth generation on the homeplace.

Some vegetables were grown on the northern portion even after the first 14 houses were built in 1955. Another 14 houses went up the next year. Nine more are planned.

The 52-unit apartment project expected to yield an income of $5,000 a month, will be completed about Sept. 1.

From a picture window on the east side of her new home, Mrs. Joseph Staelens can see the brick masons working a few feet from the windmill tower. The vine, with lavender bloom, climbs its 45-foot height.

"We'll let it stand," she said, "as long as the wisteria lives."

better equipped than many states to ride out any economic storm.

* * *

THE MACKLE system came into being in 1946 after the Mackle brothers heard a visitor from New Jersey complain:

"All my life I figured on moving to Florida when I retired. Now I find that it's not for me. This is nothing but a rich man's playground."

The Mackles ran a blind ad in a magazine and addressed several questions to people who were in the rapidly-expanding group approaching retirement age. They got 28,000 replies. The consensus: 75 per cent wanted to spend their declining years in Florida; their average retirement income was $160 a month.

* * *

THE MACKLES went on from there. Up and down both Florida coasts, they grabbed huge tracts of land before the postwar boom was to shoot prices up to high levels. On the lower Gulf Coast they acquired control of 92,000 acres, with 30 miles of Gulf of Mexico waterfront, for $30 an acre.

Then they put their architects to work, designing homes that a family with $160 a month could buy.

At the war's end, when low-income people began yielding by thousands to the seemingly universal desire to move to Florida, the Mackles were ready to accommodate them.

In eight pre-planned cities and subdivisions, they offered building lots for $10 down and $10 a month—total price $795.

* * *

LOT BUYERS could pick their own builders, if they desired. But the Mackles offered to build them houses costing as little as $6,000 for $210 down, and $46 a month.

Everything was figured down to a fine point for the family with just $160 a month to spend.

The houses were of hurricane-tested steel and concrete block construction.

By the start of 1958, the Mackles had sold 30,000 lots and built 23,000 homes and were just swinging into high gear in what has become almost a pushbutton building operation.

* * *

SOME PEOPLE who buy Mackle homes can pay cash after selling their northern properties.

Others not so fortunate are helped by the fact that there is no age limit on FHA credit in Florida. A 75-year-old man can get a 25-year mortgage and the small payments that go with it.

The government figures that the demand for the houses precludes the possibility of mortgage foreclosures. If a man dies, his heirs are sure to snap up the house—for their own retirement, for vacation use, or simply for investment.

If they don't, it can be sold for more than the mortgage.

Not all those who buy Mackle houses have low incomes. One man with a net worth of $200,000 bought the cheapest house, with one bedroom and bath.

"Acquaintances up north would descend on me like locusts if I had room for them," he said. "I want no part of that. I want to relax in peace for the first time in my life."

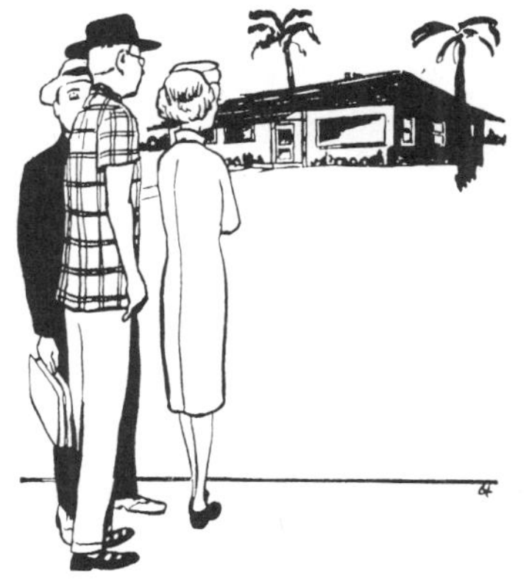

Church Aide Has Hot Time

CRAB ORCHARD, Ky.—When the Baptist Church congregation contributed a sizable collection, church treasurer Frank Burch took the money home and hid it in a waste-basket.

The next morning, unthinkingly, he carried the basket out and dumped its contents into a trash fire.

Burch suddenly remembered and jumped into the fire, scattering it right and left.

He spent the rest of the day visiting the homes of contributors, exchanging badly scorched pieces of paper for new checks.

June 28, 1958:

After nearly a century of talk, a bridge across the Straits of Mackinac is no longer a dream.

The Detroit Free Press

The Bridge: Its Arms of Steel Unite Our Mighty State

We will dedicate the Mackinac Bridge on Saturday.

But to whom or to what shall it be dedicated?

A slim, serene span—glad of its grace, superb in its strength, proud of its power to unite.

A marvelous, utilitarian monument made by men with the skills God put into their hands, with the vision He put into their minds, with the Spirit He put into their hearts.

But a monument to whom? To what?

It is a monument to many men, many things. Any or all the dedications would be graciously received.

It could be dedicated to men.

Men who dreamed, like the 1880s editor of a Traverse City newspaper who noted that all efforts to provide all-year service across the Straits had failed. There had to be "a crossing."

Like Prentiss M. Brown, who wanted the bridge a quarter century ago and who, for eight years, has been chairman of the Bridge Authority.

Like Gov. Williams, who reactivated the authority and put the wheels in motion and gave the others their chance.

Like Dr. David B. Steinman, the bridge genius —designer of the green-and-ivory span and 400 other bridges on five continents.

Like the late Charles T. Fisher, a member of the authority who brought to it a knowledge of how to get money and how best to use it.

And many thousands more.

It could be dedicated to the five workmen who gave their lives to string steel across the choppy waters that had delayed, for decades, the progress of the vast Upper Peninsula.

Frank Pepper, diver, died of the bends. James R. LaSarge fell into a caisson and was killed. Albert B. Abbott drowned in a pier cofferdam. Jack C. Baker and Robert Koppen plunged to their death from the North Tower.

It could be dedicated to them—the soldiers of construction.

It could be dedicated to intangible things.

It could be dedicated to progress—to the idea that one must go forward, or wither and die.

It could be dedicated to freedom—to the idea that the five-mile epic poem in the medium of steel could only have been built by men who were free, by men who built the Bridge because they wanted to build it, by men who knew that while they built it they were close to God.

It must be dedicated to these men, to these things—and it will.

It will be dedicated to the people of the State of Michigan and the United States of America.

With the guidance of Unseen Hands, the people built it. With His continued guidance, they will use it—for centuries.

WILLIAM SUDOMIER, Free Press staff

The Bridge stretches out from Mackinaw City across the water and grips St. Ignace.

A BEAUT!
Fair, little warmer.
High 86-90, low 68-72.

The Detroit Free Press

SATURDAY, JULY 4, 1959 — On Guard for 128 Years — Vol. 129—No. 61 — 24 Pages — Eight Cents

METRO FINAL ★ BLUE STREAK

JULY 4, 1959:

The Freedom Festival: A royal visit, thundering explosions and stalled traffic.

500,000 MOB LOOP TO VIEW FIREWORKS

We Cheer, Tired Queen Waves Back

Elizabeth Takes to Yacht --And a Bit of Rest

BY JEAN SHARLEY
Free Press Staff Writer

Pale and tired, Queen Elizabeth was cheered by thousands lining both sides of the Detroit River Friday.

Worn by a three-day tour of Ontario, Her Majesty stayed gallantly in view at the rail as the royal yacht Britannia cast off from Government Dock across from the Detroit Civic Center.

Huge crowds, including thousands of Detroiters, lined the Windsor riverfront and jammed Dieppe Gardens to greet the Queen. Windsor police estimated that 800,000 persons saw the royal visitor.

•

'OUR' MONARCH
Hearts Go Pitapat in Windsor

BY FRANK BECKMAN
Free Press Staff Writer

They came by the thousands Friday to gaze on the royal persons of Queen Elizabeth Alexandra Mary, of Great Britain and the House of Windsor, and her dashing consort, Prince Philip Mountbatten.

Flags and bunting of rich reds and yellows and blue festooned the streets and buildings of Windsor across the river and there was palpitation in every breast.

Americans, with their much younger history, came to our sister city from Texas, Nebraska, Ohio, New York and points east and west to witness the adulation of a Commonwealth for a monarch.

And if one were to guess, it would be safe to say that for every Canadian who walked the teeming streets

Turn to Page 8, Column 1

You'll Find:
Tangle Towns Tie-Breaker, P. 15

Free Press Insurance application is on Page 12.

Amusements	16
Ann Landers	9
Astrology	18
Billy Graham	10
Bonanza Bill	18
Bridge	18
Church	10-11
Comics	22-23
Drew Pearson	10
Editorials	8
Movie Guide	4
Names and Faces	16
Radio-TV	22
Sports	13-15
Town Crier	16
Want Ads	18-21
Women's Page	9
World Once Over	4

HAVE THE FREE PRESS DELIVERED AT HOME
PHONE WO 2-8900

Stock Exchanges Off for Weekend

NEW YORK—(UP)—Stock and commodity exchanges throughout the country were closed Friday for an extended Fourth of July weekend. They will reopen Monday morning.

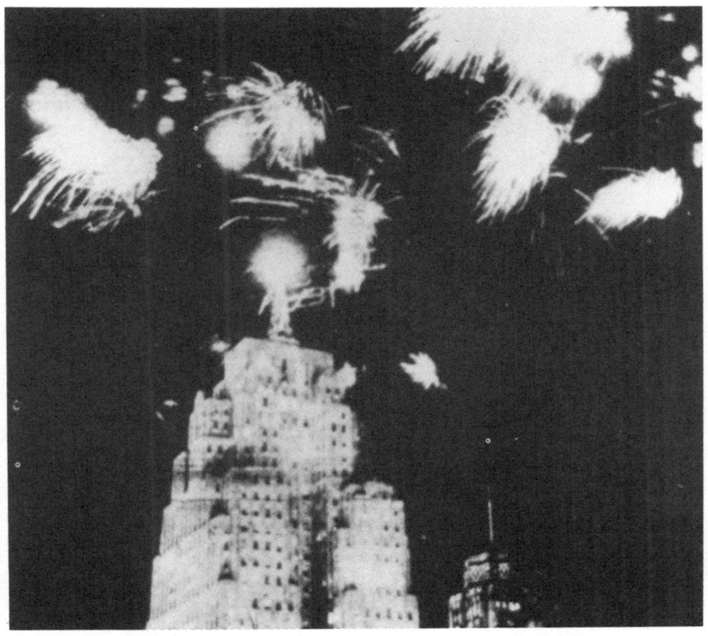

Flowery Flares, Jagged Flashes Wreathe Penobscot Building's Beacon

Among the most courtly bows made to the Queen at the Gardens ceremonies was that of Detroit Mayor Louis C. Miriani. Mrs. Miriani's curtsy was among the best the Queen had seen.

Gov. Williams, who saw the Queen last week at the St. Lawrence Seaway opening, was on hand, and will see her again Monday in Chicago.

Mrs. Williams, who is on Mackinac Island, will wave to the royal couple as the Britannia passes under Mackinac Bridge Sunday, the Governor said.

AS THE ROYAL train approached Windsor from London and Chatham, crowds stood at every railway crossing, and the Queen caught glimpses of boats bobbing along the Detroit River.

The royal train parked Thursday night in a Stratford (Ont.) siding. At 8:14 a.m. it lurched away so violently that even a

Turn to Page 17, Column 2

THE FIGHT TO GET A SEAT--AND LEAVE
Were You Part of the Mob?

BY JACK BERRY
Free Press Staff Writer

Detroiters sat on curbs and climbed atop everything that would hold still or support their weight to see Freedom Festival fireworks barrage Friday night.

Little kids sat in strollers, buried in a forest of legs, as their parents pushed toward the waterfront.

Every downtown building with windows facing south showed a solid mass of humanity gawking at the blasting pyrotechnics.

More than 10,000 persons flooded into the City-County Building. They were building workers with their families, admitted on special passes.

THE FLOODING TIDE of humanity began pouring into the loop late in the afternoon.

The old National Bank of Detroit building kept five elevators running to haul the crowds to upper floors. There were 5,000 at vantage spots there long before the first bomb let go.

The youngest and the spryest got the best seats at ground level. The railings of parking lots, the tops of telephone booths, elevated parking lot ramps, swarmed with youth.

• • •

IN THE TURMOIL, retired police Sgt. Fred Varner and his wife, of 12735 Appoline, remained in comfort on the cool stone of the Soldiers and Sailors Monument.

"I stood on this spot eight hours during the American Legion parade," he said, grinning. "It's a good spot to watch from."

Harry Roberts and his wife, of 27028 Belanger, Roseville, brought their two children along in a little red wagon.

Nearer the river, spreading away from the foot of Woodward, the sand banks along Atwater drew mobs to their summits.

Even the coal piles had a crowd of tenants.

Early comers spread newspapers and relaxed. Hundreds brought folding chairs. The waterfront became a solid mass of faces before the fireworks show began at 9:27 from barges mid stream.

• • •

THE HARRIED, sweating police strove to unwind traffic jams, but the inbound

Turn to Page 3, Column 5

About the Queen . . .
- Pages of Pictures 6, 7, 17
- Soapy Plays It Smart 5
- What a Day on River 5
- Detroit Seeks a Glimpse 5
- Ladies Swoon for Philip 9
- Chat of a Lifetime 17

Autos Create Hopeless Jam
Million See Big Display; Crowds Hamstring Police

Other pictures on Pages 3 and 24.

BY RILEY MURRAY AND DON GEEVASE
Free Press Staff Writers

Detroit's waterfront exploded Friday night in a fabulous, multi-colored spectacle of 2½ tons of bursting fireworks.

Estimates of the crowd that watched the 23-minute Freedom Festival display ranged from 500,000 to a million.

William F. Polkinghorn, Detroit Police traffic director, said the crowd may well have been closer to a million. He included the 100,000 who watched from the Windsor shore and the thousands more who started for the riverfront but didn't make it because of traffic.

Thousands looked on from their boats and from nearly every tall building in the loop.

It was described as the largest crowd ever assembled downtown for a scheduled event.

The display ended at 10 p.m. and the tremendous traffic jam that followed made it seem that everybody in Detroit with a car was downtown.

• • •

EVERY STREET and intersection was hopelessly tied up. Cars stalled. Policemen were powerless to get the traffic moving and the jam continued until nearly midnight.

Hundreds of people calling home to say they would be late resulted in a phone circuit tieup as well.

Hundreds of private boats, from expensive cruisers to row boats, anchored in the Detroit River to see the fireworks scheduled for 9 p.m.

The Coast Guard on Belle Isle said it was the largest collection of boats it had ever seen on the river.

Traffic jammed every street leading to the loop area. More than 500 policemen were assigned to crowd and traffic control. But the officers were unable to untangle some of the mixups at downtown intersections.

The Harbormaster Bureau said Belle Isle was jammed to capacity. Every inch of space along the rail of the bridge was taken early.

Traffic on E. Grand Blvd. was backed bumper-to-bumper all the way back to Gratiot.

• • •

THE HUGE display of fireworks started a half hour late, but there was little grumbling at the delay. Most of the people had been waiting for hours and 30 more minutes was of little consequence to them.

It was worth the wait.

The first exploding shell that fell into a dazzling,

Turn to Page 3, Column 5

BUT PLANS GO AHEAD
Mayor Says Nyet To Kozlov Visit

Mayor Miriani said Friday that Frol R. Kozlov, Russia's first deputy premier, is not welcome in Detroit.

At almost the same time, Kozlov's Detroit hosts released a list of places he will visit here next week.

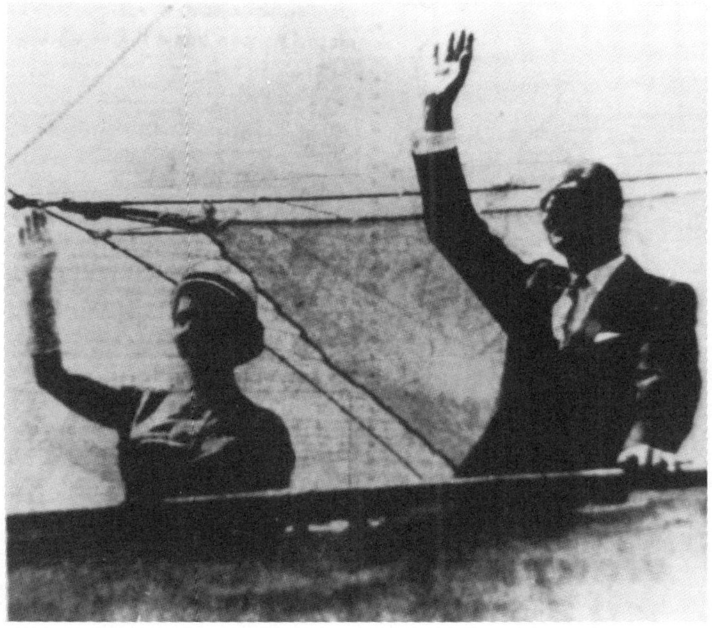

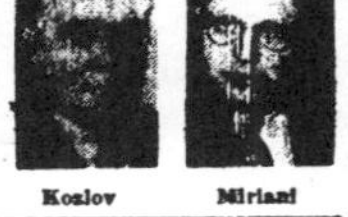

In a telegram to Secretary of State Christian A. Herter, Miriani said:

"We humbly reiterate and advise that the Russian delegate's visit to our city is not in the public interest and we trust you will inform Mr. Kozlov and his Russian delegation."

The telegram was one in a series exchanged by Miriani and the State Department after the Mayor was informed that Kozlov was to visit here.

• • •

THE EXCHANGE began June 26, when William S. B. Lacy, special assistant to Herter, telegraphed the mayor that Russia requested arrangements for a visit to Detroit.

While Miriani and the State Department swapped telegrams, Detroiters went ahead with plans for the visit.

Kozlov is scheduled to arrive in Detroit late Monday night. Tuesday morning, he will visit the Detroit Edison River Rouge plant and the Ford Motor Co. In the afternoon, he will tour the Chrysler Engine plant and

Turn to Page 3, Column 1

French A-Bomb?

PARIS—(UP)—Army Minister Pierre Guillaumat predicted Friday that France will hold its first atomic bomb tests soon.

Georgia to Say First Welcome

BRUNSWICK, Ga.—(UPI)—Georgia planned to be the first state in the nation to welcome Alaska into the Union Saturday.

Lt. Gov. Garland Byrd said he arranged to make a phone call to Alaska Gov. William Egan at 12:01 a.m.

Farewell to Windsor. It was brief visit for royal couple but one of most enthusiastic in Canada.

DEC. 22, 1959:

Charlotte Ford's debut is the party of the decade.

Detroit's Most Fabulous Party

Henry Ford's Great-Granddaughter Charlotte Bows: See Column 4; Also Pages 12, 13 and 30

The Detroit Free Press

FLAKES
Light snow, little change. High 30-34, low 23-27.

TUESDAY, DECEMBER 22, 1959 — On Guard for 128 Years — Vol. 129—No. 232 — 30 Pages — Eight Cents

METRO FINAL ★ BLUE STREAK

Firms Agree to Separate Bargaining

UNION CRACKS STEEL FRONT

OUR CHRISTMAS STORY
After Flood, People Forgot God Again

This is the fifth installment from "Our Christmas Story," a new book by Mrs. Billy Graham.

BY MRS. BILLY GRAHAM
As Told to Elizabeth Sherrill

The first sin brought unhappiness to Adam and Eve. But the unhappiness it brought them was nothing compared to the grief it brought God. Here were the creatures He had chosen out of all the universe to be His companions—and they had left Him.

He was lonely again, but now His loneliness was worse than before, because He had had children and then lost them. God, you see, still loved these people He had made. God does not change.

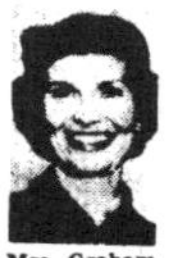

No matter how badly they had behaved, they were still His dearest creation.

Mrs. Graham

Adam and Eve had two sons, Abel and Cain. When they grew up, Cain killed his brother, and that was the first murder. Adam and Eve had more children, and those children had children until there were many people in the world—and most of them were like Cain.

Instead of living together peacefully, they quarreled with each other. Next to warn the children of Adam like noisy pleasures beat.

• • •

IN ALL, the noisy confusion no one heard God calling. No one heard Him say, over and over, that this was not the way to live, that this was not what He had made them for.

At least, very few people heard Him. In every generation there were always one or two who tried hard to shut out the din around them so that they could hear what God was saying.

One of these was Noah.

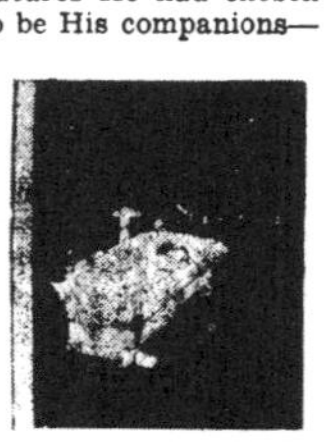

Noah lived quietly with his wife and three sons, listening all the time for God's message.

Now it happened that God had a very important message for Noah. The Bible tells us:

"God saw the wickedness of man was great in the earth, and that every imagination of the thoughts of his heart was only evil continually. And it repented the Lord that He had made man on the earth, and it grieved Him at His heart."

• • •

SO GOD decided to wash the whole earth clean with a great rain. But Noah was a good man, and God told him about the flood that was coming.

He told Noah to build an ark, a large boat with a house on its deck, big enough to hold his family and some of every kind of animal in the world.

God told Noah exactly how

Turn to Page 11, Column 1

A Sacrifice
★ ★ ★   ★ ★ ★
Many in Union Forego a Raise, Win Hike for Low Bracket

BY A. H. RASKIN
New York Times Service

NEW YORK—A New York union has used its economic strength to win a wage increase confined to Puerto Ricans and other newly enrolled workers at the bottom of its pay scale.

The beneficiaries will be 2,000 unskilled and semi-skilled members of the Millinery Workers Joint Board, an affiliate of the United Hatters, Cap and Millinery Workers International Union.

ALEX ROSE, president of the parent union, disclosed Monday night that they would receive a general pay rise of $5 a week. The pact also will establish a minimum standard of $50 for a 35-hour week.

Rose said the union's skilled members — whose wages range from $2.50 to $4 an hour — supported the decision to forego pressure for a general pay raise to concentrate on low - bracket in-

creases. The Joint Board's membership is 11,000 in the metropolitan area.

"Our membership fully understands," Rose said, "that we have a moral responsibility to protect the newcomers in our industry, who very frequently are the victims of exploitation in our community.

"We feel that to the extent we protect them we also protect the best interests of all the skilled crafts because when the wage floor rises the ceiling takes care of itself. In any event it is the duty of a union to make sure that none of its members need depend on public relief to maintain them and their families."

Million Hail Ike In Spain
Security Is Keyword In Franco Meeting

MADRID — (UPI) — President Eisenhower carried his peace mission to Spain Monday to the shouts and cheers of more than a million Spaniards who gave his bull-ring hero welcome to a handkerchief-waving hero.

Despite a cold, raw wind and a drizzle from overcast skies, Madrilenos lined 50 deep through the city to hail Mr. Eisenhower as an "ambassador of peace" in a reception so warm and enthusiastic it set back the official timetable 45 minutes.

But hordes of security guards and troops, some bearing submachine guns, kept order and there was no attempt to mob Mr. Eisenhower as there had been in New Delhi.

Security was the watchword from the moment chief of state Generalissimo Francisco Franco arrived at Torrejon American air base to welcome the President. Spanish groups opposed to Franco protested to the American Embassy against this visit—next to last on the 11-nation peace tour—but there was no sign of animosity Monday.

• • •

THE PRESIDENT'S jetliner flashed down to a landing at Torrejon while United States and Spanish honor guards snapped to attention.

Franco, in gray uniform and overcoat, saluted and shook Mr. Eisenhower's hand. The Spanish leader paid tribute to his "vigorous and moving profession of peace."

The President, standing on a platform, raised again the "peace and friendship" theme of his tour.

He said he had brought a message from the American people to the Spanish people about "a brighter future in co-operation for the noblest of all human causes. Peace and friendship in freedom."

• • •

AT A STATE dinner Monday night tendered by Franco, Mr. Eisenhower said Spain and the United States "want freedom for themselves and all nations."

Referring to Christmas, he

Turn to Page 2, Column 4

Mamie Plays Santa Alone

WASHINGTON — (UPI) — The First Lady ruled in for President Eisenhower Monday at the annual Christmas party for White House personnel.

Mrs. Eisenhower greeted members of the staff and their families in the East Room, where the White House Christmas tree is set up.

Mrs. Eisenhower, wearing a Christmas-red sheath dress and diamond earrings, gave each guest a reproduction of an Eisenhower landscape showing Mt. Eisenhower, a peak in the Canadian Rockies.

Blast Hits Plant

COLUMBIA, S.C. — (UP) — Eighty employes escaped injury when an ammonia explosion wrecked the Swift and Co. meat packing plant Monday.

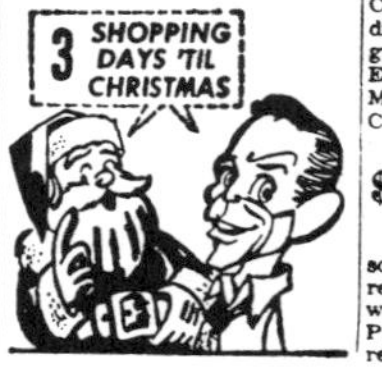

3 SHOPPING DAYS 'TIL CHRISTMAS

$1,500 Holdup

Two bandits held up Jackson's liquor store, 4101 W. Warren Monday night and escaped with $1,500, the owner, Robert P. Jackson, 38, of 1925 Edison, reported to police.

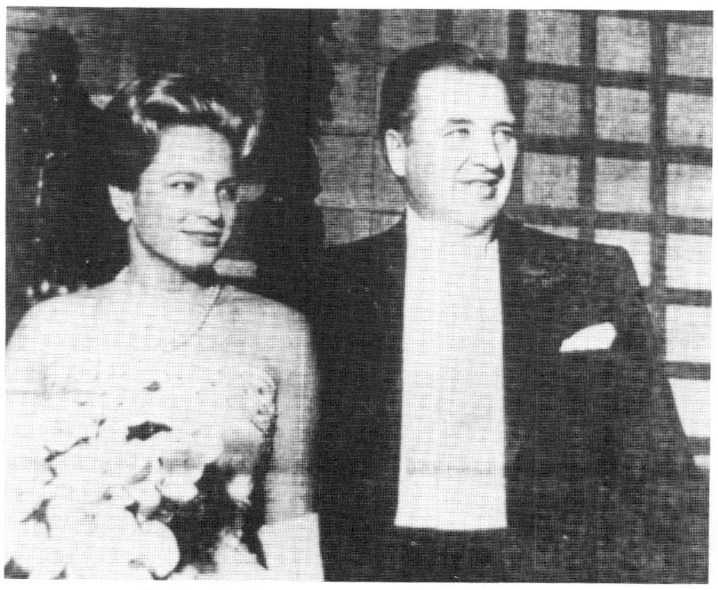

Charlotte Ford Takes Her Father's Arm For Her Big Step

A Princess Is Crowned
★ ★ ★   ★ ★ ★
Radiant Charlotte Ford Debuts Before 1,000 Guests

BY JEAN SHARLEY
Free Press Staff Writer

The family that put the world on wheels crowned a princess Monday night.

It was no solemn coronation for Charlotte Ford, Henry Ford II's blond older daughter. Champagne corks (Cuvee Dom Perignon 1949) popped till dawn at the Country Club of Detroit, the guests got progressively gayer, and by dawn the slim 18-year-old deb had danced a

• • •

THE GRANDDAUGHTER of Mrs. Edsel Ford, the great-granddaughter of Henry Ford, heiress to the world's greatest automotive fortunes, got a properly breath-taking sendoff. And she loved every minute of it.

The walls of the long gallery where the guests entered were papered with 2,000,000 magnolia leaves.

The guests walked along 150 feet of scarlet carpet, between pink-blooming rose trees and French-paneled walls to reach the French Room where the reception was held.

The Fords, the lovely Mrs. Henry Ford II in blush pink peau de soie, a gay Henry Ford II, who kissed a goodly number of the guests, and a shy but radiant deb, wearing a pink-jeweled white silk ballgown, greeted 1,000 guests.

They stood before a statue of Louis XIV riding a horse, a piece which Parisian interior decorator Jacques Frank found in the Detroit Art Institute basement, and hauled to the Country Club to oversee the French decor.

THE ROOM had trellised walls and chandeliers. Side urns were alive with flowers. The ballroom where the guests danced, many in their stocking feet, had walls paneled in 18th Century marble paper. The huge crystal chandeliers were filled with the fresh flowers of spring, carnations, tulips, calla lillies and iris, so many that by late Monday Detroit florists reported that they had no flowers for sale.

By twilight there were no evening tails for rent either.

Charlotte, wearing the scarlet can-can ruffled dress

Turn to Page 15, Column 1

PARTIES PRECEDE FORD DEBUT
Dazzling Gowns Add a Regal Touch

BY KATHIE NORMAN
Free Press Staff Writer

Beautiful women in exquisite gowns paid homage to a lovely blond princess—Charlotte Ford—at her debut ball Monday night.

The pageant at the Country Club had a royal opulence, and perhaps never again will a Motor City product be introduced with such splendor. Charlotte, a tall willowy, rather shy 18-year-old, danced the night away in a strapless white satin gown created for her by Yves St. Laurent, successor to Dior.

Mr. and Mrs. Ford dined at home, while Charlotte (in a short, shocking-pink silk faille dinner dress, also by St. Laurent) attended a gala dinner party at the Little Club, given by her aunts and uncles for some 170 of Charlotte's young friends.

VIVACIOUS Anne Ford, 16, enjoyed the "preview" of her own debut in 1961 in a white Balmain gown covered with floral patterns of shaded blue cut velvet.

Henry Ford II (looking more like her daughter's twin than ever) wore a magnificent pale pink satin ball gown, embroidered with crystals, with a bell-shaped skirt. It was designed for her by Simonetta of Rome.

Mrs. Edsel Ford, Charlotte's grandmother, wore a stunning silver lame gown, designed by Mainbocher, with a slightly full skirt, tiny shoulder straps and an oyster satin stole.

She was escorted by her cousin, Robert H. Tannahill.

Tiny, blond Mrs. William Clay Ford, Charlotte's aunt, looked delectable in an ivory satin gown by Givenchy. It was split from the floor-length hem to the knee, with a petticoat of black ruffled lace peeking through. Her accessories were black satin shoes and purse.

Mrs. Benson Ford also chose a Mainbocher original, a full-skirted, simple gown of stiff red tissue faille, set off by a diamond necklace and long white gloves.

Mrs. Walter Buhl Ford II was gowned by Clara Ray of Walton-Pierce in rose-pink cut velvet with a lily pattern. It was short in front and skimmed the floor in back.

MOST OF the 1,000 guests — including more than 100 notables from out of town — went directly to Charlotte's ball from elegant dinner parties.

One of the most lavish was hosted by the Ernest Kanz-

Turn to page 15, Column 1

New Talks To Begin On Sunday
Injunction Hearing To Be Resumed

WASHINGTON — (AP) — Industry representatives agreed Monday to hold separate company - by - company bargaining in the deadlocked steel dispute.

The decision was greeted as a victory by the United Steelworkers Union, whose President David J. McDonald said:

"What the union has been wanting right along has been agreed to."

McDonald has argued that the industry's top bargaining team, headed by R. Conrad Cooper, has lacked the power to make any concessions, so that talks with Cooper's group are hopeless.

• • •

COOPER, between meetings of Monday's negotiating session—the first in 10 days—was asked if there was any hope of early settlement. Cooper replied:

"We live in hope, but I can't say that that gives us any basis for optimism."

Under Cooper's leadership, 11 big companies have been representing almost the whole industry in bargaining talks.

Since the last joint bargaining session, McDonald not only had demanded the company-by-company talks—and threatened court action to bring them about—but also had announced new and slightly higher wage and benefit demands.

• • •

REPRESENTATIVES of the 11 big firms will meet with union leaders from their separate plants in Washington Sunday.

Executives of some of 82 smaller steel firms will meet Sunday with union local chiefs at individual company headquarters across the country.

Joseph F. Finnegan, Federal mediator, said his agency would not take part in the separate negotiations.

But he said mediation conferences will continue on a day-to-day basis in Washington he.

Turn to Page 7, Column 2

On the Inside...

- Cuban Paper Warns U.S. .... P. 5
- Nehru Hails Ike's Visit .... P. 8

Amusements	10	Stock Markets	21-23
Ann Landers	15	Town Crier	30
Astrology	28	TV-Radio	27
Auto-Business	31	Want Ads	24-26
Billy Graham	30	Women's Pages	12-15
Bridge	28	World Once Over	9
Comics	28-29		
Editorials	8		
Movie Guide	20		
Sports	17-20		

HAVE THE FREE PRESS DELIVERED AT HOME
PHONE WO 2-8800

SEPT. 6, 1960:

A crowded Labor Day in downtown Detroit gives John Kennedy's campaign a boost.

Tony Spina photostory.

Sen. Kennedy talks. Gov. Williams (left) and Sen. McNamara (above Kennedy's hands) listen as the Democratic presidential hopeful lashes at the Republicans.

Labor Day Downtown

Williams and Kennedy: They hear the cheers of 60,000 workers.

THE MAN Democrats hope will be the next President of the United States brought 60,000 people, most of them union members, downtown on a bright Labor Day. And the man, Senator John F. Kennedy, did not disappoint them. The Democratic candidate delivered a stinging speech in which he accused the Republicans of timidity and of a lack of faith that has stunted America's economic growth. Kennedy maintained a Democratic Labor Day tradition that began when Harry S. Truman launched his successful 1948 campaign in front of Old City Hall.

Free Press Photos by TONY SPINA

Labor marches in 30-minute parade to Old City Hall speeches.

Kennedy and Al Barbour, president of the Wayne County AFL-CIO, listen to a fellow Democrat

---

THE TOWN CRIER
Vacation's Wonderful, but . . .

BY MARK BELTAIRE

Now that autumn is fast acumin' in, it's time to ponder Troy Gordon's comment that a vacation is a fine place to visit but he wouldn't want to live there . . . Sign around a panhandler's neck: "If you are short of cash, I honor Diner's Club cards." . . . **Michigan State Fair's** Don Swanson has only one regret this year. He was unable to put a sign or Echo advertising his project . . . Detroit caterer **George Roumell is mighty pleased that he landed the contract to serve the food and such at the unveiling of the 1961 Ford at Flora, Ill.** . . . Bud Starwas of Flint wonders if a modern marriage is one in which the wife works so she can afford clothes to wear to the office . . . No women competitors were allowed in the recent 1960 National Championship Drag Races at the **Detroit Dragway.** One lady was admitted to competition last year after the gals howled about discrimination. There was also one accident, and guess who was involved. This year, no ladies, no howls.

Did you know that 120,000 meals a day are served at Wayne County General Hospital? . . . **George Taubeneck** tells about the little girl whose father was a judge, a position that gave the girl a certain inappropriate hauteur when she met people.

Her mother became fed up with this arrogance, told her: "Don't go around telling people you're Judge Brown's daughter. When you meet somebody, simply say I'm Marjorie Brown." Next day in a supermarket a hearty matron dashed up to the girl, boomed: "So you're Judge Brown's daughter." Said Marjorie in an equally carrying voice: "I always thought I was but mother says I'm not."

What They're Doing . . .

Within a year, researchers expect to be able to make wool a wash-and-wear fiber. Steps now being taken involve lessening shrinkage and increasing wrinkle resistance by weaving cloth from yarns in which wool fibers are relatively loosely packed, then chemically treated.

Former Detroiter **Don Stewart** has found himself an apartment in New York that is 40 feet long, three stories high, has five wood-burning fireplaces, a full basement . . . and is nine and a half feet wide!

Red and Anne Browning still bubbling over what they describe as the arrival of a "New Crew Member," **James William,** who checked in at eight pounds, 15 ounces.

If you call the Chrysler service garage on East Jefferson and get a Russell Krause on the phone, don't think you're talking to the dramatist. This one is a metal work foreman, spells his name differently (the other is Crouse) and says he's no relation.

All alumni of Boy Scout Troop 135 urged to attend the 25th reunion Sept. 14 at a dinner in Rainbow Terrace. Howard Cornfield, UN 4-1452, handling reservations . . . Scoutmaster is Irwin Ratner who has led the troop for 21 years, holds the Silver Beaver, Scouting's highest award.

Worth a Listen . . .

. . . is the advice in Catholic Digest from Sister Mary Catherine on how to help prepare your child for school.

. She urges that first of all you make every effort to convince the youngster that school is going to be a delightful experience. "Nourish the idea that he is a big boy now, that he is going to a real school with real books and a real teacher," she says. "Don't frighten him with warnings of school discipline. Instead of telling the child that the teacher will punish him if he talks in school, tell him that the teacher is there to guide and help him.

My Answer
BY BILLY GRAHAM

QUESTION: Have you any word of advice or comfort for me? I have just lost my husband, and I am too old to remarry. Life seems pretty empty. How can I adjust? —J. T.

ANSWER: It must be a pretty shattering experience to be left alone at your age. But let me offer you a little encouragement by saying that some of the happiest, and most useful people I know are widows.

During their married years they had little time to give as much time and effort to others as they would have liked. Their church had to often play "second fiddle" to home obligations. But now they find many hours to lend a helping hand to the needy, to visit with their friends, and to help in the important chores of their church.

You must not sit and brood over your sorrow. This would not help anyone, least of all, you. My advice would be—of all, you—to get involved with life. Find some noble cause to which you can give yourself. These can be the most exciting years of your life.

Enter into a partnership with God, and He will be your companion and guide.

IN GOOD OL' MICHIGAN . . .
It's Easy to Vote!

BY JUDD ARNETT

EVERY DAY or so I find a new reason for liking Michigan just a little bit better and currently I am singing our state's praises because of its enlightened voting laws.

It suddenly occurred to me the other day that if the mortgage company throws caution out the window and approves our application for a home loan, we will be switching precincts late this fall.

"Hey," I wondered out loud, "what will happen to our voting privileges? Will I lose my right to chunk one in for Wintergreen for President?"

So I called the Election Commission, and this is what they told me . . .

Moreover . . .

. . . Michigan now has a reciprocal agreement with three states: Ohio, Wisconsin and California, which provides that citizens who have moved and have therefore failed to establish minimum residency requirements, may still vote the Presidential ballot.

All they have to do is obtain a verification of their former place of residence and file it with their new Election Commission.

It is a sad commentary on the American elective system that there are not more agreements of this nature, for every year millions of our people are on the move.

The Census Bureau reports, for instance, that between March, 1957, and March, 1958, at least 5,584,000 Americans crossed state boundaries.

During that same period, 22,023,000 changed precincts. The number who lost voting rights ran into the millions.

During the . . .

. . . election of 1952 a very dear friend (then 50) was elated because for the first time he was permitted to exercise his franchise in a Presidential election.

Before this, as a member of the military and as a salesman transferred from one section to another, he had never been able to establish eligibility.

Wouldn't you know — the sonofagun turns out to be a Democrat?

Seriously, something ought to be done to standardize voting requirements and to make it easier for nomad Americans to vote.

As I was saying before being carried away on the subject, I am proud that Michigan is helping to blaze the trail.

A great state, this one!

Nov. 8, 1961:

Jerome Cavanagh upsets Louis Miriani.

The Detroit Free Press

Wednesday, Nov. 8, 1961 — On Guard for 130 Years — Vol. 131—No. 188 — Eight Cents

CHILLY Cloudy, cold, windy. High 40-44, low 30-34.

METRO FINAL ★★★ **ELECTION EXTRA**

Miriani Trounced in Upset

IT'S MAYOR CAVANAGH!

★ ★ ★ ★ ★ ★ ★ ★ ★

3 Newcomers Win Council Seats

'Unknown', 33, Beats Veteran

Hard-Hitting Campaign Pays Off for Newcomer

Other Pictures on Back Page

BY RAY COURAGE
Free Press Politics Writer

Youthful attorney Jerome P. Cavanagh parlayed a hard-hitting campaign and general unrest among Detroiters into a stunning upset victory over Mayor Miriani Tuesday.

Cavanagh, at 33, won election to a four-year term and a $25,000 salary as Detroit's chief executive.

He handed a decisive defeat to the 64-year-old Miriani, who succeeded the late Mayor Albert E. Cobo at his death and then won election to his first full term in 1957.

Cavanagh beat Miriani 200,413 to 158,778, according to final, unofficial figures.

The new mayor failed, however, to carry his own precinct.

His vote in Ward 16, Precinct 89 was 169 to Miriani's 244.

Mayor Miriani, presiding over a sorrowful group of would-be victory celebrators at Veterans Memorial, saw the handwriting on the wall minutes after the polls closed at 8 p.m.

As Cavanagh's lead continued to grow, Miriani and the 200 persons present became more dejected.

At the Pick-Fort Shelby Hotel, the scene was one of jubilant exhilaration as the young workers who comprised Cavanagh's organization began to realize they had a winner.

Cavanagh and his wife, Helen, left home before the polls closed, had one of their "dinners out" and appeared at a gathering of wives of Detroit Fire Fighters at the Labor Temple.

CAVANAGH issued a victory statement after 11 p.m. in which he said "this is not a time for gloating."

He read the statement to some 400 supporters at 11:30 p.m. and they promptly surrounded him, slapping his back and shaking his hand.

Cavanagh called on Mayor Miriani to join in "constructive efforts" to work for betterment of the City.

MIRIANI conceded and sent a congratulatory telegram to Cavanagh at four minutes after midnight.

Then he mounted the bandstand and told his audience he had lost.

He urged his workers to be "gracious in losing" and said the people obviously wanted a change "and they got it."

Cavanagh later said he had made no commitments to anyone on jobs in his new administration.

"My friends have not even asked me for jobs — except for one or two who jokingly said they'd like to be sewer commissioner."

As mayor, Cavanagh will pre-

Turn to Page 2, Column 1

Dems Win N.Y., Jersey Vote Tests

Free Press Wire Services

Democrats flying the colors of the New Frontier swept to victory Tuesday in the bellwether New Jersey and New York City elections.

In New Jersey, political novice Richard J. Hughes upset Republican James P. Mitchell, who was secretary of labor in the Eisenhower Administration.

In New York City, Mayor Robert Wagner won a third term by defeating Republican Louis Lefkowitz despite an inter-Democratic split and an all-out Republican bid for the mayoralty.

BOTH ELECTIONS were expected to have national impact and were being studied for clues as to how the political winds will blow in the 1962 congressional elections and the 1964 presidential elections.

President Kennedy had campaigned personally for both Hughes and Wagner.

New York Gov. Nelson Rockefeller had stumped extensively for Lefkowitz in New York, and former President Dwight D. Eisenhower had campaigned for Mitchell in New Jersey.

Republicans could find some consolation elsewhere around the nation. They ousted Democratic mayors in Buffalo, N.Y., Youngstown and Lorain, O., and

Turn to Page 10, Column 1

Ships Ram Off Texas, 1 Explodes

HOUSTON, Tex. (AP) — Two ships collided in the Houston ship channel Tuesday night and a tanker loaded with explosives and fuels exploded and burst into flames.

"We don't know too much about it right now, but it looks pretty bad," R. J. Marlowe of the Coast Guard operations officer in Galveston said.

The Coast Guard said there may have been some injuries. No deaths have been reported.

THE SHIPS met in open bay water about 25 miles from the heart of this industrial port city.

The Coast Guard identified the tanker as the Norwegian motor ship M. S. Bethan. The identity of the other ship, a cargo vessel was not immediately determined.

The Galveston Coast Guard sent two 40-foot utility boats equipped with fire-fighting equipment and one 125-foot cutter.

CLIP & SAVE THIS LEARN-A-LANGUAGE COUPON

For details, see Page 3

No. 11

Brickley, Wierzbicki, Ravitz In

Blanche Wise Out; Carey Tops Slate

BY FRANK BECKMAN
Free Press Staff Writer

Detroit voters, voicing a desire for change in City government by choosing a new mayor, also shook up Common Council by electing three new members and a new Council president.

The three non-incumbents swept into office were James H. Brickley, 32-year-old attorney; Anthony J. Wierzbicki, head governmental analyst of the Detroit Budget Bureau, and Dr. Mel J. Ravitz, sociology professor at Wayne State University.

They ousted incumbents Del A. Smith, Charles Youngblood and Blanche Parent Wise from the nine-member Council.

Elected Council president by capturing the most votes of the 18 candidates was Ed Carey, 56, a favorite of organized labor and Democratic organizations.

Carey, expected to provide the vigorous leadership lacking under Council President Mary V. Beck, is completing his first term as a councilman.

He is a former UAW international representative and served six terms as a Democratic State Representative, three as minority floor leader.

* * *

MISS BECK, a four-term councilman and president since 1957, slipped to sixth position behind newcomer Brickley, who showed amazing voter appeal in his first bid for elective office.

Carey's closest challenger for the presidency, which pays $2,000 in addition to the regular $12,000 Council salary, was Edward Connor, now completing his fourth term.

William T. Patrick, Jr., elected in 1957 as Detroit's

Turn to Page 2, Column 6

Lobbyists Curbed by Con-Con

Related stories on Pages 3 and 18

Lansing Bureau Staff

LANSING — The Michigan Constitutional Convention voted Tuesday to regulate lobbyists appearing before it.

It adopted a compromise three-point resolution to control agents who support or oppose any measure before the convention.

About 130 of the 144 delegates voted for the resolution. There was one dissenter.

JOHN T. KELSEY, a Warren Democrat, said he voted against the resolution because he felt that lobbyists should be permitted to come in and talk to the convention without registering.

The resolution, fourth on lobbyists to be brought before the convention's committee on rules and resolutions calls for:

• Lobbyists to register information on themselves, their firms, agencies or organizations.

• Lobbyists to file records of expenses incurred in mail, advertising or publicity intended to influence delegates.

• Lobbyists to file monthly expense statements on total amounts spent before the convention adjourns.

Lobbyists who violate the rules would be banned from Convention Hall.

The resolution could have far-reaching effects. It could, for instance, serve as a guidepost for the Legislature when it resumes in January.

Helpmate

LONDON (UPI) — Pop Singer Don Fox, who became chairman of a "Marriage Without Sex" society last weekend, resigned when his wife told him she was expecting a baby.

Special On the Inside

Sid Caesar Views TV

Visiting comedian says, "I think comedy is coming back." Page 23

TUMOR TRACERS: U-M scientists pinpoint brain tumors with "atomic cocktails." Page 3.

FARMER GETS LESS as milk prices go up, reports Drew Pearson. Page 9.

MICHIGAN-BRED footballers are now Iowa players, writes Bob Pille. Page 32.

Caesar

Amusements	24-28	Names and Faces	15
Ann Landers	21	Obituaries	25
Astrology	34	Sports	29-33
Bridge	34	Stock Markets	16
Business News	8	TV-Radio	22
Comics	33-35	Want Ads	23-27
Crossword Puzzle	34	Women's Pages	19-22
Death Notices	25	World Today	13
Drew Pearson	9		
Editorials	6	**HAVE THE FREE PRESS**	
Feature Page	9	**DELIVERED AT HOME**	
Movie Guide	35	**PHONE WO 2-8900**	

Two happy persons were Jerome Cavanagh and his wife.

Winner And New Champion

BY JACK CASEY

A wild-swinging, roughhouse campaign changed Jerome P. Cavanagh in three months from a "unknown" young lawyer into the $25,000-a-year mayor of Detroit.

The victory came in the first try for public office by the 33-year-old attorney.

When he takes oath next January he will be one of the youngest mayors of any major city in the United States.

"I'VE ALWAYS been interested in politics," Cavanagh said. "And I'll work hard at being a good mayor."

Cavanagh didn't think Miriani was a good mayor.

He said so, over and over again, at meetings, plant gates, shopping centers and in numerous newspaper, radio and television advertisements.

"Detroit has serious problems and the mayor won't admit it," Cavanagh told the voters. "I propose to do something about them."

Like candidates everywhere, Cavanagh continued to express confidence—even when he said "if I am elected mayor." Cavanagh didn't have a chance to say. When he occasionally slipped and said "if I am elected mayor," Cavanagh would catch himself, smile, and say, "WHEN I am elected mayor."

* * *

HE DECIDED to run late last July.

"I was convinced Detroit needed a new mayor," Cavanagh said. "There were other good men around, but they weren't running. So I ran."

His vigorous campaign continued through Tuesday afternoon, until just before Detroit finished voting.

Even his friends didn't think he had a chance when Cavanagh broke the news to a group of them last July 25 on the 29th floor of the Guardian Building.

But the Cavanagh enthusiasm was catching.

Many young Detroiters who

Turn to Page 2, Column 3

How He Won It: Cavanagh Wooed 'The Little Guy'

BY FRANK ANGELO
Free Press Managing Editor

Jerome P. Cavanagh was elected mayor of Detroit Tuesday because he carried his campaign to the man on the street.

Cavanagh took advantage of something which Mayor Louis C. Miriani lost sight of—that you have to be close to the little guy to win elections these days.

Miriani talked of big buildings, big ideas, efficiency in government. He talked of the fact that it takes experience to run a city and repeated constantly that running a city is like running a big business.

* * *

HE MAY have been right on every point, but in 1961 the man who wants to be president, governor or mayor must also talk to, with and about the little guy.

Miriani spoke of how the things he has done were going to help Detroit but he never quite gave his words the warmth that reached the majority of Tuesday's voters.

Cavanagh did.

Cavanagh talked about people and the problems they face in their every day life—more service on the DSR, help for the aged.

He sympathized with the unemployed and he talked to them.

* * *

[men who are considered real leaders in the Negro community by the Negroes themselves.

In some areas he got margins

Turn to Page 10, Column 1]

WINS IN POLL

Louie Does Well in School

Amid the shambles of his upset defeat, Louis C. Miriani salvaged one victory Tuesday.

He won a smashing victory in the straw ballot of Detroit public school children. The youngsters gave him 61,661 votes to Jerome P. Cavanagh's 42,722.

But it was a different story as the moms and dads cast their votes the kind that count.

The Election Story

What the new mayor faces, an editorial	Page 6
What winner and loser had to say	9
How key precincts indicated outcome	9
Amendment loses in charter vote	12
How suburbs voted in their own elections	12
City clerk and treasurer re-elected handily	12
Nedzi goes to Congress in a breeze	12
New faces for 1962 on Council	12, 14
Voters' own story of why they went for Cavanagh	14
From crankshaft inspector to council president	14
"Never had a loser," says Cavanagh's drum beater	14
Miriani in his hour of gloom	14
Meet Mrs. Cavanagh and the kids	19
Our camera catches Cavanagh	36

Complete Election Returns

MAYOR
1,145 of 1,145 precincts
Jerome P. Cavanagh ... 200,413
Louis C. Miriani ... 158,778

COUNCILMEN
1,145 of 1,145 precincts
(First nine elected)

Ed Carey	195,743
Edward Connor	187,075
William T. Patrick, Jr.	185,525
Eugene I. Van Antwerp	168,609
James H. Brickley	163,490
Mary V. Beck	159,758
Anthony J. Wierzbicki	147,025
William G. Rogell	146,138
Mel J. Ravitz	125,539
Blanche Parent Wise	123,275
Charles N. Youngblood	116,532
Del A. Smith	99,559
James A. Hoye	83,385
Terence McNamara	73,819
Edward G. Gehringer	68,713
Dale Curtiss	64,309
Stanley Novak	67,016
Frank J. O'Brien	61,794

CITY CLERK
1,145 of 1,145 precincts
Thomas D. Leadbetter ... 227,763
Edward H. Jeffries ... 61,415

CITY TREASURER
1,145 of 1,145 precincts
Charles N. Williams ... 237,031
George A. Higgins ... 55,043

CHARTER AMENDMENT
1,145 of 1,145 precincts
No ... 104,028
Yes ... 80,733

Mayor Louis Miriani was glum in defeat

The Detroit Free Press

Wednesday, Jan. 31, 1962 — On Guard for 130 Years — Vol. 131—No. 272 — METRO FINAL EXTRA — Eight Cents

FRIGID Partly sunny, cold. High 12-16, low 4-8.

JAN. 31 1962:

Tragedy strikes the world-famous Wallendas.

Two Aerialists Die in Plunge

4 ON HIGH WIRE FALL AT SHRINE CIRCUS

A Grab for Life ...

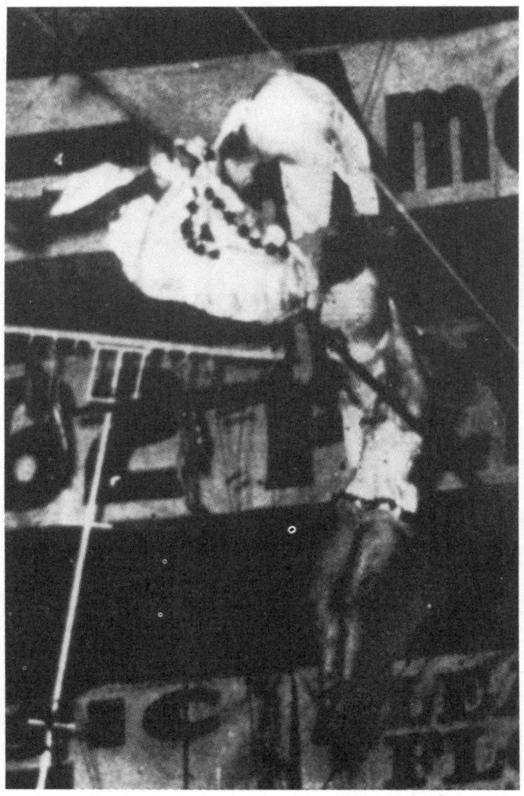

Struggling Jana Schepp was held safely on the high wire ...

IT MADE---AND KILLED---AN AERIALIST

The Tragic Trail of Love

BY RILEY MURRAY
Free Press Staff Writer

Richard Faughnan had two loves- the circus and a beautiful woman.

And it was the love of both that brought him to the high wire from which he plunged to death Tuesday night.

All his life Faughnan, 29, wanted to be a circus performer.

That desire drove him to attend every circus that came near his home town of Springfield, Mass.

He worked selling popcorn and balloons a n d programs just to be near the circus.

WHEN HE WAS 14, Faughnan met pretty Jenny Wallenda, who became his second love.

She was a bareback rider in a horse act with the Ringling Brothers Circus.

Jenny was also the daughter of the circus' high wire star, Karl Wallenda.

Faughnan told Jenny of his love of the circus, how he wanted to join a circus act. She sent him to her father.

Wallenda, impressed by his daughter's recommendation, took the boy as a pupil. Faughnan, after three years of training, was made a member of the act in 1951.

In 1955, he married Jenny Wallenda, his second love.

She collapsed Tuesday night when she was told of her husband's death. She was admitted to Highland Park General Hospital.

Circus Tragedy Stories:
- They've tempted death time and again P. 3
- Show went on to still threat of panic P. 3
- More dramatic pictures from the scene P. 32

Special On the Inside

Exhibitors' Nightmare

That's how Don Beck describes the 15-minute unloading regulation for Cobo Hall events in the fourth of a series on the problems of the big convention center. Page 3

Amusements	28	Feature Page	7
Ann Landers	19	Movie Guide	31
Astrology	30	Names and Faces	16
Auto News	13-14	Obituaries	21
Bridge	30	Sports	25-27
Business News	13-16	Stock Markets	14-15
Comics	29-31	TV-Radio	20
Crossword Puzzle	30	Want Ads	21-23
Death Notices	21	Weather	31
Drew Pearson	7	Women's Pages	17-19
Editorials	4	World Today	11

Learn a Language — See Page 29

HAVE THE FREE PRESS DELIVERED AT HOME PHONE WO 2-8000.

BY DON GERVASE AND RILEY MURRAY
Free Press Staff Writers

Two members of the famous high-wire Wallenda troupe were killed and three others were injured Tuesday night when they fell 35 feet before 7,000 horrified spectators at the Shrine Circus at the State Fair Coliseum.

Richard Faughnan, 29, was killed in the spectacular fall. He died of a skull fracture.

Dieter Schepp, 23, who fell from the wire during his first public performance on it, died early Wednesday in Highland Park Hospital.

Admitted to the hospital were Mario Wallenda, 22, in critical condition with head injuries; Schepp's sister, Jana, 17, suffering head injuries and shock, and Karl Wallenda, who suffered a pelvic injury.

Three members of the troupe grabbed the wire as they fell and were not injured.

Some of the crowd panicked when the accident occurred, but circus performers rushed into the arena and quickly restored order.

The troupe was in the middle of its act when the accident occurred. The aerialists were balanced on the wire in a pyramid, when the lead man on the wire, Deiter Schepp, lost his footing and fell.

... Then the Spectacular Plunge

... Finally dropped free after net was stretched below performers.

The head of the troupe, Karl Wallenda, told police that Schepp had complained to other members of the group of being ill, but had said nothing to him.

Wallenda said Schepp shouted, "I can't hold any more," just before he fell.

He added that Tuesday night's performance was Schepp's first in public with the troupe. Faughnan and Mario Wallenda tumbled from the wire behind him.

Gunther, Karl and Herman Wallenda grabbed the high wire as they flew by.

Miss Schepp was sitting in a chair at the top of the pyramid, 51 feet above the arena floor, when the men fell beneath her.

The three grabbed Miss Schepp as she flew by and held her until ring attendants could get a net under them.

Then they dropped the young woman to the net, climbed to the high wire and walked to safety.

MISS SCHEPP hit the net, but bounced out striking her head on the concrete floor.

The flying Wallendas are one of the most famous family circus acts in circus history. They are noted for coming up with more daring acts each circus season.

Many women and children in the audience left the arena, some of them weeping, after the accident.

Gene Randow, 46, who was waiting in the wings to go on with the other clowns, said the troupe came down "like cocoanuts falling from a tree."

"I never saw anything like it," he said.

Jenny Faughnan, 33, wife of Richard, and daughter of Karl Wallenda, was standing on a platform at one end of the wire. She gave this account of what happened:

"Dieter had the balancing poles on his fingers and I noticed before he yelled that he couldn't hold any longer. He threw the pole in the air to grip it in the center and while doing so he lost his balance. This threw everybody else off balance and down they went."

Also on the platform were Fontaine Kinkead, 19; Mike McGuire, 24, and Marty Boode, 22.

Mrs. Faughnan collapsed when she was told of her husband's death. Dr. Kenner Bell ordered her admitted to Highland Park General Hospital.

Karl Wallenda injured his left leg coming down from the wire and was treated at the same hospital.

The Wallendas were the only act performing when the tragedy occurred. They were performing over the center ring of the three-ring circus.

O. C. Hansen, 50, of 172 W Margaret, who was attending the show with his wife, said there was a "breathless gasp" from the crowd as the bodies fell through the air and hit the sawdust with a thud."

Hansen said the troupe had begun to move after Miss Schepp completed her act on the chair.

"**SUDDENLY THERE was a** slight loss of balance," Hansen

Turn to Page 6, Column 1

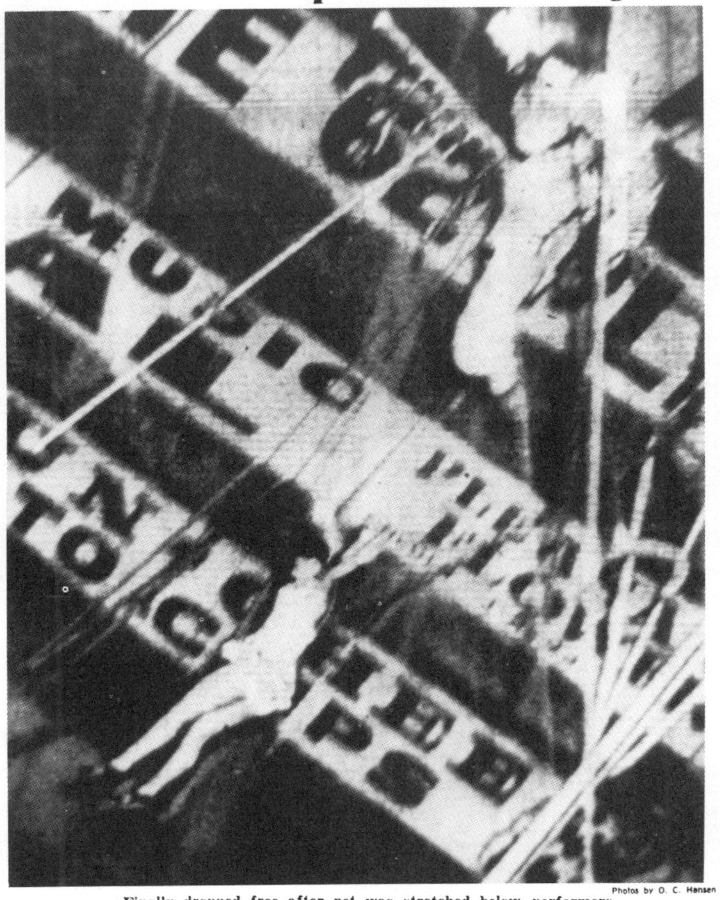

Photos by O. C. Hansen

French-Algeria Peace Expected Soon

Free Press Wire Services

PARIS—French troops and police took up positions in Paris and Algiers Tuesday night amid strongly supported reports that the seven-year-old Algerian war will end shortly.

SALISBURY, Southern Rhodesia— (UPI) — Fisherman Jan Ungerer, of Livingstone, sitting on the banks of the Zambesi River Tuesday, felt the line jerk and knew he'd hooked a big one. He was right. An enraged hippopotamus splashed out of the water and chased Ungerer away.

The reports said France and the Algerian rebels have reached final agreement on an Algerian settlement. Rebel leaders are expected to give secret approval Thursday or Friday, after which the agreement would be formally announced by both factions.

In Algeria, the French Army is understood to have been alerted for a possible emergency within the next few days. All units are under orders to keep battle ready.

COLUMNS of trucks rumbled through the deserted streets of Algiers Tuesday night, but it was uncertain whether they were connected with a ceasefire or with a possible new offensive against increasing right-wing violence and Moslem strikes.

(Attacks by the outlawed Secret Army Organization French, killed nine more persons Tuesday, and the death toll in a Secret Army bombing of Government agents' headquarters Monday was put at 18. Meanwhile, Moslem strikes crippled Algeriers docks and prisons, and students rampaged through the streets.)

In Paris, 4,200 tough troops were moved into position to guard against trouble in the city and its suburbs, where thousands of Algerians live. The new units bring Paris' security force to an estimated 26,700 men.

Despite the precautions, President Kennedy's press conference Wednesday will be telecast on Channels 2 (WJBK-TV) and 4 (WWJ-TV) at 5 p.m, and on Channel 7 (WXYZ-TV) at 7:30 p.m.

Radio stations will carry the parley at the following times:
WCAR, 4:30 p.m.; WWJ, 5 p.m.; WJBK, 6 p.m.; WKMH, 7 p.m.; WJR, 7:30 p.m.; WXYZ, 10:30 p.m.

Kennedy Broadcasts

President Kennedy's press conference Wednesday will be telecast on Channels 2 (WJBK-TV) and 4 (WWJ-TV) at 5 p.m., and on Channel 7 (WXYZ-TV) at 7:30 p.m.

This Fish Story A Real Whopper

Strange Guest

ALICANTE, Spain— (UPI) —Neighbors complained Tuesday that after Manuel Jimenez bought a burro he found he had no place to keep it, so he allowed the beast to share his fourth-floor apartment for the night.

Kennedy Backer Wins Rayburn Seat

SHERMAN, Tex.— (UPI)— A Democratic state senator backed by members of the Rayburn family Tuesday night beat a fellow-Democrat in a runoff election and won the seat held for half a century by the late Speaker Sam Rayburn.

With all but two of 207 precincts reporting in the Fourth Congressional district, Sen. Ray Roberts of McKinney had 16,151 votes to 13,474 votes for R. C. Slagle, an attorney from Sherman who also proclaimed himself a "Sam Rayburn Democrat" during a heated campaign.

Turn to Page 2, Column 3

Nov. 8, 1962:

George Romney's election as Michigan governor is overshadowed by Eleanor Roosevelt's death and Richard Nixon's bitter defeat in the race for governor of California.

"Romney Alone Amidst Dems," column two, and *"Angry Nixon Rips Reporters As He Bows Out,"* column five.

The Detroit Free Press

BLUSTERY Partly cloudy, colder. High 41-45, low 28-32.

Thursday, November 8, 1962 — On Guard for 131 Years — Vol. 132—No. 188

METRO FINAL Markets, Sports  Eight Cents

Widow of FDR Was 78
MRS. ROOSEVELT DEAD

Navy Will Check On Missile Vessels

WASHINGTON — The United States and Russia agreed Wednesday that American naval vessels will "contact" ships carrying Soviet missiles out of Cuba beginning Thursday to count the number of missiles on board.

Thus a second part of a Cuba settlement apparently had been achieved. The United States and Russia agreed earlier that International Red Cross inspectors would check Cuba-bound vessels to make certain offensive weapons were not being shipped in.

STILL UNDECIDED were two other vital questions—international inspection of the dismantled bases in Cuba, and withdrawal of Soviet jet bombers.

The United States was remaining firm on its stand that the bombers must go, but there were signs that it may drop the demand for on-site inspection of the missile bases since there may be nothing to inspect.

And in another phase of the complex negotiations, UN Secretary General U Thant denied a Soviet news agency report that he had suggested setting up UN control posts in the Caribbean and on American soil to guarantee Cuba against invasion. The United States probably would reject any such plan.

Details of the plan for contacting homeward-bound Soviet ships were not announced, but apparently they amounted to this: The missiles would be

Khrushchev announces end of Soviet A-tests Nov. 20; urges East-West accord on test ban. Page 5D.

Billie Sol Convicted; Gets 8 Yrs.

TYLER, Tex. — (UPI) — A jury Wednesday found bankrupt farm tycoon Billie Sol Estes guilty of swindling and sentenced him to eight years in state prison.

Under Texas law the jury sets the sentence in such cases.

The jury deliberated two hours and seven minutes before reaching its verdict. It asked District Judge Otis T. Dunagan three times to send various records into their chamber.

DEFENSE ATTORNEY John D. Cofer said he would file a motion for a new trial, a legal procedure which will clear the way, if refused, for an appeal to the Texas Court of Criminal Appeals.

Estes was permitted to remain free on his current $5,000 bond, pending the judge's action on the defense motion for a new trial. If the motion is refused, the judge then will pass formal sentence on Estes.

Estes' attorneys did not ask the jury for a suspended sentence. The case went to the panel with a passionate plea for acquittal.

The defendant was impassive during the reading of the verdict. He sagged momentarily with a sigh when the sentence was announced.

ESTES AND his wife, Patsy, walked arm-in-arm from the courtroom after jury foreman W. E. Florey announced the verdict. Mrs. Estes appeared to be fighting back tears.

There were three counts pending against Estes. The jury only had to find him guilty on one. Maximum sentence would have been 10 years.

It was Estes' first conviction. He awaits trial on four other charges in both state and Federal courts, including more than 30 counts of theft, swindling, mail fraud, false statements and antitrust violations.

Romney Alone Amidst Dems
He's Only Republican In the State's 'Cabinet'

BY JAMES ROBINSON
Free Press Staff Writer

George Romney, Michigan's first Republican governor in 14 years, will be surrounded by a Democratic state administration.

He will be the only Republican on the eight-member State Administrative Board over which he will preside as the chief executive.

If they want to be stubborn, the seven Democrats could make life miserable for Romney in countless ways.

The Administrative Board by law is charged with "general supervisory control over the functions and activities of all administrative departments, boards, commissioners and officers of the state, and of all state institutions."

IN HIS RELATIONS with the State Administrative Board, Romney will find that the law gives him only one vote in the determination of many important matters. Formal actions of the Board are by majority vote.

The Board, which meets twice a month, actually has functioned in recent years largely through five most important committees. The governor currently isn't a member of any committee.

The important committees each with four members, are Finance and Claims, Transportation, Education, Building and Efficiency, and Economy.

Acting largely through its committees, the Board approves such important actions as payment of claims, letting of contracts, approval of highway construction work orders, investments of state funds, leasing of building, and sale of bond issues.

It also has the function of setting quarterly allocations of state expenditures for all departments and agencies.

In the executive branch of government, the 55-year-old

Turn to Page 4A, Column 3

HE'LL NEED HELP
Romney's Task: 'Rebuild' the GOP

BY FRANK ANGELO
Free Press Managing Editor

Michigan voters got a glamorous new personality as their political leader Tuesday and they also paved the way for some major new political power lineups.

There was drama in Romney's unusual personal victory.

There will be more of the same in the weeks ahead as the political significance of the election begins to make itself felt.

OBVIOUSLY, Romney now gets a chance to go allout toward building the citizen-based type of Republican Party of which he spoke in the campaign. Practically, too, the Democrats will be looking for someone to pick up the baton for the next gubernatorial race.

The key questions thus are:
1—Will Romney be able to achieve his goal of recasting the Republican Party?
2—Who will be the man, or men, to watch in the move toward the driver's seat among the Democrats?

A post-election analysis suggests that Romney has a lot of work to do within his own party to lay the foundation for future progress.

As one wag put it, "George says he courted Lenore for more than a year and a half before he kissed her. There are some who wonder when he will get on kissing terms with the established party organization."

THE FACT that he won puts Romney in a strong position, but building a party will require a lot of doing.

The Romney volunteers gave him a good nucleus and the election begins to make

Turn to Page 5A, Column 1

Kennedy Gets Lift In Congress
Election Gives Him More Supporters

BY ROBERT BOYD AND PHILIP MEYER
Free Press Washington Bureau

WASHINGTON — If you forget about party labels, President Kennedy wound up a winner in Tuesday's elections with a slightly better chance of getting his program through the new Congress than he did the last.

Statistically, it was the biggest off-year Democratic triumph in 28 years. Over the past 50 years—except for 1934 under Franklin D. Roosevelt—the party in the White House has lost an average of 39 House seats and five Senate seats in non-presidential elections.

Tuesday the Democrats reversed the trend in the Senate, gaining four seats, and cut House losses to two. The final unofficial makeup of Congress, shows 68 Democrats and 32 Republicans in the Senate and 259 Democrats and 176 Republicans in the House.

THE SENATE, obviously, was a clear gain for the President. However, on the surface Mr. Kennedy seems to have failed in his goal of increasing the House Democratic margin.

Don't let this mislead you. Some of the new Administration really wanted was more pro-Kennedy seats, and that's what it got.

Some of those new Republican seats are from the South, and don't cost the Administration anything. Voters simply swapped anti-Kennedy Southern Democrats for anti-Kennedy Southern Republicans.

Pro-Kennedy Democrats won new seats in the North and West, particularly in California.

This means a net loss to the conservative coalition of Republicans and Southern Democrats that blocked much of the President's program.

IN EFFECT, the new Congress will have more pro-Kennedy vote, and three less anti-Kennedy votes.

The gain of these four seats makes the President eight votes stronger on close issues.

For the Republicans, it was unquestionably a day of gloom

Turn to Page 2A, Column 1

On the Inside
- Page 2B—American election results welcomed abroad.
- Page 4B—New faces gain important victories.
- Page 5B—Negroes make good showing in election.

The Election Story
- Find out how your town or ward voted Tuesday. Page 6A.
- Republican Romney to be surrounded in Lansing by Democrats. Page 1A.
- Swainson will rest, then prepare to give up office. Page 6A.
- Work faces Romney, who will also vacation. Page 6A.
- Anatomy of victory: How suburbanites and Negroes voted. Page 6A.
- Why did Detroit suburbs hold key to Romney win? Page 6A.
- Staebler is a new kind of Congressman. Page 6A.
- Democratic dominance on Supreme Court ended. Page 6A.
- Politics—not tea parties—will occupy Mrs. Romney. Page 1C.
- What do business and industry leaders think of Romney win? Page 9C.
- What can Romney expect from the new Legislature? Page 3A.
- Who will emerge as new Democratic Party leader? Page 3A.
- Complete tables on election results. Page 5D.
- Detroit elections pass stiff fairness test. Page 6A.

Mrs. Eleanor Roosevelt

End of the Line
An Angry Nixon Rips Reporters As He Bows Out

Free Press Wire Services

BEVERLY HILLS, Calif.—Richard M. Nixon admitted defeat Wednesday in his bid for California's governorship, congratulated the victor, then in an acidly bitter fashion declared: "This is my last press conference."

The former Republican vice president did not elaborate on the remark, but in view of the crushing blow dealt to his political career by his loss to Gov. Edmund G. Brown it seemed apparent he intended it to mean he is bowing out of public life.

Nixon was trailing Democrat Brown by nearly 250,000 votes when he went before news conference microphones in mid-morning and aired his views on political answers and on press and broadcast coverage of his long campaign.

Nixon started out by saying: "... Now that all the members of the press are so delighted that I have lost, I want to make a statement."

THEN, AFTER reading his statement, Nixon told a big crowd of newsmen:

"You won't have Nixon to kick around much longer."

He looked drawn, and appeared grief during most of his talk. Once or twice he smiled a quick, tight smile but his eyes at some points snapped with apparent anger. After

Turn to Page 2A, Column 4

Why Did So Many Hate Him So Much?

BY EDWIN A. LAHEY
Chief of Our Washington Bureau

WASHINGTON — Richard M. Nixon has had his seventh crisis.

The verdict:

Shock and hemorrhage—take him away.

And the answer to the most important question about Nixon will probably disappear with him as he fades on the horizon of political obscurity.

Why did so many people hate Nixon?

The spectrum of good and evil embraced by the human soul is actually pretty narrow.

DICK NIXON could not possibly have the character of total deceit attributed to him by his enemies, any more than he could be that paragon of virtue that some of his devoted followers believed he was.

A few people regarded Nixon as an innocuous bore, a chancer, an opportunist, an ambitious fellow suffering from a sense of insecurity. But he had many qualities in common with John F. Kennedy, who detests the man, and who would be the last to admit it.

If Nixon sometimes seemed a self-righteous bore, he had moments also of statesman-like grandeur. In this con-

Turn to Page 2A, Column 3

Richard Nixon

Ex-First Lady Ill 6 Weeks
Dies in N.Y. Apartment; Burial Set in Hyde Park

Other pictures and another story on Back Page. Mrs. Roosevelt and Detroit linked by bonds of affection. Page 8b.

Free Press Wire Services

NEW YORK—Mrs. Franklin D. Roosevelt, 78, widow of the 32nd President of the United States and in her own right one of the world's outstanding women, died Wednesday night.

Her heart failed under a burden of tuberculosis and anemia.

By coincidence, her death came exactly 30 years after she helped celebrate with her husband his election to the Presidency as the Democratic nominee. She spent 12 New Deal years with him in the White House until his death in 1945.

Mrs. Roosevelt was as controversial as she was prominent. She inspired deep love and affection among friends and casual admirers. She brought down the wrath of others, including political foes of her late husband. But, loved or despised, she was a woman too vital ever to be ignored.

HER INTERESTS were myriad. Almost no controversy escaped her attention—whether in international affairs or a domestic crisis involving civil rights.

On Sept. 26, Mrs. Roosevelt entered Columbia Presbyterian Medical Center, seemingly for a routine checkup. Actually, she had suffered a lung infection and anemia.

When her illness failed to yield to hospital treatment, she was discharged to her Manhattan apartment. There she gradually faded until her death at 6:15 p.m. Wednesday.

A family spokesman said that anti-tuberculosis treatment had been started at the hospital and that a rest after her return home confirmed the diagnosis.

She was too ill to take part in Tuesday's New York State election, although she had been instrumental in shaping the losing Democratic ticket. And her condition was such that she died without ever knowing the results.

With Mrs. Roosevelt besides her doctors were two sons, Franklin D. Roosevelt, Jr., and John Roosevelt, and her daughter, Mrs. Anna Roosevelt Halsted of Birmingham, Mich.

Two other sons were flying to New York. They are Rep. James Roosevelt (R., Calif.) and Elliot Roosevelt, coming from Miami.

THE BODY will be taken to the Roosevelt estate at Hyde Park, along the Hudson River above New York.

Funeral services will be held in New Hyde Park at 2 p.m. Saturday, with burial in the Rose Garden of the estate at 3 p.m.

The church service will be private. Those at the interment, in addition to the family, will include representatives of the Government, the United Nations, the State of New York and Mrs. Roosevelt's close friends.

Mrs. Halsted said that her mother had asked that her flow-

Turn to Page 4A, Column 1

America Mourns a Great Lady

Free Press Wire Services

A shocked America, mourning the death of Mrs. Eleanor Roosevelt, paid tribute Wednesday to the former First Lady as one of the great ladies in the history of the United States.

President Kennedy: "One of the great ladies in the history of this country has passed from the scene. Her loss will be deeply felt by all those who admired her tireless idealism or benefited from her good works and wise counsel."

Adlai E. Stevenson, United States ambassador to the United Nations: "Like so many others, I have lost more than a beloved friend. I have lost an inspiration. She would rather light candles than curse the darkness and her glow has warmed the world."

FORMER VICE President Henry Wallace: "It's hard to believe that one so vital is no longer with us. She represented a strong element in the Roosevelt Administration, and in a sense her death marks the end of an era."

Former President Herbert Hoover: "Mrs. Roosevelt was a lady of fine courage and great devotion to her country."

Mayor Robert F. Wagner of New York: "She was so grand a woman, so rare a person, so pure in spirit, that to judge our loss at this moment is impossible ... a light has gone out of our lives."

James A. Farley, postmaster general under Roosevelt: "As long as the memory of an American woman is recorded in our country's annals, the name of Anna Eleanor Roosevelt will be enshrined."

FORMER NEW YORK Gov. and Senator Herbert H. Lehman, long a political associate and personal friend of Mrs. Roosevelt: "There is no one anywhere in the world who will not be deeply grieved at the sad news of the passing of one of the greatest women of all time."

Canada's Lester B. Pearson, who was president of the UN General Assembly when Mrs. Roosevelt was a delegate: "She was one of the great women of our time and her contribution toward progress in her own country was only equaled by her contribution to all good international causes."

Walter P. Reuther, president of the United Auto Workers: "Mrs. Roosevelt was truly one of God's noblest creations. In her passing I have lost a close and dear friend and the world has lost a great and gracious lady who lived a life of dedication and devotion to her fellow man. Filled with compassion and human understanding, she gave unselfishly and tirelessly of herself in the search for a world of peace, freedom, justice and brotherhood. As the first lady of the world, she was a living symbol of the best in mankind and was loved and respected by people everywhere."

On The Inside
Amusements	10-11B
Ann Landers	3C
Astrology	10D
Auto News	11C
Billy Graham	12D
Bridge	10D
Business News	9C
Camera	
Comics	9-11D
Crossword Puzzle	10D
Death Notices	5D
Drew Pearson	11A
Earl Wilson	11A
Editorials	8A
Feature Page	11A
Movie Guide	11D
Names and Faces	9D
Obituaries	5D
Sports	1-4D
Stock Markets	10-11C
TV-Radio	6C
Want Ads	5-8D
Women's Pages	1-5C
World Today	8C

Double Trouble
ST. HELENS, England — Mrs. Mary Prendergast Wednesday gave birth to twins, her third pair in 34 months.

The Detroit Free Press

Thursday, April 18, 1963 — On Guard for 131 Years — Vol. 132—No. 349 — Eight Cents

DROPPING — Windy, considerably cooler. High 53-57, low 36-46.

METRO FINAL — Markets, Sports — BLUE STREAK

LIONS CRY 'DOUBLE-CROSS,' SEEK APPEAL OF PENALTIES

BY GEORGE PUSCAS
Free Press Staff Writer

Those six punished Lions feel strongly that they have been betrayed.

So they're planning a meeting with an attorney to consider all avenues of appeal and rebuttal to National Football League Commissioner Pete Rozelle, the Free Press learned Wednesday.

"ROZELLE TOLD them just a couple of weeks ago that there would be no suspensions and that nobody would be hurt," one source close to the players told the Free Press.

"Now there's this, where he (Rozelle) has come out and condemned them all without any explanations.

"Well, they want to tell their side of the story, too."

In New York, Rozelle insisted he had never made a "firm promise" that player names would not be mentioned.

He said he never intimated that their admissions would help Karras, or that there would be no suspensions.

• • •

HE REVEALED that he sent letters to all players involved, advising them that under NFL rules they were allowed to appear at a formal hearing to contest any charges against them.

"They all returned the signed waivers of a hearing, indicating that they did not want to contest the charges," Rozelle said.

NFL rules make it clear that there is no appeal possible from the $2,000 fines levied against Joe Schmidt, Wayne Walker, John Gordy, Gary Lowe and Sam Williams, and the indefinite banishment of Alex Karras.

"They scared the hell out of a couple of the kids," the source said.

"A couple of them insisted on taking lie detector tests."

SCHMIDT, captain of the Lions, did not take a lie test. He openly admitted making a $50 bet on the Green Bay-New York title game last Dec. 27, figuring it would help Karras.

"Rozelle told Schmidt he was one of the most respected people in football, and that no names would be mentioned when the investigation was finished," the source said.

Lie detector tests, it was learned, were given in Detroit and New York to a handful of players during the last three months.

Players on at least six other of the NFL's 14 teams also submitted to tests in the investigation.

Schmidt has been captain of the Lions for the last

Turn to Page 4A, Column 2

Board Delays Certification Of April Vote

Lansing Bureau Staff

LANSING—The State Board of Canvassers, locked in a partisan dispute, failed to act Wednesday on certifying the results of Michigan's April 1 election.

A day-long wrangle failed to produce agreement between the two Republican and two Democratic members on whether the board should await a decision from the State Supreme Court in a suit filed to cancel the results of the April 1 voting on the Constitution.

Chairman David Lebenbom, Detroit Democrat, and Mrs. Ester Waite, East Lansing Democrat, insisted the board wait for the Supreme Court's decision which is expected within a week.

Mrs. Zoe Burkholz, Benton Harbor Republican, and Carl Lindquist, Iron River Republican, wanted to go ahead with certification.

MRS. BURKHOLZ argued that the Board had a duty to perform and should proceed in the absence of any court order preventing certification.

Lebenbom claimed that the State boards customarily "maintain the status quo" when a decision involving their action imminent in the courts.

A motion by Mrs. Burkholz to certify that the Constitution was adopted failed to carry when the two Democrats voted against it.

THE NEW Constitution was adopted by an apparent majority of 7,829 votes.

Lebenbom said he is satisfied with the results of the canvass, except for the question of timing on the board's certification. He pointed out that the Board is given 40 days after

Turn to Page 4A, Column 1

Deadly Bet

VILA DA FEIRA, Portugal — A bet orphaned 10 children in nearby Fermil Wednesday. A farm worker, Antonio Da Silva, 50, wagered friends he could drink two gallons of wine and a quart of brandy at a sitting. He did, but died within hours.

"I SOLD

my carpet for the amount advertised, and I'm very pleased with the Free Press. I got plenty of calls and made the sale the second day this ad ran."

Mr. C. V. French

Like to have a magic wand? Try Free Press Want Ads — ideal for turning unused household furnishings into cash! Call Speedy Sales and see.

222-6800

Steel-Price Increases Snowball

Top 12 Firms Fall into Line

Free Press Wire Services

NEW YORK—Major steel producers and smaller operators jumped on the price increase bandwagon Wednesday with selective boosts.

Second-ranked Bethlehem Steel joined U. S. Steel and third-ranked Republic to bring the industry's "Big Three" into line.

THE KAISER STEEL Corp., ninth largest producer and long a maverick, ended doubts about the unity of the industry and announced an increase of $4 to $5 a ton on 19 per cent of its products. Kaiser had been the only major holdout in the upward price trend.

Kaiser refused to go along with last year's abortive price. A California firm, Kaiser lost $5.2 million in 1962.

All of the nation's top 12 steel producers have now raised some of their prices.

President Kennedy, who last week tentatively approved the "selected" price boost pattern while warning against any across-the-board hike, received a report from his economic advisers shortly after he returned to Washington from a vacation in Palm Beach, Fla. The report analyzed the economic impact of the hikes.

Walter Heller, chairman of the White House Council of Economic Advisers, gave Mr. Kennedy both an oral and written report.

A quick retort came from the Commissioner.

"This appears to be a complete disregard of the State supervisory and regulatory authority," said State Insurance Commissioner Sherwood Colburn.

Turn to Page 4A, Column 1

Blue Cross Rate Hike Approved

Blue Shield to Try June 1 Boost, Too

State Insurance Commissioner Sherwood Colburn gave approval Wednesday to a 23.4 per cent across-the-board increase in Blue Cross rates.

The off-again, on-again settlement was concluded at a meeting between Colburn and John J. Schoenenberg, Jr., Blue Cross' actuary.

Meanwhile, Blue Shield the medical insurance, announced early Thursday that effective June 1 it intends to raise its rates 19.2 per cent, Frank O. Starr, deputy executive director announced after a six-hour board meeting.

"This increase," Starr said, "is being put into effect without further notice to the State Insurance Commissioner."

Rush to Aid Sinking Ship

MIAMI—(UPI)—The Coast Guard said Wednesday night the 50-foot American research ship Nancy Queen, believed to be carrying a crew of 14, radioed it was sinking about 90 miles off Nassau.

The Coast Guard dispatched an amphibious plane carrying emergency pumps to search for the vessel. The tugboat Made was en route to the scene from Nassau.

The Coast Guard said radio messages from the ship were garbled. The word "pump" was heard several times, a spokesman said.

Auto makers are watching and waiting to see if car prices will be affected by steel price hikes. See Page 6-C.

Special On the Inside

Tigers Beat Yanks, 4-2

Detroit Takes First Place Alone as Gus Triandos Hits Homer and Double (See Page 1F)

Amusements	6-7E
Ann Landers	8E
Astrology	8F
Auto News	5B
Billy Graham	10F
Bridge	8F
Business News	5B
Camera	8F
Comics	7-9F
Crossword Puzzle	8F
Death Notices	6C
Drew Pearson	11A
Editorials	8A
Feature Page	11A
Movie Guide	8F
Names and Faces	4C
Obituaries	6C
Sports	1-5F
Stock Markets	6-7B
TV-Radio	8E
Want Ads	6-9C
Women's Pages	1-5E

HAVE THE FREE PRESS DELIVERED AT HOME — PHONE 222-6500

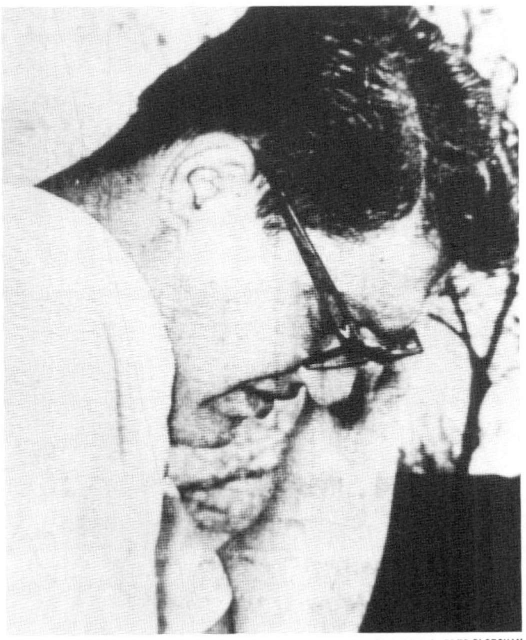

Free Press Photo by FRED PLOCHMAN
Alex Karras was shocked by news of his suspension

Southern Senators Challenge Bid to Ban Mississippi Aid

Free Press Wire Services

WASHINGTON — Southern Senators Wednesday challenged a United States Civil Rights Commission proposal urging President Kennedy to consider cutting off Federal funds for Mississippi because of racial inequality there. The state receives about $650 million a year from the Federal government.

Their denunciation of the proposal foreshadowed a fight later in Congress against the President's recommendation that the commission be given greater powers and its life extended beyond its November expiration date.

SEN. JOHN STENNIS (D., Miss.) said the "presumptuous and utterly ridiculous" proposal was "proof positive that the commission should be permitted to die its long awaited natural death later this year."

"Its report regarding the state of Mississippi is the latest example of the repeated meddling of busybodies acting beyond their assigned mission and purpose," he said in a statement.

Chairman James O. Eastland (D., Miss.), of the Senate Judiciary Committee, called the commission's proposal "the most monstrous libel that has ever been leveled against a state in this union."

SEN. JOHN SPARKMAN (D., Ala.) called the commission recommendation "absolutely absurd." He said he hoped the Executive Department would disregard it because it was "completely contrary to the intent of Congress and doesn't seem to represent clear thinking."

Sparkman said Negroes would be hurt most if Federal funds are cut off for farmers, the aged, dependent children and the school lunch program.

Northern senators took a different view of the proposal.

Sen. Philip A. Hart (D., Mich.) praised the commission for seeking to end what he termed "an intolerable irony."

And Senator Kenneth B. Keating (R., N.Y.) said he is "happy to see the recommendations and I hope they bear fruit."

SEN. Paul H. Douglas (D., Ill.) said he felt that "our southern friends" cannot continue to "flout the law and the Constitution and, at the same time, get all the favors of the national government."

In Jackson, the Mississippi Advisory Committee to the

Turn to Page 2A, Column 8

MONROE HIT HARD

Tornado, Big Hail Rip Up Property

Baseball-sized hail, severe winds and at least one tornado in southern Lower Michigan Wednesday night tore off roofs, broke windows, knocked down wires and trees and damaged cars.

The Monroe County sheriff's office said high winds ripped roofs from three homes, split one home open and flattened garages at Grand Beach, on Lake Erie, five miles north of Monroe.

DEPUTIES said more than 1,000 windows were broken by hailstones as big as baseballs. Fallen trees and tree limbs littered roads, and electricity was cut off from 1,000 Monroe County residents.

Wind-driven hail stones up to three inches in diameter pelted Milan, Pontiac, Troy and Deerfield Township, near Howell.

Police said they received hundreds of reports of dented cars and parked aircraft and torn convertible tops. Hundreds of store and home windows were broken in those areas.

A small tornado in Coldwater rolled a house trailer over

Turn to Page 2A, Column 8

Girls Smooth Mail Tempers

PARIS —(UPI)— Soft music and pretty hostesses are being introduced in Paris post-offices to speed the flow of mail and calm edgy tempers. While recorded music plays in the background, blue uniformed hostesses will help guide customers to proper windows.

Bar Karras And Hornung, Fine 5 Lions

BY GEORGE PUSCAS
Free Press Staff Writer

Detroit Lions tackle Alex Karras was suspended for at least one year—and possibly for life—Wednesday, and five other Lions and the club itself were fined a total of $14,000 in the heaviest penalties levied in the history of professional football.

Among the other Lions fined was team captain Joe Schmidt.

Schmidt and the four others — Gary Lowe, Wayne Walker, John Gordy and Sam Williams — were fined $2,000 each for betting on the 1962 championship game between Green Bay and New York.

Lions management also was fined $4,000 for neglecting action on a Detroit police report which revealed player associations with "known hoodlums."

NATIONAL FOOTBALL League Commissioner Pete Rozelle, ending one phase of his investigation into gambling, also suspended indefinitely Paul Hornung, the "golden boy" halfback of the champion Packers.

The action against the Lions, announced in New York by Rozelle, immediately brought Lion President William Clay Ford into a meeting with general manager Edwin J. Anderson, head coach George Wilson and Karras and Walker.

Karras, whose admission on a national television show that he had bet on games gave impetus to the investigation, was visibly shaken by the severity of his penalty.

"Right now I'm a bartender and a wrestler," Karras said later. "I don't know what I'm going to do about football. I might try to play in the American Football League."

ROZELLE SAID the suspensions left Karras and Hornung "legally free to play in any other league in 1963." But, in Dallas, AFL Commissioner Joe Foss said that under no circumstances would Karras and Hornung be allowed to play in his league.

Rozelle said that "indefinite suspension" meant that the cases of Karras and Hornung would not be reopened for at least a year . . . "and maybe not even then."

The commissioner said that his investigation revealed that on at least six occasions Karras had bet as much as $50 on games.

Hornung, he added, had bet as much as $500 a game on pro and college teams between 1959 and 1961.

At his Louisville home, Hornung, the NFL's player of the year in 1961 and its all-time leading scorer, said he "was expecting this."

THE PENALTIES against the five other Lions were the one genuine surprise, for there had been no inkling that Rozelle was investigating wagering by them.

Rozelle said the fines stemmed from an incident last Miami last December, when the Lions were preparing for the Pro Bowl game against the Pittsburgh Steelers.

The commissioner reported that Karras invited his teammates to watch the televised Green Bay-New York title

Turn to Page 4A, Column 4

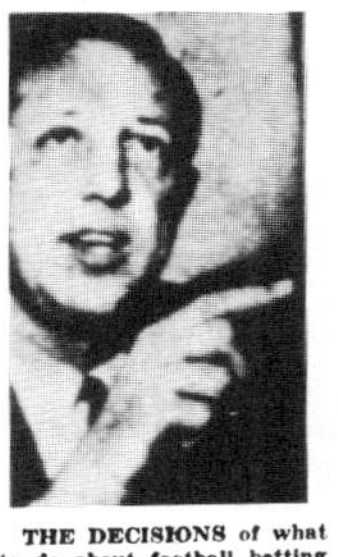

THE DECISIONS of what to do about football betting were made by Pete Rozelle, National Football League commissioner.

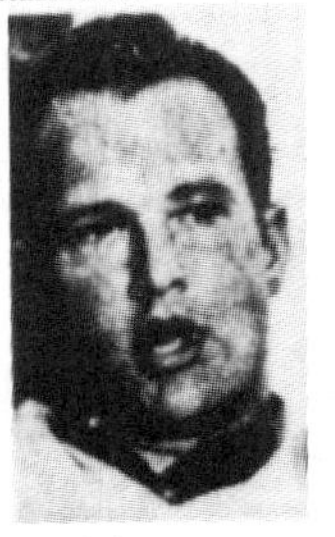

Paul Hornung

The Football Story in Full:

• Text of Rozelle statement—Page 6C.
• Players used bad judgment, says Commissioner Pete Rozelle—Page 1F.
• Karras not ashamed—Page 1F.
• Lions' brass won't appeal penalties—Page 1F.
• AFL, Canada won't accept Karras and Hornung—Page 1F.
• Karras as an athletic family—Page 1F.
• Hornung hopes he'll be reinstated in 1964—Page 2F.

APRIL 18, 1963:

The Lions are caught in a major National Football League gambling scandal.

JUNE 24, 1963:

The Rev. Martin Luther King Jr. leads the nation's largest civil rights march.

The Detroit Free Press
Monday, June 24, 1963 — On Guard for 132 Years — Vol. 133—No. 51

SUNNY Continued warm. High 86-90, low 60-64.

METRO FINAL Late News, Sports — **BLUE STREAK** — Ten Cents

125,000 WALK QUIETLY IN RECORD RIGHTS PLEA

More than 100,000 Detroiters watched and walked in orderly fashion Sunday on Woodward in a freedom march led by the Rev. Martin Luther King (arrow). This was the scene as the start of the official parade passed beyond Grand Circus Park.

Negroes Hail King Speech

Civic, Union Officials Join Woodward March

BY JEROME HANSEN AND JACK MANN
Free Press Staff Writers

A solid stream of 125,000 persons poured down Woodward Avenue Sunday and overflowed a Civic Center rally in the largest civil rights demonstration in the nation's history.

The marchers and more than 15,000 spectators jammed downtown Detroit for the Detroit Council for Human Rights' "Walk to Freedom" to demonstrate support for the Negro's fight against racial injustice and to raise funds to continue the struggle.

After the march, an audience of 25,000, more than 95 per cent Negro, packed the Convention Arena and Hall A in Cobo Hall to hear a rousing speech by the Rev. Martin Luther King, Jr.

King told the rally the "fight for freedom has caused the Negro to take new stock of himself."

"We want all of our rights and we want them now," he told the cheering, stamping, screaming crowd.

He asked for support of President Kennedy's civic rights bill and urged Negroes to use non-violence in their press for equal rights.

Detroit police officials, surprised at the size of the demonstration, said it was one of the most orderly events ever held in the city.

Only a rally for President Franklin D. Roosevelt in 1936 and some Labor Day demonstrations in the 1930's surpassed or came close to equaling Sunday's outpouring.

There were 800 extra police officers working, with 500 officers assigned specifically to the parade and rally. King and officials of the Detroit sponsoring group were unstinting in their praise of the way the officers handled the parade.

The march, originally scheduled for 4 p.m., started an hour early. Marchers and spectators began swarming into the starting area at Woodward and Adelaide shortly after noon.

• • •

HOLDING PLACARDS which read: "Evers Died for You — Join the NAACP for Him" and "We Want Freedom Now," the marchers formed from curb to curb on Woodward.

Impatient to begin, they started walking without King, who had gone from Detroit Metropolitan Airport to a suite at the Sheraton-Cadillac Hotel.

King was hustled to meet the parade front at Woodward and Cadillac Square.

He was cheered by the crowd, which surged around him. Police Commissioner George Edwards, Rev. King's escort, found no dignitaries or parade officials and took King back to Adelaide and Woodward.

There he formed a line with Mayor Cavanagh; UAW president Walter P. Reuther; former Gov. John B. Swainson; State Auditor General Billie S. Farnum; Benjamin McFall, director of the Detroit Council for Human Rights, and Rev. C. L. Franklin, chairman of the Council.

There were no serious incidents during the parade or rally.

Police arrested two drunks, who were released later, a pickpocket, and a man describing himself as a "White Muslim" who stopped a photographer's car in front of the J. L. Hudson Co. The latter was arrested for interfering with police officers when he refused to comply with a policeman's order to move.

Turn to Page 2A, Column 1

Parade pictures on 2B, 3B, Back Page

The Free Press had photographers Vince Witek, Fred Plofchan, Tom Venaleck and Jerry Heiman on the job.

More stories on Pages 3A and 2B

FBI NABS WW II VET
Prominent Dixie Racist Charged with Evers Killing

Free Press Wire Services

JACKSON, Miss. — A prominent member of Mississippi's segregationist White Citizens Council who broke with his church because of its soft stand on integration was charged Sunday with the ambush killing of civil rights leader Medgar Evers.

Byron de la Beckwith, 42, a fertilizer salesman and gun fancier, from a pioneer Greenwood (Miss.) family, was arrested Saturday night at the office of his attorney in Greenwood.

He was brought here in a three-car caravan by FBI agents early Sunday and charged with first degree murder. In addition, Beckwith faces Federal charges of conspiring to deprive the slain Negro integration leader of "free exercise and enjoyment" of his constitutional rights and privileges.

Arrest of the slim, dark-haired 160-pounder climaxed an intensive manhunt which began at 12:40 a.m. June 12 when Evers, the Mississippi field secretary of the National Association for the Advancement of Colored People (NAACP), was shot in the back by an assassin in front of his home.

Byron de la Beckwith

FBI Director J. Edgar Hoover said in Washington that a telescopic sight on a high-powered World War I vintage rifle found among honeysuckle vines near Evers' home was traced to Beckwith. Hoover also said that bureau fingerprint experts identified a print on the weapon as being from Beckwith's hand.

Attorney General Robert Kennedy told a radio-television audience Sunday night that Federal agents "have more evidence than the fingerprints on the gun."

Kennedy said, however, he was not at liberty to reveal the additional proof.

Kennedy also said the Government would defer the matter of Beckwith's trial to the state of Mississippi. The attorney general said he had talked with Jackson Mayor Allen Thompson about this.

• • •

BECKWITH turned himself in to FBI agents Saturday night in the Greenwood office of his lawyer, city attorney Hardy Lott.

Lott said Beckwith, working in another county, was tipped by neighbors that the FBI was watching his house. Beckwith contacted Lott and, after a conference

Turn to Page 4A, Column 2

---

2 Million Germans Hail JFK

Pictures on Page 1B

BONN — (AP) — President Kennedy arrived in West Germany Sunday with a pledge that the United States would never desert its allies.

He received a warmhearted, folksy and tumultuous welcome by 2 million Germans many of whom broke through police lines in their outbursts of enthusiasm.

Sunday was the start of a 12-day tour of four European nations to stress continued United States determination to defend Europe. Mr. Kennedy did it with a statement that any attack on America's European allies would be considered an attack against the United States itself.

• • •

BUT THE President told a dinner audience Sunday night that the lack of an immediate threat also posed problems for the NATO Alliance.

"If our alliance is able to stand fast in the face of immediate outside pressure, we will be the exception," he said, "and it seems to me, therefore, incumbent upon us in the '60s to jointly consider with our other allies and ourselves how we can make this alliance work while the enemy still at the gate does not present perhaps as menacing a threat as he did some time ago."

Mr. Kennedy called on NATO members to use the alliance not only for security but "from this very powerful core of Western Europe and the United States to spread out throughout the world to assist those who now occupy the battleground for freedom."

• • •

THE GREAT crowds packed to suffocation the squares in Cologne around the ancient cathedral and the City Hall in Bonn. Chants of "Ken-ne-dee" along the 40-mile parade route through both cities after he landed at Wahn

Turn to Page 2A, Column 4

Coffee Money

ADEN — (AP) — Yemen's new currency carries for the first time the seal of the republican regime. The reverse side of the new coin shows a coffee tree, representing Yemen's Mocha coffee.

Marchers Agree: 'It's a Great Day To Be Walking'

BY JOHN MUELLER AND JOHN DIEBEL
Free Press Staff Writers

The weather was perfect and the bands enthusiastic as the "Walk to Freedom" moved down Woodward Avenue and on to Cobo Hall.

Groups of marchers and spectators joined the bands in such songs as "We Shall Overcome," the "Battle Hymn of the Republic" and "We Shall Not Be Moved."

Thousands of signs and flags waved above the throng, which quietly but expectantly filled about a mile of Detroit's main street and poured solidly into the Civic Center area.

• • •

MANY OF THE marchers yelled good-naturedly at the spectators along the way.

"Come on out, it's a great day to be walking," called out one marcher to spectators.

A white youth in his early twenties was in the parade. His flag waved for the Fifteenth District Democrats. But a white man standing on the curb said he thought nothing of the demonstration.

"I'm just walking by."

The march, originally scheduled to start at 4 p.m., shifted gears and started at 3 p.m. It lasted an hour and 40 minutes. Later, the great mass of people filled and overflowed Cobo Hall.

Midway in the march, the Lodge Freeway clogged and traffic came to a standstill as people tried to get downtown to march or watch.

NO VIOLENCE of any kind was reported, although one white man tried to start something by jumping in front of a car carrying a group of press photographers.

He forced the car to a halt, screaming "I demand to see Dr. King." The man, Joseph E. Laliberte, 39, who described himself as a "White Muslim," said he wanted to tell King to slow down on integration in the suburbs.

He was forcibly removed by two uniformed police, and will be found Monday with interfering with a police officer.

THERE WAS a friendly rivalry between marchers and march watchers.

"We don't know you people out there on the sidewalks ..."

Turn to Page 4A, Column 6

REV. KING: "... the largest and greatest demonstration for freedom ever held in the United States."

"8 DOGS"
were sold through Free Press Classified. This Want Ad, costing just $1.80 on Sunday, brought a complete sellout.

Mrs. G. C. W.

Free Press Want Ads are perfect for selling premium quality goods. But Free Press rates are thrifty. Call Speedy Sales.

DIAL 222-6800

THE JOBLESS SPEAK
Why the Figures May Lie

BY SAMUEL LUBELL

Since early April this reporter has been conducting an intensive interviewing survey of jobless workers in 23 different cities. One main purpose has been to try to solve the puzzle of why the unemployment rate remains so high — 5.9 per cent of the labor force by the latest official count — in the face of record highs in production, employment and consumer spending.

I have also been hunting for answers to questions left uncovered by official government reports.

Just what is the cause of each person's unemployment? How many of the unemployed have jobs to go back to? How much actual looking around for work

The country's unemployment statistics no longer reflect the health of our economy and a drastic overhaul is needed in the nation's thinking about the unemployment problem. These are but two of the findings unearthed by public opinion reporter Samuel Lubell after extensive interviewing in 23 major cities. Following is the first of a series of articles.

is done? Are the unemployment statistics reliable? How do the jobless manage to care for themselves and their families? Three over-all conclusions stand out:

• The nature of unemployment has changed enormously since the depression of the 1930s and even since the recession of 1958.

Unless these changes are recognized and understood, efforts to overcome unemployment may only make matters worse.

• • •

IN MY SURVEY more than 350 "case histories" of men and women out of work were put together. Of this number, nearly six out of 10 did not constitute any real unemployment problem

Turn to Page 2A, Column 3

• The identical label "unemployment" is applied to so many different situations that the statistics themselves create quite misleading pictures of both the extent of the jobless problem and the human hardship involved.

Special On the Inside

Boros Takes Open

Julius Boros crushed ailing Arnold Palmer and jittery Jack Cupit with a one-under-par 70 to win the National Open Golf Championship. P. 1D.

Amusements	6C	Industrial	8C
Ann Landers	3C	Movie Guide	7D
Astrology	6D	Names and Faces	2B
Billy Graham	8D	Obituaries	4B
Bridge	6D	Sports	1-7D
Church News	3A	TV-Radio	4C
Comics	5-7D	Want Ads	4-7B
Crossword Puzzle	6D	Women's Pages	1-3C
Death Notices	4B		
Drew Pearson	9A	**HAVE THE FREE PRESS**	
Earl Wilson	6C	**DELIVERED AT HOME**	
Editorials	8A	**PHONE 222-6500**	
Feature Page	9A		

The Detroit Free Press

CLOUDY
Friday, October 11, 1963 — On Guard for 132 Years — Vol. 133—No. 160

METRO FINAL
Markets, Sports
BLUE STREAK
Ten Cents

OCT. 11, 1963:

Testimony in Washington unmasks Detroit's Mafia.

MAFIA EMPIRE IN DETROIT BARED BY EDWARDS

HITS U.S.-RED PLAN
House Votes To Ban Joint Moon Shot

New York Times Service

WASHINGTON — The House in a startling move Thursday voted to bar a joint Soviet-American manned flight to the moon.

The action was the worst rebuff of the session to President Kennedy, who told the United Nations on Sept. 20 that the United States was willing to co-operate with the Soviet Union in a joint moon project if a suitable agreement could be reached.

The amendment banning a joint Soviet-U.S. lunar expedition was offered by Rep. Thomas M. Pelly (R., Wash.). As originally written, it would have barred a co-operative flight unless the project first were approved by the Senate. The floor leader for the bill, Rep. Albert Thomas (D., Tex.), objected to the measure because it would put his appropriations subcommittee into the field of foreign affairs.

Pelly then deleted the portion of the amendment requiring Senate action and the ban was passed by teller vote.

A teller vote is a non-record one in which members are counted for and against as they pass down the center aisle.

The teller count of 125 to 110 followed only a few minutes of debate and came after an unsuccessful attempt to cut the 5.1-billion-dollar appropriations bill of the National Aeronautics and Space Administration, which governs the moon program.

The attempt to cut the moon programs by 700 million failed, 132-47, after four hours of debate begun by Chairman Clarence Cannon (D., Mo.) of the House Appropriations Committee. He termed the moon-shot program as a gigantic "moondoggle."

The space budget eventually passed as part of a $13 billion omnibus appropriation bill by a roll-call vote of 302-32.

The amendment directed that no appropriations to NASA may be used for a co-operative moon program involving any "Communist-dominated or Communist-controlled country."

It directed that no "aeronautical and space expenses which are primarily designed to facilitate or prepare for participation in such a joint manned lunar landing" be paid out of the space budget.

The vote on final passage of the measure was 302 to 32.

FOUR ASTRONAUTS sat in the gallery as the House drafted the space budget.

Accompanied by their families were Marine Lt. Col. John H. Glenn, Jr., Air Force Capt. Virgil I. Grissom, Navy Lt. Cmdr. Malcolm Scott Carpenter

Turn to Page 2A, Column 1

Dam-Flood Death Toll Over 4,000

Italy Towns Vanish; U.S. Aids Victims

Survivors tell a tale of grief. See Back Page.

Free Press Wire Services

LONGARONE, Italy — A twin landslide that thundered into an artificial lake behind the Vajont dam sent a 300-foot-high wall of water roaring through an Alpine valley and took more than 4,000 lives, authorities reported Thursday night.

Italian rescue officials said the great wave, preceded by winds that roared like a tornado, obliterated eight villages Wednesday night. The landslides splashed a torrent of water 800 feet above the lip of the dam and killed another 100 persons in four mountain hamlets overlooking the 873-foot dam. An estimated 150 million tons of water were unleashed.

BY NIGHTFALL, rescue crews including U.S. Army helicopter men from nearby NATO bases had recovered 600 bodies in this devastated village alone.

Only about 20 houses and the town hall still are standing. The rest of what was formerly a clean and prosperous mountain village is a sea of mud and slime, sprinkled with the wreckage of houses, trees and damaged cars and trucks.

Into this scene of desolation are hundreds of police, soldiers and civilian rescue workers rushed to the disaster area. Helicopters mostly manned by

Turn to Page 2A, Column 4

4,500 at Ball Fete Cavanaghs

About 4,500 persons turned out Thursday night for the Commissioners Ball at Cobo Hall honoring Mayor and Mrs. Jerome P. Cavanagh.

Couples danced to the music of four orchestras, ate sandwiches, drank coffee (there was no liquor) and shook hands with the Mayor and his wife in the reception line.

Festival Slated

ROME — (AP) — An United Arab Republic official has announced his country plans to hold its first international film festival next March.

FROM HIS SIDE of the table Chairman John McClellan looks over the Detroit police chart. In the background are Inspectors Earl Miller, Vincent Piersante and Police Commissioner Edwards, wearing glasses. — *AP Photo*

How Syndicate Works in City

Chart of the Mafia structure in Detroit. Page 7B.

BY ROBERT S. BOYD
Washington Bureau Staff

WASHINGTON — Here is how Police Commissioner George Edwards says the Mafia crime syndicate works in the Detroit area:

At the top is a "ruling council" of five bosses known as "dons."

Below them come 10 "big men," whom he described as "administrators or heirs apparent" to the leadership.

Next come 10 "chiefs," each heading an operating unit.

Below them are nine "lieutenants," and at the bottom of the pyramid are 26 "section leaders," he said.

There are also three members in a Windsor "segment," he said.

EDWARDS identified the "dons" as Joseph Zerilli, Peter Licavoli, William (Black Bill) Tocco, Angelo Meli and John (Papa John) Priziola.

Zerilli and Tocco were born in Terrasina, a little town in Sicily; Priziola and Meli were also born in Sicily, and Licavoli's parents came from Terrasina, he said.

Edwards said he thinks Zerilli has the "greatest influence" in the council, and represents Detroit at national Mafia meetings.

The function of the dons, he said, is to give racket franchises, settle disputes, discipline errant members and fix penalties for violations of the Mafia code.

The "big men" run the most profitable Mafia enterprises, Edwards said, and act as front men for the distribution and investment of Mafia funds.

They are allowed considerable discretion in their decisions, and are considered most likely to ascend to the rank of don. They are responsible for keeping order in the lower ranks.

EDWARDS LISTED the "big men" as Michael (the enforcer) Rubino, Joseph (Scarface Joe) Bommarito, Raffaele Quasarano, Salvatore Lucido, Santo (Cockeye Sam) Perrone, Anthony (Tony Jack) Giacalone, Dominic (Fats) Corrado, Michael (Big Mike) Polizzi and Vincent A. (Little Vince) Meli.

Edwards said the third rank of "chiefs" are "put forward by the Mafia as the head men in the area to deceive the local officials and

Turn to Page 10A, Column 3

Hazel Park Official Hits Edwards' Mafia Testimony

BY ROBERT PEARSON
Free Press Staff Writer

Michigan's most profitable race track was named Thursday by Detroit Police Commissioner George Edwards as "a classic example of Mafia infiltration of legitimate enterprise."

Edwards told the Senate Investigations Subcommittee in Washington that the Hazel Park Racing Association, Inc., makes "approximately $1,000,000 a year" and "much of this is available to further Mafia power in the Detroit area."

James V. Bellanca, a Detroit attorney who is board chairman of the Hazel Park Racing Association, charged Edwards with "crucifying legitimate businessmen."

"I don't think he (Edwards) knows what he is talking about," Bellanca said.

"IT IS SURPRISING to me as a businessman and a lawyer that such irresponsible statements, should be mouthed by an individual supposedly of the stature of Edwards.

"I think he has disqualified himself from becoming an appellate judge," Bellanca said that Edwards

James V. Bellanca

has failed to show any proof to back up his statement. He said that he would reserve further comment until he has read the transcript of Edwards' testimony.

Bellanca, who also serves the City of Detroit as a member of its Civil Service Commission, was the only official of the Hazel Park Racing Association who would comment on Edwards' statement.

State Racing Commissioner Berry N. Beaman said he didn't want to comment on Edwards' charges until he got more information about the testimony.

"We have heard these stories (about Hazel Park) for some time," Beaman said. "I would certainly think we have to give some thought to them now."

EDWARDS apparently bases his statement about the racing association on the relationship of some of its officers to men he has named as leaders of the Detroit Mafia.

Anthony J. Zerilli, executive vice president of the racing association, is the son of Joe Zerilli, whom Edwards named as one of the top leaders of the Detroit Mafia.

Detroit police say Jack W. Tocco, a racing association vice president and director, and Anthony J. Tocco, also a director, are sons of William (Black Bill) Tocco, named by Edwards among the top five Detroit Mafia leaders.

Other officers of the Hazel Park Racing Association are Richard A. Connell, Sr., president; Lester A. Smith, vice president; Ralph G. Matkin, treasurer, and Louis Elias, a director. None of them are known to be related to Mafia leaders named by Edwards.

THE HAZEL Park Racing Association holds thoroughbred horse races at its five-eighths mile track at Ten Mile and Dequindre in Hazel Park.

In operation for 15 years, it is the state's most profitable horse racing operation. It made $644,893 profit before Federal taxes in 1962.

It promises to make more this year as betting is running about 5 per cent ahead of last year. Horsemen's purses for the current 72-day meet at the track, which ends Oct. 19, are running a record $24,000 a day.

HAZEL PARK Harness Raceway leases the track from the Hazel Park Racing Association to hold a harness meeting there.

The Hazel Park Racing Association was the subject of several investigations by former state racing commissioner James H. Inglis, who objected to some investors as undesirables.

Inglis refused the track racing dates in 1953 and the track finally won the right to hold races in a suit before the Michigan Supreme Court.

Crime Chiefs Are Named

Mob Grosses $150 Million A Year Here, Probe Told

BY ROBERT S. BOYD
Washington Bureau Staff

WASHINGTON—Detroit Police Commissioner George Edwards tried Thursday to rip the mask of respectability from the "Jekyll and Hyde" crime bosses he said double as philanthropic executives as they run organized crime in Detroit.

Edwards said the underworld overlords, who wear gray flannel suits and live in $50,000 homes in the Grosse Pointes, run a tightly disciplined army of 250 hoodlums and gross "an absolute minimum of 150 million dollars a year" from Detroit crime.

Edwards said they had infiltrated 98 legitimate businesses worth another 50 million dollars a year, and carry on a variety of illegal enterprises ranging from gambling to prostitution to murder.

Edwards testified before the Senate Investigations Subcommittee.

Using a multi-color wall chart and a long pointer, the commissioner outlined the interlocking structure of the Detroit branch of the national crime syndicate he called the Mafia.

THE CHART showed 63 Detroit Mafia members arranged in what Edwards called "the organizational structure of this conspiracy."

(District Inspector Vincent Piersante, head of the Detroit Police Department's Criminal Intelligence Bureau, said the chart "was not a total picture of the Mafia in Detroit."

(He said a complete chart would contain about 120 names instead of 63. He said 57 names were omitted from the chart because of current investigations, lack of documentation or because the police wanted to protect some sources of information.)

Edwards described complicated marital and business relationships of those on the chart. All but one, he said, were either born in Sicily or had parents who came from Sicily.

After five hours of testimony Edwards was excused until Friday. He will return to tell the senators about Mafia-sponsored handbook and numbers operations, and the infiltration of legitimate businesses by Mafia members and their associates.

Other Stories On City Crime

• Partial text of Edwards' testimony, Page 7-B.

• A rundown on the men Edwards calls the Mafia's five top "dons" in Detroit. Page 7-B.

• The fingers of the Mafia's hand reach into Windsor, Edwards says. Page 7-B.

• On Thursday, after the testimony, the men Edwards talked about were hard to find. Page 8-B.

Hailsham — Maudling

Tories Race To Succeed Macmillan

Free Press Wire Services

LONDON — The scramble was on Thursday for Prime Minister Harold Macmillan's job.

Unofficially, odds were posted on the Tories considered to figure in the race to succeed the ailing, care-worn 69-year-old chief of government and Conservative Party leader.

Macmillan's decision to retire was announced to the Conservative Party conference in Blackpool Thursday, four hours after the 69-year-old Prime Minister successfully underwent an operation for the removal of his prostate.

No date was set for his resignation. But the announcement

Butler

Turn to Page 2A, Column 1

Tongue Tired

CANTON, N.C. — (AP) — "Even my wife can't spell my name," Eleftherios D. Appallakonnastappallious told the officer as he paid a $1 parking fine as Eli D. Stapp.

"DIDN'T
think it would happen, but the very first caller bought the furniture for the price I asked. And the ad was only in one paper: the Free Press."

Name withheld

DUNCAN Phyfe mahogany dining rm. table, 6 chairs, buffet, and china closet. $100. TU 8-0000.

The people who don't think Want Ads work are those who haven't tried the Free Press. Speedy Sales will make a believer out of you, too.

Happy Birthday, "UBY" ARNFELD—Adv.

DIAL 222-6800

Special — On the Inside
Crisis in Brazil
Max Freedman says a miracle is needed there fast to save the Western Hemisphere from a fate worse than Castro. Page 6A.

Amusements	6-7D	Feature Page	11A
Ann Landers	3C	Food Guide	5-11C
Astrology	10D	Movie Guide	11D
Auto News	4B	Names and Faces	2B
Billy Graham	12D	Sports	1-5D
Bridge	10D	Stock Markets	5-6B
Business News	4-6B	TV-Radio	8D
Comics	9-11D	Want Ads	8-11B
Crossword Puzzle	10D	Women's Pages	1-4C
Death Notices	8B		
Drew Pearson	11A	HAVE THE FREE PRESS	
Earl Wilson	11A	DELIVERED AT HOME	
Editorials	6A	PHONE 222-6500	

SAYS TEAMSTERS SHOULD BE BACK IN
Hoffa Wants Reuther to Rule AFL-CIO

James R. Hoffa

CHICAGO — (AP) — Teamsters President James R. Hoffa was quoted Thursday as saying he would like to see Walter Reuther replace George Meany as AFL-CIO president.

"In my opinion one fella who could lead the AFL-CIO would be Reuther," Hoffa said in an interview in the October issue of Playboy magazine. "I don't always agree with what Reuther is doing or how he operates, but I recognize the fact that he runs a successful union."

Hoffa said Meany's presidency is preventing the Teamsters from gaining readmission to the AFL-CIO.

"We're entitled back in, and we want in," he said. But Hoffa added that the Teamsters would be welcome "only if Meany could dictate who should be president of the Teamsters and the officers of the union."

"Meany will never retire as long as he has a breath of life in him, because he knows full well that he can't serve the interests that he serves other than by maintaining himself in office and keeping labor unions disorganized," Hoffa said. "When he retires, it'll be in a box."

Hoffa said Reuther realizes he was "stampeded into voting for the expulsion of the Teamsters because of the bad publicity we had at that time."

Walter Reuther

Carpenter — Shepard

Nov. 11, 1963:

Gordie Howe scores against Montreal to give him the National Hockey League's all-time scoring record — 545 goals.

Sports Page

BAGS ELUSIVE 545TH GOAL AS WINGS WIN

Howe Now Greatest Scorer of 'Em All

BY JACK BERRY

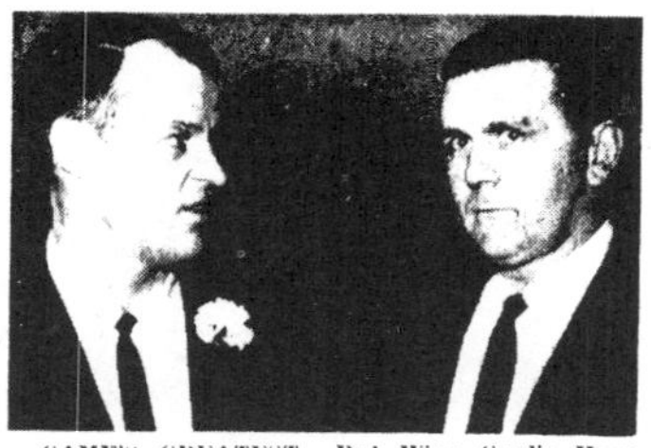

GAME'S GREATEST — Red Wing Gordie Howe (left) went to the front as the National Hockey League's top scorer Sunday when he collected goal No. 545 and broke out of a tie with Montreal's Maurice (Rocket) Richard. This picture of Howe and Richard was taken at a party honoring another hockey great — Jack Adams, former Red Wing general manager.

So much for The Rocket — now for Ol' George Hainsworth.

Gordie Howe spectacularly broke Rocket Richard's scoring record Sunday night with his 545th goal while the Red Wings were short-handed and goalie Terry Sawchuk tied Hainsworth for the most shutouts in regular season play — 94.

The twin achievements came like a double early Christmas for the sardine-packed sellout of 15,027 fans, largest since Jan. 28, 1962.

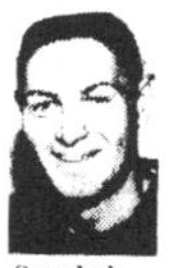

And, they saw the Red Wings' best game of the year, a hustling, muscling 3-0 victory over the Montreal Canadiens, the team of The Rocket and Hainsworth.

Howe scored at 15:06 of the second period with gentle Alex Faulkner serving a major for high-sticking Ralph Backstrom. Backstrom was cut for two stitches above the left eye at 13:57.

Manager-coach Sid Abel, who said before the game he had a premonition that Howe would score and said he would work him heavily to try and get it over with, put Howe out with Billy McNeill to kill the penalty.

McNEILL GOT the puck deep in Detroit territory at the boards and broke out with Howe on his left and defenseman Bill Gadsby on the far side.

Only two Canadiens were back—defenseman Jacques Laperriere and Dave Balon.

McNeill carried down the right side, cut in toward the middle and over the Hab blue line and slid the puck over to Howe.

Howe didn't wait, whipping a wrist shot from inside the faceoff circle, some 15 feet.

Goalie Charlie Hodge, subbing for injured Gump Worsley, hugged the goal post to his left but he wasn't there soon enough.

Howe's bullet went between him and the post and then everything broke loose.

THE OVATION lasted seven minutes and Hodge banged disgustedly at the goal post, then skated down to his bench to rest while the celebration went on . . . and on . . . and on . . . and on . . .

Faulkner was one of the first to congratulate Howe, jumping out of the penalty box and streaking down to him. The puck was retrieved and given to Howe and the applause and cheering kept coming.

It was two weeks ago, against the Canadiens, that Howe tied The Rocket with 544 goals. But that night wasn't as happy—Detroit lost, 6-4.

In this one, with Howe becoming hockey's all-time regular season champion, there was nothing but happiness.

Howe's goal was the final one of the game. Bruce MacGregor and Faulkner scored 46 seconds apart earlier in the second period.

MacGREGOR, switched to right wing on Norm Ullman's line, scored his first goal in 10 games when he batted in Andre Pronovost's sharp goal line pass at 4:49.

Faulkner, the wispy little center, slipped between the Hab defense and passed to bridegroom Lowell MacDonald — he was married Friday — and Hodge stopped MacDonald's shot. Faulkner got the rebound for his fourth goal.

Howe, MacGregor and Faulkner were the offensive heroes but their thrusts lasted just a moment. For Sawchuk it was 60 minutes and the 33-year-old veteran seldom has been better.

He made 39 saves and they were tough ones in registering his third shutout in 13 games this season.

The Habs never quit skating and Sawchuk was jumping right to the end, stopping a bouncer by Terry Harper and doing the splits beautifully on Henri Richard.

Sawchuk's 94 shutouts have been in a much faster-paced game than that of Hainsworth's days in the late 1920s and the 1930s. Hainsworth, who had 22 shutouts in 1928-29, played 10½ seasons with Montreal and Toronto.

It was appropriate that Howe broke his record and

Turn to Page 4D, Column 3

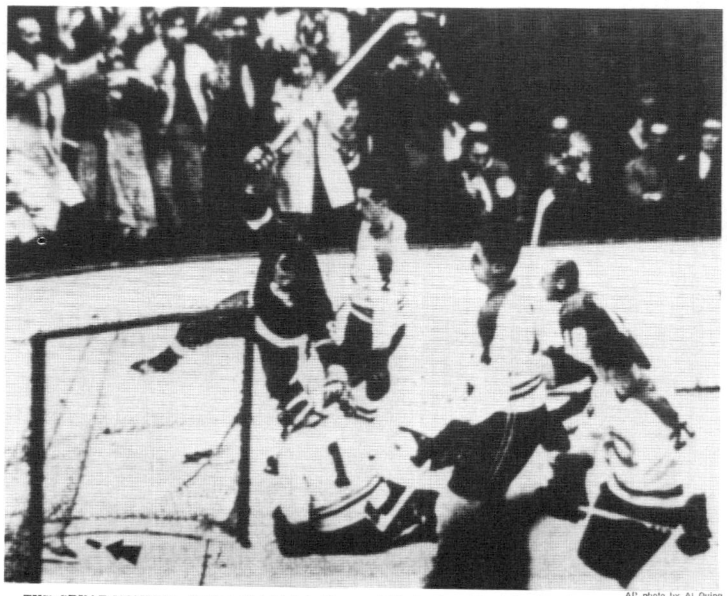

Shot Finds Police Alert

Detroit police officers on duty Sunday night learned of the historic shot at Olympia almost immediately.

The police radios in scout cars, precinct stations and patrol wagons carried this message:

"Attention, all cars. Gordie Howe's new record is 545."

That is, everyone got it but Car 54. It's off the air.

KICKED BY MARTIN

Lions Close Fast But Lose, 24-21

BY GEORGE PUSCAS
Free Press Staff Writer

BALTIMORE — The broken hearts of old Baltimore beat in wild rapture again.

For the first time, they have chilled the Lions in one of those classic battles of what must be the most exciting rivalry in pro football.

The Lions lost, 24-21, here Sunday, but there can be no tears. They gave it a battle, a whale of a battle, after being almost hopelessly beaten in the first 20 minutes of play.

DOWN 17-0, then 24-7, they came roaring back to take the play completely away from the Colts.

Three times in a pulsating final period, they stood on the brink of another of those marvelous rallies which have stunned the Colt followers for years.

A roaring crowd of 59,758 in Memorial Stadium certainly must have had in mind that 31-27 killer in 1957, that 20-15 stunner in 1960.

This one looked for a long while as though it might become a part of the storied series of Lion miracle victories.

But all three times, the Lions failed. They could not do it. And so they fell, tumbling to their fifth defeat in nine games, dropping into a tie for third place in the National Football League's Western Division.

WHAT A GAME it was! Easily the most stirring battle waged in 1963 by the sore and crippled Lions.

The Colts rubbed their pride, robbed them of the one thing which has carried the Lions along. All season, Detroit has thrived on its pass defense, allowing less than 100 yards a game.

But, largely on a phenomenal first-half performance, Johnny Unitas ruined that record. He hit the Lions for 351 yards, completing 17 of 24 passes, two of them for touchdowns.

On the scoreboard, the difference was — oh, no, not again! — a 25-yard first-period field goal by old Jim Martin.

He booted four, remember, as the Colts beat the Lions, 25-21, in Detroit a month ago.

WHILE UNITAS was brilliant, so, however, was the Lions' Earl Morrall. It was on the cool, heady play of Morrall that the Lions came back from pending rout to narrowly missing victory.

Morrall, completing 22 of 34 passes, hit for two touchdowns, and only the savagery of the Colts' rushing defense and a couple of untimely penalties prevented him from lifting the Lions to victory.

SPECIAL DELIVERY, air mail kick return is made for the Lions by Tommy Watkins Sunday at Baltimore. Watkins sped 22 yards on the ground and nearly a yard up in the air as Colt tacklers converged on him following Baltimore's opening touchdown.

The Lions, with their pass defense picked apart and the game all but gone in the early minutes, came to life

Turn to Page 4D, Column 1

	COLTS	LIONS
First downs	24	19
Rushing yardage	251	79
Passing yardage	17-34	337
Passes	2-35.8	22-34
Passes Intercepted	0	0
Punts	88	8-36.5
Fumbles lost	0	0
Yards penalized	17	82
Baltimore	0	14	7	3 — 24
Detroit	0	7	0	14 — 21

BALT—Berry 44 pass from Unitas (Martin kick).
BALT—FG Martin 25.
BALT—Mackay 42 pass from Unitas (Martin kick).
DET—Cogdill 20 pass from Morrall (Plum kick).
BALT—Moore 4 run (Martin kick).
DET—Watkins 1 run (Martin kick).
DET—Barr 19 pass from Morrall (Plum kick).

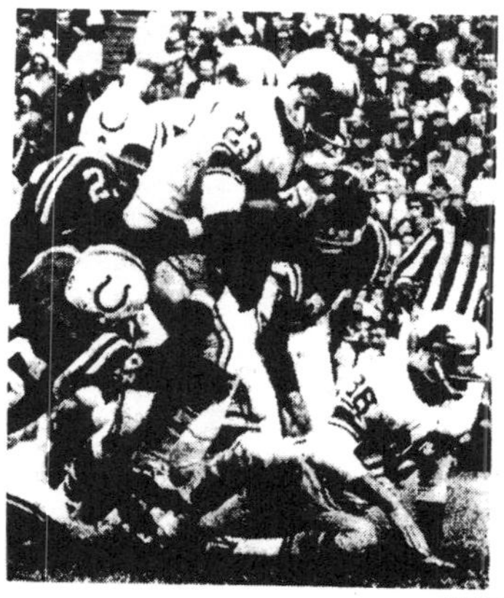

SHOWS OLYMPIC FORM

Ski Jump Champ Soars 114 Feet

Jack Charland, a 30-year-old skier from Three Rivers, Que., jumped 114 and 111 feet Sunday to win the Detroit Ski Jump meet at Light Guard Armory.

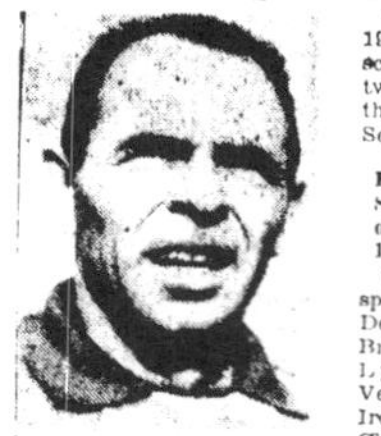

Charland, a member of the 1960 Canadian Olympic team, scored the longest jump in the two-day meet and registered the top score for style in the Senior Class.

His jumps edged Steve Reischel, of Steamboat Springs, Colo., who had leaps of 111 and 105 feet off the 130-foot scaffold "hill."

Other winners in the meet sponsored by the Metropolitan Detroit Ski Council and the Briar Hill Ski Club were John Lyons of St. Paul in the Veteran Class, Ernie Ganz of Iron Mountain in the Junior Class, and Don Olsen of St. Paul in the Class B.

Jack Charland

Helen Wears Pin Crown

MEXICO CITY — (UPI) — Helen Shablis of Detroit won the first women's world bowling tournament individual title Sunday with 4535 pins in the final eliminations.

The Schafer team star also paced the United States women's team to victory in the European-style four-woman championship, averaging 200 for six games.

Les Zekes of Chicago captured the men's title with 5519 pins Saturday night for a tournament average of 197.1. The United States won seven of the eight championships at stake in the competition.

LIKE HIS GOLF PUTTER

Ol' Davey Crackit

PALM SPRINGS, Calif. — (UPI) — Dave Hill, terrible-tempered pro golfer from Jackson, Mich., broke his putter in two Sunday when he missed a shot on the 18th green in the final round of the Frank Sinatra Open and was fined $100.

In full view of the gallery and the national television audience, Hill raised the club over his head and snapped it when he missed his third shot.

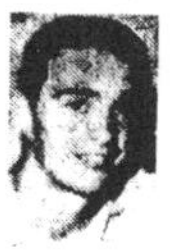

He won $272 for his 288 total in the tournament. Reduced by $100, this left him an even $172 for his effort. (Tournament story on Page 4D.)

Hill

THE GREAT MOMENT — Hockey stick high in the air, Red Wing Gordie Howe signals his record-setting 545th goal Sunday night against the Montreal Canadiens. Flat on the ice, with the puck still in the nets, is goalie Charley Hodge, who missed Howe's blazing 15-footer from the right side at the 15:06 mark of the second period. Rushing in to congratulate Howe is teammate Billy McNeill (19), who assisted on the historic play. The downcast Canadiens are Jacques LaPerriere (2), Jean Beliveau (4) and Dave Balon (20).

Packers, Bears Both Get Scares

Free Press Wire Services

GREEN BAY — Quarterback John Roach rallied a sluggish Green Bay offense and passed for three touchdowns as the Packers defeated the upstart Minnesota Vikings, 28-7, Sunday in a bruising National Football League duel.

Roach, making the most of his starting status while Bart Starr recuperates from a broken hand, fired scoring strikes to Marv Fleming, Boyd Dowler and Tom Moore as the Packers posted their eighth straight victory.

THE TRIUMPH set the stage for the showdown between the Packers and the Bears at Chicago for the Western Division lead next Sunday. The Bears defeated the Packers in the season opener.

THE VIKINGS ripped through Packer defenses for a first quarter touchdown on an 80-yard drive to take a 7-0 lead.

Fran Tarkenton, who presented a problem all afternoon for Green Bay defenses, completed three passes on the drive, with the touchdown coming on an 18-yard toss to Paul Flatley.

The Vikings' defense was outstanding and held Jim Taylor to just 37 yards in 18 carries. Taylor had entered the game as the league's second leading ground gainer with 639 yards in eight games.

FGs Win for Bears

CHICAGO — (AP) — Roger Leclerc booted field goals in the first and third quarters, and the Chicago Bears' defense did the rest in gaining a 6-0 National Football League victory over the Los Angeles Rams Sunday.

It left the Bears tied with Green Bay for the Western Division lead with 8-1 records.

AS THE BEARS' offense sputtered behind an erratic Bill Wade, such defensive giants as Earl Leggett, Bob Kilcullen, Doug Atkins and

Turn to Page 2D, Column 2

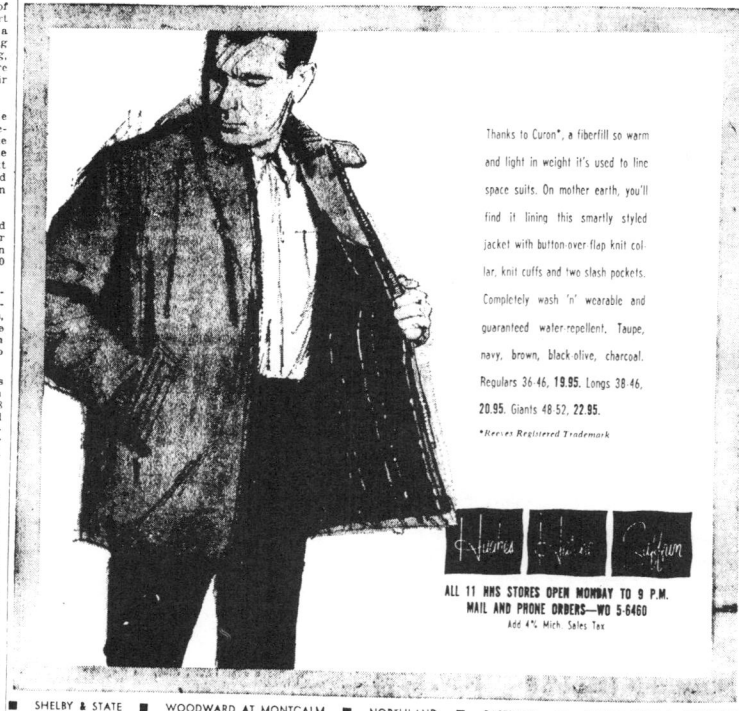

this McGregor Drizzler Ram Jet gives you warmth without weight

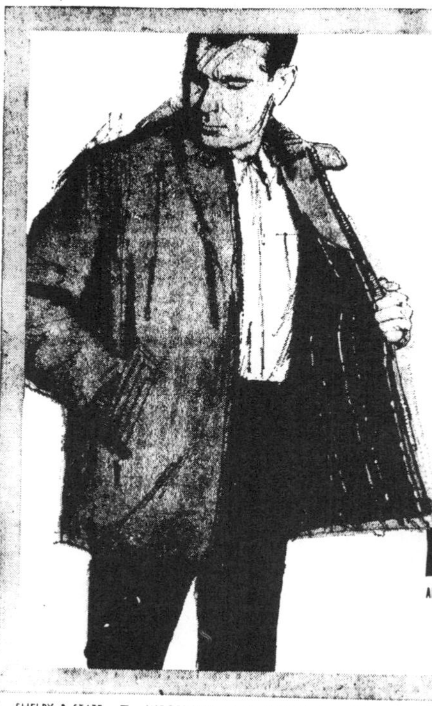

Thanks to Curon®, a fiberfill so warm and light in weight it's used to line space suits. On mother earth, you'll find it lining this smartly styled jacket with button over flap knit collar, knit cuffs and two slash pockets. Completely wash 'n' wearable and guaranteed water repellent. Taupe, navy, brown, black olive, charcoal.

Regulars 36-46, 19.95. Longs 38-46, 20.95. Giants 48-52, 22.95.

*Reeves Registered Trademark

ALL 11 HHS STORES OPEN MONDAY TO 9 P.M.
MAIL AND PHONE ORDERS—WO 5-6460
Add 4% Mich. Sales Tax

SHELBY & STATE • WOODWARD AT MONTCALM • NORTHLAND • EASTLAND • GRAND RIVER & GREENFIELD
MACK & MOROSS • WONDERLAND • WESTBORN • LINCOLN PARK • ARBORLAND • PONTIAC MALL

The Detroit Free Press

SHOWERS
Cloudy, windy, cool.
High 45-49; Low 28-32.

Saturday, November 23, 1963 — On Guard for 132 Years — Vol. 133—No. 203

METRO FINAL
EXTRA
Ten Cents

Nov. 23, 1963:

Detroit stops with the nation to mourn the dead president.

Pro-Castroite Charged in Slaying

KENNEDY MURDERED; JOHNSON PRESIDENT

IT WAS a solemn and grief-stricken moment as Vice President Lyndon B. Johnson was sworn in as President of the United States in the cabin of the Presidential plane Friday, with widowed Jacqueline Kennedy standing, tear-stained, at his side. The oath was administered by Judge Sarah T. Hughes, a Kennedy appointee to the Federal Court. This photo was made by Capt. Cecil Stoughton, official White House photographer, the only one permitted to photograph the event.

President John F. Kennedy

A Lonely Johnson Enters His White House Office

From AP, New York Times and UPI

WASHINGTON — President Lyndon Baines Johnson Friday night walked, haggard and alone, into the presidential office that now is his.

Mr. Johnson's sad journey from Dallas, where President Kennedy was slain by a sniper, ended when his helicopter landed on the White House lawn. It had brought him from Andrews Air Force Base, Md.

The new President held his wife's arm as they walked down the ramp to the lawn.

Mr. Johnson, 55, spoke with Secretary of Defense Robert S. McNamara and McGeorge Bundy, special assistant to the President for national security affairs, who flew in with him.

Then the party walked through the Rose Garden to the executive offices.

WHILE OTHERS in the party stood beneath the portico outside, Mr. Johnson walked alone through the French doors and into the White House to pick up the reins of government dropped by the lifeless hands of John F. Kennedy.

"I will do my best," the new President said. "That is all I can do. I ask for your help, and God's."

Mr. Kennedy was cut down by an assassin in Dallas, Tex., Friday and died in a hospital about 30 minutes later.

And suddenly, the full weight of the problems of a world in trouble descended on the man who was Mr. Kennedy's vice president.

Mr. Johnson immediately won a pledge of bipartisan co-operation from Congressional leaders.

The new President held a mid-evening meeting with House and Senate leaders of both parties after conferring with several top Administration officials.

HE HAD TAKEN the oath of office as 36th President of the United States at 2:30 p.m. (Detroit time) in the president's jet plane while it stood on the runway at Love Field outside Dallas.

Turn to Page 2A, Column 3

Lee H. Oswald

Suspect Once Lived In Russia

From AP and UPI

DALLAS — Lee Harvey Oswald, charged with murder in the assassination of President Kennedy Friday, is a pro-Castro Marxist who once defected to Russia.

The 24-year-old former U.S. Marine was also accused of fatally shooting a policeman who tried to grab him on a street just about the moment President Kennedy was dying with his Russian wife.

The suspect was arrogant as he was brought in for questioning. When he saw a crowd of newsmen, he raised his handcuffed hands in a clenched fist.

Police said Oswald worked at the Book Depository Building, had lived in Russia, and married the Russian woman. On Nov. 1, 1959, he had said he

Turn to Page 2A, Column 7

Body Returned To Capital in Drama of Grief

From AP, New York Times and UPI

WASHINGTON — A dead President returned Friday night to a stunned and saddened Capital.

At 6:03 P.M. E.S.T. the big Air Force I, a jet plane which had carried John F. Kennedy on so many triumphal trips, rolled to a stop at the Andrews Air Force Base 15 miles from the White House.

It was a sadly dramatic moment.

Just before the plane came to a halt all the lights were turned out and the plane pulled forward in almost complete darkness.

Only a quarter of a moon, almost obscured by clouds, shone down on the airport.

Suddenly the flood lights went on again and a cargo lift was pushed up to the rear door. A group of pallbearers from all the armed services went aboard.

But the body of the President was carried by close friends who had helped him reach his high station — Lawrence O'Brien, his legislative assistant on Capitol Hill; David Powers, his long-time personal helper, and Kenneth O'Donnell, who had played a prominent role in Mr. Kennedy's campaign for the Presidency and remained among his most trusted advisers to the end.

Then came Mrs. Kennedy, who in August suffered the shock of losing an infant son, Patrick Bouvier.

With her was the President's brother, Attorney General Robert F. Kennedy, who had boarded immediately after it stopped. He grabbed her firmly by the hand.

They rode down on the yellow cargo lift with the body in its bronze casket with a black top. Mrs. Kennedy seemed to stumble as she stepped off to the ground but quickly recovered and climbed unaided into the gray ambulance that took her husband's body to the Naval hospital in Bethesda.

A REINFORCED cordon of airmen, in dress uniform with rifles and bayonets, stood at attention. The normal

Turn to Page 2A, Column 3

The President's Death

- John F. Kennedy: An obituary. Pages 6A - 8A.
- Lyndon B. Johnson, the new President. Page 3A.
- The tragedy in Dallas. Pictures and stories. Pages 4A - 5A.
- Shock and grief stun the people of the world. Reaction from various nations, comments from world leaders, and other stories and pictures on the President and his death. Pages 2A, 9A, 12A, 13A, 14A, 15A, 16A, Back Page.

Sniper Shoots JFK, Wounds Texas Gov.

From AP, New York Times and UPI

DALLAS — President Kennedy was assassinated Friday. Lee Harvey Oswald, 24, a pro-Castro Marxist, was charged with his murder.

Texas Gov. John Connally also was wounded as he and President Kennedy rode in a motorcade through Dallas.

Officers said Oswald was the man who hid on the fifth floor of a taxtbook warehouse and snapped off three quick shots that killed the President and wounded Connally.

Police earlier had arrested Oswald for the slaying of a Dallas policeman who was shot down on the street shortly after the President's assassination.

Oswald was arraigned shortly before midnight (1 a.m. Detroit time) before Justice of the Peace David B. Johnson.

• • •

POLICE SAID Oswald, battered and sullen, denied having anything to do with the assassination, but admitted he worked in the building from which the fatal shots were fired. He would not account for his whereabouts at the time of the assassination, police said.

Oswald was arrested at a theater some four miles from the place where President Kennedy was shot. Police Capt. Will Fritz said it had been established that Oswald had been in the building from which the fatal shots came at the time they were fired.

The President suffered a massive gunshot wound in the brain and was pronounced dead at 2 p.m. (Detroit time).

At the hospital where the President was taken, Rep. Henry B. Gonzalez, of San Antonio, said he watched the nation's First Lady, spattered with blood, kiss the lifeless body of her husband on the lips in a last goodbye and take the ring off her finger and place it on his.

"I couldn't take it," Gonzalez told the San Antonio Express in a telephone call from Washington. "I walked away."

Vice President Lyndon B. Johnson, who was riding in the third car behind the President in a motorcade when the shooting took place, was sworn in as the 36th President of the United States Friday afternoon.

Mr. Kennedy, 46, was the nation's youngest elected President.

The killer fired at the President's car from a building just off the motorcade route through Dallas. The President, Connally and Johnson had just received an enthusiastic welcome from a huge crowd in downtown Dallas.

Mr. Kennedy, who apparently was hit by the first of what witnesses thought were three shots, was driven at high speed to Parkland Hospital. There, in an emergency operating room, with no one attending him but physicians and nurses, he died without regaining consciousness or uttering a word.

• • •

MRS. KENNEDY, Mrs. Connally and a Secret Service agent were in the car with the President and Connally. Two more Secret Service agents flanked the car. None of these was injured in the shooting.

Mrs. Kennedy cried "Oh, no!" and tried to hold up the President's head after the shooting.

She was in the hospital near her husband when he died, but was not in the operating room itself. She walked beside his bronze casket when it was taken from the hospital.

Just before 7 p.m., Capt. Fritz said Oswald had been identified from a police lineup as the man who shot Patrol-

Turn to Page 2A, Column 1

WELDED BY COMMON GRIEF
The Nation Comes to a Halt

From AP and UPI

The assassination of President Kennedy Friday brought forth an outpouring of grief from men in high office across the land. Lament crossed party lines and differences.

Harry S. Truman, on whom an assassination attempt was made in 1950, said at his home in Independence, Mo., the President's death was a "tragedy."

"I am shocked beyond words at the tragedy that has happened to our country and to me today," he said. "The President's death is a great personal loss to the country and to me. He was an able President, one the people loved and trusted."

Dwight D. Eisenhower, the plain President's predecessor in office, was red-eyed as he said in New York:

"I share the sense of shock and dismay that all Americans feel at the despicable act that resulted in the death of our nation's President."

Mrs. Eisenhower and I also join with all other citizens in expressing our personal grief and prayerful concern to Mrs. Kennedy and all other members of the family."

• • •

SENATOR Barry Goldwater (R., Ariz.) who had often opposed Mr. Kennedy politically, called the President's death "shocking and dreadful" and asked how "a thing like this could happen."

"The President's death is a profound loss to the nation and the free world," Goldwater said. "He and I were personal friends. It is also a great loss to me. Mrs. Goldwater and I offer our heartfelt sympathies to Mrs. Kennedy and the President's family."

Herbert Hoover, who resides in the same New York hotel in which Eisenhower was staying said: "I am shocked and grieved to learn of President Kennedy's assassination. He loved America and has given his life for his country. . . I join our bereaved nation in heartfelt sympathy to Mrs. Kennedy and their two children."

Former Vice President Richard M. Nixon, who lost the Presidency to Mr. Kennedy, said: "The assassination of

Turn to Page 2A, Column 6

MARCH 5, 1964:

Attorney General Robert Kennedy's pursuit of Teamster head Jimmy Hoffa results in a jury-tampering conviction.

The Detroit Free Press

Thursday, March 5, 1964 — On Guard for 132 Years — Vol. 133—No. 306

METRO FINAL
EXTRA
Ten Cents

FLURRIES
Cloudy, Windy and Colder
High 30-34; Low 20-24.

Faces 10 Years in Prison
HOFFA FOUND GUILTY

Says Ruby Tried For Second Shot

BY GENE ROBERTS
Free Press Staff Writer

DALLAS — A witness testified Wednesday that Jack Ruby kept trying to squeeze off a second shot after gunning down Lee Harvey Oswald and screamed in Oswald's face as Oswald lay writhing in agony:

"I hope the son-of-a-bitch dies."

Detective R. J. Leavelle, the man in the Texas-style hat whom countless Americans saw on television beside President John F. Kennedy's accused assassin as Oswald fell mortally wounded, recounted the dramatic scene in the first day of testimony at Ruby's murder trial.

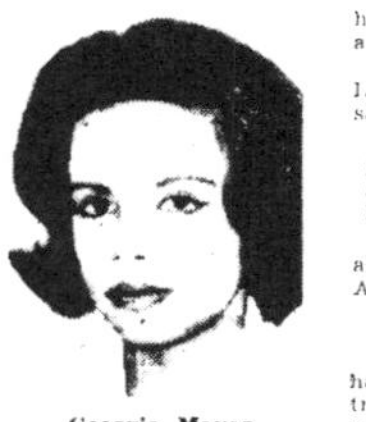

Georgia Mayor
Among first witnesses

LEAVELLE TOLD how he left the police homicide office on the third floor of the Dallas Police Station handcuffed to Oswald on their way to the Dallas County Jail.

"Two or three or four minutes later we arrived in the basement of police headquarters," Leavelle said. "Seconds after we stepped into the basement hall Ruby stepped from a crowd of newsmen and killed Oswald."

He said when he first saw Ruby he was holding a pistol in his right hand.

"I reached to catch him by his shoulder . . . but he fired anyway," Leavelle said.

When the shot was fired, Leavelle said, Oswald "grunted, said 'Oh' and sank to the floor.

"He was moaning and groaning. His voice was almost closed. I asked him if he had anything to say."

"Did he make any answer at all?" asked Assistant District Attorney William Alexander.

"No, he never did."

LEAVELLE SAID Ruby's hand was still contracting, still trying to get off a second shot as detectives wrestled him to the floor.

"His hand was convulsing," asked chief defense attorney Melvin Belli, who contends that Ruby was suffering from an epileptic fit when he shot Oswald.

"It was contracting," replied Leavelle.

A stream of prosecution witnesses described the pudgy 52-year-old operator of a striptease club as a character out of Dallas' night life who sought to ingratiate himself with police and news reporters.

Although called by the prosecution they surprisingly supported the defense's picture of Ruby as a "highly unstable, temperamental man."

RUBY, pale and 20 pounds lighter than when he fired the bullet into Oswald's stomach, stood in the courtroom as the session opened.

"How do you plead?" asked Judge Joe B. Brown, who returned to the courtroom Wednesday after a day's absence with a cold.

"Not guilty," said Ruby in a low voice.

"Not guilty for reason of insanity," corrected Belli.

"All the court is interested in," said Judge Brown, "is whether he is pleading guilty or not guilty."

Judge Brown cleared the way for testimony by overruling a series of last-ditch defense motions that would have halted or delayed the 10-day trial.

WITH ITS opening witnesses, the State sought to retrace Ruby's steps during the three days of tragic history from the moment of President Kennedy's assassination at 1:31 p.m. (Detroit Time) Nov. 22 until

Turn to Page 2A, Column 1

DFT Turns Down Plan for Teacher Joint Bargaining

BY ROBERTA MACKEY
Free Press Education Writer

Teachers' union leaders made clear Wednesday that they wanted no part of a Detroit Board of Education policy which would allow schoolteachers to be represented jointly by two organizations.

Thus it appeared that the plan was not, as board members had hoped, the answer to a threat received by the Detroit Federation of Teachers (AFL-CIO).

The plan was adopted at a special board meeting Wednesday.

THE ESSENCE of the scheme is a "Teachers' Representation Committee," which would represent both the Detroit Education Association and the DFT in dealing with the school board.

Representation on the 11-person committee would be proportionate to the number of votes received by each group in an election among the city's 10,000 classroom teachers.

The plan was presented at a special board meeting after nearly 2,100 DFT members voted last week in favor of a strike against the school system.

Mrs. Mary Ellen Riordan, DFT president, told the board, "We strongly reject the proposed resolution, which can lead only to chaos." The union has

Turn to Page 10A, Column 1

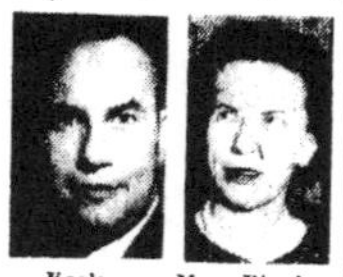

Kaste — Mrs. Riordan

On the Inside . . .

Amusements	6C
Ann Landers	3C
Astrology	10D
Auto News	9B
Bridge	9-11B
Business News	9-11B
Camera	10C
Comics	9-11D
Crossword Puzzle	10D
Death Notices	6D
Drew Pearson	15A
Editorials	8A
Feature Page	15A
Movie Guide	6C
Names and Faces	8B
Obituaries	10C
Sports	1-5D
Stock Markets	10-11B
TV-Radio	4-5B
Want Ads	6-9D
Women's Pages	1-5C

No Dice

HONOLULU — Police broke up a rolling crap game among off-duty bus drivers cruising in a Honolulu Rapid Transit Co. bus. The bus was number 711.

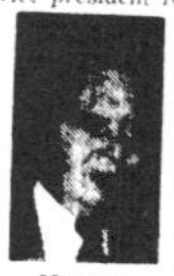

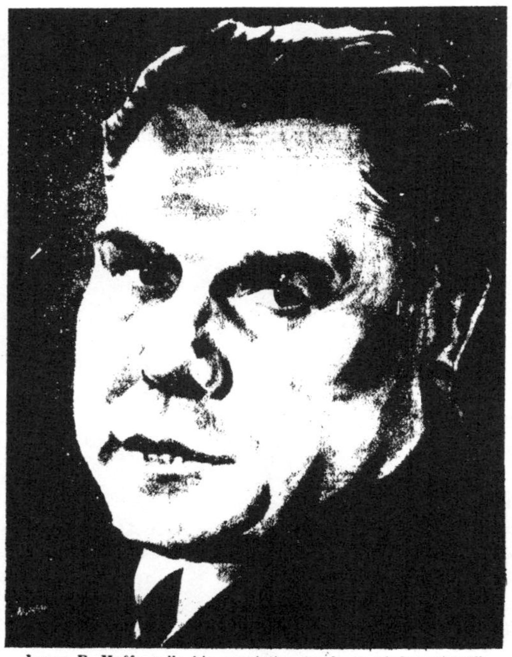

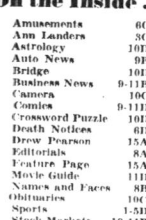

James R. Hoffa calls his conviction "a farce of democracy"

Bobby Wins Long Fight To Convict Mighty Jimmy

BY EDWIN A. LAHEY
Chief of Our Washington Bureau

WASHINGTON — Bobby Kennedy has finally gunned Jimmy Hoffa out of that driver's seat.

And some cooler-minded wolves in the International Brotherhood of Teamsters are ready to close in on Jimmy as he lies in the snow bank.

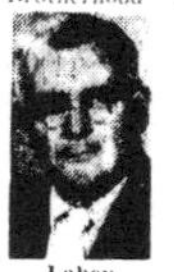

If Jimmy's conviction stands — and he goes to the $75,000-a-year job as president of the Teamsters who is not hot with the Justice Department.

The Attorney General of the United States, Robert F. Kennedy, was dedicated to Jimmy's destruction. For the past three years there has been a separate office in Jus-

Lahey

tice headed by Walter Sheridan, co-ordinating all anti-Hoffa activities.

The late President, John F. Kennedy, made Jimmy a moral and political issue. Candidates for high political

Turn to Page 6A, Column 1

many important people after his scalp.

"I Never

tried to sell anything thru a want ad before, but this one brought me $55 on the first day it ran in the Free Press."

Name withheld

DAVENPORT, chair, portable record player, reels... BR 1-0000

Ever think of how many Free Press readers scan the Want Ads regularly? One of them will pay good money for what's filling your spare room — call Speedy Sales and find a new career in selling! 222-6800.

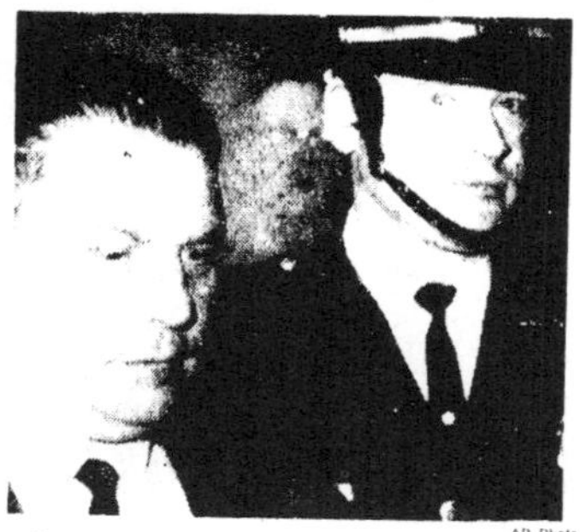

Jimmy Hoffa is led away to make bond

Ouster of Hoffa Is Up to Union

BY DON BECK
Free Press Staff Writer

CHATTANOOGA — James Riddle Hoffa may be able to keep his job as president of the 1.6-million-member Teamsters Union despite his conviction Wednesday on jury-tampering charges.

The conviction won't automatically force him out of his job because jury-tampering is not one of the crimes listed in the Landrum-Griffin Labor Reform Act which bar a person from holding union office.

The act says persons convicted of robbery, bribery, extortion, embezzlement, grand larceny, arson, narcotics violation, murder, rape or assault with intent to kill, will automatically be barred from holding office in a union.

Any move to oust Hoffa from control of the union will have to come from within the union—most likely through an ouster order by the union's 15-man Executive Board.

Hoffa's conviction is expected to be the pivot point governing his future with the Teamsters.

The sticky, pugnacious Teamster president himself conceded the importance of the jury-tampering trial by saying he was fighting "for my life."

THERE HAVE BEEN growing feelings of discontent among the Teamsters since the Justice Department first aimed its legal wrath at Hoffa.

The Justice Department, which Hoffa claims is being used by Attorney General Robert F. Kennedy to promote a "personal vendetta" against him, has obtained indictments against more

Turn to Page 4A, Column 1

Verdict Stuns Him; 3 Others Convicted

BY DON BECK
Free Press Staff Writer

CHATTANOOGA — Teamster President James R. Hoffa was found guilty Wednesday on two counts of tampering with the jury that tried him for labor conspiracy in Nashville in 1962.

Hoffa faces a maximum penalty of 10 years in prison and a $10,000 fine. The penalty is five years and $5,000 on each count.

A deputy U.S. marshal walked into the court room of Federal Judge Frank W. Wilson at 1:57 p.m. and notified the judge that the jury of eight men and four women wanted to come in.

The judge interrupted a defense mistrial motion based on what it called improper surveillance of defendants and their attorneys and the serious-faced jurors filed in from the door beside Judge Wilson's bench. They had come from the floor above.

LOOKING A LITTLE TIRED after 40 nights sequestered in a hotel, they ringed the judge's bench in the high-ceilinged room with their backs to the defendants and 100 spectators.

"Have you reached a verdict?" asked Judge Wilson.

Hoffa, with his son and married daughter sitting behind him, leaned forward tensely in his red-upholstered chair.

"Yes, your honor," replied Hal Bullen, a 69-year-old retired sales executive who served as foreman.

Wilson outlined the first count of the jury-tampering charges in which Thomas E. Parks was accused of tampering and Hoffa and Larry Campbell, a business agent for Teamsters Local 299, Hoffa's home local, were accused of aiding and abetting.

The Finding: 'Guilty'

"What is your finding as to defendant Thomas E. Parks?" asked Wilson.

"Guilty," replied Bullen in a flat, unemotional voice.

"What is your finding as to James R. Hoffa?" asked Wilson.

"Guilty," said Bullen.

Campbell got the same droned "Guilty" from foreman Bullen.

HOFFA'S FACE CRUMPLED. He looked very much older than his 51 years. But he sat silently as Wilson went through the list of defendants.

Hoffa and Ewing King, a former Nashville Teamster local president, were convicted of offering a promotion in the Tennessee Highway Patrol to a trooper whose wife sat on the Nashville jury.

Hoffa was acquitted on the third count. He was accused of aiding and abetting two businessmen in trying to rig the jury. The businessmen, Nicholas Tweel, a Huntington, W. Va., business promoter, and Allen Dorfman, a Chicago insurance broker and close friend of Hoffa's, were acquitted.

Verdict 'Thrilled My Heart'

Bullen told the Chattanooga Times Wednesday night that it was "a wonderfully arrived-at verdict. It thrilled my heart to see such unanimity. I am very proud I had the opportunity to serve on this jury."

Bullen refused to reveal, however, what went on behind closed doors as the 12 jurors decided Hoffa's fate.

"We all agreed not to discuss the deliberations," he said. Judge Wilson had cautioned the jurors to use "good common sense" in discussing their jury service.

Hoffa left the courthouse at 4:45 p.m. trailed by reporters and curiosity seekers.

Outside, the narrow street in front of the building was jammed with people, many of them teen-agers.

They swarmed around Hoffa and began asking him questions. Hoffa tried to brush aside the questions and the questioners, but there were shouts from some persons dressed in work clothes of "tell 'em, Jimmy, you tell 'em."

AT THIS POINT Hoffa started talking and said:

"Nowhere in the world has there ever been a case like this. It's a farce of democracy. You can bet your boots on that."

"You just wait," Hoffa shouted to the crowd. "There

Turn to Page 4A, Column 1

The Hoffa Story

- What Teamsters truck drivers here think of Hoffa's conviction. Page 3A.
- One Cadillac is missing at Teamster headquarters. Page 12A.
- Hoffa's jurors—who are they? Page 12A.
- Archfoe Robert Kennedy takes news quietly. Page 12A.
- Local labor leaders assess trial impact. Page 12A.
- Wife Josephine gets news in hospital. Page 13A.
- Hoffa—a colorful life of trials. Page 12D.

$2 MILLION FOR NEW PLANT
Chrysler to Expand at Trenton

Chrysler Corp. paid $500 million in wages and salaries in the Detroit area in 1963. Page 9B.

BY TOM KLEENE
Free Press Business-Industry Writer

An estimated $2 million expenditure will be made by Chrysler Corp. at its Trenton Chemical Division facilities to increase its normal production capacity for automobile brake linings and other products and reduce present heavy overtime schedules.

An 81,700-square-foot building will be erected adjacent to the present 100,000-square-foot building at 5437 W. Jefferson, Trenton, for the manufacture of brake linings.

Present facilities will be used for expanded production of Cyclewald chemical products. The expansion, fifth major construction project undertaken by the company in the Detroit area in recent months, is expected to result in a substantial increase in employment.

Thomas F. Morrow, group vice president for defense-space and diversified products, said that construction will start within this week with occupation scheduled for this summer.

OTHER PRODUCTS include approximately 300 formulations of adhesives, sealants, lubricants, paints, coatings, friction materials and specialty items will be black sold under the Cyclewald brand name to a wide variety of industries.

There are small Chemical Division operations in Detroit and Los Angeles as well as in Trenton.

Architects for the new plant are Havis-Glovinsky Associates of 14145 Puritan.

Morrow

Sumner R. Twiss, division president, said expansion of the division's facilities in each of the last five years has boosted production to more than 10 million brake linings annually, including 17 different sizes, and types.

The Detroit Free Press

Friday, July 3, 1964 — On Guard for 133 Years — Vol. 134—No. 60 — METRO FINAL — Ten Cents

FAIR A Little Cooler High 81-85; Low 61-65

JULY 3, 1964:

President Johnson hopes the Civil Rights bill will "close the springs of racial poison."

Johnson Signs Rights Bill, Vows to Enforce It

Racial Issue In the North Haunts Barry

BY EDWIN A. LAHEY
Chief of Our Washington Bureau

WASHINGTON — Senator Barry A. Goldwater dreads the possibility that his nomination for President may intensify white racism in Northern cities.

High in Goldwater's mind is the recent experience of Gov. George C. Wallace of Alabama, who frightened the Democratic leadership this spring in his invasion of the primaries in Wisconsin, Indiana, and Maryland. About 700,000 persons in those states voted for Wallace, largely because of their fears of neighborhood invasion by Negro householders.

Goldwater voted against the civil rights bill and in campaign speeches has deplored civil disobedience campaigns by civil rights groups.

But he also has consistently deplored prejudice and cited his own record of steps to end discrimination in various Arizona institutions.

* * *

WHILE GOLDWATER has seriously considered the propriety of his own role as a nominee for President, he feels his campaign has gone too far for him to pull out at this time and settle for the peace and quiet of a third term in the Senate.

The Arizonian, while officially declining to claim victory ahead of time, has nevertheless begun plans for operations after the convention.

As each day brings the convention a little closer and makes his nomination a little more probable, Goldwater has remained officially mum about his political career.

In the short time remaining before the convention opens on July 13, Goldwater probably will have a series of conferences with church leaders, including some Negroes, to discuss his problem.

* * *

INTIMATES GATHER from Goldwater that he knows the danger of white racism in the North is very real and very

Turn to Page 4A, Column 1

Senate OK's Bill to Hike U.S. Pay

WASHINGTON (AP) — The Senate passed, 58 to 21, Thursday a $564-million bill boosting salaries for Federal executives and judges, members of Congress and 1.7 million U.S. employees.

The legislation, backed by President Johnson, goes back to the House, which passed a $553-million version last month.

Forty-three Democrats and 15 Republicans supported the bill, while 12 Democrats and 9 Republicans opposed it. Senator Patrick McNamara (D., Mich.) voted for the bill. Senator Philip Hart (D., Mich.) did not vote.

Before passage, the Senate voted, 46 to 40, to cut the raises the Supreme Court justices to $2,500 a year.

The chief justice now receives $35,500 a year and the other justices $35,000. Members of congress are paid $22,500. The Senate resisted efforts to cut out, or defer until the budget is balanced, $7,500 raises for senators and representatives.

The measure carries increases of $10,000 for Cabinet members, boosting them to $35,000. Federal judges would get $7,500 increases.

The 1.1 million Civil Service workers would get raises ranging from 2.7 per cent to 22.5 per cent.

The 600,000 postal workers would receive average boosts of 5.6 per cent.

SCRANTON SAYS 'ME'

GOP Puzzle: Who Does Ike Like?

Free Press Wire Services

The split in the Republican Party over its presidential nomination widened Thursday but there was still no clear sign on whose side the party patriarch, former President Dwight D. Eisenhower, stood.

There were these developments:

● Gov. William Scranton said in Eugene, Ore., that Eisenhower "had indicated strong support for me and is sympathetic to my presidential campaign."

● The Republican National Convention's parliamentarian said Eisenhower could not, as has been suggested, nominate Scranton because he is not a delegate to the convention.

● Senate GOP leader Everett M. Dirksen, a Goldwater backer, accused Henry Cabot Lodge, a Scranton supporter, of waging a lackadaisical campaign as the Republican vice presidential nominee in 1960.

● Alf Landon, unsuccessful GOP candidate in 1936, predicted victory for Goldwater.

● Former U.S. Senator John W. Bricker, head of Ohio's 58 delegates to the Republican National Convention, said

Turn to Page 4A, Column 1

Index

Amusements	8-9A
Ann Landers	3B
Astrology	6C
Auto News	6A
Billy Graham	12C
Bridge	10C
Business News	6-8C
Comics	9-11C
Crossword Puzzle	10C
Death Notices	5B
Drew Pearson	11A
Earl Wilson	11A
Editorials	6A
Feature Page	11A
Movie Guide	11C
Names and Faces	4B
Obituaries	4B
Sports	1-4C
Stock Markets	7-8C
TV-Radio	5C
Want Ads	5-8B
Women's Pages	1-3B

HAVE THE FREE PRESS DELIVERED AT HOME PHONE 222-6500

The strain ended, the Robert Thorsons relaxed at last
Free Press Photo by VINCE WITEK

Third Trial for Thorson Ruled Out; Charge Dropped

BY JEAN SHARLEY
Free Press Staff Writer

Robert M. Thorson had occasion for a joyful explosion of animation and two trials, knew Thursday. But he didn't know what was coming. The atmosphere in Judge Elvin L. Davenport's courtroom was clearly anti-trial.

The young Birmingham stock salesman became a completely free man at 12:20 p.m. when the first-degree murder charge against him was dropped in Recorder's Court in Detroit.

"The interests of justice, common sense and decency will best be served by dismissing this case at this time, without prejudice, and we so move," Silverman said.

Thorson, sitting with his arms around his wife Joan, touched her shoulder for a moment, but showed little emotion.

He thanked Davenport for the "manner in which he conducted" the two trials —

Thorson, able to sense every aura— for or against him during the 18-month period of existence, knew what was coming. The atmosphere in Judge Elvin L. Davenport's courtroom was clearly anti-trial.

* * *

BUT THORSON didn't believe the word, he said, and he heard it— a three-page statement delivered by Assistant Wayne County Prosecutor Max M. Silverman on behalf of Prosecutor Samuel H. Olsen.

"The interests of justice, common sense and decency will best be served by dismissing this case at this time, without prejudice, and we so move," Silverman said.

Thorson, 32, was accused by police of the beating-strangulation of his wife's mother, Mrs. Dorothy Thomas, of 9173 Appoline, Dec. 3, 1962.

In June, 1963, and last month. He thanked the jurors who brought back a 10-to-2 acquittal ballot in last week's hung jury— and he thanked his wife "for being with me."

He took off his jacket and stood, with his wife at the court entrance, watching the afternoon rain, not talking, trying to unwind.

"We're pleased," Thorson finally said. "It's been a long time, a long strain."

"We tried to live normally all the time this was going on," Mrs. Thorson said. "There's still somewhat of a cloud but we're going to go on trying to live normally."

* * *

Turn to Page 4A, Column 4

Negroes Prepare to Test Bill

Two Get Service In Fla. Restaurant

From UPI, AP and New York Times

Signing of the civil rights bill by President Johnson Thursday brought a variety of reaction in the white South — ranging from ready compliance to outright defiance.

Negroes announced immediate plans to test it.

In Jacksonville, Fla., Negroes Robert Ingraham and Prince McIntosh watched President Johnson sign the bill on television Thursday night, then headed for the cafeteria where both had been arrested before when they sought service.

The Negro doorman bowed and a white woman on the serving line asked, "May I help you?"

It was the first action reported under the civil rights law in the South.

Both the Negroes are minor officials of the NAACP chapter here.

Lester Maddox, operator of a segregated restaurant in Atlanta, said he would go to jail before he would serve Negro customers. Charles Lebedin, who said demonstrators had ruined his restaurant business, displayed a huge sign in a window offering "to sell out at a reasonable figure."

Directors of the Georgia Restaurant Association vigorously opposed the bill but said with its passage "we have no alternative but to comply."

Gov. Paul Johnson of Mississippi told a news conference that "there are tremendous dangers in the enforcement of the law."

He said he felt businessmen should refuse to comply with the law until it had been tested in the courts because "many people feel it is unconstitutional."

Integrationists, he said, should move "with caution or we're going to have some chaotic days."

In South Carolina, most hotel, motel and restaurant owners who would comment indicated they would abide by the law. But one who declined to be quoted said he had no intention of serving Negroes.

Another South Carolina hotel manager who declined use of his name said he expected hotels, motels and restaurants to be tested by Negroes for compliance, "but when the tests have died down, things won't be much different from the way they have been."

Gov. George Wallace of Alabama, in reply to a television

Turn to Page 4A, Column 1

Acts 3 Hours After House

Text of President Johnson's message as he signed the civil rights bill—Page 11A.

From AP and UPI

WASHINGTON — President Johnson signed the civil rights bill Thursday night, only three hours after Congress approved it. He called on Americans to "eliminate the last vestiges of injustice."

In a historic ceremony in the East Room of the White House Mr. Johnson pledged himself to "faithful execution" of the statute and announced steps to insure its enforcement.

The measure, born in violence of the Negro protest movement, completed its congressional journey about 1 p.m. (Detroit time) when the House passed it on a 289-126 vote.

Five hours later, Mr. Johnson delivered a conciliatory message to the nation on radio and television and to more than 200 lawmakers, rival rights leaders and government officials who helped bring the legislation to enactment.

"WE HAVE COME now to a kind of testing," Mr. Johnson said.

"We must not fail.

"Let us close the springs of racial poison. Let us pray for wise and understanding hearts. Let us lay aside irrelevant differences and make our nation whole."

He appealed for voluntary compliance and predicted it would be given "because most Americans are law-abiding citizens who want to do what is right."

All provisions of the bill go into effect immediately except that barring discrimination in employment, which takes effect in one year.

Collins

IN AN EFFORT to calm the indignation of Southerners, Mr. Johnson said the bill "provides for the national authority to step in only when those responsible will not do the job."

His program of appointments included:

1. The nomination of LeRoy Collins, former governor of Florida, to the post of director of the Community Relations Service. Collins is stepping out as president of the National Association of Broadcasters to take the position.

2. Disclosing that he is appointing an advisory committee to assist Collins.

3. Announcement that other

Turn to Page 4A, Column 1

TOPLESS, BOTTOMLESS, take your pick. These two young ladies, Sheila and Sharon Heavey, 23-month-old twins, got into the swim of contemporary fashion as they cavorted in the backyard of their home in Oakland, N.J. The temperature, however, rather than the dictates of fashion governed their attire.
— AP Photo

Reuther Backs $400-a-Month Pension

BY STAN PUTNAM and GENE ROBERTS
Free Press Staff Writers

United Auto Workers President Walter Reuther committed himself Thursday to a bargaining proposal that could mean nearly $400 a month in retirement income for workers with maximum seniority in the nation's auto plants.

He called for increased pension benefits as the union opened contract talks at the Chrysler Corp.

Though Reuther did not specifically mention the $400 figure, he said the union would seek $4.25 a month in pension benefits for each year of service.

The proposal, when coupled with top Social Security benefits for a worker and his wife, would channel $381.25 a month to a worker who retired at 65 with 35 years of service.

A 63-year-old worker would get $338.25 after 35 years in plants and $296.75 after 25 years.

Another union bargaining proposal would provide a retirement bonus to workers who retire earlier than 65 in an attempt to tide them over until they qualify for Social Security payments.

THE UNION began drawing up the $400-a-month proposal two months ago as part of a compromise struck with early retirement advocates, but Reuther — until Thursday — had declined any specific comment.

However, at the opening of Chrysler negotiations he told reporters: "Lynn Townsend (the president of Chrysler) gets $198 per month in pension benefits for each year of service. All we are asking for is $4.25"

Turn to Page 4A, Column 1

What's Up?

WELL, whatever it is, it's interesting as you can tell from the It-can't-be-true expression on the face of Tommy Eckstrom, 8 months, of Lake Odessa, Mich. To find out what's up, turn to the back page.

SWAPS

are good business for both parties to the trade! As Clarence Jackson says, "This Free Press Want Ad for a swap worked out just well. I got my automatic washer the very first day the ad ran!"

WILL TRADE 21" TV for good automatic washer. 000-0000.

Want to make a trade? Call Speedy Swaps at:

222-6800

JAN. 16, 1965:

In Detroit, a black policeman becomes a precinct commander. In Dearborn, Mayor Orville Hubbard is accused of racism.

"First Negro Is Named Police Precinct Head," column five, and *"Hubbard In Rights Jam Again,"* column three.

Detroit Free Press

Page 3, Section A — THE SECOND FRONT PAGE — Saturday, January 16, 1965

Today's Chuckle
If a man removes his hat in an elevator he has one of two things—manners or hair.

Legs Paralyzed, but He's a Paul Bunyan at Heart

BY CURT HASELTINE
Free Press Staff Writer

ROSCOMMON — The snow lies deep and still in Michigan's north woods but here and there the stillness is ripped by the roar of diesel trucks and the clatter of pulpwood log loaders.

Here, amid the huge rotting stumps that speak of the state's fabulous white pine logging days, is the domain of 28-year-old Pete Legg, heir-apparent to the burly lumbering giants of yore.

Here, he has carved out an enterprise that grosses some $135,000 yearly.

A LATTER-DAY Paul Bunyan?

Hardly. Pete Legg is paralyzed from the waist down and rarely leaves his bed.

Pete is a giant only in spirit. What he lacks physically he makes up for in determination.

His paralysis stems from a neighborhood football game when Pete was 12.

An operation removed a growth from his spine but the damage had been done. Gradually he worsened.

In high school his brother, Louis, and his friends helped lug Pete from class to class. With their co-operation and his determination, he graduated.

He learned to drive a specially-equipped car with all hand controls. Even that was difficult because he had lost some of the use of his arms as well.

Meanwhile he learned the dlpwood business from his father. It was a family trade. His grandfather set up a sawmill four miles west of Roscommon and it is still owned by the family.

Pete roamed the logging trails in his special car. Those trails are rough, even for the massive diesel trucks.

ONCE HE TOOK the wrong turn down an old trail but he couldn't crawl. He couldn't get back into the car, either.

"So I just lay there all night," he recalls. "It rained and it was miserable."

He opened the car door and rolled out on the ground only to find that he couldn't crawl. He couldn't get back into the car, either.

He was stranded there most of the next day, too. His family and friends were making frantic efforts to find him.

FINALLY A CAR came bumping down the trail.

"Some fellow who had shot a deer there the previous fall was visiting at Gaylord with his wife and decided to show her where he'd got his buck."

"I figured someone up there was looking out for Pete Legg when he was too darned foolish to look out for himself. But it taught me a lesson—stay with the car."

"Things have been a bit better since I got my two-way radio setup last spring," he said.

He has a set in his car, a set on the hydraulic log loader that is the backbone of his business, a set in one of the big diesel trucks he leases and a set for his bed at home.

The radio has also simplified his job of bossing the log-loading business. With it he directs business to loading spots, handles "traffic congestion."

Turn to Page 7A, Column 6

Pete Legg: his car has special controls

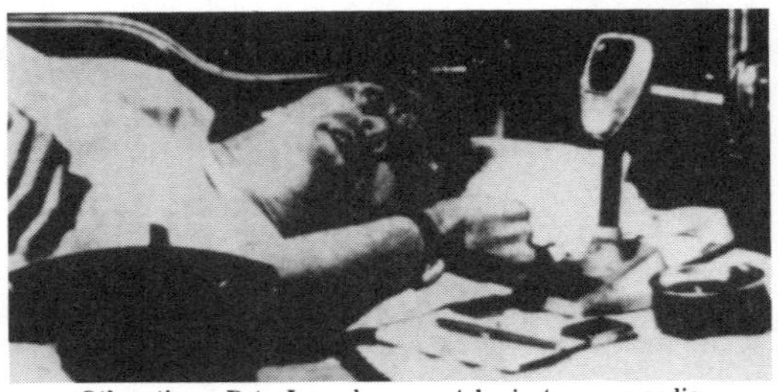

Other times Pete Legg keeps watch via two-way radio

Four Trust Funds In McKay's Will; $1 Million for U-M

BY JAMES M. MUDGE
Free Press Staff Writer

GRAND RAPIDS — A few hours before the funeral Friday of Frank D. McKay, Grand Rapids multimillionaire, his will was made public revealing the establishment of four trust funds, one of them for University of Michigan medical research.

In his will, the controversial onetime Michigan Republican party whip and power in national politics founded the Frank D. McKay and Agnes C. McKay Medical Research Fund with specific provisions.

GRANTED NOT LESS than $1 million, the trust for the U-M is for the purpose of "discovering and improving means to cure, alleviate and prevent" heart and blood diseases.

The university will be given the money after the deaths of all the annuitants.

After 20 years, the trust money may be used for "general medical research" under terms of the will.

Although the petition filed in probate court Friday estimated the McKay estate at $200,000, his local, state, national and international business holdings may be in excess of $50 million, a figure reported earlier by his associates.

McKay, who died Tuesday in the Miami (Fla.) Heart Institute at the age of 81, left the bulk of his estate to his widow.

THERE ARE no provisions in the will for a son, Frank J. McKay, or grandchildren Frank Donald McKay and Carol McKay Tetzlaff.

The former Michigan State treasurer, in leaving his son and grandchildren out of the will, said he had "made other provisions for them which I feel are ample."

McKay was entombed in a bronze casket in a Greenwood cemetery mausoleum. The financier built the tomb earlier and left $20,000 in trust for its maintenance.

Two of the trust funds are for his widow to provide "generous" care, support, comfort and pleasure."

Executors of the estate are Michigan National Bank, Alma Hermansen, his sister-in-law; and Marie Van Vliet, his personal secretary.

McKay BARRED Lee W. Finch, a Michigan National Bank vice president, from handling any details of the estate, saying in the will he "shall have no authority." There was no explanation.

Miss Hermansen is willed $150 a month, with the order that the amount be increased if needed.

Miss Van Vliet will receive $200 a week for 10 years after McKay's death and then $100 a week for her lifetime.

The will provides incomes for five relatives after the death of the widow.

Named under this provision, and the amounts each will receive are: Two nieces, Mrs. Ellen Burtt, $22,000, and Ruth Wentzler Jerio, $2,500; nephews, Donald McKay, $15,000, Gerald Young and John Dalton, each $10,000. All are of Grand Rapids.

A week after McKay's death other relatives will begin receiving incomes.

HIS DAUGHTER, Mrs. Margaret M. Poel, will get $75 a week. Three grandchildren will be given $50 a week each. They are Nancy Lou Frost Zillmer, Judith Ann Frost Timpson and Mary Margaret Frost Hall.

Mrs. Frieda Julle, a longtime employe of McKay, receives $50 a week under the terms of the will.

In addition to financial income, Mrs. McKay was given homes in Florida and Grand Rapids. She is 78 and in ill health.

Romney Sniffs Dem 'Snow Job'

Free Press Lansing Staff

LANSING — Gov. Romney said Friday he hoped he didn't have to dig out from under any Democratic "snow jobs" this year.

Romney said he was "very pleased and gratified" with the reaction of the new Democratic majority in the Legislature to his state of the state message Thursday.

Most Democrats heaped praise on the governor's proposals and summed up by saying: "He sounds just like a Democrat."

"I TRUST IT'S NOT a snow job," Romney said. He said he hopes Democrats won't try to read a different meaning into his proposals from what he intended.

"I hope I won't be confronted with a situation where it will be claimed that what is submitted to me by the Legislature is in conformance with what I proposed, if it is not in conformance," he said.

As an example of what might happen, Romney cited the proposal by some to his proposed for a study of Michigan's financial requirements for the next 10 years, as well as a survey of the tax structure and needed changes.

THE GOVERNOR proposed a $200,000 appropriation to finance a continuing study by a bipartisan commission.

Democratic critics contended it would be a needless duplication of several similar efforts in recent years.

"This will not be just another tax study or committee and made that clear in my message," Romney said. "It will be the commission's function to take a look at all needs and to say out an equitable and timely basis for meeting the essential needs that will arise."

Tax Woes? Here's How To Get Aid

Having trouble making out your 1965 Federal income tax return? The Internal Revenue Service has set up two services to help you.

EACH MONDAY between now and April 15 you can go to Room 673 in the Federal Building and an expert will assist you. The office will be open from 8 a.m. to 4 p.m.

If it is inconvenient to go downtown, you may get assistance by telephoning WO 3-5171 Monday through Friday, between 8 a.m. and 4:30 p.m.

Hubbard In Rights Jam Again

The co-chairman of the Michigan Civil Rights Commission Friday accused Dearborn Mayor Orville Hubbard of demonstrating "a lack of good faith" by resuming his practice of posting anti-Negro clippings on his City Hall bulletin board.

Damon Keith of the CRC said, however, he would not call an emergency meeting of the commission to take action on the material that was posted this week.

The full commission will meet Jan. 26 to act on the recommendation of a three-man Hubbard committee that a permanent order be issued restraining Hubbard and his aides from using the bulletin board to display anti-Negro material.

THE COMMITTEE at a hearing Jan. 4 found that the material on the bulletin board was intended to cause prejudice against Negroes.

The clippings were taken down shortly before the hearing, Dearborn City Attorney Ralph B. Guy, Jr., told the committee.

This week, however, new clippings appeared.

First Negro Is Named Police Precinct Head

Harge Given Vernor Post

BY VAN G. SAUTER
Free Press Staff Writer

Police Inspector George W. Harge, who has pioneered Negro advancement within the police department, has been named commander of the Vernor Precinct station. He is the first Negro to command a precinct in Detroit.

Commander of the Parking Enforcement Bureau since being named an inspector 18 months ago, Harge took command of the lower West Side precinct Friday afternoon.

The precinct, predominantly nonwhite and populated by minority groups, has the second highest crime rate in the city. A total of 9,677 offenses were reported there in 1964.

THERE HAD been speculation for weeks that Harge would be given a precinct command. Perhaps to prepare him for promotion to a key administrative post at the department.

"My training and experience in community relations will help a great deal in this precinct," he said. "The area includes many people on the lower end of the totem pole.

"I attach no special significance to my new assignment," said the tall, husky officer with four gold stars on his sleeve as he cleaned out his desk at the PEB.

"My primary purpose is improving conditions in that precinct for every law-abiding citizen," he said. "I'm going to spend a lot of the time in the streets."

The 43-year-old inspector, who lives at 1651 Atkinson with his wife Ruby, is a native of Waco, Tex., and the eldest of six children.

In a related action, the previous Vernor commander, Inspector Paul W. Tistle, was transferred to commander of the Parking Enforcement Bureau.

Sgt. George Bennett, 37, was transferred to the Police Academy to serve as instructor. He is the first Negro to hold a full-time instructor position in the academy.

Insp. George Harge: a precinct commander

three years of study in social sciences at Wayne State University, is considered a good policeman with administrative potential.

HARGE HOPES his promotion will encourage young Negroes to 'join the department which has experienced difficulty in recruiting Negroes. Only three per cent of the force is Negro.

Piersante Heads City Detectives

Girardin Taps Him For No. 4 Spot

BY BOB COTTER
Free Press Staff Writer

The meteoric rise of Vincent W. Piersante through the Detroit Police Department ranks continued Friday as Police Commissioner Ray Girardin tapped him to be Chief of Detectives — the fourth highest rank in the 4,200-man department.

Piersante, 45, who joined the force as a patrolman in 1941, is now under only Girardin, Supt. Eugene Reuter and Deputy Supt. James Lupton.

His latest promotion gives weight to the belief that he could eventually wind up as superintendent.

HE SUCCEEDS Thomas Cochill, a 27-year veteran who retired last week to become public safety director in Grosse Pointe Shores.

Piersante's pay in the new post is $14,487 a year. Patrolmen's new job pays about $10,000 and he draws a $1,422 annual pension from Detroit. Piersante has succeeded as deputy chief of detectives by James J. Dunleavy, 57. Dunleavy is a 30-year police veteran. Girardin announced 13 other promotions.

ARDEN DeLUCA, 55, a Detective Bureau inspector for six years, was named district detective inspector, succeeding Dunleavy, and Charles J. Kantzler, 51, was boosted to DeLuca's old job from his post as Northwest Station detective lieutenant.

Two uniform sergeants were promoted to lieutenant, Adelbert M. Welles, 41, and James H. Martin, 43, both on the force since 1942.

Detective Sgt. Jack P. Shoemaker, 41, also on the force since 1941, was promoted to detective lieutenant.

Three patrolmen were promoted to uniform sergeant. Reginald J. Burke, 36, on the force 10 years; Roy F. Snyder, 44, a 14-year veteran, and Norman E. Anderson, 41, a policeman 17 years.

Four patrolmen were promoted to detective: Glyn C. Piper and Robert F. Peterson, both 40 and both 17-year veterans, and Joseph J. Ferrick, 44, and Lawrence C. Hagen, 40, both 14-year veterans.

Vincent W. Piersante

MAESTRO RETURNS AMID SONG

A Musical Hurray for M. Paray

BY VAN G. SAUTER
Free Press Staff Writer

At the crack of dawn, in the dull and drafty Michigan Central Terminal, a small band of yawning musicians burst forth with a lusty rendition of the "Marseillaise" and halted all railroad traffic in the area.

Some weary travelers thought it had to do with installing television in the coaches and an elderly bum thawing out near a huge radiator mumbled something to a Salvation Army band convention.

But the 20 musicians from the Detroit Symphony Orchestra braved the snow to welcome back to the motor city the "Maitre," as he is known formally, or "the old man," as he is known affectionately.

"HE," IS Paul Paray, conductor-emeritus of the symphony, who returned for a four-week engagement in Detroit, and appearances with orchestras in San Francisco and Pittsburgh.

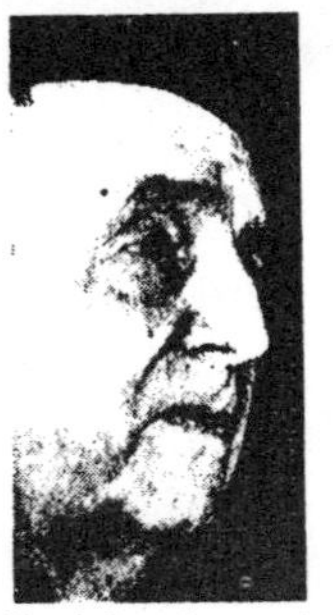

The musicians, notoriously late risers, wandered into the terminal around 7:30 p.m. and assembled on a ramp that leads down to the trains.

Violinist Jack Boesen suggested the greeting during a rehearsal break a few days ago. He stood up and said "why don't we go down to the train station and welcome the maestro?"

GUYTON AMATO, a violinist, agreed, assembled the manpower, and ordered the carnations for Madame Paray. "We're down here to show our affection for the old man. We're very sentimental about him."

Valter Poole, assistant conductor, arranged his musicians on the ramp, and explained the drum roll that would initiate the welcome. There was a short rehearsal, but Poole wondered, calling it "the wo... rehearsal in the orchestra's history."

The Wolverine from New York finally arrived, and Paray, bundled in a brown overcoat and blue scarf, walked through the doors. The orchestra burst forth with a "Marseillaise" that would be appropriate on the Champs d' Elysee on Bastille Day.

Paray, with tears in his eyes, viewed the musicians with amazement, and then threw his arms around Poole, kissing him on both cheeks.

"You've touched my heart," he said in French. "Words can't express my joy."

THE PARAYS, who now live in Monte Carlo and Paris, had 10 pieces of baggage. The musicians turned redcaps.

Paray, his hat cast at a rakish angle, moved among the crowd laughing and exchanging good wishes.

"How old is your husband?" someone asked Madame Paray.

"My husband is ageless," she said.

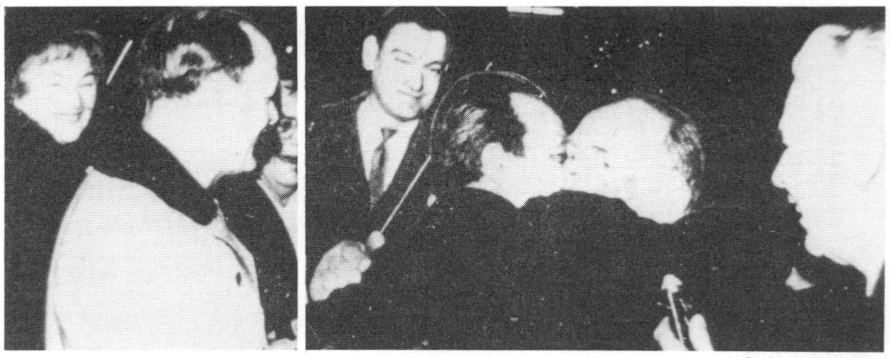

'Touched my heart...'

Paul Paray gets a welcoming kiss from musician friend which amuses his wife, left

Detroit Free Press

Vol. 134—No. 325 — On Guard for 133 Years — Friday, March 26, 1965

CLOUDY
Light Snow
High 30-34; Low 24-28

METRO FINAL ★★★
Ten Cents

March 26, 1965:

Viola Liuzzo dies working for civil rights in Alabama.

Wings Give City First Title in 8 Years

For details of Red Wings' title-clinching victory, turn to Page 1-D.

BY GEORGE PUSCAS
Free Press Staff writer

Oh the great, great glory of it all!

The Detroit Red Wings champions of the National Hockey League!

Their 7-4 victory over the New York Rangers Thursday night at Olympia ended Montreal's last flickering hope and gave Detroit its first professional sports championship since 1957.

How many tears have fallen in eight years?

How many hopes and hearts were crushed, how many careers cut short, how many teams matured since last the town knew such a moment?

City of champions! Eight years with a sunken chest.

How many heads have rolled between George Wilson and the Lions of 1957 and Sid Abel and the Red Wings of 1965?

Plenty.

The longest span of non-championship years in the lives of most Detroiters ended last night when Abel and the Red Wings won the National Hockey League championship.

Eight years without a champion, eight long years without a pennant to fly, a team to extoll, heroes to worship.

Let the champagne flow. The best sports town in the U.S. needs to celebrate.

Not since the hungry, thirsty days of the early 1930s has the city gone so long, waited so impatiently for one of its teams to rule a sport.

Scheffing Wilson

Eight years ago, Fred Zollner's Pistons moved here from Fort Wayne, Ind., having won championships in three of four previous pro basketball years.

Would you believe it? They've made the playoffs only twice since.

They went through Charley Eckman, Red Rocha, Dick McGuire, Charley Wolf, Nick Kerbawy — well, they haven't quite made it through blunders — Fred DeBusschere, Fran Smith, and they're working now on Don Wattrick and Dave DeBusschere.

The Pistons seem as far away from it as the Tigers.

Of them all, the Lions have been closest to bring home a championship.

They had three straight years 1960-61-62 of running second, but now they've slipped, George Wilson is gone.

Hail, Red Wings!

They've gone through a few, too, most notably old Jack Adams, but at last the long losing streak had ended.

Four teams over eight seasons contend for 32 championships, and now we have one.

Move over, world. It's Detroit's turn again.

Sid Abel

Detroit Woman Slain in Ala. While Aiding Rights March

Dems Ram School Aid Past Foes

House Test Vote OK's Formula

WASHINGTON —

The House tentatively approved the heart of the administration's $1.3 billion school aid bill Thursday with an impressive display of Democratic solidarity.

By a vote of 262 to 137 it turned back a Republican challenge to the formula for putting Federal funds into schools in low-income areas. Then it defeated a Republican substitute for the section by a voice vote.

* * *

A PHALANX of Democrats moved up the aisle past tellers in a nonrecord vote, crushing the opponents and increasing the prospect for passage of the bill Friday.

Once it had passed a bill granting broad Federal aid to elementary and secondary schools This one would help both public and parochial schools.

The first tip that a big majority existed came on a key amendment to the bill's formula for improving education in low-income areas.

Shortly afterward the Democrats shouted down a GOP-backed proposal to give the states $390 million in direct grants, to be used at their discretion to help poor children between the ages of 3 and 17.

The bill would make $1 billion available to help children between 5 and 17.

* * *

EACH STATE would get from the Federal government half of the average per-pupil

Turn to Page 4A, Column 8

Grissom (front), Young and their wives wave to crowds during Cape Kennedy motorcade

Astronauts Sum Up: 'Perfect'

From AP and UPI

CAPE KENNEDY, Fla. — "The spacecraft worked perfectly. We didn't expect to around the earth last Tuesday have it in good," astronaut Virgil (Gus) Grissom said Thursday in describing the press three-orbit trip of the Molly Brown.

Grissom and his copilot John Young said that money, sweat and training had paid off in space as they undergone 40 hours of medical did was as important as the Russian feat of walking in space.

Grissom and Young were plunged into several more hours of postflight conferences. Leaving the ship was a late afternoon Thursday they were hailed in phenomenal feat, but maneuvers as heroes by thousands who swung in space is quite phenomenal too.

THE MEETING with the route through the missile complex mundanes of Cape Kennedy and when they flew back to Cape Kennedy from the aircraft carrier Intrepid where they had been.

They'll be up again Friday for a 7 a.m. flight to Washington for a medal-awarding ceremony with President Johnson in the White House rose garden.

They had a happy reunion with their families and then Young said, "You can't take

King Leads 25,000 in Ala. Rally

Wallace Rebuffs Rights Delegation

Pictures on Back Page

Mood is festive as rights marchers reach goal. Page 2B.

From UPI and AP

MONTGOMERY, Ala. — Dr. Martin Luther King Jr. and United Nations Undersecretary Ralph Bunche Thursday led 25,000 flag-waving civil rights demonstrators in a historic march on the Alabama capitol, but Gov. George C. Wallace twice rebuffed delegations.

It was the most massive racial demonstration in the history of the once solidly segregated Deep South, and matched in drama the "march on Washington" by 200,000 persons in 1963.

* * *

AN AIDE of King's, Hosea Williams, said it also signaled the end of major demonstrations in this state for a while.

Williams said no additional major pushes would be attempted until after Negro leaders meet in Washington the first week in April.

Young said it was like comparing apples and oranges that both were extremely important space developments.

An intermittent rain fell during the demonstration.

With chants and "freedom songs" the demonstrators marching through his office, Wallace sent out a message saying:

"I will not, I repeat, I will not see any group of citizens whatsoever until this demonstration and march has concluded."

* * *

THE FIVE-HOUR protest finally broke up at 5:15 p.m. and a 20-man delegation, appointed during the rally, tried to see Wallace. The group was told the capitol was closed for the day. It was then after regular closing hour.

Wallace later went before the cameras of the nation's major television networks and called the march a "prostitution of lawful processes."

He said the demonstration

Turn to Page 2A, Column 4

Mother of 5 Shot in Car

Special to the Free Press

SELMA, Ala. — A Detroit woman who took part in the civil rights march from Selma to Montgomery was shot to death Thursday while returning to the state capital from Selma.

She was Mrs. Vola Gregg Liuzzo, of 19375 Marlowe.

Mrs. Liuzzo apparently was shuttling civil rights marchers back to Selma from Montgomery.

Her husband, Anthony J., a Teamster Union official, said in Detroit that Mrs. Liuzzo was a second-year sociology student at Wayne State University.

Col. Al Lingo, Alabama State Highway Patrol commander, said the woman was shot as she drove a car along US-80 on the route of the Selma-to-Montgomery march.

The shooting took place approximately 25 miles west of Montgomery and three miles west of the Lowndesboro crossing.

* * *

A PASSENGER in her car, a young Negro demonstrator identified as LeRoy Moten, told police another car pulled up beside theirs and slowed down.

He said apparently a shot was fired from a gun that was equipped with a silencer.

The Moten youth said Mrs. Liuzzo slumped over and he grabbed the wheel and fought the car to keep it on the road.

Police said she appeared to have been shot in the head on the neck.

The crossroads is in a rural section of Lowndes County. It

has two combination service stations and general store where a small crowd of white congregated two days ago to watch the marchers pass.

The Army had called out with the stronger security guards of any point along the 50-mile route But there were no incidents on the marchers' way to Montgomery.

The Highway Patrol said investigators were conducting a full probe of the slaying Selma police took five Moten youth into custody for further questioning.

LINGO SAID papers indicated the slain woman was a member of the transportation committee of the freedom march.

He said she had made one trip from Montgomery to Selma with a carload of Negroes and was returning to Montgomery with Moten.

Lingo said evidence indicated that two shots were fired at the Liuzzo car—one striking the top of the car and the other going through the window on the driver's side and hitting Mrs. Liuzzo.

The car traveled about 300 feet before stopping off the side of the road.

Liuzzo, 51, a bonding agent

Turn to Page 2A, Column 1

APPEARANCE CANCELED

Church Bars Nun's Talk to Methodists

BY HILEY H. WARD

A Detroit Catholic nun who accepted an invitation to speak at a Sunday morning Protestant service has been told to cancel her plans.

Sister Alexine, of the Sisters of St. Joseph, had planned a five-minute speech to promote an ecumenical collection Sunday, April 4, at Central Methodist Church, Woodward and Adams.

The cancellation came when Sister Alexine asked the Catholic chancery whether she could stay for the entire worship service. She was told not to go at all.

* * *

AS A SUBSTITUTE, a tape recording of Sister Alexine's message will be played at the Methodist service.

Sister Alexine, a candidate for a master's degree in nursing at Wayne State University, was to report on her work with Negro patients last week in St. John's Hospital, Selma, Ala.

The collection, itself a rarity, will go on despite the absence of Sister Alexine, said the Rev. James Laird, pastor of Central Methodist.

"I am very sorry about the turmoil this has caused in the

Sister Alexine

light of ecumenical progress," said Dr. Laird.

He called cancellation of the nun's visit a "rebuff" in church unity relations.

"I thought that it was a rather nice gesture to receive an offering in a Protestant Church for a Roman Catholic hospital doing fine, important work," he said. "I still think so in spite of the rebuff."

* * *

SISTER Alexine checked with the chancery on Wednes-

Turn to Page 4A, Column 3

WINS OVER HIS MOM

Viet GI Flays Armchair Pacifists

U.S. suffers worldwide propaganda defeat on issue of using gas in Vietnam. Page 1-B.

PLEASANTVILLE, N.Y. — Probably more than most mothers, Mrs. Betty Watson Hall understands what prompted her soldier stepson to write from Vietnam chiding Americans who want the United States to pull out.

"I know what war is and I know how deeply you can get to feel about a cause when you are right there where the cause is being fought for," said Mrs. Hall, a CBS scriptwriter who served in Greece and Scandinavia in 1939 and 1940.

MRS. HALL commented on the letter her stepson, Spec 4 Lance R. Hall, 20, sent to

Hall

her recently from Vietnam in which he took issue with the clippings from U.S. newspapers scorning our efforts in Vietnam.

"It is maddening to see so many people back home who think we ought to pull out and not be raising so much hell about it, would think twice

"I say to hell with the courageous Americans back home in the good old U.S.A. who sit around saying, 'To hell with Vietnam.'"

Mrs. Hall sent the letter to President Johnson who wrote thanking her "for sharing with me the thoughts of your fine son written thousands of miles away in Vietnam."

Mrs. Hall said that before she received the letter from her stepson, she had begun to wonder if the United States shouldn't pull out.

"Then I received Lance's letters and they told me that there was a good reason to be in Vietnam," she said.

Mrs. Hall, who has a daughter, 12, said her stepson has been in Vietnam as a radio technician for almost a year.

She now does free lance writing and authors cook books.

nam.' I don't think anyone here feels that way. It is disheartening that many back home do. I sincerely hope that you do not.

Index

Amusements	14-15C
Ann Landers	8C
Astrology	10D
Auto News	6D
Billy Graham	12D
Bridge	10D
Business News	6B
Comics	9-11D
Crossword Puzzle	10D
Death Notices	6B
Drew Pearson	15A
Earl Wilson	15A
Editorials	6A
Feature Page	15A
Food Guide	5-9C
Movie Guide	11D
Names and Faces	1A
Obituaries	6B
Sports	1-4D
Stock Markets	7-8B
Teen Page	1C
TV-Radio	12C
Want Ads	7-11B
Women's Pages	1-3C

HAVE THE FREE PRESS DELIVERED AT HOME
PHONE 222-6500

"RENTED two rooms thru this ad, and I've recommended Free Press Want Ads to my friends because of my good results."

Mrs. Claudia Hodge

Mrs. Hodge's list of friends has just expanded a bit. It now runs over half a million families. Why not enjoy the success she does thru Free Press Want Ads? For recommendation as a friend, call Speedy Sales.

Dial 222-6800

Mrs. Hall reads letter with daughter Ellen

Feb. 13, 1966:

The leader of Congregation Shaarey Zedek is gunned down in front of worshipers. A community activist involved in numerous causes, Rabbi Morris Adler dies a month later.

Detroit Free Press

CITY EDITION

Vol. 135—No. 284 — On Guard for 134 Years — Sunday, February 13, 1966 — Twenty-Five Cents

900 in Synagog See Rabbi Adler Shot

Interior of synagog, empty and silent after the shooting. At right, a bloodstained cloth on the center chair where the rabbi was shot.

Action Line — Dial 222-6464

Action Line solves problems, gets answers, cuts red tape, stands up for your rights. Write Action Line, Box 881, Detroit, Mich. 48231. Or dial 222-6464 between 8:30 a.m. and 4:30 p.m., Monday through Saturday.

Something must be done to rectify the holes that City trucks have made in our alley; they are sinking 12 to 16 inches deep. You have done such a wonderful job helping others, I am confident that you will give this your immediate attention. — Mrs. W. S.

A Street Maintenance inspector checked your alley for Action Line. It will be machine-graded in the spring, as soon as weather permits. Detroit has 1,521 miles of alleys; if yours needs fixing, call TA 6-5900.

In October, 1957, we had a residential garage addition built at a cost of $774, which was to include building permits. Last December — eight years and two months later — a city inspector came to the door, asked to look at the garage and on leaving, was asked what the builder's name. He said all he needed was the builder's name. We got a violation notice Jan. 21, ordering us to dismantle and remove the garage because no permit was secured by the contractor. We tried to locate the contractor and can't. Please, what can we do? — W. I.

Action Line has arranged for you to see Ray Goddard, building bureau chief, fourth floor of the City-County Building. If your garage meets requirements, you'll get a building permit for $12, square yourself with the City.

Action Line

My son bought a motorcycle. Now he says he's got to have a black leather jacket for safety. Is that true? — K.S.

Action Line checked with the motorcycle men of the traffic detail, who swear by 'em. They're not required by law, but the pros say nothing else offers as much protection if you take a spill on a bike. True, black leather jackets have become a symbol for hoodlum cycle jockeys, but remember: Good guys wear 'em, too, including policemen.

Your Sunday Bonus:
More Action Line — Page 12 A

When I had my driver's license renewed, the colored picture they took was the best I've ever had taken. Is there any way that I can get a copy of it? — M. R.

Police don't keep a copy and there are no negatives. It's an instant-developing process. Most people didn't want copies kept for fear the State might use the pictures somewhere else. You can take your license to a commercial photographer, have the photo copied and enlarged.

Action Line

I called a repair service to have my refrigerator door repaired. They came once, took my money and were supposed to return because they needed more parts for the door handle. My door is being closed with Scotch tape. Can you help me? — T. S.

The delay's not with the repair service but with a Westinghouse shipper who's re-ordering the part. As soon as the repairmen get it, your door will be fixed.

We are enclosing a letter from Miss Lisa Doubleday, 15930 Monica, who is interested in professional training for a career in trapeze work. We thought that your very interesting Action Line might come up with an answer for Miss Doubleday's assistance. — John M. May, Parks and Recreation, City of Detroit.

Action Line talked to Lisa, who says her heart is set on real high-wire trapeze work. No training's available in Michigan, but Florida State University has a fulltime course; students travel with the FSU circus. Dr. Harley Price is the man to write to; Lisa says she thinks her parents will let her transfer.

I am deaf so a regular alarm clock doesn't work. How can I get up on time? — S. T.

Both vibrator and electric light alarms are available for the deaf. They're deductible as medical expense on your income tax. For heavy sleepers, there's a bed vibrator ($12.50) which shakes the mattress at wake-up time. If you sleep light, a pillow vibrator ($9.95) will do. One clock turns on the lights; there's also a doorbell alarm light for the deaf that flashes when someone rings and a sound-activated device that lights up for crying babies. Call Detroit Hearing Center, 321-1436, for manufacturers' names.

Sound Off

You may be interested to know that our great efficient local government can't even get on its own elevators to the basement of the City-County Building. Unless someone in a descending car pushes the basement button, the car stops on the first floor and will go no further. Unknown man-hours of employe time are wasted daily by employes who wait hopefully in the basement, hoping someone in a descending car will push their button.

The State of Michigan should do the testing on cows instead of making the poor farmers and dealers pay high-priced veterinary bills. If the State veterinarian drew blood from animals at the auction sales, instead of sitting around doing nothing, everyone would get along better. — A group of fed-up beef and dairy raisers.

Action Line thanks you for your tremendous interest, and your patience when so many of you call at once that all our many lines are busy. If this happens to you, write us a note or postcard while your question is fresh in mind. We like mail just as much as calls. Our address: Action Line, Box 881, Detroit Mich., 48231.

Wounded Rabbi Tried to Save Boy Near Him

BY JIM TRELOAR AND GEORGE CANTOR
Free Press Staff Writers

"Get back . . . he has a gun . . . I know him very well . . ."

These were the last words uttered by Rabbi Morris Adler before he was shot Saturday by a member of his congregation attending Sabbath services at Congregation Shaarey Zedek synagog in Southfield.

"After the gunman fired the first shot," said Eugene Merkow, 37, of 22532 Greenview, who was in the congregation, "Rabbi Adler stood up and tried to shove a small boy sitting next to him out of the way."

The boy was 13-year-old Steven Frank of 19767 Cheyenne, who became Bar Mitzvah at the service and was sitting next to Rabbi Adler.

"Then the cantor (Reuven Frankel) started toward the rabbi," Merkow said, "and the youth took about three steps toward him and fired another shot.

"The bullet hit Rabbi Adler in the right temple.

"Then the youth raised the gun to his right temple and fired another shot. He started reeling, stumbling backward, went on eight feet. Then he fell on his back near the rear wall.

Blood began soaking the carpet near the pulpit. There was also blood on the carpet near where the rabbi fell in front of the chair."

"When he started talking," said Mr. Jeanette Lewis of 19464 Tracey of gunman Richard Wishnetsky who had rushed to the pulpit after Rabbi Adler had ended his sermon, "it didn't make sense . . . I thought he was a Communist.

"Then there was a shot and everybody ducked under the pews."

"I was outside in the foyer when I heard the first shot.

Turn to Page 2A, Column 5

AF Battles Meningitis Outbreak

From UPI and AP

SAN ANTONIO — The Air Force kept 16,000 recruits confined to Lackland Air Force Base Saturday in one of several stringent steps to combat an outbreak of meningitis that has killed one trainee and left five others in serious condition here.

Three Army trainees have died of the disease since the first of the year.

The Air Force also said that two squadrons of recruits have been isolated at Lackland, the world's largest air training center, and basic training of new recruits was being shifted to Amarillo Air Force Base, 300 miles to the north.

PREVENTIVE measures also were being taken at four Army bases — Ft. Gordon, Ga., Ft.

Turn to Page 8A, Column 5

Ad Placer Nets $546.40 with Sale Of Five Puppies

A $3.60 investment in an exclusive Free Press want ad returned a $546.40 profit for Miss S. T. of Detroit. She sold five German Shepherd puppies for $550. Prospective buyers began calling as soon as the ad appeared. If you have puppies for sale, the Free Press is the place to find them good homes just . . .

Dial 222-6800

Rabbi Adler: A legend in his time

Rabbi a Scholar, Leader, Legend

Rabbi Morris Adler is a man who has become a legend in his own time:

The spiritual leader of Shaarey Zedek, one of the nation's largest synagogs, with a congregation of more than 6,000 spread across the Detroit metropolitan area.

A religious scholar and teacher and author of learned tomes; an expert on Zionism and the modern state of Israel, and on the ages-old laws and practices of Judaism.

A hard-working civic leader — chairman since its founding in 1957 of the United Auto Workers union's public review board, vice president of the UAW-sponsored Community Health Association, founder and board member of the Detroit Round Table of Christians and Jews, adviser to Wayne State University's department of Near Eastern languages, member of the Governor's Committee for Higher Education, past national chairman of the B'nai B'rith Commission on Adult Jewish Education.

RABBI MEANS teacher, and Shaarey Zedek means "gates of righteousness."

Dr. Adler is a teacher and practitioner of righteousness. Steeped in the centuries-old traditions of Judaism — his father was also a rabbi — Dr. Adler has worked tirelessly for religious and racial tolerance.

He has preached to Protestant churches. He has encouraged members of other faiths to attend services at Shaarey Zedek. He has

Turn to Page 2A, Column 5

Inside the Free Press

Amusements	6-9B
Ann Landers	3C
Astrology	15D
Auto News	10-12B
Books	8B
Bridge	15C
Business News	10-12B
Chess	15C
Death Notices	8D
Dr. Pearson	3B
Editorials	2B
Heloise	2C
Movie Guide	7D
Names and Faces	10A
Obituaries	15C
Radio	12C
Sports	1-6D
Stereo	13C
Stock Markets	13-15B
Travel	16-18B
Want Ads	8-18D
Women's Pages	1-10C

HAVE THE FREE PRESS DELIVERED AT HOME PHONE 222-6500

It's Easy to Read . . .

Each Sunday the Free Press editorial page turns the spotlight on a person or issue in the news. This week education writer Roberta Mackey discusses the search for a successor to Samuel Brownell, superintendent of Detroit schools. Will the new superintendent be someone in the system or an outsider?

. . . And Easy to Find

The Spotlight articles always are on the Sunday editorial page — the second page of the Feature Section. See Page 2B.

Gunman Then Shoots Self

Gunman an intense scholar, Page 4B.

BY JEROME HANSEN AND SUSAN HOLMES
Free Press Staff Writers

Rabbi Morris Adler, 59, was shot and critically wounded Saturday during sabbath services in Shaarey Zedek Synagog, Southfield.

His assailant, a 23-year-old substitute teacher and former honor student who is a member of the congregation, then shot himself through the head.

The violent drama was played out before about 900 stunned members of the congregation.

Rabbi Adler, shot in the left side of the head and through the left arm, underwent emergency surgery in Sinai Hospital. He suffered serious brain damage.

The teacher, Richard S. Wishnetsky, of 1611 Lincolnshire, hovered near death in Providence Hospital. His brain was shattered.

Dr. Harvey Gass, the chief of neurosurgery and leader of the team of Sinai doctors that spent two hours working on Adler, said the rabbi's arm wound was relatively minor, but that there was "severe damage" from the head wound.

Dr. Gass said the bullet smashed into the skull behind the left ear, in the occipital region, and flattened itself against the heavy skull bone, shattering it and driving bone fragments into the brain.

He said there was massive bleeding in the left cerebellum and brain structures were severely damaged.

Dr. Gass would make no prediction about Rabbi Adler's condition. He was in Sinai Hospital's intensive care unit. His wife, Goldie, was at the hospital.

Wishnetsky, who had been seated among the congregation, which included his parents, Mr. and Mrs. Edward Wishnetsky, stood up just as Rabbi Adler completed his sermon shortly before noon and started striding down the main aisle.

Cantor Reuven Frankel, 35, who had started the prayers, looked up to see Wishnetsky a few feet from the platform where Rabbi Adler was seated with a

Turn to Page 2A, Column 1

Assailant Recites Confused Lament

Here is a tape-recorded transcript of the short statement Richard S. Wishnetsky made in Congregation Shaarey Zedek Saturday before he shot Rabbi Adler and then himself.

"This congregation is a travesty and an abomination. It has made a mockery by its phoniness and hypocrisy of the beauty and the spirit of Judaism.

"It is composed of people, ah, it is composed of people who on the whole make me ashamed to say that I am a Jew.

"For the most part . . . (pause, congregation silent) . . . it is composed of men, women and children who care for and love nothing except their own vain egotistical selves. With this act I protest the humanly horrifying and hence unacceptable situation. Rabbi . . ."

A shot sounded. Pandemonium broke out.

WINDSWEPT

Cloudy With Light Snow
High 36-40; Low 20-24

Action Line Dial 222-6464

Action Line solves problems, gets answers, cuts red tape, stands up for your rights. Write Action Line, Box 881, Detroit, Mich. 48231. Or dial 222-6464 between 8:30 a.m. and 4:30 p.m. Monday through Saturday.

All the culturally deprived teenagers aren't across an ocean or even in metropolitan slums. The Sault has no art galleries, museum or legitimate theater. We are trying to arrange a program of good films but I have written four times to one of the most reputable educational film producers and can't even get a reply. Can you help?—Sister Alice, Sault Ste. Marie.

Action Line has arranged for a representative of Encyclopedia Britannica Films, Inc. to call on you, make arrangements for your film series. Audio-visual division of the Dearborn Public Library is sending you a list of free or low-priced educational films. It's available free to anyone who wants one. Write the library, 4500 Maple, Dearborn; send a stamped, self-addressed envelope.

Can you put a lion and a tiger in the same cage? If they fought, which would win?—E.C.

Lions and tigers aren't natural enemies and though they're usually caged separately, they do get along in the same house. In fact, lions and tigers have been crossbred. If daddy is a lion the offspring is a liger. If Pop's a tiger, junior is a tiglon. In a fight, Detroit Zoo curator Keith Kreag puts his money on the tiger: Faster, cagier, less predictable, more irritable. Females of both species are smaller, weaker but there's not much difference in temperament. The two seldom come in contact in the wild: There are no tigers in Africa and very few lions in Asia.

What's the difference between bock beer and regular beer?—J.H.

Bock's darker, heavier, richer than regular lager. It's brewed with dark or caramel malt, sometimes with more hops. (Some breweries just add caramel coloring to regular beer, making an artificial bock.) State Liquor Control Commission regulates the period bock can be sold; this year it's Feb. 21 to Oct. 29. Traditionally, bock is brewed in the spring because it was first made to provide a more nutritious beer to supplement folks' diets during Lenten fasting. The town of Elmbock, Germany, came up with the brew, had as a trademark the head of a goat that still appears on bock bottles.

Your Action Line Bonus: Turn to Page 12A

I have a land grant made out to a John Bacon and dated Nov. 15, 1835, signed by President Andrew Jackson, for land about four miles south of Chelsea, Mich. Is it authentic?—C.N., Vernon.

Probably. Washtenaw County Register of Deeds has a grant issued by Jackson to Bacon on that date, when Michigan was still part of the Northwest Territory. Bacon sold the land almost immediately; three homes now stand on the 40 acres he owned. You've got no claim to the land, of course, but the grant might be valuable if Jackson signed it himself, worth $25 or so. Check with Clements Library at the University of Michigan in Ann Arbor.

 Action Line

There's a cat up a tree across the street from us and he's been there four days. We called the police and fire departments but they say they can't do anything. Can Action Line help?—M.H.

The cat is down. Just as Action Line swung into action — after four unsuccessful trips by the Humane Society — Jomo ambled down, is now lapping milk at home. Society's equipment goes up only 35 feet; at one time, Jomo was up 60. This is the start of the cat-up-a-tree season; call TR 2-3400 if yours climbs and quits. The Society will get him down if he's low enough. If he's not, they call a professional tree surgeon to do the job, which costs $15. Strangest case? A dog who wound up on top of a second story roof. They still don't know how he got there.

● ● ●

Dear Readers:

Today is Action Line's birthday. We're two months old.

In those 60 days, more than 100,000 people have called to ask a question, tell us about a problem or seek our help. Another 30,000 took time to write.

We've listened to every call and read every letter and we've learned something from every person who came to Action Line for help. We want you to know, most sincerely, that we're grateful.

Our only regret is that we can't reply personally to all of you, but your comments assure us that we've established an intimate, day-by-day dialog through the column.

We're thinking particularly of the people like the little girl who called and sang all three stanzas of "Jacob's Ladder," and dedicated the song to all the soldiers fighting in Vietnam. We don't know who she is, but she had a nice voice.

We're thinking of people like D. S., of Farmington, who summed up Action Line's purpose best when he wrote:

"It may sound corny, but it's good to see a champion of truth and right . . . someone who takes a few extra steps and incurs some expense to help one man and, by so doing, helps man. You're doing a good, old-fashioned job at the right time. Keep it up."

We will.

Frank Angelo
Managing Editor

Detroit Free Press

Vol. 135—No. 312 — On Guard for 134 Years — Sunday, March 13, 1966 — Twenty Five Cents

METRO FINAL

March 13, 1966:

The Free Press discovers LSD.

Students 'Take a Trip'---on LSD

'The Whole World Was WOW'

BY JIM TRELOAR
Free Press Staff Writer

"First time I got high, I walked down the street, and there was this stop light, and it was like...

". . . like all the red there ever was.

"The whole world was WOW!"

Jay blinked behind a pair of thick glasses then turned away to study the smoke from a tiny pyramid of jasmine incense.

"Then I saw the white light of pure love, and it was so beautiful I cried."

He took a gelatin capsule from a pottery tray, unscrewed the top, and poured its white powder into a Coke bottle. It fizzed, and he let the foam spray down his throat.

Daphne tried it, but missed the foam, and it boiled over onto the rug. She got down on all fours and sucked the juice from the nap.

Larry gulped his capsule, folded his legs in tight, and began reading softly from the Tibetan "Book of the Dead:"

"O Friend
*The time has come for you to seek new levels of reality.
Your ego and the game are about to cease.
You are about to set face to face with the Clear Light.*"

Friday night, in an apartment just off campus, three Wayne State University students were "taking a trip." Their fuel was an illegal drug.

The same thing is happening in beatnik pads, high school hangouts and serene suburban split-levels across metropolitan Detroit.

Police and Federal agents are going crazy trying to find these secret chapels where followers of a new cult are practicing an arcane religion.

There are an estimated 2,000 cultists at the University of Michigan alone, and an untold number among students and adults in Detroit.

Psychiatrists are becoming alarmed at the number who fail to come out of their religious trance.

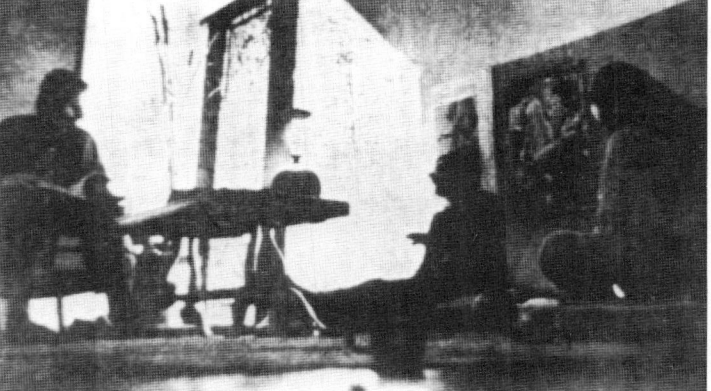

A trip on LSD: "To see what's gurgling in your subconscious"
Free Press Photo by FRED PLOCHMAN

The rites start with a jolt of LSD— lysergic acid diethylamide. Or just "acid." It is not a narcotic. It is an hallucinogen that releases secret emotions, and exaggerates what the eye sees.

It makes the world seem WOW!

● ● ●

JAY'S APARTMENT was up three flights of stairs, past a newel post which offered a burned out cigaret, a girl's comb and a Dixie Cup spoon, and down the end of the hall.

A Chinese kite—a paper fish—swam from the ceiling, incense did combat with rancid bacon fat, a six-foot stained glass window rescued from a razed church competed for attention with a picture of a woman's buttocks.

But on the bulletin board was tacked a picture of a high school sweetheart. "My contact with reality," Jay smiled.

He and his friends can buy LSD as a liquid squirted

Turn to Page 2A, Column 1

Phone Plea Fails; Dad Shoots Self

BY ROBERT DeWOLFE
Free Press Staff Writer

A police dispatcher pleaded by telephone Saturday for a young father who had threatened suicide to give up his gun and talk over his problems with police he was holding at bay outside his barricaded Sterling Township home.

Minutes after the dispatcher, Sgt. John Ruggero, of the Macomb County sheriff's department, had radioed officers that Lloyd Clayton, 23, had agreed to come out of his house, Clayton shot himself in the head. He was taken to St. Joseph Hospital in Mt. Clemens where he was reported in serious condition.

● ● ●

CLAYTON'S wife, Valerie, 21, told police her husband had been drinking. She said an argument broke out and he had forced her and their two children, Daniel, 5, and Deborah, 4, out of the house at gunpoint.

He told his wife he was going to kill himself.

Mrs. Clayton called police. Sheriff's deputies and State Police from the Warren post went to the house but Clayton refused to talk to them. They called Ruggero and asked him to try to contact Clayton by telephone.

Ruggero talked to Clayton for about five minutes. He said Clayton agreed to put down his revolver and go out and talk to police.

As police approached the house they heard a shot. Clayton was found on the floor of the living room.

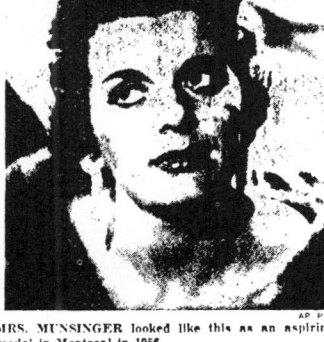

MRS. MUNSINGER looked like this as an aspiring model in Montreal in 1956.
AP Photo

Blond Is Willing To Face Spy Quiz

From UPI and AP

OTTAWA — Mrs. Gerda Munsinger, the shapely German blond who has become the central figure in Canada's boiling sex and security scandal, was reported Saturday to be preparing for a quick trip to Canada to dispute a charge that she was a spy or a security risk to a former defense official.

But Canada's Immigration Department raised a question whether she could be permitted to return to the country.

A Toronto newspaper said in a dispatch from Germany that Mrs. Munsinger planned to stay out of sight for the weekend and get her documents in order for a flight to Canada early next week.

JUSTICE MINISTER Lucien Cardin brought the affair into the open Thursday when he said a woman named Munsinger, whom he identified as an espionage agent before she entered Canada in 1955, was involved with two or more ministers in the cabinet of Prime Minister John Diefenbaker, now the Conservative Party leader.

Prime Minister Lester B. Pearson has called for an investigation and said he is ready to stake the life of the

Turn to Page 6A, Column 4

Youth Shoots At Sound, Hits Hunter

Special to the Free Press

MARQUETTE — A 14-year-old North Lake boy was critically wounded Saturday by another teen-ager in a hunting accident near his home in Marquette County.

Police said the boy, Dale Hytinen, was attempting to lure crows to a blind with a bird call when the other boy, Michael Havela, 15, shot him in the head with a .22 caliber rifle.

HAVELA, WHO was also hunting crows, said he was not aware of the other boy's presence and fired into the blind, thinking the bird cries he heard were authentic.

Hytinen is in critical condition in a Green Bay, (Wis.) hospital. Doctors said the bullet passed through the back of his head and lodged in his right eye.

MILD
Partly Cloudy
High 50-54; Low 33-37
Map and Details on Page 3A
HOURLY TEMPERATURES
3 p.m. 53   7 p.m. 45   11 p.m. 40
4 p.m. 52   8 p.m. 43   12 p.m. 39
5 p.m. 50   9 p.m. 42   1 a.m. 38
6 p.m. 48 10 p.m. 41   2 a.m. 36

38 Governors Back Johnson on Vietnam

From AP and UPI

WASHINGTON — The governors of 38 states met with President Johnson Saturday, then voted unanimously that they "wholeheartedly support and endorse" his policies in Vietnam.

The vote was announced by a Republican, Gov. John Reed, of Maine, who told reporters that he plans to get in touch with the 12 governors who were not present to seek their support for the resolution.

"There is no question in my mind they will all respond affirmatively," he said.

Gov. Romney did not attend the meeting.

Mr. Johnson said he was gratified by the vote. The resolution said:

"It is the unanimous opinion of the governors here assembled that the policies being followed by the President in pursuit of our national objectives in Vietnam be supported and the only rational policies to be followed under the circumstances."

● ● ●

THE RESOLUTION was offered by Gov. James Rhodes, a Republican, of Ohio. Seconding the resolution was another Republican, Gov. Nelson A. Rockefeller, of New York.

The President told the governors during meetings that went on through most of the day that spending in Vietnam has been running a little below earlier estimates. But he said it is too soon to decide whether higher taxes will be needed to finance the war.

Secretary of Defense Robert S. McNamara told the governors that he saw no need now to call military reservists to active duty, though he didn't foreclose the possibility later.

Referring to periodic requests for more troops by the American commander in Vietnam, Gen. William C. Westmoreland, McNamara said:

"I think we can meet Gen. Westmoreland's needs and fill our requirements without calling up the reserves."

Mr. Johnson had invited the governors to the White House to discuss, in his words, "the state of the world, the state of the nation and the state of the states."

He advised the governors that he will send briefing teams to their states, on request, to review Vietnam and

Turn to Page 2A, Column 2

Arthur A. Koscinski   Arthur J. Koscinski

Judge's Tax Muddle

Fear of His Dad Snared Koscinski

When Recorder's Judge Arthur J. Koscinski stood in Federal Court charged with failing to file income tax returns, the shadow of his late father was present.

For it was an intense loyalty to his father, a Federal Court judge, that led to Koscinski's failure to file income tax returns for 18 years.

The Free Press has learned that Koscinski 51, had such an abiding fear of his father's wrath that once he had failed to file a return it became almost impossible for him to admit his mistake.

This fear and loyalty became so overriding that, as one person described it, when it came to filing returns "it was as if his hands were tied."

Koscinski resigned Friday from the $29,000-a-year judgeship he has held since 1961.

He was charged in Federal Court March 4 with five counts of failing to file income tax returns for the years 1959 to 1963. The statute of limitations exempts him from criminal action for the years prior to 1959.

FRIENDS OF Koscinski's father, the late Arthur A. Koscinski, described the father as a fiercely proud man who was a strict jurist and a stern parent.

Arthur J. Koscinski's troubles began shortly after his discharge from the Army Air Corps in 1945.

He had dropped out of the University of Detroit Law School in 1941 to enlist. Three years later, while serving as a gunnery observer on a B-17, he was shot down over Leipzig, Germany. He was captured and imprisoned for a year.

When Capt. Koscinski was separated from the Air Corps, he was told he had to file a Federal income tax return on his accumulated service pay within 90 days.

But with the excitement of returning to civilian life and his desire to re-enter law school, Koscinski failed to follow the advice.

Turn to Page 2A, Column 2

Baby's Birth Stops Show

MEXICO CITY — (UPI) — The first thing he ever did was to show.

It was in a midtown movie house. The film "El Tragabalas," literally "bullet eater," was showing.

There were groans and screams and the lights went on as panic began to spread. Mrs. Ramona Sanchez had slipped to the floor of an aisle and a circle formed around her. There was a doctor in the house and Mrs. Sanchez brought forth a bouncing baby boy.

The mother said he would be named Tragabalas.

Among gifts showered on him will be a lifetime pass to all pictures made by the producer of the interrupted film.

'Deluge of Calls' For Ad to Rent Upper Income

"What a deluge of calls! The response was great," said Mr. L. V. of Detroit. So many readers responded to his exclusive fast-ACTION Want Ad offering an upper income for rent, he lost count of the calls. Whether you want to rent, sell, buy or trade, you'll get ACTION-packed response with Free Press Want Ads.

Dial 222-6800

Inside the Free Press

Amusements	9-12B	Names and Faces	7A
Ann Landers	3C	Obituaries	15A
Astrology	12D	Radio	15C
Auto News	14B	Sports	1-7D
Books	5B	Stereo	15C
Bridge	15C	Stock Markets	17-19B
Business News	14-19B	Travel	8-9B
Chess	4B	Want Ads	8-20D
Crossword Puzzle	14D	Women's Pages	1-13C
Death Notices	9D		
Drew Pearson	8B		
Editorials	2B		
Heloise	13C		
Home Improvem'nts	15A		

HAVE THE FREE PRESS DELIVERED AT HOME
PHONE 222-6500

MARCH 23, 1966:

GM's bungled investigation helps push Ralph Nader into the national spotlight.

"GM President Apologizes For Probe of Auto Critic," column four.

Action Line Dial 222-6464

Action Line solves problems, gets answers, cuts red tape, stands up for your rights. Write Action Line, Box 881, Detroit, Mich. 48231. Or dial 222-6464 between 8:30 a.m. and 4:30 p.m. Monday through Saturday.

To cure his snoring, my husband has started going to sleep with two mentholated candies in his cheeks. The snoring's stopped, but what will it do to his teeth? —Mrs. R. K.

He'll probably get cavities. Most people (more than 90 percent) have acidogenic bacteria in their mouths; when they eat, bacteria feeds on the food, especially sugar, to produce an acid that eats away at tooth enamel. Dentists have a special low-carbohydrate diet that stops cavities in some people for months. It's still experimental but researchers say six weeks on the diet may offer year-long protection.

Action Line

How can you call a serviceman in Vietnam? —K. W.

Detroit-Saigon calls go through the overseas operator, transmitted by radio across the Pacific. Reception's bad, depends on the weather. Calls can be made only between 6 and 10 p.m.; you make an appointment and the waiting list's two weeks long. You'll have to arrange for your party to be at a working number in Saigon. It's $12 for the first three minutes. USO had telephone service from Detroit to Saigon during Christmas season only. Now Red Cross makes 12½ minute records for families to send to boys over there, free of charge. Program started this week, ends April 2. Call "Voices from Home" at the Red Cross (961-3900, extension 357) for an appointment.

Is it true that all calico cats are females? If so, how come? —J.G.

It's true. Multicolored calicos have special genes that produce their unusual patterned fur. The gene is dominant only in the female chromosome: Hence, only females wind up calicos. It's not a breed, just results from crossing red and gray tiger cats. The same is true of two other domestic, short-haired cats: The tortoise shell and the blue-cream. Occasionally, a freak of nature produces a male calico, very rare and valuable: P.T. Barnum offered $1,000 for one and never got it. Usually the males are sterile so a permanent breed's impossible.

You've helped so many people that I wonder if you can help me. I'm trying to find out what happened to some photographs that I had taken of my baby daughter before Christmas. They've been paid for but the studio says they've already been mailed. Can you help? —Mrs. R. H., Mt. Clemens

Action Line checked, got your pictures delivered. Delay was caused by a mixup in negatives, the studio says.

We were hired by the teen club directors to play at the Anderson Junior High School dance in Berkley. They didn't pay us. Please help us get paid. —The Telstars.

Chalk it off to charity, Telstars. You weren't hired; you asked if you could play, and they did you a favor by saying yes. The dance supervisor says lots of local bands ask for tryouts. Only those contracted with in advance for special occasions get paid. Frankly, he says, the kids prefer records.

Action Line

Is it legal to make your own liquor at home in Michigan? I don't want to get anybody in trouble, but my friend does. —R.G.

If he's got a Federal permit and makes wine only, he's allowed to produce up to 200 gallons a year. Homemade beer and whisky are prohibited by the state.

I just mailed my income tax check and I put the stamp on the left hand side instead of the right. What will happen to it? —R.T.

It'll probably get there. Proper procedure is upper right hand corner but that's not a requirement for delivery. The Post Office now automated cancelling machines look for the stamp where it's supposed to be; if it's not there, the machine hands it over to a clerk who cancels it by hand. When the first auto post office opened in Providence, R.I., machines took everything, including S&H green stamps, Christmas seals, address labels, use of which is fraud, carries penalty of $500 fine, up to a year in jail.

I bought a car in February and the car is going to be delivered April 1. Am I subject to the excise tax? —E.F.

The auto excise tax dropped from seven to six percent on Jan. 1, was boosted back to seven percent effective March 16. The new tax, voted to balance the Vietnam-drained budget, applies to all cars that come off the assembly line after March 16. In other words, you pay.

Sound Off

It's a shame that a town of Detroit's size has no public clock for the convenience of its shoppers since Kern's went out of business and the old City Hall was torn down. If the downtown merchants would get together on this it could be a practical sign of appreciation for the millions of dollars spent in their stores. —M.W.

I'm a doctor visiting from Austria and have been appalled to see young mothers dragging small children by the hand, forcing them to run to keep up. This can cause a strain on the child's heart and prolonged pulling can draw the spine out of line. How would these mothers like to be dragged along the street by a giant? —F.W., Rockwood.

Detroit Free Press

Vol. 135—No. 322 On Guard for 134 Years Wednesday, March 23, 1966

METRO FINAL

Ten Cents

LBJ Still Fights Tax Increase

(C) New York Times Service

WASHINGTON — President Johnson made clear Tuesday he is not yet convinced that a tax increase is needed to slow down economic expansion and inflation.

"We don't want to act prematurely," Mr. Johnson told an impromptu news conference. "We don't want to put the brakes on too fast."

The President added, however, that he is studying the situation "every day." He did not rule out the possibility of a tax increase later on.

Mr. Johnson disclosed that spending for the Vietnam war is running "just a little" over the government's estimates for the first three months of this year.

He also noted that there had been cutbacks in the construction of housing for military dependents which "will help ease the tight supplies of building materials" and reported that the planned decline in the budget of the National Aeronautics and Space Administration will release some 50,000 to 100,000 highly skilled workers who are in great demand in private industry.

Mr. Johnson said that before any tax increase decision is reached, the Government needs to see what the effect will be of various anti-inflationary actions it has already taken.

Some of these, such as the $6 billion in Social Security taxes to finance the new program of medical care for the elderly, were not specifically designed as anti-inflationary programs, but will have that effect inasmuch as they remove money from consumers' pockets.

Mr. Johnson did not pass up the opportunity to repeat that he has asked all government departments to review their expenditures with an eye to cutting down and to note that Congress may force some increased expenditures on the Administration.

President Johnson Tuesday named Robert Komer, a top White House assistant, to be a full time specialist in "peaceful reconstruction in Vietnam."

Negro to Get High Police Job

Cushman To Take WSU Post

BY DAVID C. SMITH
Free Press Business Editor

Edward L. Cushman, key American Motors Corp. vice president, who has been on leave of absence from Wayne State University since 1954, Tuesday revealed he will return to the academic community as vice president at Wayne.

Cushman said his resignation has nothing to do with AMC's loss of sales in the automobile industry. He also emphasized he knows of no other AMC executives who are considering leaving the company.

Cushman will continue as an AMC director. There was no immediate indication whether Cushman's post as senior staff assistant to AMC President Roy Abernethy will be filled.

* * *

CUSHMAN HAS served as Abernethy's right - hand man, with over-all responsibilities for industrial relations, public relations and the corporate secretary and legal departments.

His appointment to the WSU post will become effective within the next few weeks. Cushman said. He described the new job as similar to his AMC position in that he will work in the "general administration" of the university under President William R. Keast.

Cushman's resignation surprised some auto industry observers, but not those who know him well.

"His first love always has been education," said one close friend.

Cushman, 52, joined AMC on leave from Wayne State in May, 1954, when it was formed as a result of a merger between Nash-Kelvinator Corp. and the Hudson Motor Car Co. His first job was director of

Turn to Page 2A, Column 1

Edward L. Cushman

AUTO INDUSTRY critic Ralph Nader (left) faced James Roche, president of GM (right), as Roche apologized before a Senate subcommittee. With Roche is his attorney, Theodore Sorensen. —AP Photo

GM President Apologizes For Probe of Auto Critic

Free Press Washington Staff

WASHINGTON — James M. Roche, president of the General Motors Corp., Tuesday apologized twice for his firm's investigation of attorney Ralph Nader, a critic of the auto industry.

Roche's first apology came in a prepared statement before a Senate subcommittee which has been studying traffic safety problems.

Roche acknowledged that the firm had hired private detectives who questioned between 40 and 60 of Nader's acquaintances and members of his family. The inquiry, delving into Nader's habits, his beliefs on semitism and his political views, cost GM $6,700.

ROCHE SAID in his statement, "I deplore the kind of harassment to which Mr. Nader has apparently been subjected. I am just as shocked and outraged by some of the incidents which Mr. Nader reported as members of this subcommittee.

"To the extent that General Motors bears responsibility, I want to apologize here and now to the members of this subcommittee and Mr. Nader. I sincerely hope that these apologies will be accepted."

Later, however, Vincent Gillen, head of the detective agency which investigated Nader, noted in testimony that Roche had had to be apologized if there had been harassment of Nader in the investigation.

Gillen insisted there had been no harassment.

At this, Senators Robert F. Kennedy (D., N.Y.) and subcommittee Chairman Abraham Ribicoff (D., Conn.) differed emphatically with Gillen.

"Let's get this clear," Gillen said. "Mr. Roche apologized if they happened, and they didn't happen."

* * *

RIBICOFF SAID he had interpreted Roche's statement as meaning that Roche was highly disturbed about the investigation.

Kennedy then asked Roche, who was sitting in the spectators' section, if Ribicoff's was the correct interpretation.

Roche said: "That interpretation is correct," and he asked for time at the end of the hearing to clarify GM's stand.

In his second apology, Roche said he wanted to make clear that he is taking responsibility for the actions that Nader and the committee complained about. And he said he wanted to apologize

Turn to Page 2A, Column 3

Climber Plunges to Death In Daring Swiss Alps Ascent

From UPI and AP

KLEINE SCHEIDEGG, Switzerland — American John Harlin, who moved to Switzerland because of his love of mountain climbing, fell more than 3,000 feet to his death Tuesday while attempting to climb the unconquered north wall of 13,025 - foot Eiger peak.

Triumph mingled with tragedy as two Germans in his party climbed almost to the top of the peak, unaware of the death of their 30-year-old companion.

Harlin, of Los Altos, Calif., an ex-fighter pilot, fell on the ice-covered rock he was scaling as captain of a five-man British-American team.

* * *

"WE ARE PRAYING. This is a warning," an emotion-gripped German voice crackled through the radio from a bivouac high up on the mountain.

Two days ago, the Germans and Anglo-Americans joined forces for a determined assault on the mountain.

Harlin had told his friends: "This is it. All the way to the top."

Tuesday afternoon, Harlin was a red-clad puppet hurtling down.

"I WAS WATCHING in brilliant sunshine from the Kleine Scheidegg Hotel roof," said an Austrian newspaperman. "I had just focused the telescope on Harlin, a solitary figure in red heavy - blue knapsack on his back.

"Suddenly, I saw the tiny figure throw up his arms as though in despair. A split second later he sailed through the air. It seemed a horrible eternity before the body landed at the very foot of the north wall."

This climb was to have climaxed Harlin's career as an Alpinist, adventurer and world traveller.

"Climbing is a sophistication of exploration," he said a few days ago. "This one is the biggest Alpine climb ever conceived."

A stocky, sunburned man, he loved nature, rocks, mountains, and the wind howling amidst wilderness.

Harlin was trying to join an advance team of eight West Germans and a Briton waiting in the bivouac on "The Spider," a dreaded ice field less than 3,000 feet from the summit.

Harlin, a married man with two young children, was an experienced mountaineer. He ran an international school for climbers at Leysin, Switzerland.

Minister to Aid In Racial Affairs

An outstanding Negro educator, community leader and clergyman will be named to the newly created post of administrative assistant to the police commissioner, the Free Press learned Tuesday.

The Rev. Hubert G. Locke, a counselor in the Wayne State University Office of Religious Affairs and pastor of Church of Christ of Conant Gardens, will hold the highest civilian post in the Detroit Police Department ever afforded a member of his race.

Commissioner Ray Girardin and Mayor Cavanagh are expected to make the announcement of Locke's acceptance of the job within the next few days.

Mr. Locke will be directly responsible to Girardin, working on assignment in the complex area of community and racial affairs. His appointment is comparable to that of a deputy police commissioner — a top-echelon administrative post.

Girardin said Mr. Locke's duties would include future planning for the department and many other functions — "as a matter of fact, all functions" - of the department in addition to racial affairs.

News of the expected appointment brought charges by Cavanagh's political opponents that the move is calculated to gain Negro support for Cavanagh in his try for the Democratic Senate nomination.

"He knows he made a mistake by proposing a stop-and-frisk law, and now he's trying to make up the ground he lost," one observer said.

Cavanagh will face former Gov. G. Mennen Williams in the Aug. 2 primary for the Democratic Senate nomination.

In answer to the charges, Cavanagh said:

Hubert G. Locke

"That kind of comment does great injustice to Mr. Locke. Anyone who knows this man knows he would not be used for political purposes.

"I put this job into the budget a year ago, and we've been attempting to get Mr. Locke since October, 1965. It's absurd to say it is related to politics."

WSU President William R. Keast said he was pleased that Mr. Locke had been selected for such an important position in the community.

"I am sure he will do an outstanding job," Keast said.

Turn to Page 9, Column 1

College Outlook '66

Universities Face Crisis of Numbers

In Michigan's booming higher education system, state colleges and universities are growing by leaps and bounds. Some of them are already mammoth multi-versities. In the second of four articles, Free Press Staff Writer Mary Ann Weston tells of some approaches to the problems of bigness.

BY MARY ANN WESTON
Free Press Staff Writer

Bigness is the byword of higher education in Michigan. Four of the State's universities now have more than 10,000 students - big by any standard. Most of the others expect similar enrollments.

There are now about 211,000 students at Michigan's four-year colleges and universities, about half of them in the big three — Michigan, Michigan State and Wayne. By 1975, it's expected there will be 400,000 collegians in Michigan.

One of the most knotty problems of bigness is this: How do you educate the masses while avoiding mass education?

* * *

COMPLAINTS ABOUT the intellectual and social effects of bigness—the anonymity, the atomization, the alienation — are coming louder and louder from the students, who readily remind you that it was such complaints that touched off last year's disturbances at the University of California at Berkeley.

In Michigan, giving a personal touch to education through the institutional mass is a preoccupation of many administrators. Some have come up with imaginative approaches to the problems of bigness.

At Michigan, a yet-to-be-named residential college is in the works. At Michigan State such a project is already un-

Turn to Page 8A, Column 1

Mannino Family Finds Home to Rent Through Want Ad

After a month's futile search for a home to rent, Mrs. Celeste Mannino placed an exclusive Free Press ACTION Want Ad in the Free Press and promptly found just the home her family wanted. Whether you're buying, selling or renting you'll find the kind of response you're looking for with fast-ACTION Free Press Want Ads.

Dial 222-6800

STORMY

Windy and Mild
High 56-60; Low 32-36

Name and Details on Page 11-D
HOURLY TEMPERATURES

Inside the Free Press

Is your house a target for fire? Don't answer "no" until you read Jean Carper's article on easy-to-overlook danger points. You'll find the third of her series, "Stay Alive," on Page 4C.

Easy to Read...

What is Prince Philip really like? Earl Wilson, the Free Press' New York columnist, happened in on a dinner recently and found all the lovely ladies in a flutter over their Prince Charming. Wilson concludes that Philip is a good guy.

Wilson

...And Easy to Find

Earl Wilson's column is in the Free Press every day except Sunday. Today's column will be found in its usual place, the Feature Page. It's always the next-to-last page of Section A.

Amusements	8-9C
Ann Landers	3C
Astrology	10D
Billy Graham	12D
Bridge	10D
Business News	5D
Comics	9-11D
Crossword Puzzle	10D
Death Notices	10C
Drew Pearson	15A
Earl Wilson	15A
Editorials	6A
Feature Page	2C
Heloise	11D
Movie Guide	12D
Names and Faces	5A
Obituaries	6C
Sports	1-4D
Stock Markets	6-7D
TV-Radio	8D
Travel	10-15C
Want Ads	6-7D
Women's Pages	1-5C

HAVE THE FREE PRESS DELIVERED AT HOME
PHONE 222-6500

Inside This Section...
The Inside of Sports — Page 6
Racing Results — Page 7
Michigan Outdoors — Page 8
Want Ads — Pages 9-20

Detroit Free Press
Sports — Want Ads
SUNDAY, NOVEMBER 20, 1966

SECTION C

Nov. 20, 1966:

It was the college game of the century, or the decade, or at least the year.

Sports Page

10 to 10

Why?

Q—So who's No. 1?
A—The sentiment of the writers who covered Saturday's 10-10 tie was that Notre Dame and Michigan State should share in the national championship.
A poll taken by the Free Press disclosed that 15 writers favored putting the two teams in the No. 1 spot. Seven voted for Michigan State and three for Notre Dame.

Q—What happened to Terry Hanratty and Nick Eddy?
A—Hanratty suffered a shoulder separation in Notre Dame's second series after the kickoff when tackled by Bubba Smith and Charles Thornhill.
Eddy didn't play because of a injury to his ailing shoulder. He slipped and fell when coming off the train to MSU.

Q—Why didn't the Irish use the pass-catching talents of end Jim Seymour?
A—Seymour, prized sophomore end from Royal Oak Shrine High, didn't catch a single pass. MSU safetyman Jess Phillips said the Spartans kept him covered closely on the long patterns, forcing O'Brien to throw short passes. Four passes were thrown to Seymour, he missed two and two went over his head.

Q—Why did Notre Dame run the ball instead of passing on the last six plays?
A—PARSEGHIAN: "I wasn't going to blow the game with an interception. We wanted to maintain possession. And we respected Dick Kenney's field goal kicking ability."

Parseghian, Daugherty—Both look like they're No. 2

'Conservative' Irish Irk Spartans

BY JACK BERRY
Free Press Sports Writer

EAST LANSING — Duffy Daugherty wouldn't say it but his players did.
"As far as I'm concerned," said co-captain Clint Jones, "we're No. 1. We played like champions.
"When we were in our territory and had fourth down, we gambled. We played to win and that's the only way to play the game. They played to tie.
"THEY'VE GOT a good team but I won't say that a team that eats up the clock is a great team," Jones said.
The 10-10 "Dream Game" . . . The "Game of the Century" . . . left a bittersweet taste in everyone's mouth. There was mumbling in the stands by fans from both schools, loud booes as Notre Dame killed the clock in the final minute instead of trying to pass.
"I thought they'd try to throw a long bomb, at least on that last play," said defensive star George Webster.
It was sentiment repeated throughout the Spartan dressing room.
"We were going for broke," Daugherty said, "not that ties aren't better than losing—they are."
But Daugherty wouldn't let himself get pinned into saying he was surprised that Notre Dame didn't pass at the end.
"I thought we were on top most of the game although they came back like champs."
Who does he think will be No. 1?
"It's hard to say. Probably a lot of votes will be split between us and Notre Dame and Alabama will slip in," he said, laughing somewhat wryly.
Alabama grabbed the top in the AP poll last January

ND Rally Catches Spartans

BY HAL McCOY
Free Press Sports Writer

EAST LANSING—The Football Game of the Decade the one that was to settle all debate, all prejudice all arguments, merely created more Saturday.
Which is the greater team after all? Michigan State, or Notre Dame? They could not settle it for themselves.
In a classic struggle which held a throng of 80,011 spellbound in Spartan Stadium, Michigan State and Notre Dame battled to a stunning and somewhat disappointing 10-10 tie.
Left unsolved was the great debate over which was really the foremost team in the land. There was much to recommend them both. But because of the tie, there was the threat that neither would gain acclaim as the nation's No. 1 team.
Michigan State struck out to a 10-0 lead in the first half on a four-yard smack by Reggie Cavender and a 47-yard field goal by Dick Kenney.
Notre Dame shortly chopped it to 10-7 on a 34-yard pass from Coley O'Brien to Bob Gladieux, and tied the score on the first play of the final period on a 28-yard field goal by Joe Azzaro.
The Irish left the record crowd booing at the end, however, when they finished off the final minute and 15 seconds by running six ground plays, disdaining the pass and a chance to win. Michigan State, striving desperately to win, gambled repeatedly against catastrophe by calling time outs to stop the clock while Notre Dame had the ball.
The weirdness started Friday afternoon when Notre Dame arrived in East Lansing. Star halfback Nick Eddy stumbled getting off the train and re-injured his aching shoulder. He didn't play.
Sophomore quarterback Terry Hanratty participated in two series for the Irish. On a running play, he injured his shoulder and didn't play the rest of the game.
The other half of the Notre Dame sophomore act, Jim Seymour, might as well have not played. He didn't catch a pass.
It was the same for Michigan State. Sophomore end Al Brenner didn't snare a pass until two minutes remained in the game. All-American halfback Clinton Jones was practically non-existent in the MSU offense with 21 yards in 10 carries.
Star fullback Apisa, although ready to rumble, carried two times for two yards. Cavender, his replacement, led MSU's ground assault with 36 yards in seven carries and the Spartan touchdown.

THE ONLY OFFENSIVE star in the game for either side who lived up to the monstrous pre-game buildup was MSU's end Gene Washington. He caught five passes for 123 yards and got the touchdown drive moving with a 42-yard catch.
The defenses were all they were cracked up to be

Turn to Page 2C, Column 5

	MSU	ND
First downs	13	10
Rushing yardage	142	91
Passing yardage	73	136
Passes	7-20	8-24
Passes intercepted	2	1
Punts	8-32	8-42
Fumbles lost	0	0
Yards penalized	32	5

Michigan State .... 0 10 0 0 — 10
Notre Dame .... 0 0 7 3 — 10
MSU—FG Kenney 47.
MSU—Cavender 4 plunge (Kenney kick).
ND—Gladieux 34 pass from O'Brien (Azzaro kick).
ND—FG Azzaro 28.
Attendance—80,011.

MSU—Irish Highlights
—Irish Prove Why They're Still No. 1. See Joe Falls on Page 2C.
—MSU tackle Bubba Smith nearly went to the pokey instead of to the game. Page 3C.
—How sports writers from across the nation saw the big game. Page 3C.
—Notre Dame's sub quarterback Coley O'Brien is the bright spot on glum Irish squad. Page 3C.

Photos by Free Press photographers Vince Witek, Dick Tripp, Jimmy Tafoya, Ray Glonka

Irish stew as Spartans' Regis Cavender (25) Storms in for TD

St. Ambrose Is Goodfellow Champ, 33-19

BY HAL SCHRAM

The Goodfellow charm which belongs to St. Ambrose High sparkled on a dull overcast Saturday morning at U-D Stadium.
The Cavaliers utilized both power and breaks to smother favored Denby, 33-19, before 15,000 fans at the 29th annual City football championship.
Winning this game is old hat for St. Ambrose. The Cavaliers have been in the Goodfellow classic five times in the past eight years and have never lost.

THE RECOVERY of two Denby fumbles early in both the first and third periods led to St. Ambrose touchdowns and actually decided the game.
In the opening minutes, when Denby found it difficult to hang onto the football, Doug Martinelli recovered a Tar fumble on the St. Ambrose 49. In four plays St. Ambrose went in to score.
Quarterback Greg Hacias hit Bob Walker with a 36-yard gainer on a screen pass on St. Ambrose's first play from scrimmage. Three plays later Walker broke over right tackle to score from the 10.
St. Ambrose had a 7-0 lead and was never to trail.
Early in the second period Denby got on the scoreboard when Bruce Webb scored on a 29-yard counter play to climax an 86-yard march in 10 plays.
But Pat Piper's kick was wide and St. Ambrose still held a 7-6 lead.

ST. AMBROSE came right back covering 60 yards in seven plays for its second touchdown and a 14-6 lead. The big gainers were two passes by Hacias to Gary Nowak for 19 and 23 yards. Tom Bialk scored the TD from the three.
Two long passes by Jon Rutherford got Denby back in

	ST. AMBROSE	DENBY
First downs	17	12
Rushing yardage	212	190
Passing yardage	92	54
Passes	4-10	4-15
Passes intercepted	1	0
Punts	5-32.6	4-29.5
Fumbles lost	1	5
Yards penalized	84	85

St. Ambrose .... 7 7 13 6 — 33
Denby .... 0 6 13 0 — 19
AMB—Walker, 10-run; Hacias, run.
DENBY—Webb, 29-run (kick failed).
AMB—Bialk, 3-run; Hacias, run.
DENBY—Lynch, 22-pass from Rutherford (kick failed).
AMB—Carducci, 8-fumble return (run failed).
DENBY—Webb, 35-pass from Rutherford (kick failed).
AMB—Bialk, 3-run; Walker, run.
AMB—Bommarito, 3-run (run failed).

Turn to Page 7C, Column 4

Flowery Words for Purdue

CHICAGO — (AP) — Purdue officially was designated by vote of athletic directors Saturday as the Big Ten's representative in the Rose Bowl.
The Purdue faculty will meet Monday to vote on formal acceptance.
Conference champion Michigan State, having gone to the Rose Bowl last season, was ineligible for an encore.

U-M, Detwiler Roll over Bucks, 17-3

BY JACK SAYLOR
Free Press Sports Writer

COLUMBUS, O.—So who's No. 1?
Well, in Ohio Stadium Saturday it looked a lot like Michigan's Wolverines.
Jim Detwiler held his own Columbus Day celebration as Michigan closed its season by crunching Ohio State, 17-3, in the first annual Transistor Bowl game.
It was attended by 83,403 radios, accompanied by people with two eyes on the action here and one ear tuned to "that other" game in East Lansing.
They heard an earful — but they also saw an eyeful as Michigan chewed up a vaunted Buckeye defense for 382 yards—272 of it on the ground.
It was a particularly galling loss for Ohio's Woody Hayes.
He roamed the sidelines, ranting while Michigan ripped at his proud defense. He became enraged at one clipping call and seemed ready to head for the nearby Olentangy River, short shirt-sleeves and all, as the Bucks finished with a 4-5 record—only Woody's second losing season in his 16-year tenure.
Detwiler scored his touchdown on a seven-yard sprint

	OHIO ST.	MICH.
First downs	20	21
Rushing yardage	146	272
Passing yardage	123	110
Passes	11-29	6-15
Passes intercepted	2	1
Punts	4-21.3	3-43.3
Fumbles lost	0	0
Yards penalized	38	89

Ohio State .... 0 3 0 0 — 3
Michigan .... 0 7 7 3 — 17
MICH—FG Sygar 24.
OHIO—FG Cairns 26.
MICH—Detwiler 7 run (Sygar kick).
MICH—Willhite 28 pass from Vidmer (Sygar kick).
A—83,403.

in the second quarter, breaking a 3-3 tie. The other U-M touchdown came on a 28-yard pass from Dick Vidmer to Clayton Wilhite in the third period.
Ohio State made four serious challenges to the Michigan goal as halfback Bo Rein picked up 82 yards rushing and another 59 yards on five passes from Bill Long.
But everytime the Bucks got close, the Wolverines put a watch on the Rein and Ohio had to settle for a 26-yard field goal by Gary Cairns, matching a 24-yarder by Rick Sygar as Michigan ended with a spree of broken records.

VIDMER PASSED for 110 yards, giving him a sweep of U-M game, season and career passing yardage records. He has tossed for 2,983 yards with still another season to go.
Sygar's two extra points gave him 24 for the Big Ten season— two better than Jim Brieske and Harry Allis managed.
Jack Clancy concluded his

Turn to Page 7C, Column 4

But Detroit Falls, 7-2
Wings 'Platoon' Goalies on Hawks

Special to the Free Press

CHICAGO — A noble experiment failed for the Red Wings Saturday night in the Chicago Stadium snakepit, graveyard for Detroit hockey teams in recent years.
Coach Sid Abel started out alternating his goaltenders, Hank Bassen and Roger Crozier, but junked the plan in the second period, going with Crozier.
The Hawks, however, exploded from a 2-2 tie in the third period in a five-goal flurry for a 7-2 victory.

THE HAWKS scored their five goals in the final 12 minutes of play.
Chico Maki started it and Eric Nesterenko finished the spree. In between, Dennis Hull, Bobby

Turn to 4C, Column 2

May 1, 1967:

The hippie era hits Detroit with a love-in organized by John Sinclair.

WINDY
Mostly Cloudy
High 62-68; Low 44-48
Detroit Area Forecast
See Map and Details on Page 11D

Detroit Free Press

Vol. 136—No. 361   On Guard for 135 Years   Monday, May 1, 1967

METRO FINAL

Ten Cents

Action Line solves problems, gets answers, cuts red tape, stands up for your rights. Write Action Line, Box 881, Detroit, Mich. 48231. Or dial 222-6464 between 8:30 a.m. and 4:30 p.m. Monday through Friday.

My 17-year-old nephew is critically ill in an Indianapolis hospital. He doesn't know he's dying, but has been asking to see his dad. His father remarried and moved to Seattle in 1961. We have no idea how to find him.—D. W., Lansing.

Action Line found him in a small town about 150 miles from Indianapolis, asked him to visit his son right away. He wouldn't promise to, so we did some more checking. Turns out he didn't want to be found because he's never contributed to his son's support. We explained your sister doesn't care about the money now, just wanted the boy to see his dad again. He said he'd leave immediately for the hospital.

Is there any place I could get an assortment of traffic signs? They look great in a recreation room, but I don't want to steal them.—R. S.

You'd better not. Swiping traffic signs can cost you 90 days and $500. They are a lot cheaper than that at Associated Specialties Co., 24555 W. Eight Mile. They've got everything from "No Parking" to "Don't even THINK of parking here." Signs range from $3.80 to $8.95. Make sure you get a bill in case a cop stops you. They threw the book at one guy who had 28 signs in his car.

About midnight last Friday a fair young lady approached me in a Warren bar and asked me for a donation. She had on Salvation Army garb, but what really made me suspicious was what happened when she left the bar. She got into a government-owned station wagon marked with a black X license plate. There was a nice young man driving.—I. T., Warren.

That was no nice young man, that was the lady's husband—a Salvation Army minister. His wife was making her regular Friday night tavern run collecting donations for SA's rehabilitation work in the area. Next time you see an X on a license plate, keep in mind they're also issued to non-profit organizations—like the Hazel Park branch of the Salvation Army.

I'm blind and don't get downtown very often. Last week, while standing at Woodward and Michigan, I heard chimes go off and bells sounding all around me. Could you tell me where they were coming from?—B. J.

You were smack in the middle of the chime symphony. Two acts were going, each a block away from you. One's on the top of Hudson's, the other on Bank of the Commonwealth at Griswold and Fort. Both play Westminster Chimes every hour, then bong out the time. Guy who installed Hudson's says the speakers are so good they could be turned up to broadcast two miles—right into Windsor.

My husband's going to a convention in Chicago this week. His great love is Polish food and music. We've been told that there's a Polish section in Chicago, but our Polish friends here don't know where it is.—Mrs. C. R., Harper Woods.

Neither do the Poles in Chicago. Much of the old Polish section along Division Street on the near northwest side has been bulldozed away by urban renewal. Polish Consulate suggests you try the pierogi and sauerkraut at Patryn's, 2011 North Ave. There's singing, zuppa and zywiec (beer) at Syrena's on the far south side or at Polish Villa, 1247 North Ashland. Favorite Hamtramck haunts for Detroit's 356,000 Poles: Zosia's and Martin's on Chene, Detroit Workingman's Cooperative Restaurant No. 1 on Yemans.

We've got a movie star in the family but haven't been able to prove it. My father-in-law had a part in a 1926 silent film called "A Regular Scout." No one I've asked ever heard of the movie. My five kids would certainly like to see an old picture from the film that shows their grandfather.—Mrs. R. J., Warren.

Two pictures of grandpa are on the way. If you want more, you can order them from New York's Museum of Modern Art film library at $6 each. "Scout" starred Fred Thomson, was the story of a guy who wanted revenge on a kindly old lady whose son had killed the hero's mother. His Boy Scout training trips him up, though: He ends up befriending the woman and marrying her daughter. Your father-in-law, Lewis Kirkland, had no trouble landing his part. His dad directed the film.

Sound Off!

JUST LIKE to warn prospective visitors to Expo 67 to watch out for professional pickpockets. When my sister reported the theft of her billfold to Montreal police, they said 40 such complaints had already been turned in. When we go, we're wearing travelers checks and wearing a money belt.—Mrs. R. P., Dearborn.

To Our Readers . . .

If Action Line's phones are busy when you call, remember that we like mail, too. Our address is: Action Line, Box 881, Detroit, Mich. 48231. We wish we could answer or even acknowledge each of your questions. While that isn't possible, we will check every one and print the most interesting answers every day.

Thousands Battle with Police

Belle Isle Love-In Turns to Hate

BY GARY BLONSTON AND SUSAN HOLMES
Free Press Staff Writers

The love-in that filled the Belle Isle bandstand area with brotherhood Sunday wound up as a two-part riot Sunday night.

After a day of everybody being lovable, the mood changed at 7 p.m. when a policeman arrested a motorcyclist for reckless driving, near the bandstand.

In minutes the area was transformed into a battlefield.

Witnesses said young people began cursing the policemen, pelting them with sticks, rocks, bottles, bricks and anything else that could be picked up and thrown.

Policemen promptly closed the island.

Spearheaded by the Mounted Division, the officers began to nudge the 5,000 persons at the scene, plus everybody else, across the MacArthur Bridge to Jefferson.

At the entrance to the bridge, at E. Jefferson and E. Grand Blvd., the young people — love-iners, spectators and motorcycle club members — made a stand.

Witnesses said that in this second battle between 1,000 and 2,000 were taunting and fighting the police and throwing missiles.

The Mounted Division, supported by

Turn to Page 2A, Column 3

Pictures on the Back Page

Free Press Photo by DICK TRIPP
Anything could happen—and did—at the Belle Isle love-in

Head Hippie Offers Facts On Truth, Life and Love

BY GLENNA McWHIRTER
Free Press Staff Writer

John Sinclair sits there with his wild hair and his drooping mustache, wearing painted wooden beads and silver earrings.

He looks ridiculous.

Lounging on the dusty couch at his Artist's Workshop at 4857 John Lodge, he talks about love, truth and life.

And something about him almost makes you want to get turned on and tuned in.

"Kids are beautiful, honest, trusting people," he says.

"Look at them." He nods toward a group of youngsters leafing through a stack of underground newspapers, laughing and talking without inhibition or affectation. "Now that's what's happening. Maybe it's the only reality left in our society."

Sinclair, 25, is the unofficial leader and spokesman for a loosely organized group of young people called "hippies."

JOHN Sinclair: High priest of the hippies.

HE'S THE man behind Sunday's "love-in" on Belle Isle, a defender of draft-dodging, marijuana smoking and love, both free and brotherly.

Sinclair publishes two underground newspapers — Sun and the Fifth Estate — which from time to time have been banned from the mail as obscene or pornographic.

In January Sinclair was arrested, along with 56 others, in a raid on his workshop. He was charged with possession of marijuana, the third such arrest for Sinclair in the last three years. He's free on $1,000 bond, pending trial.

Recently, the high school and college kids who cluster around Sinclair have shown a sprightly interest in publishing their own newspapers, and

Sinclair readily admits he has helped some.

"They want to know how to put a paper together, how much it will cost. We help them. It's good for kids to be discussing life, expressing and exchanging ideas. It's better than riding around in cars," he said.

The high school papers include "Yellow," (produced by Cass Tech students), "Kulcher" (Grosse Pointe High), "The Elevator" (Mumford) and "Clod and Pebble" (Lincoln Park).

Three seniors at Thurston High School, Redford Township, were suspended last week for producing another one called "Hark." And a group of Birmingham high

Turn to Page 2A, Column 1

Ford Lists 42 Percent Profit Drop

Ford Motor Co. became the third of the four major U.S. auto makers Monday to report a sharp dip in profits for the first quarter of 1967.

Ford said net income for the period was $1.10 a share, down 42 percent from the $1.89 earned during the first quarter of 1966.

General Motors last week reported its first quarter profits were down 34 percent, and Chrysler Corp. announced its profits for the period were down 70 percent.

American Motors Corp., whose quarterly report is due Monday, also is expected to show a decline in earnings.

FORD BLAMED the profit

Turn to Page 8A, Column 1

Inside the Free Press

The late Edgar Cayce, the Sleeping Prophet, had a dream that the lost continent of Atlantis would someday reappear. According to Cayce's prediction, that day is not far off. Another in a series. Pg. 4B.

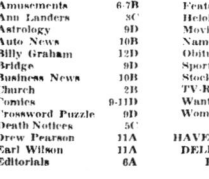

Amusements	6,7B
Ann Landers	8D
Astrology	9D
Auto News	10B
Billy Graham	12D
Bridge	9D
Business News	10B
Church	7B
Comics	9-11D
Crossword Puzzle	9D
Death Notices	5C
Drew Pearson	11A
Earl Wilson	11A
Editorials	6A
Feature Page	11A
Heloise	8C
Movie Guide	10-11D
Names and Faces	12D
Obituaries	11C
Sports	1-4D
Stock Markets	10B
TV Radio	8B
Want Ads	4-11C
Women's Pages	1-3C

HAVE THE FREE PRESS DELIVERED AT HOME
PHONE 222-6500

Tigers Triumph Without a Hit

BY GEORGE CANTOR
Free Press Sports Writer

BALTIMORE — Steve Barber was so close to the summit he could reach out and touch it.

But he came up with a handful of dirt.

Barber was one pitch away from a no-hitter against the Tigers Sunday.

But Detroit scored two ninth-inning runs without a hit to beat Barber and the Orioles, 2-1, in one of the strangest games in baseball history.

Inspired by this, Detroit exploded for a six-run inning off Jim Palmer to sweep the doubleheader. The score in the second game was 6-4.

The sweep put Detroit two games in front of Baltimore in the standings and in first place, a half-game in front of the New York Yankees.

Joe Sparma won the second game with relief help from Dave Wickersham as the Tigers wrapped it up with their fifth-inning explosion.

Al Kaline's two-run double and Norm Cash's two-run homer were the big blasts.

The Baltimore scoreboard went haywire in the middle of the Tiger rally and refused to function properly the rest of the day.

But everything was anti-climactic after the opener.

Only once before in the annals of baseball has a team won a nine-inning game while getting no hits. Cincinnati victimized Houston's Ken Johnson in this fashion in 1964.

Barber walked 10 men and hit two others. Two walks in the ninth beat him.

The tying run scored on a wild pitch with two out in the ninth and a 1-2 count on Mickey Stanley.

When Barry walked Stanley, Baltimore manager Hank Bauer took him out though he had not given up a hit.

Stu Miller retrieved him and Wes Bert smashed one of his deliveries back through the middle.

Shortstop Luis Aparicio reached it behind second base with a desperate lunge and tipped backhanded to Mark Belanger for a forceout that would have ended the inning.

But Belanger dropped the ball and pinch runner Jake Wood sped across with the winning run.

Fred Gladding took care of the Orioles in the ninth to save the victory for Earl Wilson.

Barber's performance overshadowed a superb job by the Tiger starter Wilson, who evened his record at 2-2, gave the Orioles two singles in eight innings.

The Orioles scored their lone run without a hit.

Singles by Andy Etchebarren

Turn to Page 8A, Column 2

Barber takes his loss like a man, Page 1D.

Box scores on Page 1D.

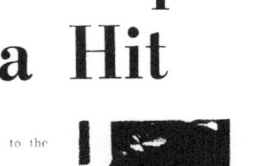

STEVE BARBER: The loser in one of the strangest games in history.

Nine Towns Hit

Tornados Kill 12 In S. Minnesota

ALBERT LEA, Minn. — At least 12 persons were killed and more than 100 injured when tornados raked at least nine southern Minnesota communities late Sunday.

Sheriff Emil Meuer of Blue Earth County reported five persons were dead at Waseca, where a tornado ripped a path two blocks wide and eight blocks long through a residential section.

Meuer could not estimate the number of injured at Waseca but said dragging operations were under way for a woman reportedly blown into a lake in the city.

Two persons died at Albert Lea, near the Iowa border, and other two at Owatonna, about 50 miles south of Minneapolis and one each at the small hamlets of Alden, the Waseca and Clarks Grove.

Tornados also struck on the outskirts of Austin and in the villages of Myrtle and Brownsdale.

"IT WAS horrible, there was no warning," said Mrs. Archie Draheim of the tornado which ripped into Waseca.

"There was this terrible rain falling, and all of a sudden I was diving along the floor with glass all around me."

The tornado ripped into the southwest edge of Albert Lea about 6:30 p.m., cutting a block wide swath through a housing development.

Newsmen estimated that as many as 80 persons were injured, in addition to the known dead.

Apparently 144 residents of a retirement home in Albert Lea escaped injury, although the home was buffeted by powerful winds.

National Guardsmen, civil defense workers, and all off-duty police were summoned to duty in Albert Lea.

GOV. ROMNEY: He marched into Georgia.

A Daring Romney Is in Dixie

BY TOM SHAWVER
Free Press Politics Writer

ATLANTA — Buoyed by a hearty reception in Arkansas, Gov. Romney marched into the Deep South Sunday and prepared to fire another volley at George Wallace's yet unborn third party.

It was a bold maneuver for Romney, who came to Georgia fully aware that this is not the friendliest part of the South for a northern, moderate Republican governor.

Georgia is one of five southern states that went for Barry Goldwater in the 1964 presidential election.

IT IS ONE that Wallace,

Turn to Page 2A, Column 1

Terrorist Mine Rips School Bus; 6 Children Die

ADEN (UPI) — A mine apparently planted by anti-British terrorists blew up under an Arab school bus Sunday, killing the driver and six schoolboys and seriously injuring 10 children.

Moslem religious leaders denounced the terrorists responsible for planting the mine.

Some observers said the mine apparently were intended for British patrol cars which use the route taken by the school bus. Several British vehicles have been blown up in the area.

Negro Leaders Plead for 'a Safe City' — See Page 3A

Detroit Free Press

Vol. 137—No. 80 — On Guard for 136 Years — Monday, July 24, 1967 — Ten Cents

NICE — Less Humid — High 76-83, Low 60-66

METRO — The Weekend In Religion — Turn to Page 2B

JULY 24, 1967:

Many Detroiters spend the first day of the riot unaware parts of town are under siege because officials convince the media to embargo news until Sunday afternoon. The Free Press won a Pulitzer Prize for its coverage of the insurrection.

Mobs Burn and Loot 800 Stores; Troops Move In; Emergency Is On

Action Line
Dial 222-6464

Action Line solves problems, gets answers, cuts red tape, stands up for your rights. Write Action Line, Box 881, Detroit, Mich. 48231. Or dial 222-6464 between 8:30 a.m. and 4:30 p.m. Monday through Friday.

We're preparing a computer exhibit which is supposed to be able to predict the next U.S. president. To do it, we have to program all kinds of voter information —including the number of registered voters in Michigan. Everyone we've talked with says they only keep track by counties.—M.E.

Feed 3½ million into the machine. Last count was in April, 1966, when 3,351,730 voters were registered. Robert Montgomery, director of state elections, says that's a good estimate. Things should be better after Oct. 1, when a new law will require cities, townships and villages to report figures to the county clerk within 15 days after registration closes. They still won't be exact, though. Since a precinct has to divide if it's over the quota (1,400 in machine precincts, 800 for paper ballots), they get lots of counts that say 799 or 1,399. Montgomery says "precinct people lie a little."

Has a woman ever been awarded the Congressional Medal of Honor?—L.W., Warren.

Once—but they took it back. Dr. Mary Walker, a surgeon for the Union Army in the Civil War, got the medal in 1866 by badgering her boss for battlefield duty. He nominated her for the medal to get her off his back. It didn't work. She was back pestering the Army a year later for a military pension, which she got in 1876. A 1916 review board scratched her—and 910 others— from the honor roll when they found out the medal had been awarded to shut her up. Mary went on to become one of the nation's first suffragettes lectured on women's rights — while wearing a frock coat and trousers.

When we opened a business on U.S. 23 we were told our neon sign had to be back at least 100 feet from the road. The other resorts in the area aren't abiding by this rule, and they're getting all the tourist business. If the rule no longer applies, we want to move our sign out to the road. Can we?—Mrs. C.S., Oscoda.

Wait till the legislature decides. A 1925 law says no commercial signs may be placed on the highway right of way. In your area, right of way varies from 100 to 150 feet—which means no signs for 50 to 75 feet on either side of the road. But when the highway department started enforcing the law by ordering the signs to be removed, owners of businesses along the highway howled. An Upper Peninsula motel owner took it to the state supreme court in 1965, which declared parts of the act unconstitutional. Real problem is that rights-of-way vary from a minimum of 66 feet to a maximum of 500—so that some people's signs can be legally closer to the road than others. Highway Department is going slow about removing signs till the legislature amends the law.

Action Line

I thought we were using zip codes on our letters because mail was being sorted by machine. Now I find out most post offices don't even have the machines. —Mrs. R.P., Roscommon.

Zip, schmip. You've just been doing it for practice! Postal service expects to have electronic scanners in every major city within two years; meanwhile, they want people to get used to using the numbers. Legally, only third-class mail is required to carry the Zip, but don't stop using it just because you don't have to. Even without the machines, Zip codes cut handling and delivery time in half. Detroit PO, which has an optical scanner, says 80 percent of letter-writers co-operate. It helps them move eight million pieces of mail a day twice as fast.

Sound Off

EVERYBODY complains about the DSR, but they sure come through in an emergency. After I'd changed buses, I realized I'd left some important papers on the other bus and told the driver about it. He radioed the dispatcher, who found the right bus and my papers. When they found out I had no car to go claim them, an investigator personally delivered them to my home. I had them two hours after I lost them. Pretty good service.—J.M.

Free Press Photo by JIMMY TAFOYA
Smoke, barricades and helmeted police: Detroit's scene of violence

Blind-Pig Raid Was Spark

From a dingy, second-floor apartment in the heart of the city's high crime area, the ugly ripples that would become Detroit's first major racial disturbance in 20 years spread like tiny tongues of gasoline, volatile and slippery.

The events that brought the city to the edge of crisis Sunday began more than six weeks ago when the 10th Precinct's clean-up squad first identified an illegal after-hours liquor operation in the apartment at 9125 Twelfth St.

ON THE SECOND floor of that building, in a vacant office, one of the dozens of blind pigs that operate in the 10th Precinct had found a home. It was placed under surveillance for the next six weeks.

Traditionally, Saturday night is a blind pig's biggest evening and the decision to raid was made on that basis. At 3:30 a.m. Sunday morning,

Aide Ready To Replace Gov. Wallace

MONTGOMERY, Ala. — (UPI)—Lt. Gov. Albert Brewer will be called on to take over as governor Tuesday unless Gov. Lurleen B. Wallace returns before then from Houston, Tex., where she is recovering from a cancer operation.

Monday will be the governor's 20th day out of the state. The Alabama constitution provides that when a governor divides that more than 20 days, the secretary of state must call on the lieutenant governor to take over.

Spokesmen for the governor say the decision on when she returns to Alabama will be made by her doctors. Mrs. Wallace left Montgomery July 4 and was operated on July 10. Doctors removed several tumors. The primary malignancy was one lodged in a coil of the sigmoid colon. A portion of the colon was also removed. Doctors predicted complete recovery.

Sgt. Arthur E. Howison and his squad entered the building and arrested more than 80 patrons who were drinking.

Squad cars and paddy wagons from the 10th Precinct made repeated runs, transporting those arrested to the precinct station to be booked and taken downtown. The process took time—too much time, it would seem later.

Howison's squad cleared the building at 4:45 a.m., 55 minutes after it had arrived. Attracted by police cruisers, a crowd had gathered on the sidewalk to taunt officers, mock friends now under arrest, giggle with girl friends.

As Howison recalled later: "They were across the street and bunched up on both sides of the building. We had no trouble with our prisoners.

Puerto Rico Votes Against Statehood

SAN JUAN—(AP)—Puerto Ricans Sunday voted solidly in favor of keeping their 15-year-old commonwealth status.

With all voting districts counted, the state election board reported that commonwealth received 425,081 votes; statehood 273,315, and independence 4,205. The total vote of 702,601 was 65.8 percent of the island's 1.1 million registered voters.

THE ISLAND has been under the jurisdiction of the United States since 1898.

Voters apparently favored statehood only in Ponce, the island's second largest city and home of industrialist Luis Ferre, a chief support of statehood.

Election officials had forecast a 70 percent turnout of the 1,067,000 registered voters. Scattered rain showers had little effect on the voting.

Before the election, it was forecast that 60 percent of the vote would go to commonwealth status, 39 percent to statehood and one percent to independence.

Just these loudmouthed onlookers who had no business being there started shouting."

As the last of the prisoners were loaded into cars, someone whose name may never be known was prompted to act. He picked an empty bottle off the street and from the protection of the crowd, hurled it toward the building. The bottle flashed in a lazy arc and smashed through the rear window of the squad car.

The crowd cheered. An incident had begun.

• • •

WITHIN moments, it seemed, the crowd began to break apart and flow like a wave down Twelfth St. More bottles flew, windows smashed and the first hands reached behind the broken glass to steal.

At 5:20 a.m., Police Commissioner Ray Girardin was called at home and told of the developing crisis. He immediately called Mayor Cavanagh.

About 6 a.m., Girardin was at work in his third-floor office, conferring with staff officers. A battle plan began slowly, hesitantly, to emerge.

Meantime, the looting on Twelfth St. had increased. At 6:30 a.m., the first fire—in a Twelfth St. shoe store—broke out.

For more than 1½ hours, firemen fought the blaze without incident. But the fire trucks awoke those who were asleep, drawing larger crowds, and producing more rumors.

At 8 a.m., firemen returned to the scene to fight a fire started in rubbish that now littered the street. This time, they were stoned.

• • •

POLICE SHIFTS in Detroit change at 8 a.m. and the 10th Precinct's crews were in the process of checking out and

Turn to Page 4A, Column 1

A-Sub Hits Buoy On Test Voyage

HINGHAM, Mass. — (AP) — The atomic submarine Greenling hit a buoy off Princess Point Sunday, but continued sea trials after a 30-minute delay, the Coast Guard said.

Adm. Hyman Rickover was reported aboard the submarine. Rickover was instrumental in developing the first atomic submarine. A spokesman said there was no damage and no injuries were reported.

Looter Killed; 724 Held as Riot Spreads

Gov. Romney called in the National Guard and clamped a state of emergency on Detroit Sunday night in an attempt to quell spreading Negro sniping, burning and looting that broke out in the Twelfth and Clairmount area on the city's West Side.

Tanks, jeeps and 2½-ton trucks moved in ahead of infantry units to clear a sealed-off area bounded by W. Grand Blvd., Chicago, Linwood and the Lodge Freeway.

The state of emergency—a step just short of martial law—was ordered by the governor at 9:05 p.m. amid reports of sporadic rifle fire throughout the city. Three looters were wounded early Monday, one fatally.

When the emergency order was issued, more than 80 stores had been looted, more than 200 persons were arrested and hundreds had been treated in hospital emergency rooms.

At 1 a.m. Monday, Police Commissioner Ray Girardin said a total of 724 persons had been arrested. This included 600 adults and 124 juveniles. The charges ranged from breaking and entering, through felonious assault to curfew violations.

After 17 hours of rampaging by Negroes, triggered by an early-morning police raid on an illegal after-hours liquor spot, the area was a shambles of shattered and demolished stores and blazing buildings.

• • •

ROMNEY SAID 700 guardsmen were in the city and 1,950 more had been mobilized for immediate call-up. In addition, the governor said, 3,000 more troops had been alerted at Camp Grayling, where they have just completed summer training.

The state of emergency, which Romney extended to cover the adjoining cities of Highland Park and Hamtramck, includes a 9 p.m. to 5:30 a.m. curfew on all but essential travel, a ban on the sale of alcoholic drinks, and a prohibition against carrying arms or flammable liquids.

"I hope we can handle this situation without resort to whole force," Romney declared. But he said he would move whatever equipment and men were needed in the city to protect life and property.

Detroit Police Commissioner Ray Girardin ordered police to return fire if they were fired on. In addition to the guardsmen and Detroit police, 370 state troopers were called in to help put down the violence.

• • •

DEAD AT Detroit General Hospital was Walter Grzanka, 45, of 641 Charlotte, who police said was shot in the chest by an unknown person as he came out of the Temple Market at Temple and Fourth. Police said the store had been looted earlier and had not been secured.

Richard Johnson, 17, of 1705 W. Philadelphia, was admitted to the same hospital suffering a bullet wound of the neck and the shoulder. Police said Johnson and two companions, who were under arrest, had been looting the Celeste Cleaners, 2588 W. Grand Blvd., when an unknown person opened fire.

Johnson's companions were identified as Victor Vernon, 17, of 3268 Clemens, and Ralph Williams, 21, of 9759 Goodwin.

In another shooting, Robert Boyd, 31, of 8201 Spokane, was admitted to Henry Ford Hospital in critical condition with a gunshot wound in the groin.

Witnesses said a crowd of looters in an alley west of Twelfth near Pingree fled when an armed private guard appeared.

Turn to Page 2A, Column 1

Violence In Detroit

Clergy maps its strategy for peace. Page 3A.

Neighborhoods burn as residents watch. Page 3A.

The meaning of Detroit's race riot. Page 4A.

Picture pages: 8B through 11B and the Back Page.

Disaster Teams Go Into Action

Sunday's rioting threw into action the police department's two command posts designed to control disasters and widespread disorders.

One post, at police headquarters, was staffed by a dozen, men under the command of District Inspector Henry Sedmak.

The second, at Herman Kiefer Hospital, nearer the trouble zone, was under the leadership of Inspector Charles Gentry.

Commissioner Ray Girardin was at the headquarters post in overall command of all defensive operations.

• • •

ALL INFORMATION, from the public and from all law enforcement forces in the field, went first to headquarters.

There calls were filtered from citizens, from policemen equipped with shoulder-radio, from police cars, as well as calls from National Guard squads in the area, from state policemen and firemen who relayed calls to' headquarters through Fire Department dispatchers.

The headquarters post took the calls and relayed orders to Gentry's post.

Gentry then sent forces where needed: Policemen to accompany firemen on runs, extra police and guardsmen to help lawmen in extreme trouble spots, and ambulances for the injured.

Race Car Kills 7

LOURENCO MARQUES, Mozambique—(AP)—Seven persons were killed and 10 injured Sunday when a car skidded on a racetrack and struck spectators.

Index

Amusements	6B
Ann Landers	10B
Astrology	9D
Billy Graham	12D
Bridge	9D
Business News	7-9D
Church	2B
Comics	9-11D
Crossword Puzzle	9D
Death Notices	6C
Drew Pearson	11A
Earl Wilson	11A
Editorials	6A
Feature Page	11A
Heloise	2C
Movie Guide	10-11D
Names and Faces	12C
Obituaries	12A
Sports	1-6D
Stock Markets	7-8D
TV-Radio	6D
Want Ads	6-12C
Women's Pages	1-5C

HAVE THE FREE PRESS DELIVERED AT HOME — PHONE 222-6500

JULY 25, 1967:

The riot intensifies on its second day.

CLEAR
Continued Warm
High 81-87; Low 60-64

Detroit Free Press

Vol. 137—No. 81 On Guard for 136 Years Tuesday, July 25, 1967

METRO
Detroit Riots Hit
NY Market Prices
See Page 9, Section C

Ten Cents

Paratroopers Roll into Riot Areas As Gun Battles & Looting Spread; 14 Killed; Damage $150 Million

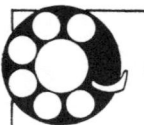

Action Line
Dial 222-6464

Action Line solves problems, gets answers, cuts red tape, stands up for your rights. Write Action Line, Box 881, Detroit, Mich. 48231. Or dial 222-6464 between 8:30 a.m. and 4:30 p.m. Monday through Friday.

Can the troubled City of Detroit use two extra hands? I'm a registered nurse. I'm not after excitement, but I would like to help while I'm in town. — Sister M. E., Seattle, Wash.

You're all set for night duty at Harper Hospital. They need four more nurses to work the 11 p.m.-7 a.m. shift during the crisis. Detroit Memorial Hospital needs at least 10. Retired, vacationing nurses should call the nursing offices: Harper at 833-400, Detroit Memorial 965-1200.

When we got back from vacation last week, we found a strange piece of metal imbedded in the backyard. It's black and oily and hit with such force it dug a six-inch hole in the ground. We're sending you a chunk of metal. Is it something from outer space? — C.M.

One of your practical jokester neighbors hoped you'd think so. He went to a lot of trouble to put together your chunk of space junk. Metallurgists at Wayne State University say its a bunch of nickel roller bearings fused together into a glob. Looks like somebody doused it with 3-in-1 oil and thumped it over your fence. If it had looked like it was for real, Aerospace Research Lab, Wright-Patterson Air Force Base, Dayton, O., would have been able to tell exactly what it was. What it is, though, is a great paperweight.

I've been trying for almost a year to get my daughter back. After we were divorced last year, my ex-husband, who's in the Army, came to Detroit and abducted the child. I've been trying to get custody of her, but the Army won't tell me where my ex-husband is. —Mrs. L.H.

Right now, he's on leave from his unit, but he's due back at the end of the month. Action Line's sending you the name of his unit and company commander at Fort Benning, Ga. Since custody wasn't decided at the time of your divorce, your lawyer is contacting a lawyer in Georgia to represent you. He'll start court proceedings to determine who gets custody of the child.

The house next to us is vacant and falling apart. The owner won't do anything; can you? — F.H.

Building and Safety inspectors went out twice for Action Line. First time, they ordered the lot cleaned, broken windows replaced. On second visit, everything was OK. Recent state law empowers cities to condemn a house if absentee landlord fails to make repairs in 90 days. Turn to violators to building inspectors, 965-4200.

We bus about 30 kids a day to a camp in Maybele, and they're high, dry and hollering. The camp bought a 50 by 25 foot cement swimming pool but the company didn't have a liner. They said we'd get it within 24 hours. That was three weeks ago.—E.A.

Your vinyl liner is being flown in from Los Angeles, should be here by today. Dealer has a guy standing by to install it. The 24 hours got stretched to three weeks because of a bum promise. Dealer had arranged to get the liner from a Detroit warehouse, but the warehouse sold it to somebody else. Company had to special order a new one from the Los Angeles manufacturer.

Our 12-year-old wears leg braces and has to use crutches. We'd like to find him some kind of electric scooter he could use to keep up with his friends on bikes. Any ideas?—Mrs. R.T., Escanaba.

How about a motorized tricycle? American Mobile Products in Lansing makes one designed for big business bosses who don't want to walk from one end of the plant to the other. It runs on a rechargeable battery, can be adapted for hand controls. Owner Richard Dinkel is calling you, says he can customize one for you at the manufacturing cost of a regular model. He made one for a little old lady in Virginia who'd been confined to her house for 20 years. Now she's zipping all over the neighborhood.

Person to Person

I've been so busy with school and sewing, I didn't have time to tell you how I made out in the sandal making business on Plum Street. I'm not only learning to make sandals, boots and dresses but I'm meeting and learning about different kinds of people. You couldn't have found me a better place to learn cobbling. — Kathy the Kobbler (as they call me now).

A Twelfth St. "reveler" takes his ease on a stolen chair after a hard day in the street
Free Press Photos by IRA ROSENBERG

Up the street, firemen fight a blaze while police check looting suspects

An Orgy of Pillage Erupts Behind Fires and Violence

By BARBARA STANTON
Free Press Staff Writer

A Negro teen-ager slid out of a darkened jewelry store at Oakman near Grand River Monday, carrying a softly gleaming silver teapot.

"What are you going to do with that?" asked a passerby.

"Make some tea," he grinned.

He was just one of thousands of looters who descended like locusts on the city's stores Sunday and Monday, grabbing and running in a sometimes senseless, sometimes calculated snatch at the good things in life.

• • •

THEY TOOK fur stoles and floor mops, diamond rings and dresses, wigs, hamburger, color TV sets, shotguns, cameras, records, cigarettes, shoes, underwear, guitars, two-pants suits, $5 Scotch and skinless hot dogs.

It began early Sunday in an orgy of flames and violence, a lust for destruction and revenge for wrongs that the rioters couldn't have named.

By Monday much of the violence was over, but the looting continued.

The daylight looters brazenly carried their booty across heavily traveled streets, smiling and nodding to office-bound drivers while burglar alarms shrilled behind them.

And as the looting spread, so did the conviction that this riot had less to do with race than with color TV sets, less with Black Power than with something for nothing.

• • •

WHITE MEN passing through some of the former riot areas were ignored or greeted with derision, but seldom menaced.

The looting, which had been incidental to the riot, became the chief reason for prolonging it. It was too sweet, too simple and too stupid not to join in.

Grand River became a grab bag from Oakman to downtown. Unabashed looters picked and chose amid acres of shattered plate glass.

At Grand River and Larchmont, four men carried a con-

Turn to Page 2A, Column 2

LBJ Vows To Resist Violence

WASHINGTON—President Johnson authorized the use of federal troops in Detroit Monday night. "We will not tolerate lawlessness," he told the American people. "We will not endure violence."

Mr. Johnson's order cleared the way for the use of not only 4,700 paratroopers flown to Detroit, but for federalization of the Michigan National Guard.

After issuing the orders, Mr. Johnson went on nationwide radio and television at midnight to tell the nation that the government could not tolerate such violence.

"IT MATTERS not by who it is done or under what slogan or banner," he said. "It will not be tolerated. This nation will do whatever is necessary to punish those responsible."

"Law and order have broken down in Detroit," the grim-faced President said. "Pillage and looting and arson have nothing to do with civil rights."

Mr. Johnson called on those involved in violence to stop immediately.

"In authorizing the use of federal troops came as the Detroit violence capped several weeks of rioting around the nation — Newark, Plainfield,

Turn to Page 2A, Column 1

Inside the Free Press

Amusements	4D	Heloise	2C
Ann Landers	3C	Movie Guide	6-7D
Astrology	5D	Names and Faces	5C
Billy Graham	8D	Obituaries	5C
Bridge	5D	Sports	1-3D
Business News	6-10C	Stock Markets	7-10C
Comics	5-7D	TV-Radio	8B
Crossword Puzzle	5D	Want Ads	4-7B
Death Notices	4B	Women's Pages	1-3C
Drew Pearson	9A		
Earl Wilson	9A	HAVE THE FREE PRESS	
Editorials	4A	DELIVERED AT HOME	
Feature Page	9A	PHONE 222-6500	

LBJ Approves All-Out Drive To End Strife

President Johnson ordered 4,700 tough Army paratroopers into Detroit riot areas Monday night as Negro snipers launched an offensive that stretched from the West Side to the Grosse Pointe borders.

Acting as commander-in-chief of the armed forces, Mr. Johnson ordered Defense Secretary Robert S. McNamara to "take all appropriate steps to disperse all persons engaged in acts of violence and to restore law and order."

• • •

MR. JOHNSON'S personal emissary, Cyrus Vance, immediately ordered 1,800 of the crack federal troops to aid Michigan National Guardsmen and state and Detroit police, who were running dangerously short of ammunition in gun battles with entrenched snipers.

Vance said the remaining 2,900 troops at Selfridge Air Force Base would move into the beleaguered city.

The presidential order authorized McNamara to:

● Use the regular federal armed forces.

● Call into active federal military service any or all units of the Army National Guard and the Air National Guard of Michigan "for an indefinite period and until relieved by appropriate orders."

● Federalize the Michigan National Guard for use when and where McNamara deemed necessary.

At 11:30 p.m. the riot toll was:

● 14 dead from gunfire, mostly looters.

● More than 800 injuries including 32 policemen and 15 firemen.

● 1,663 persons arrested.

● 731 fires including nearly 200 new ones Monday.

At least two police stations and two firehouses were besieged by snipers. Gun battles were waged between police and guardsmen in armored cars and Negro riflemen.

At Collingwood and Dexter, police forces battled nearly 10 minutes before extricating guardsmen who had been pinned down by snipers.

Police stations at Mack and Gratiot and Jefferson and St. Jean were hit by rifle fire. Firemen on runs unable to fight the rash of fires set by arsonists across the city or even escape from fire scenes.

• • •

POLICE COMMISSIONER Ray Girardin characterized Monday night's violence as "much more widespread than Sunday night."

"The bulk of the burning tonight (Monday) is on the

Turn to Page 8A, Column 1

The Riot

DEAD—14 confirmed.

INJURED—More than 800, including 32 police officers, 4 National Guardsmen and 3 state police officers, 15 firemen and 76 prisoners in hospital.

ARRESTED—1,663.

FIRES—731.

LOOTED BUSINESSES—More than 1,000.

PROPERTY LOSS—More than $150 million.

ENFORCEMENT MEN—14,800, including 8,000 National Guardsmen, 1,800 federal troops, 360 State Police and 4,400 Detroit policemen.

FIREMEN—1,200 Detroit firemen, more than 200 from 40 other departments.

REINFORCEMENTS—2,900 federal troops on standby at Selfridge Air Force Base.

Other Riot Stories

Courts get tough with rioters. Page 3A.

Fires and looting erupt in Pontiac. Page 3A.

Poverty fighters shocked by violence. Page 5A.

Tension of years echoes in the shouts of rioters. Page 6A.

How the flames have fanned across Detroit. Page 7A.

The guard: How it's doing its job. Page 5A.

Detroit's new refugees. Page 1B.

The fires — and how Mark Beltaire spent a night helping fight them. Page 2B.

Home and store owners probably will collect on their insurance policies. Page 6C.

How radio and TV delayed early coverage of the riot. Page 8B.

The sniper's sneak attack is the worst. Back Page.

PICTURES: Pages 3A, 5A through 8A, 1B, 2B, 3B and Back Page.

Inside This Section...	
Editorials	Page 6
Comment Page	Page 7
Books and Art	Page 8

Detroit Free Press
Features · Editorials
SUNDAY, SEPTEMBER 3, 1967

SECTION B

SEPT. 3, 1967:

How the riot victims died. A team of three reporters investigates the death of each person killed or fatally injured in "eight days of insanity."

Special report

The 43 Who Died

An Investigation into How and Why Detroit's Riot Victims Were Slain

Copyright 1967, The Detroit Free Press

IN THE SPACE of eight silent days and bullet-broken nights, 43 persons died or were fatally wounded on the streets of Detroit. They are explained as victims of riot, the casualties of modern civil war.

Even now, it is difficult to arrive at more satisfactory explanations. It is tempting indeed to conclude that only the riot itself can be blamed for creating the situations in which it was pathetically easy to die.

Thirty-six hours after the riot began, something more than 3,000 armed men were assigned or had access to a single 20- by 20-block area on the near West Side, a concentration of firepower paralleled only by a major military invasion force.

• • •

HUNDREDS OF regular Army paratroopers were stationed on the East Side. In the Inner City, city and state police and National Guardsmen patrolled in scout cars, paddy wagons, expressway cruisers, jeeps, trucks, personnel carriers and tanks. The armament ranged from service revolvers and M-1 rifles to privately owned sporting arms, short-barreled repeating shotguns, carbines and machine guns of up to .50 caliber.

Numbers alone made it inevitable that confrontations would occur, that incidents would result, that mistakes would be made and that ultimately, someone would die. There were too many guns and too many people for it to be otherwise.

Now the central questions are simple, though the answers are not:

● How many of the 43 deaths were necessary?
● How many could have been prevented?

The answers are individual, based on more than five weeks of independent investigation by a team of Free Press reporters assigned to examine every riot-connected death.

• • •

THE CONCLUSION reached in that investigation is inescapable:

A majority of the riot victims need not have died. Their deaths could have been—and should have been—prevented.

Fate's selection of those who would die followed no pattern and the riot victims do not fit easily into categories and classifications. Among them are the most innocent, a four-year-old girl killed by a wanton bullet, and the most guilty, a drunken sniper who died trying to take another's life. Equally various were the ways in which they died.

Eighteen of the 43 riot victims were shot and killed by Detroit police, and of that number, 14 have been confirmed as looters in the Free Press investigation. The other four are a sniper, a possible but unconfirmed arsonist and two of the three men shot and killed in the Algiers Motel.

At least six victims were killed by the National Guard, five of them innocent, the victims of what now seem to be tragic accidents.

In five more cases, both police and National Guardsmen were involved and it is impossible to say definitely whose bullets were fatal. Four of these five victims were innocent of any wrongdoing.

Two persons, both looters, were shot and killed by store-owners. Three more were killed by private citizens; murder warrants have been issued in two of those cases and a warrant decision is pending in the third. And two looters died when fire swept the store from which they were stealing.

Two victims, one a fireman, the other a civilian, were killed by electric power lines.

Five deaths remain. They are a 19-year-old boy killed accidentally by an Army paratrooper; a 23-year-old white woman shot by an unknown gunman; a Detroit fireman killed by either a hidden sniper or a stray National Guard bullet; a policeman shot as a fellow officer struggled with a prisoner; and the third victim of the Algiers Motel slayings, whose assailant is not known.

The Return to Normalcy

Hindsight is easy. The fires have gone out and the streets are quiet and in the midst of normalcy, the temptation to insist that logic and order and common sense should have prevailed throughout the riot is overwhelming, but impossible to tolerate.

No one who drove those gutted streets at midnight, when the fires still burned and the shadows hung and moved in vacant doorways, when frightened voices cried "Halt" into the silence and footsteps crunched on broken glass, will contend that men should have behaved rationally in those awful hours.

With that qualification accepted and understood, here are the general conclusions of the five-week investigation into the riot deaths:

● Both the number of snipers active in the riot area and the danger that snipers presented were vastly overstated. Only one sniper is among the riot victims and only three of the victims may possibly have been killed by snipers, two of them doubtful. In all, some 31 persons were arrested and charged with sniping; none of those cases has gone to trial.

● In the 43 deaths, criminal intent may possibly be an element in only seven—the three Algiers Motel deaths, three killings by civilians and one case, that of William Dalton, still unresolved. Free Press investigators found no evidence of deliberate or preconceived killing in the cases remaining.

● In retrospect, the performance of Michigan State and city policemen seems generally restrained and impressive. The fact that 4,400 city policemen worked for at least five days in the midst of chaos without more bloodshed is significant. There are individual incidents of poor judgment, it is true, and several regrettable instances where officers may have fired too soon, though they acted legally.

• • •

ONE MAJOR critical observation must be made. Both city and Army authorities acted to try to keep the death toll at a minimum, though they did so in different ways. In both cases, their efforts were not successful and permitted unnecessary death.

At 11:20 Monday night, within hours after the National Guard had come under Federal control, Lt. General John Throckmorton, the commanding officer, issued a general order commanding all troops under his control to unload their weapons and to fire only on the command of an officer.

Throckmorton's regular Army troops obeyed that order; only one person was killed in paratrooper territory in the five days that followed.

The National Guard did not obey, in many cases because the order was improperly disseminated and was never made clear to the men on the street. As a result, the Guard was involved in a total of eleven deaths in which nine innocent people died.

Military discipline and attention to Throckmorton's order could have avoided those deaths.

The Shooting of Looters

Within the Detroit Police Department, authorities now say that there were no standing orders on whether looters would be shot. That may be true, but both civilians and police officers had the firm and distinct impression on Sunday, the riot's first day, that looters would not be shot.

There was reason for that impression. Police officers made no secret of the fact that they were pleased with their handling of the Kercheval incident in the summer of 1966. The tactics used in that situation included no shooting and became a model for future riot control plans.

LOOTING WAS rampant Sunday and there was no shooting. The impression in the Negro community was that looters were safe.

As Commissioner Ray Girardin recalls it now, no specific order on whether looters could be shot was ever given. Officers were to use their discretion, nothing more.

The order that apparently changed the tide came from Superintendent Eugene Reuter, in response to a question on how to handle sniper incidents. Reuter gave permission for officers to return fire. The word quickly spread through the department and in the next several days, shooting increased.

The legal basis for shooting a looter is found in state law which permits officers to fire at fleeing felons after an order to halt is disregarded. Technically, most of those who were killed clearly fall in that category, though one is still left with a feeling that the thief who takes $5 worth of goods from a grocery store shelf and runs ought not to be required to pay with his life.

Nonetheless, the question of whether looters will be shot is a matter of public policy. No decision was ever made and announced publicly; as a result, the value of the law as a deterrent was minimal. Many looters certainly thought they were safe; many more would have stayed home had they known that death might be the result.

The Investigation Goes On

The official investigating agency for the riot deaths is the Detroit Homicide Bureau, which reports in turn to Wayne County Prosecutor William Cahalan, who rules on each case.

With minor exceptions, the Homicide Bureau is turning in complete and competent reports on every death. In a few cases, the investigations have been nothing short of inspired. In a few others, a reluctance to go all-out on cases involving fellow officers is understandable if not excusable.

IT IS NOT Cahalan's job to decide whether officers showed good judgment or bad, or to decide whether the deaths were necessary. Unless he finds evidence of criminal intent, Cahalan cannot act.

In most of the cases Cahalan has received so far, he has found no such evidence and where police officers are involved, has used the same citation of law over and over again. That citation reads:

"Were a man charged with crime to be held to a knowledge of all facts precisely as they are, there could be few cases in which the most innocent intention or honest zeal could justify or excuse homicide."

What the law says is simply that we cannot expect police officers to know exactly what the situation is in fact before they act. They must act as the situation appears to them at the moment and make the best judgments they can.

Forty-three are dead. In the riot's aftermath, rumor, suspicion and hatred have played equal roles in distorting the true versions of those deaths.

THE REPORT which follows is based on independent evidence and witnesses. It is as accurate as an honest regard for the facts can make it. Even now, it is impossible to arrive at complete explanations, firm conclusions or satisfactory judgments; the best that can be done is to report what is known and to suggest the probabilities that logic requires.

One conclusion must be repeated: A majority of the deaths reported here appear to be unnecessary. That price, however intolerable it may be, is part of what we have paid for eight days of insanity.

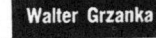

Free Press Photo by IRA ROSENBERG

1. Walter Grzanka

The first known victim of Detroit's riot was Walter Grzanka, 45, shot seconds after midnight, July 24, by an angry store manager who saw Grzanka coming through the broken window of a looted grocery.

Twenty-five minutes later, as the second day of the riot began, Grzanka was pronounced dead at Detroit General Hospital. In his pockets were seven cigars, four packages of pipe tobacco and nine pairs of shoelaces, apparently the only loot he took from the shelves of the Temple Market, 2844 Fourth.

Store manager Hamid Audish Yacoub now admits he shot Grzanka from the window of the 1965 burgundy Mustang in which he cruised the area around his store.

Yacoub did not report the shooting to the police, an omission that is technically a misdemeanor. He says he left the scene because he was frightened by the crowd that began to gather around Grzanka's body.

Yacoub is known as "Herman" in the neighborhood, where he is buying for himself the store he has worked in for several years.

There is no doubt that Grzanka was a looter, though he didn't take much. He was also unarmed and apparently was given no chance to surrender.

Investigation on the Grzanka shooting is now complete. The prosecutor's office has not yet recommended action.

2. Sheren George

The death of Sheren George, a pretty 23-year-old Detroit mother of two, may never be solved.

Mrs. George became the second known victim of the riot when a slug ripped into her chest as she was riding in her car at 11:30 p.m. on July 23, the first night of the riot.

The shooting occurred at Woodward and Melbourne, a stone's throw from the Algiers Motel where three Negroes were to die three days later.

Denizens of the area, the hangers-on and loiterers, deny any knowledge of the George shooting.

"People have got their mouths closed tight," a Negro man said. "You could hang around here a hundred years and never find out."

Mrs. George, of 17374 Riopelle, was riding in the center of the front seat of a 1959 car driven by her husband, Ross. Her brother, Paul Dimitrie, was in the right front seat, and another brother, Dennis, was in the back seat. The story police were told the night of the shooting was not changed:

The four had driven to Woodward and Grand Boulevard to drop off two Negro friends. Returning home, they were driving north on Woodward when a crowd milling in the street blocked traffic at Woodward and Melbourne.

A white man in the crowd appeared to be under attack by Negroes. Suddenly there was a loud shot, so loud it sounded as if it came from extremely close by.

Paul shouted, "Oh, my God! Sheren's been shot."

Sheren slumped in her seat and Ross drove to the Highland Park Fire Station. She was then taken to the Highland Park General Hospital.

Sheren was pronounced dead at 1:35 a.m. July 24. An autopsy disclosed she had been killed by a bullet that entered her left side about two inches below the left breast.

The bullet entered through the left rear door about two inches below the window. The slug splintered, inflicting minor wounds on Ross and Paul.

Sheren, in the center of the front seat, took the brunt of the slug in the ribs under her left arm. The slug was also fragmented in her body, breaking into several pieces.

Dr. John Burton, Wayne County Medical Examiner, said such fragmentation is typical of a .38 or .88 caliber bullet, indicating Sheren may have been killed by a pistol shot.

There was only one bullet hole in the car. Only one shot was heard. Sheren's brother, Dennis, said there were no police or Guardsmen present, and there was no other shooting.

Homicide detectives theorize the shot may have come from the Algiers Motel, where sniper fire was heard a day later. The angle of entry, on a level or nearly level plane, indicates the shot could

Turn to the following page

The Investigation Team

On the fourth day of what was to become the nation's costliest contemporary insurrection, the Free Press began an investigation into the death of each person killed or fatally injured in the riot.

For five weeks a team of Free Press reporters talked with witnesses, police officers, National Guardsmen. They talked with families of the dead, with County, State and Federal officials conducting their own investigation into the 43 deaths. More than 300 people were interviewed. Hundreds of documents — police reports, hospital records, autopsy reports, witness statements—were examined.

The riot brought to a halt every process on which our society depends. Most important, the orderly administration of justice was sidetracked by the overwhelming fact of a city caught up in civil war.

Of the 43 dead, little was known. Haste and confusion, fear and circumstance combined to make it virtually impossible for authorities — and for the public — to accurately assess responsibility for the deaths.

In the aftermath, it was essential that an accurate and dispassionate account of the riot deaths be prepared and made public. This report was initiated to satisfy that public need.

While many reporters and editors contributed to the investigation, the bulk of the work was done by three members of the Free Press staff who were assigned full time to the inquiry.

Barbara Stanton, formerly assigned to the Free Press City-County Bureau, has been a member of the staff since 1959. Born in Detroit, she is a graduate of Northwestern University and holds a master's degree in journalism from Columbia University. Her investigation of the Algiers motel deaths first revealed the circumstances that culminated in the arrest of three Detroit policemen and a private guard involved in the incident.

William Serrin joined the Free Press staff in 1966 after working for newspapers in Saginaw and Toledo. A former Army officer and member of the U.S. Special Forces reserves, Serrin, 28, was among the first newsmen at the scene when the riot began and was injured that day when he was caught and stoned by a gang of teen-age looters. Assigned to the riot area, he reported every phase of the riot's grim evolution.

Gene Goltz is 37, a veteran newspaperman who joined the Free Press early this year after 9 years experience on newspapers in Texas and New York. A winner of the Pulitzer Prize for local investigative reporting, Goltz, like Serrin, covered the riot area throughout the six days of its life.

Barbara Stanton

William Serrin

Gene Goltz

Sept. 3, 1967:

More from the special report: "A majority of the riot victims need not have died. Their deaths could have been — and should have been — prevented."

Continued from preceding page

pry the door with a hammer," the subsequent police report says.

The officers dashed from their car as the two men fled, Sims heading north, his unidentified companion north. Sims was unlucky; police chose to chase him. The other man got away.

Sims ran down an alley, then in front of the Adams house and up the driveway, trying to get in the side door. The officers, hard on his heels, ran to the foot of the driveway. They say they ordered Sims to halt several times.

Sims was shot as he struggled with the side door. He fell to the driveway, mortally wounded. He was dead on arrival at Detroit General Hospital. The time was 9 p.m.

It seems now that Sims could easily have been apprehended. The side door was locked and officers appear to have been closing in from both front and back.

But neither Sims nor the officers knew the door was locked and officers in front of the Adams house might not know about officers in back. In any case, Sims ran, a fleeing felon. The punishment was capital.

His shooting was witnessed by Mrs. Sims, although she couldn't see who the officers were taking under fire.

At the sound of gunfire, she started walking to the scene. She is partially deaf, and couldn't hear the officers telling her to stop.

"They would have shot me," she says, had a neighbor not yelled.

She watched the officers back up the ambulance, and cart the body away. She asked a neighbor who had been shot, and he replied: "They just killed your husband between those two houses."

15. Carl Smith

In fishing, playing golf or softball, Carl Smith was always the sparkplug. Around the fire station he was the take-charge guy.

"You and you and you, come with me," he would say on a fire drill exercise. "You," he would point at another fireman, "stay here." He had all the qualities of a fire chief, the men used to say jokingly, except the rank.

In his four years with the Detroit Fire Department, he was one of the hardest workers and was clearly devoted to the department.

His enthusiasm accounted in some part for his death.

Smith, of 15322 Santa Rosa, was shot through the head and killed instantly at 11:30 p.m., July 24, when he and other firemen were pinned down by sniper fire at Mack and St. Jean.

It is possible Smith was killed by a sniper. It is equally possible he was killed by a National Guard bullet.

After a thorough investigation, homicide detectives reconstructed Smith's death this way:

He was assigned to Engine Company 13, which was assembled with other fire fighting units at Mack and St. Jean. This area was being used by the Fire Department as a mobilization point.

Just before 11:30, the fire station at 8811 St. Jean (just north of Mack) was attacked by snipers. Several fire vehicles and the firemen in the street were pinned down by what was described as "heavy sniper fire."

The massive counter attack by police and National Guard undoubtedly contributed to the heavy firing. In fact, there was heavy and continuous shooting on all sides, witnesses said.

The firemen were ordered to evacuate the area.

Smith was isolated, for an unknown reason, on the southeast corner of Mack and St. Jean. His fire truck and his buddies were on the north side of St. Jean. Fellow firemen speculated later that Smith may have wanted to "see the action," and that was why he was south of Mack.

He ran north across the street toward his fire truck. As he reached the northeast intersection of Mack and St. Jean, he crouched behind a rubbish receptacle.

"At this point, Police Sgt. Roy Snyder saw Smith clasp his hand to his head and pitch forward on the sidewalk.

"Because of the heavy firing, it was 40 minutes before an ambulance could remove Smith's body.

An autopsy conducted by Dr. Joseph Jullar, assistant Wayne County medical examiner, determined that a high-powered rifle slug had passed through Smith's head on an even plane.

Detectives said police stated that sniper fire had originated from rooftops southeast of Smith, in the 11400 block of Mack. They also determined that the lethal bullet had been fired from street level near the intersection of Mack and Gladwin.

They recovered a copper jacket from a spent .30 caliber bullet which had struck a building on the northwest corner of Mack and St. Jean. The projectile was in the path of the trajectory apparently taken by the bullet that killed Smith. The lead was not recovered, but the ballistics laboratory of the police department said the jacket was fired from a .30 caliber carbine.

The National Guardsmen were equipped with both M-1 caliber rifles and .30 caliber carbines.

Smith's position was in the middle of a hail of bullets between Guardsmen and police and the snipers on the rooftops.

The detectives' report said that Smith was looking in the direction of the rooftop sniper fire — and thus in the direction from which the fatal street-level bullet came. But they do not offer any evidence to support this.

The available evidence leaves two possible conclusions: Either Smith was killed by a sniper who was on the street — at ground level — at Mack and Gladwin, unknown to anyone present — or he was killed accidentally by a National Guardsman's bullet.

16. Manuel Cosbey

Manuel Cosbey was no different than most of the people who looted during the five-day riot. He didn't start it, but as long as it was going on, Cosbey wanted his share.

Around midnight Tuesday, July 25, as the riot headed into its third day, Cosbey, 27, borrowed a tire iron and headed for the N&T Grocery, 4441 E. Nevada.

Moments later, he was trapped by a police patrol answering a radio call that announced: "Looting now." Three officers arrived in time to spot the looters.

"The defendants attempted to escape," the official report says, "when they continued to run...(one officer) fired three shots from his service revolver, inflicting the fatal wound."

Four other looters were arrested. One of them, Calvin Vance, 24, of 4804 Stockton, concedes that Cosbey was killed as he fled.

The shots were heard throughout the Sojourner Truth apartments nearby, named for the underground railway worker of the Civil War. Mrs. Roosevelt Curley, mother of the boy who had given Cosbey the tire iron, remembers being told that it was her son who was dead. She fainted, for it had been only a week before that she received word of the death of another son, Roosevelt, Jr., 19, killed in his tank in Vietnam.

Later she heard a voice from the Cosbey apartment, keening: "They've killed my brother."

17. Julius Dorsey

Julius Dorsey, had a badge, a gun and a uniform, and ultimately they cost him his life.

A Negro, Dorsey, 55, of 1026 Field, worked as a private guard. On the night of July 24, he was guarding a fruit market near his home against looters.

He had taken the job against the wishes of his common-law wife, Viola Smith, who was afraid of what the would-be looters might do.

"They wanted to jump on him," Mrs. Smith said. "I told him: You're just making enemies. He said: Maybe you're right. I'm just going to stand out there and make them."

Until midnight, it was peaceful. Once a car full of police stopped, focused a flashlight on Dorsey and told him he had better stand in the light so he would not be mistaken for a looter.

At 1:15 a.m., two Negro men and a Negro woman approached Dorsey and told him to look the other way, that they wanted to loot the market.

Dorsey refused. The looters cursed him and said they were armed. When the three continued to threaten him Dorsey drew his gun and fired three shots into the air. The looters fled south across Lafayette, breaking into the La-Field Quality Market, 716 Field, just across the street from the store Dorsey was guarding.

The three shots Dorsey fired set in motion the machinery that would kill him.

Because of Dorsey's shots, neighbors believed the looters were armed. Police broadcast that report, and both city police and National Guardsmen began to converge on the intersection.

Dorsey assured where he was, sitting on a porch next to the fruit market with a neighbor, Eugene Bailey. Police watched the intersection, ordering the looters to halt. Instead the looters fled north, toward Dorsey. A series of shots rang out; the looters escaped. But Julius Dorsey was dead.

How he was shot is not clear. Dorsey was directly in the line of fire of one group of officers who were shooting at the fleeing looters; one of those bullets may have struck him.

But Bailey says Dorsey was shot by Guardsmen driving past the house in a station wagon, just as the looters were running. Bailey then ran out and stopped another car loaded with uniformed men and told them: "You done shot a guard."

Police reports confirmed that "unidentified personnel" was shooting at the time. But their line of fire was different and if they killed Dorsey, it was because someone shot too soon.

The prosecutor has ruled that Dorsey apparently was killed accidentally by one of the original police officers firing at the looters. A memorandum notes: "Perhaps further investigation should be made to find out who fired the other shots."

18. Henry Denson

The stories of the death of Henry Denson are as opposed as their sources — police and Negroes who survived the incident.

The impressions of independent observers also differ, agreeing only on a single point: The death was unnecessary.

Here is the police version:

About 1 a.m. on July 25 — the third day of the riot—Denson, 27, and two companions, Harold Johnson, 27, and Michael Cooper, 37, all Negroes, were observed driving east on Mack, approaching a National Guard-police checkpoint just east of East Grand Boulevard.

Officers and Guardsmen stepped into the street, flashed lights at the car and ordered it to halt. The car came to a stop, but as the officers approached, the car suddenly accelerated, attempting to hit the officers and Guardsmen.

The officers and Guardsmen dodged and as the car passed two Guardsmen each fired one shot from their M-1 rifles.

Fifty feet north, on E. Grand Blvd., the car came to a stop, facing north. Denson was slumped dead in the front seat.

Officers arrested Johnson, the driver, and Cooper; Denson was taken to the Wayne County morgue, with a single gunshot that penetrated his right shoulder and exited on the left side of his neck.

Johnson and Cooper both deny the police version. Here is their story:

Shortly after midnight, Cooper called Johnson and asked if Johnson could pick him up at an East Side house. Johnson and Denson hopped in Johnson's car, a 1966 Ford convertible, picked up Cooper and were returning to the Yekel apartments, 5903 St. Antoine, where Denson and Cooper lived.

Driving east on Mack, they passed one Guard checkpoint. A Guardsman advised them to "keep it down to 10 or 15 miles an hour" because "There's a roadblock ahead."

(Most Guard checkpoints were really roadblocks. They consisted of soldiers standing in the street or at the curb, almost always without barricades.)

Driving on, Johnson stopped at a red light at Mack and E. Grand Blvd. The light turned green and Johnson started forward. A cry went out: "Halt."

Johnson stepped on the brakes. Simultaneously, the shot that killed Denson was fired. Johnson bolted out of the car, screaming: "You didn't have to shoot. We stopped. We stopped."

Johnson was arrested, charged with felonious assault for the attempt to run down police and Guardsmen, and jailed. He is now free on personal bond; examination is set for Wednesday. Cooper, who was in the back seat, was arrested but never charged.

If Johnson was in fact accelerating, why didn't he keep going? And if he was traveling at any rate of speed, why did the car halt only 50 feet beyond the intersection?

Two independent witnesses — Newsweek magazine's Chicago bureau chief, John Holt, and Newsweek photographer Joe Clark—watched the incident. They do not agree what happened.

Holt says: "As the car came across the median (on E. Grand Blvd.) there was an acceleration, or at least a lurch forward. As it turned left, they opened fire. I had the impression the car was trying to get out of there." Holt adds: "It was senseless to kill him. If they had fired over their heads, I'm sure they would have stopped."

Clark says flatly: "They never accelerated. It slowly made a left turn. Somebody yelled 'halt!' It was going five miles an hour, maybe, just rolling. Then somebody yelled 'get em.' A guy on the north side of Mack fired one shot. I don't think the car rolled five feet more.

"I just don't think the driver heard the guy yell halt. If he did, he just didn't get his foot on the brake fast enough."

Holt and Clark agree that it is inconceivable that Johnson tried to run anyone down. Nor were any firearms or loot found in Johnson's car, though technically all three men were curfew violators.

19. Ronald Evans
20. William Jones

For an armload of stolen beer from a nickel-and-dime grocery store, Ronald Evans and William Jones paid with their lives.

Evans and Jones were shot and killed by Detroit police after they broke into Bob's Market, 4100 Pennsylvania, a tiny 20-by-20-foot store on the near East Side.

Beyond doubt, both men were looters. Whether their deaths were necessary is another question.

Four Negroes participated in the break-in early Tuesday, July 25, after an evening of drinking that included curfew violations. They were Evans, 23, of 3859 Cadillac; Jones, 32, of Birmingham, Ala.; Arthur Reeves, 31, of 3482 Pennsylvania; and Walter Walker, of 3837 Montclair.

The incident was watched by at least one police officer and, though not unbiased, witnesses including two teen-age girls.

When the break-in started, a frightened tenant in a room above the store called down: "Don't burn the place, please, you men." One of the four called back: "We'll just get the some beer, man."

Minutes later, police cars and National Guard jeeps converged on the intersection from four directions. Evans and Walker, who were outside the store, apparently as lookouts, were taken at gunpoint, then spread-eagled on their faces on the sidewalk.

Moments later, Evans lurched to his feet and ran. Why he ran is not clear.

Four witnesses claim police goaded Evans into running, threatening or taunting him with language that was both harsh and obscene.

Why Evans ran, no one knows. Language, however strong, that might make one man flee could be no more than a warning to another. Presumably, any language directed at Evans applied equally to Walker and Walker stayed where he was, flat on the sidewalk and alive.

At least 20 armed men ringed the area. None of the men involved in the break-in had weapons. The chance of escape was minimal. But Evans had been drinking and certainly he was afraid. In any case, he ran.

Evans took no more than 15 steps before he fell at the curb across the street, dead of multiple gunshot wounds.

Questions remain: How, with more than a dozen officers and soldiers only inches and yards away, was Evans allowed to get to his feet at all? What attempt, short of gunfire, was made to stop him?

The police witnesses say they distinctly heard officers yell "Halt." And Evans' companion, Walker, told police that Evans had told him he would never go to jail again. From Evans, that was a strange statement: According to police records, he had never been arrested except on a traffic warrant.

After Evans died, police shot off the lock to enter the store where Jones and Reeves were cowering. Reeves crouched behind a meat counter.

The only exit was the front door. According to the police report, Jones tried to flee through that door, beyond which stood some 20 police and Guardsmen whose shots Evans had just heard.

Jones was shot twice in the chest, once or possibly twice in the abdomen, twice more in the legs. The police report explains: Jones ... "bolted from behind a counter and ran out the door."

That is wrong. Jones was shot inside the store by officers who had the doorway blocked. A dozen witnesses watched police remove the body.

21. Jerome Olshove

Patrolman Jerome Olshove died on duty, the only Detroit police officer killed during the riot. He was shot by a fellow officer's shotgun that went off in the midst of a scuffle with a prisoner arrested for looting.

In eight years on the force, Olshove, 32, had won 20 citations. He was a career police officer, studying police administration at night at Wayne State University and taking community leadership courses in his spare time. That ended early on the morning of July 25, when Olshove's car was ordered to a suspected looting at an A&P store at 121 Holbrook.

At 3 a.m. that morning, looters were active in the store. Witnesses say a car full of uniformed men cruised south on John R, spotted the looters and fired a shotgun blast into the store.

The pellets struck a man identified as Albert Phillips, 8614 Roosevelt, in the face. The car kept going and disappeared.

Minutes later, police was shot, a police car responded to a radio report that looting was underway at the A&P. The police rolled up and saw Phillips standing in front of the store with his face bleeding, the police report states. The man then collapsed and fell on the parking lot. Phillips was taken later to Detroit General Hospital and was discharged three weeks later.

Through broken windows of the store, officers said they saw two men looting. They ordered the men out of the store and the looters against the wall. Latimer obeyed and was handcuffed by Olshove. Royster hesitated, the police report says, and was pushed by Patrolman William Bolgar. The police report states that Patrolman Ray St. Onge, who was armed with a 12-gauge shotgun, assisted Bolgar.

At this point, the testimony of an eyewitness differs from the official police report. The eyewitness was Claudette Wilson, 27, who was peeking through a second-story window from her home directly across the street, at 112 Holbrook.

At a pretrial examination in Recorders Court Aug. 16, Miss Wilson said that one of the looters had come out of the store as if to surrender to police.

"But it seemed as though an officer went to hit the other man," she said. "When he tried to retaliate they began scuffling, and both men appeared to grab for the shotgun."

St. Onge said Royster had attempted to grab the gun and it went off, the shot striking Olshove. Royster was shot. No indication that he might have been injured or struck by St. Onge's gun. Nor was he treated for injuries.

The medical examiner's office said Olshove died from a shotgun wound to the abdomen, fired at fairly close range.

Latimer and Royster were both charged with first degree murder by Recorder's Court Judge Joseph A. Gillis. Latimer's attorney, Richard Zatkin, argued vainly that his client was not connected with the shooting because he was handcuffed.

Under Michigan law, a suspect involved in the act of a felony can be charged with first degree murder when a fatality occurs. Latimer and Royster are being held in the county jail. No trial date has been set.

22. Frank Tanner

While the neighbors watched, Frank Tanner died alone in someone's backyard. He was 19.

At 9:30 p.m on Monday, July 24, Tanner fled from a pharmacy at E. Grand Blvd. and Belvidere, ignoring commands to halt. He had been drinking, then looting, and as he ran, he was shot.

With a police bullet in his abdomen, Tanner ran up the alley behind the building that houses both the pharmacy and four apartments. He either vaulted or crashed through a gate of the fence behind the building, then collapsed. Police and National Guardsmen took him.

About 10 p.m., T. E. Thurston, 60, one of the building tenants, went to his window to see what had happened. Thurston says he wouldn't have stirred from his bed at all, what with all the bullets flying, but Tanner's moaning got to him.

He saw Tanner lying on his back, an arm across his face. Thurston's next-apartment neighbors, Mr. and Mrs. Harold Thompson, came into the apartment and they, too, looked out the window at Tanner's body. Mrs. Johnson says she saw him move and heard him groan.

Then the Johnsons went back to their apartment and Thurston returned to bed. No one called police, or an ambulance; no one moved to help.

They say they were too frightened to go outside, a curfew violation. The only

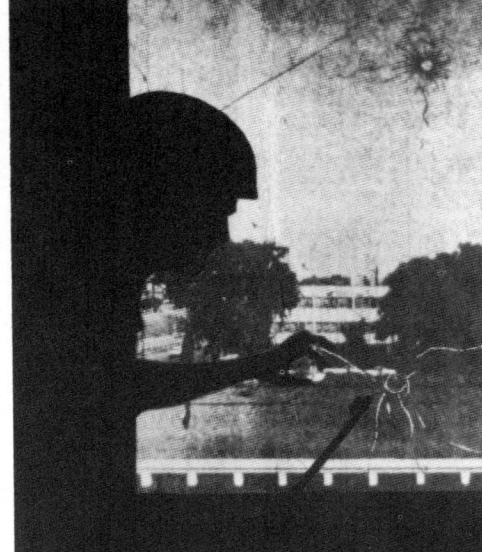

Helen Hall, No. 27, died at this bullet-riddled window

telephone in the building belonged to tenant Joseph L. Metts, 30. And he wasn't up.

About 2 a.m., four hours later, Metts woke up and stepped down the hall to the communal lavatory. He then strolled to the hall window for a breath of fresh air.

Tanner lay still. Metts woke Thurston, then called police.

At 7:45 a.m., a scout car arrived at the scene with police and Guardsmen. At 8:05 a.m., 11 hours after the shooting, Tanner was pronounced dead on arrival at Detroit General Hospital.

The shots were fired from less than 10 feet away and possibly closer than 12 inches, Dr. John Burton, the Wayne County Medical Examiner said. The wadding from the shells was imbedded in Johnson's body, causing additional wounds.

No pipe was recovered by police, but Domm said several pipes were lying on the basement floor.

The two police cars drove off. There was no explanation why they did not supervise removal of the bodies.

A short time later, at 3 p.m., a police car manned by Patrolmen Clifford Styrk and Peter McCluskui drove up and took the two bodies to Detroit General Hospital.

Police said that Styrk and McCluskui were summoned to the scene by a police radio call that two looters had been shot at the pawn shop.

However, there was no police record of such a call at that hour. Police customarily record all the radio reports in writing.

There was a call recorded from Styrk and McCluskui summoning Giacobozzi's police car to the pawn shop. There was no indication whether the pair answered the call.

Davis, from an upstairs window, heard the shots and some time later—he does not know how long—he watched the bodies being carried out. He said he was lying on the floor after the shots were fired and did not notice whether police cars were departing and arriving.

No residents of the area would admit being in the neighborhood at the time of the shootings, although a sizeable crowd reportedly watched the bodies being carried away.

25. Jack Sydnor

The Free Press investigation of the riot deaths found that only one of the 43 dead could be confirmed as a sniper.

His name was Jack Sydnor, and on the afternoon of Tuesday, July 25, he was drunk and he was dangerous.

For the riot's first two days, Sydnor, a Negro, had remained at home with his common-law wife, Zella Mallory, 27. On Tuesday, he went out, as Mrs. Mallory remembers it, "to get a loaf of bread." He returned with a companion, went out again, came back drunk.

His wife found him fingering a pistol that had long been hidden in the apartment. "I wonder if this thing will work," he mused.

It did.

At 9:15 p.m., frightened tenants called police at the Livernois Station, reporting that Sydnor was shooting onto the street from the third floor window of his apartment at 2753 Hazelwood.

Thirty minutes later, Sydnor was dead. Wounded in the chest and abdomen by police gunfire, Sydnor jumped or fell three floors, then died, probably of gunshot wounds.

Before he was killed, Sydnor had seriously wounded Patrolman Roger Poike, pinned down policemen in a two-block area and terrified his wife and neighbors. A dozen more policemen risked their lives rushing Sydnor's apartment to silence his pistol fire.

As Poike burst through the apartment door at the head of a group of officers, Sydnor fired, striking him in the abdomen. Police ripped the apartment with gunfire and hurled in tear gas.

Minutes later, sniper fire erupted from other buildings nearby—initiated perhaps by Sydnor himself. Ironically, that shooting prevented recovery of Sydnor's body until hours after his death.

26. Willie McDaniels

Willie McDaniels, who wanted to be where the action was, lost his life looking for it.

McDaniels was shot as a looter in the hot, sunny afternoon of Wednesday, July 26, when a crowd of holiday-spirited looters fled wildly from the Domestic Outfitting store at Gratiot and Canton on the near East Side.

The men who were killed were Arthur Johnson, 36, and Perry Williams, 33, of 9726 Cameron. Johnson, separated from his wife, had moved several times and his permanent address is unknown.

The men apparently were killed by police officers who shot them and then drove off. A short time later a police station wagon manned by two different policemen drove up and removed the bodies.

Homicide detectives who investigated gave this account:

Shortly before 3 p.m. on July 25 two police cars were notified by an unknown person that the pawn shop was being looted.

Patrolmen Lawrence Giacobozzi and Lawrence Pew were in one car and Patrolmen Andrew Zazula and Edward Ruppell were in the other.

The policemen, seeing the front window was broken, called for anyone inside to come out.

In an upstairs apartment over the pawn shop, Joseph Davis, 80, heard the policemen shouting, "Come out."

When no one answered, Giacobozzi and Zazula entered.

As Giacobozzi was searching the rear of the building, he said he heard a noise behind him. He said he turned and saw a man with a long, dark object in his hands.

Giacobozzi fired two shots at the man with his privately owned British Enfield .30-.30 rifle.

The medical examiner's report states that Perry Williams died of two rifle shots that went through the chest and out the back.

No club was recovered and held as evidence, although Detective John Domm of the Homicide Bureau said that Giacobozzi later recalled that the long dark object was a heavy wooden club.

After Williams was shot, Giacobozzi and Zazula began to search the basement.

Zazula said that as Giacobozzi walked past a clothing rack, Zazula saw a man emerge from between the rack carrying a long piece of pipe in his hand.

The man was Arthur Johnson. Zazula fired two shots from his privately owned 12-gauge pump shotgun.

Johnson died of two shotgun wounds that caused massive damage to his chest and abdomen, the medical examiner's office said.

McDaniels, 23-year-old Negro foundry worker and father of two, was shot by unknown persons during an exchange of fire between police and snipers.

Neighborhood residents claim there was no sniper fire in the area, and they are probably right. They claim, too, that McDaniels was not looting. About that, they are almost certainly wrong.

Despite the testimony of witnesses who deny that McDaniels was stealing, statements from another eyewitness refute that story.

An admitted looter, Elenore Evans, 2411 Belvidere, says she passed McDaniels coming out of the store as she was going in. She remembers him, she says, because they were high school classmates.

McDaniels was carrying two lamps out with him, Miss Evans says. "I wouldn't have recognized him for the lamps in front of him," she remembers," but he spoke. He said, 'Hi there, how are you all,' and then I knew him."

Miss Evans seems to have little reason to lie.

After the shooting stopped, police arrested five looters and found McDaniels lying in the street. McDaniels' companion, Edward Brewster, ran nearly a mile to McDaniels' home, 5395 Seminole, to return with his wife.

Mrs. McDaniels claims police would not let her go to her husband. "I told them I was his wife, but they wouldn't let me touch him," she has said. "They said he was stealing. We just purchased furniture from that store. Why would he want to steal?"

McDaniels died at 11:30 p.m. the next day. No weapons were found at the scene; no snipers were arrested. Almost certainly, McDaniels was shot by police as he ran. The prosecutor's office has ruled that the death was not criminal, and the case of Willie McDaniels has now been closed.

27. Helen Hall

The National Guard and Detroit police poured more than 80 rounds of ammunition into the walls and

Turn to following page

SEPT. 3, 1967:

"No one who drove those gutted streets at midnight, when the fires still burned and the shadows hung and moved in vacant doorways, when frightened voices cried 'Halt' into the silence and footsteps crunched on broken glass, will contend that men should have behaved rationally in those awful hours."

Continued from preceding page

windows of the Harlan House Motel, 6500 John Lodge Freeway, the night Helen Hall was killed.

Most of the firing was directed at the motel after she died. But the evidence leads to the conclusion that a National Guard or police bullet not a sniper ended her life.

Mrs. Hall, 50, of Oakdale, Conn., was in Detroit temporarily to help inventory some electrical supplies her firm had purchased.

She checked into the motel at 10:14 p.m. Sunday, July 23. She was killed about 1 a.m., July 26, as she stood at a fourth floor window facing north.

One shot hit her in the heart, fragmented and tore in several paths through her body. A copper jacket led to that which encases a .30 caliber rifle slug, was taken from her heart by the Wayne County Medical Examiner. A fragment of lead was taken from her liver. Other lead fragments were found in other parts of her body. They all came from the same bullet.

Two guests in the motel saw Mrs. Hall die. They were William Keller, 54, and Lisa Poirier, 24, of Montreal. Both told police Mrs. Hall was standing at the window at the north end of the hall.

A steady crackle of gunfire was heard from outside. Mrs. Hall cried to the others to come to the window and look at a tank. She pulled open the drapes and a bullet came almost instantly, hitting her chest-high and killing her almost at once.

Another bullet came at almost the same moment, passing about 12 inches over Miss Poirier's head and embedding in a wall.

There were three bullet holes in the window. The bullet that killed Mrs. Hall and the one that barely missed Miss Poirier made round holes the size of silver dollars in the window. The projectiles apparently struck straight on, and not at a sharp angle.

Moments after Mrs. Hall was shot, J. R. Glover, 47 of Washington, D. C., was packing his bags in Room 401 when he heard a shot outside his room. He crawled on the floor to the door, opened it and saw Mrs. Hall lying in the hallway.

Just then a young man brandishing a rifle burst into the room and went to the west window. Glover saw him and directed a barrage at the window. A U. S. Marine, he miraculously escaped injury and was taken into custody by police who by this time had gained entry to the motel.

Ballistics tests established that the Marine's gun did not kill Mrs. Hall, police said. They said he was on leave and just happened to be passing through Detroit. No charges were filed against him.

Because the fatal bullet seemed to have entered straight through the window, detectives investigated the possibility that the shot may have come from the National Cash Register Building. This building is on the north side of Grand Boulevard.

Between it and the window where Mrs. Hall was shot there is an annex of the Harlan House Motel which has three floors of rooms for guests and some parking space between the annex and Grand Blvd.

A part-time employe of Bowman Private Police, John W. Bryant, said in a sworn statement that he had been fired on from the building a half hour before Tonia was killed and also the night before.

Guardsmen said one of their 2½-ton trucks was under fire by a sniper who was apparently shooting from the second floor apartment where Tonia was killed. The Guardsmen said they returned the fire.

The only entrance to the roof is through a fire escape on the third floor. No spent shells were found on the roof and there was no physical evidence that anyone was up there. The building was intact all through the riots, no windows were broken, and no one reported seeing any firing coming from the building.

Detective John Jacobs of the Homicide Bureau interviewed guests and employes of Harlan House by telephone just after Mrs. Hall was shot. A few days later, Detectives Harry Hill and Robert Kanka were assigned to the case.

On the morning that Mrs. Hall was shot, however, workmen began replacing the bullet riddled window. By Wednesday afternoon, July 26—the same day of the killing a new window was in place. Thus, Hill and Kanka never saw the broken window.

They investigated the possibility that sniper fire from somewhere west of the John Lodge freeway may have killed Mrs. Hall. They concluded, and this is the official verdict, that a bullet from that area did in fact kill her.

That is inconsistent with the apparent path of the slugs that entered the window. The projectile that skimmed over Lisa Poirier's head skipped along the wall, grazing the fiberboard, and buried itself in a wall directly opposite the window where she was standing.

This bullet clearly came from a straight-in path, not angled from the west. It was fired at almost the same moment as the one that killed Mrs. Hall. Miss Poirier saw Mrs. Hall fall, heard the second bullet whiz over her head and fainted, falling back into her room.

The detectives ruled out the possibility that the fatal bullet came from the Larrow Apartments, 8647 John Lodge.

The Larrow apartment building is a full half mile, measured by a car speedometer, north of the Harlan House on the west side of the freeway.

The police say that someone with binoculars was spotted on the third floor of the building two days after Mrs. Hall was shot. An investigation brought forth several weapons. But ballistics tests disclosed that none of the weapons killed Mrs. Hall.

Furthermore, the Larrow Apartments from the fifth floor down are completely blocked from view of the fatal window by the National Cash Register Building.

The sixth and seventh floors and the roof are completely obscured by a large tree growing next to the National Cash Register Building.

A sniper could conceivably have fired wildly through the tree at a target he could not see and killed Mrs. Hall—except that the manager of the Larrow Apartments, Mrs. Mabel Baker, said the sixth and seventh floors and the roof entrances were padlocked all during the riot and were not broken into.

The sixth and seventh floors are vacant office space. No tenants live there. There are no outside entrances.

No spent shells were found in the Larrow apartment building. Mrs. Baker says no shots were fired from the building all through the riot. The Larrow apartment building must be ruled out.

Further south from the Larrow building on the west side of the freeway there is a large parking garage under construction. The shot may have originated from this area, detectives say.

There is a clear but somewhat angled view of the window from this general area. Snipers were thought to be in this area directing fire at the Henry Ford Hospital.

But a shot from that direction would have suggested a fairly sharp angle of entry through the window. The bullet holes show no indication of an angle.

Numerous witnesses inside the Harlan House testified to the deafening sound of gunfire coming from police and National Guard troops stationed all around the building.

From the fourth floor window, a person can be clearly seen from vantage points along Grand Boulevard, particularly from the sidewalk which adjoins the National Cash Register Building.

Detective Kanka said the bullet had to come from a vantage point higher than Mrs. Hall's fourth floor position because it pierced her heart and traveled downward through her liver. This would suggest a sniper from a high position on the steel girders of the unfinished parking garage west of the freeway.

But, this is a long distance—more than a quarter of a mile—furthermore, a bullet hitting a person in the heart and then the liver would have to be fired from almost directly overhead. The killer would have had to be firing from an extremely steep angle nearly straight above Mrs. Hall. There is no vantage point from which this could have happened.

Detective Kanka said the bullet had to come from a vantage point higher than Mrs. Hall's fourth floor position because it pierced her heart and traveled downward through her liver. This would suggest a sniper from a high position on the steel girders of the unfinished parking garage west of the freeway.

The Wayne County Medical Examiner, Dr. John Burton, said the bullet was fragmented. It struck something, possibly a bone, and was split into pieces and deflected so that one piece entered the liver. There is no evidence that the main path of the slug was from the heart to the liver.

Because of the angle of entry and the other inconsistencies, the theory of a shot from west of the freeway must be ruled out.

The most logical conclusion is that Mrs. Hall was killed by a bullet that was fired from the north, directly across Grand Boulevard, from ground level. This is a distance of 200 or 300 feet and would suggest a shallow trajectory approaching a level plane.

With so many police and Guardsmen at the scene, it is unlikely that a sniper was standing or crouching on the sidewalk in the midst of them.

What is likely is that a Guardsman, or more than one, saw the flashes of movement as Mrs. Hall whipped the drapes aside. He, or they, aimed and shot at the window.

Moments after Mrs. Hall was shot, when Guards and police saw the Marine with his rifle moving about in Room 401, they did the same thing.

The Marine was luckier.

Henry Heading, chief of the criminal division in the county prosecutor's office, said he believes a Guardsman shot Mrs. Hall. He is, however, continuing his investigation.

28. Tonia Blanding

Tonia Blanding, a four-year-old Negro girl, paid for the crimes and mistakes of others.

The corner of Euclid and Twelfth was like a battlefield the night of July 25.

National Guardsmen said there was sniper fire originating from the second floor of the apartment building at 1756 W. Euclid.

A part-time employe of Bowman Private Police, John W. Bryant, said in a sworn statement that he had been fired on from the building a half hour before Tonia was killed and also the night before.

Guardsmen said one of their 2½-ton trucks was under fire by a sniper who was apparently shooting from the second floor apartment where Tonia was killed. The Guardsmen said they returned the fire.

During this time, Cpl. Danny Kwiecinski reported to a tank commander, Sgt. Mortimer J. LeBlanc, 41, that he had seen a flash in the apartment window.

Huddled on the floor of the second-floor apartment were June Blanding, Valerie and William Hood, William Hood Jr., James Matthew Blanding and several other children, including Tonia. LeBlanc, while moving his tank to a position on Euclid directly opposite the apartment building, said the vehicle was under fire from the apartment. Once in position, LeBlanc flared his 50-caliber machine gun into the window as he believed the sniper fire had come from.

Occupants of the apartment said later that they were not fired on until William Hood lighted a match for a cigaret.

Detective David Mason of the Detroit Police Department investigated later and decided that the Guards' firing had been directed only at the apartment from which they believed they were fired on.

Tonia died from bullets believed fired from the machine gun.

Mason said he later found one spent .38 caliber hull next to one of the windows in the apartment and a box of .38 caliber shells with some rounds missing. Police said Hood testified he owned a .38 caliber revolver.

Mason said he found in the apartment 29 men's coats, 35 pairs of men's trousers, 40 shirts, four overcoats, 23 paint brushes, two portable record players, a tape recorder, a portable television set, three portable radios and a movie camera.

There are discrepancies between the version given by the occupants of the apartment and the National Guard investigation.

The occupants said they were not fired on until after the match was lighted, yet the guardsmen from the 2½-ton truck were reported to have fired at the apartment also.

Nowhere is it explained why the private guard, Bryant, did not report being fired on the day before from the apartment which he said he had pinpointed.

Finally, the wisdom of turning a .50 caliber machine gun, which fires a slug that will cut through quarter-inch steel, on a frame dwelling is questionable. Certainly, the men in the tank did not require protection from snipers, and no sniper was found in the building.

Police procedure calls for tear gas to be used on snipers wherever possible, a technique used on sniper Sydney. If that fails or is impossible, officers are directed to rush the building, armed with shotguns, as long as other citizens will not be endangered by their doing so.

The police were never involved in the death of Tonia Blanding. No one asked them for help.

No. 37, John LeRoy: Did someone shoot too soon?

Photo by DENNIS BRACK

29. William Dalton

William N. Dalton, a 19-year-old ex-Job Corps trainee, was killed by a police shotgun blast.

A number of witnesses claim Dalton was gunned by police into making a break, then shot when he ran. Investigators from the Detroit Homicide Bureau say the case is hardly that simple.

They say they have no doubt that Dalton was an arsonist, along with several of his companions that night. They also say that Dalton may well have been attempting to escape arrest, although this theory seems riddled when it is noted that no initial police report was ever filed on the shooting. Nevertheless, if Dalton was attempting to evade apprehension, the officer had every right to fire, the detective feels.

The investigators also note that of the number of persons who say they witnessed the incident, not one have been able to provide information that might help identify the officer they say fired the shot.

The case, subject of a 33-page report prepared by the Homicide Bureau, is being scrutinized at home this weekend by Wayne County Prosecutor William Cahalan.

The incident took place shortly after midnight on July 28, the fourth day of the riot.

According to witnesses, Dalton had been sitting on the porch of a Fernwood Street home until shortly after midnight, when he left, perhaps to go to the home of a girl friend. Marta Kitchen, 15, daughter of Mrs. Martha Kitchen, of 4871 Fernwood. The homes are just two doors apart.

As he walked between the homes, witnesses say, he was arrested by three policemen, probably as a curfew violator.

Phillip Hyde, 23, of 4852 Fernwood, who says he observed the arrest from his porch across the street, claims that the officers put Dalton against a tree and searched him. He says they "tried to make him run, but he said he wasn't going to do it."

Hyde and another witness, Willie Arnold, 26, say the officers then walked Dalton toward Grand River, and forced him to turn down an alley which runs on the south side of Grand River between Fernwood and Edmonton. He and other witnesses say they later heard a single shot.

Other witnesses say Dalton was marched to the intersection of the Fernwood-Edmonton alley with the Grand River alley, where he was forced against the wall of a warehouse, his hands on his head.

From the warehouse, witnesses say, Mrs. Alberta Jones, who lives at Grand River and Arcadia, directly across from where Dalton was shot.

She claims she saw officers take Dalton into an alley on the west side of Edmonton. There, she says, she heard Dalton cry: "I didn't set no fires. You didn't see no fires."

She says Dalton was then brought into the parking lot, where a police officer pushed him against a wall, shoving him with a shotgun.

Then, they say, officers ordered Dalton to run. They say he ran along the building and vaulted over the hood of a car. As he did, they say, a policeman raised his shotgun, and fired one shot, felling Dalton on the sidewalk in front of a cleaners.

Mrs. Jones says the officer then yelled: "Let's get out of here." She says: "Everyone jumped into their cars and went off in every direction."

She adds that she never called police about the incident. "All they would have done is relayed it to the police who did the shooting, and I didn't want no part of that," she says.

In all, witnesses say, as many as 20 police and National Guardsmen saw the shooting.

Another person who says he witnessed the shooting is Charles Hall, 25, of 4840 Edmonton.

He says he heard noise in the alley, and went to a window. In the streetlight at the intersection of the alleys, he says he saw a young Negro in a white straw hat standing with his hands on his head. That was Dalton.

He says he could not make out what the officers were saying, because their backs were turned. But he says he is sure he heard Dalton, who was facing his way, say: "Please, mister, don't do that to me."

Later, Hall says, he saw a policeman shove his shotgun at Dalton. He yelled: "Don't shoot that boy." Mrs. Jones corroborates this, saying that when Hall shouted, the officer turned in the direction of Hall's residence and shouted: "Shut up, or I'll blast your head off."

Dalton then ran, witnesses say, and was shot.

Another witness, Darryl Slater, 14, son of Mrs. Leatrice Slater, of 8680 Grand River, says he also saw officers bring Dalton out of the alley. He says he heard officers tell him to run, and saw him shot.

Dalton, a part-time milk truck helper for Twin Pines Dairy, was dead on arrival at 2:20 a.m. at Northwest General Hospital. According to Dr. John Burton, the Wayne County medical examiner, he died of shotgun wounds of the chest and abdomen. Dr. Burton estimates the wounds were inflicted by shots fired at a distance of six to 10 feet.

According to the police report in Cahalan's hands, police were unable to immediately remove Dalton's body because of heavy sniper fire.

An initial call, at 12:45 a.m. said "man down" and warned of sniper fire. The pick-up was not made until an hour or so later.

The residents, however, allege there was no fire in the area, except for the blast that killed Dalton.

And James Jones, chief of the Newsweek bureau in Detroit who arrived at the scene about 1:05 a.m., after hearing the 12:45 a.m. call, says he heard no sniper fire on Grand River as he drove to the scene, nor at the shooting site. He says Dalton was "in his death throes" when he arrived.

Dalton, who attended a Job Corps camp at Camp Kilmer, N.J., in 1966, lived with his mother, Mrs. Ethel Dalton, at 1495 Taylor, about two miles from the scene. She says that Dalton's being in the Grand River neighborhood was not unusual. She says he often spent time with friends there.

Mrs. Dalton says she first heard her son might have been killed when residents called next morning to say they thought the youth they had seen shot was her son. Some of his friends had found his white straw hat, and blood at the scene.

She says that she then saw a William M. Dalton listed in the newspapers as a riot victim, but she wasn't sure that was her son, because his middle initial is N.

That evening, she says, she went to the Wayne County Morgue, but was turned away at the door without an answer. She says she was barred from Detroit Police Headquarters by soldiers.

On Thursday, she went back to the morgue. She found that the dead youth was her son; he had been identified through fingerprints on file when he had once been arrested for reckless driving.

Victims

of the three dead youths with the consent of relatives.

Dr. Sillery concluded that all three men were shot from inside the building from a range of 15 feet or less by 12-gauge double-O buckshot. All the men were shot more than once. None could have been killed while engaged in a sniper battle with authorities outside the building.

Two of them, Temple and Pollard, were shot while lying or kneeling. The county medical examiner's autopsy reports agreed substantially with Sillery's findings.

A search of the motel annex failed to turn up any weapons.

Almost the only thing that persons in the motel and law officers are agreed on is that policemen burst into the motel about 2 a.m. The police said they were investigating sniper fire from the motel.

The motel guests said that half a dozen uniformed men broke open the front door with gun butts, burst through the building and rounded up the occupants.

The guests said they were lined up against the wall, threatened and beaten. They heard gunshots, but none said they saw any of the youths get killed, and when the police told them to leave they all fled into the night.

A pre-trial examination was begun Aug. 11 in Recorder's Court to determine whether Detroit Patrolmen Ronald W. August, 28, and Robert N. Paille, 31, should be held for trial in the killings of Pollard and Temple.

A youth who was in the motel, Michael Clark, testified that Paille and August had taken him into a room where Paille put a cocked pistol against him head and threatened to kill him.

Clark testified he later saw August take a youth into another room and that he heard a shot and someone fell to the floor.

August, charged with killing Pollard, submitted a statement that said he shot the youth in self defense when the youth tried to wrest the gun away.

August was ordered to stand trial for first-degree murder. No trial date has been set.

A National Guard warrant officer, Theodore J. Thomas, testified that he saw a policeman lead a man into a room and make him lie on the floor. Then the policeman fired a shot into the air, Thomas said. He could not identify the policeman.

He also said he saw August lead a man into a room and then heard a body fall. He said he had seen one body in Room A2 and one in A3 but did not see the other body in A3.

Paille, charged with slaying Temple, was released because of insufficient evidence. His defense attorney, Norman Lippitt, argued at the examination that all that had been proved was that Paille was in the motel that night.

No charges were filed in the death of Cooper. The evidence indicated that Cooper was the first to die in Room A2. The other two were shot later by August.

On August 24 the county prosecutor brought conspiracy charges against Paille, a private guard named Melvin Dismukes, and Patrolman David Senak. August was named as a co-conspirator but not a defendant.

Cahalan charged that some of the lawmen in the annex had beaten, intimidated and abused the witnesses. He said they had engaged in excesses in obvious violation of criminal statutes.

No trial date has been set on the conspiracy charges.

Senak was under investigation by Cahalan's office in two other riot deaths but was cleared of wrongdoing last week in the death of Joseph Chandler. Cahalan is still investigating Senak's part in the death of Fanner Gray.

Dismukes is also awaiting trial on a felonious assault charge involving the Algiers Motel.

35. Julius Lust

Julius Lust was one of two white men shot as looters.

Probably that classification is unfair. There is no proof that Lust was a looter; apparently, he was only a thief.

Lust, 26, of 13998 Mitchell, was killed in the G. & W. Auto Parts Co. junkyard at 17130 Joseph Campau, the night of July 26. Two Detroit policemen shot at him when they caught him in the yard; which bullet killed him is not known.

According to the police report of the shooting, Gary Woytalewicz, 20, and Edmund Konieki, 37, say they met at Lust's house early that evening. Lust told them he had permission to enter the junkyard to get a housing for an automatic transmission for a 1961 Ford Falcon. A junkyard employe named Dean Turley had given him permission, Lust said.

Both the yard's owners, George and Walt Wojtas, and Turley himself deny that any permission was given.

In any case, Lust, Woytalewicz and Konieki went to the yard about 9 p.m. that night, climbing over the back fence. There was a 1961 Falcon in the lot, but it was the wrong model and the part Lust sought could not be found.

Moments later, Woytalewicz spotted a police car nearby and he and Konieki ran, leaving Lust behind.

At 9:30, a private guard named James Butler hailed a passing scout car. Butler was employed to guard stores in the area, but not the junkyard. He told police, though, that he had seen four of five men enter the junkyard, including one armed with a chrome-plated revolver.

The man with the revolver was a Negro, Butler said. No Negroes, and no gunman, can be placed at the scene.

Lust, meantime, was working with a wrench on a junk motor. The fan had been taken off and Willie Thomas, 52, a junkyard clerk, theorized later that Lust was after the water pump.

At that moment, two police officers went to the front of the junkyard, another to the back. They saw Lust walking toward them and yelled halt. Lust made some sort of motion with his left hand, the officers say, began to run.

Two officers fired; one bullet struck Lust in the right side. He was dead on arrival at Detroit General Hospital.

A pool of blood was found later, within two feet of the motor Lust had been working on. If he ran, he did not run far.

Butler may have mistaken a wrench for a chrome-plated revolver; why he thought a Negro was involved is not known. Lust and his two companions were white.

The water pump Lust was working on sells for $4. The transmission housing that drew him to the junkyard costs $4.50. In fact, the junkyard's only loss was a metal lock.

Police had to shoot it off to remove Lust's body.

36. George Messerlian

They called him George, because Krikor Messerlian was quite a mouthful for his shoe repair customers. Messerlian, 68, operated a shoe repair shop at 7111 Linwood.

He worked hard and kept his own counsel. For 30 years he had mended shoes at the shop and quietly minded his own business. If other people had minded theirs, Messerlian would still be alive.

Messerlian was one of the first victims to fall in the riot. On the first day of violence, July 23, witnesses said he was beaten about the head by a Negro youth with a thick, 30-inch club. Messerlian died July 27 in Henry Ford Hospital.

Bands of looters were rampaging through the neighborhood as Messerlian was tending a closing shop next to his shoe shop. It was 4:30 p.m.

Witnesses said a gang of Negroes came along and told Messerlian to get out of the shop. Messerlian had fought for his rights and a living since he came to America in 1920. He refused.

He stood less than five feet tall and weighed 100 pounds. He took up a 20-inch saber that he kept in the shop and prepared to defend his property. Witness said Messerlian, swinging the saber, cut one youth on the right shoulder before he was felled.

A Negro youth shouted, "I'll get the old man for you," and clubbed Messerlian repeatedly before he was pulled away and disappeared into the mob, witnesses said.

On Aug. 14 police acted on a tip and arrested Darryl McCurtis, 20, of 8911 Linwood.

McCurtis was arraigned Aug. 16 on a first degree murder charge and pleaded innocent. He is being held in the Wayne County jail pending a felony examination Sept. 22.

The youth told police he had arrived in Detroit six weeks before the riot started from Birmingham, Ala.

33. Willie Hunter
34. Prince Williams

Willie Hunter and Prince Williams died by accident. There was negligence involved, but it was of their own making.

Their bodies were found Wednesday, July 26, charred and decomposing in the flooded basement of Brown's Drug store, 8202 Twelfth, by firemen called to fight a lingering rubbish fire in the building's ruins.

An autopsy showed that the men—friends and fellow auto factory workers—died of carbon monoxide asphyxiation, probably on Sunday, when the first rash of arsonist's fires swept the length of Twelfth St. There were no bullet holes or other wounds identified.

The two men were last seen by witnesses who say they were headed toward Twelfth Street from Williams' apartment at 1234 Seward. The time, as closely as it can be recalled, was about 4:30 p.m. Sunday.

Apparently they entered the store—to look or to loot—and somehow were trapped when the building burned. Perhaps the drugstore went up suddenly, ignited by a Molotov cocktail. Perhaps Hunter and Williams tempted fate, and didn't leave in time.

Hunter, 26, of 3454 Van Dyke, left a wife, a two-year-old daughter and a year-old son. Williams lived alone and seldom spoke of his family to other friends in his building. He is believed to have been separated from his wife and two daughters.

Both Negroes, the two friends left a common, stony legacy: Though their bodies were not found until Wednesday, they apparently were the first to die in the nation's deadliest riot.

37. John LeRoy

The official reports of the shooting of John LeRoy are cut and dried.

According to police and the National Guard, LeRoy, 20, of 3119 Garland, was shot when he and four companions ran a roadblock on Lycaste, near Mack. The official police report says he admitted running the roadblock when he was admitted to Detroit General Hospital with wounds to the chest, arms and stomach.

According to witnesses and survivors, the unofficial versions are untrue.

A key figure in the case is Ronald Powers, 25, of 3188 Lycaste, an employe at the Chrysler Motor Corp. Mack Ave. near Plant, and a part-time barber. He says it was because of him that the men were out after curfew. His wife was expecting a baby momentarily, he says, and he wanted to get home.

Powers says he and his companions—Edward Blackshear, 28, 1600 Blaine; Charles Glover, 36, 3322 Tyler; Charles Dunson, 32, of 5105 Garland, and LeRoy—all had been at the Dunson home the afternoon and evening of July 25, the third day of the riot. He admits they had been drinking, but insists "not much — a pint between us all day."

Shortly before midnight, he says, he decided he ought to go home. His wife, saying she was weak, had already left, he says. Dunson volunteered to drive.

All five piled into Dunson's station wagon, and left the Dunson home for Powers' apartment, some 15 blocks away.

They drove east on East Warren, then turned onto Gladwin. At Gladwin and Canfield, they were stopped at a National Guard checkpoint. They explained why they were out after curfew, and received permission to go ahead, providing they took a special route — back up Gladwin to E. Warren, over to Connor, then take Charlevoix to Lycaste.

They took off, following the Guard instructions to the letter. Powers says most of the route was dark, he recalls, with "most of the streetlights out." About 10 minutes later, Dunson turned the car off Charlevoix onto Lycaste. They drove north on Lycaste, lights on.

Midway up the street, between Charlevoix and Goethe, they spotted a National Guard jeep at the curb. Dunson says they stopped, assuming it was another checkpoint. The Guardsmen opened fire.

Standing behind trees, between houses the Guardsmen riddled the car. A Free Press reporter later counted at least 11 bullet holes, all in the front and right front.

Powers says: "We were screaming 'We didn't do anything.' But they kept on shooting." "I cut my engine off," Dunson

Turn to following page

OCT. 11, 1968:

Detroit's third World Series championship and first since 1945.

SUNNY
A Little Warmer
High: 60-67 Low: 30-38

Detroit Free Press
ON GUARD FOR 137 YEARS

Vol. 138—No. 159 — Friday, October 11, 1968

METRO
Stocks Lose
Trading Heavy
See Page 10, Section B

Ten Cents

JIM NORTHRUP

WE WIN!

MICKEY LOLICH

City Goes Wild After Tiger Victory

BY BARBARA STANTON
Free Press Staff Writer

Detroit went hell-bent for a hangover Thursday night in raucous, rowdy triumph after the Tigers won the World Series.

World champions!

At 4:06 p.m., Bill Freehan caught a pop fly in St. Louis and Detroit exploded like a magnificent firecracker.

People poured into the streets, confetti rained from the heavens, horns sang, and shrieks and squeals and sirens rose in one, great, gorgeous, swelling sound until hearts nearly burst from the joy of it.

Suddenly nothing would ever be impossible again.

The unbelievable, unpredictable Tigers had done it.

In the vain hope that the Tigers would land there, 20,000 persons jammed Metro Airport, spilling onto the runways and forcing the airport to close temporarily.

MEANWHILE the Tigers came down from the sky at Willow Run, to the dazzling glare of TV lights and the ecstatic yells of 400 fans who had guessed right.

Mickey Lolich beat the St. Louis Cardinals and unbeatable Bob Gibson, 4-1, in the final game of the World Series Thursday, bringing Detroit its first world baseball championship since the joyous days marking the end of World War II.

The sky was bluer, the sunshine brighter and the sweet madness of victory rode on the air like something you could feel, taste, touch, grasp once and hold forever, learn once in a lifetime and remember ever after.

Downtown fairly danced with delight, as a million IBM cards and tons of paper, confetti, ticker tape and shredded telephone books cascaded down from the city's skyscrapers, bedecked its lightpoles, caught at the wrists and ankles of its pedestrians, piled up in great drifts for screaming Tiger fans to toss upward again.

Grown men giggled, women cried and old, sour faces split suddenly with grins. Secretaries ran through office buildings, screaming and sobbing. Bosses mopped their brows, sighed "Oh, my God," and ran with them.

On Woodward, an elderly Negro and a white matron suddenly found themselves in step and smiling. "Everybody," giggled the man, without explanation. "Everybody." And she smiled and understood.

"This city deserved it," said a man standing outside a restaurant on Lafayette that was advertising "Today's Special: Southern Fried Cardinal."

"It really deserved it."

And it did, it did.

* * *

THE TIGERS won the World Series, and all of a sudden nine men on a grassy field in St. Louis proved that Detroit could rise again.

"Holy God, it's fantastic!" shouted Gary Scott, 28, of Lincoln Park, as he came shooting out of the Bank of the Commonwealth into a welter of ticker tape and shrieking girls. "Everybody's going crazy in there! We just took off."

Seminarians from Sacred Heart threw a classmate, Jim Stokes, 17, into the Kennedy Square pool.

Four young men swaggered down E. Jefferson swigging happily from open bottles of champagne.

The Detroit Police Department called in all three shifts to handle traffic in the churning, carnival streets.

But drunks still directed traffic, cheering teen-agers rocked cars and buses, revelers parked on Woodward sidewalks and in store doorways, the freeways were clut-

Turn to Page 2A, Column 3

AND A TROPHY TO PROVE IT! Exuberant Dick McAuliffe, left, with Jim Northrup, center, and Mickey Stanley tell it all as they display the trophy that goes to baseball's World Champions.
AP Photo

The Big Victory

George Cantor's story of the Tigers' triumph. Page 1D.

Dick Mayer's World Series. Page 3A.

Violence and vandalism mar Tiger celebration. Page 4B.

Mickey Lolich's mother has "never worried about him—even today." Page 1C.

"It's my fault . . . I misjudged Northrup's hit"— Curt Flood. Page 2D.

"I'll never forget it"—Al Kaline. Page 3D.

More pictures on Page 11C and Back Page.

Action Line
Dial 222-6464

Action Line solves problems, gets answers, cuts red tape, stands up for your rights. Write Action Line, Box 881, Detroit, Mich. 48231. Or dial 222-6464 between 8:30 a.m. and 4:30 p.m. Monday through Friday.

Any idea what we can do with a crippled cardinal we've been tending?—Frank Andrews, Director, Michigan Humane Society.

We'll keep him safe from tigers. Till he's ready to fly again, a plate glass window will protect him from big boys with baseball bats. Little boys and girls can see him, though, in Hudson's front window. He'll be closer than any other Cardinal to the World Series trophy: Hudson's has asked to display that, too, in the same window. And when your cardinal is well, he'll have a Missouri mule for permanent company. Joe Hudson Jr. won the mule in a bet with KSD-TV of St. Louis: The mule and your cardinal will live in the Children's Zoo at Belle Isle.

I just bought a German shepherd who understands only German. I can't speak a word of it. Help! If you

can find me a German trainer, I'll donate $10 to your favorite charity. — M. H., Oak Park.

Use it to buy a German dictionary to talk to your pooch. (First lesson: "Plotz!"—down!). To find out how much he knows, Charles T. Art of the Police K-9 School in Plymouth will put Nero through the paces. Art studied dog handling in Germany with the nephew of the man who developed the breed. German shepherds have been around 87 years, though not always under that name. During World War I, German - hating British called their shepherds Alsatians. Even America's World War I, star-spangled dog hero, Rin Tin Tin, was a turncoat. An Air Force colonel found the pup in a German dugout after the 1918 attack on Metz.

Help, before everyone throws away their "Sock it to 'em, Tigers!" signs. The crew of the USS Ticonderoga calls itself the Tigers, too. All of us Michigan mates sure would like to have a great big Sock It to 'em sign aboard. —Lt. j.g. Dom Mochrowiz, USS Ticonderoga, FPO San Francisco, Cal., 96601.

It's nine feet long, waterproof and printed on sailcloth. During Series week, the Sock it to 'em sign Jim Cockels is sending you hung over his bar at Russell's Steak House in Detroit. Distributors of the signs, Kramer Designs of Birmingham, are throwing in two Tiger chef's aprons and 200 "How Sweet It Is, Tigers" bumper stickers you can plaster around every port you hit.

The week of the 9th I went coho fishing. I was only supposed to be gone a couple of days, but the fish weren't biting so I stayed a week. My wife doesn't believe I was fishing all that time. She thinks I bought the prize catch I brought home. Some newspaperman from Ohio took a picture of my fish. Could you find it so she'll get off my back?—N. C., Detroit.

Hank Andrews, the Tom Opre of the Cleveland Press, will back up your fish tale. He's sending a 9-by-12 photo of you and your 18-pound coho. You're not completely off the hook, though. Conservation department says fish were biting that week and most guys got their limit in two to four days. Taking nine days to catch six coho sounds fishy to them. Maybe you were using the wrong kind of bait?

I hate to admit this, but I need help finding my jacket and car keys. I left them in a restaurant in Petoskey last weekend when my wife and I drove north to see the fall colors. All I can remember about it

Turn to Page 4A, Column 1

Tigers Avoid Welcoming Mob

Tiger fans staged such a tumultuous reception for their homecoming heroes at Metro Airport Thursday night that the World Series champions had to miss it.

Because of the crush of deliriously happy mobs that spilled in waves over airport runways, the chartered plane bringing the Tigers from St. Louis had to be diverted to Willow Run Airport, long after its scheduled 7:30 p.m. arrival.

. . .

THE MOB AT Metro ran uncontrolled. Some climbed onto the fuselage of a plane and had to be hosed off by firemen.

Runways were left a tangle of debris and broken bottles.

Television newsmen were bowled over by the crush of crowds when they tried to interview fans.

What the welcomers who turned out at Willow Run lacked in size, they more than made up for in enthusiasm.

About 400 persons crowded around the plane's gang-

way moments after it was put up to deplane the team. Some perched on the shoulders of others to see their heroes.

Young and old, men and women, they screamed their lungs out.

Some tried to scramble over the sides of the gangway to touch the players.

A cordon of police blocked the gangway but had difficulty holding back the surging crowd.

The Tigers were scheduled to land at 7:30 p.m. at Metro, but the mob of well-wishers that inundated the airport forced officials to close it to all traffic.

Auto traffic leading to Metro was backed up for 10 miles from the airport and solid masses of pedestrians—30 abreast and two miles long—left their cars to walk to the airport and swell a throng already estimated by police at 25,000.

Metro was pandemonium. Mobs ran wild across ramps and runways, scrambled over fences and in one case held up the deplaning of an incoming flight for more than an hour in the mistaken belief that the Tigers were aboard.

ONLY A SCATTERING of the fans at Metro learned that the Tiger plane had been diverted to Willow.

The Willow Run crowd went crazy when Mickey Lolich appeared at the top of the gangway, after the plane had landed at 9:25 p.m.

Just at that moment a group of persons who had been held off the runway by police lines, found a route through a hangar and ran to the plane screaming madly all the way.

Mayor Cavanagh and Gov. Romney both turned out

Turn to Page 2A, Column 1

Inside the Free Press

Amusements	6-8B	Movie Guide	10-11D
Ann Landers	3C	Obituaries	2B
Astrology	9D	Sports	1-7D
Billy Graham	12D	Stock Markets	10-12B
Bridge	9D	Teen Page	8D
Business News	9-11B	TV-Radio	5C
Comics	9-11D	Want Ads	6-11C
Crossword Puzzler	9D	Women's Pages	1-4C
Death Notices	6C		
Drew Pearson	11A	HAVE THE FREE PRESS	
Earl Wilson	11A	DELIVERED AT HOME	
Editorials	6A	PHONE 222-6500	
Feature Page	11A		

Our Man in the Bleachers

The Champions Weep in Joy

BY BOB TALBERT
Free Press Columnist

ST. LOUIS—Tears!
Big, fat, happy tears.
They didn't try to hide them.
They let them flow and kissed them away.
This was the time and this was the place.
How sweet it is for all the Tigers!
How very sweet it is for Mickey Lolich and Jim Northrup.
And Al Kaline and Bill Freehan.
And Willie Horton and Denny McLain.
And Dick McAuliffe and Norm Cash.
And Don Wert and Mickey Stanley.

AND ESPECIALLY Mayo Smith, who saw his Tigers look the brooding Moor in the eye Thursday and turn this seven-act Shakespearean tragedy into a roaring happy Tiger tale.

Bob Gibson, the man St. Louis thought could build castles with his hands and ride rockets bareback, had

Turn to Page 9A, Column 1

Detroit Free Press

MILD
Fog and Drizzle
High 42-46 Low 34-40

METRO
Stocks Gain
Trading Active
See Page 14, Section C

ON GUARD FOR 137 YEARS

Vol. 138—No. 263 — Thursday, January 23, 1969 — Ten Cents

JAN 23, 1969:

Former Gov. Romney is sworn in as Secretary of Housing and Urban Development in the Nixon administration while his successor, William Milliken, takes the oath in Lansing.

"Romney's 1st Duty Is Shaking Hands," column three, and *"Milliken Pledges Best for Michigan,"* column six.

Action Line
Dial 222-6464

Action Line solves problems, gets answers, cuts red tape, stands up for your rights. Write Action Line, Box 881, Detroit, Mich. 48231. Or dial 222-6464 between 8:30 a.m. and 4:30 p.m. Monday through Friday.

While scraping scrambled eggs out of the pan, I scraped off some of the Teflon coating. Will it hurt you if it gets into the food?—Mrs. M.T., Centerline.

It didn't faze a bunch of rats whose diet for three months was one-quarter ground-up Teflon. Dr. John Zapp at DuPont in Houston, which makes the non-stick cookware coating, says his rats proved there's no danger from eating Teflon particles. But the fumes can be deadly if you accidentally leave an empty pan smoldering on a hot burner for over an hour—particularly if there's a pet canary in the house. Birds are especially sensitive to toxic fumes, are often taken into mines to sniff out escaping gas fumes. Dr. Zapp says they've lost a few birds to Teflon fumes, but no people or rats.

Raccoons have taken up residence in our chimney. They're driving us crazy. They run around all night keeping us awake. How the heck do we get them out of the chimney?— R. S., Detroit.

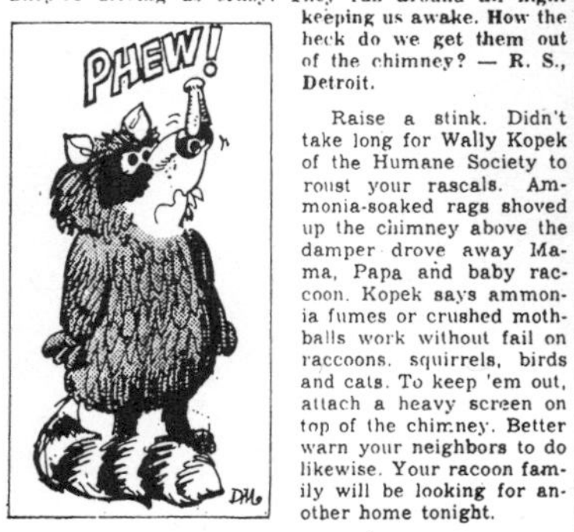

Raise a stink. Didn't take long for Wally Kopek of the Humane Society to roust your rascals. Ammonia-soaked rags shoved up the chimney above the damper drove away Mama, Papa and baby raccoon. Kopek says ammonia fumes or crushed mothballs work without fail on raccoons, squirrels, birds and cats. To keep 'em out, attach a heavy screen on top of the chimney. Better warn your neighbors to do likewise. Your racoon family will be looking for another home tonight.

My son's kindergarten teacher says she heard there are reduced-rate Shrine Circus tickets available to groups of school children, but she doesn't know where to get them or who to contact.—Mrs. G.S., Royal Oak.

A Royal Oak Shriner will provide all she needs. Special coupons can be bought for $1 from any Shriner or at the main Shrine office, 434 Temple. Coupons must be exchanged in advance at the Shrine office for regular reserved seat tickets. With the coupons, groups get bloc ticket rates for one of the 2 p.m. weekday matinee performances (regular tickets are $1.75 to $4). Better hurry; several matinee performances for the circus, at the State Fair Coliseum Jan. 31 through Feb. 16, are already sold out.

My brother was released recently from University Hospital in Ann Arbor, but he has to spend eight to 10 hours a day in an iron lung. The March of Dimes is providing the iron lung. The problem is that he's going to live with my mother in rural Kentucky, where the electricity sometimes goes off for three or four days. A power failure could kill him. We need a gasoline-driven electric generator for emergencies.—G. H. S., Wyandotte.

One is being donated by Carroll-Stuart Corp. of Ferndale, local distributors of Onan generating plants. The 1,250-watt gasoline engine produces a 10 amp current, enough to keep an iron lung going, according to experts at Herman Kiefer Hospital. Generating plant will leave today, should reach your mother's home in Fredonia, Ky., by next Wednesday. Thank General Manager Stewart Kaufman, who made all the arrangements.

Action Line

My boy, Albert, just got an induction notice to leave for the Army Jan. 31. My husband recently had a heart attack and can't work and Albert is the sole provider. We have 14 children and just can't do without him.—Mrs. J. D., Southfield.

Col. Arthur Holmes, state Selective Service director, will review Albert's case, and consider your claim that you may have to close the family store because of back debts and no one to run the place. If facts warrant it, Col. Holmes will order a postponement of the induction until Albert's local board can reconsider his case next month. Send all details to Col. Arthur Holmes, Michigan Selective Service Commission, P.O. Box 626, Lansing 48903.

Here's a switch for you: I want to GET my gas bill. I moved from Detroit to Lincoln Park three months ago and transferred my account to the new address. Four men have been out to read the meter, but every time I call the gas company for a bill they say they have no record of it. — Mrs. H.P., Lincoln Park.

It's in the mail. Gas company will set up a budget plan so you don't get socked with it all at once. They were feeding your bills into a computer, but it kept spitting them out. People you bought the house from spent winters in Florida, had a deal with the gas company that they wouldn't get monthly bills while they were out of town. Computer wasn't told about your moving, kept rejecting monthly bills for that address.

Person to Person

THANKS TO the mention in Action Line, we've sent out hundreds of free IQ3 (I Quit Smoking) and .DS (I Don't Smoke) buttons. The enclosed five-pound packet is just a sampling of the mail. Notice how many are from proud children who want to say congratulations to their newly unhooked parents and tell them how proud they are.— Michigan Cancer Foundation, 4811 John R., Detroit, 48201.

THE SUICIDE PREVENTION CENTER sends thanks for the beautiful red carpeting installed by the donor, the McNabb Carpet Company, along with the padding and labor paid for by Norman Lacoff of Detroit.—Dr. Bruce Danto and staff, Suicide Prevention Center, Detroit.

Tax Hike Seen Merely Delayed
State Gets Red-Ink Budget

IF GEORGE Romney puts half as much enthusiasm into his new cabinet job as he did Wednesday at the White House swearing-in ceremonies, he'll be a crack secretary of Housing and Urban Development. With his wife, Lenore, looking misty-eyed, and President Nixon at his side, our ex-governor snapped up his hand and swore, in no uncertain terms, to do his best.

HIS WIFE'S eyes reflected her happiness as Michigan's new governor, William G. Milliken, stood in the capitol at Lansing after taking his oath and showing that he would be as enthusiastic as the man he succeeded. "I'm ready for the job," he declared, "and eager to get started."

Romney's 1st Duty Is Shaking Hands

BY SAUL FRIEDMAN
Free Press Washington Staff

WASHINGTON — In his first day on the job Wednesday, George Romney managed to startle the federal bureaucracy.

As if he were still campaigning for something, he opened the doors to his plush 10th floor office at the Department of Housing and Urban Development to shake the hands of the more than 4,000 employees in the vast building.

All afternoon, the HUD staff members trooped across the beige carpet, most of them seeing the secretary and his office for the first time.

"I've been working for HUD since it began four years ago, and I've never seen the secretary," said a man to the woman in line ahead of him.

Personnel projected by civil service sauntered nonchalantly through the receiving line. Higher-salaried political appointees fawned a bit over Romney, trying hard to create a good impression.

"Charley says we'd better not smoke in front of him," said a lady bureaucrat to a friend. "He's Mormon, you know."

• • •

ALL MORNING the employees on the 10th floor puttered around Romney's office. They arranged his furniture, ordered books from the library to fill his shelves and thoughtfully took down a picture of Lyndon Johnson and tucked it away on the floor behind a cabinet.

Romney had already visited his wife Monday, to show his wife and children his new digs.

Although his salary will probably be raised to $60,000 a year, coming into office the pay is $35,000.

Turn to Page 4A, Column 1

Nixon Goal Is Tax Cut This Year

Pictures on Back Page

BY ROBERT S. BOYD
Chief of Our Washington Bureau

WASHINGTON — On President Nixon's orders, his new budget director is going over Lyndon Johnson's last budget hunting for savings.

If he finds enough of them, Budget Director Robert P. Mayo said Wednesday, it may be possible to cut taxes next June.

But Treasury Secretary David M. Kennedy later said the Johnson budget is "a very tight budget."

"It's going to be difficult to reduce expenditures substantially," he warned.

Mayo met reporters in the White House after being sworn in by Chief Justice Earl Warren. The swearing-in ceremony also included 11 members of Mr. Nixon's cabinet and his United Nations ambassador, Charles W. Yost.

• • •

THE CABINET held an organization meeting for three hours. It decided to meet every other week for the next two months and at least once a month after that.

Mayo said the President gave him a "mandate" to cut Johnson's $195 billion budget for fiscal 1970, the year starting July 1, "under strict control."

"We're going to look at every program individually," Mayo said. "We hope to get the total down."

If federal spending can be cut sufficiently, he said, it is "obvious" that the 10 percent federal surtax could be trimmed.

He warned, however, that the surtax "should continue as long as we have the economic and budgetary outlook of today."

• • •

THAT OUTLOOK includes the most serious inflation in half a century, and a budget that would be $5 to $7 billion in the red if it were not for the surtax.

The supposedly temporary tax, which took effect in July,

Turn to Page 3A, Column 8

Mild Weather To Continue

Detroit's weather will be cloudy, foggy and mild again Thursday with occasional light drizzle or rain expected, the Weather Bureau said.

Thursday's high temperature will be about 50 with a low Thursday night of 40. Winds will be light and out of the southeast.

Milliken Pledges Best for Michigan

BY CLARK HOYT
Free Press Staff Writer

LANSING — William G. Milliken put his left hand on a borrowed Bible just after noon Wednesday and swore to do his best as Michigan's 44th governor.

The 46-year-old Milliken, Republican lieutenant governor since January, 1965, was sworn into his new job in the green-carpeted capitol office that had been George Romney's for the last six years.

As his slender, dark-haired wife, Helen, looked on, Milliken declared: "I'm ready for the job—and eager to get started on it."

The oath-taking began at 12:03 p.m., when Mrs. Milliken picked up the worn Bible, borrowed for the occasion from the State Law Library, and Chief Justice John R. Dethmers of the State Supreme Court said: "Raise your right hand and take your oath of office."

Milliken faced the white-haired judge and swore to uphold the constitutions of the United States and Michigan.

Then he announced a pledge: "A total commitment on my part to the people of this state to work for them and with them to improve the quality of life in Michigan."

Milliken said his promise means major efforts to achieve "public order and social justice," welfare improvements, educational reforms and pollution control.

And he said, "It means a major attack on the problems of our cities."

The ceremony was all over in six minutes, and Milliken led his wife to the office reception area, where

Turn to Page 2A, Column 1

Spending To Exceed Income
Must Raid '68-'69 Surplus

BY ROGER LANE
Lansing Bureau Chief

LANSING—Michigan will spend more than it takes in under the $1.5-billion budget for 1969-70 submitted to the Legislature Wednesday.

The income this year will be $1,453,200,000 and expenditures will be $1,510,600,000.

The state's general fund will be kept out of the red only by draining the $70.3 million surplus expected at the end of the current fiscal year.

By June 30, 1970, that surplus is expected to be reduced to $13 million.

To some, it appeared that Gov. Milliken's first budget was merely delaying the day of reckoning on a tax increase.

The precariously balanced budget was unveiled by Milliken hours before he stepped into the governor's office freshly vacated by U.S. Urban Affairs Secretary George Romney.

• • •

THE BUDGET was prepared before Romney went to Washington. Both Romney and Milliken signed it.

Milliken said the budget reflected times that called for neither "standing still" nor "massive spending."

Although the total nearly doubled the $789-million general fund expenditures of 1965-66, only $10 million was recommended for genuinely new activities.

The rest of a $173 million increase over fiscal 1968-69 was for enlargement of existing programs, chiefly in education. No money was set aside for parochial state subsidies to non-public schools. Milliken already had said any

Turn to Page 5A, Column 1

Proposed State Budget At a Glance

Here is a breakdown on Gov. Milliken's proposed state budget:

SPENDING — $1,510,600,000.
REVENUES — $1,453,200,000, plus anticipated $70,300,000 surplus from current fiscal year.
TAXES—No increased or new taxes proposed.
WHO GETS WHAT — Education. $797.4 million; welfare —$261 million; mental health —$171.5 million.
WHO PAYS — Sales and use tax- $368.2 million; personal income tax—$288.3 million; corporate income tax—$270 million; corporate franchise tax—$117 million.
LEFT OVER — $12.9 million projected surplus for mid-1970.

• • •

Gov. Milliken had kind words for Michigan's cities, but little money. Page 3A.

School aid is increased $85 million in new budget. Page 4B.

Britons Can Rent Bored Soldiers

LONDON — Britain is to start a "rent-a-soldier" plan to give idle troops something to do, the government said Wednesday.

Civilians will be able to hire a soldier for a day, a week or even a month to:

• Help out in disaster areas or during emergencies.

• Work in construction, demolition or other specialized fields.

• Drive special transport units.

British Defense Minister Denis Healey pointed out that many British troops are coming back to Britain after withdrawals from foreign areas.

Healey wants to stop potential boredom and help pay the upkeep of the army.

The rental fee for a soldier was not disclosed.

Inside the Free Press

Amusements	14-15B	Food Guide	5-10C
Ann Landers	3C	Movie Guide	14-15D
Astrology	13D	Names and Faces	16D
Billy Graham	16D	Obituaries	2B
Bridge	13D	Sports	1-4D
Business News	12-16C	Stock Markets	14-16C
Camera	15B	TV-Radio	12D
Comics	13-15D	Want Ads	5-12D
Crossword Puzzle	13D	Women's Pages	1-4C
Death Notices	6D		
Drew Pearson	15A		
Earl Wilson	15A		
Editorials	8A		
Feature Page	15A		

HAVE THE FREE PRESS DELIVERED AT HOME PHONE 222-6500

Patient Wears Machine
Pump Aids Cancer Fight

BY BOYCE RENSBERGER
Free Press Science Writer

A simple windup pump that delivers cancer-killing drugs directly to tumors, bypassing other vulnerable parts of the body, is proving to be highly successful, a Detroit researcher said Wednesday.

The pump, powered by a device similar to a windup clock motor, hangs from a cord around the patient's neck. It pumps the drug through a tube leading into a blood vessel that supplies blood to the tumor area.

The device, which many Detroit-area hospitals expect to begin using, overcomes one of the major problems of drug treatment for cancer.

Drugs powerful enough to kill a tumor can also destroy healthy cells. In the past this was almost inevitable, because drugs had to be injected into the entire blood system. A dose strong enough to kill the tumor could be strong enough to kill other parts of the body.

But the new device permits drugs to be injected into the blood just upstream of the tumor. The cancer then gets a high concentration of the drug, soaks up much of the toxicity and lets a weaker concentration of the drug diffuse harmlessly into the rest of the body.

Dr. Melvin L. Reed, assistant professor of medicine at Wayne State University and a researcher at the Michigan Cancer Foundation's Daring Memorial Center, described the technique to doctors at a symposium in Detroit on cancer.

Older methods of treating liver cancer, for example, produced improvement in no better than 35 percent of

Turn to Page 5A, Column 1

March 23, 1969:

Berry Gordy's Motown Sound is heard around the world.

Sunday feature.

CHATTING ABOUT HIMSELF, MOTOWN, THE SUPREMES, HIS FAMILY

Exclusive: A Talk with Berry Gordy Jr.

This exclusive Free Press interview marks the first time Berry Gordy Jr., the Motown president, has ever sat down to talk—about anything and everything — to a reporting team from any publication. Bob Talbert and Lee Winfrey asked questions for the Free Press.

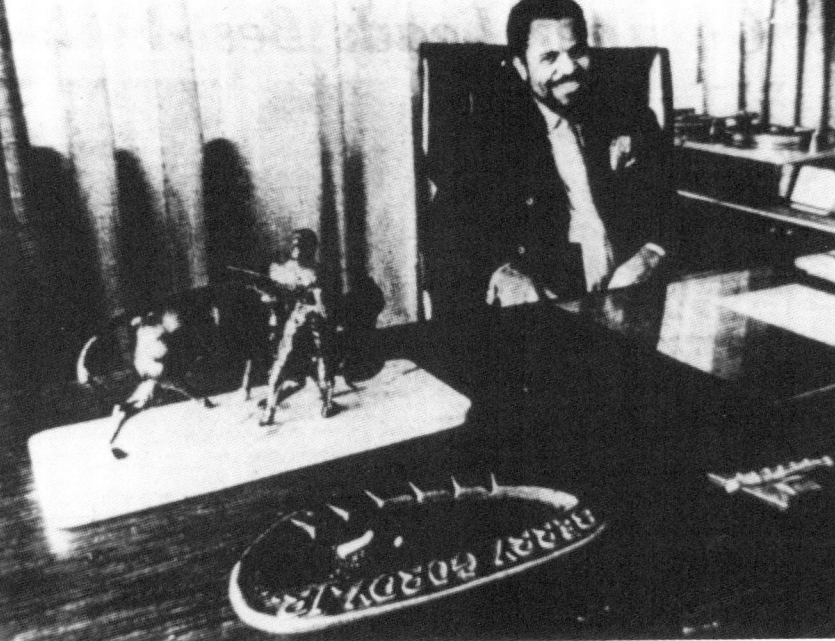

FREE PRESS: The song-writing end of the music business is the one that got you started. Have you done any serious song-writing in the last two or three years?

GORDY: Not really serious, no. I don't have time to get serious about writing any more; being a corporate president is really a full time job.

FP: Do you miss writing?

GORDY: Yes, I do. I miss all my creative activities. I fit them in whenever I can. When I started, I was doing about five per cent business and 95 per cent creative. Now I'm just the opposite. Back when we released our first record, "Way Over There," by the Miracles, we sold 60,000 and that was a mammoth hit for us. It was the first record that we'd released nationally. Now, of course, on a release of a Miracles record, in the first 30 minutes we have done a few hundred thousand.

FP: A lot of music critics and soothsayers say the Motown Sound for a few years was more mechanical than it was artistic. In other words, it seemed like Motown was just a factory turning out hit after hit after hit.

GORDY: Well, we disagree with the critics on that and obviously the public did too. Of course, there are a lot of performers who just mimic other performers. There's something lacking in this approach and the public can smell it out.

FP: You can't fool the public?

GORDY: Well, I wouldn't say that exactly. Many people do. You just can't do it for a long period of time.

FP: There have been some published reports recently to the effect that Mafia figures have some interest in Motown. Can you comment on these rumors?

GORDY: Well, there's no truth to them at all. I have never been approached by anyone whom I would consider Mafia in any way and I know a lot of people in and out of the record business. There's absolutely no truth to the rumor. We have had a policy of ignoring rumors generally because our business is really one that creates them.

FP: You have had almost as many hit rumors as hit records, haven't you?

GORDY: I can't steal that line but I will use it in the future. That's really a great line.

FP: There were reports that some syndicate figures were attempting to move in on recording contracts, perhaps two years ago, and one of the persons mentioned was Smokey Robinson. Have underworld figures, let's say, or syndicate figures ever tried to move in and get part of Smokey Robinson's contract or are an agent or something like that?

GORDY: Smokey Robinson has been approached by many people. He has been offered a million dollars cash, he's been offered all kinds of deals to leave Motown. And most of the time, he simply calls me or calls someone connected with the company and tells us about the offer. We have never made any effort to find out who and why.

He has never been under any type of pressure, because Smokey Robinson is not the type of person that you can put pressure on. He just doesn't give a damn about pressure. We all came up in the same area here in Detroit, the lower east side what is now called the ghetto, and it would be extremely hard for anybody to pressure us into doing anything, because we started with little or nothing. But our people have been approached. Some of them, of course, have not been as honorable as Smokey Robinson, but they are being approached all the time. We can only hope that they will try and be honorable enough to live up to their present contracts with us.

Smokey Robinson is perhaps our most consistent artist. He is the only artist who can have a record in the top ten that no one has ever heard of. We sometimes refer to him as the Honorable Underground. He simply has this cult of people that buy Smokey Robinson records — and every record he's put out has been on the charts, every record for the last ten years. That's pretty amazing. He's what you call a bread-and-butter artist.

FP: Mr. Gordy, where are you living now? You have this handsome home up here at Boston and Hamilton, I believe, but I understand you live mostly in California.

GORDY: That's correct.

FP: Any particular reason?

GORDY: Well, mainly my television and movie interests out there. And it's just an evolution of Motown. No real specific definite reason other than that I like it and I have a chance to move Motown into other areas.

FP: When you talk about moving Motown, you don't mean moving from Detroit?

GORDY: No. I do not mean moving it at all physically.

FP: Where is your home in Los Angeles?

GORDY: It's in the Hollywood Hills.

FP: Do you use the home here at all?

GORDY: Yes. I'm in town now and I intend to come back each year because Detroit has what we consider natural resources. We have never been able to get the sound anywhere in the world that we get here in Detroit.

FP: Is it the studios?

GORDY: Well, studios and the feeling. It's the feeling, too, of the artists and the people. It's just one of those things that clicks. The chemical contents of the people...

FP: Good vibrations?

GORDY: Yes. Generally when artists leave Detroit, they get different perspectives or something. We haven't been really able to analyze it, but Detroit is basically a sincere area and somehow it affects the ingredients of the things we're doing.

FP: Has the record industry kept Negroes from rising into corporate management and are you the only Negro to make it?

GORDY: There have been others, I think. As a matter of fact, a man who's presently working for us, Mr. Abner, was the president of a black record company called Veejay. They were the first company to handle Beatle records. However, they got into financial difficulty and went bankrupt. There are some other black companies. I don't think any are as successful as Motown.

FP: Was starting from scratch easier than working for somebody else's record company?

GORDY: No, it was never easier, never easier. I could have been very comfortable as, you know, the vice-president of another company making a tremendous salary without some of the headaches and problems that have faced me over the past ten years. No, I'm not overjoyed.

FP: Could you tell us how much of Motown you own yourself and how much additionally is held by your family?

GORDY: I'd rather not get into stock arrangements. For all practical purposes, I own Motown completely.

FP: The most sensational of your hit rumors and probably the most repeated is the one about the breakup of the Supremes, with Diana Ross going out on her own as a single artist. Would you care to comment?

GORDY: It's a rumor, but the prospects for it are in the air. It's hard to say. Diana Ross is being offered so many things. She doesn't want to leave the Supremes, but she tries to look at all sides of this. We have not come up with a definite decision about what is going to happen. Any day, of course, there could be something. There are two or three ways we can go about this thing, but then, Diana does not want to let her fans down.

FP: Do you want to get into any new areas of music—hard rock, for instance?

GORDY: Only if it's economically a sound thing to do. Many people that I talk to are amazed that we own a tune called "For Once In My Life." This tune can be done any way, psychedelic pop, many ways. Tony Bennett did it as a straight pop thing, Stevie Wonder did it as a rock and roll pop thing, Motown's Ron Miller wrote this tune. I said, well, if I put out "For Once In My Life" on our label, they're going to say, "This is just a rock and roll song, it's new." So I said, why don't we come up with another company name that sounds sort of, you know, very standard. So we called the company Stein & Van Stock and let it publish "For Once In My Life." And when the public heard it, they said, this song's been around for 20 years, great song.

FP: It sounds like a standard.

GORDY: It does sound like a standard. See, the writers of today can write tremendous songs – as good or better than some of the writers of yesteryear. But in a lot of cases they are not respected, and certainly rock and roll writers from Detroit aren't respected. Who ever heard of a rock and roll writer from Detroit writing a standard? This is what happened, and the tune became a big smash. It's been recorded by all kinds of artists.

FP: Who were the singers and musicians that you used to listen to in the old days?

GORDY: Well, jazz people. I was a Charlie Parker fan, Miles Davis. And I had this record shop down here called 3D Record Mart, and it was a very hip place. We had all the jazz albums and everything. And these people kept coming in asking for the Dominoes, Fats Domino or Johnny Ace and I couldn't understand all these droves of people coming in. I said to myself, "Hey, wait a minute, you better get some of this stuff." And I tried to sell Miles Davis. I said, "Hey look, Miles is swinging, Miles is too much, dig this." Stan Kenton was coming out with doo da da dum. They said, "Hey, look, we want Billy Ward and the Dominoes, we want B. B. King. You got a B. B. King record?"

Well, I'd heard these at parties and I always sort of looked down on them because I always figured I was sort of ultra-hip as a kid, you know, and what's this, let's listen to some jazz. But at a party somewhere they had all this other music going.

FP: At the time they called that race music, didn't they?

GORDY: Yes, rhythm and blues. I didn't know what R & B was. I didn't know until after I started in the record shop, then I finally started trying to work it. It was too late because we were doomed, we were on our way to bankruptcy and when I did finally get R & B, it was too late. But I thought about it and when I started writing tunes, I found out that's what I really felt. I didn't really feel the jazz. I tried to play jazz, I really tried. All my life I was always sort of a second jazzer. Whenever they needed another man, they let me sit in and play at some chords. But my feeling was really what I'd heard in church and the beats. Whenever I found myself playing, I really had the funky beat.

FP: Were you self taught?

GORDY: Yes, basically. I took a year of music. But then I really started feeling this beat, this feeling. So I started writing this kind of thing, and when I wrote for Jackie Wilson I was just writing what I felt and putting the beat to it. Then I met the Miracles, Smokey Robinson came to my office one day and he was a fantastic young writer who later became my protege in writing. Years back, I used to give music classes to our writers and producers and teach them what I knew. And many of them turned out fantastically well.

FP: How long have you been wearing the beard?

GORDY: I started wearing the beard probably a year ago. I went to the Bahamas for a week's rest and I didn't shave at all while I was there. And so I just said, well, I'm not going to shave for a while.

FP: Here in Detroit some businesses, like Kresge's, are moving to the suburbs, and they cite crime as one of the reasons. You have moved the opposite, you have moved Motown right downtown. Has crime been a problem, has security been an added problem?

GORDY: I have not had any real problems here that I know of. I can't compare us with other businesses. We have social problems as much as anyone else, probably more, actually.

FP: But you're pleased with your location and pleased that you made the move from Grand Boulevard?

GORDY: Oh, yes, we're very pleased we made the move. Mainly because of the fact that we're in one building rather than eight. We have so many advantages here that it would take quite a few disadvantages to disenchant us. One big problem is that we have almost outgrown the new building. Things have sort of mushroomed in many areas.

FP: Could you give us some idea of what Berry Gordy's time is like and how it is spent?

GORDY: With women, for one thing. (Smiles broadly.) And I play golf. I play a golf a lot. I've played it for three years, and I love it.

FP: How big is the course at your house?

GORDY: It's a nine-hole golf course. We have about four holes but we shoot back and forth and around to make it a nine-hole course. Very cleverly designed by my brother Robert. I get a chance to play more golf on the West Coast. The people out there are not, of course, as warm as the people in Detroit.

FP: You have something of a reputation as a gambler, too.

GORDY: Well, I have been gambling all my life one way or the other. But I am not much a big gambler. I gamble for recreation, not to win money.

FP: You don't need to.

GORDY: No. Whenever I go to Las Vegas I play and sometimes when I go to the Bahamas I play. But just for enjoyment, because whenever I go any place where it's warm, I play golf. That's my big thing. At this stage I would not consider myself a heavy gambler.

FP: Your International Management Company—is that the overall corporate parent now?

GORDY: No. Motown is a separate corporation. Jobete is a separate corporation.

FP: How many corporations are there?

GORDY: I don't know. We're pulling them together and moving them out and I'm really not certain. We have three main operations here, and we have a holding company and some other things. Mainly we manufacture records, we publish music and we develop artists. Those are our three main functions. Now, we call the companies a lot of different names. For instance, Motown has Tamla Records, Gordy Records, Soul Records. That's all Motown. We did that label-splitting years back. People told us we couldn't possibly have three hits at one time and we felt we could, so we changed the names of the labels and did have three hits at one time.

FP: You're one of the richest young entrepreneurs in the country and you've gone from poor to rich in a short period of time. Has it changed Berry Gordy?

GORDY: I hope so.

FP: What are the things that tell you you've changed?

GORDY: I think being at the top makes you more of a person, it makes you a wiser person. When you can sit on top and look at a situation and see all its angles, it makes you a wiser person.

You know, we have a very interesting situation here because of the black and white elements. It's gratifying seeing the education that each has received from the other, and it certainly has made me wiser trying to understand the problems involved. I can see both sides and look at it all from an objective view. So I have changed my understanding of a lot of things and I can see that many problems are simply caused by their context.

FP: What is the single thing that has given you the greatest pride and sense of achievement?

GORDY: The single thing, well, this is hard, but I think the single thing is the effect on my father and mother, who are both living, you know. I think that's the single thing that gives me the most pleasure.

The success story of Detroiter Berry Gordy Jr. has become a legend in its own time. He is founder and president of Motown Record Corp., and creator of what many people have called Michigan's second most famous export — The Detroit Sound. Gordy is a monumental example of how a black man can make it big in American society, and his company is on the verge of launching itself into other — and perhaps bigger — ventures.

FP: You mean because your Dad had to work hard and now he has comforts and money and things?

GORDY: No, not so much that. That's great, too, but he doesn't care about luxuries and so forth as much as he does about—

FP: —seeing his son make good?

GORDY: Well, yes. Not only that, but my parents had a lot of faith in me. My father is a very wise old man, very wise, very skeptical, very cool, very strong, very hard.

FP: What's his background?

GORDY: He's a contractor and he's always had his own business. He owned his own home on the East Side with a couple store fronts on it, and that's where I had my record shop. I never really liked to do manual labor, but I had to do it because he brought us up that way. He was a contractor and a bricklayer and he did all the work and we helped him. They paid him a little bit and he paid us less. I was a plasterer and I became a rock lath expert because he made me so good. I was very fast.

Once he had to go down South so I asked him if I could take over while he was gone. And he said, "Well, okay, but you be sure and work hard, don't waste any money," and so forth. So I took it to heart and I planned out each day so everybody would be kept working and we'd never run out of supplies. We accomplished as much in that week. When he came back I was really proud. I said, "Dad, this is the way I have arranged it, in the morning you take the supplies... and so forth and so on."

He said, "Yes, okay, go on."

Everything was great except for one thing he didn't think I was working hard enough. He kept saying you have got to work—keep busy, keep busy. So I got disenchanted. I knew I had to do something else.

FP: Is it true that all your family chipped in to get you started?

GORDY: You might say that. I borrowed $700 from the family savings organization. We all had put money into the savings account and I borrowed $700 to make a master recording.

FP: That must double your pleasure now that it's succeeded?

GORDY: Sure, especially as regards those who voted against me.

FP: Do you still go to your father and ask for advice?

GORDY: I don't have to ask for it. He's always giving it to me, he's around here. As a matter of fact, He comes in and out. He's a consultant.

FP: Is there anything you'd like to say in conclusion? We appreciate this interview because, you know, we like to be proud of Motown. Motown is in Detroit and people know about Detroit because of automobiles and Motown.

GORDY: Let me mention one thing. I read something in the Sunday Free Press a few weeks ago about a shooting here that never happened. And I can understand that kind of thing from irresponsible sources but when I saw it in the Free Press, it really shocked me.

These are the kinds of things that make our job so hard, because we have criticism from everybody anyway. You said someone quit because there was a shooting here. That's bad because other people, our employees, will not want to come to Motown, agents will not want to sign their people up at Motown. They'll say if I go up there for a meeting, I might get shot. These damaging things I regret. We have enough trouble as it is. We have trouble from competitors and in some cases from our own people, singers, artists, creative people. I mean, it's rough in Detroit, it's rough in Detroit. That is a problem.

We have tried to overcome this. In fact, I'll be coming back here very shortly for the BMI Awards Dinner for R & B songs of the year, being held here for the first time on April 15th at the Pontchartrain. It's a big industry thing. It's a big thing that's going to happen here that's never happened here before. There was a final choice between Detroit and Memphis and the board decided that based on our being here they would bring the banquet to Detroit. Next year we will be the No. 1 publisher in the business and most likely the No. 1 seller of singles.

(Later, the Free Press asked Motown for its version of the incident we reported. Motown replied:

(The incident took place during a regular work day at its offices a few weeks ago. A sharp crack was heard in a room where 10 female employes were doing clerical work. The women scattered, afraid that it might have been a shot. Motown sued Detroit police were called. They made an investigation and found a hole in one window, a hole big enough to be made by a ball-bearing, by a BB gun, or a small pebble. The hole was not big enough to be made by a bullet. The police were unable to find the object that entered through the hole, and thought it must have been a BB. Nobody quit as a result of the incident.)

FP: Could you give a ballpark figure on how many millions of dollars your company is worth?

GORDY: I would hate to say. You know, a company in this day and age really cannot afford to say. We have many plans in the financial area.

FP: Like going public?

GORDY: Something like that. It would be a natural evolution and we're of a size where we can go either way. But we're interested in expansion because we feel that we're at a plateau from which, you know, we can really move. But, of course, this would depend on meetings with my associates.

FP: How old are you?

GORDY: Thirty-nine. I'm nearing 40, unfortunately. All this was a lot of fun when I was a kid.

"I was a Charlie Parker fan, Miles Davis fan. And I had this record shop down here called 3D Record Mart, and it was a very hip place. We had all the jazz albums and everything. And these people kept coming in asking for the Dominoes, Fats Domino or Johnny Ace and I couldn't understand all these droves of people coming in. I said to myself, 'Hey, wait a minute, you better get some of this stuff.'"

BERRY GORDY JR.: "My parents had a lot of faith in me. My father is a very wise old man, very wise, very skeptical, very cool, very strong, very hard."

Neil Armstrong

*'That's One Small Step for Man
—One Giant Leap for Mankind'*

—Neil Armstrong as he stepped onto moon

Edwin Aldrin

JULY 21, 1969:

The moon walk.

SUNNY
High 76-81 Low 58-64

Detroit Free Press
ON GUARD FOR 138 YEARS

Vol. 139—No. 78   Monday, July 21, 1969

METRO
Bob Talbert's Detroit
Page 15, Section A
Ten Cents

Man Walks on Moon!

Crash Averted
Man Excels Machine in Touchdown

BY RICHARD POTHIER
Knight Newspapers Writer

HOUSTON — In the end, man was on his own.

The wondrous machine he had built to ride to a safe landing on the moon just was not as versatile as man himself.

As Neil Armstrong and Buzz Aldrin descended toward the moon's craggy surface on a column of flame Sunday afternoon, the machine—built as well as modern science could build—was leading them into danger.

So, Armstrong and Aldrin stepped in to rescue Apollo 11 and perhaps save themselves. Man, even before the lunar module (LM) was built, knew the machine could not be trusted to go all the way down by itself.

Flying by hand and eye, peering through the tiny triangular windows in the lunar module Eagle, Armstrong and Aldrin saw that the Eagle's automatic targeting system was guiding them into a crater the size of a football field, filled with boulders large enough to tip them over.

So Armstrong took semi-automatic control of the spacecraft, using an alternative—computer Program 66—to glide the Eagle away from disaster. P-66, as the program is known, allows pilot control of some systems while other navigation aids continue to operate automatically.

Controlling the craft himself, through a toggle switch on the computer, Armstrong manually cut down the rate of descent. He never actually stopped the spacecraft, but slowed it to allow its forward motion—a few miles an hour—to carry it beyond the crater onto flatter land.

"HE PICKED a spot he liked and set it down right there," flight director Gene Kranz said shortly after the heart-stopping 12-minute, 39-

Turn to Page 7A, Column 1

Dramatic moment for astronauts after planting U.S. flag on moon

First Words from the Moon

With the calmness of two commuters taking a bus ride, and their voices only occasionally betraying their emotions, astronauts Neil Armstrong and Col. Edwin Aldrin gave the world a guided tour of the moon Sunday night.

With mounting excitement, millions listened as the taciturn civilian and the slightly more voluble Air Force colonel talked each other down to and across the moon's pitted face.

Sitting on the moon, only minutes away from stepping onto it, the two voyagers talked:

ALDRIN—Sure takes it (the pressure) a long time to get all the way down, doesn't it?
ALDRIN—Let me see if it'll open now.
ARMSTRONG—OK.
ALDRIN—It's unlocked . . . it'll pop open . . .
HOUSTON—What is your status on the hatch opening? Over.
ARMSTRONG—Everything is go here. We're just waiting for cabin pressure to bleed to a low enough pressure to open the hatch.
HOUSTON—We're showing a relatively static pressure on your cabin. You think you can open the hatch with a pressure of about point 1 PSI.
ARMSTRONG—We're gonna try it.
HOUSTON—Roger.
ARMSTRONG—The hatch is coming open.
ALDRIN — Now up by the DSKY, forward now. Now you're clear. Forward toward me. Plenty of me. You're lined up nicely. Toward me a little bit. Down. OK, now you're clear. You're touching the first edge a little.
ARMSTRONG—What edge?
ALDRIN—Roll to the left. Now you're clear. You're lined up on the platform. To the right a little bit. That's good. Roll left.
ALDRIN—OK, now I'm gonna kick past here.
ALDRIN—OK, you're not quite squared away. Roll right a little. Now you're even.
ARMSTRONG—That's OK.

Turn to Page 6A, Column 1

SWEATING OUT the moon landing at Mission Control is astronaut Alan L. Bean, a member of the next Apollo flight.

Inside the Free Press

Amusements	10A	Drew Pearson	15A
Ann Landers	8C	Editorials	4A
Astrology	7D	Feature Page	15A
Billy Graham	10D	Movie Guide	8-9D
Bridge	7D	Names and Faces	10D
Business News	6C	Obituaries	12A
Comics	7-9D	Sports	1-6D
Consumers	5C	Television	13A
Crossword Puzzle	7D	Want Ads	2-8B
Death Notices	2B	Women's Pages	1-4C

Action Line---Page 3A

Down Ladder To a Dream

While the people of earth watched a quarter-million miles away, man set his foot on the moon.

At 9:56:31 p.m. Detroit time Sunday, July 20, Apollo 11 commander Neil A. Armstrong stepped from the last rung on the ladder that led him downward to realization of a dream as old as humanity.

Stiffly, he said the first words: "That's one small step for man—one giant leap for mankind."

For two hours and 13 minutes, Armstrong walked, talked and worked on a land that may never before have known life. An American flag, stiffened with a rod to stand out in the airless lunar environment, watched the boy from Wapakoneta talk his buddy, Edwin (Buzz) Aldrin, down the Eagle's ladder to join him on the moon.

At times, they seemed almost like schoolboys lumbering about in their bulky suits and bouncing in the light pull of gravity.

An anxious planet watched and slowly relaxed. When the two men returned safely to their ship, they were crowding the deadline and seemed not to want to return.

The mood was in sharp contrast to the tension that greeted Armstrong's abrupt appearance in the living rooms of the world.

Moments earlier, Armstrong had emerged from the tiny door in the spaceship Eagle, shuffling backward across the porch and down the ladder. He pulled the D-ring that yanked open the scientific-experiments package and suddenly, on television screens throughout the world, an estimated half-billion people saw man on the moon — upside down.

At Mission Control, technicians flipped the electronic image right side up and Armstrong's figure took on shape and form, his left foot bouncing up and down on the surface as he made sure he could reclimb the ladder if necessary.

ARMSTRONG stepped first onto one of the four saucer-like footpads of his spacecraft, standing in the bitter cold of the 260-degree below zero lunar shadows.

He said the surface was "fine and powdery. I can pick it up loosely with my toe. It does adhere in fine layers like powdered charcoal to the sole and inside of my boots."

Armstrong picked up a piece of the moon and stuffed it in his pocket, making sure that Apollo 11 could not return home empty-handed. He moved slowly and carefully in the moon's gravity, only one-sixth that of the earth, but had no difficulty doing so.

Looking at the moonscape, he said: "It has a stark beauty all of its own. It's much like the desert of the

Turn to Page 6A, Column 2

Moonshot Awesome To Earth

LONDON — (AP) — Crowds screamed joyously in Trafalgar Square, people danced in Chile, a Russian yelled, "Hooray."

Almost everyone on earth was somehow touched by man's arrival on the moon.

Pope Paul praised America's three astronauts as "conquerers of the moon" minutes after the Eagle spacecraft touched down on the lunar surface. He said man faces "the expanse of endless space and a new destiny."

Soviet media did not dramatize the landing. Reports of the touchdown were buried in Soviet television and radio broadcasts behind other news of the day.

But individual Muscovites cheered and expressed congratulations to Americans in the Soviet capital. "Hooray," one yelled. Another shouted "It's a great day."

In the war-torn Middle East, Arab radio stations interrupted their bulletins of a major air battle over the Suez Canal to acclaim the event and praise Edwin Aldrin and Neil Armstrong for "making history."

THE STREETS of some of the world's largest cities — Mexico City, Oslo, Belgrade, Rome — were nearly deserted as millions stayed home glued to their television screens.

One Yugoslav teen-ager said: "They have stolen the romance out of the moon and it will never be the same again. Now the moon is real, and lovers won't have it for themselves alone any more."

In the middle of a war broadcast from Beirut the announcer said: "Ladies and gentlemen. The moon is now within man's grasp." Then Ferous, one of the Middle East's top singers, began crooning "Oh, Moon, I am with you."

Poles jammed the lobby of the U.S. Embassy in Warsaw, while a crowd of hundreds applauded outside.

In Guayaquil, Ecuador, fire-

Turn to Page 2A, Column 5

Police Chief Arena

Kennedy's Crash Still A Puzzle

Special to the Free Press

EDGARTOWN, Mass.—The Edgartown police chief said Sunday he will attempt to prosecute Sen. Edward M. Kennedy for leaving the scene of an accident in which a pretty Washington secretary was killed.

The senator remained in seclusion Sunday after issuing one brief statement which still left several major questions unanswered.

Kennedy has admitted driving the car that plunged into a pond sometime before 1 a.m. Saturday, drowning Mary Jo Kopechne, a 28-year-old blonde who formerly worked for his late brother Robert.

Kennedy did not report the accident for more than eight hours. He described himself as "in a state of shock" and a family physician said Sunday he suffered a mild concussion in the accident.

"I am firmly convinced that there was no negligence involved," said the Edgartown police chief, Dominic J. Arena. Arena sent Kennedy formal notice, however, that he will seek to prosecute him for leaving the scene.

ARENA SENT Kennedy notice of his complaint by reg-

Turn to Page 2A, Column 2

Other Moon Stories

Astronauts go exploring on the moon. Back Page.

Astronauts' wives lead cheers. Page 7A.

President Nixon calls lunar landing "the greatest moment of our time." Page 9A.

Michael Collins, the loneliest astronaut. Page 11A.

Wapakoneta goes wild for favorite son Armstrong. Page 12A.

Two wives go to church, but it was a private day for Jan Armstrong. Page 14A.

The heartbeats that will be remembered. Page 8C.

Now, to Get Back Down to Earth . . .

BY RICHARD POTHIER
Knight Newspapers Writer

HOUSTON — Beyond man's greatest adventure, a critical step remains. The men of Apollo 11 have traveled to another world. Now they must come home.

Barring adjustments in the Apollo time sequence, Neil Armstrong and Edwin Aldrin will attempt at 12:51 p.m. Detroit time Monday to fire the tiny engine that will power them to rendezvous with the command module Columbia, circling in orbit 69 miles above.

The Voyage of Apollo 11

If the engine does not fire, the astronauts are doomed. No rescue is possible. The command module cannot land.

The LM ascent engine is one of the most reliable in the world, every part and process duplicated twice to provide a back-up system to counter any breakdown. Its thrust is only 3,500 pounds, barely enough to lift a car on earth but capable of lifting six times that weight on the moon.

The ascent engine is located in the top half of the lunar module. The bottom half will serve as the launch pad for the Eagle's upper section and will stay behind on the moon.

The engine burns liquid fuels — volatile compounds that burst into violent flame when they touch each other. They're called "hypergolic" fuels and are the most reliable rocket fuels in the world.

Instead of worrying about providing a flame or some other ignition source to keep the rocket going, the National Aeronautics and Space Administration (NASA)

Turn to Page 6A, Column 1

OCT. 16, 1969:

Detroiters protest the Vietnam war.

RAIN
Cloudy and Cool
Highs 52-58 Lows 35-40

Detroit Free Press
ON GUARD FOR 138 YEARS

Vol. 139—No. 165   Thursday, October 16, 1969

METRO
Stocks Mixed
Trading Heavy
See Page 10, Section D
• • •
Ten Cents

Millions Join Unique Peace Bid
War Protests Resound Across U.S.

Action Line
Dial 222-6464

Action Line solves problems, gets answers, cuts red tape, stands up for your rights. Write Action Line, Box 881, Detroit, Mich. 48231. Or dial 222-6464 between 8:30 a.m. and 4:30 p.m. Monday through Friday.

I paid $75 to Skyroamers Ltd. for membership in their "fabulous travel club," which supposedly owns a plane and schedules trips at low rates. Well, I've yet to see the plane, let alone the world, and their phone's disconnected. What happened?—P. L. Mt. Pleasant.

You're now a Sky Hopper. Skyroamers, a New York flying club, sold 400 memberships in the Detroit area before they realized they couldn't afford to expand. A clause in the contract says membership fees are non-refundable. Skyroamers sold your names for five bucks each to a new club, the Sky Hoppers, who are giving you all free memberships. They have a real DC7 parked at Metro and offices at 24600 Plymouth Rd. (537-2930). First trip to Miami leaves today. Between now and Christmas, plane will fly to the Bahamas, Reno, Acapulco, Mexico and Venezuela at less than half commercial rates.

Please help me win $10 from a nonbeliever who says there are only half a million Volkswagens in the U.S. I say it's closer to a million.
—V.J., St. Clair Shores.

Bug invasion is even greater than that. Beetle people say they've sold 3½ million in the U.S. since 1949, when the first two chugged into Big Three country. They were a matched pair black, said a Volkswagen spokesman fondly. Company's been searching futilely for them for ten years (Price up to $110). Guggenheim was official photographer for Robert Kennedy's campaign, sifted through 50,000 feet of film, including some from the Kennedy family, to make "Remembered." Premiere showing at the convention brought a standing ovation and spontaneous singing of the "Battle Hymn of the Republic," which Andy Williams sang at Kennedy's funeral.

Is it true we have to pay workmen's compensation for bands that play in our bar? My insurance man says it's a new law and my premium will be $250. I don't consider those kids my employes and I can't see how they'll hurt themselves unless they get a finger stuck in their instruments.—Mrs. E. J., Flint.

Law's the same as always, but since the state upped workmen's compensation benefits in 1965, insurance companies are taking more notice. Besides your regular employes, you're responsible for band members while they're in the bar if the group doesn't have its own insurance. Before 1965, an injured employe without dependents could collect $33 a week, and one with five or more dependents, $57 a week. Now it's up to $69 and $98. Best way to get around stiff premiums is to hire only bands that carry their own workmen's comp.

Black walnuts are ruining me! I'm nuts about them but I can't get the black stains off my hands. I'm a salesman and my boss won't hear of me calling on customers in this condition.—W. J. A., Ypsilanti.

Use strong powdered bleach (chlorine or sodium perborate) and water. Mix to a thick paste. Wash it off quickly as you can. Folks don't mind stains if they sell black walnut timber. Price is $2 for a square foot, an inch thick. During World War I wood was used for propellers, and in World War II demand for walnut gunstocks drained the country's supply. Led to launching in 1943 of a drive by American Walnut Manufacturers Association to plant walnut seedlings over the entire country.

The Act wouldn't give our pet raccoon a rabies shot because we don't have a permit from the state to keep him. Where do you get one?—E. R., Garden City.

Usually, for $1 a year from the Department of Natural Resources, Game Division, Mason Bldg., Lansing. But since you didn't get your 'coon from a game breeder, the state won't give you one. State says animals found in the wild belong to everybody and must be allowed to run free. Give yours to a local conservation officer, who'll turn it loose if it can fend for itself, put it in a zoo if it can't. Even a permit wouldn't entirely clear you with the law. Garden City ordinance says you can't keep wild animals in captivity.

Anti-war marchers swarm down Griswold Wednesday between Fort and Congress streets

Detroiters Jam Kennedy Square

Thousands of Detroiters, most of them young people, jammed Kennedy Square in downtown Detroit Wednesday in a Moratorium Day anti-Vietnam war protest.

The temper of the crowd changed frequently during the day-long demonstration, turning alternately from youthful exuberance to sober seriousness. For some, the day was a chance to finally protest the war on a personal basis. For others, it was a golden opportunity to skip school.

Police estimates of the crowd ranged up to 13,000.

THE SMASHING of windows in several downtown stores and the attempted looting of a sporting goods store on Griswold prompted Gov. Milliken to put 1,600 to 2,000 National Guard troops on alert in the area.

The alert was called off at 9:30 p.m., seven hours later. Neither guardsmen nor state police who also were alerted were required to control the sporadic outbreaks.

Detroit police were held four hours beyond their normal 4 p.m. quitting time. They were on a "tactical alert" with policemen in outlying parts of the city ready to come downtown if help were needed.

Several incidents of looting and window smashing took place after police ordered the moratorium rally in Kennedy square ended at 6 p.m. But by 8:30 p.m. downtown Detroit was quiet.

During the rally, and at a score of other smaller rallies across the city, speakers denounced U.S. involvement in the Vietnam War and called for immediate troop withdrawal.

REP. JOHN Conyers, D-Mich., told the crowd he will vote against all military appropriation in Congress "until the Nixon administration shows some re-organization of priorities and some humanities."

William Keast, president of Wayne State University who led a march of 5,000 persons from the school to Kennedy Square, called the draft system a "profound error."

He urged his youthful audience to broaden the peace movement by bringing their parents and friends into it.

"This war should be stopped because it is draining America of its resources and of its goodwill and of its confidence and faith," Keast said.

A potentially explosive confrontation between demonstrators and police came shortly before 6 p.m. when a crowd of about 75 young Negroes pushed into a plate-glass window at the Body Shop, a mod clothing store at 515 Park, then invaded the store.

The owner said the group stole $1,000 to $1,500 worth of merchandise.

AFTER THE Kennedy Square rally, police, who remained well disciplined throughout the rally, had several small fights with lingerers when they ordered the square cleared.

About 200 youths left the square and began walking in a group north on Woodward.

Several ran into the Sanders candy store at 1037 Woodward and came out with looted baked goods and candy.

In the next block, they knocked down a middle-aged

Turn to Page 11A, Column 1

The Moratorium Story

In Michigan, Moratorium Day drew thousands of people to demonstrations in all major cities. Page 3A.

Senate leaders assail North Vietnamese letter supporting Moratorium Day. Page 1B.

Moratorium activities in the suburbs were generally successful. Page 6B.

Seven major peace plans are floating around Washington. Page 9B.

Some GIs wear black armbands in support of Moratorium Day. Page 16B.

More pictures on Back Page.

A Point of View
Youth's Protest: Innocence Is Lost

MEDITATION and the flag and a quiet moment during the Moratorium Day rally settle over this young couple.

BY GARY BLONSTON
Free Press Staff Writer

America, especially young America, has lost a lifetime of innocence since those halcyon days last year when Gene McCarthy was going to make everything better.

The thousands of young people who massed in downtown Detroit Wednesday have outrun their 1968 delusions.

The Washington cast has changed, but the war goes on, and the debate has turned into a fight, regularly on the campuses, occasionally in the streets. McCarthy talks about 1972 when he talks at all.

BUT THE people in Kennedy Square talked about Now. This Week. This Month. And underlying their presence and their anti-war outrage was something different from democratic hope.

The serious ones talked about collision—between alienated and established, young and old, in and out, militant and pacifist. For all their exuberance, they were grim, and straight people by and large kept their distance in homes and offices and on the fringes of the crowd.

It was not necessarily the issue that kept them away. Sprinkled through the throng were plenty of neckties — though there were more Roman collars — and women with children, some baby-buggy new.

It was, as one rally speaker said, fear and apathy, plus the requirements of a job and maybe an aversion to the style of the young New Left that kept the Detroit moratorium rally from swelling in numbers sufficient to corroborate pollsters' readings of war opposition.

The language in the crowd of young whites and blacks was rough and the revolutionary sloganeering of some of the kids drew only silence

Turn to Page 12A, Column 1

Debates Point Up Division

Little Violence Is Reported

From New York Times and AP

Demonstrations ranging from noisy street rallies to silent prayer vigils, and involving a broad spectrum of the population, were held across the nation Wednesday in display of the deep and growing public opposition to the war in Vietnam.

Only scattered incidents of violence marred the outpourings of the crowds, which small some vast.

The black armband was the standard symbol.

THE VIETNAM moratorium — which began as a national protest by college students and came to include such diverse groups as the United Automobile Workers and the Pittsburgh City Council—was called an overwhelming success by its planners, the youthful members of the Vietnam Moratorium Committee.

And it demonstrated the American divisions in American society that have been worsened, if not created, by the prolonged American involvement in Southeast Asia.

The demonstrations spawned counter-protests in some areas and some supporters of the war who had been quiet for months spoke out in anger.

It was the largest of many public protests against the Vietnam war, and historians in the Library of Congress said that as a nationally coordinated anti-war demonstration it was unique.

There was no way to estimate immediately the number of persons involved, but—counting the demonstrators, the children who stayed out of school, workers who did not report for their jobs, those who did and wore armbands, and those who prayed in homes and churches — possibly millions participated.

The demonstrations drew largely on students and other youths, the middle class and professional groups. Such unions as the UAW and the United Shoeworkers of America endorsed the moratorium. In a number of communities, blue-collar workers made up the active opposition.

REGIONALLY, the biggest and most enthusiastic demonstrations occurred in the Northeast and on the West Coast. For example, the police in Boston estimated that close to 100,000 jammed the Boston Common.

In the South and Middle West, the demonstrations tended to be somewhat subdued.

Although some communities were cool or hostile to the moratorium, it reached unexpected places with unexpected impact, such as conservative, pro-war Orange County, Cal., the birthplace of President Nixon.

The concrete campus of California State College, which had never seen a demonstration, echoed with chants of "Peace now" and "Hell no, we won't go!"

Across the nation, the mo-

Turn to Page 2A, Column 1

UAW Strikes AMC Plants After Talks Break Down

RACINE — The United Auto Workers (UAW) early Thursday struck American Motors Corp. auto plants in Milwaukee and Kenosha, Wis., where the two sides failed to reach agreement on a new contract.

The strike involved some 9,000 production and maintenance workers in the two cities. The walkout was delayed a day at the firm's plant in Brampton, Ontario, because the contract there expires a day later.

Company and union negotiators recessed contract talks until 9 a.m. Thursday after failing to come anywhere near a settlement in negotiations that opened last August.

THE UAW'S two-year contract with American Motors expires at 12:01 a.m. Thursday in the Wisconsin plants. Picket lines went up at the struck plants where only a few hundred employes were on duty on the night shift.

The company made two non-contract offers Wednesday.

The first was a two-year offer carrying an estimated 56 cents-an-hour increase in wage and fringe benefits. The union rejected that offer saying it would settle for nothing less than 12 months.

The company then made a second offer for a one-year pact worth 36 cents an hour. This offer included a three percent — or nine cents-an-hour — wage increase on Nov. 25 and an immediate raise of five cents an hour for production workers and 15 cents an hour for skilled tradesmen.

These increases would have brought AMC workers up to levels of the Big Three auto companies.

In addition the offer provided for eight cents-an-hour cost-of-living increase and for three-cents-an-hour in additional contributions for the Supplemental Unemployment Benefit (SUB) fund.

The second offer also included an 11th paid holiday.

The big disagreement reportedly was over pension and insurance benefits.

Inside the Free Press

Amusements	17B	Death Notices	12C	Sports	1-8D
Ann Landers	3C	Earl Wilson	19A	Stock Markets	10-12D
Astrology	12D	Editorials	8A	Television	14D
Billy Graham	18D	Feature Page	19A	Want Ads	11-19C
Bridge	15D	Food Guide	6-10C	Women's Pages	1-5C
Business News	9-12D	Movie Guide	16-17D		
Camera	12-13D	Names and Faces	18D	HAVE THE FREE PRESS	
Comics	15-17D	Obituaries	6B	DELIVERED AT HOME	
Crossword Puzzle	15D	Opinion	8C	PHONE 222-6500	

SOCIAL JUSTICE CONCERNED HIM MOST
Reuther: A Born Battler for Labor's Causes

MAY 11, 1970:

Remembrances of UAW leader Walter Reuther, who dies in a plane crash in northern Michigan.

By JAMES DEWEY
Free Press Staff Writer

Walter Philip Reuther, one of the foremost leaders of the American labor movement and the innovative chief architect of union commitment to social justice, was born on the eve of Labor Day, Sept. 1, 1907, in Wheeling, W. Va.

Bred in the rough - and - tumble of the organizing efforts of the Depression years he welded an innate shrewdness and mental brilliance to a fiery rhetoric to serve a singleness of purpose.

THE SON OF a socialist German immigrant, he was, in the words of his brother, Victor, "born into the labor movement." He lived every minute of it.

For nearly two decades Mr. Reuther was a dominating force on the American labor and political scene.

He was first and foremost a labor organizer with an overpowering sense of social justice that shaped his controversial, temperamental, combustible, even at times unrelenting character.

To the scorn of some critics and the admiration of supporters he was a voice of conscience crying out in matchless oratory on every problem of contemporary America — peace, disarmament, civil rights, dissent, student unrest, housing, education and health.

He preached that the bread box was inseparable from the ballot box.

"You can," he said, "win a principle or a program in the bargaining room one day and lose it the next in the legislative halls."

It was to prevent the erosion of worker gains that he developed a political-action arm of his 1.8 million member United Automobile, Aerospace and Agricultural Implement Workers union (commonly known as the United Auto Workers union). And it was a testament to his political effectiveness that he helped reshape Michigan politics and wielded extensive power in Washington.

He was a democrat among autocrats of labor.

At a skilled trades conference in Cincinnati last year he was walking down a hall in the convention hotel with Regional Director Marcellius Ivory, a Negro, who had had a fatiguing day.

MR. REUTHER noticed the fatigue in the face of the black man. "Marc," he said, "You have had a rough day. Let me carry your bag."

At the UAW convention in Atlantic City last month facing his first opposition as UAW president in 21 years, he waived convention rules to let the opposition present its case.

If the demonstration that followed his nomination was contrived it was nevertheless enthusiastic, enough so to attract the attention of veteran labor newspaper reporters who had passed up Mr. Reuther's keynote speech but returned to marvel at the acceptance.

They saw Mr. Reuther willingly pose with delegates for pictures and, severe as he was in his personal life, even with a leggy blond delegate who put an arm around him, grinning broadly and turning so she could be photographed with the union chief.

And reporters saw for the first time in memory rank and file delegates lined up at the rostrum to get Mr. Reuther's autograph.

Yet he sought to dispell any hint of the veneration some supporters sought to cloak him in and was annoyed when delegates twice addressed him from the floor as "Mr. Reuther."

"Please don't say that," he said, admonishing them to use the convention union hall form of address: "Brother Reuther."

The broad scope of Mr. Reuther's interests and activity complicated his relationship with industrial management which preferred to deal with a union advocate with more limited aims. But it vastly enlarged the role of his union.

The UAW through its huge staff at Solidarity House, its Detroit headquarters, is active in a host of community-wide programs, to reflect Mr. Reuther's concept of the role of a labor union—an organization not only to represent the worker on the job but also to develop the "inner man."

But it was at the collective bargaining table that Mr. Reuther's impact was greatest. A leader of the UAW practically since its inception in the mid-1930s, he was the heart and brain of its impressive achievements in the post-World War II period.

IN 1948 UAW pressure with a plan by then General Motors Corp. President Charles E. Wilson brought the annual improvement factor and cost-of-living escalator clauses in auto industry contracts.

Then came pensions, insurance and broader seniority protection.

In 1955 Mr. Reuther achieved two signal victories that had enormous significance not only for the UAW but for the entire labor movement.

With the auto industry enjoying its best year in history Mr. Reuther negotiated first at the Ford Motor Co. and then at the other auto companies a supplemental unemployment benefit plan which has served as a model for dozens of other labor-management agreements.

It was Mr. Reuther's mastery of the bargaining table that once prompted GM's president Charles E. Wilson to say:

"I'd like to get in a poker game with you when the stakes weren't a billion dollars."

Later in 1955, as president of the Congress of Industrial Organizations (CIO), Mr. Reuther was a principal architect of the merger of the American Federation of Labor (AFL) and the CIO into a single organization representing 15 million of the nation's 18.5 million organized workers.

He was a prodigious worker and possessed of unflagging energy.

His day—when he was in Detroit—most often began with a study of reports and correspondence while he was being driven from his closely-guarded, Reuther-designed and largely Reuther-built home in suburban Rochester to his office in Solidarity House.

HE LUNCHED generally on a single glass of milk at his kidney-shaped desk—another product of his home woodwork shop—and he rarely finished the day's business by dinner time.

There were few vacations and even these were utilized for union business. One fishing trip remembered by an associate found Mr. Reuther showing up with a briefcase full of economic studies.

Puritan in his personal conduct, he was devoted to his wife, May, and daughters, Linda May and Elizabeth Ann. He neither smoked, nor drank, and his social activities were all but non-existent.

He bought his suits off the rack and lived simply in his creek-side home. His address was never publicized because of a 1948 assassination attempt.

A tool-and-die worker by trade and a skilled woodworker, his home was filled with his handicraft. A visitor once described the home as "early Yamasaki and late Reuther."

He spent much of his time flying to speaking engagements, union meetings or congressional or national economic meetings.

One trip he disliked was to the annual winter meeting of the AFL-CIO Executive Council, held each January or February in Miami Beach or some other southern pleasure city.

"They (executive council members) always stayed in the plush hotels in Miami Beach, discussed a few meaningless resolutions in the morning, then adjourned to spend the afternoon at the race track," he once said.

Walter Reuther: 1907-1970
Free Press Photo by Chief Photographer TONY SPINA

When Mr. Reuther was 15 he dropped out of high school to work for the Wheeling Steel Corp. as an apprentice tool and die maker.

He was fired in 1926 for organizing co-workers in a protest over Sunday and holiday work.

In February, 1926, Mr. Reuther came to Detroit. He worked for Briggs Co., General Motors, Coleman Tool and Die Co. and finally Ford, where he was employed in the tool and die room at the Rouge Plant for six years.

DURING HIS years at Ford he completed high school and went to Wayne where he organized a Social Problems Club devoted to the study of the campus Reserve Officers Training Corps (ROTC) program abolished.

He customarily returned to the AFL-CIO the expense money it advanced for trips to federation meetings. And for many years he returned thousands of dollars in speaker's fees to a scholarship fund for needy students at Wayne State University, where he studied for three years.

As a speaker he was tireless, articulate, and forceful. He was constantly in demand and, properly inspired, at a UAW convention for instance, he could talk and hold his audience for extended periods.

He was a resourceful coiner of phrases, although some suffered from repetition.

UAW demands through the years were most often characterized as "economically sound, morally right and socially responsible."

Workers, he said, too often were paid in the "wooden nickel of inflation." The nation's security at times was jeopardized by "guided missiles in the hands of misguided men."

MR. REUTHER'S training started in his early childhood. His father, Valentine, was president of the Ohio Valley Trades and Labor Assembly and for many years worked as an international organizer of the United Brewery Workers.

The father gave his four sons — Theodore (Ted); Walter, Victor and Roy — their first training in debating and public speaking.

Evenings and Sundays father and sons would often gather in an upstairs bedroom for debate on social problems.

Roy and Victor both later became officials of the UAW and Roy died in January, 1968. Theodore is an accountant for a Wheeling steel company.

Walter was the second son. A sister, Christine, now Mrs. Eugie Richey, was born in 1922.

At the new union's first convention in South Bend, Ind., he was elected to the executive board.

Thereafter for nearly five years, Mr. Reuther was in the forefront of often bloody and riotous organizational strikes. In one 12 - month period in 1936-1937 there were 825 authorized sitdown strikes in Detroit alone, plus hundreds more wildcat strikes.

The year 1937 was a decisive one for Reuther and the notorious "Battle of the Overpass" at the Ford Rouge plant gained his national publicity.

In that incident Mr. Reuther and Richard Frankensteen, a UAW official, were beaten by Ford hired toughs when they tried to distribute handbills at the plant gates.

Two years later Mr. Reuther led the important "strategy strike" at General Motors.

The brothers toured Siberia, China and Japan and somewhere on his world travels Mr. Reuther contracted malaria, a disease that was to plague him until the 1950s.

In the fall of 1935 the two brothers worked their way back to the United States as seamen on a tramp steamer.

Back in Detroit, Mr. Reuther joined the UAW, then an affiliate of the American Federation of Labor, and worked in tool and die shops.

In 1936 he was elected president of West Side Local 174, which represented workers in tool and die shops.

IN AN ASTOUNDING burst of organizing energy, Mr. Reuther boosted the local's strength from 178 to 30,000 in one turbulent year.

He was a man to be reckoned with when the UAW that year walked out of the AFL and into the newly organized CIO.

THE GM STRIKE had the additional result of destroying the rebellious Homer Martin faction which had begun setting up shop as a competing union under the AFL banner.

Martin, the UAW's first president, had been the center of bitter factional controversies from 1936 through 1939. Just a few months before the UAW's victory at GM, Martin was ousted and R.J. Thomas named as his successor.

In its early years the UAW was torn with factional strife. More than one promising young unionist lost his way in the rapid grouping and re-grouping.

But Mr. Reuther, his trained eye on the ultimate goal, kept his balance.

One of his severest struggles was with the communists, who had contributed heavily to the union's early growth and expansion.

For years Mr. Reuther and the communists had alternately fought and worked together under an uneasy truce.

A member of the UAW executive board since 1936, Mr. Reuther scored a major victory over his rivals when in 1942 he gained the vice-presidency. By 1945 he was a powerful force in the union and he started the final climb that was to win him the UAW presidency.

In mid-September, 1945, Mr. Reuther announced his plan to blockade General Motors unless it granted a 30-percent pay increase to auto workers. In his plan, the other auto manufacturers would be assisted by the union in capturing the postwar market.

It was a bold plan. Its announcement flooded Detroit with the greatest influx of out-of-town newspaper reporters the city had ever seen.

Then head of the union's GM department, Mr. Reuther battled management down to the wire and, in November, 1945, called the strike that shut down GM from coast to coast and idled nearly a half million workers for 113 long and hungry days.

With 250,000 workers on the sidewalk and a strike fund that totaled only $900,000, Mr. Reuther appealed to his friends for help. One was Mrs. Eleanor Roosevelt, wife of President Franklin D. Roosevelt.

"I was able," Mr. Reuther later recalled, "to ask Mrs. Roosevelt to head up a Citizens Committee to support the strikers and their families, and they raised from public sources a million dollars."

The strike ended just 10 days before the UAW convention in 1946. The settlement was worth 18½ cents.

Reuther did not enter the convention as a conquering hero. The strike settlement had been dictated by GM pretty much on the company's terms.

Not until three days before the convention opened in Atlantic City did he formally announce he was a candidate for the presidency. Then he suddenly attacked.

He boldly washed the union's dirty linen in public, calling Thomas an incompetent and a communist stooge.

By the narrow margin of 124 votes, Mr. Reuther led the important "strategy strike" at General Motors.

Mr. Reuther's election was both cheered and booed in a stormy scene climaxed by several fist fights on the convention floor. It was the wildest convention ever staged by the country's most tumultuous union.

In years to come Mr. Reuther would work indefatigably to oust the so-called "goons"—the bully boys and muscle men—from the UAW.

For the next 19 months after his election to the presidency Mr. Reuther was saddled with an executive board that outvoted him 14 to 8.

Balked at every turn at the top level, he zealously worked the union's precincts, aided chiefly by his brother, Victor.

The results were startling.

IN NOVEMBER, 1947, he smashed his opposition and won control of the board, 18 to 4.

The old left-wing was riddied and helpless. Never again was Mr. Reuther's supremacy in the UAW challenged.

On the CIO level, Mr. Reuther worked with Phil Murray to clean the big unions of communist influence.

In 1949 that fight was climaxed when the CIO convention bounced 12 unions, accused of communist leadership.

The struggle he waged on all fronts was not without peril to Mr. Reuther.

On the night of April 20, 1948, he was nearly assassinated.

After a UAW executive board meeting, Mr. Reuther was chatting with his wife in the kitchen of their home when a would-be assassin blasted his right arm and chest with a shotgun.

The gunman was never caught.

From that time on, Mr. Reuther's steps were shadowed by at least one, and usually two, bodyguards.

For years after the shooting Mr. Reuther's wife, May, whom he married in 1936, and their two daughters, Linda and Elizabeth, also were guarded closely.

In 1952, Mr. Reuther succeeded the late Phil Murray as president of the CIO and quickly began working with AFL President George Meany on a merger of the two labor groups.

The merger took place in December, 1955.

WHILE MR. Reuther and Meany worked well together in the early years—particularly in dealing with corrupt unions in the federation — their relationship later became unsatisfactory to Mr. Reuther.

He was impatient with what he felt was the lack of energy and initiative on the part of Meany and other AFL leaders.

The federation, he felt, was sapping its strength with petty internal arguments over jurisdiction while millions of workers were waiting for organization.

In 1968, charging that the AFL-CIO had stagnated under George Meany, Mr. Reuther led the auto workers out of the giant federation.

He said the AFL-CIO had failed to "organize the unorganized" and that its hierarchy ignored the pressing social problems of the day.

A bitter critic of American involvement in Vietnam, Mr. Reuther said the federation leaders were "hawks" and their support of the war policy delayed the time when the nation should face up to domestic problems.

IN JULY, 1968, Mr. Reuther and Frank E. Fitzsimmons, acting president of the 2.1 million member Teamster Union, announced formation of the Alliance for Labor Action (ALA). When two other unions subsequently joined the ALA it became a rival federation of the AFL-CIO.

Mr. Reuther was a believer in strong secondary and tertiary leadership. He envisioned the sprawling Black Lake Family Education Center as a place where the new generation could be inculcated with the trade union tradition.

The union convention last month voted to rename the Black Lake facility the Walter P. Reuther Family Education Center. But the resolution specified that the name was not to be changed until Mr. Reuther had completed his last incumbency.

The Beginning

In 1937, Walter Reuther was 30, just elected to a UAW executive board allied with the newly organized and militant CIO, and ready to go to war. The times were bloody and tumultuous as the nation's most powerful industrialists fought demands that the working man have a voice in the operation of the factories. The same year, Reuther and UAW co-officer Richard Frankensteen were beaten bloody in the famed Battle of the Overpass when they tried to distribute handbills at the gates of Ford's Rouge Plant.

JULY 16, 1970:

The slaying of three Chrysler workers sparks controversy after James Johnson claimed he acted in a psychotic rage caused by intolerable working conditions. A jury found him not guilty by reason of insanity, and Chrysler later was ordered to pay him workers' compensation.

Detroit Free Press

ON GUARD FOR 139 YEARS

Vol. 140—No. 73 — Thursday, July 16, 1970

WARM — Less Humid — Highs 78-83, Lows 57-62

METRO — Stock Market Up Sharply — See Page 8, Section D — Ten Cents

Ousted Worker Kills Three In Chrysler Plant Shooting

2 Foremen, Bystander Are Slain

Rifle Smuggled Into Building

BY JOHN GRIFFITH AND LOUIS HELDMAN
Free Press Staff Writers

A Chrysler worker, enraged over being suspended, sneaked into the company's Eldon Ave. axle plant with an M-1 carbine Wednesday and shot and killed three workers, including the foreman who laid him off for insubordination.

Witnesses said James Johnson Jr., 36, of 8859 Clarion first killed his foreman, Hugh M. Jones, 45, of 16222 Muirland.

Then he killed Gary L. Hinz, 32, of 21810 Stephens, St. Clair Shores, also a foreman, and Joseph Kowalski, 53, of 3433 Comstock, Hamtramck before he fled the plant, a brake-shoe department.

He surrendered to a UAW steward after first trying to kill the union official, who was saved because Johnson ran out of ammunition.

The union official escorted Johnson to security guards at a plant gate where Detroit police took him into custody and held him for murder. Police said he offered no resistance.

Witnesses said Johnson fired from eight to 12 bullets in the plant.

Jones and Kowalski were dead on arrival at Henry Ford Hospital. Jones had multiple gunshot wounds and Kowalski was killed by a single bullet that entered the left part of his back.

Hinz was dead on arrival at Detroit General Hospital with two gunshot wounds to the chest.

Three workers were injured slightly when they and fellow employes scrambled for cover as Johnson shot his way through the east-side factory at 6700 Lynch at the corner of Eldon.

JOHNSON, A conveyer loader in the plant's brake-shoe department, had worked at the plant since May, 1967. He had returned to his job in June after a four-month layoff.

He was suspended Wednesday for insubordination after refusing to obey orders. He was sent home at 3:47 p.m.

About an hour later Johnson showed up at the plant's east gate on Lynch and told a security guard he was late for work.

The guard called the plant general foreman and learned Johnson had been suspended and was not to be admitted to the plant. The guard took Johnson's plant badge and told him he could not enter.

Johnson went to a plant parking lot on Jordan and got into the brake-shoe department a fence.

At 4:55 p.m. he appeared in the brake-shoe department. Witnesses said they heard him ask: "Where's Jones?"

Edward Lacey, 34, of 6367 Selkirk, a worker, said later he saw Johnson when he first

Turn to Page 11A, Column 1

Legal Abortion May Cost More Than Illegal One

NEW YORK—(AP)— Abortions performed under New York's two-week-old abortion on demand law are often more expensive than they were when the operation was illegal, a city health department hearing.

State Assemblyman Franz S. Leichter warned that a proposed amendment to the health code which would restrict abortions to hospitals and clinics, could jack up costs and "drive certain people back to their back alley abortionists." Backers of the amendment are trying to outlaw abortions in doctors' offices.

The handshake of UAW president Leonard Woodcock (right) and GM's Earl Bramblett begins the talks

NEGOTIATIONS BEGIN

Auto Talk Key: Living Costs

BY RALPH ORR AND EDWARD SHANAHAN
Free Press Staff Writers

The battle was joined Wednesday between General Motors Corp. and the UAW as their top strategists shook hands across a glistening oak table over which they hope to hammer out a new labor contract will be negotiated.

Two things became clear when the negotiators emerged 90 minutes later from the 8th-floor room in the GM Building:

● An early, peaceful settlement hinges on management's disposition on the issue of unlimited cost-of-living index.

● Both sides have agreed to step up the tempo of the bargaining, with a view to reaching a final agreement before the present contract expires Sept. 14.

Surrounded by their entourages of specialists and technicians, UAW President Leonard Woodcock and GM Vice-president Earl Bramblett repeated the hand-shaking routine four times for a horde of photographers and television cameramen.

Each time they grinned broadly and exchanged pleasantries.

A member of the UAW team tugged at one of the gold drapes drawn across the room's windows and whispered:

"See those? Some time before..."

Turn to Page 6A, Column 1

Viet Peace Seen Vital To Colleges

BY WILLIAM VANCE
Free Press Washington Bureau

WASHINGTON — President Nixon's Commission on Campus unrest was warned Wednesday that there is little chance for cooling off student protests until the United States get out of Southeast Asia.

In a moment of frustration during the panel's long first day of hearings, chairman William Scranton said with a sigh that the commission may have to find a way to end the Indochina war before it can recommend ways to bring peace to the campus.

The comment by the former Pennsylvania governor reflected the view of witness after witness that until the fighting stops in Southeast Asia there's going to be trouble in the halls of ivy.

For example, University of Michigan President Robben Fleming told the nine-member commission:

"No set of recommendations that this commission or any other can come up with will cause the problem to disappear."

BUT FLEMING said there were at least three ways to bring campus unrest "within tolerable limits:"

His list, like those of many others Wednesday, begins with "an unwavering, completely credible and rapidly implemented commitment to end the presence of our troops in Vietnam."

Fleming also suggested "a major financial commitment" to end racial inequality and a "refurbishing" of the images of both political parties "to capture the imagination and support of the young."

Scranton was mildly critical of Fleming for limiting his statement to "problems outside the student body" and

Turn to Page 16A, Column 1

David Eberhard

COUNCILMAN'S PLAN

25-Cent Toll to Enter City?

BY TIM HOLLAND
Free Press Staff Writer

The Rev. David Eberhard, a minister - turned - councilman, wants to put "collection baskets" at the city limits of Detroit.

Drivers entering or leaving Detroit would be required to make a 25-cent "donation" under Eberhard's plan.

To pay for its bridge and tunnel costs, river-bound Manhattan charges at least 50 cents to any vehicle entering from New Jersey through one of six portals.

New York politicians have at times suggested putting up toll booths on all bridges—not just the New Jersey ones — and using the revenue for general fund services.

"As a councilman I have to propose something to come up with some money for the city," said Eberhard, beaming.

"And this is what I'm proposing."

The councilman's proposal is perhaps unique among schemes for financing city government in the United States. However, New York City, as a practical matter, charges tolls to many visitors.

Eberhard asked the corporation counsel, city controller and auditor general during a meeting of Common Council Wednesday to determine whether it would be feasible to put the "collection baskets" and toll gates at each street which crosses the city limit.

"I don't know if legally it can be done," Eberhard said.

A staff member of the Southeast Michigan Transportation Authority (SEMTA) doubted the legality of such a toll, particularly on state roads and expressways.

Pupils' Bus Dives Down Hill; 7 Die

From UPI and AP

ALLENTOWN, Pa.—A chartered bus carrying school children on a tour of the Pennsylvania Amish country skidded in a rainstorm and rolled over a 50-foot embankment Wednesday, pinning dead and injured in the wreckage.

Seven children were killed and 51 persons were injured, spokesmen at three hospitals said.

LOADED WITH children and counselors from the Hillel School, a private Jewish day school in Lawrence, N.Y., the bus skidded on a slight curve on rain-slick U.S.-22, 10 miles west of Allentown.

The bus ripped through guardrails, fell nose first down the hill, flipped over

Turn to Page 13A, Column 1

Police remove an injured student from wrecked bus in which seven children were killed

---

Action Line solves problems, gets answers, cuts red tape, stands up for your rights. Write Action Line, Box 881, Detroit, Mich. 48231. Or dial 222-6464 between 8:30 a.m. and 4:30 p.m. Monday through Friday.

When my former husband went bankrupt, the creditors came and took our furniture. Now my seven kids have to take turns sleeping on one bed. We're managing to buy two sets of bunk beds, and I can't find a store that sells that cheap. — Mrs. G., Detroit.

Kids are off the floor. Wayne County welfare people gave you names of three stores that would meet pre-inflation welfare allowances. To give kids a little breathing space, Statler Hotel threw in a roomy double bed. Rules say $139 is the most state can give you, and money must buy TWO sets of beds. Families of six or more with troubles like yours must also find bargains like these: A 12-cubic-foot refrigerator (for maximum) $147, a stove for $107 and a wringer washer for $82.50.

Our lovely flowers are being crowded out by hundreds of little mushrooms. For every 100 we dig out, 200 pop up the next day. How can we get rid of them once and for all? — L. S., Pontiac.

By getting rid of railroad ties around your flower beds. Decorative border is source of fungi's favorite food — rotting wood compost. Tiny type in your garden is easy to live with compared to native Michigan "puffball." Variety's been known to reach 50 pounds. Biggest one found in recent years was ripe 21-pounder northwest of Ann Arbor. At first folks thought mammoth mushroom was a meteor, but thing finally wound up in the larder of Detroit family of fungus-fanciers that polished it off in a week.

My niece was born with a veil over her face — isn't this supposed to be lucky? — Mrs. G. K., Detroit.

According to Scottish legend, veil (called a caul) is actually membrane that nourishes child before birth. It was believed to give child psychic powers, especially if birth date was a Friday. Superstition spread around Europe, along with notion that a caul brought good luck to sailors by preventing shipwreck and drowning. Veil definitely brought luck to parents who get a good price for it from gullible sailors. But it didn't do much for a French girl who got kidnapped twice by sailors who figured having the whole kid was luckier than caul alone.

The 50-year-old Thomas Edison phonograph I just bought is in perfect condition except for the needle. Do you know where I can get one? — A. H., Farmington.

From Thomas Pollard, 3300 Fairway Dr., Soquel, Cal. 95073. He specializes in needles for old phonographs. If you send reproducer (part that holds needle), he'll fix you up for about $5. If anything else goes wrong, call Keith Dunnigan of Utica (731-4651). Dunnigan's hobby is fixing mechanical phonographs and music boxes for Henry Ford Museum, Greenfield Village. Pollard was green with envy when he heard you paid $15 for phonograph in man who was cleaning out his attic. He says old talking machines can bring $75 and up, depending on condition.

Action Line

When the $30 worth of gifts I ordered from J. C. Penney didn't come in time for Christmas, I canceled my order. I told them I wanted my money back in January, but still no check. What's the story? — S. K., Grand Haven.

Tale of two cities. Credit department in Chicago said Milwaukee catalog headquarters never relayed order to refund your money. But credit manager agreed you'd waited long enough and wrote refund check while folks in Milwaukee tried to figure out where they slipped up.

The owner of the junkyard across the street must really have it in for us. He piles his stuff so close to the fence it spills over into our yard, and the dust is unbelievable. Can Action Line get through to him? — Miss I.W., Detroit.

Junk won't spoil your view from now on: owner's raising his fence. And Wayne County air pollution inspector paid a surprise visit to make sure dust pollution was within bounds. Though he didn't find a violation that day, he said he'd be back to make sure guy doesn't get careless.

THE QUESTION

Do you agree with groups that have proposed the U.S. and Canada merge to form one country?

HOW YOU VOTED

NO, 55.7 percent. COMMENTS: "We're Canadians and proud of it." . . . "The larger a country, the harder it is to govern." . . . "It must have been you Americans with your big egos that proposed it." . . . "We're two great countries living side by side in peace. Let's leave it that way." . . . "Canada would be crazy to hand over its natural resources and get all your problems in return."

YES, 44.3 percent. COMMENTS: "No two countries ever had so much in common." . . . "We need their land and resources and they need our money and industry." . . . "We could learn something from Canada about living in peace." . . . "To dissolve boundaries instead of creating them would set an example for the world."

TOMORROW'S QUESTION

Should the public schools be on a year-round schedule instead of having summer vacation?

To Vote YES — Call 961-3211
To Vote NO — Call 961-4422

HAVE THE FREE PRESS DELIVERED AT HOME — PHONE 222-6500 — Or Your Local Free Press Number

---

Index	
Amusements	11D
Ann Landers	3C
Astrology	13D
Billy Graham	16D
Bridge	13D
Business News	7-10D
Camera	13D
Comics	13-14D
Crossword Puzzle	13D
Death Notices	7B
Earl Wilson	15A
Editorials	4A
Feature Page	13A
Food Guide	6-10C
Movie Guide	14-15D
Names and Faces	16D
Obituaries	6B
Opinion	15B
Sports	1-6D
Stock Markets	8-9D
Television	12C
Want Ads	7-12B
Women's Pages	1-5C

Detroit Free Press

WARMER
Partly Cloudy to Fair
High 82-87 Low 60-65

ON GUARD FOR 139 YEARS

Vol. 140—No. 97   Sunday, August 9, 1970

METRO
John S. Knight's Notebook Page 2B

Thirty Cents

AUG. 9, 1970:

The Goose Lake music festival is Michigan's Woodstock.

FREE FOOD RUNNING OUT
200,000 Jam Rock Festival

The huge crowd of fans listens to rock music at Goose Lake. The stage is at the right.

Onion Stew Rushed to Ease Crisis

Two Injured In Accidents

BY GEORGE CANTOR AND HOWARD KOHN
Free Press Staff Writers

GOOSE LAKE—A food crisis threatened the mammoth Goose Lake Rock Festival on Saturday as the gates remained open to all comers and 200,000 people, most of them young, swarmed into the 370-acre park.

The free kitchen operated by Open City reported that it had exhausted all its supplies by Saturday morning and had been given no extra money by the promoters to buy more. Open City is a Detroit-based underground service organization.

"They told us to prepare food for 60,000 people," said Jim Bungard of the Open City steering committee. "We served that many Thursday and Friday alone.

"The festival advertised free food and a lot of these kids didn't bring money with them."

Panhandlers were prevalent Saturday along the main walkways of the sprawling park as hungry rock fans tried to scrape together funds to buy food from the dozens of vendors.

Late in the afternoon Open City did put together a stew made of onions and brown rice. But the supply was quickly exhausted, and many youths who had counted on eating at the free kitchen went back to their sleeping bags hungry.

DESPITE the food shortage, the first two days of the three-day affair near Jackson were more peaceful and accident-free than other festivals around the nation in recent months.

Tom Neumaier, 18, of Bloomfield Hills, suffered the most serious injuries when he jumped off a 40-foot amplifier tower Saturday. He was rushed by helicopter to University Hospital in Ann Arbor, and was admitted to the intensive care unit suffering from shock and severe bruises.

An unidentified youth was taken to Foote Hospital in Jackson with a severe neck sprain after falling off the park's giant slide. And a 2-year-old girl was hospitalized after she drank several ounces of gin.

The medical tent was dispensing tetanus shots to persons cut on the barbed wire fence.

DRUGS circulated freely throughout the grounds, but officials insisted that no one had been arrested for narcotics use inside the park. Dozens of youngsters, however, were arrested on drug charges en route here.

The park hospital and the Open City medical tent treated cases of overdose and bad trips throughout the day.

Festival sponsors emphasized at a noon press conference that no one would be allowed into the park without a ... chip—a policy ... edly was to have

Turn to Page 4A, Column 1

Action Line solves problems, gets answers, cuts red tape, stands up for your rights. Write Action Line, Box 881, Detroit, Mich. 48231. Or dial 222-6464 between 8:30 a.m. and 4:30 p.m. Monday through Friday.

A drunk on our block is terrorizing the whole neighborhood. He peeps in our windows, swears at our kids, has even threatened to kill us. He's made our lives pure hell for six years and the police can't do anything about it. Can you help?—Neighbors, Northeast Detroit.

He's sobering up in the Wayne County Jail. Detectives from the 15th precinct finally got all of you together in the prosecutor's office and got the warrant. Loudmouth will be out of circulation for 90 days if he's convicted on charge of using indecent language to a woman. Hard as he was to live with, guy's committed only misdemeanors and cops' hands are tied if they don't catch him in action or get witnesses to sign complaints. One woman who moved out of your neighborhood when he made sexual threats to her five-year-old didn't even bother to report it to police.

I was in the ladies' room at the Top of the Flame restaurant for the first time and couldn't believe it. The whole wall is windows! I felt as though the whole city was watching me. —Mrs. B., Mt. Clemens.

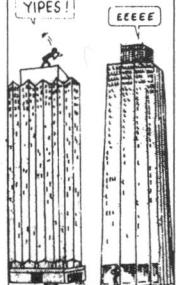

Action Line spies have completed an undercover investigation from the Pontchartrain Hotel roof, say even there it would take binoculars to ogle ladies visiting their private room on the 26th floor of the Gas Building. City inspectors say interiors of restrooms must be screened from view, but don't think law applies to birds and rooftops. Since Gas Building was built before the Pontch, nobody figured on skyscraper peepers and so far nobody's tried it. Flame manager William Hare says he'll pull the shades, but expects to catch the devil from the guys who insist you don't get a panorama of Southwest Detroit, the river and Canada in just any old ladies' room.

The Coast Guard is getting rid of the old Huron Lightship north of Port Huron. I've watched it from our cottage since I was a kid. Can you get me aboard once before they scrap her?—J.B., Detroit.

Coast Guard has a lump in the throat too, will toss a party aboard the floating lighthouse for folks like you. When ship ends its half-century of service on the Great Lakes Friday morning, hands will play. She'll be tied up at the Port Huron dock and stay open to sentimental visitors till Sunday. Lightship spent her last 30 years warning ships of dangerous Corsica Shoals where the southern tip of Lake Huron narrows into the St. Clair River. The 97-foot ship, manned by a crew of 11, is being replaced by a buoy and shore-based radio station. City of Port Huron is dickering to buy the old craft as a tourist attraction.

I sent $20 last April 1 to Winter Wonderland, a hockey school for kids. They never told me if I was accepted but they still have my money. It sure is tough about my "personal problem," but I'd have to pay full fare on the fourth bus. Was he right or just nasty?—Mark T., Livonia.

And you will. Winter Wonderland isn't cheating little boys, just forgot how tough it is to wait for something you want real bad. They've set up classes, but never got around to telling budding Gordie Howes like you when to show up. With teachers like Doug Roberts, Paul Popiel, Wayne Connelly and Jimmy Peters Jr., school's filled till February, but it welcomes boys six to nine to try out for the Tri-County League. League starts playing September 1 at 16611 Schoolcraft. Call BR 3-0050 for schedules.

Action Line

I can't drive because of a handicap, so I depend on buses more than most people. I had to take four buses the other day to get where I was going. On the third bus the driver grabbed my transfer and said it was tough about my "personal problem," but I'd have to pay full fare on the fourth bus. Was he right or just nasty?—J. E., Detroit.

Both. DSR General Manager Ernest Knox will give the driver a talking-to and refund your fare just to make up for the rude treatment. Nickel transfer only buys two extra rides in the same direction; besides, it can't be used for return trips on the same line. Knox says frequent lectures on courtesy just don't sink in with just a few of their 1,580 drivers. Their Complaint Bureau (925-2600) wants to hear about bad guys.

What would happen if the sun went out?—T.J., Mt. Clemens.

To you? You'd die. Air holds in heat, so it wouldn't get deathly cold instantly. But plant life would be killed by frost in just a few days, leaving animals and people to die of starvation. Our planet would become a ball of ice as the atmosphere froze into layers of nitrogen and oxygen. Some very simple life forms might survive. Earth's core, which is not dependent on the sun, would continue to glow. Experts say not to worry about it, though. They expect the sun to keep shining, add that even the next ice age isn't due for 10,000 years.

THE QUESTION

Should entertainment establishments like Disneyland refuse to admit people because of their hair or clothing?

HOW YOU VOTED

NO. 54 percent. COMMENTS: "People shouldn't be judged by appearance. These kids aren't violating any laws of decency" . . . "Some of this country's worst enemies are people who dress and act in the most conservative fashion" . . . "It's as ridiculous as refusing them because of their color or their religion or their name" . . . "With the get-up's some of our middle-aged tourists wear on vacations, we've got a nerve criticizing the kids" . . . "Why should they care? All they're after is money."

YES, 46 percent. COMMENTS: "It'll keep their foul mouths out, too. Most of the visitors are children who shouldn't have to see or hear that kind of behavior" . . . "Freedom works two ways. People who bathe regularly and dress and act decently have rights, too" . . . "Hippies have already taken over and ruined Yosemite Park for decent people. It's time somebody stopped them" . . . "It's the beginning of stopping these kids from destroying the nation."

TOMORROW'S QUESTION

Would a tough, national gun control law prevent incidents like the San Rafael, Calif., courthouse shootings?

To Vote YES Dial 961-3211   To Vote NO Dial 961-4422

Nerve Gas Will Roll Monday

By United Press International

The Army went ahead Saturday with plans for shipping 12,500 nerve-gas rockets to an Atlantic Ocean burial ground despite criticism from the United Nations and charges by Congress that it had indulged in "heavy-handed blackmail."

Shipments will roll by rail Monday from Army arsenals at Anniston, Ala., and Richmond, Ky. Loading of the Anniston rockets was completed Friday, but officials said preparations for movement of the Richmond shipment would not be finished until Sunday.

Army officials have warned that some of the rockets are leaking and all must be disposed of. The six-foot-long rockets, designed to be fired from airplanes, have been encased in concrete vaults and reinforced with steel.

The Army contends that chances of anything going wrong during shipment are virtually nil, but it has taken elaborate precautions.

Helicopters and empty pilot trains will precede the gas trains — each of which will be a sort of rolling military command with its own disaster unit aboard.

THE TRAINS will make their way to Sunny Point, N.C., a distance of about 600 miles in both instances, where the rockets will be loaded aboard an old ship hull. The hull will be towed to

Turn to Page 2A, Column 3

'Freedom' Is the Lure

BY GEORGE CANTOR
Free Press Staff Writer

GOOSE LAKE—What is the lure that has attracted 200,000 people to this meadow in the middle of Michigan?

The attractions range from the ready availability of drugs to something that sounds like a distant echo of Huckleberry Finn.

ALL THE THINGS that would get a youngster hustled — or spanked — in the outside world are standard behavior here. And even though it's all been done before and clucked at and analyzed and deplored elsewhere, the kids seem to want and expect it when they come to an event like Goose Lake.

"I know this sounds trite but I think it's beautiful," said Jim Fine of Bradley University as he sat on a blanket in the midst of the jammed concert bowl Saturday.

"I'd have been disappointed if it wasn't just like this. I saw the movie 'Woodstock,' and that's the way every rock festival should be. I'd have been crushed if I came here and saw everyone sitting in nice neat rows."

Linda Ruse of Toledo said the only thing that surprised her at Goose Lake was that there were so many trees. "This is my first rock festival and it's just like I thought it'd be," she said. "Except I

thought it would be just one big, open field."

Woodstock was a big, open field.

STEVE MEYERS of Columbus, O., liked the idea that "there's nobody here to tell you what to do or when to do it. If you want to sleep on the ground, that's all right, and if you don't feel like brushing your teeth you don't have to.

"This is somewhere where it's all for real," he said.

"I like the idea of people being able to police themselves," said Dayton University student Phillip Krajcovic.

Mary Ann Priami of Redford Township

Turn to Page 4A, Column 2

MEANWHILE, IN MONTE CARLO...
The 'Beautiful People' Meet

BY FREDERICK M. WINSHIP

MONTE CARLO — (UPI) — The Beautiful People are flocking to Monte Carlo again, and it makes all the difference to the Riviera resort that was more "out" than "in" during the 1960s.

The Beautiful People of the 1970s are a heady mixture of capitalists, socialites, European aristocracy and leaders in the creative arts and luxury trades. They're all on a first-name basis, at home in a half dozen countries, and will greet their worst enemies with a kiss (two if they're European).

They prefer French period furniture or a French-modern mix, European cars, European food, tennis, skiing and yachting, privacy except at show-off time and the company of their peers.

Phony titles are tolerated but not phony jewels, unless they are by Kenneth J. Lane.

They take themselves seriously as social leaders but would rather be quoted as agreeing with Cleveland Amory that society is dead.

They refer to themselves as "BPs" as sort of a perverse put-down, but believe they must be doing something right because the communications media celebrate their beauty, wealth, wit, naughtiness and talent, however small.

They're also taken quite seriously by the commercial world which uses Beautiful People as a sales pitch for resorts, fashions, home decor, hair-styling, restaurants, cosmetics and liquor.

A press release on the re-

"I see every hippie as an enemy," said one BP. "They can't fool me. They simply want what we've got...."

cent Monaco Red Cross gala, hosted annually by Princess Grace, dutifully reported that the glamorous Princess Lalla Nezah of Morocco attended wearing coiffure by Sebour of the House of Revlon.

And reports that the ilk of 10,000 or so BPs and you'll find a hard-core egotist run-

York financier Henry Ittleson and dancer Rudolf Nureyev find annual August nesting at the Hotel de Paris can do that hostelry no harm.

SCRATCH ANY one of the 10,000 or so BPs and you'll find a hard-core egotist run-

ning scared of a social revolution. Many Americans among them already prefer to live abroad and have gradually transferred their assets to Switzerland, Liechtenstein, the Bahamas, or some other "safe" haven. There's no panic, but the prevailing BP philosophy is "live for today, for tomorrow..."

Unlike people who are born into the Social Register, Burke's Peerage, or Italy's Blue Book, Beautiful People are virtually the creation of the age of jet plane travel.

Prior to World War II summer might have me...

Turn to Page 2A, Col...

Terrorists Threaten Execution

MONTEVIDEO, Uruguay — (UPI) — The Tupamaros terrorists announced Saturday night that their plan to execute kidnaped U.S. public safety adviser Dan Mitrione at noon Sunday (10 a.m. Detroit time). The terrorists allowed Mitrione to send a last letter to his wife and children.

Uruguayan police said they had confirmed the execution threat as genuine. The threat was in a communique signed by the organization and sent to a radio station earlier in the day.

The U.S. embassy here seriously by the commercial world which uses Beautiful announced that Mitrione, 50, of Richmond, Ind., had been permitted to send a letter to his wife, Henrietta, expressing his love for her and their children. A spokesman said the letter also urged Amba...

Dan Mitrione

...ador Charles Adair Jr. to do all he could to obtain Mitrione's release.

Meantime, Uruguayan President Pacheco Areco met with his top advisers Saturday night. Foreign Minister Jorge Peirano Facio told newsmen after the meeting that the government would take unspecified "new measures" to try to rescue Mitrione and two other hostages.

The two others are Claude L. Fly, 65, of Fort Collins, Colo., and Brazilian Consul Aloysio Dias Gomide, 41.

The Tupamaros had set midnight Friday as the deadline for government compliance with their demand that all political prisoners in Uruguay be freed in exchange for the three men.

The communique released Saturday said the guerillas had decided "to execute Mr. Dan Mitrione" because the

government refused to meet their demands.

"The execution will take place at noon Sunday, Aug. 9," it said.

Neither the communique nor the warning mentioned either Fly or the Brazilian.

CONCERN about the fate of comrades arrested during the search for the kidnapers possibly prompted the guerillas' warning, a police official said.

"Faced with the eventuality of crimes, tortures and death being inflicted on our companions, severe reprisals will be taken against the repressive forces, representatives of the oligarchy and foreign diplomats," said the earlier note, also delivered to a radio station.

Index

Amusements	6-8B
Ann Landers	10D
Astrology	17C
Books	5B
Bridge	15D
Business News	11-16B
Crossword Puzzle	15D
Death Notices	9C
Editorials	2B
Movie Guide	9B
Names and Faces	17A
Obituaries	8C
Outdoors	7C
People Page	17A
Sports	1-8C
Travel	14D
Want Ads	9-17C
Women's Pages	1-13D

HAVE THE FREE PRESS DELIVERED AT HOME PHONE 222-6500 Or Your Local Free Press Number

AUG. 20, 1970:

John Norman Collins is convicted of murdering an 18-year-old woman, the last of seven slain in and around Ann Arbor and Ypsilanti within two years.

CLOUDY
Less Humid
High 78-84 Low 55-61
Map and Details on Page 15-D
HOURLY TEMPERATURES

Detroit Free Press
ON GUARD FOR 139 YEARS
Vol. 140—No. 108
Thursday, August 20, 1970

METRO
Mart Rally Continues
See Page 11, Section D
Ten Cents

FACES LIFE IN PRISON

Collins Is Guilty of Murder

Action Line
Dial 222-6464

Action Line solves problems, gets answers, cuts red tape, stands up for your rights. Write Action Line, Box 881, Detroit, Mich. 48231. Or dial 222-6464 between 8:30 a.m. and 4:30 p.m. Monday through Friday.

I was a Democratic write-in candidate for precinct delegate in Dearborn. I won the election, but the Election Commission just informed me by registered mail that I'm the REPUBLICAN precinct delegate. The state Democratic convention is this weekend—what can I do?—E.G., Dearborn.

Get a court order and have machines opened for a recount. Dearborn Elections Director William Karr admits tired election workers might've goofed after working 16 straight hours. But his hands are tied by state law that forbids opening machines till Board of Convassers certifies the election in two or three weeks. What might have happened: Four people who voted for you pulled the Republican handle and then wrote in your name. Michigan primaries don't allow split tickets, so machine made you a Republican. Another disgruntled candidate once accused Dearborn elections people of cheating him when he lost. His wife and friends all told him they voted for him, but when ballots were checked it turned out the only vote he got was his own.

I've always wondered — where did the tooth fairy come from? — F.G., Detroit.

North Carolina, Illinois, Kentucky or Tacoma, Wash. —take your pick. Traditions of several states include exchange of money for tooth left under your pillow, but not all of 'em give the fairy credit. Some claim moneybags is a mouse. WSU folklorist Ellen Stekert told Action Line custom probably goes back to ancient belief that children are especially susceptible to harmful spirits, and that parts of their bodies like teeth and clipped hair must be hidden from folks who'd use them to cast spells. More North Carolina lore: Bury an extracted tooth under a rock, because if a dog steps on it, a hound's tooth will grow in its place.

What's the story on army surplus motorcycles? I'd like to buy one, but every place I call tells me to forget it.—B.S., Detroit.

Good advice. Department of Defense Surplus Center in Battle Creek, major DLS outlet, says it's sold five in the past 20 years—all in rotten shape. To get on mailing list that advertises sale of old jeeps and motorcycles, write: Director of Marketing, Defense Logistics Services Center, Federal Center, Battle Creek 49016. But don't expect much. Army and Navy think of it this way—if it's salvagable, it's not surplus.

Action Line

My doctor says I have to stay in bed for a few weeks because I suffered a mild heart attack. But I'm involved in community work and I don't want to get behind. Can Action Line get an extension phone installed in my bedroom right away? —P.S., Detroit.

We did, but you could have done it yourself by calling Bell's business office. Tougher problem for Bell servicemen came up after they installed an extension phone at horseback level in the stables of the Bloomfield Open Hunt Club. New phone let riders gab without dismounting, but horses found phone cords so tasty they gobbled up four of 'em.

A friend of mine says he goes to a potato festival up north every year. Is he putting me on?—D.S., St. Clair.

Potato fete is Sept. 6-13 this year in Posen. Little town (pop. 400) drew 20,000 spud fanciers to last year's bash. Folks lined up for half a mile for potato pancake orgies. First day, oldtimers (over 70) get treated to free lunch. Other attractions: Fashion show, costume ball, antique car show, beauty contest, fair and fireworks. Posen farmers started celebrating 19 years ago when spud was the only crop, "and the potato is still king in these parts," Chamber of Commerce says.

THE QUESTION
Sound Off
Do you approve of the action taken by the sergeant who ordered 15 airmen to clip a general's picture from 10,000 papers?

HOW YOU VOTED

NO, 65.4 percent. COMMENTS: "It seems to me that they'd have something better to do" . . . "They could've used 10,000 airmen to each cut one picture" . . . "Too bad we can't get people in there who are interested in ending the war" . . . "Nothing the military does surprises me—or pleases me" . . . "Just playing games as usual" . . . "Biggest waste of time I've ever heard of" . . . "It's nice to know where the taxpayers' money goes."

YES, 34.6 percent. COMMENTS: "The sergeant was just doing his duty" . . . "The military exists because orders can be passed down and followed" . . . "It didn't hurt the boys and kept them occupied" . . . "When you're in the service you take orders—period" . . . "They have to learn to take all orders so they won't be killed in combat."

TOMORROW'S QUESTION
Do you believe copper bracelets help people with arthritis and other aches and pains feel better?

To Vote YES Call 961-3211
To Vote NO Call 961-4422

Mrs. Collins (right) and her sister Doreen leave the courthouse

Tearful Mother Vows Fight to Free Her Son

BY WILLIAM SCHMIDT
Free Press Staff Writer

ANN ARBOR — Mrs. Loretta Collins sat in the rectory of St. Thomas Church and pressed a crumpled handful of Kleenex into her face.

"I know my son didn't do it," she repeated over and over again through her tears. "I know he's innocent, I just know he is."

After a year and 19 days of waiting, Mrs. Collins had just heard a jury of six men and six women pronounce her son John guilty of murder. For some — the police and the family of the slain girl — the wait apparently was over. But for Mrs. Collins, it would not end here.

"I'm going to fight this every step," she said, shaking her head. "I'm not going to let them keep my son. I want John home with me."

Her daughter Gail sat stoically next to her, her eyes red with the tears that had begun when jury foreman William Billmeier stood

> "I'm not going to let them keep my son. I want John home with me."

at 9:34 a.m. to announce that the 23-year-old former student was guilty of the torture murder of Karen Sue Beineman.

MRS. COLLINS' sister, Doreen, and a young girl friend of John's also were there, sitting in stiff-backed chairs under the picture of Christ that hung on the rectory's north wall.

There was no sound in the room except for

Turn to Page 16A, Column 1

Kent Troops Felt Danger, Ohio Guard Chief Claims

From UPI and AP

KENT, O. — The commander of Ohio's National Guard said Wednesday he is "certain" his troops fired into students at Kent State University because they felt their lives were endangered.

Adjutant Gen. S. T. Del Corso told the President's Commission on Campus Unrest that the guardsmen who killed four Kent State students during a demonstration May 4 were authorized to fire weapons as a "last resort" when they felt in danger.

WHEN ASKED how guardsmen decide their lives are threatened, Del Corso replied: "This is basically a self determination. We can't control the mind of the individual. It's conceivable individual soldiers might be assaulted while in troop formation and fire back, and I am certain that's what happened here."

He added: "I can visualize

S. T. DEL CORSO: "I can visualize no commander giving an order to fire into a crowd."

no commander giving an order to fire into a crowd."

Del Corso told the commission, which is opening three days of hearings on the Kent State shootings, that the guardsmen would continue to be armed when called to quell campus disturbances, but he would prefer that most troops be equipped with shotguns and use birdshot for ammunition.

He told the commission Ohio guardsmen do not fire warning shots "because this can be dangerous." He added that warning shots pose a potential danger to innocent bystanders.

DEL CORSO was accompanied by an attorney, Charles Brown, who objected to

Turn to Page 4A, Column 4

Lawyers Plan Appeal

BY WILLIAM SCHMIDT and TOM DeLISLE
Free Press Staff Writers

ANN ARBOR — A jury of six men and six women, after four days of agonizing deliberation, found John Norman Collins guilty of first-degree murder in the sex-slaying of Karen Sue Beineman.

The verdict, announced at 9:34 a.m. after 34 hours of sometimes heated arguing, carries a mandatory life prison sentence.

UNDER MICHIGAN law, Collins, a 23-year-old former Eastern Michigan University student, cannot be paroled and must spend 20 years in prison before he is eligible to apply for commutation of the sentence (pardon) by the governor.

The defense said it would appeal after Washtenaw County Circuit Judge John W. Conlin, who presided over the lengthy trial, sentences Collins Aug. 28.

Collins showed no emotion when the verdict was announced by jury foreman William G. Billmeier of Ann Arbor.

Court aides said he later broke down and cried when closeted with his mother, Mrs. Loretta Collins of Center Line, who was allowed to visit and comfort her son after the verdict was announced.

Collins, who did not take the stand to testify in his own behalf during the trial, made no public comment.

JURORS, contacted at their homes later, also refused comment.

In Grand Rapids, Mrs. Roland Beineman, the mother of the dead girl, praised the verdict and said: "God was on the jury. I'm convinced He was the main member of the jury."

Miss Beineman, a petite 18-year-old Grand Rapids girl, was a freshman at Eastern Michigan University where Collins was a senior. She was the seventh and last young woman slain under similar circumstances in a two-year period around the twin university towns of Ann Arbor and Ypsilanti.

No one has been charged in the other deaths.

Gov. Milliken said in Lansing after the verdict was announced that he had not made

Collins heads back to jail

any decision on whether Collins will be extradited to California to stand trial there.

Authorities in Monterey County, Cal., said Wednesday they will begin extradition proceedings within 10 days to bring Collins to trial there.

Collins faces death in the gas chamber if he is convicted in California of the murder last June of 17-year-old Roxie Ann Philips of Milwaukie, Ore.

Asked whether Collins' conviction cleared up in his mind the entire series of Ann Arbor-Ypsilanti area murders, Milliken said:

"I don't know. I'm sure there will remain in many people's minds the question of the other murders."

The jury had only the choice of conviction of first-degree murder or acquittal. Lesser charges of second-degree murder or manslaughter were ruled out by Judge Conlin in his instructions to the jury last Thursday.

Washtenaw County Prosecutor William F. Delhey and his assistant, Booker T. Williams, who conducted the case against Collins, said they were pleased with the verdict.

"WE FELT quite convinced in our own minds about his guilt," Delhey said. The prosecutor congratulated defense attorneys Neil H. Fink and Joseph W. Louisell on conducting a "gentlemanly trial."

Delhey said the trial was "a credit to our judicial system."

Louisell, the chief defense attorney, was not present when the verdict was returned. He had not been in the courtroom since the jury got the case at 11:35 a.m. Tuesday.

"I think it was a very good, fair jury and a well tried case on both sides," Judge Conlin said.

After failing to reach a verdict Tuesday

Turn to Page 12A, Column 1

Karen Sue Beineman

ABM Wins Final Vote In Senate

From AP and UPI

WASHINGTON — Defenders of President Nixon's Safeguard anti-missile system repulsed a final Senate attack Wednesday 53 to 45.

The vote climaxed a three-week debate marked chiefly with contention over Safeguard's usefulness as a bargaining chip in arms talks with the Soviet Union.

The Nixon administration holds that since attempts to limit Safeguard's expansion have been defeated, the entire system can be bargained out of existence to win concessions on mutual arms limitations.

The final round of this year's Safeguard battle came

Turn to Page 2A, Column 1

Nerve Gas Intact On Ocean Floor

ABOARD THE USS HARTLEY — Sample water tests indicated Wednesday that no nerve gas escaped when the liberty ship LeBaron Russell Briggs crunched to the floor of the Atlantic after being scuttled Tuesday.

The impact knocked out two radio beacons whose signals were to pinpoint the Briggs' location for scientists who plan to check on the site again in October.

FORD TO USE IT
New Lock Makes Driver Buckle Up

BY TOM KLEENE
Free Press Automotive Writer

LAS VEGAS, Nev. — Ford Motor Co. is rushing development of a device which would prevent drivers from starting their cars unless their safety belts are buckled.

Lee A. Iacocca, one of three Ford group presidents, said he has been driving a Continental Mark III equipped with the device and that "it's terrific."

Iacocca said at Ford's 1971 model press preview here Wednesday that the company hopes to put the device on at least one of its car lines by next year — possibly during the '71 model year on a limited basis.

Ford recently proposed to the National Highway Safety Bureau that the device be accepted as an alternative for controversial air bags scheduled to become mandatory on 1973 cars.

Ford proposed that a new car buyer have a choice between

Turn to Page 2A, Column 1

Inside the Free Press

Amusements	8D	Names and Faces	16D
Ann Landers	3C	Obituaries	11B
Astrology	13D	Opinion	11B
Billy Graham	16D	Sports	1-7D
Bridge	13D	Stock Markets	10-12D
Business News	10-12D	Television	8D
Camera	2B	Want Ads	3-11B
Comics	13-15D	Women's Pages	1-4C
Crossword Puzzle	15D		
Death Notices	6B	HAVE THE FREE PRESS	
Earl Wilson	15A	DELIVERED AT HOME	
Editorials	6A	PHONE 222-6500	
Feature Page	15A	Or Your Local	
Food Guide	7-15C	Free Press Number	
Movie Guide	14-15D		

Detroit Free Press
Features – Editorials
SUNDAY, NOVEMBER 8, 1970

SECTION B

In This Section
Editor's Notebook Page 2
Amusements Pages 6-10
Business Report Pages 13-18

Nov. 8, 1970:

The mystery of who killed the Robisons never has been solved.

Sunday feature

ROBISON, 42

MRS. ROBISON, 40

After two years, the murders of the six members of the Richard C. Robison family remain unsolved. Following a month-long investigation, much of it independent of police sources, Free Press Staff Writer William Schmidt and veteran reporter and free-lancer Al Koski assembled this review of the case, revealing important factors never before published. Portions of their report might never have been disclosed, were it not for a Grand Rapids furniture dealer who last year bought a filing cabinet from Robison's office at an Internal Revenue Service auction. Koski purchased the contents of that cabinet for $10 and found information among Robison's records that provides surprising new insights into the character of the dead man.

GARY, 17

RANDY, 12

SUSAN, 8

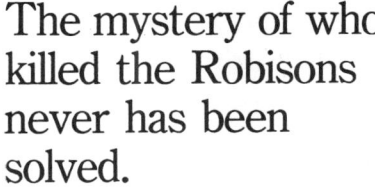
RICHARD JR., 19

The Unsolved Robison Case

A New, Startling Report on the Bizarre Events And Strange Dealings That Foreshadowed Murder

BY WILLIAM SCHMIDT AND AL KOSKI

For the past two years, Joseph Raymond Scolaro III has been a watched man.

When he goes on a trip, the police know where he is. When he buys a new car, the police write down its license number. And when he talks about Dick Robison, his former business associate, the police listen carefully to every word.

By his own admission, Joe Scolaro, 33, is the major suspect in the June, 1968, slaying of Richard C. Robison, his wife and four children.

"The police told me I did it. And they said if I didn't pull the trigger, I know who did," Scolaro has said.

He said police have already given him two lie detector tests. They told him the results of both were "inconclusive."

And in September, 1969, Scolaro said that for seven hours police led him to believe he had been arrested for the murders when he was picked up and held overnight on a bad check charge.

The charge was dismissed less than two months later in Southfield District Court.

The $15,000 Robison cabin near Goodhart on the Lake Michigan shore, scene of the tragic murders of all six members of the family in June, 1968. (The structure has since been torn down.)

Through all of this, Joe Scolaro has maintained his innocence. He says flatly he does not know who is responsible for the Robison family murders at their $15,000 northern Michigan summer cabin. And he says he does not know why they were killed.

For their own reasons, however, the police keep coming back to Scolaro.

LAST JANUARY, detectives presented Emmet County Prosecutor Donald C. Noggle with a 700-page summary of their 19-month-investigation.

However, both Noggle and Attorney General Frank Kelley refused to issue any warrants, pending a review of the case.

That review — the lengthy investigation before it — has focused on Robison's convoluted business dealings, and on the man who was Robison's successor and closest business confidant — Joe Scolaro.

And though police won't spell it out, money seems to be the root of the killings, the catalyst that brought about the fatal meeting between Robison and his murderer.

If a calculated business swindle or double-cross was the only reason for the crime, however, police might have had their warrant months ago.

But there are other elements confusing the case, strange reflections on a man who was regarded by friends and admirers as the perfect family man, churchman and businessman.

Before he was murdered, Robison:

● Dramatically increased both the give-away circulation and number of pages of his so-called magazine of the arts, Impresario. Most of the increase resulted from full page airline advertising that had been planted without authorization to make the magazine look more prosperous than it really was.

● Promoted a mysterious $100-million scheme that was to include everything from computerized warehouse operations to airport cultural centers. After two years of investigation, police have never found any proof of the project's existence beyond the simplest schematic drawings.

● Involved himself with a half-dozen mysterious people who made up his real or imagined netherworld of big business and high finance. Police have never found any of the people, and do not know if they even exist.

● Made two unexplained and solitary visits during the three weeks before his murder to hotels in San Francisco and at Detroit's Metro Airport.

● Wore a strange religious medallion police found around his neck, upon which was carved the name of "Roebert," apparent leader of Robison's invisible business empire.

The six members of the Richard C. Robison family were murdered on a Tuesday, June 25, 1968, while vacationing at their summer home near Goodhart, about 25 miles north of Petoskey on the Lake Michigan shoreline.

The family had traveled up to the cabin in two separate cars on June 16.

Their bodies were not discovered until July 22 — about a month later — when Chauncey A. Bliss and Nuvo Shenanaquet, an Ottawa Indian, answered neighbors' complaints that a foul odor was coming from the cabin. Bliss had helped build.

Nearby neighbors assumed the Robisons were out of state on a business trip. A note taped on a window over broken glass that later turned out to have been shattered by bullets read: "Be Back 7-10. Robison."

Since there had been some talk of the Robisons taking a trip to Florida and Kentucky, even the presence of both of the family's dust-covered autos alongside the lacquered log cabin did not make anyone suspicious.

In fact, when Bliss first responded to the complaint about the odor, he assumed a raccoon or some other animal had crawled up under the house and died.

But when Bliss and Shenanaquet unlocked the bolted cabin door, the first thing they saw was the body of Shirley Robison, partially covered with a blanket and sprawled face down on the cabin floor.

Police and crime lab technicians wearing gas masks combed every square inch of the cabin. The bodies were transported in plastic bags to Little Traverse Hospital, where authorities refused them. They were finally transferred to the 4-H Fairgrounds where autopsies were performed in a chicken coop.

The odor was so foul and the flies so thick that Shenanaquet was sickened and said he could not eat dinner that night.

Police speculate it was all over within 20 minutes — including the time the killer took to carefully drag most of the bodies out of sight into a back hallway and pull all the window draperies shut and lock the cabin door.

THERE WERE few clues. Police sawed a small section out of the cabin's wooden floor where they found what appeared to be a bloody bootprint and also collected several .22 caliber and .25 caliber cartridge casings from the cabin.

Police also found a hammer they suspected the killer had used to hit little Susan Robison in the head. If there were any fingerprints on it, however, they were lost when the Emmet County undersheriff wrapped a handkerchief around the handle so he could hold it up for a newspaper photographer.

A $9,000 diamond ring belonging to Shirley Robison was missing, and relatives were never able to find a set of colored pearls and an emerald brooch that belonged to the dead woman.

But four cameras and a light meter left in the cabin appeared to be untouched and $90 in cash was found on the victims.

And then there was the note taped over the bullet holes in the window. It is reasonable to suspect that the note was written by the killer.

Two tree trimmers who were working near the cabin on Wednesday — June 26 — remembered seeing the note and broken glass when questioned by police a month later.

AS A RESULT, police pinned the day of the murder as June 25. It could have occurred no earlier. On the morning of June 25, Robison exchanged several calls with his office, and made two calls to his bank. He also talked to Joe Scolaro.

Later on June 25 — sometime near dusk — Mr. and Mrs. William R. Freeman, who lived a quarter-mile down the beach from the Robisons, heard gunshots.

"We just heard a series of shots ... one with a little short pause ... and then there were others after that," remembered Mrs. Freeman. "It was still light enough so we thought that somebody was shooting gulls on the beach at the time."

When he was shot, police speculate, Dick Robison was sitting in an easy chair. A volley of bullets came from outside the cabin, shattering the window. Two caught him squarely in the chest.

A stray bullet from the same volley must have hit his son, Gary, 17, in the back as he sat at a table near his father and played double-solitaire with his older brother, Richard Jr., 19.

The boys broke for a back closet, where the family kept a .22 caliber rifle. So quickly had they reacted, they had carried their playing cards with them as they fled.

Police found them with the cards strewn around their bodies.

Randy Robison, 12, was shot and dragged into the hallway alongside the body of Susan, 8, the Robison's only daughter.

The killer then dragged Robison's body into the hallway with his children and gruesomely positioned the body of his wife, Shirley, 40, near the sofa so she appeared to have been sexually assaulted.

Then the killer or killers pumped one .25 caliber bullet into the head of each victim.

On the day of the murder, Joe Scolaro got up early and by 8 a.m. he was at the office, a one-story red-brick building at 28081 Southfield Rd.

Robison had built the office building in the early sixties. It was only several blocks from the $50,000, one-story gray-brick home at 18790 Delores where he and his family had lived since moving to Lathrup Village.

The office housed Robison's two principal businesses — his advertising agency, R.C. Robison & Associates, and his publishing firm, Village House Publishing, Inc., which published Impresario.

The agency and publishing house had been a one-man show until December, 1965, when Scolaro came to work for Robison.

Scolaro had a background in advertising and had been a space buyer for several publications, including the Birmingham Eccentric.

Robison admired Scolaro for his memory, friends recalled, and credited Scolaro with having almost total recall.

He earned Robison's trust quickly, and in late 1967, Robison was considering cutting Scolaro in for 20 percent of his business.

DURING THE few months before the murder, in fact, Scolaro virtually ran Robison's office. Robison himself was out of town much of the time — in Hawaii, Florida, New York, San Francisco and, in June, up north with his family.

And in the few weeks before the murder, Scolaro and Robison had a big raise from Robison. His salary was also up from about $300 a week to almost $1,000.

A few months before the murder, Scolaro also had done a favor for Robison. A gun enthusiast, Scolaro bought two matching .25 caliber Berettas automatics and gave one to Robison.

That Beretta was never found and is believed to be the weapon the killer or killers used to shoot each of the Robisons in the head.

Scolaro's purchase of Robison's two firms after the killings was co-ordinated by National Bank of Detroit officials who handled the estate and was based on accounting statements prepared by Calvin Mackey, Robison's former accountant. The statements showed that Robison's businesses were losing money, and Scolaro took over everything for $3,500.

Scolaro then moved in with Adrian, in return for stacks of unpaid printing bills. Scolaro is still associated with Impresario as its advertising director.

The poor health of Robison's business at the time of the killings was a surprise to many people. When Philip Skillman, a Bloomfield Hills insurance man, prepared an estate analysis for Robison eight months before the murders, Robison valued the two firms together at more than $600,000.

At about 9 a.m. on the day of the murder, Frank Joity, the manager of the National Bank of Detroit branch just six blocks south of Robison's office, came into his paneled office.

At 9:30 a.m., just as the bank doors were opening to admit the first customers of the day, Joity's phone rang. It was Dick Robison, calling from Goodhart.

"He asked me first if someone from the West Coast had deposited $200,000 in his account," said Joity, who has been manager of the colonial, red-brick bank branch since 1966.

Police later suspected the $200,000 may have had something to do with the mysterious warehouse-cultural center business deal Robison was plotting at the time he was killed.

"When I told him no money had been deposited, he asked for the balance in his account," Joity said.

Joity told him the balance was about $15,000. "Then he asked me to stop payment on all checks," Joity said.

"I questioned him about it," said Joity, who had found Robison in some sort of financial bind. "Dick said he would check back with me in a few minutes."

Robison called his office, one of several such calls made there that morning. Then he called back Joity. "Pay the checks," Joity was told.

There were several phone calls that morning between Robison and Scolaro, the last one at about 10:30 a.m. Scolaro said they didn't talk about anything important, and there was no conversation he could remember about the balance in the agency account.

THE POLICE have checked Scolaro's actions carefully during the remainder of the day. Time is important, since the trip to Goodhart from Southfield is a journey of some 275 miles. A round trip would take between ten and twelve hours.

Scolaro said he left the office on Southfield Road before noon, and drove downtown to the plumbing convention at Cobo Hall.

"Dick told me during one of our phone conversations to go down to the convention," said Scolaro, who claimed the visit was part of keeping up good relations with Robison's chief client—Delta Faucet.

Scolaro said he walked around the convention for a while, and then went across the street to the Pontchartrain Hotel. He said he had two drinks at the Salamander Bar.

Then he walked over to Hudson's and Crowley's and shopped. He did not buy anything. When he left to go home, Scolaro said, he was in the middle of a pounding rainstorm.

"By the time I got home, there was water in my trunk and my taillights had water inside them," said Scolaro.

Before he went home to his two-story white frame house in Birmingham, he said he stopped in at Robison's house to check the basement for flooding.

Scolaro had been given a key to Robison's house before the family left to go up north about 10 days earlier.

He said there was little water in the basement. He left the Robison house and arrived home sometime between 10 p.m. and 11 p.m., although police cannot pin down the exact time.

During the 10 or 11 hours between the time he left his office in Southfield and returned to his house in Birmingham,

Turn to Page 4B, Column 1

---

tipoff
inside the news with the people who make it.

Whose Opinion?

Market-Opinion Research, the Detroit firm that does election polling for the Detroit News and the Michigan Republican Party, has been told by Republican leaders it must stop working for one or the other.

GOP leaders were infuriated when, on the Sunday night before the Nov. 3 election, Fred Currier, president of Market-Opinion Research, appeared on Lou Gordon's television show and called the governor's race too close to call, with a trend running toward Democrat Sander Levin. Currier was pulled on the Gordon show as the News pollster. The Republicans thought he should have watched out for their interests and called Milliken a winner.

When the Son Shines Bright . . .

Good old Sonny Elliot, the TV weatherman, was in a hurry to vote and he gone Tuesday, and like everybody else at his Lafayette Park polling place, he was dismayed at the long line of people he found waiting.

So good old fast-talking Sonny told the election ladies who he was and how important his time was, and they let him vote ahead of all those other people.

By the time good old Sonny left, he was about as popular as a stationary cold front.

Stick-to-it-tiveness

Detroit's computer foul-up was not unique in the state. Flint had problems, too, and among them was one created by a city commission candidate who hadn't even made it through the August primary.

He waged a write-in campaign and distributed stickers with his name on them to facilitate the write-in. They were supposed to be stuck on the write-in section of the ballot envelope, but a lot of people slapped them right on the computer punch card ballots, sometimes on top of the holes they had punched for other races.

Police Power

Remember how it was back in those little towns where the police knew everybody and took an interest? There is still at least one such town left in the Detroit area—Pleasant Ridge, Oakland County Prosecutor Thomas Plunkett lives there, and he was pleased to be on the receiving end of what he says is standard police procedure in his town. Police rushed his son to the hospital several weeks ago with a bad cut. "Not only did they insist that the boy be treated quickly," he says, "but they stop by every week to see how he's doing."

Fort WJBK

Revolution-modern architecture is spreading even to deepest Southfield. Employees of Storer Broadcasting Co.'s WJBK who have seen their station's new facilities near Northland say they looked over the sprawling brick building with gunslit windows and high chain-link fence, pondered their station's conservative politics and quickly dubbed their new quarters "Fort Storer."

Sonny

Plunkett

"When he was shot, police speculate, Dick Robison was sitting in an easy chair. A volley of bullets came from outside the cabin, shattering the window. Two caught him squarely in the chest."

MARCH 7, 1971:

Detroit fought the nickname "Murder City" after its homicide rate soared.

Sunday feature

Detroit Free Press

Features-Editorials
SUNDAY, MARCH 7, 1971

SECTION **B**

In This Section
- Editor's Notebook — Page 2
- Amusements — Pages 6-10
- Business Report — Pages 11-16

Why Detroit's Homicide Rate Is Skyrocketing: A Look Beyond the Statistics

BY GARY BLONSTON
Free Press Staff Writer

Homicides are not like other crimes. People seldom make money simply by killing other people, and there is little purely physical gratification that comes of taking a life. Sometimes killing is an act of survival, but most often it is an act of rage.

That is why a 50 percent increase in Detroit's homicide rate since the first of the year seems such an unfathomable change in the pattern of life, and of death, in the city.

It is as if 50 percent more people cannot cope, as if 50 percent more people cannot back off, as if 50 percent more people must push simple human relations problems to illogical, fatal conclusions.

IT IS TEMPTING to think of the killings as part of an overall street crime problem, and to a degree that is true. The number of killings related to drug traffic is increasing, and so is the number of deaths that occur during robberies. But fully two-thirds of the homicides that have occurred this year follow the classic formula — friend against friend, relative against relative.

And no one can say how many of those killings born of passion rather than crime might have been avoided if a few dozen of Detroit's 1.5 million people had, at given moments, been in different places, away from the lethal, spur-of-the-moment confrontations that claimed them.

Given all that, Detroit's increase in homicides is not necessarily any kind of measure of Detroit's level of crime. It is more accurately a reflection of the quality of life in the city — a gauge of stress and friction and frustration, and a reading on the violent potential of people under pressure.

There is no mysterious new force at work in the city, turning more and more people into killers and victims. There are just all the old forces, becoming inexorably more potent as years go by without major improvement in the harried lives of hundreds of thousands of Detroiters, some of them seemingly destined to be future murderers.

It isn't surprising that most homicides recorded this year, as in the past three decades, have occurred in certain specific sections of the black inner city.

For it is in those same neighborhoods that housing is the worst, that health is the poorest, that unemployment is the highest, that poverty is most rife, that under-education is most common, that drug use is greatest, that family disruption is most widespread, that inadequate policing is most likely, that insecure, aggressive behavior is most open, that personal fear is deepest.

POLICE WILL SAY that "people just don't seem to respect human life any more." Psychologists add an important explanation: People who don't respect human life are people who probably don't respect themselves either, and life in a city slum can be a profoundly cheapening experience.

It creates a community where many, many men have very little by which to prove themselves, very limited opportunities to assert themselves as individuals. So an old-style, tough-guy, frontier aggressiveness becomes an important, sustaining way of life.

Arguments become violent faster, personal offenses are countered more quickly. Fists and knives fly at less provocation. And there are all those guns.

Any petty argument can end in a shooting. Any minuscule difference of opinion can be settled by a killing. People in Detroit have died over the price of a pair of shoes, the results of a penny-ante card game, the volume of a radio, the severity of a frown, "silly things" as one police officer put it.

They also have died at the hands of thieves in increasing numbers. The deaths attributable to drug traffic have increased drastically in the past two years. Shoot-outs between grocers and bandits have become almost commonplace.

SOME OF THOSE killings might have been prevented. But scores of the 127 deaths that occurred in January and February couldn't have been, until the moment a knife flashed or a gun went off.

And that will be true of most of the deaths yet to come as well. Statistically, most homicides are committed by young black men with guns. But statistics don't reveal what goes on inside a given head in the moment before a life is ended, or how to pin-point the people most murder-prone.

And they don't shed any light on the cosmic averaging that seems to determine how much squeeze a community can take before its weakest, least restrained members begin to crack in numbers that end up being called a homicide wave.

But those communities most vulnerable are being squeezed these days, and by the time the year is out, 700 or 800 people will have died of the pressure. Murder is not like other crimes.

Weekend of Death: How 11 Victims Died In a Strange Pattern of Sudden Violence

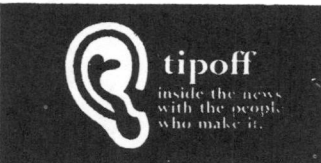
tipoff
inside the news with the people who make it.

Judging the Judge

A number of Detroit judges are unhappy with the recent nomination of Recorder's Court Judge Robert J. DeMascio as federal district judge for eastern Michigan. Members of the bench in both District and Recorder's Courts expressed dismay at DeMascio's nomination by GOP Senator Robert Griffin. "I can think of at least 25 judges in Detroit who are more qualified than Bob," one judge said.

What Else Is New?

After a year's study, the 19-member Michigan Welfare Study Commission came out with an 83-page report on the state's welfare program. One of the conclusions: "... the Commission believes that the basic problem of welfare clients is the lack of sufficient income."

Bars Checked

The day Mayor Gribbs made his tour of new downtown Detroit bars, city hall and police department investigators checked each of the four establishments on his itinerary for possible Mafia connections. All four bars passed the test.

Hood Winked

Common Councilman Nicholas Hood may be getting slightly carried away with his legislative power—or he may just be mixing his elected job with his role as an ordained minister.

Griffin   DeMascio   Hood

At any rate, last week Hook told a city official about to address the Council that he could: "Either stand, sit or kneel."

Running a Railroad

Add this to your collection of ways not to run a railroad. When a Free Press photographer went to Michigan Central station recently to take a picture, he was told he would have to get permission from a sergeant of the railroad police. The sergeant sent him upstairs to the captain, who sent him down the hall to the station manager, who sent him upstairs to the administrative assistant, who sent him down who said he would have to call Chicago. Chicago told him he would have to sign a form which they would mail and which he would probably get in two days.

In 36 hours last weekend, 11 persons were killed in Detroit. It may have been the most murderous two-day period in Detroit history. The circumstances of last weekend's deaths were not necessarily representative of the way most homicides occur, but they tell much about the randomness and unpredictability of violent death. Free Press reporters Julie Morris, Tom Ricke and Edward Shanahan spent last week examining those weekend killings, learning how the victims came to be where they were killed and, when possible, why they died.

On the last Friday night in February, people were dying in Detroit at the rate of one per hour.

The last deaths that night were perhaps the most tragic. The victims apparently were killed mistakenly by a friend because they were kidding around.

It began about 11 p.m. when construction worker Harvey Plant got up to leave a small gathering at his sister's house on Stanley. Plant, his sister, Annie Rooker, and her boyfriend, Jack Wilson, had spent the evening sitting around the dining room table drinking. They had finished a pint of whisky among them.

Plant agreed to drive with Wilson to Flat Rock the next morning to work on a car and bail Wilson's brother out of jail.

Plant said his goodbys and walked alone to his car, which was parked at the end of the block near the corner of Fourteenth and Stanley.

Within minutes, two cars pulled next to Plant. Four men got out and surrounded him.

Fourteen-year-old Lee Rooker looked out the dining room window, across the junk-filled vacant lot, and down to the dark street corner where she saw his uncle walking to his car.

He said the four men shouting his uncle and he yelled: "Uncle Harvey's getting it. They're ganging up on Uncle Harvey."

"I'm going to help him," Wilson said. He appeared on the front steps of the house a few seconds later holding a 30-caliber carbine.

"Next thing you know," Harvey Plant said, "I was just standing there and there were bullets and cement flying all around us. Guys were falling one by one. First Tommy, then the others."

Plant was shot in the leg, but he managed to get to the unregistered .38 revolver which he had kept in his car's glove box since he was beaten and robbed three years ago.

Wilson stopped shooting to reload and Plant fired three shots at him from his .38. The last bullet hit Wilson in the chest. He dropped the rifle and fell to the ground.

When police arrived a few minutes later, there were six men lying on Stanley Street with bullets in them.

Soon it became apparent that Wilson had made a tragic error. The four men who had surrounded Harvey Plant were his cousin, Mack Heard, and three brothers, Evert, Thomas and Charles Plant.

Wilson knew all the Plants. He came to Detroit from the same small town they had come from, Okolona, Miss. But in the dark he could not recognize them.

Thomas Plant and Mack Heard died of their wounds. They died because they were kidding Harvey Plant about driving home to Mount Clemens. They told Harvey he couldn't leave because they had just arrived and they wanted to visit with him. Kidding and pushing as they had done since they were boys growing up in a close family in Okolona.

The corner of Fourteenth and Stanley is not well lighted and it was natural for the people in the house at 2234 Stanley that night to assume that Harvey Plant was being robbed on that corner. It happens around there all the time.

Wilson was charged with two counts of manslaughter.

Plant and Heard were the fourth and fifth persons to die in a five-hour period that evening.

THE THIRD may have been a 30-year-old salesman from

Turn to Page 4B, Column 4

"It is tempting to think of the killings as part of an overall street crime problem, and to a degree that is true ... But fully two-thirds of the homicides that have occurred this year follow the classic formula — friend against friend, relative against relative." (The picture above is of an actual victim — from a photographer's files. This victim was carrying a gun. Protection or provocation?)

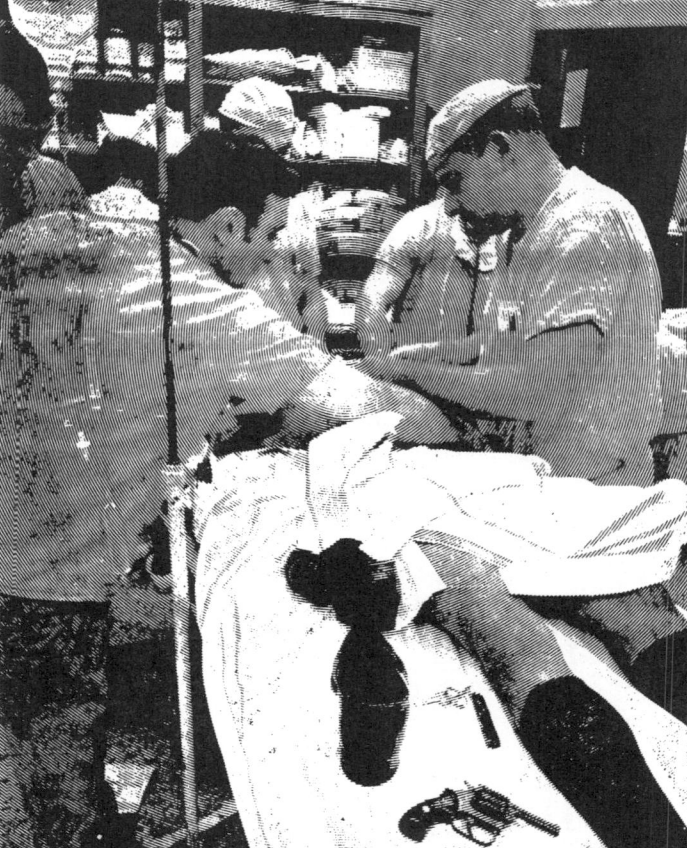

Free Press Photos by IRA ROSENBERG

'A VICIOUS CIRCLE OF FEAR'
Detroit's Home Arsenals

BY TOM DeLISLE
Free Press Staff Writer

You can buy them at stores downtown; in gun shops in the suburbs. Many are sold on the sly; some are stolen or smuggled items that come cheap. Ask around, they're not hard to find.

You don't want to use a gun. But it's nice to know you've got it the next time somebody messes with your property. Keep it hidden in your home. Away from the kids, of course. Or the glovebox of your car is a good place. Just let some guy try to rob you or get smart with your wife.

There is a vicious circle of fear that runs through Detroit. It's almost an arms race, a threat-protection cycle. Its evidence is an awesome group of statistics that can be boiled down to signify violence and death.

More than 80 percent of the stunningly high number of murders in Detroit are committed with handguns. There are an estimated 500,000 handguns in circulation in the city. More than 20 percent of the other murders involve the use of rifles and shotguns.

The number of long weapons in the city is unestimable, but it is likely that, lumping them with handguns, there are more firearms in the Motor City than cars. The Auto Club estimates 700,000 vehicles within the city limits. Guns are easily a bigger item.

And they are easy to purchase.

TO BUY a handgun you must be 21 years old with no felony convictions. You apply for a permit and are fingerprinted. You are granted the permit. You buy the gun of your choice.

To buy a rifle you don't need a permit. You fill out an affidavit at the store swearing you are not a felon.

To buy any type of ammunition you must show your driver's license.

To carry a gun you must apply for a Wayne County permit. You can get one for business reasons or to protect yourself. About 700 concealed weapons permits are granted monthly.

But, since only an estimated one of every four guns is registered with Detroit police, the rules of gun procurement and use matter little. They are obtained and they are carried in large numbers illegally.

A DETROIT couple who live in the Virginia Park area are an example of the 1,000 people who apply monthly for legal gun permits.

"I need it for protection," the man said. "We have quite a bit of trouble in the neighborhood. I need a handgun for my wife. I'm worried."

"We applied first last year," his wife said, "but we decided not to get the gun. We were afraid of having one. I was scared our kids might get hold of it. But now we need it.

"I'll probably carry it at times because you can't walk alone at night without getting beat up. I'm afraid of having one — I've never shot one — but I don't understand what's happened

Turn to Page 4B, Column 5

It is likely there are more firearms in the Motor City than cars. But gun shop owners, such as Santo Carollo, above, say it is not gun sales that cause the problem. "The trouble," he says, "is with the courts not enforcing present gun restrictions."

Detroit Free Press

Vol. 141—No. 128 Friday, September 10, 1971

COOLER — Showers or Thunderstorms. Highs 80-85, Lows 60-65.

METRO — Mart Slips at Lack Of Nixon Surprises. See Page 8, Section B

SEPT. 10, 1971:

The Ku Klux Klan, active in Michigan for decades, is implicated in the bombing of Pontiac school buses.

KLAN'S GRAND DRAGON INCLUDED

6 Arrested in School Bus Bombings

Legislators OK School Aid Bill

Senate Agrees To Big Cut

BY DAVID COOPER AND ROGER LANE
Free Press Lansing Staff

LANSING — The Michigan Legislature, rushing toward adjournment, took a major step Thursday night toward completing the big state budget by passing a $1.06 billion school aid bill.

Final action on the hill by both the House and Senate represented a $23.4 million cut in the school aid bill as it was originally adopted by the Senate.

Some legislators angrily fought the cuts, designed to help balance Michigan's long-delayed new budget, but the Senate gave final passage to the bill on a 21-9 vote.

PASSED EARLIER by the House Thursday, on a 64-37 vote, the bill now goes to Gov. Milliken for his expected approval.

With legislators already nine weeks past the normally start of the 1971-72 fiscal year, House and Senate leaders raced for a Friday adjournment and are expected to reconvene Oct. 28.

With school aid out of the way, the big state welfare bill and state aid to cities remained as the major items left to be resolved.

The Senate earlier Thursday cut a House-passed $534 million welfare bill by $31.5 million and sent it back to the House.

House Speaker William Ryan, D-Detroit, said he was prepared to adjourn without passing any welfare bill until October unless legislators could agree on removing some of the money cut from the bill.

In a tense struggle, the Senate accepted the school aid compromise over the strong objections of its Education Committee Chairman, Sen. Gilbert Bursley, R-Ann Arbor, and the lobbyist for Detroit's school system, Assistant Superintendent Richard Smith.

The fight in favor of the compromise was led by Sen. Robert VanderLaan, R-Kentwood, Republican Senate leader, and Sen. Coleman A. Young, D-Detroit, Democratic floor leader.

Both argued that despite shortcomings, the bill, with its $111 million increase over 1970-71 school aid subsidies,

Please turn to Page 4A, Col. 1

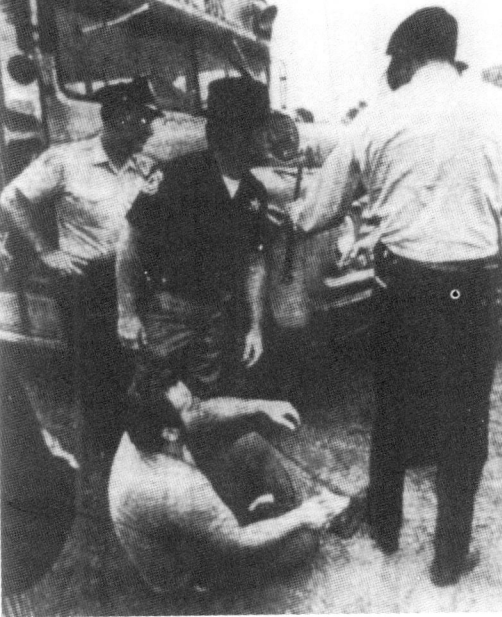

Free Press Photo by Chief Photographer TONY SPINA

Alexander J. Distel Jr., one of six men arrested Thursday, sits on the road Tuesday morning after he was allegedly bumped by a school bus trying to leave the Pontiac bus lot. Distel, who was among about 70 persons trying to block the buses the first day of school, said he hurt his ankle in the accident.

Hurricane's Rains Rake Texas Coast

Pictures on Back Page

GALVESTON, Tex.—(AP) — Hurricane Fern lashed the coastal area of Texas with heavy rains Thursday night as she moved toward shore after losing some of the blustery winds built up at sea.

"She barely has hurricane force winds now," said Dave Benton, chief meteorologist for the National Weather Service here.

Fern's winds dropped from 90 miles an hour to 80 m.p.h. Thursday afternoon. When her vanguard began raking the Texas mainland Thursday night, winds dropped to 70 to 75 m.p.h.

"We can't count on the wind diminishing further," Benton said, "but it should after it gets well over land."

AS THE FRONT edge of the storm began moving ashore, heavy rains hit the coastal area, with weathermen predicting as much as four to eight inches of rain before Fern dies.

The National Weather Service reported that at 8 p.m. the storm was about 40 miles off Galveston, moving at eight to 10 m.p.h.

A Coast Guard cutter searched 17 miles offshore for a shrimp boat which had reported it was in distress.

The Galveston causeway was closed, although the San Luis Pass Bridge remained open between Galveston Island and Freeport. These are the only bridges to Galveston Island.

Winds at the Galveston airport were gusting to 65 m.p.h. as the storm began moving ashore. Winds in the Houston area, 50 miles to the north, were gusting to between 35 and 40 m.p.h.

The National Weather Service
Please turn to Page 8A, Col. 1

FBI Cracks Pontiac Case

BY WILLIAM SCHMIDT
Free Press Staff Writer

Six persons, including the grand dragon of the Michigan Ku Klux Klan, were arrested Thursday in the bombing of 10 Pontiac school buses Aug. 30.

The six were charged with conspiracy to violate federal bomb laws, conspiracy to obstruct federal court orders and conspiracy to violate the 1968 Civil Rights Act.

The U.S. Department of Justice said the arrests followed an intensive FBI investigation into the bombing of the school buses which the Pontiac Board of Education planned to use to carry out a federal court school desegregation order.

ARRESTED were Robert Miles, 46, a Howell insurance salesman and head of the KKK in Michigan; Wallace Fruit, 29, of Drayton Plains, a state officer of the Michigan Klan; Alexander J. Distel Jr., 28, of Clarkston; Dennis C. Ramsey, 24, of Drayton Plains, Raymond Quick Jr., 24, of Pontiac and Edmund Reimer of Howell.

Miles and Reimer were arrested on Miles' farm home by FBI agents and state police who swooped down on the farm in a helicopter and in 40 cars.

The government said the alleged conspiracy involving the six men began at a statewide meeting of the KKK near Odessa in Vassar, Mich., July 4.

It charged that a number of other meetings were held and the bombing was planned by the six. It said a report on the bombing was made at a regularly scheduled meeting of the Michigan Klan at Miles' farm home last Sunday.

Three days later, the government said, the six accused men and others who were unnamed met and discussed additional acts of violence and destruction involving the school buses.

The complaint prepared by the FBI and sworn to before U.S. Magistrate Paul J. Komives, was signed by special FBI agent Philip L. Mercado, who the government said is a material witness.

It has long been known that the FBI keeps watch on the Ku Klux Klan through undercover agents.

THE 10 PONTIAC school buses were destroyed by bombers who cut their way into a school bus parking lot about 10 p.m. Aug. 30.

Fifty-seven buses were parked in the lot and 44 new ones had been ordered to help implement the busing program which has divided the city.

Six bombs were placed on the tops of bus gas tanks before
Please turn to Page 2A, Col. 2

Pontiac cracks down on disruptions of court-ordered busing. Page 3A.

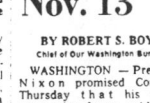

KLAN leader Robert Miles, who was arrested Thursday.

Freeze Will End Nov. 13

BY ROBERT S. BOYD
Chief of Our Washington Bureau

WASHINGTON — President Nixon promised Congress Thursday that his 90-day wage-price freeze will end Nov. 13. He announced he will begin consultations Friday with labor, business and agriculture to plan a more permanent system of "wage and price stabilization."

In a rare appearance before a joint session of Congress, the President won thunderous applause with a vow to put America's interests ahead of foreign nations' desires for trade and aid.

He plugged for prompt passage of his three tax-cut proposals, but cautioned the Democratic controlled congress against the "temptation" of cutting taxes even further.

In the only real news of his 30-minute address, he said he will send Congress next year a new program of "tax reform to create jobs."

THE PRESIDENT gave no details, but he may have been referring to the "human investment" program he suggested in his 1968 campaign, but never achieved.

It would offer tax incentives to companies which hire and train unskilled workers and
Please turn to Page 2A, Col. 1

U.S. sees drop in jobless rate, but compensation stays the same. Page 6C.

Action Line Dial 222-6464

Action Line solves problems, gets answers, cuts red tape, stands up for your rights. Write Action Line, Box 881, Detroit, Mich. 48231. Or dial 222-6464 between 8:30 a.m. and 4:30 p.m. Monday through Friday.

Our work with Indians in the Upper Peninsula is being held back because we don't have a truck to transport the donations we get. Sometimes we even have to turn down donations that are badly needed. Can Action Line Help? — American Foundation, Grosse Ile.

Program will get in gear in about six weeks when anonymous donor delivers converted three-ton utility van. Students from a Detroit high school will keep van in running shape. Foundation managed to help out poverty-stricken Chippewa tribe this summer even without truck. Volunteers gave up vacations to repair and insulate houses and fix roofs in Sault Ste. Marie area. Three Detroit doctors donated time to give free physical exams that turned up cases of TB and one boy who needed open heart surgery. To donate food, clothing, building supplies or money to Michigan tribes, write Foundation at 26265 W. River Rd., Grosse Ile 48138.

I collect rocks from all over the country for my patio and my favorites are white beach rocks from Cape Cod. Pollution is turning them gray. What can I do? — R.V., Lansing.

Try coating them with liquid silicone. Stuff available at hardware stores seals up rock pores so gray gunk won't stick. Stone phony of all time, 10-foot, 3,000-pound Cardiff Giant, was result of 1866 argument between Connecticut farmer George Hull and an Iowa minister over Bible passage "There were giants in the earth in those days." Reverend thought it meant men used to be taller, wouldn't agree passage 10 years later on the same reservation.

My father died in May and mom had to go on ADC. She's been trying since then to get glasses for my sister and brother, but the social worker is stalling. Please help, they've got to start school and won't be able to see. — A.C., Detroit.

Check is in the mail. When Action Line called, caseworker claimed "a lot of weird things" delayed your mom's claim. After your mom got eye prescriptions, Social Services medical division refused to accept them since they couldn't read doctor's writing. Next foul-up was when new prescription got lost in the mail. After that, caseworker delivered it by hand.

Action 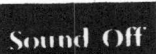 Line

My cousin is on emergency leave from Marine Corps because his father is in the hospital. My uncle isn't recovering well but Emanuel's request for extra leave was turned down. Can Action Line help? — J.S., Detroit.

Leave's longer. Action Line called Red Cross' Detroit director of Services to Military Families. Call to commanding officer at Camp Le Jeune, N.C., netted your cousin an extra week's leave when situation was explained. Any serviceman with legitimate reason for requesting extended leave can get help from the Red Cross by calling 961-3900.

Sound Off

THE QUESTION

Do you wish Gordie Howe would say it isn't so?

HOW YOU VOTED

YES, 67.7 percent. COMMENTS: "He's the only living legend Detroit has"... "Even at his age he's our best player the Red Wings have"... "If he'd only wait till he hits 800 goals I wouldn't mind as much"... "My father almost cried when he heard the news"... "I'm not even interested in hockey if Gordie isn't playing"... "Just one more game for your fans!"

NO, 32.3 percent. COMMENTS: "Gordie is a superstar not superman"... "He couldn't stand that punishment forever"... "I'm glad he's quitting while he's on top"... "Just wish he'd become a coach for the Red Wings"... "I want to remember him as he is"... "He sure earned a rest so let's just thank him for the past 25 years."

TOMORROW'S QUESTION
Do you approve of co-educational dormitories?

To Vote YES Call 961-3211
To Vote NO Call 961-4422

A Wife's Lonely Vigil

Mrs. Patricia Zuder of Muskegon keeps an anguished watch as divers search for the body of her husband, Curtis M. Zuder, 25, who drowned Wednesday afternoon while swimming in Lake Michigan off a Muskegon beach. His body was recovered 2½ hours later. Zuder, a recently discharged Vietnam veteran, and his 24-year-old wife were married in May.

Index

Amusements	3-5B
Ann Landers	3C
Astrology	7D
Billy Graham	10D
Bridge	7D
Business News	6-9B
Comics	7-8D
Crossword Puzzle	7D
Death Notices	7C
Earl Wilson	11A
Editorials	6A
Feature Page	11A
Movie Guide	6-8D
Obituaries	9B
Names and Faces	10D
Opinion	7A
Sports	1-4D
Stock Markets	7-8B
Television	4C
Want Ads	7-11C
Weekend Calendar	8C
Women's Pages	1-3C

HAVE THE FREE PRESS DELIVERED AT HOME PHONE 222-6500 Or Your Local Free Press Number

DEC. 12, 1971:

Gas explosion kills 17, traps workers in Lake Huron tunnel.

Detroit Free Press

MILD Considerable Cloudiness. Highs 35-40 Lows 22-27

ON GUARD FOR 140 YEARS

Vol. 141—No. 221 Sunday, December 12, 1971

METRO John S. Knight's Notebook See Page 2, Section B

Thirty Cents

NINE BADLY HURT, 14 SAFE

Blast Kills 17 in Lake Tunnel

Rescuers help a stumbling survivor of explosion Saturday in tunnel under Lake Huron
Free Press Photo by ALAN KAMUDA

Gas Fumes Explode at Port Huron

Crew Trapped In Water Tube

BY MICHAEL MAIDENBERG AND JAMES HARPER
Free Press Staff Writers

PORT HURON — A roaring gas explosion ripped through a water tunnel being built under Lake Huron five miles north of here Saturday, killing 17 workers and seriously injuring nine.

Fourteen other workers who were in the tunnel when the shattering blast occurred at 3:11 p.m. escaped injury and walked out of the death trap.

"There are people lying under pieces of metal who are cut in half," said a rescue worker. "I saw a rock that blew a man's head off. There are arms and legs lying around down there."

Two doctors who crawled through piles of debris to reach the victims said they had difficulty freeing workers from twisted metal. They feared to use torches because of gas fumes still lingering in the tunnel.

The blast was believed caused by gas that trapped the men as they were pouring concrete on steel forms just where the six-mile-long tunnel burrows under the lake-shore bed, about a mile from the tunnel shaft entrance. The tunnel is about 20 feet in diameter.

BOB MEESE, a Burtchville fireman who aided in rescue efforts, said the force of the blast had blown "hard hats and lunch boxes" a mile from the blast scene to the foot of the elevator entrance shaft on Metcalf Rd. between State and Lake Shore.

"There are a lot of dead men down there," Meese said. "It's a mess."

Firemen said it would take until Sunday to get the bodies from the tunnel. All electric lines were knocked out and rescuers worked by flashlight. Gas hampered the efforts.

The cause of the blast was not officially determined, but natural gas seepage from the shale surrounding the tunnel was suspected.

One worker who was in the tunnel but escaped injury said the blast "sounded like a tornado."

"It picked me up and threw

Please turn to Page 2A, Col. 1

Action Line Dial 222-6464

Action Line solves problems, gets answers, cuts red tape, stands up for your rights. Write Action Line, Box 881, Detroit, Mich. 48231. Or dial 222-6464 between 8:30 a.m. and 4:30 p.m. Monday through Friday.

I work at the Chrysler Eldon Avenue Axle Plant. You wouldn't believe the filth the employes have to put up with in the plant cafeterias. They don't even wash the cooking utensils, and rats scamper around picking up garbage while we're eating. Can you get this place cleaned up? — Anonymous Employe.

City health inspector visited all seven cafeterias in your plant, slapped Chrysler with a list of health code violations in cafeterias A, B and C. List includes dirty floors, dirty fixtures, dirty equipment, dirty tables and dirty chairs. The "rats" you saw are mice, but health inspector doesn't like them either, ordered Chrysler to step up extermination. (He also suggested you guys stop feeding them out of your lunch bags.) Inspector will be back in a week to haul company into court if place isn't shipshape. Inspector says Chrysler "has had general housekeeping problems, but they're just going to have to keep on top of it."

I'm a New Yorker and I can't convince my stubborn midwestern wife that fleas can do tricks. I used to go to a flea circus in a building on 42nd street — right downstairs from the tattooed lady. Can you convince her? — F.W., Midland.

Smallest show on earth played 42nd street for 31 years. Hubert's Museum was billed as the last flea circus in the country when ringmaster Roy Herbert Heckler, who inherited the circus from his father, retired in 1956. Heckler provided his audience with magnifying glasses to watch mini-stars with tiny collars around their necks tug on their desk-top show. Seven act program included chariot races, football, dancing, juggling and star Paddy carrying a flag. Show featured European fleas who passed Heckler's flea intelligence test. American fleas are too lazy, Heckler said. Took him three weeks to train a "bright flea" — and two years to train a human to train fleas.

My buddy is one of those guys who says labor unions run the country. He says more than half of American workers belong to unions. Is he right? — R.R., Detroit.

Far from it. In American labor force of 85.9 million, 21.2 million workers or 24.7 percent belong to unions. Union membership's down from 35 percent of the total work force ten years ago. Industrial unions account for 9.2 million workers. Another 9.2 million belong to non-industrial labor organizations, and 2.3 million government employes have organized at local, state and federal levels. Only labor organizations that boast over a million members are the nation's largest, the Teamsters, with 1.8 million members and the UAW with 1.5 million.

GOT A YEN this year to gather together with people and sing the songs of Christmastime? Action Line does, and we'd like to sing with you. The sixth Action Line Christmas Carol Sing is coming up next Monday, December 20, at 7:30 p.m. at Kennedy Square. Please join us and J.P. McCarthy, Jimmy Clark at the Grinnell organ, Fat Bob the Singing Plumber and Don Large and his University of Detroit Chorus. Don't worry about the hungries or the chills: Hot dogs will be on Hygrade's; hot coffee on ARA Services.

Dear Readers

Action Line editors consider every request you send us. We publish the most interesting and helpful answers. We regret that we cannot answer, or even acknowledge, individual requests.

THE QUESTION

A Birmingham Santa charges $10 to make a Christmas morning house call to wake up kids and give them presents. Would you hire him?

HOW YOU VOTED

NO. 60.8 PERCENT. COMMENTS: "I live in the ghetto and I don't think he'd come here for $10"... "You don't have to pay the real Santa Claus"... "My dad's been doing that for years without getting paid"... "Christmas is already too commercial"... "Ho, Ho, Ho, now give him the dough."

YES, 39.2 PERCENT. COMMENTS: "The gleam in my kids' eyes would be worth the $10"... "It's a great idea"... "It's in keeping with the spirit of Christmas"... "Only if the $10 includes the price of the reindeer"... "If you pay him $10, he'll come even if the kiddies aren't good little boys and girls."

TOMORROW'S QUESTION

Mrs. Philip A. Hart said she favors a mandatory two-year conscription of young men and women to work in humanitarian projects. Are you in favor of this program?

To Vote YES — Call 961-3211
To Vote NO — Call 961-4422

Tunnel Survivor — a Witness to Death

BY WILLIAM SCHMIDT
Free Press Staff Writer

PORT HURON — One of the eight survivors of the underwater tunnel explosion lay in his hospital bed Saturday night with a broken arm and talked about being a witness to death.

"One minute I was working, the next minute listening to everybody scream."

Francis M. (Rick) Hamrick, 28, of Lexington, was being treated for the broken arm and other possible injuries at Port Huron Hospital. He had been working on forming the wall of the tunnel with concrete when the explosion occurred.

"Who knows what happened?" Hamrick said. "I never heard anything at all.

All of a sudden everything was gone and it was black."

ANOTHER survivor, Richard M. Green of Carsonville, said: "People and bodies went flying everywhere, just like a bomb."

As Hamrick lay on his back on his hospital bed, two nurses sponged dirt and dried blood from his face, some of it from a cut above his right eye.

Someone had already stitched up a cut under his chin and set up the intravenous feeding equipment.

Hamrick said he doesn't remember losing consciousness, but he does remember waking up later in the tunnel. "I opened my eyes and everything was dark," he said. "Another guy was somewhere near me hollering."

Hamrick said he stood up, but someone (presumably a rescuer) came along in the darkness and told him to sit down.

Hamrick said he was paid about $5.75 an hour for a 48-hour work in the tunnel. But the work is so hot and wet that the men — usually in crews that average about 25 in number—wear only rain

Please Turn to Page 2A, Col. 2

BLAST survivor Larry Vernor: "It picked me up and threw me about 10 feet through the air."

Indians Near Dacca

From UPI and AP

Thousands of Indian paratroopers launched an airborne assault on the outskirts of the East Pakistani capital of Dacca on Saturday, seeking to knock out the city's outer defenses and clear the way for ground forces closing in.

An Indian army spokesman indicated that a forward elements of the ground forces were now within 15 miles of Dacca.

India's army commander broadcast an appeal to the estimated 30,000 to 50,000 Pakistani troops there to surrender and "avoid unnecessary deaths of many of your soldiers."

A Pakistani spokesman confirmed that the Indians had made massive troop landings but said most of the paratroopers had been wiped out. However, he added: "The general situation remains grim."

There were reports in London that the military governor of East Pakistan, Maj. Gen. Forman Ali Khan, had offered to surrender to India under certain conditions, but that the Pakistani government had blocked the move.

Ali was said to have told United Nations officials in Dacca that he would surrender to the Indian army but would have no dealings with the Bangla Desh guerrillas.

He also insisted that West Pakistan civilians and troops be evacuated and that East Pakistan be put in the hands of leaders of the Awami League, a Bengali political movement which has had representatives elected to the Pakistan National Assembly.

An All-India Radio broadcast Saturday night said: "Operation Dacca is in full swing." It said India forces, working closely with Mukti Bahini "freedom fighters," had crippled and routed the

Please turn to Page 15A, Col. 1

India Mothers A New Nation

This is the first report from Saul Friedman of the Free Press Washington Staff, who is covering the India-Pakistan conflict in the war zone.

BY SAUL FRIEDMAN
Free Press Washington Staff

JESSORE, East Pakistan — The road to Jessore, like an umbilical cord, is giving life from India's belly to a new nation.

Along that 100 miles of road, with its blown-up bridges and debris of war, flow the blood and sinew for what is becoming Bangla Desh.

Once, when the British ruled it, the area was called East Bengal, home of the fabled Bengal Lancers. After the British gave it up in 1947, the area became East Pakistan.

Saul Friedman

Now, about nine months after West Pakistan began a reign of terror to keep its eastern half in line, Indian troops and local guerrillas are closing in on the last of the Pakistanis at Dacca, the capital of the area. They are assuring that the new state — Bangla Desh, which means "Bengali nation"—will live.

In aiding Bangla Desh, India for the first time is playing a military and power politics role in the subcontinent. And it is about to win.

BUT EVEN in the euphoria of winning and the beginning of a new state, India is risking danger. Bengal has traditionally been hostile toward India, and the hostility may erupt if India attempts to ... Muslim, and deep-rooted rivalries still exist ... and Hindus in the new country are due in the new country ...

West Bengal, a state ... communist move ... ments which now could ... to India's

Please turn to ...

Inside the Free Press

Amusements	7-11B	People Page	18A
Ann Landers	5C	Radio	6B
Astrology	19D	Sports	1-8D
Books	5B	Stock Markets	16-18C
Bridge	6B	Travel	8-11D
Business News	15-19C	Want Ads	12-19D
Crossword Puzzle	8B	Women's Pages	1-14C
Death Notices	12D		
Editorials	2B	HAVE THE FREE PRESS	
Movie Guide	12B	DELIVERED AT HOME	
Names and Faces	18A	PHONE 222-6500	
Obituaries	20B	Or Your Local	
Opinion	3B	Free Press Number	
Outdoors	8D		

The workmen's families wait in quiet anguish. Page 3A.

CITY WANTS ROCK PALACE SHUT

Drug Sales Boom at Eastown

BY JOHN WEISMAN AND JIM NEUBACHER
Free Press Staff Writers

More than a dozen dope dealers are operating a veritable drug supermarket every weekend on the mezzanine of the Eastown Theater, openly and with almost no fear of the management, the theater's security force or the Detroit police.

In past months, Detroit's foremost rock and roll palace has become more than just a place to hear music. For hundreds of young people, that once-lavish old movie house at 8041 Harper near Van Dyke has become a place to buy, sell and use drugs.

A city hearing examiner, after taking testimony from a number of police officers, recommended Friday that Mayor Gribbs lift the licenses of the Eastown for reasons ranging from overcrowding to missing rest-room doors.

Oddly in the testimony, the only mention of drug abuse involved the pervasive smell of marijuana in the theater and two narcotics arrests, both made in 1970 and both made while there were no crowds in the theater.

Bob Bageris, the 24-year-old promoter who is co-owner of the Eastown, says: "The Eastown is not a place for dope. I try to keep dope out."

And his attorney, David Fried, says: "If there was (a serious drug problem), I would think the police would have been more active than they have ... From the testimony presented in the hearing, drugs are not the problem the public was led to believe."

NEVERTHELESS, ON THREE successive nights late last month, Free Press reporters mingled with the young people patronizing the dealers on the Eastown mezzanine, watched dozens of sales, and found it a simple matter to buy pills and powder hawked as mescaline, amphetamines, barbiturates, LSD, cocaine and heroin.

Some of the drugs were proved in laboratory tests to be the real thing. Others were phony. And one batch of purported heroin turned out to be an insoluble substance that could kill anyone who injected it.

It is no secret that the Eastown has become a drug center. Detroit police know about it, but fear that any move to stop the drug traffic will provoke a riot among the hundreds of people who pay $5 each to attend rock concerts there.

City officials know about it, too, but after a year of trying, they still have not been successful in closing the place and may

Please turn to Page 8A, Col. 1

Schmidt Quits, Lions Hunt Coach
Details On Page 1D

COOL
Scattered Sunshine
High 30-36 Low 20-27
Map and Details on Page 9-D

Detroit Free Press
ON GUARD FOR 141 YEARS

Vol. 142—No. 250   Saturday, January 13, 1973

METRO
Inflation Fears
Send Market Skidding
See Page 2, Section C

15c
6-Day Home Delivery—75c

JAN. 13, 1973:

Hayward Brown, one of three men sought in the shooting of an undercover Detroit police unit, is captured.

STRESS Suspect Captured

Action Line
Dial 222-6464

Action Line solves problems, gets answers, cuts red tape, stands up for your rights. Write Action Line, Box 881, Detroit, Mich. 48231. Or dial 222-6464 between 8:30 a.m. and 4:30 p.m. Monday through Friday.

My daughter has been separated from her husband for a year. He's been harassing us with phone calls night and day ever since. He calls my 85-year-old mother and stepfather at all hours too. We have no proof, but we're sure it's him. He's threatened us many times. The phone company and the police say they can't help. He's on probation on a marijuana possession charge now, so his probation officer should have some control over him. That ends next month, and we're afraid of what will happen. Please don't dismiss this as just another family fight.— J. A., Detroit.

Change your mind about changing your phone number. That was the first relief Ma Bell offered. Bell officials checked records, found you'd refused help from the Annoyance Call Bureau. Before you can do anything about annoyance calls to your telephones, you've got to have some proof. Bureau will help you get it. His probation officer knows about threats too, said he has a surprise for phantom caller at his February 16 probation hearing. Officer will ask for a one-year extension of his probation. That means if you and Bell can prove phone harassment or other wrongdoing, his magic dialing fingers will cool in jail.

My dad and I saw a girl with a far-out hat, and he said it reminded him of "whoopie hats" of the 1930s. My mother doesn't remember them, and neither do my older profs at Wayne. Is this a put on?—J. P., Detroit.

All your dad put on was a whoopie hat, like every other Depression era swinger. Large headpiece, felt and floppy, went for about two bucks. Hat made its debut with Eddie Cantor underneath it in 1928 Broadway musical review "Whoopie." Cantor donned the hat to sing title song "Making Whoopee." Style lasted until 1935 when whoopie hats went the way of bathtub gin. By the way, whoopie hats were for men. Their feminine companions stuffed their hair into snoods, a '30s revival of a Victorian era fashion with one notable exception. Gone were jewels and fancy embroidery that marked a more prosperous era.

Action Line

Last March I paid $319 for a couch and chair at Center Road Discount in Essexville. By June the cushion covers started to fall apart and the couch sinks in when you sit on it. Every time I call, they promise a factory representative will be right out. Nobody ever calls or comes. Can you get them to at least look at my furniture? — G. O., Bay City.

First you have to get their attention. Center Road ignores calls and letters — even the two Action Line asked attorney general's Consumer Protection Division to send — but it perks up when a lawsuit's in the wind. Suits in Small Claims Court have worked for six other unhappy customers since June, 1970. Action Line helped you file yours last week. Hampton Township official who's fielded other gripes like yours said ignoring customer complaints "seems to be a general policy of the store." Bay County prosecutor Eugene Penzien has a complaint too. Center Road hasn't filed as a business with county or state. Penzien will inform store it can file or face criminal prosecution.

THE QUESTION
A new state law allows snowmobilers to use the far right of the right-of-way of any highway except for limited access roads like freeways. Do you favor this law?

HOW YOU VOTED
NO, 75.5 percent. COMMENTS: "People will do anything to avoid exercise. Why don't they try walking to get from one place to another" . . . "Our highway death toll is horrible now. Just wait until this starts." . . . "Snowmobiles should be banned as a menace in the tri-county area" . . . "It certainly is a good way to reduce the population."

YES, 24.5 percent. COMMENTS: "Snowmobiles have just as much right in the road as cars" . . . "We pay gasoline and highway taxes too" . . . "I've been dodging the cops for three years. I'm glad I'll be legal" . . . "Some snowmobilers are good, cautious people."

TOMORROW'S QUESTION
Lions head coach Joe Schmidt resigned Friday, saying, "The game just isn't fun anymore." Are you glad to see Joe go?

To Vote YES   To Vote NO
Call 961-3211   Call 961-4422

Dear Readers
Action Line editors consider every request you send us. We publish the most interesting and helpful answers. We regret that we cannot answer or acknowledge individual requests.

Brown... Police Knew Him Well

BY WILLIAM SCHMIDT
Free Press Staff Writer

Of the three suspects being sought in the recent STRESS shootings, none was better known to police than Hayward Brown.

Brown, 18, had been arrested by police 14 times as a juvenile, then twice more within the last year — once in June for armed robbery and again in September on a concealed weapons charge.

He was being sought on both of those warrants when he was named as one of three suspects in the Volkswagen sedan who opened fire on a Detroit STRESS team early Dec. 4 near the University of Detroit. Four policemen were wounded.

WHILE THE other two suspects — Mark C. Bethune, 22, and John Percy Boyd Jr., 23 — have had few brushes with police, Brown's name and face were well known to officers in

Please turn to Page 2A, Col. 1

—UPI Photo by JOHN ANDERSON

Two views of Hayward Brown as he arrived for his arraignment in Detroit Recorder's Court.

Free Press Photo by IRA ROSENBERG

Wild Chase Near WSU

One of three suspects sought by police in the recent STRESS shootings was captured Friday afternoon following a running gun battle that apparently began when a wild scheme to rob a Woodward Ave. bank went awry.

Hayward Brown, 18, was captured on Trumbull Av. near Warren after police exchanged gunshots with him during a 20-block chase south of Wayne State University.

Brown was first spotted by police after two or more men tossed at least three fire bombs into an upstairs office at 3750 Woodward in an apparent "diversion" to rob a bank directly downstairs.

ONE OF THOSE men was Brown, police said. A second man was identified by witnesses as John Percy Boyd, 23, also a suspect in the STRESS shootings, police said. A third man believed to have been involved has not been identified. At least one witness said that a fourth man also may have taken part in the fire bombings.

Police reported that the third suspect in the STRESS shootings, Mark Clyde Bethune, 22, was seen by witnesses in the area.

A high-ranking police official said police after his capture Brown told police he was "trying to get money to buy clothes so he could

Please turn to Page 10A, Col. 1

Fire-bombing causes panic. Page 3A.
Diagram of chase is on Back Page.
Council split on STRESS hearing. Page 5C.

LIKE BEING DEAD
Captives Tell of B52 Terror

SAIGON — (AP) — Being caught by a B52 bomb strike is "like being dead for three seconds," says Le Van Hieu. He lived through six of them.

Truong Van Thang, who has survived a dozen B52 strikes, reports: "Too many times and you lose your mind."

Strikes by the giant bombers are the most feared of American air attacks. But Hieu and Thang say ground soldiers, in fact, well-trained and lucky, can live with them.

THE WAR IS over for these two men, ex-officers from North Vietnam. Both surrendered last year and are undergoing indoctrination at an Open Arms center in Saigon.

Their memories are vivid.

Hieu, in 22 years of communist service, and Thang, in 13, saw B52 strikes, eard the whistle of bombs falling six miles through the air and the thunder when they hit. Each B52 in a three-plane mission spreads more than 100 bombs—25 to 30 tons of explosives—over a swath half a mile wide and a mile long. The curtain of black smoke looks from afar like a forest fire.

"My first experience with the B52s was in December, 1965," said Thang, 32. "It was near Plei Me, in the central highlands.

"When the spotter planes leave and the jungle goes quiet you know the B52s are coming. But you don't know when until the first bomb explodes.

"One bomb hit about 10 yards from a cave where I was hiding. Blood poured out of my ears. I was deaf for a month."

Hieu, 41, recalled his last B52 experience, in the Mekong Delta last November. "I was caught in the open when the first string of bombs hit. It was like a great wind. I was able to run to a bunker that the second string hit closer, about 100 yards away.

"You hear nothing. You are deaf and blind. You have no thoughts, no sensations, no feelings."

Please turn to Page 7A, Col. 1

B52s bomb red buildup near Saigon. Page 7A.

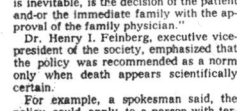

LE DUC THO, Hanoi's chief negotiator, smiled and waved as he arrived for Friday's peace talks with Henry Kissinger in Paris. Tho and Kissinger conferred for more than six hours, then agreed to meet again Saturday. (Story on Page 7A)

AP Photo

Corsetti   Oliphant

Two Tell Of Brush With Death

BY MICHAEL GRAHAM
Free Press Staff Writer

Robert Oliphant was almost ashen Friday afternoon as he recounted his brush with death at the hand of one of Detroit's most wanted men, Hayward Brown, who has been sought in connection with recent December police shooting incidents.

Oliphant, 24, a tall, reed-thin, bespectacled patrolman with the Wayne State University Department of Public Safety, has been fired at three times in his year and a half as a campus cop, but Friday was the worst.

Oliphant and fellow WSU Patrolman Leonard Corsetti agreed Friday afternoon that they are lucky to be alive after Brown tried to shoot both of them within a span of a few minutes on the fringes of the university.

"I had Bob Edge in the car with me, and at 12:43 p.m. we were on routine patrol going north on Woodward between Selden and Alexandrine," Oliphant said.

Edge, 22, a civilian dispatcher with the public safety department, was riding with Oliphant to familiarize himself with the neighborhood.

"When we got to the front of 3750 Woodward, we saw a group . . . flagging us down."

Please turn to Page 2A, Col. 1

Patient's 'Right to Die' Upheld by NY Doctors

NEW YORK — (AP) — Terminally ill patients have "the right to die with dignity" and may decide with a physician to discontinue extraordinary means of prolonging life, under a new policy of the New York State Medical Society.

The policy statement rules out the use of euthanasia, so-called "mercy killing." The 62-word statement, adopted by the society's board of governors Dec. 21 but just disclosed, reads:

"The use of euthanasia is limited to the province of the physician. The right to die with dignity, or the cessation of the employment of extraordinary means to prolong the life of the body when there is irrefutable evidence that biological death is inevitable, is the decision of the patient and/or the immediate family with the approval of the family physician."

Dr. Henry I. Fineberg, executive vice-president of the society, emphasized that the policy was recommended as a norm only when death appears scientifically certain.

For example, a spokesman said, the policy could apply to a person with terminal cancer who decides with his doctor to forgo some treatment that might prolong his life for days or weeks.

I'd Do It All Over Again...
---Quints' Mother

CHICAGO —(UPI)— The 26-year-old mother of week-old quintuplets said Friday that their birth was a "shocking" experience but that she "would do it all over again if I had to."

Mrs. Lynn Baer, looking healthy and happy in a bright red robe over a yellow nightgown, met the press for the first time since the two boys and three girls were born one month prematurely on Jan. 5.

Doctors at Evanston (Ill.) Hospital said the babies are recovering from a touch of jaundice and are "doing fine." Mrs. Baer, who is in Highland Park Hospital, has not even them since their birth but her husband, James, 30, views them every day.

"He says they're all very active, knocking each other around and fighting," Mrs. Baer said, laughing.

"I haven't seen them since they were born and then I was awake but kind of foggy-eyed. I remember a vision, or rather a blur of pink," she said.

THE BABIES were rushed to Evanston Hospital soon after birth because it has better facilities for handling emergencies.

Please turn to Page 7A, Col. 1

Mr. and Mrs. Baer grin as they discuss being parents of quints

AP Photo

Index

Amusements	6D
Ann Landers	8A
Astrology	7D
Billy Graham	10D
Bridge	7D
Business News	1-3C
Comics	7-9D
Crossword Puzzle	7D
Death Notices	5C
Editorials	6A
Feature Page	9A
Movie Guide	8-9D
Names and Faces	10D
Obituaries	5D
Real Estate	1-9B
Religion	9C
Stock Markets	1-3C
Television	10B
Want Ads	5-10C
Women's Page	8A

Feb. 23, 1973:

Introducing Michigan's first millionaire lottery winner, Hermus Millsaps.

Detroit Free Press

CLOUDY Light Snow High 25-29 Low 14-19

ON GUARD FOR 141 YEARS

Vol. 142—No. 291 — Friday, February 23, 1973

METRO Upturn Fails On Big Board — See Page 6, Section B

15c — 6-Day Home Delivery—75c

CHRYSLER WORKER WINS LOTTERY

From $176 a Week to a Million Bucks!

Action Line — Dial 222-6464

Action Line solves problems, gets answers, cuts red tape, stands up for your rights. Write Action Line, Box 881, Detroit, Mich. 48231. Or dial 222-6464 between 8:30 a.m. and 4:30 p.m. Monday through Friday.

We applied for a federal urban renewal loan last July to fix up our house. The Urban Renewal office in Center Line told us our loan was approved in September, but that's all anybody knows. When will we get our money?—W.B., Center Line.

You can pick up your $17,000 this morning. Your application has been lying around since September—everything was go except the money. Congress voted the funds for HUD 312 loans like yours in July, but money didn't reach HUD's coffers until this month. People who live in designated urban renewal areas in approved cities are eligible for government home improvement loans or outright grants. Grants go to families whose gross income is under $3,000 a year or whose housing cost equals 25 percent of income. Everyone who lives in a designated area is eligible for a home improvement loan of up to $17,000 at three percent interest. Program's available in parts of 18 Michigan cities—Detroit, Benton Harbor, Muskegon, Muskegon Heights, Jackson, Saginaw, Ann Arbor, Flint, Lincoln Park, Ferndale, Center Line, Alma, Benton Township, Clinton Township, Hamtramck, Madison Heights, Pontiac and Highland Park. See city Urban Renewal officials for information.

Last night my boyfriend and I had a big fight. He went home mad, and I brooded all night. This morning I wrote him a letter and said a lot of things I shouldn't have. Five minutes after I mailed it, he called to apologize. If he gets that letter, we'll be finished. The mailman wouldn't give it back to me. Can you save me?—R.M., Detroit.

Letter's dead. Romance is alive, U.S. Postal Service realizes there are times when mail must not go through. Call main post office at 226-6545 if you get a sick feeling in the pit of your stomach as you walk away from a mailbox. Describe the envelope, and postal authorities will contact branches where letter might be and intercept it. If letter's been airmailed or sent to another country, there's a 20 cent fee. After letter's corralled, you'll have to fill out recall form to get it back. Without signed authorization, mail can't be given to anyone but addressee. Post office spokesman said it gets about 10 requests a day from secretaries who mail things their bosses didn't want sent, or short-tempered employes who changed their minds about that nasty note headed for the boss. Make sure you have a valid reason for wanting a letter back—post office warns it can only intercept mail in "extreme" cases.

Action Line

Last fall, three friends and I worked for the Garrison House Organization in Garden City. The owner, George L. Noble, still owes me $140 in back wages. He owes my friends money, too. The place was closed in early January, and some employes were notified to attend a hearing in bankruptcy court February 23. My friends and I weren't contacted — does this mean we won't get our money?—J.K., Garden City.

Only thing it means is that mistake was made when your names were left off of list of Garrison House creditors sent to the court. Court records department supervisor said you're still entitled to appear at hearing in Room 1057 of the Federal Building at 10 a.m. You also have 30 days after hearing to send in proof of claim form and be eligible for payment even if you can't attend Friday session. Garrison House filed for reorganization under Chapter 11 of Federal Bankruptcy Code. If judge at Friday's hearing thinks plan is workable, hall will stay open under court supervision. This way business doesn't fold and creditors have better chance to get all their dough. If judge decides Garrison House has to file for bankruptcy, creditors have 60 days to file claims and share in company assets. Other Garrison House creditors can contact bankruptcy records office at 133 Federal Building to file claims.

Dear Readers

Action Line editors consider every request you send us. We publish the most interesting and helpful answers. We regret that we cannot answer or acknowledge individual requests.

THE QUESTION

President Nixon predicts history will prove him right for "sticking out" the war in Vietnam. Do you agree?

Sound Off

HOW YOU VOTED

NO, 60.9 percent. COMMENTS: "We didn't get peace with honor. We bought ourselves a little time to get out" . . . "Nixon stuck out the war until election day" . . . "We should have listened to MacArthur back in the early 1950s" . . . "History will prove Nixon a lot of things, but right isn't one of them."

YES, 39.1 percent. COMMENTS: "After Nixon's gone we'll appreciate how great he is" . . . "Those draft dodgers and commie-lovers will be sorry one day" . . . "Without U.S. efforts to save Southeast Asia, communism would have taken over the world."

TOMORROW'S QUESTION

Recorder's Court judges will decide whether to authorize a one man grand jury investigation of the drug traffic in Detroit. Should the court okay this dope probe?

To Vote YES Call 961-3211

To Vote NO Call 961-4422

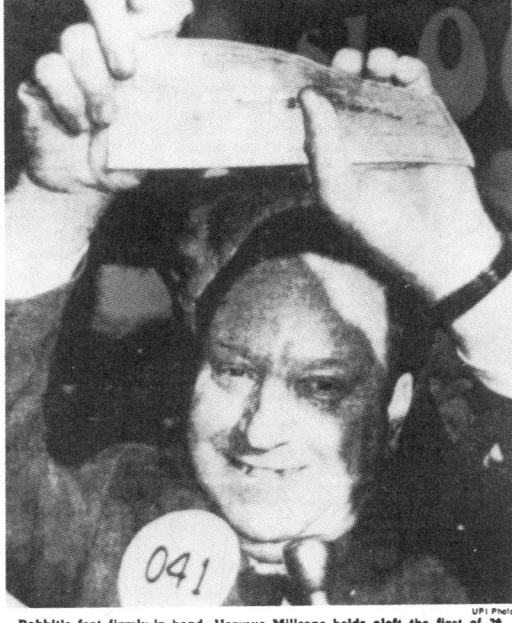

Rabbit's foot firmly in hand, Hermus Millsaps holds aloft the first of 20 $50,000 checks he will receive as Michigan's first lottery millionaire.

Airline Pilot Ignored Warning, Israelis Say

From AP and UPI

TEL AVIV — Israel's air force chief and the fighter pilots who shot down a Libyan airliner said Thursday the pilots were only trying to force the plane to land but it restate's laws as presently writing to escape.

Defense Minister Moshe Dayan told newsmen that the Israeli decisions in the incident were taken through normal military channels below the government level and had "no political significance whatsoever."

The Soviet Union, which backs the Arab countries in the Middle East conflict, declared through official news media that Israel was attempting to wreck a settlement.

APPARENTLY, 105 persons died in the crash Wednesday of the Libyan Airlines Boeing 727 jet in the Israeli-occupied Sinai Desert. Libyan officials said the three-jet plane had 112 aboard. Israel reported nine survivors were pulled from the wreckage but two of these, both women, later died.

"We tried desperately to force it down, not to shoot it down," the air force chief, Maj. Gen. Mordechai Hod, told reporters. He added: "The more the pilot objected and the more he tried to get away, the more suspect he became."

Israeli pilots said that before firing they confronted the French captain of the airliner face to face at less than 15 feet and tried in vain with hand signals and wing-wagging to get him to land.

But in Cairo, the plane's in—

Please turn to Page 2A, Col. 1

New Dem Chairman Bombs In First Meeting with Press

BY DAVID COOPER and REMER TYSON Free Press Staff Writers

LANSING — Morley Winograd, Michigan's new Democratic chairman, called a briefing for newsmen Thursday to announce a new party press policy. Instead, he:

● Tore up the notes of a reporter, who shouted that Winograd also struck him.

● Tried to hold the meeting with newsmen on an "off-the-record" basis, then lost his temper when some refused to agree to that.

● Answered "no comment" 16 times when asked on-the-record for his views on a party controversy between a labor leader and a black leader.

● Shifted the site of his "press briefing" in the Capitol at the last moment in an effort to avoid television cameras.

● And, finally, stalking angrily out of his own meeting before it even got started.

All in all, it was quite a first meeting with the news media for the 30-year-old Winograd,

Please turn to Page 16A, Col. 4

Democratic Chairman Morley Winograd just smiles and refuses to answer reporters' questions Thursday.

TV Adopts Medicine Ad Code

WASHINGTON — (AP) — Television industry leaders Thursday announced strong and sweeping rules regulating the TV advertising of non-prescription medications, starting next Sept. 1.

The rules adopted by a unanimous vote of the nine-member Television Code Review Board of the National Association of Broadcasters prohibit:

● On-camera taking of pills or capsules.

● Advertising in or adjacent to programs designed primarily for children.

● The use of children in presentations on behalf of non-prescription medications intended for adults.

● Personal testimonials or endorsement of products by "authority figures or celebrities."

● Approaches commonly associated with the "drug culture" or which imply a casual attitude toward the use of drugs and medications.

● References to non-prescription medications as "non-habit forming" or "non-addictive."

All 396 TV stations that subscribe to the NAB code are bound by the rules. And since the three National TV networks also are bound by the rules most of the 372 stations that do not subscribe to the code will, in effect, be following the ruler.

THE CODE board chairman, Max Bice, vice president and general manager of KTNT, Tacoma, Wash., said:

"In these actions today, the code board demonstrated again that voluntary, self-regulation machinery can protect the public interest by dealing effectively with difficult issues. The important and extensive changes adopted today will be visible to television viewers this fall."

Bice said the NAB code authority will hold a workshop for broadcasters to discuss the rules. It will be held in New York City at a date to be announced.

BY WILLIAM MITCHELL Free Press Staff Writer

LANSING—With his fingers crossed and holding a 50-cent lucky rabbit's foot, a 53-year-old auto plant worker from Taylor became the first million dollar winner in the Michigan lottery at a drawing here Thursday night.

Hermus Millsaps, who said he makes $176.80 a week sawing wood in a Detroit Chrysler Corp. plant, received a check for $50,000 immediately and will receive a check for the same amount every year for the next 19 years.

"I'm pretty shook right now," Millsaps said, as his number was drawn for the big prize in the three-month-old lottery. "God bless everybody, God bless you.

"I'm going to pay off my house, get the bill collectors off my back and get straight for a change," Millsaps said following the drawing.

MILLSAPS WON out of a field of 10 finalists who had been selected from 120 semifinalists Thursday night. The remaining nine finalists won amounts ranging from $5,000 to $100,000. Millsaps said he and his wife, Ann, 47, took a bus to Lansing from their home because

his 1961 model car had "bad tires."

"It's not going to change my life at all," his wife told reporters. "I like to sew, I like to cook, I like to work in the garden. We've always been kind of poor, and this isn't going to change things that much," she said.

But later, as she sat drinking a screwdriver with her husband in the Filibuster Bar of the downtown Lansing Olds-Plaza Hotel, Mrs. Millsaps said, shaking her head:

"I never thought things like this happened to people like us." Her husband sat drinking a beer—Miller High Life.

Mrs. Millsaps was a widow before they were married. She has two children from her first marriage. Both children are now grown. Millsaps has three children from a previous marriage, which ended in divorce. He said two of the children are grown and he makes $18 -a-week child support payments for the care of the third, a 14-year-old son.

MILLSAPS SAID HE was in debt $24,000 but that now he is thinking of buying a new car. He said he didn't think he would go to work Friday.

The names of seven of the 10 finalists were

Please turn to Page 16A, Col. 1

U.S.-China Ties Expand; Peking To Free 2 Yanks

WASHINGTON — (UPI) — The United States and China announced Thursday they will open liaison offices in each other's capitals, a step just short of full diplomatic relations, to arrange a vast expansion of trade, scientific, cultural and journalistic contacts between the two countries.

White House adviser Henry A. Kissinger said that as a further gesture of goodwill, Premier Chou En-lai had informed president Nixon that China in the next few weeks will release two American pilots downed and captured when they penetrated Chinese territory during Vietnam bombing raids.

THE PROMISED release of Navy Lt. Cmdr. Robert J. Flynn of Salt Lake City, who has been held since Aug. 21, 1967, and Air Force Maj. Philip Smith of Victorville, Cal., captured Sept. 20, 1965, would leave only one American known to be imprisoned in China.

He is John Thomas Downey of New Britain, Conn., acknowledged recently by the President to have been a CIA agent, who was captured Nov. 29, 1952 on an intelligence mission in China.

His life sentence was commuted to five years, apparently in connection with Mr. Nixon's trip to China a year ago.

Kissinger said Chou informed him during his recent four days of talks in Peking that Downey's sentence would be reviewed the second half of this year on the basis of his "exemplary" behavior.

Kissinger briefed reporters and congressional leaders at the White House at the same time that Washington and Peking issued a joint communique declaring that "the time was appropriate for accelerating the normalization of relations."

He said he and Chinese leaders agreed that the existing channel of communications in Paris was inadequate, and that the two countries would establish "moderate-sized" offices in Washington and Peking in the next few weeks.

THESE LIAISON offices will handle trade matters and the "whole gamut of relationships" between the United States and China, Kissinger said.

The representatives would lack formal diplomatic status but would enjoy traditional diplomatic privileges, including immunity from arrest and the right to use secret codes in communicating with their home governments.

"Our contacts with the People's Republic of China have moved from hostility towards normalization," said Kissinger, who returned Tuesday from a two-week tour of Bangkok, Vientiane, Hanoi, Hong Kong, Peking and Tokyo.

It would be the first time since the communists seized power in 1949 that China and the United States have established a formal, working contact, and the first time that China has had official representation in the capital of a country which recognizes the rival Nationalist Chinese regime on Taiwan.

Kissinger said Peking's reversal of policy on the issue of

Please turn to Page 5A, Col. 2

3 Federal Judges Strike Down State Anti-Abortion Law

BY JUDY DIEBOLT Free Press Staff Writer

Michigan's 127-year-old abortion law was struck down as unconstitutional by another court Thursday.

This time, a three-judge panel from U.S. District Court in Detroit, adopting the language of a recent U.S. Supreme Court decision, said Michigan's restrictive abortion law "cannot survive the constitutional attack made upon it here."

The decision was handed down by U.S. Circuit Court of Appeals Judge George C. Edwards and U.S. District Judges Thomas P. Thornton and John Feikens.

Their decision came in response to a lawsuit filed by an Ingham County woman identified under the fictitious name of "Nancy Poe" who was seeking an abortion in Michigan.

Mrs. Poe subsequently had to go to another state to obtain an abortion.

Other parties in the lawsuit were four doctors who claimed they are being denied constitutional rights to the full practice of medicine as they see fit.

The U.S. Supreme Court ruled on Jan. 22 that states cannot prohibit voluntary abortions during the first three months, however, states may point in a pregnancy the decision belonged to the women and her doctor, the court said.

During the remaining six months, however, states may regulate abortion procedures in ways reasonably related to the mother's health. For the

Please turn to Page 16A, Col. 1

Index

Amusements	5-8C
Ann Landers	2C
Astrology	13D
Business News	4-8B
Comics	13-15D
Death Notices	8D
Editorials	8A
Movie Guide	14-15D
Obituaries	8D
Opinion	9A
Sports	1-6D
Stock Markets	5-8B
Television	7D
Want Ads	8-12D
Weekend Calendar	4C
Women's Pages	1-4C

Winning Numbers

156 819

If you have 156 or 819, you win $25 and qualify for a million dollar drawing. If you have 156 819 or 819 156, you qualify for a super-drawing at which you will win at least $10,000 and perhaps as much as $200,000. All winners should contact one of the 7,000 lottery agents for the location of the nearest claim center. Take your winning ticket to the claim center for verification. The next weekly drawing will be at 9:45 a.m. Thursday in the Fashion Mall at Saginaw. Tickets for that drawing are on sale until Tuesday morning.

SHOWERS
Cloudy and Cool
High 61-69 Low 47-49
Map and Details on Page 9D
HOURLY TEMPERATURES

Detroit Free Press
ON GUARD FOR 142 YEARS

Vol. 143—No. 162 Saturday, October 13, 1973

METRO
NYSE Scores
Slight Gain
See Page 7, Section A
15c
6-Day Home Delivery—75c

OCT. 13, 1973:

Gerald Ford, of Grand Rapids, replaces Spiro Agnew as vice-president.

HOUSE REPUBLICAN LEADER

Gerald Ford Picked for V-P

Action Line
Dial 222-6464

Action Line solves problems, gets answers, cuts red tape, stands up for your rights. Write Action Line, Box 881, Detroit, Mich. 48231. Or dial 222-6464 between 8:30 a.m. and 4:30 p.m. Monday through Friday.

My son went to Europe in the spring of 1972 and brought back some novelty and gift items to sell. He had to post a $2,000 cash bond with U.S. Customs. The merchandise has long since been sold but Customs hasn't returned the bond payment. All they'll say is that Washington has to release the money. How long will that take? — L.S., Southfield.

Check for $1,975 — minus $25 broker's fee — arrived yesterday. Joseph Rychlicki, chief inspector at the U.S. Customs office in Detroit put tracer on son's file, located it gathering dust in Washington. Everything was in order so regional finance office in Chicago was able to issue check immediately. Customs holds onto bond money to guarantee payment of duty. Sometimes merchandise brings bigger profit than at first anticipated and customs keeps money in hand to make sure it gets fair share. All imports over $500 require a bond. Your son actually got his money back quicker than most. Normal waiting period for Customs refund is two years and some take up to three years to process.

Is it possible to get pet insurance in Michigan? I just spent $100 trying to save my cat from acute anemia and figure that insurance might save me a similar expense in the future. — S.S., Fraser.

"Pet-care" insurance is a thing of the past in Michigan. Insurance companies claim pet owners felt payment of health care premiums on cats and dogs just wasn't worth it. You might try asking your insurance agent if his company would be interested in setting up pet insurance program. If company agrees to petition state for that right, all insurers has to do is notify State Insurance Bureau of Fido's policy and he's covered. Coverage comes under cold heading of "miscellaneous property." One pet who never had need for health insurance was a pampered female German Shepherd owned by an eccentric South Carolinian. When the guy grew tired of his luxurious Lincoln Continental he turned it into a four-wheeled kennel for the dog. Dog got so homey that she gave birth to a healthy litter in the back seat.

The Warren Jaycees are sponsoring haunted house tours from October 19-30. We'd like to treat some underprivileged children to a free tour on the 18th, complete with a magic show and refreshments. Can you find 100 kids who would like an evening of fun? — I.E., Warren.

Big cheer went up at St. Francis Home for Boys and St. Vincent-Sarah Fisher Home for Children when kids got your invitation. Jaycees will hold pre-Halloween open house each evening from 6 p.m. to 9 p.m. at that spooky looking place on the corner of Chicago and Mound Roads in Warren. Creaking door opens to the public on October 19 and admission is 25 cents.

On North Territorial Road in Chelsea, midway between M52 and the Huron River, are two, large handpainted signs that state "Trespassers will be shot." Are these signs legal? — J.O., Hazel Park.

Distasteful—but not illegal. Washtenaw County Sheriff Fred Postill told Action Line that what a person posts on his own property is his business, as long as it isn't obscene — or in this case, as long as artist doesn't make good on threat. County Road Commission can only control road "right of way" — the property extending 33 feet to both sides of highway center line. If you see sign on commission territory that's offensive, ask to have it removed.

Culver Sales and Service in Mt. Morris has had our lawnmower since April. We know the parts necessary to fix it weren't sent to Culver until July, but it shouldn't take over two months to repair one lawnmower. — R.G., Flushing.

Mower's back home in time for last few cuts before winter. Store owner Charles Culver admitted he'd just let grass grow under his feet on repairs, said you'd been more than patient with him. Your machine was fixed and returned 24 hours after Action Line's call.

THE QUESTION
Agnew was allowed to plead no contest to the charge of tax evasion and to accept a $10,000 fine and probation in exchange for his resignation. Do you think he should have been forced to stand trial and answer for his misdeeds?

HOW YOU VOTED

YES, 74.3 percent. COMMENTS: "We have two separate laws, one for the rich and one for the poor"... "Agnew should have got 10 years"... "Anyone who'd hang around with a guy like Sinatra was no good from the beginning"... "If I'd have done that, they'd have locked me up and thrown away the key."

NO, 25.7 percent. COMMENTS: "Isn't it enough that he quit?"... "If Kennedy can get away with murder, Agnew can get away with this"... "But I think Nixon should stand trial for the way he avoided paying taxes."

TOMORROW'S QUESTION
Lee Iacocca, president of Ford Motor Co., said recently that efforts to save gasoline and cut down on pollution are threatening the basic American right to move about freely. Do you think that mobility is a more basic right than cleaner air?

To Vote YES Call: 961-3211
To Vote NO Call 961-4422

Gerald Ford acknowledges the applause as he stands by Mr. Nixon after the announcement
AP Photo

Court Says Judge Can Hear Tapes

BY ROBERT S. BOYD
Chief of Our Washington Bureau

WASHINGTON—The U.S. Court of Appeals ordered President Nixon on Friday to surrender his Watergate tape recordings to District Judge John J. Sirica.

The 5-2 decision was a serious but not unexpected setback for the President.

The President's lawyers were given five days to appeal the decision to the Supreme Court. Mr. Nixon has promised to obey only a "definitive order" of the highest court, but has not defined "definitive."

The appeals court order went beyond Sirica's ruling of Aug. 29 against Mr. Nixon.

Sirica had only asked to hear the controversial tapes himself so he could decide what parts to turn over to the Watergate grand jury. The appeals court said Sirica may let special prosecutor Archibald Cox listen to them too, if he chooses, to help the judge decide what evidence is essential to the prosecution.

Cox had asked that unedited tapes be presented directly to the Grand jury.

ALL FIVE judges who ruled against Mr. Nixon are Democrats. Two Republicans, both Nixon appointees, agreed with the Democratic majority that the courts have jurisdiction in the historic struggle over the tapes. But they sided with the President that he should not be forced to turn over the tapes in this case.

The majority opinion rejected the President's two major arguments: That he is absolutely immune from com-

Please turn to Page 2A, Col. 1

Nixon Taps Michigander

From UPI and AP

WASHINGTON — President Nixon, declaring it "time for a new beginning for America," tapped House Republican leader Gerald R. Ford of Michigan Friday night to be vice-president — a choice that brought cheers from Congress.

Two days after Spiro T. Agnew resigned in disgrace, Mr. Nixon told dignitaries at the White House and a nationwide broadcast audience that he had chosen the Grand Rapids congressman because "we need strong, effective leadership" to keep world peace and halt inflation.

Ford, 60, said he was "deeply honored, extremely grateful and I terribly humble." He pledged to work with Mr. Nixon and Congress to "make America a united America."

Ford said he assured Mr. Nixon that he would not seek the presidency in 1976.

Mr. Nixon decided on Ford early Friday, but did not tell him until about 7:30 Friday evening, 90 minutes before the announcement was made.

But the well-kept secret became obvious to the East Room crowd when the President said his nominee had served 25 years in the House of Representatives.

The large congressional delegation leaped to its feet in applause and cheers.

AGNEW WAS absent from the room and his name was never mentioned. He resigned Wednesday, pleaded no contest to a single charge of income tax evasion and was placed on three years' probation and fined $10,000 — the first vice-president in history forced from office.

Ford, a staunch conservative, is popular among members of Congress and his confirmation is virtually certain.

The nomination will go to both houses of Congress on Saturday. Under the 25th Amendment to the Constitution, adopted six years ago, confirmation requires a simple majority vote in each house.

Initial reaction among members of Congress was overwhelmingly favorable toward Ford. Most of those who commented, both Republicans and Democrats, predicted easy confirmation. A few, however, said Congress would not be stampeded into acting without full deliberations.

Mr. Nixon said Ford met the qualifications he had set for Agnew's successor. He said the new vice-president had to be "qualified to be president," a person who shared Mr. Nixon's own views "on the critical issues of foreign policy and national defense," and one

Please turn to Page 5A, Col. 6

The super-square Ford is a safe way out of a dilemma for Nixon, Page 10B.

How the President came to his decision. Page 3C.

Agnew will make television address Monday to explain his resignation. Page 3C.

More pictures on the Back Page.

SEN. VANDERLAAN:
The favorite for Ford's seat?

Election Would Fill Ford Seat

If Rep. Gerald R. Ford Jr.'s nomination as vice-president is approved by Congress, Gov. Milliken plans to call a special election immediately to fill Ford's seat in the U.S. House of Representatives.

Ford represents the Fifth District, of which Grand Rapids is the center.

Republican leaders expect one of the leading candidates to succeed Ford, if he becomes vice-president, will be State Sen. Robert Vanderlaan, the Senate Republican leader.

MILLIKEN HAS the option of calling a special election or waiting until the next regular election in 1974 to fill a congressional seat vacancy.

A spokesman for the Republican governor said Thursday night that Milliken would call a special election.

Milliken said of Ford's nomination:

"It was a good choice for America and a proud moment for Michigan. Gerald Ford is a man of great experience and great dedication to public service. I share his wish for a united America."

George Weeks, Milliken's press secretary, said Thursday night that contrary to reports published earlier, Ford's name had been among those Milliken recommended to replace Spiro Agnew.

Weeks said Milliken's list in

Please turn to Page 5A, Col. 5

Rep. Ford Ambitious, But a Team Player

BY REMER TYSON
Free Press Politics Writer

Rep. Gerald Rudolph Ford Jr. is a rough-and-tumble Midwestern Republican who believes in football, a strong military force, conservative public fiscal policy and getting ahead in life.

He has sought the vice-presidency twice, in 1960 and 1964, and has been a close friend of President Nixon since they served together in the U.S. House of Representatives in 1948.

Ford, 60, has always been an ambitious politician on the look-out for advancement, but he also is a team player.

HIS FIRST notice outside of his hometown of Grand Rapids, a western Michigan city steeped in Republicanism and the Dutch Reformed Church, came in the early 1930s when he played center and linebacker at the University of Michigan.

Ford, a broad-shouldered, blond, six-footer, was a mediocre football player, but the team's record was so bad in 1934 that he was named the university's outstanding player. Michigan won one game and lost seven that year.

In 1932 and 1933, Michigan was unbeaten, tying only one of 16 games, but Ford wasn't a starter on those teams.

Over the years, his football record has been embellished to where he is commonly referred to as one of Michigan's best-known All-Americans.

Ford likes his football-hero image.

THE OTHER big team in Ford's life has been the Republican Party, where he rose in the top by knocking off the old GOP leadership in the U.S. House of Representatives to become a national figure on Jan. 4, 1965.

Throughout his political career he has attached himself to established or rising political figures who have helped him move up to the nomination for the No. 2 office in the country.

The first was the late Sen. Arthur H. Vandenberg, a Republican from Michigan who served as speaker pro tempore of the U.S. Senate and was an architect of the bipartisan U.S. foreign policy of World War II years.

Vandenberg encouraged Ford to run for Congress in 1948 to oppose another Republi-

Please turn to Page 2A, Col. 3

SYRIA DENIES REPORT

Israeli Tanks Near Damascus

From UPI and AP

Israeli tanks drove to within artillery range of Damascus Friday, closing to a point less than 20 miles from the Syrian capital in a drive to annihilate Syria's armed forces, an Israeli spokesman said.

Syria denied the report, and said its forces were continuing fierce battles on the Golan Heights to the south. It said Israelis were retreating.

The Israeli military command also said its forces clashed with Iraqi troops for the first time inside Syria.

On the other front, Egypt said it had wiped out an Israeli flotilla in the Gulf of Suez and blasted apart an Israeli armored column in the Sinai desert.

The Soviet news agency Tass said a Soviet merchant ship was sunk by an Israeli attack on the Syrian port of Tartus. It warned that Israel would face "grave consequences" if such incidents continued.

The Tass statement said Israeli shelling of Tartus caused the sinking of the ship, Ilya Mechnikov, which was unloading equipment for a hydroelectric project. The Soviets reported no further details but Syrian government sources said the ship was set afire during Israeli shelling. All crewmen reportedly escaped injury.

OFFICIAL ISRAELI sources said lead elements of Israel's two-day-old armored thrust into Syria had advanced up the Damascus road in bitter fighting to a point where it was possible for Israel's longest gun, the U.S.-supplied 175mm cannon, to bombard the city's defenses.

The Israelis said their pilots shot down 29 Syrian MiGs. Syria said it shot down 35 Israeli warplanes.

An Israeli spokesman said the first of two defense lines before Damascus had been cleared. The second one, on the capital's doorstep, is anchored by a brigade under command of the brother of Syrian president Hafez Assad.

The burst through the first Syrian defense line put Israel on the outskirts of Qatana, which a spokesman described as a "bristling" military installation 12 miles outside Damascus.

Syrian officials, however, denied Israel's claims and maintained that the Syrians were still besieging the Golan Heights town of Qneitra. They said fierce tank and artillery battles were in progress.

ON THE SINAI front behind the Suez Canal, an Egyptian

Please turn to Page 2A, Col. 2

Kissinger clears Soviets of urging Arab attack. Page 3C.

Wholesale Fuels Rationed

WASHINGTON — (UPI) — The Nixon Administration, hoping to stave off fuel shortages this winter, ordered mandatory allocations of jet fuel, diesel oil and fuel oil for home heating. Airlines immediately announced a cutback in flights.

The Interior Department will administer the program, which will allow wholesalers to purchase as much of the oil as they purchased during the 1972 calendar year. If there is not as much diesel oil and fuel oil available, they will receive a sup-

ply proportional to their share last year.

THE CIVIL Aeronautics Board promptly authorized airlines "to consider schedule adjustments to the extent necessary to accommodate the President's fuel adjustment program."

Trans World Airlines said it would cut about five percent from its daily schedule, about 40 flights. Other airlines are expected to announce cutbacks shortly.

In Michigan, a spokesman

for a state agency working to resolve the fuel oil shortage said he hoped the administration's program would set up a system of even distribution.

"It will take time for us to assess what this new allocation program means," said Richard K. Helmbrecht, state Commerce Department director and head of Gov. Milliken's task force on fuel supply.

"But hopefully, it will im-

Please turn to Page 2A, Col. 3

Index

Amusements	2C
Ann Landers	9A
Bridge	7D
Business News	6-8A
Classified	3-10C
Comics	7-9D
Crossword Puzzle	7D
Death Notices	2C
Editorials	4A
Feature Page	9A
Horoscope	7D
Modern Living	1-8B
Movie Guide	8-9D
Names and Faces	2A
Obituaries	2C
Religion	1-5D
Sports	1-5D
Stock Markets	6-8A
Television	5A

Nov. 7, 1973:

Coleman Young promises "freedom and equality for all" upon his election as Detroit's first black mayor.

CLOUDY
Chance of Snow
High 36-39 Low 26-29

Detroit Free Press
ON GUARD FOR 142 YEARS

METRO
Rally Fades;
DJIA Loses 6
See Page 8, Section C

Vol. 143—No. 187 — Wednesday, November 7, 1973 — 15c — 6-Day Home Delivery—75c

NICHOLS LOSES CLIFF-HANGER

Young Elected City's 1st Black Mayor

6 Stay on Council; 3 Newcomers Win

BY JULIE MORRIS
Free Press Staff Writer

All six incumbents in the Detroit Common Council race won re-election Tuesday and the three open council seats were taken by Clyde Cleveland, Maryann Mahaffey and Jack Kelley.

With more than 99.9 percent of all city precincts counted early Wednesday morning, incumbent Carl Levin became the new council president as the highest vote getter among 18 candidates.

He was followed, in order of vote totals, by incumbents Nicholas Hood, Erma Henderson and Ernest C. Browne Jr. and newcomers Cleveland and Mahaffey. Following them were incumbents William G. Rogell and David Eberhard.

Kelley, who has run for and missed council seats three times in the past, took the ninth seat, finishing ahead of state Sen. Stanley Novak and former Council President Ed Carey. The top nine finishers were elected.

PERHAPS THE biggest surprise of the council outcome was the 14th place finish by Katherine Gribbs, the wife of outgoing Mayor Roman Gribbs, who had placed seventh in the Sept. 11 primary election.

The order of finish among the council candidates following Carey was: Michael W. Kerwin, George Van Antwerp, Mrs. Gribbs, State Rep. Frank Wierzbicki, Barbara-Rose Collins, Ted Sikora and Harold Varner, in last place.

Carl Levin, 39, a Harvard-educated attorney, practiced law in the Public Defender's Office and was general legal counsel for the Michigan Civil Rights Commission until he followed a Levin family tradition by entering political life four years ago.

A liberal who is proud of a reputation as a tough fighter on issues, Levin scored victories in curbing phosphate-based detergent sales in the city and drew attention to little noticed aspects of the HUD housing scandal.

A west sider, Levin wore an Abe Lincoln style beard for some months but later returned to his clean-shaven image.

Levin sometimes described as looking like "an impish choir-boy," served the first half of his eight years on council as the only black member and was elected council president pro tem in 1969.

As a church pastor first in New Orleans and since 1958 in Detroit, Hood has built a reputation as a moderate, progressive civil rights advocate, a housing development expert. He has been the council's resident wit, occasionally quoting the Bible to make a point and generally voting with the liberal side.

Ernest C. Browne Jr., a career city employe specializing in budget analysis, was elected to the council four

Please turn to Page 10A, Col. 3

Action Line
Dial 222-6464

Action Line solves problems, gets answers, cuts red tape, stands up for your rights. Write Action Line, Box 881, Detroit, Mich. 48231. Or dial 222-6464 between 8:30 a.m. and 4:30 p.m. Monday through Friday.

I'm a member of the Volunteer Chaplain Corps of the Greater Detroit Association of Evangelicals. We have pledged our counselling services to the Hazel Park, Utica and Shelby police departments to help them with their law enforcement programs. Starting today, we are supposed to be on 24 hour call. However, the beepers we ordered so we would be in constant contact with the police aren't ready and won't be for weeks. Can you help us get beepers so our program will get off on the right foot? — J.E., Utica.

Evangelicos won't miss a beep. Ram Broadcasting of Michigan, Inc. in Southfield dug up necessary beepers on short notice to put your operation in gear. When your services are necessary, police will be able to contact you via short wave signals. Beep is your cue to call in and see what problem is. Volunteers will deal basically with family stress situations, suicide attempts or any conflict in which religious counselling would be beneficial.

There's a group of guys at Jackson Parkside High School trying to organize a rugby league. We've got our teams all picked and everyone has a uniform. The only thing we're missing is a rugby ball. Can Action Line find one for us? — R.N., Jackson.

It's debatable a ball's really even necessary in most rock 'em, sock 'em rugby melees — but if you insist, Schneider's Sport Shop in Ann Arbor has a faster version of our football. Game of rugby was conceived during English soccer match in 1823 when a player ran with the ball instead of kicking it. A set of rules was then made up to allow handling of the ball, which is forbidden in soccer. Like football, rugby's objective is to score by crossing the goal line or booting the ball through the uprights. Play is virtually continuous and there are no substitutions allowed during match's two 40 minute halves.

Each morning on the way to work, I drive by the Fair Lane mansion on the U-M Dearborn campus. I notice the gardens are going to pot. They must have really been beautiful once — why are they being neglected? — J.S., Dearborn.

Upkeep was too expensive. During height of Fair Lane glory estate had six gardens in full bloom — one of them a 2½ acre rose garden containing 12,000 rose bushes of 300 different varieties. Spokesman for U-M told Action Line it would cost $150,000 annually to maintain garden and money just isn't available for such an expense. Fair Lane is former home of the Henry Fords. Constructed in 1915 at cost of $1,032,000, the mansion has 56 rooms, 15 baths, a swimming pool and a bowling alley. U-M now uses it as a conference and cultural center.

The street light pole in front of my house is two inches from

Please turn to Page 2A, Col. 1

THE QUESTION

Do you think the news media have been fair to President Nixon in their handling of the Watergate and related affairs?

HOW YOU VOTED

NO, 61.9 percent. COMMENTS: "As fair as a lynch mob" . . . "We'd like facts, not fiction" . . . "The news media are so vindictive" . . . "No, but he doesn't deserve fairness" . . . "The press is trying to play God" . . . "Does the sun rise?"

YES, 38.1 percent. COMMENTS: "You've treated a crook like a crook" . . . "Too fair" . . . "Old Tricky Dicky has gotten just what he deserves" . . . "Three cheers for the press"

TOMORROW'S QUESTION

A New Jersey man, who had killed his paralyzed brother after the brother begged for death, was acquitted of murder charges Monday by reason of temporary insanity. Do you feel mercy killings are ever justified?

To Vote YES — Call 861-3211
To Vote NO — Call 961-4422

Arms thrust in a victory salute, Coleman Young greets cheering supporters at the Detroit Hilton Hotel.

New Charter Adopted By Voters In Detroit

JIM NEUBACHER
Free Press Staff Writer

A new charter for the City of Detroit won the approval of 56.8 percent of the voters Tuesday.

With 99.9 percent of Detroit precincts reporting in the unofficial vote count, the charter had 185,885 votes in its favor, with 141,066 opposing.

The new charter—the constitution of city government—had been endorsed by a wide coalition of community leaders. An earlier charter proposal was defeated narrowly by the voters last November.

At the campaign headquarters of the Coalition to Support the Charter, commissioners and staff workers lifted champagne-filled glasses Tuesday night to celebrate a successful end to three years of work that went into the drafting of the new city charter.

THE NINE-MAN commission that wrote the new city charter was elected by the voters. The nine held many public

Please turn to Page 10A, Col. 6

Levin Tops Council Field, Pledges to Unite the City

BY JULIE MORRIS
Free Press Staff Writer

Carl Levin, an energetic, curly-haired attorney in his first term on Detroit's Common Council, won the council presidency Tuesday as the highest vote-getter among 18 candidates in the race.

Levin was followed closely in the balloting by incumbent Councilman Nicholas Hood. Late Tuesday night Levin said: "My first task will be to move with the entire council to unite this city. That is our first priority for the short term. Obviously, the (election) returns show we have a divided city."

CARL LEVIN: "My first task will be to move . . . to unite this city."

Levin, who is white, referred to the close vote between mayoral candidates Coleman Young, a black, and John Nichols, a white, and racial divisions among voters.

"I campaigned on my record of improving neighborhoods," Levin added. "In the long term, I predict the council will move toward more attention to neighborhood improvement."

LEVIN, 39, came to the council four years ago on the strength of his family's recognizable political name and with a reputation as a liberal and aggressive young attorney.

He set out immediately after the election to prove himself a doer in city politics and campaigned this time on his record of successful proposals as an "action" councilman.

Attentive to details, Levin rarely sits down at the council table without a fat stack of files covering major issues scheduled for discussion that day.

Levin zeroed in during his first term on high downtown parking prices, phosphate-based detergents, HUD housing abuses, juvenile vandalism, city courts and endangered species of animals.

He proposed a tough new city law against truckers who strew debris on city streets; led a major volunteer cleanup of Belle Isle last spring and recently proposed a broad anti-discrimination law designed to protect handicapped Detroiters.

Levin often researches his proposals for months before unveiling them in public and normally will criticize only in private proposals made by other council members.

A graduate of Swarthmore College and Harvard Law School, Levin practiced law in the Public Defender's Office and was the first general legal

Please turn to Page 10A, Col. 4

Balloting Split On Race Lines

BY REMER TYSON
Free Press Politics Writer

State Sen. Coleman A. Young was elected Detroit's first black mayor Tuesday and pledged that "I'm not mad with anyone, I'm not going to punish anyone, but I'm going to insist on equality."

Alabama-born Young, flanked by black Michigan Congressman Charles Diggs and other supporters, told a cheering crowd in the Detroit Hilton ballroom at midnight:

"We have won our place in the sun."

THE ELECTION between Young and former Police Commissioner John F. Nichols was in doubt until about midnight when Young pulled ahead by more than 14,000 votes, 231,815 to 217,433.

Until then, Nichols supporters thought he had won.

The final vote was not as close as the 1969 mayor's election, decided by 6,194 votes.

A few blocks away from Young's headquarters, supporters of John Nichols were dancing and throwing confetti just before midnight, believing their man was in.

The Nichols campaign headquarters had a report of only 86 percent of the vote, with Nichols still leading.

But Young pulled ahead with less than one percent of the vote to be counted.

It was at that point when Young, closely guarded by volunteer Detroit policemen, made his victory appearance.

"IT'S BEEN a long night," hoarsely proclaimed the weary Young. "It's been a long fight. But we can see daylight."

Young told his cheering supporters:

"I think we can say safely that Detroit has come alive. Detroit has shown the country that we are ready to move ahead."

Young thanked his supporters for the "blood, sweat, tears, and the money, and the effort that went into this. I don't think only we won. All of Detroit won."

"Detroit shall again be the great city with freedom and equality for all," Young declared.

His election, Young said, was of overriding importance to the city's younger generation "seeking reassurance that we can make it in America through the democratic process."

In his concession speech to his supporters, Nichols said: "We must now unite and support the government headed by Coleman Young."

Vote returns indicated that the balloting in Tuesday's election was along much sharper racial lines than the city's mayoral election four years ago.

The result suggested that, after years of political speculation, the decisive balance of power in Detroit's elections indeed has moved from the city's white working-class neighborhoods in the inner and middle city.

YOUNG BEAT Nichols in a bitterly fought contest that focused on the city's high crime rate and operation of the police department.

The Alabama-born state senator had accused Nichols of heading a police department that had controlled the city by "blackjack rule."

Nichols had defended the "police culture" during his losing campaign.

It is significant that Young got proportionately fewer white votes on Tuesday than Richard Austin, a black candidate, received four years ago when he lost narrowly to outgoing Mayor Roman Gribbs.

Austin received about 15 percent of the white vote when he lost to Gribbs, who did not seek re-election this year.

Young got less white support than that, but still defeated Nichols.

The former police commissioner received overwhelming votes in Democratic, blue-collar white areas on the city's northeast side.

In most of those areas, Nichols received more than 90 percent of the votes.

BUT YOUNG's vote in the

Please turn to Page 10A, Col. 8

Sirica Summons Nixon Aide

WASHINGTON — (UPI) — President Nixon's personal secretary, Rose Mary Woods, has in her possession, including six given to her on Monday, a White House aide testified Tuesday.

Chief U.S. District Judge John J. Sirica ordered Miss Woods to testify after an earlier witness indicated she still might have eight tapes which she first obtained during the weekend of Sept. 29 at Camp David, Md.

The White House gave no indication of whether the president would allow her to testify.

AT A FEDERAL court hearing into the alleged nonexistence of two crucial Watergate tapes, John C. Bennett, a dep-

Please turn to Page 5A, Col. 1

Golightly, Temple Win
—Page 10A

Suburban Elections
—Page 11A

The Winners

These are the certain winners in Detroit in Tuesday's election as based on returns from Free Press indicator precincts:

Mayor
Coleman A. Young

Council
(Nine to be elected)
Carl Levin
Nicholas Hood
Erma Henderson
Ernest C. Browne Jr.
Maryann Mahaffey
Clyde Cleveland
William G. Rogell
David Eberhard
Jack Kelley

Clerk
James Bradley

Treasurer
Robert J. Temple

School Board
C. L. Golightly

Regions put six new members on board. Page 1A.

Charter
(Pass or fail)
Passed

Democrats win New Jersey governorship; GOP leads in Virginia. Page 11C.

Index
Amusements	7-8D
Ann Landers	1C
Bridge	6-10C
Business News	9D
Classified	11-15C
Comics	9-11D
Crossword Puzzle	5C
Death Notices	11C
Editorials	8A
Food Guide	1-8B
Horoscope	9D
Movie Guide	10-11D
Obituaries	3C
Opinion	7A
Real Estate	10C
Sports	1-4D
Stock Markets	7-10C
Television	11B
Women's Pages	1-4C

Richardson: Nixon Must Tell It All

WASHINGTON — (UPI) — Former Attorney General Elliot L. Richardson called on President Nixon on Tuesday to turn over all Watergate-related evidence to the new special prosecutor.

Richardson said such a total presidential commitment was the only way Nixon could restore "deeply eroded public confidence" and silence the cries for his resignation or impeachment.

In testimony before the Senate Judiciary Committee, Richardson asked Nixon should give the committee a "written commitment to 'waive' executive privilege and surrender all documents, memos, notes or tapes requested.

He said such a commitment could be a prerequisite to Senate confirmation of Jaworski or even Nixon's nominee for attorney general, Sen. William B. Saxbe, R-Ohio.

Richardson said the events of the past few weeks "have so severely damaged public confidence" in Nixon "that this is necessary to repair it."

"I see no other way at this juncture to provide reassurances to the American people that the special prosecution is going to get to the bottom of this."

"We have reached a point where any further discussion of executive privilege . . . ought to be eliminated."

Richardson opposed a bill introduced by Sen. Birch Bayh, D-Ind., and sponsored by 55 other senators, to create a court-appointed special prosecutor.

He said the proposal had constitutional flaws, and if it were enacted and then overturned by the Supreme Court, any indictments the prosecutor obtained would be invalid. He said he believed that Watergate defendants would "in due course" raise the issue in the

Please turn to Page 2A, Col. 1

HUMID	**Detroit Free Press**	METRO	# AUG. 9, 1974:
Chance of Rain High 80-83 Low 64-67	ON GUARD FOR 143 YEARS	Big Board Rally Crumbles See Page 4, Section B	
Vol. 144—No. 97	Friday, August 9, 1974	15c 6-Day Home Delivery—90c	Nixon clears the way for Gerald Ford to become president.

Ford Will Be 38th President

Nixon Resigns

EPILOGUE

Nixon's Fate Is Ironic Twist Of History

BY JAMES RESTON
New York Times Service

WASHINGTON — In the long ironic history of America, events have kept unfolding contrary to the expectation of her greatest leaders and thinkers, but seldom has there been such an example of the irony and incongruity of political life as the case of Richard Milhous Nixon.

The journalists have now written his political obituary and passed him on to the historians — who will probably treat him more kindly — but he remains a tragic tangle of contradictions, and will have to be left in the end to the dramatists, novelists and psychologists.

THERE IS SOMETHING uncanny about the twists and accidents of this fantastic story, which may baffle even the mystery writers: The piece of tell-tale white tape placed the wrong way on the Watergate doors; the almost accidental discovery, in a throw-away question by a minor attorney, that rooms had been bugged and conversations recorded; the sudden appearance of two superb young reporters on the Washington Post; the appointment of two stern judges — John Sirica and Gesell — to hear the cases; and the astonishing decision to raise, launder and conceal campaign funds that were not really needed.

Constantly, the president and his men almost seemed to create the things they feared the most, by assuming the worst in everybody. Nixon's intent all along, he has explained, was to protect and strengthen the presidency, but the result was to weaken it and revive the confidence and authority of Congress.

He set an electronic trap to father evidence for the prosecution of his enemies, and produced instead evidence for his own impeachment and conviction.

He campaigned for the presidency on a platform of law and order, appealing for "a new morality" and the end of "permissiveness," and was brought down by the disorder, lawlessness and moral squalor of his triumphant team.

He blamed his plight on his political enemies in the press and Congress, and asked the people to trust him and believe he had told the truth, but he didn't even trust his own aides or lawyers, and was finally repudiated by most of his own supporters and by a Supreme Court that included four of his own appointees.

THERE SEEMS NO end to the irony of this drama, and so many odd and unexpected revelations and punishments have come about that it almost sustains the moral interpretation of history. The men who gave their loyalty to him rather than to their oath of office, hoping for personal success through their association with power, were destroyed in the process — and they will never be the same even if he pardons them.

Even the man he admired the most and hoped might succeed him in the White House, John Connally of Texas, finds himself in the ironical position of being abandoned by his old friends in the Democratic Party, rejected by his new colleagues in the Republican Party and under indictment in the courts.

In his first Inaugural Address, Nixon said that perhaps the greatest crisis he faced upon taking office was a "crisis of the spirit" in America. And after he had won a second term by the largest margin in the history of the presidency, his administration summed up its achievement of the past:

"Perhaps his greatest achievement," the administration said of Nixon, "was his success in helping the nation find an 'answer of the spirit' within itself. In the past four years, a new sense of calm and confidence has begun to grow up in America. A nation that had grown skeptical, accustomed to promises which outran reality, has been learning to trust its institutions again . . . . A nation that had become divided, with a waning sense of common purpose, has begun to pull itself back together. . . ."

John Ehrlichman made this theme more specific on Sept. 7, 1972. "After the history of this first term is written and you look back," he said, "you're going to see that, compared to other administrations or by any other standard you'd want to apply, that it has been an extraordinarily clean, corruption-free administration, because the president insists on that."

Nevertheless, perhaps the greatest irony of all is that the nation has come out of this nightmare reasonably united. By his tragic blunders and lonely conspiracies, Nixon has finally kept his promise to the little girl with the sign in Ohio. He has "brought us together," not for his leadership and his tactics but against them.

It has been a terrible time, and but for this extraordinary combination of accidental disclosures it might have been much worse, but the long agony has not been without its advantages. It took the Civil War to get rid of slavery, two apocalyptic world wars to put American power behind peace and order in the world, a wasting economic depression to reform the social structure of America, and Vietnam and Watergate to bring excessive presidential power under control.

There will be reforms now that will reform campaign financing, protect the privacy of our people, control the presumptions and power of White House officials and bring the public's business more into the open. Nothing has been solved, but everything has been changed in subtle ways, and for the better. The tragedy has been Nixon, and the essence of the tragedy is that he was not faithful to his better instincts, or even to his trusting friends.

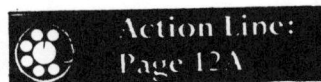
Action Line:
Page 12A

President Nixon reveals his resignation in TV address to the American people

What Happens Now?

Q — Who will pick the new vice-president?
A — President Gerald Ford will nominate a man to assume the vice-presidency, but confirmation of that nominee by the Senate is required under the 25th Amendment before he can assume office. The procedure is the same that was used when Ford himself was elevated to replace Spiro Agnew.

Q — To whom does Nixon resign? Can his resignation be refused?
A — Secretary of State Henry Kissinger accepts the resignation. It cannot be refused.

Q — What about Nixon's cabinet members? Will they all resign? Will Kissinger quit?
A — The cabinet members will submit resignations as a matter of form, but Ford plans to keep some of them. He already has said he wants Kissinger to stay. Others, among them Secretary of Defense James Schlesinger, probably will be replaced.

Q — Has any other president resigned or been removed from office before?
A — No.

Q — Will impeachment proceedings continue even after the president's resignation?
A — Probably not, but they could. There is precedent for continuing an impeachment action in cases against lower federal officers who already have resigned, for the sake of completing the record of the case against them.

Q — What about prosecution of Nixon as a private citizen for crimes he may have committed as president?
A — That is possible, but there is substantial sentiment against it, both in Congress and in the public at large, because of the view that Nixon will have been punished enough by being forced from office. It will be up to Congress, the Justice Department and Ford to give that question a final answer.

Q — Does that mean Nixon might never go to court for any of the allegations against his administration?
A — No. It is almost certain that he will be called as a witness for either the defense or the prosecution in the so-called cover-up trial of six Nixon aides, including John Mitchell, John Ehrlichman and H.R. Haldeman.

Q — What is his financial situation?
A — His resignation leaves him in much better shape than impeachment and removal from office would have. First, he will receive a pension of $60,000 a year for the rest of his life, which, he would have lost if he had been removed, and he will be spared the high cost of defending himself in a Senate trial. He owes more than a quarter of a million dollars on his California home in San Clemente and has promised to pay $148,000 in back taxes from 1969. Still, a book contract could be worth a fortune to him and might even make him a millionaire.

Q — Besides the pension, what other benefits due to a former president will he receive?
A — Secret Service protection, $96,000 a year for staff costs, free office space, postal franking privileges and some other items, all for the rest of his life.

Q — Where will he live?
A — The family is leaving Friday morning for San Clemente.

Q — How does Nixon feel?
A — A congressional delegation who visited him earlier in the week described him as "serene" and he himself has talked about the "serenity" he has maintained through this trying period. Nixon always has prided himself on his toughness and has consistently contended that his only errors in regard to Watergate were errors of judgment, not impeachable acts. He is inclined to let history be his judge.

Ford to Take Oath Today

BY ROBERT S. BOYD
Chief of Our Washington Bureau

WASHINGTON—Richard M. Nixon, the first president in history to be forced from the White House, told the nation Thursday that he is quitting for the good of the country.

In a calm and conciliatory television address, America's 37th president said he will resign "with great sadness" at noon Friday.

Gerald R. Ford Jr. will immediately be sworn into office as Nixon's successor.

CHIEF JUSTICE Warren E. Burger will administer the oath of office to the 38th president in the Oval Office.

Ford, a 61-year-old former congressman from Grand Rapids, Mich., immediately pledged to carry on Nixon's major foreign and domestic policies.

At the Capitol, legislators of both parties expressed solid support for Ford, the former House Republican leader, and a tinge of sadness at Nixon's departure. "The long, dark night is over," said Sen. Frank Church, D-Idaho.

The momentous but peaceful transfer of authority from the scandal-tinged Nixon to his chosen successor will occur as the outgoing president and his family swing westward to their estate in San Clemente, Calif.

In a brief address to a worldwide television audience, Nixon apologized for "mistakes in judgement" and said he deeply regretted any injuries he may have caused.

He called on the nation to give its "help and support" to the new president and to put "the bitterness of the recent past behind us."

"I feel great sadness that I will not be in his office working on your behalf," he said. "But I know the leadership of America will be in good hands."

"I have never been a quitter," Nixon said. "To leave office before my term is completed is abhorrent to every instinct in my body."

But to continue the fight for his personal vindication, he said, would have absorbed the attention of the president and Congress when they should be concentrating on peace abroad and prosperity at home.

"I would have preferred to carry through to the finish, whatever the personal agony it would have involved.

"My family unanimously urged me to do so, but in the interest of the nation must always come before personal considerations . . . Therefore,

Please turn to Page 13A, Col. 1

• Michigan's reaction to the resignation, Page 3A.

• Chronology of the Watergate affair, Page 6A.

• Nixon's last stand: the fight over the tapes, Page 7A.

• Text of President Nixon's resignation address, Page 11A.

• A quiet dinner, routine tasks. Back Page.

• Ford faces early task of picking a vice-president, Page 14A.

Swearing-In Set for TV

Tentative plans late Thursday for Detroit area television coverage of the swearing-in ceremony Friday of Gerald R. Ford called for it to begin at 7 a.m. on Channel 4 (NBC) and run continuously until 12 noon, the actual time of the ceremony.

CBS (Channel 2) and ABC (Channel 7) are to begin coverage at 9 a.m.

CKLW (Canadian Broadcasting Co.), Channel 9, said it would begin coverage at 11:30 a.m.

Nixon's Last Day: A Loner to the Very End

BY CLARK HOYT
Free Press Washington Staff

WASHINGTON — At the final hour, Pennsylvania Avenue was jammed with a horn-honking, dancing, cheering celebration. The flag-waving presidential supporters who had earlier stood singing the "Battle Hymn of the Republic" were gone.

Inside the high black fence, across the tree-shaded expanse of lawn and red geraniums, where the sounds from the street barely penetrated, Richard Nixon spent his last day in intense privacy.

Once, when he walked the few short yards across a driveway from his Executive Office Building hideaway to his family quar-

In White House offices Thursday there were few tears, only the sad realization that the end had come.

ters, the press corps was locked up inside the press room to prevent them from glimpsing the chief executive.

It was the president's penchant for isolation, many had felt, that finally helped bring him down. But it was too late for any change of personal style.

As an ironic footnote to his ultimate rupture with Congress,

the reason Nixon gave for stepping down — he made perhaps his last official act a veto.

He rejected the appropriations bill for the Department of Agriculture and the Environmental protection Agency, declar-

Please turn to Page 13A, Col. 1

KISSINGER TO STAY ON

Ford Praises Nixon 'Sacrifice'

GERALD FORD, after the resignation: ". . . one of the very saddest incidents . . ."

ALEXANDRIA, Va. — (AP — Gerald R. Ford said Thursday night that President Nixon "made one of the greatest personal sacrifices for the country" by resigning as president.

Appearing outside his home shortly after Nixon's announcement, Ford said he plans to continue Nixon's foreign policies with Henry A. Kissinger remaining as secretary of state.

"I want him to be my secretary of state and I'm glad to announce he will be secretary of state," said the man who at noon Friday will succeed Nixon as the nation's 38th president.

FORD SAID he expects "a spirit of co-operation between the new president and the Congress."

"I've been very fortunate in my lifetime in public office to have a great many adversaries in the Congress," he said. "But I don't think I have any enemies in the Congress."

Ford said in praising Nixon that "I think the president of the United States has made one of the greatest personal sacrifices for the country and one of the finest personal decisions on behalf of all of us as Americans."

Ford emerged from his brick and white-frame house at 514 Grand View Drive about 15 minutes after Nixon finished his televised address.

Standing in a light drizzle, the vice-president spoke without notes and told the crowd of newsmen and about 200 onlookers that he considered this "one of the most difficult and very saddest periods and one of the very saddest incidents I have ever witnessed."

Ford spoke for 10 minutes. He emphasized that his administration would pursue peace, praised Kissinger as "a very

Please turn to Page 8A, Col. 1

Index

Amusements	6-9C
Business News	2-5B
Classified	11-15C
Comics	5-7D
Crossword Puzzle	10A
Death Notices	11C
Editorials	5C
Garden	5D
Horoscope	5D
Obituaries	7B
Opinion	11A
Sports	1-4D
Stock Markets	3-5B
Television	10C
Weekend Calendar	1C
Women's Pages	1-4C

Details of Thursday's lottery winners are on Page 7B.

AUG. 1, 1975:

Former Teamsters President Jimmy Hoffa disappears.

Detroit Free Press
ON GUARD FOR 144 YEARS

Vol. 145—No. 88   Friday, August 1, 1975

HOT Humid High 93-96 Low 69-72

METRO Farm Price News Kills Market Rally See Page 8, Section C — 15¢ — 6-Day Home Delivery—90¢

LAST SEEN OUTSIDE RESTAURANT
Jimmy Hoffa Is Missing

Investigators Probing Mystery Appointment

Former Teamsters President James R. Hoffa is missing.

He was last seen standing outside the Machus Red Fox restaurant, on Telegraph Road near Maple in Bloomfield Township, at 1:30 p.m. Wednesday.

Police found his 1974 Pontiac in the restaurant parking lot at approximately 10 a.m. Thursday.

He was reported missing by his family after failing to come home Wednesday night.

"I know the police suspect foul play," said Oakland County Prosecutor L. Brooks Patterson. "Jimmy never stayed out this long before reporting in."

Hoffa's disappearance follows a series of violent events which have plagued the embattled Teamsters Local 299 — Hoffa's home local — in the past month.

Bloomfield Township Police Lt. Curtis F. Grennerei said Hoffa left his home in Lake Orion between 1 and 1:30 p.m. Wednesday for a 2 p.m. meeting at the fashionable suburban restaurant.

Bloomfield Police Chief Robert Snell said two witnesses, whose names he withheld, saw Hofa standing on a curb at the side of the restaurant at about 2 p.m.

BOTH WITNESSES said they recognized Hoffa and exchanged greetings with him. Hoffa was alone — without a bodyguard — and was wearing a dark blue sports shirt, dark blue trousers, and sunglasses. They said he appeared to be waiting for someone.

At 2:30 p.m., Hoffa called home, saying that the person he expected had not arrived. Lt. Grennier said Hoffa asked his wife if he had gotten any calls about the missed meeting and she said she had not.

When asked whom his father might have been meeting, his son, James P. Hoffa, told a reporter: "I'd rather not say who. I can't say anything."

Lt. Grennier said only that "there's a lot of speculation to give to whom he may have been going to meet," adding that police want to contact "five or six" persons.

In Grand Rapids, Gov. Milliken told newsmen he understood Hoffa had intended to meet Anthony Giacalone Wednesday night.

Giacalone, named in 1963 U.S. Senate testimony as a kingpin in the Detroit Mafia, is a close and well-trusted friend of the Hoffa family.

Lt. Grennier said the family

Please turn to Page 4A, Col. 3

Pictures on Back Page

Betty Ford jokingly scolds Finnish President Urho Kekkonen for suggesting that he accompany her home. Mrs. Ford told him she did not think it was a good idea—at which the president let out a laugh. The Fords were attending a reception for heads of state in Helsinki Thursday night.

James R. Hoffa in a 1974 photo

New Turk Arms Bill Is Stalled by House

WASHINGTON — (AP) — A new effort to renew U.S. arms sales to Turkey was narrowly approved by the Senate Thursday night but was blocked from being considered by the House until September.

House Rules Committee chairman Ray J. Madden, D-Ind., said he would not clear the bill for House action until Sept. 9, when Congress returns from its August vacation.

Shortly before midnight, House Minority Leader John J. Rhodes, R-Ariz., said he was abandoning his efforts to win approval of the measure before Congress departs Friday for its month-long recess.

THE SENATE approved a conditional lifting of the six-month-old ban on arms aid to Turkey by only one vote, 47 to 46. Supporters of the bill in the House forced six roll call votes against House adjournment so the bill could be considered late Thursday.

But Madden steadfastly refused to clear the measure for consideration. One resolution to replace Madden with a temporary Rules Committee chairman to get action on the bill was ruled out of order by Speaker Carl Albert, D-Okla.

However, the vote in the Senate represented something of a victory for the Ford administration. Administration sources said they wanted to have one house of Congress on record in favor of resuming aid in hopes this would bolster U.S. diplomatic efforts to restore good relations with Turkey.

The Senate vote came after the Ankara government rejected an offer by President Ford earlier in the day to give the Turks $50 million in arms if Turkey would reactivate U.S. military bases there.

Secretary of State Henry A. Kissinger said Demirel rejected the offer as contradictory.

"Turkey takes the position that it is contradictory to give $50 million as a gift when it can't buy arms or take delivery on arms already purchased," the secretary told a news conference.

Nevertheless, the secretary went on, "It is our impression that the situation is recoverable. That is, the bases can be substantially restored if the House reverses itself."

MEANWHILE, the Soviet news agency Tass reported that Demirel had met with Soviet Communist party chief Leonid I. Brezhnev and For-

Please turn to Page 8A, Col. 1

He Has Pride
HELSINKI — (UPI) — Secretary of State Henry Kissinger, leaving the morning session of the European Security Conference, encountered three reporters who asked him to "please say something historical."

"Not to such a small group," he said, laughing.

"It is our impression that the situation is recoverable. That is, the bases can be substantially restored if the House reverses itself."
—*Secretary Kissinger*

Index
Amusements	10-13C
Business News	6-8C
Classified	5-8D
Comics	9-11D
Death Notices	5D
Editorials	6A
Garden	4C
Horoscope	9D
Obituaries	14A
Sports	1-4D
Stock Markets	8-9C
Television	10A
Weekend Calendar	5C
Women's Pages	1-4C

Action Line — Dial 222-6464

Action Line solves problems, gets answers, cuts red tape, stands up for your rights. Write Action Line, Box 881, Detroit, Mich. 48231. Or dial 222-6464 between 8:30 a.m. and 4:30 p.m. Monday through Friday.

The Dearborn Heights police gave my mother-in-law a ticket for overgrown weeds, trees and shrubs in her yard and an adjoining lot she owns. She survives on an allotment from Social Security and can't afford to have the work done. She's worried sick that the police are going to come back and give her trouble. Is there anything you can do?—D.D., Dearborn Heights.

Action Line took problem straight to Mayor John Harris of Dearborn Heights, received promise city wouldn't hassle mother-in-law about growth. Harris said that while city money's not supposed to be used for jobs on private property, authorities try to give senior citizens and other hardship cases a break. Many times means lining up volunteer help from outfits like Lions Club and Boy Scouts. Some day Action Line called, crew was dispatched to prune overgrown greenery on mother-in-law's property. Cops got involved because of complaints by neighbors, issued standard warning that gives property owners 10 days to comply. City ordinance violations included vegetation growing over property lines and weeds exceeding 12-inch limit.

I live in East Lansing, which is pretty close to Howell. So why is it that I can't grow melons that taste as good as those grown in Howell?—S.S., East Lansing.

Resident Howell sod buster told Action Line secret is extra tender loving care locals put into melon growing, but folks in the know say delectability results from good soil, low humidity and fact Howell has one of highest elevations in state. About 200,000 melons are harvested each August — season for Howell Jaycee Melon Festival. This year's 16th annual bash will be held weekend of August 22-24. Goings-on include square dancing and Oktoberfesting (sampling gourmet goodies from Oktoberfest tent). Howell growers will also send best-of-bunch melon shipment to White House.

I've worked at Biff's on Telegraph near Five Mile Road for just a short time, but two of my paychecks have already turned out to be worthless. Detroit Bank and Trust cashed the checks for me because I had an account there, but now they're after me for the money. What should I do?—R.M., Detroit.

Return to bank with $76.42 money order prior from Biff's. DB&T said bank tried to put through one check three times and the other twice, but Biff's bank account was never quite up to handling amount. Action Line went to restaurant manager who agreed to give you money order if bank would turn loose checks. Action Line explained that bank couldn't release checks because it wouldn't have proof of paying out cash in first place. Manager saw light, handed over dough to cover bum checks. Once DB&T completes paperwork on transaction, checks will be returned.

Action 😊 Line

Last August 1 I shot a hole-in-one at the Traverse City Golf and Country Club. Because I was a member of the Hole-In-One Club of New York, I was supposed to get a new set of golf clubs as a prize. The club acknowledged my ace, but that's the last I heard. Can you find out what's going on?—E.P., Traverse City.

Like most outfits offering rewards for aces, Hole-In-One Club ended up in rough. Club telephones were disconnected, but Action Line tracked down former vice-president who related sad details. Principle remaining stockholder is presently attempting to negotiate sale of assets, but new buyers don't intend to honor old claims. Ace clubs sold memberships for about $29, hoped to turn profit after paying off to golfers who potted tee shot. Sounded like easy money, since odds against amateur holing one during round is 10,738 to one. However, reports of aces poured in from members—some of which were questionable but verified by others in foursome—and clubs got drowned in red ink.

THE QUESTION
Former President Richard Nixon is asking $1 million to appear on television to discuss his life. Would you care to see a TV interview with Nixon?

HOW YOU VOTED
NO, 79.5 percent. COMMENTS: "I'd like to forget the bad things in life"... "I've already seen the Al Capone story and the 'Godfather,' which is enough gangster entertainment for me"... "Only if they do the interview in jail where he should be"... "I don't care to waste my time listening to his lies"... "There'll probably be an 18-minute interruption in the interview."

YES, 20.5 percent. COMMENTS: "Why not? Nixon was the greatest president we ever had"... "Let's see what he has to say. Maybe he will admit his guilt to the Watergate case"... "As long as it isn't taped or edited by him"... "Let the man give his side of the story and stop this public execution"... "It sure would be interesting."

TOMORROW'S QUESTION
A Chicago attorney has suggested a plan to unify the U.S. on its 200th birthday by having a chain of Americans clasping hands from coast to coast next July 4. Would you like to take part in such an event?

To vote YES   To vote NO
Call 961-3211   Call 961-4422

Beating Victim In Livernois Violence Dies

Marian Pyszko, a beating victim in Monday night's disturbance in northwest Detroit, died Thursday morning of a crushed skull. He had never regained consciousness.

Pyszko, on his usual way home from work, was pulled from his auto and clubbed in the head with a piece of concrete before he ever reached the main disturbance area on Livernois.

The 54-year-old immigrant baker's helper was the second fatality in three days of unrest which started when Obie Wynn, 18, was shot and killed by a Livernois Avenue bar owner around 8:30 p.m. Monday.

Since then police have arrested some 93 adults and 20 juveniles, mostly for malicious destruction of property along Livernois and the fire department has recorded 30 incidents of arson, including an attempt at burning the bar where Wynn was shot.

The situation was cooled considerably by civilian and police co-operation on Wednesday, and police, who had been working 12-hour shifts, were ordered late Thursday night to return to regular eight-hour shifts beginning at 8 a.m. Friday.

But the special Livernois and headquarters command posts set up during the disturbances were to continue operations until further notice, a police teletype order said.

Earlier Thursday, Mayor Young, who had spent three nights keeping peace on the streets, spent an hour at noon consoling the families of both dead men.

AFTER THOSE meetings Young said: "Both the mother and whole were very understanding, and I believe they represent the majority of the

Please turn to Page 8A, Col. 1

Five Die In Attack On Irish Bandsmen

BELFAST — (UPI) — Five men, including three members of the Irish Republic's best known dance band, were killed Thursday in a bomb and bullet attack near the border town of Newry, 30 miles southwest of Belfast. The other two victims were identified as officers of the Ulster Volunteer Force (UVF), an extremist Protestant group.

Police said the bus carrying the Miami Show Band back to Dublin after a show in Northern Ireland was stopped on a rural road about 2 a.m. by a patrol in Army-type uniforms.

THE MEMBERS of the band were lined up along a hedgerow and asked their names and addresses. Then there was a burst of gunfire and an explosion.

The three members of the band shot to death were Fran O'Toole, a television award-winning singer; Brian McCoy, and Anthony Geraghty. A fourth member, Steven Travers, was wounded.

The attack was reported by another member of the band, Desmond McAlea, after he recovered consciousness and got a ride to the police station at Newry.

An organization calling itself the Ulster Central Intelligence Agency and claiming to represent paramilitary Protestant groups, named the other two men killed as Maj. Harris Boyle and Lt. Wesley Sommerville of the UVF.

The Ulster agency said the UVF patrol stopped to search the bus when an explosion occurred and shooting broke out.

---

2 MEN WOUNDED; SUSPECT HELD
Doctor Slain at Ypsi Ford Plant

BY TOM HENNESSY
Free Press Staff Writer

YPSILANTI — A Ford Motor Co. plant physician was killed Thursday and two other persons were seriously wounded by a gunman who allegedly surrendered meekly to police minutes after the shootings.

Bewildered police and Ford representatives could give no motive for the shootings, which took place shortly before 9:30 a.m. in the administration building of the sprawling Ypsilanti Ford parts plant, located near the Huron Street exit of I-94.

Police said the suspect in their custody would be arraigned late Thursday or early Friday. He was identified as J.C. Vinson, 27, of Ypsilanti, a Ford employe for the past six years and an assembler on the plant's shock-absorber line.

KILLED WAS DR. ROBERT Watling, 37, of Dearborn, Watling, married and the father of four children, joined Ford nine years ago and had been plant physician at Ypsilanti for the past two years.

Seriously wounded were Alton Emerine, 45, of Clinton in Lenawee County, a labor relations supervisor, and Charles Seed, 48, of Bay Village, Ohio, an employe of a vending machine firm that services the plant.

Emerine was reported in fair condition at St. Joseph Mercy Hospital, Ann Arbor, with a gunshot wound in the chest. Seed was in serious condition at University of Michigan Hospi-

DR. WATLING, who died in his office at the hands of a gunman.

Ypsilanti Police Lt. Kenneth J. Holder escorts shooting suspect J.C. Vinson, 27.

Please turn to Page 2A, Col. 1

Detroit Free Press

CLOUDY
Chance of Showers
High 53-55 Low 33-35

ON GUARD FOR 144 YEARS
Vol. 145—No. 192   Wednesday, November 12, 1975

METRO
Dow Average Gains 3.07
On Moderate Trading
See Page 8, Section D

Nov. 12, 1975:

The wreck of the Edmund Fitzgerald.

ORE BOAT SINKS IN LAKE SUPERIOR

Life Rafts Empty—Hope Dim for 29

Action Line
Dial 222-6464

Action Line solves problems, gets answers, cuts red tape, stands up for your rights. Write Action Line, Box 881, Detroit, Mich. 48231. Or dial 222-6464 between 8:30 a.m. and 4:30 p.m. Monday through Friday.

My brother is critically ill at Veterans Hospital in Allen Park and we don't think he's going to make it. His stepmother and three stepbrothers are now living in Baltimore, but I don't have their address or phone number and can't locate them. I think they should know about my brother as soon as possible so they can get here to see him. Can you help find them?—S.L., Livonia.

Stepmother reached you same day, after Action Line found Baltimore residence and relayed message. Only clue to work with was fact you knew she was receiving veteran's benefits in name of your father, who died at Johns Hopkins Hospital in Baltimore in 1972. VA said it couldn't help track down stepfather's kin unless his social security number was furnished. Call to Johns Hopkins secured number, which VA fed into computer. Administration was then able to contact stepmother with information that Action Line was attempting to reach family. She called short time later and was informed of stepson's condition.

Stepparent said she lost touch with Detroit-area branch of family when you moved last year without leaving forwarding address.

This past summer I got hooked on the sound of my bedroom air conditioner. Now I can't get to sleep unless it's on. Since the weather no longer calls for air conditioning, can Action Line find me something that simulates the sound? Please—I need a good night's sleep!—R.A., Royal Oak.

Norman Dine Sleep Center in New Jersey has gadget called "Sleep Conditioner" that should drone you into dreamland during winter. Sleep conditioners sell from $25 to $90, emit "white sounds"—frequency that's supposed to be relaxing and conducive to sleep. Machines range from one-sound units to super-deluxe models which simulate sound of things like falling rain and ocean surf. Dine got started in sleep-inducing business 40 years ago after he had trouble nodding off night after night. Besides conditioners, Dine also markets other sleep-related items, such as ear plugs, sleep masks and anti-snoring face coverings. Catalog of Dine's offerings is available by writing Norman Dine Sleep Center, c/o Robert Wiensch's, 33 Halstead, East Orange, N.J. 07018. Dr. Donald Caldwell of Lafayette Clinic Sleep Center in Detroit told Action Line your problem isn't all that uncommon, is simply matter of becoming used to everyday sound. Doctor said most folks are able to get over sound reliance in time without use of gadgetry.

Action Line

On July 18, I returned a catalog order to Montgomery Ward in Chicago and ordered different items in exchange, enclosing a check for $37.82 to cover the increased amount of the new order. I've yet to receive any of the merchandise or a refund. Since I'm a widow trying to make ends meet on social security, I can't afford to lose this money. Can you help straighten this out for me?—N.L., Oscoda.

Check for $53.18 was in mail to you after Action Line's call to Montgomery Ward Catalog House. Customer adjustment department said total amounted to full refund since that's option you preferred. Ward rep told Action Line that when original order was returned, request for new items didn't include catalog numbers. Back in September, company sent questionnaire requesting you specify order with numbers, said it never came back. Company claims next it heard of problem was when Action Line called.

Dear Readers

Action Line editors consider every request you send us. We publish the most interesting and helpful answers. We regret that we cannot answer or acknowledge individual requests.

THE QUESTION
The San Diego police recently completed a successful experiment where patrolmen stressed helping people on their beats rather than "preventive patrolling." Do you think a system like this could work in Detroit?

Sound Off

HOW YOU VOTED

YES, 55.3 percent. COMMENTS: "Helping people has always been the primary role of the patrolman." ... "Police should be considered friends rather than enemies." ... "There'd be a lot less crime." ... "It's high time Detroit police got back on the streets where they belong." ... "It would help community relations."

NO, 44.7 percent. COMMENTS: "It's too dangerous to help people nowadays, and that's a sad thing." ... "San Diego isn't the murder capital of the world." ... "We don't have enough policemen to control crime, much less help people."

TOMORROW'S QUESTION
Dr. Joyce Brothers says that cars express our image of ourselves. Does your car reflect your personality?

To vote YES   To vote NO
Call 961-3211   Call 961-4422

Hearings Ordered on Future U.S. Role in UN

By JAMES McCARTNEY
Free Press Washington Staff

WASHINGTON — The Senate Tuesday voted to reassess further U.S. participation in the United Nations General Assembly in the wake of a UN resolution labeling Zionism as racism.

In a voice vote just 22 minutes after the chamber opened for business, with about eight senators present, a resolution was approved ordering immediate hearings on the question. There was no opposition.

A similar resolution in the House bogged down when Rep. Robert Kastenmeir, D-Wis., demanded clarifications.

He said the resolution did not make clear whether it meant to suggest withdrawal from the UN as a whole.

THE SENATE vote was one of a series of sharp reactions here Tuesday to the Arab-sponsored UN resolution, approved late Monday night by a 72 to 35 margin, with 32 abstentions.

The UN action touched off a flood of angry statements in the Senate and the House, many of which asked for a sweeping re-examination of U.S. relations with the UN.

But there were no demands for a total U.S. pullout and the Ford administration, while angrily criticizing the UN vote, avoided threats of wholesale retaliation.

A White House statement said President Ford deplored the UN resolution as a "wholly unjustified action," but made no further threat.

When White House spokesman William Greener was asked if the president still sought passage of his request for $750 million in economic aid for Egypt, which voted for the UN resolution, Greener replied: "Yes."

State Department spokesman Robert Funseth said reports were not correct that the U.S. was considering a cut in finances to support the UN.

He said the U.S. "will review carefully" the "implications" of the UN vote, in a search for an "effective response."

But he also made clear that the U.S. believes the UN performs some valuable functions, including the maintenance of peacekeeping forces in the Middle East.

UN troops, for example, will have a major role in the new Sinai desert disengagement agreement between Egypt and Israel. UN forces also separate Syrian and Israeli forces on the Golan Heights.

IN THE UN debate over the Zionism resolution, the U.S. and much of the industrialized West and Japan found themselves overwhelmingly outvoted by underdeveloped nations of the so-called Third World.

Zionism is the concept that a Jewish national homeland exists in the Middle East to which Jews historically are entitled. It is the philosophic base for the modern Israeli state.

Arabs argue that Zionism is implicitly racist because, they say, hundreds of thousands of Palestinian Arabs have been

Please turn to Page 2A, Col. 1

Photo by BERT EMANUELE
The 729-foot ore boat Edmund Fitzgerald

Rights Unit To Mount Integration Offensive

WASHINGTON — (AP) — The U.S. Commission on Civil Rights announced Tuesday a new nationwide effort to defend school desegregation.

The chairman, Arthur S. Flemming, said anti-busing attacks in Congress threaten the whole civil rights movement.

The announcement came on a day when the Senate Judiciary Committee held an afternoon hearing on proposed constitutional amendments against busing to achieve school desegregation.

ALSO, THE Supreme Court agreed Tuesday to consider desegregation issues affecting private and public schools. A decision in one of the cases, involving Pasadena, Calif., could affect how long school districts may be kept under court supervision in desegregation cases.

The Civil Rights Commis-

Please turn to Page 2A, Col. 1

UPI Photo
Life preservers from the freighter Edmund Fitzgerald, found in Lake Superior, are unloaded at the Coast Guard base in Sault Ste. Marie.

Rescuers Find No Survivors

BY JAMES HARPER AND RONE TEMPEST
Free Press Staff Writers

SAULT STE. MARIE — Searchers held out little hope Tuesday of finding any of the 29 crewmen who went down with the Edmund Fitzgerald when the huge ore boat sank during a raging storm in the numbing waters of Lake Superior.

Coast Guard rescue teams said all three of the ship's life rafts were found empty.

Although Coast Guard spokesmen said they would continue their search Wednesday, they were skeptical of the crew's chances.

"It's pretty hopeless about finding any survivors," Coast Guard Captain Charles Millradt said Tuesday afternoon. "We've combed the area pretty thoroughly and its been 20 hours."

"Their percentage of survival is pretty nil — three to four hours in Lake Superior waters."

The water temperature Tuesday was 50 degrees in Whitefish Bay near where the Fitzgerald went down Monday night.

"The widows are calling now," said Chief Warrent Officer Hal Robbins at the Sault Ste. Marie Coast Guard station where the search is being coordinated.

Robbins said he had received four calls from crew members' families, including one call from a father in Ohio who said he would come here Wednesday to join in the search.

The Fitzgerald sank in a vicious storm, with waves reaching 25 feet and hurricane force winds over 80 miles an hour, as it was making its way toward the Soo Locks 15 miles northwest of Whitefish Point near the entrance to Whitefish Bay.

The 729-foot vessel, the largest ore boat on the Great Lakes when it was built in the River Rouge Great Lakes Engineering Works in 1958, was 15 miles from shelter when it last made radio contact with the ore boat Arthur M. Anderson at 7:10 p.m.

The Anderson was following 10 miles behind the Fitzgerald. Anderson skipper Jessie Cooper told the Coast Guard that he was contacted by Fitzgerald Captain Ernest McSorley at that time and McSorley told him his ship had lost two ventilator covers and was taking water and operating at a slight list.

Cooper told the Coast Guard that there was no panic in McSorley's voice and there was no distress signal. Shortly after that the Fitzgerald disappeared from the Anderson's radar screen and failed to respond to radio calls.

The water in that section of Lake Superior is more than 500 feet deep, one of the deepest areas in the lake.

ALL DAY Tuesday, seven Coast Guard and private vessels, as well as six Coast Guard, Air National Guard and Canadian aircraft scoured the waters of the lake searching for survivors.

But the search took on an especially gloomy note late in the afternoon when the Coast Guard announced all three of

Please turn to Page 12A, Col. 1

Disaster has sailed the Great Lakes since 1679. Back Page.

AP photo
ARTHUR BURNS: "They (New York) haven't done enough, but they have done a great deal."

Burns Says He's Closer To Urging NYC Aid

WASHINGTON —(AP)— Declaring that "my concern has deepened," Chairman Arthur F. Burns of the Federal Reserve Board said Tuesday he is closer than ever before to recommending federal help for New York City.

Burns said, "While I've not yet reached the conclusion that federal financial help is necessary, I'm perhaps closer to that conclusion than I have been."

MEANWHILE, the House Judiciary Committee started work on a bill to change federal bankruptcy laws to help guarantee essential services in New York City if it does default on its debts. Burns said he supports the proposed changes.

Burns made it clear to a meeting of House Republicans that his main worry is over the possible impact of a New

Please turn to Page 5A, Col. 1

BLACKS UNHAPPY

Board Seeks Busing Changes

BY WILLIAM GRANT
Free Press Education Writer

The Detroit Board of Education Tuesday agreed to try to pressure U.S. District Judge Robert E. DeMascio into developing a more "just" school integration plan.

The decision came in a voice vote after school board President C. L. Golightly criticized the student busing plan ordered by DeMarcio last week and suggested the board petition the judge for changes.

The black majority of the city school board is generally unhappy with the DeMascio order and believes the judge has shown too much concern for those white parents who are opposed to busing.

There is an "increasing pattern" in the judge's thinking, Golightly said, with "more emphasis on discipline and on neighborhood stability than on justice and equality."

DeMascio, Golightly said, "has acted as if Milliken were the plaintiff and Bradley the defendant."

The city school integration suit is officially titled Bradley V. Milliken. It was filed five years ago by the NAACP in the name of Ronald Bradley and other specific plaintiffs. Gov. Milliken, the state and city school boards are defendants.

THE BLACK school board members are particularly angry at the portions of Judge DeMascio's order that would increase the percentage of white students at Finney and Pershing high schools by sending some black students who now attend those two schools to virtually all-black high schools.

Golightly called this phase of the court order "resegregation" and said "DeMascio is just digging himself into a hole."

Golightly said he hopes the school board "can redirect the thinking of the judge" and "save him being overturned."

The NAACP has appealed Judge DeMascio's integration orders and a hearing before the U.S. 6th Circuit Court of Appeals in Cincinnati is expected late this year or early in 1976.

Golightly said Tuesday he will not at this point encourage his fellow board members to also appeal because "in a spirit of cooperation we will petition the judge to make changes."

Golightly would not say, however, what position the board will take on the student busing plan if DeMascio refuses to make the requested changes.

THE FORMAL action the school board took Tuesday asks the school administration to make an analysis of the student

Please turn to Page 12A, Col. 1

Senate Foes Muzzled In Picket Bill Fight

From UPI and AP

WASHINGTON — The Senate Tuesday swept aside a filibuster of a labor-backed bill that would expand the picketing power of union construction workers.

Opponents threatened another filibuster. The vote on cloture was 66 to 30, six more votes than needed to halt debate.

The bill, known as "Common Situs Picketing," would allow picketing building trades workers to close down an entire construction site in a dispute against one subcontractor.

SENATE DEMOCRATIC Leader Mike Mansfield, who initiated the cloture motion, accused opponents of the measure of "obstructionism."

Sen. Paul Laxalt, R-Nev., who was leading the filibuster, replied that the Senate should not consider the bill, because it has more important issues to handle. He noted that situs picketing legislation has been "kicking around the Congress for 25 years."

The debate was particularly heated. Opponents describe the

Please turn to Page 12A, Col. 1

Inside the Free Press

Amusements	5-8C	Horoscope	11D
Ann Landers	2C	Movie Guide	12-13D
Business News	6-10D	Obituaries	10C
Classified	16-15C	Real Estate	14D
Comics	11-13D	Sports	1-5D
Death Notices	10C	Stock Markets	8-9D
Editorials	8A	Television	9C
Food Guide	1-11B	Women's Pages	1-4C

JULY 4, 1976:

The Bird was the Word during his sensational rookie year.

Sports Page

In This Section
Sports on Television — Page 2
Travel — Pages 9-10
Radio — Page 11

Detroit Free Press

Sports

SUNDAY, JULY 4, 1976

SECTION **D**

Bird Swoops Down on O's, 4-0...
And 51,032 Tiger Fans Go Wild

Joe Falls

Fabulous Fidrych: He Gives Off Sparks

Imagine winning on cue? Imagine a ball player taking curtain calls?

Imagine — if you can — Mark Fidrych.

It is almost impossible to believe what this youngster is doing. They come out expecting a big show from him and he delivers it.

Babe Ruth called one shot. The kid is starting to do it every time he goes to the mound.

It's incredible. Nobody is supposed to win on cue. Or take bows after a game.

That's what's been happening around here and seldom has the old game been more fun.

They filled the ball park Saturday night and The Bird didn't let them down. He went through all the moves, all the gyrations and all the antics which have made him one of the most talked about players in baseball since Henry Aaron was going for No. 715.

Fidrych also had all the pitches as he blanked the Baltimore Orioles on just four hits. The score was 4-0 and it was an evening that won't soon be forgotten.

The players even gagged it up by putting a phone in front of Fidrych's locker, as though the President was ready to call at any moment. Or maybe the Pope.

You don't suppose he was expecting a call from...

Naw. Not yet. Soon, maybe, but not just yet.

Nobody can be expected to perform when his every move is cheered mightily by the mobs.

As Fidrych opened some of the letters before the game, he came across one from 1600 Pennsylvania Ave., Washington D.C.

The Bird's eyes widened.

Did he know a Gerald Ford? No. But he read the letter anyway.

It was a prank since everyone knows that Presidents use the telephones and not the mails to talk to their athletes. Who can trust the mails these days.

He's on Top Step for Anthem

This is what Fidrych is facing, though. The spotlight is on his every move.

Do you believe they gave him a standing ovation for nearly three minutes when his name was announced before the game? That's never happened in this old ball park.

Even the enemy — the Orioles — were anxious to get their first look at The Bird.

"I've talked to a lot of quality people and they tell me he's for real," said Reggie Jackson. "They say he keeps the ball low and he's a very enjoyable person and I'm looking forward to facing him."

"So he's supposed to be crazy, eh?" smiled Earl Weaver, the O's manager. "All I know is that he's already writing down the attendance figures in front of his locker, so how crazy can he be?"

The amazing thing about Fidrych is that he affects so many people around him. It's not just the fans who are ga-ga over him. It's his own teammates.

The Bird gives off sparks and they catch fire.

No sooner had Fidrych worked out of a bases-loaded jam Saturday night than Jason Thompson came up in the bottom of the inning and nearly hit one out of the ball park, the ball bouncing off the roof in rightfield.

Fidrych has put a charge in everyone. The electricity crackles in the air. Let him flex his shoulder blades and they go berserk. Let him smooth out the mound and they are in utter ecstasy.

They even thrill to him racing back to the dugout as he tries to be the first one home. He made it every time Saturday night.

The kid knows just how to play it, too. He was standing on the top step of the dugout as they played the National Anthem. He had his hat over his heart, as any red-blooded American youth would do on the eve of the Fourth of July.

And then, when the anthem had ended, he took off for the pitcher's mound — but not before rolling the warmup ball down the top of the dugout to some unbelievably lucky fan.

The question is, how long can he keep his act going? It is almost too much to ask anyone — much less a 21-year-old rookie — to take hold of an entire town the way Fidrych has and maintain his poise.

All Eyes Are Glued on Mark

The Tigers are enjoying his astounding success, especially when it comes to counting the dollars, but they also know what a terrible spot the young man is in.

They don't want to do anything to spoil him. They want him to be himself — as flaky as that might be. But at the same time, they don't want him to get carried away with all of the hoopla and forget the main reason he is here — to pitch baseball.

Fidrych's sudden success has put Ralph Houk in a tough spot. He admits he has never seen anything like this in all his days in baseball, and this is a man who knew Joe DiMaggio, Mickey Mantle, Yogi Berra, Whitey Ford, Roger Maris and all of the other great Yankees.

"I've just told him to be himself but I want him to concentrate on pitching on the nights he's supposed to pitch," said Houk.

In other words, no running all over the ball park making radio tapes, TV interviews and answering the questions of the writers.

"Now I didn't tell him he couldn't talk to the press," said Houk, a man who is very crafty about his profession.

Fidrych got the message, though — and he was non-committal before Saturday night's game, giving out only nods and grunts to anyone who came by his locker. This may be the only way he can survive.

You find you can't take your eyes off him. Never before have I ever watched a pitcher warm up in the bullpen. I mean, watch his every pitch. I did Saturday night.

And even from high in the press box you could see why Fidrych has pitched as well this season. Even when he is facing nobody, he keeps the ball down — pitch after pitch.

"I don't know why everyone's taken to him the way they have . . . we just talk about it a lot," said coach Dick Tracewski. "Maybe it's because we haven't been a bundle of joy around here in recent years . . . or maybe the fans are ready for someone like him."

"All I know is I saw Sandy Koufax pitch and he never got the reception this kid gets."

The President. The Pope. Sandy Koufax. That's just about covers all the political and religious angles. Denny who?

BY JIM HAWKINS
Free Press Sports Writer

They flocked to Tiger Stadium by the thousands, and the tens of thousands, again Saturday night. They came for only one reason — to see Mark Fidrych perform.

And, The Bird definitely didn't let them down.

By the end of the evening, the Tigers' frizzy-haired phenom had the near-capacity crowd of 51,032 fans in an absolute frenzy as he shut out the Baltimore Orioles on four well-scattered hits, 4-0.

They came to see a show — and baseball's brightest new star gave them one.

THEY ROARED FOR MORE than 3 minutes when Fidrych was introduced before the game, and they yelled themselves hoarse during the final two innings, urging on their gangling, 21-year-old idol with a chant of "Go, Bird, Go!"

And The Bird was simply his usual fantastic self.

In spite of all the pressure that was obviously on him as he personally packed the house for the second time, Fidrych was sensational as he turned in his first shutout of his brief but brilliant career.

And so the legend of Mark Fidrych continues to grow.

There obviously is a lot more to this remarkable young man than just his antics on the mound and his peculiar conversations with the baseball.

He's also one helluva pitcher.

WHEN SATURDAY'S game ended and Fidrych left the field,

Fidrych is AL Player of the Month
— Page 4D

The Bird doesn't chirp in the dugout
—Page 4D

Fidrych has now won eight in a row and nine for the year, compiling all but one of his 10 starts. His earned run average is a miniscule 1.85 and he is a cinch to make the All-Star team, if not to start the game.

after first shaking hands with each of his teammates, the exuberant fans refused to leave their seats.

Instead, they stood and chanted, "We Want The Bird, We Want The Bird," until Fidrych finally emerged from the dugout after more than three minutes to take a curtain call.

If he hadn't, they might have stayed there all night...

"In all my years in baseball, I've never seen anything like this," admitted Tiger manager Ralph Houk. "This stirs me up. It's gotta stir up all the players."

"That's how much Mark Fidrych has turned on this town.

"I wanted him to win so darn bad. The kid's so energetic, so enthused. Everything goes together.

"Mickey Mantle used to draw crowds, but I've never seen a rookie do anything like this," the Tiger manager added. "I don't think I've ever enjoyed anything like this in my life."

FIDRYCH HAS NOW drawn a total of 95,887 cash customers the last two times he has pitched. And it can safely be said that at least half that number paid their way into the park solely to see him.

And he'll get a chance to improve on that total when he faces Kansas City here Friday night.

Fidrych was in trouble only once Saturday night — and he

Please turn to Page 4D, Column 7

Mark (The Bird) Fidrych fires plateward against Baltimore, then tells the ball exactly where to go on the next pitch

Bird Dazzled By Success

BY CHARLIE VINCENT
Free Press Sports Writer

Mark Fidrych bounced around the Tiger dressing room like a man trying to find his way out of a maze.

He held a Stroh's in one hand, but broke through a ring of reporters to go grab a Lite.

He shook hands with every teammate within sight. He took a giant poster with a caricature of himself from John Hiller's locker and moved it against the wall. He stalked around in circles, going nowhere in particular, running his fingers through his sweat-soaked locks.

Plainly, Mark Fidrych cannot believe what is happening to him.

"I don't know what to say . . . I just don't know what to say," he said over and over.

"Why don't you go and talk to the other guys. I shouldn't even talk to you," he told the reporters. "I shouldn't say anything, they're the ones who are doing it."

THE BIRD, THE HOTTEST property in the American League at the moment, had just won his ninth game of the season and he got his first major league shutout in the process — blanking Baltimore, 4-0, before 51,032.

"Hell, yes, the shutout means a lot to me," he said. "It feels good . . . it feels real good, but I just hope it doesn't crack.

"I think about it when I go out there. I know it might go like this," he said, making a diving gesture with his right hand. "I just hope when it happens, it goes like this," he said, making

Please turn to Page 4D, Column 4

Fidrych, usually incessantly vocal, sits quietly in the dugout.

Borg Is King At Wimbledon

From AP and UPI

WIMBLEDON, England — Bjorn Borg, deciding "attack was the best form of defense," against the artistry of Ilie Nastase cut the temperamental Romanian down in straight sets Saturday to become the youngest Wimbledon champion in 45 years, despite playing with three cortisone injections to ease a painfully strained stomach muscle.

He is the first Scandinavian ever to win Wimbledon.

The athletic Swede raced about the Wimbledon center court and hit top-spin forehands like a demon to crush Nastase 6-4 6-2 9-7 in the men's singles final.

He went through the whole tournament without dropping a set.

AT 20 YEARS and one month, Borg is the fourth youngest men's champion since Wimbledon started 99 years ago. Three 19-year-olds have won the title — Wilfred Baddeley of Britain in 1891, Rene Lacoste of France in 1925 and Sidney Wood of the United States in 1931.

While Borg struck a blow for youth, Billie Jean King at 32 failed in a bid to make history. She needed to win the women's doubles with Betty Stove of The Netherlands to break the all-time record of 19 Wimbledon titles she shares with Elizabeth Ryan.

Chris Evert, this year's women's singles champion, and the exiled Czech, Martina Navratilova, beat the King-Stove team 6-1 3-6 7-5 in the final.

King has won six singles and 13 doubles titles since 1961.

Please turn to Page 2D, Column 3

Detroit Free Press

MILD
Chance of Showers
High 70-74 Low 45-49

ON GUARD FOR 145 YEARS

© 1977, Detroit Free Press, Inc.

Vol. 146—No. 347

Saturday, April 16, 1977

METRO
Stock's Week
Best in a Year
See Page 6, Section B

15¢
6-Day Home Delivery — 90¢

APRIL 16, 1977:

The beginning of a hoped-for renaissance.

5½-YEAR MIRACLE DEDICATED
Detroit Hails City Renaissance

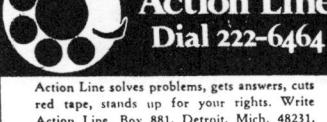

Action Line Dial 222-6464

Action Line solves problems, gets answers, cuts red tape, stands up for your rights. Write Action Line, Box 881, Detroit, Mich. 48231. Or dial 222-6464 between 8:30 a.m. and 4:30 p.m. Monday through Friday.

In February I ordered some photographic equipment from Frank's Highland Park Camera in Los Angeles. I chose this particular company because they advertised "superfast, same day shipping," if I sent them a certified check or money order, which I did. I've never received my merchandise, nor a good reason why not. I'm going home from school for the summer in less than a month, and am anxious to get this resolved. Can you? — M.V., Ann Arbor.

Frank's Highland Park Camera got the picture. Photo gear finally found it's way to Ann Arbor after call from Action Line. Store manager launched intensive search for neglected order, saying that orders "probably got mixed up." Manager fingered back-order with equipment manufacturer as largest contributor to delay, adding that you weren't only one to wait. All merchandise went out in following morning's mail, arrived in time for your end-of-semester move.

I've always been interested in the art of mime. For years I've studied classical ballet, but my real passion is mime. My problem is I'd like to take some classes and haven't been able to find any. Can you find someone in the area that teaches mime? — L.G., Dearborn Heights.

Put on a happy face. You're in luck because the Mime Ensemble, Michigan's only professional mime troupe, will be holding classes this summer in metro Detroit area. Tom Aston, Mime Ensemble director, told Action Line that workshop is still in planning stage, so dates, location and fees for classes will be set later depending on response to program. Those interested in participating can contact Aston by calling 375-0505 in Rochester, or writing to P.O. Box 151, Bloomfield Hills 48013. Aston said course will begin with fairly strenuous exercise program to get body in shape. Then basic isolation moves, like walking, running and climbing in place, will be taught. Mime is thought to pre-date language as a means of communication between early tribes of man. As an art form, mime appeared on Greek and Roman stages, centuries before Christ.

Action Line

We have an unusual problem and need help fast. We don't have an organ in our church because it was stolen, and our piano is in such terrible shape it's not playable. Well, we have a young member of our congregation who's getting married this Saturday, and right now it looks like it will be a musicless wedding — unless you can find an organ that we can use for the day. Can you? — N.C., Detroit.

Dearly beloved . . . joyous strains of "Wedding March" will be heard in Highway Baptist Church in Detroit tonight, thanks to goodwill of Anderson Music. Action Line put in call to 'owner of Detroit area stores Richard Anderson who said he'd be glad to help make young couple's wedding complete, said loan of organ is free of charge. He also made arrangements for delivery and pick-up of instrument.

When I needed emergency X-rays last October at Ferguson-Droste-Ferguson Hospital in Grand Rapids, my medical coverage so I paid $47.50 on the spot. Despite paying off, in November I got a bill from their radiology department for $20. I've been trying ever since to convince them that I paid for all of the services, but the bills keep on coming. Can you put a stop to this? —C.S., Hobart.

Dunning's been halted. Bill sent to you in March will be last after Action Line called Ferguson-Droste-Ferguson credit manager James Beecroft. Beecroft pulled file for close inspection, discovered that $20 radiology fee had never been transferred to separate records maintained by X-ray department. He said money would be credited to radiology immediately, adding that he would be penning letter of apology to you for credit department error.

Action Line

The intersection of Leslie and Stratford Streets in Oak Park is quite a hazardous. There aren't any "Stop" or "Yield" signs, and cars often go racing through in both directions. There have been so many near misses that I'm afraid for the drivers and the many children who play in the area. Isn't there a law that requires some kind of traffic signs to be posted? — M.A., Oak Park.

No, but if intersection proves dangerous enough it could convince Oak Park authorities to place signs there. Hazardous intersections should be brought to attention of your mayor and City Council. Complaint would then be referred to engineering and civil defense departments for traffic study. Report would be filed back to council for ultimate decision. City spokesman, however, checked records for Leslie and Stratford and said no accidents have occurred there this year, and only one minor mishap occurred last year. Apparently corner's safe, or maybe speeding drivers have been lucky so far.

THE QUESTION
Convinced that the nation's economy is on the rebound and worried a tax rebate might be inflationary, President Carter has withdrawn his $50-a-person tax rebate proposal. Can you do without the $50?

HOW YOU VOTED
NO, 61.9 percent. COMMENTS: "I've spent it already" . . . "Congress gave themselves a pay raise and forgot the people of America again" . . . "With both me and my husband working we still need the $50" . . . "I need all of the money that I can get" . . . "Why doesn't Carter give it to everyone and let those who don't need it send it back?"

YES, 35.1 percent. COMMENTS: "It would only make inflation worse" . . . "We should support President Carter as much as possible" . . . "I can do without the fifty dollars but these tax increases are killing me" . . . "I'll stick behind Jimmy Carter all the way."

TOMORROW'S QUESTION
Organized labor is pressing for tighter limits on imported shoes, clothing and TVs, claiming the imports make up too much of the domestic market. Do you favor tighter import restrictions on these goods?

To vote YES Call 961-3211
To vote NO Call 961-4422

The achievement and hope symbolized by Renaissance Center are affirmed by Mayor Young and Henry Ford II. The photos in this montage were taken Friday by Free Press Chief Photographer Tony Spina during the formal dedication of the $337 million complex.

What Has Center Wrought? Jobs, Hope – and Doubts

BY PETER C. GAVRILOVICH
Free Press Staff Writer

A News Analysis

And finally, the doors to Renaissance are open. There it stands, $337 million worth of ambition and hope, 2.4 million square feet of office space, another 350,000 square feet of retail space, a 1,400-room hotel and a sight for sore eyes.

Already crowds flock to the concrete caverns on weekends to gawk and stroll or sip drinks while slowly spinning around a dark pool of water.

But sections of land in downtown still stand naked. Still there is blight and decay. What has Renaissance Center done, if anything, to date?

IT CERTAINLY has created more jobs, 1,700 at the hotel alone. And restaurant business is reported brisk at some eateries downtown.

Mayor Young, during a dedication press conference Friday, spoke of "considerable acreage now being designed" for high-rise housing west of Cobo Hall. But financier Max Fisher, a partner in that project, has yet to announce when the $100-million development will begin. Young indicated Friday that Fisher is seeking private funding.

Both Young and Henry Ford II spoke Friday of nearly $603 million worth of development going on around metropolitan Detroit since Renaissance Center was announced nearly six years ago. Some of that construction, most notably the Woodward Ave. shopping mall, will occur downtown.

Yet, Renaissance Center — a multiphase development — will still stay as it is for now. Phase II and Phase III of the project, which include posh condominiums and other housing

Please turn to Page 2A, Col. 1

More pictures on Back Page

BY SUSAN WATSON
AND PETER C. GAVRILOVICH
Free Press Staff Writers

Henry Ford II, Mayor Young and a retired laborer who migrated to Detroit 30 years ago to seek a better life were among the hundreds of people who joined together Friday for the formal dedication of Renaissance Center — the towering symbol of what is hoped to be Detroit's new lease on life.

The center's four office buildings and the 72-story hotel had cost $337 million to construct and had taken nearly 5½ years to grow from an idea in Henry Ford's head to concrete and steel reality.

A crowd of 800 people was friendly and appreciative as the dignitaries — including Ford, Young and the mayor of Florence, Italy — spoke at the brief dedication at the E. Jefferson entrance to the center.

THE REV. MALCOLM CARRON, president of the University of Detroit, blessed the complex where, he said, "we join together as brothers and sisters in the renaissance of our city."

Then Father Carron, Ford and Young stepped over to a large, royal blue curtain, grabbed a gold braid and together unveiled three bronze plaques listing the 51 names of the partners in the center.

After that, Ford invited the crowd into the center for "free champagne."

The hotel served 14 cases of Mums Cordon Rouge and Blanc de Blanc to its guests and also supplied 200 dozen cookies, made in the shape of the center towers.

During the dedication and at a press conference immediately preceding the dedication, Ford spoke of the center as a catalyst for the renewed growth of Detroit.

"I personally feel Detroit has reached the bottom and is on the way up," Ford said.

"If we all co-operate together and do things together, we can once again make this the great city it was during World War II," he said.

Ford said the center already has served as a catalyst, citing the fact that $603 million in new construction and expansion has been completed or launched in Detroit in the last

Please turn to Page 4A, Col. 3

President Aims At Inflation Rate Of 4% in 1979

From AP, UPI and Free Press
Washington Staff

WASHINGTON — President Carter said Friday that he will aim at reducing the nation's six percent inflation rate to about four percent by the end of 1979 without using wage and price controls.

Except for saying that George Meany and Reginald Jones will work with the administration on its anti-inflation program, there was little in Carter's program that had not been revealed previously. Meany heads the AFL-CIO, and Jones is chairman of the General Electric Co.

Treasury Secretary W. Michael Blumenthal said he will meet early next week with Meany and Jones to talk about ways to reduce inflation and provide more jobs.

Carter's program lays considerable stress on reducing government paperwork and regulations that push up prices and provides for a strengthened Council on Wage and Price Stability to study price behavior and possible industry bottlenecks.

"Most importantly, this joint effort must be voluntary and co-operative and not be based on coercive or self-defeating controls," Carter said.

Carter pledged again to balance the budget by fiscal 1981 and said his administration will announce a "hospital-cost-containment program" later this month to slow spiraling medical costs.

He also said he would veto a permanent tax reduction, favored by congressional Republicans, in the unlikely event that it passes Congress.

CHARLES L. SCHULTZE, the chairman of Carter's Council of Economic Advisers, said the administration's interim economic targets will be to reduce inflation to between four and 4.5 percent by the end of 1979 and unemployment to between five and 5.5 percent.

Recent inflation statistics show consumer prices rising at an annual rate of about nine percent, but Carter said the underlying inflation rate is around six percent. Unemployment was 7.3 percent in March.

Prices increased 4.8 percent

Please turn to Page 12A, Col.

Michael Blumenthal   Charles Schultze
Carter aides ponder reporter's question at briefing

Murder Suspect Shoots 2 Officers, Flees Apartment

BY JULIE MORRIS AND ROBERT DeWOLFE
Free Press Staff Writers

A murder suspect firing through a closed trapdoor in an east side apartment building wounded two Detroit policemen Friday night before making his escape, police said.

The officers, both shot while investigating an earlier homicide, were taken by surprise about 7:50 p.m and did not see their assailant, police said

Officers Walter Williams, 29, and Gregory Falconer, 29, both six-year police veterans, were treated at nearby St. Joseph Mercy Hospital and released. The dead man, victim of an earlier 5:20 p.m. shotgun slaying, was identified as Henry Sims, 36, of 5343 Field.

Police are seeking Hardy Bowlden, 40, of 1340 E. Grand Blvd. for both shooting incidents.

A second suspect, James Moora, 26, 1282 E. Grand Blvd., has been charged with murder in connection with the first shooting.

The first shooting stemmed from an argument in Moora's apartment, police say.

The argument moved into the street and a scuffle ensued between several passersby including Sims, according to witnesses. Bowlden and Moora returned to the apartment building, and Moora came outside once again with a handgun, followed by Bowlden with a shotgun.

One of the women on the street, Roberta Armstrong, 20, told police she heard Sims yell "Duck!" and then heard a shotgun blast, which caught Sims in the face. Sims later died at Detroit General Hospital.

Two-and-a-half hours later, with Moora already in custody, officers Williams and Falconer were walking up the stairs in Moora's two-story apartment building when they were met with "four or five" blasts from a 12-gauge shotgun fired through a closed trapdoor above their heads.

Police believe Bowlden fired at the two officers, then fled across the roof. Despite an intensive search with police dogs, officers were unable to find Bowlden.

U.S.-British Flights Periled

WASHINGTON — (AP) — Transportation Secretary Brock Adams said Friday there is a "realistic" possibility that all commercial air traffic between the United States and Great Britain could be grounded on June 22 unless the two countries reach a new air treaty agreement by then.

Britain has renounced a 31-year-old air treaty between the countries, saying it wants a larger share of the market now divided by the airlines of the two countries.

Two American carriers, Pan Am and Trans World Airlines carry two-thirds of the North Atlantic traffic between the United States and Britain. State-owned British Airways handles one-third of the traffic. Some three million persons traveled these routes last year.

Adams also said the issue of the Anglo-French Concorde supersonic aircraft had been injected into the talks. But he did not say in what form, adding only that the issue has not complicated the matter.

One of the British demands, he said, is that only one airline from each country "be allowed to fly passengers between any two cities. They also have proposed the two nations' airlines

Please turn to Page 11A, Col. 1

Index
Ann Landers	15A
Bridge	13C
Business News	6-8B
Classified	8-12C
Comics	13C
Crossword Puzzle	13C
Death Notices	8C
Editorials	8A
Entertainment	8-7C
Feature Page	15A
Horoscope	13C
Modern Living	1-5B
Movie Guide	14-15C
Names and Faces	16C
Obituaries	8C
Sports	1-9C
Stock Markets	6-8B
Television	10A

RECORD $970,000
Ford Execs' Pay Tops GM

GM CHAIRMAN Thomas Murphy — his $950,000 finished third in 1976.

BY TOM KLEENE
Free Press Automotive Writer

The two top officers of the Ford Motor Corp. topped General Motors Corp's highest paid executive in 1976 salaries and bonuses in a reversal of the normal pattern.

According to the two companies' proxy statements, released late Friday, Chairman Henry Ford II and President Lee A. Iacocca each drew $970,000, while GM chairman Thomas A. Murphy received $950,000.

In a year when record profits for the two automakers generated unusually hefty bonuses, all three men topped the industry's previous highest figure of $823,000 earned by former GM chairman Richard C. Gerstenberg during 1973.

The proxy statements were mailed to Ford and GM shareholders in preparation for their annual meetings — Ford on Thursday, May 12, and GM on Friday May 20.

The bonuses of the three substantially exceeded their salaries for the year. Ford and Iacocca each drew $610,000 in incentive pay and $360,000 in salary while Murphy received $625,000 in bonuses and $325,000 in salary.

GM President E.M. Estes and Vice-President Richard L. Terrell followed Murphy with earnings of $885,000 and $860,000, respectively.

Please turn to Page 4A, Col. 3

DEC. 11, 1977:

The disappearance of east side neighborhoods was a story that took years to unfold.

Sunday feature

In This Section
Editorials — Page 2
Books — Pages 5-6
Entertainment — Pages 7-13
Art — Page 15

Detroit Free Press

Features—Editorials
SUNDAY, DECEMBER 11, 1977

SECTION B

Seven pounds per dip — how much have YOU moved?

Know Your Enemy

BY PETER C. GAVRILOVICH
Free Press Staff Writer

The Eskimo, as we all know, has several dozen different words for snow. The Detroiter has two, and only one of them is printable.

That's obviously because Eskimos know a lot more about snow than Detroiters. If Detroiters knew more about snow, they might have several dozen words for snow, too, though it might remain true that only one was printable.

In any case, here are a lot of things to know about snow, starting with:

What's good about snow?

Two things: Snow blankets grass and plants, insulating them from bitter winter cold. That's important to some farmers, like winter wheat growers in southern lower Michigan. Without a good blanket of snow, their fall plantings will die of exposure. And of course, snow replenishes water basins. Up north, in country of tall pine where forest floors of ferns and matted needles form runoffs, melting snow in spring trickles to brooks and creeks which feed streams and rivers, which run to lakes, which wind up in water glasses.

How does snow happen?

Snow forms in clouds where temperatures are constantly cold. The same clouds bring rain in the summer — but rain starts as snow. The snow forms in small ice crystals, too tiny for the naked eye to see. They're six-sided crystals, usually polygons, stars or spangles. Often the crystals are needle-like, with the ends of them forming hexagons. They are translucent — clear. So in a sense, where there's a storm cloud over Michigan, whether it's February or August, there's snow up there.

Rain starts as snow?

Yep. When the crystals begin to fall and pass through warmer air, they melt and hit ground as raindrops.

What's sleet, and what's hail?

Sleet forms when falling snow crystals begin to melt, but are held up in colder air layers by updrafts of wind. While they hover, dropping slowly, they melt and refreeze, hitting earth as sleet. Hail hovers longer, collecting more and more layers of ice before it begins its downward plummet.

What makes snow white?

The crystals collide as they fall, forming snow flakes, which reflect light and make snow appear to be white. Actually, snow is clear.

What's this malarky about no two snowflakes being alike?

Fact. Not even two snow crystals are alike, much less two snow flakes, which are made up of crystals. Figure it this way: A snow crystal is made up of several million molecules of water. A snow crystal is .000005 centimeters wide. A good size snow flake could be up to one centimeter wide. The possibilities are endless.

Is our snow in Michigan any different than, say, the snow in Denver?

Nope. Temperature controls snow. Wet snow in large flakes falls when temperatures are about 28 degrees and above. Drier, more powdery snow, falls at colder temperatures. It can never get too cold to snow.

What's the equivalent of snow in rain?

About six inches of wet snow equals an inch of rain. The snow that bombarded Detroit and southern lower Michigan last week was a wet snow. Depending on how cold it is, 30 inches of dry snow could equal an inch of rain.

That snowstorm Monday — why wasn't it a blizzard?

Definition. The National Weather Service calls storms "blizzards" when winds stay above 35 miles an hour and temperatures stay below 20 degrees. "Snowstorms" are storm systems expected to

Please turn to Page 4B, Col. 3

Charting the Tragedy Of the Lower East Side— A Fifth of It Has Vanished

Free Press Staff Writers Jim Neubacher and Ellen Grzech have inspected literally every residential block of a 14-square-mile area of Detroit's lower east side to produce this comprehensive assessment of that deteriorating area's present and future. They looked at 45,600 properties, counted 10,000 razed or abandoned parcels and found no one who could tell them what Detroit is going to do about what they saw. Here is their report.

BY JIM NEUBACHER
AND
ELLEN GRZECH
Free Press Staff Writers

ON A COLD FALL DAY when a light snow covers the bare ground, the land looks much as it must have looked 150 years ago, when a Frenchman named St. Jean owned it. Except for the refrigerator.

The ungainly box lies on its side, rust showing through the white enameled exterior. Ahead, looking south, is a house, quiet on a quiet morning. Too quiet. The windows and doors of the house are covered with plywood.

To the left is a long, open and unobstructed line of sight. Homes that once stood in the way are gone now.

Across the street, to the right, is a house at 1607 Illibridge. It is not boarded up, it is burned and charred, and open to the elements. A rookie fireman died in that house in October, fighting the fire that gutted the structure.

To the north? More and more and more of the same.

IT IS THE HEART of a 14-square mile area on Detroit's lower east side, an area characterized by pervasive blight, decay and poverty. No other large section of the city is so dismal.

In these neighborhoods are 9,000 vacant lots; nearly 20 percent of the once-occupied residential land in the area is empty.

In the same area, another 1,000 homes—enough to populate 25 square blocks of the city—stand vacant and boarded up. They exist on the hope someone will once again occupy them before they are vandalized, burned or ultimately demolished like the thousands before them.

In some large areas within this section of Detroit, vacant homes and vacant lots now account for four of every 10 parcels.

"It looks like Hiroshima out there," said one city official.

Once a Population The Size of Battle Creek

In better Detroit days, on almost all of those 9,000 vacant lots stood homes and flats, built all at once in a city that grew all at once in the automobile-spawned boom after World War I.

Today, those homes and more have been forsaken by people who are unable—or unwilling—to live in them.

The vacant and demolished homes in the lower east side area once housed a population of 40,000, the equivalent of a city the size of Battle Creek.

The 9,000 empty parcels—if they were put together—would cover an area of almost two square miles, or more than Belle Isle.

In the area surveyed by the Free Press, no house or lot is more than 3.5 miles from either the affluent Grosse Pointes or the Renaissance Center. Five minutes to the north is the convenience of the Ford Freeway. Five minutes to the south are the pleasures of the river and Belle Isle.

Indian Village and several other elegant subdivisions are in this area of Detroit. A half-dozen parks dot the river front.

Yet within the last three years some land in this area has changed hands for the equivalent of an incredibly low $500 an acre. There is no visible, realistic market for much of the land in this section of Detroit, and much of it has fallen into the hands of the owner of last resort—the public.

THERE IS SO MUCH vacant land in Detroit that city officials admit candidly that they not only don't know what to do with it, they are not even sure where it all is. Russ Chambers, property inventory manager for the city's Community and Economic Development Department (CED), says an estimated 35,000 of the 425,000 assessable parcels of land in Detroit are believed to be vacant.

He estimates the city owns 10,000 of these, and says another 100 a month are coming into city hands just from the U.S. Department of Housing and Urban Development — the bitter fruits of a spectacularly unsuccessful federal home-loan insurance program.

The amount of vacant land on the lower east side will continue to grow for years. There is no significant amount of money available to carry out an east side redevelopment plan, say Chambers and Tom Cunningham, CED's community development co-ordinator.

And, they add, there is no plan, either.

Without a plan for the future of the lower east side there can be no predictions of any certainty about the future of Detroit, or even the chances for successful reconstruction of other decayed urban areas in Michigan and the U.S.

The manner and degree in which the lower east side is redeveloped will affect the city for generations. The mix of races, economic classes, business and residences that results will set a pattern that will have an impact into the next century.

HERE ARE SOME of the factors that could determine what the future will hold:

• The city government will undoubtedly have an upper, if not ruling, hand in the redevelopment process. Private developers are almost totally hamstrung by policies, laws and economics that prevent them from undertaking even modest-sized redevelopment programs.

Prior to 1973, an opinion by the city corporation counsel—the city's own attorney—said it was illegal for the city to "landbank," acquire land without a definite and declared purpose in mind.

That opinion changed in 1973, however, clearing the way for the city to receive thousands of property deeds that were flooding the scandal-ridden HUD office in Detroit. Until that arrangement with HUD, the federal agency was desperately attempting to reduce its inventory of properties by selling vacant lots to the first comer for a minimum bid of $50. Speculators bought many of the lots at the minimum price.

An inspection of neighborhoods on the east side and discussions with private and public real estate men give no indication that any major private assemblage of land or rebuilding occurred because of that program. So far, no one has made any financial killing in HUD lots.

A Dampening Effect On Private Investment

And since mid-1975, those lots have been coming directly to one landlord—the city of Detroit. Not only has this stopped acquisition of HUD lots by all but a few private citizens, it has dampened private speculation and investment in much of the city and particularly on the lower east side.

There are least two reasons for this: An investor who tied up all but the 1,000 vacant parcels in one neighborhood would have to deal with the city, largely on city terms, before he could acquire the rest of the land. While that may not be all bad, some developers don't consider it to be all good, either.

One east side developer, who would like very much to build a community of townhouses along one of the canals that leads to the Detroit River, says that even if he managed to acquire all the privately-owned land along the canals—a difficult task—he would have to find some way to acquire the city-owned land.

If he approached the city, officials could not merely sell sell the land to him on request. It would have to be put out for bids, or the area would have to be designated as official renewal area. In the latter case, the townhouse project would have to meet with citizen approval, as well as follow city, state and even federal guidelines covering almost every conceivable aspect of the development.

Secondly, says the same developer, city homeowners on the lower east side who have watched the "total clearance/

Please turn to Page 4B, Col. 3

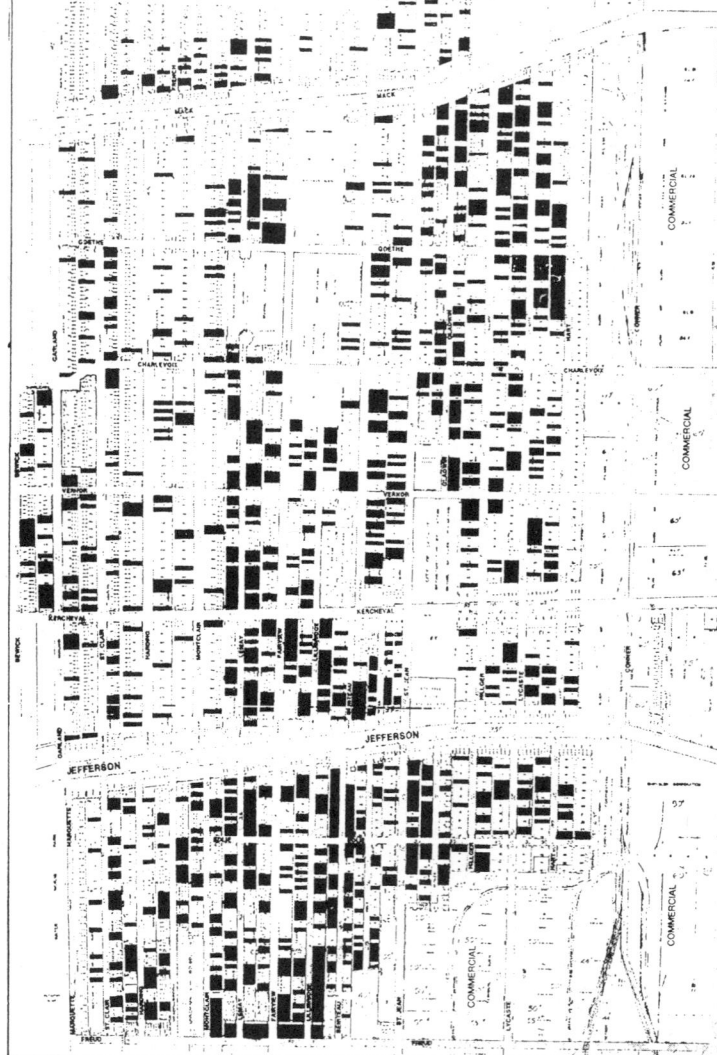

Each of the 1,500 blacked-out lots on this detailed map of a portion of east side Detroit (see black inset in map at left) is empty residential property, either unused or, in most cases, leveled. In all, these properties represent 30 percent of the 5,000 lots in the area, but they are only a small part of the record of inertia and decay assembled by Free Press Staff Writers Jim Neubacher and Ellen Grzech in a painstaking survey of 14 square miles of residential east side neighborhoods (see gray portion of map at left). Neubacher and Grzech personally looked at 45,000 plots of residential land and found fully 9,000 of them — 20 percent — vacant. Another 1,000 were occupied by abandoned, boarded-up homes. One of the hardest hit sections is the area in the map above, bounded by Waterworks Park and Garland on the west, Mack Avenue on the north, the Conner Industrial corridor on the east and Freud near the river on the south. While no massive, organized clearance program has affected this area, some of its neighborhoods are more than 40 percent empty.

In This Section		Detroit Free Press	SECTION	DEC. 18, 1977:
Editorials	Page 2	**Features—Editorials**	**B**	
Books	Pages 5, 16	SUNDAY, DECEMBER 18, 1977		The PBB story: A catalog of heroes and villains.
Entertainment	Pages 7-14			Sunday feature

Bureaucrats and Bad Meat – the PBB Story

How Much Harm? By Next Year We Might Know

"I didn't personally actually sneak in and mix up that compound one night in the chemical company shop. I didn't do that. But there are people who would have you believe this governor did it . . . but I've tried in a responsible and honest way to cope with it. And I don't claim it was done perfectly. Not for one minute."

— Governor William G. Milliken;
Free Press interview, Dec. 13, 1977

BY KATHY WARBELOW AND ELLEN GRZECH
Free Press Staff Writers

Sometime in January, a high-powered team of medical researchers will begin to roll up the sleeves of 3,000 Michigan citizens and draw the first vials of blood, launching a multi-million dollar testing program to see if PBB has made us sick.

With microscopes and sophisticated testing equipment, they will look for damaged white blood cells, unusual enzyme levels, and abnormal antigens — evidence of the kinds of illness they already have found among 1,029 farmers who consumed meat and milk from PBB-poisoned dairy herds and among the chemical workers who made PBB.

What they want to know is whether Michigan citizens who have been eating food tainted with lower levels of PBB than that are running risks of the same health problems the farmers appear to have:

• Damaged immunological systems that make them more susceptible to disease and infection.
• Damaged livers.
• Impaired neurological functions.
• The brooding possibility that years from now they may have a greater chance of developing cancer.

BY SEPTEMBER 1978, the researchers could have some of the answers for the people waiting to hear them. Then, for the first time — an incredible five years after the chemical accident that poisoned the state's food chain — we may finally know just how much damage PBB has done to the health of nine million Michigan people; not to mention the unknown number of Americans outside Michigan who may have eaten tainted beef.

The PBB experience has already resulted in a devastating toll: Hundreds of Michigan farms touched by the contamination; more than 30,000 cattle shot and buried in a mass grave; a Canadian boycott of Michigan beef that is costing $1 million a year; the contamination of a 30-mile stretch of the Pine River by the Velsicol Chemical Corp., the firm that made the PBB responsible for the disaster.

And the damage continues. Last month, the federal Farmers Home Administration began foreclosing on three PBB-affected farms because of delinquent mortgages. Those proceedings had been suspended out of sheer charity.

On Jan. 3, 1978, however, auctioneers will sell Eli Argersinger's farm near Cadillac to pay off a mortgage he has been unable to meet in more than two years.

Since they see no other answer, the Argersinger's neighbors have threatened to protect the couple's farm with the only dependable weapon they know — their shotguns.

In February, 300 more contaminated cows will be shot and buried in a 50-foot deep pit lined with a 20-foot thick layer of clay near Mio, evidence that PBB still contaminates the state's farms and animals.

SOMETIME IN 1978, Velsicol Chemical and Farm Bureau Services, Inc., which operated the feed mill that mistakenly distributed the PBB (polybrominated biphenyl) as cattle feed, will go to trial in a Grand Rapids federal court on criminal charges for causing the disaster. Even if they are convicted, however, the companies will only have to pay fines of $1,000 because the charges are misdemeanors.

Around June, 1978, federal agents expect to conclude an investigation into other possible criminal actions in the PBB episode, including allegations that quarantined cattle destined for the Kalkaska burial pit were instead illegally sold for food.

The scars of the PBB tragedy will be with us for a long time, just as official action to finally contain the problem and help its victims has been a long time — undoubtedly much too long — coming.

For three-and-a-half years, Gov. Milliken, the Legisla-

First the farmers lost their cattle. Now some may lose their farms. But the loss could have been far worse without the efforts of people like the four pictured below.

ture, and key state and federal officials grossly underestimated the scope of the disaster, ignored initial complaints by farmers that PBB was making them sick, and refused to do anything to help those farmers who became PBB's major victims.

Heroes and Culprits In The PBB Tragedy

It took the persistent, even brave efforts of a few individuals to shake the politicians and bureaucrats out of their inertia and make them confront the full meaning of the crisis.

In the absence of official action, the people of Michigan owe a debt to these individuals:

• Fred Halbert, the Battle Creek farmer who spent $5,000 of his own money to test contaminated feed in early 1974, and whose efforts led to identification of PBB as the contaminant.

• Dr. Thomas Corbett, an Ann Arbor anesthesiologist who was the first to warn that PBB could hurt people and pressed public officials to keep PBB-tainted food off the market.

• Dr. Alpha Clark, a dedicated, slightly eccentric northern Michigan veterinarian who mobilized farmers into action when state officials refused to help them and who refused to be intimidated when they tried to silence him.

• Dr. Irving Selikoff, the mild, portly New York medical researcher who volunteered to test Michigan farmers in 1976, did so at no cost to anyone but his own research program, and was the first to document that PBB had probably made them sick. His work jolted state officials into action and led to the general population study that the Legislature has approved to begin in January.

• Edie Clark, a 31-year-old aide to state House Speaker Bobby Crim who adopted PBB as her personal crusade and fought like a mongoose to get bills through a sometimes recalcitrant state Legislature. She listened to the farmers when no one else at an official level would and brought Selikoff here in 1976.

• Gary Schenk, a cocky, brilliant Grand Rapids attorney who gave up a lucrative corporate law practice to represent 100 farmers who have filed damage suits against Velsicol and Farm Bureau Services. He has spent most of 1977 trying the first case; there are more than 80 others to go.

• Hundreds of Michigan farmers, who kept the PBB issue alive when state officials were trying to bury it, even when it meant dumping dead cattle on the Capitol steps or shooting the farmers' own cows so we would not have to eat them.

JUST AS THERE ARE heroes in the PBB problem, there are culprits. Who is to blame for the PBB disaster and the fact that it wasn't halted much sooner?

• Velsicol Chemical Corp. (formerly Michigan Chemical Co.) of St. Louis, Mich. The firm made more than 12 million pounds of PBB, which is supposed to be used as a fire retardant, without telling its own workers the firm believed the chemical was dangerous. In 1973, it sent a load of PBB to Farm Bureau Services in Battle Creek in bags so poorly marked that Farm Bureau employes did not know they were mixing poison into feed for dairy cattle.

• Farm Bureau Services, which failed to tell state officials in late 1973 that farmers had reported that the feed in question was making cows sick and even killing them. That failure alone delayed discovery of the accident and its extent for nearly a year, a period in which the contamination spread throughout the state's food chain and citizens unwittingly ate most of the hundreds of pounds of PBB that were dumped into the system.

• The U.S. Food and Drug Administration, which allowed us to eat the food tainted with PBB instead of banning the chemical from food until it could determine if the food was safe. Farmers who complained that the level of PBB the FDA said could be permitted in food was too high were branded by FDA as liars and frauds. The FDA attacked the later health studies by Selikoff and even sent a spy to Grand Rapids last November when Selikoff examined farmers there.

The FDA refuses, even today, to lower the level of PBB it will permit in food in the face of mounting clinical and laboratory evidence that PBB is dangerous to people. Under 1977 legislation, the state's standards are now much stricter than the federal standards.

Alan Hoeting, district director of the FDA, admitted during a recent interview that "ideally, we wouldn't have permitted any of it (PBB) in the food chain."

But Hoeting defended the amount allowed by the FDA, which is 15 times higher than the amount now allowed under Michigan law, and said that food contaminated below the FDA level is safe to eat.

"We've said that in 1975 and 1976 and 1977. This is what our people have concluded," he said.

Milliken calls the FDS's insistence on maintaining a three-year-old standard for PBB in food "astounding," says he regrets relying on that standard as long as he did.

But Hoeting insists he is satisfied with the job his agency has done in Michigan.

Please turn to Page 4B, Col. 3

Dr. Tom Corbett
An early warning

Dr. Irving Selikoff
Tests on his own time.

Edie Clark, who
brought Selikoff in.

Attorney Gary Schenk
Working for the farmers.

Cuba Si, Yankee Si, Si — Havana Opens for Business

BY ELIZABETH O'BRYAN VENANT
Free Press Travel Editor

At the world famous Tropicana nightclub the show girls strut once again in plumes and chiffon. The Floridita Bar where Hemingway drank is open for business with a fresh coat of paint. The white sand and aquamarine waters shine as they always have.

But after 18 years of communism, Cuba has changed. Tourists who remember the pre-Castro glitter — the hum of casinos, the tuxedoed nightclub crowds, will be disappointed. Those who expect a grim-faced Communist regime will be surprised. Cuba today is no longer a swank resort; nor is it an armed camp.

On Dec. 22, Americans will be able to travel to Cuba again on regularly scheduled tours arranged by the tour, Sunflight Holidays. What will they find when they arrive? Last Monday 157 Midwest travel agents flew from Detroit and several other cities into Havana to find out. I went along.

AT 1:40 P.M. our DC8 charter jet landed at San Jose Airport and we filed through the small cement building into Cuba. For the Cuban government, our arrival was an important event. It was the largest group of travel agents to visit the country since the ban on American travel to Cuba was lifted last March. And representatives of Cubatur, the government tourist agency, were eager to please.

"They greeted us with the kind of luxury we didn't expect: five air-conditioned tour buses, stocked with free beer, rum and Cuban cigars, and an official reception at the nearby beach resort of Santa Maria del Mar.

The rum flowed freely, the buffet tables were laden with ham, roast beef and pineapple, and a band played loud and lively Cuban music. Outside the pine trees waved in a warm December breeze and blue-green waves rolled in on a wide sand beach. "What begins well must end well," a Cubatur guide announced.

It was in the tour buses, however, that we first

The Sunflight Holidays tour of Cuba will be an eight-day/seven-night excursion. It will include two nights in Havana, three nights at Cienfuegos, a southern coastal resort, and two nights at Varadero. The price from Metro Airport is $489, including three meals a day at the hotels. After the initial December 22 departure, tours will be scheduled weekly February through April. They can be booked through local travel agents.

saw what life in Cuba really is like. The signs of old and new Cuba spread over the countryside. There were the expected blocks of cement prefabricated buildings — stark and cold monuments of Cuba's construction programs. Some of the buildings were schools, others were factories, youth recreation camps, or military installations. Individually, they were indistinguishable.

As our buses rolled through the afternoon, we passed neatly laid out citrus groves, the site of a shopping in Varadero, no tennis courts, no golf courses. And, with the exception of fish and fresh fruit, food is mediocre at best. "After a couple of days here, they'll be crawling up the walls," one agent complained.

A peasant on horseback galloped across a newly-paved road, one of the many highways that now crisscross the island. A soldier in brown khaki uniform chatted with an elderly woman on the porch of a pastel house. An ancient Buick sat in the drive. And children in burgundy school uniforms laughed and waved as our bus went by. American tourists in Cuba are a novelty.

Our guides were not selling us communism. They did say that Cubans have free medical care and education, that they pay only 6 percent of their salaries for rent and 4 percent for furniture. And the rate of illiteracy has been slashed from 33 to 3 percent. But there was no propaganda.

WHAT THE CUBANS are selling are their beach resorts. Varadero Beach, billed as Cuba's most luxurious resort, was our first stop.

In pre-Castro days, Varadero was the watering hole of the rich. The Dupont's had an estate there; so did Batista. Today the Dupont house is a museum and restaurant, Batista's mansion is used for official Communist party functions, and the private homes of the wealthy have been converted to hotels for workers.

For the foreign tourist, a half-dozen pre-revolution hotels have been taken out of mothballs. Their doors seem to open on the same interiors they closed on 18 years ago.

The **Hotel Internacional** is typical. Our rooms were large and clean, but sparsely furnished. In places the plaster was peeling, and in modern bathrooms the plumbing was not always working.

A trio of Canadian tourists said you forgot about the discomforts after a day or two. There was the wide sand beach to lie on, the sun to soak up, local restaurants for dining, and evening entertainment at the hotels.

The American travel agents were not convinced. Except for a hotel souvenir shop, there is no shopping in Varadero, no tennis courts, no golf courses. And, with the exception of fish and fresh fruit, food is mediocre at best. "After a couple of days here, they'll be crawling up the walls," one agent complained.

But for the moment, at least, Americans traveling to Cuba have no other choice. They must go on tours that dictate where they stay and, in large measure, the cities they visit. According to the Cuban government, all persons must obtain immigration passes to travel from one town to another. But a long-time Cuban resident shrugs the idea off. "You can go anywhere you want," he said. He seems to be right.

THE BAY OF PIGS is an hour and half drive from Varadero across the agricultural province of Matanzas. On the morning of our second day in Cuba, three of us, escorted by a Cubatur guide, hired a taxi to go there. Marcelino, the driver, pointed his Dodge 500 due south and floored it. He never stopped grinning and he rarely lifted his foot from the accelerator pedal. Marcelino, the Cubatur guide explained, had a sharp nose for cops.

The last community before the Bay of Pigs is a crossroads village called El Palpite. On one side of the road is an old country school house; on the other, there is a large billboard that announces, "This is as far as the mercenaries got." The sign is three miles from where the Cuban exiles landed.

On April 15, 1961, when American-supported Cuban exiles launched their pre-dawn attack, there were no roads to lead them inland. They had intentionally chosen a remote landing point. The Bay of Pigs is a swamp named for the wild boars that inhabit it.

Today a two-lane road leads to the bay. Along the road, tombstones have been erected in honor of the Cuban soldiers who died repelling the invaders.

At the bay itself the only relic of aborted attack is a rusting anchor of one of the ships. The Bay of Pigs today is a peaceful beach resort. Cubans sip orange juice at a refreshment stand. A tanned lifeguard with peroxided hair patrols the beach. And gentle ripples of water lick the sand.

The Bay of Pigs round-trip for four cost $98. There are no car rentals in Cuba. The only inter-city alternative is the bus. I tried that, too, but not intentionally.

When our tour buses left Varadero for Havana Tuesday afternoon, I was down at the beach.

To go to Havana, I took a cab and a bus. Jose, my taxi driver, considered my situation highly amusing. We laughed about it a lot on the shore road from Varadero to Matanzas, the nearest large city. We laughed because we couldn't talk much in the same language.

In a sign language that we developed, we did spend some time comparing the quality of American and Cuban cigarettes. Tipping in Cuba is not accepted, but gifts of such things as cigarets are appreciated. A pack of Populares Superfino, one of the better Cuban brands, cost $2. I offered Jose a pack of NOWs; he smoked one and told me he would just as soon pay the Populares price.

When we reached Matanzas it became clear that although I was going to Havana, Jose was not. We had reached the outer perimeter of his taxi service. But he had no intention of dropping me unattended at a bus stop. From a gas station to police headquarters to a Cuban world friendship office, Jose drove in search of an English-speaker. At the friendship office, we met Senor Graciar, the second deputy, who spoke a few words of English. Senor Graciar escorted me to the bus station. And despite my protests, he waited with me on the platform for over an hour. Only when my bus for Havana pulled out of the station and, like a fond relative, he had waved goodby to me, did Senor Graciar turn to go.

The bus trip took two hours and cost $2.

At the Tropicana nightclub a dozen tour buses lined the drive. "This is paradise under the sky," my cab driver said with pride. Like the Lido in Paris and the floorshows in Vegas, the Tropicana is show biz on a spectacular scale. A band plays Cuban music à la Desi Arnaz, colored steam jets shoot into the palm trees like fountains, and show girls prance and swirl. But unlike the chorines of the 50s, the dancers are well covered now. And the audience dress code has changed. The few Cubans in the audience wore sports shirts and slacks.

It was an odd mix of old-time glamor and new-style socialist restraint. All Havana reflects that. It is a city divided.

One side is colonial and mellow, the other is prefab cement. A tour of the city takes in both. I skipped the new and took the old in at my leisure.

AT THE LOVELY OLD Plaza de Armas, our first stop in old Havana, the Cubatur guide enumerated the functions and facts of a Spanish fortress, a neoclassical monument, and various Cuban heroes on pedestals. As he was telling how the cobble-

Please turn to page 4B, Col. 3

JAN. 24, 1979:

The Republicans pick Detroit for their convention, and "the city that was supposedly dead" gets national recognition.

Mays named to baseball's Hall of Fame
Details on Page 1D

Detroit Free Press

Volume 148, Number 265   ON GUARD FOR 147 YEARS   Wednesday, January 24, 1979

metro
Snow likely
High 34, Low 20
Details on Page 13D

15¢

'A CITY WITH A NEW VITALITY'
GOP Picks Detroit for Convention

action line
dial 222-6464

Action Line solves problems, gets answers, cuts red tape, stands up for your rights. Write Action Line, Box 881, Detroit, Mich. 48231. Or dial 222-6464 between 8:30 a.m. and 4:30 p.m. Monday through Friday.

Last February we ordered a set of custom-made, $300 fireplace doors from Fireplace 'N' Things at Lakeside Mall. We were told it would take about six months to get the doors, so we didn't expect to have them until this winter. It has been almost a year since we placed the order, however, and all we can get are promises. Can you do better?
— J.J., Sterling Heights

Hearth is fully equipped now. Results came after we applied six weeks of heat to Daryl Hickman, owner of two Fireplace 'N' Things outlets. Hickman said 300 door orders were delayed last year when his New York supplier fell through and Hickman set up his own factory locally. Your doors were finally installed couple of weeks later, but first fire after that almost brought tragic consequences. Shortly after fire was lit, one pane of glass exploded, slightly injuring your nine-month-old baby who was crawling nearby. Hickman wasn't surprised, saying he's had five panels explode out of 800 his factory has put out. He said explosions are caused by defects in glass that slip by inspection, and added that if there is problem, it would show up during first couple of fires. Hickman had replacement pane made for your door and you report no problem with this one. Action Line took story of exploding glass to Consumer Product Safety Commission and investigator contacted Hickman to discuss matter. CPSC rep said full investigation would be made.

I've been worried ever since I read the story last week about the policeman who got in trouble for having a stuffed eagle in his home. About 12 years ago I purchased several whale teeth to make into scrimshaw jewelry. I'm worried that I might get in trouble with the federal government because whales are now on the endangered species list. Should I quietly drop the evidence off the Belle Isle bridge?
— S.W., Dearborn

No need to deep-six whale teeth. According to Detroit agent of U.S. Fish and Wildlife Service, you won't have to worry about admiring scrimshaw form behind bars since your ownership predates Endangered Species Act of 1973. Act made it federal offense to possess, buy, sell, import or export products made from animals on list. Burden of proof has not been violated lies with feds. Because of embargo on whale parts, scrimshaw, which was started by whalers in 1800s who carved designs in teeth, is now created from bone or ivory. As an indication of how tedious art form is, word scrimshaw comes from French root s'escrimer" — to work hard for small results.

In 1960, my family sold a small wedge of land to the Wayne County Road Commission. The land was supposed to be part of a park, but the park never came to be. Since we still own property on both sides of the piece we sold the county, we asked if we could buy the land back. At first we were told we could, then the county changed its mind and said sale was doubtful. We have a buyer interested in the property, but only if it's in one piece. Can you find out if Wayne County intends to sell us that land?
— J.F., Dearborn

Prognosis isn't good. According to spokesman for Wayne County Road Commission, sale of land back to you has been rejected because property is in flood control area. Flood control lands are those areas adjacent to streams which tend to flood when water level rises. If land is developed, it could cause flooded basements and health hazards in area, Department of Natural Resources oversees all flood control areas and rep there said state law prevents selling the land without DNR's permission. Although WCRC has nixed your original request, you still have right to appeal decision to three-person board, which acts as final arbitrator on disputes involving road commission.

sound off

The question
To boost the declining birth rate in France, a woman is paid $375 during pregnancy and then $80 a month after the baby is born. Would this be an incentive for you to have more children?

How you voted
NO, 72.7 percent. COMMENTS: "You don't have children for money"... "France should be glad the birthrate is dropping"... "I already have eight children and there isn't enough money in the world to get me to have more"... "Having children is supposed to be beautiful, not profitable."

YES, 27.3 percent. COMMENTS: "Money is the only thing stopping me from having a child"... "Parents need some help supporting kids"... "Money talks, even if it wears diapers"... "Children are wonderful, as long as you can afford them"... "I could use something to supplement my income."

Tomorrow's question
According to a recently released University of Michigan study, Americans worry more now than they did 20 years ago over such things as jobs, their community and their lives in general. Do you worry a lot?

To vote YES   To vote NO
Call 961-3211   Call 961-4422

Carter plugs U.S. goals, world peace

By SAUL FRIEDMAN
Free Press Washington Staff

WASHINGTON — President Carter Tuesday night asked the Congress and the nation to help lay "a new foundation" for a stable American economy and a peaceful, prosperous world.

"Our children born this year will come of age in the 21st century," he told the glittering joint session of Congress in his second State of the Union appearance.

"The challenge to us is to build a new and firmer foundation for the future—for a sound economy, for a more effective government, for political trust, and for a stable peace—so that the America our children inherit will be even stronger and better than our own."

THE PRESIDENT'S SPEECH on the state of the union, a report to the nation required by the Constitution, lacked new proposals and avoided the soaring promises, pledges and requests for new programs traditional in the annual addresses.

Instead, it was a plea from Carter, the engineer, to manage "the good programs more effectively and weed out those which are wasteful or unnecessary."

Only in foreign affairs did the president argue with any emotional rhetoric for innovation. He called forcefully for American friendship with the People's Republic of China, a strategic arms limitation treaty (SALT) with the Soviet Union and negotiations to curb atomic weapons generally.

"In this year, 1979, nothing is more important than that the Congress and the people of the United States resolve to continue with me on that oath of nuclear arms control and peace," the president said.

On domestic affairs, however, the president's speech was a low-key effort to explain and justify the unprecedented departure of his administration from traditional Democratic programs for solving problems, programs

See **CARTER**, Page 12A

Highlights of Carter address

WASHINGTON — (AP) — Here are the highlights of President Carter's State of the Union speech, delivered Tuesday night before a joint session of Congress.

New Foundation — The president introduced the term "new foundation" and said: "Tonight I want to examine in a broad sense the state of our American union — how we are building a new foundation for a peaceful and prosperous world."

Myths — Saying the nation must not "substitute myths for common sense," Carter cited as persistent myths the idea that "we must choose endlessly between inflation and recession" or that the government must choose "between compassion and competence."

Budget — "The 1980 budget provides enough spending restraint to begin unwinding inflation, but enough support to keep American workers productive and to encourage investment to provide new jobs."

Program — Key issues being given top priority include legislation to hold down hospital costs; efforts to deregulate the rail, bus and trucking industries; extension of government reorganization to encompass education, economic development and natural resource management; limited public financing of congressional elections, and enactment of a national sunset law "so that when government programs have outlived their value they will automatically be terminated."

Foreign Policy — Carter urged support for "the strong defense budget I have proposed" and said: "We have no desire to be the world's policeman. America does want to be the world's peacemaker."

Arms Limitation — Carter said that "if the Soviet Union continues to negotiate in good faith, a responsible (strategic arms limitation) agreement will be reached."

Rep. Diggs will yield House post

From AP and UPI

WASHINGTON — Rep. Charles C. Diggs, D-Mich., announced Tuesday he would not seek re-election as chairman of a House subcommittee on Africa while appealing his three-year prison sentence conviction.

Diggs voluntarily relinquished the post "to avoid a confrontation" that he said could work against African interests.

Despite Diggs' peace overture, House members from both parties vowed to pursue issues affecting the congressman.

Diggs, convicted on payroll-kickback charges, made the announcement in a letter to Rep. Clement Zablocki, D-Wis., chairman of the full House International Relations Committee.

DIGGS decided to relinquish his Africa subcommittee after being told by House Speaker Thomas P. O'Neill Monday night that failure to do so could result in his being stripped of the post, sources said.

He previously had given up his chairmanship of the full House Committee on the District of Columbia. Sources also said O'Neill urged Diggs to refrain from voting while

See **DIGGS**, Page 15A

inside today

ANN LANDERS	9C	REAL ESTATE	6D
BUSINESS NEWS	7-10D	SPORTS	1-6D
CLASSIFIED	11-16C	STOCK MARKETS	8-10D
COMICS	11-13D	TELEVISION	6C
DEATH NOTICES	11C	THE WAY WE LIVE	1-4C
EDITORIALS	8A		
ENTERTAINMENT	10-11B		
FOOD GUIDE	1-9B		
MOVIE GUIDE	12-13D		
OBITUARIES	10C	TUESDAY	057

William Brock, Republican national chairman, announces the selection of Detroit as the site of the party's 1980 convention. Applauding is Mary Crisp of Arizona, deputy national chairman.

1980 primary politics hinted by a challenge from Sunbelt faction

By WILLIAM J. MITCHELL
Free Press Washington Staff

WASHINGTON — Detroit was selected as the site for the 1980 Republican National Convention Tuesday after it withstood a spirited, last-minute attack from the Sunbelt faction of the party's national committee.

Variously described as depressing, dangerous and Democratic, Detroit nonetheless emerged victorious from a two-hour debate that may have foreshadowed the politics of the 1980 GOP presidential primaries.

The victory was finally insured by a mysteriously changed vote that broke a 73-73 tie. Detroit eventually won the designation by a final vote of 95-52.

"The turning point was the city's technical ability to perform," GOP National Chairman William Brock said after Detroit's selection by the national committee. But he also noted the political statement involved in choosing a city that he said "is in the midst of a renaissance, is on its way back and is a city with a new vitality and spirit and a strong minority and ethnic presence."

Detroit won over six other locations: Dallas, New Orleans, New York City, Miami Beach, Minneapolis-St. Paul and Kansas City.

Although Democrats have not yet selected a committee to look for a site, Detroit is also seeking their convention. The television networks are urging the parties to simplify TV coverage of conventions by choosing the same city.

So far, leading contenders for the Democratic convention appear to be Detroit and Houston with Detroit the favorite.

Michigan Republican Party Chairman William McLaughlin described Tuesday's meeting here as "the most exciting and most nervous national committee meeting of my life."

When the fight was over, he boasted that the Detroit convention "will be so great that the candidate we nominate will be the next president of the United States."

That prompted the first sustained applause of the day, and it was deafening compared with the two or three delegates who applauded the selection committee's earlier declaration of Detroit as its choice.

The national committee traditionally accepts the site committee's recommendation, and Tuesday's floor fight was the first in the memory of Republicans interviewed later.

IN ADDITION to regional preferences, the debate spotlighted the split between moderate Midwestern Republicans and Southern conservatives.

Choosing Detroit represents a return to the Republican heartland, where the party of Lincoln was founded. It was under an oak tree in Jackson, Mich., that the party met to organize its fight against slavery.

McLaughlin said there has never before been a major

See **REPUBLICANS**, Page 15A

• Cabbies, bellmen jubilant over prospect of Republican tips. Page 3A.

• Detroit will woo the Democrats, too, but they don't have a site committee yet. Page 4A.

• John Connally expected to announce for the presidency Wednesday. Page 10A.

• Mississippi Republican says he meant no racial slur. Page 13A.

> The convention represents an unparalleled opportunity for Detroit . . .
>
> See the Back Page

Non-partisan delight greets site selection

By JULIE MORRIS and TIM KISKA
Free Press Staff Writers

A laughing, smiling Mayor Young, posing with a photograph of himself riding an elephant, Tuesday hailed the choice of Detroit as host of the 1980 Republican National Convention as "a tremendous shot in the arm and a real tribute to the turning around of this city."

Young, clearly delighted by the vote of the Republican National Committee, said the choice of Detroit signaled "official recognition across the nation that the city that was supposedly dead is now among the prime convention cities in the nation."

A LIFELONG Democrat and member of the Democratic National Committee, Young said he set aside partisan considerations in joining the Detroit pitch to get the GOP meeting and added: "I'm a Democrat with a big D and a small D. I can deal with Republicans as long as they're spending money and going home."

An aide propped the elephant picture up beside Young during a press conference. The photo showed the mayor riding a small elephant — symbol of the GOP — during opening ceremonies at the Belle Isle Children's Zoo in 1976.

Young's elation was shared Tuesday by dozens of other political, civic and business leaders who joined in a year-long campaign to woo the GOP to Detroit for the first major political convention ever held in the city.

The chairmen of General Motors Corp. and the Ford Motor Co. released statements cheering the announcement, and people in downtown Detroit gossiped over lunch about the big announcement, which brought calls of congratulation flooding into the city's convention bureau headquarters.

"We got it! We got it! We got it!"crowed William B. Browning, owner of the Bob-Lo Co. and immediate past chairman of the Metropolitan Detroit Convention & Visitors Bureau, was nearly speechless with excitement Tuesday, right after he got the news via a telephone call from Washington, D.C., where the choice was announced.

Mayor Young's smile says it all Tuesday.

See **REACTION**, Page 15A

McLAUGHLIN'S FINAL BATTLE
GOP chief savors victory

By REMER TYSON
Free Press Politics Writer

WASHINGTON — Contraband Cuban cigars, a foreign country, a Texas judge throwing around $1,000 bills and a political party bent on changing its losing image figured into Detroit getting the next Republican presidential convention.

The choice was a victory for many in Detroit and the rest of Michigan, but it was a personal triumph for the state's retiring Republican chairman, William McLaughlin.

The nation's senior Republican state chairman, McLaughlin had led the fight for more than 10 years against the GOP's political right. McLaughlin attended his final meeting as a member of the Republican National Committee Tuesday, ending his career there with one of his few victories over the years.

McLAUGHLIN'S 10 years of toil against the Republican conservatives began leading toward his biggest payoff when Republican National Chairman William Brock named Ody Fish of Wisconsin to direct the day-to-day operations of the seven-member site selection committee.

Fish is a Republican moderate and had been in many fights alongside McLaughlin against the conservatives.

When Fish flew into Detroit to look over the city as prospective national convention site, McLaughlin met his political cohort at the airplane. They walked to the baggage pickup at Metro Airport and just as they stepped up to it, Fish's bag popped out of the chute into his hand.

It was only a chance happening that Fish did not have to wait for his baggage and that his bag was the first one to be delivered at the pickup.

Although flabbergasted at the fortunate timing, McLaughlin said to Fish, "We know how to handle baggage in Detroit."

Later during that visit, Fish wanted to tour Windsor to inspect hotel facilities there.

FISH LIKES GOOD, big cigars, but he loves Havana cigars, which are banned in the U.S. because the federal government forbids their importation from Cuba. But Canada's trade with Cuba includes importation of Havana cigars. Fish was delighted.

When they drove back through the tunnel to Detroit, the U.S. Customs official at the border asked: "Do you have

See **CIGARS**, Page 15A

sports
Detroit Free Press

U-D coach job-hunting
Dave Gaines is one of the finalists for the job of head basketball coach at San Diego State University. — Page 2

Bird has no words
All-American Larry Bird took the loss to Michigan State hard, so hard he refused to appear at the postgame press conference. — Page 3

Tuesday, March 27, 1979

SPORTS PEOPLE	2
STANDINGS	3
HORSE RACING	4
COMICS	5-7

D

March 27, 1979:

Michigan State and Magic Johnson win the NCAA crown.

Sports Page

EARVIN'S WIZARDRY CLIPS THE BIRD'S WINGS

Spartans No. 1 in the land, 75-64

By CURT SYLVESTER
Free Press Sports Writer

SALT LAKE CITY — Call it magic if you want, but while you're at it, you can also call Michigan State the best college basketball team in the country.

The Spartans proved it once and for all Monday night, claiming the school's first NCAA basketball championship ever, with a 75-64 victory over previously undefeated Indiana State.

It wasn't the classic showdown between Michigan State's magical Earvin Johnson and Indiana State's college player of the year Larry Bird.

The defenses on both sides were just too tough to let it happen the way so many in the crowd of 15,410 at the University of Utah's Special Events Center and a national television audience had anticipated.

The Spartans ganged up on Bird to hold him to 19 points (nine below his average) and only two assists. He was strong underneath at times, but he was not the dominating do-it-all star who had led Indiana State to 33 consecutive victories.

Every where he went he found himself pestered by one, or more often two, and frequently three MSU defenders.

When it was over, the senior from little French Lick, Ind., sat on the bench in tears.

JOHNSON, WHO HAD BEEN so spectacular through the Spartans' drive to the championship game, did not have his most spectacular game either. All night long he had either Brad Miley dogging his steps or Leroy Staley attacking him frenetically.

But it was the Magic Man who hit eight of 15 shots, scored 24 points, grabbed seven rebounds and added five assists, and it was he — not Bird — who was the deciding factor in the game.

And after he had delivered the final assist of the season — a court-long pass to Gregory Kelser who finished the game with a tremendous flying one-hand slam dunk, Johnson laughed and danced and absorbed every single delight of the victory the Spartans have been working for all season.

As a matter of fact, they all did — Kelser, Mike Brkovich, Terry Donnelly, Ron Charles, Jay Vincent and all the others who brought Michigan State from a disastrous 4-4 start in the Big Ten to the national championship.

KELSER WAS also outstanding with 19 points, eight rebounds and nine assists. Donnelly, the lowest scoring and least publicized starter on the MSU team, scored 15 points, only one below the junior guard's high for the season. And Vincent came off the bench with his hurting foot to help Charles work on Bird defensively.

"We've been playing so well, I thought that if we stuck to our game plan and followed the coach's plan to contain Larry Bird, we'd win," said Johnson, who may have been playing his final game for MSU if he decides to accept a pro offer this spring.

The Spartans stuck to the defensive plan Heathcote

See **MSU**, Page 3D

George Puscas

A-a-men! Spartans hit the basketball heights

SALT LAKE CITY
Maybe there have been more delightful moments. Perhaps there have been more delicious moments. But never ever could there have been a more wild, delirious moment in Michigan State's long athletic history, than the one its magic basketball team produced here Monday night.

The Spartans are champions of college basketball. They completed a miraculous turnaround from midseason despair to whip unbeaten and No. 1-ranked Indiana State, 75-64, and all the joy championships can produce burst from them.

They swarmed over each other on the floor of the jammed Utah Sports Arena, pounded, hugged and even kissed each other, and up in the stands, some 2,500 who had followed them here burst out in song.

"A-a-men! A-a-men!" they chorused.

They waved and tossed their green and white ponpons in the air and danced in the aisles and seemed likely to cascade down the chairs in unrestrained celebration.

It was as wild a scene as you are likely to see in any basketball arena.

Coach Jud Heathcote and his players gathered in a circle at midcourt, knelt, clasped hands all around and seemed to be chanting a prayer of some kind. A moment of sobering thanks, so it appeared.

It was no prayer. It was a chant, the chant the team has created and used as its inspirational rallying signal since mid-January.

They sang it out like a college cheer. They spelled:
"P-O-T-E-N-T-I-A-L!" Potential.

It has been their motivation. They knew they had it in them to do great things, even while they were on the verge of collapse weeks ago, if only they persisted. Now here they had done it all, completing one of the grandest comebacks from near disaster in the history of the NCAA tournament.

Kelser's dunk was the icing

They won't forget their hour here. It was an incredible scene from the instant Magic Man Earvin Johnson fired a pass from under one basket far up floor, where Greg Kelser gathered it in, took a flying leap and slam-dunked the ball for the final score of the game.

It was typical of this Spartan team. They always have been very quick, opportunistic, destructive, and especially dramatic, and here was Kelser delivering the hammer blow to a proud Indiana State team that had not lost in 33 previous games.

This wasn't an easy victory for the Spartans. Far from it. There were several moments when they seemed likely to put Indiana State to the same kind of rout they had applied to all others enroute to the championship finals.

They couldn't manage it. Indiana State stayed threateningly close, close enough to suggest right up until the final two minutes this game still could be plucked away from the Spartans.

As we mentioned here Monday, the one element that could ruin the Spartans in this showdown was fouling. It came perilously close to happening.

They got in foul trouble early and it restricted their play the remainder of the game. Except for some careful play by Johnson, and Kelser, too, the mounting fouls could have proved disastrous.

Most of the fouls were worth it, because the majority of 'em came as the Spartans battled heavily under the boards to control Indiana State's driving offense.

Coach Jud Heathcote gambled with that. There had been a suspicion he would let Indiana State's marvelous Larry Bird roam fairly free and do his thing, which is score, while shutting down all the other Sycamore shooters.

Heathcote decided to concede nothing to Bird. The sharpshooter who had averaged better than 29 points a game came away with merely 19.

Magic wins the matchup

The Spartans threw their scissor-tight three-man zone around Bird, shutting off passes from the front and behind. They kept him frustrated from start to finish, and that was the decisive stroke in thwarting the Sycamores.

"We won it with our defense, no question about it," said Heathcote, who had ranted on the sidelines while penalties continued to mount against the Spartans.

"The penalties limited the things we could do on offense, and so we had to play conservatively, more conservatively than we like. But that's the way the game developed."

The heralded matchup of MSU's Earvin Johnson and ISU's Larry Bird, the two best players in college ball this year, was clearly won by the Magic Man.

Johnson not only outscored Bird, 24-19, he produced more assists, ran the Michigan State game on offense and defense as if his every move had been choreographed, and he kept Indiana State at a distance and under control at all times.

"Coach came up with a great game plan to stop Larry Bird," said Johnson, "and it really worked. Larry's a great player, but we did a job on him."

The Magic Man was mainly responsible for that. Most of the game, he was in Bird's face, with either Kelser, Ron Charles or Jay Vincent at his back, and one or the other shutting off Bird so he could not slip through the vice.

And of such strategy are championships won.

Gregory Kelser

On the business end of the alley-oop, Michigan State's Gregory Kelser says dunk you very much.

Ringed by his stars, Jud finally twinkles

SALT LAKE CITY — (AP) — Michigan State coach Jud Heathcote, his stars wreathed with basketball nets representing NCAA victory, said it will be some time before he realizes the enormity of the Spartans' accomplishment.

No. 3-ranked Michigan State got 24 points from All-American Magic Johnson and 19 from Gregory Kelser in winning the tough NCAA title game, 75-64, over No. 1-ranked Indiana State.

"Down the line I'm going to feel this is a great personal goal," Heathcote said. "But right now, I feel that it's the players that have accomplished so much.

"That was a very hard-fought game and we feel fortunate to win. We lost a little of our offensive punch in the second half when Kelser got in foul trouble, but our defense kept us in the game. The Magic Man directed the show and we got good basketball out of the rest of the team."

KELSER, WHO LIKE Johnson sat at the postgame news conference with a basketball net draped around his neck, put the difference in the outcome of the game in succinct terms.

"Our shots were dropping and theirs weren't, and that was the difference in the ball game," Kelser said. The Spartans outshot Indiana State from the field 60 percent to 42 percent.

Heathcote said he told his players before the game that whenever Sycamore All-American Larry Bird got the ball, he was to have one man guarding him. But if Bird put the ball on the floor, one of the Michigan State guards was to double-team him.

See **CELEBRATE**, Page 3D

CLOSE FRIEND REVEALS PRICE
$3 million for Magic Man?

By CURT SYLVESTER
Free Press Sports Writer

SALT LAKE CITY — If the National Basketball Association wants Earvin (Magic) Johnson next season, it's probably g'g'ng to take $3 million dollars to get him.

That's what Dr. Charles Tucker, the confidante and personal adviser to the Johnson family, believes Earvin is worth if he decides to pass up his final two seasons at Michigan State for a professional contract.

"Three million (dollars) over . . . say, six years," said Tucker, "with incentives to compensate for inflation.

"A market value for a player like that should be in that area. Somebody like Larry Bird (of Indiana State) would probably be in the area of about $4 million.

"It's not just that they put the ball in the hole, it's the charisma they have. And that's what the NBA needs now. White fans like Earvin and black fans like Larry, and that's what the NBA needs now — to please people.

"Earvin can say — like Dr. J (Julius Erving) did, that he's going to pack the stadiums," continued Tucker. "With a team like Detroit, they can pay everybody's salary for six years, because they're going to have 27,000 people every night.

"He's got that charisma. It's like going to see a show when you go to see people like Earl Monroe and Julius."

See **JOHNSON**, Page 3D

The Magic Man soars through the air with the greatest of ease as he goes in for a layup. Earvin had 24 points to lead the Spartans to their first NCAA championship.

Back spasms push back Fidrych's comeback

By BRIAN BRAGG
Free Press Sports Writer

CLEARWATER — The long-running, soap opera saga of Mark Fidrych and his two-year battle with a series of physical ailments has taken another melodramatic twist: The Bird is out of action again.

Fidrych had been scheduled for his second exhibition-game duty of the spring here Monday, but he was suddenly stricken with muscle spasms in his lower back. He now faces another indeterminate period of enforced idleness.

If the problem persists for more than a day or two, it is almost certain Fidrych will not be ready to pitch when the regular season begins. In that case, he would likely be placed on the 15-day disabled list when the Tigers head north.

The latest setback came, most inappropriately, just as Fidrych had been progressing nicely in the rehabilitation of a sore shoulder that sidelined him most of last season.

"It's a tough thing, dammit!" grumped manager Les Moss. "This has definitely set him back, no question about it. The rainout (last Friday when The Bird had planned to pitch) had set him back to start with, and now this."

FIDRYCH EVIDENTLY encountered the back spasms after doing his prescribed running Sunday afternoon. He was given a muscle relaxant and Tigers' trainer Bill Behm applied heat to the affected area.

When Fidrych arose Monday morning, there was still some tightness in his back. Behm applied more heat and told The Bird to take it easy the rest of the day.

Fidrych did not make the trip here with his teammates, who played the Philadelphia Phillies.

"We'll take care of it with the normal heat and rest," said

See **FIDRYCH**, Page 2D

SEPT. 30, 1979:

Henry Ford II ends an era by resigning from the company his grandfather started.

Special section

Henry Ford II
DETROIT FREE PRESS

Born to rule: He could have chosen a life of idle wealth but instead fought to rescue the failing company his grandfather founded. Page 2.

Sunday, Sept. 30, 1979
HIS COMPANY	2-3
HIS PERSONAL LIFE	4-5
COMMENT ON HFII	7

G

Farewell to an era

Monday, for the first time in 34 years, Henry Ford II won't be running Ford Motor Co. Though his retirement as chief executive officer takes effect that day, he remains for many millions of people throughout the world the embodiment of the American industrialist.

His career and personal life — his great strengths and appetites — recall a vanishing time when powerful men built private empires in their own names and controlled the destinies of thousands.

In his own way, Henry Ford II, as his grandfather before him, has been as influential as presidents and popes.

His decision in Detroit to build a factory could change a whole nation's economy in Asia, Africa or South America.

His decision to build the Renaissance Center in Detroit may have changed the world's view of the city and the city's view of itself.

This section is not a tribute to Henry Ford II; it presents him in all his facets. And it's not a eulogy, because the evidence is that Ford will continue to wield great influence in his company and the world.

Rather, it is a retrospective of a powerful man's life. It is, if you will, a farewell to an era.

A patrician with the common touch

Free Press photos by Chief Photographer TONY SPINA

His name is on the building, Henry Ford II liked to remind associates, and from his 12th floor office, he ruled a $42.8 billion enterprise.

By ALEX TAYLOR
Free Press Business Writer

A longtime friend, George Kennedy, was apologizing to Henry Ford II over lunch for missing the wedding of Ford's younger daughter, Anne, a few weeks earlier.

The wedding had been a typical Ford celebration of the 1960s. There was a party the night before at Delmonico's in New York City with 445 guests, 100 magnums of Piper-Heidsieck champagne and a big society orchestra. Ford himself was on the dance floor until 3 a.m.

He politely told Kennedy, then chairman of Kelsey-Hayes Co., a Ford Motor Co. supplier, "I missed you." Kennedy explained that because he was approaching 70, he didn't like to stay up half the night drinking and partying any longer.

"Well, George," said Ford with a smile, "we really didn't miss you."

HENRY FORD II has hobnobbed with kings and princes. Yet, he has acquired — and never lost — an open, direct manner that occasionally raises hackles but is treasured by his close friends.

He can be plainspoken to the point of bluntness. "A man etched with candor" is how he is described by Ford Foundation executive Fred Friendly. Gossip columnist Liz Smith, on the other hand, has sometimes found his behavior "vulgar."

Although his acquaintances include some of the world's richest and most sophisticated people (he puts his own wealth at $70 million), Ford has been known to use the coarse language of the streets and pick his teeth with a paper match torn from a monogrammed pack.

"He's really a patrician, but a patrician with the common touch," says Ford Motor Co. president Philip Caldwell.

His sudden, well-publicized firings of high company executives explained with throwaway phrases, his "never complain, never explain" when caught in an indiscreet situation — all are part of the personal style of the man known as Hank the Deuce.

Cosmopolitan in many ways, Ford speaks French, owns a number of Impressionist paintings, has collected antique furniture, rare porcelains and jewelled snuffboxes and thinks enough of his wine cellar to have called on a wine expert once to help him move it.

But he also can be very down-to-earth. Although he flew his family to England for Christmas one year and recently chartered a 160-foot yacht, he is capable of remarking about an acquaintance, "How can he afford that? That's an awful lot of money."

He possesses a legendary temper. "He seethes inside and he stays sore for a long time," says John Bugas, a friend and business associate for three decades. And he has no patience with those he perceives as poseurs. "One thing he can't stand is a phony," says Detroit financier Max Fisher, who has known Ford for 25 years. "He can spot them a mile away."

At the same time, he is capable of great personal warmth and kindness. "I think it's common knowledge that Anne (Ford's first wife) was supposed to get a certain amount of money on her divorce and Henry said, 'That's not enough,'" said a close friend to both.

Despite upheavals in his business and personal life, he has maintained a strong sense of his own self — totally unpretentious about his own shortcomings. When Fred Friendly, meaning to compliment him, told Ford he was "a very visceral man," Ford responded unself-consciously, "What the hell does 'visceral' mean?"

His friends are intensely loyal. They treasure his handwritten notes, telephone calls on birthdays and anniversaries, tie clasps, key chains and money clips he distributes at Christmas.

Unlike other rich men in the public eye, Ford has shunned bodyguards, apparently a reaction from his youth when security men drove him to grade school and lived next to him in college. Although he has a company chauffeur and his home is looked after by security personnel, he ventures out in public without protection.

STANDING JUST UNDER six feet tall, Ford presents a solid, commanding figure in person. His taste in clothing runs to suits of traditional fabric with an extra flair, such as a double vent and a colored silk handkerchief protruding from the breast pocket. Like his shoes, the suits are custom-made in England. His shirts, often pink in color and carrying a discreet HF II on the left breast, come from Hong Kong and cling tightly to his ample middle.

Though he affects medium-length sideburns, he still wears his hair combed back closely against his skull with a high part — a style associated with an older generation.

See **STYLE**, Page 8G

The Henry I know...

"Henry and I have been friends since he was eight or nine. We rode horseback and went to nature study class together at our parents' summerhouses in Seal Harbor, Maine. He was pudgy then but so was I.

I guess we both feel the same way about having a famous family name and inherited wealth: There are pluses and minuses but the pluses outweigh the minuses."

— **David Rockefeller, chairman, Chase Manhattan Corp.**

Q: Any second thoughts?
A: No, none whatsoever

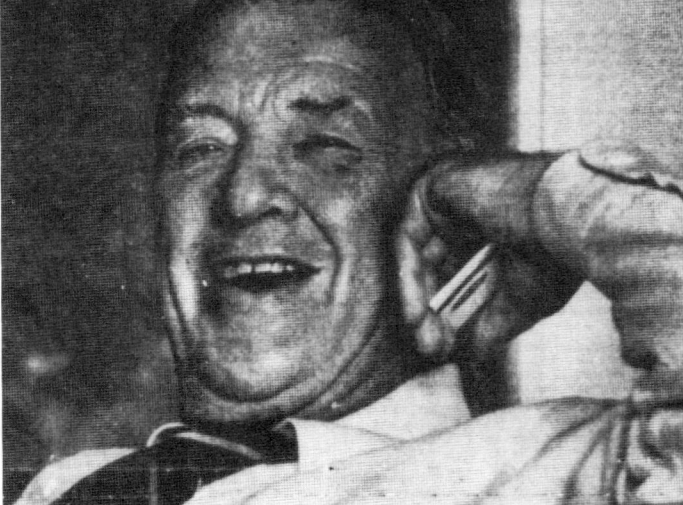

He plans a farewell tour of Ford facilities around the world and then isn't sure what he'll do.

By TOM KLEENE and DONALD WOUTAT
Free Press Automotive Writers

Two days after his 62nd birthday, Henry Ford II took off his jacket, lit his customary cigar and talked for an hour about the past, present and future — his own and that of the company he ran for 34 years.

The conversation took place in Ford's large, uncluttered, earth-tone office on the top floor of Ford Motor Co. headquarters in Dearborn. It is the office to which Philip Caldwell is moving his antique furnishings, replacing the modern motif Henry Ford prefers.

WEARING A SOFT-PINK shirt and seated at a small marble-topped conference table, the retiring chief executive:

• Said his company is guilty of poor planning and has been out-maneuvered during the 1970s by General Motors Corp. on diesel engines, V6 engines and front-wheel-drive cars.

• Raised the prospect Ford Motor would have to quit being a full-line car company in North America and said he is "apprehensive" about his company's plans for the 1980s.

• Said he has no intention of writing his memoirs because he hasn't saved his personal papers and "I can't write my name . . . and I don't want to try to go back and try to remember a lot of stuff."

What follows is an edited transcript of the Free Press Interview with Henry Ford II:

Q — You once told me that your original plans as you joined the company were to retire at 40.

A — I did say that. That's correct.

Q — How come you stayed so long? What were the things that changed you?

A — Well, I can't really remember so I'll have to think up something. I guess I just wasn't ready to quit at 40. We still had a lot of things to do, still do, of course. But, ah, I guess when I got to be 40, I just wasn't ready to quit.

Q — Well, now four months have passed since you announced that you were stepping down as the chief executive officer on October 1. Do you have any second thoughts about this decision?

A — No, none whatsoever. It was the right decision, the right time, good time and I don't have any second thoughts about it at all.

Q — When you were asked last May what you had in mind for spending your spare time, you didn't really know.

A — That's still the case. I don't really know. As you know, my schedule's pretty full right up through the first of the year, and so I'm just going to have to wait and see what happens when I don't have a reasonably full schedule. I'm going to England in December sometime and speak to the British Ford dealers as part of this total program of visiting all — what I'm going to do is to visit each one of our locations all around the world and speak to the dealers and people that work in management and bankers and all the people that we deal with — sort of a good-bye tour. It's going to take about — well it's gonna take a year-and-a-half anyway to do it all. I don't want to rush it. I'm gonna take a little time doing it.

See **Q & A**, Page 6G

Action line ... does a model job in getting a refund. Page 15A		Tigers win Schatzeder downs the Angels, 6-1. Page 1G.		A town lab Tecumseh undergoes a huge health study. Page 1C.	the way we live	MAY 11, 1980:

Detroit Free Press

thundershowers
High 70, low 49
Showers Monday
Details on Page 2A

sunday
50¢
metro

Volume 150, Number 7   ON GUARD FOR 149 YEARS   Sunday, May 11, 1980

Lee Iacocca hammers out the Chrysler bail-out plan in the depths of the Michigan recession.

Q.

Arab TV ally

Rep. Broomfield

A television "docu-drama" based on the execution of a Saudi Arabian princess and her lover for adultery has provoked an angry protest from the Saudi government. The film, "Death of a Princess," is scheduled for showing on more than 100 public television stations (including WTVS, Channel 56 in Detroit) from 8 to 10 p.m. Monday. Yielding to apparent Saudi pressure, the State Department has urged the Public Broadcasting System to withdraw the film. Mobil and Exxon, two of PBS' major sponsors, also have asked the network to cancel the show. And in Congress, Rep. William Broomfield, R-Mich., the ranking GOP member of the House Foreign Affairs Committee, has expressed his reservations about the program.

By TOM HUNDLEY
Free Press Staff Writer

Q — Why shouldn't PBS show this film?

A — PBS has every right to show the film if they think it's in good taste. However, I feel that it will adversely affect our relations with Saudi Arabia.

Q — Why is that?

A — The Saudi Arabian government has already indicated the film was offensive to them, and they've already asked our government to intervene in the showing of this film.

Q — Have you seen the film yourself?

A — No, I have not seen the film. I don't think that's the question anyway. I think the main thing is that the Saudis feel it's in bad taste.

Q — I am told by some of my friends that this film has been circulated among the upper classes in Saudi Arabia — for a very high price — and those who have seen it are saying privately that it is an accurate and fair portrayal of the events. Why are the Saudis so sensitive about letting us see it?

A — I have no idea, but apparently they feel it runs contrary to their moral values and is not an accurate portrayal of their true feelings.

Q — Would you say you are "pressuring" PBS — which depends on public funds and corporate contributions — not to show this film?

A — Not at all. I'm asking them to evaluate the showing of the film in terms of the best interests of this country. I'm not denying their right to show the film if they don't feel it will hurt our relations with Saudi Arabia . . . (but) Public Broadcasting has to look beyond its immediate audience and see the broader implications of showing this film.

Q — What about some of your colleagues in Congress who suggest that leaning on PBS in this way runs counter to the spirit of 1st Amendment guarantees of free speech and freedom of the press?

A — As I said, I'm not denying PBS' right to show the film. I think that the world situation is so serious that the issues have to be weighed in this context. What I'm trying to get across is that the PBS people have to look at this film in terms of the interests of this country. They have to ask themselves how this will affect our foreign relations in a time when things are in such disarray. I find the whole issue very difficult because I know the rights of public broadcasting, but I'm appealing to them to look at how this affects our foreign relations at a time when we have serious problems in the Middle East.

Q — Some people would say our interests are again being held hostage by the oil barons of the Middle East.

A — I don't feel that Saudi Arabia is holding us hostage. I haven't heard them make any threats about cutting off oil supplies over the film. The Saudis are good friends and important allies, and I don't think this is a good way to treat an ally. We would still be on gas lines if we didn't have the Saudis. We just don't have that many friends left in the world.

Chris Stuehr and Lee Winfrey discuss the issue in detail on Page 1H.

Sputtering along with the auto industry

First of a series

By JOHN HYDE
Free Press Lansing Staff

The Michigan economy, that magnificent, gasfueled, high-powered engine that made the state's residents among the best paid people on earth, is sputtering along on three cylinders.

A year ago 366,000 people were looking for jobs in Michigan. Today 523,000 are unemployed, almost one of every eight workers in the state.

A year ago, the average Michigan manufacturing worker was making $375.74 a week, which amounted to $177 in 1967 dollars. Today that worker is earning $375.38, which is about $154 in 1967 dollars.

Annual car production, the single most important indicator of economic health in Michigan, stood at 8,051,000 a year ago. Today, seasonally adjusted, car production is 7,048,000. Truck and bus production has been cut in half.

hard times:
a report on Michigan's economy

More than one out of four auto workers who had jobs last summer — when they were bargaining over paid personal holidays and increased pension benefits — is on indefinite layoff now.

A year ago, Michigan was issuing building permits at a rate of more than 54,000 a year. Today that figure has fallen to 19,800.

About one out of 10 Michigan families — one out of four families in Detroit — now receives some form of welfare.

IN SHORT, the Michigan economy has hit the skids. Politicians comparing the nation's seven percent unemployment rate to Michigan's 12.4 percent are starting to talk of a "regional depression."

Most economists would not say that. Depression is a scary word that conjures up a time of bank panics and soup lines. The built-in safeguards that now protect the American economy — unemployment compensation, bank guarantees and welfare, for example — at least provide a floor on which to survive.

But there is little disputing state Budget Director Gerald Miller, who said, "We are in a very severe recession. In terms of the well-being of the state, our purchasing power and the ability of people to get by, it is the worst time since the Great Depression."

Miller has been saying for weeks that Michigan's economy is in worse shape than that of any state in the nation.

There have been bad times before, of course. Even mild national recessions strike a blow to Michigan's economy, with its heavy reliance on hard durable-goods manufacturing. The boom-and-bust cycle is part of the Michigan psyche, like long winters and hating Ohio State.

"Times will get better. They always do," said Robert Kleine, chief analyst of the state Department of Management and Budget. "But right now things look awfully bleak."

Unemployment in Michigan reached 14.4 per-

See **ECONOMY**, Page 15A

Chrysler Swings U.S. Aid Deal

Reagan is wooing Jerry

By REMER TYSON
and SAUL FRIEDMAN
Free Press Staff Writers

Ronald Reagan is trying to persuade Gerald Ford, the Republican president he tried to knock out of the White House four years ago, to become the point man in Reagan's fall presidential campaign.

Ford, who said in March that Reagan's conservative appeal was too narrow for him to win the presidency, has indicated a willingness to play a leading part in Reagan's campaign in exchange for assurances from Reagan about foreign policy and other issues.

A Michigan Republican close to both the Reagan organization and Ford said Reagan is eager for the former president to take a major role in the fall campaign, but Reagan still has "one hell of a selling job to do on Ford."

Reagan, seeking to broaden his appeal to establishment Republicans in the Midwest and the Northeast, is prepared to meet Ford more than half way on issues, said Reagan's campaign leaders probably will offer Ford the opportunity to become the 1980 vice-presidential candidate.

FORD IS expected to reject second place on the ticket with Reagan, although some Republicans think Ford might accept. More likely, Ford would accept the title of honorary national campaign chairman for Reagan and would campaign across the country for Reagan and for Republican congressional and state candidates.

Despite Ford's feeling that he would prob-

See **REAGAN**, Page 5A

Ronald Reagan (left) wants Gerald Ford on his team (a 1976 photo).

George Bush, campaigning in Detroit, talks about Chrysler aid. Page 1A.
Complete list of Michigan's Democratic delegates. Page 11A.
A rundown on Reagan's economic policies. Page 5B.

Free Press Photos by AL KAMUDA

They're all gussied up

Why does Tiger have a ribbon in his hair, and what is Schultz doing in that funny hat? The pets of Mary Ellen Hoerig, of Warren (left), and Joan Edem, of Warren, are dolled up for a big event. To see what was going on, see the picture on Page 3A.

Officials hail bail-out news

By PATRICIA CHARGOT and JACK KRESNAK
Free Press Staff Writers

Reaction to Treasury Secretary G. William Miller's announcement Saturday that $1.5 billion in federal aid had been approved for the Chrysler Corp. was immediate, with Chrysler Chairman Lee A. Iacocca calling the long-awaited decision "good news for Chrysler and for the entire country."

"It will help establish Chrysler Corp. as a strong competitor in the market of the 1980s, and it signals the first step in a program to beat the foreign imports in the marketplace with all-new, fuel-efficient, Chrysler-built cars," Iacocca said.

UAW President Douglas Fraser reiterated his faith in the ailing automaker at a press conference at Detroit's Pontchartrain Hotel.

Prefacing his remarks with the admission, "I was beginning to doubt it would ever happen," Fraser called the federally guaranteed loans "essential to the survival of the corporation."

"Had it (the negotiations) gone on another week, it would have been too late."

Fraser said he disagreed with Republican presidential candidate George Bush's initial reservation against the loans on the ground that they would only provide Chrysler with temporary financial relief, possibly causing the automaker to find itself once again on the brink of bankruptcy two or three fiscal quarters down the road.

"You're going to see a different company, a smaller company with fewer car lines," he said. "The whole structure has been redesigned to avoid that eventuality."

See **REACTION**, Page 4A

All-night talks end in success

By DONALD WOUTAT
and WILLIAM VANCE
Free Press Staff Writers

WASHINGTON — The year-long struggle of Chrysler Corp. to win financial aid from the U.S. government ended in success Saturday after Chairman Lee A. Iacocca bargained the final pieces together in an all-night session at a Toronto hotel.

The last-minute negotiations with reluctant Ontario politicians broke up shortly after dawn, clearing the way for the announcement at 4 p.m. in Washington that the U.S. Chrysler Loan Guarantee Board had approved the automaker's pleas for $1.5 billion in federally-guaranteed loans.

The stamp of approval by the loan guarantee board means Chrysler should have access to the money by May 27, which the company says is soon enough to rescue it from bankruptcy.

Treasury Secretary G. William Miller, in announcing the approval, said that without federal aid, "quite frankly . . . the resources of Chrysler would be exhausted this month."

AUTO INDUSTRY analysts say the infusion of cash — Chrysler is expected to immediately borrow $500 million — virtually guarantees Chrysler's survival for up to a year. The company's ultimate success remains highly questionable, particularly because of the slump in the entire industry.

Miller, who chairs the guarantee board, said the board projects Chrysler will lose $1.05 billion in 1980. Chrysler said it

See **CHRYSLER**, Page 6A

Posse seizes bank bandits after a 40-mile gun battle

FONTANA, Calif. — (AP) — A daring bank holdup followed by a Wild West-style chase marked by gunplay, explosions and three deaths, ended in slow-motion Saturday as three tired, dirty and wounded men were taken into custody without a shot fired. A fourth, armed fugitive was shot dead after disobeying an order not to move issued by police who surrounded him, authorities said.

The fourth man, Manny Delgado, 21, was spotted by a helicopter equipped with a device used in the Vietnam War to detect human body heat, police said. Delgado, who was believed to be from Westminster, was found in a rugged area high in the San Gabriel Mountains.

Authorities earlier said he was dead when they found him.

A TRACKING TEAM that moved up the craggy, brush-covered slopes spotted one of the men Saturday morning. Within a half-hour they surrounded and captured him and then saw two others, who gave up without resistance.

The three men each had a handgun, said sheriff's deputies. Two of the men, described as long-haired, with beards and mustaches and in their 30s and 40s, were wounded, authorities said.

The three were identified as Christopher Harven, 29, of Mira Loma, who had a bullet wound in the back; his brother Russell, 26, of Cypress, who was not hurt; and Gregory Smith, 27, of Mira Loma, who had a bullet wound in the groin, deputies said. Two of them were reportedly wounded, but it was not immediately known which ones.

FIVE BANDITS IN ski masks, believed to be members of the "Two-Minute Gang," burst into the Security Pacific National Bank in Norco on Friday just before closing time. They ordered bank workers and patrons to lie face down on the floor and scooped up $19,000 from teller's cash drawers, stocked

See **HEIST**, Page 4A

inside today

ANN LANDERS	2C
BOOKS	6B
BRIDGE	11H
BUSINESS NEWS	1-7F
CLASSIFIED	1-16E
CROSSWORD PUZZLE	11H
EDITORIALS	2B
ENTERTAINMENT	1-8H
HOROSCOPE	11H
MOVIE GUIDE	9H
OBITUARIES	7A
RADIO PAGE	10H
TRAVEL	1-11D
TV CHANGES	8A

SATURDAY 773

inside Detroit's schools

Free Press staff writers Susan Brown (left) and Donna Britt (right) went undercover in the Detroit public schools recently — Brown posing as a substitute teacher and Britt posing as an 11th-grade student. They lived for several weeks in that world of trouble and promise, and today they tell what they saw from their very different perspectives. Look for their stories on page 1B.

JULY 15, 1981:

Police evict parishioners from Detroit's Immaculate Conception Church to make way for GM's Poletown plant.

Detroit Free Press

Coming up: A freeway crawl — Page 3A

partly cloudy
High 81, low 58
Showers possible Thursday
Details on Page 11F

wednesday
20¢
metro final

Volume 150, Number 72 — Wednesday, July 15, 1981

Will our TVs spy on us?

John Wicklein

John Wicklein, a former television news executive and dean of the School of Public Communication at Boston University, fears that the technological advancements that will turn televisions into all-encompassing home communications systems could also lead to censorship and an erosion of personal privacy. He has written a book on the subject, "Electronic Nightmare."

By JOE URSCHEL
Free Press Staff Writer

Q — What kind of communications hardware do you foresee?

A — All communications systems are coming together into a single medium that will combine print, television, entertainment and information and home services in a single set ... two-way cable systems... In a two-way system it can be either a television picture or text on the screen. You can call up your own television picture, or you can reply to questions that are asked of you, or you can take part in a public meeting by way of this two-way system.

Q — How will it work?

A — The set eventually will contain a return audio and a return video. It will have a small camera in it. So you could take part in a public meeting and in effect be present at the discussion. You can also attach a small keyboard ... that will contain a typewriter keyboard that will permit you to send messages via the system and receive messages ... You could put in your credit card number for something you saw on the screen and the order would be made automatically, and you would be billed automatically by the two-way system ... Electronic funds transfer is also part of the system — and the two-way systems are already thinking of doing it — in which money is transferred out of your bank account into the bank account of a store from whom you are purchasing something.

Q — Is this an Orwellian nightmare — 1984 with Big Brother watching us through our television screens?

A — I am rather concerned about using the term Orwellian ... I don't believe there is one big brother coming to supervise our every action, but I do think there are a lot of smaller dangers ... If all these systems come together, who is going to control what goes into that set? That could be a media conglomerate, that could be AT&T, it could be a government agency. They could ... keep information from us or put in only the information they would like us to have.

Q — How can you ensure privacy, keep someone from getting into your bank account?

A — It is going to be extremely hard to prevent breaking into systems ... almost any encoding system that you can devise can be broken down ... there is no legislation existing that says ... the operators of the system couldn't take all of the information that you put into that system, for instance the amount of your bank account, the amount of your indebtedness to credit cards, the kind of replies you make in a public affairs program, what your predilections are for looking at movies ... A candidate might be very upset to find that his opponent has learned through the two-way system that he has been watching pornographic movies every night. All that information is available ... and they can conceivably construct dossiers on you ... operators of that system could take the information and put it together and sell it to an investigating agency.

Q — When will all this be available?

A — it will be quite possible for everyone to have a home communications system ... within 10 or 15 years.

The final hours
Reporter's log of parish and precinct

By MARIANNE RZEPKA
Free Press Staff Writer

It is 1:30 a.m. Tuesday when the phone rings. Debra Choly, a legal aide for the Poletown Neighborhood Association, says she has been tipped that police are going to move into Immaculate Conception Church at 5 a.m. and evict the protesters who have been staying in the church basement for 28 days, trying to stop it from being torn down.

About 12:30 a.m., she tells a reporter, two policemen had pounded on the church door, saying that they had to get in. The people would not unlock the door, Choly says; as the policemen left, she said, someone had overheard them saying, "Well, I guess they know what is going to happen."

Later, a woman had come to the door with a message: The police would come at 5 a.m.

The protesters — 15 men and women, aged 23 to 71 — are not sure they can trust the warnings. But just in case, they start moving church files into a car outside.

Meanwhile, night-duty personnel at the 7th (Mack) Precinct, where the church is located, tell

Free Press reporter Marianne Rzepka, who has covered the effort to save Immaculate Conception, joined the protesters in the church basement at 2 a.m. Tuesday and stayed with them until they were released by police.

the Free Press that they know nothing of an eviction plan.

2:30 a.m.: In the faint glow of candles and gas lanterns, some protesters are trying to sleep on a battered gym mat. Others chatter quietly — about lottery numbers, marriage, the church. Choly is on the phone, trying to find out if the rumor is true. No one seems to know.

5:20 a.m. Most of the group are nodding back to sleep when Jeanne Wylie, a Poletown activist, comes to report that policemen are gathering on the Ford Freeway service drive, about three blocks away.

Quietly, the protesters knot near the green metal door and try to figure out what they will do when the police come.

A few minutes later, as dawn breaks, Deputy Police Chief Richard Dungy comes to the basement door. "I want to advise you that you are trespassing, and I urge you to leave," he says through the door.

Two of the protesters go up into the choir loft

See **VIGIL**, Page 11A

At left, a protester, Josephine Jakubowski, 70, stands in the back of a police van after being evicted from Poletown's Immaculate Conception Church. Seated in the van at right is Marie Grucz, 71. The officer is not identified. Below, a crane lifts a ball from the now-empty church. (More pictures on Back Page.)

Free Press TARO YAMASAKI

Church Faithful Out, Wrecking Crew Moves In

Wreckers Tuesday began the demolition of a church building on the Poletown site where General Motors plans to build an assembly plant. Earlier, 12 persons, 11 holding a vigil and a newspaper reporter, were ordered to leave and then taken into police custody.

This story was reported by Harry Cook, Tom Hundley, Luther Jackson, Patricia Montemurri, Mary Anne Stanley, Joe Swickard and Michael Wagner and was written by Cook.

Six women taken into custody were later released from the Seventh (Mack) Precinct without charges being brought. Six men who were taken to Recorder's Court also were released when the Wayne County Prosecutor's Office refused to issue warrants charging them with a crime.

Twenty-six Detroit policemen arrived about 5:30 a.m. to remove protesters, who had been holding a vigil in the basement of the former Immaculate Conception Church since the city of Detroit took possession from the Detroit Archdiocese June 18.

But the 15 protesters inside the church, who fought for months to save it from the wrecking ball, said they had been tipped by unidentified policemen shortly after midnight that other police would come at dawn to attempt to remove them.

The protesters secured inside doors and refused to leave when ordered to do so by Deputy Police Chief Richard Dungy.

"We asked them at least four different times," Dungy said, "and when they continued to refuse we hooked up a tow-truck cable to the door and pulled it off. Then we went in, and I personally asked each person to please leave peaceably. When they didn't, we had no choice but to arrest them."

A 16th person inside the church, Free Press reporter Marianne Rzepka, who was covering the protest, was one of the 12 persons who were directed to get into a police van and taken to the 7th (Mack) Precinct. Four others in the church chose not to be arrested and left the area. The six men taken by police were later brought to Recorder's Court, where warrants were sought from Prosecutor William Cahalan's office.

A SPOKESMAN for Cahalan said warrants were denied because "there is some question of the actual criminal intent involved." The men were released before noon Tuesday. Several of the detained women protesters demanded of the police that they be arrested, too.

"We should be treated the

See **CHURCH**, Page 7A

Cigaret shortage irritates Polish ills

WARSAW, Poland — Near the end of his 2½-hour address to the emergency party congress at the Palace of Culture Tuesday, the leader of the Polish Communist Party said he wished it weren't so tough to find a pack of cigarets around here.

"I realize that smoking isn't healthy," Stanislaw Kania acknowledged, "but it would be much better to solve that problem (after) we have some cigarets in the shops."

IT WAS the kind of remark you'd expect a politician to make at some point in a speech of such length, if only to give his listeners the chance to laugh or smile or duck out for a smoke.

But Kania, a solid look-alike for Ed Asner whose head seems connected to his shoulders without benefit of a neck, made the comment with all the seriousness with which he had denounced "the enemies of socialism" about 40 minutes earlier in his speech.

In fact, the shortage of cigarets is no joking matter in a nation where men, women and very young adolescents spend hours waiting in line for a pack of

William J. Mitchell in Poland

whatever they can get.

More significantly, however, First Secretary Kania's remark provided a vivid illustration of the task facing the party trying to lead this country out of its various crises: There are so many problems, where do we begin?

In this case, should the government-run economy try to solve the shortage of paper and glue, to satisfy the popular demand for cigarets, or should the government deal with the health hazards of tobacco?

DESPITE POLAND'S national smoking habit, the cigaret shortage was among the least of Kania's problems here Tuesday.

Struggling to satisfy both the Soviet Union's demand for Communist discipline and the demands of millions of Polish workers, Kania delivered a middle-of-the-road report to the congress that seemed aimed at keeping both sides reasonably happy and himself in his job.

Reaffirming the Polish party's com-

See **POLAND**, Page 7A

Kania urges a "fighting party." 7A

inside today

ANN LANDERS	2C	FOOD GUIDE	1-8D
BILLY GRAHAM	9F	HOROSCOPE	9F
BUSINESS NEWS	1-5B	MOVIE GUIDE	10-11F
CABLE/PAY TV	7F	OBITUARIES	8F
CLASSIFIED	1-8E	STOCK MARKETS	2-5B
COMICS	9-11F	TELEVISION	7F
CROSSWORD PUZZLE	9F		
DEATH NOTICES	2E		
EDITORIALS	8A		
ENTERTAINMENT	9-10C		
FEATURE PAGE	11C	TUESDAY	35¢

AFSCME now faces 600 layoffs by city

By KEN FIREMAN
City-County Bureau Chief

City officials now have plans to lay off nearly 600 members of the American Federation of State, County and Municipal Employees (AFSCME) at the end of the month in order to balance the city's 1981-82 budget and preserve Mayor Young's fiscal bailout program.

When the layoff plan was first formulated last week, 428 AFSCME members were slated to be furloughed. But Budget Director Walter Stecher said Tuesday a closer examination has revealed that close to 600 layoffs will be necessary to keep the budget in balance.

Stecher said the exact number of layoffs would not be determined until Friday, when notices are scheduled to be delivered to the affected employees.

NEGOTIATORS FOR the city and AFSCME will resume bargaining Thursday morning in an effort to fashion a new agreement

See **AFSCME**, Page 11A

CIA deputy out after charges of stock deals

By MICHAEL J. SNIFFEN
Associated Press

WASHINGTON — Max Hugel, an outsider whose appointment irked career intelligence officers, resigned Tuesday as director of the CIA's spy network hours after a newspaper reported he slipped inside information about a firm he once headed to two Wall Street brokers.

Meanwhile, it was learned that U.S. District Judge Charles E. Stewart Jr. ruled May 19 in New York that Hugel's boss, CIA Director William J. Casey, knowingly misled potential investors when he and others tried to raise capital for an unsuccessful farming corporation in 1968.

Hugel called the allegations in Tuesday's Washington Post by two former business associates "unfounded, unproven and untrue."

"These allegations have become a burden which I no longer believe is fair to impose on the administration, the agency, my family and the splendid men and women who work with me," he added in a letter of resignation to Casey.

Casey accepted Hugel's resignation with "deepest regret" and immediately named career CIA official John Stein as his successor.

Max Hugel

See **CIA**, Page 11A

Full Super Bowl story in 2 Sports sections

Detroit Free Press

snow
High 16, low 1
Partly sunny Tuesday
Details on Page 11A

Volume 151, Number 266 — ON GUARD FOR 150 YEARS — Monday, January 25, 1982

monday
20¢
metro final

JAN. 25, 1982:

San Francisco wins Michigan's first Super Bowl.

Super Day for 49ers!

Is television bad for sports?

David Halberstam

David Halberstam is best known as the author of "The Best and the Brightest," about how the United States became involved in Vietnam, and "The Powers That Be," about the powerful media organizations in the U.S. He recently completed "The Breaks of the Game," which describes the year he spent traveling with professional basketball's Portland Trail Blazers. An atypical Detroit visitor last week, he passed through but didn't stay for Super Bowl XVI.

By CHARLIE VINCENT
Free Press Sports Writer

Q — You're a sports fan. Why aren't you staying for the Super Bowl?

A — For one thing, the game is almost invariably a disappointment... But what I really dislike is the almost pagan ritual leading up to it. It's about corporate status, Lear jetting, who can give the biggest brunch. It's the Enshrining of (National Football League Commissioner Pete) Rozelle Week. It's bizarre. I think that overt materialism hurts sport.

Q — Will you watch it on television?

A — Oh, yes, but I've got to figure out how to just see the game and not all that buildup... This is crazy. It's just a game.

Q — "The Breaks of the Game" dealt with professional basketball, but it really wasn't about basketball, was it?

A — It was a book about America. I could have done a book about Reagan vs. Carter; they were playing the same season (the election of 1980). But I don't think that would have been nearly as good.... By doing this book, and by doing what television does with its commercialism, I was able to show that, like a lot of things in America, with television there was more but there was less.

Q — You seem to see television as evil.

A — It enhances but it potentially distorts.... We know tennis because of television; but also because of television, (John) McEnroe is allowed to behave like a punk because TV likes punks. Television ... dramatically raises the level of commercialism.

Q — And that's something you think we'll see manifested more and more?

A — With this new competitiveness between the networks for college basketball games, I think so. I think you'll see, instead of the natural rivalries, the networks battling to schedule games between teams that are big attractions. And in four or five years you'll see a quantum increase in recruiting violations, not necessarily among the larger schools but from the new instant outlaw colleges who are going to make themselves an instant reputation because of the bigger money....

Q — You've got some strong opinions, too, on what we perceive as stars, don't you?

A — For one thing, I think Magic Johnson's contract (with the Los Angeles Lakers) is the reflection of an egocentric owner who made himself a star by being the man to pay Magic Johnson $1 million a year.

Free Press Photos by MARY SCHROEDER and DAVID C. TURNLEY

San Francisco 49ers Coach Bill Walsh, above, got a victory ride on the shoulders of his team, and quarterback Joe Montana, right, won the Most Valuable Player award for their Super Bowl efforts Sunday. That's the Super Bowl trophy Montana is admiring.

For fans: It was great — or awful

By PATRICIA MONTEMURRI and RICK RATLIFF
Free Press Staff Writers

There were the rich in their private suites with catered plates of boiled shrimp, and the less affluent in the bleachers eating hot dogs and drinking beer from plastic cups.

There were the Cincinnati Bengals fans in their frizzy orange-and-black wigs, and the San Francisco 49ers backers in their designer jackets.

There were 81,270 fans at the game, and their styles contrasted as garishly as the mismash of colors many sported — 49er red and Bengal orange.

But by the end of the game it was the Bengals fans who were red-faced, after their heroes had fallen, 26-21.

Post-game reaction was subdued. Bengals and 49ers fans rubbed elbows and shook hands as the hordes snaked their way out of the building. Few fans charged onto the field, and many 49ers fans didn't even stick around after the victory.

"NOBODY'S FIGHTING. Nobody's even cheering," said Pontiac police officer Gene Ortman shortly after the game ended. "I don't understand why it's so quiet."

But a 49ers season ticket holder for the last five years, Toss Garcia, 28, of San Francisco, told how he felt:

"It was heaven," he said, swigging a bottle of Courvoisier. "There's been a lot of years with 2-14 seasons, and here we got everything."

Said one true fan: "I've been hiking 3½ miles through the snow, and I love the whole wad."

Bob Benestelli, 28, of Pittsburgh, had been rooting for Cincinnati. But 30 minutes after the game, he stood despondent on an exit ramp, holding a cup of Stroh's and chanting, "Let's go, Bungles."

"Unfortunately, we were cheering for Cincinnati," he said.

Fans for both sides were excited at first. But when San Francisco jumped to a 20-0 lead at halftime, Cincinnati fans grew quiet. They roared back when their team rallied in the fourth quarter — and moaned when San Francisco's

See FANS, Page 10A

Little aid to jobless

Reagan's actions belie his words

By DAVID HOFFMAN
Free Press Washington Staff

WASHINGTON — President Reagan says unemployed Americans should turn to help-wanted ads to find work, and that's precisely what Barbara Ruby did recently when she was laid off from her waitress job.

Ruby, 28, went to job interviews in her hometown of Kokomo, Ind., a factory town that has suffered heavy layoffs, and she was surprised. "There's 100 people when you go to a job interview," she recalled. In many cases, the job seekers lacked skills for the work being offered.

As the recession deepens and un-

See CONTRADICT, Page 11A

analysis

The Reagans return to snowy Washington from a weekend at Camp David.

Day workers in Detroit feel sting of recession. Page 3A.

inside today

ANN LANDERS	2C
BRIDGE	10F
BUSINESS MONDAY	1-6D
CABLE/PAY TV	7C
CLASSIFIED GOLD ADS	7-12D
COMICS	10-11F
CROSSWORD PUZZLE	11F
DEATH NOTICES	8F
EDITORIALS	8A
ENTERTAINMENT	9F
FEATURE PAGE	11C
HOROSCOPE	11C
MOVIE GUIDE	10-11F
OBITUARIES	8F
TELEVISION	8C
THE WAY WE LIVE	1-3C

Congress returns to stormy issues

By DAVID HESS
Free Press Washington Staff

WASHINGTON — Some members of the 97th Congress had hoped the second session, which opens today, would be a refreshing respite after last year's marathon that wrought wrenching changes in federal programs.

But there will be little rest for the 535 lawmakers who reconvene here after their midterm recess.

They will be faced on the one hand with a host of contentious holdover issues.

On the other, they will have to deal with new issues that have

See CONGRESS, Page 4A

Baker says president will spurn excise hike. Page 7C.

The hype and hoo-ha are history

Finally...

Super Bowl XVI, the event of excesses dedicated to the so-called "game of inches," roared into reality Sunday.

A crush of 81,270 jostled into the Silverdome to see the Cincinnati Bengals and the San Francisco 49ers bruise their way through four quarters of football.

The final score: 49ers 26, Bengals 21.

The 49ers leaped to a 20-0 lead in the first half, setting two Super Bowl records: largest half-time lead (bigger than Miami's 17-0 lead over Minnesota in Super Bowl VIII) and longest drive for a touchdown, 92 yards for the second touchdown. The old record was held by Dallas with an 89-yard drive in Super Bowl XIII.

In the second half, Cincinnati bounced back with three touchdowns to threaten the 49ers' lead. However, San Francisco managed to stay ahead with the help of two field goals kicked by Ray Wersching in the final quarter.

Satisfied that they had seen a terrific game, fans left the stadium quietly and retrieved their cars in 8-degree darkness. Despite the crush of traffic, Pontiac police said there were no unexpected tie-ups.

Hotels also reported few problems Sunday night; most of their Super Bowl guests checked out Sunday morning or had decided to leave today.

High winds restricted flights departing from

See SUPER!, Page 10A

This story was reported by Free Press staff writers Laura Berman, Andrea Ford, Tim Kiska, Glen Macnow, Patricia Montemurri, Joyce Walker-Tyson and Gerald Volgenau. It was written by Volgenau.

Super Bowl inside

☐ When the big game began, Motown turned into a ghost town. See Page 10A.
☐ Guindon's view of the Super Bowl and Spectator Sports are on Page 1C.
☐ TV's Super Bowl performance is viewed by Mike Duffy and Joe Lapointe on Page 6C.
☐ On Page 9F Diane Haithman tells how non-football fans spent the day.
☐ And on the Back Page are pictures showing faces in the Super Bowl crowd.

Showing the form that made him most valuable is 49er star Joe Montana.

APRIL 15, 1982:

The J.L. Hudson Co. decides to close its downtown store after 101 years.

 **Car sales worse than expected** Story on Page 8D.

Tigers lose in 9th Details on Page 1F.

 **Tiger Stadium ready for opener** Story on Page 1F.

sunny skies High 65, low 42 Scattered thundershowers Friday Details on Page 13A

Detroit Free Press

thursday 20¢ **metro final**

Volume 151, Number 346 — ON GUARD FOR 150 YEARS — Thursday, April 15, 1982

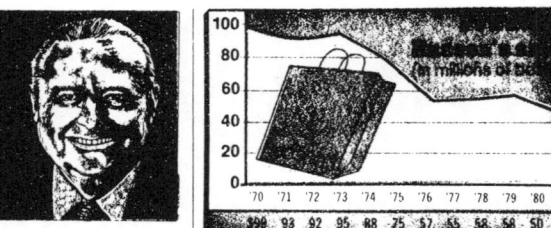

Bottom row shows exact sales figures per year. Chart by Free Press artist NOLAN ROSS

Hudson's Giving Up On Downtown Store

What was your toughest call?

Tigers scorer

Ed (Big Ed) Browalski, 62, baseball writer for the Polish Daily News since 1951, is the official scorer for 90 percent of Tigers home games. Browalski is chairman and secretary of the Baseball Writers Association of America's Detroit chapter. Today's game will be his 37th opening day.

By BILL McGRAW
Free Press Sports Writer

Q — What's your most memorable opening day?

A — It was 1962. The temperature was around 36 degrees, and the game was delayed because of snow. The Tigers finally won 5-3, but (pitcher) Frank Lary was never the same after that. We assume (he hurt his leg) because of the cold weather.

Q — How many games have you seen?

A — I'm official scorer in the National Fastball League, the Michigan-Ontario League and world softball tournaments. In both amateur and major leagues, I've probably scored over 5,000 games.

Q — What's your toughest call?

A — The toughest call is the ball hit at somebody. The rule is "ordinary effort." (It's an error if the ball could have been handled with ordinary effort.) It's up to you to decide if it's ordinary effort or extraordinary effort. I've scored two no-hitters, Steve Busby, in April 1973, and Nolan Ryan that July.

Q — What was the most complicated play you ever scored?

A — In a game against the Minnesota Twins. The bases were loaded, and it turned out to be a double play with seven people handling the ball. When I made the announcement, I got applause from the press box media.

Q — Do you ever change your mind?

A — A couple times after consulting with the umpire on wild pitches and passed balls. Those are tough to see because the catcher blocks off your view. I don't use the TV camera because the TV camera angle creates an untrue view.

Q — Do you get any guff from the players?

A — Occasionally, but not to a great extent. I've gotten some. One I remember is, Ike Brown was playing third base for the Tigers and there was a rundown play between third and second and he hit the runner in the back, so I charged him with an error. After the game he came up and said, "Big Ed, did I see right? You charged me with an error." "Yeah," I said. "It was not my fault," (Brown) said, "He got in my way."

Q — Does a fielder have to touch a ball to commit an error?

A — No. If he loses it in the sun, I rule it a solar double (chuckle). One time a player lost it in the lights and I ruled it a lunar double. I added my own designations.

Q — Once in a while fans boo your calls. What's your reaction then?

A — They see it from a different angle. I see it from one angle. And I have to make my decision from that angle. Players see it from another angle.

Q — Who was the crankiest player you ever met?

A — There's a few. The modern players are crankier than the older players. They're a different breed today. They're interested more in individual statistics than team statistics.

Q — Do you think the Tigers get overly favorable coverage in the local media?

A — No, I don't think so. I think we've got pros and cons on all the papers and the outstate papers. They call 'em as they see 'em.

Memories

It was THE store, in any department

By BARBARA STANTON
Free Press Associate Editor

For decades, when Detroiters said "Let's go downtown," what they meant was: "Let's go to Hudson's."

The flagship store of the J. L. Hudson Co. once reigned over Woodward Avenue and the city like a grand and gracious lady, the arbiter of taste, the purveyor of fashion and the epitome of service. Downtown Hudson's was bigger than Marshall Field and more elegant than Macy's, and it dominated Detroit retailing completely, its hold on its customers as much a sentimental phenomenon as a commercial one.

There has been a Hudson's downtown for 101 years, but in the minds of Detroiters now living, the store probably reached its apogee in the period between the 1920s and the 1950s, a time when a visit to Hudson's was as much a social occasion as a shopping trip.

THOSE WERE the days when women wore hats and pearls to shop and little girls put on their patent leather Mary Jane slippers and white string gloves to accompany them. The Hudson's they entered, debarking from buses and streetcars on Woodward and Gratiot and Grand River, was a spacious, high-ceilinged place laid out in the days before sales were calculated by square foot of selling space.

Detroiters came downtown to Hudson's in March or April for their Easter outfits, in June to see the six-story flag hung out for Flag Day, in July in later

See MEMORIES, Page 13A

Free Press Photo by CRAIG PORTER

It was a sunny day Wednesday, but the future looked bleak for Hudson's downtown store.

Company report tells the story

By BETSEY HANSELL
Free Press Marketing Writer
Copyright 1982, The Detroit Free Press

The J.L. Hudson Co., conceding it can't solve the financial problems of its landmark downtown store, has "initiated efforts" toward closing it, according to a confidential report made last January by Hudson's president P. Gerald Mills.

"Hudson's management has concluded that the downtown store does not represent a viable part of our long-range strategy," said the report, which Mills presented to the board of directors of Dayton-Hudson Corp., Hudson's parent company.

Mills acknowledged the report, a copy of which was obtained by the Free Press. In an interview Wednesday, Mills said no timetable had been set for closing the store, once the premier shopping place for generations of Detroiters. He said the store's continued operation is being evaluated on a "month-to-month basis."

In the interview, Mills also said he thinks the Cadillac Center shopping mall, a vision of shopping center developer A. Alfred Taubman, city officials and Hudson's itself, "is not a viable project for the foreseeable future."

"We had hopes of that," he said, referring to Hudson's plans to build a new 320,000-square-foot store in the mall. He said the hopes had been dimmed by the "deepening depression," developers' failure to attract two other anchor stores crucial to the success of the mall, and delays in downtown residential projects.

"MR. TAUBMAN has brought me up to date on what the past has been," Mills said. "There is really nothing to discuss" about the future.

The mall, to be built on the Kern Block directly south of the 70-year-old, 25-story Hudson's store, was to have been the centerpiece of several

See HUDSON'S, Page 13A

Downtown retailers still optimistic. Page 12A.

Photos trace Hudson's 101-year downtown tradition. Back Page.

School board's lame ducks get junket

By GLEN MACNOW
Free Press Education Writer

Twenty of Detroit's regional school board members whose posts will be eliminated this fall will spend $24,000 in tax money this weekend to attend an Atlanta convention.

The regional board members will attend the National School Boards Association convention despite the state Legislature's vote last week to recentralize the Detroit School District. As of November, that will eliminate the city's eight regional boards, along with the 32 regional board posts.

At least 28 city school officials will fly to Georgia, which will give Detroit a delegation much larger than school districts of comparable size. The 42d annual convention will focus on ways local districts can cope with tight budgets and federal aid cutbacks.

THE CONVENTION is expected to cost the financially beleaguered Detroit district at least $31,000. About $24,000 of that will go to providing transportation, registration fees, food and lodging for the regional board members.

Two members of the city's central Board of Education will attend as representatives of other organizations. Ida Murray will be sponsored by the National Caucus of Black School Board Members and will be attending at no expense to Detroit taxpayers.

Mary Blackmon is being sponsored by the Wayne County Intermediate School District and will be funded by county tax revenues.

Despite the high cost of the convention, Detroit school spokesman Stephen Chennault this week defended the trip of regional board members to attend.

"Logically, their tenure doesn't run out until November," he said. "They are still, theoretically, justified in their reasons for wanting to go. For the time being, they still have the right to do that."

THE ATLANTA MEETING will be the nation's

See JUNKET, Page 7A

Freedom day with the queen

TORONTO — Sandra Hilliard ruefully admits she paid scant attention to Canada's new constitution until she was asked to dine with a queen.

"I knew the constitution was coming home, but I never thought it would make much difference to me," the 19-year-old Toronto student said.

But Hilliard, a self-confessed monarchist, said the official proclamation of Canada's full independence by Queen Elizabeth is offering her "the opportunity of a lifetime."

"Meeting the queen is about the most exciting thing that has happened to me. My whole family is excited," Hilliard said.

HILLIARD IS one of 282 young Canadians — chosen for their educational achievements — who will dine in regal elegance with Queen Elizabeth and Prince Philip Friday as part of the four-day celebration of Canada's new constitution.

She is one of the few non-politicians in Canada to take part in the pomp and circumstance as the queen, who arrives in Ottawa today, officially cuts Canada's last colonial link with Britain.

Canada was created and governed under the British North America Act, passed by England's Parliament in 1867. It never had its own constitution.

See CANADA, Page 6A

Susan Brown Canada

Toronto Star photo via Canadian Press

Sandra Hilliard, above, confides that the invitation to dine with the queen is "about the most exciting thing that has happened to me."

Mosque attack brings protests in many lands

Associated Press

Millions of Muslims throughout the world staged a general strike Wednesday to protest the attack on the Dome of the Rock in Jerusalem, one of Islam's holiest shrines.

Air and rail traffic was disrupted in several Middle East countries, and major banking centers were closed. The flow of oil was unaffected, despite a call by Iran to "unsheath the oil weapon" against Israel.

King Khaled of Saudi Arabia, the world's largest oil exporter, sponsored the one-day strike in his capacity as custodian of Islam's holy shrines.

KUWAIT, BAHRAIN, Qatar, the United Arab Emirates, Iraq, Jordan, Syria, Lebanon, Libya, Morocco and the Palestine Liberation Organization shut down business totally. So did Iran, Pakistan and Bangladesh.

In Algeria, work stopped for 15 minutes. South Yemen, however, ordered double shifts to raise money for "Palestinians in revolt." In the Greek sector of Cyprus, Larnaca's airport was

See MUSLIMS, Page 12A

inside today

ANN LANDERS	2D
BRIDGE	10F
BUSINESS NEWS	8-12D
CABLE TV	6B
CAMERA	8-7C
CLASSIFIED GOLD ADS	13D-8E
COMICS	10-11F
CROSSWORD PUZZLE	11F
DEATH NOTICES	12D
EDITORIALS	10A
ENTERTAINMENT	4-5B
FEATURE PAGE	11C
HOROSCOPE	11C
MOVIE GUIDE	11F
OBITUARIES	12D
STOCK MARKETS	9-12D
TELEVISION	8-7C
THE WAY WE LIVE	1-5D

WEDNESDAY 299 and 4001

breezy, warmer
High 44, low 35
Partly cloudy Monday
Details on Page 2A

Carter signs with the Panthers — Page 1F
M*A*S*H — Farewell and Amen — Page 1C

Detroit Free Press

Volume 152, Number 299 ON GUARD FOR 151 YEARS Sunday, February 27, 1983

sunday 50¢ metro final

FEB. 27, 1983:

Among many West Germans, Detroit is seen as a leading symbol of social and economic failure in America.

"Care packages for Detroit," column two.

Thieves find gusher in nation's oil fields

By GARY BLONSTON
Free Press Western Bureau

DENVER — Ever since there was an oil industry, people have been lying, cheating and stealing to get their hands on oil money.

In the oil boom of the last five years, talented thieves, frauds and embezzlers have made hundreds of millions of dollars — maybe even billions — stealing crude oil, refined petroleum products and drilling equipment from U.S. oil companies.

Today, drilling activity is off substantially in the western U.S., and economic signs point to reductions in the price of foreign and domestic oil. But, to some leading members of the country's small, specialized band of oil-crime investigators, those trends suggest that the theft problem is only going to get worse — at a sizable cost to consumers, investors and government at every level, in virtually every state.

"The general trend is that, when times get harder, everybody starts scrambling," says Union Oil Co.-Texas' highly respected chief of security, Leonard Wood, "and that includes thieves."

Stolen tools shelved

Richard Goins, a veteran private investigator in Oklahoma City, says, "They're going to continue stealing crude oil. As the price goes down, the demand is not going to decrease, and people getting this easy money aren't going to stop."

And, Goins says, "as more people associated with the petroleum industry lose their jobs, then I think you'll find a larger percentage are going to turn to dishonest acts."

Houston-based security consultant Joe Dickerson says that even though the legitimate demand for drilling gear has fallen dramatically in the past year, costly equipment thefts are still occurring, possibly for a new reason. Says Dickerson:

"Organized crime is buying everything it can get its hands on and putting it on the shelf," in anticipation of a day when the market for oil-field equipment booms once again.

"And thieves are having to steal more, because they're selling cheaper, to maintain their standard of living."

Much theft goes undetected

They have been maintaining that lifestyle at a cost to many groups of people who aren't even aware of it — among them some people who run oil companies.

That is because so much of the theft occurs at the well site, often with the complicity of company employes who divert oil as soon as it leaves the earth and then underreport the well's production. The result, says Dickerson: "Our experience is that 90 percent of crude oil theft goes undetected. The company never knew it had it."

Whatever the known losses, the costs are generally passed on — to consumers who pay higher prices, to investors who receive lower earnings, to landowners who cash smaller royalty checks, to governments that lose sizable tax revenues.

Citing Department of Commerce figures for industrial theft costs in general — direct losses, insurance premiums, security system expenses and the like — Dickerson estimates that 17 cents of every dollar spent at retail on petroleum products is the price of experiencing and combatting oil crime.

Many oil companies are loath to admit the scope of the crime problem, though.

As Goins says, "They're very sensitive from a public image point of view. They have to go to the outside for their investment money."

And there is nothing more discouraging to investors than a company that doesn't seem to manage its prime assets carefully.

Implications boggling

Oil company security is a historic problem. Goins says, "When the price of oil was $3 or $3.25 (per barrel), they had just as many problems as when it was $40. There wasn't enough margin of profit to provide security, and local law enforcement has never been able to support the oil industry the way it needed."

Though there is more security these days, the implications for oil-industry loss in 1983

See THIEVERY, Page 8A

West Germans filled this container with food, clothing and other aid for Detroit. Trude Wendlinger, a Pan Am employe who helped organize the effort, checks the container at the Frankfurt airport. It was flown to Detroit Saturday.

Care packages for Detroit
Germans really want to help, but politics keeps creeping in

By WILLIAM J. MITCHELL
Free Press Europe Bureau

FRANKFURT, West Germany — Sixty-eight care packages from West Germany left here Saturday for poor people of Detroit, in the most dramatic installment yet of a curious international tale of poverty, politics and the press.

Stuffed with vitamins and clothing as well as such foods as rice, beans, powdered milk and chocolate bars, the packages were prompted by West German television and newspaper reports of needy people filling Detroit's unemployment lines and soup kitchens.

Many of the West German donors received CARE packages from Americans after World War II and regard their efforts to help Detroiters as a simple gesture of appreciation.

BUT THIS IS NOT simply the story of a helping hand extended back across the ocean.

Several leaders in the various aid-for-Detroit campaigns under way here have coupled their charity with commentary aimed at embarrassing the Reagan administration.

Among many West Germans, in fact, Detroit has emerged as the leading symbol of social and economic failure in America. Why doesn't Washington provide jobs and support for the people of Detroit? they ask.

German views of the United States have become especially important here in the context of next Sunday's national elections, which in many ways have turned into a referendum on just how closely West Germany should align itself with the U.S.

Critics of the conservative incumbent chancellor, Helmut Kohl, have held up Detroit as a warning of what can happen to a society that spends too much money on arms and not enough on social welfare.

The popular German magazine Quick described the German care package program for Detroit as "a bitter pill for the most powerful country in the world."

In an economic analysis published last week, former German Chancellor Helmut Schmidt said, "If soup kitchens have to be set up in Detroit, it amounts to a depression there."

Describing Detroit's situation as an indicator of more widespread economic problems, Schmidt added: "Such a state of affairs (in Detroit) is unbelievable. It is grotesque to think of German automobile workers sending packages to Detroit."

A fundraising drive launched by a Protestant minister in northern Germany — which has already raised nearly $10,000 for Detroit — contains this declaration in its organizing petition: "We don't conceal our concern that President Reagan is driving not only the American people but all mankind into permanent misery."

The spokesman for a group of German auto workers who contributed nearly $20,000 said: "We criticize the social policy of the Reagan administration and we say his policy of armaments does no good for the social situation of all American workers — not just auto workers."

WHATEVER their politics, nearly everyone here seems to

See GERMANS, Page 11A

Harold Washington, Democratic nominee for Chicago mayor, waves as he visits his high school alma mater.

Winds of change in the Windy City

By KEN FIREMAN
City-County Bureau Chief

CHICAGO — The students poured out of their classrooms, hundreds strong, determined to see, hear and touch the man likely to become the first black mayor of Chicago.

"Haa-rold! Haa-rold! Haa-rold!" they chanted. "We want Washington!"

Harold Washington, class of '42, had returned to DuSable High School in the city's gritty South Side ghetto, and his presence nearly touched off a small riot.

It was less than 48 hours after Washington's upset victory Tuesday in Chicago's Democratic mayoral primary, and the two-term congressman was a hero in his old neighborhood.

Excited students crowded so closely around Washington that aides and bodyguards feared for his safety. They linked arms and surrounded the candidate to protect him during a noisy, chaotic

See CHICAGO, Page 8A

inside today

ACTION LINE	6C		
ANN LANDERS	2G	SATURDAY	
BOOKS	5D		
BRIDGE	9D		
BUSINESS NEWS	1-8D		
CLASSIFIED GOLD ADS	1-13E	OBITUARIES	3C
CLASSIFIED GOLD ADS	8-9H		
CROSSWORD PUZZLE	9D		
DEATH NOTICES		SPORTS	1-9F
EDITORIALS	1C		
ENTERTAINMENT	1-7C		
		HOROSCOPE	9D

Decontrol Gas Prices — Reagan

By JAMES GERSTENZANG
Associated Press

WASHINGTON — President Reagan said Saturday he will ask Congress to remove all controls from the natural gas market over the next three years "to ensure abundant supplies ... at reasonable prices."

At the same time, the Reagan plan would cap consumer prices through Jan. 1, 1986, allowing increases based only on inflation, unless a government agency approved higher fees. On that date, all price controls would be removed.

"The key to cheaper, more abundant energy for all Americans is a policy that combines consumer protection, incentives to produce and efficient economic use of our resources," the president said in his weekly radio address to the nation, broadcast from the Oval Office. "That's what our program will do."

THE PRESIDENT said the Energy Department estimates the plan will reduce prices 10 cents to 30 cents per 1,000 cubic feet of natural gas in the first year.

Larry Speakes, the chief deputy White House press secretary, said Reagan would send the proposal to Congress Monday and Energy Secretary Donald Hodel has reported, on the basis of preliminary consultations, that congressional reaction "has been far better than expected."

"There seems to be a consensus that something has to be done," Speakes said, in reference to complaints about increases in natural gas prices that have driven bills up 20 percent to 40 percent in some areas this winter.

SINCE 1978, the average residential customer of Michigan Consolidated Gas Co. has seen bills rise by 96 percent. The average Consumers Power Co. customer pays 50 percent more. Yet both are using an average of 14.5 percent less gas.

Sen. Howard Metzenbaum, D-Ohio, an opponent of decontrolling natural gas prices, said he believed the Senate would defeat Reagan's proposal.

"The gas industry itself has

See GAS PRICES, Page 4A

Anne Burford: Charges of blocked funding for political purposes.

EPA aides say director stalled aid

By GREGORY GORDON
United Press International

WASHINGTON — Environmental Protection Agency chief Anne Burford blocked funding until after the November election for a California toxic waste cleanup package — to justify her decision — effectively stalled action at a Minnesota site for up to a year, agency officials charged Saturday.

The officials said they were told Burford and aides were worried that release of $6.1 million to California might benefit the Democratic Senate campaign of Gov. Edmund Brown.

In contrast to normal routine, only top-level agency officials were allowed to handle much of the paperwork on funding for the Stringfellow Acid Pits in Glen Avon, Calif., near Los Angeles, agency sources said.

ONE OFFICIAL said that, when he asked last June about progress on the cleanup package, he was told, "We don't think we can fund it because Jerry Brown will beat up on it" in his campaign. Brown, who lost to Sen. Pete Wilson, R-Calif., made the environment a

See EPA, Page 9A

Of gossip, drugs, sex in Ludington

By THOMAS BeVIER
Free Press Staff Writer

LUDINGTON — Fred Slimmen was barbering in a shop at Seven Mile and Prevost in Detroit in 1971 when he decided he'd had all he could stand of the city's racial tension and violence. He sold his house and moved to this western Michigan town of 9,000 on Lake Michigan and opened the Golden Razor barbershop.

Small town life appealed to Slimmen, now 44. He became active in the Optimist Club and helped raise money for charity; one Christmas season, the Salvation Army gave him a plaque as Bell Ringer of the Day. People liked him for his outgoing personality and his outspokenness, even if the things he said sometimes seemed excessive.

Fred Slimmen became a force to be reckoned with in Ludington, especially after he formed the Mason County Citizens for Justice in 1975 and started taking out after judges and lawyers. He bantered charges of misconduct within the legal establishment, of illicit drug dealing and loose moral standards on the part of prominent citizens. People listened to him, even though most of what he said could not be confirmed, even by his good friend and ally Mason County Sheriff Walter Carrier, whom Slimmen says he helped get elected in 1976.

"I just got tired of seeing the crap that goes on in this

See LUDINGTON, Page 11A

Barber Fred Slimmen, whose campaign against those in positions of authority has shaken up Ludington.

Oct. 15, 1984:

The Roar of '84: The Tigers' incredible season ends with Kirk Gibson dancing on the baseline and fans partying in the streets.

The Ford-UAW deal
— Story, Page 3A

A 2d Front Page on 3A today

foggy, showers
High 69, low 55
Mostly cloudy Tuesday
Details on Page 2A

Detroit Free Press

Volume 154, Number 164 · ON GUARD FOR 153 YEARS · Monday, October 15, 1984

monday
20¢
metro final

Gr-r-reat!

The culmination of an incredible season, the high point of a still-young career: Kirk Gibson after his second home run Sunday.

Fans go wild over Tigers

By MARTIN F. KOHN
Free Press Staff Writer

Five or so ounces of cork wound in twine and wrapped in sewn white leather settled into the glove of a man named Larry Herndon, and the baseball season of 1984 settled into the massive mitt of History.

The Tigers, the come-from-ahead ball club from the coming-from-behind town, won the World Series, beating the San Diego Padres 8-4 before Vice-President George Bush and a home crowd of 51,901 who hollered themselves hoarse and waved themselves silly and, years from now, can show their ticket stubs to their grandchildren and say they were there.

Playing no favorites, President Reagan telephoned both locker rooms after the game to congratulate the players.

For Detroit, for Michigan, for the Midwest, for everybody who has been with the Tigers in spirit, the victory was a moment to cherish in a season to savor.

Starting in the Tigers locker room and spreading out in immeasurable waves wherever fans of the home team gathered, it was "cel-e-brate good times, come on!" and dancing in the streets.

BUT IT wasn't all fun. At least four police cars were damaged at Michigan and Trumbull; another was set afire and destroyed, and a private car also was set afire.

Emergency Medical Services ambulances had trouble reaching at least one accident victim, police said.

Souvenir vendors near the stadium had their remaining wares stolen.

Many bottles were thrown at police officers. No serious injuries had been reported within the first couple of hours after the game.

For the most part, though, just as it happened 16 years ago, when the Tigers last won the Series, hearts swelled and spirits lifted. Banished for the moment were thoughts of crime and unemployment, recession and soup kitchens. The Tigers were world champions, and all things good suddenly had become possible, or even likely.

See **WORLD SERIES**, Page 15A

the roar of '84

- Game story and special Series Report, Section F.
- More pictures, Page 12F.
- Talbert's Tiger diary, 7E.
- Series Sidelights, 1E.

The naturals win in maverick way

Mike Downey

They won it, just the way everybody in Detroit thought they would.

They won it, in a way nobody thought they could.

They won it on a sacrifice fly to second base.

They won it on a pinch-hit, bases-loaded pop-up by Rusty Kuntz.

They won it on a wild run for the money by Kirk Gibson, who tagged up and scored on a ball that might not have gone 25 feet onto the outfield grass.

They did it with two Gibson home runs, one of which opened the scoring, one of which closed it.

They won it.

The World Series.

THE DETROIT Tigers became the undisputed best team in baseball Sunday, beating the San Diego Padres, 8-4, for their fourth world championship since joining the American League in 1901. When Willie Hernandez got Tony Gwynn on a short fly to left field for the final out, the crowd of 51,901 stormed onto the Tiger Stadium field, as did thousands of non-paying customers outside the park who didn't want to be left out.

They couldn't restrain themselves. The Tigers had won it.

They won it with Gibson tying into a Mark Thurmond pitch in the first inning and sending it halfway to Hamtramck. The two-run homer landed in the upper deck in right-center.

They won it because another San Diego pitcher failed to last beyond the first inning. Thurmond threw only 15 pitches and faced only six batters.

They won it even though the Padres put together a rally that knocked out Dan Petry and tied the game at 3-all.

See **DOWNEY**, Page 15A

State wraps up Tiger ticket sale investigation — 3A

Dow Jones index flirts with another record — 8C

FEB. 9, 1985:

Stroh's announces the end of 135 years of brewing beer in Detroit.

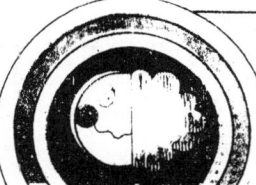

partly cloudy
High 25, low 10
Cloudy, chance of snow Sunday
Details on Page 2A

Detroit Free Press

Volume 154, Number 281 — ON GUARD FOR 153 YEARS — Saturday, February 9, 1985

saturday 20¢ **metro final**

Free Press Photo by IRA ROSENBERG

Stroh Won't Brew Here Anymore

U.S. asks recall of 2 million GM cars

By MARCIA STEPANEK
Free Press Automotive Writer

Federal safety authorities are asking General Motors Corp. to recall almost two million of its midsized A cars from 1982, 1983 and 1984 because of an alleged tendency for the rear brakes to lock up too soon and cause severe skidding in normal braking.

That is the same kind of problem the government has said plagues GM's 1980 X cars. But GM has said both models are safe. The 1,903,000 A cars involved in the government's request are the Chevrolet Celebrity, Pontiac 6000, Buick Century and Oldsmobile Cutlass Ciera models.

"WE BELIEVE a significant safety problem exists among the cars that involves the potential for rear-brake lock-up, vehicle control loss and personal injury — such as sliding sideways down the road and spinning 180 degrees," the National Highway Traffic Safety Administration wrote GM in a Jan. 3 letter.

Philip Davis, acting director of the traffic safety administration's Office of Defect Investigations, emphasized that the action is a request for a recall, not an order. He said the letter "essentially says we will upgrade our investigation and start taking the necessary steps to formally order such a recall if GM doesn't recall the cars on its own."

Davis said the agency has linked 448 complaints, 69 accidents, 23 injuries and "88 incidents of vehicle control loss" to the alleged lock-up problem. No deaths were reported to the government. The Center for Auto Safety, an auto safety lobby based in Washington, D.C., said it has received 500 complaints alleging 91 accidents, 48 injuries and three deaths.

See **GM**, Page 11A

End of the X-car

☐ GM will quit building the X-body compacts in May, about a year earlier than planned, because publicity over alleged safety defects in earlier models has hurt sales. Page 8C.

Peter Stroh: "This was one of the most difficult decisions we ever made . . ."

Mayor Young: "It is painful to know that . . . Stroh must close down . . ."

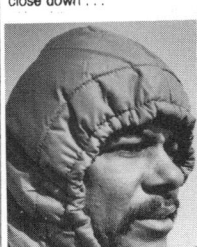
Tyrone Lewis, who earns $13.50 an hour driving a forklift truck on the brewery's loading dock: "It's bad, brother . . . makes you want to cry." His wife said that if he brings another bottle of Stroh's into the house "I'll break it over his head."

James Scott, a bartender at Nemo's: "I'm sorry to see it go. They've done a lot for the city."
Free Press Photo by PAULINE LUBENS

By PETER GAVRILOVICH and TERESA BLOSSOM
Free Press Staff Writers

Stroh's will stop brewing beer in Detroit sometime this spring — ending a 135-year tradition.

Catching civic leaders by surprise and angering many employes, Peter Stroh, chairman of Stroh Brewery Co., announced Friday that the family-owned company would close its Detroit brewery — the oldest and least efficient of its seven plants — but would maintain its corporate headquarters on the riverfront.

"THIS WAS one of the most difficult decisions we ever made," said a visibly shaken Stroh, considered by many local government and business leaders to be a major booster of Detroit.

The announcement comes at a time when Detroit is battling a sour national image.

Robert McCabe, chairman of Detroit Renaissance, said: "The symbolism of another major facility becoming obsolete in the inner city has its negative image connotation. . . . It makes revitalization of the city tougher. At the same time, fortunately, they have not said that (they are leaving). And they are continuing to invest in the city."

Business leaders said they understood, from a business perspective, why the brewery will close operations, a move scheduled to be completed this spring.

"Stroh's has not attempted to steal away in the dead of night," Mayor Young said Friday evening. "It's not easy to take, but it's not all negative."

Young stressed that Stroh will maintain a corporate presence here as well as its ice cream operations, but said the decision to close the brewery "is not good news."

After Vernors announced recently it was leaving the city, Stroh was quoted in the Feb. 3 Detroit News as saying: "As long as I'm running things, Stroh's will never move out of Detroit."

THE CLOSING stunned the company's 1,190 brewery employes, most of whom are unlikely to be hired at other Stroh plants. About 750 corporate employes will remain at Stroh headquarters.

See **STROH CLOSING**, Page 4A

A four-page report inside

☐ *Business, political and civic leaders lament Stroh Brewery Co.'s decision to close its downtown Detroit plant, but hail word that its headquarters will remain.* 4A.

☐ *Businesses in the shadow of the brewery say they'll miss their neighbor.* 5A.

☐ *Industry analysts explain the problems that led to the closing.* 5A.

☐ *The brewery closing as seen from the barstools.* 5A.

☐ *Stroh Brewery Co.: A history in words and pictures.* 6A.

☐ *People who know Peter Stroh say the decision must have been agonizing.* 6A.

Closing is a bitter brew for longtime employes

By JOHN SAUNDERS and DAVID EVERETT
Free Press Staff Writers

Tyrone Lewis figured the worst part of his day would be trying to revive his battered '71 Mercury Marquis, stalled in a subzero windchill in the Stroh brewery parking lot. Then he got the news on the radio.

"It's bad, brother," he said. With three children and a $330-a-month mortgage, Lewis may be joining as many as 1,190 other Stroh employes looking for work this spring.

After 10 years of bottling Stroh beer, Lewis earns $13.50 an hour. The paychecks will continue at least a few more months. But there was no definite word on how many Detroit workers would be offered jobs at Stroh operations in other cities when the hometown brewery shuts down.

"WE ARE exploring that intensively," Stroh Chairman and Chief Executive Officer Peter Stroh told a news conference, "to make sure as many as possible are absorbed at other plants."

Many employes voiced anger

See **EMPLOYES**, Page 7A

It's not a brewery closing down, it's a part of the city

Neal Shine

We ripped the back porch off our house on Wayburn one Saturday afternoon in the summer of 1949 to rebuild the foundation.

The long-forgotten workers who built the original a few decades earlier celebrated its completion by finishing a few Stroh's and tossing the empty bottles in the dirt before building the porch over them.

It seemed only right, that warm day, to repeat the pageantry and contribute our own Stroh's empties to those already lying there.

Who knows, we thought then, when some archeological explorers on an urban dig would find them and report to the world that the favorite beer of this porch-building people was something called Stroh's.

If we were going to be remembered in history at all, then let us be remembered for our sophistication in choosing our beer rather than for the quality of our cement-block foundations.

It went without saying that long after the old porch had fallen in on itself, Stroh Brewery Co. would still be making beer in Detroit, just like always.

THERE IS SOME indefinable point in the history of a company when it stops being a business and becomes part of a place. Identified not just by the product it makes but by the friends it makes.

Not a symbol, really, the way the ball on the Penobscot Building or the fountain at Belle Isle are symbols. Something more substantial than that.

Something that makes you think that losing Stroh's is

See **SHINE**, Page 5A

Medicaid passes physical, president's panel reports

By DAVID HESS
Free Press Washington Staff

WASHINGTON — In a startling departure from the usual conservative complaint that Medicaid is riddled with fraud and abuse, the President's Council of Economic Advisers gives the program a clean bill of health.

Charges, chiefly by conservatives, that the medical aid program for poor people is abused widely by users and health-care providers, are not substantiated by facts, the council said.

"In fact, Medicaid has successfully met its legislated objectives," the council said in its report to Congress this week.

The 20-year-old program is the largest federal grant program. This fiscal year, states and local governments will receive nearly $23 billion to help pay for the medical needs of about 22 million people. States and localities will spend another $19 billion.

The council does not contend the program is free of fraud or other abuse. But it said abuse is not rampant.

See **MEDICAID**, Page 11A

Inside today

ANN LANDERS	7B
BRIDGE	6D
BUSINESS NEWS	8-11C
CLASSIFIED GOLD ADS	1-5B
COMICS	6-7D
CROSSWORD PUZZLE	7D
DATELINE MICHIGAN	12C
DEATH NOTICES	2B
EDITORIALS	8A
ENTERTAINMENT	6-7C
FEATURE PAGE	7B
HOROSCOPE	6D
MOVIE GUIDE	7D
OBITUARIES	12C
TELEVISION	5C

FRIDAY CARD GAME 013 and 6133 8¢ and 5¢
LOTTO JACKPOT $2 million

To place a classified ad, call 222-5000, Monday-Friday 8-6, Saturday 9-5 and Sunday 10-4.

Mother gets jail in bank robbery

Despite a plea from a prosecutor, a Macomb County judge has sentenced a woman with five children to serve as many as five years in jail for robbing a bank with a toy gun. Page 3A.

Friends say social worker is unlikely slaying suspect

By BRIAN FLANIGAN and SANDY McCLURE
Free Press Staff Writers

To friends and associates, Victor Malone is a "bright, caring, creative" social worker who holds a master's degree from the University of Michigan.

To psychiatrists who have examined him, Malone has "dull normal" intelligence and is "psychotic, schizophrenic and sociopathic."

To Detroit police, Malone is a man with a lengthy criminal record who is charged with murdering one woman and is the prime suspect in the slayings of at least 10 other women.

"I don't believe it, to be honest with you," Dr. Howard Brabson, a U-M associate professor of social work, said Friday. "I've seen him inside and I've seen him outside and I just don't believe it."

BUT BRABSON'S assessment is not necessarily shared by Detroit police homicide investigators, who since Thursday morning have been pulling files on unsolved slayings of women to determine if Malone can be connected to them.

See **SLAYINGS**, Page 11A

OCT. 31, 1985:

Long a Detroit tradition, mischief on Devil's Night turns violent.

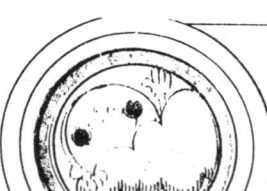

Joke's on us: Wings win one
Also: Isiah Thomas (right) tells how he refused to sell out to college bidders' cash offers — 1E

Net-as-chic fashions from Paris — 1C

cloudy
High 57, low 52
Rain likely Friday
Details on Page 2A

Detroit Free Press

thursday
20¢
metro final

Volume 155, Number 180 — ON GUARD FOR 154 YEARS — Thursday, October 31, 1985

© 1985, Detroit Free Press, Inc.

Three Soviets freed unhurt

By IHSAN A. HIJAZI
New York Times

BEIRUT, Lebanon — Three Soviet Embassy employes were freed unharmed Wednesday, a month after they and a colleague were kidnapped in west Beirut. The fourth Soviet was found shot dead two days after he was abducted.

The Soviet Embassy confirmed the release Wednesday night and said the three were safe at the embassy. It gave no details.

A Muslim fundamentalist faction calling itself the Islamic Liberation Organization announced in a statement delivered to a Western news agency here that it had freed the three officials. They are Valery Mirkov, the embassy's commercial attache; Oleg Spirin, the press attache, and Dr. Nikolai Sversky, the embassy physician.

The body of the fourth Soviet, Arkady Katkov, the 38-year-old consular attache at the embassy, was recovered on Oct. 2 from an empty lot near the Beirut stadium.

The Islamic Liberation Organization said in its statement that it had

See SOVIET, Page 10A

Two slain, 8 wounded at Pa. mall

UPI and AP

SPRINGFIELD, Pa. — A woman in Army fatigues and black boots went to a suburban Philadelphia mall Wednesday with a semiautomatic rifle and opened fire on shoppers, killing two people and wounding eight others before she was subdued by a man who sneaked up behind her, police said.

Sylvia Seegrist, 25, of Crumlyn, was taken into custody after the 4 p.m. shooting rampage at the Springfield Mall in Delaware County, Police Chief George Hill said. Police then closed the shopping center.

Seegrist got out of her car at an entrance to the mall and began shooting the .22-caliber rifle at a woman using an automatic bank machine, but missed her, Hill said.

"Then she began firing at everybody and anybody who got in her path," he said.

A two-year-old boy was killed near the entrance to the mall, Hill said.

See SHOOTINGS, Page 4A

Free Press Photo by WILLIAM ARCHIE
Eastwood near Chalmers: Forty neighbors chipped in to help extinguish this garage fire on the city's northeast side. A puppy was killed when the garage collapsed.

All-out offensive
City's Devil's Night plan began 3½ months ago

By PATRICIA EDMONDS
Free Press Staff Writer

City officials began meeting 3½ months ago to plan an all-out offensive against Devil's Night crime and arson.

"And the first thing we did was pray that it rained," said Charlie Williams, chairman of the Devil's Night task force formed by police and fire and other city officials in July.

"But since we don't control that, we thought we'd better be prepared."

The team's task: to isolate areas where pranksters and arsonists had wrought the most damage in past years, and to map a strategy for heading off the mayhem and destruction.

The planning would take into account a thousand Devil's Night contingencies — everything from how to deploy 8,000 law officers and citizens to where a brimming dumpster might draw a firebug.

THE FORCE INCLUDED assistants to Mayor Young, Police Chief William Hart, Fire Commissioner Melvin Jefferson and Fire Marshal Donald Robinson as well as officials of the Department of Public Works, the Engineering Department and the Buildings and Safety Engineering Department.

Young appointed Williams — director of the Water and Sewerage Department and Young's campaign treasurer-chairman.

The first step, Williams said, was to assemble demographic data about Devil's Night 1984, when what Young called an "unprecedented" mobilization of police, fire fighters and citizens did not stem the arsons.

The task force started with the fire marshal's report for the 48 hours between 12:01 a.m. Oct. 30 and midnight Oct. 31. Williams said that report showed 215 false

See PLAN, Page 11A

Detroit fights Devil's Night

Photo by Free Press Chief Photographer TONY SPINA
Euclid at Beaubien: Two homes burn uncontrollably near the New Center area. A third home was damaged in the blaze.

Young: Plans reduced arson

While Mayor Young proclaimed a victory over Devil's Night vandals — a reduction from last year's fiery incidents by about 30 percent — weary fire fighters methodically battled the last of hundreds of blazes early today.

Although there was no pattern to the fires Wednesday and this morning, they appeared to be concentrated in southeast and southwest Detroit and dotted other portions of the 139.6-square-mile city.

At least 20 people were forced to flee their burning homes, and there was significant property damage through-

■ **Full coverage of Devil's Night, 11A.**

out the city, officials said, but no serious injuries or deaths were reported.

YOUNG'S PRESS secretary, Robert Berg, said 24 people were arrested. Berg said seven were arrested for arson, seven for malicious destruction of property, eight for curfew violations, one for interfering with an arson investigator and one for turning in a false fire alarm.

Young, who had ordered a task force 3½ months ago to study how to combat what has become Detroit's traditional night of arson, said he was "very satisfied" with the reduction in arson this year from 1984.

Young said information probably would not be available until today on how many fires were in structures, both occupied and abandoned. He said computer failures complicated tabulation of the statistics, but added that a hand count of fire reports indicated "we have clearly attained our goal of 25 percent reduction, and we might have done much

See DEVIL'S NIGHT, Page 11A

Tempers flare with the flames for those left homeless

By ERIC KINKOPF and JACK KRESNAK
Free Press Staff Writers

Despair and anger rose as high as the flames on Detroit's near southwest side Wednesday night when three homes on Lansing were hit by a Devil's Night fire, leaving at least 20 people homeless.

"I got no f------ place to go," said Gary Davis, 29, whose home in the 1500 block of Lansing was seriously damaged by a fire that began in a house next door. "I ain't got money for a motel room. Nothing."

"I ain't got nowhere to live," said Frankie Armstead, 36, who said she left to take her six children to a Halloween party only to return and find her home leveled by fire.

Neighbors said the fire broke out at Armstead's house 15 minutes after she left with her children.

"What am I going to do?" asked Ethel Davis, 19. "I don't got no idea, sweetheart."

MARGARET BOLING, 36, who hugged some warmth into her chilled body with a blanket as she watched the fire lick at her home, took her frustration out on a bystander and almost set off a brawl that had to be broken up by police.

A relative, Joni Boling, was kneeling on a tree lawn, facing away from the flames, crying.

"This guy was laughing about my house being on fire," said Boling, who chased the man across the street. "I hit him with my fist."

Boling said that she lived at her home with four other relatives.

A police officer said that when he got there Boling and the other residents of her home were trying to put out the fire at the home next door with pans of water and garden hoses.

Residents said that the fire broke out about 7:45 p.m., when what they described as a firebomb was thrown through a front window of Armstead's home.

MUCH OF the residents' anger and

See TEMPERS FLARE, Page 11A

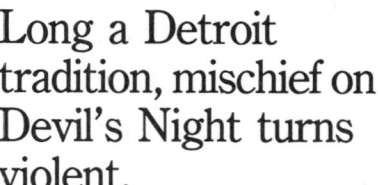

A rich land?
Life-styles Spartan in wealthy Japan

By SUSAN CHIRA
New York Times

TAMAGAWAJOSUI, Japan — Japan is a wealthy nation whose citizens do not enjoy many of the amenities of wealth.

Only 34 percent of Japanese communities have modern sewer systems, compared with 85 percent in the United States. Just 51 percent of Japanese roads are paved, compared with a 1981 figure of 85 percent in the United States. And the average size of homes built in Japan in 1983 was 932 square feet compared with 1,450 square feet last year in the United States.

There would seem to be plenty for people here to buy, particularly given Japan's $50 billion trade and capital surplus.

For many Japanese, national wealth has brought little sense of personal entitlement.

BUT THE AVERAGE Japanese still seems attuned to the realities of the postwar era and the need to sacrifice comforts so the nation could rebuild. For many, national wealth has brought little sense of personal entitlement.

Shihoko Sugimoto's house would be Spartan by American standards. By Japanese standards, it borders on the luxurious.

She has no sewers, central heating,

See JAPAN, Page 8A

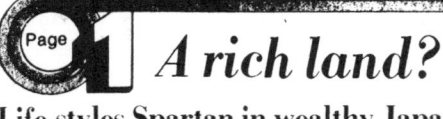

LOTTO 1, 5, 8, 20, 27, 34
WEDNESDAY 882 and 8410

inside today

ANN LANDERS	2B
BRIDGE	8E
CAMERA	18-19A
CLASSIFIEDS	6-10C, 2-7D
COMICS	8-9E
CROSSWORD PUZZLE	9E
DATELINE MICHIGAN	13A
DEATH NOTICES	6C
ENTERTAINMENT	4-5C
FEATURE PAGE	11C
HOROSCOPE	8E
MOVIE GUIDE	5C
OBITUARIES	6C
TELEVISION	16-17A

To place a classified ad, call 222-5000, Monday-Friday 8-6, Saturday 9-5 and Sunday 10-4

■ **Sky King dies.**  6C.

U.S., Soviets discuss a second summit

AP, Free Press Washington Staff and New York Times

WASHINGTON — The United States and the Soviet Union have begun "preliminary discussions" about a second summit meeting between President Reagan and Soviet leader Mikhail Gorbachev, even as preparations proceed in both capitals for the first summit next month, an administration official disclosed Wednesday.

Although no decision has been made, Secretary of State George Shultz intends to pursue the subject when he visits Moscow on Monday for talks with Gorbachev and Soviet Foreign Minister Eduard Shevardnadze, the official said.

The idea would be to make the Nov. 19-20 summit in Geneva "the start of a dialogue" between the two leaders, said the official, who insisted on anonymity. That, he said, long has been the U.S. intention, and "in a preliminary way has been discussed with the Soviets."

The conversations, through diplomatic channels, have not yet focused on a time or place for a second summit meeting. Such a

See SUMMIT, Page 8A

Three of a kind
Projects strengthen hand of development in city

By RICK RATLIFF, JEANNE MAY and W. KIM HERON
Free Press Staff Writers

New places to live, to work and to shop in downtown Detroit were in various stages of blossoming Wednesday.

The place to live is the Heritage Hotel, on Grand Circus Park, where work will start today on turning the building into a luxury apartment house with a 400-car parking building.

The place to work is the Metropolitan Center for High Technology, near the Masonic Temple, which Wednesday celebrated the beginning of an $8.2 million renovation designed to pull in new companies.

And the place to shop is Phase II of Trappers Alley, in Greektown, with more shops and offices — and maybe even a new Attic Theatre — scheduled to open in a month or two.

The specifics:

• The long-abandoned Heritage Hotel is to be turned into 334 one- and two-

See DEVELOPMENT, Page 10A

THE JOA

APRIL 15, 1986:

Detroit's two major newspapers, at war for decades, say the Free Press is failing, and ask the federal government to approve a joint operating agreement.

Agreement caps long-running rivalry

Free Press older than Michigan

By PATRICIA CHARGOT
Free Press Staff Writer

The Detroit Free Press is older than the state of Michigan, with a proud history stretching back 154 years.

When the first paper hit the streets May 5, 1831, Michigan was a territory and Detroit was a frontier town with 2,500 residents. But what began as a four-page weekly — and then a daily paper in 1835 — has grown into the 10th largest daily-circulation newspaper in the United States.

Originally called the Democratic Free Press and Michigan Intelligencer, the paper was founded by Sheldon McKnight, who started publishing with one printer and an apprentice. Michigan's oldest newspaper supported the drive for statehood, established a national reputation by deploying reporters to the Civil War battlefield, and helped form the Western Associated Press, a precursor of the Associated Press, the world's largest news-gathering agency.

In May 1940, the Free Press was bought by John S. Knight and associates and became part of Knight Newspapers Inc. Knight merged with Ridder Publications Inc. in 1974 to become Knight-Ridder Newspapers Inc.

The Free Press has won numerous prizes for outstanding journalism, including six Pulitzer Prizes:
• In 1932, by W.C. Richards, D.D. Martin, F.D. Webb, J.N.W. Sloan and J.S. Pooler, for reporting on a huge parade during an American Legion convention in Detroit.
• In 1945, for an investigation of graft and corruption in Lansing.
• In 1955, by Royce Howes, for an editorial analyzing the responsibility of labor and management in a major automobile strike.
• In 1956, by Lee Hills, for reporting UAW negotiations with Ford Motor Co. and General Motors Corp.
• In 1968, for coverage of the 1967 Detroit riots.
• In 1981, by Taro Yamasaki, for a photographic essay on life inside the State Prison of Southern Michigan at Jackson.

In the late 1960s, the Free Press gained a reputation editorially as the more liberal of the city's two major newspapers because of the strong stand taken by then-Editor Mark Ethridge Jr. against the Vietnam war, and later because of the editorial board's stand on such issues as affirmative action, school desegregation and freedom of choice on abortion.

Higher prices expected

By STEPHEN ADVOKAT
Free Press Communications Writer

If history is any guide, advertisers and subscribers to the Detroit Free Press and the Detroit News will have to pay more.

In markets where newspapers publish under joint operating agreements, studies have shown ad and subscription rates far exceed those in markets where newspapers are competing.

"You have to assume that one of the first things they will do is raise their ad rates," said Peter Appert, a media analyst with New York-based C.J. Lawrence Inc. "And I'd imagine they'll reconsider to raise their circulation prices, too."

History tends to support Appert's view.

Shortly after the Gannett Co. bought the Cincinnati Enquirer in June 1979, it signed an agreement with Scripps-Howard for the Cincinnati Post and the Enquirer to enter into a JOA.

Gannett, long viewed as an aggressive pricer in the industry, raised the daily price of the Post and Enquirer to a quarter each from 15 cents and 20 cents, respectively. In June 1984 the price of the two Cincinnati papers rose to 35 cents each daily. The Sunday Enquirer costs $1.

Based on 1982 figures, the average cost of one line of display advertising among JOA papers was $20.20. Competing papers charged $11.21, adjusted for circulation.

The Detroit Free Press building under construction on Feb. 4, 1925. Construction had reached the 11th floor.

News sale may have sealed pact

By LYNNELL MICKELSEN
Free Press Staff Writer

For the Detroit News, the joint operating agreement announced Monday was another dramatic turn for a newspaper that in the last year has undergone a tumultuous bidding war and corporate takeover by Gannett Co. Inc.

It may mark another step away from an 112-year history of independence that began when its founder, James Scripps, broke away from his partners and launched an evening newspaper for working class families Aug. 23, 1873.

Suspicious of outsiders, Scripps included a provision in his will to keep the Evening News Association in family hands — and he was largely successful, despite the company's growth and diversification over the next 100 years.

THE SCRIPPS tradition of refusing to concede ground to the competition was so strong that, many observers believe, the proposed agreement would not have been considered by the former family owners, even though both the News and the Free Press had suffered losses for years.

"Pride precluded either party from initiating the (joint operating agreement) issue," said Ralph Booth, a relative of the founder, and president of Booth-American Co. Last year, Booth sold his five percent of Evening News Association stock to Gannett. "Clearly, the change of players (from the family-owned Evening News Association to Gannett) has been fundamental to bringing this about. A JOA has been in the best interests of the stockholders throughout this so-called newspaper war for a long, long time."

From the beginning, Scripps concentrated on producing short, lively news stories and underselling the competition. The first edition of the News sold for two cents — three cents less than any other Detroit newspaper. The paper merged with several rivals over the years. The last major consolidation was in 1960 when the paper purchased the assets and subscription list of the Detroit Times.

From then on, the major rival of the News was the Free Press. The News kept the lead in circulation, although competition was fierce. The most recent audit of circulation of the two newspapers showed 645,016 for the daily News and 634,466 for the Free Press. On Sundays, the News has 837,821 circulation to the Free Press 754,615.

THE NEWS WON two Pulitzer Prizes, journalism's highest honor — the first in 1942 for a photograph of a riot at the Ford River Rouge plant, the second in 1982 for a series on the mysterious death of a Michigan man in the Navy.

Analysts predicted that the standoff between the papers could last for years, citing both companies' pride and "deep pockets." But in 1984, investors began pursuing the ENA stock in the belief it was undervalued. Stock prices, which had been languishing for years, suddenly shot up. When longtime family members put a substantial portion of stock on the market to take advantage of the high prices, the company became a target for takeover.

After a bidding war, the company averted a hostile takeover by asking Gannett — the nation's largest newspaper group — to buy it out. The $717 million purchase was ratified by ENA stockholders in December.

At the time of the purchase, Gannett Chairman Allen Neuharth would not speculate on the possibility of a joint agreement with the Free Press.

The newspaper war was long and bloody

WAR, from Page 1A

said Bill Giles, former editor of the Detroit News.

The rivalry stopped short of homicide, but not much. It ranged from the front page to the bottom line, bleeding both newspapers so badly in the last five years that at times the contest seemed to be not who would win but who would lose less.

Over the years, when the Free Press offered free papers to breakfasters at McDonald's, the News gave away copies at Burger Chef. When the Free Press started its Action Line help column in the 1960s, the News responded with Contact 10. This year, when the News began touting its Super Sports section, the Free Press fought back with Sports Bonus.

By the time your daily Detroit paper plopped on your porch, morning or afternoon, there was more passion and energy and sometimes outright pain invested in it than in a week's worth of soap operas.

IN THE SMOKY grotto on West Lafayette known as the Anchor Bar, where staffers from both papers regularly trade boasts and rumors, Free Press reporters brag of the paper's six Pulitzer Prizes to the News' two. Detroit News editors, on the other hand, were gleeful that they won their 1982 Pulitzer by beating the Free Press up and down on a story the Free Press reported first — the brutal disciplinary methods in the Navy that cost a Detroit-area sailor his life.

When the Gannett chain, new owner of the News, announced a few weeks ago it was dropping the price of the News outstate from 20 cents back to 15 cents, the Free Press followed suit within hours — an unheard-of move for a paper that admitted it was losing millions of dollars a year. The Free Press still says 20 cents on the masthead, but in Lansing, Saginaw, Grand Rapids and Traverse City, readers get it for a nickel less, courtesy of the great newspaper war.

YOU MIGHT trace the origins of this conflict back to August 23, 1873, when the first issue of the Detroit News appeared on city streets where the forerunner of the Free Press, a paper called the Democratic Free Press and Michigan Intelligencer, had been a fixture since 1831.

In 1976, the News muscled in on the Free Press' morning franchise by launching an early morning edition of its own. The News also built a plant near Lansing, to better woo outstate readers, a field that the Free Press had long found fertile.

Last week, the Free Press took on the News toe-to-toe in the city of Detroit, challenging the News' dominance in center city circulation with a special Free Press weekly section dubbed Detroit Plus.

The Free Press, stalking readers wherever it could find them, added Pope John Paul II as a columnist; the pope's superior being unavailable as a columnist, the News settled for Lee Iacocca, instead.

But the real heating-up began in 1960, when the Detroit News bought the assets of the Detroit Times and — so the News thought — perpetual dominance of the Detroit newspaper market. Instead, executives at the News — a sedate, wealthy, conservative paper known around town as the "old gray lady" — found they had bought a 26-year-long circulation war with a scrappy, feisty Free Press.

For a brief moment in 1960, before the death of the Times, the Free Press led the News in circulation by 2,177 readers. By 1963, the News had absorbed enough Times readers to pull ahead of the Free Press by 214,163 subscribers. The News had more pages, more political influence, more advertising; the News is still dominant in advertising.

What the smaller Free Press had was an irreverent disdain for trying to be a newspaper of record and an emphasis, instead, on sprightly stories, sharp writing, talked-about features. The Free Press also had that magical thing called momentum: Every year, the circulation of the two papers grew, but the circulation of the Free Press grew faster, abetted by the swing in readers' tastes to a morning newspaper, rather than an afternoon one.

As of Friday, the Detroit News' lead over the Free Press had narrowed to less than 11,000 daily, a razor-thin margin in the more than 1.2 million copies sold by both papers daily. The News still held a substantial lead over the Free Press on Sundays — 837,821 to the Free Press 754,615.

NOW GANNETT, owner of the Detroit News, and Knight-Ridder, the parent corporation of the Free Press, have announced they will join in a venture called the Detroit Newspaper Agency, in which the advertising and circulation operations of the two papers will be combined. The rivalry on the news side will remain.

Executives of the two parent corporations described the joint venture as a means to insure the survival of two strong newspapers and two strong, independent editorial voices in Detroit and Michigan for a hundred years. They say it has averted the tragedy of one newspaper having to die before the other could become prosperous.

Not everybody agrees. There are those who would rather have had a clean victory of one paper over the other, those who argue the Detroit metro market was rich enough ground to support two newspapers if the parent corporations had not engaged in cutthroat price-cutting in advertising and circulation.

"There is nothing operating here except corporate appetite," Kurt Leudtke, former executive editor of the Free Press, said of the joint agreement. "It's bad for everybody but the stockholders."

But Al Stark, former city editor and now columnist for the News, says the competition was so emotional, it got "cuckoo" and distorted both newspapers' priorities at times.

"It was pretty cutthroat," Stark said. "It diverted both papers from the good things that we independently would have thought of to do, because everything had to be judged and assessed on the basis of the newspaper war. Can we relax now? I hope so."

Both papers lost a bundle fighting, but Free Press lost more

By REMER TYSON
Free Press Staff Writer

Both Detroit daily newspapers lost millions of dollars during the past five years, but only the Free Press will file as a "failing newspaper" in the application for a proposed joint operating agreement that was announced Monday.

"There is no precedent of having two (failing newspapers) file with the Justice Department) and the Free Press qualifies," said Alvah Chapman Jr., chairman and chief executive officer of Knight-Ridder Newspapers Inc., owner of the Free Press. "There was no reason to break new legal ground."

The joint operating agreement proposed by the owners of the Free Press and the Detroit News requires approval by the U.S. attorney general under the federal Newspaper Preservation Act of 1970. The law also requires that a Justice Department inquiry conclude at least one of the newspapers is in danger of failing financially.

Knight-Ridder and Gannett Co. Inc., owner of the News, plan to file in about two weeks for permission to form a joint agreement under the act.

IF BOTH newspapers filed as "failing," said Calvin Collier, Knight-Ridder's legal counsel in Washington, D.C., "the burden of the inquiry would simply be doubled. It is a burden that is not assumed lightly."

"The failing newspaper will bear the burden of proving the qualification," Collier said. "The burden is significant. There can be an inquiry into all sorts of details."

Chapman said the Free Press qualifies as a "failing newspaper" because its financial losses have been larger and its share of revenue smaller than the News'.

Financial data provided Monday by Knight-Ridder and Gannett indicated that over the past five years the Free Press lost about $35 million and the News lost about $20 million.

OFFICERS OF both corporations refused to disclose 1985 financial results for the two newspapers, but general information they provided indicated that the Free Press lost more than $8 million last year and the News made a small profit.

Chapman said the Free Press has been "losing between $8 million and $10 million a year for the past three years."

Charles Overby, a Gannett spokesman, quoted Allen Neuharth, chairman and chief executive officer of Gannett, as saying the News was "marginally profitable last year."

Both parent corporations reported substantial 1985 profits, according to their annual reports. Knight-Ridder had 1985 gross operating revenue of $1.7 billion, with net income of $133 million.

Gannett reported 1985 gross operating revenue of $2.2 billion and net income of $253 million.

THE HEALTHY financial condition of the parent corporations would not affect the proposed joint operating agreement in Detroit, Chapman said.

"That point of law has already been proved," the Knight-Ridder chairman said.

The last two major joint operating agreements approved by the Justice Department involved some of the nation's largest financially sound media corporations, including Knight-Ridder and Gannett. Chapman said.

Knight-Ridder is involved in a joint operating agreement with Hearst Newspapers in Seattle, and Gannett has such an agreement with Scripps-Howard Inc. in Cincinnati.

Proceedings leading to the attorney general's approval of the Cincinnati and Seattle agreements took more than two years, Collier said. In Seattle, he said, public representatives intervened to contest the agreement.

"Of the Detroit proposal, Collier said, "We are confident of the conclusion"

This night view of the Free Press building was taken in 1938.